Sociology Now

Sociology
Now
Census Update

Michael Kimmel *Stony Brook University*

Amy Aronson *Fordham University*

With the assistance of Jeffery Dennis, Wright State University

Allyn & Bacon

Boston ■ Columbus ■ Indianapolis ■ New York ■ San Francisco ■ Upper Saddle River

Amsterdam ■ Cape Town ■ Dubai ■ London ■ Madrid ■ Milan ■ Munich ■ Paris ■ Montreal ■ Toronto

Delhi ■ Mexico City ■ Sao Paulo ■ Sydney ■ Hong Kong ■ Seoul ■ Singapore ■ Taipei ■ Tokyo

Senior Acquisitions Editor: Brita Mess
Senior Development Editor: Jessica Carlisle
Editorial Assistant: Seanna Breen
Senior Marketing Manager: Kelly May
Senior Production Project Manager: Donna Simons
Cover Administrator: Linda Knowles
Manufacturing Buyer: Megan Cochran
Editorial Production Service: PreMedia Global
Electronic Composition: PreMedia Global
Project Manager: Susan McNally
Copy Editor: Margaret Pinette
Interior Designer: Carol Somberg
Illustrator: Mapping Specialists, Ltd.
Photo Researchers: Laurie Frankenthaler, Naomi Rudov
Cover Designer: Susan Paradise, Joel Gendron

For related titles and support materials, visit our online catalog at www.pearsonhighered.com.

ISBN-10: 0-205-18106-6   ISBN-13: 978-0-205-18106-3

Library of Congress Cataloging-in-Publication Data was not available at press time

Photo credits appear on page 717, which constitutes an extension of the copyright page.

10 9 8 7 6 5 4 3 2 1   CRK   15 14 13 12 11

Brief Contents

Contents

PART ONE Foundations of the Field

chapter 1

What Is Sociology?   2

chapter 4

How Do We Know What We Know? The Methods of the Sociologist   102

chapter 5

Socialization   138

Deviance and Crime 166

PART TWO Identities and Inequalities

Stratification and Social Class 204

chapter **12**

The Family 380

Sociology of Environments: The Natural, Physical, and Human Worlds 616

Maps

Features

Sociology and Our World

How Do We Know What We Know?

Try It

What Do You Think?

Preface

I am a sociologist—both by profession and by temperament. It's what I do for a living and how I see the world. I consider myself enormously lucky to have the kind of job I have, teaching and writing about the world in which we live.

I love sociology. I love that it gives us a way to see the world that is different from any other way of seeing the world. It's a lens, and when I hold that lens up to the world, I see shapes and patterns that help me understand it, colors and movement that enable me to perceive depth and shading. I love sociology because when I see those shapes, those patterns, and those shades of gray, I feel hopeful that we can, as citizens and sociologists, contribute to making that world a better place for all of us.

Teachers in general are a pretty optimistic bunch. By working with you to develop your own critical engagement with the world—developing ideas, using evidence to back up assertions, deepening and broadening your command of information—we believe that your life will be better for it. You will: get a better job, be a more engaged and active citizen, maybe even be a better parent, friend, or partner than you might otherwise have been. We believe that education is a way to improve your life on so many different levels. Pretty optimistic, no?

In this book, we have tried to communicate that way of seeing and that optimism about how you can use a sociological lens.

Why Study Sociology?
A Message to Students

So, what did people say when you told them you were taking sociology?

They probably looked at you blankly, "Like, what is sociology?" They might say, "And what can you do with it?" Sociology is often misunderstood. Some think it's nothing more than what my roommate told me when I said I was going to go to graduate school in sociology. (He was pre-med.) "Sociology makes a science out of common sense," he said dismissively.

It turns out he was wrong: what we think of as common sense turns out to be wrong a lot of the time. The good news is that sociologists are often the ones who point out that what "everybody knows" isn't necessarily true. In a culture saturated by self-help books, pop psychology, and TV talk shows promising instant and complete physical makeovers and utter psychological transformation, sociology says "wait a minute, not so fast."

Our culture tells us that all social problems are really individual problems. Poor people are poor because they don't work hard enough, and racial discrimination is simply the result of prejudiced individuals.

And the "solutions" offered by TV talk shows and self-help books also center around individual changes. If you work hard, you can make it. If you want to change, you can change. Social problems, they counsel, are really a set of individual problems all added together. Racism, sexism, or homophobia is really the result of unenlightened people holding bad attitudes. If they changed their attitudes, those enormous problems would dissolve like sugar in your coffee.

Sociology has a different take. Sociologists see society as a dynamic interaction between individuals and institutions, like education, economy, and government. Changing yourself might be necessary for you to live a happier life, but it has little impact on the effects of those institutions. And changing attitudes would make social life far more pleasant, but problems like racial or gender inequality are embedded in the ways those institutions are organized. It will take more than attitudinal shifts to fix that.

One of sociology's greatest strengths is also what makes it so elusive or discomforting. We often are in a position in which we contrast American mythologies with sociological realities.

I remember a song as I was growing up called "Only in America" by Jay and the Americans, which held that only in this country could "a guy from anywhere," "without a cent" maybe grow up to be a millionaire or president. Pretty optimistic, right? And it takes a sociologist, often, to burst that bubble, to explain that it's really not true—that the likelihood of a poor boy or girl making it in the United States is minuscule, and that virtually everyone ends up in the same class position as their parents. It sounds almost unpatriotic to say that the single best predictors of *your* eventual position in society is the education and occupation of your parents.

Sociology offers some answers to questions that may therefore be unpopular—because they emphasize the social and the structural over the individual and psychological, because they reveal the relationship between individual experience and social reality, and because structural barriers impede our ability to realize our dreams.

This often leads introductory students to feel initially depressed. Since these problems are so deeply embedded in our society, and since all the educational enlightenment in the world might not budge these powerful institutional forces—well, what's the use? Might as well just try and get yours, and the heck with everyone else.

But then, as we understand the real mission of sociology, students often feel invigorated, inspired. Sociology's posture is exactly the opposite—and that's what makes it so compelling. Understanding those larger forces means, as the Who put it, "we won't get fooled again!"

What also makes sociology compelling is that it connects those two dimensions. It is *because* we believe that all social problems are really the result of individual weaknesses and laziness that those social problems remain in place. It is *because* we believe that poverty can be eliminated by hard work that poverty doesn't get eliminated. If social problems are social, then reducing poverty, or eliminating racial or gender discrimination, will require more than individual enlightenment; it will require large-scale political mobilization to change social institutions. And the good news is that sociologists have also documented the ways that those institutions themselves are always changing, always being changed.

Why Study Sociology Right Now? A Message to Students and Instructors

Understanding our society has never been more important. Sociology offers perhaps the best perspective on what are arguably the two dominant trends of our time: globalization and multiculturalism.

Globalization refers to the increasingly interlocked processes and institutions that span the entire world rather than in one country. Goods and services are produced and distributed globally. Information moves instantly. You want to know how much things have changed? More than 2,000 soldiers in both the Union and Confederate armies were killed in the summer of 1865—that is, *after* the Civil War had ended. Why? Because no one had told them the war was over.

Globalization makes the world feel smaller, leaves us all far more intimately connected. And since people all over the world are wearing the same sneakers, eating the same fast food, and connecting by the Internet and texting each other, we are becoming more and more similar.

On the other hand, multiculturalism makes us keenly aware of how we are different. Globalization may make the world smaller, but we remain divided by religious-inspired wars, racial and ethnic identities, blood feuds, tribal rivalries, and what is generally called "sectarian violence."

Multiculturalism describes the ways in which we create identities that at once make us "global citizens" and also, at the same time, local and familial, based on our membership in racial, ethnic, or gender categories. Here in the United States, we have not become one big happy family, as some predicted a century ago. Instead of the "melting pot" in which each group would become part of the same "stew," we are, at our best, a "beautiful mosaic" of small groups which, when seen from afar, creates a beautiful pattern while each tile retains its distinct shape and beauty.

Globalization and multiculturalism make the world feel closer and also more divided; and they make the distances between us as people seem both tiny and unbridgeably large.

Globalization and multiculturalism are not only about the world—they are about us, individually. We draw our sense of who we are, our **identities,** from our membership in those diverse groups into which we are born or that we choose. Our identities—who we think we are—come from our gender, race, ethnicity, class, sexuality, age, religion, region, nation, and tribe. From these diverse locations, we piece together an identity, a sense of self. Sometimes one or another feels more important than others, but at other times other elements emerge as equally important.

And these elements of our identities also turn out to be the bases on which social hierarchies are built. Social inequality is organized from the same elements as identity—resources and opportunities are distributed in our society on the basis of race, class, ethnicity, age, sexuality, gender, and so forth.

A sociological perspective has never been more important to enabling us to understand these problems, because sociology has become the field that has most fully embraced globalization and multiculturalism as the central analytic lenses through which we view social life.

Why Use *Sociology Now?*
A Message to Instructors

The field of sociology has changed enormously since I first went to graduate school in the mid-1970s. At the time, two paradigms, functionalism and conflict theory, battled for dominance in the field, each one claiming to explain social processes better than the other. At the time, symbolic interactionism seemed a reasonable way to understand micro-level processes.

That was an era of great conflict in our society: the civil rights, women's, and gay and lesbian movements, protests against the Vietnam war, hippies. On campuses these groups vied with far more traditional, conservative, and career-oriented students whose collegiate identity came more from the orderly 1950s than the tumultuous 1960s.

Just as the world has changed since then, so, too, has sociology—both substantively and demographically. New perspectives have emerged from older models, and terms like rational choice, poststructrialism, collective mobilization, cultural tool kit—not to mention multiculturalism and globalization—have become part of our daily lexicon.

Demographically, sociology is the field that has been most transformed by the social movements of the last decades of the twentieth century. Because sociology interrogates the connections between identities and inequalities, it has become a home to those groups who were historically marginalized in American society: women, people of color, gays and lesbians. The newest sections in the American Sociological Association are those on the Body, Sexualities, and Race, Class, and Gender; the largest sections are no longer Medical Sociology and Organizational Sociology, but now Sex and Gender, Culture, and Race.

It turned out that symbolic interactionism was resilient enough to remain a theoretical lens through which social interaction and processes can still be understood. That's largely because the old textbook model of "three paradigms" placed the three in a somewhat stilted competition: conflict and functionalism were the macro theories; interactionism stood alone as a micro theory.

Themes: Exploring the Questions of Today

One of the biggest differences you'll see immediately in *Sociology Now* is that we have built on older functionalism–conflict theory–interactionism models with a contemporary approach. We no longer believe these paradigms are battling for dominance; students needn't choose between competing models. Sociology is a synthetic discipline—*for us the question is almost never "either/or," and thus the answer is almost always "both/and."*

Sociology is also, often, a debunking discipline, rendering old truisms into complex, contextualized processes and interactions. What "everybody knows" to be true often turns out not to be. We didn't learn everything we needed to know in kindergarten. It's more complicated than that!

And using globalization and multiculturalism as the organizing themes of the book helps to illustrate exactly how "both/and" actually works. The world isn't smaller or bigger—it's both. We're not more united or more diverse—we're both. We're not more orderly or more in conflict—we're both. And sociology is the field that explains the way that "both" sides exist in a dynamic tension with each other. What's more, sociology explains why, and how, and in what ways they exist in that tension.

This way of expressing where sociology is now turned out to be quite amenable to the traditional architecture of a sociology textbook. The general sections of the book, and the individual chapter topics, are not especially different from the chapter organization of other textbooks.

There are, however, some important differences.

First, **globalization** is not the same as cross-national comparisons. Globalization is often imagined as being about "them"—other cultures and other societies. And while examples drawn from other cultures are often extremely valuable to a sociologist, especially in challenging ethnocentrism, globalization is about processes that link "us" and "them." Thus, many of our examples, especially our cultural references, are about the United States—in relation to the rest of the world. This enables students both to relate to the topic, and also to see how it connects with the larger, global forces at work.

Globalization is woven into every chapter—and, perhaps more important, every American example is connected to a global process or issue.

Second, **multiculturalism** is not the same as social stratification. Every sociology textbook has separate chapters on class, race, age, and gender. (We have added a few, which I will discuss below.) But in some books, that's about as far as it goes—chapters on "other topics" do not give adequate sociological treatment to the ways in which our different positions affect our experience of other sociological institutions and processes.

Multiculturalism is used as a framing device in every chapter. Every chapter describes the different ways in which race, class, age, ethnicity, sexuality, and gender organize people's experiences within institutions.

Within Part Two on "Identities and Inequalities," we deal with each of these facets of identity—age, class, race, ethnicity, gender, sexuality—separately, of course. But we are vitally concerned, also, with the ways in which they intersect with each other. When, after all, do you start being middle class and stop being Black? Contemporary sociological inquiry requires that we examine the *intersections* among these various elements of identity and inequality, understanding how they interact, amplify, and contradict each other.

These aspects of identity both *unite us (as elements of identity)* and *divide us— into groups that compete for scarce resources. These are the dimensions of social life that organize inequality. Thus we explore both—identity and inequality.*

Multiculturalism requires not just that we "add women (or any other group) and stir"—the ways that some courses and textbooks tried to revamp themselves in the last few decades of the twentieth century to embrace diversity. Multiculturalism requires that we begin from questions of diversity and identity, not end there. This book attempts to do that.

Organization

We've added two chapters to the standard sociology textbook configuration, and we've revamped four others fundamentally. While some other books have one or two of these, none has them all.

- **Chapter 10, Sexuality.** We have included this chapter not because it's trendy, but because it's sociologically accurate. Over the past several decades, sexuality has emerged as one of the primary foundations of identity, while inequalities based on sexuality have emerged as among the nation's (and the world's) most charged arenas of inequality. And sociologists were at the forefront of the effort to identify sexuality as a primary foundation of identity.

  Students today are eager to discuss these issues. Textbooks developed in the late twentieth century have not fully taken account of the massive changes that our current interest in sexuality has wrought.

  When I was a sociology student in the 1970s, we were asking very different questions in my coeduational dorm: Could we use the same bathrooms? What impact does feminism have on women's sexuality? Are gay people "normal"? Students today are more likely to be debating transgenderism and what bathrooms are appropriate for the intersexed, hooking up, and the effectiveness of abstinence pledges. Sexuality deserves its own chapter.

- **Chapter 18, Mass Media.** Again, we have included this chapter not to be trendy, but because the world has changed so enormously in the past few decades, and the media have been among the most important causes, and consequences, of those changes. Few institutions are more centrally involved in both globalization and multiculturalism.

  And, again, it has been sociologists who have come to see the increased centrality of the media in both the creation of identity and the global distribution of information. Sociologists have insisted that media (and peer groups) must take their place as equally important agents of childhood socialization as the former "big three"—family, religion, and education. And while some of us are zooming down the information superhighway; others are stuck on barely passable dirt tracks.

We have also reconceptualized the standard way of organizing four other chapters. We feel that these changes will more accurately reflect where sociology is *now* and the interests of our students, and thus more adequately prepare students to engage with sociological ideas.

- **Chapter 11, Age: From Young to Old.** Most other textbooks have a chapter on age. They deal exclusively with aging—that is, with old people. Now, I have nothing against old people—I am, or will soon be, one myself! But students often feel the age chapter is not about them, but about their parents or grandparents, about "other people."

  Of course this chapter retains the sociological treatment of aging, but we've also added new material on youth. Half the chapter focuses on youth as an identity and as a source of inequality. After all, when we discuss age stratification, it is *both* old and young who experience discrimination. Our students know this: we should acknowledge it in our textbooks. And, again, it has been sociologists who have been at the forefront of exploring and understanding youth—as identity and as a basis for inequality.

- **Chapter 15, Religion and Science.** We often think of religion and science as competitors, even as enemies. After all, both seek answers to life's big questions, but they use very different methods and come up with different answers. Sociologically, they exhibit many formal similarities—hierarchies of positions, organizational networks, hierarchies of knowledge. Both guide social action, offering normative claims derived from their respective "truths."

  More than that, students often feel that they must choose between the two. But religious belief and scientific knowledge co-exist. In fact, the United States is simultaneously one of the most scientifically advanced and one of the most deeply religious countries in the world. The same person may be both religious and scientific in different situations. Most clergy in the U.S. keep up with advances in medicine and law in order to minister to their congregations effectively, and many, if not most, scientists attend church or temple. Students are eager to talk about religion, although some may feel initially uncomfortable discussing it sociologically. Placing the discussion alongside an equally sociological discussion of science will facilitate the sociological conversation about both subjects.

- **Chapter 16, The Body and Society: Health and Illness.** Virtually every textbook has a chapter on health and medicine, which discuss both our experience of health and illness and the social institutions that engage with us in those experiences. We've organized this chapter to include far more about the body—that is, the "social body," the ways in which our experiences of our bodies are socially constructed.

  Students are eager to discuss the other sociological aspects of the body besides, for example, the sick role. Body modification (tattoos, piercing, cosmetic surgery) lends itself to marvelous class discussions about the construction of identity through the body, and the ways we assert both individuality and conformity. This discussion connects well with traditional discussions of health and illness. And, once again, sociologists have been among the more visible researchers in this new and growing field of interest, as the newest section of the ASA on the Sociology of the Body attests.

- **Chapter 19, Sociology of Environments: The Natural, Physical, and Human Worlds.** Few issues are more pressing to the current generation of college students than the environment. Yet, while many textbooks discuss aspects of the environment, they typically focus on the "human" environment (chapters on demography and population) or the "built" environment (a chapter on urbanization). While fundamental and necessary, these books often leave out the third element of the environmental equation: the natural environment.

By reconceptualizing the chapter on the environment, we focus on all three elements: human, built, and natural. It is, after all, the interaction among these three elements that structures the sorts of issues we face, and constructs and constrains the sorts of policy options available to meet environmental needs. We believe that this framing will better equip a new generation of sociology students to understand and engage with the vital environmental issues of our time.

Finally, the chapter on methods has been moved from its more common place as Chapter 2 to Chapter 4. That is not because we have somehow "demoted" methods to a less-important place in the sociology curriculum. In fact, it's because we see it as that much more important.

- **Chapter 4, How Do We Know What We Know: The Methods of the Sociologist.** We believe that methods don't exist in a conceptual vacuum. Strategies of researching sociological problems only come after one has a problem to investigate. We have placed the discussion of classical and contemporary theory (Chapter 1) and of the conceptual foundations of sociology—culture, society, organization, interaction—before the discussion of methods because, we believe, it's more sociological to do so. When sociologists do research, they don't begin with a method and then go looking for a problem. They begin with a problem, drawn from the conceptual foundations of the field, and then determine the sorts of methodological strategies that they might use to comprehend it.

  What's more, we believe that sociological methods are so important that we should not end our discussion of methodology with the individual methods chapter. One of the distinctive elements of *Sociology Now* is the "How Do We Know What We Know?" feature box. In each substantive chapter, we stop and ask exactly *how* sociologists have come to know what we know about a certain topic. That is, we discuss different methods used in sociological research. Thus the discussion of methods is woven into each chapter, and it is woven in *in context* with substantive sociological questions.

Distinctive Features

The "How Do We Know What We Know?" box is only one of several features of *Sociology Now* that are fresh and exciting for students, enhancing their enjoyment of the text without sacrificing any of the substance.

▶ **Did You Know?** Each chapter is punctuated by several "Did You Know?" boxes. These are generally short sociological factoids tidbits of information that are funny, strange, a little offbeat, but illustrate the sociological ideas being discussed.

For example, did you know that the notion that the Eskimos have 24 different words for snow is a myth? Did you know that at the turn of the last century, baby boys were supposed to be dressed in red or pink, and little girls in blue?

You won't draw their attention to all of these factoids, but the students are going to enjoy reading them. And, we guarantee that there are at least a few that you didn't know!

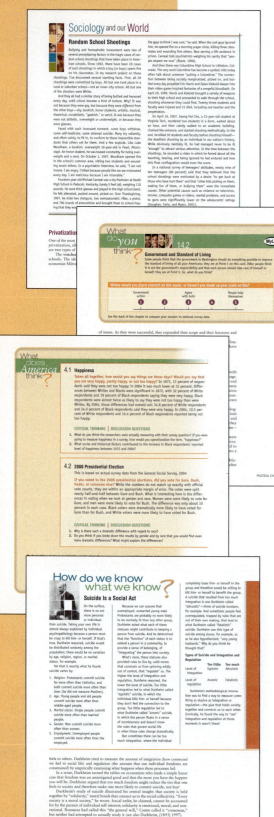

▶ **Sociology and Our World.** Among the most exciting and rewarding parts of teaching introductory sociology is revealing to students how what we study is so immediately applicable to the world in which we all live. Thus each chapter has at least two boxes that make this connection explicit. They're there to help the student see the connections between their lives, which they usually think are pretty interesting, and sociology, which they might, at first, fear as dry and irrelevant. And these boxes also are there to facilitate classroom discussions, providing only a couple of examples of what could be numerous possibilities to apply sociology to contemporary social questions.

▶ **What Do You Think? and What Does America Think?** Part of an introductory course requires students to marshal evidence to engage with and often reevaluate their opinions. Often our job is to unsettle their fallback position of "this is just my own personal opinion"—which floats, unhinged from any social contexts. We ask that they contextualize, that they refer to how they formed their opinions and to what sorts of evidence they might use to demonstrate the empirical veracity of their position. How they came to think what they think is often as important as what they think.

But students often benefit enormously from knowing what *other people* think as well. What percentage of Americans agree with you? Throughout each chapter, we've included a boxed feature that asks students questions taken directly from the General Social Survey. At the end of the chapter, we provide the information about what a representative sample of Americans think about the same topic, to give a student a sense of where his or her opinion fits with the rest of the country. Critical-thinking questions based on the data encourage students to think about how factors like race, gender, and class influence our perceptions and attitudes.

▶ **How Do We Know What We Know?** As mentioned above, this feature enables us to show students how methods actually work in the exploration of sociological problems. Instead of confining methods to its own chapter, and then ignoring it for the remainder of the book, we ask, for example, how sociologists measure social mobility (Chapter 7), or how we use statistics to examine the relationship between race and intelligence (Chapter 8), or how participant observation studies of gangs have changed our views of inner-city life (Chapter 6).

Sometimes, we show how *bad* methods have been used to support various arguments, such as nineteeth century arguments against women entering higher education (Chapter 9), the notion that men experience a "midlife crisis" (Chapter 11) or even the recent claim by economist Steven Levitt that the legalization of abortion in 1973 led to the decline in violent crime two decades later (Chapter 6).

In this way, students can see method-in-action as a tool that sociologists use to discover the patterns of the social world.

▶ **Try It** These exercises, based on real classroom experience and contributed by sociology instructors across the country, provide opportunities for active learning. One "Try It" exercise per chapter directs students to perform an activity—individually or in a group, inside or outside of class—that illustrates a sociological concept. Activities include asking students to apply theories of deviance to what they see in the news (Chapter 6), to think sociologically about the lifespan (Chapter 11), and to consider and apply the concept of population pyramids (Chapter 19).

▶ **An Engaging Writing Style** All textbook writers strive for clarity, a few even reach for elegance. This book is no exception. We've tried to write the book in a way that conveys a lot of information, but also in a way that engages the students where *they* live. Not only are concepts always followed by examples, but we frequently use examples drawn from pop culture—from TV, movies, and music—and even from videos and video games.

This will not only make the students' reading experience seem more immediate, but should also enable the instructor to illustrate the relevance of sociological concepts to the students' lives.

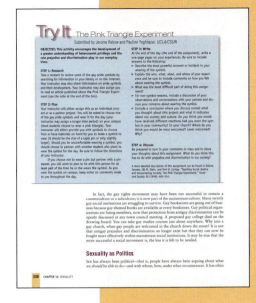

Acknowledgments

To say that every book is a conversation is true, but insufficient. Every book is many conversations at once. To be sure, it's a conversation between authors and readers, and it's designed to stimulate conversations among readers themselves. But writing a book is itself saturated with other conversations, and though I cannot possibly do justice to them all, it is important to acknowledge their presence in this process.

First, there is my conversation, as an author, with my chosen field, my profession. How have I understood what others have written, their research, their way of seeing the world? How can I best communicate that to a new generation of students encountering sociology for the very first time?

I've had conversations with dozens of other sociologists who have read these chapters and provided enormously helpful feedback. Their candor has helped us revise, rethink, and re-imagine entire sections of the book, and we are enormously grateful.

Manuscript Reviewers

Boyd Bergeson, Oregon Health and Sciences University
Susan Blackwell, Delgado Community College
Ralph Brown, Brigham Young University
Philip J. Crawford, San Jose Community College
Kris de Welde, University of Colorado at Boulder
Brenda Donelan, Northern State University
Catherine Felton, Central Piedmont Community College
Dian Fitzpatrick, East Stroudsburg University
Risa L. Garelick, Coconino Community College
Ann Marie Hickey, University of Kansas
Candace L. Hinson, Tallahassee City College
Michael L. Hirsch, Huston-Tillotson University
Amitra Hodge, Buffalo State College

Lynette F. Hoelter, University of Michigan
Amy Holzgang, Cerritos College
William Housel, Northwestern Louisiana State University
H. David Hunt, University of Southern Mississippi
Judi Kessler, Monmouth College
Amy Manning Kirk, Sam Houston State University
Jennifer Lerner, Northern Virginia Community College
Ami Lynch, George Washington University
Karen E. B. McCue, University of New Mexico
Shelley A. McGrath, Southern Illinois University
Abigail McNeely, Austin Community College
Stephanie R. Medley-Rath, University of West Georgia
Sharon Methvin, Clark College
Barbara J. Miller, Pasadena City College
Beth Mintz, University of Vermont
Monique Moleon-Mathews, Indian River Community College
Adam Moskowitz, Columbus State Community College
Elizabeth Pare, Wayne State University
Joseph Keith Price, West Texas A&M University
Cynthia K. S. Reed, Tarrant Community College
Susan Smith-Cunnien, University of St. Thomas
Ryan Spohn, Kansas State University
Marybeth C. Stalp, University of Northern Iowa
Kell J. A. Stone, El Camino College
Richard Valencia, Fresno City College
Dean Wagstaffe, Indian River Community College
Georgie Ann Weatherby, Gonzaga University
Pamela Williams-Paez, Canyons College
S. Rowan Wolf, Portland Community College

A number of instructors were kind enough to share some of their favorite class-tested learning activities for the feature in this book called "Try It": these make more concrete and experiential some of the themes we discuss in the chapters, enabling the students to gain some hands-on sociological experience. Thanks to Katherine Rowell of Sinclair Community College for her valuable work in assembling, editing, and contributing many of these; other contributors include:

Amy Agigian, Suffolk University
Sharon Barnartt, Gallaudet University
Michelle Bemiller, Kansas State University
Casey J. Cornelius, Delta College
Jeff Dixon, Indiana University
Meredith Greif, Cleveland State University
Amy Guptill, SUNY–Brockport
Jonathan Marx, Winthrop University
Jerome Rabow and Pauline Yeghnazar, University of California, Los Angeles

In addition, each chapter includes two boxes called "What Do You Think?" and two end-of-chapter exercises called "What Does America Think?"—all of which were contributed by Kathleen Dolan of North Georgia College and State University. These help the students gauge their own opinions next to the results of GSS and other surveys of Americans' opinions. Such a gauge is pedagogically vital. Often my students begin a response to a question with a minimizing feint: "This is just my own personal opinion. . . . " What a relief and revelation to see their opinions as socially shared (or not) with others. I'm grateful to Kathleen for her efforts to contextualize those "personal opinions."

I've also carried on a conversation with my colleagues at SUNY, Stony Brook, where I have been so fortunate to work for two decades in a department that strongly values high quality teaching. In particular, I'm grateful to my chair, Diane Barthel-Bouchier, for managing such a diverse and collegial department where I have felt so comfortable. Every single one of my colleagues—both past and present—has assisted me in some way in the work on this book, guiding my encounter with areas of their expertise, providing an example they have used in class, or commenting on specific text. I am grateful to them all.

There has also been an ongoing conversation with my students, both graduate and undergraduate, throughout my career. They've kept me attentive to the shifts in the field and committed to working constantly on my own pedagogical strategies to communicate them. My teaching assistants over the years have been especially perceptive—and unafraid to communicate their thoughts and opinions!

I have spent my entire career teaching in large public universities—UC Berkeley, UC Santa Cruz, Rutgers, and now Stony Brook—teaching undergraduate students who are, overwhelmingly, first generation college students, and most often immigrants and members of minority groups. They represent the next generation of Americans, born not to privilege, but to hope and ambition. More than any other single group, they have changed how I see the world.

Many other sociologists have influenced my thinking over the years. I suspect I may be a rather impressionable guy, because were I to list them all, I think the list would go on for pages! So I will only thank some recent friends and colleagues who have contributed their advice, comments, or criticisms on specific items in this book, and those old friends who have shared their passion for sociology with me for decades: Elizabeth Armstrong, Troy Duster, Paula England, Cynthia and Howard Epstein, Abby Ferber, John Gagnon, Josh Gamson, Barry Glassner, Erich Goode, Cathy Greenblat, Michael Kaufman, Mike Messner, Rebecca Plante, Lillian Rubin, Don Sabo, Wendy Simonds, Arlene and Jerry Skolnick, Jean-Anne Sutherland, and Suzanna Walters.

For the rest of my far-flung friends and colleagues, I hope that you will find the fruits of those conversations somewhere in these pages.

One person stands out as deserving of special thanks. Jeffery Dennis began his career as my graduate student—an enormously gifted one at that. We engaged Jeff as a colleague to work with us to develop this book—to help us develop chapters, explore arguments, clarify examples, track down obscure factoids, organize thematic presentations—and with everything we asked of him, he delivered far more than we hoped. He's been a most valued contributor to this project, and a major participant in its conversations.

A textbook of this size and scale is also the result of a conversation between author and publisher—and there we have been enormously lucky to work with such a talented and dedicated team as we have at Allyn and Bacon. As the editor, Jeff Lasser does more than acquire a book, he inhabits it—or, more accurately, it inhabits him. He thinks about it constantly and engages with the authors with just the right balance of criticism and support. He knows when to push—and when not to.

Jessica Carlisle has been simply the ideal development editor. Her instincts were almost always flawless—she held aloft a concern for both the form and the content of this book in equal measure, helping us revise, trim, cut, and add in a way that made the book better, stronger and tighter.

The rest of the production team, including Donna Simons and Susan McNally, were as professional and dedicated to the project as we were.

At the beginning of this preface, I said I was really lucky because my job is so amazingly rewarding, and because I get to do something that is in harmony with my values, with how I see the world.

But I'm also really lucky because I get to do virtually everything—including the writing of this book—with my wife, Amy Aronson. Amy is a professor of Journalism and Media Studies at Fordham University; she comes to her sociological imagination through her background in the humanities and her experiences as a magazine editor (*Working Woman*). In the writing of this book, we have been completely equal partners—this is the only part I have written myself. (Don't worry: she edited it!)

Amy thanks her colleagues at Fordham University, Lincoln Center, for their support and various helpful comments. She's grateful always to Robert Ferguson for his unwavering encouragement over the years.

And we both thank our respective families—Winnie Aronson, Nancy Aronson, Barbara and Herb Diamond, Sandi Kimmel and Patrick Murphy, Ed Kimmel, Bill Diamond, Jeff Diamond, Leslie and Bruce Hodes, and Lauren Kaplan—for believing in us and cheering us on.

And we thank Zachary, our son. At age 8, he's been a lively critic of some of our ideas, a curious listener, and a patient family member. (He helped pick some of the pictures!) Every single day, when he recounts the day's events at school, or is at soccer or ice hockey practice, or observes something in the neighborhood, or asks a question about the news—he reminds us of the importance of a sociological perspective in making sense of the world.

And finally I thank Amy. As partners in our lives, as parents to our son, and in our collaboration on this and other books, we work toward a marriage of equals, in which the idea of gender equality is a lived reality, not some utopian dream.

Michael Kimmel

To learn more about this text and the authors, watch video of Michael Kimmel and Amy Aronson discussing *Sociology Now* at www.ablongman.com/kimmelpreview.

About the Authors

Michael Kimmel, Professor of Sociology at Stony Brook University, is one of the pioneers in the sociology of gender and one of the world's leading experts on men and masculinities. He was the first man to deliver the International Women's Day lecture at the European Parliament; was the first man to be named the annual lecturer by the Sociologists for Women in Society; and has been called as an expert witness in several high-profile gender discrimination cases. Among his many books are *Men's Lives*, *The Gendered Society*, *Manhood in America*, and *Revolution: A Sociological Perspective*. He is also known for his ability to explain sociological ideas to a general audience. His articles have appeared in dozens of magazines and newspapers, including the *New York Times*, *The Nation*, the *Village Voice*, the *Washington Post*, and *Psychology Today*.

Amy Aronson is Assistant Professor of Journalism and Media Studies at Fordham University. She is the author of *Taking Liberties: Early American Women's Magazines and Their Readers* and an editor of the international quarterly, *Media History*. She has co-edited several books, including a centennial edition of Charlotte Perkins Gilman's *Women and Economics* and the two-volume *Encyclopedia of Men and Masculinities*, which was honored by the New York Public Library with a Best of Reference Award in 2004. A former editor at *Working Woman* and *Ms.*, her work has also appeared in publications including *Business Week*, *Global Journalist* and the Sunday supplement of *The Boston Globe*.

A Note from the Publisher about Supplements

Instructor Supplements

Unless otherwise noted, instructor's supplements are available at no charge to adopters and available in printed or duplicated formats, as well as electronically through the Pearson Higher Education Instructor Resource Center (www.pearsonhighered.com/irc).

Instructor's Manual *(Jennifer E. Lerner, Northern Virginia Community College, Loudoun)*   For each chapter in the text, the Instructor's Manual provides chapter summaries and outlines, learning objectives, key terms and people, teaching suggestions (which include film suggestions, in-class activities, and projects and homework exercises), and references for further research and reading. The Instructor's Manual also includes the "Try It" activities from the text, along with notes for the instructor.

Test Bank *(Elizabeth Pare, Wayne State University)*   The Test Bank contains approximately 90 questions per chapter in multiple-choice, true-false, short answer, fill-in-the-blank, essay, and open-book formats. The open-book questions challenge students to look beyond words and answer questions based on the text's figures, tables, and maps. All questions are labeled and scaled according to Bloom's Taxonomy.

Computerized Test Bank   The printed Test Bank is also available through Pearson's computerized testing system, TestGen EQ. This fully networkable test-generating software is available for Windows and Macintosh. The user-friendly interface allows you to view, edit, and add questions, transfer questions to tests, and print tests in a variety of fonts. Search and sort features allow you to locate questions quickly and to arrange them in whatever order you prefer.

PowerPoint™ Presentation *(Kell Stone, El Camino College)*   These PowerPoint slides on a CD, created especially for *Sociology Now*, feature lecture outlines for every chapter and many of the tables, charts, and maps from the text. PowerPoint software is not required, as a PowerPoint viewer is included.

Student Supplements

Study Guide *(Shelly McGrath, Southern Illinois University)*   The Study Guide is designed to help students prepare for quizzes and exams. For every chapter in the text, it contains a chapter summary, lists of key terms and people, a practice test with 25 multiple-choice questions and an answer key, and a set of PowerPoint lecture outlines. We have also included a list of videos, simulations, and other activities students can find in MySocLab for further exploration of topics in each chapter. Packaged at no additional cost on request with the text.

Online Course Management

The MySocLab Census Update   MySocLab Census Update gives students the opportunity to explore 2010 Census methods and data and apply Census results in a dynamic interactive online environment. It includes:

- a series of activities using 2010 Census results
- video clips explaining and exploring the Census
- primary source readings relevant to the Census
- an online version of the 2010 Census Update Primer

MySocLab Census Update is available at no additional cost to the student when packaged with a *MySocLab Student Access Code Card* (ISBN 0-205-21389-8).

WebCT and Blackboard Test Banks   For colleges and universities with WebCT™ and Blackboard™ licenses, we have converted the complete Test Bank into these popular course management platforms. Adopters can request a copy on CD or download the electronic file by logging in to our Instructor Resource Center.

Additional Supplements

***A Short Introduction to the 2010 U.S. Census,* by John Carl (ISBN 0-205-21325-1)**
A Short Introduction to the 2010 U.S. Census presents a brief seven-chapter overview of the Census, including important information about the Constitutional mandate, research methods, who is affected by the Census, and how data are used. Additionally, the primer explores key contemporary topics such as race and ethnicity, the family, and poverty. The primer can be packaged with any Pearson text at no additional cost, and is also available via MySocLab, MySocKit, and MySearchLab.

The Allyn and Bacon Social Atlas of the United States (*William H. Frey, University of Michigan, with Amy Beth Anspach and John Paul DeWitt*)   This brief and accessible atlas uses colorful maps, graphs, and some of the best social science data available to survey the leading social, economic, and political indicators of American society. Available for purchase separately or packaged with this text at a significant discount.

Additional Acknowledgments

Many sociology instructors were consulted about this text in various ways, and at various stages of development. The following people were interviewed by telephone, filled out a survey, or participated in a focus group. The information they shared with us—what they like and don't like about their textbooks; what goes on in their classroom; what matters most to their students, and to sociologists today—all contributed to the making of *Sociology Now*.

Gabriel Acevedo, University of Texas at San Antonio

Anora Ackerson, Kalamazoo Valley Community College

Isaac Addai, Lansing Community College

Francis Adeola, University of New Orleans

Bob Alexander, North Hennepin Community College

Sarah Allred, Berry College

Sandra Alvarez, Shippensburg University

Sine Anahita, University of Alaska, Fairbanks

Judy Andreasson, North Idaho College

Karl-Erik Andreasson, North Idaho College

Amy Armenia, Hofstra University

Matt Aronson, Colorado State University

Grace Auyang, University of Cincinnati

Carl Backman, Auburn University

Deborah Baiano Berman, Framingham State College

Parris Baker, Gannon University

Dorothy Balancio, Mercy College

Anthony Balzano, Sussex County Community College, Newton

Heidi Barajas, University of Minnesota, Minneapolis

Nielan Barnes, California State University, Long Beach

Cynthia Barnett, Moorpark College

Angel Basabe, Milwaukee Area Technical College

Diane Bates, The College of New Jersey

Timothy Baylor, Lock Haven University

Todd Bernhardt, Broward Community College

Sheli Bernstein-Goff, West Liberty State College

Terry Besser, Iowa State University

Chris Biga, University of Wisconsin, Milwaukee

Debbie Bishop, Lansing Community College

Dorothy Blackman, Cuyahoga Community College, Metro

Daniel Boudon, Hofstra University

Karen Boyd, Indiana University, South Bend

Robert Brainerd, Highland Community College

Jennifer Brennom, Kirkwood College

Jack Brouillette, Colorado State University

Ralph Brown, Brigham Young University

Valerie Brown, Cuyahoga Community College, Metro

Ryan Caldwell, Texas A&M University

Walt Calgaro, Prairie State College

Thomas Calhoun, Southern Illinois University, Carbondale

Roberta Campbell, University of Cincinnatti

Allison Carey, Shippensburg University

Michael Carolan, Colorado State University

Mark Carpenter, Columbus State Community College

Ellen Casper-Flood, Dutchess County Community College

Bruce Chadwick, Brigham Young University

Brenda Chaney, Ohio State University

Brenda Chappell, University of Central Oklahoma

Janet Christopulos, Milwaukee Area Technical College

Jean Christy, Delaware Technical and Community College, Stanton Campus

Kristi Clark-Miller, Montana State University

Katherine Clifton, Edison Community
College

Langdon Clough, Community College of
Rhode Island

Karen Cohen; Macomb Community
College

Mary Cole, East Tennessee State University

Tom Conroy, Lehman College

Jonathan Cordero, California Lutheran
University

Janet Cosbey, Eastern Illinois University

Susan Cox, Bellevue Community College

Cynthia Crisel, Arkansas State University
Mountain Home

CJ Crivaro, Northern Essex Community
College

Mary Croissant, Front Range Community
College

Karen Dalke, University of Wisconsin-
Green Bay

Dianne Dentice, Stephen F. Austin State
University

Michelle Dietert, Texas Women's
University

Keri Diggins, Scottsdale Community
College

Yanyi Djamba, Auburn University

Raymond Dorney, Merrimack College

Dennis Downey, University of Utah

Gregory Dunaway, Mississippi State
University

Al Dunkleman, Cleveland Community
College

Rick Duque, Louisiana State University

Isaac Eberstein, Florida State University

Jean Egan, Asnuntuck Community College

June Ellestad, University of Montana

Leslie Elrod, University of Cincinnati,
Raymond Walters College

Deborah Engelen-Eigles, Century College

Rebecca Fahrlander, University of
Nebraska at Omaha

Roya Falahi-Kharaghani, Joliet Junior
College

Charles Faupel, Auburn University

Heather Feldhaus, Bloomsburg University

Kathryn Feltey, University of Akron

Juanita Firestone, University of Texas,
San Antonio

Karen Fischer, Fingerlakes Community
College

Rosalind Fisher, University of West Florida

Cynthia Flores-Martinez, San Antonio
College

Patrick Fontane, St. Louis College
of Pharmacy

Rebecca Ford, Florida Community College
at Jacksonville

Craig Forsyth, University of Louisiana,
Lafayette

Mark Foster, Johnson County Community
College

Tony Foster, Kingwood College

Lori Ann Fowler, Tarrant County College

Robert Freymeyer, Presbyterian College

Risa Garelick, Coconino Community
College

Patricia Gibbs, Foothill College

George Glann, Fayetteville Technical
Community College

Cara Gluskoter, Miami-Dade Community
College, North

Marcie Goodman, University of Utah

David Greenwald, Bloomsburg University

Leonard Goodwin, South Carolina State
University

Maia Greenwell-Cunningham, Citrus
College

Sue Greer-Pitt, Southeast Kentucky
Community and Technical College

Laura Gruntmeir, Redlands Community
College

Bram Hamovitch, Lakeland Community
College

Rudy Harris, Des Moines Area
Community College

Anne Hastings, University of North
Carolina, Chapel Hill

Anthony Hatch, University
of Maryland, College Park

Cynthia Hawkins, Hillsborough
Community College, Dale Mabry

Sheldon Helfing, College of the Canyons

Joshua Heller, Fingerlakes Community
College

Lynn Hempel, Mississippi State University

Vicky Herbel, St. Charles Community
College

Idolina Hernandez, Cy-Fair College

Wendell Hester, East Tennessee State
University

Robert J. Hironimus-Wendt, Western
Illinois University

Bruce Hoffman, Ohio University, Athens

Amy Holzgang, Cerritos College

Larry Horn, Los Angeles Pierce College

William Housel, Northwestern Louisiana
State University

Hua-Lun Huang, University of Louisiana,
Lafayette

Jean Humphreys, Dallas Baptist University

Lorraine Ito, Mt. San Antonio College

Carol Jenkins, Glendale Community College

Gaye Jenkins, Pennsylvania College of Technology

Meigan Johnson, Shorter College

Elizabeth Jones, California University of Pennsylvania

Ella Faye Jones, Mississippi Gulf Coast Community College

Kathleen Jones, East Carolina University

Dian Jordan-Werhane, University of Texas at Permian Basin

Judy Kairath, San Jacinto College

Peter Karim-Sesay, Columbus State Community College

Anna Karpathakis, Kingsborough Community College

Mark Kassop, Bergen Community College

Donna Kauffman, Bowling Green State University

Jo Anna Kelly, Walsh University

Dean Ketchum, University of Oklahoma

Bill Kimberlin, Bowling Green State University

Donald King, Dordt College

Theresa Kintz, Wilkes University

Kathleen Korgen, William Paterson University

Vicky Knickerbocker, Inver Hills Community College

Rosalind Kopfstein, Western Connecticut State University

Kathleen Korgen, Millersville University

Susan Krook, Normandale Community College

Lawrence Leavitt, Holyoke Community College

Thomas Lehman, Tallahassee Community College

Donovan Leigh, Anoka Technical College

Jason Leiker, Utah State University

Lora Lempert, University of Michigan, Dearborn

Joseph Lengermann, University of Maryland, College Park

Tunga Lergo, Santa Fe Community College

Charles Levy, Mt. San Antonio College

Jonathan Lewis, Benedictine University

Nkrumah Lewis, University of North Carolina at Greensboro

Marci Littlefield, Indiana University Purdue University Indianapolis

William LoPresti, Hofstra University

Joanna Maatta, Pennsylvania State University

Dennis MacDonald, Saint Anselm College

Ross MacMillan, University of Minnesota

Scott Magnuson-Martinson, Normandale Community College

Kristy Maher, Furman University

Dennis Malaret, Grand Valley State University

Don Malone, St. Peter's College

David Manning, Santa Fe Community College

Kristen Marcussen, Kent State University

Michele Marion, Paradise Valley Community College

Brent Marshall, University of Central Florida

Rosanne Martorella, William Paterson University

Raymond Matura, University of Rio Grande

Marcia Maurycy, Sage College of Albany

Martha Mazzarella, Bowling Green University

Layne McAdoo, Central New Mexico Community College

Kevin McElmurry, University of Missouri

LaDorna McGee, The University of Texas at Arlington

Shelly McGrath, Furman University

Lisa McMinn, George Fox University

Marian McWhorter, Houston Community College, Central

Dave Medina, Mt. San Antonio College

Stephanie Medley-Rath, University of West Georgia

Peter Meiksins, Cleveland State University

Hector Menchaca, Tarrant County College, Southeast

Sarath Menon, Houston Community College, Central

Greta Meszoely, Suffolk University

Kathleen Miller, University at Buffalo

Richard Miller, Missouri Southern State University

Janice Milner, Century College

Monique Moleon-Matthews, Indian River Community College

Tina Mougouris, San Jacinto College

Kelly Moore, University of Cincinnati

Madeline Moran, Lehman College

Amanda Moras, University of Connecticutt

Adam Moskowitz, Columbus State Community College

Tina Mougouris, San Jacinto College

Ken Muir, Appalachian State University

Jeff Mullis, Emory University

Margaret Munro, San Antonio College

Annalyssa Gypsy Murphy, North Shore Community College
Scott Myers, Montana State University
Nader Naderi, Lee College
Art Nishimura, City College of San Francisco
Gwen Nyden, Oakton Community College
Kwaku Obosu-Mensah, Lorain County Community College
Zacchaeus Ogunnika, Virginia State University
Kimberly O'Toole, Mountain State University
Amy Palder, Georgia State University
Wendy Pank, Bismarck State College
Krista Paulsen, University of North Florida
Robert Payne, Mesa Community College
Bennie Perdue, Miami Dade Community College, North
Berry Perlman, Community College of Philadelphia
Jack Peterson, Mesa Community College
Candy Pettus, Orange Coast College
Kim Phillips, Long Beach City College
Candace Pierce, Pulaski Technical College
Wilford Pinkney, John Jay College
Rebecca Plante, Ithaca College
Dwaine Plaza, Oregon State University
Scott Potter, Marion Technical College
Rod Powell, California State University, Long Beach
Saundra Regan, University of Cincinnati
Jo Reger, Oakland University
Paul Rhoads, Williams College
Fernando Rivera, University of Central Florida
Larry Rosenberg, Millersville University
Pamela Rosenberg, Shippensburg University
Nicholas Rowland, Pennsylvania State University, Altoona
Maggie Rubio, Miami-Dade Community College
Ken Rudolph, Asheville Buncombe Technical College
Ivanka Sabolich, Kent State University
Ishmail Said, Macomb Community College
Rita Sakitt, Suffolk County Community College
Ronald Severtis, Jr., Ohio State University
Susan Sharp, University of Oklahoma
Steve Shuecraft, St. Charles Community College
Daniel Schultz, Cayuga Community College
Laurence Segall, Housatonic Community College

Steve Severin, Kellogg Community College
Regina Sewell, Ohio State University at Newark
Stuart Shafer, Johnson County Community College
Nadia Shapkina, Georgia State University
Shanta Sharma, Henderson State University
Susan Sharp, University of Oklahoma
Jerry Shepperd, Austin Community College
Robert Shirilla, Cuyahoga Community College, Metro
Ed Silva, El Paso Community College
Toni Sims, University of Louisiana, Lafayette
Karl Smith, University of Maryland, Eastern Shore
Michelle Smith, Lakeland Community College
William Snizek, Virginia Polytechnic Institute and State University
Brian Matthew Starks, Florida State University
Evelina Sterling, Chattahoochee Technical College
Gail Stewart, Tacoma Community College
George Stewart, Santa Rosa Junior College
James Stewart, Columbus State Community College
Terrence Stewart, Charles S. Mott Community College
Beverly Stiles, Midwestern State University
Steven Stoll, Flagler College
Kell Stone, El Camino College
Brooke Strahn-Koller, Kirkwood Community College
Jolene Sundlie, St. Paul College
Teresa Swartz, University of Minnesota, Minneapolis
Kenneth Szymkowiak, Portland Community College
S. Alexander Takeuchi, University of North Alabama
Zongli Tang, Auburn University at Montgomery
Cheray Teeple, William Paterson University
Mary Jo Tenuto, College of Lake County
Robert Thornburrow, Paris Junior College
Ronald Thrasher, Oklahoma State University
Gary Titchener, Des Moines Area Community College
Robert Torrisi, Cayuga Community College
Elizabeth Tracy, Rhodes State College

Robert Transon, Milwaukee Area Technical College

Anne Tsul, City College of San Francisco

David L. Tutor, Oakland Community College

Alalazu Ugoji, Bishop State Community College

Jodie Vangrov, Chattahoochee Technical College

Connie Veldink, Everett Community College

Dennis Veleber, Michigan State University, Great Falls College of Technology

Daniel Vieira, Moorpark College

Joel Villademoros, El Paso Community College, Valle Verde

Andrea Wagganer, University of South Florida

Dean Wagstaffe, Indian River Community College

Thomas Waller, Tallahassee Community College

Sheryl Walz, Citrus College

Kat Warner, Green River Community College

Margaret Weinberger, Bowling Green State University

George Weiner, Cleveland State University

Donald Wells, Henderson State University

Stephen Wieting, University of Iowa

Matthew Williams, Boston College

Pamela Williams-Paez, College of the Canyons

Debra Williamson, Lansing Community College

George Wilson, University of Miami

Loren Wingblade, Jackson Community College

Helen Wise, Louisiana State University, Shreveport

Sandra Woodside, Modesto Junior College

S. Rowan Wolf, Portland Community College

LaQueta Wright, Richland College

Lenard Wynn, Moraine Valley Community College

Lissa Yogan, Valparaiso University

Brenda Zicha, Charles S. Mott Community College

Herbert Ziegler, Chesapeake College

John Zipp, University of Akron

Sociology Now

chapter 1

It was the best of times, it was the worst of times, it was the age of wisdom, it was the age of foolishness, it was the epoch of belief, it was the epoch of incredulity, it was the season of Light, it was the season of Darkness, it was the spring of hope, it was the winter of despair, we had everything before us, we had nothing before us, we were all going direct to Heaven, we were all going direct the other way—in short, the period was so far like the present period . . . .

— Charles Dickens (1859)

THESE ARE THE FIRST LINES of one of Western literature's greatest novels, *A Tale of Two Cities* by Charles Dickens. In it, Dickens recounts the saga of the French Revolution, at once one of the most exciting, hopeful, and momentous events in history, and among its most bloody, cruel, and tragic, a period of unparalleled optimism about the possibilities of human freedom and some of the most barbaric and repressive measures ever taken in the name of that freedom.

But which is it: best or worst, wisdom or foolishness, light or darkness? Dickens insisted that it was

What Is Sociology?

both—and there lies the essence of sociological thinking. It's difficult to hold both ideas in our heads at the same time. More often, we take a position—usually at one extreme or the other—and then try to hold it in the face of evidence that suggests otherwise. We find it easier to take an extreme position than to occupy a vague middle ground of ambivalence. [doubt]

Sociology is a way of seeing the world. It takes us beyond the "either/or" framing of common sense, and looks at how most social issues are really "both/and."

Besides, logic and common sense insist that it can't possibly be both.

That's what makes sociology so fascinating. Sociology is constantly wrestling with two immense and seemingly contradictory questions: social order and social disorder—how it often feels that everything fits together perfectly, like a smoothly functioning machine, and how everything feels like it's falling apart and society is coming apart at the seams. If every single individual is simply doing what is best for him- or herself, why is there any social order at all? Why are we not constantly at war with each other? And how is order maintained? How is society possible in the first place?

On the other hand, why does it often seem that society is falling apart? Why do so many people in society disobey its laws, disagree about its values, and differ about the political and social goals of the society? Why is there so much crime and delinquency? Why is there so much inequality? Why does society keep changing?

These sorts of giant questions are what sociology sets out to answer. Sociologists analyze the ways that institutions like family, marketplace, military, and government serve to sustain social order and how problems like inequality, poverty, and racial or gender discrimination make it feel as if it is falling apart. And it turns out that most of the answers aren't so obvious or commonsensical after all.

Sociology as a Way of Seeing

If you're like most people, you know that sociology is "the study of society." But we don't typically know much more than that. What is society? And how do we study it?

Unlike other social sciences, the field of sociology is not immediately evident from just its name, like economics or political science. Nor are there many TV or movie characters who are sociologists, as there are psychologists (like Dr. Phil), psychiatrists (Frasier), or anthropologists (Indiana Jones or Lara Croft). In the popular movie *Animal House* (1979), the protagonist encounters two sorority girls at a party. The writers wanted to portray these girls as gum-chomping, air-headed idiots. So what are they majoring in? Right—sociology.

Those who don't know about sociology also tend to dismiss it as not worth knowing about. "Sociology only makes a science out of common sense," was the way it was presented to us when we were students. But, as you will soon see, sociology is far more than that. In fact, what common sense tells us is true often turns out not to be. Sociology may be the field that overturns what we already "know" because of "common sense." It helps us comprehend our world—and understand our place in it.

Sociology sets for itself the task of trying to answer certain basic questions about our lives: the nature of identity, the relationship of the individual to society, our relationships with others. Sociologists try to explain the paradoxes that we daily observe in the world around us: for example, how globalization brings us closer and closer, and, at the same time, seems to drive us further and further apart into smaller religious, tribal, or ethnic enclaves. Or we observe that society is divided into different unequal groups based on class, race, ethnicity, and gender, and yet, at the same time, everyone's values are remarkably similar.

Sociology is both a field of study and a way of seeing. As a field, perhaps the pithi- est definition was written 50 years ago, by C. Wright Mills (1959), a professor at

Columbia University. Sociology, he wrote, is an "imagination," a way of seeing, a way of "connecting biography to history." What Mills means is that the sociological imagination sees our lives as *contextual* lives—our individual identities are sensible only in the social contexts—such as family, or our jobs, or our set of friends—in which we find ourselves. A sociological perspective is a perspective that sees connections and contexts. Sociology connects individuals to the worlds in which we live. Stated most simply, sociology *is the study of human behavior in society.*

Beyond Either/Or: Seeing Sociologically

To help orient you to the field of sociology, read again the quote that begins this chapter. Now, take a look at your local daily newspaper or watch your local TV news. Most of the time, they're telling you how things are getting worse, much worse than they've ever been. Crime waves threaten our safety; dramatic rises in teenage drinking and drug use threaten the survival of the nation; and fundamentalist fanatics make
→ person who
adhere to strict
basic ideas or
principles

the entire world unsafe. We worry about the spiraling divorce rate, the rate of teen pregnancies, the collapse of marriage. We worry about "new" diseases, like SARS; of "old" diseases like smallpox being unleashed as weapons; about costs of prescription medicines; and about the microbial dangers lurking in our food. We fret about the collapse of morality, the decline in religion, the collapse of law and order. We're shocked, outraged, and often frightened when we hear of someone being pushed under a train in a busy New York City subway station. Is the country falling apart?

Perhaps the opposite is true. We're also equally bombarded with stories about the enormous social changes that have made the world a smaller and smaller place, where millions of people can communicate with one another in an instant. Dramatic technological breakthroughs expand the possibilities for trade, cultural exchange, economic development. Scientific advances make it possible to live longer, healthier lives than any people who have ever lived. The mapping of the human genome may enable scientists to eliminate many of the diseases that have plagued human beings for millennia while the rise of the Internet will enable us to communicate that knowledge in a heartbeat. Americans are going to college in greater numbers, and today we have women, African American, Asian American, Hispanic, and gay CEOs, corporate board members, and business owners. Freedom and democracy have spread throughout the world. Is society getting better and better?

Typically, we vacillate between these positions. Sometimes, when it suits us, as when we are examining the behavior of other people, we say that things are getting

fluctuate

worse. This is especially true when older people look at the things that younger people are doing. "When I was a kid . . ." they'll say, "things were a lot better." Other times, often when we are examining our own behavior, we say that things are getting better. "Every day in every way I am getting better and better" is how the mantra of the recovery movement goes. Young people often have to remind older people of all the technological break-throughs that have made their lives healthier, wealthier, and more fun.

To the sociologist, neither of these polar positions is completely true. The sociologist is as concerned about the collapse of traditional social institutions and values as he or she is about the extraordinary ways society is improv-ing. A sociologist is as interested in how things are held together as he or she is in how things are falling apart. Sociologists see *both* sides at once. They don't think in "either/or"; they usually think in "both/and." And what's more, sociologists don't see the glass half full or half empty, as the classic for-mulation of optimist or pessimist goes. Sociologists see the glass half full—and want to know about the quality of the air in the glass. They see the glass half empty and want to know about the quality of the water as well.

For example, as you'll see in this book, most sociologists believe our identities come from *both* nature and nurture; that people are getting *both* richer and poorer (it depends on which people in what places); that our racial and ethnic identities *both* draw us closer together and further fragment us.

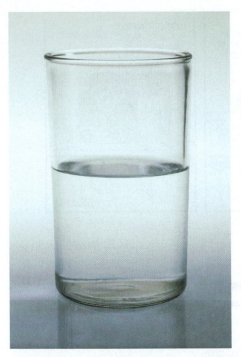

▲ Half full or half empty? We often think we have to choose, but sociologists see the glass as both half full and half empty—and explore the relationship between them.

Making Connections: Sociological Dynamics

The sociologist is interested in the connections between things getting better and things getting worse. In our globalizing world, where daily the farthest reaches of the world are ever more tightly connected to every other part, where changes in one remote cor-ner of Earth ripple through the rest of society, affecting every other institution—in such a world, the sociologist attempts to see both integration and disintegration and the ways in which the one is related to the other.

Take one example. In New York City, we are occasionally aghast that some inno-cent person, calmly waiting for a subway train, is pushed in front of an oncoming train and killed—all for apparently no reason at all. On the freeway, we daily hear of cases of "road rage" that got a little out of control. Instead of merely being con-tent with cutting each other off at more than 70 miles an hour, playing a sort of "free-way chicken" game, or giving each other the finger and cursing at the tops of our lungs, occasionally someone gets really carried away and pulls a gun out of the glove compartment or from the passenger seat and opens fire on a stranger, whose only "crime" might have been to have cut in front of the first driver. Immediately, the head-lines blare that society is falling apart, that violence is on the rise. Psychologists offer therapeutic salve and warn of the increasing dangers of urban or suburban life. "It's a jungle out there," we'll say to ourselves. "These people are nuts."

But sociologists also ask another sort of question: How can so many people drive on clogged freeways, on too-little sleep, inching along for hours, surrounded by mani-acs who are gabbing on their cell phones, ignoring speed limits and basic traffic safety—many also going either toward or away from stressful jobs or unbalanced home lives? How can we stuff nearly two million human beings, who neither know one another nor care very much for any of them, into large metal containers, packed like sardines, hurtling through dark tunnels at more than 60 miles an hour? How is it possible that these same people don't get so murderously angry at their conditions that people aren't pushed in front of subway trains at every single subway stop every single day of the year? How come more people aren't driving armed and dangerous, ready to shoot anyone who worsens an already difficult morning commute?

To a sociologist, social *order* is as intriguing as social breakdown. Sociologists want to know what keeps us from fragmenting into 280 million different parts, and, at the same time, we want to know what drives us in so many millions of directions. We want to know what holds us together and what drives us apart. How is social order possible—especially in a nation in which we believe that each individual is completely free to do as he or she sees fit, where we're all supposed to be "looking out for number 1"? How come, despite all our protests, we also tend to "look out for number 2"?

Is it simply the threat of coercion—that we'd all simply be wreaking murder and mayhem if we weren't afraid of getting caught? We think it's something more, and that's what sociology—and this book—is about.

Sociological Understanding

Our interest is not entirely in social order, nor is it entirely social disintegration and disorder. Let's return for a moment, to that person who pushed someone in front of a subway train. Sure, that person probably needs to have his or her head examined. But a sociologist might also ask about governmental policies that deinstitutionalized millions of mentally ill people, forcing them onto ever-shrinking welfare rolls and often into dramatically overcrowded prisons. And perhaps we need also to examine the dramatic income disparities that collide in our major cities—disparities that make the United States the most unequal industrial country in the world and the modern city as the world's most heterogeneous collection of people from different countries, of different races, speaking different languages in the entire world.

And what about that person who opened fire on a passing motorist? Can we discuss this frightening event without also discussing the availability of guns in America and the paucity of effective gun control laws? Shouldn't we also discuss suburban and urban sprawl, the sorry state of our roads and highways, overwork, the number and size of cars traveling on roads built for one-tenth that many? Or maybe it's just those shock jocks that everyone is listening to in their cars—the guys who keep telling us not to just get mad, but get even?

A comparison with other countries is usually helpful. No other industrial country has this sort of road rage deaths; they are far more common in countries ruled by warlords, in which a motorist might unknowingly drive on "their" piece of the highway. And though many other industrial nations have intricate and elaborate subway systems, people being pushed in front of trains is exceedingly rare. And are those same countries far more homogeneous than the United States with well-financed institutions for the mentally ill or with a more balanced income structure? Or maybe it's that people who live in those countries are just more content with their lives than we are.

These are just two examples of how a sociologist looks at both social order and social breakdown. There are many others that we will discuss in this book. For example, the much-lamented decline in marriage and increase in divorce is accompanied by a dramatic increase in people who want to marry and start families (like lesbians, gay men, and transgendered people) and the dramatically high percentage of people who remarry within three years of divorce—which indicates that most people still believe in the institution. The oft-criticized decline in literacy and "numeracy" among

▲ Order and chaos: Cars proceed in an orderly way on this freeway in Manila, Philippines, despite the "creative" lanes the drivers have developed.

American teenagers is accompanied by equally astonishing increases in competition at America's most elite schools—so much so that many who attended elite schools in the past would not be admitted now.

Doing Sociology

Sure, sociology is an academic field, with a clear object of study and theories that inform that inquiry and various methods that we use to understand it. But just as important, sociology is a kind of posture, a perspective, a way of seeing the world.

Take a look at the course offerings in your school's catalog. Most courses in most fields seem to present part of the field's object of study—except sociology. While about half of our course offerings are about what sociology *is* and *does*—that is, about sociological theory, methods, and specific areas of study—the other half are often listed as what we might call the "sociology ofs"—they offer a sociological perspective on other fields. So we have sociology of: alcohol, art, crime, culture, delinquency, drugs, gender, literature, mass communications, media, music, science, sexuality, and technology.

Sociology is, of course, also a defined subject—and as such it uses theoretical models of how the world works and various methods to understand that world. But sociology is equally a "way of seeing"—a way of organizing all these seemingly contradictory trends—indeed a way of looking at the objects of study of all the other disciplines. The sociological perspective itself is dynamic. It is a difficult position to maintain in the wake of moral certainties asserted from both sides. But it is precisely the fact that such moral certainties are asserted from both sides that makes the mapping of relationships—seeing vices as well as virtues, stability as well as change, order as well as disintegration—that much more imperative. Sociologists see both trends simultaneously, as well as seeing how they are interrelated. ↘ *necessary*

The sociological perspective is not avoidance, nor is it an unwillingness to take a position. In fact, sociologists are involved in designing policies to ameliorate many of the world's most pressing problems. Nor is it the same thing as moral relativism, which is a form of apolitical resignation. Most sociologists have strong political commitments to using their research to make other people's lives better, though they inevitably disagree about what "better" might mean and how best to accomplish it. Finally, the sociological perspective is not to be confused with indifference. Seeing problems as analytically complex doesn't mean that one is uninterested in solving them. *→ become better* *→ not political*

To be a sociologist is to recognize the social complexity of problems—the events we seek to understand have many parts, each connected to the others. It requires that we step back from the immediate pulls of political positions and take into account larger contexts in which problems take shape. And it requires a certain intellectual humility, to acknowledge that none of us can completely grasp the fullness of any problem because the parts are so connected. None of us can see the complete picture.

You probably recall the famous story of the blind men asked to describe an elephant. (The story originated in India, but there are also versions of this folktale in ancient China, twelfth-century Islam, and nineteenth-century England, which gives you the idea that it's a parable that strikes a cross-cultural nerve.) In the story, each man touches a different part of the elephant, and then each, in his arrogance, describes the entire animal. One declares the elephant to be a tree (he felt the leg), another a wall (the side), and others declare it a spear (the tusk), a snake (the trunk),

Thinner and fatter: Only by understanding the global sociology of race, class, and gender can we explain the patterns of both increased starvation and increased obesity. ▼

and so forth. The sociologist realizes that his or her view is partial, and we rely on the perceptions and observations (research) of other social scientists to complete our understanding of the whole picture.

→ inconsistent

Patience and humility are temperamental qualities that are in relatively short supply these days. But they are necessary. The alternatives are even less pleasant: a retreat to idealized and nostalgic notions of moral certainty (which certainly never existed as we romantically recall them now) or some uncritical embrace of the new that leads to a frantic, headlong rush into an uncertain future.

Recall the way you may have argued with your parents. You try to persuade them with what you consider to be reasoned logic ("it makes sense for me to have the keys to the car") or with social trends ("all the other parents let their kids have the keys to the car"). If the argument seems to be going your way, they may retreat to their parental authority as the only way to meet your arguments. "Because I said so, that's why," or "Because I'm the dad." When authority figures retreat to such traditional arguments they may get their way—you may not get to use the car—but you have also won a major ideological victory, forcing them to rely on that tired and soon-to-be-outmoded form of authority instead of meeting your logic with an equally compelling logic of their own.

But should you reply to their rational arguments with equally time-oriented dismissals—such as "it's just the way we do things now" or "that may have worked in your day, but everything is different now"—you may succeed in making them feel older than they actually are, but you've lost the high ground, being unable to meet their idea of reason with reason of your own.

As a sociology professor, I often hear a variant of these positions from students. When presented with evidence of some social problem, they may say, "Well, there's nothing you can do about it. It's always been that way." In the next minute, when confronted with some other evidence about another problem, they're just as likely to say, "Well, the data you have are from 2002. That's old. It's completely different now."

It's not that the students are wrong half the time. It's that we *use* these sorts of statements to avoid dealing with the issues that are presented to us. They're evasions, and we use both of them as the situation seems to warrant. They enable us to avoid any genuine productive engagement with the problem before us.

The sociological perspective accepts neither "timeless" truisms nor constant flux as the grounds for the positions we take. Nor are they adequate as the foundations for understanding social life.

Sociology and Science

Sociology is a social science. To some, this phrase is an oxymoron—a phrase where the terms are opposites, sort of like "jumbo shrimp." It's true that the social sciences cannot match the predictive power of natural science, because people don't behave as predictably as rocks or bacteria or planets. But that doesn't mean that we cannot test hypotheses to discern patterns of behaviors, clusters of attitudes, and structures and institutions that make social life possible.

practical

Some sociologists would not look out of place in a science department: They create hypotheses based on empirical observations of social phenomena, then test them. In other words, they are looking for scientific facts. Other sociologists would not look out of place in a humanities department: They ask open-ended questions to find out what it feels like to belong to a certain social group. In other words, they are looking for the human spirit.

"I'm a social scientist, Michael. That means I can't explain electricity or anything like that, but if you ever want to know about people I'm your man."

One sort of sociologist believes that social phenomena like race, class, deviance, and injustice are as real as natural phenomena and should be studied just as objectively. The other sort believes that social phenomena exist only through human interaction, so they can't be studied objectively at all. One uses numbers (quantitative methods), and the other uses words (qualitative methods). They have different theories. They publish in different journals. Sometimes departments are split into two camps, each accusing the other of not doing "real sociology."

different sides on whether or not sociology should be objective

1 2

no choice/ free will

However, a sociologist who sits down to compare research methods with a chemist or even biologist will find substantial differences. Other scientists work with objects (carbon isotopes, microorganisms) that have no volition, no motivation, no emotion. OK, maybe the higher mammals do, but even they have no hidden agenda, they don't care about presenting themselves in the best possible light, and simply being observed doesn't make them reevaluate their lives. When the object of study is intelligent and aware, you need different techniques and different propositions. For this reason, sociology is a *social* science.

On the other end of the conference table, the sociologist talking to the humanities scholar will also find substantial differences. Humanities scholars look at texts (books, movies, art, music, philosophical treatises) for their own sake. The artists may have described the society they lived in, but the description is always an artistic vision, not meant to be taken as real life. Sociologists try to get at the real life. They engage in systematic observation and hypothesis testing, draw a representative sample. They worry about validity and reliability. And they claim that their research has revealed something about what it was really like to live in a past society (or in a contemporary society). For this reason, sociology is a social *science*.

Some of the questions that sociology poses for itself also distinguish it from the other social sciences. For example, economists follow the processes of individuals who act rationally in markets, such as the labor market. Sociologists are interested in such rational economic calculation but also study behavior that is not rational and that is collective—that is, sociologists typically understand that behavior cannot be reduced to the simple addition of all the rational individuals acting in concert. Psychologists may focus on those group processes—there are branches of psychology and sociology that are both called "social psychology"—but our everyday understandings of psychology are that the problems we observe in our lives can be remedied by adequate therapeutic intervention. Sociologists think these "private troubles" actually more often require social solutions. For example, your individual income may be enhanced by working harder, changing your job, or winning the lottery, but the social problem of poverty will never be solved like that—even if every person worked harder, switched jobs, or won the lottery.

Getting beyond "Common Sense"

However, sociology is not just "common sense"—the other rhetorical retreat from engagement with complex social issues. In fact, very often what we observe to be true turns out, after sociological examination, not to be true. Commonsense explanations trade in stereotypes—"women are more nurturing"; "men are more aggressive"—that are never true for everyone. What's more, common sense assumes that such patterns are universal and timeless—that, for example, men and women are from different planets (Mars and Venus) and that we're programmed somehow to be completely alien creatures. But what if you actually decide you want to be different—that you want to be an aggressive woman or a nurturing man? Can you? Commonsense explanations have no room for variation, and they have no history. And they leave no room for freedom of choice.

You know that old, tired, argument between "nature" and "nurture"? It describes a debate about whether we behave the ways we do because our biology, our "nature," determines our actions—as they say, because we are "hardwired" to do so—or because our ancestors millions of years ago found it to their evolutionary advantage to behave in such a way to ensure their survival? Or, in contrast, do we do the things we do because we have been taught to do them, socialized virtually from the moment we are born by institutions that are bigger and more powerful than we are?

To the sociologist, the answer is clear but complex. Our behavior does not result from *either* nature *or* nurture; our behavior results from *both* nature *and* nature. Looking through a sociological lens reveals that it's not a question of either/or. It's all about seeing the both/and and investigating how that relationship is playing out. Of course the things we do are the result of millennia of evolutionary adaptation to our environments, and of course we are biologically organized to do some things and not others. But that environment also includes the social environment. We adapt to the demands and needs of the social contexts in which we find ourselves, too. And we frequently override our biological drives to do things that we are *also* biologically programmed to do. Just as we are hardwired to preserve ourselves at all costs, we are also biologically programmed to sacrifice our own lives for the survival of the group or for our offspring. Were that not true, all those firefighters who ran up the twin towers of the World Trade Center acted against their "nature."

But to the sociologist, the two sides of the nature–nurture debate share one thing in common: They make the individual person a passive object of larger forces, with no real ability to act for him- or herself and therefore no role in history. According to nature lovers and nurturers, we can't help doing what we do: We're either biologically destined or socially programmed to act as we do. "Sorry, it's in my genes!" is pretty much the same thing as "Sorry, I was socialized to do it!"

Neither of these positions sees the *interaction* of those forces as decisive. That is the domain of sociology.

What makes a more thorough analysis of social life possible and makes the sociological perspective possible is the way we have crafted the lens through which we view social problems and processes. It is a lens that requires that we set events in their contexts and yet remain aware of how we, as individuals, shape both the contexts and the events in which we participate.

A sociological perspective helps you to see how the events and problems that preoccupy us today are timeless; they do not come from nowhere. They have a history. They are the result of the actions of large-scale forces—forces that are familial, communal, regional, national, or global. And they enable you to see the connections between those larger-scale forces and your own experience, your own participation in them. Sociologists understand that this history is not written beforehand; it is changeable, so that you can exert some influence on how it turns out.

That's why Mills's definition of the sociological imagination, the connection between biography and history, is as compelling today as when it was written half a century ago. Sociology connects you, as an individual, to the larger processes of both stability and change that compose history.

▲ Nature and nurture: Sociology explores how we construct our individual identities through the interaction of our biological inheritance with social categories such as race, class, and gender.

Sociology and our World

More than Just Common Sense

Does sociology merely give a scientific face to what we already know? Actually, it turns out that many of the things we know by common sense are not true at all. It may be that sociology's single most important contribution is to debunk (disprove) those common-sense ideas.

For example, a large majority of Americans believe the following statements to be true:

1. The United States is a meritocracy, in which any individual can rise to the top as long as he or she works hard enough.
2. The poor are poor because of individual factors, such as laziness, lack of thrift, poor money management skills, or lack of effort or talent.
3. Men are from Mars and women are from Venus—that is, there are fundamental, unchanging, biologically based differences between women and men.
4. Most welfare recipients are minorities who live in large cities.

5. People who live together before they get married are less likely to get divorced because they have already had a "trial marriage."
6. There is very little racial discrimination remaining in the United States, and the racism that remains is because of racist individuals who give everyone else a bad name.
7. Women and men are just about equal now, and so there is no need for feminists to complain all the time.
8. A woman who is beaten up or abused in her relationship has only herself to blame if she stays.
9. Only people who are unstable mentally commit suicide.
10. The person most likely to rape or sexually assault a woman is a stranger on a dark street.

It turns out that every one of these commonsense assumptions is empirically false. (Each one of them is discussed in the chapters of this book.) As a result, very often the task of sociology is not only to understand why these "facts" are untrue. Sociologists also try to understand why we want so much to believe them anyway.

Where Did Sociology Come From?

The questions that animate sociology today—individuals, progress, freedom, inequality, power—were the founding ideas of the field. Sociology emerged in Europe in the early nineteenth century. At that time, European society had just passed through a calamitous period in which the Enlightenment, the French Revolution, and the beginnings of the Industrial Revolution had dramatically transformed European society.

Before Sociology

Even in the seventeenth and eighteenth centuries, philosophers were attempting to understand the relationship of the individual and society. Political revolutions and intellectual breakthroughs led to this period being called "The Age of Reason" or the "Enlightenment." Theorists challenged the established social order, like the rule of the monarchy and hereditary aristocracy, and the ideas that justified it, like the "divine right of kings"—that kings ruled because they were ordained by God. British, French, and eventually American social thinkers began to envision a society as a purposeful gathering together of free individuals, not the result of birth and divine mandate. It was during the Enlightenment of the seventeenth and eighteenth centuries that the idea of the "individual" took shape, and philosophers came to understand the individual as the foundation of society.

John Locke (1632–1704), for example, believed that society was formed through the rational decisions of free individuals, who join together through a "social contract" to form society. Society permits and even facilitates the free movement of goods, making life easier and more predictable. The purpose of government, Locke argued ([1689] 1988), was to resolve disagreements between individuals, and ensure people's rights—but that's all. If the government goes too far, Locke believed, and becomes a sort of omnipotent state, the people have a right to revolution and to institute a new government.

In France, meanwhile, Jean-Jacques Rousseau (1712–1788) had a rather different perspective. Rousseau ([1754] 2004) believed that people were basically good and innocent, but that private property creates inequality, and, with it unhappiness and immorality. Rousseau believed that a collective spirit, what he called the "general will," would replace individual greed and that through social life people could be free—but only if they were equal.

These two themes—Locke's emphasis on individual liberty and Rousseau's idea that society enhanced freedom—came together in the work of Thomas Jefferson, when he penned the Declaration of Independence in 1776, the founding document of the United States. That document asserted that all men are equal in rights and that government is the servant, not the master, of human beings. Jefferson fused Rousseau's vision of a community with Locke's ideal of individual freedom, limited government, and free exchange of ideas into a document that continues to inspire people the world over.

These ideas—"discovery" of the individual, the relationship of the individual to society, and the regulation of individual freedom by governments—were the critical ideas circulating in Europe on the eve of the nineteenth century. And these were among the fundamental questions addressed by the new field of sociology.

The Invention of Sociology

The economic and political changes heralded by the American Revolution of 1776 and the French Revolution of 1789 were in part inspired by the work of those Enlightenment thinkers. Between 1776 and 1838, European society had undergone a dramatic change—politically, economically, and intellectually. The American and French Revolutions replaced absolutist kings with republics, where power rested not on the divine right of kings but on the consent of the people. The Industrial Revolution reorganized the production and distribution of goods from the quaint system of craft production, in which apprentices learned trades and entered craft guilds, to large-scale factory production in which only the very few owned the factories and many workers had only their ability to work to sell to the highest bidder.

The foundation of society, one's identity, the nature of politics, and economics changed fundamentally between the collapse of the "old regime" in the late eighteenth century, and the rise of the new "modern" system in the middle of the nineteenth century (Table 1.1).

The chief sociological themes to emerge from these changes included:

1. *The nature of community*. What does it mean to live in a society; what rights and obligations do we have to each other?

2. *The nature of government*. Should power reside in the hands of a king who rules by divine right, or in the people, who alone can consent to be governed?

TABLE 1.1

Contrasting the "Old Regime" and the New Social Order		
	OLD REGIME	NEW ORDER
Basis of economy	Land	Property
Location of economic activity	Rural manors	Urban factories
Source of identity	Kinship	Work
	Status/caste	Class
Ideology	Religion	Science
Type of government	Monarchy	Republic
Basis of government	Divine right	Popular consent

3. *The nature of the economy.* Should only a few people have most of the wealth and most of the people have very little, or should it be more fairly distributed?

4. *The meaning of individualism.* What rights and responsibilities does an individual have toward him- or herself and to others?

5. *The rise of secularism.* How can religious ideas about God and morality be reconciled with scientific beliefs about rationality and economic ideas about the marketplace?

6. *The nature and direction of change.* Where are we heading? Is it, as Dickens said, writing about this very time, the best of times or the worst of times?

This dramatic change in American and European society—the Industrial Revolution, the political revolutions in America in 1776 and France in 1789—changed the way we saw the world. Even the language that we used to describe that world was transformed. It was during this era that the following words were first used with the meaning they have today: *industry, factory, middle class, democracy, class, intellectual, masses, commercialism, bureaucracy, capitalism, socialism, liberal, conservative, nationality, engineer, scientist, journalism, ideology*—and, of course, *sociology* (Hobsbawm, 1962). Politically, some revolutionists thought we should continue those great movements; conservatives thought we'd gone too far, and it was time to retreat to more familiar social landscapes.

Sociologists both praised and criticized these new developments.

Classical Sociological Thinkers

The word *sociology* itself was introduced in 1838 by a French theorist, Auguste Comte. To him, it meant "the scientific study of society." Most of the earliest sociologists embraced a notion of progress—that society passed through various stages from less developed to more developed and that this progress was positive, both materially and morally. This notion of progress is central to the larger intellectual project of "modernism" of which sociology was a part. *Modernism*—the belief in evolutionary progress, through the application of science—challenged tradition, religion, and aristocracies as remnants of the past and saw industry, democracy, and science as the wave of the future.

Auguste Comte. Comte (1798–1857) believed that each society passed through three stages of development based on the form of knowledge that provided its foundation: religious, metaphysical, and scientific. In the religious or theological stage, supernatural forces are understood to control the world. In the metaphysical stage, abstract forces and what Comte called "destiny" or "fate" are perceived to be the prime movers of history. Religious and metaphysical knowledge thus rely on superstition and speculation, not science. In the scientific, or "positive," stage (the origin of the word *positivism*) events are explained through the scientific method of observation, experimentation, and analytic comparison.

Comte believed that, like the physical sciences, which explain physical facts, sociology must rely on science to explain social facts. Comte saw two basic facts to be explained: "statics," the study of order, persistence, and organization; and "dynamics," the study of the processes of social change. Comte believed that sociology would become "the queen of the sciences," shedding light on earlier sciences and synthesizing all previous knowledge about the natural world with a science of the social world. Sociology, he believed, would reveal the principles and laws that affected

▲ Auguste Comte coined the term *sociology* as the scientific study of society.

the functioning of all societies. Comte hoped that the scientific study of society would enable sociologists to guide society toward peace, order, and reform (Comte, 1975).

Comte's preoccupation with sociology as a science did not lead him to shy away from moral concerns; indeed, Comte believed that a concern for moral progress should be the central focus of all human sciences. Sociology's task was to help society become better. In fact, sociology was a sort of "secular religion," a religion of humanity, Comte argued. And he, himself, was its highest minister. Toward the end of his life, he fancied himself a secular prophet and signed his letters "the Founder of Universal Religion, Great Priest of Humanity." (Some sociologists today also suffer from a similar lack of humility!)

After Comte, the classical era of sociological thought began. Sociologists have never abandoned his questions: The questions of order and disorder, persistence and change, remain foundations of contemporary and classical sociological thought.

Alexis de Tocqueville. Alexis de Tocqueville (1805–1859), a French social theorist and historian, is known for studies of American democracy and the French Revolution. Tocqueville saw the United States as the embodiment of democracy. Without a feudal past that tied us to outdated ideas of kingship or aristocracy and with nearly limitless land on which the country could grow prosperous, democracy flourished. But democracy contains tensions and creates anxieties that European societies did not face.

Tocqueville's greatest insight is that democracy can either enhance or erode individual liberty. On the one hand, democracy promises increasing equality of conditions and increasingly uniform standards of living. On the other hand, it also concentrates power at the top and weakens traditional sources of liberty, like religion or the aristocracy (which he believed were strong enough to protect individuals from encroachments by the state). Democracies can lead to mass society, in which individuals feel powerless, and are easily manipulated by the media. As a result, democratic societies are faced with two possible outcomes, free institutions or despotism. When he tried to predict the direction America was heading, he thought it depended on Americans' ability to prevent the concentration of wealth and power and on the free spirit of individuals. And the solution, he believed, lay in "intermediate institutions"—the way that Americans, as a nation of "joiners," developed small civic groups for every conceivable issue or project.

Karl Marx. Karl Marx (1818–1883) was the most important of all socialist thinkers. He was also a sociologist and economist who supported himself by journalism but lived the life of an independent intellectual and revolutionary. Marx's greatest sociological insight was that class was the organizing principle of social life; all other divisions would eventually become class divisions.

Marx's great intellectual and political breakthrough came in 1848 (Marx and Engels, [1848] 1998). Before that, he had urged philosophers to get their heads out of the clouds and return to the real world—that is, he urged them towards "materialism," a focus on the way people organize their society to solve basic "material" needs such as food, shelter, and clothing as the basis for philosophy, not "idealism," with its focus on society as the manifestation of either sacred or secular ideas. As revolutions were erupting all across Europe, he saw his chance to make that philosophy into a political movement. With Engels, he wrote *The Communist Manifesto*. Asserting that all history had "hitherto been the history of class

Did you know?

Tocqueville's most famous book, *Democracy in America* (1835), is perhaps the most famous analysis of American society ever written. But it actually happened by accident. Tocqueville came to the United States to study a major innovation in the American penal system that he regarded as especially enlightened. The reform? Solitary confinement, which was initially a reform that would give the otherwise "good" person a chance to reflect on his actions and begin to reform himself.

Did you know?

To earn enough money to write his books, Marx also served as a journalist. His coverage of the American Civil War, which he saw as a clash between the feudal South and the capitalist North, was published all over Europe.

Kirk Anderson, www.kirktoons.com. Used by permission.

▲ **Karl Marx argued that as capitalism progressed, the rich would get richer and the poor would get poorer—until it exploded in revolution.**

struggles," the *Manifesto* linked the victory of the proletariat (the working class) to the development of capitalism itself, which dissolved traditional bonds, like family and community, and replaced them with the naked ties of self-interest.

Initially, Marx believed, capitalism was a revolutionary system itself, destroying all the older, more traditional forms of social life and replacing them with what he called "the cash nexus"—one's position depended only on wealth, property, and class. But eventually, capitalism suppresses all humanity, drowning it in "the icy waters of egotistical calculation." We are not born greedy or materialistic; we become so under capitalism.

His central work was *Capital*, a three-volume work that laid out a theory of how capitalism worked as a system. His central insight was that the exchange of money and services between capital (those who own the means of production) and labor (those who sell their "labor power" to capitalists for wages) is unequal. Workers must work longer than necessary to pay for the costs of their upkeep, producing what Marx called "surplus value." And because of competition, capitalists must try to increase the rate of surplus value. They do this by replacing human labor with machines, lowering wages (and cutting any benefits) until workers can't afford even to consume the very products they are producing, and by centralizing their production until the system reaches a crisis. Thus capitalists are not only fighting against labor, but they are also competing against each other. Eventually, Marx believed, it would all come tumbling down.

This work inspired socialists all over the world who saw the growing gap between rich and poor as both a cause for despair about the conditions of the poor, and an occasion for political organizing. Marx believed that the "laws of motion" of capitalism would bring about its own destruction as the rich got so rich and the poor got so poor that they would revolt against the obvious inequity of the system. Then workers would rise up and overthrow the unequal capitalist system and institute communism—the collective ownership of all property.

Marx believed this would take place first in the industrial countries like Britain and Germany, but the socialist revolutions of the twentieth century that used Marx as inspiration were in largely peasant societies, like Russia and China, for example. Nowhere in the world has Marx's political vision been implemented. His economic theory that the development of capitalism tends to concentrate wealth and power, however, has never been more true than today, when the gap between rich and poor is greater than ever in U.S. history. Currently, the richest 1 percent of people in the world receive as much income as the bottom 5 percent. Globally, the United States has the most unequal distribution of income of all high-income nations (UC Atlas of Global Inequality, 2007).

Emile Durkheim. Emile Durkheim (1858–1917) was a master of sociological inquiry. He searched for distinctly social origins of even the most individual and personal of issues. His greatest work, *Suicide* (1897), is a classic example of his sociological imagination. On the surface, suicide appears to be the ultimate individual act. Yet Durkheim argued that suicide is profoundly social, an illustration of how connected an individual

How do we know what we know?

Suicide Is a Social Act

On the surface, there is no act more personal or individual than suicide. Taking your own life is almost always explained by individual psychopathology because a person must be crazy to kill him- or herself. If that's true, Durkheim reasoned, suicide would be distributed randomly among the population; there would be no variation by age, religion, region, or marital status, for example.

Yet that is exactly what he found; suicide varies by:

1. *Religion*. Protestants commit suicide far more often than Catholics, and both commit suicide more often than Jews (he did not measure Muslims).
2. *Age*. Young people and old people commit suicide more often than middle-aged people.
3. *Marital status*. Single people commit suicide more often than married people.
4. *Gender*. Men commit suicide more often than women.
5. *Employment*. Unemployed people commit suicide more often than the employed.

Because we can assume that unemployed, unmarried young male Protestants are probably no more likely to be mentally ill than any other group, Durkheim asked what each of these statuses might contribute to keeping a person from suicide. And he determined that the "function" of each status is to embed a person in a community, to provide a sense of belonging, of "integrating" the person into society.

What's more, these statuses also provided rules to live by, solid norms that constrain us from spinning wildly out of control, that "regulate" us. The higher the level of integration and regulation, Durkheim reasoned, the lower the level of suicide. Too little integration led to what Durkheim called "egoistic" suicide, in which the individual kills him- or herself because they don't feel the connection to the group. Too little regulation led to what Durkheim called "anomic" suicide, in which the person floats in a sense of normlessness and doesn't know the rules that govern social life or when those rules change dramatically.

But sometimes there can be too much integration, where the individual completely loses him- or herself in the group and therefore would be willing to kill him- or herself to benefit the group. A suicide that resulted from too much integration is one Durkheim called "altruistic"—think of suicide bombers, for example. And sometimes people feel overregulated, trapped by rules that are not of their own making, that lead to what Durkheim called "fatalistic" suicide. Durkheim saw this type of suicide among slaves, for example, or, as he also hypothesized, "very young husbands." Why do you think he thought that?

Types of Suicide and Integration and Regulation

	Too little	Too much
Level of integration	Egoistic	Altruistic
Level of regulation	Anomic	Fatalistic

Durkheim's methodological innovation was to find a way to measure something as elusive as integration or regulation—the glue that holds society together and connects us to each other. Ironically, he found the way to "see" integration and regulation at those moments it wasn't there!

---

feels to others. Durkheim tried to measure the amount of integration (how connected we feel to social life) and regulation (the amount that our individual freedoms are constrained) by empirically examining what happens when those processes fail.

In a sense, Durkheim turned the tables on economists who made a simple linear case that freedom was an unmitigated good and that the more you have the happier you will be. Durkheim argued that too much freedom might reduce the ties that one feels to society and therefore make one *more* likely to commit suicide, not less!

Durkheim's study of suicide illustrated his central insight: that society is held together by "solidarity," moral bonds that connect us to the social collectivity. "Every society is a moral society," he wrote. Social order, he claimed, cannot be accounted for by the pursuit of individual self-interest; solidarity is emotional, moral, and non-rational. Rousseau had called this "the general will," Comte called it "consensus," but neither had attempted to actually study it (see also Durkheim, [1893] 1997).

In traditional society, solidarity is relatively obvious: Life is uniform and people are similar; they share a common culture and sense of morality that Durkheim characterizes as **mechanical solidarity**. In modern society, with its division of labor and diverse and conflicting interests, common values are present but less obvious. People are interdependent, and Durkheim calls this **organic solidarity**.

Durkheim's influence has been immense, not only in sociology, where he ranks with Marx and Weber as one of the founders of the discipline, but in anthropology, social psychology, and history. Durkheim's use of statistics was pioneering for his time, and his concept of the "social fact," his rigorous comparative method, and his functional style of analysis have been widely adopted (Durkheim, [1895] 1997). His emphasis on society as a moral entity has served as a powerful critique of abstract individualism and rationality and of a definition of freedom that places human liberty in opposition to society.

Max Weber. Max Weber (1864–1920) was an encyclopedic scholar whose expertise left hardly a field untouched. But his chief interest in all his studies was the extraordinary importance of "rationality" in the modern world. His major insights were that rationality was the foundation of modern society and that while rationality organized society in more formal, legal, and predictable ways, it also trapped us in an "iron cage" of bureaucracy and meaninglessness.

To understand society, Weber developed a sociology that was both "interpretive" and "value free." Weber's interpretive sociology understands social relationships by showing the sense they make to those who are involved in them. Weber also insisted that experts separate their personal evaluations from their scientific pronouncements because such value judgments cannot be logically deduced from facts. By protecting science from the taint of ideology, Weber hoped also to protect political debate from unwarranted claims by experts. "Value freedom" does not mean sociologists should not take political positions but that we must use value judgments to select subjects deemed worthy of research and must engage with the minds and feelings of the people being studied.

Weber's most famous work, *The Protestant Ethic and the Spirit of Capitalism* (1904, 1905), was a study of the relationship of religious ideas to economic activity. What made European capitalism unique, he argued, was its connection to the ideas embodied in the Protestant Reformation, ideas that enabled individuals to act in this world. Essentially, Weber argued that the Puritan ethic of predestination led to a deep-seated need for clues about whether one is saved or not. Seeking some indication, Protestants, particularly Calvinists, began to value material success and worldly profit as signs of God's favor.

At the end, however, Weber was pessimistic. Rationality can free us from the theocratic past but also imprison us in an "iron cage"—an utterly dehumanized and mechanized world. Like Marx, Weber believed that the modern capitalist order brought out the worst in us. "In the field of its highest development, in the United States, the pursuit of wealth, stripped of its religious and ethical meaning, tends to become associated with purely mundane passions, which often actually give it the character of sport."

And like Marx, Weber believed that, in the long run, class was the most significant division among people. But Weber had a more complicated understanding. At any one moment, he wrote, there are other, less economic, factors that divide people from each other, as well as unite them into groups. To class, Weber added the idea of "status" and "party." "Party" referred to voluntary organizations that people would enter together to

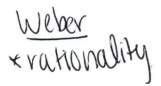

Weber
+ rationality

Max Weber introduced purely social processes, like charisma and status, as sources of identity and inequality. ▼

make their voices heard collectively because individually we would be unable to affect real change.

While one's class position was objective, based on the position in the labor market, status groups were based, Weber believed, on social factors—what other people thought about one's lifestyle. Class is based on one's relationship to production; status is based on one's relationship to consumption. While people really couldn't do much about class, they can definitely try to transform their status, since it depends on how others see them. The desire to have others see one as belonging to a higher status group than one actually belongs to leads to extraordinary patterns of consumption—buying very expensive cars and homes to "show off" or "keep up with the Joneses," for example.

In later writings, Weber argued that the characteristic form of modern organization—whether in the state, the corporation, the military, university, or church—is bureaucratic. Whereas Marx predicted a revolution that would shatter capitalism, and Durkheim foresaw new social movements that would reunify people, Weber saw a bleak future in which individual freedom is increasingly compressed by corporations and the state.

Weber's often dense and difficult prose was matched by the enormous range of his writings and the extraordinary depth of his analysis. He remains the most deft thinker of the first generation of classical theorists, both appreciating the distinctiveness of Western society's promotion of individual freedom and deploring its excesses, celebrating rational society, and fearing the "iron cage" of an overly rational world.

Georg Simmel. Georg Simmel (1858–1918) is among the most original and far-ranging members of the founding generation of modern sociology. Never happy within the academic division of labor, he contributed to all of the social sciences but remained primarily a philosopher.

Simmel was in quest of a subject matter for sociology that would distinguish it from the other social sciences and the humanistic disciplines. He found this not in a new set of topics but in a method, or rather, in a special point of view. The special task of sociology is to study the *forms* of social interaction apart from their content. Simmel assumes that the same social forms—competition, exchange, secrecy, domination—could contain quite different content, and the same social content could be embodied in different forms. It mattered less to Simmel what a person was competing about, or whether domination was based on sheer force, monetary power, or some other basis: What mattered to him was the ways that these forms of domination or competition had specific, distinctive properties.

Forms arise as people interact with one another for the sake of certain purposes or to satisfy certain needs. They are the processes by which individuals combine into groups, institutions, nations, or societies. Forms may gain autonomy from the demands of the moment, becoming larger, more solid structures that stand detached from even opposed to, the continuity of life. Some forms may be historical, like "forms of development"—stages that societies might pass through. Unlike Marx, Durkheim, or Weber, then, Simmel never integrated his work into an overarching scheme. Instead he gathered a rich variety of contents under each abstract form, allowing for new and startling comparisons among social phenomena.

While this all sounds somewhat "formal" and abstract, Simmel's major concern was really about individualism. His work is always animated by the question of what the social conditions are that make it easier for persons to discover and express their individuality. In modern society, with its many cultural and social groups, individuals are caught in crosscutting interests and expectations. We belong to so many groups, and each demands different things of us. Always aware of the double-edged sword that characterizes sociology, Simmel saw both sides of the issue. For example, in his major philosophical work on money, he argued that money tends to trivialize human relationships, making them more instrumental and calculable, but it also enlarges the possibilities of freedom of expression and expands the possibilities for action.

Like a good sociologist, Simmel argued that money is neither the root of all evil nor the means to our emancipation: It's both.

American Sociological Thinkers

Three American sociologists from the first decades of the twentieth century took the pivotal ideas of European sociology and translated them into a more American version. They have each, since, joined the classical *canon* or officially recognized set of foundational sociologists.

Thorstein Veblen. Thorstein Veblen (1857–1929) is best known for his bitingly satirical work, *The Theory of the Leisure Class* (1899). Here, he argued that America was split in two, between the "productive"—those who work—and the "pecuniary"—those who have the money. That is, he divided Americans into workers and owners, respectively. The wealthy, he argued, weren't productive; they lived off the labor of others, like parasites. They spent their time engaged in competitive displays of wealth and prestige, which he called "conspicuous consumption"—consumption that is done because it is visible and because it invites a certain social evaluation of "worth." One comes to advertise wealth through wasteful consumption.

He also saw a tension between the benevolent forces of technology and the profit system that distorts them. He contrasted the rationality of work, of the machine process and its personnel, to the irrational caprices of speculators, financiers, and the wealthy who squander valuable goods so as to win prestige. Modern society was neither a simple Marxian class struggle between the malevolent wealthy owners and their naïve and innocent workers, nor was technology inevitably leading to either social uplift or social decay. It was not a matter of the technology but of its ownership and control and the uses to which it was put.

Lester Ward. Lester Ward (1841–1913) was one of the founders of American sociology and the first to free it from the biological fetters of the Darwinian model of social change. Ward rebelled against **social Darwinism**, which saw each succeeding society as improving on the one before it. Instead, Ward stressed the need for social planning and reform, for a "sociocratic" society that later generations were to call a welfare state. His greatest theoretical achievement, called the theory of "social telesis," was to refute social Darwinism, which held that those who ruled deserved to do so because they had "adapted" best to social conditions (Ward, [1883] 1969).

Ward argued that, unlike Darwinist predictions, natural evolution proceeded in an aimless manner, based on adaptive reactions to accidents of nature. In nature, evolution was more random, chaotic, and haphazard than social Darwinists imagined. But in society, evolution was informed by purposeful action, which he called "social telesis."

Ward welcomed the many popular reform movements because he saw enlightened government as the key to social evolution. Education would enable the common man and woman to participate as democratic citizens. The bottom layers of society, the proletariat, women, even the underclass of the slums, are by nature the equals of the "aristocracy of brains," he wrote. They lack only proper instruction.

George Herbert Mead. George Herbert Mead (1863–1931) studied the development of individual identity through social processes. He argued that what gave us our identity was the product of our interactions with ourselves and with others, which is based on the distinctly human capacity for self-reflection. He distinguished between the "I," the part of us that is inherent and biological, from the "me," the part of us that is self-conscious and created by observing ourselves in interaction.

The "me" is created, he said, by managing the **generalized other**, by which he meant a person's notion of the common values, norms, and expectations of other people in a society. Thus Mead developed a distinctly *social* theory of the self (the "me")—one that doesn't bubble up from one's biology alone but a self that takes shape only through interaction with society (Mead, 1967).

This "pragmatic" approach—in which one examines social phenomena as they occur—actually made Mead optimistic. Mead believed that each of us develops through play, first by making up the rules as we go along, to later being able to follow formal rules, and still later by learning to "take the role of the other"—to put ourselves in others' shoes. The ability to step outside of ourselves turns out to be the crucial step in developing a "self" that is fully able to interact with others. Mead's work is the foundation for much of the sociological research in interactionism.

The "Other" Canon

Thus far, you've probably noticed, the classical **canon** of sociology has consisted entirely of White males. And for many years, American sociology listed only these great pioneers as the founders of the field. Others, equally influential in their time, were either ignored or their contributions downplayed. In the 1930s, as sociology was seeking legitimacy as an academic discipline, theorists who had emphasized inequality and diversity were marginalized and excluded from the canon of the field's pioneers, but they first pointed out the ways in which inequality and identity are both derived from race, class, ethnicity, and gender. As a result, to discuss them now is not to capitulate to some form of political correctness; it is instead an effort to return them to their earlier prominence and recognize that at any moment in history—including the present—there are many competing theoretical models.

Two theorists, one British and one American, brought women's position and gender inequality into the center of their writing. Mary Wollstonecraft (1759–1797), a passionate advocate of the equality of the sexes, has been called the first major feminist. Many of her ideas, such as equal education for the sexes, the opening of the professions to women, and her critique of marriage as a form of legal prostitution, were shocking to her contemporaries but have proven remarkably visionary. In her classic book, Wollstonecraft argued that society couldn't progress if half its members are kept backward, and she proposed broad educational changes for both boys and girls.

But she also suggested the problems are cultural. Women contribute to their own oppression. Women accept their powerlessness in society because they can use their informal interpersonal sexual power to seduce men, an enterprise that is made easier if they also deceive themselves. Men who value women not as rational beings but as objects of pleasure and amusement allow themselves to be manipulated, and so the prison of self-indulgence corrupts both sexes. Wollstonecraft was the first classical theorist to apply the ideas of the Enlightenment to the position of women—and find the Enlightenment, not women, to be the problem!

Margaret Fuller (1810–1850) was America's first female foreign correspondent. Her book *Woman in the Nineteenth Century* (1845) became the intellectual foundation of the American women's movement. The book is a bracing call for complete freedom and equality, a call that "every path be open to woman as freely as to man." Fuller calls on women to become self-reliant and not expect help from men and introduces the concept of sisterhood—women must help one another, no matter whether they are scholars, servants, or prostitutes. Her research documents women's capabilities from an immense catalogue of mythology, folklore, the Bible, classical antiquity, fiction, and history. She explores the image of woman, in all its ambiguity, within literature and myth,

> ## Did *you* know?
>
> Mary Wollstonecraft's daughter, Mary, married the great British poet Percy Shelley. Mary Shelley was the author of the classic gothic horror novel *Frankenstein*.

▲ **W. E. B. Du Bois identified racism as the most pressing social problem in America—and the world.**

Charlotte Perkins Gilman argued that defining women solely by their reproductive role is harmful to women—as well as to men, children, and society. ▼

and asserts "no age was left entirely without a witness of the equality of the sexes in function, duty, and hope." She also calls for an end to sexual stereotyping and the sexual double standard.

Frederick Douglass (1817–1895) was the most important African American intellectual of the nineteenth century. He lived 20 years as a slave and nearly 9 as a fugitive slave, and then achieved international fame as an abolitionist, editor, orator, and the author of three autobiographies. These gave a look into the world of oppression, resistance, and subterfuge within which the slaves lived.

↳ deception/ cheat

Sociologically, Douglass's work stands as an impassioned testament to the cruelty and illogic of slavery, claiming that *all* human beings were equally capable of being full individuals. His work also reveals much about the psychological world of slaves: its sheer terror but also its complexities. Its portraits of slave owners range from parody to denunciation and, in one case, even respect, and all serve Douglass's principal theme: that slaveholding, no less than the slave's own condition, is learned behavior and presumably can be unlearned.

W. E. B. Du Bois (1868–1963) was the most articulate, original, and widely read spokesman for the civil rights of black people for a period of over 30 years. A social scientist, political militant, essayist, and poet, he wrote nineteen books and hundreds of articles, edited four periodicals, and was a founder of the NAACP and the Pan-African movement. His work forms a bridge between the nineteenth century and the Civil Rights movement of the 1960s. Today he is recognized as one of the greatest sociologists in our history, and the American Sociological Association recently voted to name the annual award for the most influential book after him.

Du Bois believed that race was the defining feature of American society, that, as he put it, "the problem of the twentieth century was the problem of the color line," and that, therefore, the most significant contribution he could make toward achieving racial justice would be a series of scientific studies of the Negro. In 1899, he published *The Philadelphia Negro*, the first study ever of Black people in the United States; he planned an ambitious set of volumes that would together finally understand the experiences of the American Negro (Du Bois, [1903] 1999).

Du Bois also explored the psychological effects of racism, a lingering inner conflict. "One feels ever his two-ness—an American, a Negro, two souls, two thoughts, two unreconciled strivings; two warring ideals in one dark body, whose dogged strength alone keeps it from being torn asunder." His work defines a "moment in history when the American Negro began to reject the idea of the world belonging to white people." Gradually disillusioned with White people's resistance to integration, Du Bois eventually called for an increase in power and especially economic autonomy, the building of separate Black businesses and institutions.

Most readers who know Charlotte Perkins Gilman (1860–1935) at all know her for her short story "The Yellow Wallpaper" (1899), or for her novel, *Herland* (1915). But sociologists know her for her groundbreaking *Women and Economics* (1898), a book in which she explores the origin of women's subordination and its function in evolution. Woman makes a living by marriage, not by the work she does, and so man becomes her economic environment. As a consequence her female qualities dominate her human ones, because it is the female traits through which she earns her living. Women are raised to market their feebleness, their docility, and so on, and these qualities are then called "feminine."

Gilman was one of the first to see the need for innovations in child rearing and home maintenance that would ease the burdens of working women. She envisaged

↓ agreement

↓ imagined

Try It Historical Figures in Sociology Examined

OBJECTIVE: Explore one of the historical figures in sociology and examine his or her significance to sociology.

STEP 1: Plan
Your instructor may assign each student a historical figure to examine in more detail.

STEP 2: Research
Search the Internet and other library resources to find detailed information on your historical figure. Include information like:
▶ Name, date, and location of birth and death
▶ Picture (if you can locate one)

▶ Educational background and a list of significant writings
▶ Brief discussion of most important sociological contribution
▶ Critiques of this historical figure and obstacles faced by this historical figure
▶ List all resources used in this project

STEP 3: Discuss
▶ Be prepared to either turn in your findings or share them in class.

housework as being like any other kind of work—as a public, social activity no different from shoemaking or shipbuilding. In her fiction she imagines a range of institutions that overcome the isolation of women and children, such as communal kitchens, day care centers, and city plans that foster camaraderie rather than withdrawal. For women, as well as for men, she wrote in her autobiography, "[t]he one predominant duty is to find one's work and do it."

One of the important commonalities among these founders of sociological thought was that because they were minorities or women, they were constantly defiled and denounced because of their views. Margaret Fuller and Mary Wollstonecraft were denounced as "feminists," their reputations sullied by their personal relationships. Du Bois and Gilman were denounced because each gave such weight to economic independence for Blacks and for women; they were accused of reducing social issues to simple economic autonomy. And Frederick Douglass was consistently denounced because he extended his cry for Black freedom to women as well. It was Douglass who provided the oratorical support for the suffrage plank at the first convention for women's rights in Seneca Falls, New York, in 1848—for which he was denounced the next day as an "Aunt Nancy man," the nineteenth-century equivalent of a wimp.

Doing sociology is not always comfortable, nor is sociology done only by those whose material lives are already comfortable. Sometimes sociology challenges common sense and the status quo.

MyLab Log on to www.MySocLab.com for more resources that will help you complete this Try It activity.

(handwritten margin notes)
imposing → Corrupted / soiled

Frederick Douglass
* all humans capable of being full individuals

Du Bois
* Blacks identity split—Negro / American
* color line = problem

Gilman
* orgin of women's subordination and its function in evolution

Contemporary Sociology

Contemporary sociologists return constantly to the ideas of its founders for inspiration and guidance as they develop their own questions about how society works—and doesn't work. Classical theories provide orientation for the development of sociological thinking.

In the United States, sociology developed as an academic field in the period between 1930 and 1960. It promised to be a social science that could explain the historical origins and dynamics of modern society. Two questions dominated the field: What could sociology contribute to the study of the self? And what processes ensure social order? Stated differently, the first question was about the distinction of sociology from psychology: What is the self, and how is it different from what psychologists call

(handwritten note) * making housework easier—more communal (ex: daycare)

"personality"? And the second question was really about why there had been such dramatic political upheavals in Europe (Nazism, Fascism, Communism) and why, despite the terrible ravages of the great Depression and the instability of the world war, the United States remained relatively stable and orderly.

Symbolic Interactionism and the Sociology of the Self

The creation of a stable social "self" rested on interest in microlevel interactions, interactions among individuals, and sociologists who called themselves "symbolic interactionists." **Symbolic interactionism** examines how an individual's interactions with his or her environment—other people, institutions, ideas—help people develop a sense of "self." The "symbolic" part was the way we use symbol systems—like language, religion, art, or body language and decoration—to navigate the social world. Symbolic interactionists follow in the sociological tradition of George Herbert Mead.

Erving Goffman, an influential symbolic interactionist, used what he called a *dramaturgical* model to understand social interaction. Like an actor preparing to perform a part in a play, a *social* actor practices his or her part "backstage," accumulating props and testing out different ways to deliver one's lines. The actual "frontstage" performance, in front of the intended audience, helps us refine our presentation of self: If the people we want to like us do, in fact, like us, we realize that our performance is successful, and we will continue it. But if they reject us, or don't like us, we might try a different strategy, rehearse that "backstage," and then try again. If that fails, our identity might get "spoiled," and we would have to either change the venue of our performance, alter our part significantly, or accept society's critical reviews.

In one of Goffman's most important works, he looked at what happens to individuals' identities when all their props are removed and they are forced to conform to an absolutely rigid regime. In *total institutions* such as prisons, mental hospitals, and concentration camps, Goffman discerned that individuals are routinely stripped of anything that identifies them as individuals. And yet, still, they try to assert something that is theirs alone, something that enables them to hold on to their individual senses of themselves.

In his conclusion to his book *Asylums* (1961), Goffman describes this dynamic. He writes that

> . . . without something to belong to, we have no stable self, and yet total commitment and attachment to any social unit implies a kind of selflessness. Our sense of being a person can come from being drawn into a wider social unit; our sense of selfhood can arise through the little ways in which we resist the pull. Our status is backed by the solid buildings of the world, while our sense of personal identity often resides in the cracks. (Goffman, 1961, p. 320)

Structural Functionalism and Social Order

At the larger, structural, or "macro" level, sociologists were preoccupied with political and social stability and order. Following the great Harvard sociologist, Talcott Parsons (1902–1979), sociologists explored what they called **structural functionalism,** a theory that social life consisted of several distinct integrated levels that enable the world—and individuals who are within it—to find stability, order, and meaning. Functionalism offers a **paradigm,** a coherent model of how society works and how individuals are socialized into their roles within it (Parsons, 1937, 1951).

While Talcott Parsons was, perhaps, the central figure of structural-functionalist analysis, his work today is sometimes characterized as anachronistic, naïve, and written in a style so dense that it defies comprehension. This is unfortunate, because

Parsons exhibited an unparalleled enthusiasm for the possibility of sociological understanding to make sense of the world.

Parsons believed that like most natural phenomena, societies tend toward balance—balance within all their component parts and balance within each individual member of society. The functionalist model stresses balance and equilibrium among the values of the society, its norms, and the various institutions that develop to express and sustain those values over time.

According to this perspective, every institution, every interaction has a "function"—the reproduction of social life. Thus, for example, educational institutions function to ensure the steady transmission of social values to the young and to filter their entry into the labor force until the labor force can accommodate them. (If every 18-year-old simply went off to work, more than half wouldn't find jobs!) Families "function" to regulate sexual relationships and to ensure the socialization of the young into society.

▲ The British say the king (or queen) "reigns, but does not rule." To the sociologist, the monarchy symbolically represents the nation, providing a sense of unity and shared purpose.

It was left to Robert K. Merton (1910–2003), Parsons's former student and colleague, to clarify functionalism and also extend its analysis. Like Parsons, he argued that society tends toward equilibrium and balance. Those processes, events, and institutions that facilitate equilibrium he called "functional," and those that undermine it he called "dysfunctional." In this way, Merton understood both the forces that maintain social order and those that do not (Merton, 1949).

Merton argued that the functions of any institution or interaction can be either "manifest" or "latent." **Manifest functions** are overt and obvious, the intended functions, while **latent functions** are hidden, unintended, but nonetheless important. For example, the manifest function of going to college used to be that a person educated in the liberal arts would be a better, more productive citizen. The latent function was that going to college would also enable the graduate to get a better job. However, that's changed significantly, and the manifest function for most college students today is that a college education is a prerequisite for getting a good job. Latent functions today might include escape from parental control for 2 to 4 years or access to a new set of potential dating partners, because many people meet their future spouses in college.

As they cast their eye back to classical theorists, functionalists followed Durkheim's idea that society was held together by shared beliefs. More than that, they believed that every social institution helped to integrate individuals into social life. What *was*, they argued, "was" for a reason—it worked. When there was a problem, such as, for example, juvenile delinquency, it was not because delinquents were bad people but because the system was not socializing young boys adequately. Poverty was not the result of the moral failings of the poor but a systemic incapacity to adequately provide jobs and welfare to all. Although functionalism was criticized for its implicit conservatism—if it exists it serves a purpose and shouldn't be changed—the theory also expressed a liberal faith in the ability of American institutions to eventually respond to social problems.

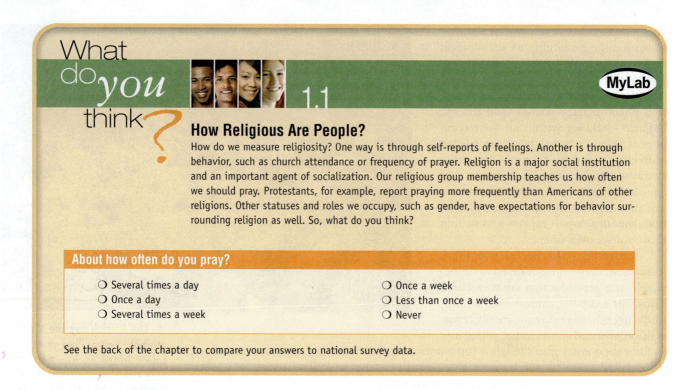

MyLab Log on to www.MySocLab.com to participate in these polls and view your class's responses.

Functionalism was, itself, "functional" in explaining society during a period of stability and conformity like the 1950s. But by the end of the decade there were rumblings of change—from individuals and groups who came to believe that what functioned for some groups wasn't so functional for other groups. They pushed sociologists to see the world differently.

Conflict Theories: An Alternative Paradigm

In the 1960s, many sociologists, inspired more by Marx and Weber than by Durkheim and Parsons, argued that this celebrated ability of American institutions to respond to social problems was itself the problem. American institutions did not solve problems; they caused them by allocating resources unequally. The United States was a society based on structural inequality, on the unequal distribution of rewards. The rich got richer and the poor got poorer—and the institutions of the economy, the political process, and social reforms often perpetuated that inequality.

Generally, these sociologists adopted a theoretical paradigm that was called **conflict theory**—a theory that suggested that the dynamics of society, both of social order and social resistance, were the result of the conflict among different groups. Like Marx and Weber before them, conflict theorists believed that those who had power sought to maintain it; those who did not have power sought to change the system to get it. The constant struggles between the haves and the have-nots was the organizing principle of society, and the dynamic tension between these groups gave society its motion and its coherence. Conflict theories included those that stressed gender inequality (feminist theory), racial inequality (critical race theory), or class-based inequality (Marxist theory or socialist theory).

For two decades, the 1970s and 1980s, these two theories, functionalism and conflict theory, were themselves in conflict as the dominant theoretical perspectives in sociology. Were you to pick up an introductory sociology textbook originally written in the last two decades of the twentieth century, between 1980 and 2000, it would likely describe these two theoretical perspectives (as well as symbolic interactionism to describe microlevel social interactions) as the dominant and competing perspectives of the field.

Today there is some debate about whether these paradigms continue to compete for dominance in the field. The dramatic global economic and political shifts of the past decades, the rise of new transnational institutions like the EU and trade agreements like NAFTA, and the rise of new social movements based on ethnicity or religion to challenge them require that sociologists shift the lenses through which they view the social world.

▲ Conflict theorists argue that society is held together by the tensions of inequality and conflict. Rich and poor, powerful and powerless, struggle for resources and goods. In 2004, a Sudanese policeman controls access to the distribution of food and clothing to hungry refugees in Darfur.

The three dominant sociological theories of the second half of the twentieth century all addressed similar sorts of questions:

- What holds society together? (the problem of social order)
- How are individuals connected to larger social processes and institutions? (the relationship of the individual to society)
- What are the chief tensions that pull society apart? (social disorganization, tension)
- What causes social change? (progress)

The answers to these questions led sociologists to different answers to the major questions about where society is heading and what we can do to improve the lives of people in it.

Globalization and Multiculturalism: New Lenses, New Issues

The events of the past few decades have seen these older divisions among sociologists subsiding, and the incorporation of new lenses through which to view sociological issues. Probably the best terms to describe these new lenses are globalization and multiculturalism. By **globalization,** we mean that the interconnections—economic, political, cultural, social—among different groups of people all over the world, the dynamic webs that connect us to one another and the ways these connections also create cleavages among different groups of people. By **multiculturalism,** literally the understanding of many different cultures, we come to understand the very different ways that different groups of people approach issues, construct identities, and create institutions that express their needs.

Globalization focuses on larger, **macrolevel analysis,** which examines large-scale institutional processes such as the global marketplace, corporations, and transnational institutions such as the United Nations or World Bank. Multiculturalism stresses both the macrolevel unequal distribution of rewards based on class, race, region, gender, and the like, and also the **microlevel analysis,** which focuses on the ways in which different groups of people and even individuals construct their identities based on their

TABLE 1.2

Major Sociological Theories, 1950–2000

THEORY	LEVEL OF ANALYSIS	ORDER: WHAT HOLDS SOCIETY TOGETHER?	INDIVIDUAL TO SOCIETY	CHANGE	DIRECTION OF CHANGE
Structural-functionalism	Macro	Society is a stable system of interrelated elements—shared values, institutions—and there is general agreement (consensus) about how society should work.	Individuals are integrated into society by socialization.	Incomplete integration leads to deviance. Change is progressive.	Positive Society is evolving to more and more equality.
Conflict theory	Macro	Society is a dynamic tension between unequal groups marked by an unequal distribution of rewards and goods.	Individuals belong to different groups that compete for resources.	Groups mobilize to get greater goods.	Short term: conflict Longer term: greater equality
Symbolic interactionism	Micro	Society is a set of processes among individuals and groups, using symbolic forms (language, gestures, performance) to create identity and meaning.	Individuals connect to others symbolically.	Tension between institutions and individual identity.	No direction specified

membership in those groups. For example, the globalization of the media industries allows books, magazines, movies, television programs, and music from almost every country to be consumed all over the world. A macrolevel analysis of globalization might point to ways global information exchange promotes interconnection and mutual understanding. A microlevel, multiculturalist analysis might point out, however, that the flow of information is mostly one way, from the West and particularly the United States into other countries, dominating other cultures, reinforcing global economic inequalities, and promoting a homogeneous, Westernized global society (Figure 1.1). Or a multiculturalist might argue that global media, particularly the Internet, are playing a role in reinvigorating local cultures and identities by promoting mixing and fusion and by allowing a diversity of voices—including "alternative" and "radical" ones—to be heard (Williams, 2003).

Globalization and Multiculturalism: Interrelated Forces. Today the world often seems to alternate between feeling like a centrifuge, in which everything at the center is

FIGURE 1.1 An Alternative View of the World

MyLab Log on to www.MySocLab.com to further explore maps and data using Google Earth applications and exercises.

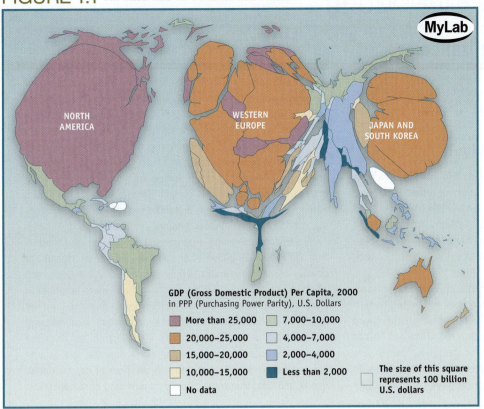

GDP (Gross Domestic Product) Per Capita, 2000
in PPP (Purchasing Power Parity), U.S. Dollars

- More than 25,000
- 20,000–25,000
- 15,000–20,000
- 10,000–15,000
- No data
- 7,000–10,000
- 4,000–7,000
- 2,000–4,000
- Less than 2,000

The size of this square represents 100 billion U.S. dollars

Source: From United Nations Environment Programme/GRID–Arendal website, maps.grids.no. Cartogram reproduced by permission of the authors, Vladimir Tikunov (Department of Geography, University of Moscow) and Philippe Rekacewicz (Le Monde diplomatique, Paris).

scattered into millions of individual, local particles, and a great gravitational vacuum that collects all these local, individual particles into a congealing center.

There are numerous, formerly unimaginable changes that go under the heading of "globalization"—scientific advances, technological breakthroughs that connect people all over the globe, the speed and integration of commercial and economic decisions, the coherence of multinational political organizations and institutions—like the recently "invented" European Union and G8 organizations, not to mention the older and venerable organizations like the United Nations (founded in 1945) and NATO (founded in 1950). The increased globalization of production of the world's goods—companies doing business in every other country—is coupled with increasingly similar patterns of consumption as teenagers all over the world are listening to Eminem or Britney Spears, on portable stereo equipment made in Japan, talking on cell phones made in Finland, wearing clothing from Gap that is manufactured in Thailand, walking in Nikes or Reeboks, shopping at malls that feature the same boutiques, which they drive to in cars made in Germany or Japan, using gasoline refined by American or British companies from oil extracted from the Arabian peninsula.

Just as our societies are changing dramatically, bringing the world closer and closer together, so too are those societies changing, becoming multiracial and multicultural. Increasingly, in industrial societies, the old divisions between women and men, and among various races and ethnicities, are breaking down. Women and men are increasingly similar: Both work, and both care for children, and the traits that were formerly associated with one sex or the other are increasingly blurred. Most of us know that we possess both the capacity for aggression, ambition, and technical

Sociology and our World

Defining Globalization

There are many definitions of globalization. The one here is from the Carnegie Endowment for International Peace, a major research and policy institution.

What Is Globalization?

Globalization is a process of interaction and integration among the people, companies, and governments of different nations. The process is driven by international trade and investment and is aided by information technology. Its effects extend from the environment, to culture, to political systems, to economic development and prosperity, to human physical well-being in societies around the world.

Globalization is not new. For thousands of years, people—and, later, corporations—have been buying from and selling to each other in lands at great distances, such as through the famed Silk Road across Central Asia that connected China and Europe during the Middle Ages. Likewise, for centuries, people and corporations have invested in enterprises in other countries. In fact, many of the features of the current wave of globalization are similar to those prevailing before the outbreak of the First World War in 1914.

But policy and technological developments of the past few decades have spurred increases in cross-border trade, investment, and migration so large that many observers believe the world has entered a qualitatively new phase in its economic development. Since 1950, for example, the volume of world trade has increased by twenty times, and from just 1997 to 1999 flows of foreign investment nearly doubled, from $468 billion to $827 billion. Distinguishing this current wave of globalization from earlier ones, author Thomas Friedman has said that today globalization is "farther, faster, cheaper, and deeper."

Globalization is deeply controversial. Proponents of globalization claim that it allows poor countries and their citizens to develop economically and raise their standards of living. Opponents of globalization argue that the creation of an unfettered international free market has benefited multinational corporations in the Western world at the expense of local enterprises, local cultures, and common people. Resistance to globalization has therefore taken shape both at a popular and at a governmental level as people and governments try to manage the flow of capital, labor, goods, and ideas that constitute the current wave of globalization.

competence, as well as the ability to be compassionate and caring. Industrial countries like the United States, or the nations of Europe, are increasingly multicultural: Gone are the days when to be American meant being able to trace your lineage to the Mayflower or when to be Swedish meant uniformly blond hair and blue eyes. Today, even the U.S. Census cannot keep up with how much we're changing: The fastest-growing racial category in the United States in the year 2005 was "biracial." Just who are "we" anyway?

At the same time that we've never been closer or more similar to each other, the boundaries between us have never been more sharply drawn. The collapse of the former Soviet Union led to the establishment of dozens of new nations, based entirely on ethnic identity. The terrifying explosion of a murderous strain of Islamic fundamentalism vows to purify the world of all nonbelievers. Virtually all the wars of the last two decades have been interethnic conflicts, in which one ethnic group has attempted to eradicate another from within the nation's borders—not necessarily because of some primitive bloodlust on the part of those neighboring cultures but because the political entities in which they were forced to live, nation-states, were themselves the artificial creations of powerful nations at the end of the last century. The Serbian aggression against Bosnia, Croatia, and Kosovo, the Hutu and Tutsi in Rwanda, the past or current tribal civil wars in Somalia or Congo, plus dozens of smaller-scale interethnic wars have given the world a new term for the types of wars we witness now—*ethnic cleansing.*

The drive for uniformity as the sole basis for unity, for sameness as the sole basis for security, leads to internal efforts at perpetual self-purification—as if by completely excluding "them," we get to know what "us" means. Such efforts are accompanied by a dramatic (and often violent) restoration of traditional roles for women and men. Women are "refeminized" by being forced back into the home, under lock and key as well as under layers of physical concealment; men are "remasculinized" by being required to adopt certain physical traits and return to traditional clothing and the imposition of complete control over women.

Religion, blood, folk, nation—these are the terms we use to specify who we are and who they are not. The boundaries between us have never been more sharply drawn—nor have they ever been so blurred.

These trends play themselves out not only on the global stage but also within each society. In the economic North, there are calls for returns to some idealized visions of pristine purity of racial bloodlines, to religious fundamentals, to basics like the '50s vision of the family—the 1850s, that is. And in many societies in Africa or Latin America, there are signs of increased multiculturalism, tolerance for difference, the embracing of technological innovation and secular humanist science. Neither side is as monochromatic as stereotypes might imagine it to be.

We often imagine the past and the present as a set of opposites. The past was bucolic, stable, unchanging; society today is a mad rush of dizzying social changes that we can barely grasp. But neither vision is completely true. "Just as there was more change among past peoples than often meets the eye," writes sociologist Harvey Molotch, "so there is more stability in the modern world than might be thought" (Molotch, 2003, p. 94).

And most of us adopt an idiosyncratic combination of these trends. The terrorists of al-Qaeda, who seek a return to a premodern Islamic theocracy, keep in touch with wireless Web access and a sophisticated technological system while Americans, their sworn archenemy, the embodiment of secularism, stream to church every Sunday in numbers that dwarf those of European nations. We speak with patriotic fervor of closing our borders to non-Americans, while we merrily consume products from all over the world. (I recently saw a bumper sticker that said "Buy American"—on a Honda Civic.)

Global Tensions. These two master trends—globalization and particularism; secular, scientific, and technological advances and religious fundamentalism, ethnic purification and local tribalisms—these are not simply the final conflict between two competing worldviews, a "clash of civilizations" as one eminent political scientist calls it. Such a view imagines these as two completely separate entities, now on a collision course for global conflagration, and ignores the ways in which each of these trends is a reaction to the other, is organized in response to the other, is, in the end, *produced* by the other. And such a view also misses the ways in which these master trends are contained within any society—indeed, within all of us.

Globalization is often viewed as increasing homogeneity around the world. The sociologist George Ritzer calls it **McDonaldization**—the homogenizing spread of consumerism around the globe (1996). *New York Times* columnist Thomas Friedman (2000) once predicted that "no two countries which both have a McDonald's will go to war with each other."

Friedman's prediction turned out to be wrong—in part because he saw only that part of globalization that flattens the world and minimizes cultural and national differences. But globalization is also accompanied by multiculturalism, an increased awareness of the particular aspects of our specific identities, and a resistance to losing them to some global identity, which most people find both grander and blander. In the words of political scientist Benjamin Barber (1996), our world is characterized by *both* "McWorld" and "Jihad"—the integration into "one commercially homogeneous network" and also increased tribalization and separation.

▲ Religion can bring us together in joy and song . . .

▲ . . . or drive us apart in anger and hatred.

Globalization and multiculturalism express *both* the forces that hold us together—whether the repression of armies, police forces, and governments or the shared values of nationalism or ethnic pride—*and* the forces that drive us apart. These are, actually, the same forces.

For example, religion both maintains cohesiveness among members and serves as one of the principal axes of division among people in the world today. Ethnicity provides a sense of stable identity and a way of distinguishing ourselves from others, as well as a way that society unequally allocates resources. Gender, race, youth/age, and social class also contribute to stable identity and can help us feel connected to groups, but they similarly serve as major contributors to social inequality, thus pulling society apart.

One impetus for the recognition of globalization and multiculturalism as among the central organizing principles of society is the continued importance of *race, class,* and *gender* in social life. In the past half century, we've become increasingly aware of the centrality of these three categories of experience. Race, class, and gender are among the most important axes around which social life revolves, the organizing mechanisms of institutions, the foundations of our identities. Along with other forms of identity and mechanisms of inequality—ethnicity, sexuality, age, and religion—they form a matrix through which we understand ourselves and our world.

Sociology and Modernism

One of the central themes of virtually all of the classical sociological theories was an abiding faith in the idea of progress. This idea—that society is moving from a less developed to a more developed (and therefore better) stage—is a hallmark of the idea of **modernism.** In classical sociological theory, modernism was expressed as the passage from religious to scientific forms of knowledge (Comte), from mechanical to organic forms of solidarity (Durkheim), from feudal to capitalist to communist modes of production (Marx), from traditional to legal forms of authority (Weber). In the twentieth century, structural functionalists hailed the movement from extended to nuclear family forms and from arbitrary rule by aristocrats to universal legal principles as emblems of social progress.

Yet many of the founders of sociology were also deeply ambivalent about progress. Tocqueville saw democracy as inevitable but potentially dangerous to individual freedom. Durkheim saw that organic solidarity required constant effort to maintain the levels of integration that individuals would feel, so they would not drift away from social life. Marx bemoaned the fact that the working class would have to experience great deprivation before they would rise up against capitalism. And Weber saw the very mechanism of individual freedom, rationality, coming back to trap us in an iron cage of meaninglessness.

Today, we live in an age in which the very idea of progress from one stage to the next has been called into question. For one thing, it's clear that no society ever passes from one stage fully into the next. We can see pieces of both mechanical and organic solidarity all around us. In the most advanced societies, kinship, "blood," and primordial ethnic identity continue to serve as a foundation for identity; in some of

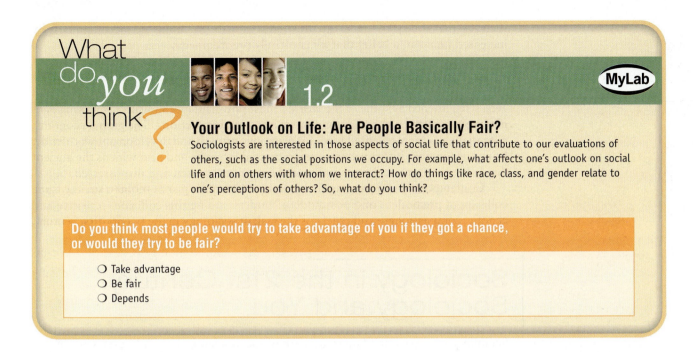

What do *you* think 1.2

Your Outlook on Life: Are People Basically Fair?

Sociologists are interested in those aspects of social life that contribute to our evaluations of others, such as the social positions we occupy. For example, what affects one's outlook on social life and on others with whom we interact? How do things like race, class, and gender relate to one's perceptions of others? So, what do you think?

Do you think most people would try to take advantage of you if they got a chance, or would they try to be fair?

○ Take advantage
○ Be fair
○ Depends

the least developed countries, young people are using the Internet and hanging out on Facebook. Societies maintain both feudal relations and capitalist ones—including those countries that call themselves communist! We are governed by authorities that rely on traditional, charismatic, and legal rationales.

What's more, the world has become so interdependent that one society cannot exist in isolation from others. The development of one society toward different ways of organizing social life (replacing tribal elders with elected representatives, for example) is heavily influenced by the global marketplace, by transnational organizations like the United Nations, and by ideas that circulate over the globe via transportation, telecommunications, and the media faster than any classical theorist could ever have imagined. We no longer see less-developed societies as the image of our past, any more than they see Europe or the United States as an image of their future.

Sociology remains a deeply "modern" enterprise: Most sociologists believe that science and reason can solve human problems and that people's lives can be improved by the application of these scientifically derived principles. Yet sociologists are also reexamining the fixed idea of progress and seeing a jumble of conflicting possibilities that exist at any historical moment rather than the inevitable unfolding of a single linear path. As a concept, postmodernism originated in architecture, as a critique of the uniformity of modern buildings. Using elements from classical and modern, postmodernists prefer buildings that are not fixed and uniform but rather a collage, a collision of styles in a new form.

In sociology, **postmodernism** suggests that the meaning of social life may not be found in conforming to rigid patterns of development but rather in the creative assembling of interactions and interpretations that enable us to negotiate our way in the world. In the postmodern conception of the world, the fundamentals of society—structure, culture, agency—are all challenged and in flux. Thus we are simultaneously freer and more creative and also potentially more frightened, more lost, and more alone.

In the face of these postmodernist ideas, the modern world has also witnessed a rebirth of "premodern" ideas. Premodern ideas—kinship, blood, religion, tribe—were the ideas first challenged by the Enlightenment view of the world, from which sociology emerged in the nineteenth century. The increased freedom of postmodern

MyLab Log on to www.MySocLab.com to participate in these polls and view your class's responses.

society—the ability to make up the rules as you go along—is accompanied by increased fatalism, a belief that all is entirely preordained.

There has been a dramatic increase in religious beliefs, New Age consciousness, and other nonscientific way of explaining our lives and our place in the universe. The forces that were supposed to disappear as the bases for social life have remained and even strengthened as some of the world's most powerful mechanisms for uniting people into connected clans and dividing us into warring factions. The global economy, potentially an unprecedented force for economic growth and development worldwide, brings us together into a web of interconnected interests and also widens the ancient divide between rich and poor, haves and have-nots, chosen and dispossessed.

Contemporary society consists of all these elements; just as modern society is the collision of premodern and postmodern. Understanding this collision—creative and chaotic, compassionate and cruel—is the task of sociology in the twenty-first century.

Sociology in the 21st Century, Sociology and You

Sociologists are part of a larger network of social scientists. Sociologists work in colleges and universities, teaching and doing research, but they also work in government organizations, doing research and policy analysis; in social movements, developing strategies; and in large and small organizations, public and private.

Sociologists reflect and embody the processes we study, and the changes in the field of sociology are, in a way, a microcosm of the changes we observe in the society in which we live. And, over the past few decades, the field has undergone more dramatic changes than many of the other academic fields of study. Sociology's mission is the understanding—without value judgments—of different groups, and, as you will see, to understand the dynamics of both *identity* and *inequality* that belonging to these groups brings, as well as the different institutions—the family, education, workplace, media, religious institution, and the like—in which we experience social life. It makes a certain logical sense, therefore, that many members of marginalized groups, such as racial, sexual, and ethnic minorities and women, would find a home in sociology.

Once, of course, all academic fields of study were the dominion of White men. Today, however, women and racial, ethnic, and sexual minorities have transformed collegiate life. Not that long ago, women were excluded from many of the most prestigious colleges and universities; now women outnumber men on virtually every college campus. Not that long ago, racial minorities were excluded from many of America's universities and colleges; today universities have special recruiting task forces to insure a substantial minority applicant pool. Not that long ago, gays and lesbians, bisexuals, and transgendered people were expelled from colleges and universities for violating ethics or morals codes; today there are LGBT (Lesbian, Gay, Bisexual, Transgender) organizations on most college campuses.

Sociology has been one of the fields that has pioneered this inclusion. It is a source of pride to most sociologists that today sociology is among the most diverse fields on any campus.

In the past 50 years (since 1966), the percentage of B.A. degrees in sociology awarded to women has increased 98.7 percent, while the percentage of M.A. degrees rose 336.9 percent, and the percentage of Ph.D. degrees rose a whopping 802.5 percent. At the same time, the percentage of African American Ph.D.s in sociology has more than doubled, while the percentage of Hispanic Ph.D.s nearly tripled in the same period, and Asian American degrees more than doubled—all of these are the highest percentages of any social science (American Sociological Association, 2007).

We live in a society composed of many different groups and many different cultures, subcultures, and countercultures, speaking different languages, with different kinship networks and different values and norms. It's noisy, and we rarely agree on anything. And yet we also live in a society where the overwhelming majority of people obey the same laws and are civil to one another and in which we respect the differences among those different groups. We live in a society characterized by a fixed hierarchy and in a society in which people believe firmly in the idea of mobility, a society in which one's fixed, ascribed characteristics (race, class, and sex) are the single best determinants of where one will end up, and a society in which we also believe anyone can make it if he or she works hard enough.

This is the world sociologists find so endlessly fascinating. This is the world about which sociologists develop their theories, test their hypotheses, and conduct their research. Sociology is the lens through which we look at this dizzying array of social life—and begin to try and make sense of it. Welcome to it—and welcome to sociology as a new way of seeing that world.

Chapter Review

1. *What is sociology?* Sociology is a field of study and way of thinking that helps us to understand the world around us and how we fit into it by looking at the construction and development of identity, society, relationships, and inequality. Sociologists don't think in terms of either/or; rather, they examine social issues and problems in terms of both/and, interconnectedness, and always within a larger social context.

2. *What does it mean to "do" sociology?* Sociology is both an academic field and a way of seeing the world. It uses theoretical models and standardized research methods to understand social phenomena. Sociologists understand that things are complex and that the individual view is incomplete, so they always try to see the bigger picture and look at issues from various angles.

3. *Where did sociology come from?* During the Enlightenment period in Europe, there was a general shift from a geocentric to a heliocentric world view—from religion to science as the source of knowledge and explanations of reality. Sociology began as an attempt to understand the changes society was undergoing. These changes led to the sociological inquiry of the nature of community, government, and the economy, the meaning of individualism and increased secularism, and the nature and direction of change.

4. *What did the early sociologists think?* Considered the founder of sociology, August Comte believed that society's development was based on forms of knowledge—religious, metaphysical, and scientific—and how they explain the world. Thus, as forms of knowledge changed, society changed accordingly. Alexis de Tocqueville showed how democracy both enhances and erodes individual liberty, while Karl Marx saw class as the organizing principle of social life. Emile Durkheim used his study of suicide to show how the bonds between the individual and society affect human behavior, and Max Weber studied the importance of rationality in the modern world and developed a sociology that was both interpretive and value free. Weber also expanded Marx's analysis of social stratification by adding status and party to social class as determinants of social status. Georg Simmel showed how forms of social interaction are used by individuals to combine into groups.

5. *How did sociology develop beyond the main thinkers?* Early sociologists in the United States included Thorstein Veblen, who argued that the wealthy were not productive and instead engaged in what he coined "conspicuous consumption." Lester Ward was the first sociologist to reject the evolutionary model of social change; he believed that social change should be planned and that society should be reformed into a welfarelike state, and George Herbert Mead showed how individuals developed through social processes and self-reflection. Not all sociologists were White or male; Mary Wollstonecraft was the first major feminist. She argued that women

should be educated the same as men or society would never progress. Frederick Douglass, a former slave and prolific author, was very influential in the abolitionist movement, while W. E. B. Du Bois founded the NAACP and wrote 19 books on race. He is now considered one of the greatest sociologists in history.

6. *What are the major contemporary sociological perspectives?* Three main paradigms, or ways of thinking, have dominated sociological inquiry. Symbolic interactionists explain how interactions with the environment help people develop a sense of self. Structural functionalists stress equilibrium in society and examine how institutions function to reproduce social life. Conflict theorists believe that society evolves from conflict among groups. Today, sociologists increasingly view the world through the lenses of globalism and multiculturalism. Globalization, or the economic, political, cultural, and social interconnectedness among people around the world, spreads culture and values and has both positive and negative consequences. Using the multicultural lens, sociologists understand the different ways that people see the world, construct selves, and create institutions. Today's sociologists understand that race, class, gender, and sexuality are intersections of identity, and one cannot be studied without taking the others into account.

Key Terms

Canon (p. 21)
Conflict theory (p. 26)
Generalized other (p. 21)
Globalization (p. 27)
Latent functions (p. 25)
Macrolevel analysis (p. 27)
Manifest functions (p. 25)

McDonaldization (p. 31)
Mechanical solidarity (p. 18)
Microlevel analysis (p. 27)
Modernism (p. 32)
Multiculturalism (p. 27)
Organic solidarity (p. 18)
Paradigm (p. 24)

Postmodernism (p. 33)
Social Darwinism (p. 20)
Sociological imagination (p. 5)
Sociology (p. 5)
Structural functionalism (p. 24)
Symbolic interactionism (p. 24)

What does America think?

1.1 How Religious Are People?

This is actual survey data from the General Social Survey, 2004.

About how often do you pray? Almost 60 percent of respondents reported praying at least once a day. Women were more likely than men to pray several times a day or once a day. Results for examining by race were also striking, with 55 percent of Black respondents praying several times a day as compared to 27 percent of White respondents.

CRITICAL THINKING | DISCUSSION QUESTION

1. What social and cultural factors do you think account for the gender differences in reports of prayer frequency? What about the race difference?

1.2 Your Outlook on Life: Are People Basically Fair?

This is actual survey data from the General Social Survey, 2004.

Do you think most people would try to take advantage of you if they got a chance, or would they try to be fair? Half of all respondents thought most people would try to be fair, and 40 percent thought they would try to take advantage of others. Nine percent said it depended. Social class differences in responses were striking, with those in the lower class being most likely to think people would try to take advantage and least likely to think people would try to be fair. Those in the middle class were most likely to think people would try to be fair. When examined by sex, the range in responses was small, but when examined by race, Black respondents (58.8 percent) were far more likely than White respondents (34.4 percent) to say people would try to take advantage of others.

CRITICAL THINKING | DISCUSSION QUESTIONS

1. Half of all respondents thought most people would be fair. Is that more or less than what you expected? How do you explain these results?
2. While gender did not appear to have an effect on respondents' perceptions of others, social class and race had a striking effect. Looking at these differences and thinking about positions, why do you think these differences exist?

▶ Go to this website to look further at the data. You can run your own statistics and crosstabs here: **http://sda.berkeley.edu/cgi-bin/hsda?harcsda+gss04**

REFERENCES: Davis, James A., Tom W. Smith, and Peter V. Marsden. General Social Surveys 1972–2004: [Cumulative file] [Computer file]. 2nd ICPSR version. Chicago, IL: National Opinion Research Center [producer], 2005; Storrs, CT: Roper Center for Public Opinion Research, University of Connecticut; Ann Arbor, MI: Inter-University Consortium for Political and Social Research; Berkeley, CA: Computer-Assisted Survey Methods Program, University of California [distributors], 2005.

chapter 2

ONE OF THE MOST POPULAR SONGS of the past quarter-century was "We Are the World," written in 1984 by Quincy Jones and Michael Jackson to raise money for starving children in Africa and originally sung by some of the biggest stars in the musical pantheon. It expresses a feeling that we're all one, that people are people everywhere, and that we're all the same.

And yet you might well find yourself feeling uncomfortable, in a class or in casual conversation, if someone were to actually ask you a question based on that idea. "Well, how do you Asian Americans feel about that?" or "Well, as a woman, don't you agree that . . .?" At those moments, you aren't likely to feel very much like "we are the world." You're more likely to say, "Well, I can't speak for all of them, so this is just my own personal opinion."

Culture and Society

We sometimes feel like we vacillate between abstract universalism (we are the world) and very specific particularism (it's just me). Neither is wrong, but neither is the whole story. It's the mission of sociology to connect those two levels, those two experiences, to connect you as a discrete individual with the larger society in which you live.

As we saw in the last chapter, one of the most concise yet profound definitions of sociology is C. Wright Mills's idea that sociology "connects biography and history"—that is, it

What makes human life different from other species is that we alone have a conscious "history," a continuity of generations and a purposive direction of change. Humans have culture.

connects you, as an individual, to the larger social *contexts* in which you find yourself. This connection raises important questions for us: How much "free will" do I actually have? Can I control my own destiny or am I simply the product of those larger contexts? Both—and neither. We have an enormous amount of freedom to choose our paths—probably more than any entire population in history. And yet, as we will see, those choices are constrained by circumstances that we neither chose nor created. Another way of saying this is found in the first paragraphs of a book by Karl Marx (1965):

> Men make their own history, but they do not make it as they please; they do not make it under self-selected circumstances, but under circumstances existing already, given and transmitted from the past.

It is this connection—between the personal and the structural—that defines the sociological perspective. The sociological perspective enables us to see how nature and nurture combine, how things are changing and how they are eternal and timeless, how we are shaped by our societies and how we in turn shape them—to see, in essence, how it can be both the best of times and the worst of times.

[handwritten: ✳ we have the freedom to choose but only under existing circumstances]

Culture

[handwritten: ✳large institutions= offer the larger, general pattern ✳ agency = shaping our own destiny]

Sociology uses specific terms and concepts that enable us to see those linkages discussed above and to make sense of both ourselves and the world we live in—and the connections between the two. Every academic field uses certain concepts as the lenses through which it sees and therefore understands the world, much like the lenses of eyeglasses help us see what we need to see much more clearly. For example, psychologists might use terms like *cognition, unconscious,* or *ego;* economists would use terms like *supply and demand, production cycle,* or *profit margins.*

The lenses through which sociologists see the world are broad terms like *society* and *culture;* structural terms like *institutions;* and cultural terms like *values* and *norms.* Larger structures—institutions and/or organizations like the economy, government, family, or corporation—offer the larger, general patterns of things. And *agency* stresses the individual decisions that we make, ourselves, to create and shape our own destiny.

What makes us human? What differentiates human life from other animals' lives? One answer is culture. **Culture** refers to the sets of values and ideals that we understand to define morality, good and evil, appropriate and inappropriate. Culture defines larger structural forces and also how we perceive them. While dogs or horses or chimpanzees live in social groupings, they do not transmit their culture from one generation to the next. Although they learn and adapt to changing environmental conditions, they do not consciously build on the experiences of previous generations, transmitting to their children the wisdom of their ancestors. What makes human life different is that we alone have a conscious "history," a continuity of generations and a purposive direction of change. Humans have culture.

[handwritten: difference from animals →]

Culture is the foundation of society—both the material basis for social life, and the ideas, beliefs and values that people have. **Material culture** consists of the things people make, and the things they use to make them—the tools they use, the physical environment they inhabit (forests, beaches, mountains, fertile farmlands, or harsh desert). **Nonmaterial culture** consists of the ideas and beliefs that people develop about their lives and their world. Anthropologists have explained how people who live near dense forests, where animals are plentiful and food abundant, will develop very different cultural values from a culture that evolves in the desert, in which people must constantly move to follow an ever-receding water supply.

Our culture shapes more than what we know, more than our beliefs and our attitudes; culture shapes our human nature. Some societies, like the Yanomamo in Brazil, "know" that people are, by nature, violent and aggressive, and so they raise everyone to be violent and aggressive. But others, like the Tasaday tribe in the Philippines, "know" that people are kind and generous, and so everyone is raised to be kind and generous. In the United States, our culture is diverse enough that we can believe both sides. On the one hand, "everybody knows" that everyone is only out for him- or herself, and so it shouldn't surprise us that people cheat on exams or their taxes or drive over the speed limit. On the other hand, "everybody knows" that people are neighborly and kind, and so it doesn't surprise us that most people *don't* cheat on exams or their taxes and they drive under the speed limit.

Cultural Diversity

Cultural diversity means that the world's cultures are vastly different from each other. Their rich diversity sometimes appears exotic, sometimes tantalizing, and sometimes even disgusting. Even within American culture, there are subcultures that exhibit beliefs or behaviors that are vastly different from those of other groups. And, of course, culture is hardly static: Our culture is constantly changing, as beliefs and habits change. For example, in the early nineteenth century, it was a common prescribed cultural practice among middle-class New Englanders for a dating couple to be expected to share a bed together with a board placed down the middle, so that they could become accustomed to each other's sleeping behavior but without having sex. Parents would welcome their teenage children's "bundling" in a way they might not feel particularly comfortable doing today.

Often, when we encounter a different culture, we experience culture shock, a feeling of disorientation, because the cultural markers that we rely on to help us know where we are and how to act have suddenly changed. Sometimes, the sense of disorientation leads us to retreat to something more comfortable and reassert the values of our own cultures. We find other cultures weird, or funny, or sometimes we think they're immoral. In the 2003 movie *Lost in Translation*, Bill Murray and Scarlett Johansson experience the strange limbo of living in a foreign culture during an extended stay at a Tokyo hotel. They develop an unlikely bond of friendship, finding each other as a source of familiarity and comfort. Sometimes, culture shock is expressed in rather strange behaviors: The first time I ever lived abroad, as a high school

Oppressed or free? To many Westerners, these Afghan women are oppressed by traditional cultural practices. But they describe themselves as free and full participants in their culture. (These women are standing in line to vote in Afghanistan's first direct presidential election in 2004.). ▼

student, I suddenly started taking about four showers a day, and brushing my teeth half a dozen times a day, just to regain my sense of center and control.

That condemnation of other cultures because they are different is called ethnocentrism, a belief that one's culture is superior to others. We often use our own culture as the reference point by which we evaluate others. William Graham Sumner, the sociologist who first coined the term, described ethnocentrism as seeing "[o]ne's own group is the center of everything, and all others are scaled and rated with reference to it" (Sumner, 1906, p. 12). Ethnocentrism can be relatively benign, as a quiet sense of superiority or even cultural disapproval of the other culture, or it can be aggressive, as when people try to impose their values on others by force.

Sociologists must constantly guard against ethnocentrism, because it can bias our understandings of other cultures. It's helpful to remember that each culture justifies its beliefs by reference to the same guiding principles, so when Yanomamo people act aggressively, they say, "Well, that's just human nature," which is exactly what the Tasaday say when they act kindly toward each other. Because each culture justifies its activities and organization by reference to these universals—God's will, human nature, and the like—it is difficult for any one of us to stand in judgment of another's way of doing things. Therefore, to a large extent, sociologists take a position of cultural relativism, a position that all cultures are equally valid in the experience of their own members.

At the same time, many sociologists also believe that we should not shy away from claiming that some values are, or should be, universal values to which all cultures should subscribe. For example, the ideals of human rights that all people share—these are values that might be seen as condemning slavery, female genital mutilation, the killing of civilians during wartime, the physical or sexual abuse of children, the exclusion of married men from prosecution for rape. Some have suggested that these universal human rights are themselves the ethnocentric imposition of Western values on other cultures, and they may be. But they also express values that virtually every culture claims to hold, and so they may be close to universal. Cultural relativism makes us sensitive to the ways other people organize their lives, but it does not absolve us from taking moral positions ourselves.

Cultures vary dramatically in the ways they go about the most basic activities of life: eating, sleeping, producing goods, raising children, educating them, making

Try It — Thinking about Culture in Everyday Life

Modified from an activity submitted by Jonathan Marx, *Winthrop University.*

OBJECTIVE: Understand the importance of culture in everyday life.

STEP 1: Plan
Your instructor will either ask you to think about something that represents your culture/subculture or you may be asked to bring a material artifact (food, clothing, music, photo, or other object) that would help someone understand your culture.

STEP 2: Share
Briefly share what first came to mind (or the actual object). Identify yourself by name and talk about the cultural/subcultural group(s) you represent.

STEP 3: Evaluate
As students in your class are presenting, make a note of each culture/subcultural group mentioned. Are you surprised by the diversity or lack of diversity in your class? Why or why not?

STEP 4: Discuss
After everyone has presented, your instructor may lead the class in further discussion of culture.

friends, making love, forming families. This diversity is sometimes startling, and yet, every culture shares some central elements. Every culture has history, a myth of origin, a set of guiding principles that dictates right and wrong, with justifications for those principles.

Subcultures and Countercultures

Even within a particular culture there are often different subgroups. Subcultures and countercultures often develop within a culture.

Subcultures. A **subculture** is a group of people within a culture who share some distinguishing characteristic, beliefs, values, or attribute that sets them apart from the dominant culture. Some groups within a society create their own subcultures, with norms and values distinct from the mainstream, and usually their own separate social institutions. Roman Catholics were once prohibited from joining fraternal organizations such as the Masons, so they founded their own, the Knights of Columbus. Ethnic and sexual minorities often appear in mass media as negative stereotypes, or they do not appear at all, so they produce their own movies, novels, magazines, and television programs.

Subcultures arise when a group has two characteristics, prejudice from the mainstream, and social power. *Prejudice* (literally "prejudging") refers to beliefs about members of another group based on stereotypes or falsehoods that lead one to diminish that other group's value. Without prejudice, people will have no motive to produce subcultures. And without social power, they won't have the ability. Subcultures are communities that constitute themselves through a relationship of *difference* to the dominant culture. They can be a subset of the dominant culture, simply exaggerating their set of interests as the glue that holds them together as a community. So, for example, generation Y is a youth subculture, a group for which membership is limited to those of a certain age, that believes it has characteristics that are different from the dominant culture. Members of a subculture are part of the larger culture, but they may draw more on their subcultural position for their identity. Membership in a subculture enables you to feel "one" with others and "different" from others at the same time.

Countercultures. Subcultures that identify themselves through their *difference and opposition* to the dominant culture are called countercultures. Like subcultures, **countercultures** offer an important grounding for identity, but they do so in opposition to the dominant culture. As a result, countercultures demand a lot of conformity from members because they define themselves in opposition, and they may be more totalistic than a subculture. One can imagine, for example, belonging to several different subcultures, and these may exist in tandem with membership in the official culture. But countercultural membership often requires a sign of separation from the official culture. And it would be hard to belong to more than one.

As a result, countercultures are more often perceived as a threat to the official culture than a subculture might be. Countercultures may exist parallel to the official culture, or they may be outlawed and strictly policed. For example, the early Christians thought they were a subculture, a group with a somewhat separate identity from the Jews (another subculture) and the Romans. But the Romans were too threatened, and they were seen as a counterculture that had to be destroyed.

Like subcultures, countercultures create their own cultural forms—music, literature, news media, art. Sometimes these may be incorporated into the official culture as signs of rebellion. For example, blue jeans, tattoos, rock and rap music, leather

Sometimes a countercultural movement can change a society. In 1989, writer Vaclav Havel led the "Velvet Revolution" in Czechoslovakia and became the country's president.

jackets, and wearing black pants and shirts together all have their origins as signs of countercultural rebellion from the hippie, ghetto, or fringe sexual cultures. But they were incorporated into consumerism and have now achieved mainstream respectability.

The term *counterculture* came into widespread use during the 1960s to describe an emerging subculture based on age (youth), behaviors (marijuana use, psychedelic drug use, "free" sexual practices), and political sensibilities (liberal to radical). Gradually, this subculture became well-defined in opposition to the official culture, and membership required wearing certain androgynous fashions (tie-dyed shirts, sandals, bell-bottom blue jeans, "peasant" blouses), bodily practices (everyone wearing their hair long), musical preferences, drug use, and anti–Vietnam War politics. Other countercultures sprang up in many other countries, and some, like those in the Czech Republic and Poland, even became the dominant political parties during periods of radical reform.

Countercultures are not necessarily on the left or the right politically—what they are is oppositional. In the contemporary United States, there are groups such as White Supremacist survivalists as well as back-to-the-land hippies on communes: Both represent countercultures (and, given that they tend to be rural and isolated, they may also be neighbors!).

When you have a geographic territory occupied by people who have the same culture and the same social institutions, you have a *society* (discussed more fully in Chapter 3). More or less, there will always be subcultures within the society with distinctive norms and values, as well as people who slip through the cracks of the social institutions and hold different values.

Elements of Culture

All cultures share six basic elements: material culture, symbols, language, rituals, norms, and values.

Material Culture

As we mentioned earlier, material culture consists of both what people make and what they make it with. Every society must solve basic needs of subsistence: provision of food, shelter from the elements for both the person and the family (shelter and clothing). We organize our societies to enable us to collectively meet these basic subsistence needs for food, clothing, and shelter. We develop different cultures based on the climate, the available food supply, and the geography of our environment.

This much we share with animals. But it's equally important for human societies to solve a need that is different from basic subsistence or survival: the basic human need for meaning. We do the things we do not only because we must do them to survive, or because we have been routinely trained to do them, but also because we *want* to do them, because we believe that what we do is part of a larger scheme of things. Human beings also create a culture that enables us to attempt to answer the great unknowable questions of existence: Why are we here? Where are we going? What happens to us when we die? (As far as we know, we are the only animal species that is troubled by such questions.)

Symbols

As human wrestle with the meanings of their material environment, we attempt to represent our ideas to others. We translate what we see and think into symbols. A **symbol** is anything—an idea, a marking, a thing—that carries additional meanings beyond itself to others who share in the culture. Symbols come to mean what they do only in a culture; they would have no meaning to someone outside. Take, for example, one of the most familiar symbols of all, the cross. If one is Christian, the cross carries with it certain meanings. But to someone else, it might be simply a decoration or a reference to the means of execution in the Roman era. And to some who have seen crosses burning on their lawns, they may be a symbol of terror. That's what we mean when we say that symbols take on their meaning only inside culture.

Symbols are representations of ideas or feelings. In a single image, a symbol suggests and stands in for something more complex and involved. A heart stands for love; a red ribbon signifies AIDS awareness and solidarity; the bald eagle represents the American national character.

Symbols can be created at any time. Witness the recent and now widely known red AIDS ribbon or the pink ribbon for breast cancer awareness. But many symbols developed over centuries and in relative isolation from one another. In the case of older symbols, the same ones may mean completely different things in different cultures. For example, the color red means passion, aggression, or danger in the United States while it signifies purity in India and is a symbol of celebration and luck in China. White symbolizes purity in the West, but in Eastern cultures is the color of mourning and death.

Symbols are not always universally shared, and many cultural conflicts in society are over the meaning and appropriateness of certain symbols. Consider flags, for example. Many people around the world feel deeply patriotic at the sight of their nation's flag. My grandfather would actually often weep when he saw the American flag because it reminded him of his family's arduous journey to this country as an immigrant and the men who fought and died alongside him in World War I. Flags are important symbols and are displayed at solemn ceremonial moments and at festivals and sports events. Is burning the American flag a protected form of speech, a way for Americans to express their dissent from certain policies, or is it the deliberate destruction of the symbol of the nation, tantamount to an act of treason? And what about waving the flag of a different nation, like the one where your ancestors may have come from? To some, it's harmless, an expression of ethnic pride, like waving Irish flags on St. Patrick's Day; but others think it borders on treason, like waving the flag of the former Soviet Union or the Iraqi flag at a demonstration. To some, waving the Confederate flag is a symbol of civic pride, or of Southern heritage, while to others the Confederate flag is a symbol of racism.

These examples illustrate how symbols can often become politicized, endowed with meaning by different groups, and used as forms of political speech. Symbols elicit powerful emotions because they express the emotional foundations of our culture.

Flags can be powerful cultural symbols, eliciting strong emotions. To some, the Stars and Bars (a battle flag of the Confederate states during the Civil War) is a symbol of Southern heritage; to the majority of Americans (and people around the world), it is a symbol of racism and a reminder of slavery. ▼

*need language to survive as seen through Frederick II's experiment, babies raised by animals, and isolates

*Edward Sapir / Benjamin Whorf —

Sapir-Whorf hypothesis- language shapes our perception ex: Hopi Indians + tenses

Language

Language is an organized set of symbols by which we are able to think and communicate with others. Language is also the chief vehicle by which human beings create a sense of self. It is through language that we pose questions of identity—"Who am I?"—and through our linguistic interactions with others that we constitute a sense of our selves. We need language to know what we think as well as who we are.

In the thirteenth century, Frederick II, Emperor of the Holy Roman Empire, decided to perform an experiment to see if he could discover the "natural language of man." What language would we speak if no one taught us language? He selected some newborn babies and decreed that no one speak to them. The babies were suckled and nursed and bathed as usual, but speech and songs and lullabies were strictly prohibited. All the babies died. And you've probably heard those stories of "feral children"—babies who were abandoned and raised by animals became suspicious of people and could not be socialized to live in society after age 6 or so. In all the stories, the children died young, as do virtually all the "isolates," those little children who are locked away in closets and basements by sadistic or insane parents (Pines, 1981). We need to interact with other people to survive, let alone thrive. And language enables us to accomplish this interaction.

Language is not solely a human trait. There is ample evidence that other animals use sounds, gestures, facial expressions, and touch to communicate with each other. But these expressions seem to always relate to events in the present—nearby food sources, the presence of danger—or immediate expressions of different feelings or moods. What makes the human use of language different from that of animals is that we use language to transmit culture, to connect us to both the past and the future, to build on the experiences of previous generations. Even the most linguistically capable chimps cannot pass that kind of language on to their offspring.

Language does not merely reflect the world as we know it; language actually shapes our perceptions of things. In 1929, two anthropologists, Edward Sapir and Benjamin Whorf, noticed that the Hopi Indians of the Southwest seemed to have no verb tenses, no ways for them to state a word in the past, present, or future tense. Imagine speaking to your friends without being able to put your ideas in their proper tense. Although common sense held that the function of language was to express the world we already perceived, Sapir and Whorf concluded that language, itself, provides a cultural lens through which people perceive the world. What became known as the **Sapir-Whorf hypothesis** states that language shapes our perception.

Sociologist Eviatar Zerubavel (1991) noted that, in English, there are different words for "jelly" and "jam," while Hebrew, his native language, did not distinguish between the two and had only one word. Only when he learned English, he writes, did he actually "see" that they were different. Having the language for the two things made it possible for him to see them. In France, there is a specific ailment called a pain in the liver, a *crise de foie*. Americans find the idea strange because that sort of pain is given a generic "stomach ache." (In fact, when I lived in France, I found it somewhat amusing to think that they knew exactly which internal organ was in pain!) And there is no word for "gentrification" in Spanish. An Argentine colleague of mine first heard the word when he moved to New York City, and when he returned to Buenos Aires, he couldn't believe how different the city looked to him, now that he had the language to describe the changes he saw. Ask yourself or anyone you know who speaks more than one language about how different things actually *are* different when you speak Chinese, or Russian, or French, or Spanish.

untamed/ Animal/ savage

cruel

renovation to improve property values (mcmansions)

Language is a conceptual framework for understanding our social world. Every culture transmits its values through language. ▼

We often say that we'll "believe it when we see it"—that empirical proof is required for us to believe something. But it's equally true that we "see it when we believe it"—we cannot "see" what we don't have the conceptual framework to understand.

Because language not only reflects the world in which we live but also shapes our perception of it, language is also political. Consider, for example, the battles over the implicit gender bias of using the word *man* to include both women and men, and the use of the masculine pronoun *he* as the "inclusive" generic term. Some words, such as *chairman* or *policeman* make it clear that the position carries a gender—whether the occupant of the position is male or female.

Even the appellation for women and men was made the object of political struggle. While referring to a man as "Mr." indicates nothing about his marital status, appellations for women referred only to their status as married (Mrs.) or unmarried (Miss). To create a neutral, parallel term for women, Ms., took several years before it became commonplace. In the 1970s, one could occasionally read an article in the *New York Times* quoting feminist leader Gloria Steinem as "Miss Steinem, editor of *Ms.*" (the *Times* changed its policy in 1986). While some resist the change, most social institutions (corporations, schools, and the like) have replaced gendered language with neutral terms.

Similarly, language conveys cultural attitudes about race and ethnicity. This happens not simply through the use of derogatory slang terms, but also in the construction of language itself. Adjectives or colloquial phrases may convey ideas about the relative values of different groups, simply through the association of one with the other: "a black mark against you," "good guys wear white hats," "a Chinaman's chance," or "to Jew someone down" all encode stereotypes in language.

The idea of a single unifying language has also become a hot-button issue in the United States. If language is central to the smooth functioning of society, what does it imply about that unity when "only" 82 percent of Americans speak only English at home, and more than 17 percent speak a different language (10 percent of them speaking Spanish)?

Ritual

Shared symbols and language are two of the most important processes that enable cultures to cohere and persist over time. Another process is rituals, by which members of a culture engage in a routine behavior to express their sense of belonging to the culture. Rituals both symbolize the culture's coherence by expressing our unity and also create that coherence by enabling each member to feel connected to the culture.

Consider just two cultural rituals that some Americans engage in on an almost daily basis: the recitation of the Pledge of Allegiance and the singing of "The Star-Spangled Banner," our national anthem. The Pledge of Allegiance opens the school day in virtually every public school in the country. The national anthem is sung at the beginning of most major professional events (although not at the beginning of NASCAR, tennis, or boxing matches), and major college athletic events. In both cases, we're celebrating the flag, the symbol of our country ("the republic for which it stands"). These rituals are rarely, if ever, performed in other countries and would be unimaginable before a professional soccer match in Latin America or Europe, for example.

also Mr. / Miss + Mrs.

← constant

↳ name

Ex. / "black" mark against you

Ex. the Pledge of Allegiance

English as the Official Language

Although the majority of people living in the United States speaks English, the question of whether or not to make it the official language is one that elicits strong emotions and arguments on both sides. Those who are against a single official language argue that the United States is a multicultural country that should have space for more than one language, that the rest of the world is multilingual, and that an official language is exclusionary. Those in favor of an official national language maintain that the policy does not mean an English-only nation, that it's cost-effective, and that such a policy will unite Americans. So, what do you think?

Do you favor or oppose making English the official language of the United States?

○ Favor
○ Oppose

See the back of the chapter to compare your answers to national survey data.

Norms

[handwritten note: ex: Ten Commandments / = no texting at the dinner table]

Norms are the rules a culture develops that define how people should act and the consequences of failure to act in the specified ways. Cultural "norms" and cultural "values" are often discussed together; values are the ideas that justify those standards, or norms. We'll discuss them in the next section. Norms prescribe behavior within the culture, and values explain to us what the culture has determined is right and wrong. Norms tell us *how* to behave; values tell us *why*. Norms and values not only guide our own goals and actions but also inform our judgments of others.

The basic set of norms in Western societies was set down in the Ten Commandments and other ancient texts and include prescriptions to remain humble and religiously obedient to both God and one's parents, as well as normative prohibitions on theft, adultery, murder, and desiring what you don't have. The New Testament is filled with values as well, such as reciprocity ("do unto others as you would have them do unto you") and "let he who is without sin cast the first stone," which implies self-knowledge, restraint, and refusal to judge others. *[handwritten note: ↳ mutual exchange]*

Like the other components of culture, norms and values vary from place to place. What might be appropriate behavior in one culture, based on its values, might be inappropriate, or even illegal, in another. While eating together in a restaurant, for example, Americans might feel insulted if they didn't get to order their own meals. Individual choice is very important, and often others (the waiter, our dining companions) will compliment us on our choice. In China, the person at the top of the hierarchy typically orders for everyone, and it is assumed the food will be shared. Individual choice matters little; self-esteem is gained through group participation, not individual choice.

Similarly, in China, if one is opening a new restaurant, the owner typically will invite local leaders, including police, the tax collector, and political officials, for free meals. It is understood that in exchange for these free meals, the officials will treat the new business kindly. This is because the culture stresses social reciprocity and mutual obligations to each other. In the United States, however, such behavior would be seen as corruption, attempted bribery, and both the restaurant owner and the officials who accepted such "gifts" would be breaking the law.

Norms and values also vary within cultures. For example, while images of wealth and success may be inspiring to some Americans, Hispanics tend not to approve of overt materialistic displays of success. While Americans over the age of 40 might find it inappropriate for you to text message in a social situation, younger people often feel virtual relationships are just as important and "present" as interpersonal ones right in the same room (Twenge, 2006). Enforcement varies, too. Teenagers, for example, may care deeply about norms and standards of their peers but not about the judgment of others.

Norms also change over time. For example, not that long ago, norms surrounding the use of telephones included not calling someone or talking on the phone during the dinner hour unless it was an emergency. Now telemarketers target that time slot as a good time to call people because they are likely to be home from work, and people routinely talk on cell phones right at the dinner table, even in restaurants. People check voice mail and text message each other during college classes (!) and during business meetings, when it used to be considered highly inappropriate to initiate or allow interruptions in these settings, again, except in an emergency. People walk around plugged into iPods and MP3 players even on the job, at museums or other cultural events, and in social groups.

Technology has been a major driver of new norms and new mores over the last several decades. After all, technological inventions have created some entirely new social situations, new kinds of encounters and relationships, which have spawned new social norms and mores to organize them. Think about it—there are sets of informal rules about appropriate behavior on elevators, in airplanes, or at urinals, to name just a few examples. The Internet has spawned a particularly wide range of new norms, mores, and language. "Netiquette" is now so elaborate that book-length manuals are written about it, and magazines frequently offer service features to help their readers avoid a Web faux pas (Table 2.1).

Norms consist of folkways, mores, and laws, depending on their degree of formality in society. Folkways are relatively weak and informal norms that are the result of patterns of action. Many of the behaviors we call "manners" or etiquette are folkways. Other people may notice when we break them, but infractions are seldom punished. For example, there are no formal laws that prohibit women from wearing white to a wedding, which is informally reserved for the bride alone. But people might think

Each culture develops norms surrounding basic life experiences. For example, table manners—how we dress, the utensils we use, and dining etiquette—vary considerably from one culture to the other. ▼

TABLE 2.1

Internet Slang

Many of the English speakers on the Web (366 million of them!) use and invent Internet slang—shortcuts and stylized renderings of common expressions. Popular terms include:

10X	Thanks
LOTI	Laughing on the inside
2U2	To you, too
2L8	Too late
TMI	Too much information
IRL	In real life
O Rly	Oh, really
JOOC	Just out of curiosity
BTDT	Been there, done that
SCNR	Sorry, could not resist
W/E	Whatever!
CU	See you (later)
: -)	smile or happy
: - (	frown or sad
: - 0	surprised
: - D	open-mouthed smile, "rly" happy

[handwritten: translations]

you have bad taste or bad manners, and their informal evaluation is often enough to enforce those unwritten rules.

[handwritten: ex: wet hair at an interview]

Mores (pronounced more-ayz) are stronger norms that are informally enforced. These are perceived as more than simple violations of etiquette; they are moral attitudes that are seen as serious even if there are no actual laws that prohibit them. Today, some would argue that showing up for a college interview wearing flip-flops or with hair still wet from a shower violates mores; it doesn't break any laws, but it would probably sink your application.

[handwritten: ex: no theft]

Laws are norms that have been organized and written down. Breaking these norms involves the disapproval not only of immediate community members but also the agents of the state, who are charged with punishing such norm-breaking behavior. Laws both restrict our activities, prohibiting certain behaviors (like theft, for example), and enhance our experiences by requiring other activities. For example, the Social Security law requires that both employers and employees contribute to their retirement funds, whether they want to or not, so that we will have some income when we retire.

Laws are enforced by local, state, and federal agencies that impose specific penalties for breaking certain laws. These penalties are called sanctions. Positive sanctions reward behavior that conforms to the laws, and negative sanctions punish those who violate laws. Some sanctions are informally applied for violations of mores; other sanctions are applied by formal institutions and agencies.

Sociology and our World

Changing Mores around Smoking

In the 1950s and 1960s, smoking was permitted virtually everywhere—in restaurants and bars, in airplanes, and offices. Elevators had ashtrays because it was assumed people would smoke there. If you held a dinner party in the 1950s, you would have been seen as an inconsiderate host if you failed to put out a box or holder containing cigarettes for your guests. All the movie stars smoked. It was cool. Glamorous. Sexy. Smoking was a socially desirable thing to do.

Since the 1980s, though, smoking has been increasingly proscribed, both by informal mores that suggest that people who blow smoke in your direction are inconsiderate and by formal laws that restrict where you can and cannot smoke. Today, in your college or university, people are probably prohibited from smoking in their own offices.

This significant change occurs because our understanding of the effects of smoking have changed and also because our values have changed. Today, we might place health higher than pleasure on a hierarchy of values, and we believe that the rights of those who do not smoke are more significant than the rights of those who do.

Values

Values are the ethical foundations of a culture, its ideas about right and wrong, good and bad. They are among the most basic lessons a culture can transmit to its young because values constitute what a society thinks about itself. (The process of value transmission is called *socialization*, discussed in Chapter 5.)

[handwritten note: ex: valuing women's rights unlike 40 years ago → prohibit]

As such, values are the foundation for norms, and norms express those values at different levels of complexity and formality. When members of a culture decide that something is right or wrong, they often enact a law to prescribe or proscribe it. Less than 100 years ago, women were not permitted to vote, because they were not considered rational enough to make an informed decision or because, as married women, they were the property of their husbands. Less than 40 years ago, women were prohibited from service in the nation's military, police forces, and fire departments. Today, our values have changed about women's abilities, and discriminatory laws have been defeated.

Values respond to norms, and changes in our laws are often expected to produce a change in values over time. When our values about racial equality began to change, laws were enacted to prohibit discrimination. These laws were not completely popular when they were first enacted, but over time our values have shifted to better conform to the laws. Seat belt and helmet laws were incredibly unpopular when they were first passed, over significant resistance from both individuals and the automobile manufacturers. But now most Americans conform to these laws, even when there are no police around to watch them.

Even the values we hold are more fluid than we often think. Values are both consistent abstract ethical precepts *and* convenient, fluid, and internally contradictory rationalizations of our actions. Sometimes we consider them before we act; other times we apply them after the fact. In that sense they're more like contradictory childhood aphorisms—"he who hesitates is lost" versus "look before you leap"—than they are the Ten Commandments.

[handwritten note: → a short general truth]

How do we know
what we know ?

Our Values—and Others' Values

We often think of our values as a consistent set of ethical principles that guide all our actions, but the reality is more complex. Anyone who has ever made, but not kept, a New Year's resolution knows that there are often big gaps between our values and our actions. As a result, sociologists point to a difference between "ideal" cultures, the values, norms, and ideals to which we aspire, and "real" cultures, which represent those ideals as we enact them on a daily basis. It turns out we are quite forgiving of our own failures to live up those ideal values, although we are often less forgiving of others' failures. We hold others to higher standards than we hold ourselves. And we also believe that we live closer to our values than others do.

For example, the Pew Research Center, a research and charitable foundation, completed a survey in which Americans were asked about their own values and the values they perceive that others hold. An overwhelming majority of Americans said responsibility (92 percent), family life (91 percent), and friendship (85 percent) were their primary guiding principles. But they also felt that less than half of other Americans felt that way. Over two-thirds listed generosity (72 percent) and religious faith (68 percent) as guiding principles for themselves, but only about one-fifth (20 percent) for their fellow citizens. By contrast, only 37 percent of these same Americans thought prosperity and wealth were important values for them but for 58 percent of others (Pew, 2006). Perhaps we consider ourselves more moral than other people; perhaps we just let ourselves off the hook more readily. Or perhaps, it's a little bit of each.

(handwritten margin notes, left side)

American values
* freedom
* justice
* unity
* equality

(handwritten margin note, vertical) Calculated/listed

What Are American Values? In the United States, many of our values are contained in the Pledge of Allegiance: political unity in the face of a crisis ("one nation," "indivisible"), religious belief ("under God"), freedom and equality ("with liberty and justice for all"). And like all such statements, there are inconsistencies, even within the "one nation." For example, to be free implies the absence of restraints on individual behavior, as in doing whatever you please to the environment or underpaying workers in the name of making money. But "justice for all" may require just those constraints so that each person would have an equal chance.

In his famous studies of American values, sociologist Robin Williams Jr. (1970) enumerated a dozen "core" American values. These are:

1. *Achievement and success.* Americans highly value personal achievement—succeeding at work and at school; gaining wealth, power, and prestige; and successfully competing with others.

2. *Individualism.* The individual is the centerpiece of American life. Individuals take all credit and all responsibility for their lives. Individualism is, according to another study of American values, "the very core of American culture" (Bellah et al., 1985, p. 142).

3. *Activity and work.* Americans believe one should work hard and play hard. One should always be active. Americans work longer hours with fewer vacations than any other industrial society, and this gap is growing. We believe that hard work pays off in upward mobility.

4. *Efficiency and practicality.* Americans values efficient activity and practicality. Being practical is more highly valued than being intellectual.

(handwritten margin note, vertical) imperceptible

5. *Science and technology.* We are a nation that relies daily on scientific break-throughs, supporting research into the furthest recesses of outer space and infinitesimal subatomic particles for clues about our existence and tiny genetic markers for cures for illness.

6. *Progress.* Americans believe in constant and rapid progress, that everything should constantly be "new and improved."

7. *Material comfort.* Americans value living large; we believe that "living well is the best revenge."

8. *Humanitarianism.* We believe in helping our neighbors, especially during crises, and value personal kindness and charity.

9. *Freedom.* Americans believe that freedom is both the means and the end of a great society. We resist any limitations on our freedom and believe that the desire for freedom is a basic human need, which may even justify imposing freedom on others.

10. *Democracy.* Americans believe in a "government of the people, by the people, and for the people," a government that represents them. Democracy also entails the right to express your own opinion.

11. *Equality.* Americans believe that everyone is created equal and entitled to the same rights that everyone else enjoys.

12. *Racism and group superiority.* At the same time as we believe in equality of opportunity, we also believe that some people are superior to others. Usually, we assume that "our" group is superior to the others. Historically, the dominant group—men, Whites, heterosexuals—has assumed it was superior, but in recent years, some Blacks, women, and homosexuals have professed that their marginality gives them a "special" angle of vision and that they are, in fact, superior.

You'll notice that these values are internally inconsistent: The beliefs in equality and group superiority, for example, or humanitarianism and achievement, can be contradictory. In fact, we might even say that Americans hold the opposite of these twelve values at the same time. For example, these *also* seem to be American values:

1. *Luck and pluck.* We value success, but we may not care how one achieves it. Mobsters are folk heroes and even TV celebrities. Over 90 percent of Americans gamble; in 1993, we spent over $500 billion on illegal and legal gambling—a 1,900 percent increase since 1976. Americans buy more lottery tickets than any other country; casinos are a growing industry; Americans gamble on sports and horse racing and in organized gambling arenas.

2. *Community.* Americans may believe in individualism, but we are also a nation of civic-minded volunteers, animated by a spirit of community, who help out our neighbors in times of crisis. No other nation has so many volunteer fire departments, for example.

3. *Leisure and cheating.* While we value affluence, we often don't really want to work very hard to achieve it. We claim to believe in honest toil, but an enormous → hard work number of Americans cheat on their income tax, and more than one-third of Americans steal at least occasionally on their jobs (Overell, 2003, p. 4). We believe that honesty is the best policy but also that, as French philosopher Blaise Pascal said, "Mutual cheating is the foundation of society."

4. *Luxury.* We also believe that indulging in luxury is a sign of virtue as well as a vice. We are often willing to pay double the price for an article of clothing or a car if it has the right designer label on it. We like bling.

5. *Religion.* And we are also a nation that is three times more likely to believe in the virgin birth of Jesus (83 percent) as in evolution (28 percent). Ninety-four percent of adults believe in God, 86 percent believe in miracles, 89 percent believe in heaven, and 73 percent believe in the devil and in hell. (Ninety-one percent of Christians believe in the virgin birth, as do 47 percent of non-Christians [Kristof, 2003, A-25].)

6. *"Karma."* While we believe in science and progress, 51 percent of us also believe in ghosts and 27 percent believe in reincarnation. "What goes around comes around."

7. *Distrust the rich.* Although it's true that we value the good life, we also believe that the rich are immoral and probably unhappy. "The best things in life are free"; "money is the root of all evil"; and "it's easier for a camel to go through the eye of a needle than a rich man to enter the kingdom of heaven" are the sorts of phrases one is likely to hear in such discussions.

8. *Entitlement.* Our culture values "looking out for number one" and making sure that we do what we believe will make us feel good. Everyone feels entitled to the good life. Everyone has a right to his or her own opinion—even if that opinion is wrong.

9. *Tolerance has its limits.* Americans believe in tolerance, especially for themselves. We support diversity, but live near, work with, and marry those who are most similar to ourselves. We believe people should be free to do whatever they want in the privacy of their own homes, as long as they don't flaunt it in public.

Americans both love and distrust the rich and famous. We both emulate them and often take a secret pleasure in their downfall. Here, celebrity Paris Hilton greets fans as she leaves prison, June, 2007. ▼

environmentalism but also contradicted by wanting to do things like driving a (nicer) car with low mpg

10. *Security over democracy.* Freedom may be <mark>curtailed</mark> in the name of security. Recent surveys and the enactment of the Patriot Act of 2002 severely limit Americans' freedoms, but many Americans see that as a small price to pay for security from terrorist attack.

cut short ↑

11. *Inequality.* Americans also believe that unequal incomes and experiences are the result of individual effort, and so they are justified. We tolerate inequality by seeing it as a by-product of unequal individual efforts.

12. *We're all just people.* Americans don't like to be seen as members of a group, although they like to see others that way.

Emerging Values. Values aren't timeless; they all have histories. They change. As a result, there may be some values that are emerging now as new values. Some of these may become core values; others may be absorbed or discarded. Those recently observed by sociologists include physical fitness, environmentalism, and diversity/multiculturalism. And yet each of these emerging values may actually contradict others: We want to stay in shape but do not want to work hard at exercise or diets; we want to protect the environment but not at the expense of developing roads, housing, and extracting natural resources or driving the cars we want to drive; we believe in multiculturalism but oppose political efforts that would force different groups of people to go to school together or live closer to each other. Though we believe that everyone is equal, we increasingly marry people with similar education levels and befriend people whose backgrounds are similar to our own (Brooks, 2003, pp. 30–31).

Changing and Contradictory Values. One good example of this difference is Americans' attitudes about homosexuality. Most Americans agree with the statement that homosexuality is "wrong" and have felt that way for the past 40 years. In 1991, the General Social Survey (GSS), perhaps the most definitive ongoing study of Americans' attitudes, found that 71 percent said gay sex was always wrong. By 2002, the percentage of Americans who felt that homosexuality was always wrong had fallen to 53 percent—barely a majority.

Yet few would disagree that Americans' attitudes about homosexuality have changed dramatically in those 40 years. The difference is that most Americans are unlikely to apply that "ideal" value to their own interactions. So most Americans may hold an opinion that homosexuality is wrong, but they also believe that their gay or lesbian friend, colleague, or relative should be free to pursue his or her life without discrimination.

On the other hand, the recent visibility of homosexuality—the Supreme Court's decision striking down <mark>antisodomy</mark> laws, the popularity of gay-themed television shows, the ordination of an openly gay Episcopal bishop, and the debate about gay marriage—has led to a slight downturn in support for equality. Support for equality for gays and lesbians seems to stop at the marriage altar.

American attitudes about heterosexual sex often show a similar pattern. In 1972, the GSS found that 37 percent of Americans felt sex before marriage is always wrong. By 1996, that figure had dropped to only 24 percent. Yet nonmarital sex has become an accepted feature of American life during the past 25 years (Figure 2.1). The number of cohabitating couples has grown 1,000 percent in the United States since 1960, with more than 4.7 million couples currently living together. Between 1965 and 1974,

* homosexuality
* premarital sex

ant-sex involving anal oral

only 10 percent of marriages were preceded by a period of cohabitation. But between 1990 and 1994, that number increased to 57 percent, and it remains there today. Nonmarital sex is a standard plot element routinely portrayed in American TV programs, movies, books, even commercials, with little public outcry.

There are two consequences of holding such contradictory and inconsistent values. For one thing, it means that values are less the guiding principles of all our actions and more a sort of collection of attitudes we can hold situationally to justify and rationalize our belief and actions. And it also means that we become a deeply divided nation, in which clusters of attitudes seem to cohere around two separate poles. In the 2004 presidential election, these were the "red" states (those that voted for George W. Bush) and the "blue states" (those that voted for John Kerry) (Figure 2.2).

Sometimes expressed as a "culture war" between the left and the right, liberals and conservatives, these clusters suggest that the United States is a deeply and fundamentally divergent society, in which attitudes and behaviors tend to revolve around two opposing positions. Many different groups may also hold different sets of values.

beliefs revolve around 2 opposing views in U.S. (think democrats and republicans)

Cultural Expressions

Cultures are the sets of symbols and rituals that unite groups of people, enable them to feel part of something bigger and more enduring than just their own individual existence. Despite the remarkable diversity in the world's cultures, they also share certain features in common.

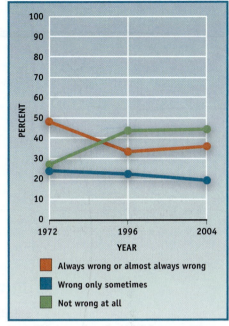

FIGURE 2.1 **American Attitudes about Nonmarital, Heterosexual Sex, 1972–2004**

Legend:
- Always wrong or almost always wrong
- Wrong only sometimes
- Not wrong at all

Notes: Women consistently think it is more wrong; White people are more likely than Black people to say it is wrong; and the upper-class is least likely to think it is wrong.
Source: General Social Survey Data, 1972–2004

culture makes us feel part of something bigger

FIGURE 2.2 **2004 Presidential Election: Red vs. Blue**

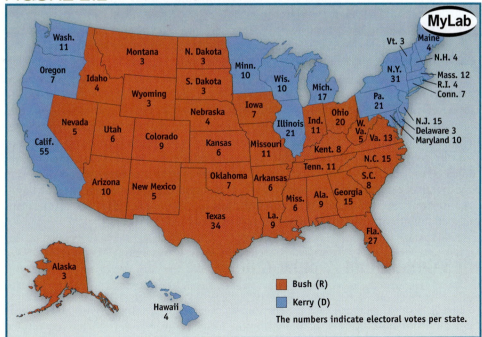

MyLab

Bush (R)
Kerry (D)
The numbers indicate electoral votes per state.

TABLE 2.2

> **Cultural Universals**
>
> Contemporary anthropologists have identified these categories of cultural universals:
>
> 1. *Material Culture*—food, clothing (and adornment of the body), tools and weapons, housing and shelter, transportation, personal possessions, household articles
> 2. *The Arts, Play, and Recreation*—folk art, fine arts, standards of beauty and taste
> 3. *Language and Nonverbal Communication*—nonverbal communication, language
> 4. *Social Organization*—societies, families, kinship systems
> 5. *Social Control*—governmental institutions, rewards and punishments
> 6. *Conflict and Warfare*
> 7. *Economic Organization*—trade and exchange, production and manufacturing, property, division of labor, standard of living
> 8. *Education*—formal and informal education
> 9. *World View*—belief systems, religion

Source: George P. Murdock, "On the Universals of Culture," in Linton, *The Science of Man in the World Crisis,* (1945); *Universals of Culture,* Alice Ann Cleveland, Jean Craven, and Maryanne Danfelser: Intercom, 92/93

Universality and Localism

Culture is both universal and local. Every culture has families, legal systems, and religion. All cultures engage in sports and music, dancing and jokes. All cultures prescribe some forms of bodily rituals—from adorning the body to styling the hair to transforming the body. The specific forms of these universals may vary from one culture to another, but all cultures exhibit these forms.

The anthropologist George Murdock (1945) identified 67 **cultural universals**— that is, rituals, customs, and symbols—that are evident in all societies (Table 2.2). What purpose do these rituals serve that they would appear everywhere? Another anthropologist, A. R. Radcliffe-Brown (1952), argued that these cultural universals permit the society to function smoothly and continuously. Other sociologists have disputed the inevitability of some universals, arguing that some may have been imposed from outside through conquest or even cross-cultural contact.

Cultural universals are broad and basic categories, allowing for significant variation as well. Although all cultures manifest religious beliefs, some may lead to behaviors that are tolerant and peace loving, while others may lead to violence and war. Cultural universals are expressed locally, experienced at the level of families, communities, and regions in ways that connect us not only to large and anonymous groups like our country but also to smaller, more immediate groups. Culture is not *either* universal or local; rather, to the sociologist, culture is *both* universal *and* local. Sometimes we feel our connection more locally and resent efforts to connect us to larger organizations. And then, often at times of crisis like September 11, 2001, Americans put aside their cultural differences and feel passionately connected.

High Culture and Popular Culture

Typically, when we hear the word culture, we think of an adjective describing someone (a "cultured" person) or a possession, as in a line in a song by Paul Simon, "the man ain't got no culture." In the common usage, culture refers to having refined aesthetic sensibilities, knowing fine wines, classical music, opera, and great works of literature. That is, the word culture is often synonymous with what we call *high*

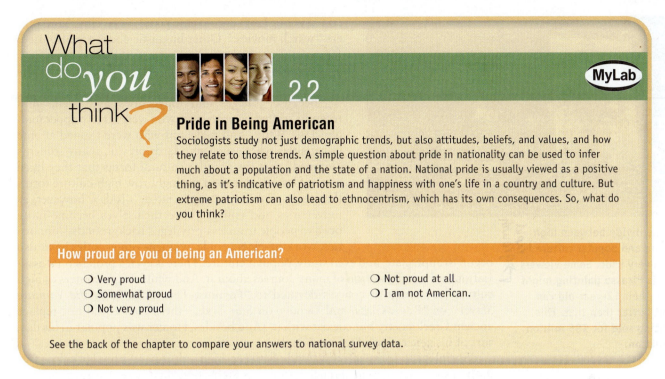

What do you think? 2.2

Pride in Being American

Sociologists study not just demographic trends, but also attitudes, beliefs, and values, and how they relate to those trends. A simple question about pride in nationality can be used to infer much about a population and the state of a nation. National pride is usually viewed as a positive thing, as it's indicative of patriotism and happiness with one's life in a country and culture. But extreme patriotism can also lead to ethnocentrism, which has its own consequences. So, what do you think?

How proud are you of being an American?

○ Very proud   ○ Not proud at all
○ Somewhat proud   ○ I am not American.
○ Not very proud

See the back of the chapter to compare your answers to national survey data.

---

culture. High culture attracts audiences drawn from more affluent and largely White groups, as any visit to a major art museum will attest.

High culture is often contrasted with "popular culture," the culture of the masses, the middle and working class. **Popular culture** includes a wide variety of popular music, nonhighbrow forms of literature (from dime novels to comic books), any forms of spectator sports, and other popular forms of entertainment, like television, movies, and video games. Again, sociologists are interested less in what sorts of cultural activities are classified as high or low and more interested in the relationships between those levels, who gets to decide what activities are classified as high or low, and how individuals negotiate their way through both dimensions. And sociologists are interested in the way that certain cultural forms shift their position, from low to high or high to low. Notice, for example, how comic books have been the subject of major museum shows in recent years, and they are now being seen as high culture *and* popular culture.

The connection between high and low culture is often expressed through comedy because comedy can painlessly reveal our own cultural biases. For example, the actress Lily Tomlin used to delight her audiences with a clever critique of this distinction. Portraying a homeless "bag lady," she professed confusion about modern culture. She held up a picture of a big Campbell's soup can. "Soup," she said. Then she held up a poster of the Andy Warhol painting of that same soup can—a poster from the Museum of Modern Art. "Art," she said. Back and forth she went. "Soup." "Art." "Soup." "Art." Confusing, huh?

→ Charged

This contrast is not only confusing, but often value laden, as if it is somehow morally superior to attend an opera sung in a language you do not understand than it is to go see a performance by the Dixie Chicks, or somehow better to view modern art in a museum than to watch NASCAR on television. (Or better to do anything than to watch television!) The split between high culture and popular culture is often

* culture is often synonymous with high culture and high culture is typically contrasted by popular culture

▲ The divide between high culture and popular culture is often very wide. Some viewers of this Picasso painting might think their 12-year-old can paint better than that. This painting sold for $85 million at auction.

rapid growth

coded in our language—some people "see films" and others "watch movies." Other linguistic codes are also used; for example, only the upper class uses the word "summer" as a verb, as in, "We summer in Maine." One rarely says he or she "summers" in Toledo.

Because colleges and universities had been, until recently, staffed by professors who were largely upper middle class, White, and male and who were trained at elite universities where such standards prevail, many students "learned" that the popular cultural forms that they liked were of lesser value than the highbrow high-culture forms that their professors "appreciated." Today, however, as universities and colleges have themselves become more open to people from less-privileged backgrounds—minorities, working-class people, women—universities have also begun to appreciate, and even study, popular culture. There is even a professional association and a proliferation of many courses about it. And while the promoters of high culture may cringe at courses devoted to "Feminist Themes in *Buffy the Vampire Slayer*" or "Race, Class, and Gender on *Star Trek*," these courses do not replace ancient Greek poetry but coexist with it. (And besides, Homer was popular in his day, sort of his generation's Stephen King!)

Sociologists approach this divide between high culture and popular culture as, itself, a sociological issue. French sociologist Pierre Bourdieu (1984) argued that different groups possess what he called "cultural capital," a resource that those in the dominant class can use to justify their dominance. **Cultural capital** is any "piece" of culture—an idea, an artistic expression, a form of music or literature—that a group can use as a symbolic resource to exchange with others. If I have access to this form of culture, and you want to have access to it, then I can "exchange" my access to access to those forms of capital that you have.

* elites "gatekeep" who is allowed to know higher culture (typically based on class)

If there is a divide between high culture and popular culture, Bourdieu argues, then the dominant class can set the terms of training so that high culture can be properly appreciated. That is, the proper appreciation of high culture requires the acceptance of certain rules, certain sets of criteria for evaluation. And this establishes certain cultural elites with privileged knowledge: the proper ways to like something. These elites are cultural "gatekeepers" who permit entry into high culture circles only to those whom the elites have deemed worthy of entry. Such gatekeeping is far less about aesthetic taste and far more about social status.

Actually, both high and popular culture consumption has such rules for appreciation. For example, imagine someone who doesn't know these rules attending the opera in the way he or she might attend a U2 concert: singing along loudly with each aria, holding up a lighter at the end of a particularly good song, standing on his or her chair, and swaying to the music. Now, imagine an opera buff attending a U2 concert, sitting politely, applauding only at the end of the concert, and calling out "bravo" to the band. Both concertgoers will have got it wrong—both of them will have failed to express the appropriate ways to show they like something.

The sociologist tries to make no value judgment about which form of culture one appreciates—actually, virtually all of us combine an appreciation of both popular and high culture at various times and places. And both carry specific norms about value and criteria for evaluating whether something is good or not. To the sociologist, what is interesting is how certain cultural forms become established as high or popular and how they change, which groups promote which forms of culture, and the debates we have about whether something is really art—or a can of soup.

Sociology and our World *suitable*

The High Culture–Low Culture Divide

The divide between popular culture and high culture is not nearly as clear as we like to think. In fact, the strict separation is bad history, because many of those cultural products that are now enshrined in "high culture" were originally popular forms of entertainment. Take Shakespeare, for example. Did you know that originally, Shakespeare's plays were performed for mass audiences, who would shout out for the performers to do encores of their favorite scenes? In fact, Shakespeare himself added a little blood and gore to his tragedies to appeal to the mass audience. Opera also was originally a mass entertainment, which was appropriated by music critics in the nineteenth century, when they developed rules for appreciating it that excluded all but the richest and most refined (see Levine, 1988).

Some popular culture can become high culture. Recall Andy Warhol's painting of a soup can. Similarly, jazz was initially denounced as racially based, sexually charged popular culture. Now some people believe you need a Ph.D. in music theory just to "appreciate" John Coltrane or Miles Davis.

Equally, some elements of high culture can become part of popular culture. For example, various fashion styles of upper-class life—for example, collared "polo" shirts, even those decorated with little polo players—are worn by large numbers of people who would never set foot in the upper-class arena of the polo field.

Forms of Popular Culture

Popular culture refers not only to the forms of high culture (like art, music, or literature) that are enjoyed by the middle and working classes. Popular culture also refers to those objects, ideas, and values that people may hold at a specific moment. While we have seen that high culture changes, one of popular culture's defining qualities is its fluidity: It is constantly changing, constantly establishing new trends and discarding old ones. We can differentiate between two types of popular culture trends: fads and fashions. → *fluid/constantly changing*

Fads. Fads are defined by being short-lived, highly popular, and widespread behaviors, styles, or modes of thought. Often they are associated with other cultural forms. They are often created and marketed to generate "buzz" because if they catch on, they can be enormously profitable. Sociologist John Lofland (1993) identified four types of fads:

1. *Objects.* These are objects people buy because they are suddenly popular, whether or not they have any use or intrinsic value. Hula hoops, yo-yos, poodle skirts, mood rings, Day-Glo, Beanie Babies, Cabbage Patch Kids, Furbies, Pokemon, or Yu-Gi-Oh! trading cards, and various children's confections are often good examples of object fads. (Because they are often associated with children, they are deliberately created by marketers and carefully placed in films and accompanied by aggressive marketing campaigns. For example, Ewoks were introduced in *Star Wars* because they would make superb cuddly stuffed animals.)   *candy*   *ex: Beanie Babies*

2. *Activities.* These are behaviors that suddenly everybody seems to be doing, and you decide to do it also, or else you'll feel left out. These can include various risk-taking behaviors—car surfing—or sports like rock climbing or simply going to a certain tourist destination that is suddenly "in." Dances like the Moonwalk, the Bump, the Hustle, and before them the Swim, the Twist, and the Watusi are activity fads. Diets are top examples of activity fads today.   *ex: diets*

3. *Ideas.* Sometimes an idea will spread like wildfire, and then, just as suddenly, slip out of view. The Celestine prophesy, beliefs in UFOs, various New Age ideas, and everything you needed to know you learned in kindergarten are examples of idea fads.

4. *Personalities.* Some celebrities burst on the scene for their accomplishments, for example, athletes (Tiger Woods, Lebron James) or rock stars (Norah Jones, Bono, Eminem). Yet others are simply "famous for being famous"—everyone knows about them and seems to care about them, but few actually know what they've actually done to merit the attention. Anna Nicole Smith, Paris Hilton, and Jessica Simpson are examples of the latter.

Today there are also Internet fads, sometimes called "Internet memes," which suddenly circulate wildly and/or draws millions of hits through the World Wide Web. Internet memes, defined as "self-propagating units of culture," include people (like Mr. T, the A-Team actor who is considered one of the earliest Internet fads), video, audio and animation segments, and various websites and blogs that suddenly become "in" places to read and post.

Fashion. A **fashion** is a behavior, style, or idea that is more permanent than a fad. It may originate as a fad and become more widespread and more acceptable over time. For example, the practice of tattooing, once associated with lower-class and even dangerous groups, became a fad in the 1990s, but is, today, an accepted part of fashion, with over one-fourth of Americans under 25 years old having at least one tattoo.

Fashions involve widespread acceptance of the activity, whether it is music, art, literature, clothing, or sports. Because fashions are less fleeting than fads, they involve the cultural institutions that mediate our relationships with culture. Fashions may become institutionalized and aggressively marketed to ensure that people know that, unless you subscribe to a particular fashion, you will be seen as an outsider. While fads may appear to bubble up from below, fashions are often deliberately created. (In reality, fads are also likely to have been created.)

proliferating

control / intervene with

The Politics of Popular Culture

Most cultural elites are culturally conservative (regardless of how they vote or what sorts of policies they favor). That is, they wish to conserve the cultural forms that are currently in place and the hierarchies of value that are currently given to them. The status quo, as Bourdieu argued, reproduces their cultural dominance. As a result, changes in popular culture typically come from the margins, not the center—from those groups who have been excluded from the cultural elites and thus develop cultural expressions that are, at least in part, forms of cultural resistance.

Take clothing, for example. Blue jeans were once a workingman's attire. In fact, Levi Strauss invented blue jeans to assist gold miners in California in their muddy work. Appropriated by the youth culture in the 1960s as a form of clothing rebellion against the bland conformity of 1950s campus fashion, blue jeans were considered a fad—until kids' parents started to wear them. Then fashion designers got into the act, and the fad became a fashion. Today these symbols of a youthful rejection of materialism can cost up to $500 a pair.

Trends in clothing, music, and other tastes in popular culture often originate today among three marginalized groups: African Americans, young people, and gay men and lesbians. As we've seen, blue jeans were once a youthful fashion statement of

* ideas often taken from marginalized groups who rebel against status quo (elites)

ex: hoodies (originally Black inner-city youth and now fashion)

Think: margin to center

rebellion. Many men's fashions in clothing or accessories often have their origins among gay men (clothing styles, pierced ears) or Black inner-city youth (hoodie sweatshirts, skater shoes and pants). White suburban embrace of hip-hop and rap echoes the same embrace of soul and R&B in the 1960s (see the movie *Animal House*), or even the same embrace of jazz and bebop in successive generations. Clever marketers are constantly on the lookout for trends among the marginalized groups that can be transformed into luxury items. If you want to know what White suburban boys will be wearing and what music they'll be listening to in 5 years, take a look at what Black teenagers or gay men are wearing and listening to today.

The Globalization of Popular Culture

It's not just American teenagers who are dressing in the latest fashions. Tourists in other countries are often surprised at how closely the fashion styles in other cultures resemble those in the United States. Interestingly, this occurs both through the deliberate export of specific cultural items and also through the ways in which cultural forms of resistance are expressed by young people and minorities.

Sometimes culture is exported deliberately. Popular culture—movies, music, books, television programs—is the second largest category of American export to the rest of the world (the first is aircraft). Large corporations like Nike, Disney, Coca-Cola, and Warner Brothers work very hard to insure that people in other countries associate American products with hip and trendy fashions in the States.

Some see this trend as a form of cultural imperialism, which is the deliberate imposition of one's country's culture on another country. The global spread of American fashion, media, and language (English as the world's lingua franca in culture, arts, business, and technology) is often seen as an imposition of American values and ideas as well as products. Cultural imperialism is not usually imposed by governments that require citizens to consume some products and not others. It is cultural in that these products become associated with a lifestyle to which citizens of many countries aspire. But it is criticized as imperialist in that the profits from those sales are returned to the American corporation, not the home country.

On the other hand, cultural transfer is not nearly as one directional as many critics contend. There are many cultural trends among Americans that originated in other countries. Imported luxury cars, soccer, reggae, wine, beer, and food fads all originate in other countries and become associated with exotic lifestyles elsewhere.

And sometimes, global cultural trends emerge from below, without deliberate marketing efforts. In the 1970s, when I was doing my dissertation research in Paris, I kept seeing young men wearing navy blue V-neck sweaters with UCLA imprinted on the chest. Since I was a student at Berkeley, UCLA was familiar (even though a rival), and so one day I approached one guy and asked, in French, if he had gone to UCLA. He looked blankly at me. I asked again, pointing to his sweater. He shrugged his shoulders and said what sounded like "oooo-klah?" a reasonable French phonetic pronunciation. He had no idea it was a university, but it was simply the fashion among French students to wear "American-style" sweaters. Even today, you can see sweatshirts on Europeans that advertise incorrectly "University of Yale" or "California University."

▲ Often members of the dominant culture appropriate cultural styles of marginalized groups because they believe them to be more authentic and slightly transgressive.

Did you know?

During the Prayer Book Rebellion of 1549, the English state sought to suppress languages other than English in the *Book of Common Prayer*. By replacing Latin with English and suppressing Catholicism, English was effectively imposed as the language of the Church, with the intent of its becoming the language of the people. At the time many people in England did not speak English, but they soon had no other choice.

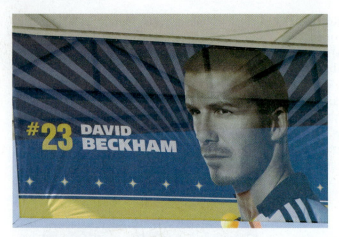

▲ Cultural artifacts are often exported to other societies, which tend to incorporate them into their own culture. As much a "brand" as a player, David Beckham was exported by Europe to the L.A. Galaxy in 2007 with the hopes that he could invigorate professional soccer in the United States.

Culture as a Tool Kit

The social movement of popular culture from margin to center reveals a final element in the sociological approach to culture. Culture is not a thing one does or does not have, nor is it a level of refinement of taste and sensibility. It is not a constant throughout our lives, and it doesn't simply evolve and grow as we mature and develop.

Culture is a complex set of behaviors, attitudes, and symbols that individuals *use* in their daily relationships with others. It is, as sociologist Ann Swidler (1986) calls it, a "tool kit," a sort of repertoire of habits, skills, and styles from which people construct their identities. Culture is not passively inherited, transmitted from one generation to the next through various institutions, so that each generation eventually obtains all the requisite symbols, linguistic skills, and values of the society. Culture is diverse, and one uses different parts of it in different circumstances with different groups for different reasons.

Cultural Change

Cultures are dynamic, constantly changing. Sometimes that rate of change may seem faster or slower than at other times. And sometimes change feels sudden and dramatic, producing conflict between those who support change and those who resist it. Culture wars often are symbolic clashes—of ideas, symbols, values—between groups who support certain changes and those who want to resist change. And while some change is inevitable, not every change is necessarily beneficial.

Although cultures are constantly changing, all the elements of culture do not change at the same time or in the same ways. In some cases, as we saw, changes among some marginalized groups become fashions for the mainstream after a period of time. It is often the case that changes in material culture—the level of technology, material resources—change more rapidly than changes in cultural institutions like the family or religion. At those moments, societies experience what sociologist William Ogburn called culture lag—the gap between technology and material culture and its social beliefs and institutions.

At those times, the beliefs and values of a society have to catch up to the changes in technology or material life (Ogburn, [1922] 1966). For example, changes in communication technology have dramatically transformed social life, but our values have failed to keep pace. Cell phones, text messaging, and instant messaging, combined with e-mail and other Internet-based modes of communication have dramatically altered the ways in which people interact. Yet the cultural mores that govern such interaction—etiquette, manners, norms governing appropriate behavior—have not yet caught up to the technology. Occasionally, this results in confusion, discomfort, or conflict. We're constantly creating new norms to respond to these changes—like laws regarding cell phone use while driving or policies on text messaging in class.

My grandfather once told me that the single greatest change in his lifetime was not television, but the introduction of the radio when he was a child. The invention of the radio completely changed his life in the city. Before the radio, the streets of the city were teeming with people sitting outside in the evening, talking, discussing, and arguing about current events and gossiping about their neighbors. Suddenly, the streets were deserted, as everyone stayed home to listen to this new invention. To him, television just added pictures, but staying home with the family had already been

material culture changes faster

ex: technology has developed faster than the manners that go with it established by radio. (This example also suggests that the cultural norm of "family time" in the evenings is also a historical product.)

Culture lag is a relatively gradual process by which nonmaterial elements of culture catch up with material culture. In this instance, we can also speak of **cultural diffusion,** which means the spreading of new ideas through a society, independent of population movement. As the impact of the technological innovation ripples through the rest of society, eventually a new equilibrium will be reached (Figure 2.3). Then all goes smoothly until the next technological breakthrough.

But sometimes, technological breakthroughs also enable groups within a society, or an entire society, to impose its values on others. Cultures can change dramatically and suddenly by conquest as well as by diffusion. The impact is often stark, sudden, and potentially lethal. Sometimes conquest can deliberately transform the culture of the colonized, as when missionaries force conquered groups to convert to the religion of the conqueror or be put to death. In those instances, the entire belief system of the culture, its foundation, is dismantled and replaced by a foreign one.

▲ Cultures do not change uniformly. Culture lag describes how changes in material culture (like technology) outpace the values and norms of the traditional culture, which attempts to incorporate them.

FIGURE 2.3 Cell Phones per 1,000 People

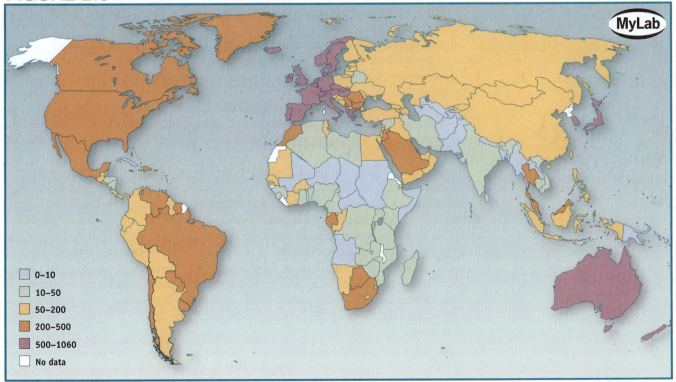

MyLab

- 0–10
- 10–50
- 50–200
- 200–500
- 500–1060
- No data

Source: From United Nations Environment Programme/GRID–Arendal website, http://maps.grida.no. Cartogram reproduced by permission of the authors, Vladimir Tikunov (Department of Geography, University of Moscow) and Philippe Rekacewicz (*Le Monde diplomatique,* Paris).

In other cases, it is less immediate or direct, but no less profound. The first European colonists who came to the New World in the sixteenth century were able to subdue the indigenous peoples of North America by superior technology (like muskets and artillery), by the manipulation of religious beliefs about the potential benevolent foreigners, and by the coincidental importation of diseases, like syphilis, which killed millions more Native Americans than the colonists' bullets. It is possible that other food-borne diseases, like avian flu and mad cow disease, could have an almost equally devastating impact on local cultures today.

Intercultural contact need not be accomplished through force. Today, global cultural forms are emerging that diffuse across national boundaries and are incorporated, unevenly and incompletely, into different national and local cultures. These often result in odd juxtapositions—a consultant in rural Africa talking on a cell phone or downloading information from a laptop standing next to a woman carrying a pail of water on her head. But these are no odder than a scene you might well have witnessed in many parts of the United States just 70 years ago—cars speeding past homes with outhouses and outdoor water pumps. Culture spreads unevenly and unequally and often is accompanied by significant opposition and conflict.

Culture in the 21st Century

Concepts such as culture, values, and norms help orient the sociologist, providing a way to understand the world he or she is trying to study. They provide the context, the "field" in which myriad individual experiences, motivations, and behaviors take place. They are necessary to situate our individual experiences; they are the concepts by which sociologists connect individual biography and history. They are the concepts that we'll use to understand the forces that hold society together and those that drive it apart.

Cultures are constantly changing—from within and through their contact with other cultures. A global culture is emerging of shared values and norms, shared technologies enabling common behaviors and attitudes. Increasingly, we share habits, fashions, language, and technology with a wider range of people than ever in human history. We are in that sense all becoming "one." And, at the same time, in our daily lives, we often resist the pull of these global forces and remain steadfastly loyal to those ties that bind us to local cultural forms—kinship and family, our ethnic group, religion, or community.

The cultural diversity that defines most industrialized societies also defines American society, and that diversity will continue to provide moments of *both* combination *and* collision, of separation and synthesis. Most people are rarely "all-American" or feel completely like members of one ethnic or racial subculture. We're both. To be a hyphenated American—an Asian-American or Italian-American, for example—is a way of expressing the fact that we don't have to choose. Sometimes you may feel more "Italian" than American, and other times you may feel more "American" than Italian. And then, finally, there are times when you feel specifically Italian-American, poised somewhere between, distinct and unique, and yet not completely fitting into either. As Bono sings in the U2 song "One": "We're one but we're not the same."

1. *How do sociologists see culture?* Culture is the connection between the personal and the structural, between how we are shaped by our society and how we are in turn shaping it. It is both the material basis for social life and the ideas, beliefs, and values that guide social life. Most people think their culture is "normal," and this belief can lead to culture shock when they are exposed to unfamiliar cultures and to ethnocentrism, which involves condemning other groups for being different. Even within a single culture, there are differences between groups that lead to the formation of subcultures (groups that are part of the larger culture but have distinct characteristics) and countercultures (subcultures are in opposition to the larger culture).

2. *What are the elements of culture?* All cultures share five basic elements. Material culture is what people make (food, clothing, tools, and the like) and the things they use to make it. The next universal element is symbols, or things that represent something else and have a shared social meaning. Language is how we think and communicate with others and the way we create a sense of self; it both reflects how we see the world and shapes how we see it. The last universal element is rituals, which are routinized behaviors that express belonging to a culture.

3. *How is culture expressed in a society?* Cultural universals are those components of culture that exist in all societies. They include material culture, the arts and play, language and nonverbal communication, social organization, a system of social control, conflict and warfare, economic organization, a system of education, and a shared worldview. But these broad, basic categories include a lot of variation. Sometimes the word culture

is used to describe the high culture of arts and literature. High culture is contrasted with popular culture, which is more inclusive. Pierre Bordieu described how knowledge of high culture, or cultural capital, is used to reinforce social status. Popular culture often occurs as trends like fads and fashions, which spread worldwide through globalization.

4. *What is the difference between norms and values?* The core elements of culture are norms and values. Norms are expectations for behavior, and values are the ideas that justify those expectations. Norms are based on one's status and establish one's role in society. Norms and values are transmitted through socialization and vary by culture and by groups within a culture. They also change over time. Norms come in various stages of seriousness of transgression and consequences. Values are ethical ideas about what is right or wrong, good or bad. They are shared by members of a society. Values and norms interact and change each other. Laws, which are formal norms, are expected to change values. Often, though, there are big gaps between values and actions, between "ideal" and "real" cultures.

5. *How does culture change?* Cultures are constantly changing. Changes in ideas, symbols, or values often ensue in a symbolic clash called culture wars. Technological changes can happen faster than social ideas change, which can lead to a culture lag, which results often in confusion or discomfort. Technological changes often spread quickly in what is called cultural diffusion. Cultures change in other ways as well, such as after a conquest or simply through the increased interaction of globalization. In addition, a global culture is developing where we share technology, fashion, and values.

Key Terms

Countercultures (p. 43)
Cultural capital (p. 58)
Cultural diffusion (p. 63)
Cultural diversity (p. 41)
Cultural imperialism (p. 61)
Cultural relativism (p. 42)
Cultural universals (p. 56)
Culture (p. 40)
Culture lag (p. 62)

Culture shock (p. 41)
Ethnocentrism (p. 42)
Fads (p. 59)
Fashion (p. 60)
Folkways (p. 49)
Language (p. 46)
Laws (p. 50)
Material culture (p. 40)
Mores (p. 50)

Nonmaterial culture (p. 41)
Norms (p. 48)
Popular culture (p. 57)
Rituals (p. 47)
Sapir-Whorf hypothesis (p. 46)
Subcultures (p. 43)
Symbol (p. 45)
Values (p. 51)

What does *America* think?

2.1 English as Our Official Language

This is actual survey data from the General Social Survey, 2004.

Do you favor or oppose making English the official language of the United States? Overall, slightly more than three-quarters of the U.S. population favors English as the official language of the United States. There are significant class differences in this, with those who identify as lower class being less likely than other groups to be in favor.

English as Official Language, by Social Class, Percent

	Lower	Working	Middle	Upper	Row Total
Favor	70.2	75.8	79.8	78.4	77.5
Oppose	29.8	24.2	20.2	21.6	22.5

CRITICAL THINKING | DISCUSSION QUESTIONS

1. How can we explain the social class differences in responses to this survey question?
2. How do you think the results might have differed had we looked at them by race or by gender?

2.2 Pride in Being American

This is actual survey data from the General Social Survey, 2004.

How proud are you of being an American? An overwhelmingly high proportion of respondents said they were very proud to be an American (89 percent). Less than 3 percent of respondents said they were not very proud or not proud at all to be American. Those who identified as working class were the least likely to say they were very proud to be American.

Pride in Being American, by Social Class, Percent

	Lower	Working	Middle	Upper	Row Total
Very proud	85.3	76.9	79.7	85.1	79.0
Somewhat proud	10.2	18.6	16.1	14.9	16.8
Not very proud	4.5	1.0	2.2	0.0	1.8
Not proud at all	0.0	0.3	0.4	0.0	0.3
Not American	0.0	3.1	1.5	0.0	2.0

CRITICAL THINKING | DISCUSSION QUESTIONS

1. While the class difference in responses was not that great, it is still interesting. Why do you think those who identify as lower class and those who identify as upper class were most likely to report being very proud to be American? Why do you think those who identified as middle class were least likely to report being very proud?

2. The number of Americans who are proud to be American is very high. Why do you think this is so? Do you think pride in country is as high in other countries? Why or why not? Give examples.

▶ Go to this website to look further at the data. You can run your own statistics and crosstabs here: **http://sda.berkeley.edu/cgi-bin/hsda?harcsda+gss04**

REFERENCES: Davis, James A., Tom W. Smith, and Peter V. Marsden. General Social Surveys 1972–2004: [Cumulative file] [Computer file]. 2nd ICPSR version. Chicago, IL: National Opinion Research Center [producer], 2005; Storrs, CT: Roper Center for Public Opinion Research, University of Connecticut; Ann Arbor, MI: Inter-University Consortium for Political and Social Research; Berkeley, CA: Computer-Assisted Survey Methods Program, University of California [distributors], 2005.

chapter 3

IN THE BEGINNING of the last chapter, we saw how people feel both separate *and* connected, both different and the same. Sometimes, we want to "fit in," be just like everyone else—for example, when your professor scans the classroom looking for someone to call on for a question, and you put your eyes down, hoping not to be seen, to disappear into the class, to fit in without ever being noticed. Yet when you approach your professor at the end of the semester and ask for a letter of recommendation, you would feel a bit uncomfortable if your professor were to say, "You're just like all the other students." At that moment, you are likely to protest that you are a "unique individual," and that you cannot be seen as just like everyone else. You want to "stand out in the crowd." Or, when you create a page for yourself on Facebook, you are

Society: Interactions, Groups, and Organizations

doing it because everybody is doing that these days, to fit in, to be in step with others, to be one of the crowd. Yet when you design it, you also want to stand out, to grab people's attention, so you will be seen as a unique person.

Sociologists do not want you to have to choose between "fitting in" and "standing out." You couldn't if you tried. We spend our lives both trying to fit in and trying to stand out; sometimes we succeed, and sometimes we fail. What's interesting to a sociologist is the choices you make about where to fit in or stand out, how you decide to go about fitting in or standing out, what

What's interesting to a sociologist is the choices you make about where to fit in or stand out, what the formal and informal criteria are for fitting in or standing out, and who gets to decide if you've been successful in the position you want to take.

the formal and informal criteria are for fitting in or standing out, and who gets to decide if you've been successful in the position you want to take. Fitting in and standing out are similar, after all. Both refer to something outside yourself. Both assume that you are referring to an "other"—another group or person that you either want to accept you or from which you want to separate yourself. You want to be seen as special, different, worth knowing and being with because you are *you*, and you don't want to be seen as *too* different, weird, or strange, because then people won't want to be with you.

Society: Putting Things in Context

Sociology is a way of seeing that can be described as "contextualizing"—that is, sociologists try to understand the social *contexts* in which our individual activity takes place, the other people with whom we interact, the dynamics of interaction, and the institutions in which that activity takes place. Sociologists are less concerned with the psychological motivations for your actions and more concerned with the forces that shape your motivation, the forces that push you in one direction and pull you in another, other people with whom you interact, and meanings you derive from the action. Understanding social behavior is a constant process of "contextualizing" that behavior—placing it in different frameworks to better understand its complexity. (The importance of the term *context* cannot be overstated. The American Sociological Association's new magazine, designed to present sociology's message to the wider public outside the field, is called *Contexts*. When this title was announced, the universal praise among sociologists indicated a collective nod of understanding.)

The chief context in which we try to place individuals, locate their identity, and chart their experiences is generally called society. But what is this thing called "society" that we study?

Some people don't even believe it exists. In 1987, British Prime Minister Margaret Thatcher caused an uproar when she told an interviewer "There's no such thing as society. There are individual men and women, and there are families" (Keay, 1987). Is society simply a collection of individuals, or is it something more than that?

Society can be defined *an organized collection of individuals and institutions, bounded by space in a coherent territory, subject to the same political authority, and organized through a shared set of cultural expectations and values.* But what does that mean? Let's look look at each element:

- *Organized collection of individuals and institutions.* Society isn't a random collection but purposive and organized, composed not only of individuals but of all the institutions (family, economy, religion, education) in which we find ourselves.
- *Bounded by space in a coherent territory.* This adds a spatial dimension to society. Society exists someplace, not only in our imaginations.

Did *you* know?

While no one can say for sure where society originated, human beings are, by definition, social creatures, so the origin of society is the origin of human life. But we can say where the word *society* came from: France. It comes from the French word *société*. This term has its origins from the Latin word *societas*, a "friendly association with others."

- *Subject to the same political authority.* Everyone in the same place is also subject to the same rules.
- *Organized through a shared set of cultural expectations and values.* Our behaviors are not only governed by what people expect of us but also motivated by common values.

The definition of society here is somewhat top heavy—that is, it rests on large-scale structures and institutions, territorial arrangements, and uniform political authority. But society doesn't arrive fully formed from out of the blue: Societies are made, constructed, built from the bottom up as well. In this chapter, we will look at the basic building blocks of society from the smallest elements (interactions) to coherent sets of interactions with particular members (groups) and within particular contexts (organizations). From the ground up, societies are composed of *structured social interactions*. Again, let's look at each of these terms individually:

- *Structured* means that our actions, our interactions with others, do not occur in a vacuum. Structured refers to the contexts in which we find ourselves—everything from our families and communities, to religious groups, to states and countries, and even to groups of countries. We act in the world in ways that are structured, which makes them (for the most part) predictable and orderly; our actions are, in large part, bound by norms and motivated by values.
- *Social* refers to the fact that we don't live alone; we live in groups, families, networks. Sociologists are interested in the social dynamics of our interaction, how we interact with others.
- *Interaction* refers to the ways we behave in relation to others. Even when we are just sitting around in our homes or dorm rooms with a bunch of friends, "doing nothing," we are interacting in structured, patterned ways.

These two definitions are complementary; they are the micro and the macro levels of society. Sociologists believe that society is greater than the sum of its parts. Sociologists examine those parts, from the individual to the largest institutions and organizations. Sociologists have discovered that even a small group of friends makes different decisions than the individual members would alone. And it doesn't end there. Groups are embedded in other groups, in social institutions, in identities, in cultures, in nation-states, until we come to that enormous edifice, society. It turns out to be not a mass of individuals at all but an intricate pattern of groups within groups. What's more, it's not the mere *fact* of different types of groups but how we interact with others in society that structures our behavior, our experiences, and even our selves.

Since the early twentieth century, sociologists have attempted to understand exactly how we "construct" a sense of self, an identity through our interaction with the world around us. Instead of being a "blank slate" on which society imprints its dictates, sociologists see individuals as actively engaged in the process. We create identities through our interactions with the world around us, using the materials (biological inheritance, cultural context, social position) that we have at hand. Our identities, sociologists believe, are socially constructed.

Sociologists use certain conceptual tools to understand the ways in which we construct these identities. Some, like *socialization,* refer to processes by which the culture incorporates individuals, makes the part of the collectivity. Other terms, like *roles, statuses, groups,* and *networks,* help us understand the ways in which individuals negotiate with others to create identities that feel stable, consistent, and permanent. Finally, other terms, like *organizations* and *institutions* describe more formal and stable patterns of interactions among many individuals that enable us to predict and control behavior. *Society* refers to the sum of all these other elements.

Societies cohere through social structure. **Social structure** is a complex framework, or structure, composed of both patterned social interactions and institutions that together both organize social life and provide the context for individual action. It consists of different positions, resources, groups, and relationships. Social structure is both formal and informal, fluid and fixed. It is both a web of affiliations that supports and sustains us and a solid walled concrete building from which we cannot escape.

The Social Construction of Reality

Social life is essentially patterns of social interaction—behaviors that are oriented toward other people. Other people are also interacting as well, and these near-infinite interactions cohere into patterns. While we are performing in the gigantic drama of social life, everyone around is also performing, trying to present the best role possible and trying to avoid losing face. Because everyone has different ideas, goals, beliefs, and expectations, how does it all fit together into a social world with some semblance of order? Commonsense knowledge—things that we take for granted as "obvious"—differs among people from different cultures and even among different people within the same culture. Even empirical data—what we see, hear, smell, and taste—differ. One person may watch a movie and be thrilled, another bored, and a third outraged.

There is no objective social reality, no one "true" way of interpreting the things that happen to us. The job of the physical scientist is to find out what is "true" about the physical world, but with no "true" social world, the job of the social scientist is to find out how people come to perceive something as true.

According to Peter Berger and Thomas Luckmann (1966), we "construct" social reality through social interaction. We follow conventions that everyone (or almost everyone) in the group learns to accept: that grandmothers and buddies are to be treated differently, for instance, or that teachers like students who express their own opinions. These conventions become social reality, "the way things are." We do not challenge them or even think about them very much.

Cooley and the Looking-Glass Self

One of the first sociologists to argue that the identity is formed through social interaction was Charles Horton Cooley (1864–1929), who coined the term **looking-glass self** to describe the process by which our identity develops (Cooley, 1902). He argued that we develop our looking-glass self or mirror self in three stages:

1. *We imagine how we appear to others around us.* We think other people see us as smart or stupid, good or bad. If a teacher scolds me for not knowing the answer, I will believe that the teacher thinks of me as stupid. Our conclusions do not need to be accurate—perhaps the teacher thinks that I am exceptionally intelligent and is just frustrated that I do not know the answer this time. Misinterpretations, mistakes, and misunderstandings can be just as powerful as truthful evaluations.

2. *We draw general conclusions based on the reactions of others.* If I imagine that many people think I am stupid, or just one important person (like a teacher or a parent), then I will conclude that I am indeed stupid.

3. *Based on our evaluations of others' reactions, we develop our sense of personal identity.* That is, I imagine that many people think I am stupid, so I "become"

FIGURE 3.1 Cooley's Looking-Glass Self

stupid or at least hide my intelligence. A favorable reaction in the "social mirror" leads to a positive self-concept; a negative reaction leads to a negative self-concept.

This is never a finished process. We are constantly meeting new people and getting new reactions, so we are revising our looking-glass self throughout our lives (Figure 3.1).

George Herbert Mead (1863–1931), a sociologist, believed that our self arises through taking on the role of others. Mead used interaction as the foundation for this theory of the construction of identity: We create a "self" through our interactions with others. (We will discuss Mead further in Chapter 5.) Mead said that there were two parts of the self, the "I" and the "me." The "I" is the self as subject, needs, desires, and impulses that are not channeled into any social activity, an agent, the self that thinks and acts. The "me" is self as object—the attitudes we internalize from interactions with others, the social self. We achieve our sense of self-awareness when we learn to distinguish the two.

Goffman and the "Dramaturgical" Self

Erving Goffman (1922–1982) went beyond the concept of the looking-glass self. He believed that our selves change not only because of other people's reactions but also because of the way we actively try to present ourselves to other people. Early in life, we learn to modify our behavior in accordance with what particular people expect of us. Perhaps when I am with my buddies, I tell vulgar jokes and playfully insult them, because they approve of this sort of behavior as a form of male bonding. However, I would never consider such behavior when I am visiting my grandmother: Then I am quiet and respectful. Goffman calls this **impression management** (1959). I am not merely responding to the reactions of others. I am actively trying to control how others perceive me by changing my behavior to correspond to an ideal of what they will find most appealing.

We change our behavior so easily and so often, without even thinking about it, that Goffman called his theory **dramaturgy**. Social life is like a stage play, with our performances changing according to the characters on stage at the moment. Everyone tries to give the best performance possible, to convince other "characters" that he or she is corresponding to an ideal of the best grandchild, buddy, or whatever role is being played.

Our attempt to give the best possible performance is called **face work**, because when we make a mistake or do something wrong, we feel embarrassed, or "lose face." We are always in danger of losing face because no performance is perfect. We may not fully understand the role, we make be distracted by another role, or others may have a different idea of what the role should be like.

For example, students who come to the United States from some Asian countries often "lose face" in class because they believe that the "ideal student" should sit quietly and agree with everything the professor says, whereas in American colleges the "ideal student" is expected to ask questions, share personal opinions, and perhaps disagree with the professor. Potential pitfalls are endless, and we learn to avoid them only through years of observation and experimentation.

If we have little to lose during the scene, if the other "characters" are not very important to us or we don't have a lot of emotional investment in the role, we often "front," simply pretend to have a role that we do not. We may pretend to be an expert on gourmet cuisine to impress a date or a high school sports hero to impress our children. But the more important the role, the more adept we must become in playing the role.

How do we interact? What tools do we use?

Nonverbal Communication

One of the most important ways of constructing a social reality is through nonverbal communication: our body movements, gestures, and facial expressions, our placement in relation to others. There is evidence that some basic nonverbal gestures are universal, so they may be based in biological inheritance rather than socialization. Ekman and Friesen (1978) studied New Guinea natives who had almost no contact with Westerners and found that they identified facial expressions of six emotions (happiness, sadness, anger, disgust, fear, and surprise) in the same way that Westerners did. Later, they discovered that the facial expression associated with another emotion, contempt, was not culture specific either; it was recognized by people from Germany, Hong Kong, and Italy to West Sumatra, as well as the United States (Ekman and Friesen, 1986).

However, most facial expressions must be interpreted depending on social situations that vary from culture to culture and era to era and must be learned through socialization: a New Guinean and a Westerner would certainly disagree over what sort of smile people use when they are pretending to be unhappy over an incident but are really thrilled, or when they have hurt feelings but are trying not to show it.

Through socialization, observing and experimenting in a wide variety of social situations, we learn the conventions of nonverbal communication. What is a comfortable distance for standing near another person? It differs depending on whether the person is a friend, relative, or stranger, male or female, in private or in public. People raised in the Middle East are socialized to want a very close speaking distance, so close that you can feel the breath of your partner, and they often find people raised in the United States, accustomed to a farther distance, cool and unfriendly. One of my dorm mates in college, from India, sat so close that our knees or thighs touched, even when there was plenty of room. In the United States, that degree of closeness means romantic intimacy, or at least flirting, but he intended only a comfortable distance for talking. Fortunately, some strange looks (and perhaps a harsh word or two) soon socialized him into keeping his distance.

Did *you* know?

The rules of body language and gestures change from culture to culture, so it is understandable that mistakes happen. Sometimes they can ruin a cross-cultural friendship or business deal, or even cause a war:

- The "thumbs up" gesture is obscene in Australia and New Zealand.
- In Japan, the "OK" gesture is a request for money. It's obscene in Russia, Turkey, Greece, and Italy, and in France it signifies that you believe the speaker is "worthless."
- In the Middle East, it is rude to sit cross-legged (keep both feet on the ground) or to point with the index finger (use your fist instead).

Source: Axtell, R. E. *Do's and Taboos around the World*. New York: John Wiley & Sons, 1985.

Here's a good example of how nonverbal communication is a form of social "glue" that holds us together as a group and maintains social cohesion even in groups that are based on inequality: laughing. Theorists have often misunderstood laughter, assuming that it was a cognitive reaction: You hear a joke, you get the joke, you laugh at it—because the joke is funny. Laughter is not about getting the joke. It's about getting along. Researchers have found that about 80 to 90 percent of the time, laughter is social, not intellectual. Laughter is a powerful bonding tool that is used to signal readiness for friendship and reinforce group solidarity by mocking deviants or insulting outsiders. It also expresses who belongs where in the status hierarchy. Women tend to laugh more than men, and everyone laughs at jokes by the boss—even if the jokes he or she tells aren't funny. Maybe *especially* if they aren't funny (Tierney, 2007)!

[margin notes: unity/ coherence; mental; "abnormals/differents"]

▲ Successful social interactions are governed by cultural conventions that are often unstated. If this theatre were nearly full, it would be perfectly acceptable to sit next to any of these people. But with the theatre nearly empty, it would be seen as a violation of personal space.

Verbal Communication

[margin note: insignificant]

Nonverbal communication is so subtle that it requires a great deal of socialization, but talking is not straightforward. Even the most inconsequential statements, a "hello" or "How are you?," can be full of subtle meanings. Harold Garfinkel (1967) asked his students to engage in conversations with family and friends that violated social norms. People frequently ask us "How are you?" as a polite greeting, and they expect to hear "Fine!" as a response, even if we are not fine at all (those who are really interested in our condition might ask "How are you feeling?" instead). But Garfinkel's students took the question at face value and asked for clarification: "How am I in regard to what? My health, my finances, my peace of mind? . . ." Their "victims" usually became annoyed or angry, without really knowing why: The students had violated a convention of social interaction that we depend on to maintain a coherent society. Garfinkel eventually developed an entire sociological tradition called **ethnomethodology** in which the researcher tried to expose the common unstated assumptions that enable such conversational shortcuts to work.

*[margin note: * subtle norms ex: "How are you?" "fine." (know not to say how you actually are)]*

Patterns of Social Interaction

There are five basic patterns of social interaction, what sociologist Robert Nisbet (1970) calls the "molecular cement" that links individuals in groups from the smallest to the largest:

[margin note: payback/revenge]

1. *Exchange.* According to sociologist Peter Blau (1964), exchange is the most basic form of social interaction: We give things to people after they give things to us or in expectation of receiving things in the future. In traditional societies, the exchange can take the form of extravagant gifts or violent retribution, but most often in modern societies, the exchange is symbolic: Smiles or polite words symbolize welcome or friendship , and vulgar gestures or harsh words are exchanged to symbolize hostility. Individuals, groups, organizations, and nations keep an informal running count of the kindnesses and slights they have received and act according to the "norm of reciprocity."

[margin note: ex: you smile- I smile.]

▲ Group participation often leads individuals to do things they wouldn't ordinarily do. More than 5,000 Santas participated in the Santa Dash in Liverpool, England, in December 2006 to raise money for charities.

Ex: driving the speed limit for the good of all people! no ticket

2. *Cooperation.* The running counts of good and bad exchanges are forgotten when we must work together toward a common goal: growing food, raising children, and protecting our group from enemies. And building civilizations: Without cooperation, social organization more complex than a small group of family and friends would be impossible. In modern societies, our jobs are usually a tiny part of an enterprise requiring the cooperation of hundreds or thousands of people. Sometimes we can even be persuaded to abandon our own goals and interests in favor of group goals. Soldiers, police officers, and others may even be asked to sacrifice their lives.

3. *Competition.* Sometimes the goal is not one of common good: Several advertising agencies may be interested in a prized account, but only one will get the contract. When resources are limited, claimants *A person who makes a claim* must compete for them. In modern societies, competition is especially important in economies built around capitalism, but it affects every aspect of social life. Colleges compete for the best students; religious groups compete for members.

4. *Conflict.* In a situation of conflict, the competition becomes more intense and hostile, with the competitors actively hating each other and perhaps breaking social norms to acquire the prized goal. In its basic form, conflict can lead to violence, in the form of schoolyard fights, terrorist attacks, or the armed conflicts of nations. However, sociologist Lewis Coser argued that conflict can also be a source of solidarity. In cases of conflict, the members of each group will often develop closer bonds with each other in the face of the common enemy. Conflict can also lead to positive social change, as groups struggle to overcome oppression (Coser, 1956).

5. *Coercion.* The final form of social interaction is coercion, in which individuals or groups with social power, called the **superordinate**, use the threat of violence, deprivation, or some other punishment to control the actions of those with less power, called the **subordinate** (Simmel, 1908). Coercion is often combined with other forms of social interaction. For instance, we may obey the speed limit on the highway through coercion, the threat of getting a traffic ticket, as well as through cooperation, the belief that the speed limit has been set for the public good. A great deal of our interactions are coercive, though very often the threat is not violence but being laughed at, stared at, or otherwise embarrassed. Think of how hard you might find it to be friends with uncool people—not because you don't want to but because peer pressure is a powerful form of coercion.

Elements of Social Structure

Social life requires us to adopt many roles. We must behave according to the role of "parent" around our children, "student" while in class, and "employee" at work. We know the basic rules of the each role: that "students" sit in chairs facing a central podium or desk, keep quiet unless we raise our hands, and so on—but we also have a great deal of freedom, and as we become more experienced in playing the role, we can become quite creative. The particular emphasis or interpretation we give a role, our "style," is called **role performance**.

Sociologists use two terms, *status* and *role,* to describe the elementary forms of interaction in society.

Status

In everyday life we use the term *status* to refer to people who have a lot of money, power, and influence. But sociologists use **status** to refer to any social identity recognized as meaningful by the group or society. A status is a position that carries with it certain expectations, rights, and responsibilities. Being a Presbyterian, an English major, or a teenager are statuses in contemporary American society, but having red hair or liking pizza are not. Many statuses are identities that are fixed at birth, like race, sex, or ethnicity; others we enter and exit, like different age statuses or, perhaps, class.

ex: age/race/ethnicity

Statuses change from culture to culture and over time. Having red hair was once a negative status, associated with being quick tempered, cruel, and possibly demonic. When pizza was first introduced into the United States in the early 1900s, only a few people knew what it was, and "liking pizza" was a status. Many statuses are identical to roles—son or daughter, student, teacher—but others, like residents of Missouri or cyberathlete, are more complex, based on a vast set of interlocking and perhaps contradictory roles (Merton, 1968). There are two kinds of statuses.

Ascribed Status. An **ascribed status** is a status that we receive involuntarily, without regard to our unique talents, skills, or accomplishments: for instance, our place of birth, parents, first language, ethnic background, gender, sexual identity, and age. Many ascribed statuses are based on genetics or physiology, so we can do little or nothing to change them. At various times in our lives, we will have an ascribed status based on our age, as child, teenager, young adult, and so on, whether we want it or not. We have the ascribed status as "male" or "female," whether we want it or not. Some people do expend a great deal of time and effort to change their appearance and physiological functioning, but they end up with a new ascribed status of "transsexual."

ex: gender

Sociologists find ascribed statuses interesting because they are often used to confer privilege and power. Some statuses (White, native born, young, male, heterosexual) are presented as "naturally" superior and others (non-White, immigrant, elderly, female, gay, or lesbian) as "naturally" inferior so often and so effectively that sometimes even people who have the "inferior" statuses agree with the resulting economic, political, and social inequality. Just what statuses are presented as superior and inferior differ from culture to culture and across eras.

Though we usually cannot change our ascribed statuses, we can work to change the characteristics associated with them. If being female or African American, both ascribed statuses, are negatively valued, then people can mobilize to change the perception of those statuses. Many of the "new social movements" of the twentieth century, such as the Civil Rights movement, the women's movement, and the gay/lesbian movement, were dedicated to changing a negative ascribed social status.

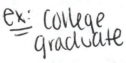

Did *you* know?

In the United States, the status of "elderly" is often negative, associated with being weak, feeble-minded, decrepit, and useless, but in China, the status is associated with wisdom and strength, so you might call a 25-year-old teacher "old teacher" to indicate respect.

Achieved Status. An **achieved status** is a status that we attain through talent, ability, effort, or other unique personal characteristics. Some of the more common achieved statuses are: being a high school or college graduate; being rich or poor; having a certain occupation; being married or in a romantic relationship; belonging to a church or club; being good at a sport, hobby, or leisure pursuit; or having a specific point of view on a social issue. If you like big band or heavy metal music, for instance, you have an achieved status.

ex: college graduate

ex: female being hired for child care

Achieved statuses are often dependent on ascribed statuses. Fans of big band music tend to be considerably older than fans of rap. Some ascribed statuses make it more difficult to achieve other statuses. Race, gender, and ethnicity all affect our abilities to achieve certain statuses. The status of "male" vastly increases your likelihood of being hired as an airline pilot or dentist, and the status of "female" vastly increases your potential of being hired for a job involving child care. In the United States, while we profess a belief that achieved statuses should be the outcome of individual abilities, ascribed statuses continue to exert a profound influence on them. Social movements for equality often organize around a sense of injustice and seek to reduce the importance of ascribed statuses.

We are able to change achieved statuses. We can change jobs, religions, or political affiliations. We can learn new skills, develop new interests, meet new people, and change our minds about issues. In fact, we usually do. I have most of the same ascribed statuses now that I did when I was 16 years old (all except for age), but my achieved statuses are dramatically different: I have changed jobs, political views, taste in music, and favorite television programs.

In traditional societies, most statuses are ascribed. People are born rich or poor and expect to die rich or poor. They have the same jobs that their parents had and cannot even think of changing their religion because only one religion is practiced throughout the society. They dress the same and listen to the same songs and stories, so they can't even change their status based on artistic taste. However, in modern societies, we have many more choices, and more and more statuses are attained.

ex: cancer patient

Master Status. When ascribed or achieved status is presumed so important that it overshadows all of the others, dominating our lives and controlling our position in society, it becomes a **master status** (Hughes, 1945). Being poor or rich tends to be a master status because it dramatically influences other areas of life, such as education, health, and family stability. People who have cancer or AIDS often find that all of the other statuses in their lives become subsidiary. They are not "college student" or

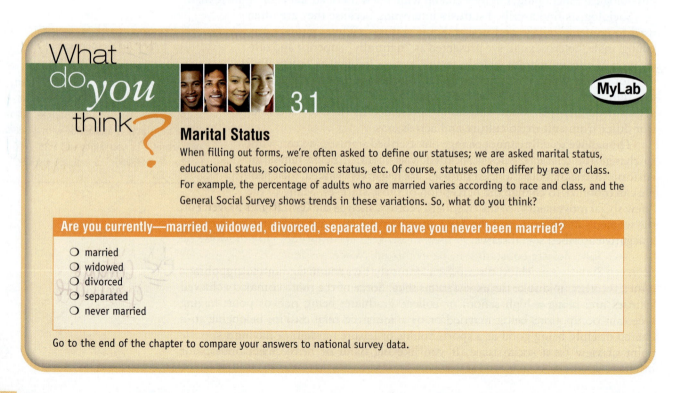

What do *you* think? 3.1 — MyLab

Marital Status

When filling out forms, we're often asked to define our statuses; we are asked marital status, educational status, socioeconomic status, etc. Of course, statuses often differ by race or class. For example, the percentage of adults who are married varies according to race and class, and the General Social Survey shows trends in these variations. So, what do you think?

Are you currently—married, widowed, divorced, separated, or have you never been married?

○ married
○ widowed
○ divorced
○ separated
○ never married

Go to the end of the chapter to compare your answers to national survey data.

"Presbyterian" but "college student with cancer," "Presbyterian with cancer," or just "cancer patient." People who suddenly become disabled find that co-workers, acquaintances, and even their close friends ignore all their other statuses, seeing only "disabled." Other common master statuses are race, ethnicity, religion, and sexual identity (Figure 3.2). Members of ethnic, religious, and sexual minorities often complain that their associates treat them as representatives of their status rather than as individuals, asking "What do gay people think about this?" or "Why do Muslims do that?" but never about last night's ball game. Occupation may also be a master status; the first question you are likely to be asked at a gathering is, "What do you do for a living?"

Roles

Social **roles** are sets of behaviors that are expected of a person who occupies a certain status. In the dramaturgical analogy, a social role is like the role an actor plays in a drama: It includes the physical presentation, props, and costume; the actor's motivation and perspective; and all the actor's lines, as well as the physical gestures, accent, and timing.

As in the theatrical world, our experience of roles is a negotiation between role *expectations* and role *performances*. We learn what sorts of behaviors are expected from specific roles, and then we perform those roles in conformity with those expectations. Our roles are constantly being evaluated: When we do them right, we may receive praise; when we do them wrong, we may be admonished or even punished. And if we begin to dislike the expectations that accompany a role, we may try to modify it to suit our needs, convince others that our performance is better than the expectations, or even reject the role altogether. Role expectations may be independent of the individuals who play them, but each individual does it slightly differently.

Because roles contain many different behaviors for use with different people in different situations, sometimes the behaviors contradict each other. We experience **role**

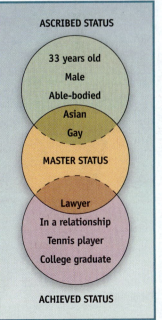

FIGURE 3.2 Ascribed, Achieved, and Master Statuses

ASCRIBED STATUS

33 years old
Male
Able-bodied
Asian
Gay

MASTER STATUS

Lawyer
In a relationship
Tennis player
College graduate

ACHIEVED STATUS

strain when the same role has demands and expectations that contradict each other, so we cannot possibly meet them all at once. For instance, the role of "student" might ask us to submit to the professor's authority *and* exercise independent thought. How can a single behavior fill both demands? In my first teaching job, I was 21 years old, and my students were middle-aged policemen. I noticed the students were having a tough time figuring out how to relate to me. On the one hand, they were students and I was the professor, so they knew they should act deferentially toward me. On the other hand, I was the age of their children, so they expected me to act deferentially toward them.

Role strain makes us feel worried, doubtful, and insecure, and it may force us to abandon the role altogether. Goode (1960) found that we often solve the problem of role strain by *compartmentalizing*, depending on subtle cues to decide if we should submit or exercise independent thought *right now* and often never even noticing the contradiction.

A related problem, **role conflict,** happens when we try to play different roles with extremely different or contradictory rules at the same time. If I am out with my buddies, playing the cool, irreverent role of "friend," and I see my teacher, who expects the quiet, obedient student, I may have a problem. If I suddenly become polite, I will lose face with my friends. If I remain irreverent, I will lose face with my teacher. Because everyone is playing multiple roles all the time, role conflict is a common problem. Once a student who came to my office to discuss a test grade brought her toddler twins with her. It was fascinating to watch her trying to balance the contradictory roles of "student" and "mommy" without losing face in either.

What happens when we must leave a role that is central to our identity? **Role exit** describes the process of adjustment that takes place when we move out of such a role. Sometimes we leave roles voluntarily: We change jobs or religions, get divorced and leave the "married" role, and so on. Sometimes we leave roles involuntarily: We change age groups (suddenly our parents say "You're not a kid anymore"), get arrested, get fired. Whether we leave voluntarily or involuntarily, we are likely to feel lost, confused, and sad. Helen Rose Fucs Ebaugh (1988) notes four stages in voluntarily exiting from significant social roles:

1. *Doubt.* We are frustrated, burned out, or just unhappy with our role.

2. *Search for alternatives.* We observe people in other roles or perhaps try them out ourselves temporarily. This may be a lifelong process.

3. *Departure.* Most people can identify a turning point, a specific moment or incident that marked their departure from the role, even though they might continue to play it for some time.

4. *New role.* It is very important to find a new role to take the place of the old. People who leave a role involuntarily must start the search for alternatives after departure, and it is quite likely that they will try out several new roles before finding one that they like.

Roles and statuses give us, as individuals, the tools we need to enter the social world. We feel grounded in our statuses; they give us roots. And our roles provide us with a playbook, a script, for any situation. We are ready to join others.

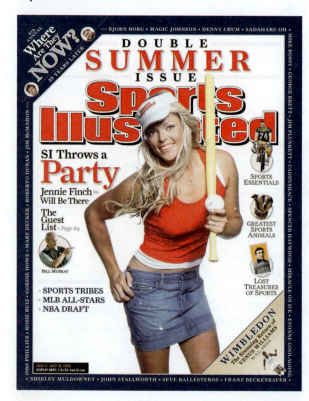

Ballplayer or babe? Women who enter traditionally male domains—from the operating room to the boardroom to the sport stadium—must constantly negotiate between different sets of role expectations. Jennie Finch may be an Olympic softball gold medalist and the holder of the NCAA record for most consecutive wins, but she still has to look like a cover girl to reaffirm traditional gender expectations. ▼

Groups

"The world is too much with us," the great British poet William Wordsworth once complained. He believed that immersion in the world kept us from the divine realm of nature. But sociologists are more likely to side with John Donne: "No man is an island, entire of itself . . ."

Even by yourself, sociologists believe, you are "in society." Brought up within culture, the very ideas you carry around about who you are and what you think and feel—these are already conditioned and shaped by society. It is our experience in society that makes us human.

Apart from individuals, then, the smallest unit of society is a group. To sociologists, a **group** is any assortment of people who share (or believe that they share) the same norms, values, and expectations And the smallest group is a **dyad,** a group of two. Anytime you meet with another person, you are in a group. And every time the configuration of people meeting changes, the group changes. Two different classes may have the same professor, the same subject matter, and most of the same students, but they comprise different groups, and they are often completely different environments. Groups can be formal organizations, with well-defined rules and procedures, or they may be informal, like friends, co-workers, or whoever happens to be hanging around at that moment.

A group can be very small, such as your immediate family and friends, or very large, such as your religion or nation, but the most significant groups in our lives are the ones so large that we don't personally know everyone, but small enough so we can feel that we play an important role in them: not your occupation, but your specific place of business; not all skateboarders in the world, but your specific skateboarding club.

Passengers on the airplane or the customers in a restaurant are not a group. Strictly speaking, they are a **crowd,** an aggregate of individuals who happen to be together but experience themselves as essentially independent. But the moment something goes wrong—the flight is cancelled or the service is inexplicably slow—they will start looking to each other for validation and emotional support, and chances are they will become a group. On the TV series *Lost*, an airplane crashes on a mysterious island in the South Pacific, and the survivors band together to fight a series of weird supernatural threats. On the airplane, they had been reading, napping, or staring into space, basically ignoring each other, but now they are becoming a group.

Groups differ from crowds in their **group cohesion,** the degree to which the individual members identify with each other and with the group. In a group with high cohesion, individual members will be more likely to follow the rules and less likely to drop out or defect to another group. Because every group, from business offices to religious cults to online newsgroups, wants to decrease deviance and keep the members from leaving, studies about how to increase cohesion have proliferated. It's not hard to do: You need to shift the group importance from second place to first place, transforming the office or cult into "a family," by forcing members to spend time together and make emotional connections. Wilderness retreats and "trust exercises" are meant to jump-start this connection. And you need to find a common enemy, a rival group or a scapegoat, someone for the group members to draw together to fight. The survivors on *Lost* have little to do but establish emotional intimacy, and they have a common enemy, the mysterious Others from the other side of the island.

Groups and Identity

Everyone belongs to many different groups: families, friends, co-workers, classmates, churches, clubs, organizations, plus less tangible groups. Are you a fan of blues music?

▲ **Even though this man may identify himself as a tennis player, co-workers, acquaintances, and even his close friends may ignore all of his other statuses, seeing only disabled, and thus force him to root his identity more firmly in that group.**

David Beckham? Even if you never seek out an organized club, you belong to the group of blues fans or soccer fans. Do you favor gun control? Even if you don't feel strongly about the issue, you belong to the group of people who favor gun control. Your gender, sexual orientation, race, ethnicity, age, class, nationality, and even your hair color place you in groups and form part of your identity. Often our membership in a group is a core element of our identities. And other times, other people assume that just because we are members of a particular group, that this membership forms that core of identity—when it may, in fact, do nothing of the sort. Imagine an Asian American gay man who is an avid mountain biker. So avid, in fact, that he joins every mountain biking club in his community and is a central person in all its activities. It is the core of his identity, he believes. But without his bicycle, other people assume that the core of his identity is his membership in a racial and sexual group. "I'm a mountain biker, who happens to be Asian American and gay," he insists, "not a gay Asian American who happens to be a mountain biker." The various elements of our identity may fit together neatly or we may struggle to integrate them. And the rest of society must see our priorities the way we do, or we will experience conflict.

What's visible and invisible to us as a facet of our identity is often related to the organization of society. I recently asked my students in an introductory sociology class to list the five most important elements of their identities on a piece of paper. Every African American student listed their race as the first or second item, but not one White student listed being "White" anywhere on their answers. Every woman listed being a woman, but only 10 percent of men thought to put "male." And every gay or lesbian student listed sexual identity, but not one heterosexual student did. Virtually every student put his or her ethnicity, especially those who were Latino or Asian; among European Americans, only the Italian, Irish, and Russian put their ethnicity (no Germans, Swedes, French, or Swiss). The majority of Jews and Muslims listed religion; half of all Protestants put "Christian," but only 2 percent listed a denomination. And only a quarter of the Catholics listed Catholic.

Why would that be? Sociologists understand that identities based on group membership are not neutral, but hierarchically valued. Those identities that are most readily noticeable are those where we do not fit in with others, not those in which we are most like everyone else. We're more aware of where we stand out as different, not where we fit in.

Types of Groups

There are many different types of groups, depending on their composition, permanence, fluidity of boundaries, and membership criteria. You are born into some groups (family, race). In other groups, you may be born into the group, but membership also depends on your own activities and commitments, like ethnic or religious groups. Some are based entirely on expression of interest (clubs, fans), and others based on formal application for membership.

Primary and Secondary Groups. Small groups (small enough so that you know almost everybody) are divided into two types, primary and secondary. According to the sociologist Charles Horton Cooley (1909), **primary groups,** such as friends and family, come together for *expressive reasons:* They provide emotional support, love,

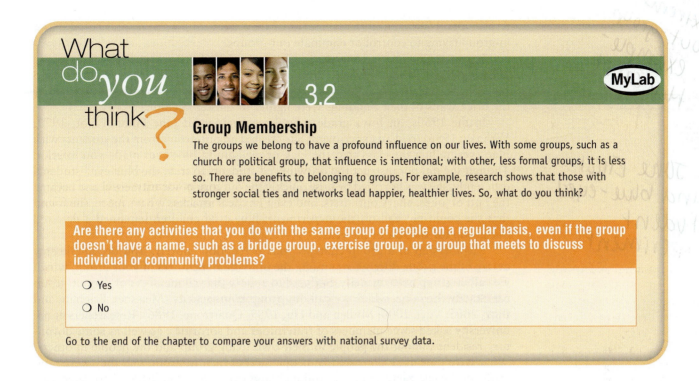

Group Membership

The groups we belong to have a profound influence on our lives. With some groups, such as a church or political group, that influence is intentional; with other, less formal groups, it is less so. There are benefits to belonging to groups. For example, research shows that those with stronger social ties and networks lead happier, healthier lives. So, what do you think?

Are there any activities that you do with the same group of people on a regular basis, even if the group doesn't have a name, such as a bridge group, exercise group, or a group that meets to discuss individual or community problems?

○ Yes

○ No

Go to the end of the chapter to compare your answers with national survey data.

companionship, and security. **Secondary groups,** such as co-workers or club members, come together for *instrumental reasons:* They want to work together to meet common goals. Secondary groups are generally larger and make less of an emotional claim on your identity. In real life, most groups have elements of both: You may join the local chapter of the Green Party because you want to support its political agenda, but you are unlikely to stay involved unless you form some emotional connections with the other members.

In-Groups and Out-Groups. William Graham Sumner (1906) identified two different types of groups that depend on membership and affinity. An **in-group** is a group I feel positively toward and to which I actually belong. An **out-group** is one to which I don't belong and do not feel very positively toward. We may feel competitive or hostile toward members of an out-group. Often we think of members of out-groups as bad, wrong, inferior, or just weird, but the specific reactions vary greatly. An avid tennis player may enjoy a wonderful friendship or romance with someone who hates tennis, with only some occasional teasing to remind that friend that he or she belongs to an out-group.

Sometimes, groups attempt to create a sense of superiority for members of the in-group—or to constitute themselves as an in-group in the first place. For example, members of a club want to create an aura of importance to their weekly meetings. They may charge a massive "initiation" fee that only other rich people could afford to pay or insist that membership is only open to graduates of an Ivy League college. Creating an in-group can be conscious and deliberate. But for the in-group to be successful, members of the out-group (those not in the in-group) must actually want to join. Otherwise all those secret codes and handshakes just look silly.

Sometimes, however, especially when in-groups and out-groups are divided on the basis of race, nationality, gender, sexuality, or other ascribed status, reactions become more severe and violent. The Holocaust of World War II, the ethnic cleansings of

out-group-
not liking tennis
amongst people
who do

Armenia and Serbia, and the lynchings of the American South were all based on an in-group trying to control or eliminate out-groups.

In-groups and out-groups do not have to be built around any sort of socially meaningful characteristic. Gerald Suttles (1972), studying juvenile groups in Chicago housing projects, found that boys formed in-groups and out-groups based on whether the brick walls of their buildings were lighter or darker in color.

In the 1960s, an Iowa grade school teacher named Jane Elliot (Elliot, 1970; Verhaag, 1996) tried an experiment: She created an out-group from the students with blue eyes, telling the class that the lack of melanin in blue eyes made you inferior. Though she did not instruct the brown-eyed students to treat the blue-eyed students differently, she was horrified by how quickly the out-group was ostracized and became the butt of jokes, angry outbursts, and even physical attacks. What's more, she found that she could not call off the experiment: Blue-eyed children remained a detested out-group for the rest of the year!

Membership in a group changes your perception entirely. You become keenly aware of the subtle differences among the individual members of your group, which we call **in-group heterogeneity**, but tend to believe that all members of the out-group are exactly the same, which we call **out-group homogeneity** (Meissner, Brigham and Butz, 2005; Voci, 2000; Mullen and Hu, 1989; Quattrone, 1986). Researchers at my university asked some members of fraternities and sororities, as well as some dormitory residents, about the people in their own living group and the people in others. What were they like? Consistently, people said of their in-group that they were "too different," each member being "unique" and everyone "too diverse" to categorize (in-group heterogeneity). When asked about the other groups, though, they were quick to respond, "Oh, they're all jocks," or "That's the egghead nerd house" (out-group homogeneity).

The finding that we tend to perceive individual differences in our in-group and not perceive them in out-groups holds mainly in Western societies. It doesn't hold, or it holds only weakly, for China, Korea, and Japan. The Chinese, in particular, tend to believe too much that everyone is alike to perceive subtle differences (Quattrone, 1986; Quattrone and Jones, 1980).

Reference Groups. Our membership in groups not only provides us with a source of identity, but it also orients us in the world, like a compass. We *refer* to our group memberships as a way of navigating everyday life. We orient our behavior toward group norms and consider what group members would say before (or after) we act. A **reference group** is a group toward which we are so strongly committed or one that commands so much prestige that we orient our actions around what we perceive that group's perceptions would be. In some cases the reference group is the in-group, and the rest are "wannabes."

Ironically, one need not be a member of the reference group to have it so strongly influence your actions. In some cases, a reference group can be *negative*—as in when you think to yourself that you will do everything that the members of that other group do not like or when your identity becomes dependent on doing the opposite of what members of a group do. Some of these may be political (Nazis or the Ku Klux Klan are familiar negative reference groups), or simply competitive, like a neighboring clan, a fraternity, or students at another school.

In other cases, your reference group can be one to which you aspire. For example, assume that you have decided that despite your poor upbringing in rural Kentucky, you know you will eventually be one of the richest people in the world and will eventually be asked to go yachting with European aristocracy. You may feel this so strongly that you begin, while in college, to act as you imagine those in your reference group act: You wear silk ascots and speak in a fake British accent. Despite the fact that your classmates might think you're a little bit strange, you are developing a reference group. It just happens to be one that no one else around you shares. In these cases, reference groups do not just guide your actions as a member of a group but guide your actions as a *future* member of a different group.

Your reference group and your membership groups are thus not always the same. Both reference groups and memberships groups will change over the course of your life, as your circumstances change as well.

▲ One of the best illustrations of group dynamics is the high school clique. Cliques are organized around inclusion and exclusion—and who has the power to enforce it. In the hit movie *Mean Girls* (2004), Lindsay Lohan is reminded that only the most popular girls can eat their lunch at this table.

Cliques. One of the best illustrations of group dynamics is the high school clique. All across the United States, middle and high school students seem to form the same groups: jocks, nerds, preps, skaters, posers, gang-bangers, wannabes, wiggers, princesses, stoners, brainiacs (Milner, 2006). Cliques are organized around inclusion and exclusion. Ranked hierarchically, those at the bottom are supposed to aspire to be in the cliques at the top. Cliques provide protection, elevate one's status, and teach outsiders a lesson. Many high schools are large enough to accommodate several cliques, and not belonging to the social pinnacle is not so painful, because there are so many other cliques to which you can belong (and you can more easily say you don't care what those people think). In smaller schools, though, exclusion from the most popular group may be a source of significant pain. In the late 1940s, sociologist James Coleman studied high school cliques and found, much to his distress, that popularity was not at all related to intelligence, that student norms, and clique composition, were the result of social factors alone. The "hidden curriculum" of social rankings continues today. Being smart may make you popular, but it is just as likely to have nothing to do with it. In fact, being smart can make you extremely unpopular.

Group Dynamics

Groups exhibit certain predictable dynamics and have certain characteristics. Often these dynamics are simply a function of formal characteristics—size or composition—and other times they are due more to their purpose.

When it comes to groups, size matters. Small groups, in which all members know each other and are able to interact simultaneously, exhibit different features than larger groups, in which your behaviors are not always observed by other members of your group. Large groups may be able to tolerate more diversity than small groups, although the bonds among small groups may be more intense than those in larger groups. Small groups may engage us the most, but larger groups are better able to influence others.

Every group, even the smallest, has a structure that sociologists can analyze and study. There is always a leader, someone in charge, whether that person was elected, appointed, or just informally took control, and a small number of hardcore members,

* groups = size matters

those with a great deal of power to make policy decisions. Leaders and hardcore members spend an enormous amount of time and energy on the group; it forms an important part of their identity. As a consequence, they have a vested interest in promoting the norms and values of the group. They are most likely to punish deviance among group members and to think negatively about other groups. Ordinary members split their time and energies among several groups, so they are not as likely to be strongly emotionally invested. They are more likely to commit minor acts of deviance, sometimes because they confuse the norms of the various groups they belong to and sometimes because they are not invested enough to obey every rule.

Conformity. The groups we belong to hold a powerful influence over our norms, values, and expectations. Group members yield to others the right to make decisions about their behavior, their ideas, and their beliefs. When we belong to a group, we prize conformity over "rocking the boat," even in minor decisions and even if the group is not very important to us.

Conformity may be required by the norms of the group. Some groups have formal requirements: For example, cadets at military schools often have their heads shaved on their enrollment, and members of some groups wear specific clothing or get identical tattoos. If you do not conform, you cannot be a member. Other times, however, we volunteer our conformity. We will often imitate the members of our reference group and use it as a "frame of reference" for self-evaluation and attitude formation (Deux and Wrightsman, 1988; Merton, 1968), even if we don't belong to it. For instance, you may have paid special attention to the popular clique in high school, and modeled your dress, talk, and other behaviors on them. Other common reference groups are attractive people, movie stars, or sports heroes. Marketing makes use of this dynamic, aiming to get the "opinion leaders" in selected reference groups to use, wear, or tout a product, in the hopes that others will imitate them (Gladwell, 1997; PBS, 2001). The most familiar example of group conformity is peer pressure.

How do we know what we know?

Group Conformity

How can we observe these processes of conformity to group norms? In a classic experiment in social psychology (Asch, 1955), a group of strangers was gathered together under the pretense of testing their visual acuity. They were shown two cards, one with one line and one with three lines of different lengths. (In the group, however, only one person was really the subject of the experiment; all the rest were research assistants!) The group was then asked which of the lines on the second card matched the line on the first. When the subject was asked first, he or she answered correctly. (It didn't matter what others said.) But when the first group members to respond were the research assistants, they gave wrong answers, picking an obviously incorrect line and insisting it was the match.

Surprisingly, the test subjects would then most often give the wrong answers as well, preferring to follow the group norm rather than trust their own perceptions. When asked about it, some claimed that they felt uncomfortable but that they actually came to see the line they chose as the correct one. Psychologist Soloman Asch concluded that our desire to "fit in" is very powerful, even in a group that we don't belong to.

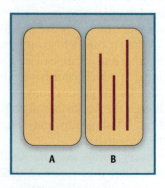

Psychologist Irving Janis called the process by which group members try to preserve harmony and unity in spite of their individual judgments groupthink (Janis, 1982). Sometimes groupthink can have negative or tragic consequences. For example, on January 28, 1986, the Space Shuttle *Challenger* exploded shortly after take-off, killing the seven astronauts aboard. A study afterward revealed that many of the NASA scientists in charge of the project believed that the O-ring seal on the booster rocket was unstable and that the shuttle was not ready to be launched, but they invariably deferred their judgments to the group. The project went on according to schedule (Heimann, 1993).

Diffusion of Responsibility. One of the characteristics of large groups is that responsibility is diffused. The chain of command can be long enough, or authority can seem dispersed enough that any one individual, even the one who actually executes an order, may avoid taking responsibility for his or her actions. If you are alone somewhere and see a person in distress, you are far more likely to help that person than if you are in a big city with many other people streaming past.

This dynamic leads to the problem of bystanders: those who witness something wrong, harmful, dangerous, or illegal, yet do nothing to intervene. In cases where there is one bystander, he or she is more likely to intervene than when there are more bystanders. In some cases, bystanders simply assume that as long as others are observing the problem, they are no more responsible than anyone else to intervene. Sometimes, bystanders are afraid that if they do get involved the perpetrators will turn on them; that is, they will become targets themselves. Bystanders often feel guilty or sheepish about their behavior.

In one of the most famous cases, a woman named Kitty Genovese in a quiet residential neighborhood in New York City was murdered outside her apartment building in 1964. Though she screamed as her attacker beat and stabbed her, more than 30 people looked out of their apartment windows and heard her screaming, and yet none called the police. When asked later, they said that they "didn't want to get involved" and that they "thought someone else would call the police, so it would be OK."

Stereotyping. Stereotyping is another dynamic of group life. Stereotypes are assumptions about what people are like or how they will behave based on their membership in a group. Often our stereotypes revolve around ascribed or attained statuses, but any group can be stereotyped. Think of the stereotypes we have of cheerleaders, jocks, and nerds. In the movie *High School Musical* (2006), members of each group try to downplay the stereotypes and be seen as full human beings: The jock/basketball star wants to be lead in the school play; his Black teammate is a wonderful chef, who can make a fabulous crème brûlée.

Sometimes you don't even need a single case to have a stereotype; you can get your associations from the media, from things people around you say, or from the simple tendency to think of out-groups as somehow bad or wrong. In Jane Elliott's experiment, the blue-eyed students were not associated with any negative characteristics at all until they became an out-group. Then they were stereotyped as stupid, lazy, shiftless, untrustworthy, and evil.

Stereotypes are so strong that we tend to ignore behaviors that don't fit. If we have a stereotype of teenagers as lazy and irresponsible, we will ignore hardworking,

(handwritten margin note:) ex. = Kitty Genovese murder

▲ Group conformity and large bureaucratic organizations can often lead to a diffusion of responsibility—which leads people to claim they were "just following orders." Here, Field Marshal William Keiter testifies at the Nuremberg trials in 1946. He was hanged as a war criminal.

Sociology and our World

Groups in Cyberspace

Newsgroups and bloggers often rail against "old media" as elitists and insiders who rely on status and social networks to get and do their jobs, keeping out the voices of "regular people." But are online groups such liberated spaces, where members are free of stifling norms and conformity to group behavior?

Sociologists find that group behavior in cyberspace can be just as patterned and policed as it is in the "real" social world. And newsgroups themselves can be among the strongest shapers of cybernorms and practices deemed appropriate for group membership. McLaughlin, Osborne, and Smith (1995) found that newsgroups consciously develop specific types of acceptable group behavior, and anyone who persists in "reproachable" acts will be threatened with expulsion and may ultimately be kicked out of the group.

Newsgroups, in fact, are such powerful enforcers of their own group norms that the vast majority of subscribers never venture beyond being "lurkers" who read postings but do not endeavor to respond with a message of their own. (One widely held newsgroup norm, in fact, is to follow a group for some time first, learning about its traditions and agenda before posting a message.) New members typically receive support materials that contain both technical advice and social instruction on appropriate conduct within the group. Files of "frequently asked questions" often strive to prevent new subscribers from cluttering up the network with queries or challenges to standards of group behavior (Croteau and Hoynes, 2003).

Such practices, McLaughlin and her colleagues (1995) argue, help reinforce the collective identities of electronic communities and protect them from newcomers who may pose a threat to them or the stability of the group.

---

responsible teenagers, maybe thinking of them as exceptions to the rule. Stereotypes are a foundation of *prejudice,* where we "prejudge" people based on their membership in a specific group. (We will discuss this more fully in Chapter 8.)

Social Networks

A **network** is a type of group that is both looser and denser than a formal group. Sociologist Georg Simmel used the term *web* to describe the way our collective membership in different groups constitutes our sense of identity.

Sociologists often use this metaphor to describe a network as a web of social relationships that connect people to each other, and, through those connections, with other people. A network is both denser than a group, with many more connecting nodes, and looser, in that people who are at some remove from you exert very little influence on your behavior.

Networks and Social Experience

The social connectedness of certain groups in the society can produce interaction patterns that have a lasting influence on the lives of people both within and without the network. For example, prep schools not only offer excellent educations but also afford social networks among wealthy children who acquire "cultural capital" (those mannerisms, behaviors, affectations that mark one as a member of the elite, as we discussed in Chapter 2) that prepares them for life among the elite (Cookson and Persell, 1985). Sociologist G. William Domhoff found that many of the boards of directors of the largest corporations in the world are composed of people who went to prep school together, or at least who went to the same Ivy League college (Domhoff, 2002).

Social networks provide support in times of stress or illness; however, some research finds that social networks are dependent on people's ability to offer something in exchange, such as fun, excitement, or a sparkling personality. Therefore, they tend to shrink precisely during the periods of stress and illness when they are needed the most (Fisher, 1982). If you are sick for a few days, you may be mobbed by friends armed with soup and get-well cards. But if your sickness lingers, you will gradually find yourself more alone.

Networks exert an important influence on the most crucial aspects of our lives; our membership in certain networks is often the vehicle by which we get established in a new country or city, meet the person with whom we fall in love, or get a job. Examine your own networks. There are your friends and relatives, your primary ties. Then there are those people whom you actually know, but who are a little less close—classmates and co-workers. These are your secondary ties. Together they form what sociologist Mark Granovetter (1973, 1974) calls your "strong ties"—people who actually know you. But your networks also include "weak ties"—people whom you may not know personally, but perhaps you know *of* them, or they know *of* you. They may have strong ties to one of your strong ties. By the time you would calculate your strong and weak ties, the numbers might reach into the thousands.

Interestingly, it is not only your strong ties that most influence your life, but possibly, centrally, your weak ties. Granovetter (1995) calls this "the strength of weak ties." While one might think strong interpersonal ties are more significant than weak ones because close friends are more interested than acquaintances in helping us, this may not be so, especially when what people need is information. Because our close friends tend to move in the same circles that we do, the information they receive overlaps considerably with what we already know. Acquaintances, by contrast, know people whom we do not and thus receive more novel information. This is in part because acquaintances are typically less similar to one another than close friends and in part because they spend less time together. Moving in different circles from ours, they connect us to a wider world.

For example, let's take two life-changing decisions: finding a romantic partner with whom you fall in love and getting a job. How do people typically find the person they expect to spend the rest of their lives with? Most often it is through being "fixed up" with a "friend of a friend"—a network in action. If that date works out, you are likely to thank your friend for the networking on your behalf; if it doesn't work out . . . well, let's just hope it works out. When initiating a job search, you won't typically find a job from a close friend or family member but again through a friend of a friend. This is why job search consultants stress the importance of networking.

Some new Internet companies, such as Match.com and Monster.com, seek to expand the range of your networking for jobs and romantic partners. In fact, young people have become network experts, having devised new and innovative ways to expand and manage their networks through interfaces with technology. Friendster, Facebook, MySpace, and other networks utilize the ever-expanding web of the Internet to create new network configurations with people whom you will never meet but rather get to know because they are a friend of a friend of a friend of a friend of—your friend.

Networks and Globalization

New technology, such as text messaging, satellite television, and especially the Internet, has allowed us to break the bounds of geography and form groups made up of people from all over the world. The Internet is especially important for people with very specialized interests or very uncommon beliefs: You are unlikely to find many people in your hometown who collect antique soda bottles or who believe that Earth is flat, but you can go online and meet hundreds. People who are afraid or embarrassed to discuss their interests at home, such as practitioners of witchcraft or S&M, also find that they can feel safe in Internet message boards and chat rooms. However, there are also thousands of Internet groups formed around more conventional interests, such as sports or movie thrillers.

Message boards and chat rooms allow us more creativity in playing roles than we have in live interaction. Even in everyday social interactions, we often engage in impression management (Goffman, 1959), emphasizing some aspects of our lives and minimizing or ignoring others. We may pretend to have beliefs, interests, and skills that we do not, to fit better into a role. For instance, we may put "fluent in French" on our resumé to impress potential employers, when actually we can barely manage to ask for directions to the nearest Métro station. However, online we can adopt completely new roles and statuses, changing not only our skills and interests, but our age, ethnicity, gender, and sexuality at will. Researchers are still studying the impact of this fluidity on the sense of self.

Social networks sustain us; they are what communities are made of. At the same time as our networks are expanding across the globe at the speed of light, there is also some evidence that these networks are shrinking. A recent study by sociologists found that Americans are far more socially isolated than we were even in the 1980s. Between 1985 and 2004 the size of the average network of confidants (someone with whom you discuss important issues) fell from just under three other people (2.94) to just over two people (2.08). And the number of people who said that there is no one with whom they discuss important issues nearly tripled. In 1985, the modal respondent (the most frequent response) was three; in 2004, the modal respondent had no confidants. Both kin (family) and nonkin (friendship) confidants were lost (McPherson, Smith-Lovin, and Brashears, 2006).

The sociological consequences of such increasing isolation are significant. Historically, we have seen cities as dangerously large and alienating, where individuals have to struggle to build networks of support. By contrast, rural life has been seen as sustaining us in the support networks of kin and friends in small towns. It is therefore surprising that in the United States suicide rates are significantly higher per capita in rural areas than in urban ones (Butterfield, 2005). Remember that Durkheim might have predicted this; because cities have greater "density," they offer more opportunities for sustaining support and social interaction.

On the other hand, in some ways, young people today are far *less* isolated than their parents might be. The Internet has provided users with a dizzying array of possible communities of potential confidants, friends, and acquaintances. People who have never met find love, romance, sex, and friendship in cyberspace. Some specific forums have been created to assist us—from finding potential cybersex partners to marriage-minded others. People report revealing things about themselves that they might not even tell their spouse. And some participants in these forums actually meet in person—and a few actually marry! Some sites, like Friendster, simply provide a network of people who know other people who know other people who . . . know you.

MySpace and other networks utilize the ever-expanding web of the Internet to create new communities of "friends" whom you will never meet and to offer an opportunity to create the identity you want to present to the world. ▼

Source: Homepage from MySpace website, www.Myspace.com
<http://www.Myspace.com>. Reprinted by permission.

Sociology and our World

Facebook

Have you heard of Facebook? Probably. Millions of high school and college students are using the Facebook website. If they're a little younger, they might try MySpace.com, which accepts middle schoolers. Or they can use Friendster.com, tribe.net, or ConnectU. If they want more control over their online relationships, there's Ning, Vox, eSnips, or Dogster. All of these Internet services allow users to create online social circles by posting their photographs (and video clips), personal information, tastes, interests, blogs, and comments on everything from world events to music. They can search for others with similar tastes and interests, anywhere in the world, and others can search for them, adding them to their "Favorites," "List of Friends," and "Fans." They can join groups of the like minded: Facebook offers every conceivable group, from "Cracklin' Oat Bran Is [Good]" to "We Need to Have Sex in Widener [Library at Harvard University] before We Graduate." They can even engage in online, real-time chatting and arrange to meet each other in person.

According to a recent study, 87 percent of Americans between 12 and 17 years old are online, and more than half have uploaded personal information of some sort. Meeting people through clubs and sports has not gone out of style, but high schoolers today are just as likely to have friends who live a thousand miles away, whom they have never met in person (and probably never will). The Internet sites allow for the expression of unusual interests and opinions and allow for people who would be ostracized and alone at their high schools in "the middle of nowhere" to find a community.

Organizations

Organizations are large secondary groups designed to accomplish specific tasks in an efficient manner. They are thus defined by their (a) size—they are larger, more formal secondary groups, (2) purpose—they are purposive, intent to accomplish something, and (3) efficiency—they determine their strategies by how best to accomplish their goals. We typically belong to several organizations—corporations, schools and universities, churches and religious organizations, political parties. Organizations tend to last over time, and they are independent of the individuals who compose them. They develop their own formal and informal organizational "culture"—consisting of norms and values, routines and rituals, symbols and practices. They tend to maintain their basic structure over a long time to achieve their goals.

Types of Organizations

Sociologists categorize organizations in different ways. One of the most common is by the nature of membership. Sociologist Amitai Etzioni (1975) identified three types of organizations: normative, coercive, and utilitarian.

Normative Organizations. People join a normative organization to pursue some interest or to obtain some form of satisfaction that they consider worthwhile. **Normative organizations** are typically voluntary organizations; members receive no monetary rewards and often have to pay to join. Members therefore serve as unpaid workers; they participate because they believe in the goals of the organization. They can be service organizations (like Kiwanis), charitable organizations (like the Red Cross), or political parties or lobbying groups. Many political organizations, such as the Sierra Club, AARP, or the National Rifle Association are normative organizations: They seek to influence policies and people's lives.

Race, ethnicity, gender, and class all play a part in membership in voluntary organizations. In fact, many such organizations come into being to combat some groups' exclusion from other organizations! For example, the National Women's Suffrage Association came into being in 1869 to oppose the exclusion of women from the voting booth, just as the Congress for Racial Equality (CORE) was formed in 1942 to press for removal of racial discrimination in voting in the segregated South. Other organizations, such as the Ku Klux Klan in the late nineteenth century, were founded for the opposite reason, to keep newly freed Blacks from exercising their right to vote.

Because these organizations make no formal claims on one's time or energy, people tend to remain active members only as long as they feel the organization is serving their interests. With no formal controls, they may lose members as quickly as they gain them. Sometimes the groups dissolve when their immediate objectives have been secured, and individual members drift off to find other groups to join and other causes to embrace. The National Women's Suffrage Association had little reason to exist after women's suffrage was won in 1920; members became involved in other campaigns and other organizations.

Coercive Organizations.
There are some organizations that you do not volunteer to join; you are forced to. **Coercive organizations** are organizations in which membership is not voluntary. Prisons, reform schools, and mental institutions are examples of coercive institutions. Coercive organizations tend to have very elaborate formal rules and severe sanctions for those seeking to exit voluntarily. They also tend to have elaborate informal cultures, as individuals try to create something that makes their experience a little bit more palatable.

Coercive institutions are sometimes what sociologist Erving Goffman (1961) called **total institutions**. A total institution is one that completely formally circumscribes your everyday life. Total institutions cut you off from life before you enter and seek to regulate every part of your behavior. They use what social theorist Michel Foucault called a "regime of surveillance"—constant scrutiny of everything you do.

Total institutions are fairly dichotomous: One is either an inmate or a "guard." Goffman argued that total institutions tend to follow certain methods to incorporate a new inmate. First, there is a ceremonial stripping of the "old self" to separate you from your former life: Your head may be shaved, your personal clothes may be replaced with a uniform, you may be given a number instead of your name. Once the "old" self is destroyed, the total institution tries to rebuild an identity through conformity with the institutional definition of what you should be like.

Goffman suggested, however, that even total institutions are not "total." Individuals confined to mental hospitals, prisoners, and other inmates often find some clandestine way to hold onto a small part of their prior existence, to remind them that they are not only inmates but also individuals. Small reminders of your former life enable inmates to retain a sense of individuality and dignity. A tattoo, a cross, a family photo—any of these can help the individual resist the total institution.

Total institutions use regimentation and uniformity to minimize individuality and replace it with a social, organizational self. ▼

Utilitarian Organizations.
Utilitarian organizations are those to which we belong for a specific, instrumental purpose, a tangible material reward. To earn a living or to get an advanced degree, we enter a corporation or university. We may exercise some choice about which university or which corporation, but the materials rewards (a paycheck, a degree) are the primary motivation. A large

business organization is designed to generate revenues for the companies, profits for shareholders, and wages and salaries for employees. That's what they're there for. We remain in the organization as long as the material rewards we seek are available. If, suddenly, businesses ceased requiring college degrees for employment, and the only reason to stay in school were the sheer joy of learning, would you continue reading this book?

This typology distinguishes between three different types of organizations. But there is considerable overlap. For example, some coercive organizations also have elements of being utilitarian organizations. The recent trend to privatize mental hospitals and prisons, turning them into for-profit enterprises, has meant that the organizational goals are changed to earning a profit, and guards' motivations may become more pecuniary.

Also, individual motivations for entering the organizations may vary. For example, my stepbrother once joined several charitable organizations that were composed largely of wealthy supporters of women's rights. These were clearly normative organizations. When I asked him why he had joined (he wasn't particularly interested in women's rights), he replied that these organizations were known to have really pretty women members and "they give really good parties." The organization may have been normative; his motives were altogether utilitarian.

Are We a Nation of Joiners?

In his nineteenth-century study of America, *Democracy in America*, the French sociologist Alexis de Tocqueville called America "a nation of joiners." It was the breadth and scale of our organizations—everything from local civic organizations to large formal institutions—that gave American democracy its vitality. A century later, the celebrated historian Arthur Schlesinger (1944, p. 1) pointed out that it seems paradoxical "that a country famed for being individualistic should provide the world's greatest example of joiners." That is another sociological paradox: How we can be so individualistic *and* so collective minded—at the same time?

But recently it appears this has been changing. In a best-selling book, *Bowling Alone* (2000), political scientist Robert Putnam argued that the organizations that once composed daily life—clubs, churches, fraternal organizations, civic organizations—had been evaporating in American life. In the 1950s, two-thirds of Americans belonged to some civic organization, but today that percentage is less than one-third. It is especially among normative organizations that membership has decreased most dramatically.

For example, if your parents were born and raised in the United States, it is very likely that *their* parents (your grandparents) were members of the PTA and regularly went to functions at your school. It is very likely that your grandparents were members of local civic organizations, like Kiwanis, or a fraternal organization (like Elks or Masons). But it is far less likely that your parents are members. And very *unlikely* that you will join them.

Organizations: Race and Gender and Inequality?

We often think that organizations and bureaucracies are formal structures that are neutral. They have formal criteria for membership, promotion and various rewards, and to the extent that any member meets these criteria, the rules are followed without prejudice. Everyone, we believe, plays by the same rules.

What that ignores, however, is that the rules themselves may favor some groups over other groups. They may have been developed by some groups to make sure that they remain in power. What appear to be neutral criteria is also socially weighted in favor of some and against others.

▲ Bureaucratic organizations are both rational systems and engines of inequality. Through formal rules, clear lines of authority, and structured roles, the "old boys' network" appears to be based strictly on merit.

To give one example, membership in a political party was once restricted to those who could read and write, who paid a tax, and whose fathers were members of the party. This effectively excluded poor people, women, and Black people in the pre-Civil Rights South.

Sociologists of gender have identified many of the ways in which organizations reproduce gender inequality. In her now-classic work, *Men and Women of the Corporation*, Rosabeth Moss Kanter (1975) demonstrated that the differences in men's and women's behaviors in organizations had far less to do with their characteristics as individuals than it had to do with the structure of the organization. Organizational positions "carry characteristic images of the kinds of people that should occupy them," she argued, and those who do occupy them, whether women or men, exhibited those necessary behaviors. Though the criteria for evaluation of job performance, promotion, and effectiveness seem to be gender neutral, they are, in fact, deeply gendered. "While organizations were being defined as sex-neutral machines," she writes, "masculine principles were dominating their authority structures." The "gender" of the organization turns out to be male.

Here's an example. Many doctors complete college by age 21 or 22 and medical school by age 25 to 27 and then face three more years of internship and residency, during which time they are occasionally on call for long stretches of time, sometimes even two or three days straight. They thus complete their residencies by their late 20s or early 30s. Such a program is designed not for a doctor, but for a *male* doctor—one who is not pressured by the ticking of a biological clock, for whom the birth of children will not disrupt these time demands, and who may even have someone at home taking care of the children while he sleeps at the hospital. No wonder women in medical school—who number nearly one-half of all medical students today—often complain that they were not able to balance pregnancy and motherhood with their medical training.

Bureaucracy: Organization and Power

When we hear the word *bureaucracy*, we often think it means "red tape"—a series of increasingly complex hoops through which you have to jump to realize your goals. In our encounters with bureaucracies, we often experience them as either tedious or formidable obstacles that impede the purpose of the organization.

In a sense we're right. When we encounter a bureaucracy as an applicant, as one who seeks to do something, it can feel like the bureaucracy exists only the thwart our objectives. But if you were at the top of the bureaucracy, you might experience it as a smoothly functioning machine in which every part fits effortlessly and fluidly into every other part, a complex machine of rules and roles.

The sociologist is interested in both aspects of bureaucracies. A **bureaucracy** is a formal organization, characterized by a division of labor, a hierarchy of authority, formal rules governing behavior, a logic of rationality, and an impersonality of criteria. It is also a form of domination, by which those at the top stay at the top and those at the bottom believe in the legitimacy of the hierarchy. Part of the reason those at the bottom accept the legitimacy of the power of those at the top is that bureaucracy appears to be simply a form of organization. But, as the great sociologist Max Weber understood, it is by embedding power in formal rules and procedures that it is most efficiently exercised. Bureaucracies are thus the most efficient organizations in getting things done *and* for maintaining the power of those at the top.

Characteristics of Bureaucracies. Max Weber is credited with first describing the essential characteristics of bureaucracies (Weber 1978 edition). While these characteristics are not necessarily found in every single bureaucratic organization, they represent the *ideal type* of bureaucracy, an abstract mental concept of what a pure version of the phenomenon (in this case a bureaucracy) would look like:

> ## Did *you* know?
>
> Although the French invented the word *bureaucracy*, the Chinese are credited with perfecting the practice. During the Song dynasty (AD 420–479), the emperor developed a centralized bureaucracy, staffed with civilian scholar-officials. This led to a much greater concentration of power than had ever been achieved before.

1. *Division of labor.* Each person in a bureaucratic organization has a specific role to play, a specific task to perform. People often become specialists, able to perform a few functions exceptionally well, but they might be unable to do what their colleagues or co-workers do.

2. *Hierarchy of authority.* Positions in a bureaucracy are arranged vertically, with a clear reporting structure, so that each person is under the supervision of another person. Those at the top have power over those below them, all along what is often called the "chain of command." The chain of command is impersonal; the slots held by individuals are independent of the individual occupying the position. If your supervisor leaves a position to move to another part of the company, you no longer report to that person. You report to the new holder of the position of supervisor. The hierarchy of a bureaucratic organization often resembles a pyramid (Figure 3.3).

3. *Rules and regulations.* Those in the hierarchy do not exert power on a whim: They follow clearly defined rules and regulations that govern the conduct of each specific position in the organization and define the appropriate procedures for the function of each unit and the organization as a whole. These rules and regulations are formalized, "codified" (organized into a coherent structure), and written down, which further reduces the individual discretion supervisors may have and increases the formal procedures of the organization.

4. *Impersonality.* Formal and codified rules and regulations and a hierarchy of positions (instead of people) lead to a very impersonal system. Members of bureaucratic organizations are detached and impersonal, and interactions are to be guided by instrumental criteria—what is the right and appropriate decision for the organization, according to its rules, not how a particular decision might make you feel. There is a strict separation of personal and official business and income.

5. *Career ladders.* Bureaucratic organizations have clearly marked paths for advancement, so that members who occupy lower positions on the hierarchy are aware of the formal requirements to advance. They thus are more likely to see their participation as "careers" rather than as "jobs" and further commit themselves to the smooth functioning of the organization. Formal criteria govern promotion and hiring; incumbents cannot leave their positions to their offspring.

6. *Efficiency.* The formality of the rules, the overarching logic of rationality, the clear chain of command, and the impersonal networks enable bureaucracies to be extremely efficient, coordinating the activities of a large number of people.

FIGURE 3.3 Hierarchy of Authority

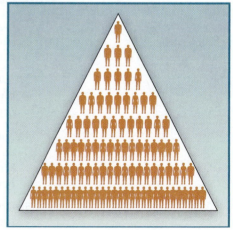

How do we know what we know?

Do Formal or Informal Procedures Result in Greater Productivity?

Does the informal culture of bureaucracy enhance or detract from worker productivity? In a classic study of a Western Electric factory in Hawthorne, Illinois, in the 1930s, Elton Mayo and W. Lloyd Warner found that the informal worker culture ran parallel to the official factory norms. In the experiment, a group of 14 men who put together telephone-switching equipment were paid according to individual productivity. But their productivity did not increase because the men feared that the company would simply raise the expectations for everyone (Mayo, 1933; Roethlisgerberger & Dickson, 1939).

In another classic study, though, Peter Blau (1964) found informal culture increased both productivity and effectiveness. Blau studied a government office charged with investigating possible tax violations. When agents had questions about how to handle a particular case, the formal rules stated they should consult their supervisors. However, the agents feared this would make them look incompetent in the eyes of higher-ups. So, they asked their co-workers, violating the official rules. The result? Not only did they get concrete advice about ways to solve the problem, but the group then began to evolve a range of informal procedures that permitted more initiative and responsibility than the formal rules did, probably enhancing the quantity and quality of work the agents produced.

Formal procedures, according to Meyer and Rowan (1977), are often quite distant from the actual ways people work in bureaucratic organizations. People will often make a show of conforming to them and then proceed with their work using more informal methods. They may use "the rules" to justify the ways a task was carried out, then depart considerably from how things are supposed to be done in actually performing the tasks at hand.

Why do our experiences with bureaucracies often feel so unsatisfying? Why do we commonly criticize bureaucracies as too large, too unwieldy, and too impenetrable to be efficient forms of organization?

Problems with Bureaucracy

Bureaucracies exhibit many of the other problems of groups—groupthink, stereotypes, and pressure to conform. But as much as they make life more predictable and efficient, bureaucracies also exaggerate certain problems of all groups:

1. *Overspecialization.* Individuals may become so specialized in their tasks that they lose sight of the larger picture and the broader consequences of their actions.

2. *Rigidity and inertia.* Rigid adherence to rules makes the organization cumbersome and resistant to change and leads to a sense of alienation of personnel. This can make bureaucracies inefficient.

3. *Ritualism.* Formality, impersonality, and alienation can lead individuals to simply "go through the motions" instead of maintaining their commitment to the organization and its goals.

4. *Suppression of dissent.* With clear and formal rules and regulations, there is little room for individual initiative, alternate strategies, and even disagreement. Often bureaucracies are characterized by a hierarchy of "yes-men"; each incumbent simply says "yes" to his or her supervisor.

5. *The bureaucratic "Catch-22."* This phenomenon, named after a famous novel by Joseph Heller, refers to a process by which the bureaucracy creates more and

more rules and regulations, which result in greater complexity and overspecialization, which actually reduces coordination, which results in the creation of contradictory rules.

As a result of these problems, individual members of the bureaucratic organization may feel alienated and confused. Sociologist Robert Merton (1968) identified a specific personality type that he called the **bureaucratic personality** to describe those people who become more committed to following the correct procedures than they are in getting the job done. At times, these problems may drag the bureaucracy toward the very dynamics that the organization was supposed to combat. Instead of a smoothly functioning, formal, and efficient organizational machine, the bureaucracy can become large, chaotic, inefficient, and homogeneous.

Bureaucracy and Accountability. The mechanisms that enable bureaucracies to be efficient and formal enterprises also have the effect of reducing an individual's sense of accountability. In a chilling example, psychiatrist Robert Jay Lifton (1986) studied doctors who worked at the Nazi death camps. His work shows how bureaucratic organizations can create a sense of alienation that shields people from the consequences of their own actions. In the massive bureaucratic death camps, where processing inmates for extermination was the "business" of the organization, doctors focused on (1) the internal formal administrative tasks that were germane only to their position in the hierarchy (making sure everything went smoothly), and (2) the informal culture of personal relationships among staff. Lifton describes how these doctors would often come home to their families after a "hard day at the office" and complain only about how a nurse wasn't feeling well or that another doctor was boasting about his car. In this way, Lifton says, the bureaucratic organization led the doctors to experience a form of "psychic numbing"—a psychological distancing from the human consequences of their actions—especially since their "day at the office" consisted of participation in mass murder.

Recall the last few times you've dealt with a bureaucracy. You may have pleaded your case and had a really, really good reason why you were asking them to bend a rule a little bit. And remember how frustrated you were when they waved you away, saying there is "nothing I can do," "my hands are tied," "I'm only following orders."

If you have ever been on the other side of the desk, though, and faced someone who is trying to plead an excuse, recall how comforting it might have felt that you could refer to specific rules in turning them down and how it supported you in doing your job. It may also have absolved you from feeling bad about it: "I would if I could, honest."

Bureaucracy and Democracy. Weber also identified another potential problem with bureaucracies: a formal structure of accountability that is, ironically, undemocratic. Elected officials are accountable to the public because they have fixed terms of office. They must stand for reelection after a specified term. But officeholders in a bureaucracy tend to stay on for many years, even for their entire careers. (Of course, you can be fired or dismissed by those above you, but your clients or subordinates have no power to remove you.)

There is another reason that bureaucracies do not tend to be democratic organizations. While the formal rules and regulations govern the conduct of each officeholder, at every rank, these rules are rarely applied at the top, where more informal and personal rules might apply. For example, those at the top of a bureaucratic hierarchy are likely to forgive minor transgressions when they are performed by their

Did *you* know?

Sociologists have found that two of our most "commonsense" adages about bureaucracy are mostly false: the "Peter Principle," which holds that "people rise in an organization to their level of incompetence" (Peter and Hull, 1969) and "Parkinson's Law," which holds that "work expands to fill the time available for its completion." Each may contain a grain of truth, but if they were right, most bureaucratic organizations would fail. Yet bureaucracies are generally successful. Evans and Rauch (1999) studied governments of 35 developing countries and found prosperity developed in those with central bureaucracies, so long as they hired on the basis of merit and offered workers rewarding work.

immediate colleagues and friends but are likely to punish underlings quite severely for the same infractions.

In addition, "old boys' networks" can circumvent the formal procedures of the bureaucracy, making sure that personal connections—the children of the bosses' friends or those who went to prep school with them—are favored candidates for jobs, promotions, or plum assignments. In this way, informal networks and cultures within bureaucracies, which can sometimes work to humanize conditions or enhance productivity, can in other situations perpetuate race, class, and gender inequalities. When questioned, the personnel department can point to the formal requirements for the job and declare that the person who got hired was simply the "best qualified" for it.

Bureaucracies appear rational and impersonal, and the criteria they employ are thought to be applied equally and uniformly. But that turns out to be more true at the bottom than at the top (Weber, 1978).

The "Iron Cage" of Bureaucracy. As a result of this difference between appearance and reality, Weber was deeply ambivalent about bureaucracy. On the one hand, bureaucracies are the most efficient, predictable organizations, and officials within them all approach their work rationally and according to formal rules and regulations. But on the other hand, the very mechanisms that make bureaucracies predictable, meaningful, efficient, and coherent, and enable those of us who participate in them to see clearly all the different lines of power and control, efficiency and accountability often lead those organizations to become their opposites. The organization becomes unpredictable, unwieldy, and unequal; officials become alienated, going through the motions with no personal stake in the outcome. The very things we thought would give meaning to our lives end up trapping us in what Weber called the "iron cage." The iron cage describes the increasing rationalization of social life that traps people in the rules, regulations, and hierarchies that they developed to make life sensible, predictable, and efficient. Ironically, mechanisms such as bureaucracies, which promised to illuminate all the elements of an organization, make life more transparent, and enable us to see with greater clarity could end up ushering in the "polar night of icy darkness." They could crush imagination and destroy the human spirit (Weber, 1958, p. 128).

▲ Bureaucracies depend on the impersonal application of rules. In the 2002 film *John Q*, a young father (played by Denzel Washington) is nearly driven to violence when his son needs a heart transplant and is denied treatment by a hospital administrator because the family has surpassed its annual limit on health insurance coverage. The father points to her heartlessness; the administrator points to the rules and believes her hands are clean.

Globalization and Organizations

In large complex societies, bureaucracies are the dominant form of organization. We deal with bureaucracies every day—when we pay our phone bill, register for classes on our campus, go to work in an office or factory, see a doctor, or have some interaction with a local, state, or federal government. And when we do, we act as *social actors*—we adopt roles, interact in groups, and collectively organize into organizations.

Groups and organizations are increasingly globalized. Global institutions like the World Bank, or International Monetary Fund, or even private commercial banks like UBS or Bank of America, are increasingly the institutional form in which people all over the world do their business. It is likely that if you have a checking account, it is at a major bank with branches in dozens of countries; 50 years ago, if you had a checking account at all, it would have been at the "Community Savings and Loan," and your banker would have known you by name. Most of your bank transactions will be done online, and if you call your bank, you'll probably be speaking to someone in another city—probably in another country. Political institutions like the United

Nations, or regional organizations like the European Union, attempt to bring different countries together under one bureaucratic organization and even a single monetary system (the euro).

And, of course, even the reactions *against* globalization use the forms and institutions of globalization to resist it. Religious fundamentalists or political extremists who want to return to a more traditional society all use the Internet to recruit members. Global media organizations like Al Jazeera (a global Arabic Muslim media source, with TV and online outlets) spread a specific form of Islam as if it were the only form of Islam—and Moslems in Indonesia begin to act more like Moslems in Saudi Arabia. Every antiglobalization political group—from patriot groups on the far right to radical environmentalists on the far left—uses websites, bloggers, and Internet chat rooms to recruit and spread its message. Globalization may change some of the dynamics of groups and organizations—some new ones emerge and others fade—but the importance of groups and organizations in our daily lives cannot be overstated.

Groups 'R' Us: Groups and Interactions in the 21st Century

Although we belong to fewer groups than our parents might have, these groups may also be increasingly important in our lives, composing more and more the people with whom we interact and the issues with which we concern ourselves. We're lonelier than ever, and yet we continue to be a nation of joiners, and we locate ourselves still within the comfortable boundaries of our primary groups.

We live in a society composed of many different groups and many different cultures, subcultures, and countercultures, speaking different languages, with different kinship networks and different values and norms. It's noisy, and we rarely agree on anything. And yet we also live in a society where the overwhelming majority of people obey the same laws and are civil to one another and in which we respect the differences among those different groups. We live in a society characterized by fixed, seemingly intransigent hierarchy and a society in which people believe firmly in the idea of mobility; a society in which your fixed, ascribed characteristics (race, class, sex) are the single best determinants of where you will end up and a society in which we also believe anyone can make it if they work hard enough.

It is a noisy and seemingly chaotic world and also one that is predictable and relatively calm. The terms we have introduced in these two chapters—culture, society, roles, status, groups, interaction, and organizations—are the conceptual tools that sociologists use to make sense of this teeming tumult of disparate parts and this orderly coherence of interlocking pieces.

 Chapter Review

1. *What do sociologists think about society?* Sociologists try to see the social context of individual lives. They look at how society influences people and how people construct society, as well as the interactions among individuals and the institutions in which these take place. These institutions, along with social interactions, form a social structure that organizes and provides context for social life.

2. *What is the social construction of reality?* Sociologists believe that there is no such thing as an objective reality. Instead, according to Berger and Luckman, we

construct reality through interaction. Cooley called the process by which our identity develops the looking-glass self. In his model, we develop our identity based on our evaluation of others' reactions. Goffman said we purposely try to control others' opinions of us through impression management. We also construct reality through communication, both verbal and nonverbal.

3. *What are the elements of social structure?* Social life is composed of statuses and roles. A status is a position in a group, and a role is the expectations for behavior that go along with a status. We have no choice over some statuses. These ascribed statuses include one's race and gender and are often used to justify inequality. Other statuses are achieved; that is, we attain them ourselves, although they are often dependent on ascribed statuses.

4. *What are groups?* A group is any assortment of people who share norms, values, and expectations. They can be large or small, formal or informal. Our group memberships are among the defining features of our lives, both for our definitions of self and others' ideas of who we are. Groups are primary, coming together for expressive reasons, or secondary, coming together for instrumental reasons. We also see groups in terms of in-groups, to which we belong, and out-groups, to which we do not belong. In-group–out-group rivalry can lead to dire consequences.

5. *How do groups function?* Groups often function based on their size, composition, and purpose. Groups have a powerful influence over their members, and a certain degree of conformity is required to be part of a group. Sometimes group membership leads to phenomena such as groupthink, diffusion of responsibility, and stereotyping, all of which can have negative consequences.

6. *What are organizations?* Organizations are large secondary groups that work efficiently toward a specific goal. If one joins because of interest, it is a normative organization, and participation is voluntary. However, some organizations are coercive, and they are often total institutions with formal rules. Organizations we belong to to attain a specific goal are called utilitarian organizations. Bureaucracies are a specific type of formal organization, with a division of labor, a hierarchy, formal rules, impersonality, and rationality. Bureaucracies have problems such as overspecialization, rigidity, and ritualism.

Key Terms

Achieved status (p. 77)
Ascribed status (p. 77)
Bureaucracy (p. 94)
Bureaucratic personality (p. 97)
Coercive organizations (p. 92)
Crowd (p. 81)
Dramaturgy (p. 73)
Dyad (p. 81)
Ethnomethodology (p. 75)
Face work (p. 74)
Group (p. 81)
Group cohesion (p. 81)
Groupthink (p. 87)
Hardcore members (p. 85)

Impression management (p. 73)
In-group (p. 83)
In-group heterogeneity (p. 84)
Leader (p. 85)
Looking-glass self (p. 72)
Master status (p. 78)
Network (p. 88)
Normative organizations (p. 91)
Organizations (p. 91)
Out-group (p. 83)
Out-group homogeneity (p. 84)
Primary groups (p. 82)
Reference group (p. 84)
Roles (p. 79)

Role conflict (p. 80)
Role exit (p. 80)
Role performance (p. 76)
Role strain (p. 79)
Secondary groups (p. 83)
Social interaction (p. 72)
Social structure (p. 72)
Society (p. 70)
Status (p. 77)
Stereotypes (p. 87)
Subordinate (p. 76)
Superordinate (p. 76)
Total institutions (p. 92)
Utilitarian organizations (p. 92)

What does America think?

3.1 Marital Status

These are actual survey data from the General Social Survey, 2004.

Are you currently—married, widowed, divorced, separated, or have you never been married? According to the General Social Survey, in 2004 about 60 percent of

U.S. adults were married. However, this varied dramatically by social class. Those in the upper class were far more likely to be married (79 percent) than those in the lower class (36.2 percent) and the results for those who were never married were inverse, 30.1 percent for lower class and 7.9 percent for upper class. With regard to race, White respondents were far more likely to be married (63.3 percent) then were Black respondents (41 percent).

CRITICAL THINKING | DISCUSSION QUESTIONS

1. Why does marital status vary by social class? What cultural values and experiences might contribute to the differences?
2. Why does marital status vary by race? What cultural values and historical experiences might contribute to the differences?

3.2 Group Membership

These are actual survey data from the General Social Survey, 2004.

Are there any activities that you do with the same group of people on a regular basis even if the group doesn't have a name, such as a bridge group, exercise group, or a group that meets to discuss individual or community problems?
Almost three-quarters of respondents reported not being part of a regular informal group. White respondents (29.3 percent) were more likely than Black respondents (19.1 percent) to be part of such a group. Those who were of another racial classification were least likely to report being part of a group (14.1 percent). There was no difference in group membership by gender.

CRITICAL THINKING | DISCUSSION QUESTIONS

1. Were you surprised that so few respondents report being members of informal groups? Do you think these numbers reflect reality? Why do you think so few people belong to groups? Why do you think Black respondents were less likely to report belonging to an informal group than were White respondents?
2. What other benefits are there to group membership? Think about what kinds of groups you belong to and how you benefit from them.

▶ Go to this website to look further at the data. You can run your own statistics and crosstabs here: **http://sda.berkeley.edu/cgi-bin/hsda?harcsda+gss04**

REFERENCES: Davis, James A., Tom W. Smith, and Peter V. Marsden. General Social Surveys 1972–2004: [Cumulative file] [Computer file]. 2nd ICPSR version. Chicago, IL: National Opinion Research Center [producer], 2005; Storrs, CT: Roper Center for Public Opinion Research, University of Connecticut; Ann Arbor, MI: Inter-university Consortium for Political and Social Research; Berkeley, CA: Computer-Assisted Survey Methods Program, University of California [distributors], 2005.

chapter 4

How Do We Know What We Know? The Methods of the Sociologist

EVERYBODY KNOWS THAT DIVORCE IS BAD for children. It's a daily staple on TV talk shows that children of divorced parents are less emotionally well-adjusted and have lower rates of achievement in school, poorer grades, lower self-esteem, and higher rates of depression than kids from intact families.

What everybody knows is based on two sorts of studies. First, child psychologists indicate that the majority of the kids they see are children from families of divorce. And studies comparing the experiences and achievements of children from divorced families are compared with children from intact families. Therefore, we are constantly advised, parents should stay together "for the good of the children."

To a sociologist, though, both sources of data are riddled with problems. How does the population of children in therapy compare with the population of children who are not in therapy? Could it be that children whose parents are divorcing are sent to therapists by courts or mediators? Could it be that whatever problems children might have, they are attributed to the divorce by well-meaning therapists—even if the problems have nothing to do with the divorce?

And comparing children from families of divorce with children in intact families compares two incomparable groups. After all, divorce is not an alternative to marriage, it's an alternative to an *unhappy* marriage. And if you were to compare children from families of divorce with children from

It turns out that much of what passes for common sense turns out to be wrong. Sociology enables us to use scientific thinking to see the complexity of various issues.

intact families in which there was a lot of conflict between the parents, the children from divorced families actually are doing *better*!

It turns out, in a sense, that what "everybody knows" is wrong. Sociologists Paul Amato and Paul Booth found that children from intact high-conflict families fare worse than children in intact, low-conflict families and children from divorced families. And while we would never prescribe divorce "for the sake of the children," it's clear that the impact of divorce is far more complicated, and children far more resilient, than many popular pundits might imagine (Booth and Amato, 2001; Amato, 2000).

How could these conclusions have been so wrong? It turns out that the populations they chose for their sample, the way they constructed comparisons, and the manner in which they analyzed data led the researchers down an errant path. Most researchers are honest and well-intentioned. But the methods they choose can often lead them astray.

This example shows how false it is to dismiss sociology as simply "making a science out of common sense." It turns out that much of what passes for common sense turns out to be wrong. Sociology enables us to use scientific thinking to see the complexity of various issues.

Why Sociological Methods Matter

Sociology is a "social science," a phrase that requires some consideration. As a social *science*, sociology, like economics or political science, uses methods derived from the natural sciences to study social phenomena. Sociologists study group dynamics as an economist might study price fluctuations: When a new variable is introduced to the situation, we can measure its direct impact on its surroundings.

But sociology is also a *social* science, like anthropology or history, attempting to study human behavior as it is lived by conscious human beings. As a result of that consciousness, human beings don't behave in exactly the same ways all the time, the ways that natural phenomena like gravity, or planetary orbits, might. People possess **subjectivity**—a complex of individual perceptions, motivations, ideas, and really messy things like emotions. "Imagine how hard physics would be if particles could think" is how the Nobel Prize–winning physicist Murray Gell-Mann once put it.

Thus, sociology uses a wide variety of methodologies—perhaps a greater variety than any other academic field. The range of different methods sociologists use extends from complex statistical models, carefully controlled experiments, and enormous surveys to such methods as the literary analysis of texts, linguistic analysis of conversations, ethnographic and field research, "participant observation," and historical research in archives.

That is because the range of questions that sociologists pose for research is also enormous. Instead of being forced to choose between qualitative and quantitative methods, field research or textual analysis, students of sociology should be exposed to a wide variety of methodologies. The method we use should depend less on some preexisting prejudice and more on what we want to study.

You might think that the choice of method and the type of data that you use are of little importance. After all, you might say, if you are trying to find out the truth, won't every method basically get you to the same results? In fact, though, the methods we use and the kinds of questions we ask are often so important that they actually lead to some answers and away from others. And such answers have enormous implications for public policy.

Here's a recent example. For centuries people have argued about "nature" versus "nurture." Which is more important in determining your life course, heredity or environment? In recent years, the argument has been tilting increasingly toward nature. These days, "everybody knows" intelligence is largely innate, genetically transmitted. The most famous—or, to schoolchildren, "infamous"—test of all is the IQ test, a test designed to measure your "innate" intelligence, or aptitude, the natural, genetically based ability you have to understand things. Sure, good schools and good environments can help, but most studies have found that about 75 percent of intelligence is hereditary. Typically, these sorts of studies are used by opponents of affirmative action to argue that no amount of intervention is going to help those at the bottom—they're at the bottom for a reason.

It turns out, though, that this "fact" was the result of the methods being used to find it out. Most of the data for the genetic basis for intelligence are based on studies of twins. Identical twins share exactly the same DNA; fraternal twins, or other siblings, share only half. Researchers have thus taken the finding that the IQs of identical twins were more similar than for nonidentical twins and other siblings as a demonstration that heredity determines intelligence.

But recently, Eric Turkheimer (Turkheimer et al., 2003, 2005) and his colleagues reexamined those studies and found a curious thing. Almost all the studies of twins were of *middle-class* twins (poor people tend not to volunteer for research studies). When he examined the results from a massive study of more than 50,000 children and factored in the class background of the families, a startling picture emerged. For the children from wealthy families, virtually all the differences in IQ could be attributed to heredity. But among poor children, the IQs of identical twins varied a lot—as much as the IQs of fraternal twins.

The impact of growing up in poverty (an environmental effect) completely offset the effects of heredity. For the poor, home life and environment are absolutely critical. "If you have a chaotic environment, kids' genetic potential doesn't have a chance to be expressed," Turkheimer told a journalist. "Well-off families can provide the mental stimulation needed for genes to build the brain circuitry for intelligence" (Turkheimer, cited in Kirp, 2006).

The other great set of experiments that proved that heredity trumped environment was studies of biological offspring versus adoptive children in the same family. By comparing them, assuming that the environment was constant for both, differences between the children could be attributable to heredity. Which is true—but, again, only for wealthier families. French researchers found some cases of children from middle-class homes who were adopted by poorer ones and found that regardless of their birth, children who grew up in wealthier families—who were raised in a "richer" intellectual environment—had significantly higher IQ scores (Capron and Duyme, 1989).

Is intelligence the result of nature or nurture? Both. Class matters also. Poor twins show greater differences in IQ than do middle class twins, whose IQs are very similar. ▼

What's more, children who were adopted from crisis circumstances—abused or neglected—did better after adoption. This disproves the notion that IQ is stable throughout your life. But what was really interesting is that the IQs of those who went to wealthier homes went up significantly more than those who went to more modest families (see Kirp, 2006).

Eric Turkheimer's experiment [It turns out that the relationship between heredity and environment, between nature and nurture, is far more complex than anyone imagined: A certain environmental threshold has to be reached before heredity can kick in and "determine" anything. Only under some environmental conditions can the genetic ability emerge. It is a clear indication that it's rarely either/or—either nature *or* nurture. It's almost always both. But it took careful methodologists to see the methodological shortcomings in those previous studies and help to correct the misunderstanding that resulted. And think, then, of the potential geniuses whose environments have never enabled their ability to emerge!

Sociology and the Scientific Method

As social scientists, sociologists follow the rules of the scientific method. As in any argument or debate, science requires the use of evidence, or data, to demonstrate a position. The word **data** refers to formal and systematic information, organized and coherent. (The word *data* is the plural of *datum*.) Although the 1991 Nobel Prize winner in economics, Ronald Coase, once famously quipped, "the plural of anecdote is data," data are more than a collection of impressions, assumptions, commonsense knowledge. Data are not simply a collection of anecdotes; they are systematically collected and systematically organized.

To gather data, sociologists use a variety of methods. Many of these methods sociologists share with other social scientists, such as anthropologists, psychologists, or historians. To the sociologist, the choice of method is often determined by the sorts of questions you want to answer. Some sociologists perform experiments just as natural scientists do. Other times they rely on large-scale surveys to provide a general pattern of behaviors or attitudes. They may use historical materials found in archives or other historical sources, much as any historian would. Sociologists will reexamine data from other sources. They might analyze systematically the content of a cultural product, such as a novel, a magazine, a film, or a conversation. Some sociologists rely on interviews or focus groups with particular kinds of people to understand how they see things. Another sociologist might go into the field and live in another culture, participating in its customs and rituals much as an anthropologist might do.

Some of these research methods use **deductive reasoning** in that they logically proceed from one demonstrable fact to the next and deduce their results. These are more like the methods of the natural sciences, and the results we obtain are independent of any feelings that we or our research subjects may have. It's often impossible to then reason from the general to the specific: If you were to find out that a majority of American teachers supported the use of corporal punishment in the schools, you wouldn't be able to predict what your

"Are you just pissing and moaning, or can you verify what you're saying with data?"

own teacher will do if you misbehave. (Don't worry, it's not true: Most teachers oppose it.)

In other situations, the feelings of our research subjects are exactly what we are trying to study, and we will need to rely on **inductive reasoning,** which will help us to understand a problem using our own human capacity to put ourselves in the other person's position. In this case, the research leads the researcher to a conclusion about all or many members of a class based on examination of only a few members of that class. For example, if you want to understand *why* teachers support corporal punishment, you might interview a few of them in depth, go observe their classrooms for a period of time, or analyze a set of texts that attempt to explain it from the inside (Figure 4.1).

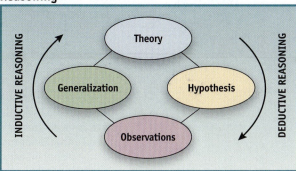

FIGURE 4.1 Deductive and Inductive Reasoning

Loosely, inductive reasoning is reasoning from the specific to the general. This is what Max Weber called **verstehen,** a method that uses "intersubjective understanding." By this he meant that you use your own abilities to see the world from others' point of view. Sometimes sociologists want to check all emotions at the door of their research lab, lest they contaminate their findings with human error. At other times, it is our uniquely human capacity for empathic connection that is the source of our understanding.

Sociologists study an enormous range of issues. Virtually every area of human behavior is studied, from the large-scale activities of governments, corporations, and international organizations like the European Union or the United Nations, to the most minute and intimate decision making about sexual practices or conversations or self-presentation. As a result, the methods that we use to study sociological problems depend more on the kind of problem we want to study than whether one method is better than any other. Each method provides different types of data, and each type can be enormously useful and illuminate a different part of the problem.

Research methods are like the different ways we use glass to see objects. Some of us will want a magnifying glass, to bring the object so close that we can see every single little feature of the particular object. Others will prefer a prism, by which the object is fragmented into hundreds of tiny parts. A telescope is useful if the object is really far away but pretty useless if you need to see what's happening next door. Bifocals are best if you want to view both close and distant objects through the same lens.

Each of these ways of seeing is valuable. A specific method may be inappropriate to adequately study a specific problem, but no research method should be dismissed as inadequate or inappropriate in all situations. It depends on what you want to know.

The Qualitative/Quantitative Divide

Most often we think that the real divide among social science methods is between quantitative and qualitative methods. Using **quantitative methods,** one uses powerful statistical tools to help understand patterns in which the behaviors, attitudes, or traits under study can be translated into numerical values. Typically, quantitative methods rely on deductive reasoning. So, for example, checking a box on a survey that gives your sex as "male" or "female" might enable the researcher to examine the relative percentages of men and women who subscribe to certain ideas, vote a for a particular political party, or avoid certain behaviors.

Qualitative methods often rely on more inductive and inferential reasoning to understand the texture of social life, the actual felt experience of social interaction. Qualitative methods are often derided as less scientific, as quantitative researchers often assume that their own methods eliminate bias and that therefore only quantitative methods are scientific.

What do *you* think?

4.1

Happiness

Sociological research has many applications. Large-scale, representative surveys can tell us a lot about our population, about social trends, and about attitudes, behaviors, and beliefs. They also give us results that we can generalize to the larger population. For example, researchers might want to know how happy a population is. One way to find that out is to directly ask a representative sample how happy they feel. Researchers can then generalize their findings to the larger population. For example, national survey data tell us that, in general, Americans say they are happy. So where do you fit in that survey?

Taken all together, how would you say things are these days? Would you say that you are very happy, pretty happy, or not too happy?

- ○ Very Happy
- ○ Pretty Happy
- ○ Not Too Happy

See the back of the chapter to compare your answers to national survey data.

Social surveys generate large bodies of data for quantitative analysis. ▼

These are convenient myths, but they are incorrect; they are, themselves, the result of bias. Both quantitative and qualitative methods are capable of understanding social reality—although each type of method illuminates a different part of that reality. Both types of methodology have biases, but qualitative methodologists struggle to make their biases explicit (and thus better control them), while quantitative researchers, assuming they have no biases, sometimes don't see them. Personal values always influence the sorts of questions we ask, the hypotheses we develop and test, and the interpretation of the results.

After all, most great scientific discoveries initially relied on simple and close observation of some phenomenon—like the apple falling on the head of Sir Isaac Newton leading to his "discovery" of gravity. Gradually, from such observations, other scientists are able to expand the reach of explanation to include a wider variety of phenomena, and these are then subject to more statistical analysis.

Here's perhaps the classic example. You study a random sample of glasses with water in them, and you discover that the average level of water in the glasses is at about 50 percent. Is the glass half full or half empty? Every single interpretation of data contains such biases.

Try another, less conventional example. Recently, a study found that nationally, 72 percent of the girls and 65 percent of the boys in the high school class of 2003 actually earned their diplomas and graduated from high school (Lewin, 2006). One can interpret this in several different ways: (1) Things are going well, and the overwhelming majority of boys and girls do earn their diplomas; (2) things are going terribly for everyone because nearly one in every three high school students did not earn his or her diploma; (3) things are going significantly worse for boys than for girls, as there is a significant "gender gap" in high school graduation. (Each of these interpretations was made by a different political group.)

Debates among sociologists and other social scientists often focus on which method leads to the "truth." But the correct answer is *both* methods lead us to the "truth"—that is, each method is adept at revealing a different part of the entire social experience.

Doing Sociological Research

The research method you use usually depends on the question you want to address in your research. Once you have formulated your research question, you'll begin to think about the best method you can use to generate the sort of information you will need to address it. And once you've chosen the method that would be best to use, you are ready to undertake the sociological research project. Research in the social sciences follows eight basic steps (Figure 4.2):

▲ **Observational methods enable qualitative researchers to explore subtleties of interaction.**

1. *Choosing an issue.* What sort of issue interests you? What do you want to know about? Sometimes sociologists follow their curiosity, and sometimes they are invited to study an issue by an agency that will give them a grant for the research. Sometimes sociologists select a problem for research in the hopes that better understanding of the problem can lead to the formulation of policies that can improve people's lives.

   Let's take the example that we used at the beginning of this chapter. Let's say you've read an article in the newspaper in which a politician said that we should make divorce more difficult to obtain because divorce always harms children. This is interesting, you might think. What is the impact of divorce on children?

2. *Defining the problem.* Once you've chosen the issue you want to understand, you'll need to refine your questions and shape them into a manageable research topic. Here, you'll have to decide what sorts of impacts divorce may have on children you might want to explore. How do these children do in school? What is the likelihood that such children would, themselves, have their marriages end in divorce? How do they adjust to divorce socially and psychologically?

FIGURE 4.2 Research in the Social Sciences

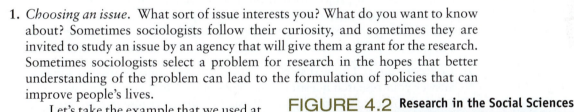

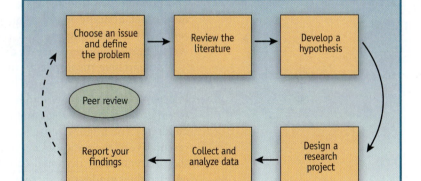

3. *Reviewing the literature.* Chances are that other social scientists have already done research on the issue you're interested in. You'll need to critically read and evaluate the previous research on the problem to help you refine your own thinking and to identify gaps in the research. Sometimes a review of the literature will find that previous research has actually yielded contradictory findings. Perhaps you can shed a clearer light on the issue. Or perhaps you'll find the research has

already been done conclusively, in which case you'll probably want to find another research question.

4. *Developing a hypothesis.* Having now reviewed the literature, you can state what you anticipate will be the result of your research. A **hypothesis** predicts a relationship between two variables, independent and dependent. An **independent variable** is the event or item in your experiment that you will manipulate to see if that difference has an impact. If it does, it will affect what's called the dependent variable. The **dependent variable** gets its name because it depends on, or is caused by, the independent variable. The dependent variable is what gets measured in an experiment; it's the change to the dependent variable that constitutes your results.

   In our example, you might develop a hypothesis that "children from divorced families are likely to have more psychological problems and lower school achievement than children in intact families." In this case, the marital status of the parents—whether or not they are divorced—is the independent variable. That's the aspect you would manipulate to see if it causes change in the dependent variable(s). The psychological and educational consequences are those dependent variables; changes in those areas are the things you would measure to get your results.

5. *Designing a project.* Now that you've developed a hypothesis, you are ready to design a research project to find out the answer. There are numerous different methods. Choose the one best suited to the question or questions you want to ask. Would quantitative or qualitative methods be more appropriate to address this question? What sorts of data might enable you to test your hypotheses?

6. *Collecting data.* The next step of the research is to collect data that will help you answer your research question. The types of data that you collect will depend a lot on the research method you will use. But whatever research method you use, you must ensure that the data are valid and reliable. *Validity* means that your data must actually enable you to measure what you want to measure. And *reliability* means that another researcher can use the same data you used and would find similar results. (We discuss validity and reliability later in this chapter.)

   Researching the impact of divorce on children, you might design a survey that would assess whether divorce has any impact on school achievement or psychological problems. (You would have to ensure that the participants represent all different groups, so that you don't inadvertently measure the effect of race or class on children.) You might choose several different schools (to make sure they were representative of the nation as a whole) and would code all the children as to whether their parents were divorced or not. Then you could see if there were any differences in their grades or if there were any differences in how often they were reported to the school principal for disciplinary problems. You might find that there already was a survey that had questions that could address your research question. Then you would use the existing data and look for those variables that would describe the impact of divorce. (This secondary analysis of existing data might sound like duplication, but it also ensures that the data you use will be valid and reliable.)

   You might decide to use more qualitative methods and do in-depth interviews with children of divorced parents and children from intact couples to see if there were any differences between them.

7. *Analyzing the data.* There are several different ways to analyze the data you have collected, and the technique you choose will depend on the type of method you have adopted. Large surveys need to be coded and analyzed statistically, to

discern whether there are relationships among the variables that you predicted in your hypotheses and, if there are such relationships, how strong they are or whether they might have been produced by chance. If you've used qualitative techniques, interviews would need to be coded for their narrative content, and observational field notes would need to be organized and systematically examined. Data analysis is often the most cumbersome and tedious element in the research process, whether you are "crunching the numbers" or transcribing interviews. Data analysis requires care and precision, as well as patience.

8. *Reporting the findings.* No research project, no matter how small, is of much use unless you share it with others. Typically, one seeks to publish the results of research as an article in a peer-reviewed journal or in an academic book, which also passes peer review. Peer review is a process by which others in the field are asked to anonymously evaluate the article or book, to make sure the research meets the standards of adequate research. Peer review is essential because it ensures the acceptance of the research by one's colleagues. More than simple gate-keeping, peer review provides a valuable service to the author, enabling him or her to see how others read the work and providing suggestions for revision.

Even a student research project needs to experience peer review (as well as review by professors). You should plan to distribute your research projects to other students in the class, to see how they reacted to it and to hear their advice for revision.

Sociological research is a statement in a conversation between the researcher and the public. One needs to report one's findings to a larger community to get their feedback as part of a dialogue. Sometimes, that community is your fellow students or other sociologists. But sometimes, one also shares the findings with the larger public, because the public at large might be interested in the results. Many sociologists also make sure to share their findings with the people they studied, because the researcher might feel that his or her research might actually be useful to the subjects of the study.

Types of Sociological Research Methods

Sociologists typically use one of two basic types of research methods. One type of method relies on observation of behavior, either in a controlled setting, like a lab, or in its natural setting, where people usually do the behavior you're studying (what we call the "field"). Another type relies on analysis of accumulated data, either from surveys or from data already collected by others. Each of these basic types is composed of several subtypes.

Students often use the term *experiment* to refer to any kind of research, but in fact experiments require a very specific procedure: You have to divide the research subjects into two or more groups, make sure that they are similar for the purposes of the experiment, and then change the conditions in some specified way for one group and see if that results in a change. For instance, does heating coffee cause it to boil? Get two pots of coffee, put one on the burner and the other in the freezer, and check it out.

What social scientists call *variables* help us measure whether, how, and in what ways, something changes (varies) as a result of the experiment. There are different kinds of variables. The independent variable is the agent of change, the element that you predict is the cause of the change, the ingredient that is added to set things in motion: the lit stove in the example above. The dependent variable is the one that changes, the variable whose change "depends" on the introduction of the independent variable: the coffee in the pot.

These are the key types of variables. But there are others. There are **extraneous variables**, which may influence the outcome of an experiment but are not actually of interest to the researcher. Extraneous variables might include the material the coffeepot is made of and whether your stove uses gas or electricity. (These might influence the speed of the boiling, or how high the temperature is, but they're not what you are interested in.) And there are **confounding variables** that may be affecting the results of the study but for which you haven't adequately accounted. Again, in the example above, the intelligence of the researcher to correctly sort the pots might confound, or complicate, the result.

Sociologists rarely conduct experiments: It's too hard to change the independent variable. Say you want to know if children of divorced parents are more likely to become juvenile delinquents. You can hardly divide children into two groups and force the parents of the first to divorce and the second to stay together.

Instead of experiments, sociologists are likely to engage in the following types of research:

- *Observation.* Observing people in their natural habitat, joining their clubs, going to their churches, getting jobs in their offices. This is usually called "participant observation."
- *Interviews.* Asking a small group of people open-ended questions, such as, "Can you describe your last road rage experience?"
- *Surveys.* Asking a lot of people closed-ended questions, such as, "How many times have you got angry in traffic in the last month?"
- *Content analysis.* Analyzing artifacts (books, movies, TV programs, magazine articles, and so on) instead of people.

What about going to the library and looking things up in books? Isn't that doing research? Sociologists would call that an incomplete literature review. A real **literature review** needn't perform any original or new research, but it must carefully examine all available research already done on a topic or at least a systematic sample of that research, through a specific critical and theoretical lens.

Let's look at each of these methods in a bit more detail.

Observational Methods

In all observational studies, we directly observe the behavior we are studying. We can do this in a laboratory, conducting an experiment, or we can do it in the place where it more "naturally" occurs. When we observe phenomena, we do more than just watch—we watch scientifically, testing hypotheses against evidence.

Experiments. An **experiment** is a controlled form of observation in which one manipulates independent variables to observe their effects on a dependent variable. To make an experiment valid, one typically uses two groups of people. One is the **experimental group**, and they are the group that will have the change introduced to see what happens. The other is the **control group**, and they will not experience the manipulation of the variable.

A control group enables us to compare the outcomes of the experiment to determine if the changes in the independent variable had any effects on the dependent variable. It is therefore very important that the experimental group and the control group be as similar as possible (by factors such as age, race, religion, class, gender, and so on) so that we can reduce any possibility that one of these other factors may have caused the effects we are examining.

In one of the most famous, or infamous, experiments in social psychology, Stanley Milgram (1963, 1974) wanted to test the limits of people's obedience to authority. During the trials that followed the end of World War II, many Nazis defended themselves by claiming that they were "only following orders." Americans were quick to assume that this blind obedience to some of the most horrifying orders was a character trait of Germans and that such obedience could never happen in the United States. Milgram decided to test this assumption.

He designed an experiment in which a subject was asked to participate in an experiment ostensibly about the effects of negative reinforcement on learning. The "learner" (a colleague of the experimenter) was seated at a table and hooked up to a machine that would supposedly administer an electric shock of increasing voltage every time the learner answered the question wrong. The "teacher" (the actual subject of the experiment) sat in another room, asked the questions to the learner, and had to administer the electric shock when the learner gave the wrong answer.

The machine that administered the shocks had a dial that ranged from "minor" at one end of the dial to a section marked in red that said "Danger—Severe Shock." And when the teacher reached that section, the "learner" would scream in apparent agony. (Remember, no shocks were actually administered; the experiment was done to see how far the teacher would go simply by being told to do so by the experimenter. The experimenter would only say, "Please continue," or, "The experiment requires that you continue.")

What would you have done? What percentage of Americans do you think administered a shock to another human being simply because a psychologist told them to? And what percentage would have administered a potentially lethal electric shock? What would you do if your sociology professor told you to give an electric shock to the person sitting next to you in class?

The results were startling. Most people, when asked, say they would be very unlikely to do such a thing. But in the experiment, over two-thirds of the "teachers" administered shocks that would have been lethal to the learners. They simply did what they were told to do, despite the fact that they could hear the learners screaming in pain, and the shocks were clearly labeled as potentially fatal. (After the experiment was over, the teacher and learner met, and the teachers were relieved to realize that they did not actually kill the learners.) And virtually no one refused to administer any shocks to another person. From this, Milgram concluded that Nazism was not the result of a character flaw in Germans but that even Americans, with their celebrated rebelliousness and distaste for authority, would obey without much protest.

Let's look at an equally startling but far less controversial experiment. In the late 1960s and early 1970s, sociologists Robert Rosenthal and Lenore Jacobson decided to test the *self-fulfilling prophesy*—the idea that you get what you expect or that you see what you believe (Rosenthal and Jacobson, 1992). They hypothesized that teachers had expectations of student performance and that students performed to those expectations. That is, the sociologists wanted to test their hypothesis that teachers' expectations were actually the cause of student performance, not the other way around. If the teacher thinks a student is smart, the student will do well in the class. If the teacher expects the student to do poorly, the student will do poorly.

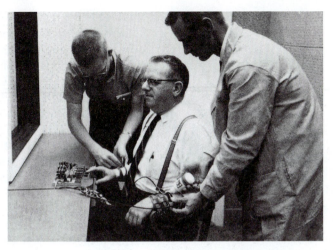

▲ In the "Obedience to Authority" studies, social psychologist Stanley Milgram pretended to attach electrodes to his associate to administer increasingly painful electric shocks when he answered questions incorrectly. Two out of every three test subjects (65 percent) administered shocks all the way up to the maximum level.

Rosenthal and Jacobson administered an IQ test to all the children in an elementary school. Then, without looking at the results, they randomly chose a small group of students and told their teachers that the students had extremely high IQs. This, Rosenthal and Jacobson hypothesized, would raise the teachers' expectations for these randomly chosen students (the experimental group), and these expectations would be reflected in better performance by these students compared with other students (the control group).

At the end of the school year, Rosenthal and Jacobson returned to the school and administered another IQ test to all the students. The "chosen few" performed better on the test than their classmates, yet the only difference between the two groups was the teachers' expectations. It turned out that teacher expectations were the independent variable, and student performance was the dependent variable—not the other way around.

(Before you blame your teachers' expectations for your own grades, remember that professors have been made aware of these potential biases and have, in the past 40 years, developed a series of checks on our expectations. Your grades probably have at least as much to do with your own effort as they do your professors' expectations!)

Neither of these experiments could be conducted in this way today because of changes in the laws surrounding experiments with human subjects. Thus, sociologists are doing fewer experiments now than they once did.

Field Studies. Many of the issues sociologists are concerned with are not readily accessible in controlled laboratory experiments. Instead, sociologists go "into the field" to conduct research among the people they want to study. (The field is any site where the interactions or processes you want to study are taking place, such as an institution like a school or a specific community.) In observational studies, we rely on ourselves to interpret what is happening, and so we test our sociological ways of seeing.

Some observational studies require **detached observation,** a perspective that constrains the researcher from becoming in any way involved in the event he or she is observing. This posture of detachment is less about some notion of objectivity—after all, we are relying on our subjective abilities as an observer—and more because being detached and away from the action reduces the amount that our observation will change the dynamic we're watching. (Being in the field, even as an observer, can change the very things we are trying to study.)

For example, let's say you want to see if there is a gender difference in children's play. If you observe boys and girls unobtrusively from behind a one-way mirror or screen, they'll play as if no one was watching them. But if they know there are grownups watching, they might behave differently, and you might not see what you needed to see. Another way to do this detached and unobtrusive observation is to blend into the crowd and not call attention to yourself as a researcher. Sociologist Barrie Thorne (1993) did this for her study of children's play in several California schoolyards. She walked around the playground, as did other adults (teachers and school monitors), and recorded her observations quietly. After a while the children barely paid any attention to her, and she gained their trust and asked questions.

Detached observation is useful, but it doesn't enable you as a researcher to get inside the experience, to really get your hands dirty. For that you'll have to participate in the activities of the people you are studying. **Participant observation** requires that the researcher do both, participate and observe. Many participant observers conceal their identity to blend in better with the group they're studying.

Juggling these two activities is often difficult. In one famous case, Leon Festinger (1957) studied a cult that predicted the end of the world on a certain date. All cult members were required to gather at the leader's house and wait for the end of the world. Festinger participated in the group's activities and every hour or so rushed to the bathroom to record what he was observing. Other cult members assumed he had some digestive distress!

In another famous study, Laud Humphreys (1970) was interested in the negotiation of anonymous homosexual sex in public restrooms. He volunteered to act as a lookout for the men who waited at a rest stop along the New Jersey Turnpike, because it was against the law to have sex in public restrooms. As the lookout, he was able to observe the men who stopped there to have sex and jotted down their license plate numbers. Later, he was able to trace the men's addresses through their license plate numbers and went to their homes posing as a researcher doing a general sociological study. (This allowed him to ask many questions about their backgrounds.) His findings were as astonishing as they were controversial. Most of the men who stopped at public restrooms to have sex with other men were married and considered themselves heterosexual. Most were working class and politically conservative and saw their behavior simply as sexual release, not as an expression of "who they really were."

Humphreys's research has been severely criticized because he deceived the men he was studying, and he disguised his identity. As a result, universities developed institutional review boards (IRBs) to insure that researchers comply with standards and ethics in conducting their research. But Humphreys was also able to identify a population of men who had sex with other men who did not identify as gay, and this was thought to be one of the possible avenues of transmission for HIV from the urban gay population into heterosexual suburban homes.

Increasingly, field researchers use the ethnographic methods of cultural anthropology to undertake sociological research. **Ethnography** is a field method used most often by anthropologists when they study other cultures. While you don't pretend to be a participant (and you identify yourself as a researcher), you try to understand the world from the point of view of the people whose lives you are interested in and

▲ Ethnography enables researchers to see people's worlds up close, in intimate detail, bringing out both subtle patterns and structural forces that shape social realities. Here you can see an ethnographer talking with villagers in Bundu Tuhan, Malaysia.

attempt, as much as possible, to put your own values and assumptions about their activities "on hold." This avoids two extreme outcomes: (1) If you try to forget your own cultural assumptions and immerse yourself, you risk "going native"—which means you uncritically embrace the group's way of seeing things. (2) If you see the other group only through the filter of your own values, you impose your way of seeing things and can't really understand how they see the world. At its most extreme, this is a form of cultural imperialism—imposing your values on others. Ethnographers attempt to steer a middle path between these extremes.

Ethnographers live and work with the group they're studying, to try to see the world from the others' point of view. Two of the most famous of such studies are William F. Whyte's *Street Corner Society* ([1943] 1993) and Elliot Liebow's *Tally's Corner* (1968). Both studies examined the world of working-class and poor men; Whyte's subjects were White and Italian in Boston; Liebow's were Black men in Washington, D.C. In both cases, readers learned more about the complexity in these men's lives than anyone had ever imagined.

Recent field work among urban minorities has echoed these themes. Martin Sanchez Jankowski (1991) lived with Latino gangs in Los Angeles. Contrary to popular assumptions that might hold that gangs are composed of children from broken homes, adrift and delinquent because they are psychologically maladjusted, Sanchez Jankowski found that most came from intact families, were psychologically better

*[handwritten margin note: Researchers immersing themselves... * being part of a gang]*

Try It   Investigating Interviews and Surveys

Adapted from submission by Meredith Greif, *Cleveland State University*

OBJECTIVE: Investigate how to develop interview questions and explore how research connects to sociological content.

STEP 1: Plan
Identify a research question that would require you to interview college students. There are numerous topics that would work for this project, but when in doubt be sure to check with your instructor about your research question. After you have identified your topic of interest, take a moment to identify your dependent variable. After you have identified your dependent variable, think about how you might measure it and develop six questions that you would ask in an interview to address your research question. Your instructor may have an example to help you with this process. Write out your research question, dependent variable, and interview questions.

STEP 2: Collect Data
The next step is to find a student in your sociology class to interview. It is best to partner with another student and to share interviews. As you are interviewing your partner student, not only pay attention to the responses but also think about how well your interview questions allowed you to really explore your research question. Make notes about what questions were not understood by your interviewee

or what questions did not really result in the information you were hoping to gain from the student. After completing the interview, review your questions and revise them. As you are revising them, explain briefly why you revised each question.

STEP 3: Write
After completing this activity, you may be asked to submit a short reflection paper including the following items. First, explain the research questions you chose for the project and discuss the dependent variable you were hoping to measure. Second, include your original list of interview questions and briefly explain what information you were hoping to learn in your interview. Third, discuss what happened in your interview and what you learned from the experience. Finally, include a list of your revised questions and provide a detailed explanation of why you revised your questions. Your instructor will give you further details on the length of this paper and may include other topics in this paper.

STEP 4: Discuss
At some point, your instructor may lead the class in a discussion of survey research, and you could be asked to share your experiences with this project. Please note that there are numerous variations of this activity, and your instructor may have further directions.

adjusted than non–gang members, and saw gang membership as a reasonable economic alternative to unemployment and poverty. Gangs provided good steady jobs, high wages (with high risks), and the rich social relationships that come from community. Similarly, Elijah Anderson's research on young black men in the inner city (1992, 2000) gave a far deeper understanding of the complex of meanings and motives for behavior that had often been reduced to rather one-dimensional stereotypes.

Ethnography taxes our powers of observation and stretches our sociological muscles to try to see the world from the point of view of other people. Philippe Bourgois (2002) lived for three years in New York City's Spanish Harlem, studying the culture of crack dealers. Loic Wacquant (2003) trained for over three years right alongside local boxers in a training gym in Chicago's South Side. Nancy Sheper-Hughes (1992) studied the poor in Brazil, revealing the physical and psychological violence that permeates their everyday lives and structures social interaction. Javier Auyero (2000) studied clients' own views of the patronage systems that sustain survival in shantytowns on the outskirts of Buenos Aires, Argentina. Chen Hsiang-Shul (1992) studied the transnational worlds of Taiwan immigrants in New York. Ethnographic methods enable us to see people's worlds up close, in intimate detail, bringing out both subtle patterns and structural forces that shape social realities.

Interview Studies. The most typical type of qualitative study uses interviews with a small sample. These studies use a **purposive sample,** which means that respondents

How do we know
what we know?

Measuring Attitudes with a Likert Scale

The Likert scale is the most widely used scale in survey research. Developed by Rensis Likert (1932), it is a technique that presents a set of statements on a questionnaire, then asks respondents to express levels of agreement or disagreement with these statements. Their responses are given numerical value, usually along a five-point or a seven-point scale. By tallying these numeric values, sociologists can gauge people's attitudes.

Likert scales can be used to gauge many types of attitudes, from agreement or disagreement to relative importance, likelihood, quality, or frequency. Some Likert scales provide a middle value that

is neutral or undecided; others use a "forced-choice" scale, with no neutral value, that requires respondents to decide whether they lean more toward agreement or disagreement.

For example, let's say you are doing a survey examining employee self-esteem. You want to gauge levels of self-satisfaction in the workplace. You might present people with a series of statements such as, "I feel good about my work in school on the job," and "I can tell my co-workers respect me," among others. Then you would ask respondents to record the extent of their agreement or disagreement with these statements along a Likert scale. The scale could look something like this:

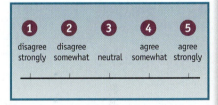

Or, they could record their answers on a "forced-choice" scale that looks more like this:

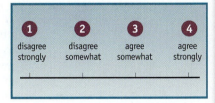

You would take the different scaling structure into account when analyzing and reporting your results. But in either case, the Likert scale would help you to see the extent or intensity of attitudes—more or less, stronger or weaker, bigger or smaller—registered by your survey subjects.

are not selected randomly and not representative of the larger population but selected purposively—that is, each subject is selected precisely because he or she possesses certain characteristics that are of interest to the researcher.

One problem with interview studies is not the size of the sample but the fact that the sample is not a probability sample—that is, it is not a random sample, but rather the sample is selectively drawn to make sure that specific characteristics are included or excluded. Purposive samples do not allow sociologists to generalize about their results as reliably as they can with random samples. However, they do enable researchers to identify common themes in the data and can sensitize us to trends in attitudes or behaviors among specifically targeted groups of people.

For example, let's say you wanted to study feelings of guilt among new mothers, to see how much these feelings were influenced by television shows and magazine articles that instruct women on how to be good mothers. It wouldn't make much sense to conduct a random sample, because you wouldn't get enough new mothers in the sample. You could use a "snowball" technique—asking one new mother to refer you to others. Or you could draw a random sample from a nonrandom population—if, for example, the manufacturers of baby foods could be persuaded to give you their mailing lists of new mothers and you selected every hundredth name on the list. (We discuss sampling further below.)

All the methods above involve actually interacting with real people—either in a controlled environment or in their natural habitat. These methods give us a kind of up-close and personal feel to the research, an intimate knowledge with fine nuance and detail.

You know the old expression of being unable to see the forest for the trees. Field methods such as ethnographies are often so focused on the minute patterns of leaves and bark on an individual tree that they lose a sense of the shape and size of the forest. Because the researcher wants to understand broad patterns of behaviors and attitudes, sociologists also use more quantitative methods involving our interaction not with people but with data. Of course, these methods might reveal the larger patterns, but it's hard to make out the nuances and subtleties of the individual trees.

Analysis of Quantitative Data

Quantitative data analysis involves the use of surveys and other instruments to understand those larger patterns mentioned previously.

Surveys. Surveys are the most common method that sociologists use to collect information about attitudes and behaviors. For example, you might be interested in how religion influences sexual behavior. A survey might be able to tell you whether one's religious beliefs influence whether or not an adolescent has had sex (it does), or if a married person has committed adultery (it doesn't). Or a survey might address whether being a registered Republican or Democrat has any relationship to the types of sports one likes to watch on television (it does).

To construct a survey, we first decide the sorts of questions we want to ask and how best to ask them. While the simplest question would be a dichotomous question, in which "yes" and "no" were the only choices, this form of question can provide only limited information. For example, if you asked, "Do you believe that sex before marriage is always wrong?" you might find out some distribution of moral beliefs, but such answers would tell you little about how people *use* that moral position, whether they apply it to themselves or to others, and how they might deal with those who transgress.

Usually, we ask questions that can be graded on a scale. The most common form is a **Likert scale** that arranges possible responses from lowest to highest. Instead of a simple "yes" or "no" answer, we are asked to place ourselves on a continuum at one of five points or one of seven points. When we answer a question on a survey by saying whether we "strongly agree," "agree," "neither agree nor disagree," "disagree," or "disagree strongly," the researchers are using a Likert scale.

Once we've decided what questions to ask, we have to decide to whom to ask them. But you can't ask everyone: It would cost too much, take too long, and be impossible to analyze. Sociologists take a **sample** (or a subset) of the population they want to study. (We've already discussed the purposive sampling of interview studies.) This is usually done by telephone or by mail. If you want to know what Americans think about an issue, you can't ask all of them. A **random sample** asks a number of people, chosen by an abstract and arbitrary method, like tossing a piece of paper with each person's name on it into a hat or selecting every tenth name in a telephone book or every thousandth name on the voter registration list. In this way, each person has an equal chance of being selected.

When you take a random sample, you assume that those not in the population from which you are choosing your sample are themselves random. For example, choosing from the phone book would exclude those people who don't have telephones (who tend to be rural and conservative) as well as those who use only their cell phones and are not listed (who tend to be urban and liberal). Using voter registration rolls would exclude those who are not registered, but researchers assume an equal number of liberals and conservatives are not registered.

Often the differences between different groups of people are what you actually want to study. In that case, you'd take a **stratified sample**, in which you divide people into different groups before you construct your sample and make sure that you get an adequate number of members of each of the groups. A stratified sample divides the sample into proportions equal to the proportions found in the population at large.

Let's say you wanted to do a study of racial attitudes in Chicago Heights, Illinois. (Chicago Heights is 38 percent African American, 37 percent White, 24 percent Hispanic, 13.5 percent other, 2.7 percent multiracial, 0.8 percent Native American.) A random sample might actually give you an inaccurate portrait because you might, inadvertently, have an unrepresentative sample, with too few or too many of a particular group. What if your random sample was gathered through voter records, a common method? You'd lose all those residents who were not registered to vote, who tend to be concentrated among minorities and the poor, as well as the young (and the median age in Chicago Heights is 30.6 years old.) What if you called every one-hundredth number in the phone book—you'd lose all those who were unlisted or who don't have landline phones, and overrepresent statistically those who have several numbers (and would therefore stand a higher chance of being called). So your random sample could turn out to be not very representative. A stratified sample would enable you to match, in the sample, the percentages in the actual population, making the data much more reliable.

Another type of sample is a **cluster sample**. In these, the researcher might choose a random sample of neighborhoods—say every tenth block in a town—and then survey every person in that "cluster." This sort of sample often provides a richer "local" feel to a more representative sample.

Surveys are extremely common in the contemporary United States. There are dozens of organizations devoted to polling Americans on every possible attitude or behavior on a daily basis. Politicians rely on survey data to tailor their policies and shape their message. These are often so targeted and biased that they may make the politicians feel more comfortable, but they may tell us little about what the actual

How do we know
what we know ?

Finding Hard-to-Get Answers through Sampling

Calculating the number of deaths as a consequence of war is a gruesome but difficult task. We might know how many troops armies have, but what about civilian casualties? In Iraq, for example, different sources of data—hospital records, media reports, police reports, or mortuary data—all provide conflicting numbers. (These numbers are low because many people don't go to hospitals, are buried by their families, and are not reported to the media or police. What's more, Iraq has never had a national census, so random sampling would be uncertain because the lists of residents from which such a sample might be drawn would be incomplete.)

Demographer Gilbert Burnham and his colleagues at the Johns Hopkins School of Public Health conducted cluster samples in which they picked out neighborhoods at random and surveyed all the people living in them. They examined data from 47 neighborhoods, each of which had about 40 residents living in it. They asked residents whether anyone had died since the U.S. invasion and what the cause of death was and certified over 90 percent of the deaths. They compared this to data from before the invasion, and they calculated that about 650,000 more people had died than would have died had the war never begun, a number significantly higher than earlier estimates (*The Economist*, October 14, 2006, p. 52).

The statistical methods we use often have significant impact on how we perceive an event.

citizenry thinks about a particular issue. Some surveys are created by websites or popular magazines, and these sometimes get attention for their results even though most fail to use valid methods of sampling and questioning. Still, numerous surveys that we see, hear, or read about are developed and privately administered by bona fide research organizations like Roper or Gallup; other sound surveys are publicly financed and available to all researchers, such as the General Social Survey at the National Opinion Research Center in Chicago.

Survey Questions. Surveys are the mainstay of sociological research, but coming up with good survey questions is hard. The wording of the question, the possible answers, even the location of the question in the survey questionnaire can change the responses.

Take a classic example from 1941 (Rugg, 1941). In a national survey, respondents were asked two slightly different questions about freedom of speech:

- Do you think the United States should forbid public speeches against democracy?
- Do you think the United States should allow public speeches against democracy?

When the results came in, 75 percent of respondents would *not allow* the speeches, but only 54 percent would *forbid* them. Surely *forbid* and *not allow* mean the same thing in practice, but the wording changed the way people thought about the issue. Psychologists, sociologists, and statisticians are still trying to figure how to avoid this problem.

Have you ever shoplifted? No? Well, then, have you ever taken an object from a store without paying for it? Respondents are much more likely to answer "yes" to the second version because it somehow doesn't seem as bad, even though it's really the same thing.

Do you think women should have the right to have an *abortion*? How about the right to *end their pregnancy*? You guessed it—far more respondents favor the right to end a pregnancy than to have an abortion.

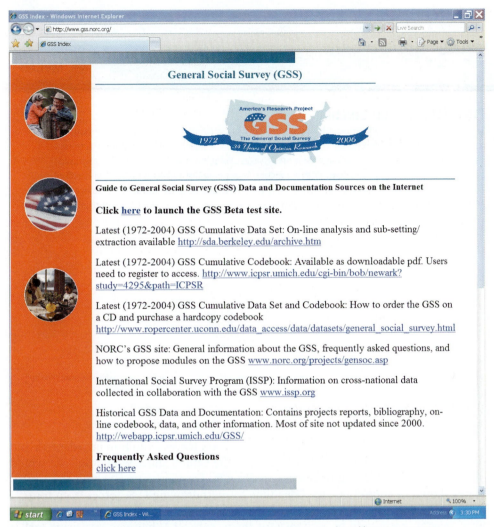

General Social Survey (GSS)

America's Research Project
GSS
The General Social Survey
1972 34 Years of Opinion Research 2006

Guide to General Social Survey (GSS) Data and Documentation Sources on the Internet

Click here to launch the GSS Beta test site.

Latest (1972-2004) GSS Cumulative Data Set: On-line analysis and sub-setting/extraction available http://sda.berkeley.edu/archive.htm

Latest (1972-2004) GSS Cumulative Codebook: Available as downloadable pdf. Users need to register to access. http://www.icpsr.umich.edu/cgi-bin/bob/newark?study=4295&path=ICPSR

Latest (1972-2004) GSS Cumulative Data Set and Codebook: How to order the GSS on a CD and purchase a hardcopy codebook http://www.ropercenter.uconn.edu/data_access/data/datasets/general_social_survey.html

NORC's GSS site: General information about the GSS, frequently asked questions, and how to propose modules on the GSS www.norc.org/projects/gensoc.asp

International Social Survey Program (ISSP): Information on cross-national data collected in collaboration with the GSS www.issp.org

Historical GSS Data and Documentation: Contains projects reports, bibliography, on-line codebook, data, and other information. Most of site not updated since 2000. http://webapp.icpsr.umich.edu/GSS/

Frequently Asked Questions
click here

◀ **The General Social Survey has been surveying American attitudes and behaviors since 1972.**

Source: From the homepage of General Social Survey website, www.gss.norc.org <http://www.gss.norc.org>. Reprinted by permission of General Social Survey.

The possible answers also affect responses. On June 27, 2006, two different newspapers reported the results of two different polls about the U.S. occupation of Iraq:

- *USA Today*'s headline read: "Most in Poll Want Plan for Pullout from Iraq." This story reported a *USA Today*/Gallup poll in which 50 percent of the respondents say they want all U.S. troops home from Iraq within 12 months, and 57 percent say that Congress should pass a resolution outlining plans for a troop withdrawal (Page, 2006).
- That same day, the *Washington Post*'s report of their poll (with ABC News) read "Nation Is Divided on Drawdown of Troops"; in this story, 51 percent of the respondents say that the Bush administration should not set a deadline for withdrawing U.S. troops from Iraq (Balz and Morin, 2006).

Why the difference? It could be the way in which the questions were posed. The *USA Today*/Gallup pollsters asked respondents to pick a plan for U.S. troops: "Withdraw immediately," "withdraw in 12 months' time," "withdraw, take as many years as needed," or "send more troops." The *Washington Post*/ABC pollsters, on the other hand, asked more open-ended questions: "Some people say the Bush administration

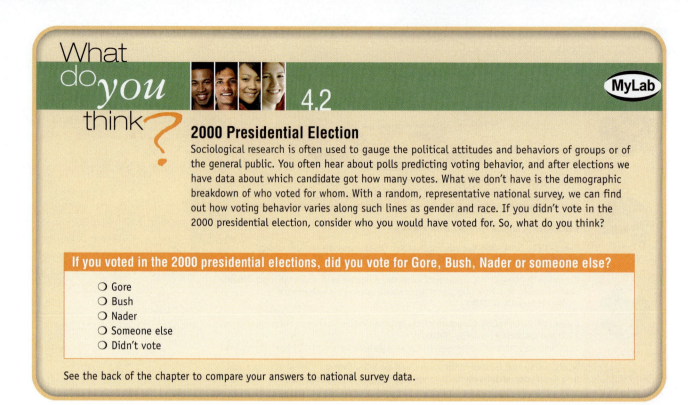

See the back of the chapter to compare your answers to national survey data.

should set a deadline for withdrawing U.S. military forces from Iraq in order to avoid further casualties. Others say knowing when the United States would pull out would only encourage the anti-government insurgents. Do you yourself think the United States should or should not set a deadline for withdrawing U.S. forces from Iraq?"

In other words, the *Post* asked, should we get out just to save American lives, even if that would be a victory for the terrorists? What was surprising is that 47 percent of the respondents still said that some timetable is better than no timetable.

How about the placement of the question in the survey? Respondents are much more likely to respond honestly to the shoplifting question if it's near the end of the survey. When sensitive or embarrassing questions come early, respondents are put off, wondering how intimate the questions are going to get. After they get a little practice by answering questions about their gender, race, age, and occupation, then they are able to handle the tough questions more readily.

Secondary Analysis of Existing Data. Given the enormous amount of time and money it takes to conduct a survey from scratch, many sociologists rely on the survey data previously collected from others. They may perform **secondary analysis** of already existing data. Secondary analysis involves reanalyzing data that have already been collected. Often this new analysis asks different questions of the data than the original researcher asked.

Others may need to use existing historical data. After all, if you're interested in political debates in seventeenth-century France, you can't very well conduct a survey or interview the participants. Still others use content analysis to explore what people actually mean when they give the sorts of responses they do.

Sociology and our World

How to "Read" a Survey

- Four out of five doctors recommend Zytrolvan.
- Forty-three percent of Americans support the president's policy.

We hear statements like these all the time. But what do they mean?

According to the American Association for Public Opinion Research, an intelligent analysis of survey results requires that you know some minimal information:

- Who sponsored the survey, and who conducted it?
- What is the population being studied?
- What is the sample selection procedure?

- What is the size of the sample, and the completion rates?
- What is the wording of the questions?
- What are the method, location, and dates of data collection?
- How precise are the findings, including weighting or estimating procedures and sampling error?
- Are some results based on parts of the sample rather than the whole sample?

Unfortunately, very few of the survey results you hear about in the mass media (or, for that matter, in many textbooks) include all of the necessary information. Therefore you cannot be sure of their accuracy. If the accuracy of the numbers is important to you, look up the references. If there are no references, start to worry.

For example, let's say you were interested in the effect of political persuasions on moral attitudes and behavior. Perhaps your hypothesis was that the more conservative one is politically, the more conservative one might be morally. You've operationalized your variables on political persuasion by assuming conservatives are registered Republican and liberals are registered Democrat and that morally conservative people will disapprove of divorce and be less likely to get a divorce. You decide to test the hypotheses that because Republicans are less likely to approve of divorce than Democrats are, then Republicans are less likely to get divorced (attitudes lead to behavior).

You find that a reputable social scientific researcher had done a survey of a sample of Americans, but this researcher was interested only in gender and racial differences in moral attitudes and behavior. It's possible that the research contains other background variables, such as age, political persuasion, educational background, or occupation. Secondary analysis of the existing data will enable you to answer your questions. In addition, you might be able to find data on statewide divorce rates and statewide political attitudes; while these will not answer the question at the more individual level, they can point to broad patterns about whether conservatives are true to their beliefs and so less likely to divorce. (The answer is apparently no; states that voted Republican in the last two presidential elections have higher divorce rates than states that voted Democratic, with eleven "red states" recording higher divorce rates than any "blue state") (Crary, 1999; Dossier: Red State Values, 2006).

Also, there may be different forms of data you can use. Sometimes, for example, researchers will conduct an *interview* and use only a numeric scale to register responses. But then certain answers to certain questions might prompt the interviewer to ask for more information. These responses may be written down as notes or sentences on the initial interview forms. Going back to these forms might require you to do content analysis of the narrative responses people gave to the questions.

For example, one of my students was perplexed by an apparent discrepancy in the research on date and acquaintance rape. The National Crime Victimization Study (NCVS) found that 25 percent of all college-age women had experiences that met the

▲ Content analysis of national magazines can be used to chart the differences in gender ideals. Women today are less likely to be defined only as mothers, or in relation to their husbands' occupations, and more likely to be seen as independent and complex individuals.

legal definition of rape ("being forced to have sex against your will"), but only between 27 and 46.5 percent of those women whose experience did meet this definition actually defined what happened to them as rape. Is it still rape if you don't perceive it as rape? Karen Weiss (2006) decided to look at the original questionnaires administered in the survey, because when the respondent said that she had had sex against her will, the interviewer stopped and asked the woman to describe what happened and wrote it down. By undertaking an analysis of the narratives of these experiences, Weiss was able to understand under which circumstances women are more likely to see their experiences as qualifying as rape (if they didn't know the guy before, or had never dated him, or didn't really want to date him) and under which circumstances they were likely to see the experience as something other than rape.

While field studies do not permit exact replication—the cultural group you study is indelibly changed by the fact that you have studied it—one can reasonably "replicate" (reproduce) a field study by careful research. For example, if you are in the field, doing an ethnography, and you keep a running record of both your observations and the research strategies and decisions you made while in the field, other researchers can follow your decision making and attempt to understand a similar phenomenon.

Here's another good example. One of my graduate students had gone to college at the University of New Mexico. As an undergraduate, one of her professors told me, she had done a marvelous ethnographic study of local "taggers"—kids who develop elaborate signatures in writing graffiti on walls and public buildings. For several months she hung out with these taggers and interviewed many of them. Just after she wrote her honors thesis, she discovered that someone had just published an ethnographic study of taggers in Denver (Ferrell and Stewart-Huidobro, 1996). She was heartbroken to discover that their conclusions were similar to her own; as she saw it, they had "scooped" her, beaten her to the punch. But her professor explained that actually each researcher had replicated the study of the other researcher, and thus their conclusions were supported, not weakened. This student's work had been validated, not undermined. Although they were not identical, the fact that two teams researching two different examples of a phenomenon in two different cities came to similar conclusions actually strengthens the **generalizability** of the findings of each. We can learn a great deal by such replication because it suggests the extent to which the results of a study can be generalized to other circumstances.

Content Analysis

Content analysis is usually not a quantitative method but instead involves an intensive reading of certain "texts"—perhaps books, or pieces of conversation, or a set of articles from a newspaper or magazine, or even snippets from television shows. Some content analysis involves taking a random sample of such pieces of conversation, or media representations, and then develops intricate coding procedures for analyzing them. These answers can then be analyzed quantitatively, and one can generate observable variations in the presentations of those texts.

If you want to know if the media images of girls or boys have changed much over the past ten years, then content analysis might enable you to do this. You might choose ten magazines, the five most popular among boys and girls of a certain age. Then you might look at all the issues of those magazines in the month of August of every year for the past ten years and look at the sections called "Back-to-School Fashions." You could devise a coding scheme for these fashions, to judge whether they are more or less gender conforming in terms of style, color, and the like. Then you could see if the race or class of the models who are wearing those clothes changes.

How do we know what we know?

Balanced Reporting and the Value of Content Analysis

Many news programs brag that they give you "balanced reporting" and "both sides of the story," when actually they are manipulating the statistics.

Say proposition *X* is up for voting. The reporters will interview one person who approves of it and another who disapproves, giving viewers the impression that the population is divided equally, when actually 90 percent or more of the population may approve, and fewer than 10 percent disapprove.

For some "issues," the percentage is closer to 99.9 percent. Smoking causes cancer. Saturated fat increases blood cholesterol. It's hard to find a physician who will disagree with these statements, but in the interest of "balanced reporting," reporters will still scour the countryside to find one.

The great example is global warming. Top climate change scientists from around the world have produced numerous major reports in the past decade that assert a remarkably high level of scientific consensus that (1) global warming is a serious problem with human causes, and (2) it must be addressed immediately (Adger et al., 2002). In 1997, the head of the U.S. National Oceanic and Atmospheric Administration said "there is a better scientific consensus on [global warming] than on any issue I know—except maybe Newton's second law of dynamics" (Warrick, 1997, A1). Yet America's major papers, including the *New York Times, Washington Post, Los Angeles Times*, and *Wall Street Journal*, continue to report on the supposed "uncertainties" about global warming among scientists. Content analysis studies find one reason for inaccuracy is methodological—the journalistic norm of "balanced" reporting actually creates this bias in the content presented (Boykoff and Boykoff, 2004; Stamm, Clark and Eblacas, 2000; Zehr, 2000).

Oddly enough, many people fall for this phenomenon, concluding that the issue in question is subject to controversy when there really isn't one, or that "nobody really knows," when in fact almost everybody knows. Sometimes it isn't enough to see the numbers; you have to also understand how the numbers are used.

Making the Right Comparisons

No matter what research method we choose, it is always important to make sure we are comparing things that are, in fact, comparable (Table 4.1). Otherwise, one risks making claims that turn out not to be true. For example, as we saw at the beginning of the chapter, it is often assumed that divorce has negative consequences for children, both in terms of their school achievement and in terms of their psychological health. But such studies were based on comparisons of children from divorced and married parents and never examined the quality of the marriage. Then, as we saw, children from intact *but unhappy* marriages actually do worse (have lower grades and more psychological problems) than children from divorced families!

Such an example reminds us that researchers in this case needed to distinguish between two types of married parents, happy and unhappy. Policies derived from the original study would have disastrous results for the children who lived in families in which there was a lot of conflict and the parents were really unhappy—even worse consequences than had the parents divorced (Booth and Amato, 2000).

Take another example of how researchers compared the wrong groups. You've probably heard the idea that homosexuality is often the result of a certain family dynamic. Specifically, psychiatrists found that the gay men they saw in therapy often had overdominant mothers and absent fathers (which, the theory goes, caused their homosexuality by preventing the men from making the healthy gender transition away from mother and identifying with father [Bieber et al., 1962]). Such a dynamic would, the researchers believed, keep them "identified" with their mothers, and therefore "feminine" in their psychological predisposition. For decades, this family dynamic was the foundation of the psychological treatment of homosexual men. The problem was in the comparative group. The gay men in therapy were compared with the family arrangements of heterosexual men who were not in therapy.

It turned out, though, that the gay men who were not in therapy did not have overdominant mothers and absent fathers. And it also turned out that heterosexual men in therapy *did* have overdominant mothers and absent fathers. In other words, having an overdominant mother and an absent father didn't seem to be the cause of homosexuality but was probably a good predictor of whether a man, straight or gay, decided to go into therapy.

TABLE 4.1

Research Methods

RESEARCH METHOD	KEY POINTS
Experiments	Some variables can be tightly controlled and monitored, but it's difficult to control the independent variable.
	Replication is easy and convenient.
	Ethical considerations prevent many experiments with human subjects.
Field studies	Sociologists can conduct research directly with the people they want to study.
	Researchers can often tease out both subtle patterns and structural forces that shape social realities.
Interview studies	A carefully selected sample makes it easy to identify common themes and highlight trends and behaviors within a very specific group.
	Generalizing about results is not reliable because the sample group is so targeted.
Surveys	It is easy and convenient to collect large amounts of data about equally large numbers of people.
	Data may be corrupt due to poor methodology, including poorly worded questions and question ordering.
Secondary analysis of existing data	It is often easier and cheaper to rely on information collected by others; sometimes it's the only way to "replicate" a field study.
	You are completely dependent on the original sources and can't use common follow-up methods.
Content analysis	A researcher can quantitatively analyze an existing text and make generalizable observations based on it.

Social Science and the Problem of "Truth"

One thing that is certain about social life is that nothing is certain about social life. Sociology is both a social *science*, sharing basic strategies and perspectives with the natural sciences, and a *social* science, attempting to study living creatures who often behave unpredictably and irrationally, for complex rational, emotional, or psychological reasons. Because a single "truth" is neither knowable nor even possible, social scientists approach their research with the humility of the curious, but armed with a vast array of techniques that can help them approach "truths."

Even if truth is impossible, we can approach it. Like all other sciences, we approach it through addressing two central concerns, predictability and causality. **Predictability** refers to the ability to generate testable hypotheses from data and to "predict" the outcomes of some phenomenon or event. **Causality** refers to the relationship of some variable to the effects it produces. According to scientific requirements, a cause is termed "necessary" when it always precedes an effect and "sufficient" when it initiates or produces the effect.

cause/effect

Predictability and Probability

Everybody knows, for example, that *Titanic* (1997), with Leonardo DiCaprio and Kate Winslet as passengers on the doomed ship, is a "chick flick": Women love it, and men don't. But when I invite 300 women to a free screening, something remarkable happens: Only 80 percent of them love it. What's wrong with the other 20 percent?

Auguste Comte (1798–1857), often considered the founder of sociology, actually founded something that he called "social physics." He believed that human society follows permanent, unchangeable laws, just as the natural world does. If they know just two variables, temperature and air pressure, chemists can predict with 100 percent certainty whether a vial of H_2O will be solid, liquid, or gas. In the same way, social physicists would be able to predict with 100 percent certainty the behavior of any human population at any time. Will the crowd outside the football game get violent? What political party will win the election? Will women like *Titanic*? The answer should be merely a matter of analyzing variables.

For 50 years, sociologists analyzed variables. They made a lot of predictions. Some were accurate, many not particularly accurate at all. It turns out that human populations have many more variables than the natural world. Yet predictability is of central concern to sociologists because we hope that if we can understand the variations of enough variables—like race, ethnicity, age, religion, region, and the like—we can reasonably guess what you would be more likely to do in a particular situation. And that—being able to use these variables to predict future behavior—is the essence of predictability.

Why do 20 percent of the women in my study dislike *Titanic*? Maybe gender is not the only variable that can be the cause of the desired effect. So I also ask their age, race, socioeconomic class, and sexual orientation. Of women who are aged 18 to 25, White, middle class, and heterosexual, 95 percent like *Titanic*. But that still leaves 5 percent who do not; I still can't predict whether any particular woman will like *Titanic* with 100 percent accuracy.

What other potential variables are there? Who knows? Maybe one woman doesn't like *Titanic* because her uncle drowned, and the movie brings back unhappy memories.

Another had a boyfriend who looked like Leonardo DiCaprio. Another is a film buff and prefers the 1953 version starring Barbara Stanwyck.

The number of predictive variables increases dramatically as the group gets bigger and the behavior more complex, until the sociologist has no chance of ever finding them all. But even if we could, predicting human behavior would still be inaccurate because of the observer effect: People *know* that they are being studied. Maybe some of the women watching *Titanic* are aware of its reputation as a "chick flick," and they don't want to be stereotyped, so they deliberately look for things not to like. People change their behavior, and even their beliefs and attitudes, based on the situation that they are in, so the variables that are predictive today may not be tomorrow, or even five minutes from now.

So sociologists—and other social scientists—can never hope to attain the 100 percent certainty of the natural sciences. Instead, we use probability. If you are a White, middle-class, heterosexual woman aged 18 to 25, you will probably like *Titanic*. But we can offer no guarantees.

Causality

Students who take a foreign language in high school tend to be less xenophobic (fearful or suspicious of people from foreign countries). Does taking a foreign language decrease their level of xenophobia, or are xenophobic people less likely to sign up for foreign language classes?

In 1958, marriage between men and women of different races was illegal in many states, and, according to the Gallup Poll, 96 percent of the population disapproved of it. Then the Supreme Court legalized interracial marriage in the *Loving v. the Commonwealth of Virginia* decision (1967). In 1978, only 66 percent of the population disapproved. Did legalization change people's minds, or did the Supreme Court base its decision on changing mores of the society?

Causality attempts to answer the question we have asked each other since primary school: Which came first, the chicken or the egg? Which "caused" which to happen? Which is the independent variable (the cause), and which is the dependent variable (the effect)?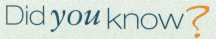

In quantitative research, variable *A* is supposed to have a causal impact on variable *B*, but it is not always easy to decide which is the cause and which is the effect. Scientists use a number of clues. Let's look at the old saw that watching violence on television and in the movies (variable *A*) makes children violent (variable *B*).

Imagine I place 50 children at random into two groups. One group of 25 children watches a video about bears learning to share, and the other watches a video about ninjas chopping each other's heads off. I then monitor the children at play. Sure enough, most of the children who watched the sharing video are playing nicely, and the ones who watched the ninjas are pretending to chop each other's heads off. Can I establish a causal link?

The answer is a resounding "maybe." There are several other questions that you have to answer:

1. Does variable *B* come after variable *A* in time? Were the children calm and docile until after they watched the ninja video?

2. Is there a high correlation between variable *A* and variable *B*? That is, are all or almost all of the children who watched the ninja video behaving aggressively and all those who watched the bear video behaving calmly?

Did *you* know?

Actually, scientists have answered the question of which came first. Because living things evolve through changes in their DNA, and because in each animal the DNA is the same in every single cell (beginning with the first cell in reproduction, the zygote), then chickens evolved from nonchickens through a series of tiny changes caused by mutations in the male and female DNA in the process of reproduction. Such changes would only have an effect when a new zygote was created. So, what happened was that two nonchickens mated, but the zygote contained the mutations that produced the first "chicken." When it broke through its shell—presto, the first chicken. So the egg came first.

3. Are there any extraneous variables that might have contaminated the data? Maybe the sharing bears were so boring that the children who watched them are falling asleep.

4. Is there an observer effect that might be contaminating the data? Maybe I'm more likely to classify the behaviors of the ninja video kids as aggressive.

Any or all of these questions might render your assertion that watching ninja videos "causes" violent behavior unreliable. Sociologists must constantly be aware of possible traps and biases in their research—even in a controlled experimental setting like this one.

One must also always be on guard against logical fallacies that can lead you in the wrong direction. One problem is what is called the "compositional fallacy" in logic: comparing two groups that are different, assuming they are the same, and drawing an inference between them. Even if all members of category A are also members of category B doesn't necessarily mean that all members of category B are members of category A. In its classic formulation: Just because all members of the Mafia (A) are Italian (B) doesn't mean that all Italians (B) are members of the Mafia (A). Just because virtually all those arrested for child sexual abuse are heterosexual men doesn't mean that all heterosexual men are child abusers.

Issues in Conducting Research

No research project involving human beings is without controversy. Debates have always raged about the validity of studies, and we often come to believe that we can explain anything by statistics. That may be true—that you can prove even the most outrageously false things by the use of statistical manipulations—but not all "proofs" will be equally valid or hold up in the court of review by other social scientists. Most sociological research is published in academic or scholarly journals—such as the *American Sociological Review, Social Problems, Social Forces*, or the *American Journal of Sociology*. The American Sociological Association sponsors several "flagship" journals and controls the selection of editors to ensure that the entire range of topics and perspectives is covered. Each subfield of sociology has its own journals, devoted to those specific areas of research. In the sociology of gender alone, for example, there are dozens of journals, including *Gender & Society* or *Men and Masculinities*, a scholarly journal that I edit.

In all such reputable journals, articles are subject to "peer review"—that is, each article is evaluated by a set of reviewers who are, themselves, competent researchers in that field. Peer review

"That's the gist of what I want to say. Now get me some statistics to base it on."

© The New Yorker Collection, 1977. Joseph Mirachi, from cartoonbank.com. All Rights Reserved. Reprinted with permission.

accomplishes two tasks: (1) It ensures that the research is evaluated by those who are competent to evaluate it and assess the adequacy of the research, and (2) it ensures that the editor's own particular biases do not prejudice her or him in the decision to accept or reject the article. Peer review is the standard model for all serious academic and scholarly journals.

In completing the research, there are three issues that you always needs to keep in mind.

Remain Objective and Avoid Bias

You must strive for objectivity, to make sure that your prejudices and assumptions do not contaminate the results you find. That is not to say that your political persuasion or your preconceived assumptions cannot guide your research: They can. Indeed, they will even if you don't want them to. You'll invariably want to do research on something that interests you, and things usually interest us because we have a personal stake in understanding or changing them.

Despite these assumptions, though, you must be careful to construct the research project so that you find out what is really there and not merely develop an elaborate way to confirm your stereotypes. The research methods you use and the questions you ask have to allow for the possibility that you're wrong. And you, as a researcher, have to be prepared to be surprised, because we often find things we didn't expect to find.

There are two kinds of bias that we must be aware of:

1. There are your own sets of assumptions and values, your political positions on specific issues. Everyone has these, as they are based on widely held cultural values (although, as we saw in the first chapter, they are often contradictory). These may determine what you might be interested in studying, but this kind of bias should not make it impossible for the results to surprise you.

2. A second kind of bias is not the values that inform your choice of subject but biases *in the research design itself* that corrupt your results and make them unreliable and invalid. One must be sure to be as conscientious as possible in the integrity of the research design to avoid excluding specific groups from your sample.

For example, if you are vehemently antichoice, you might decide to research the moral and religious status of women who have abortions. You might hypothesize that abortion is morally wrong and those women who had an abortion were not informed by morality or committed to any religion. That research question is informed by your biases, which is fine. But if you do a survey of women who have had abortions and find out that about a quarter of them did so even though they claimed that it was morally wrong or that nearly one-fifth of them were born-again or evangelical Christians, you are obligated by your commitment to science to report those findings honestly. (Incidentally, that is what you would find were you to study the question [Alan Guttmacher Institute, 1996; Henshaw and Kost, 1996; Henshaw and Martire, 1982; Medical World News, 1987].)

If you find that most women don't regret their decision, and then readminister the survey this time only to women who identify as evangelicals and exclude any women who voted Democratic in the last election, you might find the results you were hoping for. But now your survey would be biased, because you systematically excluded some particular group, which skews the results.

Objectivity doesn't mean not having any values; it means being aware of them so that we are not blinded by them.

Avoid Overstating Results

Overstating one's findings is one of the biggest temptations to any sociological researcher. Findings are often not "newsworthy" unless you find something really significant, and funding sources, such as governmental research institutes and private foundations, often link continuing funding to such glamorous and newsworthy findings. Even when you do your first research project, you'll likely be tempted to overstate your results, if for no other reason than to impress your professor with some "big" finding and get a better grade.

But there are temptations to overstate within the research methodologies themselves. In ethnographic research, for example, one can say a lot about a little—that is, one's insights are very deep, but one has only examined a very small phenomenon or group of people. One cannot pretend that such insights can be generalized to larger populations without adequate comparisons. In survey research one can say a little about a whole lot: Through good sampling, one can find out the attitudes or behaviors of Americans, but one cannot explain why they hold such beliefs or take such actions, nor can one explain how they "use" their beliefs.

Researchers must be cautious about inferring why something happens from the fact that it does happen. A **correlation**, or some relationship between two phenomena, doesn't necessarily mean that one is the *cause* of the other. A correlation between a dependent variable and an independent variable tells you that they are related to each other, that one varies when the other varies. Finding a relationship between two variables tells you nothing about the *direction* of that relationship. And it doesn't tell you *why* they both vary together.

For example, there is a strong correlation between the amount of ice cream sold in the United States and the number of deaths by drowning. The more ice cream sold, the higher the number of drowning deaths. Does eating ice cream lead to drowning?

Sociology and our World

Major League Baseball Prevents Divorce?

I recently read in the "relationships" section of my Internet server's webpage that cities with major league baseball teams have a lower divorce rate than those that do not. Cities that introduced teams in the past decade have seen their divorce rates decline up to 30 percent. This led a University of Denver psychologist to claim that having a major league baseball team leads to greater compatibility among couples. "One way to get going is to head for your nearest ballpark," he said (Snyder, 2006).

A simple correlation between two variables—in this case rates of divorce and proximity to major league baseball teams—is often offered as "proof" that going to major league baseball games helps to sustain marriages. (This might prompt some government agency to give away a lot of tickets to struggling marriages!) But for what other reasons might there be a correlation between baseball teams and low divorce rates?

Could it be that baseball teams are located in major cities, which have lower divorce rates than the suburbs or rural areas? Could those cities also be places where there are a lot of *other* things going on (theater, movies, concerts, and the like) that enrich one's life? Don't those cities also have basketball teams and football teams? Or major symphonies and large libraries? Could it be that cities with major league teams are also those with the lowest rates of *marriage*? Could it be that those cities that introduced teams in the past decade are those in the Sun Belt where many retirees live—that is, people who are unlikely to get divorced?

It's also true that cities with major league baseball teams are in the North, where there are far more Catholics and Jews, who have lower divorce rates than Protestants who are the overwhelming majority in the South, where there are fewer teams.

And besides, the divorce rate in the United States has been declining *overall* since 1992, so it's no surprise that those cities with new teams would also have a decline in the divorce rate.

Of course not. Both ice cream sales and deaths by drowning happen during the summer, when the temperature gets hot and people eat more ice cream and go swimming more often. The temperature causes both, and so it appears that there is a relationship between them.

Here's another example. Reports of domestic violence apparently increase during the Super Bowl. Does watching the Super Bowl cause violence? Not really. More people are home for a longer period of time on a winter weekend—rates of domestic violence (violence in the home) go up when more people are home. In addition, people drink a lot more during the Super Bowl than during a typical football game, since the game, and the pregame and halftime shows, last several hours longer than typical football Sunday afternoons. It turns out that on any day that a lot of people are home, drinking a lot, rates of domestic violence go up. They could be watching SpongeBob SquarePants.

Another potential problem is that events in society are not isolated from other events. To measure the impact of one variable on another might be possible in a social vacuum, but in real life, there are so many other things that might get in the way of accurate measurement. Confounding variables need to be assessed in some fashion— by trying to measure them, by minimizing their impact, or by assuming that they confound everything equally and therefore can be safely ignored.

As a result of all these potential problems, researchers must be careful not to overstate their information and aware of a variety of possible explanations for the results they find.

Maintain Professional Ethics

The researcher must also be ethical. As scientists, sociologists are constantly confronted with ethical issues. For example, what if you were interested in studying the social impact of oil drilling in the Alaska wilderness on indigenous people who live near the oil wells? And suppose that the research would be funded by a generous grant from the oil companies who would profit significantly if you were to find that the impact would be either minimal or beneficial. Even if your research were completely free of corporate influence, people would still be suspicious of your results. Research must be free of influence by outside agencies, even those that might provide research grants to fund the research. And it must be free of the perception of outside influence as well, which means that much research is funded by large foundations or by government agencies.

The most important ethical issue is that your research should not actually hurt the people you are researching. A recent scandal among anthropologists concerned a researcher who introduced guns into a primitive culture and changed the hierarchy among the men by enabling a less-successful hunter to suddenly become very successful. Recall the example of psychologist Stanley Milgram's experiment on obedience to authority in which one subject administered "shocks" to another.

The psychological consequences of deceptive experiments led to significant changes in research ethics. An act of Congress in 1970 made "informed consent" a requirement of research. Only after all adult subjects of an experiment (or the parents of minors) are clearly

One of the most infamous research studies in U.S. history was the Tuskegee experiment, in which nearly 400 African American men with late-stage syphilis were deliberately left untreated to test what the disease would do to them. ▼

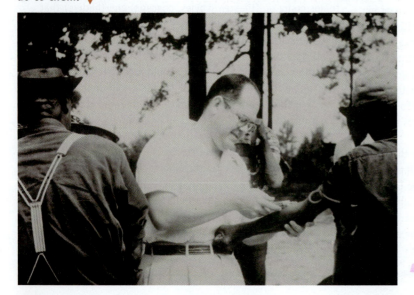

informed about the object of the experiment and assured of confidentiality can they consent to the experiment. And only then can the experiment proceed. Today, all major research universities have a Committee on Research Involving Human Subjects (CORIHS) or an Institutional Review Board (IRB) that oversees all research undertaken at the university.

The Institutional Review Board

When people find out that you are a sociologist, they immediately assume that you're using them in some crazy research project, and in a few weeks you'll be on *Oprah*, talking about their childhood bed-wetting (with their picture, name, and phone number prominently displayed). They don't realize that every research project that goes through a university must pass the inspection of an institutional review board (IRB), which has strict guidelines to protect test subjects. The researcher cannot even begin the data collection unless he or she can guarantee:

- *Informed consent.* Test subjects must be informed, in advance, of the nature of the project, what it's about, what they will have to do in it, and any potential risks and benefits they will face. It's possible to waive informed consent, but only under extreme circumstances; for instance, if you want to study hired killers who would kill you if they discovered that they were being studied.
- *Continuous consent.* Test subjects must be informed that they can back out of the project at any time for any reason, no questions asked.
- *Confidentiality.* Any information that would allow the subject to be identified must be stored separately from the other test data, and it must never be published.
- *Anonymity.* Test subjects must be anonymous. Pseudonyms must be used instead of real names, and if there is any question, even the respondents' biographical data must be modified.
- *Freedom from deception.* Test subjects must not be deceived unless it is absolutely necessary, the deception is unlikely to cause major psychological trauma, and they are debriefed immediately afterwards.
- *Freedom from harm.* Test subjects must not be subjected to any risk of physical or psychological injury greater than they would experience in real life, unless it is absolutely necessary—and then they must be warned in advance. "Psychological injury" extends to embarrassing questions like "Have you ever been pregnant?"
- *Protected groups.* Children and adolescents, college students, prisoners, and other groups have a protected status, because they cannot really give consent (children are too young, and college students may believe that they must participate or their grade will suffer). The IRB requires special procedures for studies involving these groups.

In recent years, IRBs have expanded the scope of their review to include any research that involves human subjects in any way whatever. Sometimes, this has resulted in oversight leading to "overreach." For example, one review board asked a linguist studying a preliterate culture to "have the subjects read and sign a consent form." Another IRB forbade a White student studying ethnicity from interviewing African American Ph.D. students "because it might be traumatic for them" (Cohen, 2007, p. 1).

ex: not letting a white student interview a black doctor

But what if the questions you want to answer are answerable only by deception? Sociologist Erich Goode undertook several research projects that utilized deceptive research practices (Goode, 1996a, 1996b, 2002). Refusing to submit his research proposals to his university's CORIHS guidelines, he took personal ads in a local magazine to see the sorts of responses he would receive. (Though the ads were fictitious, the people responding to them were real, and honestly thought they were replying to real ads. They thus revealed personal information about themselves.)

He took out four ads to determine the relative importance of physical attractiveness and financial success in the dating game. One was from a beautiful waitress (high attractiveness, low financial success); one was from an average-looking female lawyer (low attractiveness, high success). One was from a handsome male taxicab driver (high attractiveness, low success), and the final one was from an average-looking male lawyer (low attractiveness, high success). While about ten times more men than women replied to the ads at all, the two ads that received the most replies from their intended audience were for the beautiful waitress and the average-looking male lawyer. Goode concluded that in the dating marketplace, women and men often rank potential mates differently, with men seeking beauty and women seeking financial security.

While these were interesting findings, many sociologists question Goode's research methods (Saguy, 2002). Goode defended his behavior by saying that the potential daters didn't know that they were responding to fake ads, and that therefore, no harm was done, because people often receive no reply when they respond to ads. But ask yourself: Did he have to deceive people to find this out? How else might he have obtained this information? Do you think he crossed a line?

In every research project, you must constantly balance the demands of the research (and your own curiosity) against the rights of the research subjects. This is a delicate balance, and different people may draw their lines in different places. But to cause possible harm to a research subject is not only unethical; it is also illegal.

Social Science Methods in the 21st Century: Emergent Methodologies

New technologies provide opportunities for new research methods. For example, a new methodology called "field experiments" combines some of the benefits of both field methods and experimental research. On the one hand, they are experiments, using matched pairs and random assignment, so that one can infer causality. On the other hand, they take place "in the field," that is, in real-life situations. You've probably seen field experiments reported on television, because they often reveal hidden biases in employment, housing markets, or consumer behavior.

Here are some examples of how field methods reveal biases and discrimination in employment, housing, and consumerism. Matched pairs of prospective "car buyers" go to an auto showroom, or prospective "tenants" walk into a real estate office, or "job seekers" answer a "help wanted" ad. In each case, the prospects consist of a White couple and a minority couple, or a man and a woman. They go to the same showroom, and look at the same cars, and get very different price quotes. Or the White couple is shown several houses that are listed with the real estate broker, but the Black couple is told they've been rented or sold. And while a male and female applicant answered the same job ad, the male job applicant is told about a managerial opening and the female applicant is given a typing test. Because the experiment was conducted in real time in real life, the discrimination is readily evident, because the only variable that was different was race or gender. (When shown on TV, the news reporter will often go back to the car showroom or real estate office with videotape made by the participants and confront the dealer or agent with the evidence of their discrimination.) Recently, field experiments have revealed what minorities had long suspected but could never prove: They are discriminated against by taxi drivers who do not stop for them (Ayres and Siegelman, 1995; Cross et al., 1990; Yinger, 1995).

Just as social scientists are finding new methods, they are always trying to refine older survey techniques to obtain the most accurate data. For example, surveys of sexual behavior always find that people are somewhat self-conscious about revealing their sexual behaviors to strangers talking to them on the phone—let alone someone sitting across from them in a face-to-face survey interview. Researchers have developed a new survey technology—telephone audio computer-assisted self-interviewing—that greatly reduces the requirement of revealing your sexual behavior to a stranger. And some of the results indicate that a significantly higher percentage of Americans report same-sex sexual behavior than previously estimated (Villarroel et al., 2006).

Perhaps the most significant new technology is the proliferation of Internet chat rooms and listservs that has created virtual online communities of people who are drawn to particular issues and interests. If you want to study, for example, collectors of Ming dynasty pottery or buffalo head nickels, you would find several chat groups of such people online. Imagine how much time and energy you would save trying to track them down! They're all in one place, and they all are guaranteed to be exactly what you are looking for. Or are they?

Here's a good example. For the past few years, I have been doing research on White supremacist and Aryan youth in the United States and several European countries. There are many Internet chat rooms and portals through which one can enter the virtual world of the extreme right wing. Online, I can enter a place where eight White supremacists, neo-Nazis, and White power young people are discussing current events. I can listen in, perhaps even participate and ask them some questions. (Professional ethics require that whenever you are doing research you must disclose to them that you are doing research.) I could get some amazing "data" that way. But how can I be sure it's reliable?

After all, what if several of them aren't really White supremacists at all, but a couple of high school kids goofing around, a couple of graduate students in anthropology or sociology doing their "field work," or even a student in an introductory sociology course doing research for a term paper for my class? Have you ever gone online and pretended to be someone you weren't? How many people do you know who have done that?

Obviously, one cannot rely solely on the information gathered in such chat rooms. (In my case, I decided I had to interview them in person.) But any new method can be embraced only with caution and only when accompanied by research using more traditional methodologies.

In fact, it is often the combination of different methods—secondary analysis of already existing large-scale survey data coupled with in-depth interviews of a subsample—that are today providing the most exciting research findings in the social sciences. You needn't choose one method over another; all methods allow you to approach social life in different ways. Combined in creative combinations, research methods can shed enough light on a topic that many of its characteristics and dynamics can become clear.

Chapter Review

1. *Why do sociological methods matter?* Sociological methods are the scientific strategies used to collect data on social happenings. The methodology one chooses has an effect on the questions one asks and the answers one gets from research. Sociologists follow the rules of the scientific method; this means their arguments must be backed up by data that are systematically collected and analyzed. Research is also divided between quantitative research, which is statistically based, and qualitative research, which is used to understand the texture of social life and is text based.

2. *How do sociologists do research?* Sociological research follows eight basic steps. First, choose an issue. Then

define your topic in a meaningful and manageable way. Next, review the literature to see what has been done on the subject and what gaps exist in the research, and if you are engaging in deductive research, develop a hypothesis. Design your project based on the most suitable methodology. Collect data; then analyze the data using a method appropriate to your data collection strategy. Finally, report your findings.

3. *What types of research do sociologists do?* Sociologists use one of two basic types of research methods, one that involves observation of behavior, and one that involves analysis of accumulated data. Participant observation involves observing behavior in real-life situations, where the researcher relies on himself to interpret what is happening while trying to see phenomena from the point of view of those being observed. Sometimes a researcher will live for a period with the group she is studying; this is called ethnography. Interviews involve asking a small group of individuals who are purposively sampled with open-ended questions. Surveys are characterized by asking a large number of people closed-ended questions; the results are used to analyze patterns and to generalize to the larger population. Content analysis involves looking at objects such as text, photos, books, and the like.

4. *How does social science handle the problem of "truth"?* Sociologists try to approach truth by addressing predictability and causality. Predictability is important to social scientists because if we can understand how variables affect behavior, attitudes, and beliefs, then we can predict how one will act, think, or feel. Predictability is never completely accurate, so sociologists speak in terms of probability. Causality refers to one event being the direct result of another event or variable. In order to have causality, you must have certain conditions. First,

variable *B* has to come after variable *A* in time. Next, there must be a high correlation between variable *A* and variable *B*. Also, one must account for any possible extraneous variables that might be having an effect on variable *B*. Finally, one must look to see if there is an observer effect contaminating the data.

5. *What are some issues sociologists encounter in conducting research?* If statistical data can be manipulated to support any point of view, then how do we know what reports to trust and what not to trust? Sociologists publish their research results in peer-reviewed journals. In addition to peer review, sociologists strive to be objective and to avoid bias. This means making sure your own prejudices and assumptions do not contaminate your research. In addition to the possibility of your own bias contaminating the research, the research design itself may be biased, which means it may corrupt your results and make them invalid. To counter this, sociologists avoid overstating their results, avoid attributing causality to a correlation, and maintain professional ethics.

6. *What methodologies are emerging in sociology?* Technology is constantly advancing, and research methods keep pace. Telephone sampling has moved from using a random sampling of names listed in the phone book to random-digit dialing by computer. Field experiments use matched pairs and random assignment to infer causality. This type of study is often used to uncover hidden biases. In addition to developing new methodologies, social scientists are using new technology to refine and improve old methodologies. The Internet probably provides the best possibilities for new data collection and research techniques, as it provides unprecedented access to data and to individuals.

Key Terms

Causality (p. 127)	Experiment (p. 112)	Predictability (p. 127)
Cluster sample (p. 119)	Experimental group (p. 112)	Purposive sample (p. 117)
Content analysis (p. 124)	Extraneous variables (p. 112)	Qualitative methods (p. 107)
Confounding variables (p. 112)	Hypothesis (p. 110)	Quantitative methods (p. 107)
Control group (p. 112)	Generalizability (p. 124)	Random sample (p. 119)
Correlation (p. 131)	Independent variable (p. 110)	Sample (p. 119)
Data (p. 106)	Inductive reasoning (p. 107)	Secondary analysis (p. 122)
Deductive reasoning (p. 106)	Interviews (p. 112)	Stratified sample (p. 119)
Dependent variable (p. 110)	Likert scale (p. 119)	Subjectivity (p. 104)
Detached observation (p. 114)	Literature review (p. 112)	Surveys (p. 118)
Ethnography (p. 115)	Participant observation (p. 114)	Verstehen (p. 107)

4.1 Happiness

Taken all together, how would you say things are these days? Would you say that you are very happy, pretty happy, or not too happy? In 1971, 17 percent of respondents said they were not too happy; in 2004 it was much lower at 12 percent. Differences between Whites and Blacks were significant in 1972, with 32 percent of White respondents and 19 percent of Black respondents saying they were very happy. Black respondents were almost twice as likely to say they were not too happy than were Whites. By 2004, those differences had evened out; 34.8 percent of White respondents and 34.0 percent of Black respondents said they were very happy. In 2004, 10.5 percent of White respondents and 16.4 percent of Black respondents reported being not too happy.

CRITICAL THINKING | DISCUSSION QUESTIONS

1. What do you think the researchers were actually measuring with their survey question? If you were going to measure happiness in a survey, how would you operationalize the term, "happiness?"
2. What social and historical factors contributed to the increase in Black respondents' reported level of happiness between 1972 and 2004?

4.2 2000 Presidential Election

This is based on actual survey data from the General Social Survey, 2004

If you voted in the 2000 presidential elections, did you vote for Gore, Bush, Nader, or someone else? While the numbers do not match up exactly with official vote counts, they are within an appropriate margin of error. The votes were split nearly half-and-half between Gore and Bush. What is interesting here is the differences in voting when we look at gender and race. Women were more likely to vote for Gore, and men were more likely to vote for Bush. The difference was only about 10 percent in each case. Black voters were dramatically more likely to have voted for Gore than for Bush, and White voters were more likely to have voted for Bush.

CRITICAL THINKING | DISCUSSION QUESTIONS

1. Why is there such a dramatic difference with regard to race?
2. Do you think if you broke down the results by gender and by race that you would find even more dramatic differences? What might explain the differences?

▶ Go to this website to look further at the data. You can run your own statistics and crosstabs here: **http://sda.berkeley.edu/cgi-bin/hsda?harcsda+gss04**

REFERENCES: Davis, James A., Tom W. Smith, and Peter V. Marsden. *General Social Surveys 1972–2004:* [Cumulative file] [Computer file]. 2nd ICPSR version. Chicago, IL: National Opinion Research Center [producer], 2005; Storrs, CT: Roper Center for Public Opinion Research, University of Connecticut; Ann Arbor, MI: Inter-University Consortium for Political and Social Research; Berkeley, CA: Computer-Assisted Survey Methods Program, University of California [distributors], 2005.

chapter 5

IN MY HIGH SCHOOL YEARBOOK, probably the single most common inscription from friends and classmates was a variation of, "Stay the same great guy you are now. Don't ever change." Yet countless conversations from college on have charted exactly such a trajectory of change. "Well, when I was younger I felt this way. But *now* I see it differently!" And how many relationships pivot on whether or not someone will "change"—either to stop doing something hurtful or bad or to start doing something better? How many self-help books are written to help us change? Or maybe the fact that there are so many self-help books to help us change actually indicates that we really want to change but actually can't!

On the one hand, we are constantly growing and changing. On the other hand, we believe we have a core self, something constant and unchanging, a place deep down that is who we "really are."

Sociologists are interested in "both" of you—the part that feels eternal and constant and the part that is constantly changing. In fact, sociologists may believe that you're not schizophrenic but that these two parts are actually the same person.

Socialization

Most of the time, we think of our "self," our identity, as a thing that we possess, like a car. I might decide to hide my "true self," "who I really am," in some situations and reveal it in others. But is there really a single, permanent true self, buried deep inside our minds or our souls? Is there really a "who I really am"?

The sociological perspective sees identity not as a possession but as a process, not a thing that you have, but a collection of ideas, desires, beliefs, and behaviors that is constantly changing

The sociological perspective sees identity not as a possession but as a process, not a thing that you have, but a collection of ideas, desires, beliefs, and behaviors that is constantly changing as we grow, experience new situations, and interact with other people. We are different today than we were ten years ago, or even last month, and we will be different tomorrow. We are different at home and at school, when talking to our boss and when talking to our grandmother: not just a different front on a "true self," but a different self, a different person. Our identity is a process, in constant motion.

The sociological perspective may make us feel more creative because we are constantly revising our identity to meet new challenges, but it may also make us feel more insecure and unstable because it argues that there is nothing permanent or inevitable about the self. Change means creative potential, but it also means instability and the potential for chaos.

Socialization and Biology

Our identity is based on the interplay of nature and nurture. *Nature* means our physical makeup: our anatomy and physiology, our genes and chromosomes. *Nurture* means how we grow up: what we learn from our physical environment and our encounters with other people. Nature and nurture both play a role in who we are, but scientists and philosophers have debated for centuries over how much each contributes and how they interrelate.

Before the Enlightenment of the seventeenth and eighteenth centuries, nature was supreme: Our identity was created by God along with the natural world and could not be changed by mere circumstances. Nurture played virtually no part at all: As many fairy tales assure us, a princess raised in poverty was still a princess. Theologian John Calvin taught that we were predestined to be good or evil, and there was nothing we could do about it. But in the seventeenth century, British philosophers like John Locke rejected the idea that nature is solely responsible for our identity, that biology or God places strict limits on what we can become. They went in the other direction, arguing that we are born as *tabula rasa*—blank slates—and our environment in early childhood determines what we become.

The French philosopher Jean-Jacques Rousseau proposed a compromise. He argued that human beings do inherit identities: All children, and adults in their natural state, are "noble savages," naturally warm, sociable, and peace loving. However, their environment can also change them. Cold industrial civilization teaches children to become competitive, belligerent, and warlike. Thomas Jefferson based his ideas for the American experiment on Locke and Rousseau: "All men are created equal," that is, they derive some basic qualities from nature. However, some are more civilized than others.

In the nineteenth century, the nature side of the debate got a boost when Charles Darwin observed that animal species evolve, or change over time. He was not aware of genetic evolution, so he theorized that they develop new traits to adapt to changing food supplies, climates, or the presence of predators. Because human beings, too, are the result of millions of years of adaptation to the physical changes in their world, identity is a product of biological inheritance, unchangeable (at least during any one individual's lifetime).

But growing up in different environments changes our ideas about who we are and where we belong without having to wait millions of years. For example, a person who grows up on an Artic tundra, with rough weather and scarce food, will think and act differently from a person who grows up in a tropical paradise, where the weather is mild and food is abundant. The former might consider the world harsh, a struggle for survival, and human nature communal and cooperative. The latter might think life is easy, and it is human nature to compete with everyone else to see who can gather the most coconuts. Or, it could go the opposite direction: The tundra dweller might think life is so harsh that you need to compete with everyone else to even have a chance at survival, and the tropical paradise resident might think life is so easy that one can lie back on a hammock, with a pina colada in hand, and wait for the coconuts to drop.

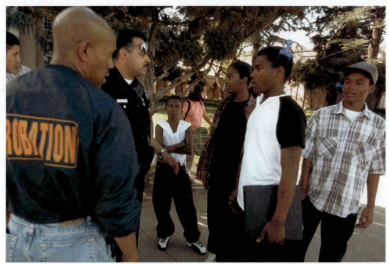

▲ Socialization varies significantly by race, class, or gender. When White middle-class people see a police officer, they are likely to feel safer; when Black people see a police officer, they often feel more vulnerable—as these California high school boys express (even when confronted by a Hispanic police officer and a Black probation officer).

The type of environment doesn't determine what sort of "human nature" you will think you have, but the environment definitely plays a part in calculating it. Even identical twins, separated at birth and raised in these two different areas, would think and act differently (Farber, 1982; Loehlin and Nichols, 1976; Wright, 1997).

The choice is not *either* nature *or* nurture, but both; our biological inheritance, physical surroundings, history, civilization, culture, and personal life experiences all interact to create our identity. Sociologists tend to stress nurture, not because we think nature unimportant but because the ongoing interaction with people and objects in the real world throughout our life course has a profound impact on the creation of individual identity. Biology and the physical world give us the raw materials from which to create an identity, but it is only through human interactions that identity coheres and makes sense to us.

Socialization is the process by which we become aware of ourselves as part of a group, learn how to communicate with others in the group, and learn the behavior expected of us: spoken and unspoken rules of social interaction, how to think, how to feel. Socialization imbues us with a set of norms, values, beliefs, desires, interests, and tastes to be used in specific social situations.

Socialization can take place through formal instruction, but usually we are socialized informally by observing other people's behaviors and reactions. If you are rewarded for a behavior (or see someone else rewarded for it), you will tend to imitate it. If you are punished for a behavior (or see someone else being punished for it), you will tend to avoid it.

Socialization is at its busiest during childhood, but it also happens throughout our lives. Every time we join a new group, make new friends, change residences or jobs, we are being socialized, learning new expectations of the group and modifying our behavior, thoughts, and beliefs accordingly. And others are being socialized by watching us.

Socialization in Action

Most animals are born with all of the information they need to survive already imprinted in their brains. But some, especially the mammals, are born helpless and must spend some time "growing up," learning how to find food and shelter, elude predators, and get along with others. The period of learning and growth usually lasts

▲ Socialization extends long after early childhood. In college, students learn group norms and adopt new identities—in this case, as Florida Gators.

for just a few months, or in the case of the higher primates, a few years. But human beings need an extraordinary amount of time, over a third of our lives.

Compare a horse and a human. If you have ever watched a pony being born, in real life or on film, you will recall that it will try to stand up on its wobbly legs shortly after birth. It can walk and run on its own by the next day. After a few weeks, the pony can forage for its own food without depending on its mother's milk. It still has some growing to do, but it is basically as capable as an adult horse.

Human babies do not begin to crawl until about eight months after birth, and they do not take their first hesitant steps for about a year. They can walk and run on their own by the time they are 2 or 3 years old, but they are still virtually helpless, dependent on their parents for food, shelter, and protection from predators (or other dangers) for at least another ten years. If suddenly abandoned in a big city without any adult supervision, they would be unable to survive. Even after puberty, when they have reached physical adulthood, they are often unprepared to buy their own groceries or live by themselves until they have graduated from high school, college, or even graduate school! By that time, about a quarter of their life is over.

Why do human beings require so many years of dependency? What are they learning during all those years? Of course they are developing physically, from childhood to full-grown adulthood, but they are also learning the skills necessary to survive in their community. Some of the instruction is formal, but most of it is informal, through daily interactions with the people and objects around them and learning an ever-changing array of roles and expectations. Socialization works with the basic foundation of our biology to unleash (or stifle) our individual identity.

Feral Children

In Edgar Rice Burroughs's novel *Tarzan of the Apes* (1912), the infant Lord Greystoke is orphaned on the coast of Africa and raised by apes. A childhood without human contact does not affect him at all; the adult Tarzan is fluent in English, French, and many African languages and fully comfortable in human society. But real "feral children," who spend their toddler years in the wilderness, are not so lucky.

Other than Romulus and Remus, who were raised by wolves, according to the folktale, and grew up to found the city of Rome, the most famous feral child was the "Wild Boy of Aveyron," probably 12 years old when he was discovered in the woods of southern France in 1800. No one knew where he came from or how long he had been alone. He was unable to speak or communicate, except by growling like an animal. He refused to wear clothes. A long, systematic attempt at "civilizing" him was only partially successful. He was toilet trained, and he learned to wear clothes. He exhibited some reasoning ability. But he was not interested in ordinary childhood pastimes like toys and games, and he never learned to speak more than a few words (Lane, 1979; Shattuck, 1980).

Other so-called feral children have been discovered from time to time, but some scientists dispute their authenticity. Infants and toddlers would surely die in the wilderness, they argue. Many of the cases misidentified as feral children were probably children with mental deficiencies abandoned much later at the age of 10 or 11 (Newton, 2003).

Did *you* know?

In December 1971, kangaroo hunters on the Nullabor Plain in Australia saw a half-naked woman living in the wild with kangaroos. Rupert Murdoch's newspaper *The News* immediately dispatched a photographer, and for weeks, virtually every English-language newspaper in the world ran stories about this feral creature. It turned out she was a 17-year-old model performing in a hoax thought up by hotel managers to draw tourists to the area.

Isolated Children

Though feral children may be largely a myth, some children have been isolated from almost all human contact by abusive caregivers. They can also be studied to determine the impact of little or no early childhood socialization.

One of the best-documented cases of an isolated child was "Isabelle," who was born to an unmarried, deaf-mute teenager. The girl's parents were so afraid of scandal that they kept both mother and daughter locked away in a darkened room, where they had no contact with the outside world. In 1938, when she was 6 years old, Isabelle escaped from her confinement. She was unable to speak except to make croaking sounds, she was extremely fearful of strangers, and she reacted to stimuli with the instinct of a wild animal. Gradually she became used to being around people, but she expressed no curiosity about them; it was as if she did not see herself as one of them. But doctors and social scientists began a long period of systematic training. Within a year she was able to speak in complete sentences, and soon she was able to attend school with other children. By the age of 14, she was in the sixth grade, happy and well-adjusted. She managed to overcome her lack of early childhood socialization, but only through exceptional effort.

Studies of other isolated children reveal that some can recover, with effort and specialized care, but others suffer permanent damage. It is unclear exactly why, but no doubt some contributing factors are the duration of the isolation, the child's age

How do we know
what we know ?

Maternal "Instinct"

When a mother sees her newborn baby for the first time, we expect her to feel a special bond of love and devotion: The maternal "instinct" has kicked in. If she had planned to give the baby up for adoption, she might suddenly change her mind. Even after the child grows up and moves away, she may feel a pang whenever the child is lonely or upset. Suddenly her career, her other relationships, and her other interests dim into insignificance against a life fully and completely devoted to caring for the child. The Romantic poet William Wordsworth said that "maternal sympathy" is a "joyless tie of naked instinct, wound about the heart." But how instinctive is it?

In *Mother Nature: A History of Mothers, Infants, and Natural Selection* (1999), Sarah Hrdy points out that little actual research has been done on mothers and children. Scientists assume that they have an instinct bond based on millions of years of evolution and leave it at that. But even in the animal kingdom, many mothers neglect or abandon their offspring. Rhesus monkeys who have been raised in isolation, without seeing other monkeys mothering their offspring, refuse to nurse or interact with their own. Among humans, women raised by abusive parents tend to be abusive to their own children, and women raised by indifferent parents tend to be indifferent.

Social expectations also play a role in how mothers respond to their children. In some human cultures, mothers are supposed to be cool and unfriendly to their children. In others, they are not supposed to know them at all. Children are raised by uncles and aunts, or by strangers, and the biological mother ignores them. In *Death Without Weeping: The Violence of Everyday Life in Brazil* (1992) Nancy Scheper-Hughes examines a culture of such grinding poverty that children often die at an early age, and she wonders why their mothers seem indifferent. She concludes that maternal devotion is a luxury that only the affluent can afford. Every now and then the newspapers in India report of parents who deliberately disfigure their children to make them more hideous looking and thus more pitifully "attractive" beggars.

Mothers are certainly capable of profound love and devotion to their children, but so are fathers, grandparents, uncles, aunts, brothers, sisters, and adults who have no biological connection at all. And not every mother is capable of such devotion. Biological instinct may play a part in the bond between mother and child, but early training at home and social expectations later in life make all the difference.

when the isolation began, the presence of some human contacts (like Isabelle's mother), other abuse accompanying the isolation, and the child's intelligence (Birdsong, 1999; Candland, 1993; Newton, 2003). But lack of socialization has serious consequences; it is socialization that makes human beings human.

Primates

Obviously children can't be deliberately raised in isolation for the sake of scientific research, but we can study primates, who require the longest period of socialization other than humans. Psychologists Harry Harlow and Margaret Harlow studied rhesus monkeys raised apart from others of their species and found severe physical and emotional problems. The monkeys' growth was stunted, even when they received adequate nutrition. They were fearful of others in their group and refused to mate or associate with them socially. Those returned after three months managed to reintegrate with the group, but after six months the damage was irreparable. The females who gave birth (through artificial insemination) neglected their offspring, suggesting that "maternal instincts" must be learned through the experience of being nurtured as a child. (Harlow, Dodsworth, and Harlow, 1965; Griffin and Harlow, 1966; Harlow, Harlow, Dodsworth, and Arling, 1966; Harlow and Suomi, 1971).

Stages in Socialization

Socialization doesn't happen all at once but proceeds in stages. Similarly, the construction of our identities also develops through definable stages. Sociologists have identified these stages of socialization.

Mead and Taking the Role of Others

Imitation is not only "the sincerest form of flattery," it is also a crucial element of socialization, according to George Herbert Mead. Children imitate the behaviors, and adopt the prejudices, of their parents. ▼

George Herbert Mead, whose notions of the difference between the "I" and the "me" we discussed in Chapter 3, developed a stage theory of socialization, stages through which children pass as they become better integrated into society. As young children, we picture ourselves as the focus of everything and are virtually incapable of considering the perspectives of others. As the self develops, we still have a tendency to place ourselves at the center of the universe, but we are increasingly able to understand the reactions of others.

Children develop this ability gradually. Before the age of 8, they may imitate the behavior of others, playing with toy cars to pretend they are driving or dolls to pretend that they are caring for babies, but they are not yet able to "take on the role of the others," to try to understand what it is really like to drive a car or care for a baby. As their play becomes more complex, they can take on the roles of significant others, people they know well, such as parents and siblings. Later, they can "internalize" the expectations of more and more people, until eventually they can take on the role of their group as a whole—the **generalized other** of their neighborhood, their school, their religion, their country, or all of humanity.

Mead argued that there are three stages in the development of the perspective of the other:

1. *Imitation.* Children under the age of 3 can imitate others, but they cannot usually put themselves into the role of others.

2. *Play.* Children aged 3 to 6 pretend to be specific people or kinds of people that they think are important (their parents, doctors, firefighters, Batman). They say and pretend to do things that these people might say and do. But they are learning more than a repertoire of behaviors. Mead saw children's play as crucial to the development of their ability to take the perspective of others. They must anticipate how the people they are pretending to be would think, feel, and behave in various situations, often playing multiple roles: As "parents," for instance, they may play at disciplining their "children," first playing a parent who believes that a misdeed was deliberate, and then a child who insists that it was an accident.

3. *Games.* In early school years, children learn to play games and team sports. Now they must interpret and anticipate how other players will act, who will do what when the ball is hit, kicked, passed, or thrown. Complex games like chess and checkers require strategy, the ability to anticipate the thoughts of others. And, perhaps most important, the children are learning to place value on actions, to locate behavior within a sense of generalized morality (Mead, 1934).

Piaget and the Cognitive Theory of Development

Swiss psychologist Jean Piaget (1896–1980) studied children of different ages to see how they solve problems, how they make sense of the world. (Piaget, 1928, 1932, 1953, 1955). He argued that their reasoning ability develops in four stages, each building on the last (Table 5.1).

In the *sensorimotor stage* (birth to age 2), children experience the world only through their senses. They do not recognize themselves as beings distinct from their environment; they will not realize that the hand they see is part of their body. They are not usually able to draw abstract conclusions from their observations; they are initially not afraid of heights, for instance, because they do not correlate the objects

TABLE 5.1

Piaget's Cognitive Stages of Development		
STAGE	**AGE RANGE**	**CHARACTERISTICS**
Sensorimotor stage	Birth–2 years	Still in the sensory phase; can understand only what they see, hear, or touch
Preoperational stage	2–7 years	Capable of understanding and articulating speech and symbols, but can't understand common concepts like weight
Concrete operational stage	7–12 years	Causal relationships are understood, and they understand common concepts, but they can't reach conclusions through general principles
Formal operational stage	12 years and up	Capable of abstract thought and reasoning

they have seen falling with the possibility that they might fall. Eventually they learn to differentiate people from objects and to classify some as important (perhaps the faces of their parents) and to minimize or ignore others (the faces of strangers). And they develop depth perception.

In the *preoperational stage* (about ages 2 through 7), children can draw a square to symbolize a house or a stick with a blob at the end to symbolize a tree. Perhaps they even learn the more complex symbols necessary for reading and writing. But they are not yet able to understand common concepts like size, speed, or weight. In one of his most famous experiments, Piaget poured water from a short, fat glass into a tall, skinny glass. Children at the ages of 5 and 6 were unable to determine that the glasses contained the same amount of water; when they saw higher, they thought "more." In this stage they are egocentric, seeing the world only from their position in it.

In the *concrete operational stage* (about ages 7 through 12), children's reasoning is more developed; they can understand size, speed, and weight; they can use numbers. They can perceive causal connections. But their reasoning is still concrete; they can tell you if a specific statement is true or false, such as, "This is a picture of a dog," when it is really a picture of a cat, but they can't explain why it is true or false. They can learn specific rules, but they are not able to reach conclusions based on general principles.

In the *formal operational stage* (after about age 12), children are capable of abstract and critical thinking. They can talk about general concepts like "truth." They can reach conclusions based on general principles, and they can solve abstract problems.

Piaget believed, along with other social scientists, that social interaction is the key to cognitive development. Children learn critical and abstract thinking by paying careful attention to other people behaving in certain ways in specific situations. Therefore, they need many opportunities to interact with others.

Kohlberg and Moral Development

According to Piaget, morality is an essential part of the development of cognitive reasoning. Children under 8 have a black-and-white view of morality: Something is either good or bad, right or wrong. They can't see "extenuating circumstances," acts that could be partially right, partially wrong, or right under some circumstances, wrong under others. As they mature, they begin to experience moral dilemmas of their own, and they develop more complex reasoning.

Lawrence Kohlberg built upon the ideas of Piaget to argue that we develop moral reasoning in three stages:

1. *Preconventional (birth to age 9).* In this stage, morality means avoiding punishment and gaining rewards. A child who gets away with a misdeed will not perceive it as bad—the wrongness lies in the punishment, not in the deed itself.

2. *Conventional (ages 9 to 20).* Conventional morality depends on children or teenagers' ability to move beyond their immediate desires to a larger social context. They still want to avoid punishment and gain rewards, but they view some acts as essentially good or bad. It is their "duty" to perform good acts, whether or not there are any immediate rewards, and when they perform bad acts, they feel "guilt," whether or not there is any immediate punishment.

In his studies of the development of moral reasoning, psychologist Lawrence Kohlberg argued that an abstract "ethic of justice," as in this symbol of American jurisprudence, was the highest form of ethical thought. His student, Carol Gilligan, disagreed, arguing that just as important, though not as recognized, was an "ethic of care," in which people's moral decision making is based on how it will actually affect people. ▼

3. *Postconventional (older than 20).* In this stage, we are able to see relative morality, viewing acts as good in some situations but not others, or acts that are not all good or all bad, but somewhere in between. Kohlberg's famous test of postconventional moral reasoning set up this scenario: Your wife is sick, and you cannot afford the necessary medication. Should you break into the pharmacy and steal it? Stealing is wrong, but does the situation merit it anyway? (Kohlberg, 1971).

In her book *In a Different Voice* (1982), psychologist Carol Gilligan wondered why women usually scored much lower than men on Kohlberg's morality scale. Were they really less moral? As a student of Kohlberg's, she realized that Kohlberg assumed a male subject. He interviewed only men, made up a story about a man breaking into the pharmacy, and assumed that moral reasoning was dictated by masculine-coded justice, asking "What are the rules?," instead of by feminine-coded emotion, asking "Who will be hurt?" She argued that there is a different guide to moral reasoning, one more often exhibited by women, called "an ethic of care," which is based on people sacrificing their own needs and goals for the good of people around them. While all of us exhibit characteristics of both justice and care as ethical systems, women tend to gravitate toward care and men toward ethics. Gilligan's argument is that by focusing only on justice, we will miss an equally important ethical system.

Most social scientists do not believe that women and men have completely different forms of moral reasoning. Both women and men develop ethics of care and ethics of justice. These systems are not gender specific. They are simply different ways of solving moral dilemmas.

Freud and the Development of Personality

Psychiatrist Sigmund Freud (1856–1939), the founder of psychoanalysis, believed that the self consisted of three elements. Of course, they are always interrelated:

1. *The id.* The inborn drive for self-gratification, the **id** is pure impulse, without worrying about social rules, consequences, morality, or other people's reactions; so if unbridled, it could get you into trouble. If we were pure id, we would go into a restaurant and grab anything that looks good, even if it was on someone else's plate, or proposition sexual favors from anyone we found attractive, regardless of the social situation.

2. *The superego.* The **superego** is internalized norms and values, the "rules" of our social group, learned from family, friends, and social institutions. It provokes feelings of shame or guilt when we break the "rules," pride and self-satisfaction when we follow them. Just as pure id would be disastrous, pure superego would turn us into robots, unable to think creatively, make our own decisions, or rebel against unjust rules.

3. *The ego.* The balancing force between the id and the superego, or impulses and social rules, the **ego** channels impulses into socially acceptable forms. Sometimes it can go wrong, creating neuroses or psychoses (Figure 5.1).

FIGURE 5.1 The Human Psyche According to Freud

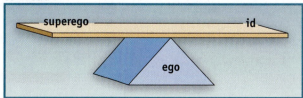

Since the id can never have everything it wants, the task of socialization is twofold. First the ego must be strong enough

Although Freud's theory stated that homosexuality was the result of the failure of the child to adequately identify with the same-sex parent and was therefore a problem of gender identity development, he did not believe in either the criminal persecution or psychiatric treatment of homosexuals. In fact, when Freud was contacted by a woman whose son was homosexual, he explained why he did not think her son needed to be "cured":

Homosexuality is . . . nothing to be ashamed of, no vice, no degradation; it cannot be classified as an illness; we consider it to be a variation of the sexual function . . . Many highly respectable individuals of ancient and modern times have been homosexuals, several of the greatest men among them . . . It is a great injustice to persecute homosexuality as a crime—and a cruelty too . . . (1960, p. 419)

It took another 40 years before the American Psychiatric Association declassified homosexuality from being labeled a mental illness.

Source: Sigmund Freud. *Letters of Sigmund Freud,* 1873–1939. London: Hogarth Press, 1960, p. 419.

---

to handle being rebuffed by reality and able to find acceptable substitutes for what the id originally wanted. (Psychoanalysis is supposed to strengthen the ego to handle this task.) And second, the superego must be strong enough to prevent the id from going after what it wants in the first place. Thus, the superego is the home of guilt, shame, and morality. In one of his most famous passages, Freud described this process:

The ego, driven by the id, confined by the superego, repulsed by reality, struggles to master its . . . task of bringing about harmony among the forces working in and upon it, and we can understand how it is that so often we cannot suppress a cry, "Life is not easy!"

Freud believed that each child passes through three stages of development to become a healthy adult man or woman. These stages are based on the strategies that the ego devises to obtain gratification for its bodily urges.

1. *The oral stage.* At birth, the infant derives gratification from breast-feeding, which Freud regards as a sensually pleasurable activity.

2. *The anal stage.* After being weaned, the baby derives gratification from urination and defecation. These bodily functions are a source of pleasure, until we are toilet trained (repressed).

These two stages are the same for both boys and girls. In the beginning of the third stage, though, they separate. Both boys and girls continue to see their mothers as the source of gratification and also as the object of identification. But their tasks diverge sharply.

3. *The Oedipal stage.* The boy desires his mother sexually and identifies with her. Fearing his father's wrath at this sexual competition, the boy renounces his identification with her, identifies with his father, and thus becomes "masculine." He is now capable of maturity as a man and, simultaneously, will be heterosexual.

The girl's tasks are different. She must sustain her identification with her mother and come to see that her source of gratification is not in having sex but in making a baby. By remaining identified with her mother, she becomes "feminine"; and by renouncing her "masculine" sexual drives, she will be capable of heterosexuality as well.

The key insight from Freud's stage theory is that we understand sexual orientation to be linked to gender. We assume that effeminate men and masculine women are gay or lesbian. Whether or not that is true (it's actually not), we owe that stereotypic assumption to Freud.

Problems with Stage Theories

Stage theories are extremely popular. Many best-sellers describe the "seasons of a man's life," "passages," or "the fountain of age." And we often use stage theory to describe a problem, preferring to believe that someone will "grow out of" a problematic behavior than to believe that such a behavior is part of who they "really are." It is interesting, and often amusing, to try to fit our own experiences into the various theorists' stages of human development, but the whole idea of stages has some problems in the real world:

■ The stages are rigidly defined, but many of the challenges are lifelong. Erikson (1959) puts the conflict between being part of a group and having a unique identity in adolescence, but every time we join a new club, get a new job, move to a new town, or make new friends, we face the same conflict, even in old age.

- It is not clear that failure to meet the challenges of one stage means permanent failure. Maybe we can fix it during the next stage?
- The theorists usually maintain that the stages are universal, but do people in all cultures and all time periods really develop in the same way? In cultures where there are no schools, is there a preadolescence? In many parts of the world, the life expectancy is about 40; are middle adulthood and old age the same there as in the United States, where we can expect to live to about 80? Even within the same culture, people do not develop in the same way. Piaget argued that the formal operational stage of abstract reasoning begins during adolescence, but Kohlberg and Gilligan (1971) found that 30 percent of the U.S. population never develop it at all.

Two other problems with stage theories result from the fact that we assume that one passes through a stage fully and never returns to that stage. But we are also constantly cross-cutting stages, moving back and forth. Socialization turns out to be a lifelong and fluid process.

There are two other socialization processes that are important to consider.

Anticipatory Socialization. Even while you occupy one status, you may begin to anticipate moving to the next stage and begin a future-oriented project of acting *as if* you were already there. **Anticipatory socialization** is when you begin to enact the behaviors and traits of the status that you expect to occupy. For example, young adolescents might decide to begin drinking coffee, in anticipation of the onset of adulthood, when they will drink coffee the same as grownups do. Often people begin to imitate those who occupy the statuses *to which we believe we will eventually belong.* This can result in some confusion and even some anger from your friends, especially if you start acting like a "snob" or "putting on airs" because you are anticipating becoming rich when you win the lottery.

Resocialization. Moving from one stage to another doesn't happen easily, but we often have to relearn elementary components of the role when we enter a new status. **Resocialization** involves learning new sets of values, behaviors, and attitudes that are different from those you previously held. Resocialization is also something that happens all through your life, and failure to adequately resocialize into a new status can have dire consequences. For example, let's say you are a happy-go-lucky sort of person, loud and rambunctious, and you are arrested for speeding and sent to jail. Failure to resocialize to a docile, obedient, and silent prisoner can result in serious injury. New parents are also suddenly resocialized.

One of the more shocking moments in resocialization happens to college students during their first year in school. Expectations in college are often quite different from high school, and one must adjust to these new institutional norms. Many arrive at a college having already been at the top of their class, excelling in school, achieving good grades, and standing out in the crowd. Suddenly, however, they are in a new group in which virtually everyone else is at that same level. They must resocialize into being "one of the pack."

We also socialize ourselves in anticipation of the positions we hope to occupy. This woman, fresh out of college, is on her way to a job interview on Wall Street—and she already looks the part. ▼

When resocialization is successful, one moves easily into a new status. When it is unsuccessful, or only partially realized, you will continue to stick out uneasily. For example, if you intend to make a lot of money after you graduate from college, don't begin to act like you are one of the Fortune 500 wealthiest individuals just yet. You're likely to lose most of your friends. Even after you make your fortune, you might consider a more subtle resocialization path. The nouveau riche are usually scorned by those who inherited their money.

Agents of Socialization

Agents of socialization are people, groups, or social institutions that socialize new members, either formally (as in lessons about traffic safety in school) or informally (as in cartoon characters on television behaving according to social expectations). **Primary socialization,** which occurs during childhood, gives us basic behavioral patterns, but allows for adaptation and change later on. **Secondary socialization** occurs throughout life, every time we start a new class or a new job, move to a new neighborhood, make new friends, or change social roles, allowing us to abandon old, outdated, or unnecessary behavior patterns, giving us new behavioral patterns necessary for the new situation.

Socialization is not necessarily a positive ideal, helping the child adjust to life in the best of all possible worlds. Some of the norms we are socialized into are oppressive, shortsighted, and wrong. We can be socialized into believing stereotypes, into hating out-groups, into violence and abuse. "You've got to be taught to hate and fear" is a well-known line from a song in the Broadway musical *South Pacific* (1958). Children of different cultures might be curious about differences they see, even somewhat uneasy, but they aren't biologically programmed to commit genocide as adults. That is learned.

For a long time psychologists and sociologists argued that the major agent of primary socialization was the family, with school and religion becoming increasingly important as childhood proceeded. These three institutions—family, school, religion—and the three primary actors within those institutions—parents, teachers, clergy—were celebrated as the central institutions and agents of socialization.

Of course, they are central; no institutions are more important. But from the point of view of the child, these three institutional agents—parents, teachers, clergy—are experienced as "grownups, grownups, and grownups." Asking children today about their socialization reveals that two other institutions—mass media and peer groups—are also vital in the socialization process. These two institutions become increasingly important later in childhood and especially in adolescence. Later, as adults, government, the workplace, and other social institutions become important. Agents of socialization tend to work together, promoting the same norms and values, and they socialize each other as well as the developing individual. It is often impossible to tell where the influence of one ends and the influence of another begins, and even a list seems arbitrary. (Each of these institutions is so important that we return to each one in a separate chapter.)

Socialization is not always positive. One can be socialized to hate and fear; indeed, you can be socialized to be a ruthless killer as were many child soldiers in the ethnic conflict in Sierra Leone. ▼

Family

There are many different child rearing systems in cultures around the world. In the United States, we are most familiar with nuclear families (father, mother, children) and extended families (parents, children, uncles, aunts, grandparents), but in some cultures everyone in the tribe lives together in a longhouse; or men, women, and children occupy separate dormitories. Sometimes the biological parents have little responsibility for raising their children or are even forbidden from seeing them. But there is always a core of people, parents, brothers, sisters, and others, who interact with the children constantly as they are growing, giving them their first sense of self and setting down their first motivations, social norms, values, and beliefs. From our family we receive our first and most enduring ideas about who we are and where we are going in life.

Our family also gives us our first statuses, our definitions of ourselves as belonging to a certain class, nationality, race, ethnicity, religion, and gender. In traditional societies, these remain as permanent parts of our self-concept. We live in the same village as our parents, work at their occupation, and never aspire to an economic success greater than they enjoyed. In modern societies, we are more likely to be mobile, choosing occupations and residences different from those of our parents, having different political and religious affiliations, changing our religions. But even so, the social statuses from our childhood often affect the rest of our lives. People raised in the Methodist Church who later join the Roman Catholic Church usually think of themselves not as "Catholic" but as "ex-Methodist, now Catholic."

Studies show that different sorts of families socialize their children in different ways. Melvin Kohn (1959, 1963, 1966, 1983, 1986, 1989, 1993) found that working-class families are primarily interested in teaching the importance of outward conformity—of neatness, cleanliness, following the rules, and staying out of trouble—while middle-class families focus on developing children's curiosity, creativity, and

How do we know what we know?

"Be Like Me/Don't Be Like Me"

For decades, sociologists believed that parents socialized their children to grow up like them; that is, parents saw themselves as positive role models for their children. And that was true for middle-class parents. Middle-class fathers see themselves as role models for their children, saying, in effect, "You can grow up to be like me if you study and work hard."

But this isn't true for the working class. In a landmark study, *The Hidden Injuries of Class* (1967), sociologists Richard Sennett and Jonathan Cobb interviewed hundreds of working-class women and men, many of whom were immigrants or children of immigrants. They found that these people felt inadequate, sometimes like frauds or imposters, ambivalent about their success. They had worked hard but hadn't succeeded, and because they were fervent believers in the American Dream—where even a poor boy can grow up to be the president—they blamed themselves for their failure. Sennett and Cobb attributed this to "status incongruity"—living in two worlds at the same time.

And how did they manage to ward off despair when they were at fault for their own failures? They deferred success from their own lives to the lives of their children. They worked at difficult, dirty, and dangerous jobs not because they were failures, but because they were sacrificing to give their children a better life. They were noble and honorable.

But they saw themselves not as role models to be emulated but as cautionary tales to be avoided. "You could grow up to be like me if you don't study and work hard," they were saying. It turns out that whether you see yourself as a positive or a negative role model depends on what class you belong to (Sennett and Cobb, 1967).

▲ One of the chief socializing institutions is religion. Here, a Jewish family celebrates Passover, which requires the telling of the story of Exodus to each generation.

good judgment. Lower-class families are similar to working-class families in favoring conformity and obedience, and the affluent follow the middle class in favoring creativity and good judgment. Kohn (1977) found that these differences are determined by the pattern of the parents' jobs. Blue-collar workers are closely supervised in their jobs, so they tend to socialize their children into the obedience model, but skilled tradesmen, who have more freedom, tend to socialize their children into the creativity model.

Socialization in the family is rarely the result of intentional training but rather happens through the kind of environment the adults create. Whether children see themselves as smart or stupid, loved or simply tolerated, whether they see the world as safe or dangerous, depends largely on what happens at home during the first few years of their lives.

Education

In modern societies, we spend almost a third of our lives in school. Seventy-five percent of the U.S. population graduates from high school after 12 or 13 years of education, and 25 percent completes four or five years of college. Graduate school or professional school can add another five to ten years. During this time, we are learning facts, concepts, and skills, but education also has a latent function, a "hidden curriculum" that instills social norms and values, such as the importance of competition. Education has an enormous impact on our sense of self, and it is nearly as important as family in instilling us with our first social statuses. For example, high school curricula are typically divided into "academic" and "practical" subjects. Most students are channeled into one or the other on the basis of their race or class, thus ensuring that White middle-class children prepare for college and middle-class careers, while non-White and working-class children prepare for working-class jobs.

Education socializes us not only into social class, but into race, gender, and sexual identity statuses. Jonathan Kozol (1967) documented the "destruction of the hearts and minds" of African American children in the Boston public schools in the 1960s, where teachers and administrators were overtly prejudiced, but even teachers and administrators who are not prejudiced privilege in-groups and marginalize or ignore out-groups, often in the interest of "not rocking the boat."

Religion

The United States is the most religious nation in the Western world: 40 percent of the population attends religious services every week, and nine out of ten have a weekly conversation with God. (Nearly 60 percent pray every day or several times a day—higher for Blacks and Latinos (Pew Forum, 2007). But we are socialized into religious belief in many places besides churches, mosques, and temples. Often we pray or hear religious stories at home. Nearly two-thirds of Americans with Internet access have used it for religious purposes (Hoover, Clark, and Rachie, 2004). In school, we recite the Pledge of Allegiance, which since the mid-twentieth century has included the phrase "one nation under God," and increasingly school boards are requiring that biblical creation be taught along with (or instead of) evolution in science class as an explanation for the origin of the world. Every political candidate is expected to profess publicly his or her religious faith; an atheist would have a very difficult time getting elected to any office. (In fact, a Gallup poll found that more people say they'd vote for a homosexual for president than would vote for an atheist; [Adler, 2006].)

Religion is an important agent of socialization because it provides a divine motivation for instilling social norms in children and adults. Why do we dress, talk, and behave in a certain way? Why do we refuse to eat pork, when our neighbors seem to like it? Why are we not allowed to watch television or go to school dances? Why are men in charge of making money, and women in charge of child care? Why are most of the elite jobs occupied by White people? Religion may teach us that these social phenomena are not arbitrary, based on outdated tradition or on in-groups competing with out-groups. They are based on God's law. However, when we are socialized into believing that our social norms come directly from God, it is easy to believe that the social norms of other groups come directly from the devil. Sometimes we even receive formal instruction that members of out-groups are evil monsters.

In traditional societies, religious affiliation is an ascribed status. You are born into a religion, and you remain in it throughout your life, regardless of how enthusiastically you practice or how fervently you believe (or if you believe at all). Several of the religions practiced in modern societies continue to be ascribed. For instance, if you are born Roman Catholic and later decide that you don't believe in the Roman Catholic Church anymore, you are simply a "lapsed Catholic." However, in modern society religions operate in a "religious marketplace," with hundreds and even thousands of different groups competing for believers and the freedom to select the religious group that will best fit into our other social roles.

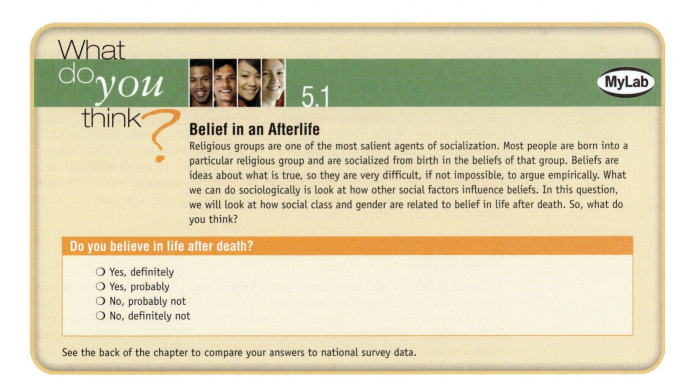

What do *you* think?

5.1

MyLab

Belief in an Afterlife

Religious groups are one of the most salient agents of socialization. Most people are born into a particular religious group and are socialized from birth in the beliefs of that group. Beliefs are ideas about what is true, so they are very difficult, if not impossible, to argue empirically. What we can do sociologically is look at how other social factors influence beliefs. In this question, we will look at how social class and gender are related to belief in life after death. So, what do you think?

Do you believe in life after death?

○ Yes, definitely
○ Yes, probably
○ No, probably not
○ No, definitely not

See the back of the chapter to compare your answers to national survey data.

Peers

At school, in the neighborhood, at our clubs, and eventually at work, we develop many groups of friends, wider groups of acquaintances, and a few enemies. In modern societies, our **peer groups** (the friends) are usually age specific—a third grader hardly deigns to associate with a second grade "baby" and would be ostracized by a group of fourth graders. As adults, we expand the boundaries of age a bit, but still, 50-year-olds rarely buddy around with 30-year-olds. Peer groups also tend to be homogeneous, limited to a single neighborhood, race, religion, social class, gender, or other social status. The smart kids may sit at one table in the cafeteria, the jocks at another, and the heavy metal fans at a third.

Peer groups have an enormous socializing influence, especially during middle and late childhood. Peer groups provide an enclave where we can learn the skills of social interaction and the importance of group loyalty, but the enclaves are not always safe and caring. Peers teach social interaction through coercion, humiliation, and bullying as well as through encouragement, and group loyalty often means being condescending, mean, or even violent to members of out-groups (Figure 5.2).

Sometimes peer groups resist the socialization efforts of family and the schools by requiring different, contradictory norms and values: rewarding smoking, drinking, and vandalism, for example, or punishing good grades and class participation. But more often they merely reinforce the socialization that children (and adults) receive elsewhere. Barrie Thorne (1993) looked at gender polarization (separating boys and girls) among elementary school students and found that peer groups and teachers worked together. The teachers socialized gender polarization by rewarding boys for being "masculine"—aggressive, tough, and loud—and girls for being "feminine"—shy, quiet, and demure. During masculine-coded math and science classes, they gave boys a lot of extra help and were short and impatient with girls, assuming that they wouldn't know anyway; but during feminine-coded English and art classes, girls got the extra help, and boys were ignored. The peer groups merely reinforced gender polarization. Boys' groups rewarded athletic ability, coolness, and toughness; and girls' groups rewarded physical appearance, including the ability to use makeup and select fashionable clothing.

We continue to have peer groups throughout adulthood. Often we engage in anticipatory socialization, learning the norms and values of a group that we haven't joined yet. For example, we may mimic the clothing style and slang of a popular peer group in the hope that we will be accepted.

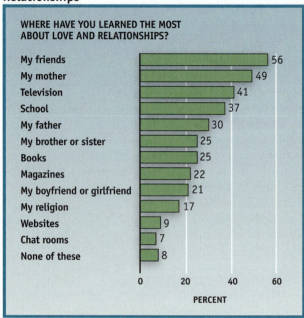

FIGURE 5.2 Peer Socialization and Love Relationships

WHERE HAVE YOU LEARNED THE MOST ABOUT LOVE AND RELATIONSHIPS?

	PERCENT
My friends	56
My mother	49
Television	41
School	37
My father	30
My brother or sister	25
Books	25
Magazines	22
My boyfriend or girlfriend	21
My religion	17
Websites	9
Chat rooms	7
None of these	8

Source: *Harris Interactive YouthQuerySM Monthly Omnibus,* December 2002 data, published in the *Trends & Tudes* Newsletter, Feb. 2003, "Love and Romance and America's Youth," Harris Interactive Inc. All rights reserved. Reprinted with permission.

Mass Media

We spend all day, every day, immersed in mass media—popular books and magazines, radio, television, movies, video games, and the Internet. While media use varies somewhat with race and ethnicity, gender, education and income, overall young people in the United States spend about six and a half hours every day with one form or another of mass media (Kaiser Family Foundation, 2004). It is an important agent of socialization from childhood right through adulthood.

Sociology and our World

Race, Gender, and Peer Approval

What we do in our leisure time depends in large part on what we think our peers think of that activity. If we think they approve, we're more likely to do it; if we think they disapprove, we're less likely to do it.

But our judgment depends a lot on race and gender. Researcher Steven Philipp surveyed 421 eleventh and twelfth graders in a school district in Florida. He asked them to evaluate which leisure activities they thought were approved by their peer groups. Philipp found significant racial differences for half the items. Blacks showed stronger peer approval for playing basketball, going to the mall, singing in a choir, and dancing; White adolescents showed stronger approval for playing soccer, horseback riding, waterskiing, camping, fishing, and golfing. Blacks and Whites had equally strong approval for watching television, and the groups had equally strong negative ratings for bowling, reading, using a computer, collecting stamps, playing a musical instrument, and going to a museum.

Gender differences were much higher between White girls and boys than between Black girls and boys. It may be that for White adolescents, gender is a more important agent of peer socialization, while for Black adolescents, race may be more important (Philipp, 1998).

Television is probably the dominant form of mass media across the world. Viewing is dependent on status: Generally, the higher the socioeconomic class, the less television viewing. Women watch more than men, African Americans more than White Americans. But children of all classes, races, and genders watch the most: The Kaiser Family Foundation says that of the five and a half hours that children aged 2 through 18 spend consuming mass media every day, nearly three hours are spent watching television (the rest of the time is devoted to listening to music, reading, playing video games, and using the computer).

Many scholars and parents are worried about the impact of heavy television watching, arguing that it makes children passive, less likely to use their imagination (Christakis, 2004; Healy, 1990), and more likely to have short attention spans. But other scholars disagree. Television has been around for over 50 years, so the worried parents watched themselves, when they were children, with no catastrophic loss of creativity or rise in mass murder; in earlier generations, similar fears were voiced about radio, movies, comic books, and dime novels.

Video games are increasingly becoming an important form of mass media. The vast majority of players are children and teenagers, making video games nearly the equal of television in popularity. (The genres aren't strictly separate; the same characters and situations may appear in television, movies, comic books, and video games simultaneously.) Adult observers have the same sorts of concerns as they have with television: lack of creativity and decreased attention span, plus rampant sexism. (Women are usually portrayed as passive victims who must be rescued, and those who are competent adventurers, such as Lara Croft, Tomb Raider, are leggy supermodels rather than competent adventurers.) But some studies show that video games develop logic, reasoning, and motor reflexes, skills useful in a technological future (Johnson, 2005).

For teenagers, music and magazines play as great a role as television in socialization. Popular songs, aimed mostly at a teenage audience, socialize expectations regarding gender and sexual expression, and magazines aimed mostly at girls are full of articles expressing gender polarization and compulsory heterosexuality: They are mostly about how to select fashions, use makeup, and date boys.

Did you know?

The average American home has more television sets than people—there are 2.73 sets in a typical American home and only 2.55 people—plus 1.8 VCRs, 3.1 radios, 2.6 tape players, 2.1 CD players, 1.4 video game players, and at least one computer. Fifty-eight percent of families with children have the TV on during dinner, and 42 percent of families with children are "constant television households"—that is, they have a TV on virtually all day, whether or not anyone is actually watching it.

FIGURE 5.3 Internet Distribution around the World

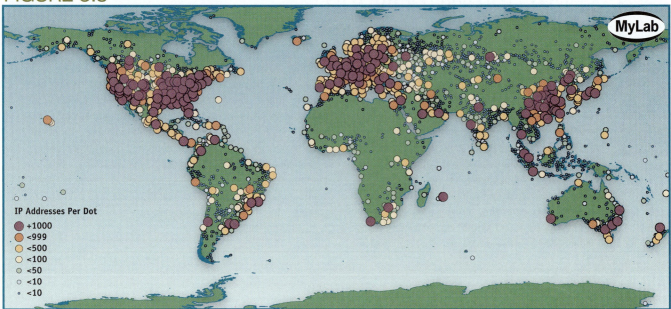

IP Addresses Per Dot
- +1000
- <999
- <500
- <100
- <50
- <10
- <10

Source: From Ipligence.com, 2007 (ipligence.com/worldmap/).

The media perfectly illustrate the dynamic tensions of globalization and multiculturalism. On the one hand, media are so complex and diverse that different groups can engage almost exclusively with "their" media: There are television networks, radio stations, video games, computer websites, magazines, and newspapers for just about every single "demographic" imaginable. So, it appears that multiculturalism in the media is really the fragmentation of media into a plentiful array of demographic niches.

But, on the other hand, people all over the world are increasingly meeting in computer chat rooms, on Facebook and other global media network sites, on global access computer gaming sites, in video conferences, and on global telephone connections (Figure 5.3). The media bring us together across every conceivable boundary and also *at the same time* fragment us into discrete subgroups.

The Workplace

We spend about one-third of our lives in the workplace, and we often define ourselves most essentially by our jobs: If you ask someone "What are you?" he or she will probably reply "I am an architect" or "I am a factory worker" rather than "I am somebody's brother." In traditional societies, your job was less a symptom of identity because there were only a few specialized jobs: a religious sage, a tribal chief, and perhaps a few skilled artisans. Everyone else in the community did everything necessary for survival, from gathering crops to spinning cloth to caring for the children.

In modern societies we receive specialized training, and we have jobs that usually require us to leave home and family and spend all day in a workplace (although staying home to take care of the household is often considered a job, too). In many ways, workplaces are similar to schools: Supervisors assign tasks like teachers, and there are peer groups (those we interact with all the time), acquaintances, and sometimes enemies. We are expected to behave in a "professional" and "businesslike" fashion, but depending on the social class of the job, what that means varies tremendously.

Try It   Self Image and Socialization

Adapted from submission by Michelle Bemiller, *Kansas State University.*

OBJECTIVE: Understand that your image(s) of self have developed through interactions that occur with agents of socialization (media, peers, family, and the like) and that experiences with significant others have also played an important role in developing your sense of self.

STEP 1: Develop
Buy poster board to complete this project. (Your instructor may give you specific directions on what size of poster board.) Place a picture of yourself in the middle of the board (be sure to write your name on the top of the poster board). The rest of the board should be dedicated to photos, magazine pictures, words, phrases, and so on that help tell your story. Be creative and have fun, but make sure that none of your photos or the language used on your board could be offensive to others.

STEP 2: Write
Write a short reflection paper explaining what the poster is supposed to be communicating about you. Explain in detail what agents of socialization shaped your view of your self (for example, family, media, peers, education). How did these agents influence you? Include and discuss all the agents that apply. Choose two specific others within the agents of socialization and recount a specific experience where these individuals had an impact on your sense of self (this could be positive or negative). Your instructor will give you further guidelines on the expected length of this paper and other expectations such as grading. Be detailed and relate your paper to this textbook chapter on socialization. Be prepared to share your poster in class and to submit your paper to your instructor.

STEP 3: Discuss
Depending on the size of your class, your instructor may have you share your poster either with another student or with the entire class.

In a hospital, the maintenance workers might be expected to tell dirty jokes and discuss their sexual exploits; someone who does not may be rejected as unfriendly. But doctors would be rejected for the same behavior.

Socialization and the Life Course

Some of the transitions we experience throughout our lives are biologically fixed and marked by physiological changes: Puberty marks the beginning of adolescence, for instance, and menopause or gray hair the beginning of old age. But the stages of the life course are primarily social constructions, differing widely from culture to culture and strongly influenced by statuses like race, class, gender, and nationality and by material circumstances. For instance, in some cultures 15-year-olds are considered fully grown adults and in others still children. In some cultures people in their 40s are considered elderly and in others still in the prime of their life. Even the physiological changes differ: The age of menarche (the first menstruation) in girls has been steadily decreasing throughout the twentieth century, and in modern societies, old age no longer begins at the age of 40. (We detail each of these stages in significantly more detail in the chapter on aging.)

Childhood (Birth to Puberty)

In modern societies, we think that we can instantly distinguish children from other sorts of people, and not only because they are smaller. We assume that they have interests, abilities, beliefs, and goals that differ

Did *you* know?

When Moses led the Hebrews out of Egypt, they wandered for 40 years before they reached the Promised Land, which was not all that far away. (They had created a golden calf and worshipped it while Moses was off getting the Ten Commandments, and God was punishing them.) Why 40 years? Why not 25 or 35? Because in those times, 40 years was a lifespan, ensuring that no one who left Egypt with Moses was still alive when they made it to the Promised Land. Only those who were born en route made it.

tremendously from those of teenagers and adults. They do not work; they have no interest in dating or romance; they play with toys and go to school. They are fragile and innocent. They must be shielded from the bad aspects of life, like sex and death. They need constant adult supervision and care.

Although this notion of childhood seems like common sense, it is not universal. It does not occur in every culture, and even in the modern West, it has evolved relatively recently, during the past few centuries. In earlier eras, children were considered miniature adults. As soon as they were able to walk, they went to work alongside the adults, merely getting more difficult and complex tasks as they grew older. There are countries in the world today where children still work full time, sometimes in physically demanding and dangerous jobs.

There was no knowledge considered inappropriate for the children of earlier eras. Sex and death happened openly, in front of them, and sometimes with them. Aries (1962) records that when King Louis XIV of France (1638–1715) was a child, the courtiers openly engaged in sexual horseplay with him, grabbing and fondling his private parts and discussing their sexual function. Today they would be required to register as sex offenders, but in the seventeenth century it was considered completely appropriate.

Industrialization changed the way we see childhood. No longer were children seen as "little adults" but as innocents, needing protection and guidance. Without their parents—without socialization—they would not grow up to be healthy grownups. And thus parents were seen as having specialized knowledge and heightened responsibilities. Some observers suggest that modern media, television, video games, and the Internet are shrinking childhood itself, so soon there may again be no knowledge that is considered inappropriate for children.

Adolescence (Roughly the Teen Years)

Biological changes that occur in puberty are universal, but the timing changes from culture to culture and over time. A century ago, most girls did not experience menarche (their first menstruation) until they were 17 or 18, but today it often comes at age 11 or 12. The cultural boundaries of adolescence are even more variable.

Psychologists early in the twentieth century began to define adolescence as a stage of life in modern societies, when children, especially from affluent groups, need training to compete in specialized job markets, so they stay out of the workforce for several years past puberty. During this time, they have a great deal of freedom to make their own choices about their friends and activities, and they often explore their political, social, sexual, and religious identities: You are more likely to leave your religion, or convert to a new religion, in adolescence than at any other time in your life. But they still must live under the supervision of adults, parents or guardians, who have the final say in decisions. They do not have the responsibilities of adults, nor do they enjoy many adult privileges. In the United States, most adolescents do not work full time; their criminal acts receive different punishments from those of adults; and they are forbidden from marrying, having sexual relations, signing contracts, purchasing real estate, entering military service, and drinking alcohol.

In earlier eras, a girl became a woman when she married, usually in her early 20s, and a boy became a man when he entered the working world—on the farm, in the factory, or apprenticed to a trade. This usually occurred before his fifteenth birthday. As late as 1920, only 16 percent of

Sociology and our World

The Violent Years?

Adolescence is often portrayed as a time of turmoil and uncertainty, as people who used to be children but are not yet adults struggle to find their place in the world. The generation gap between adolescents and adults has been bewailed for centuries. In the 1960s, commentators often countered complaints that contemporary youth were uniquely crazy by quoting this passage:

Our youth today now love luxury; they have bad manners, contempt for authority, disrespect for older people. Children nowadays are tyrants, they no longer rise when elders enter the room, they contradict their parents, they chatter before company, gobble their food and tyrannize their teachers. They have execrable manners, flout authority, have no respect for their elders. What kind of awful creatures will they be when they grow up?

The "punch line" was that the passage was written by Socrates, about 500 BCE.

Ever since G. Stanley Hall's massive, two-volume tome, *Adolescence: Its Psychology and Its Relation to Physiology, Anthropology, Sociology, Sex, Crime, Religion and Education* (1904) mapped out a distinct period for these postchild/preadult youths, parents and psychologists have worried that adolescence is a conflict-ridden stage of psychological development, filled with emotional upheaval and seismically shifting emotions. After World War II, the din of concern reached a crescendo in the national consciousness when near-universal high school attendance, suburbanization, and the new affluence of the Eisenhower years all converged to create a definable new segment of society, "teenagers" (the term was first used in 1944).

However, numerous studies show that most adolescents are no more uncertain than adults, and their lives are not particularly tormented (Males, 1996, 1998; Offer, 2004). With the support of parents, other adults, and peers, they move easily and happily from childhood to adulthood.

17-year-old males—one in six—graduated from high school. Yet increasingly, high school became the defining experience for children of the middle and professional classes. Between 1880 and 1900, the number of public high schools in the United States increased by more than 750 percent.

The boundary between childhood or adolescence and adulthood is marked by many milestones, called rites of passage. In early societies, rites of passage were grueling endurance tests that took weeks or months. Modern societies tend to make them festive occasions, ceremonies like the Bar and Bat Mitzvah for Jewish 13-year-olds, or parties like the *quinceañera* for 15-year-old Hispanic girls. There are also many symbolic rites of passage, like getting a driver's license and graduating from high school.

Adulthood

Most social scientists measure the transition to adulthood by the completion of five demographic markers: (1) Complete your education; (2) get a job; (3) get married; (4) leave your parents' home and move into your own; and (5) have a baby. Fifty years ago, all these transitions would have been accomplished by the early 20s. But today, they are more likely to be completed by one's early 30s. So developmental psychologists have identified a new stage of development, *young adulthood*, that is perched between adolescence and full adulthood.

Young adulthood (from the late teens to about 30) has no roots in physiological growth. It is a social category, based on the modern need to postpone full adulthood for years past adolescence. The first young adults were college and professional students, who would not work full time or marry until they reached their mid-20s, but

▲ Old age was historically a stage of life characterized by boredom, loneliness, and poverty. As people are living longer, they are also re-creating communities, and, in those countries with adequate social security, living happier and healthier—as well as longer—lives.

in contemporary society many people feel a sort of adolescence until they reach their 30s, or even longer (Goldschneider and Waite, 1991): They are not "settled down" into permanent careers, residences, and families. They are still exploring their sexual, political, and religious affiliations.

In contemporary society many people change careers several times during their lives, each requiring new periods of training, moves to new cities, and new sets of social acquaintances, so the stability and long association we expect from "adulthood" may be replaced by constant beginnings.

From young adulthood, one passes into "middle age," roughly from age 30 to age 60. Today, there is more anxiety and tension surrounding middle age than in the past. When so much mass media glorify youth, it is easy for people in middle age to think of themselves as deficient or diminished.

In earlier times, middle-aged persons maintained closer connections with kin and followed the routines of work that were the same as those around them. Now, we tend to go out on our own, choosing careers different from those of our kin and living far away. Our interpersonal connections depend on individual initiative, not on parents, community, and tradition, and it is easy to get lost along the way.

Above age 60 has generally been referred to as "old age." In earlier cultures, few people lived to see their old age, and those who did were revered because they had the job of passing on the wisdom of earlier generations to the later. To call someone "Grandfather" or "Grandmother" was to put them at the pinnacle of social status. In industrialized societies, their children were usually working at jobs they knew nothing about, using technology that didn't even exist when they were young, so they tended to lack social status. Nowadays, we may say, "Get out of the way, Grandpa!" as an insult to an older person who is moving too slowly for us. On *The Simpsons*, Homer's father Abraham is constantly ridiculed for his physical disabilities and for being forgetful, longwinded, narrow minded, and fantasy prone.

Because older people often move to retirement communities and nursing homes far from their children, grandchildren, and friends, they must make social connections all over again, and many find old age to be the loneliest time of their lives. It is also the poorest, because they are not working, and their only source of income may be a small pension or Social Security check.

The longevity revolution in industrialized countries means that most people can expect to live 20 or more years in old age. Sixty-five no longer seems doddering and decrepit, and the mandatory retirement age has been raised to 70 in some states or eliminated altogether. Will such a long life span transform old age, restoring to it some of its lost prestige? The longevity revolution has ushered in new terms for the aged, as we will see later in this book, from the "young old" to the "old old." If 30 is the new 20, then today 90 is the new 70.

Gender Socialization

We are not only socialized into the norms and expectations of age categories. We are socialized into all of our roles and statuses. When we get a new job, we are socialized into the spoken and unspoken rules of the job: Do you eat your lunch at your desk, in the employee lounge, or out at a restaurant? Are you supposed to discuss

Caring for Others

Socialization touches every aspect of our lives. It's through socialization that we learn the norms, values, and beliefs of our culture and the groups we belong to. Agents of socialization such as the family, religion, and peers teach us how to live in the world and how to view the world, but not everyone is socialized the same. One thing we learn from those around us is how much we are supposed to care about others versus how much we should invest in self-interest. Men and women are socialized to care in different ways and to express concern for others in different ways, as well. So, what do you think?

People need not worry about others.

○ Strongly agree
○ Agree
○ Neither agree nor disagree
○ Disagree
○ Strongly disagree

See the back of the chapter to compare your answers to national survey data.

your personal life with your co-workers or limit your interaction to polite greetings? Should you profess an interest in opera or the Superbowl? The socialization is usually into what "should" be done, not what "must" be done. You will not be thrown out onto the street for mentioning the Superbowl when the social norm is to like opera, but you will find your prestige lessened. You will be less likely to belong to the most coveted peer groups and less likely to rise to positions of leadership in the group.

Socialization into gender is one of the most profound and thorough, occupying a great deal of the time and energy of a great many agents of socialization throughout the life course. From the moment babies return from the hospital in pink or blue blankets, or wear their first outfits marked with "Daddy's Little Princess" or "Daddy's Little Slugger," they undergo **gender socialization** to accept two entirely different sets of social norms. Boys are expected to be tough, aggressive, loud, and athletic; and girls to be sensitive, passive, quiet, and nonathletic.

◀ Boys may be called "sissies" when they defy gender expectations (as in this image from the movie *Billy Elliot*) and girls called "tomboys." But sanctions for gender nonconformity are more severe for boys than for girls.

How do we know what we know?

Gender and the Boy Code

In their best-selling books about boys, psychologists such as William Pollack (1998), James Garbarino (1999), Michael Thompson, Dan Kindlon (2000), and others argue that from an early age, boys are taught to refrain from crying, to suppress their emotions, never to display vulnerability. As a result, they argue, boys feel effeminate not only if they express their emotions, but if they even feel emotions.

Young boys begin to embrace what Pollack calls "the boy code" by age 4 or 5, when they enter kindergarten, and they get a second jolt when they hit adolescence. Think of the messages boys get: "Stand on your own two feet! Don't cry! Don't be a sissy! Don't be a mama's boy!" As one boy in Pollack's book summarizes it: "Shut up and take it, or you'll be sorry."

Consider the parallel for girls. Carol Gilligan (1982) describes how assertive, confident, and proud young girls "lose their voices" when they hit adolescence. At the same moment, Pollack notes, boys become more confident, even beyond their abilities. You might even say that boys find their voices, but they are inauthentic voices of bravado, risk-taking, and foolish violence. The boy code teaches them that they are supposed to be in power, and they begin to act like it. What is the cause of all this posturing and posing? It's not testosterone, but privilege. In adolescence both boys and girls get their first real dose of gender inequality. Therefore, girls suppress ambition, boys inflate it.

The boy code leaves boys disconnected from many of their emotions and keeps them from sharing their feelings with their peers. As they grow older, they feel disconnected from adults, as well, unable to experience the guidance toward maturity that adults can bring. When they turn to anger and violence it is because they believe that these are the only acceptable forms of emotional expression.

Where do they learn the boy code (or, as teenagers and adults, the guy code)? From teachers and parents certainly, but mostly from their peers. The guy code offers a specific blueprint for being accepted as a guy. But just as "the first rule of *Fight Club*" (1996)—perhaps the touchstone text for thousands of guys—says, "You can tell no one about Fight Club," the guy code is never written down or verbalized. Rather, it is passed from guy to guy in locker rooms and gyms, bars and frat houses, workplaces and churches, all across the nation. The guy code teaches exaggerated versions of the ideology of masculinity, with certain modifications: "Be tough! Be strong! Laugh at weakness! Do not feel!"

Throughout childhood, both groups are punished for transgressions by every agent of socialization: parents, teachers, peers. Perhaps the boys get more punishment. Girls who are tough, aggressive, loud, and athletic are labeled "tomboys," while boys who are sensitive, passive, quiet, and not good at sports are labeled with the much worse term "sissies." The difference is one of gender privilege. Because "masculine" things are powerful, girls who do "masculine" things may be praised as just trying to increase their prestige, but boys who do "feminine" things are "acting like a girl"; that is, they get less prestige.

Growing up does not lessen the intensity of gender socialization. We are bombarded with media images every day about appropriate masculinity and femininity. On television, Jerry Seinfeld orders salad on a date; his friends ridicule him, and he is refused a second date because "real men" order steak. Our romances are expected to be gender polarized, with heterosexual men from Mars, heterosexual women from Venus, and gay men and lesbians the reverse, even in such trivialities as handling the television remote (men flip quickly from channel to channel, women stick with one channel). Our churches and temples are sites of performing gender, our jobs dependent on demonstrating that we are "real men" and "real women." Even at home, among our friends, we cannot relax: Our peer groups are constantly enforcing the rules, policing everyone and punishing any transgression with snubs, stares, jokes, or ostracism.

Socialization in the 21st Century

The socialization process is dynamic and continuous. Across the life span, more and different agents of socialization can come into play. One never achieves or reaches a "true" identity but is always interacting and reacting to create what can only be a temporary or partial "self." While this complex process potentially offers us constant opportunities for self-creation and growth, it is also rife with tensions between autonomy and belonging, individuality and group identification. As the sociologist Erving Goffman captured it:

> Without something to belong to, we have no stable self, and yet total commitment and attachment to any social unit implies a kind of selflessness. Our sense of being a person can come from being drawn into a wider social unit; our sense of selfhood can arise through the little ways in which we resist the pull. Our status is backed by the solid buildings of the world, while our sense of personal identity often resides in the cracks. (1961)

Next time someone gives you his or her yearbook to inscribe, consider writing, "Change! And keep changing! For the rest of your life!"

Chapter Review

1. *How do sociologists see the relationship between socialization and biology?* Both nature (biology) and nurture (socialization) play a role in how we are made and how we develop. Before the Enlightenment, nature ruled, and identity was thought to be preordained by God along with the natural world. During the Enlightenment, the idea emerged that our environment shapes who we are. Rousseau argued a compromise and said human beings do inherit identities, but the environment changes them. That is the view sociologists take, although they tend to focus on the nurture aspect, because interaction with others is ongoing and affects who we are. Learning from interactions with others, or socialization, is the process by which we become aware of ourselves as part of a group, learn how to communicate, and learn expectations for behavior.

2. *How does socialization work?* Humans require more years of dependency and socialization than other species. We are learning the skills necessary not just to survive in the physical world but also to survive in the social world.

3. *What are the stages of socialization?* George Herbert Mead developed a theory about how we learn to see others' points of view gradually as children as the internalized expectations of what he called the "generalized other." Mead said this happened in three stages, including imitation, play, and games, in which children learn to anticipate the thoughts of others. Jean Piaget theorized that reasoning ability develops in four stages. In the first stage, children experience the world through their senses; in the second, they learn to use symbols; in the third, they develop reasoning; and in the fourth, they become capable of abstract thinking. Lawrence Kohlberg built on that theory and added that we develop moral reasoning in three stages. In the first, we are motivated by reward and punishment. In the second, we see the larger social context. In the third stage, we see relative morality. Stage theories have problems: The stages are rigidly defined, it is not clear if one must complete each stage in order, and the stages are not necessarily universal.

4. *What are agents of socialization?* Agents of socialization are those people, groups, or institutions that socialize new members. Socialization is not always positive and varies in relative importance at different times of life. One of the most important agents of socialization is the family. Education is another major agent of socialization. At school, we learn facts, concepts, and skills but also are exposed to a hidden curriculum instilling social norms and values. Religion provides a divine motivation and rationalization for norms and values, and through

peer groups we learn skills such as social interaction and group loyalty. The media are also pervasive agents of socialization, touching on all areas of our lives.

5. *How does socialization occur over the life course?* Although the stages of the life course are a social construction, they provide a useful way of looking at how humans make their way through life. Childhood is the period from birth to puberty. Our notion of childhood is not universal, nor has it remained the same historically. The idea of adolescence emerged along with the development of specialized job markets; young people needed specialized education. Adulthood is often marked by completion of one's education, getting a job, getting married, moving into one's own home, or having a baby. The transition from adolescence to adulthood is occurring later in life now, when people are in their 30s instead of in their 20s.

6. *How are we socialized into gender?* We are socialized into all of our roles and statuses, including gender. Gender-role socialization permeates all aspects of our lives and is ongoing throughout the life course. Even before birth, parents choose colors and clothing based on gender. Boys and girls are socialized into two different sets of norms, and this socialization is pronounced during childhood. Gender transgressions are punished by every agent of socialization. As children grow into adolescents and adults, they continue to be socialized by these agents on what is appropriate for males and females in different situations and at different stages of the life course.

KeyTerms

Agents of socialization (p. 150)
Anticipatory socialization (p. 149)
Ego (p. 147)
Gender socialization (p. 161)

Generalized other (p. 144)
Id (p. 147)
Peer groups (p. 154)
Primary socialization (p. 150)

Resocialization (p. 149)
Secondary socialization (p. 150)
Socialization (p. 141)
Superego (p. 147)

What does *America* think?

5.1 Belief in an Afterlife

These are actual survey data from the General Social Survey, 1998.

Do you believe in life after death? Data from the General Social Survey for the 1990s show the following: More than half of the respondents definitely believed in life after death, and another one-fifth probably did. Only slightly more than 20 percent did not believe in life after death. More women than men believed in an afterlife (59.3 percent versus 53.3). Social class differences were not that marked.

CRITICAL THINKING | DISCUSSION QUESTIONS

1. From the GSS data seen above, it appears that Americans in general tend to believe in life after death. How does this reflect the character of American society and core American values?
2. Each religion has different ideas about the afterlife. How do history and culture affect how a religious group conceives its ideas about an afterlife?
3. This is one topic where there seems to be very little deviation with regard to either social class or gender. Why do you think that is?

5.2 Caring for Others

These are actual survey data from the General Social Survey, 2004.

People need not worry about others. One-quarter of respondents either agreed or strongly agreed with this statement. Another quarter was neutral. One-half disagreed or strongly disagreed. The gender differences in responses were striking. Men were far more likely to agree with the statement than were women. Almost 32 percent of the men agreed or strongly agreed, in contrast to almost 20 percent of the women.

CRITICAL THINKING | DISCUSSION QUESTIONS

1. How much we think we should care for others versus care for ourselves is heavily influenced by how we are socialized. One level of socialization is that of the larger culture. What core values do you think Americans in general hold that might help explain these survey results?
2. What do you think lies behind the variation of responses with regard to gender? What stereotypically masculine qualities might make men report that they are less worried about the needs of others than women are? What stereotypically feminine qualities might teach women that it is appropriate to care for others? Where do we learn these qualities?

▶ Go to this website to look further at the data. You can run your own statistics and cross tabs here: **http://sda.berkeley.edu/cgi-bin/hsda?harcsda+gss04**

REFERENCES: Davis, James A., Tom W. Smith, and Peter V. Marsden. General Social Surveys 1972–2004: [Cumulative file] [Computer file]. 2nd ICPSR version. Chicago, IL: National Opinion Research Center [producer], 2005; Storrs, CT: Roper Center for Public Opinion Research, University of Connecticut; Ann Arbor, MI: Inter-university Consortium for Political and Social Research; Berkeley, CA: Computer-Assisted Survey Methods Program, University of California [distributors], 2005.

most prisoners are paroled before they serve their full terms. In other respects, America is hard on crime: It is the number one jailer in the world and the only industrialized nation that still has the death penalty. It seems to be a matter of working very hard to achieve very limited results. In fact, we are both soft *and* hard on crime; to the sociologist what is most interesting is the how and why of that "softness" and "hardness" and measuring the effectiveness of the institutions that are designed to handle deviance and crime.

What Is Deviance?

Breaking a social rule, or refusing to follow one, is called **deviance**. Deviant acts are not just illegal; they can also violate a moral or a social rule that may or may not have legal consequences. This week, many of you will do something that could be considered deviant—from the illegal behaviors we just mentioned to arriving at a party too soon or leaving too early.

More involving acts of deviance, like being a nudist or organizing a hate group, are another matter. I know full well that walking around naked or pronouncing irrational prejudices in public may get me shunned, screamed at, or beat up, so I don't bring it up in casual conversation or on the train ride to work in the morning. I might reveal this only within a group of other nudists or bigots, or very close friends or family, or not at all.

We can also be considered deviant without doing, saying, or believing anything bad or wrong but just by belonging to a stigmatized minority group (Hispanic, gay, Jewish, for example) or by having some status that goes against what's considered "normal" (mentally ill, disabled, atheist). There is even deviance by association: If you have a friend who belongs to the stigmatized minority group, or a family member with a deviant status, you may be labeled as deviant just for being seen with him or her.

Most deviance is not illegal, and many illegal acts are only mildly deviant or not deviant at all. But when lawmakers consider a deviant act bad enough to warrant formal sanctions, it becomes a *crime*, and the full force of the government goes into regulating it. Some common sexual practices—like oral sex or masturbation—are illegal in a number of states because lawmakers at one time found them sufficiently deviant to be criminal and wanted anyone who committed them to "pay his or her debt to society" with fines or prison terms.

Some sociologists study minor forms of deviance, like appearing in public without your corset, but most are interested in the

"Lizardman" is deviant because he breaks or refuses to follow social norms about appearance. Most deviance in society is not illegal. ▼

Sociology and our World

Crazy Laws

What we consider deviant changes over time, as people change their ideas of what is normal and what is wrong. As a result, laws prohibiting certain acts are often enforced long after most people in the society stopped considering them deviant. Men were fined for going topless on the beach as late as the 1930s. As of this writing, it is illegal for a man and a woman who are not married or relatives to share a hotel room in Florida (though the police look the other way during spring break). Some of these laws are still enforced—sometimes when the local police chief has had a bad day—but many others are unenforced and probably unenforceable. They are relics of long-vanished values, acts that some lawmakers considered deviant enough to warrant legal penalties:

- In Alabama, it is illegal to buy peanuts at night.
- In Colorado, it is illegal for a man to kiss a woman while she is asleep.
- In Florida, unmarried women are prohibited from skydiving on Sunday.
- In Boston, Massachusetts, it is illegal to take a bath unless you are under physician's orders.
- In New Mexico, it is illegal for women to appear in public with unshaven legs.
- In Tulsa, Oklahoma, heterosexual kissing is permitted, as long as it lasts less than three minutes.
- In Oregon, a man may not purchase alcohol without the written consent of his wife.

(All are from Davidson, 1998.)

---

major forms of deviance. These are acts that can get you shunned and screamed at or labeled an "outsider" (Becker, 1966); or they are the sorts of crimes that get you thrown in prison. These are not matters of mere carelessness: The rules come from many important agents of socialization, and the penalties for breaking them are high. With some, like burglary or fraud, you have to consciously plan to commit the act, and the law distinguishes between those crimes that are the result of intention and those that could be the result of negligence or even an accident (and we adjust our penalties accordingly). So why do people break them? And why don't most of us break them all the time? What makes a deviant or a criminal? What can we do about it? These are the central questions to a sociologist because they illustrate our concern for social order and control—both when they are present, and people obey the rules and when they are absent, and people feel unconstrained by those same rules.

In the first chapter of this book, we suggested that sociologists are always interested in both sides of this question: How is society possible in the first place (social organization) and why does it often feel that society is "breaking down" or some institution is on the verge of collapse (social disorganization)? Recall the example of the New York City tabloid newspapers featuring screaming headlines about a person being pushed to his or her death on the subway tracks at rush hour. On the one hand, sociologists ask: What could possibly bring someone to push someone else, a stranger, in front of an oncoming subway train? Society, we fear, is breaking down right in front of our eyes. And yet, at the same time, more than one million strangers ride in those metal tubes going 75 miles an hour underneath the streets of New York City every day—crowded conditions with people you don't know, don't especially like, and all sleep deprived and buzzed on coffee. Sociologists also ask: Why aren't more people pushed in front of oncoming trains every day? We're interested in both questions: Why do most of us conform to social norms most of the time, and why do most of us decide to break some of them at other times? We want to know: What accounts for conformity? What accounts for deviance? And who decides which is which?

Conformity and Social Control

Each culture develops different types of rules that prescribe what is considered appropriate behavior in that culture. They vary by how formalized they are, how central to social life, and the types of sanctions that are threatened should you break them:

1. **Folkways** are routine, usually unspoken conventions of behavior; our culture prescribes that we do some things in a certain way, although other ways might work just as well. For example, we face forward instead of backward in an elevator, and answer the question "How are you?" with "Fine." Breaking a folkway may make others in the group uncomfortable (although they sometimes don't understand why they're uncomfortable), and violators may be laughed at, frowned on, or scolded. Folkways are rarely made into laws.

2. **Mores** are norms with a strong moral significance, viewed as essential to the proper functioning of the group: We absolutely should or should not behave this way. You might break a *mos* (the singular form of mores) by assaulting someone or speaking abusively to someone. Breaking mores makes others in the group upset, angry, or afraid, and they are likely to consider violators bad or immoral. Mores are often made into laws.

3. **Taboos** are prohibitions viewed as essential to the well-being of humanity. To break a taboo is unthinkable, beyond comprehension. For example, Sigmund Freud considered the incest taboo—one should not have sex with one's own children—to be a foundation of all societies. If parents and children had sex, then lines of inheritance, family name, and orderly intergenerational property transfer would be completely impossible. Taboos are so important that most cultures have only a few. In the United States, for instance, murder and assault break mores, not taboos. Breaking taboos causes others to feel disgusted. The violators are considered sick, evil, and monstrous. Taboos are always made into laws, unless they are so unthinkable that lawmakers cannot believe that anyone would break them.

Stigma

If some part of you—your race or sexuality, for example—is considered deviant, without your actually having to do anything, you would be considered "stigmatized." The sociologist Erving Goffman (1963) used the term **stigma** to mean an attribute that changes you "from a whole and usual person to a tainted and discounted one." Deviant behavior or a deviant master status creates stigma, although not in every case. Other people might ignore our deviance, or "forgive" it as an anomaly. Goffman believed that people with stigmatized attributes are constantly practicing various strategies to ensure minimal damage. Because being stigmatized will "spoil" your identity, you are likely to adopt one of three strategies to alleviate it.

Goffman identified three strategies to neutralize stigma and save yourself from having a spoiled identity. He listed them in order of increased social power—the more power you have, the more you can try and redefine the situation. (These terms reflect the era in which he was writing, since he obviously uses the Civil Rights movement as the reference.)

What do *you* think

MyLab

6.1

Censoring Perceived Deviance

All groups have tendencies toward social control. The desire to censor people or ideas we think are deviant is strong, especially when those ideas seem in opposition to widely held values. At the same time, America prides itself on being a free country, and free speech is protected by the U.S. Constitution. Let's look at how you and other Americans feel about an antireligionist, a homosexual, and a racist teaching college or having books in the library. So, what do you think?

1. Should someone who is against all church and religion be allowed to teach in a college or university, or not?
   ○ Allowed
   ○ Not allowed

2. And what about a man who admits he is a homosexual?
   ○ Allowed
   ○ Not allowed

3. Should a person who believes Blacks are genetically inferior be allowed to teach?
   ○ Allowed
   ○ Not allowed

4. Should an antireligion book be removed from the library?
   ○ Remove
   ○ Don't remove

5. What about a book written in favor of homosexuality?
   ○ Remove
   ○ Don't remove

6. What about a book that suggests Blacks are inferior?
   ○ Remove
   ○ Don't remove

See the back of the chapter to compare your answers to national survey data.

---

1. *Minstrelization:* If you're virtually alone and have very little power, you can over-conform to the stereotypes that others have about you. To act like a minstrel, Goffman says, is to exaggerate the differences between the stigmatized and the dominant group. Thus, for example, did African Americans overact as happy-go-lucky entertainers when they had no other recourse. A contemporary example might be women who act ultrafeminine—helpless and dependent—in potentially harassing situations. Note that minstrels exaggerate difference in the face of those with more power; when they are with other stigmatized people, they may laugh about the fact that the powerful "actually think we're like this!" That's often the only sort of power that they feel they have.

2. *Normification:* If you have even a small amount of power, you might try to *minimize* the differences between the stigmatized groups. "Look," you'll say, "we're the same as you are, so there is no difference to discriminate against us." Normification is the process that gays and lesbians refer to when they argue for same-sex marriage or that women use when they say they want to be engineers or physicists. Normification involves exaggerating the similarities and downplaying the differences.

3. *Militant chauvinism:* When your group's level of power and organization is highest, you may decide to again *maximize* differences with the dominant group. But militant chauvinists don't just say "we're different," they say "we're also better."

For example, there are groups of African Americans ("Afrocentrists" or even some of the Nation of Islam) who proclaim black superiority. Some feminist women proclaims that women's ways are better than the dominant "male" way. These trends try to turn the tables on the dominant group. (*Warning:* Do not attempt this if you are the only member of your group in a confrontation with members of the dominant group.)

These three responses to stigma depend on the size and strength of the stigmatized group. If you're all alone, minstrelizing may be a lifesaving technique. If there are many of you and you are strong, you might try to militantly turn the tables.

Deviant Subcultures

A **subculture** is a group that evolves within a dominant culture, always more or less hidden and closed to outsiders. It may be a loose association of friends who share the same interests, or it may be well organized, with its own alternative language, costumes, and media. While most subcultures are not deviant, the separation from the dominant culture allows deviant subcultures to develop their own norms and values. For a deviant subculture to develop, the activity, condition, identity, and so on must meet three characteristics:

1. It must be punished but not punished too much. If it is not punished enough, potential recruits have no motivation to seek out the subculture. If it is punished too much, the risks of membership are too great.

2. It must have enough participants but not too many. If it has too few participants, it will be hard to seek them out locally. If it has too many, it would be pointless.

3. It must be complex but not too complex. If it is not complex enough, you could engage in it by yourself. If it is too complex, it could exist only within a counterculture or dominant culture: You would need a college degree.

Notice that each of these criteria is not a simple either/or proposition, but rather the achievement of a balance or middle way between heavy punishment and leniency and between size and complexity.

Deviants or Folk Heroes? Jesse James and the Black Panthers were considered criminals by law enforcement agencies, but they were folk heroes in their communities, celebrated in folk songs and tributes. ▶

Youth Gangs as Deviant Subculture. Youth gangs are a good example of a deviant subculture. Before the 1950s, we often considered youth gangs as relatively innocent. Their deviance consisted of swiping apples from fruit stands and swimming in the East River in spite of the "no trespassing" signs. Meanwhile they helped out mothers and friends in distress and sometimes even cooperated with the police. They were juvenile delinquents with hearts of gold, mischievous but not bad. It was the adult gangsters who posed a threat, trying to seduce them into lives of adult, hard-core crime.

Today, though, our image of youth gangs is quite different, closer to the film *Boyz in the Hood* (1991). And they no longer swipe the occasional apple. There are some 24,000 youth gangs in the United States, with 760,000 members, a figure that doesn't even include informal ganglike cliques, crews, and posses (Snyder and Sickmund, 2006). Nearly eight in ten cities with populations of 50,000 or more now have a "gang problem." For example, nearly one-quarter of high school students surveyed in Virginia belonged to a gang and another 18 percent to a ganglike group. Minority students and those in urban schools have a higher proportion of gangs. Sometimes gangs can be distinguished from other sorts of groups by their distinctive marks of membership: symbols on clothing, dress styles and colors, or tattoos. However, many high school and junior high "wannabes" with no gang ties adopt gang symbols and styles anyway, in an attempt to be cool.

Most gangs are composed of poor or working-class adolescents, typically male (Jankowski, 1991). Members are startlingly young, often preteen when they start, and they generally retire (or go to prison or die) by their mid-twenties. Ethnic minorities are overrepresented, in part because, as numerical minorities, they often feel a stronger need to belong to a group that can provide identity and protection. The National Youth Gang Survey found that 49 percent of gang members are Hispanic, 37 percent Black, 8 percent White, 5 percent Asian, and 1 percent all others (Snyder and Sickmund, 2006). The racial composition of gangs, however, reflects the characteristics of the larger community and so varies considerably with location (Howell, Egley, and Gleason, 2002).

While females represent a small proportion of youth gang members, their numbers have been increasing in recent years (Moore and Hagedorn, 2001; National Youth Gang Center, 2007). As young teenagers, roughly one-third of all youth gang members are female (Esbensen and Winfree, 1998; Gottfredson and Gottfredson, 2001); however, females tend to leave gangs at an earlier age than males (Gottfredson and Gottfredson, 2001; Thornberry, Krohn, Lizotte, et al., 2003). Emerging research has begun to suggest that the gender composition of a gang affects its delinquency rates. In one study, females in all- or majority-female gangs had the lowest delinquency rates, whiles both males and females in majority-male gangs had the highest—including higher rates than males in all-male gangs (Peterson, Miller, and Esbensen, 2001).

Why do adolescents join gangs? Sociologists have conducted many interviews with gang members, and the reasons most commonly given are friends and relatives who already belong to the gang, a desire for excitement, a need for protection, and the availability of money, drugs, and alcohol. While earlier psychological research suggested that gang membership was "irrational"—leading to high arrest rates, likelihood of dying a violent death, chronic physical danger, instability—sociologists also stress that in some circumstances, gang membership can be a rational decision. Sociologist Martin Sanchez-Jankowski interviewed gang members in New York and Los Angeles, and he found that their motivations were similar to any underemployed job seeker: Gang membership provided economic opportunities to support a family, opportunities of career enhancement (moving up the ladder), feelings of belonging and camaraderie in a hostile world, and status to attract girls (Sanchez-Jankowski, 1991).

Youth Gangs Today. Today youth gangs are well-armed and financed because of their involvement in drug trafficking. In some communities, offences are more violent, and they now interact with members of organized crime (National Youth Gang Center, 2007). In one nationwide study of high-crime areas, gang members reported committing large percentages of various types of youth crimes. In Rochester, gang members admitted committing 68 percent of all violent crimes by adolescents; Seattle gangs self-reported committing 85 percent of adolescent robberies; Denver gangs admitted to 79 percent of all serious violent crimes by adolescents (Howell, 2006). Prison terms, usually shorter for minors, give youth gang members the opportunity to form alliances with older criminals and learn from them (Greene and Pranis, 2007).

▼ Youth gangs are seen as deviant subcultures, with their own norms, values, and rules of conduct. The number of female gang members has been increasing, but most gang members are male.

Gangs are a new form of organized crime—less organized but more violent than the Mafia ever was. Their agenda is usually purely financial, but some commentators worry about the implications if well-armed, highly organized gangs acquire a political agenda. For instance, the FBI is particularly worried about the Mara Salvatrucha, a gang based in northern Virginia. Its membership is drawn not only from local youth but from former paramilitary guerilllas who came north from Central America. They still have ties in Central America, which facilitate a brisk traffic in guns and drugs (*The Economist, 2005*).

However, most disturbing to the FBI are reports that gang members have met with al-Qaeda members in El Salvador (*The Economist, 2005*). Potential links between American gangs and international terrorist groups fuel much of the current concern about gangs.

Most gangs are not involved in such far-ranging criminal activities. Most provide a sense of belonging and connection for members, protection against perceived hostility, and a sense of menace to those who are not in the gang. Most important to some is that they have good parties, provide easy access to alcohol and drugs, and "know how to have fun," as one gang member told me.

Deviance and Social Coherence

Because there is always deviance in society, some sociologists ask what purpose it might serve. One of the founders of modern sociology, Émile Durkheim, wrote that having some members of a society castigated as deviant actually helps the society maintain itself as a coherent entity (Durkheim, 1964a,b). Durkheim argued that deviance is useful to society in four ways:

1. *It affirms cultural norms and values.* Without defining what is wrong, we do not know what is right: There can be no good without evil, no justice without crime. Deviance is needed to define and sustain morality.

2. *It clarifies moral boundaries.* We don't really know what the rule is until we see someone breaking it. Deviance lets societies draw a clear distinction between good and bad, right and wrong. If there are no clear distinctions, the society falls victim to *anomie* (normlessness).

3. *It heightens group solidarity.* When someone commits an act of major deviance, other people in the society react with collective anger: They are outraged. In responding to the deviant, they reaffirm the moral ties that bind them together.

4. *It encourages social change.* Someone who breaks a social rule makes us wonder if the rule is all that important after all. Deviant people push moral boundaries, suggesting alternatives to the status quo. Today's deviance can be tomorrow's morality (Durkheim, 1964a,b).

Deviance is socially useful because it reminds "us" that we are "normal"—it's *they* who are different and deviant.

Explaining Deviance

Durkheim's explanation explains what deviance *does* for the larger society, but it doesn't explain why deviance happens, especially major acts of deviance that will result in major punishment.

Differential Association. Edwin H. Sutherland's theory of **differential association** (1940) suggests that it is a matter of rewards and punishment: Deviance occurs when an individual receives more prestige and less punishment by violating norms rather than by following them. What is deviant to one group might be something that enhances our status in another group. For example, students who behave in an irreverent, disrespectful fashion in class may be seen as deviant by the teachers and even punished for it, but they might also receive a great deal of prestige from their peers. They may calculate that the benefit (increased prestige) is better than the minor punishment they might receive. Thus, Sutherland argued, individuals become deviant by associating with people or joining groups that are already deviant and therefore are in the position to award deviant behavior (Sutherland, 1940).

Sutherland's theory helps to explain the way we sometimes have multiple moral voices in our heads—like the little devil and angel versions of ourselves often depicted on TV—and why sometimes we choose to be deviant. But the theory does not explain how the "carriers of criminality" became deviant in the first place. It also does not explain acts that occur without a community, when everyone around disapproves, or when no one is even aware of the deviance.

Try It Applying Theories to Deviance in the News

Contributed by Katherine Rowell, *Sinclair Community College.*

OBJECTIVE: Apply what you have been learning about theoretical explanations of deviance to the real world of deviance and crime.

STEP 1: Research
Search for examples of news articles that demonstrate each of the above theoretical perspectives of deviant behavior (you will have three different articles and are not permitted to use the same article twice). There are numerous ways to find the news in our world today, and for this project you may use news sources online or your local newspaper.

STEP 2: Compile Information
After finding the three news articles, complete the following information for each one. If your news article is not

available on the Internet, you will need to make a copy of it to attach to your completed information sheet.
For each news article, provide the following information:

1. Title of article
2. Author
3. Date and specific citation information
4. An explanation of why you think this particular news article demonstrates the particular theory. Please note you will have one newspaper article for each theory. Complete these four questions for each theory/newspaper article.

STEP 3: Discuss
Be prepared to share your results in class. Please note that some instructors may collect this activity for a grade.

Control Theory. Travis Hirschi (1969; Gottfredson and Hirschi, 1995) argued that people do not obey lots of hidden forces: They are *rational*, so they decide whether or not to engage in an act by weighing the potential outcome. If you knew that there would be absolutely no punishment, no negative consequences of any sort, you would probably do a great many things that you would never dream of otherwise, like propositioning an attractive co-worker or driving like a maniac. You are constrained by the fear of punishment.

Hirschi imagined that people do a "cost-benefit analysis" during their decision-making process, to determine how much punishment is worth a degree of satisfaction or prestige. In a cost-benefit analysis, you weigh the respective costs of doing something (the likelihood or severity of punishment, for example) against the benefits of doing it (like the money you might get, the increased prestige, the thrill of doing it in the first place). People who have very little to lose are therefore mostly likely to become rule-breakers because for them the costs will almost always be less than the potential benefits.

According to **control theory,** an assembly-line worker whose job training has been significantly less, and who earns considerably less money, might make a different calculation, and get into the fight and risk losing the job, figuring that at such a low wage, one can easily get a comparable job.

Of course, we often fail to break rules even when the benefits would be great and the punishment minimal. I often arrive on campus at 6:00 a.m., before dawn, and just inside, I usually have to stop at one of those stoplights that feels as if it takes five minutes to change from red to green. I could easily run it. There would be a substantial benefit, in arriving at the office five minutes early and not wasting the gas and oil it takes to just sit there. There would be no punishment: No one is around, and I am certain that no police officers are monitoring a deserted intersection from a hidden camera. I do not even agree that the rule is just; stoplights are a good idea in general, but forcing a driver to wait five minutes to cross a deserted street is idiotic. Nevertheless, in spite of my objections, in spite of the benefits and lack of punishment, I always just sit there.

Walter Reckless (1973) would suggest that I am subject to **social controls.** If I really think that a police car is lying in wait to give me a traffic ticket, I am subject to *outer controls:* family, social institutions, and authority figures (like the police) who influence us into obeying social rules (Costello and Vowell, 1999). But even when my mother can't see me, I am subject to *inner controls:* internalized socialization, religious principles, my self-conception as a "good person" (Hirschi, 1969; Rogers and Buffalo, 1974).

Inner and outer controls do their job in four ways:

1. *Attachment.* Strong attachments encourage conformity; weak attachments encourage deviance.

2. *Commitment.* The greater our commitment to the norms and values of the group, the more advantages we derive from conforming, and the more we have to lose through deviance.

3. *Involvement.* Extensive involvement in group activities—job, school, sports—inhibits deviance.

4. *Belief.* A strong belief in conventional morality and respect for authority figures inhibits deviance.

Control theory suggests that deviants/delinquents are often individuals who have low levels of self-control as a result of inadequate socialization, especially in childhood.

Labeling Theory. We used to think that the wrongdoing in deviance resided some-where in the wrongdoer: You break a social rule because you are "that kind of person," with faulty genes, a criminal personality, or a defective soul. But now we know that wrongdoing is not inherent in an act or an actor, but in the social context that determines whether an act is considered deviant or not and how much punishment it warrants.

Howard Becker (1966) used the term labeling theory to stress the relativity of deviance. Labeling describes a relationship between a dominant group and the actor. For something to be deviant, it has to be labeled as deviant by a powerful group—a group powerful enough to make that label stick. (If you do something wrong and your little sister declares it deviant, it doesn't have the same sort of weight as if all your friends label it deviant, or, even more, if the police and the juvenile courts call it deviant.) Labeling theory understands deviance to be a *process*, not a categorical difference between the deviant and the nondeviant. The label depends on the group's relative amount of power.

The same act might be deviant in some groups and not in others. It might be deviant when one person commits it but not when another person commits it. In fact, an action, belief, or condition is neutral in itself. It only becomes "deviant" when someone decides that it is wrong, bad, or immoral and labels it as deviant. For example, think of women who are sexually aggressive or enjoy pornography. Society might call them "sluts" and shun them. But if a man did any of those things, other men might call him a "stud" and perhaps hang out with him.

But deviance does not only reside in whether other people apply the label "deviant" to your acts. To become a deviant actor, you also have to believe the deviant label; you have to to agree with the labels other people ascribe to you.

Edwin Lemert (1972) theorized that most acts, which he called **primary deviance**, provoke very little reaction and therefore have little effect on your self-concept. If I decide one day to run that red light on campus at 6:00 a.m., a passing police office may label me as reckless and irresponsible, but I am unlikely to believe it. Only when I repeatedly break a norm, and people start making a big deal of it, does **secondary deviance** kick in. My rule breaking is no longer a momentary lapse in judgment, or justifiable under the circumstances, but an indication of a permanent personality trait: I have acquired a deviant identity. Finally, sociologists also have identified **tertiary deviance**, in which a group formerly labeled deviant attempts to redefine their acts, attributes, or identities as normal—even virtuous. John Kitsuse (1980) and others point to the ways some formerly deviant groups have begun to stand up for their rights, demanding equality with those considered "normals." Similar to "militant chauvinism" defined by Goffman when discussing stigma, examples might include the disability rights movement, which has attempted to redefine disabilities from deviant to "differently abled."

Deviance and Inequality

Some sociologists argue that deviance is not solely a product of "bad" people or "wrong" behaviors but also of the bad, wrong, and/or unfair social conditions of people's lives. What is labeled as deviant is applied differently to different people. The powerful and the privileged escape the label and the punishment. Therefore, deviance in itself is the product of social inequality.

In a groundbreaking article entitled "Nuts, Sluts, and Perverts: The Poverty of the Sociology of Deviance" (1972), Alexander Liazos noted that the people commonly labeled deviant are always powerless. Why? The answer is not simply that the rich and powerful make the rules to begin with or that they have the resources to avoid being labeled deviant. The answer lies in the fact that those who have the power can make us believe that the rules are "natural" and "good" to mask their political agenda. They can then label actors and acts deviant to justify inequalities in gender, sexual orientation, race, ethnicity, and social class (Daly, 1989; Daly and Chesney-Lind, 1988; Goode, 2005; Hagan and Peterson, 1995; Lang, 2002).

In a classic study of a suburban high school, there were two "gangs" of boys, what the researcher called the "Saints" and the "Roughnecks." The Roughnecks were working-class boys, who were in the vocational track and not college bound. Teachers thought of them as deviant, and they wore clothing styles like those in the movie *Grease*—black leather jackets, jeans, and white T-shirts. They were known to commit petty crimes and were called "hooligans" by the school administrators. The "Saints," by contrast, were middle-class boys, and they dressed the part—crew cuts, button-down "preppy" shirts, and penny loafers. They played sports, were popular, and were headed for college. They also spent their weekends breaking into people's homes and committing serious burglaries. But they were not considered deviant because they were "wholesome" and middle class (Chambliss, 2000).

Ironically, the relationship of inequality and deviance often leads us to see and punish the behaviors of the less fortunate and forgive the behavior of the more fortunate. From this perspective, it is more likely that a poor person who stole a few dollars from a company would end up in jail than a CEO who steals millions of dollars from millions of shareholders.

Deviance and Crime

Most theories of deviance also apply to crime, which is simply a legally regulated form of extreme deviance. Crime can be defined as any act that violates a formal normative code that has been enacted by a legally constituted body. Simple violation of a more or folkway may not be a crime, unless you violate a formal code. Likewise, you can commit a crime (actually break a law) and not be seen as deviant if other people see your act as acceptable. Sometimes, people commit crimes and are seen as heroes, like Robin Hood.

Some crimes are defined by being bad in and of themselves—bad because they violate formal group norms—like homicide, rape, or assault. Other crimes are not as obvious violations of group norms and are considered bad mostly because they have been prohibited. In some cultures or contexts they might not be crimes at all, but because they are illegal, they are crimes.

For example, smoking marijuana is illegal in the United States, yet public opinion polls show many Americans don't see it as "bad" at all times and favor its legal use for medical purposes. Internationally, some countries, including Japan, Thailand, and Hondoras, maintain strict laws against pot use for any reason, while others, have more relaxed attitudes about pot use, especially for medical purposes. In the Netherlands, pharmacies have been legally obliged to stock and dispense medical marijuana since 2003.

The efforts to control and punish crime have become so extensive and the institutions that have developed—prisons, courts, police, to name a few—so large, that the

Religious observance, medical therapy or crime? Different cultural groups construct some behaviors differently, as these participants at a pot festival might attest. But who gets to decide if they go to jail? ▼

study of crime, criminology, has developed into a subdiscipline separate from the sociology of deviance, with its own special theories about the causes and consequences of different kinds of crime.

What causes crime?

Strain Theory

Robert K. Merton (1957) argued that while some deviance benefits society, some deviance also puts an enormous *strain* on social life. He argued that excessive deviance is a by-product of inequality. When a society promotes certain goals but provides unequal means of acquiring them, the result is anomie, a conflict between accepted norms and social reality. This is called **strain theory.**

For instance, in the United States, and to some degree in all industrialized societies, we promote the *goal* of financial success and claim that it can be achieved through the *means* of self-discipline and hard work. But these qualities will lead to financial success only when channeled through a prestigious education or network of prestigious social contacts, advantages that many people do not have. They will therefore feel pressured to use alternative *means,* legitimate or illegitimate, to reach the goal (Merton, 1967).

According to Merton, there are five potential reactions to the tension between widely endorsed values and limited means of achieving them:

1. *Conformists* accept both the means and the values, whether they achieve the goal or not. They may not achieve financial success, but they will still believe that it is important and that self-discipline and hard work are appropriate means of achieving it. Most people are conformists.

2. *Innovators* accept the values but reject the means. They believe that financial success is an important goal but not that self-discipline and hard work are effective means of achieving it. Instead, they seek out new means to financial success. They may try to win the lottery, or they may become con artists or thieves.

3. *Ritualists* accept the means but reject the values. They follow rules for their own sake, conforming to standards even though they have lost sight of the values behind them. They will work hard but have no aspirations to financial success.

4. *Rebels* reject both the means and the values and substitute new ones. Instead of financial success, for instance, they may value the goal of spiritual fulfillment, to be achieved not through hard work but through quiet contemplation.

5. *Retreatists* reject both the means and the values and replace them with nothing. They do not accept the value of working hard, and they have not devised any alternative means. They have no aspirations to financial success, or any alternative goal, such as spiritual or artistic fulfillment.

Critics of strain theory point out that not everyone shares the same goals, even in the most homogeneous society. There are always many potential goals, conflicting and sometimes contradictory. And while strain theory may adequately explain some white-collar crime, such as juggling the books at work, and some property crimes, such as stealing a television set, it is less effective when explaining those crimes that lack an immediate financial motive.

Broken Windows Theory

Social psychologist Philip Zimbardo (1969) proposed the **broken windows theory** to explain how social controls can systematically weaken, and minor acts of deviance can spiral into severe crime and social decay. He placed cars without license plates and with their hoods up, but otherwise in good condition, in two different social settings, one in wealthy, mostly white Palo Alto, California (the home of Stanford University, where he worked), and the other in a poor, mostly black neighborhood in the Bronx, in New York City. The social class and race of passersby made no difference: In both sites, cars were quickly gutted. One person would conclude that the car was abandoned and "no one cared," and break a side window. The next person would see the side window broken and feel it was acceptable to smash the windshield.

The pattern would continue and escalate from there. Zimbardo concluded that breaking more windows, committing more serious crimes and acts of deviance, is a rational response to situations of social disorder. Later, James Q. Wilson (1985) expanded this thesis to conclude that community characteristics, such as decayed housing, preexisting crime, and the like, contributed to increased crime. Crime rates go up, he argued, in blighted areas where people think no one cares and no one is watching.

The societal response has been proactive: policing directed at maintaining public order. However, the flaw is that the police are left to identify "social disorder" however they want. Without more systematic definition, police can see almost anything as a sign of social disorder and almost anyone as a threat.

Criminal Subcultures

In 1955, juvenile delinquency was getting a lot of publicity in the United States. Albert Cohen wondered why young people, mostly working-class and poor boys, were spurning the values of the dominant society and committing so many crimes. After studying working-class and poor youth gangs, he concluded that strain theory wouldn't work: As lower-class youths, they had the least opportunity to achieve economic success, but their crimes were usually not economically motivated. They were not trying to get rich (1955).

Cohen drew upon Edward Sutherland's theory of differential association (which we discussed earlier in the chapter) to propose that the gang members were not being socialized with the same norms and values as lower class non–gang members or the middle class. They were being subjected to differential association, socialized into a new set of norms and values that allowed them to succeed on their own terms. Cohen listed their five most important values as:

1. *Nonutilitarianism.* They had no economic motive, or any other sort of motive, for committing their crimes. They committed crimes "for the hell of it."

2. *Maliciousness.* They valued being just plain mean. The meaner gang members enjoyed considerable prestige, and the "nice" ones were deviant.

3. *Negativism.* They were aware of the norms of the dominant culture and valued doing the exact opposite. If the dominant culture disapproved of smoking, they smoked.

4. *Short-run hedonism.* They valued getting immediate gratification and disapproved of members who waited patiently, saved their money, and so on.

5. *Group autonomy.* They defied or ignored authority figures. Even within the gang, the leaders had little power. They resisted any attempt to control their behavior, except as imposed informally by gang members acting as a group.

Walter B. Miller (1970) agreed, but he argued that it is not just lower-class boys in gangs whose norms and values differ from those of the dominant society; it's the entire lower class. In other words, behavior that the main society might consider deviant actually reflects the social norms of the lower-class *subculture*. They have six core values that differ from those of the main society:

1. *Trouble.* The subculture has trouble, chronic and unsolvable: for men, fights; for women, pregnancy. They value ways of avoiding or getting out of it.

2. *Toughness.* People in the subculture are constantly facing the challenges of fights or physical deprivation, and they value physical prowess, bravery, stoicism.

3. *Smartness.* The subculture does not value "book smarts," intellectual knowledge about the world. But it values "street smarts," the ability to avoid being duped, outwitted, and conned and to successfully dupe, outwit, and con others.

4. *Excitement.* The subculture values looking for thrills, flirting with danger, risk taking.

5. *Fate.* In the dominant culture, people believe that they are responsible for their own destiny. In the subculture, people value the idea that most of their everyday activities are determined by forces beyond their control.

6. *Autonomy.* Although their fate is determined by forces beyond their control, the members of the lower-class subculture resist authority figures much more often and vigorously than members of the dominant culture. The police are the enemy. Social workers, case workers, and sociologists asking questions have a shady hidden agenda.

Miller implied, therefore, that lower-class culture was conducive to crime, despite the overwhelming number of lower-class people who are law-abiding, decent citizens and the many upper-class people who reverse Robin Hood's ethic and rob from the poor to give to themselves.

Cohen's and Miller's theories of crime rely on the public outcry about juvenile delinquency in the 1950s. Today, sociologists find this work less compelling in an era of organized gangs of lower-class males, whose motivations may be far more rational than malicious pleasure and group cohesion.

Opportunity Theory

Richard Cloward and Lloyd Ohlin (1960) argued that crime actually arises from opportunity to commit crime. **Opportunity theory** holds that those who have many opportunities—and good ones at that—will be more likely to commit crimes than those with few good opportunities. They agreed, with Merton, that those who don't have equal access to acceptable means to achieve material success may experience strain, but that doesn't explain why most poor people are not criminals. In fact, studies show that most are "conformists," with the same values and goals as the dominant society.

Cloward and Ohlin emphasized *learning*—people have to learn how to carry out particular forms of deviance, and they must have the opportunity to actually deviate.

They revised differential association theory to propose several different types of deviant subcultures based on the opportunities to deviate:

1. In stable neighborhoods where most people know each other throughout their lives, *criminal subcultures* develop, devoted to such activities as burglary and theft. Young men can rely on social contacts with experienced older men to learn the roles of being a criminal, and the older men in turn can depend on the availability of younger protégés as they go to prison or retire.

2. In unstable neighborhoods where people are constantly moving in and out, there are few opportunities to learn about burglarly and theft, and boys who are mostly strangers to each other must find some way to establish dominance. They develop *violence subcultures,* gaining tough reputations through fighting and assaults.

3. In neighborhoods too disorganized for either crime or violence to succeed, people withdraw from society altogether through the use of alcohol and drugs. They develop *retreatist* subcultures.

These are not necessarily exclusive groups. A gang that may start out as part of a violent subculture in an unstable neighborhood may become a criminal subculture as the members become involved in more stable criminal activities like protection rackets and drug trafficking and begin recruiting younger members.

Some aspects of opportunity theory have been confirmed by subsequent research (Allan and Steffensmeier, 1989; Uggen, 1999). But as with many typologies, the theory ignores the interrelation of types of crime: Drug dealers and users often depend on property crime to finance their drug use and violence for territorial defense; violence often occurs in tandem with property crime. Also, the theory defines deviance in a way that targets poor people—if we include white-collar crimes like stock fraud, neighborhood dynamics become much less significant.

Conflict Theory

We may condemn the unequal application of the law, but we give little thought to whether the laws themselves are inherently unfair. Conflict theories of crime resemble inequality theories of deviance—they rest on a larger structural analysis of inequalities based on class, or race, or gender for their explanation of crime. Richard Quinney (1977) argued that the dominant class produces deviance by making and enforcing laws that protect its own interest and oppress the subordinate class. Law becomes an instrument of oppression, designed to maintain the powerful in their privileged position (Chambliss, 1999). It's not simply that basically neutral and equal laws are applied unequally, meaning that poor people get longer and harsher sentences when they commit the same crimes as upper-class people. That's true. But it's also that the laws themselves are designed to make sure that the rich stay rich and the poor stay poor.

When I was in college, a student who lived in my dorm was arrested very early one morning for stealing some fresh-baked bread that had been delivered to a local grocery store. (The bread was baked by a local bakery, and then left on the steps of the store at around 4 a.m. to wait for the owner to arrive to open the store.) When he was arraigned, the local magistrate looked at him sternly. "I assume this is a fraternity prank," the magistrate said, "and so I'm going to let you go with a warning. If this had been a real crime, if you had really needed the bread, you'd be going to jail for 10 years for theft."

Types of Crimes

There are many different types of crimes. Some are crimes against other people; others are crimes against property. They are handled differently by the police, courts, and penal system, depending on how serious the society believes the crime to be. In the United States, crimes against people are almost always heard in criminal court, while crimes against property may be heard in criminal or civil courts.

Sociologists study all types of crimes, from crimes against other people, like homicide, assault, and rape, to crimes against property, like burglary, motor vehicle theft, and arson. **Violent crime** consists of four offenses, according to the FBI's definitions: murder and nonnegligent manslaughter, forcible rape, robbery, and aggravated assault. **Property crime** includes offenses like burglary and motor vehicle theft, where the object is the taking of money or property, but there is no force or threat of force against the victims (Figure 6.1).

Crime at Work

Theft at work, whether simply pocketing office supplies or exercising the "100% employee discount" at the department store, costs U.S. employers nearly $20 billion a year (National Retail Federation, 2007). But there are many other crimes that you can commit at work, using the authority of your position, with the direct or indirect consent of the boss. In 1940, Edwin Sutherland introduced the term **white-collar crime** for the illegal actions of a corporation or people acting on its behalf (Sutherland, 1940).

Some white-collar crimes are **consumer crimes** such as credit card fraud, in which the criminal uses a fake or stolen credit card to buy things for him- or herself or for resale. Such purchases cost both retailers and, increasingly, "e-tailers" over $1 billion per year, or nearly 5 cents for every dollar spent online (Berner and Carter, 2005).

White-collar criminals might commit **occupational crime**, using their professional position to illegally secure something of value for themselves or the corporation. Some of the more common occupational crimes include income tax evasion, stock manipulation, bribery, and embezzlement. Media entrepreneur Martha Stewart went to prison for insider trading when she used her fame to find out that a company whose stock she owned was about to suffer a significant setback; she sold her stock the day before its price collapsed. (She claimed it was a coincidence.) Periodically, a famous Wall Street tycoon will be arrested for manipulating stocks or fraudulently reporting distorted earnings.

Or they might commit **organizational crime**, illegal actions committed in accordance with the operative goals of an organization. Some of the more common organizational crimes are stock manipulation, antitrust violations, false advertising, and price fixing. Periodically, some corporate whistle-blower notices the remarkable coincidence that all the gasoline companies charge about the same amount for their gas, despite the fact that they are supposed to be competing with each other. In 2002, several corporations, including Enron and WorldCom, went bankrupt when they revealed they had manipulated their records to boost the stock prices. Some of the executives of the companies floated to financial safety through a "golden parachute" of hundreds of millions of dollars; their employees, who often took raises and bonuses in stock options, lost everything.

Such high-profile arrests for white-collar crime may provide the rest of us with the illusion that the system works, that criminals always get caught, and that

Did you know?

When women commit fraud, they are most likely to cheat banks through bad credit cards or loans or the government by garnering benefits to which they aren't entitled. Crimes such as advertising fraud or insider trading are almost exclusively committed by men—because they still have far greater access to the high-level jobs that offer opportunities to commit such crimes (Daly, 1989).

FIGURE 6.1 Selected Types of Violent Crimes, and Property Crimes, in the United States, 1986–2005

¹ The murder and nonnegligent homicides that occurred as a result of the events of September 11, 2001, are not included in this table.

² The 2004 crime figures have been adjusted.

Source: Crime in the United States, U.S. Department of Justice, 2005.

the "little guy" can beat the corporations. In fact, these high-profile cases are rare. And it is exceptionally rare for corporate violators to ever spend a day in jail (Hagan and Parker, 1985; Sasseen, 2006). The convictions of Enron's top executives were notable because they broke precedent rather than sustained it.

The cost of white-collar crime is substantial—$400 billion per year in the United States, which is far more than the "paltry" $15 billion for "regular" street crime (Livingston, 1992; Zeune, 2001). And of course, corporate officers or their agents are breaking the law, and they can be subject to criminal prosecution. Yet most cases of white-collar crime go unpunished. Many white-collar crimes are settled out of court and never become part of the public record.

In rare cases when white-collar criminals are charged and convicted, odds are almost 50-50 that they will not go to jail. White-collar offenders are more likely to receive fines than prison sentences. Amitai Etzioni (1990) found that in 43 percent of incidents, either no penalty was imposed or the company was required merely to cease engaging in the illegal practice and return any funds gained through illegal means. Even if they do go to jail, white-collar criminals are typically sentenced to terms averaging less than 3 years (Pizzo and Muolo, 1994).

Cybercrime

Cybercrime—the use of the Internet and World Wide Web to commit crime—is a relatively new form of crime. Some of these crimes involve fraudulent maneuvers to get victims to reveal personal information that can then be used to commit crimes; others involve theft of cyber-identities. Some cybercrime is simply the adaptation of old crimes to new technology—the fraudulent messages, called *phishes,* designed to get you to part with credit card information or to make bogus purchases, are simply the latest version of an old telephone scam that preyed especially on retirees.

For example, I often bid on items online through eBay, and when I win, I pay with PayPal, a service that transfers the money directly from my checking account to the seller's. No checkbook, no stamps, no envelopes, and my item is shipped immediately. One day I received an e-mail receipt from PayPal indicating that I had paid $248 for a Myst game! I never bought a Myst game. At the bottom of the e-mail was a link to the PayPal security center.

Yeah, right. I typed in the PayPal address manually, and there was no payment for a Myst game. The e-mail was a fraud—a phish—and the perpetrator was hoping that I would be so dismayed that I would click on the link immediately, whereupon all of the personal information stored on my computer would be uploaded into the hands of some cyber-criminal. Virtually every university student and employee gets these messages. Sometimes they purport to come from the University Computer Center, or from people I know—actually they're from address books copied by Trojan horse viruses.

The rise of personal computers and the Internet have made some criminal activities, such as money laundering and fraud, easier, and it has spawned a whole new field of crime. Internet-based crime is the fastest growing category of crime in the United States. The year 2006 marked the seventh year in a row that identity theft topped the list of consumer complaints with the U.S. Federal Trade Commission, accounting for 36 percent of the total (Federal Trade Commission, 2007). An estimated 8.3 million Americans were victimized by consumer fraud and identity theft, at a cost of $1.1 billion. Much of the victimization occurs when people willingly give out the information, either believing they are about to receive a massive windfall of cash or that they've already paid that $248 for a Myst game, so they panic and "click here immediately."

But hackers are often responsible. Hackers have tapped into customer information as well as proprietary company information stored online by credit bureaus, marketing agencies, banks, credit card companies, and other financial services firms. Of the top global financial services organizations, 83 percent had some kind of hacker attack on their computer information systems in 2004, up 39 percent over a year earlier (Deloitte Global Security Survey, 2004). By 2005, the number of security breaches

▲ In 2006, Kenneth Lay, CEO of Enron Corporation, was found guilty of 11 counts of securities fraud in a corruption scandal that bankrupted the company, costing 20,000 people their jobs and many of them their life savings. Investors lost billions.

TABLE 6.1

Computer Crimes, 2005

INCIDENT	DOLLAR COST
Virus	$42,787,767
Unauthorized access	$31,233,100
Theft of proprietary information	$30,933,000
Denial of service	$7,310,725
Insider Net abuse	$6,856,450
Laptop theft	$4,107,300
Financial fraud	$2,565,000
Misuse of public Web application	$2,227,500
System penetration	$841,400
Abuse of wireless network	$544,700
Sabotage	$340,600
Telecom fraud	$242,000
Web site defacement	$115,000

Source: CSI/FBI Computer Crime Security Survey, 2005.

fell to 30 percent due to government attention and company actions (Deloitte Global Security Survey, 2005). Forty-three percent of these intrusions go unreported because private companies fear undermining the confidence of their customers and shareholders (Computer Crime and Security Survey, 2005). (Table 6.1).

There can be considerable variation in the types and dollar costs of computer crime from year to year. In 2003, for example, theft of proprietary information was the top hacker target, which accounted for losses of over $70 million (Computer Crime and Security Survey, 2003).

Hate Crime

A **hate crime** is a criminal act committed by an offender motivated by bias against race, ethnicity, religion, sexual orientation, or disability status. Anyone can commit a hate crime, but perpetrators usually belong to dominant groups (white, Christian, straight) and victims to disenfranchised groups (black, Jewish, Muslim, or gay). The FBI records over 7,000 hate crimes per year, but because state and local law enforcement agencies differ in their reporting procedures, and some do not report at all, this number is no doubt extremely low. Bias based on race seems to be the largest motivating factor in hate crimes (51 percent of cases), followed by religion (18 percent), sexual orientation (16.5 percent), ethnicity (14 percent), and disability (less than 1 percent).

Legislators approve of hate crime legislation sometimes and disapprove at other times. In 2001, 43 states increased their penalties for hate crimes. However, in October 2004, leadership in House of Representatives stripped language that would have expanded current federal hate crime protection from a defense bill, the Local Law Enforcement Enhancement Act, after it was approved in Congress.

Advocates of these laws argue that hate crimes affect not only the individual but the entire community, so they should be punished more harshly than ordinary crime. The lynchings in the American South were used not only to victimize an individual but to terrorize the entire Black population, and contemporary antigay hate crimes are not meant to express hatred of a single gay person but to demonstrate to all gay people that they are unwelcome and unsafe in the community.

But opponents of these laws argue that they punish attitudes, not actions. Why does the motivation of a crime matter? If I am planning to commit a robbery, I may select a gay man, believing the stereotype that he is fragile and weak and therefore unlikely to resist. My prejudice didn't motivate the crime, merely my choice of an appropriate victim.

Crime in the United States

In 2005, the violent crime rate in the United States was 21 victims per 1,000 people, and the property crime rate was 154 victims per 1,000 people, according to the Justice Department. While these statistics are considerably lower than they were 30 years ago, the United States still has higher crime rates than many other countries in the world: It ranks third in drug offenses per capita, fifth in assaults, eighth in murders with firearms, ninth in rape, eleventh in robberies, and sixteenth in burglaries.

When compared with most other advanced countries, the United States stands out for its very high homicide rates (Van Kesteren, Mayhew, and Nieuwbeerta, 2000; Kurki, 1997). With six murders for every 100,000 people, the rate of lethal violence in America is nearly five times higher than that of France, Germany, or England (van Kesteren, Mayhew, and Nieuwbeerta, 2000; Wacquant, 2006; Zimring and Hawkins, 1997).

What social factors explain our rates of crime? And why would we feel so safe, considering that our violent crime rate is so high?

Sociologists have considered three explanations:

1. American culture emphasizes on individual economic success as *the* measure of self-worth, at the expense of family, neighborhood, artistic accomplishment, and spiritual well-being (Currie, 1985).

2. Not everyone has a high standard of living. The United States has one of the largest income differentials in the world. When the gap begins to shrink, as it did during Clinton-era prosperity, the crime rate declines (Martens, 2005).

3. Guns—that is, the easy availability of guns and the lax enforcement of loose gun control measures, coupled with an American value system that places gun ownership as a sacred right—are a contributor to the crime rate.

Despite the fact that our overall crimes rates are higher than some other advanced countries, such as Ireland and Austria, and our outsize homicide rate distinguishes the United States from all of Western Europe (Wacquant, 2006), it is also true that crime rates in the United States have been falling. The National Crime Victimization Survey (2005), which addresses victims of crime (and therefore leaves out murder), reports that the violent crime rate has dropped by 58 percent and the property crime rate has dropped by 52 percent since 1973. Violent crime dropped 14 percent in just *two years*, between 2001 and 2003, and stayed the same between 2004 and 2005 (U.S. Department of Justice, 2005). (Figure 6.2).

So sociologists have to ask two questions: Why are some of our crime rates so high? And why should the crime rate be falling? Research by sociologists and

How do we know what we know?

Abortion and the Crime Rate

Did the legalization of abortion cause the decline of crime? In the book *Freakonomics* (2005), economist Steven Levitt and journalist Stephen Dubner suggest the controversial idea that the legalization of abortion in 1973 meant that far fewer unwanted children were born, and that these children would have had few economic opportunities and lower levels of education and employ-ment. They would have become adults in the mid-1990s—which is exactly when the crime rate began to decline. Thus, many would-be criminals—those with the demographic "profile" of criminals—were never born. Some disagree with their calculations (Foote and Goetz, 2005).

This is a marvelous example of what sociologists call a specious correlation. Sure, the two variables may be correlated, but there are so many intervening variables, not to mention 20 years of other factors that might have influenced things, that one cannot possibly say with any certainty that this one variable caused another. For one thing, how do we know that the fetuses that were aborted were more likely to be criminals? Or that the legalization of abortion was not also connected to a larger set of social and economic reforms that reduced the crime rate? Do you think, perhaps, that all the recent efforts to make abortions more difficult will result in a dramatic increase in crime 20 years from now? I doubt it.

FIGURE 6.2 Violent Crime Offense: A Five-Year Trend

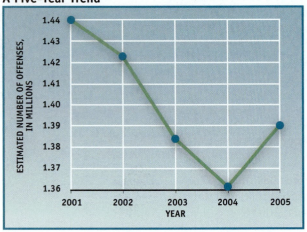

Source: Crime in the United States, U.S. Department of Justice, 2005.

criminologists has identified a legion of factors that contributed to the drop in crime, including:

- An expanding economy (and thus more legitimate opportunities for employment)
- An aging population (more older people means crime rate goes down)
- An increase in the number of police officers
- A decrease in the number of young males in their late teens and early 20s
- Longer jail sentences for hard-core criminals
- Declining sales of crack cocaine and the violence associated with the drug trade
- An increase in immigration by females, especially from Russia and China
- The legalization of abortion
- The "little-brother syndrome" by which younger boys did not grow up to become criminals after witnessing what happened to their older mentors (Bourgois, 1995; Fox, 2000; Freeman, 2000; Greene, 1999; Jackall, 1997; Kelling and Souza, 2001; Wacquant, 2006)

The decline of these "little brothers" is pronounced. During the 1980s, a great deal of violent crime was concentrated in inner-city neighborhoods. Studies find that in some of those areas, significant numbers of young boys saw the consequences of older boys' actions and opted not to follow in their footsteps to prisons or graveyards. Crime rates came down when the younger boys reached the peak age for involvement in crimes (Blumstein and Wallman, 2000; Glassner, 1999; Wacquant, 2006).

Crime and Guns

The United States has the weakest laws on handgun ownership in the industrialized world. As a result, there are as many guns as there are people, and it shows in crime statistics. Four million Americans carry a gun on a daily basis. Half of all U.S. households have a gun at home (Wacquant, 2006). Nearly 70 percent of murders, 42 percent of robberies, and 20 percent of aggravated assaults are committed with guns (U.S. Department of Justice, 2005).

Globally, the United States ranks in the middle of all countries' rates of deaths by guns (Figure 6.3). But no other industrialized country comes close to the U.S.; indeed our rate is nearly double that of our nearest 'rival.' The United States has had difficulty passing minimal regulations to monitor the distribution of guns. Federal efforts to institute simple safeguards such as criminal background checks on prospective gun owners have met with fierce opposition from gun lobbyists. Many efforts—such as attempts to block convicted criminals from obtaining guns or to revoke the licenses of gun dealers who break the law—remain under attack by gun advocates. In fact, since approximately 2000, some of the scattered state laws that had been in effect for a decade or more have been weakened or repealed, particularly in the South (Hemenway, 2005). For example, although criminologists have shown that limiting volume purchases of handguns is effective at stemming illegal gun trafficking, South Carolina abolished a one-per-month purchase rule in 2004 that had been in place for nearly 30 years. That same year, the state of Virginia weakened a similar law that had been on the books since 1993 (Wirzbicki, 2005). Despite stupendous rates of violent crime involving guns, America has seen a general relaxing of gun regulation so far in the twenty-first century (Hemenway, 2005).

FIGURE 6.3 Guns: The Global Death Toll

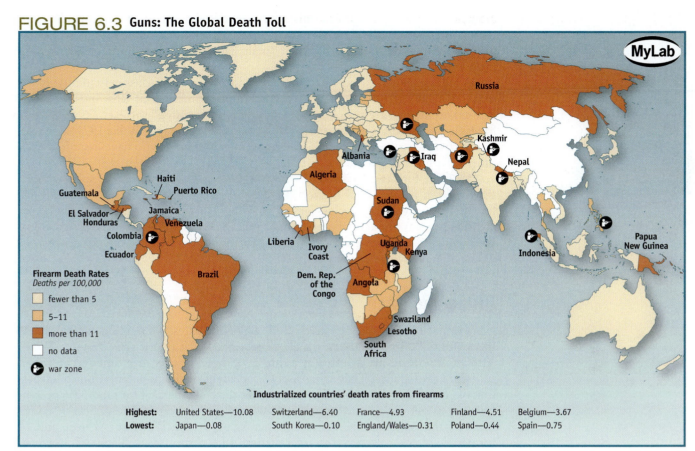

Firearm Death Rates
Deaths per 100,000

- fewer than 5
- 5–11
- more than 11
- no data
- war zone

Industrialized countries' death rates from firearms

Highest:	United States—10.08	Switzerland—6.40	France—4.93	Finland—4.51	Belgium—3.67
Lowest:	Japan—0.08	South Korea—0.10	England/Wales—0.31	Poland—0.44	Spain—0.75

Source: Newsweek, April 30, 2007.

Crime and Gender

When looking at crime statistics, we are often astonished by the gender gap. In the United States in 2003, only 23 percent of people arrested for all crimes were women. The gender gap narrowed only in three white-collar crimes—forgery, fraud, and embezzlement—and women outranked men in prostitution and runaways. Otherwise, women were significantly less likely to be arrested, less likely to be convicted, and less likely to serve sentences. And yet the United States has the largest female arrest and conviction rate in the world: 8.54 per 1,000, nearly double the United Kingdom and four times higher than Canada (Justice Policy Institute, 2005; Schaffner, 2006). Nonetheless, when we say *crime,* we might as well say *male.*

The gender gap may be influenced by the "chivalry effect": police, judges, and juries are likely to perceive women as less dangerous and their criminal activities less consequential, so they are more often let go with a warning (Pollak, 1978). Women who belong to stigmatized groups, who are Black, Hispanic, or lesbian, are more likely to be arrested and convicted, perhaps because they are not granted the same status as women in the mainstream. Feminists note that women receive harsher treatment when their behavior deviates from feminine stereotypes, that is, when they "act like a man" (Edwards, 1986).

But even when we take the chivalry effect into account, men still commit more violent crimes and property crimes than women. Some criminologists argue that biologically, males are a lot more aggressive and violent, and that explains the high levels of assaults and other violent crimes. However, this biological theory does not explain why crime (or at least criminal arrests) occur primarily in working-class and poor communities. Middle-class men have testosterone, too; shouldn't they be committing assault and murder? Nor can "male aggression" explain the gender gap in property crime.

A more sociological explanation is the model of working-class masculinity: In the working-class and poor subcultures where most crimes (or at least most criminal arrests) occur, men are socialized to believe that "defending" themselves, violently if necessary, is appropriate masculine behavior (see, for example, Willis 1977). On television, *Judge Joe Brown* is quite lenient on men and boys who have assaulted each other: "Part of being a man is learning how to fight," he intones.

Men are further socialized to believe that they must provide the sole financial support in a heterosexual household. Judge Joe Brown is constantly berating his litigants (mostly working class or poor) when a man allows his mother, wife, or girlfriend to pay some of the household bills: "Be a man!" he yells. "Take care of your women!" And when no legitimate opportunity is available, "taking care of your women" may involve property crime.

Crime and Race

If we were to judge solely by arrest and conviction rates, we might conclude that if the gender of crime is male, the race of crime is Black (Pettit and Western, 2004). African Americans are arrested at a rate two, three, or even five times greater than statistical probability: They comprise 12.5 percent of the population but 54.5 percent of arrests for robbery, 48.5 percent for murder, 33.3 percent for rape, 32.6 percent for drug use. And they are considerably more likely to become the victims of crime. In 2003, the violent crime rate was 29 per 1,000 for Blacks, 22 for Whites, and 16 for people of other races. Of murder victims 48.6 percent were Black, 47.3 percent White, and 4.1 percent other races or unknown (U.S. Department of Justice, 2005) (Table 6.2).

Black overrepresentation does not happen only in America. In the United Kingdom, Blacks are three times more likely than Whites or Asians to be arrested. In Britain, however, Blacks and Whites are equally likely to be crime victims, and it is Asians who face a significantly higher risk (*Home Office*, 2004).

But it isn't just African Americans; Latinos are overrepresented in the U.S. criminal justice system as well. While Latinos make up about 13 percent of the U.S. population, they are 31 percent of those incarcerated in the federal system. Latino defendants are imprisoned three times as often as Whites and are detained before trial for first-time offenses almost twice as often as Whites, despite the fact that they are the least likely of all ethnic groups to have a criminal history (Walker, et al., 2004). They are also disproportionately charged with nonviolent drug offenses and represent the vast majority of those arrested for immigration violations (HRW, 2002; National Council of La Raza, 2004; Weich and Angulo, 2000).

What is the link between crime and race? Each of the theories we have discussed in this chapter offers a perspective on this issue:

1. *Strain theory*. It's really a matter of social class, not race. Most Blacks are poor, and poor people living amidst affluence are more likely to perceive society as unjust and turn to crime (Anderson, 1994; Blau and Blau, 1982). This theory fails to

TABLE 6.2

Percentage of Arrestees Who Were Black, 2005	
OFFENSE	PERCENTAGE
Gambling	71.1%
Robbery	56.3%
Murder	48.6%
Rape	32.7%
Burglary	28.5%
Drug offenses	33.9%
Vagrancy	38.4%
Loitering	35.5%
Disorderly conduct	33.6%

Blacks represent 12% of the U.S. population.
Source: Crime in the United States, U.S. Department of Justice, 2005.

Sociology and our World

"DWB"

The perceived connection between race and crime is often painful to those who are targeted. African Americans sometimes refer to the phenomenon of being constantly stopped by the police as "DWB"— "driving while Black." Studies of traffic stops have found that while 5 percent of the drivers on Florida highways were Black or Latino, nearly 70 percent of those stopped and 80 percent of those searched were Black or Latino.

A study in Maryland found that although Blacks were 17 percent of the motorists on one freeway, they were also 73 percent of those stopped and searched. A study in Philadelphia found that 75 percent of the motorists were White and 80 percent of those stopped were minorities (Cannon, 1999; Cole, 1999). Stopping and searching minorities is a form of "racial profiling" in which members of minority groups are seen as "more likely" to be criminals and therefore stopped more often. It's more a self-fulfilling prophecy: Believing is seeing.

---

take into account the fact that even within the lower classes, Blacks are significantly more likely to be arrested and sentenced than Whites.

2. *Differential opportunity.* Black children are much more likely to be raised by single mothers than are White children. They receive less supervision, so they turn to crime. But the vast majority of children raised by single parents (mostly mothers) do not turn to crime. No significant correlation has been found between growing up in single-parent households and juvenile or adult crime.

3. *Labeling.* Being Black is a master status, automatically labeled deviant, equated with violence and criminality. So people (Black or White) tend to view Black behavior as more threatening and report on it more often, police officers (Black or White) tend to arrest Blacks more often, and juries (Black or White) tend to give them stiffer sentences.

4. *Conflict.* The crime records omit fraud, income tax evasion, embezzlement, and other crimes that are more often committed by Whites, thus producing misleading statistics.

> ## Did *you* know?
>
> Latinos have a one in six chance of being incarcerated in their lifetime. Black men have a one in three chance. White men have a one in 17 chance of ever serving time (Bureau of Justice Statistics, 2003).

Crime and Age

When we say *crime*, we might also say *young.* Since the rise of the first adolescent subcultures in the 1940s, minors have been committing far more than their share of crimes. In 2000 and 2001, 15- to 24-year-olds constituted 14 percent of the U.S. population but 47 percent of arrests for property crime, and 39 percent of arrests for violent crime.

In search of explanations, many sociologists point to gang activity, which has infiltrated every aspect of community life. Also, because most of the youthful offenders are male, the culture of masculinity may also be at fault: A 15 year-old boy can hardly demonstrate his "masculine" toughness, aggression, and control through academic or artistic accomplishments. He can go out for sports, but in the inner city, school sports have substandard facilities and underpaid staff, and there are few private after-school programs. He proves his masculinity by violence and crime.

Certainly, there are female gangs, and crimes by young females have increased in recent decades. But even the phrase "prove your femininity" is hard to translate into a provocation to crime. And the data make it clear that crime is largely an activity of young males—and it has been for some time. Figures 6.4 and 6.5 show data on age and gender of homicide rates in two different places, England and Chicago, separated

FIGURE 6.4 Criminal Offenders by Age and Gender, England and Wales, 1842–1844

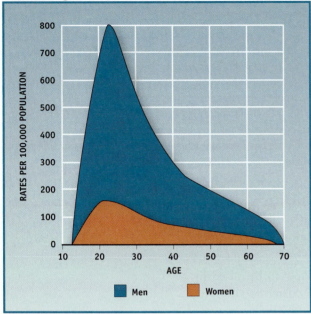

Source: Based on data from F.G. P. Neison, *Contributions to Vital Statistics . . .* , 3d ed. (London, 1857), 303–304, as plotted by Travis Hirschi and Michael Gottfredson, "Age and the Explanation of Crime," AJS 89 (1983): 556.

FIGURE 6.5 Homicide Rates by Age and Gender, Chicago, 1965–1990

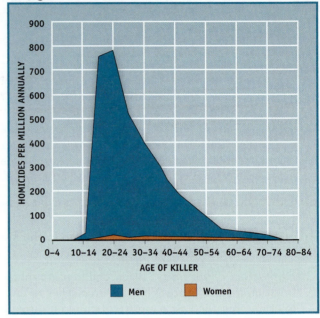

by more than a century—midnineteeth century to the late twentieth century. And yet the charts look very familiar—as they would virtually anywhere.

Just because other males are the most frequent victims of violent crimes doesn't mean that girls are not also vulnerable. They are. In 2005, according to the FBI, 2,053 boys under the age of 18 were arrested on charges of rape and sexual assault (9.5 percent of the total). Over 30 percent (632) were under the age of 15. There are over 1,000 treatment programs in the United States devoted solely to treating youthful sex offenders. Psychologists believe that these boys are still developing their notions of appropriate sexual behavior, so their preference for coercive and violent sexual activity is capable of change.

But college students are old enough to have already developed their sexual "scripts"—their cognitive map about how to have sex and with whom—and they sometimes exhibit a similar interest in sexual coercion. According to a 2003 Bureau of Justice Statistics study, rape is the most common violent crime at colleges and universities in the United States; 2.8 percent of college women experience either a completed rape or an attempted rape every year, most often by a male peer, boyfriend, or classmate (90 percent of college women know their assailants) (Bureau of Justice Statistics, 2003; Cole, 2006). Another 13 percent of college women have been stalked, as compared with 8 percent of women of all ages. Aggression and control seem still integral to hegemonic masculinity in young adulthood.

Crime and Class

Historically, those with less power in society—women, minorities, young people—have been more likely to be arrested. So, too, with class. The poorer you are, the more likely that you will be arrested for a crime. While the crime rate goes up as the person's socioeconomic status goes down, this may be caused less by economic deprivation—people stealing because they are hungry or don't have enough money to pay their rent—and more because their crimes are more visible and their "profile" is more likely to fit a criminal profile. When the poor rob the rich, it makes the papers; when the rich rob the poor, it's often called "business."

Equally, the poorer you are, the more likely you are to be the victim of crime. The wealthy are more insulated in their neighborhoods, better served by the police, and more likely to press charges in assaults.

The Criminal Justice System

"In the criminal justice system, there are two separate but equally important groups: the police who investigate crimes and the district attorneys who prosecute the offenders. These are their stories." So says the narrator at the beginning of each episode of *Law and Order,* the most successful crime series in television history.

It's mostly right. The criminal justice system is a complex of institutions that includes the police and the courts, a wide range of prosecuting and defense lawyers, and also the prison system.

Police

The number of police officers in the United States has roughly doubled over past 30 years. In 2005, there were nearly 582,000 full-time law enforcement employees in the United States, or about three for every 1,000 people (Crime in the United States, 2005; U.S. Department of Justice, 2005). This is more than most countries: France has 2.06, Japan 1.81, and Canada 1.73.

But police officers actually spend only about 20 percent of their time in crime-fighting activity. A surprising amount of their daily routine involves completing departmental paperwork: arrest and accident reports, patrol activity reports, and judicial statements. Their "on time" mostly involves routine public order activity and communicating information about risk control to other institutions in society (insurance companies, public health workers, social welfare agencies, and schools). Today the police have become "knowledge workers" as much as they are "crime fighters" (Ericson and Haggerty, 1997): They offer tips and techniques, such as "stay in well-lighted areas," but in the end you are responsible for your own safety.

The police have a split image. To some people, seeing a police officer on the street makes them feel safe and secure, as if no harm will come to them. To others, seeing that same police officer is a terrible threat, and they might feel that they are in danger of being arrested or killed simply for being there. Some people see the police as protection, others see them as an occupying army.

The police understand this dichotomy. In many cities, like Los Angeles, their motto is "to protect and to serve"—they want people to feel safe, and they want to be of service to those who feel threatened. The most important trends in police forces across the country have been to embed the police within the communities they serve; to encourage more minority police, especially in minority areas; and also to train new groups of female officers, especially to respond to complaints about domestic violence. Since the 1990s, the number of female and minority police officers has increased.

> Did *you* know?
>
> Americans say they feel safer than almost anyone in the world: 82 percent report that they feel safe walking after dark, second only to Sweden. Seventy-eight percent feel that they are not at risk or only slightly at risk for burglary, compared to 58 percent in the United Kingdom and 43 percent in France (U.N. International Crime Victim Survey, 2001).

"You look like this sketch of someone who's thinking about committing a crime."

Source: © The New Yorker Collection 2000. David Sipress from cartoonbank.com. All Rights Reserved. Reprinted by permission.

Minority representation among local police officers increased from 14.6 percent in 1987 to 23.6 percent in 2003. Women's representation increased from 9 percent in 1990 to 11.6 percent in 2005 (National Center for Women and Policing, 2002; U.S. Department of Justice, 2005).

Courts

The court system is an important arena of the criminal justice system. In criminal court, the district attorney's office prosecutes those arrested by the police for criminal offenses; the accused are defended in adversarial proceedings by a defense attorney. Thus, criminal proceedings pit the government (its agents, the police, lawyers, and the like) against a defendant, unlike civil courts in which the court is an arbiter of arguments between two individuals or groups. While the criminal courtroom drama is a staple of American movies and television, over 90 percent of criminal cases never go to trial. Instead, most are resolved by plea bargaining or pleading guilty to a lesser crime.

In the early 1990s, mandatory sentencing rules were enacted across the United States. These laws applied to about 64,000 defendants a year and required certain sentences for certain crimes, allowing no room for discretion. The laws were supposed to be tough on crime and eliminate bias in prosecutions and sentencing. However, the main result has been an explosion in the prison population. Bias remains in both arrests and prosecutions. Only under mandatory sentencing judges couldn't take circumstances—which could help the poor, minorities, mentally unstable, the sick or addicted—into account. In early 2005, the Supreme Court ruled that federal judges no longer must abide by the guidelines, saying they violated a defendant's right to a fair trial.

Punishment and Corrections

Today the United States has 2.2 million people in jail or prison, 7.1 per 1,000 people, many more than any country in the world (Figure 6.6). Russia is in second place, with 5.8. The United States has four times more prisoners than the world average, four to seven times more than other Western nations such as France, Germany, Italy, and the United Kingdom, and up to 32 times more than nations with the lowest rates, Nepal, Nigeria, and India (National Council on Crime and Delinquency, 2006). We imprison three times more people per capita than Iran, five times more than Tanzania, and seven times more than Germany. We also imprison at least three times more women than any other nation in the world (Hartney, 2006). And it's not because the United States has higher crime rates; with the single exception of incarceration rates in Russia for robbery, we lock up more people per incident than any other country in the world (National Council on Crime and Delinquency, 2006).

When we add the 4.8 million people on probation or parole, we come up with an amazing statistic: 3.2 percent of the adult American population is currently immersed somewhere in the criminal justice system. And the numbers are increasing dramatically (Figure 6.7). Since 1995, the number of people in jail has increased by an average of

4 percent per year, in prison 3.4 percent per year, and on probation 2.9 percent per year (Bureau of Justice Statistics; *New York Times*, 2004). The American prison system now employs well over half a million people and costs $57 billion a year to maintain (Bureau of Justice Statistics, 2003).

Prisons. People convicted of crimes may be asked to pay fines and restitution to victims or to engage in community service, but for most offenses, the main penalty is incarceration: jail or prison terms of up to 84 months for violent crimes, 48 months for drug crimes, and 41 months for property crimes (not including those rare instances when life in prison or the death penalty is imposed). But criminologists, lawgivers, and private individuals have often wondered *why*: What are the goals of incarceration, and are they being achieved? Four goals have been proposed (Goode, 2004; Siegel, 2000):

1. *Retribution.* People who break rules must be punished; they "owe a debt to society." Children who break their parents' rules are often grounded, temporarily losing their liberty and some of their privileges (the freedom to watch television or play video games, for instance). In the same way, adults who break laws can be effectively punished through the loss of their liberty and some of their citizenship privileges (the freedom to vote, sign contracts, take gainful employment, and so on).

    A problem with the retribution goal is that we believe that the punishment should fit the crime: The greater the degree of social harm, The worse the punishment. However, incarceration can only be extended, not worsened. Also, justice is not blind: Prison terms are longer for minorities than Whites, and for men than for women, even when both have been convicted of the same offense (Mustard, 2001).

2. *Deterrence.* Children may not understand or agree with the reasoning behind their parents' rules, but threat of grounding deters them from most rule breaking in the first place, and the memory of punishment is sufficient to hinder future rule breaking. In the same way, the threat of prison decreases the likelihood of a first offense, and the memory of prison is assumed to deter people from future crimes.

    But does it? Between 30 and 50 percent of people released from prison commit new crimes, often of the same sort that got them the prison sentence in the first place. Criminologists have found that fear of prison itself plays virtually no role in the decision-making process of either first-time or repeat offenders, although quality of life in prison can affect criminal behavior (Katz, Levitt, and Shustorovich, 2003). To people who belong to subcultures, prison is seen as an occupational hazard. Inside or out makes little difference in their social network, their norms and values, their goals, their problem-solving techniques, their social

FIGURE 6.6 Selected Comparative International Incarceration Rates, 2006

Country	Incarceration Rate
Nepal	28
India	31
Pakistan	57
Iraq	60
Japan	62
Sweden	78
Egypt	87
France	88
Turkey	91
Germany	95
South Korea	97
Italy	102
Canada	107
Philippines	108
China	118
Saudi Arabia	132
Zimbabwe	139
Spain	145
United Kingdom	145
Colombia	152
Lebanon	168
Brazil	191
Mexico	196
Iran	206
Libya	207
Israel	209
United Arab Emirates	250
Taiwan	259
South Africa	335
Botswana	339
Singapore	350
Ukraine	360
Cuba	487
Russian Federation	607
United States of America	738

INCARCERATION RATE
(PER 100,000 POPULATION)

Note: Rates, as opposed to actual prison population, allow for comparisons across time as populations change or across nations with different populations. Rates are calculated by dividing the prison population by the general population and multiplying by 100,000.
Source: National Council on Crime and Delinquency, 2006.

FIGURE 6.7 Incarceration Rates for Men in Federal and State Prisons, 1925–2005

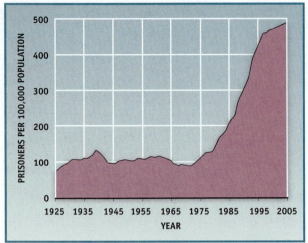

Source: From "NCCD Fact Sheet, U.S. Rates of incarceration: A Global Perspective" by Christopher Hartney, November 2006. Data from International Centre for Prison Studies, 2006. *World Prison Brief Online* version. London: University of London, Kings College London, International Centre for Prison Studies. Used by permission of National Council on Crime and Delinquency.

Did *you* know?

The American prison system has become partially privatized. That means that prisons are run like a business, with an eye toward profits. The more prisoners, the more profit. And the cheaper it is to house them—food, computers and television, libraries—the higher the profit. A large number of people now have a vested interest in making the prison system even bigger and perhaps also less "hospitable."

world. In some ways, inside is even preferable, offering regular meals and free medical care.

3. *Protection.* When we "take criminals off the streets," they will not be able to commit further crimes (at least, not on the streets), and society is protected.

However, only a few of the most violent criminals stay off the streets forever. The average time served in a county jail is 7 months, and in a state prison 2 years and 3 months. Many social scientists argue that during those months the criminals are in "crime school," with seasoned professionals teaching them how to commit more and better crimes (Califano, 1998).

4. *Rehabilitation.* Criminals lack the skills necessary to succeed (or even survive) in mainstream society. The National Literacy Survey of 16,000 inmates found that 63 percent were at the lowest levels of functional illiteracy. Less than half have high school diplomas or GEDs. So prison time can be used for rehabilitation. They can get drug and alcohol therapy, learn a trade, get their GED, and even take college classes. A four-year study conducted by the Department of Education found that inmates who participate in any education program are 23 percent less likely to be reincarcerated. A CUNY study at Bedford Hills Correctional Facility, New York's only maximum-security women's prison, found that prisoners who took college courses were over 60 percent less likely to return than those who did not (Clark, 1991).

But prisons actually offer few rehab programs, and those available are seriously understaffed and underfunded. Most prisoners do not receive counseling or drug and alcohol therapy, and budget cuts terminated almost all of the prison education programs in 1994. Those prisoners who do take classes often find that they have not acquired the skills for real-world jobs, nor have they received any training on how to find work.

The Death Penalty. In 1998, Estonia, Canada, and the United Kingdom abolished their death penalties. Malta followed in 2000 and Cyprus in 2002. In 2004, Bhutan, Samoa, Greece, Senegal, and Turkey joined the 99 countries worldwide that ban executions for all crimes (128 countries are abolitionist in practice, having not carried out an execution in 10 years or more) (Amnesty International, 2005). Fewer than half of the countries in the world (69) currently have death penalties—countries like Algeria, Benin, China, Mongolia, Thailand, and Uganda. There is none in the industrialized West. The European Union will not accept as a new member any country that has the death penalty.

This means the United States could not become a member of the EU. As of this writing, the death penalty exists in all but 12 of the states. In 2004, it was declared unconstitutional in Kansas and New York. That same year, the United States was fourth in the number of executions, after China, Iran, and Vietnam (Amnesty International, 2005).

What crimes are heinous enough deserve death? Most countries that have capital punishment invoke it only for extraordinary crimes (murder or war-related crimes),

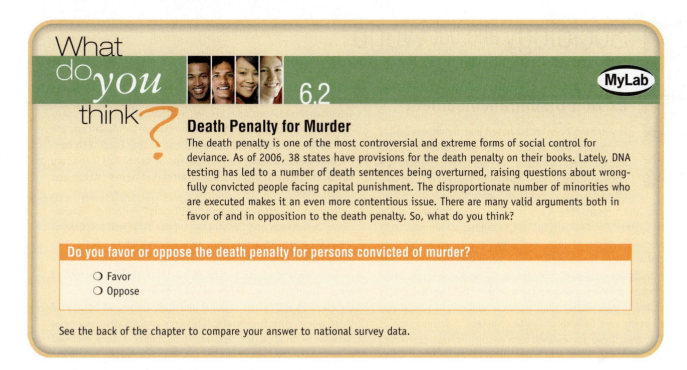

What do *you* think? 6.2

Death Penalty for Murder

The death penalty is one of the most controversial and extreme forms of social control for deviance. As of 2006, 38 states have provisions for the death penalty on their books. Lately, DNA testing has led to a number of death sentences being overturned, raising questions about wrongfully convicted people facing capital punishment. The disproportionate number of minorities who are executed makes it an even more contentious issue. There are many valid arguments both in favor of and in opposition to the death penalty. So, what do you think?

Do you favor or oppose the death penalty for persons convicted of murder?

○ Favor
○ Oppose

See the back of the chapter to compare your answer to national survey data.

while others, like China, Malaysia, Saudi Arabia, and Singapore, use it for some business and drug-related offenses. In the United States, it is usually invoked only in cases of murder and treason.

Who can be executed? In 1989, the Supreme Court decided that it was constitutional to execute John Paul Penry, a 44-year-old man who had the reasoning ability of a 6-year-old. However, in 2002, the Supreme Court reversed its earlier ruling and held that the death penalty constituted "cruel and unusual punishment" for mentally retarded persons.

What about kids? It was once commonplace to execute children as young as 12 or 13 for everyday sorts of crimes; in 1944, George Junius Stinney, age 14, was electrocuted in South Carolina. In 1988, the Supreme Court determined that it was unconstitutional to administer the death penalty to persons aged 15 or younger at the time of the crime, but, the court ruled, 16 and 17 were acceptable. In 2005, the Supreme Court outlawed the death penalty for crimes committed by persons under the age of 18, leaving only two countries in the world where juvenile executions are still legal (Iran and Congo).

The American public generally favors the death penalty for adult offenders—by about two to one, with more support among men than women, and more among Whites than among minorities. They typically cite the death penalty's value in deterring crime. However, as we have seen, few, if any, offenders actually stop to consider the prospect of being executed before committing the crime. Many violent crimes are committed in the heat of passion, when rational calculation is largely or entirely blocked by emotion (Bouffard, 2002). Besides, for deterrence to work, the punishment must be swift and certain. Neither is the case in the U.S. criminal justice system.

Many scholars have noted that the death penalty is unjustly applied. Race plays a major factor: Blacks convicted of murdering Whites are most likely to get the death penalty, and Whites convicted of murdering Blacks are the least likely (Baldus and Woodworth, 1998; General Accounting Office, 1990). Location also plays a factor. Some states, such as Illinois and New York, have strong public defender offices with sufficient financial resources to attract the top lawyers. Cases can then be assured of

Sociology and our World

After Prison: Parolee and Ex-Con Disenfranchisement

If you have been incarcerated and are released after completing your sentence, your punishment may still not be over. Virtually all released prisoners are released before their complete sentence is served, often for "good behavior," and they are placed on parole, which means they are still under the surveillance of the penal system. Parolees are subject to regular screenings, must find specific types of jobs, and may have travel restrictions placed on them. They are also often prohibited from socializing with their old "criminal" friends. Rarely do parolees get state support or counseling to help them; more often they are simply punished if they violate their parole. Violations of parole may mean being sent back to prison to complete their sentence.

But even if you are released from prison and have completed parole, you still may not have all your citizenship rights restored—even if you have "paid your debt to society." "Felon disenfranchisement" is the denial of the right to vote because of having been convicted of a felony. There are 5.4 million Americans—that's one out of every 40 voting age adults—who are denied the right to participate in democratic elections because of a past or present felony conviction. The vast majority of these disenfranchised Americans are not in prison (Manza and Uggen, 2006). More than half of these disenfranchised Americans are African American; in several states, one in four Black men cannot vote due to a felony conviction. The United States is the only nation that disenfranchises nonincarcerated felons (Manza and Uggen, 2006).

Is felon disenfranchisement "politically" motivated? Sociologists Jeff Manza and Christopher Uggen examined the data in the 2000 presidential election, an election that was decided by a tiny margin in the state of Florida. Manza and Uggen used voter registration and election data to calculate that 35 percent of these disenfranchised felons would vote in any given presidential election and, given national and state trends, 74 percent of them would vote Democratic. (That's a conservative estimate: Nationwide, in 2000, the Democratic candidate, Al Gore, received more than 90 percent of the African American vote.) In Florida, there would have been a net Democratic gain of 63,079 votes and a Gore margin of victory of 62,542. Al Gore would have been elected president had the disenfranchised felons been able to vote (Uggen and Manza, 2002).

---

vigorous defense through several appeals. Other states, such as Texas and Alabama, do not coordinate public defense or fund it at the state level—the judge appoints a lawyer, who is paid on a fixed scale that does not cover federal appeals.

Cases there are represented by inexperienced lawyers who often lack the resources to mount a vigorous defense and the incentive to stick through the appeals process. As a result, a crime committed in Texas is much more likely to get a conviction than the same type of crime committed in Illinois, where two-thirds of capital cases are overturned (Liebman, Fagan, and West, 2000).

Finally, the death penalty, once applied, is irreversible, leading to worries that innocent people might be wrongly executed. In the twentieth century, at least 18 executed offenders were later found innocent (Radelet and Bedau, 1992), and today new techniques of DNA analysis are thinning the ranks of death row.

Globalization and Crime

Every day I receive an e-mail message informing me that I've won a national lottery in England, giving me a hot stock tip, or saying that the wife of a dearly departed African dictator would like my help in spiriting away several million dollars (for which I will be handsomely compensated). These are phishes, and they originate in many different crime cells all over the world.

While the Internet may have expanded the global networks of crime, crime as a global enterprise has a long history, from ancient slave traders (who kidnapped their

How do we know what we know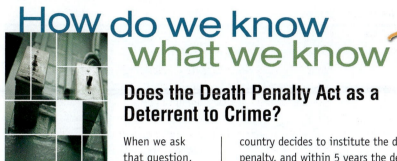

Does the Death Penalty Act as a Deterrent to Crime?

When we ask that question, we are really concerned with causality: Does knowing about the possibility of going to the gas chamber or electric chair *cause* people to reconsider their murder plans?

The best way to determine causality is through experiment: Introduce variable A into a situation and determine if variable B results. If B only happens after A is introduced, and never before A or without A, then can we state with some certainty that A caused B.

But sociologists obviously can't turn the death penalty on and off to look at the results. Instead, we turn to the somewhat riskier business of correlation. We look at places where the death penalty has ended, or where it has been instated, to see what happens to the serious crime rate.

Imagine a country that has no death penalty and a murder rate of 0.10 per 1,000 people, significantly higher than that of the United States (0.04). The country decides to institute the death penalty, and within 5 years the death penalty drops 10 percent, to 0.09. Sociologists all over the world would stare at the statistics in amazement: The death penalty (variable A) is correlated with a decrease in the murder rate (variable B)! Is it possible that someone stops to consider the consequences before he sets out to shoot his nuisance of a brother-in-law?

Maybe. Correlation cannot prove causality. Maybe the country is enjoying a period of remarkable economic prosperity, so there is less crime in general. Maybe it has instituted strict gun control laws, so there is no way for anyone to shoot his brother-in-law. Maybe the population is aging, and murder is mostly a young person's activity. We can never know for sure that the death penalty, and not other intervening variables, caused the drop in the murder rate.

Even though a positive correlation is not always a good indication of a causal relationship, the *lack* of correlation is a pretty good indicator of *a lack* of causality. If B happens sometimes before A, sometimes after A, and sometimes without A, we can be reasonably sure that the two variables are not causally linked. When real-life countries and states put in a death penalty, or revoke one, the rate of murder and other serious crime does not go up or down in any systematic fashion. There is no significant correlation.

In fact, it might actually seem to go the other way. Florida and Texas, the two states with the highest numbers of executions, actually have a higher murder rate than states with no death penalty or death penalties on the books but few or no executions. Is there another variable behind both the executions and the murder rate?

Of course, no one would seriously make the argument that the death penalty *causes* murders! But neither can anyone make a convincing argument that the death penalty deters murder either.

Therefore, despite what "everybody knows" sociologists conclude that the death penalty has no significant effect on serious crime. What "everybody knows" in this case turns out to be wrong.

"cargo") to criminal networks operating in many different countries. There were pirates on the seven seas, hoisting their proverbial black flags beyond territorial waters; and there are contemporary pirates who operate in countries where it is legal to steal and duplicate material from the Internet or to ransack corporate funds into offshore bank accounts.

Today, global criminal networks operate in every arena, from the fake Gucci handbags for sale on street corners to the young girls who are daily kidnapped in Thailand and other countries to serve as sex slaves in brothels around the world; from street gangs and various ethnic and national organized crime networks (the "Russian Mafia," the Italian Mafia) to the equally well-organized and equally illegal offshore bankers and shady corporate entities that incorporate in countries that have no regulations on toxic dumping, environmental devastation, or fleecing stockholders.

And yet much crime also remains decidedly "local"—an individual is assaulted or robbed, raped or murdered in his or her own neighborhood. Despite the massive networks of organized global crime, it is still true that the place where you are most likely to be the victim of a violent crime is your own home (Bureau of Justice, 2005; National Crime Victimization Survey).

FIGURE 6.8 **Death Penalty Executions in the United States**

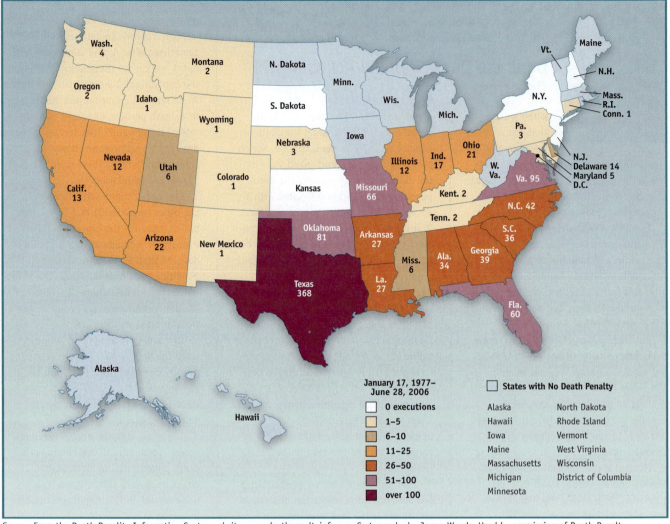

January 17, 1977–
June 28, 2006

- ☐ 0 executions
- ☐ 1–5
- ☐ 6–10
- ☐ 11–25
- ☐ 26–50
- ☐ 51–100
- ☐ over 100

☐ **States with No Death Penalty**

Alaska	North Dakota
Hawaii	Rhode Island
Iowa	Vermont
Maine	West Virginia
Massachusetts	Wisconsin
Michigan	District of Columbia
Minnesota	

Source: From the Death Penalty Information Center website, www.deathpenaltyinfo.org. Cartography by James Woods. Used by permission of Death Penalty Information Center and James Woods.

Deviance and Crime in the 21st Century

I still wait each morning at 6:00 a.m. for that red light on campus to change to green. I stare at my watch. One minute. Two minutes. Today I'm going to run it. There are no police cars around. There are no cars around at all. Three minutes. I'm going to run it. I'm really going to run it. I'm a rebel—I make my own rules! Four minutes. There are no hidden cameras. There will be no punishment. I'm going to run it. Just watch me!

Five minutes. The light turns green. I say a bad word under my breath and drive through the intersection.

The main question in deviance and crime is not why so many people break the rules. It's also why so many people don't. The question of order is the flip side of the question of deviance—and both are of significant interest. We may all be deviants, but we're also, most of the time, law-abiding citizens. And we obey the law not only because we are afraid to get caught but because, deep down, we believe that the system of laws is legitimate and that we all will benefit somehow from everyone obeying them.

In the future, we'll continue to obey most of the rules and also decide which ones we can break and legitimate their breaking to ourselves. Our society will likely continue its anticrime spending spree, and the number of prisoners will continue to spiral upward. The crime rate will shift unevenly; some crimes will increase and some decrease. And we'll continue to debate the age-old questions of guns and the death penalty.

The sociological questions will remain the same: How do people make the sorts of decisions about what laws to obey and which ones to break? Who decides what laws are, how they are to be enforced, and how equally the law is to be applied? How does our understanding of deviance and crime reflect and reinforce the inequalities of our society even as the institutions that administer them—the police, courts, and prisons—also reflect and reinforce those inequalities? What are the possibilities of more equitable understandings and policies?

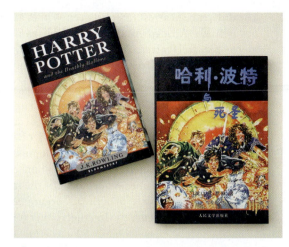

▲ **Global crime occurs in every arena, from fake Harry Potter books made in China, to cybercrime rings that steal identities or financial information, to young girls kidnapped to serve as sex slaves around the world.**

Chapter Review

1. *How do we define deviance?* Deviance is any failure to follow a norm, or social rule. Deviance sometimes takes the form of behavior and other times is as simple as group membership.

2. *What is social control?* Following or breaking norms often leads to reactions called sanctions. Sanctions can be positive or negative and formal or informal. As a mechanism of social control, sanctions are used to get individuals to follow the rules, and like norms, they exist in degrees. The sanction for breaking a folkway will be informal (such as a smile or a frown) while the sanction for breaking a law will be formal (such as jail or a fine). Because social control contributes to smooth social functioning, all groups and societies have some form of it.

3. *How do sociologists explain deviance?* *Differential association* explains deviance as an excess of definitions. When an individual sees that there is a reward for deviance, the deviance is defined as rewarding. *Control theory* assumes that individuals are rational actors and weigh the costs and benefits of any action. If benefit outweighs cost, an individual is more likely to be deviant. The more connected individuals are with others and with institutions, the less likely they are to engage in deviance. Inner and outer controls work through attachment, commitment, involvement, and belief. According to labeling

theory, something or someone has to be labeled as deviant before it is considered deviant. Once a person is labeled as a criminal, he or she will always be viewed as one. *Conflict theory* explains reactions to deviance in terms of inequality, as those with more power are less likely to suffer negative consequences.

4. *How do sociologists explain crime?* Crimes are violations of norms that have been codified in law. *Strain theory* explains crime as a result of a tension between the accepted goals of society and the accepted means of obtaining those goals, means to which everyone does not have equal access. Possible reactions to the strain include conformity, innovation, ritualism, rebellion, and retreat. The *broken windows theory* of crime holds that minor acts of deviance spiral into more serious ones. *Opportunity theory* shows how crime is related to specific opportunities and availability. *Conflict theory* says that crime is a result of inequality.

5. *How is deviance related to gender, race, and age?* Most people arrested for crimes are male, especially those who are arrested for blue-collar crimes. Women are less likely to be arrested, to be convicted, and to serve time. At the same time, the United States arrests and convicts more women proportionally than the rest of the world. Most arrests, however, are among working-class and poor men.

The difference in arrest rates between Whites and minorities is huge. African Americans and Hispanics are far more likely to be arrested for crime and also more likely to be the victims of crime. Individuals who are arrested are also more likely to be young than old.

6. *What types of crimes are there?* Crimes occur against people or against property. The FBI categorizes crimes as violent crimes or as property offenses; the difference is force or threat of force. Some crimes are workplace crimes, including white-collar, consumer, and occupational crimes, which benefit the individual. Organizational crimes benefit an organization as a whole. Cybercrimes use the Internet, either for personal gain or to cause trouble, as with viruses. Crimes are classified as hate crimes when the act was motivated by bias based on one's social group membership.

7. *What role does the criminal justice system play?* Police are responsible for fighting crime, protecting citizens, and serving their communities. The court system is responsible for prosecuting crimes. Jails and prisons are responsible for punishment and correction. The United States has a higher incarceration rate than the rest of the world. Incarceration is used for restitution, deterrence, protection of potential victims, and rehabilitation. The criminal justice system is the main mechanism for social control in any society.

KeyTerms

Broken windows theory (p. 180)
Conflict theory (p. 182)
Consumer crime (p. 183)
Control theory (p. 176)
Crime (p. 178)
Cybercrime (p. 185)
Deviance (p. 168)
Differential association (p. 175)
Folkways (p. 170)

Hate crime (p. 186)
Labeling theory (p. 177)
Mores (p. 170)
Occupational crime (p. 183)
Opportunity theory (p. 181)
Organizational crime (p. 183)
Primary deviance (p. 177)
Property crime (p. 183)
Secondary deviance (p. 177)

Social controls (p. 176)
Stigma (p. 170)
Strain theory (p. 179)
Subculture (p. 172)
Taboos (p. 170)
Tertiary deviance (p. 177)
Violent crime (p. 183)
White-collar crime (p. 183)

What does *America* think?

6.1 Censoring Perceived Deviance

This is actual survey data from the General Social Survey, 1972–2004.

1. **There are always some people whose ideas are considered bad or dangerous by other people. For instance, somebody who is against all churches and religion . . . Should such a person be allowed to teach in a college or university?** Data from 2004 show the following: 65.1 percent said yes, 34.9 percent said no. The percentage of people saying yes has steadily increased from 1972, when data showed 41.9 percent of respondents saying yes and 58.1 percent saying no. The current percentage of 65.1 is the highest it has been since the survey started in 1972.

2. **What about a man who admits that he is a homosexual? Should such a person be allowed to teach in a college or university?** Data from 2004 show the following: 80.1 percent said yes, 19.9 percent said no. The percentage of people who agree that a homosexual should be allowed to teach has been steadily increasing from 1973, when 49.4 percent of the respondents said yes, and 50.6 percent said no.

3. **Should a person who believes that Blacks are genetically inferior be allowed to teach in a college or university?** Data from 2004 show the following: 47.8 percent said yes, 52.2 percent said no. There has been very little variation in responses since the question was first asked in the 1976 survey.

4. **If some people in your community suggested that a book written against churches and religion should be taken out of your public library, would you favor removing this book?** In 2004, the responses were 25.3 percent to remove the book and 74.7 percent to not remove it. Attitudes have changed somewhat since 1982, when 40.2 percent said to remove the book.

5. **If some people in your community suggested that a book written in favor of homosexuality should be taken out of your public library, would you favor removing this book?** In 2004, 26.4 percent of respondents said remove the book and 73.6 percent said don't. The percentage of people advocating removing the book has been in a steady decline since 45 percent said remove in 1973.

6. **If some people in your community suggested that a book that said Blacks are inferior should be taken out of your public library, would you favor removing this book, or not?** In 2004, 32.9 percent of respondents said they would be in favor of removing the book, while 67.1 percent said they would not. Although those numbers have remained pretty steady since the 1970s, the percentage of people wanting to remove the book peaked in 1982 at 40.4 percent.

CRITICAL THINKING | DISCUSSION QUESTIONS

1. It appears that American's attitudes toward censoring unpopular ideas have changed significantly in the past 30 years. How does this change reflect changes in American society and in American values?
2. Why do more Americans seem to be tolerant of books in the library having perceived deviant views than they are of college teachers having perceived deviant views?
3. What does it say about American values that more Americans would censor an antireligion point of view than a prohomosexual view?

6.2 Death Penalty for Murder

This is actual survey data from the General Social Survey, 2004.

Do you favor or oppose the death penalty for persons convicted of murder? In 2004, almost 70 percent of respondents were in favor of the death penalty. When we look at the responses by race, though, we see a very large and significant difference. Seventy-two percent of White respondents favor the death penalty for murder, while only 40 percent of Black respondents do so.

CRITICAL THINKING | DISCUSSION QUESTION

1. How can we explain the difference in White and Black responses to the survey question?

▶ Go to this website to look further at the data. You can run your own statistics and crosstabs here: **http://sda.berkeley.edu/cgi-bin/hsda?harcsda+gss04**

REFERENCES: Davis, James A., Tom W. Smith, and Peter V. Marsden. General Social Surveys 1972–2004: [Cumulative file] [Computer file]. 2nd ICPSR version. Chicago, IL: National Opinion Research Center [producer], 2005; Storrs, CT: Roper Center for Public Opinion Research, University of Connecticut; Ann Arbor, MI: Inter-University Consortium for Political and Social Research; Berkeley, CA: Computer-Assisted Survey Methods Program, University of California [distributors], 2005.

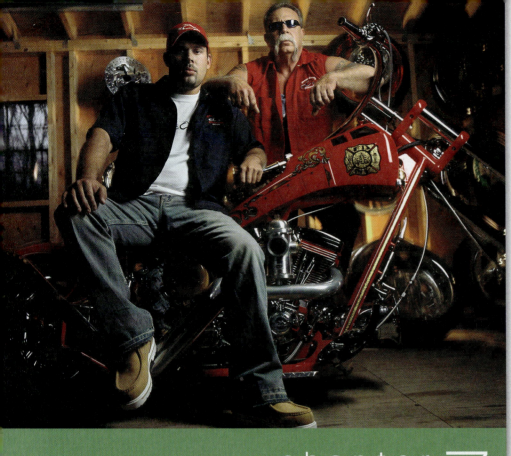

chapter 7

THERE'S AN OLD BRITISH JOKE that goes something like this:

Two Oxford professors, a physicist and a sociologist, were walking across a leafy college green.
"I say, old chap," said the physicist, "What exactly do you teach in that sociology course of yours?"
"Well," replied the sociologist, "This week we're discussing the persistence of the class structure in America."
"I didn't even know they had a class structure in America," said the physicist.
The sociologist smiled. "How do you think it persists?"

Stratification and Social Class

Most countries are aware of their own class structure—the physics professor didn't need a sociology course to know that England has social classes—but in the United States, class seems to be invisible. Many people don't even believe it exists. Surely, they say, we're an equal-opportunity country. Class is a relic of old European monarchies, where princes scandalize the media by consorting with commoners.

But the United States does have a class structure. Every country does; social class is present in some form in every human society. Even the Old Order Amish, perhaps the most egalitarian society that has ever existed, have three social classes ranked by occupational prestige: traditional farmers, business owners, and day laborers (Kraybill, 2001). The details may shift and change somewhat over time, but class structure is omnipresent, always operating in our lives,

Although it seems invisible, social class remains the single best indicator of . . . the sort of life you are likely to have—where you will go to school, what you think, and even whom you will marry (or if you will) and how you like to have sex!

and, paradoxically, especially powerful in countries where people don't believe it exists. Their inability to "see," as the joke suggests, helps class persist from generation to generation.

Although it seems invisible, social class remains the single best indicator of your "life chances"—of the sort of life you are likely to have—where you will go to school, what you think, and even whom you will marry (or if you will) and how you like to have sex! Even focusing so much on your individual choices and individual talents is a reflection of your class position. (Middle-class people believe in the meritocracy more than upper-class people.)

This chapter will explore the importance of class in our society—both as a source of identity and as a structure of inequality.

What Is Social Stratification?

The system of structured social inequality and the structure of mobility in a society is called **social stratification**. Stratification is concerned with the ranking of people. Social stratification takes its name from geology: Imagine a society looking very much like the side of a mountain made of sedimentary rock: each layer—or "stratum"— carefully demarcated and sitting on the top of another well-defined layer.

All societies rank people. The criteria for the ranking varies: In the contemporary United States, perhaps it's the size of your bank account; in traditional societies, perhaps it's the size of your yam crop. But once you are ranked, you enjoy benefits and rewards "appropriate" to your social location. You get more or less money, fame, prestige, and power throughout your life, regardless of your individual talent, intelligence, and drive to succeed.

In almost every society, an entrepreneurial genius born in a hovel dies in a hovel, and a person of, shall we say, limited ability, born in a palace dies in a palace. Nobody moves from hovel to palace, except in fairy tales. Your social position is a matter of birth, passed on from parents to children, from generation to generation. Some societies, mostly extremely wealthy ones, like our own, allow for some social mobility, so entrepreneurial geniuses born in hovels can found megasuccessful corporations, or the children of solidly middle-class shop owners can find themselves punching time clocks. But even where social mobility is possible, most people remain at the same social location throughout their lives. If your father was a janitor, it is very unlikely that you will one day be the president—even if you get the right education.

Social stratification involves inequalities not only in wealth and power but also in belief systems. It gives some people more benefits and rewards than others and also defines the arrangement as fair, just, and reasonable. The explanation offered for *why* it is fair, just, and reasonable differs from society to society. Often no explanation is offered at all: Both the "haves" and the "have-nots" accept the system without question (Crompton, 1993; Kerbo, 1996; Saunders, 1990).

Why Do We Have Social Stratification?

What purpose does stratification serve? Classical sociologists disagreed on this question. Some, like Durkheim, believed that stratification was a necessary organizing principle of a complex society and that it served to create interdependence among society's members, so that everyone "needed" the activities of everyone else (Filoux, 1993). Marx, on the other hand, stressed the ways the stratification system benefited those at the top—at the expense of those at the bottom. He spoke of oppression and exploitation, not integration and interdependence (Resnick and Wolff, 1987).

In the middle of the twentieth century, many sociologists followed Durkheim, saw stratification as integrative, and claimed that it allowed for significant mobility. For example, Kingsley Davis and Wilber Moore (1945) argued that as long as some degree of social mobility was possible, stratification is essential to the proper functioning of a society. Some jobs (say, brain surgeon) are extremely important, and other jobs (say, serving hamburgers at the student union) are relatively unimportant. Social stratification creates a **meritocracy**, a system in which those at who are the most "meritorious" will rise to the top, and those who are less so will sink to the bottom. Meritocracy is the rule by those who deserve to rule. The greater the functional importance of the job, the more rewards it brings, in salary, perks, power, and prestige. Therefore people will work better, longer, and harder in hopes of getting a high-prestige job. Of course, some will not succeed; *most* will not succeed. But the society benefits from everyone working very hard. If a brain surgeon and a burger flipper suddenly started getting the same salary, perks, and prestige, no one would be motivated to work hard. Severing rewards from performance leads to low quality and low productivity.

However, those arguments came at a far more optimistic time in American society; today, the persistence—and even the intensification—of class-based inequalities has rendered that vision obsolete. Sociologists now understand that social mobility occurs in only a few societies, and it is not common anywhere.

Social stratification divides us far more than it unites us. Stratification is a form of inequality. Elites maintain inequality for their own advantage, prohibiting many of the most talented and intelligent people from making favorable contributions to the society and giving less talented, less intelligent people tremendous amounts of power. Even where some people do get to move up in the rankings, it is so infrequent that elites still manage to retain control, and the possibility of mobility ensures that the disenfranchised remain docile: They assume that if they don't succeed, it's their own fault (McAll, 1990).

Systems of Stratification

Societies reproduce social stratification in different ways. Sometimes boundaries are relatively fluid, and sometimes they are etched in stone. The most common forms of stratification are the caste system, feudalism, and class.

Castes. Castes, found in many traditional agricultural societies, divide people by occupation: farmers, merchants, priests, and so on. A **caste system** is fixed and permanent; you are assigned to your position at birth, without any chance of getting out. Perhaps the most famous example of a caste system has been India. India had four castes, or *Varnas: Brahmin* (priests), *Kshatriyas* (warriors and other political elites), *Vaishyas* (farmers and merchants), and *Shudras* (servants), plus

This woman is an Untouchable, one of the 160 million people who occupy India's lowest caste. No matter how hard or diligently she works, she won't escape the poverty and discrimination into which she was born. ▼

Sociology and our World

Apartheid

Apartheid is a caste system in which the basis of the caste designation is race. The term is derived from the Dutch term for "separate," and politically it involved the geographic, economic, and political separation of the races. It was the common, if informal, system in the southern United States through the first half of the twentieth century, maintained legally by "Jim Crow" laws.

In South Africa, the most famous case of apartheid, the ruling party, descendents of Dutch immigrants, enacted apartheid laws in 1948. People were required to register as White (someone who was "in appearance obviously a White person"), Black (a member of an African tribe), or Colored (of mixed descent, plus South and East Asians). Blacks were forced to live in four

separate Bantustans, or "homelands" with 13 percent of South Africa's area, even though they comprised about 75 percent of the population. When they came to "White" South Africa, they had to carry passports and identification papers.

Protests against apartheid began almost immediately, among both Blacks and Whites. (In 1976, more than 600 high school students were killed in the African townships of Soweto and Sharpesville, when the police responded to their protests with bullets.) Finally, after years of protests, riots, strikes, and states of emergency, former dissident Nelson Mandela was elected president in 1994, the homelands were dismantled, and apartheid laws were removed from the civil code. Of course, racial prejudice still exists; some newspaper commentators argue that the end of apartheid has exacerbated racial tensions, as Whites who believe that they are now discriminated against in jobs and housing are likely to lash out against Blacks (Clark and Worger, 2004).

---

the untouchables, a "casteless" group at the bottom of the society. Your *varna* determined not only your occupation but where you could live, whom you could talk to on the street (and the terms you would use to address them), your gods, and even your chances of a favorable afterlife: Only a Brahmin could hope to escape samsara, the cycle of endless deaths and rebirths. Modern India prohibits discrimination on the basis of caste, and reserves a percentage of government jobs and university admissions to untouchables. However, the traditional system is still strong, especially in rural areas (Gupta, 2000).

Feudalism. In medieval Europe, between the eleventh and sixteenth centuries; in nineteenth-century Japan; and in a few other regions, there were a few merchants and "free men," but most of the population consisted of peasants and serfs who worked the estates belonging to a small group of feudal lords. Feudalism was a fixed and permanent system: If you were born a lord or a serf, you stayed there your whole life.

The classic feudal relationship was one of mutual obligation. The feudal lords housed and fed serfs, offered protection inside the castle walls, and decided on their religion and on whether they would be educated. Peasants had no right to seek out other employment or other masters. In effect, they were property. Their only avenue to social advancement was to enter a convent or monastery (Backman, 2002).

Feudalism endured in Germany through the nineteenth century and in Russia until the Bolshevik Revolution of 1917. A person's wealth—and the taxes owed to the Tsar—was gauged not by how much land that person owned but by how many serfs (or "souls") he owned.

Feudalism began to disappear as the class of free men in the cities—artisans, shopkeepers, and merchants—grew larger and more prosperous, and the center of society began to shift from the rural manor to the urban factory. Industrial society dispensed with feudal rankings and ushered in the modern class system.

Class. Class is the most modern form of stratification. Class is based on economic position—a person's occupation, income, or possessions. Of the major forms of stratification, class systems are the most open—that is, they permit the greatest amount of **social mobility,** which is the ability to move up—or down—in the rankings. **Class systems** are systems of stratification based on economic position, and people are ranked according to achieved status (as opposed to ascribed status). Each system of stratification creates a belief system that declares it legitimate, that those at the top "deserve" to be there through divine plan, the natural order of things. Class systems "feel" the most equitable to us today because they appear to justify one's ranking solely on his or her own initiative, hard work, and talent.

Social Class

Many Americans believe that a class system is a relic from our European past and that it exerts far less influence—if any—in the modern world. After all, the very idea of American democracy is that an individual should be able to rise as far as his or her talents, aspirations, and hard work can take that person. And, since we believe we are capable of virtually unlimited upward mobility, we believe that we can leave our "class of origin" (the class we are born into) behind and easily join a higher class.

We also have seen ample evidence that the importance of class is increasing. The recent commentary, for example, on the rescue and cleanup efforts in New Orleans in the aftermath of Hurricane Katrina exposed persistent class and racial inequalities. And sociologists also understand that class remains the single best predictor of one's "life chances"—one's eventual place in the economic and social hierarchy.

If we credit class at all, it is the class to which we are aspiring, not the class into which we were born. But it turns out your class of origin is a very reliable measure of where you will end up. Your class background is just about the best predictor of many things, from the seemingly important—what college you go to (or if you go to college at all), what job you have—to the seemingly trivial—what your favorite sexual position is, what music you like, and even what you probably had for dinner last night.

Class also operates on the global level. Just as there are upper-, middle-, and lower-class people, there are upper-, middle-, and lower-class countries. These, too, shift and change over time—a tycoon country today might be a pauper country tomorrow—but the hierarchy of rich and poor, weak and strong, high status and low status doesn't seem to go away.

◄ Class inequality often combines other forms of inequality to create a complex hierarchical order. The government's response to Hurricane Katrina in 2005 exposed persistent class and racial inequalities in the United States.

Theories of Social Class

The analysis of social stratification in general, and class in particular, is one of the defining interests of the founders of sociology—as well as a central concern among sociologists today.

Marx and Class. Karl Marx (1818–1883) was the first social scientist to make class the foundation of his entire theory. Marx argued that human survival depends on producing things. How we, as a society, organize ourselves to do this, and how we distribute the rewards, is what Marx called the mode of production—the organization of society to produce what people need to survive.

There are many ways to do this. We could imagine a system in which one person owns everything, and everyone else works for him or her. Or we could imagine a system in which everyone owns everything, and you simply take what you need—and leave the rest for others. Or we could imagine a system in which a very few people had far more than they could possibly ever need, and the large majority had very little, but, instead of giving the rest away to others who need it, the wealthy would simply throw it away. All of these are systems that organize production, the creation of the goods we need for survival, and the relations of production—the relationships people enter into to facilitate production and allocate its rewards.

Marx argued that, historically, it has always been the case that some people own means of production—the cornfields, the cows, and the factories—and everyone else works for them. With ownership comes control: If you own the only cornfield in town, everyone else has to listen to you or go without corn. Therefore there are two types of people, the owners and workers.

In Marx's day, capitalists or the **bourgeoisie** owned the means of production, only now they owned factories instead of farms, and the lower classes or the **proletariat** were forced to become wage-laborers or go hungry. They received no share of the profits and lived in perpetual poverty. Ironically, they used their wages to buy the very products that they were helping to manufacture.

Marx believed that this system was inherently unfair. He also believed that classes were in intractable and inevitable conflict. He predicted that eventually the proletariat would organize, rebel, and overthrow capitalism altogether in favor of a socialist economy where the workers owned the means of production (Smelser, 1975).

Weber and Class. Max Weber (1864–1920) doubted that overthrowing capitalism would significantly diminish social stratification. It might address economic inequality, but what about other forms of inequality? In one of his most celebrated essays, "Class, Status and Party," Weber argued that there were three components to social class: economic (class position), social (status), and political (power). Often they were interrelated, but sometimes they operated independently: You could be at the top of the economic ladder, but at the bottom of the social ladder, and somewhere in the middle of the political ladder. So are you a member of the upper, middle, or lower class? Or all three? Social class, it turns out, is a complex, multidimensional hierarchy.

In Weber's theory, stratification is based on three dimensions: class, status, and power:

1. *Class position*. It can determine whether you are an owner or a worker; how much money you make (your income); your property, stocks, bonds, and money in the bank (your wealth). Wealth is more important than income because the legal system, with its laws concerning private property and inheritance, ensures that wealth will pass on to your heirs and endow them with a class position similar to yours—or higher. Class is based simply on your relationship to production—what you do for a living and what you earn.

2. *Status*. Social prestige is what other people think of you. If class is based on your relationship to production, **status is based on your relationship to consumption: your** lifestyle. People see what you have and how you live and make judgments about how much wealth and power you have. This results in people often buying higher-priced luxury goods—status symbols—even if they have a hard time paying for them.

People with higher class positions tend to enjoy higher status, but not necessarily: In the United States, college professors enjoy high status, but (unfortunately) they don't make much money, compared to other high-status professions. Accountants have a relatively low status, but they tend to command high salaries. High and low status differs from society to society and changes over time. (Table 7.1) Status does not pass from generation to generation automatically, like wealth, but it can still be transmitted. Upper-class parents teach their children the social skills expected of people with high status, perhaps an appreciation for classical music or modern art, and send them to exclusive schools and colleges where they can prepare for high-status lives. Meanwhile lower-middle-class and working-class parents teach their children the skills necessary for lives of somewhat lower expectations.

3. *Power*. **Power is the ability to do what you want to do.** This may mean a certain amount of control over your own working situation. People in higher class or status positions can set their own hours, disregard punching time clocks, and work to their own rhythm.

TABLE 7.1

Occupational Prestige: 27 Year Trend

BASE: ALL ADULTS	1977 %	2006 %	CHANGES SINCE 1977 %
Doctor	61	58	–3
Nurse	NA	55	NA
Scientist	66	54	–12
Teacher	29	52	+23
Police Officer	NA	43	NA
Priest/Minister/Clergyman	41	40	–1
Engineer	34	34	0
Athlete	26	23	–3
Lawyer	36	21	–15
Entertainer	18	18	0
Accountant	NA	17	NA
Banker	17	17	0
Journalist	17	16	–1
Business executive	18	11	–7

Note: Prestige is rated on a scale from 100 (most prestigious) to 0 (least prestigious).
Source: Adapted from *Introduction to Sociology, 6th ed.,* by Thompson and Hickey, p. 204.

Sociology and our World

Prestige Means Not Having to Deal with People

In *The System of Professions: An Essay on the Division of Expert Labor* (1988), sociologist Andrew Abbott noticed an interesting workplace phenomenon: the more prestigious the job, the less contact with real, live human beings.

When you go to the doctor's office, a receptionist (low prestige) greets you, asks you to fill out some forms, and creates a file for you. Then a nurse (medium prestige) records your weight, temperature, and blood pressure in the file that the receptionist prepared and informs the doctor that you're there. Finally, a doctor (high prestige) swoops in, examines you briefly, and gives directions to the nurse, who completes your treatment. On your way out, the receptionist talks to you again to take your payment and set up the next appointment. You've spent about 60 percent of the visit with the receptionist, 35 percent with the nurse, and 5 percent with the doctor.

When you walk into a fast-food restaurant for lunch, the person who takes your order (low prestige) will probably take a thousand other orders that day. If you are dissatisfied with your order, you will go to the manager (medium prestige), who determines the work schedules, checks on the supplies, and handles complaints, but never takes orders from customers. Meanwhile, somewhere far away in a glass-and-steel tower, the CEO (high prestige) makes high-level policy decisions and never sees a customer.

We can find so many examples that it seems almost a workplace rule: the higher your prestige, the less you actually have to deal with people.

To Weber, power also denoted people working together to achieve a certain goal. Typically, Weber believed, people would form political coalitions to accomplish some limited political end—putting up a stop light on a corner, obtaining more funding for a school program—despite the fact that they are from different classes and status groups. These sorts of political pressure groups formed at the local level are often thought to ensure that individuals are not trampled by the will of the majority.

Power also resides in your ability to influence the actions of others. People with high power dictate, order, command, or make "requests" that are really commands issued in a nice way, as when a police officer "asks" to see your driver's license. People can have a great deal of power but low class position or social status. (Weber, 1958).

As with status, people with higher class positions and social status tend to have more power. As the tyrannical king tells us in the *Wizard of Id* comic strip, "Remember the Golden Rule: He who has the gold, makes the rules."

Class position, status, and power remain the major components of social class, but sociologists after Max Weber have continued to postulate new ones: your social connections, your taste in art, your ascribed and attained statuses, and so on. Because there are so many components, sociologists today tend to prefer the term **socioeconomic status** over social class, to emphasize that people are ranked through the intermingling of many factors, economic, social, political, cultural, and community.

Prestige or status operates somewhat differently from class. Some of the occupations that have high status are not exceptionally well paid, and other well-paid jobs don't have the highest status. But, in the long run, as Weber argued, class and status tend to go together.

Socioeconomic Classes in the United States

Karl Marx divided the world into two simple classes, the rich and the poor. But the sweeping economic and social changes of the past century and the recognition of multiple components to socioeconomic status have pushed sociologists to redefine these class categories and to further delineate others (Grusky, 2000; Lenski, 1984).

Today most sociologists argue for six or more socioeconomic classes in the United States. They are usually divided on the basis of household income because that information is easily obtained in census reports, but bear in mind that there are many other factors, and income is not always the best indictor (Figure 7.1).

The Upper Upper Class. These are the superrich, with annual incomes of over $1 million. They include the older established wealthy families, born into massive fortunes that their ancestors amassed during the industrial boom of the nineteenth-century Gilded Age. While the original fortunes were amassed through steel, railroads, or other industries, recent generations depend on extensive worldwide investments. They are neither the "haves" nor the "have nots"—they are the "have mores."

Many of the superrich amassed their fortunes recently, during the information revolution, in computers and other

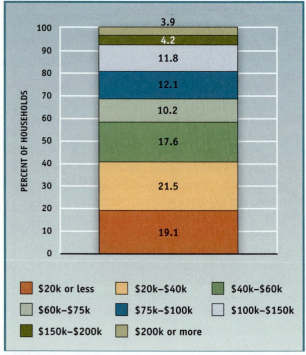

FIGURE 7.1 Household Income in the United States

Legend:
- $20k or less
- $20k–$40k
- $40k–$60k
- $60k–$75k
- $75k–$100k
- $100k–$150k
- $150k–$200k
- $200k or more

Bar values (bottom to top): 19.1, 21.5, 17.6, 10.2, 12.1, 11.8, 4.2, 3.9

Source: U.S. Census Bureau, 2010.

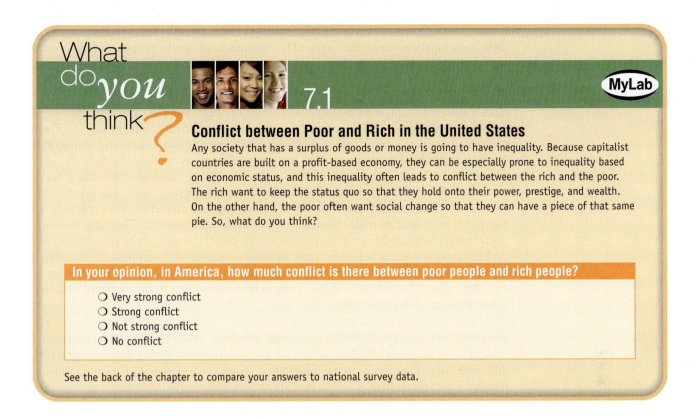

What do you think? 7.1

MyLab

Conflict between Poor and Rich in the United States

Any society that has a surplus of goods or money is going to have inequality. Because capitalist countries are built on a profit-based economy, they can be especially prone to inequality based on economic status, and this inequality often leads to conflict between the rich and the poor. The rich want to keep the status quo so that they hold onto their power, prestige, and wealth. On the other hand, the poor often want social change so that they can have a piece of that same pie. So, what do you think?

In your opinion, in America, how much conflict is there between poor people and rich people?

○ Very strong conflict
○ Strong conflict
○ Not strong conflict
○ No conflict

See the back of the chapter to compare your answers to national survey data.

---

technology. Bill Gates came from an elite background but was nowhere near even the top 10 percent in income in 1975, when he dropped out of Harvard to found Microsoft. Today, Gates's fortune tops $40 billion, and *Forbes* magazine named him the richest person in the world.

Other billionaires who didn't inherit most of their fortunes come from entertainment and sports. A blockbuster movie can shoot actors to the ranks of the superrich almost overnight, after years of financial hardship. (Of course, it usually doesn't; the mean salary for working actors in 2006 was $36,790.)

The superrich are usually invisible to the rest of the world. They have people to do their shopping and other chores. They have private jets, so they rarely stand in line at airports.

Lower Upper Class. With annual household incomes of more than $150,000 but less than $1 million, the lower upper class are the "everyday" rich. They tend to have advanced degrees from high-ranking colleges. Though they have substantial investment incomes, they still have to work: They are upper-level CEOs, managers, doctors, and engineers. Much more visible than the superrich, they still protect their privacy. They do not participate extensively in civic and community organizations. They live in gated communities, vacation at exclusive resorts, and send their children to prestigious private schools.

Upper Middle Class. With household incomes above $80,000 but less than $150,000, these are the high-end professionals and corporate workers. Most have college degrees. Only a small percentage of their

Did you know?

In J. K. Rowling's popular book series, Harry Potter finds out not only that he is a wizard but also that his parents left him a sizeable fortune. Daniel Radcliffe, who plays Harry Potter in the films based on the books, had a similar experience. A middle-class boy from Fulham, England, the 11-year-old child landed the lead in the guaranteed hit *Harry Potter and the Sorcerer's Stone* (2001) and subsequent films. Daniel received a salary as well as a percentage of the gross profits, and, in 2004, he became the richest teenager in Britain, with a fortune of over $11,000,000.

income comes from investments. They tend to be community leaders, very active in civic organizations and the arts. The audience in performances of the local philharmonic is likely to be mostly upper middle class (the upper class is in Vienna, and the lower middle and working classes are at home watching television).

Middle Middle Class. With household incomes between $40,000 and $80,000, these are the "average" American citizens. Most hold white-collar jobs: They are technicians, salespeople, business owners, educators. However, many blue-collar workers and high-demand service personnel, such as police, firefighters, and military, have acquired incomes large enough to place them in the middle class. Most have attended college, and many have college degrees. They have very little investment income but generally enough savings to weather brief periods of unemployment and provide some degree of retirement security. They are also in a precarious position: Shrewd career decisions could propel them into the upper middle class, while a few faulty career decisions could send them plummeting down to the working class. However, they are usually able to buy houses, drive new cars, and send their children to college. They tend to have small families and are very active in community civic life.

Working Class. Also called "lower middle class" to avoid the stigma of *not* being middle class in America, this group has a household income of between $20,000 and $40,000. They tend to be blue-collar workers, involved in manufacturing, production, and skilled trades, but there are also some low-level white-collar workers and professionals (such as elementary school teachers) and some high-level clerical and service industry workers, especially those in two-income households.

They make things and build things. They usually have high school diplomas, and many have been to college. Their savings accounts are usually minimal, so a few missed paychecks can be devastating, and for retirement they will have to depend on government programs such as Social Security or union pensions. Nevertheless, they can often buy houses, drive inexpensive cars, take occasional vacations, and send their children to public college.

They are not heavily involved in local civic and community organizations; instead, their social lives revolve around home, church, and maybe some hobby or sports groups. Extended family appears to be extremely important, more significant in the daily lives of the working class than of the middle class or upper class, who usually live hundreds or thousands of miles away from aunts, uncles, and cousins.

Lower Class. Also called the "working poor" to avoid the stigma of being called lower class, this group has a household income of less than $20,000 per year. They have unskilled and semiskilled jobs: They are service workers, maintenance workers, clerical workers. They deliver pizzas, wait on customers at retail stores, and clean homes and offices. Most do not have high school diplomas: They have an average of 10.4 years of education, as compared with 11.9 for the working class, 13.4 for the middle class, and 14.3 for the upper class.

It's hard to accumulate any money on $20,000 per year, so they usually live from paycheck to paycheck, and even a brief period of unemployment can be catastrophic. And because service jobs rarely include health benefits, illnesses and accidents also have a devastating effect. They often cannot afford houses or cars or college educations for their children. They are not heavily involved in any activity besides making ends meet.

The Underclass. The underclass has no income and no connection to the job market. Their major support comes from welfare and food stamps. Most live in substandard housing, and some are homeless. They have inadequate education, inadequate nutrition, and no health care. They have no possibility of social mobility, and little chance of achieving the quality of life that most people would consider minimally acceptable. Most members of the underclass are not born there: They grow up working poor, or working class, or middle class, and gradually move down through a series of firings, layoffs, divorces, and illnesses.

America and the Myth of the Middle Class

Generally, Americans believe that class is even less important than ever and that most Americans are middle class. On the other hand, class inequality has never been greater, and it is growing wider, not narrower. How can it be both?

Since the turn of the twentieth century, the middle class has expanded dramatically, and the classes of the very rich and the very poor have declined. Home ownership has risen, incomes have risen, and many more people own stock through mutual funds, pensions, and retirement accounts than ever before. They thus own at least a fraction of the means of production—and identify not with workers but with owners.

Today most people in the United States define themselves as middle class, even if they have to resort to creative redefinitions. Forty-second President George W. Bush's father was the ambassador to the United Nations, director of the CIA, and finally president of the United States. Like his father and grandfather, George W. Bush attended an elite prep school, and graduated from Yale. His family bought him the Texas Rangers baseball franchise as his first job, and he was elected governor of Texas before running for president. Yet even he insists that he is middle class!

At the same time that boundaries of the middle class are expanding to the breaking point, with almost everyone thinking that they are middle class (or upper middle class or lower middle class), fully invested in the system, the lifestyle associated with middle class is in obvious decline: less money, a smaller house or no house, a worse job or no job, and less financial security.

Sociology and our World

The Hidden Injuries of Class

In 1969 and 1970, sociologists Richard Sennett and Jonathan Cobb interviewed working class and poor men and women whose jobs were difficult, demeaning, low-paying, and dead-end. Sennett and Cobb expected to hear about hardship and deprivation, but they also heard working-class men judging themselves by middle-class standards. They believed in the American dream, where a poor boy can grow up to be president, where all it takes to get rich is perseverance and hard work. Yet they weren't rich—and they blamed themselves. They thought their "failure" was a matter of laziness, lack of ambition, or stupidity.

How did they ward off despair, when they believed themselves fully to blame for their lives of deprivation? They deferred success from their own lives onto the lives of their children. They were working at difficult, dirty, and dangerous jobs not because they were failures, but because they were sacrificing to give their children a better life. They were noble and honorable. Middle-class fathers tried to be role models to their children, saying, in effect, "You can grow up to be like me if you study and work hard." But working-class fathers tried to be cautionary tales: "You could grow up to be like me if you *don't* study and work hard."

Living through one's children proved to be enormously damaging. Fathers were resentful if their children were successful and perhaps even more resentful if they weren't, and all of the deprivation was for nothing. Successful children felt ashamed of their parents, and unsuccessful children felt guilt and despair of their own. Following the American Dream can also produce painful feelings.

How do we know what we know?

The General Social Survey

The U.S. Bureau of the Census can tell us people's income, occupations, household size, and college degrees, but for more subtle analysis of socioeconomic status, we need a lot more information. We need to conduct a survey; we need to select a random sample or stratified random sample of people, telephone them or knock on their door, and start asking questions: What sort of neighborhood do you live in? What are your tastes in music, art, and literature? How much time do spend every week in religious observation, clubs, business organizations, and community activities?

If you are interested only in a single college, a single neighborhood, or even a single city, you will have to conduct the survey yourself. However, if you are interested in the U.S. population as a whole, the work may already have been done for you. Dozens of social science organizations conduct national surveys every year. The most extensive, the General Social Survey (GSS), has been conducted by the National Opinion Research Center (NORC) almost every year since 1972, with 43,000 cases per year. All of the respondents are over 18 years old, and the results are valid only in nationwide analysis, but where else are you going to find information like:

- Have you ever done any active work in a hobby or garden club? (62 percent yes)
- In the last year, have you attended an auto race? (15 percent yes)
- Did your mother work outside the home? (58 percent yes)
- How often do you watch TV dramas or sitcoms? (21 percent daily, 37 percent several times a week)
- Do high school students spend too much time reading "classics" that are irrelevant to today's world? (38 percent agree)
- What social class would you say you belong in? (3 percent upper, 46 percent middle, 46 percent working, 5 percent lower)

The results of the GSS are available at a number of websites, including the NORC headquarters (http://webapp .icpsr.umich.edu/GSS/) and the University of California at Berkeley (http://sda .berkeley.edu:/cgi-bin/hsda?harcda+ gss04). You can browse the results; perform correlations and regressions; limit results by race, gender, or age; or download data sets to use later.

In the United States and other high-income countries, college is a necessary prerequisite for a middle-class life, but no longer guarantees it. ▼

Economist Michael Lind (2004) argues that the middle class has always been a product of social engineering by the government. Today's middle class emerged during the "New Deal" of the 1930s when technological innovation, a home front relatively unscathed by war, and a large population of young, well-educated people led to a climate just right for an unprecedented expansion of the middle class. But this

was only temporary, and today two of the most important factors, a superior education and a favorable investment climate, have declined in significance. The increases in the percentage of the labor force with college degrees has slowed to less than 5 percent, and America's massive trade deficit ($1.4 trillion) and the supercharged economies of Asia make America less attractive for investment. And white-collar jobs are in steady decline. Knowing about computers is no longer key to instant success. The jobs with the biggest numerical gains in the next 10 years are expected to be in food service, customer service, retail sales, clerical work, and private security. We may be seeing the rise of a new feudalism, with a few elites sitting in their skyscraper condos while the rest of the population—the new serfs—cook, clean, park the cars, and patrol the grounds.

Income Inequality

At the same time that most people believe that they are middle class and believe that the system works for them, the United States is increasingly a nation of richer and poorer. Sociologists measure the income inequality in a society by comparing the top incomes with the bottom incomes. In the United States, the top 5 percent earn an average of 11 times more than the bottom 20 percent—this is the most extreme example of income inequality in the developed world. In contrast, the top 20 percent in Sweden earn less than four times the bottom 20 percent, and in Japan, it's three to one (Economic Policy Institute, 2007). In fact, the income gap in the United States is the widest of any industrialized country among all countries included in the Organization for Economic Cooperation and Development (OECD), an international organization that measures and assists in economic development (Figure 7.2).

The income gap in the United States actually seems to be widening: The gap between rich and poor more than doubled between 1980 and 2000. The richest 1 percent have more money to spend after taxes than all of the bottom 40 percent. The richest 10 percent of Americans control

"*The poor are getting poorer, but with the rich getting richer it all averages out in the long run.*"

FIGURE 7.2 Share of U.S. Median Income Received by Low- and High-Income OECD Households, 2000

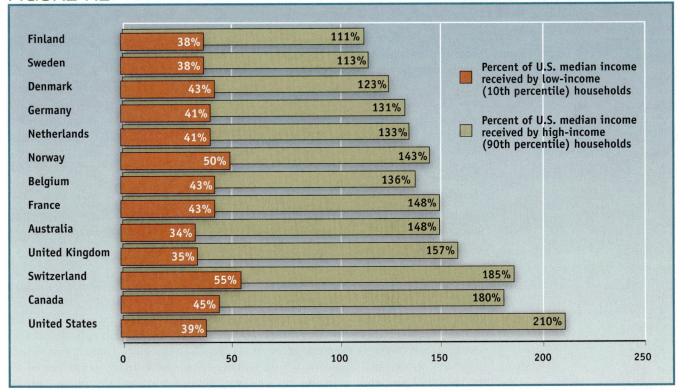

Country	Percent of U.S. median income received by low-income (10th percentile) households	Percent of U.S. median income received by high-income (90th percentile) households
Finland	38%	111%
Sweden	38%	113%
Denmark	43%	123%
Germany	41%	131%
Netherlands	41%	133%
Norway	50%	143%
Belgium	43%	136%
France	43%	148%
Australia	34%	148%
United Kingdom	35%	157%
Switzerland	55%	185%
Canada	45%	180%
United States	39%	210%

Note: These relative income measures compare the gap between the top 10 percent and the bottom 10 percent of household income in each country to the U.S. median income in purchasing-power-parity terms.

Source: Smeeding and Rainwater (2001) and Smeeding (2006). Figure 8D, taken from the Economic Policy Institute's *State of Working America 2006/2007*, available at www.epi.org

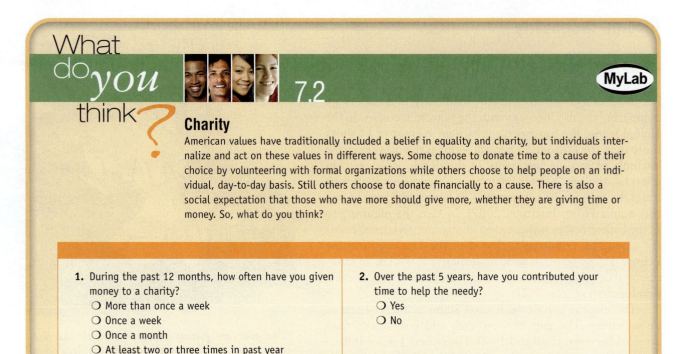

Charity

American values have traditionally included a belief in equality and charity, but individuals internalize and act on these values in different ways. Some choose to donate time to a cause of their choice by volunteering with formal organizations while others choose to help people on an individual, day-to-day basis. Still others choose to donate financially to a cause. There is also a social expectation that those who have more should give more, whether they are giving time or money. So, what do you think?

1. During the past 12 months, how often have you given money to a charity?
   ○ More than once a week
   ○ Once a week
   ○ Once a month
   ○ At least two or three times in past year
   ○ Not at all in past year

2. Over the past 5 years, have you contributed your time to help the needy?
   ○ Yes
   ○ No

See the back of the chapter to compare your answers to national survey data.

34 percent of the nation's wealth (up a few percentage points since 1990), and the bottom 10 percent virtually none (Economic Policy Institute, 2007).

Even at the top, the gaps are growing enormously. Between 1972 and 2001, the wages and salary of the 90th income percentile (the top 10 percent) grew 34 percent—about 1 percent a year. That means that being in the top 10 percent did not pay off handsomely. But income at the 99th percentile (the top 1 percent, or about $400,000 a year) rose 181 percent during that same period. And income at the 99.99th percentile (the top one-hundredth of 1 percent) rose 497 percent. That's for those earning over $6 million a year (Krugman, 2006). An old expression tells us, "A rising tide lifts all boats." But it seems that nowadays the rising tide lifts only the yachts.

These averages mask even greater disparities between Whites and people of color. The median wealth (net worth less home equity) of White households is $18,000, while that of African American households is a modest $200 and of Hispanic households, zero (Gates, 1999).

Class and Race

Class position is based on your position in the economic world. And while it is more flexible than your race or gender statuses that are fixed, or ascribed, at birth it is also less an achieved status than our ideology would often imagine. There is less than a 2 percent chance that someone whose parents are in the bottom 60 percent of all incomes will ever end up in the top 5 percent. And if you are born in the bottom 20 percent, you have a 40 percent chance of staying there (Hertz, 2007).

This means that the historical legacy of racism has enormous consequences for class position. Given how little mobility there actually is, the descendents of poor

Sociology and our World

CEO Compensation

The income gap between rich and poor is evident in the corporate world. Between 2001 and 2003, corporate profits increased 87 percent, while workers' wages and salaries enjoyed only a 4.5 percent cost of living increase. Average CEO pay today is $10.5 million a year, compared with just $28,310 for the average American worker. In 1970, the average CEO made 28 times what the average worker earned; today it is 400 times more (up from 282 times more in 2001).

And the gap is particularly big in the United States America's chief executives earn almost twice as much as their European counterparts (Towers Perrin, 2006).

HIGHEST-PAID CEOs in 2004

Executive	Company	Annual Compensation
Terry S. Semel	Yahoo!	$120,100,000
Lew Frankfort	Coach	$ 58,700,000
C. John Wilder	TXU	$ 54,900,000
Ray R. Irani	Occidental Petroleum	$ 37,800,000
Paul J. Evanson	Allegheny Energy	$ 37,500,000
Robert I. Toll	Toll Brothers	$ 36,400,000
Bruce Karatz	K.B. Home	$ 34,500,000
James E. Cayne	Bear Stearns	$ 32,600,000
Edward J. Zander	Motorola	$ 32,300,000

(*Source:* "A Payday for Performance," *Business Week*, April 18, 2005)

---

slaves were unlikely to rise very much in the class hierarchy—even over several generations. Race and class tend to covary—being African American is a good predictor of a lower-class position than being white.

Yet a few do make it, and at the same time as African Americans are over-represented among the poor, there is also a growing Black middle class, a class of professionals, corporate entrepreneurs, and other white-collar workers. While the existence of this Black middle class reveals that there is some mobility in American society, its small size also illustrates the tremendous obstacles facing any minority member who is attempting to become upwardly mobile.

And, on the other side, there is a significant number of poor Whites in America. Largely in rural areas, former farmers, migrants, and downsized and laid-off White workers have also tumbled below the poverty line. In cities like Flint, Michigan, where a large GM auto manufacturing plant closed, former workers, both White and Black, were suddenly and dramatically downwardly mobile. Race may be a predictor of poverty, but poverty surely knows no race.

Globally, poverty is also unequally distributed by race. The economic south, largely composed of Africans, South Asians, and Latin Americans is the home to more than four-fifths of all the world's poor—and a similar percentage of the world's people of color. On the other side of the global divide, the predominantly White nations of Europe are among those with the highest standards of living and the lowest levels of poverty.

Poverty in the United States and Abroad

In 1964, when President Lyndon Johnson declared "war on poverty" in the United States as part of his dream of a Great Society, he asked economist Mollie Oshansky to devise a poverty threshold, a minimum income necessary to not be poor. She decided that poverty meant "insufficient income to provide the food, shelter, and clothing needed to preserve health." Minimal requirement of shelter and clothing was hard to gauge, but not food: The Department of Agriculture prescribed several diets that provided minimal nutritional requirements. So she took the least expensive of the diets, multiplied it by three (one-third food, one-third shelter, one-third clothes), and voila! She estimated the poverty threshold—or the **poverty line.** Anyone who fell below it was categorized as poor (Andrew, 1999).

This system is not without its problems. First, its calculations are amazingly low, because shelter and clothing cost far more than food. In 2005, it was $9,570 for an individual (about $4.60 per hour), and $19,350 for a family of four (about $4.65 per hour if two adults work).

The calculations also don't take into account significant differences in cost of living in various regions of the United States: In Omaha, groceries cost 24 percent less than they do in Chicago, 22 percent less than in Boston, and 30 percent less than in Queens, New York. Housing in Omaha runs half of the average price in Chicago and 53 percent less than in Boston or Queens. But the same poverty threshold is used to determine who is poor and who isn't in all four cities (CNN has a city and state calculator for cost of living at http://cgi.money.cnn.com/tools/costofliving/costofliving.html).

The poverty line doesn't take into account things besides food, shelter, and clothes that are equally necessary to preserve health—things like child care, medical care, and transportation. The Economic Policy Institute offers a basic family budget calculator, including all of these necessities. For Omaha, it comes to $31,000 for a four-person household (two adults, two children). For Nassau-Suffolk County (part of New York City), it comes to $52,114. And the percentage of the population that can't meet the budget increases to 23.4 percent and 37.5 percent, respectively.

Yet these statistics are still sobering. The United States has the highest GDP in the world and the second highest GDP per capita (after Luxembourg), yet even 12.6 percent of its people fall below the poverty threshold—more than Croatia (11 percent) or Syria (11.9 percent), only a little less than Thailand (13.1 percent) (U.S. Census Bureau, 2006; CIA World Factbook, 2006; World Bank, 2006). ("GDP per capita" is the gross domestic product, the total value of all goods produced in the country divided by the number of inhabitants—a standard measure of the total wealth and economic development of a country. GDP per capita tells us little about the *distribution* of that wealth—whether one family owns everything or whether it's distributed exactly equally to everyone.)

Recently, sociologist Fred Block began to calculate somewhat different measures to illustrate poverty and standards of living. Instead of the "poverty line," Block calculated the "dream line"—estimates of the cost of a no-frills version of the American dream for an urban or suburban family of four (Figure 7.3). This includes the "four H's"—housing (owning a single-family home), high-quality child care, full health coverage, and higher education (enough savings to make sure that both

FIGURE 7.3 The Dream Gap

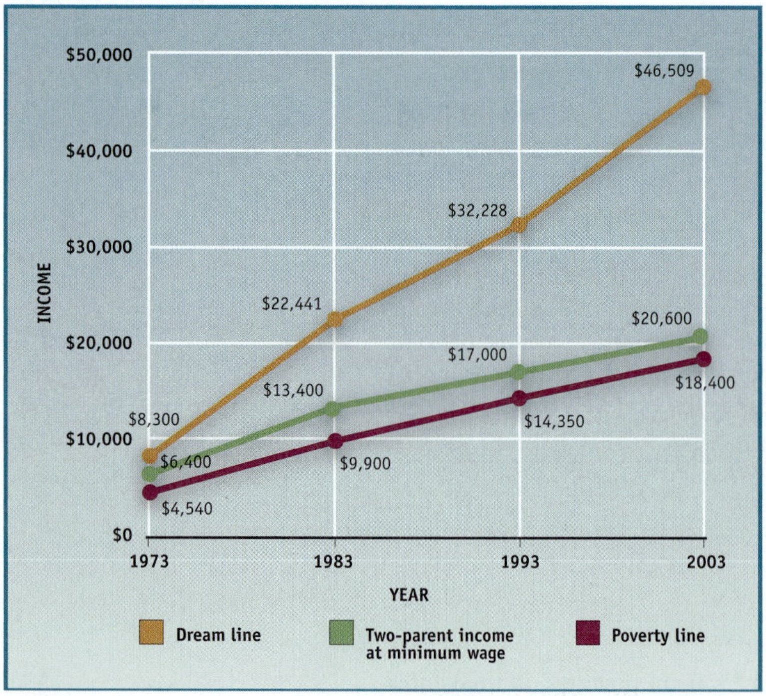

Source: From "Is the American Dream Dying?" by Fred Block, as appeared on Longview Institute website, www.longviewinstitute.org. Reprinted by permission of the author.

children can attend a public, four-year college or university). The "dream line" comes out to $46,509—and that estimate is low, because it's a national average and cannot even approach what people pay for these services in major metropolitan areas. Currently, if both parents work at minimum wage jobs, they earn $20,600—less than half of the American dream. It appears that the American dream is out of reach for many Americans.

What's worse, the American dream is harder to achieve than it was a generation ago. Between 1973 and 2003, housing costs increased by 515 percent, child care by 736 percent, higher education by 679 percent, and health insurance by 1,775 percent. During this same period, the average income for a family of four increased by 21.9 percent. It is hardly surprising that more American children live in poverty than in any other industrial nation except Russia (Luxembourg Income Study, 2007).

Who Is Poor in America?

The poor are probably not who you think they are. Contrary to stereotypes and media images:

- *Not all poor people are ethnic minorities.* The poverty *rate* for Whites is a low 11.7 percent, compared to that of blacks (25.8 percent), Native Americans (27.3 percent), Hispanics (23.5 percent), and Asians (11.4 percent). However, 26.2 million Whites were living in poverty in the United States in 2009, nearly 12 percent of the total 224.3 million (American Community Survey 2009).

- *Not all poor people live in the inner city.* In fact, the highest percentages of poor people live in the rural South. In 2002, Arkansas, Mississippi, and West Virginia had a poverty rate of 18 percent, compared to 12 percent in the urban North. The rural poor are less skilled and less educated than their urban counterparts, and the jobs available to them pay less than similar jobs in urban areas (Dudenhefer, 1993). And their numbers are increasing: Between 2000 and 2005, rural child poverty increased nearly 5 percent in Arkansas and Tennessee and more than 6 percent in Mississippi and North Carolina. Overall, rural poverty among children increased in 41 of the 50 U.S. states during that time (O'Hare and Savage, 2006).

- *Not all poor people are unemployed.* A 2005 Department of Labor report found that one in five poor people were in the labor force, but their incomes still did not lift them above the official poverty line. Of these "working poor," three out of five worked full time (U.S. Department of Labor, 2005).

- *Children are more likely than others to be poor.* Thirteen million American children under the age of 18 live in families with incomes below the poverty line. Some five million of them live in families with incomes less than half the official poverty level—and the numbers are increasing (Fass and Cauthen, 2006). Children suffer more than adults from limited health care, poor nutrition, and unsanitary living conditions. We can see the effects of poverty in the infant mortality rate, a measure of how many children survive their first year of life, and how many die from malnutrition, disease, accidents, and neglect. The lowest infant mortality rates are found in highly industrialized states like Sweden (2.77 deaths per 1,000 infants), Japan (3.28), and Spain (4.48). The United States, at 7.00, has a higher rate than any industrialized country, and it has increased by 8 percent since 2002.

It costs more to be poor. Strange as it sounds, the poor must pay more for essential goods and services:

- *Housing.* Renting rooms by the week or apartments by the month costs more than signing a lease.
- *Food.* Cheap housing has no kitchen, so you must subsist on more costly takeout. If you have a kitchen, supermarkets are often miles away, so you have to buy your food at expensive convenience stores.
- *Furniture.* Without a credit card, you can't buy furniture or appliances, so you rent them, for two or three times the price.
- *Money.* You probably can't get a checking account, and so you cash your checks at a check-cashing service and pay your bills with money orders (for hefty fees).

- *Mothers are more likely than others to be poor*. The poverty rate among female-headed households is more than double that of married couple families. Nearly half of all poor families are depending on a mother alone to support them (American Community Survey 2009).

- *The elderly are less likely than others to be poor.* A generation ago, in 1967, 30 percent of Americans over the age of 65 were living in poverty. By 2004, government intervention through such programs as Social Security, subsidized housing and food, and Medicare lowered the poverty rate to 9.8 percent, a little less than the elderly population in general (12.4 percent). Another 20 percent are "nearly poor," according to the Roper Poll. However, poverty places more of a burden on elderly people than others. They are more likely to suffer from chronic illnesses that require expensive treatment (my mother takes a dozen pills a day, and if she had no health insurance, her monthly pharmacy bill would run about $1,000). They are more likely to live alone and lack the social support networks that other poor people use to get by. And, as the population ages and people live longer, the government subsidy safety nets will be strained to the breaking point.

The Feminization of Poverty

Social scientists often argue that poverty is also being increasingly "feminized"—that is, women compose an increasing number of poor people. The image of the itinerant (male) pauper has largely faded, replaced today by a single mother. This **feminization of poverty has never been more obvious;** of the poor over the age of 18, 61 percent are women and 39 percent are men. Of all poor families, women head 51 percent. During the past 40 years, the number of single-parent families headed by women has more than doubled (U.S. Bureau of the Census, 2006). In 2000, 11 percent of all families in the United States lived in poverty, but 28 percent of families headed by single mothers did so (Dalakar, 2001). Supporting a family is difficult for single mothers because women's salaries are often lower anyway, and many single mothers have left the labor force or paused their education when they had children. The lack of adequate child supports in the United States—from parental leave to affordable day care to adequate health care—exacerbates the problem (McLanahan and Kelly, 2006). For women of color and their children, these problems can be even more acute (U.S. Census Bureau, 2006).

This disparity is echoed in the global arena. In poor countries, women suffer double deprivation, the deprivation of living in a poor country and the deprivation imposed because they are women. In high-income countries, women live much longer than men: 8.26 years in France, 7.35 years in Switzerland, 6.55 years in the United States. But in low-income countries, the gap in life expectancy is much narrower: 3.20 years in Zaire, 2.40 years in Sudan, 1.10 years in India. In Nepal and Guinea, the gap is even reversed: Men live slightly longer than women. Some commentators believe that the reason for the narrowed gap in life expectancy is a high death rate among the *men*, due to high levels of crime, occupational accidents, and chronic warfare. But certainly women suffer in societies where their life chances are composed entirely of bearing and raising children.

The "feminization of poverty" is a global phenomenon. In rich, poor, and emerging economies worldwide, women are over represented among the impoverished. ▼

Explaining Poverty

Why are poor people poor? Is it because they are born into poverty, or because they don't work hard enough to get themselves out of it, or because they have some physical, intellectual, or emotional problem that prevents them from getting out?

Personal Initiative. One common explanation is that people are poor because they lack something—initiative, drive, ambition, discipline. A question in the General Social Survey asks, "Differences in social standing between people are acceptable because they basically reflect what people made out of the opportunities they had" and 74 percent of respondents agreed. They were expressing a long-standing belief that people are poor because they are unmotivated and lazy. They do not try hard enough. They don't want to work. While we often excuse widows, orphans, children, and the handicapped—the "deserving poor"—who can't help it (Katz, 1990), most Americans believe that the vast majority of poor people are "undeserving" poor.

Sociologists, however, understand poverty differently—as a structural problem, not a personal failing. In fact, it's often the other way around: People are unmotivated and lack ambition *because they are poor*, not poor because they lack ambition. No matter how hard they try and how motivated they are, the cards are so heavily stacked against them that they eventually give up—as would any sensible person. In *Nickel and Dimed* (2001), renowned journalist Barbara Ehrenreich tried an experiment: to live on minimum wage for a year. "Disguised" as a poor person, she applied for and received jobs as a waitress in Florida, a maid in Maine, and a Wal-Mart employee in Minnesota. At first she worried that she would not be able to maintain the ruse: Surely co-workers would notice her superior intelligence and competence and realize that she wasn't "one of them," or else the boss would notice and fast-track her into a managerial position. But neither happened. She was no smarter and *less* competent than anyone else in minimum wage jobs. Back home as a renowned journalist, she had to conclude that her privileged lifestyle had a little to do with her drive, ambition, intelligence, and talent, and a lot to do with her social location. Anthropologist Katherine Newman found that poor people actually work harder than wealthy people—often in two demeaning, difficult, and exhausting dead-end jobs (Newman, 1999).

The Culture of Poverty. In 1965, sociologist Oscar Lewis introduced the influential culture of poverty thesis (Lewis, 1965) that argued that poverty is not a result of individual inadequacies but of larger social and cultural factors. Poor children are socialized into believing that they have nothing to strive for, that there is no point in working to improve their conditions. As adults, they are resigned to a life of poverty, and they socialize their children the same way. Therefore poverty is transmitted from one generation to another.

This notion of resignation has often been challenged. For example, the General Social Survey states: "America has an open society. What one achieves in life no longer depends on one's family background, but on the abilities one has and the education one acquires," and 76 percent of lower-class respondents agree, only a little less than the working-class (84 percent), middle class (87 percent), or upper class (80 percent). Certainly these percentages don't indicate any culture of complacency.

Structures of Inequality. Today sociologists know that poverty results from nationwide and worldwide factors that no one individual has any control over, such as economic changes, globalization, racism, and government policies (the minimum wage, Social Security, publicly funded or subsidized health care and day care, and other antipoverty initiatives). Today we also understand that though people living in poverty are not necessarily resigned to their situation, they face structural disadvantages that are nearly impossible to overcome. They would like to lift themselves out of poverty and lead better lives, but they suffer from:

- Poor education
- Higher rates of chronic diseases
- Poor or nonexistent health care
- Inferior housing
- A greater likelihood of being victimized by crime and a greater likelihood of being labeled criminals

Did *you* know?

For generations, almost every American child has grown up hearing that in America "you can grow up to be President of the United States." As proof, we hear of Abraham Lincoln (1809–1865), who was born in a log cabin and did his school work on the back of a shovel because he couldn't afford paper. According to *Abraham Lincoln: The Man behind the Myths* (Oates, 1994), Lincoln was indeed born in a log cabin near Hodgenville, Kentucky. But he was anything but destitute: Log cabins were common on the frontier, and his was set on a 238-acre farm. His father was one of the largest landowners of the area. And he definitely had paper and pencils for his homework.

We may believe that wealth or poverty are attributes of individuals—those who work hard enough and sacrifice enough get ahead, and those who don't, well, don't—wealth and poverty are actually structural features of society. Your relative wealth or poverty depends on who you are, more than on how hard you work.

What's more, wealth and poverty are related to each other. Sociologists have argued that the poor are poor *because* the rich are rich. Maintaining a wealthy (or middle-class) lifestyle requires that some people be poor.

Poverty leads to reduced life chances, limited opportunities for securing everything from health care to education, from job autonomy to leisure, from safety at home to the potential for a long life. People at the top of the social hierarchy have resources that enable them to respond to opportunities when they arise, like choosing a prestigious internship or job even if it doesn't pay, or relocating to an expensive city or area in order to garner better education or experience. What's more, their superior resources allow people at the top to weather problems, from illnesses to accidents to lawsuits to unemployment, that ruin the already precarious lives of the poor. Advantages start early and persist throughout life. And they are virtually invisible—unless you don't have them.

Poverty on a World Scale

Half the world's population—three billion people—live on less than $1 a day (Table 7.2). The gross domestic product of the poorest 48 nations in the world—that is,

TABLE 7.2

Share of People Living on Less than $1 a Day (%)								
REGION	**1981**	**1984**	**1987**	**1990**	**1993**	**1996**	**1999**	**2001**
East Asia and Pacific	56.7	38.8	28.0	29.5	24.9	15.9	15.3	14.3
Europe and Central Asia	0.8	0.6	0.4	0.5	3.7	4.4	6.3	3.5
Latin America and Caribbean	10.1	12.2	11.3	11.6	11.8	9.4	10.5	9.9
Middle East and North Africa	5.1	3.8	3.2	2.3	1.6	2.0	2.7	2.4
South Asia	51.5	46.8	45.0	41.3	40.1	36.7	32.8	31.9
Sub-Saharan Africa	41.6	46.3	46.9	44.5	44.1	46.1	45.7	46.4
World	40.4	33.0	28.5	27.9	26.3	22.3	21.5	20.7

Source: World Bank, 2005.

25 percent of the world's nations—is less than the wealth of the world's three richest *people* combined (Shah, 2007).

And yet the actual number of the world's poor has actually been declining. In 2001, there were 390 million *fewer* people living in poverty than 20 years earlier. What happened?

For one thing, China happened. There are 400 million fewer poor people in China today than in 1981. China's growth, coupled with the growth of the economies of East and South Asia, has shifted the global distribution of poverty, so that today the region with the greatest depth of poverty is sub-Saharan Africa. By 2015, that region will be the epicenter of world poverty (Chen and Ravallon, 2006).

Reducing Poverty

When President Johnson declared a "war on poverty" in 1964, he assumed, optimistically, that it was a war that could be won. The ensuing half century has shown that poverty is a more difficult enemy than anyone originally believed—not because poor people have it so good that they don't want to work to get themselves out of poverty, but because the structural foundations of poverty seem to be so solidly entrenched.

A greater proportion of families and children in America today live in poverty (12.6 percent) than in 1973—when the 11.1 percent poverty figure was the lowest ever on record (Eberstadt, 2006). Dramatic structural, demographic, and policy shifts keep the number of poor high but also obscure just how many poor people have struggled to get themselves out of poverty.

Different societies have tried different sorts of strategies to alleviate poverty. Virtually all industrial nations have a welfare system that guarantees all citizens the basic structural opportunities to work their way out of poverty: free education, national health care, welfare subsistence, housing allowances. Only the United States does not provide those basic structural requirements, and so poor people spend most of their money on housing, health care, and food. As a result, the United States has the highest percentage of poor people of all industrialized countries. While many Americans believe, as the Bible says, "blessed are the poor," the country, as a whole, does little more than bless them and send them on their way.

Global efforts to reduce poverty on a global scale have historically relied on "outside" help: the direct aid of wealthier countries, global organizations devoted to the issue, or large-scale philanthropic foundations. The United States spends billions in direct aid to poor nations. And the World Health Organization, the Red Cross and Red Crescent, and other global organizations channel hundreds of billions of dollars to poorer nations. Finally, foundations such as the Ford and Gates Foundations and the Open Society Institute funnel massive amounts of aid to poor nations to improve health care and education and to reduce poverty, disease, and violence. In 2001, the United Nations announced the "Millennium Project"—a global effort to identify the causes of poverty and to eradicate extreme poverty and hunger by 2015.

This strategy is vital in creating the infrastructure (roads, hospitals, schools) and sustaining agricultural food production (irrigation, seed technologies) that will enable nations to combat poverty. Yet this strategy of direct payments to governments has also received criticism because some of these funds have been terribly misspent by corrupt political regimes, and often little of the money collected actually reaches the poor themselves.

Several newer strategies target local people more directly. In the poorer rural areas of Latin America, the governments of Mexico and Brazil, for example, have embraced "conditional cash transfer schemes" (CCTS) by which the government gives direct payments to poor families of about $50 a month. This may mark the difference

▲ Microcredit helps individuals pull themselves out of poverty by providing tiny loans—some as little as $9—that enable borrowers to start businesses. Most micro-credit participants worldwide are women.

between too little food to feed the family and just barely enough. CCTS are "conditional": In return the beneficiaries must have their children vaccinated, their health monitored, and keep them in school. ("New Thinking about an Old Problem," 2005).

In Pakistan, economist Muhammad Yunus has developed a system of "microcredit" by which his bank lends tiny amounts to local poor people. Initially, as a young professor, he loaned a group of women $27 to buy straw to make stools. Over the past 30 years, Grameen Bank has lent $5.72 billion to 6.61 million borrowers—some loans as low as $9—including beggars who wanted to start small businesses or a group of women who needed start-up funds to start a cell phone business or to buy basket-weaving supplies. The bank claims a 98% repayment rate (Moore, 2006).

In 2006, Yunus received the Nobel Peace Prize in recognition of his work to end poverty one person at a time.

Social Mobility

Social mobility means the movement from one class to another. It can occur in two forms: (1) *intergenerational*—that is, your parents are working class, but you became lower, or your parents are middle class, but you became upper class; and (2) *intragenerational*—that is, you move from working to lower, or from middle to upper, all within your lifetime. Social mobility remains one of America's most enduring beliefs, but it is far less common in reality than we imagine. One of the hallmarks of American sociology has been to measure social mobility—and the persistence of our beliefs in it. One of the most important studies of mobility was undertaken in the 1960s by Peter Blau and Otis Dudley Duncan (Blau and Duncan, 1967). In their studies of the American occupational structure, they found actually very little mobility between classes, although they found a lot of mobility within any particular class. People moved up or down a little bit from the position of their parents, but movement from one class to another was extremely rare.

Intergenerational mobility seems to have increased since Blau and Duncan. Hout (1984) found that 65 percent of sons were not in the occupational category of their fathers. And Solon (1992) found that while intergenerational mobility was less than he originally expected, it was still significant. Generations do seem to be mobile, but almost as many went from riches to rags as went from rags to riches.

Whatever the American dream may promise about equal opportunity and pulling yourself up by your bootstraps, it is actually far more likely that either you are born with opportunity or you aren't. Most of the sons stayed squarely in the social class of their fathers. Although America doesn't have the same rigid standards as some other societies, it still makes the primary determinant of your social class your parents.

Dynamics of Mobility

Much of the upward mobility that Blau and Duncan found was *structural mobility*—a general upward trend of the entire society, not the result of either intergenerational or intragenerational mobility. **Structural mobility** means that the entire society got

Try It   Living on an Impoverished Salary

Contributed by Jeff Dixon, *Indiana University.*

OBJECTIVE: While no activity can truly help you totally understand what it is like to live in poverty, this activity will give you a sense of what it might be like to be poor in the United States and also what it might be like to be poor in a developing country in the world.

STEP 1: Research

Review the following two scenarios before moving to Step 2.

▶ *Scenario 1: Single mother with one child in the United States.* Go to the Economic Policy Institute website (www.epi.org) and search for "family budget calculator." Note what a livable family budget would look like for this family in your geographic location. Assume that this mother is earning minimum wage in your state and works 35 hours a week as a part-time worker with no benefits. Assume her child is 4 years old and that this mother must pay for child care when she works. Next assume that there is no other financial support.

▶ *Scenario 2: Single mother with one child in Haiti.* Go to globalissues.org and read about global poverty and what it means to live on less than $2.00 a day. Using Google.com as your search engine, type in the words "Poverty" and "Haiti." Review some of the websites that deal with Haitian poverty. Assume that this mother is currently unemployed and that she is unable to find a regular job. She is able to find periodic day labor and makes the

equivalent of $1.00 a day. Assume that her child is 4 years old and that there are relatives who help with child care. Next assume that there is no other financial support.

STEP 2: Plan

Using the information provided in Step 1, prepare a monthly budget for each scenario. When in doubt about information, estimate your figures and explain the reasons for your estimation.

STEP 3: Explain

After looking at the budgets for each scenario, briefly explain what life would be for families in both Scenario 1 and Scenario 2.

STEP 4: Theories

Examine what theories in this chapter offer the best explanations for poverty in the two scenarios and provide an explanation of your responses.

STEP 5: Discuss

Be prepared to discuss your responses and to turn in your budgets for each scenario, your explanations of what life would be like, and your theoretical explanations.

---

wealthier. Because of the post–World War II economic boom, many working-class families found themselves enjoying middle-class incomes. Similar structural mobility occurred during the Industrial Revolution, when the labor force shifted from farming/agriculture to manufacturing.

More recently, the pattern has been downward mobility, caused by the decline in manufacturing jobs (40 percent disappeared between 1970 and 2000), coupled with the growth of service jobs. Service jobs tend to pay low wages (averaging about half the wages of manufacturing jobs) and offer few or no benefits (averaging 60 percent less than manufacturing jobs). As a result, many people who grew up or spent most of their lives in the middle class find themselves working class or even working poor (Uchitelle, 2006).

Many Americans are underemployed—highly educated and qualified for positions higher than the ones they occupy. On *The Simpsons*, the proprietor of the comic book store defends his bitter outlook on life by saying, "I have a master's degree in Folklore and Mythology." Millions of Americans have had similar experiences. They acquire college degrees, with dreams of a white-collar job and a middle-class lifestyle, only to find that the jobs simply aren't there. So they take jobs for which they are vastly overqualified in the service industry or as clerical workers, with low salaries, no benefits, and no possibility of career advancement, and join the ranks of the working poor.

How do we know what we know?

Mobility Studies

The classic study of intergenerational mobility was by Peter Blau and Otis Dudley Duncan. In their effort to understand the *American Occupational Structure* (the title of their 1967 book, which summarized two decades of research), they created a "path diagram" of American mobility using four key variables: father's level of education, father's occupation, son's level of education, and son's occupation. (These questions were asked only of White men.) One version is shown in the diagram.

Here, the son's education and occupation depend on both ascriptive characteristics (father's occupation and education are fixed, and you are born

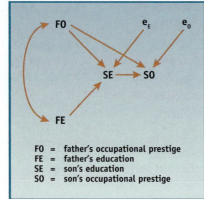

FO = father's occupational prestige
FE = father's education
SE = son's education
SO = son's occupational prestige

with them) and achieved characteristics (the "e" refers to external factors). The son's education is seen as an intervening variable because it affects occupation all by itself, as well as being influenced by father's education and occupation.

Blau and Duncan were interested in the relative weight of these ascribed or achieved characteristics to measure the "openness" of the American class system and the amount of mobility in it. One of their key findings was that the effects of father's occupation and education were both direct and indirect. They directly confer some advantages and also indirectly enhance their sons' education, which furthers the sons' success as well.

Among their key findings were that 40 percent of the sons of blue-collar workers *moved up* to white-collar jobs. Perhaps even more intriguing, almost 30 percent of the sons of white-collar workers *moved down* to blue-collar jobs. Today, though, we would also question the idea that we can chart "American" mobility patterns by using data drawn only from White men.

Another way to move down from the middle class is to become a permanent temp or part-time worker. Employers prefer temporary employees, even for contracts that will last years, because "temps" command lower salaries and receive neither benefits nor severance pay. Sometimes, employers demote full time employees to a "part time" status of 38 hours per week, because employment laws require benefits to be offered only to full-time employees. The result is that employees suffer from the reduced salary and benefits but corporate profits increase (Cummings, 2004).

Mobility takes place largely within groups, not between them. Between 1980 and 2000, the lower class saw an income increase of 15 percent. The middle and working classes saw gains of around 20 percent. The upper middle and upper class enjoyed an increase of 59 percent. But the superrich of the income scale saw a windfall. They were earning an average of $132,000 in 1980, and in 2000 they were earning $500,000, *an increase of 400 percent* (Neilsen and Alderson, 1997; U.S. Census Bureau, 2001). The poor are staying poor, but the superrich are getting superricher (Economic Mobility Project, 2006). This is the result of a general relaxation of regulations placed on corporations, increasing profits massively, and the suppression of wages, part-time work, and the decrease in the power of unions to protect workers.

Mobility is also affected by race and ethnicity. White people have higher upward mobility. With the economic boom in the 1980s and 1990s, some people of color were able to move up the socioeconomic ladder, but not many. In 2000, African American households earned 64 percent of the average White household, about the same share as in 1970. Hispanic households actually lost ground: In 1975, they earned

67 percent of the income of White households, and in 2000 they earned 66 percent (Featherman and Hauser, 1978; Pomer, 1983; U.S. Census Bureau, 2001).

Historically, women have had less opportunity for upward mobility than men because of the types of jobs they were permitted: mostly clerical and service positions that do not offer many opportunities for promotion or increased responsibility. And when they married, they were expected to quit even those jobs or else decrease their hours to part time.

Today, many middle-class women still do not pursue careers that afford middle-class lifestyles because they curtail career ambitions for household and child care responsibilities. As a result, if they divorce, they experience downward mobility. Not only do they lose the second (and often higher) income from their husband, they also lose benefits like health care and insurance (Weitzman, 1996).

Social Mobility Today

Since the beginning of the twenty-first century, the United States has become less mobile than it has ever been in its history. According to a recent survey, Americans are more likely than they were 30 years ago to end up in the class into which they were born. Rates of mobility are about the same as France or England—countries with hereditary aristocracies and, in the case of Britain, a hereditary monarch. American levels of mobility are significantly lower than Canada and most Scandinavian countries (Economic Mobility Project, 2006).

That doesn't mean that Americans have stopped believing in mobility, though. A recent poll in *The New York Times* found that 40 percent of Americans believed that the chance of moving up from one class to another had risen over the last 30 years—the same period when those chances were actually shrinking (Scott and Leonhardt, 2005).

Global Inequality

Global inequality is the systematic differences in wealth and power among countries. These differences among countries coexist alongside differences within countries. Increasingly the upper classes in different countries are more similar to each other—especially in their patterns of consumption—than they are to the middle classes in their own countries. The world seems to be developing a global class structure.

The same processes we observed in the United States are happening on a world scale. For example, over the past 30 years, the overall standard of living in the world has risen. Illiteracy is down, the infant mortality rate is down, the average income is up, and life expectancy is up. But many of these gains are in countries that were high or middle income to begin with, such as the advanced industrial economies of Europe. The standard of living in many of the poorest countries has actually declined. Rich countries are getting richer; poor countries are getting poorer.

The income gap between rich and poor that we see in the United States is becoming the pattern worldwide. The richest 20 percent of the world's population receives about 80 percent of the global income and accounts for 86 percent of total private consumption, while the poorest 20 percent survives on just 1 percent of the global income and accounts for 1.3 percent of private consumption (Figure 7.4). Actually, the three richest U.S. individuals together—Bill Gates, Warren Buffett, and Paul Allen—earn as much as the annual economic output of the world's 48 poorest countries (Miller and Serafin, 2006).

FIGURE 7.4 Where the Money Is

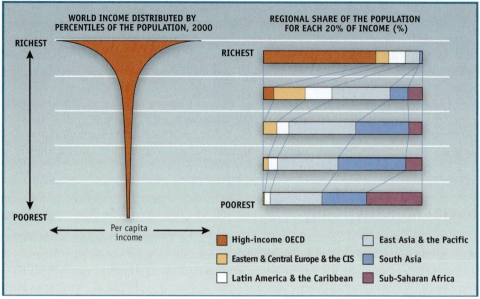

Source: From "Trends in Global Income Distribution 1970–2015" by Yuri Dikhanov, *Human Development Report 2005*, p. 37. Reprinted by permission of Yuri Dikhanov, www.hdr.undp.org.

Globalization has increased the economic, political, and social interconnectedness of the world. It has also resulted in both unthinkable wealth and widespread poverty and suffering. Three decades ago, the richest 20 percent was 30 times better off than the poorest 20 percent. By 1998, the gap had widened to 82 times (Gates, 1999).

Classifying Global Economies

Social scientists used to divide the world into three socioeconomic categories:

- *The First World* includes wealthy, industrialized, capitalist countries: the United States, Canada, Western Europe, Australia, and New Zealand. It is the equivalent of the upper class.
- *The Second World* is made up of less wealthy, less industrialized, socialist countries: the Soviet Union, Eastern Europe, China, Cuba, and a few countries in Africa. It is the equivalent of the middle or working class.
- *The Third World* includes poor, nonindustrialized countries, usually colonial or postcolonial states: Africa, Asia, Latin America, and Oceania.

But that classification is now considered outdated, ethnocentric, and way too broad to be useful (there are over 100 countries in the "Third World"). Today we tend to use the terms *developed, developing,* and *underdeveloped,* or else the World Bank's classification by economic and social indicators, listed below, that suggest a high or low quality of life (Figure 7.5):

- *Gross domestic product (GDP),* the annual production of goods and services, averaging $8,200 per capita worldwide in 2004. High-income countries account for about 80 percent of the world's GDP and low-income countries about 2 percent (World Bank, 2006).
- *Work,* or the percentage of the population engaged in agriculture versus industry. Because agricultural work is usually at subsistence level—that is, farmers

FIGURE 7.5 The World by Income

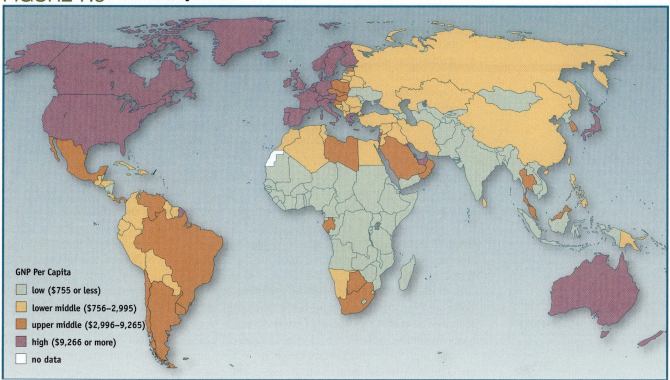

GNP Per Capita

- low ($755 or less)
- lower middle ($756–2,995)
- upper middle ($2,996–9,265)
- high ($9,266 or more)
- no data

Note: This map presents economies classified according to World Bank estimates of 1999 GNP per capita. Not shown on the map because of space constraints are French Polynesia (high income); American Samoa (upper middle income); Fiji, Kiribati, Samoa, and Tonga (lower middle income); and Tuvalu (no data).
Source: From The World Bank website, http//go.worldbank.org. Reprinted by permission of the International Bank for Reconstruction and Development/The World Bank.

produce about as much as they need to survive, barring droughts, pestilence, and flood—industrial work is associated with a higher quality of life. In poor countries, most people use muscle or animal power, so complex machinery is rare.

- *Life expectancy.* During the last 30 years, better nutrition and advanced health care have increased the mean life expectancy around the world by a decade, to 64. But in low-income countries, it's still hovering around 50.
- *Infant mortality rate.* Better nutrition and advanced health care have had an impact on infant mortality as well: It's currently about 50 deaths per 1,000 births. But it's much higher in low-income countries, much lower in high-income countries.
- *Literacy rate,* the population over the age of 15 who can read and write, about 77 percent worldwide.
- *Percentage of children aged 10 to 14 in the labor force.* Child labor is illegal in most high-income countries because when children are working, they cannot be in school, learning the skills necessary to overcome poverty. In addition, most of the unskilled and semiskilled jobs children are qualified for are too strenuous for growing bodies.

The World Bank also classifies quality of life based on:

- *Birth rate.* Poor countries usually have the world's highest birth rates. In traditional societies, children are an important economic asset because they can assist in farming. But in urban societies, they are an economic liability because they are dependent, can't work, and must be fed and clothed. Thus, the more children you have, the poorer you are. Furthermore, an expanding population limits the opportunities for economic improvement.

- *Distribution of wealth.* Every country has rich and poor people, but inequality is more pronounced in poor countries: In India, the middle-class elite buy magazines about the latest diet fads, while outside their windows, people are starving to death.
- *Gender inequality.* Poor countries usually depend almost entirely on male labor and limit the opportunities for women (this usually means that they stay at home, and the birth rate is very high). Many analysts conclude that raising the living standards in a country depends on getting women in the workforce.

High-Income Countries. There are about 40 high-income countries, including the United States ($37,800 per capita GDP), Switzerland ($32,600), Japan ($28,000), and Spain ($22,000). These countries cover 25 percent of the world's land surface and are home to 17 percent of its population. Together they enjoy more than half of the world's total income and control the world's financial markets. Most of these nations' populations live in or near cities. Industry is dominated by large-scale factories, big machinery, and advanced technology; however, these countries are also at the forefront of the Information Revolution, with most companies that make and sell computers and most computer users; 53 percent of the United States' population and 33 percent of Switzerland's is on the Internet. Because they have access to better nutrition and expert medical care, residents of these countries tend to have high life expectancies (80.8 in Japan) and low infant mortality rates (4.43 per 100,000 in Switzerland). Because the population is mostly urban and well educated, the birth rate tends to be low (10.1 per thousand in Spain), and the literacy rate high (99 percent in Switzerland).

Middle-Income Countries. There are about 90 middle-income countries, divided into high middle-income countries like Portugal ($18,000 per capita GDP), Uruguay ($12,600), and South Africa ($10,700), and low middle-income countries like Brazil ($7,600), Libya ($6,400), and China ($5,000). These countries cover 47 percent of Earth's land area and are home to more than half of its population. Only two-thirds of the people live in or near cities. There are many industrial jobs, but the Information Revolution has had only a minor impact: Only 7 percent of Portugal's residents and 4 percent of South Africa's is on the Internet. Demographic indicators vary from country to country: In South Africa, the life expectancy is very low (43.3), but in China it is quite high (71.6). The infant mortality rate is 4.92 deaths per 1,000 births in Portugal and 27.62 in Brazil. Middle countries are not staying in the middle: They are getting either richer or poorer. (And in those countries, the rich are also getting richer and the poor are getting poorer.)

Low-Income Countries. There are about 60 low-income countries, including Jamaica ($3,800 per capita GDP), India ($2,900), Kenya ($1,000), and Somalia ($500). These countries cover 28 percent of the world's land area and are home to 28 percent of its population. Most people live in villages and on farms, as their ancestors have for centuries; only about a third live in cities. They are primarily agricultural, with only a few sustenance industries and virtually no access to the Information Revolution: There are 45,000 Internet users among Kenya's 30 million people and 200 among Somalia's 7.4 million. They tend to have low life expectancies (46.6 in Somalia), high infant mortality rates (62.6 deaths per 1,000 births in Kenya), high birth rates (40.13 per thousand in Kenya), and low literacy rates (52 percent in India). Hunger, disease, and unsafe housing frame their lives (CIA, 2007).

Explaining Global Inequality

For many years, sociologists weren't worried about the causes of global inequality as much as its cure, how to help the underprivileged countries "get ahead." Today, social scientists are less optimistic and are at least equally concerned with what keeps poor countries poor.

Market Theories. These theories stress the wisdom of the capitalist marketplace. They assume that the best possible economic consequences will result if individuals are free to make their own economic decisions, uninhibited by any form of governmental constraint; government direction or intervention, the theorists say, will only block economic development. However, they shouldn't make just any economic decisions: The only avenue to economic growth is unrestricted capitalism (Berger, 1986; Ranis and Mahmood, 1991; Rostow, 1962).

By far the most influential market theory was devised by W. W. Rostow, an economic advisor to President Kennedy. His **modernization theory** focuses on the conditions necessary for a low-income country to develop economically. He argued that a nation's poverty is largely due to the cultural failings of its people. They lack a "work ethic" that stresses thrift and hard work. They would rather consume today than invest in the future. Such failings are reinforced by government policies that set wages, control prices, and generally interfere with the operation of the economy. They can develop economically only if they give up their "backward" way of life and adopt modern Western economic institutions, technologies, and cultural values that emphasize savings and productive investment.

According to Rostow's theory, countries desiring to break out of poverty must go through four stages:

1. *Traditional economy.* This is the "starting point" of impoverished countries, characterized by a lack of a work ethic and a fatalistic worldview that encourages people to accept hardship and suffering as the unavoidable plight of life. They are therefore discouraged from working hard and saving their money.

2. *Takeoff to economic growth.* When the people in impoverished countries begin to jettison their traditional values and start to work hard and save money to invest in the future, they begin to experience some economic growth. Wealthy countries have an essential role to play in assisting this growth: They can help control the population by introducing birth control and family planning techniques, increase food production by introducing modern agricultural techniques, and provide investment capital or low-cost loans for roads, airports, new industries, and so on. Perhaps most importantly, they can teach the values and ideals of modern capitalism.

3. *Drive to technological maturity.* Wealthy countries still play an important role, providing both financial assistance and training in modern values, as the impoverished countries slowly climb to an increased level of economic functioning ("cruising altitude"). Gradually they improve their technology, reinvest their recently acquired wealth in new industries, and adopt the institutions and values of the wealthy countries.

4. *High mass consumption.* Finally, people in the impoverished countries would enjoy the fruits of their labor by achieving a standard of living similar to that of the wealthy countries.

It is somewhat difficult to believe that the people of Somalia, with per capita income of about $500, or Mali, at $900, fail to stash their money in savings accounts and IRAs because they are so eager to consume or that their path to economic solvency lies in abandoning their traditional laziness for good old Yankee elbow grease. Sociologists have been quick to criticize this theory for its ethnocentrism (using the United States as the "model" for what development should look like), its suggestion that people are responsible for their own poverty, and for its curious assurance that wealthy countries act as benevolent Big Brothers to the rest of the world, when in fact they often take advantage of poor countries and block their economic development. Besides, it is not simply a matter of "us" versus "them," rich and poor countries occupying separate social worlds: In a global economy, every nation is affected by the others.

Nevertheless, Rostow's theory is still influential today (Firebaugh, 1996, 1999; Firebaugh and Beck, 1994; Firebaugh and Sandu, 1998). It is sometimes argued that global free trade, achieved by minimizing government restrictions on business, will provide the only route to economic growth. Calls for an end to all restrictions on trade, an end to minimum wage and other labor laws, and an end to environmental restrictions on business are part of this set of policies.

State-Centered Theories. Perhaps the solution is not the market, operating on its own, but active intervention by the government (or by international organizations). State-centered theories argue that appropriate government policies do not interfere with economic development but that governments play a key role in bringing it about. For proof, they point to the newly developed economies of East Asia, which grew in conjunction with, and possibly because of, government intervention (Appelbaum and Henderson, 1992; Cumings, 1998). The governments have acted aggressively, sometimes violently, to ensure economic stability: They outlaw labor unions, jail labor leaders, ban strikes, repress civil rights. They have been heavily involved in social programs such as low-cost housing and universal education. The costs have been enormous: horrible factory conditions, widespread environmental degradation, exploitation of female workers and "guest workers" from impoverished neighboring countries. But the results have been spectacular: Japan enjoyed an economic growth of 10 percent per year through the 1960s, 5 percent through the 1970s, and 4 percent through the 1980s (followed by a slowdown to 1.8%). It has a national reserve of $664 billion and has donated $7.9 billion in economic aid to other countries.

Dependency Theory. **Dependency theory** focuses on the unequal relationship between wealthy countries and poor countries, arguing that poverty is the result of exploitation. Wealthy countries (and the multinational corporations based in them) try to acquire an ever-increasing share of the world's wealth by pursuing policies and practices that block the economic growth of the poor countries. Capitalist countries exploit worker countries, just as Karl Marx predicted, thereby ensuring that the rich get richer and the poor get poorer.

The exploitation began with **colonialism**, a political-economic system under which powerful countries established, for their own profit, rule over weaker peoples or countries (Cooper, 2005). The most extensive colonialism occurred between 1500 and 1900, when England, Spain, France, and some other European countries exercised control over the entire world—only Ethiopia, Japan, and Thailand were free of European domination throughout the 400 years. Europeans immigrated in large numbers only to regions with low native populations—the Americas, southern Africa, Australia, and New Zealand—which soon became colonial powers in their own right. Other nations were merely occupied and mined for the raw materials necessary to maintain European wealth—petroleum, copper, iron, sugar, tobacco, and even people (the African slave trade was not finally outlawed until 1830).

After World War II, colonialism gradually ended, today only a few colonial possessions are left, mostly small islands (Bermuda, Guam, Martinique). However, the exploitation did not end. Transnational (or "multinational") corporations, often with the support of powerful banks and governments of rich countries, established factories in poor countries, using cheap labor and raw materials to minimize their production costs without governmental interference. Today corporations engage in "offshoring," setting up factories in poor countries where the cost of materials and wages are low.

The exercise of power is crucial to maintaining these dependent relationships on the global level. Local businesses cannot compete with the strength of multinational corporations, and former self-subsisting peasants have no other economic options but to work at near-starvation wages at foreign-controlled mines and factories. In 2001, the average Mexican maquiladora worker (employee of a foreign corporation) earned the equivalent of $5.31 per day (with benefits) or $3.56 (without).

Sometimes individual economic pressure is backed up by force. When local leaders question the unequal arrangements, they are suppressed. When people elect an opposition government, it is likely to be overthrown by the country's military—backed by armed forces of the industrialized countries themselves. For example, the CIA played a major role in overthrowing the Marxist governments of Guatemala in 1954 and Chile in 1973 and in undermining the leftist government of Nicaragua in the 1980s.

Dependency theory has been criticized for being simplistic and for putting all blame for global poverty on high-income countries and multinational corporations. Some social scientists, such as Enrique Fernando Cardoso (also a past president of Brazil) argue that, under certain circumstances, poor countries can still develop economically, although only in ways shaped by their reliance on wealthier countries (Cardoso and Faletto, 1978).

World System Theory. **World system theory** draws on dependency theory but focuses on the global economy as an international network dominated by capitalism. It argues that the global economy cannot be understood merely as a collection of countries, some rich and some poor, operating independently of each other except for a dynamic of exploitation and oppression: It must be understood as a single unit. Rich and poor countries are intimately linked.

Immanuel Wallerstein, who founded world system theory and coined the term *world economy* (1974, 1979, 1984, 2004), argued that interconnectedness of the world system began in the 1500s, when Europeans began their economic and political domination of the rest of the world. Because capitalism depends on generating the maximum profits for the minimum of expenditures, the world system continues to benefit rich countries (which acquire the profits) and harm the rest of the world (by minimizing local expenditures and therefore perpetuating poverty).

According to Wallerstein, the world system is composed of four interrelated elements: (1) a global market of goods and labor; (2) the division of the population into different economic classes, based loosely on the Marxian division of owners and workers; (3) an international system of formal and informal political relations among the most powerful countries, who compete or cooperate with each other to shape the world economy; and (4) the division of countries into three broad economic zones—core, periphery, and semiperiphery.

The *core countries* include Western Europe and places where Western Europeans immigrated in large numbers: the United States, Canada, Australia, New Zealand, South Africa, plus Japan, the only non-European country to become a colonial power in its own right. These are the most advanced industrial countries, and they take the lion's share of profits in the world economic system. Goods, services, and people tend to flow *into* the core.

The *periphery* is the opposite zone, corresponding roughly with the Third World, and includes countries that were under Western European domination but did not receive many permanent settlers: sub-Saharan Africa (other than South Africa), India and Pakistan, parts of Latin America, most of East and Southeast Asia, and Oceania. These countries are low income, largely agricultural, and often manipulated by core countries for their economic advantage. Goods, services, and people tend to flow *away from* the periphery.

Finally, the *semiperiphery* is an intermediate zone between the core and the periphery. This includes the former Soviet Union, Eastern Europe, countries that were under Western European domination only briefly (the Middle East, parts of East Asia), or countries that received a substantial number of immigrants but not as many as the core (parts of Latin America). These are semi-industrialized, middle-income countries that often form their own local core-periphery systems. For example, goods and services flow *into* Russia from its own periphery states in Eastern Europe, the Baltic, and Central Asia, but they also flow *from* Russia into Western Europe and the United States. The semiperiphery functions much as the middle class does in any country: It both is a buffer zone between rich and poor and exhibits elements of both rich and poor, depending on the position of the other country it is dealing with.

World system theory emphasizes **global commodity chains**—worldwide networks of labor and production processes, consisting of all pivotal production activities, that form a tightly interlocked "chain" from raw materials to finished product to retail outlet to consumer (Gereffi and Korzeniewicz, 1993; Hopkins and Wallerstein, 1996). The most profitable activities in the commodity chain (engineering, design, advertising) are likely to be done in core countries, while the least profitable activities (mining or growing the raw materials, factory production) are likely to be done in peripheral countries. Some low-profit factories (or "sweatshops") are appearing in core countries, often underground to avoid minimum wage laws, but paradoxically, they tend to employ mostly immigrants from peripheral countries, who are willing to settle for the poor pay (still better than they would get at home), minimal or nonexistent benefits, and terrible working conditions.

How does the world economy make peripheral countries dependent on the core countries? There are three major factors:

- *Narrow, export-oriented economies.* A huge percentage of the peripheral state's economy is based on a few products or even just one product (palm oil in Malaysia, hardwoods in the Philippines) for export to the core states. If the core states decrease their demand by only a little, the economy is ruined.

- *Lack of industrial capacity.* Peripheral states lack major industries, so they sell their raw materials inexpensively to the core states. Then they are forced to buy expensive manufactured goods back from them.

- *Foreign debt.* Unequal trade patterns keep peripheral states constantly in debt to core states. For instance, Gabon (periphery) has a federal reserve of $268 million and an external foreign debt of $3.8 billion. Burma (periphery) has a federal reserve of $590 million and an external foreign debt of $6.7 billion. France (core) has a federal reserve of $70.7 billion and no foreign debt (Walton and Ragin, 1990).

The world system theory has been criticized for depicting the process as only one way, with goods and services flowing from

Globalization has increased the economic, political, and social interconnectedness of the world. It has also increased some staggering inequalities between the world's rich and its poor. ▼

Sociology and our World

Prostitution and the World System

In the world system, it is not only goods and services that flow from periphery to core. People do, too, in the form of slaves, foreign workers, and prostitutes (or sex workers). Interviews with sex workers in dozens of countries around the world reveal that in Japan (core), they tend to come from Korea (semiperiphery) or the Philippines (periphery). In Thailand (semiperiphery), they tend to come from Vietnam or Burma (periphery). In France (core), they tend to come from Turkey or North Africa (semiperiphery). In Germany, they tend to come from Bosnia, Slovenia, or the Czech Republic (semiperiphery). However, in the Czech Republic, they tend to come from Poland, Slovakia, and Hungary (semiperiphery).

Why does a country in the semiperiphery draw sex workers from the semiperiphery? Perhaps the answer lies in relative wealth: The average GDP per capita in the Czech Republic is $15,700, compared to $13,900 in Hungary, $13,300 in Slovakia, and $11,000 in Poland. Or perhaps it lies in the mechanics of global sex tourism, in which people (mostly men) from the core take vacations in periphery or semiperiphery states with the intention of having sex, either with prostitutes or with impoverished local "friends" willing to spend the night in exchange for dinner or gifts. Prostitution in the Czech Republic really means Prague, about 2 hours by train from Dresden and 4 hours from Munich, a perfect distance for German businessmen to get away for a weekend sex holiday (Kempadoo, Saghera, and Pattanaik, 2005).

---

periphery to core. However, some goods and services flow from core to periphery, and of course states within a zone trade with each other. There are innumerable currents, eddies, undertows, and whirlpools in the economic sea.

Global Mobility

Just as people can move up and down the socioeconomic ladder from generation to generation, and even within a single generation, rich countries can become poor, and poor countries can become rich. Great Britain, the richest country in the world a century ago, today ranks number 19 in per capita GDP (not exactly poor, but moving toward middle income). The United Arab Emirates, impoverished peripheral sheikdoms before the discovery of oil, now rank higher than New Zealand (core). A generation ago, the Soviet Union was an economic and political superpower. But the collapse of communism and the move to a capitalist economy had a devastating impact. In 2004, 25 percent of the population of Russia lived below poverty level, and its per capita GDP ranked below its former satellite states, Poland, Slovakia, Slovenia, and the Czech Republic, just a little above Botswana. Times change, economies change, the world system changes.

Recently there has been a trend of newly industrializing economies (NIEs), countries that move from poor to rich in a matter of a few years. Japan was the first, beginning in the 1950s, and now most of East Asia and Southeast Asia have moved up to middle income, and Hong Kong, Japan, South Korea, Singapore, and Taiwan have moved up to high income (Brohman, 1996). Several of these have risen not because of valuable raw materials but because these former colonial trading centers easily adapted to become large-scale manufacturing and global financial centers.

Did you know?

Depending on where you work, wages will vary enormously. For example, if we compare the hourly wages for various white-collar positions in India and the United States, we can also see the incentive to "outsource" these jobs:

Financial analyst: $33–34 U.S., $6–15 India

Payroll clerk: $15 U.S., $2 India

Programmer: $29 U.S., $3–6 India

Telephone operator: $13 U.S., $1 India

Source: U.S. Department of Labor, Fisher Center for Real Estate and Urban Economics

But Japan was never a European colony and in fact had its own colonial empire before World War II. None of these countries received significant European economic assistance until the Cold War, when the world was taking up sides in the apocalyptic conflict between the United States and the Soviet Union. Japan, South Korea, and Taiwan, just a few miles from the Communists, could function as political (and symbolic) bulkheads of democracy, so the United States and its allies poured money and military aid into them. Later, when increasingly efficient global transportation and communication systems made importing manufactured items from long distances economically viable, they began aggressively exporting locally produced merchandise, until "made in Japan" and "made in Korea" became clichés for cheap, mass-produced articles. Once, when I was in Paris, I picked up a cheap ceramic gargoyle in one of the tourist kiosks that line the Left Bank. It wasn't until I got back to my hotel that I checked the bottom, and saw the words—in English: "Made in Japan."

Class Identity and Class Inequality in the 21st Century

Today, class continues to have a remarkable impact in our lives—from the type of education or health care you receive to the type of job you'll have, whom you'll marry, and even how long you'll live and how many children you'll have. The decline in social mobility in the United States makes America increasingly a nation of rich and poor, as in every country there are rich people and poor people, as well as rich countries and poor countries. The gap grows daily. As a result, "being born in the elite in the U.S. gives you a constellation of privileges that very few people in the world have ever experienced," notes David Levine, an economist who researches social mobility and class in America. But, comparatively, "being poor in the U.S. gives you disadvantages unlike anything in Western Europe and Japan and Canada" (cited in Scott and Leonhardt, 2005).

Just as class increases in importance and class inequality increases in its impact on our everyday lives and our society, so too do Americans continue to disavow its importance. We may be becoming a nation of rich and poor, but we continue to assert that we're all middle class, and that class has little bearing on our lives. Perhaps that Oxford professor was onto something.

 Chapter Review

1. *What is social stratification, and why does it exist?* All societies are stratified into layers, with those on top generally having more power, privilege, and prestige than those on the bottom. Stratification is often based on wealth, income, or birth. A society's system of stratification is often accompanied by a justifying ideology that is accepted by most people.

2. *What does social stratification look like?* The main two forms of social stratification are caste and class. In a caste system, one is born into a group and can never leave that group. Class is the most common modern form of stratification and is based on wealth, income, and, to some extent, birth. A class system allows for social mobility, or movement up or down the social class

ladder, although most individuals remain in or near the class position they are born into.

3. *How do sociologists explain social class?* Marx explained social class as derived from one's relationship with the means of production. People were divided into owners, who had capital, and workers, who had labor to sell. According to Marx, the owners, or bourgeoisie, exploited the workers, or proletariat, for profit. Weber said social class depended on economics, status (or prestige), and power.

4. *How does class manifest in the United States?* Social class in the United States is based on income. The upper classes are the superrich, a tiny proportion of the population. The lower upper class is usually well educated with upper-level jobs and incomes. The upper middle class consists of white-collar managers and community leaders. The middle middle class is viewed as the "normal" Americans; they hold white-collar jobs, own small businesses, or have good-paying blue-collar jobs. The working class has steady jobs as blue-collar or low-level white-collar workers. The lower class, or working poor, live precariously on the edge, while the underclass are very poor.

5. *What does poverty look like in the United States?* Poverty rates for racial minorities are much higher than those for Whites. Rural poverty is increasing and is more difficult to emerge from as jobs, transportation, and the economy in general are depressed in rural areas. Many poor Americans work, and many work full time.

6. *Why are people poor?* The culture of poverty theory argues that poor people live in a culture that does not allow them to get out of poverty and that socializes them to continue to be poor. Modern sociologists look at other social and structural factors in addition to culture. These include globalization, market forces, racism, and government; sociologists understand that poverty reduces one's life chances. That is, it is not impossible to escape poverty, just difficult.

7. *What is social mobility?* Class systems allow for individual and group mobility up and down the social class ladder. Intergenerational mobility refers to a movement between generations, while intragenerational mobility refers to a movement between classes in one's individual lifetime. Intergenerational mobility is common, but it is common both ways—groups move up the class ladder while other groups move down the class ladder—and tends to even out.

8. *What does global inequality look like, and how do sociologists explain it?* Trends in global inequality mirror those within countries such as the United States, as the rich countries are gaining more wealth and power and the poor countries are declining in the same. Theories of global inequality include market theories, which are based on capitalism; state-centered theories, which are based on government and development; and dependency theories, which focus on inequality between the poor and rich countries. World systems theory combines some of these other theories and focuses on the global economy in terms of capitalism and interconnectedness of nations.

KeyTerms

Bourgeoisie (p. 210)
Caste system (p. 207)
Class (p. 208)
Class system (p. 209)
Colonialism (p. 234)
Culture of poverty (p. 223)
Dependency theory (p. 234)
Feminization of poverty (p. 222)

Feudalism (p. 208)
Global commodity chains (p. 236)
Global inequality (p. 229)
Meritocracy (p. 207)
Modernization theory (p. 233)
Poverty line (p. 220)
Power (p. 211)
Proletariat (p. 210)

Social mobility (p. 209)
Social stratification (p. 206)
Socioeconomic status (SES) (p. 212)
Status (p. 211)
Structural mobility (p. 226)
Underclass (p. 214)
World system theory (p. 235)

7.1 Conflict between Poor and Rich in the United States

This is actual survey data from the General Social Survey, 1972–2004.

In all countries, there are differences or conflicts between different social groups. In your opinion, in America, how much conflict is there between poor people and rich people? In the 2000 General Social Survey, more than half of all respondents said they thought there was either strong or very strong conflict between the rich and the poor. Those who identified as lower class were far more likely than others to say there was strong (47.1%) or very strong (39.2%) conflict. With regard to race, Blacks were far more likely than Whites to report they thought there was strong (42.9%) or very strong (27.3%) conflict.

CRITICAL THINKING | DISCUSSION QUESTIONS

1. The social class difference in responses was significant. Almost 90 percent of those who identified as lower class reported thinking there was strong or very strong conflict, while only about 60 percent of those who identified as upper class reported the same. What explains the social class differences?

2. Black Americans were far more likely than White Americans to report thinking there is strong or very strong conflict between the rich and the poor. In sociology, we study the intersections between race, class, and gender. How does the intersection of race and class help explain these survey results?

7.2 Charitable Giving

This is actual survey data from the General Social Survey, 1972–2004.

During the past 12 months, how often have you given money to a charity? Over the past 5 years, have you contributed your time to help the needy? Data from 2002 show that most individuals gave money to a charity in the year prior to the interview. Breakdown by social class shows the higher the social class, the greater the likelihood of giving. The responses for giving time to help the needy broke down in a similar way by social class. In addition, individuals were more likely to have given money in the past year than time in the past 5 years.

CRITICAL THINKING | DISCUSSION QUESTIONS

1. Why do you think the social class differences exist? They are easy to explain away by saying that richer people have more money to give to charity, and poor people need their money for basic necessities. What other sociological explanations can you come up with?

2. The differences among social classes for giving money to charity were much greater than the differences for contributing time to help the needy. What might explain that?

3. Many people reported not giving money and not giving time for charity. What are some commonly held stereotypes about the needy that might hold people back from giving or at least give them justification for not giving?

▶ Go to this website to look further at the data. You can run your own statistics and crosstabs here: **http://sda.berkeley.edu/cgi-bin/hsda?harcsda+gss04**

REFERENCES: Davis, James A., Tom W. Smith, and Peter V. Marsden. General Social Surveys 1972–2004: [Cumulative file] [Computer file]. 2nd ICPSR version. Chicago, IL: National Opinion Research Center [producer], 2005; Storrs, CT: Roper Center for Public Opinion Research, University of Connecticut; Ann Arbor, MI: Inter-University Consortium for Political and Social Research; Berkeley, CA: Computer-Assisted Survey Methods Program, University of California [distributors], 2005.

chapter 8

WHEN WE THINK ABOUT RACE, we typically think of the most primordial and basic attributes of a person, fixed and permanent, a foundation of identity. We assume that race is carefully bounded, with no overlap—as my grade school social studies textbook taught me. The chapter on "race" discussed only three: "Negroid, Mongoloid, and Caucasoid." Nobody could be a member of any other race, and nobody could belong to more than one race.

To me, the most interesting part of the book chapter was the illustrations. There were three: a black guy in a loincloth, holding a spear, standing in front of a grass hut; an Asian guy in a silk kimono, holding some sort of scroll, standing in front of a pagoda; and a white guy in a business suit, holding a briefcase, standing in front of a skyscraper. All were men. We were supposed to classify the three races, from least to the most civilized, technologically sophisticated, inventive, and intelligent. It doesn't take a genius to figure out which of the three "races" the illustrator belonged to.

How do sociologists think about race?

Race and Ethnicity

Sociologists tend not to see fixed, immutable biologically based characteristics but the ways in which we have come to see those characteristics as timeless and universal. Race is less fixed than fluid, less eternal and more historical. In fact, race is relatively recent, an invention of Europeans in the eighteenth century. Rather than immutable, it is among the parts of our identity that is in greatest flux at the present, as individuals are increasingly biracial or even multiracial. With race, as with other features of social life, believing is seeing: When we believe that there are only a certain number of races, then we will "see" those, and only those, races.

Race is more than a system that categorizes people according to physical characteristics. It is a foundation of our identity and a basis for social inequality.

To a sociologist, race is more than a system of classification, a system that categorizes people. Race is also one of the bases on which our society perceives, rewards, and punishes people. Being from different races is often a primary marker of structured social inequality and a justification for discrimination. Race is among the foremost predictors of your experience in society.

As with class, gender, age, and ethnicity, race is a foundation of identity and a basis for social inequality.

Distinguishing between Race and Ethnicity

Race and ethnicity are sometimes used interchangeably, but actually they are based on two different assumptions. **Race** depends on an assumption of biological distinction. You can be Black or White and live in any country in the world, have any religion, and speak any language. All that matters is your skin color and whatever other physical trait counts. However, **ethnicity** depends on an assumption of cultural distinction. You can belong to any race and have a Swedish ethnicity—if you speak Swedish at home, attend the Swedish Lutheran Church, eat lutefisk (cod soaked in lye and served with bacon fat), and celebrate St. Lucia's Day on December 13 by dancing with lit candles on your head, as many do in Sweden.

Or if you do none of those things at all. Few Swedish American students at undergraduate colleges today eat lutefisk or wear crowns of candles! There are likely few, if any, cultural differences between Swedish students and everyone else on campus. In fact, you'd probably never know they are Swedish, except for last names like "Swenson" and a few Swedish flags on dorm room walls. Their Swedish ethnicity resided entirely in how their ancestors might have lived.

Like race, ethnicity has no basis in any empirical fact.

Yet race and ethnicity are the single most predictive factors in determining a person's eventual social position. Race and ethnicity can be used to predict how you vote, whom you will marry, and what sort of job you will have when you graduate from college. Race and ethnicity can predict your attitudes on birth control, your musical tastes, and whether or not you go to church. They can even be used to predict what church you go to! In spite of repeated, extensive attempts at racial integration, Americans tend to live in segregated neighborhoods, go to segregated churches, make friends almost entirely within their own race or ethnic group, and date almost entirely within their own race or ethnic group. (There's an old joke among Protestant clergy that the most segregated time in American history is 10 a.m. every Sunday.)

Students often say they are amazed at how race and ethnicity are experienced in class. Students may sit anywhere they wish, but by the third day of the semester the African American, White, and Hispanic groups are as strictly segregated as if they had been assigned that way. If forced to integrate, they will separate again as soon as they are divided into small discussion groups. Why?

How can a category be nothing and so obviously something, at the same time?

Sociology and our World

Why Do All the Black Kids Sit Together in the Cafeteria?

Psychologist Beverly Daniel Tatum (1997) noticed black and white kids separating in classes, in clubs, and in tables in the cafeteria, even when there seemed to be little bad feeling between the groups, even when the teachers encouraged them to "not notice" race at all. In *Why Are All the Black Kids Sitting Together in the Cafeteria?*,

she argues that this separation is not always a bad thing. White privilege so pervades our society that the Black kids tend to grow up with internalized oppression, a negatively stereotyped "ethnic self." Even if few of the White people around are actively trying to be racist, being the "only one" invariably leads to feelings of isolation and lower self-worth. Minorities must find ways to be in the majority, to be the "norm" some of the time, in order to establish and affirm a positive identity. So they seek each other out in the classroom and the cafeteria.

What Is Race?

To this day, we still do not have a good definition of race. Some textbooks say, "a set of obvious physical traits singled out by members of a community or society as socially significant." Others say "a set of social relationships that allows attributes or competencies to be assigned on the basis of biologically grounded features." But what's "obvious," and what features are "biologically grounded"? Head shape? Eye color? Earwax? There are only two major types of earwax, and according to the experts who study such things, about 90 percent of Asians and Native Americans but less than 20 percent of other racial groups have the type known as *gray-grainy*. No other "biologically grounded feature" appears nearly as often, although no one has ever suggested that earwax is an indicator of cultural superiority!

What about skin color? In the United States we assign people to "white," "black," and "yellow" categories, but in Central and South America, there are a dozen or more shades (in Brazil, over 40), and we can perceive thousands of color gradients. Even within a single individual, skin color can change daily, darkening or lightening due to such factors as diet, exposure to the sun, or age. Trying to pinpoint a race based on skin color is absurd.

This is why sociologists have come to understand that race as a biological distinction has no basis in any empirical fact. To sociologists, race is more of a social construction than a biological fact.

Most cultures divide people into good and bad types on the basis of their cultural traits, usually "us," the real people, against "them," the cannibals (who eat the wrong food), barbarians (who speak the wrong language), or infidels (who worship the wrong God). But physical appearance rarely enters the equation. Historically, the word *race* meant the same thing as *culture*: the French "race" lived in France and spoke French, and the Russian "race" lived in Russia and spoke Russian.

Not until the eighteenth century did physical attributes become determining factors in "race." In the United States, debates about the morality of "Negro slavery" indicated a concern for skin color that was more important than the very different cultures from which those Negro slaves came. By the nineteenth century, "race

Differences within racial categories are often greater than differences between them—even among beauty queens. ▼

science" tried to give the real people/barbarian division a scientific-sounding gloss arguing that some "races" of people were more highly evolved than others, just as mammals are more highly evolved than reptiles and fish. And, just as mammals are physiologically different from reptiles and fish, the more highly evolved races differed from the less highly evolved, not only culturally, but physiologically.

It turns out that the race scientists got it wrong. People are actually far more physiologically similar than different to suggest we are from different races. Genetic makeup, blood type, facial type, skin color, and every other physical attribute vary more within the groups we call races than between them. You can get distinct races only if a group is isolated for many generations, which prevents any forms of cross-breeding. No human group has ever been isolated long enough (the Australian aboriginals come closest, cut off from the mainland of Asia for 40,000 years, but they're still 100,000 or more years short).

Sociologically, then, race isn't "real"—that is, there are no distinct races that are pure and clearly demarcated from others. And there haven't been such things in millennia. However, it is a sociological maxim (first offered by sociologist W. I. Thomas in 1928) that "things that are perceived as real are real in their consequences." Most people believe there are distinct races, with distinct characteristics, and therefore social life is often arranged as if there were. It's less that we believe it when we see it, and more that we see it when we believe it.

Biraciality and Multiraciality

There is no such thing as a "pure" race. Every human group has mixed ancestry. An estimated 30 to 70 percent of North American Blacks have some White European ancestors (Herskovits, 1930; Roberts, 1975), and 30 to 50 percent of North American Whites have some Native American ancestors (Table 8.1). Even so, interracial romantic relationships have often been considered deviant and forbidden. Such relationships were labeled *miscegenation* and punishable by prison sentences in all but nine states until 1967 (Sollors, 2000). Lawmakers argued that they were against nature and against God's law, that they were an insult to the institution of marriage and a threat to the social fabric. Children of mixed-race unions were called half-breeds, or to be more precise, mulattos (Black–White) or mestizos (White–Indian), and considered morally and intellectually inferior to members of both races. Novelists and

TABLE 8.1

Multiracial Identification by Race: People Recorded as One Race Who Are Also Recorded as One or More Other Races			
	RACIAL IDENTIFICATION (MILLIONS)	MULTIRACIAL IDENTIFICATION (MILLIONS)	PERCENT MULTIRACIAL
White	216.5	5.1	2.3%
Black	36.2	1.5	4.2
Asian	11.7	1.4	12.4
Other	18.4	3.0	16.4
American Indian and Alaska Native	3.9	1.4	36.4
Native Hawaiian or other Pacific Islander	0.7	0.3	44.8

Source: U.S. Census, 2000

FIGURE 8.1 Percentage of Americans in Couples Married to or Cohabiting with Someone of a Different Race

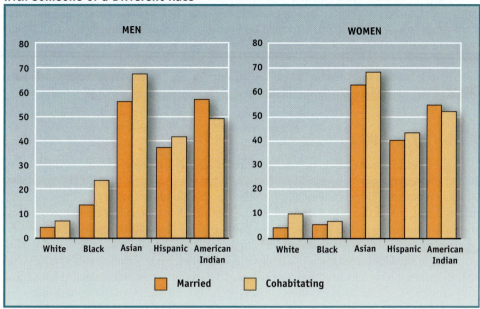

Source: U.S. Census, 2000.

screenwriters often made their villains "half-breeds" as a shorthand way of denoting that they were morally depraved and not to be trusted.

The legal restrictions against intermarriage have been gone for nearly 40 years, and popular support has shifted considerably: In 1958, 96 percent of Whites disapproved of Black–White intermarriage, but in 1997, 77 percent *approved* (Kristof, 2004) (Figure 8.1). Although they have increased in recent years, intermarriage and interracial romantic relationships are still stigmatized. It is interesting that just as magazine articles and dire warnings were given to White Americans at the turn of the last century about "race suicide," now some popular magazine articles and films suggest that a Black person who dates or marries a White person is betraying his or her race. On MTV's *The Real World: Philadelphia*, Karamo, who is Black, is outraged when a White guy and a Black girl start dating; he even threatens, "jokingly," to cut the White guy's throat. But then he dates a Latino with impunity, perhaps thinking that it is acceptable because they are gay and will not produce children.

In the 2000 census, there were at least 7 million of those children: Of the population, 2 percent was identified as biracial and multiracial. Half were under the age of 18, so it is evident that the population will grow. Perhaps *biracial* will become a new ethnicity. In the past, people of mixed races usually just "picked one."

The Sociology of Race and Ethnicity

Sociologists see race and ethnicity as two of the ways that many societies organize the allocation of goods and resources. Some people are set apart for unequal treatment, receiving more or less political power, economic resources, and social prestige. Assumed physical or cultural characteristics called "race" or "ethnicity" are arbitrary markers that serve to legitimate social inequality.

Yet race and ethnicity are not all about inequality. They also give us a profound sense of identity. If you are African American, you have access to an enormous infrastructure of political, social, and economic organizations, churches, colleges, fine arts, and mass media that you might not want to give up even if your race became irrelevant. People lacking recognizable ethnic heritages often envy those whose grandparents told stories about the old country, or who can plan a visit overseas to connect with their roots, or who can point to a famous novel and say "it's about us." The story of being a racial or ethnic minority in America is as often a story of pride as it is of prejudice.

Minority Groups

A racial or ethnic minority group is not defined strictly by being a numerical minority. In fact, there are more "minorities" in the United States than the "majority" population. Blacks constitute 71 percent of the population of Allendale County, South Carolina, and 0.3 percent of the population of Blaine County, Montana, but no one would say they are a minority group in only one of those places. And not all groups that are few in numbers are necessarily minorities. There are only 2.8 million people of Swedish ethnicity in the United States, a relatively small number, but according to the 2000 Census, 27 percent have graduated from college, 33 percent are in managerial/professional jobs, and their median household income is $42,500, all higher than the national average. Clearly, they are not subjected to significant amounts of discrimination.

For a race or ethnic group to be classified as a **minority group**, it needs to have four characteristics:

1. *Differential power.* There must be significant differences in access to economic, social, and political resources. Group members may hold fewer professional jobs and have a higher poverty rate, a lower household income, greater incidence of disease, or a lower life expectancy, all factors that point to lifelong patterns of discrimination and social inequality.

2. *Identifiability.* Minority group members share (or are assumed to share) physical or cultural traits that distinguish them from the dominant group.

3. *Ascribed status.* Membership is something you are born with. Membership is not voluntary. You are born into it, and you cannot change it. Affiliation in many ethnic groups is a matter of choice—you can decide how much of your French heritage, if any, you want to embrace—but you can't wake up one morning and decide to be Japanese.

4. *Solidarity and group awareness.* There must be awareness of membership in a definable category of people, so that there are clearly defined "us" and "them." The minority becomes an **in-group** (Sumner, 1906), and its members tend to distrust or dislike members of the dominant **out-group.** When a group is the object of long-term prejudice and discrimination, feelings of "us versus them" can become intense.

Majority Groups

Minority groups and **majority groups** are often constructed in the United States not so much through race as through skin color: dark people versus light people, people "of color" versus people who are "White." In an interesting linguistic experiment called the Implicit Association Test, students were given word association tests, and all of them, regardless of their own race, tended to associate "White" with purity, goodness, and happiness, and "Black" with corruption, evil, and sadness (Greenwald, McGhee, and Schwartz, 1998; Hofmann et al., 2005). Within racial groups, people who are lighter are privileged over people who are darker (Greenwald and Farnham, 2000; Greenwald, 1998). When the African American sports legend O. J. Simpson was arrested on suspicion of murdering his estranged wife and her companion, he appeared on the cover of *Time* magazine. The photograph was manipulated to make him look considerably darker than he did in real life.

Whiteness becomes the standard, the "norm," like being male and heterosexual. It is invisible, at least to those who are White (or male or heterosexual). A number of years ago, in a seminar, we were discussing whether all women were, by definition, "sisters," in spite of race and ethnicity, because they all had essentially the same life experiences and because all women faced a common oppression by men. A White woman asserted that simply being women created bonds that transcended racial differences. A Black woman disagreed.

"When you wake up in the morning and look in a mirror, what do you see?" she asked the White woman.

"I see a woman," replied the White woman.

"That's precisely the problem," responded the Black woman. "I see a *Black* woman."

The White woman saw only *woman*, not *White*, because she enjoyed privilege—such as never having to think about the implications of being White or the impact race had on her everyday interactions. "Whiteness" was invisible to her, just as "maleness" is invisible to men, and "heterosexuality" invisible to heterosexuals. The Black woman saw race because race was how she was *not* privileged; it was there in every interaction every day, in every glimpse in the mirror (Kimmel, 1996).

How We Got White People. The privilege of Whiteness does not depend on your skin color. It has a history and is the result of political positioning. During the nineteenth century, ethnologists, anthropologists, and sociologists traveled around the world, dividing people into races, ordering them from the most to least intelligent, moral, interesting, and evolved. They found hundreds of races, divided into ten broad categories (Table 8.2).

Teutonic people (from England, Germany, and Scandinavia) were defined as White, but people from other parts of Europe were not. The U.S. Census separated them on forms. Magazine illustrations, popular songs, and sociology textbooks characterized these "others" as savage, lazy, sexually promiscuous, born criminals, and responsible for the "social disintegration" of the slums. They were denied jobs and places to live. In the South, many were lynched along with Blacks.

The furor of racial classification in the late nineteenth century and the "discovery" that Europe had inferior and superior races was directly related to a fear of immigration. Established groups from northern Europe were afraid of being overrun by immigrants from southern Europe.

Before 1880, most European immigrants were German, French, English, or Scots-Irish.

TABLE 8.2

Discredited Pseudo-Scientific Racial Categories

FAMILY	LOCATION	MEAN CRANIAL CAPACITY
Teutonic family	Northern Europe	92
Semitic family	Middle East	89
Celtic family	Northern Europe	87
Pelasgic family	Southern Europe	84
Chinese family	East Asia	82
Polynesian family	Polynesia	86
Native African family	West Africa	83
Nilotic family	East Africa	80
Toltecan family	Central America	79
Australian (aboriginal) family	Australia	75

Source: Gould, 1995: 55

They were mostly middle class and Protestant, and they settled in small towns, where they assimilated quickly into the middle-class, Protestant population. But between 1880 and 1920, 23 million immigrants came to the United States, too fast to disperse and blend. Instead they piled up in cities; in 1900, immigrants and their children made up more than 70 percent of populations of New York, Boston, Philadelphia, and Chicago. They were primarily working class and poor; they spoke Italian, Polish, or Yiddish; and they were more often Catholic or Jewish (Van Vugt, 1999; Walch, 1994).

The U.S.–born English-German, Protestant, small-town elite feared these new "primitive" groups (Roediger, 1991). By 1924 the door to immigration from most of Europe (not England) slammed shut (Saxton, 1971, 1990). Because the immigrants tended to have larger families than the native elites, President Theodore Roosevelt raised the alarm of "race suicide" and urged Anglo-Saxon women to have more children, just as poor and immigrant families were advised to limit the number of children they had. By the 1920s and 1930s, scientists developed theories of *eugenics*, the science of "breeding," and encouraged laws that would help the country breed a superior race (Mowry, 1958; Selden, 1999).

By the 1920s, racialist "science" was being taught as fact in American universities. Some early sociologists and anthropologists attempted to demonstrate that these immigrants from "primitive" societies were inferior to native-born Americans (Schwendinger and Schwendinger, 1974).

But gradually the Irish, the Italians, the European Jews, and other European ethnic groups became categorized as "White." The 1930 census distinguishes ten races (White, Negro, American Indian, Chinese, Japanese, Korean, Filipino, Hindu, Mexican, and Other) and further classifies White people into only three types: native White with native White parents; native White with immigrant parents; and immigrant White. The 1940 census distinguishes only native White and immigrant White. How did that happen? Was it because many had become middle class? Or did expanded versions of Whiteness mean that employers and apartment owners took the "No Irish Need Apply" or "No Bohunks Allowed" placards from their windows, allowing the middle class to enter? (A "Bohunk" is an immigrant from central Europe, a combination of "Bohemian" and "Hungarian.")

Both, and neither. Historian Noel Ignatiev maintains that the Irish deliberately positioned themselves in opposition to Blacks, visibly participating in the massive anti-Black violence in the northeastern United States in the 1840s, to posture for a place at the table of "Whiteness." Anthropologist Karen Brodkin (1999) similarly maintains that Jews began to "speak of a mythic whiteness" that both they and the Anglo-Saxons participated in, transcending the separate categories that scientific racism put them in. The Irish and the Jews "chose" to be White and then set about trying to convince native-born Protestant Whites that they were White.

We also can't discount the 1930s rise of Nazi Germany, where race science was taken to its logical conclusion: the Aryan "master race" protecting its "stock" with military aggression and death camps. By the time Ashley Montagu published *Man's Most Dangerous Myth: The Fallacy of Race* in 1942, a book that declared "race science" to threaten the foundations of modern society itself, race science had the taint of Nazi tyranny, and using ethnography to analyze culture was gaining ground over measuring skull capacity to prove biological distinction. Instead of dirty and dangerous "races" that must be kept separate, immigrants became "ethnic groups" who could easily assimilate into the mainstream. Instead of a nation of Northern European Protestants worried about race mixing or "mongrelization," the United States became a *melting pot*, with immigrant economic and social success praised as a triumph of democracy over the superstition of race science.

However, the melting pot seemed to work only with Europeans and with some drawbacks: Assimilation meant abandoning cultural traditions. Immigrant parents punished their children for speaking the language from back home, and in a generation or two an entire cultural heritage was nearly forgotten. That was the price they paid for becoming white.

Prejudice

Prejudice is a set of beliefs and attitudes that cause us to negatively "prejudge" people based on their social location. In the classic work on the subject, psychologist Gordon Allport defined prejudice as "a pattern of hostility in interpersonal relations which is directed against an entire group, or against its individual members; it fulfills a specific irrational function for its bearer" (Allport, 1954, p. 12). For example, you may decide not to sell your car to an Asian American because you believe they are bad drivers, or you may decline to rent an apartment from a Hispanic owner because you believe the building would be sloppily maintained.

[handwritten note: Ex: not selling your car to an Asian-American because you think they are bad drivers]

Stereotypes

Often prejudices are based on **stereotypes,** generalizations about a group that are oversimplified and exaggerated, and fail to acknowledge individual differences in the group. For instance, if you believe the stereotype that Asians are gifted in science, you will believe that it is true of all Asians, without exception. You will believe that any Asian selected at random will be able to answer scientific questions, and will score better on science exams, than any person randomly selected from another race. Most likely, however, you will not reason it out in any systematic way: You will just ask an Asian when you have a scientific question or be surprised when you meet an Asian who is an art history major.

[handwritten note: Ex: Asians are gifted in science.]

Recently I saw a scene in a movie in which a Black guy invited a White guy to his house for dinner and announced that they were having chicken. "Oh, I love fried chicken!" the White guy responded, associating "Black" with "fried chicken" as a stereotype even though he knew, logically, that enjoying fried foods is not a racially specific characteristic. In this case, they were actually having chicken curry.

Most stereotypes, like the association of "Asian" and "science" or "Black" and "fried food," refer to traits that only a small percentage of group members actually possess, or that are no more common to group members than to anyone else, so they are simply inaccurate and unfair. However, some stereotypes are downright wrong: No one (or almost no one) in the group possesses the trait.

In the early 1960s, Bull Connor, a sheriff in Alabama, commented that "Blacks are intellectually inferior" and that therefore integration would fail. In the 1980s, Al Campanis, an official with the Los Angeles Dodgers, commented that "Blacks are better athletes." One occasionally hears that Blacks are more "naturally" gifted basketball players but that White players are "smarter" or "have a better work ethic." And for years, football quarterbacks were White, on the assumption that you had to be a brilliant tactician, not a powerful athlete, to play the position. There have also been several celebrated cases in which public speakers spoke about these stereotypes, indicating that they believe them to be true, that races and ethnic groups *are* signifi-

Talk radio star Don Imus lost his job in 2007 after calling the Rutgers women's basketball team "nappy-headed ho's." ▼

cantly different in their strength, physical power, intelligence, musical ability, or other characteristics. Sometimes these public pronouncements cost them their jobs.

Today, such arguments have become more subtle and sophisticated, but no less stereotypic, with "culture" merely substituted for "biology" as an explanation of the differences. For instance, they argue that because of social discrimination, Blacks have less stimulating intellectual environments than Whites during their formative years, so they end up with lower intelligence. Or their parents reward playing basketball instead of cracking books, while the parents of White children reward academic skills, so the Black children grow up better athletes. This is still stereotyping. No study has demonstrated that Black parents regularly discourage their children from getting good grades, or that White parents are never obsessed with their children's sports accomplishments.

Sociologists are fascinated by the phenomenon of stereotypes: People seem to believe them regardless of the utter lack of supporting evidence and in spite of evidence to the contrary. When one explanation of a stereotype fails, they look for another, trying anything they can think of to support and legitimate their prior beliefs. In a classic illustration of this, Gordon Allport reports the following conversation with an anti-Semite:

Mr. X: The trouble with the Jews is that they only take care of their own group.

Mr. Y: But the record of the Community Chest campaign shows that they give more generously, in proportion to their numbers, to the general charities of the community, than do non-Jews.

Mr. X: That shows they are always trying to buy favor and intrude into Christian affairs. They think of nothing but money; that is why there are so many Jewish bankers.

Mr. Y: But a recent study shows that the percentage of Jews in the banking business is negligible, far smaller than the percentage of non-Jews.

Mr. X: That's just it; they don't go in for respectable business; they are only in the movie business or run night clubs (Allport, 1954: 13–14).

Racism

Racism describes a set of attitudes; racism is prejudice that is systematically applied to members of a group. It can be **overt racism**, in speech, manifest in behaviors such as discrimination, or a refusal to associate with members of that group; it can also be **subtle racism** and even unconscious, simply a set of mental categories that we possess about the "other" based on stereotypes.

Racism is a particularly powerful form of prejudice, not only a belief in general stereotypes but a belief that one race (usually White) is inherently superior to the others. It is not necessary to belong to the "superior" race to buy into racism. Race science, with its "evidence" of the superiority of White people, was quite common 50 or 60 years ago and still pops up from time to time in academic or popular discussions (along with its opposite, "evidence" of the superiority of Black people).

We still hear racist sentiments from time to time. A few years ago in an introductory sociology class, I mentioned that by 2050, White people will be a numerical minority in the United States. A student gasped. "That's terrible! Doesn't that scare you?" It didn't scare me at all, so I said, "What's the problem? America will still be here." She responded, "Yeah, but it won't be our America!" I doubt that she had ever heard of race science, but she was expressing the same fear of losing "our" country to the incursion of minorities that prompted the immigration quotas 70 years ago, or that politician Pat Buchanan expresses in *The Death of the West* (2002), about the decline of "our America" due to immigration and low birth rates among White people.

Discrimination

Discrimination is a set of actions based on prejudice and stereotypes. They often, but need not, negatively affect the group in question. For instance, if I believe that Asians are academically gifted, I may ask Asian students more questions in class, assign them more difficult projects, or grade their papers more leniently, giving them the "benefit of the doubt." But I may also be especially aware of an Asian student who is disruptive in class.

Some acts of discrimination are responses to specific stereotypes, like vigilance in response to the stereotype of violence, but more often discrimination occurs as general negative treatment. A waiter or waitress may exercise discrimination against minority customers by waiting on nonminority customers first, rushing them out when they have finished eating, or behaving in an unfriendly or hostile manner. Of course, the victims never know for sure if they are facing discrimination or just bad service. Minority students who get low grades on tests might suspect that the professor is discriminating, but they will never know for sure unless they do some detective work and uncover a pattern of low grades for minority students.

Prejudice and discrimination are not always causally connected. I can be prejudiced but not discriminate, if none of my friends is discriminating and I don't want to appear different or do something socially unacceptable. Or I can discriminate without being prejudiced, if all of my friends are discriminating, if I believe that it is "the thing to do." Studies show that many of the perpetrators of hate crimes are no more prejudiced than those who do not commit hate crimes: They are just "going along for the ride" (Boyd, Berk, and Hamner, 1996; Craig and Waldo, 1996; Morsch, 1991). Sociologist Robert Merton divided prejudice and discrimination into four categories:

> *(unfairly)*
> → person who dislikes another person/people

1. *All-weather bigots* are prejudiced against some minority groups, and they discriminate against group members. If they do not discriminate in certain social situations, it is because they do not care to, not because they are worried about losing face. They may even take pride in their prejudice. They might tell a racist joke, for instance, even if they know that the people around them will disapprove, to demonstrate their "heroic" refusal to be swayed by politically correct tolerance.

2. *Fair-weather bigots* are prejudiced against some minority groups, but they do not discriminate when there may be negative consequences. This category includes most prejudiced people: They may dislike minorities, but they will not show it when they have something to lose. They will tell a racist joke only when they are sure they will receive a positive reaction.

3. *Fair-weather liberals* are not prejudiced, but they do discriminate when it is profitable for them to do so. They will not tell a racist joke, but they may laugh at one to avoid being embarrassed or starting an argument.

4. *All-weather liberals* are not prejudiced and do not discriminate. They adhere to the American ideal of equal opportunity for all, regardless of the situation. They will not tell a racist joke or respond favorably to one. (Merton, 1949)

This typology assumes that prejudice is a quality that you have—you are either prejudiced or not—and that discrimination consists of specific, deliberate acts. However, there is a great degree of variation in prejudice and discrimination. Many people who would never dream of telling or laughing at a racist joke, and who fully support equal rights for minorities, still harbor prejudices—they believe, perhaps subconsciously, that being White is just better than being something else. Similarly, many acts of discrimination are so subtle, almost unconscious, that we are barely aware of them. Even in a social climate where open acts of discrimination are frowned upon, members of minority groups suffer many acts of personal discrimination every day, ranging from hostile or frightened stares to unconscious stereotyping to insults and jokes and sometimes to violence. When discrimination comes from someone with power, the power to give you a job, an apartment, a good grade, or a speeding ticket, it is especially damaging.

A recent case on the TV program *The People's Court* involved the owner of an apartment house who contracted a realtor to provide potential renters. The realtor was asked to "screen the applicants," so she did, ensuring that they had good jobs, good credit histories, and references from previous landlords. But when she brought the first applicant around to view the apartment, she discovered that the owner meant something else entirely. He said: "That applicant is Black! You were supposed to screen applicants!" The realtor quit (and was sued for breach of contract). One wonders how many other realtors do not quit, how often unwritten and unspoken agreements allow discrimination to continue.

Institutional Discrimination

Screening out Black applicants for an apartment or house is illegal in the United States. I may be free to behave in a hostile or impolite fashion toward anyone I choose, but I may not deny members of certain minority groups equal access to housing, jobs, public services, and selected social rewards. Nevertheless, unequal access continues to be common.

Institutional discrimination is the most subtle and pervasive type of discrimination, deeply embedded in such institutions as the educational system, the business world, health care, criminal justice, and the mass media. These social institutions promote discriminatory practices and traditions that have such a long history they just "seem to make sense," and minority groups become the victims of systematic oppression, even when only a few people, or none at all, are deliberately trying to discriminate. If unchecked, institutional discrimination undermines the very idea of a society based on individual achievement, merit, and hard work. Democracies must institute laws that prevent it and provide remedies when it happens.

The Fair Housing Act of 1968 banned discrimination in housing, but institutional discrimination persists. African Americans and Latinos are turned down for home loans twice as often as Whites with the same qualifications. The HUD Housing Discrimination Study of 2000 found that adverse treatment against Black applicants occurred in 22 percent of cases and against Hispanic applicants in 26 percent of cases: They were less likely to be told that a unit was available, were less likely to be offered a unit for inspection, and were quoted higher rents. The discrimination rate varied from city to city, from 14 percent in Chicago to 30 percent in Atlanta for Black renters, and from 15 percent in Denver to 32 percent in Chicago for Hispanic renters.

Segregation and Integration

For many years in the United States, physical separation between the White majority and the minority groups (especially African Americans), or segregation, was law. Discrimination means unequal treatment, and in the 1896 *Plessy vs. Ferguson* decision, the Supreme Court ruled that "separate but equal" accommodations for Blacks

How do we know what we know?

Changing Racial Attitudes

One way to find out whether our society has made racial progress is to track racial attitudes over time. In the 1920s, sociologist Emory Bogardus devised a *social distance scale* to measure the extent to which we use racial and ethnic categories in the choices we make about our social life (Bogardus, 1925, 1933). He asked a national sample of college students, aged 18 to 35 (about 10 percent of his respondents were Black) a set of questions designed to measure their distance from other groups. These included whether you would make personal friends with them, accept them as neighbors on your street, work in the same office, and date or marry someone from that group. Bogardus predicted that the social distance among groups would decline.

Every 10 years, these questions have been asked of a national sample, and the students ranked their preferences among 30 different groups—mostly Europeans, but also Black Americans, Canadians, Japanese Americans, and various Asian groups. There was some fluctuation over this half-century of surveys. Blacks, for example, moved up from the bottom to the middle of the group. But generally the rankings listed White Americans, Canadians, Northern and Western Europeans in the top third, South and Central and Eastern Europeans in the middle third, and racial minorities in the bottom third. (Italians were the only Southern European group to make the top 10 eventually.) Americans were surprisingly consistent.

In 2001, sociologists Vincent Parillo and Christopher Donoghue updated these categories and administered the survey again to a large national sample of college students. It was administered in the 6 weeks following September 11. Italians had jumped to second place, even ahead of Canadians and the British, and Blacks had cracked the top 10. The last two categories now were filled by Muslims and Arabs (Parillo and Donoghue, 2005; Parillo, 2006).

and Whites were not discriminatory. In fact, they were necessary to cater to the different needs of the races and ensure racial harmony. There were separate neighborhoods, separate businesses, separate sections on buses and in restaurants, separate schools and colleges, even separate washrooms and drinking fountains. In mainstream (that is, White) movies, Blacks appeared only as servants and entertainers, but in their own "separate but equal" movies, they played rugged action heroes, mystery sleuths, romantic leads, every imaginable role.

Usually, however, the "separate" meant "inferior." Black schools received only a fraction of the resources of White schools. The Black section of the bus was at the back. The Black section of the restaurant was in the kitchen.

In the case of the system of apartheid, that inferiority was institutionalized and legal. **Apartheid** means "separation" (think: apart-ness), and it was a system that mandated segregation of different racial groups. In South Africa, apartheid was a political system institutionalized by the White minority in 1948, and all social life was determined by whether you were one of four races: White, black, "coloured" (mixed race), or Indian (South Asian). There were separate schools, restaurants, hospitals, churches, drinking fountains—and even separate buses and bus stops. Apartheid remained in effect until 1990, when Nelson Mandela, the leader of the African National Congress, was freed from prison and soon elected president of South Africa.

In 1954, the Supreme Court heard the *Brown vs. the Board of Education* case and reversed its decision, concluding that "separate but equal" was never equal. So segregation was replaced by legal **integration**, physical intermingling of the races, which presumably would lead to cultural intermingling and racial equality. Fifty years later, integration has not been entirely achieved. We have integrated washrooms and drinking fountains in the United States, but most people, especially poor Blacks and

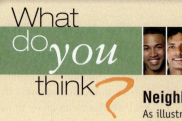

rich Whites, continue to live in same-race neighborhoods and attend same-race schools. Segregation continues to separate poor people of color from education and job opportunities and isolate them from successful role models, helping to create a permanent minority underclass (Massey and Denton, 1993).

Affirmative Action or "Reverse Discrimination"?

In 1965, President Lyndon Johnson asked employers to "take affirmative action to ensure that applicants are employed, and that employees are treated . . . without regard to their race, color, creed, or national origin." He established the Equal Opportunity Commission, which administers many **affirmative action** programs to ensure that minorities get fair treatment in employment applications.

Affirmative action programs are controversial. Opponents complain that minority applicants are "stealing jobs" from more qualified White applicants, a sort of "reverse discrimination." Recently I appeared on a television talk show opposite three "angry White males" who felt they had been the victims of workplace discrimination. The show's title, no doubt created to entice a large potential audience, was "A Black Woman Stole My Job." In my comments to these men, I invited them to consider what the word "my" meant in that title. Why did they believe the job was "theirs" to begin with? Why did they feel entitled to it? When a Black female applicant was hired instead, was she really stealing it from them? Why wasn't the title of the show "A Black Woman Got *the* Job" or "A Black Woman Got *a* Job"?

One might even say that White males have been the beneficiaries of a 2,000-year "affirmative action" policy that favored them. In an article in *The Nation* a few years ago, the eminent historian Eric Foner ruminated on his own college experience as a beneficiary of that version of affirmative action:

> Thirty-two years ago, I graduated from Columbia College [the undergraduate college at Columbia University]. My class of 700 was all-male and virtually all white. Most of us were young men of ability; yet had we been forced to compete for admission with women and racial minorities, fewer than half of us would have been at Columbia. None of us, to my knowledge, suffered debilitating self-doubt because we were the beneficiaries of affirmative action—that is, favored treatment on the basis of our race and gender . . . [In fact], I have yet to meet a white male in whom favoritism (getting a job, for example, through relatives or an old boys' network, or because of racial discrimination by a union or an employer) fostered doubt about his own abilities. . . .

"Despite our rhetoric," Foner concludes, "equal opportunity has never been the American way. For nearly all our history, affirmative action has been a prerogative of white men" (Foner, 1995).

In 1978, the Supreme Court heard the case of Allan Bakke, a white premed student who was twice denied admission to the University of California-Davis Medical School, even though his test scores were superior to many Black students who were admitted. A 5-4 split decision acknowledged that race was a legitimate determining factor in medical school admission but held that strict racial quotas were unconstitutional. That is, admissions departments can take race into account as a factor in admission but cannot reserve a set number of places for any particular group.

Today, around 2 percent of the 91,000 cases of job discrimination pending before the Equal Opportunity Commission are for reverse discrimination, and state affirmative action measures have been abolished in California, Washington, and Florida (for college admissions only). In 2003, the Supreme Court ruled in a 6-3 decision that the University of Michigan's affirmative action policy in undergraduate admissions, which awarded 20 extra points to Black, Hispanic, and Native American applicants, was unconstitutional (though it was allowed to remain in place in the Law School).

Sometimes affirmative action programs can lead to tokenism, in which a single member of a minority group is present in the office, workshop, or the classroom. When you are a *token*, you occupy a curious position. You are simultaneously invisible and hypervisible. You are a representative of your race, ethnicity, gender, or sexual identity—not a person. Nobody sees you, everybody sees your characteristics, and they are using those characteristics to form new stereotypes of your group. Your individual quirks and shortcomings will become stereotypes of the entire group. This is a huge responsibility. You have to be on your best behavior and be very careful to not do anything that might support a stereotype. This can lead to social paralysis: You are afraid to speak or act because everyone is watching and making conclusions about your group.

Although racial discrimination is illegal, research experiments have shown that minorities continue to face subtle discrimination in housing, employment, and other areas. ▼

Hate Groups

People join hate groups to promote discrimination against ethnic and other minorities, usually because they feel that the main society is not doing a very good job of it.

The Know-Nothing Party was formed in 1849 to promote anti-Catholic and anti-immigrant legislation. The Ku Klux Klan (KKK), formed shortly after the end of slavery in 1863, tried to prevent newly freed blacks from acquiring social equality with both political legislation and the more immediate tactics of violence and intimidation. When open discrimination is commonplace in the main society, these groups can acquire a great deal of political power. The Know-Nothings managed to dominate several state legislatures, including Massachusetts, and promoted the sitting president, Millard Fillmore, in the 1852 presidential election (he lost, but not due to an anti-immigrant agenda). At its height in the 1920s, the second Ku Klux Klan had over 4,000,000 members and was praised by many public figures, including President Warren Harding.

When open discrimination is frowned upon in the main society, it becomes more difficult for hate groups to get laws passed or sponsor successful political candidates. Former KKK Grand Wizard David Duke rose highest, when he captured 55 percent of the White vote in the 1989 Louisiana gubernatorial election, although he had to explain that his KKK membership was a "youthful mistake." Hate groups today usually do not hope to legislate discriminatory policies. Instead, they want to make their presence known, win supporters, and promote individual acts of discrimination, especially violence.

In the twenty-first century, many hate groups have moved beyond marching in strange costumes or starting fistfights on talk shows to using up-to-date tools of mass media and marketing: attractive, professionally produced books, music, and Web pages that hide their racist beliefs under a veneer of respectability. In public presentations, they never use racist slurs. They say that they are interested in science, Christianity, or patriotism rather than racism. A student once wrote on a paper that Blacks are 730 percent more likely to murder Whites than the other way around. When I questioned him about this curious statistic (and weird way of expressing it), he said that he got from keying "statistics," "Black," and "crime" into an Internet search engine. The first website that appeared was bankrolled by a hate group, and sadly, an intelligent college student believed it because it looked so scientific and official. It is hard to imagine how many other young, inexperienced, non–media-savvy people key into hate group websites and acquire new prejudices or find their old ones validated.

There are only perhaps 50,000 hard-core members of hate groups and no more than 500,000 "fellow travelers," people who read the literature, browse the websites, and agree with racist ideologies (Potok, 2006). A more subtle threat of hate groups is to draw attention away from everyday forms of prejudice and discrimination. After listening to the outrageous statements of a hate group, or seeing their ultraviolent behavior, people may believe that their own prejudice is harmless and inconsequential. After all, they do not believe that non-White people are children of Satan, and they would never dream of bombing a Black church, so what does it matter if they feel uncomfortable in a Black neighborhood?

Although membership in organized hate groups is relatively low, there is an alarming increase in violent crimes in which the victim was chosen because of his or her membership in some minority group (Figure 8.2). In 2005, the FBI documented 7,163 hate crimes. The most (2,630) were against Blacks, and 828 were against Whites. The second highest group, however, was anti-Jewish (848). There are more anti-Semitic crimes than against all other religious groups combined. The 128 anti-Islamic crimes, however, are by far the fastest growing type of bias crime (FBI Hate Crimes Statistics, 2005).

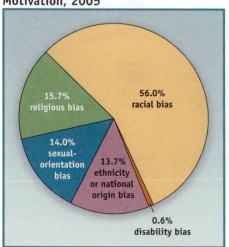

FIGURE 8.2 **Offenses by Bias Motivation, 2005**

56.0% racial bias

15.7% religious bias

14.0% sexual-orientation bias

13.7% ethnicity or national origin bias

0.6% disability bias

Source: Based on data from *Crime in the United States,* U.S. Department of Justice, 2005.

Theories of Prejudice and Discrimination

Social scientists and philosophers have wondered about prejudice for centuries. Why does prejudice exist? Why are we prejudiced against some groups and not others? Why do we believe certain stereotypes and not others? And most importantly, what can we do about it?

The **primordial theory** suggests that a conflict exists between in-groups and out-groups, but doesn't explain how some groups come to be classified as out-groups. Is there any evidence that we have an "innate preference for people like us"? Often we prefer people who are not at all like us. In fact, "opposites attract": We tend to select friends and romantic partners who complement our personalities or physical attributes. It is not unusual to see athletes paired with couch potatoes, supermodels paired with faces that would stop a clock, trust fund babies paired with steelworkers, people so light they burn under fluorescent lamps paired with people so dark that they can spend the entire day at the beach without reaching for the sunblock. More importantly, these "innate" theories disregard the political, social, and economic processes behind individual prejudices. People can and do become racist through deliberate choice and socialization, not through any innate preferences.

According to *frustration-aggression theory*, people are goal directed, and when they can't reach their goals, they become angry and frustrated. If they cannot find the source of their frustration, or if the source is too powerful to challenge, they will direct their aggression toward a **scapegoat**, a weak, convenient, and socially approved target. Considerable evidence shows racial and ethnic hostility increases during periods of economic instability (Blackwell, 1982). Sometimes people may become convinced that the scapegoat is actually the cause of their frustration—for instance, that they are unemployed because illegal immigrants have stolen their job—but often they are just lashing out at someone convenient. This theory does not explain why some groups become scapegoats and others do not or why we are prejudiced against groups who are not immediately visible.

Conflict theory suggests that prejudice is a tool used by the elites, people at the top of the social hierarchy, to "divide and conquer" those at the bottom, making them easier to control and manipulate (Pettigrew, 1998). Racial and ethnic stereotypes are used to legitimate systemic inequality. For instance, if blacks are really lazy, we can explain why there are so few working in high-power corporate jobs without having to deal with institutional discrimination. This theory is supported by research suggesting that prejudice decreases when racism is not institutionally supported (Pettigrew, 1998), but it ignores the role of race in the lives of those at the bottom of the hierarchy.

In the United States and worldwide, members of minority groups are often prejudiced against other minority groups, and they can harbor their own stereotypes about the elites (Kinloch, 1999; Phinney, Gerguson, and Tate, 1997; Tsukashima, 1983). For example, Puerto Rican shopkeepers who own small neighborhood bodegas are deeply suspicious that the Asian greengrocers have been supported by the city's wealthy to drive the Puerto Ricans out of business. Cross-cultural historical studies show that racial and ethnic minorities often promote prejudice against other minorities to try to increase their own wealth, power, and privilege (see, for example, Dreier, Mollenkopf, and Swanstrom, 2005).

Feminist theory considers how the category of race overlaps with other social categories, especially gender but also sexual orientation, social class, religion, age, and ability status. Stereotypes about stigmatized groups in all of these categories are remarkably similar: They are almost always illogical, emotional, primitive, potentially

FIGURE 8.3 Matrix of Domination

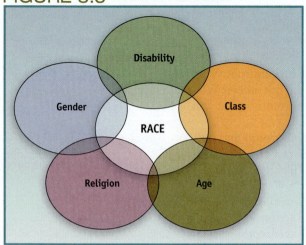

violent, and sexually suspect. Consequently, they often combine, and the effects of racism are compounded by the effects of classism, sexism, heterosexism, and the other "isms." Together, these are what Patricia Hill Collins (1990) calls a **matrix of domination**—an interlocking system of control in which each type of inequality reinforces the others so that the impact of one cannot be fully understood without also considering the others (Figure 8.3).

Doing Something about It

Finding out what causes prejudice is not as important as finding out how to combat it. Early social scientists argued that prejudice could be changed by exposure to members of minority groups (Allport, 1954). We might believe that Italians are passionate, Blacks are lazy, or Jews are greedy because we haven't met enough members of these groups who don't fit the stereotypes. A few handshakes, therefore, will end the prejudice.

During the 1960s and 1970s, a huge amount of time and money was invested in busing students from segregated schools, not only to equalize instruction but to introduce Black and White students to each other. It didn't work: Contact alone does not diminish prejudice. People who have never met even one member of another particular group may not be prejudiced, while people who are surrounded by members of the minority group may still be prejudiced. In *Searching for Aboriginal Languages* (1983), linguist John Dixon finds that many of the White residents of Queensland, Australia, are prejudiced against the aboriginals and believe they are more sexually promiscuous. Dixon found that aboriginals actually select romantic partners on the basis of a very complex system of clans, kinship roles, and informal alliances dating back hundreds of years. The White residents saw aboriginals every day, talked to them, and worked with them, but were completely oblivious to anything except "jumping into bed."

Social psychologist Mark Snyder (1987) found that even awareness of prejudice and desire to change were insufficient. You can realize that prejudice is wrong, and you can try to stop, but you might still believe stereotypes: They are beyond the reach of reason and goodwill. You will tend to notice and remember the ways in which a person from a minority group seems to fit a stereotype, whether you want to or not.

One of the problems in combating prejudice is that it is not merely a matter of individual perceptions. Gordon Allport (1954) called prejudice "a self-fulfilling prophecy." We see what we expect to see and don't see what we don't expect to see. Thus, what we see "fulfills" our expectations, and the stereotypes are confirmed.

In this model, discrimination is simply a form of socialization, and the targets of any discrimination can be socialized into believing that the stereotypes are accurate and behave accordingly. I will then see them behaving according to the stereotypes and be socialized into more discrimination. In the 1960s, Harvard psychologists Robert Rosenthal and Lenor Jacobson entered elementary school classrooms and announced that certain children could be expected to show dramatic academic improvement over the course of the year. No one knew that they actually selected the children at random. Some were good students to begin with, and some were not. But by the end of the year, all of them made clear gains in test performance. What happened was positive stereotyping. The teachers saw only evidence that the children were "gifted" and ignored everything else, and treated them accordingly. Soon the children were behaving as if they actually were gifted, studying more and working harder (Rosenthal and Jacobson, 1968).

How do we know what we know?

Race and Intelligence

In 1994, Harvard psychologist Richard Herrnstein and public policy analyst Charles Murray stirred up a cloud of controversy with their book *The Bell Curve: Intelligence and Class Structure in American Life*. They argued that intelligence—measured by the speed with which you learn new skills and adapt to new situations—is the key to social success and that low intelligence is an important root cause of crime, poverty, unemployment, bad parenting, and many other social problems. In other words, intelligent people succeed more often than stupid people.

But the controversy came when Herrnstein and Murray presented the results of their research to demonstrate that this essential intelligence is correlated with race: African Americans on the average scored significantly lower than White Americans on standard intelligence tests. Scientists have known about racial differences on intelligence tests for many years and explain that they are due to cultural bias in the testing instrument or social inequality during the crucial period of primary socialization, rather than to differences in the way brains actually process information. But Herrnstein and Murray argue that intelligence is 40 to 80 percent inherited, based in genetics.

Now people got angry. Murray was labeled "America's most dangerous conservative" by the *New York Times Magazine* (Herrnstein died in 1994). When conservative columnist Andrew Sullivan published an excerpt in the magazine *The New Republic*, the entire editorial board vehemently protested. When *The Bell Curve* was assigned to a class, some students refused to read it, and some complained of racism to the dean.

But the most important objection to *The Bell Curve* is that it is just bad science. In *Inequality by Design: Cracking the Bell Code Myth*, sociologists Claude Fischer and Mike Hout and their colleagues show the methodological flaws in the bell curve research: Neither "intelligence" nor "race" is a purely biological phenomenon, so their correlation cannot be purely biological either. Plus, as we saw in the methodology chapter, demonstrating correlation between two variables cannot tell you the direction or cause of the relationship.

And how can we account for the impact of institutional racism, the structures of discrimination that have nothing to do with individual abilities? Social structures set "the rule of the game" whereby individual differences matter. If you have high intelligence but no access to the elite education necessary for social prestige, you might learn the skills of drug dealing or adapt to the new situation of a federal penitentiary rather than going for a Berkeley Ph.D. On the other hand, if you have low intelligence but the right social connections, you just might inherit the family fortune.

The same expectation effect can happen on the job, among friends, in families, and among strangers—even within the group that has been negatively stereotyped. We tend to modify our beliefs and behaviors to correspond to a social role, even if that role is a negative stereotype. In 1997, John Ogbu, an anthropologist at the University of California, Berkeley, wondered why middle-class African American students in affluent Shaker Heights, Ohio, got lower grades than their White classmates (an average of C instead of B). Usually such disparities are explained by economic and social inequalities, but in this case, both groups of students were attending well-funded middle-class schools. He concluded that the Black students were afraid of being labeled as "acting White" if they studied too hard or got good grades (Ogbu, 1997). Sociologist Pedro Noguera (2004) found that young Black men are so disconnected from school that they are the only group for whom there is no positive correlation between self-esteem and academic achievement.

More recent research in inner-city schools suggests an even more compelling picture. It turns out that black *girls* who do well in school are indeed accused of "acting White," but Black boys who do well are accused of "acting like girls" (Ferguson, 2001; Fordham, 1999). Collins's "matrix of domination" suggests a correlation between gender and racial oppression: For these boys, being seen as a girl is even worse than being seen as White.

Overcoming Prejudice

In spite of institutional discrimination and patterns of racism and White privilege that go far beyond any individual's actions, there is hope. People can and do decrease their prejudice. Mere contact is not enough, but when people of different groups must work together toward a common goal (Miller and Brewer, 1984), most measures of prejudice decrease. Other important factors are strong role models that contradict the stereotypes and a decrease in institutional forms of discrimination that make inequality seem normal and natural.

Sometimes, the most significant changes happen at the interpersonal level. One of the more promising indications of the decline in prejudice that I saw recently was when I watched two people, one White and one Black, discussing a minor traffic accident. Well, not exactly "discussing." The veneer of civilized communication vanished as they screamed at each other, using every name they could think of. There were insults about parentage, intellectual capacity, and waist size and invitations to sexual practices with each other's mothers. But there were no racial slurs. Evidently it never occurred to them, even in their most unguarded and outraged moments, to use race as the basis of an insult.

However, other evidence suggests that many people are just learning what answers look best on surveys, regardless of how they really feel or react. Discrimination, especially of the backhanded "have a nice day" sort, seems to be on the rise. In a 1997 Gallup poll, 79 percent of Whites believed that Blacks and Whites were always treated equally, but only 49 percent of Blacks agreed. Thirty percent of Black respondents said that they had encountered discrimination during the last month, while shopping, at work, while dining out, while using public transportation, or with the police. The percentage increased to 70 percent for young Black men, who were especially likely to experience discrimination while shopping (45 percent) and in interactions with the police (35 percent). A 1995 survey of the racial climate at Indiana State University (Terre Haute, Indiana) found that 64 percent of Black students had heard racial jokes or seen racial graffiti, 55 percent felt they had been left out of social activities, 48 percent had been insulted intellectually, and 47 percent had been called names or racial slurs. Most surprisingly, 40 percent had been insulted in class by a teacher.

Ethnic Groups in the United States

Every group has some distinctive norms, values, beliefs, practices, outlooks, and cultural artifacts, but when they emerge historically and tend to set the group apart from other groups, physically and culturally, they can be called an **ethnicity**. In some ways, ethnicity is like race in that you belong to it whether you want to or not. If you have a Pakistani ethnicity, you will never acquire a Swedish ethnicity, even if you become a citizen of Sweden, learn to speak fluent Swedish, join the Swedish Lutheran Church, write 12 books on Swedish culture, and claim to love lutefisk. But in other ways, ethnicity and race are different. Because ethnicity is not based on biological difference (or the myth of biological difference), it can change from generation to generation, as culture becomes more or less significant. People "decide" just how "ethnic" they want to be. Immigrant groups find their ethnicities fading away, as children and grandchildren grow in the new country with fewer and fewer ties to home.

Ethnic groups share a common ancestry, history, or culture. They share similar geographic origins, language, cultural traditions, religion, and general values. When asked, "What ethnicity are you?" people whose families have lived in the United States for more than a few generations usually cannot answer. If they are White, they assume that their ancestors came from "somewhere in Europe," but English, French, Swiss, Prussian, Belgian, and Dutch immigrants intermingled so freely that they simply forgot about the homeland and its customs.

The United States is called a "nation of immigrants." Ever since the founding of the East Coast colonies by immigrants who had been thrown out of England for being too religious and "puritanical," different ethnic groups have not only "enriched" American life, but make that life possible in the first place. President John F. Kennedy characterized the country's greatness as based on this fact, that America is "a society of immigrants, each of whom had begun life anew, on an equal footing." This was, he continued, the "secret" of America: "a nation of people with the fresh memory of old traditions who dared to explore new frontiers."

What are the origins of this nation of ethnic immigrants?

People from Europe

In the 2010 Census, 74.8 percent of the U.S. population was identified as White, most of European ancestry. The largest ethnic groups were German (11.4 percent), Irish (7.5 percent), Italian (4.5 percent), Polish (2.2%), and French (1.8 percent). We may now call them "European Americans" as a matter of convenience, but really we are saying "White people," referring to race rather than ethnicity. The differences today among many of these groups are far smaller than they once were. The White European population will experience only a 7 percent increase during the next 50 years, increasing from 195.7 million in 2000 to 210.3 million in 2050.

People from North America

Native Americans (once called "Indians") were the original inhabitants of North America, present from at least 40,000 BC. When the first Europeans and Africans arrived, there were between 2,000,000 and 10,000,000 people living north of the Rio Grande, divided into around 800 linguistic and cultural groups. Some were the nomadic hunter-gatherers of Hollywood-movie myth, but many were settled and agrarian, living in villages as large and prosperous as any villages among the European settlers. Still, the early European settlers usually approached the Native Americans through stereotypes: They were "noble savages," living without sin in a sort of Garden of Eden, or they were "wild savages," uncivilized and bestial. They were systematically deprived of their land and herded onto reservations, if not hunted and killed outright. William Henry Harrison and Andrew Jackson were both elected to the presidency primarily on their prestige as "Indian fighters." Political slogans and illustrations of the day showed them as noble, heroic White men "saving" America from the savage Indian threat. This threat was contrived as the excuse to appropriate Native American land and natural resources, and especially to clear a path for the transcontinental railroad. The stereotype of the Native American as uncivilized is still intact today, though it has changed from "violent" to "intuitive." Now movies have Native American sages teaching the White characters about listening to their hearts and staying close to nature.

Native Americans have long been used as mascots for sports teams. Did you know that half of all high school, college, and professional teams that used Native American mascots in 1960 have changed their mascots? Despite claims that these mascots are signs of "respect" for the tenacity and ferocity of the Native American tribes— tribes upon whose appropriated land the colleges and universities may actually have

TABLE 8.3

Selected Colleges and Universities That Changed Their Mascots

COLLEGE	FORMER MASCOT	CURRENT MASCOT	DATE CHANGED
Dartmouth College, NH	Indians	Big Green	1969
Marquette University, WI	Warriors	Golden Eagles	1994
Northeastern State University, OK	Redmen	Riverhawks	2007
Seattle University, WA	Chieftains	Redhawks	1999
Shippensburg University, PA	Red Raiders	Raiders	2006
Simpson College, IA	Redmen	Storm	1992
Southeast Missouri State University	Indians	Redhawks	2004
Southern Nazarene University, OK	Redskins	Crimson Storm	1998
Southern Oregon University	Red Raiders	Raiders	1980
St. Bonaventure University, NY	Brown Indians	Bonnies	1979
Stanford University, CA	Indians	Cardinal	1972
Syracuse University, NY	Orangemen	Orange	1978
University of Massachusetts, Amherst	Redmen	Minuteman	1972
West Georgia University	Braves	Wolves	2006

been built—most Native Americans feel such mascots are insulting and perpetuate racial stereotypes. (Table 8.3).

In the 2010 Census, only about 0.8 percent of the population identified as Native American (alone or in combination with other races), but many more people have some Native American ancestry (most tribes require one-quarter ancestry to declare an official tribal affiliation). About half live in rural areas, mostly on reservations, and the rest are concentrated in big cities, especially Los Angeles, New York, Seattle, Chicago, and Houston. The largest Native American nation, the Navajo or Dine of Arizona and New Mexico, has 269,000 members and many distinctive cultural institutions, including its own newspaper, radio station, and college. Its language is thriving. But most of the other Native American cultures are slowly dying out. Before the Europeans arrived, California was home to some 300 languages, more than the whole of Europe. Today 50 remain, though they are spoken by only a few people, almost all of them elderly.

The history of contact between European immigrants and Native Americans left many tribes destroyed, decimated, or displaced onto "reservations" (which were ironically conceived as places to "protect" the Native Americans from further harm, by Whites who were stealing their land). As a result, today, Native Americans are worse off than other minorities in many measures of institutional discrimination:

- A 65 percent high school graduation rate and 9 percent college attendance rate, far below the national average
- A poverty rate of 25.9 percent, higher than any other ethnic group
- The highest rate of suicide in the 18- to 24-year-old age group
- A lower percentage of "current drinkers" than Whites and Hispanics, yet a higher rate of alcoholism
- A lower life expectancy than the nation as a whole (U.S. Census Bureau, 2005).

Reservation life has grown mean and difficult, and funds are scarce for needed services. Many Native American cultures have taken advantage of tax and legal opportunities to open casinos (because reservations are not legally restricted from gambling) as a way to raise money, since federal and state funds have all but dried up. This presents Native tribes with a cynical "choice": Either open a casino and feed the nation's gambling addiction or fail to provide needed services for their people.

Nonetheless, many Native Americans continue to embrace their cultural heritage. *Pan-Indianism* today emphasizes common elements that run through Native American cultures, creating an identity that goes beyond the individual nations.

People from Latin America

In the 2000 census, 12.5 percent of the U.S. population declared that they were Hispanic or Latino/Latina, with ancestry in Latin America (the Caribbean, Mexico, and Central and South America). They are now the largest ethnic minority group in the United States, and they are growing almost three times faster than the population as a whole (2.9 percent per year

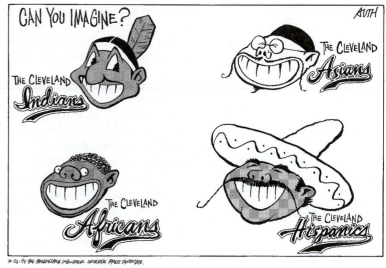

versus 1 percent per year in the general population), due both to immigration and higher birth rates (Figure 8.4). By 2050, the Hispanic population will nearly triple, from 35.6 million to 102.6 million.

Because these regions were originally settled by Native Americans, Europeans, Africans, and Asians, Hispanics may be of any race. Most speak Spanish at home, but they may speak Portuguese, French, Creole, Japanese, Italian, or an Indian language. Most are Roman Catholic, but they can be Protestant (usually Pentecostal), Jewish, Muslim, or followers of an Afro-Caribbean religion like Santería. Some do not approve of dozens of distinct cultures being lumped together into people from a continent, so they prefer to be called Mexican Americans (or Chicanos), Cuban Americans, and so on.

Latinos in the United States come from various countries of origin:

- *From Mexico: 34.3 million.* This is the most established of the Hispanic subgroups: Just 36 percent are foreign born, and many have had ancestors in California, Arizona, or Texas since those states were part of Mexico.
- *From Central America: 2.3 million, mainly from El Salvador, Guatemala, Honduras, and Nicaragua.* These people live mostly in California, Texas, Florida, and New York. They tend to be foreign born (71 percent), and 34 percent immigrated within the last decade. About 22 percent fall beneath the poverty line.
- *From South America: 1.7 million, mainly from Colombia, Ecuador, and Peru.* They tend to be foreign born (74 percent), and 33 percent immigrated within the last year. Many are well educated and belong to the middle class. About 35 percent of the foreign born have college degrees.
- *From Cuba: 1.2 million.* Of this group, 68 percent are foreign born, but most arrived more than a decade ago. Most settled in Florida. They tend to be more affluent than other Hispanic subgroups. About a third of the foreign-born adults have some college.
- *From the Dominican Republic: 912,000.* Over half live in New York. They are among the most impoverished of the Hispanic subgroups; 36 percent fall below the poverty line.

We are a nation of immigrants. President John F. Kennedy said this was the "secret" of America: "a nation of people with the fresh memory of old traditions who dared to explore new frontiers." Latinos represent the nation's largest ethnic minority. (Spanish Harlem, New York City.) ▼

- *From Puerto Rico: about 3.5 million (not counting the 3.8 million in Puerto Rico itself).* About a third live in New York. They are among most impoverished of the Hispanic subgroups: more than 30 percent are below poverty line (Passel and Suro, 2005; U.S. Census Bureau, 2004).

Hispanic Americans are not only the fastest-growing minority group in the United States: They also have the fastest-growing affluence. Their disposable income is expected to top $1 trillion by 2010 (Humphreys, 2006), and marketing executives have noticed. Hispanic people appear regularly on television commercials as purveyors of "traditional American values." Ten years ago, when Mexican American actor Mario Lopez starred in the teen sitcom *Saved by the Bell*, his character had to be made Anglo: Executives feared that no one would watch a show "with a Mexican in it."

Today, Hispanic actors are still mostly assigned to play gangsters, thugs, and servants, or else asked to play Anglo, but some, such as Antonio Banderas and Jennifer Lopez, are "going mainstream": They not only refuse to hide their ethnicity, they celebrate it. In South Florida, cable TV offers three all-Spanish channels, but they are not marketing only to the Hispanic community. The most popular *telenovelas* (prime-time soap operas) come with English-language subtitles so Anglos can watch too.

FIGURE 8.4 Second-Generation Latinos

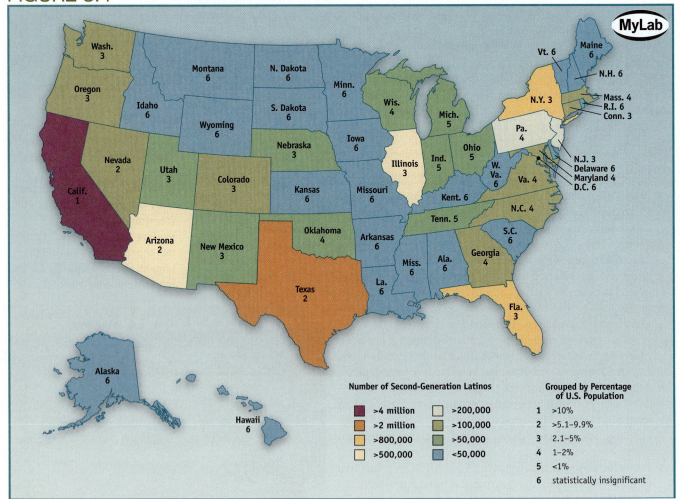

Source: From "2nd Generation Latinos—Focus on an Untapped Market," *DiversityInc.*, September 2005, p. 34.

People from Sub-Saharan Africa

In the 2010 Census, 12.4 percent of the U.S. population was identified as Black or African American, with ancestry in sub-Saharan Africa. The two terms are often used interchangeably, but technically *Black* is a race that includes Andaman Islanders, Australian aboriginals, and other people from outside sub-Saharan Africa and does not apply to the White, Asian, and Khoisan residents of Zimbabwe or Zaire. African American is an ethnicity, referring to the descendants of Black Africans who came to North America as slaves between 1500 and 1820 and after slavery were subject to "Jim Crow" laws that kept Blacks and Whites separate and unequal. They therefore do share a history and cultural traditions. African Americans are the only group to immigrate to the United States against their will, as they were forcibly abducted to serve as slaves in the South and in the Caribbean.

To reinforce that common cultural tradition, some have invented new holidays like Juneteenth and Kwaanza. Some have fashioned a distinctive dialect of English, called "Ebonics," with some terms and grammatical structures borrowed from West African languages. The creation of new, and distinctly African American, names is also an invented way to "preserve" traditions. (Historically, slaves were named by their masters and likely to bear Anglo names like Sally and Bill; the power to name your child a more African-sounding name, like, say, Shaniqua or Kadeem, illustrates the power to control the fate of that child.)

Thus, in the process, they transformed race into ethnicity in its own right. (These invented traditions are controversial in the African American community itself because they replace more Christian holidays like Christmas.) Contemporary immigrants from Nigeria or South Africa may be Black, White, or Asian, but they would not be African American.

The African American population is expected to experience modest growth by 2050, growing from 195.7 million to 210.3 million.

At the turn of the last century, the great African American sociologist W. E. B. DuBois said that "the problem of the twentieth century is the problem of the color line." There are many racial and ethnic minority groups in the United States, and African Americans are not even the largest, yet they have always been the "standard" minority. Studies of prejudice and discrimination often concentrate on White and Black, ignoring everyone else, and indeed most of the racist legislation in the United States has been directed primarily if not exclusively against African Americans. The Civil Rights movement of the 1960s did not need to be more specific: Everyone realized that it was about the civil rights of African Americans.

Today, African Americans have achieved some measure of political and economic success. There is a sizeable Black middle class, with educational background and earnings comparable to those of middle-class Whites. Overall, however, African Americans lag behind White non-Hispanic Americans in high school graduation rate by 15 percentage points (Mishel and Joydeep, 2006) and college graduation rate by 20 percentage points (*Journal of Blacks in Higher Education,* 2007). Black men's median earnings are 75 percent of what White men earn (women are roughly equal) (*State of Black America,* 2007). Nearly 26 percent of Black families and 11.7 percent of White families are below poverty level (American Community Survey 2009). Young Black men are nine times more likely to be murdered than are White men, and Black women three times as likely as White women (*State of Black America,* 2007). In the mass media, Black actors continue to be segregated, playing streetwise, inner-city thugs, cops, and other raw or rebellious types, except in movies and television programs aimed at a Black audience (Hill and Hill, 1985; Marchioso, 2001).

Did *you* know?

The words *hip-hop, hippie,* and *hip* all come from the African American *hep,* "cool" or "up to date," which ultimately derives from the Yoruba *hipikat,* "one who is aware, finely tuned to his or her environment." Other words and phrases derived from West African languages include *guy* (gay, "people"), *dig* (dega, "understand"), *jamboree* ("gathering"), *bug* ("bother"), *bogus* (boku, "fraud"), and *kick the bucket* (*kikatavoo,* "die").

In recent years, there has been much debate about paying "reparations" to the descendants of former slaves because they worked for no payment and had their lives torn apart through slavery. (Jews have received reparations from the German and Swiss governments that profited from seizing their assets during World War II, and Black South Africans have received reparations for what was lost during apartheid.) Opponents claim that it would be too costly and would result in profiteering by minorities.

People from East and South Asia

About 3.6 percent of the U.S. population traces its ancestry to East, Southeast, or South Asia. These groups include China (22 percent), the Philippines (15 percent), India (15 percent), Korea (10 percent), Vietnam (10 percent), and Japan (9 percent). Harsh quotas limited immigration before the 1960s, so most are recent immigrants. They differ tremendously in language, religion, and culture, and often they have long-standing ethnic and national conflicts back home (Korea versus Japan, China versus Vietnam, and so on) that make the umbrella term *Asian American* problematic.

Even within a nationality, there are many ethnic differences. People from China may speak Mandarin, Cantonese, or any of a dozen other varieties of Chinese or a hundred local languages. People from India may be Hindu, Muslim, Christian, Buddhist, Sikh, Jain, or atheist. People from Mindanao, the largest and most industrialized island of the Philippines, may look down on people from other islands as uncouth and uncivilized. So even *Chinese American*, *Indian American*, and *Filipino/a* become a problem. The Asian American population is expected to triple by 2050, rising from 10.7 million to 33.4 million, primarily due to immigration (U.S. Census Bureau, 2005).

Asian Americans are often depicted as "the model minority." Many measures of discrimination are significant only for Blacks and Hispanics (like school achievement, college enrollments, prison populations); Asian Americans score the same as Whites, or surpass them. They have the highest college graduation rate of any ethnic group. Though Asian Americans are only 5 percent of the total population, they comprise 15 percent of all U.S. physicians and surgeons, 15 percent of all computer and mathematical occupations, 10 percent of all engineers, and 16 percent of the student body at Ivy League colleges (Kim, 2006). They are less likely to become victims of racially motivated hate crimes than any ethnic group except Whites.

▼ Athletes like 2007 All-Star Game MVP Ichiro Suzuki defy stereotypes of Asians as weaklings and submissive nerds.

Even the stereotypes of Asian Americans are somewhat different. Prejudiced beliefs about Blacks and Hispanics mark them as barbaric, unpredictable, violent, and sexually dangerous. *The Bell Curve* and other works claimed that African Americans were genetically inferior to whites, had a lower native intelligence—that is, the arguments were about "nature" and no amount of "nurture" could compensate for their natural inferiority (Hernnstein and Murray, 1996). Prejudiced ideas about Asian Americans mark them as weak, passive, and asexual. In the mass media, they commonly appear not as thugs and drug dealers but as mystical sages and science nerds—stereotypes that are equally unfair but not nearly as threatening (Hamamoto, 1994). The success of Asian Americans, though, is attributed to their incredible work ethic, discipline, and parental influence—that is, as the result of "nurture." Few would be so consistent as to posit that Asian Americans were genetically superior to other groups. Of course, all of these are broad and false stereotypes. The point is that racist arguments are inconsistent; people refer to whichever one suits their purposes.

Scholars wondering about the "success" of the Asian American population have come up with several explanations. First, most Asian immigrants belonged to the

Try It The Media and Racial and Ethnic Relationships

OBJECTIVE: Use sociology to think about the ways race and ethnic relationships are portrayed in the media.

STEP 1: Collect Data

To collect some data, plan to watch one hour of television.

Your best bet is to watch one of the major networks like ABC, NBC, or CBS. Unlike much of cable broadcasting, these three networks are specifically designed to target a larger audience. Record the date and time you watched television. For each television show or commercial you observe during this one-hour period, record the number of characters portrayed by their racial/ethnic heritage. In other words, how many White people appeared? How many African Americans? What other groups were portrayed? You may also want to note gender and social class for a more detailed analysis. List not only the shows but also the commercials during this time period. Take notes on a separate piece of paper and then transfer the totals to a grid like the one below.

Be sure to include the following information in your final results.

Your name: _____

Date and time you completed project: _____

Name of network: _____

How many television shows did you watch during this period? _____

List the name of the show(s): _____

_____

How many commercials? _____

List the products sold in each commercial: _____

_____

_____

	African American	White	Other/Note the Ethnicity
1. Number of people or characters from each category			
2. The central figure, star, leader, or most important person in each scene			
3. The "bad guy," criminal, or other person shown in a negative role			
4. The number in each category appearing as wealthy or of higher social class			
5. The number of females in each category			
6. The number of males in each category			
7. The number in each category appearing as poor or lower social class			
8. The number in each category interacting with members of a different racial/ethnic category			
9. The number of times shown in nonstereotypical roles			
10. The number in each category appearing as the "good guy" or good person			

STEP 2: Evaluate

Think about what your results have to say about the issues of prejudice, discrimination, and institutional discrimination. Did you notice patterns? If so, please explain. If you do not notice any patterns, you may need to extend the time period of your television viewing.

STEP 3: Discuss

Be prepared to share your results in class.

middle class in their home country, so they find it easier to enter the middle class in the United States. They are more likely to be fluent in English. Because there are relatively few of them, they are unlikely to live in segregated neighborhoods, and much more likely to marry someone of another racial/ethnic group (Asian American Cultural Center, 2005; Wong, 1986). Finally, if prejudice often boils down to light versus dark, they may profit by being relatively light skinned.

People from the Middle East

The U.S. Census does not give them a separate category, but about 2 million people in the United States trace their ancestry to the Middle East or North Africa. About 1,500,000 are recent immigrants who have arrived since 1970. About one-third of these are Iranian, one-third Turkish, and the other one-third are Arabs, Israelis, Cypriots, and others. There have been two broad migrations of Middle Easterners to the United States:

- Between 1880 and 1920, refugees came here from the failing Ottoman Empire, especially Lebanon, Cyprus, Syria, and Armenia. They were mostly working class and poor, about 75 percent Christian and the rest Muslim or Jewish. They settled primarily in the industrial Northeast and Midwest.
- After 1970, many middle-class Israelis, Arabs, and Iranians immigrated to America. Of there, 73 percent were Muslim. They settled primarily in large cities, especially Los Angeles, New York, Chicago, Houston, and Washington, D.C.

Members of the first wave of immigration were assimilationist; like most other immigrants of the period, they hid or minimized their Middle Eastern ancestry and sought to fit in. During the last 50 years, there has been an increase in efforts to retain separate identity as Muslims.

Like Asian Americans, Middle Eastern Americans tend to be a "model minority." They are the most well-educated ethnic group in the United States: Half have college degrees, as opposed to 30 percent of White non–Middle Easterners. The median salary of Middle Eastern men is slightly higher than the national mean. However, nearly 20 percent live below the poverty level (U.S. Census Bureau, 2005).

Stereotypes about Middle Easterners tend to be more extreme, and more commonly believed, than stereotypes about other minority groups. Many Americans unaware of the political, cultural, and religious differences in the Middle East tend to believe that all Middle Easterners are Arabs, Muslims, or even Bedouins, who live in tents and ride camels. The men are stereotyped as wide-eyed terrorists; the women as subservient chattel. Even the hero of Disney's *Aladdin* (1993), who was an Arab but evidently not "as Arab" as everyone else, complains of the barbarity of his country: "They'll cut off your nose to spite your face, but hey, it's home." The conventional movie villain was once German, then Russian, then "Euro-terrorist;" now he is a Middle Eastern Arab.

Prejudice and discrimination against Middle Easterners, Arabs, and Muslims have increased significantly in the last decade, and especially after the 9/11 terrorist attacks. According to the Pew Forum on Religion and Public Life, 38 percent of respondents would not vote for a well-qualified Muslim for president (a higher percentage than for any minority except gays) and half believe that half or more of all Muslims are anti-American (Pew Forum on Religion and Public Life, 2003). The FBI documented an increase of 1,600 percent in hate crimes against Arabs in 2001, jumping from 28 reported crimes in 2000 to 481 in 2001. The number is second only to anti-Jewish crimes, which tower atop the list at 1,043 reported crimes (U.S. Department of Justice, 2005). In most countries of the European Union, intolerance has also increased significantly, first

Did *you* know?

The first building in the United States designed for exclusive use as a mosque was constructed in Cedar Rapids, Iowa, in 1934. It was sold in 1971, becoming a youth center and a church, and then abandoned. In 1990, the Islamic Council of Iowa acquired and restored the building, and the "Mother Mosque" is now listed on the National Register of Historic Places as an "essential piece of American religious history."

Sociology and our World

"Choosing" One's Ethnicity

Although we often experience ethnicity as a "primordial" essential and biologically based category, sociologists are also aware that ethnicity can be more flexible than that. In her book, *Ethnic Options* (1990), Mary Waters describes the ways that different ethnic groups either exaggerate or downplay their ethnicity, depending on the situation.

Sometimes ethnicity can be rather confusing—to ourselves and to others. One of my colleagues, Pat Pugliani, had several children. Pat was from an Italian background and, at the time, a stay-at-home mom, and she spent a good deal of time preparing Italian food, celebrating traditional holidays, and the like. When Sara, her youngest, was in elementary school, the class was doing a unit on ethnicity, and the kids had to do a report on their ethnic background. One day, Pat got a concerned phone call from the teacher. "I think we have a problem with Sara," the teacher said.

Sara was doing a report about Italy, the teacher said. "Well, what's wrong with that?" Pat asked. "But, but . . ." the teacher stammered. "She's Asian!"

Sara was indeed of Korean origin, and Pat and her husband had adopted her. And though they spend some time learning about Korea, Sara also identified with the ethnicity of her family.

Sara's teacher informed Pat on the phone that Sara should do a report about Korea. So she did. That week, the children were all supposed to bring in a dish that was representative of their culture. Pat found a recipe for *bulgogi*, a Korean barbecue steak, and brought it to class.

Now the teacher was again shocked—this time seeing a non-Asian parent! Ever the sociologist, Pat patiently explained to the teacher the difference between race and ethnicity, and that we can often choose our ethnicity from a range of options.

---

following September 11 and then spiking in different countries in the aftermath of incidents there. Eighty percent of Muslims in the United Kingdom said they had experienced discrimination in 2001, a jump from 45 percent in 2000 and 35 percent in 1999; hostility increased in Spain and Germany after the Madrid train bombing and in the Netherlands after the murder of filmmaker Theo van Gogh, both in 2004 (International Helsinki Federation for Human Rights, 2006).

Ethnicity and Conflict

Ethnicity is fluid; sometimes ethic identification is stronger than at other times. For some groups, for whom discrimination has largely disappeared, such as the Irish and the Italians, ethnic identity has become mostly a choice (Gans, 1962; Waters, 1990). Ethnicity becomes "situational"—to be asserted in times and situations when it will increase their prestige and downplayed or ignored when it may decrease their prestige. Or it becomes symbolic ethnicity, something to participate in on special occasions, like St. Patrick's Day or Passover, but ignored the rest of the time. Just as old ethnicities can fade away, new ethnicities can emerge. Members of the Yoruba, Ibo, Fulani, and other West African ethnic groups transported to the United States during the slavery era were forcibly stripped of their distinctive cultures, until only a few customs remained, but they banded together to form a new ethnic group, African American.

When several different ethnic groups are present in a single nation, they often compete for power and resources. Because there are around 5,000 ethnic groups in the world trying to share 190 nations, ethnic conflict is common, ranging from discrimination to violence and sometimes even civil war. Since 1945, 15 million people have died in conflicts involving ethnicity to some degree (Doyle, 1998).

At its most brutal, ethnic conflict can result in **genocide**, the planned, systematic destruction of a racial, political, or cultural group. The most infamous modern example of genocide is the Nazi massacre of 6 million Jews, Gypsies, gays, and other "undesirables" during World War II, but there have been a number of others. Between 1915 and 1923 the Turkish elite of the Ottoman Empire killed over 1 million ethnic

Armenians. In the 1990s, the dominant Hutu ethnic group killed hundreds of thousands of minority Tutsi in Rwanda and Burundi, and a new euphemism for genocide arose, "ethnic cleansing," when majority Serbs killed hundreds of thousands of minority Muslims in Bosnia. War in Kosovo in 1999 was prompted by the charges that Serbian forces were engaging in "ethnic cleansing" of the Kosovar Albanians.

Why do ethnic minorities live in relative harmony in some countries, while in others, they are at each other's throats? There are no easy answers, but one factor appears to be heterogeneity. If there are many ethnic groups in the country, it is less likely that any one will dominate, and the others feel left out. However, if there are only two or three, it is easy for them to characterize each other as demonic. Another factor is the rights and privileges given to minorities. In countries where ethnic minorities are accepted as ordinary parts of the political structure, they are less likely to compete for resources, real or imagined, and ethnic conflict is less common (Gurr, 2000; van Amersfoort, 1982).

Melting Pot (Assimilation) and Multiculturalism (Pluralism)

My grade school social studies textbook—that same one with the pictures illustrating the three races—glowingly described America as a *melting pot*. The United States was praised for its acceptance of difference, lack of prejudice, and our ability to melt down all cultural differences into a single, savory American soup.

Sociologically, this process seems unlikely because the dominant groups are rarely willing to let their characteristics melt away into the pot. Instead, the minority groups were subject to **assimiliation**, nearly abandoning their cultural traditions altogether and embracing the dominant culture. Only a few of their traditions entered the pot, mostly food (like pizza) and slang terms (like *pal* for friend, from the Romany word for "brother"); most traits and traditions were left behind. It was Italian Americans in the process of assimilating, not Italy, that gave us pizza—it was unknown in Palermo until a Pizza Hut franchise opened there. Besides, only White Europeans were invited to melt down. Asians, Native Americans, and Blacks weren't even given the option.

Some immigrant groups felt that assimilation was not desirable. They didn't want to lose their distinctive customs, social norms, language, and religion. Why couldn't they continue to speak their native language, read newspapers from home, eat the same food they ate at home, and still be Americans? Maybe in the nineteenth century, when the journey from the homeland to the United States took months and there was little chance of ever returning, assimilation made sense, but now the homeland was only a short plane flight away, and friends and relatives back home as close as a telephone call or e-mail message.

During the 1980s and 1990s, many minority groups proposed pluralism as an alternative to the melting pot. **Pluralism** maintains that a stable society need not contain just one ethnic, cultural, or religious group. The different groups can treat each other with mutual respect instead of competing and trying to dominate each other. Thus, minority cultures can maintain their own distinctiveness and still participate in the greater society without discrimination.

At its most stable, pluralism becomes multiculturalism, in which cultural groups exist not only side by side but equally. Real multiculturalism seems to be rare—one language, religion,

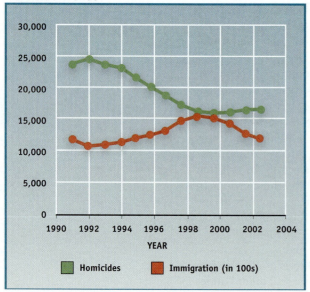

FIGURE 8.5 **Immigration Flows and Homicide Trends**

Source: From "Open Doors Don't Invite Criminals" by Robert J. Sampson, *New York Times* March 11, 2006.

or culture will usually dominate, either by numbers or by prestige, and people will be drawn to it, even in the absence of institutional discrimination. India has 22 official languages, but official communication in the national arena must be conducted in Hindi or English, and for everyday communication, people tend to prefer English.

Advocates of multiculturalism like to point out the case of Switzerland, where four linguistic and cultural groups enjoy complete equality under the law. But are they really equal in everyday life? Nearly two-thirds (65 percent) of the population speaks German, 18 percent French, 10 percent Italian, and 0.8 percent Romansch (descended from Latin). Street signs are usually in the local language and German. In Parliament, speeches may be given in any of the national languages, but most politicians choose German, even if they speak something else at home. All schoolchildren must learn a second national language, but schools usually offer only German and French, so learning Italian or Romansch is not an option. People outside of the German-speaking cantons often pretend that they do not understand German at all, as a way of resisting what they feel is linguistic imperialism by the "dominant" linguistic group. Clearly, the other languages do not enjoy the same prestige.

Bilingualism

The assimilation model meant that English was preferred by society at large to the home language. The dominant culture expected that immigrants would enroll in English classes the moment they arrived, and even if children were not punished for using their parents' birth language, they might grow up thinking that it was old-fashioned and outdated, a relic of their parents' generation. Today, however, many immigrants continue to speak their "native" language. Spanish is especially popular.

The Hispanic preference for speaking Spanish has led to some controversy that speakers of Bengali, Muong, and Byelorussian do not generate. In the United States, 29 million people use Spanish as their everyday language, more than any non-Spanish nation in the world, yet 23 states have laws declaring English their official language and permitting only English in official documents.

But even when English is not legalized, many people believe that "our" only language should be English. Recently I was talking to a man who said he traveled across the United States, and there was one thing he wondered: "Why isn't Spanish taught in every grade level, from kindergarten on?" I replied that Spanish classes were offered in many elementary schools. But he meant something different. "They've taken over!" he shouted. "Why don't we just admit it, and start teaching all classes in Spanish!" I was amazed at how bitter he was, connecting speaking Spanish with a foreign invasion and English with patriotism.

Race and Ethnicity in the 21st Century

Like class, or gender, race and ethnicity are vital elements of our identity and also the basis for discrimination and inequality. Every one of us constructs our identities, at least in part, through race and ethnicity. It is one of the most important foundations of identity, an anchor that ties us to family, tradition, and culture. And yet virtually every one

We tend to believe that increased immigration leads to increases in the crime rate, both because of the increased ethnic tension that increases hostility and potential violence and because the immigrants are often poorer and therefore turn to crime to enhance their class position. But if we thought that, we would be wrong (Figure 8.5). Research by Robert Sampson found that Mexican American immigrants in Chicago were 45 percent less likely to commit violence than third-gener-ation Americans. He found that "immigrants appear in general to be less violent than people born in America, particularly when they live in neighborhoods with high numbers of other immigrants." Perhaps instead of moving from the multi-cultural city to the more homo-geneous suburbs to avoid crime and violence, we should move to an immi-grant neigh-borhood. They're safer (Sampson, 2006)!

3. *What is prejudice?* Prejudice is a set of beliefs and attitudes that cause us to prejudge others based on their social location. Prejudice is based on stereotypes, which are broad generalizations about a group that are applied to all individuals in that group. Racism is systematic prejudice applied to groups. It is very powerful and can be overt or subtle, and even groups victimized by racially based attitudes often believe in the underlying stereotypes.

4. *What is discrimination?* Discrimination is a set of actions based on prejudice and stereotypes. Prejudice and discrimination are not always causally related. Deeply embedded in the institutions of society, discrimination often results in systematic oppression. Laws against institutional discrimination often have some effect but are not always useful.

5. *How do sociologists explain prejudice and discrimination?* Sociologists are interested in combating prejudice. Awareness of prejudice and a desire to stop it still require a suspension of belief in stereotypes to be effective. Discrimination is a form of socialization, as stereotypes can become self-fulfilling prophecies. The primordial theory holds that innate conflict exists between in- and out-groups. The frustration-aggression theory says that individuals direct frustration at their own personal lives toward a scapegoat. According to conflict theory, prejudice is a tool used by the elites to control those at the bottom of the social hierarchy.

Feminist theory looks at the intersections of race, class, gender, sexual orientation, and so on.

6. *What ethnic groups exist in the United States?* Ethnic groups are those who share a common ancestry, history, or culture. According to the 2000 U.S. Census, 75 percent of the U.S. population is White, or of European ancestry. Native Americans comprise 1.5 percent of the population and are worse off than other minority groups with regard to poverty and other social ills. Of the population, 12.5 percent is Hispanic, or Latino, with roots in Latin America; 12.5 percent is Black, or African-American; and 3.6 percent is Asian. There are about 2 million individuals from the Middle East and North Africa in the United States.

7. *How does ethnicity relate to conflict?* Racial terminology defines us to ourselves and to others. There is conflict between and within groups over racial terminology, and the acceptability of racial terms changes over time and by group. Ethnic groups also compete over power and resources, and at their starkest they can result in genocide. The United States is often called a melting pot society, and there is disagreement over whether assimilation or pluralism best describes U.S. society. Assimilation occurs when the minority group fits into the majority group, pluralism is ethnic diversity with mutual respect among groups, and multiculturalism is marked by groups living side-by-side in equality.

KeyTerms

Affirmative action (p. 256)
Apartheid (p. 255)
Ascribed status (p. 258)
Assimilation (p. 272)
Differential power (p. 248)
Discrimination (p. 253)
Ethnicity (pp. 244, 262)
Ethnic groups (p. 262)
Genocide (p. 271)
Identifiability (p. 258)

In-group (p. 248)
Institutional discrimination (p. 254)
Integration (p. 255)
Matrix of domination (p. 260)
Majority group (p. 248)
Minority group (p. 248)
Out-group (p. 248)
Overt racism (p. 252)
Pluralism (p. 272)
Prejudice (p. 251)

Primordial theory (p. 259)
Race (p. 244)
Racism (p. 252)
Scapegoat (p. 259)
Segregation (p. 254)
Stereotypes (p. 251)
Subtle racism (p. 252)
Tokenism (p. 257)

What does *America* think?

8.1 Neighborhood Segregation

This is based on actual survey data from the General Social Survey, 2004; cumulative data.

Please respond to the following statement: White people have the right to keep Black people out of their neighborhoods if they want to, and Black people should respect that right. Seventy-five percent of respondents disagreed either slightly or strongly. Almost 80 percent of Black respondents disagreed strongly, as opposed to 45 percent of White respondents. Only about 11 percent of respondents agreed strongly.

CRITICAL THINKING | DISCUSSION QUESTIONS

1. Why do you think 10 percent of black respondents agreed that White people should be allowed to keep Black people out and that Black people should respect that right? Do you think those same individuals feel that Black people should be able to keep White people out of their neighborhoods?
2. How do you think responses to this question would differ by social class? By geographical region? How would you explain those potential differences?
3. Seventy-five percent of respondents disagreed with White-imposed neighborhood segregation. What percent of respondents do you think would have disagreed had this survey been given in 1850? In 1950? Explain your answers.

8.2 The Melting Pot

This is based on actual survey data from the General Social Survey, 2004.

Some people say that it is better for a country if different racial and ethnic groups maintain their distinct customs and traditions. Others say that it is better if these groups adapt and blend into the larger society. Which of these views comes closer to your own? The responses to this question were split almost in half. Slightly more than 50 percent of respondents thought it was better if groups adapted and blended into the larger society. White respondents (55.4%) were more likely to think that than were Black respondents (52.8%), and those who identified as other race were least likely to feel groups should assimilate (45.7%).

CRITICAL THINKING | DISCUSSION QUESTIONS

1. Why do you think there were only very small differences in responses by racial classification?
2. In many areas of the world, the question of assimilation and group difference leads to civil war and even genocide. Why do you think that does not happen in the contemporary United States?

▶ Go to this website to look further at the data. You can run your own statistics and crosstabs here: **http://sda.berkeley.edu/cgi-bin/hsda?harcsda+gss04**

REFERENCES: Davis, James A., Tom W. Smith, and Peter V. Marsden. General Social Surveys 1972–2004: [Cumulative file] [Computer file]. 2nd ICPSR version. Chicago, IL: National Opinion Research Center [producer], 2005. Storrs, CT: Roper Center for Public Opinion Research, University of Connecticut; Ann Arbor, MI: Inter-University Consortium for Political and Social Research; Berkeley, CA: Computer-Assisted Survey Methods Program, University of California [distributors], 2005.

chapter 9

"MEN ARE FROM MARS, WOMEN ARE FROM VENUS." This phrase, now part of our everyday language, is the title of John Gray's book, perhaps the most successful bestselling self-help book in world history. It has also been the title of a movie, a television show, and a board game. It expresses what many people have come to believe is a basic and simple truth: Men and women are so different that we might as well be from different planets. As Gray puts it, women and men "think, feel, perceive, react, respond, love, need and appreciate differently" (1992, p. 5). Seen this way, communication between women and men is an event of cosmic proportions, a moment of intergalactic understanding.

Yet, despite these differences, you are probably reading these words at a coeducational school, where you sit in the same classes, live in the same dorms, eat in the same cafeteria, listen to the same lectures, read the same texts, take the same tests, and are graded (you hope) by the same criteria as members of the opposite sex. At home, we live in the same houses, prepare and eat

Sex and Gender

the same meals, use the same bathrooms, and often watch the same television programs as our opposite-sex family members or spouses. And I'll bet none of you has ever considered going to the dean of students to complain that because you are a Martian and your professor is a Venusian that you should receive extra credit, or at least the school should provide an interplanetary translator.

We live in a world of *both* gender difference and gender similarity. Women and men do often appear to be completely different creatures, and yet we are also able to work together and even live together.

We live in a world of *both* gender difference and gender similarity. Women and men do often appear to be completely different creatures, and yet we are also able to work together and even live together.

Gender is one of the foundations on which we build our identities. It is also one of the major ways in which societies organize themselves. Sociologists are interested in both gender identities and gender inequality.

Gender is one of the fundamental ways in which we develop an identity. Every society in the world classifies people by whether they are male or female, and a host of social roles and relationships are prescribed as a result. And virtually every society assumes that, in some basic ways, women and men are different (see Kimmel, 2003).

And in virtually every society, women and men are not equal. Gender inequality is a nearly universal phenomenon: To be a man or a woman means not only difference but also hierarchy.

Why does virtually every society differentiate people on the basis of biological sex? And why is virtually every known society also based on gender inequality, on the dominance of men over women? These are the two questions that animate the sociological study of gender.

To many observers, the answer to the second question derives from the answer to the first: Men dominate women because men and women are so different. Biological differences between women and men lead inevitably to different political, social, and economic outcomes. Men and women are unequal because nature made them different.

But sociologists take a different view. Sociologists believe that if gender inequality were simply the product of gender difference, then gender inequality would look pretty much the same everywhere. And, as we will see, gender inequality varies enormously from one culture to another. Plus, if gender difference itself were simply a reflection of natural differences, then these differences, too, would be universal. As we will see, they are far from universal.

Sex and Gender: Nature *and* Nurture

Sociologists begin by distinguishing sex and gender. When we refer to **sex** we refer to the biology of maleness and femaleness—our chromosomal, chemical, anatomical organization.

Gender refers to the meaning that societies give to the fact of biological difference. What is the significance of biological difference? Does it mean that you must—or must not—perform certain tasks, think certain thoughts, or do certain things? Sex is male and female; gender is the cultural meanings of masculinity and femininity.

This distinction is now even noted in our law. In a 1994 case, Justice Antonin Scalia of the U.S. Supreme Court wrote:

> The word gender has acquired the new and useful connotation of cultural or attitudinal characteristics (as opposed to physical characteristics) distinctive to the sexes. That is to say, gender is to sex as feminine is to female and masculine is to male. (Scalia, 1994)

Biological sex varies little—males everywhere have a Y chromosome, for example—but gender varies enormously. Specifically, gender varies in four crucial ways:

1. *Gender varies from culture to culture.* What it means to be a man or a woman in one culture may be quite different from in another. In some cultures, women are thought to be passive and dependent; in other cultures decisive and competitive. In some cultures men are supposed to be aggressive and stoic; in others, caring and emotionally responsive.

2. *Definitions of gender change over time.* What it may mean to be a man or a woman in the United States today is different from what it meant in 1776. Take hairstyles, for example—at that time, the "in" style was for men to wear their hair set in ringlets or in a windswept look of loose confusion on top, with locks falling over the forehead—that is, if they didn't wear a longish wig with a pony-tail down the back (the style for many white-collar professionals).

3. *Definitions of gender vary within a society.* Within any one society it may mean different things to be a man or a woman depending on race, religion, region, age, sexuality, class, and the like (see Kimmel, 2003). Imagine, for example, two "American" women: One is 22 years old, wealthy, Asian American, Buddhist, heterosexual, and living in suburban San Francisco; and the other is a poor, White, 75-year-old Irish Catholic in Boston. Do you think they would have the same idea of what it means to be a woman?

4. *Gender varies over the life course.* What it means to be a man or a woman at age 20 is probably quite different from what it will mean to you at age 40 or at age 70. These ages correspond to changes in our life experiences, and masculinity and femininity will mean different things if you are entering the labor force or if you are retiring from it, if you are prepubescent, a young parent, or a grand-parent (Rossi, 1985).

Each of the social and behavioral sciences contributes to the study of gender. Anthropologists can help illuminate the cross-cultural differences, while historians can focus our attention on the differences over time. Developmental psychologists explore how definitions of masculinity and femininity vary over the course of one's life. And it has been sociology's contribution to examine the ways in which our different experiences, based on other bases of identity—class, race, and the like—affect our definitions of gender.

Gender identity refers to our understanding of ourselves as male or female, what we think it means to be male or female. Sociologists are aware that other identities, like class or race, dramatically affect gender identity. Sociologists who observe the *intersection* of these identities speak, then, of gender identities as plural: *masculinities* and *femininities*. In fact, the differences *among* men and *among* women are often greater than the differences that we imagine *between* women and men. So, for example, although there are small differences between girls and boys in math and language abilities, we all know plenty of boys who are adept at languages and can barely learn the times tables and plenty of girls who whiz through math class, but can't conjugate a Spanish verb.

▲ Falling outside of your culture's standard definitions of masculinity or femininity can by uncomfortable at best. Often the consequences are severe and can affect your relationships, job opportunities, and quality of life.

Making the terms plural indicates how different groups of men or women might have different identities. Recognition of the gender identities as plural enables us to see how conflicts between different groups—say, for example, Whites and Blacks or rich and poor—may also be expressed in gender terms. So, for example, racists declare that minority men are not "real men" because they don't possess certain traits or because they possess too many of other traits. Sociologists today study the intersections, or the **intersectionality** of these forms of identity—race, class, sexuality, age, religion, region, and so on.

The other major aspect of gender is inequality. **Gender inequality** has two dimensions: the domination of men over women, and the domination of some men over other men, and some women over other women. Making the category of identity plural doesn't mean that all masculinities or femininities are considered equal.

All known societies are characterized by some amount of gender inequality, in which men dominate women (see Coult, 1965). This is called male domination, or patriarchy. **Patriarchy** literally means "the rule of the fathers," and while fathers don't rule in every case, men do hold power over women.

And most societies also grant more power and resources to some men and some women. One definition of masculinity or femininity comes to dominate and becomes the standard against which everyone comes to be measured and to measure themselves. This is where race and class and the other bases of identity and inequality come in.

In 1963, the sociologist Erving Goffman described masculinity in the United States this way:

> In an important sense, there is only one complete unblushing male in America: a young, married, white, urban, northern, heterosexual, Protestant, father, of college education, fully employed, of good complexion, weight and height, and a recent record in sports. (p. 128)

In the next sentence, Goffman described what it feels like to *not* have all those characteristics. "Any male who fails to qualify in any one of these ways is likely to view himself—during moments at least—as unworthy, incomplete, and inferior." Because it is certain that all males will, at some point, fail to measure up to all those criteria, what Goffman is saying is that *all* males will, at some point, feel "unworthy, incomplete, and inferior."

But why do men and women in every country seem to be so different from each other? And why do we everywhere observe gender inequality?

The Biology of Sex and Gender

Most everyday explanations of gender identity and gender inequality begin—and often end—with biology. The observed biological differences between women and men are thought to lead naturally, and inevitably, to the inequality we observe. Because we're different, the argument goes, we shouldn't try to be similar. And if these differences are natural, gender inequality is inevitable; changes in male–female relations contradict nature's plan and are therefore best avoided. (This is, of course, the "nature" side of the debate; we will also discuss the "nurture" side.)

Biological arguments rest on three types of evidence: the demands of evolution, different brain structures and chemistry, and hormonal differences. Sociologists must be aware of these sorts of arguments because sociological perspectives on sex and gender often run counter to them.

Evolutionary Imperatives

All creatures evolve and adapt to changing environments. The differences we observe between women and men are the results of thousands of years of evolutionary adaptation (Daly and Wilson, 1999; Dawkins, 1989). Because the chief goal of all living creatures is to reproduce themselves, males and females developed different "reproductive strategies" to ensure that this happens and that they are able to pass on their genetic material to the next generation. This is called the **evolutionary imperative.**

According to this school of thought, we can see the origins of both gender differences and gender inequality in the different strategies males and females develop to reproduce. Biologically, the male's part in reproduction ends at ejaculation. He produces millions and millions of sperm cells, and his goal is to inseminate as many females as possible, increasing his chances that his offspring will survive. Evolutionary biologists argue that men are "naturally" promiscuous and extremely reluctant to commit to a relationship.

The female's part in reproduction really begins at conception. Females release only one egg at a time and require only one successful mating for conception. They must invest a significant amount of energy to ensure that their offspring is born and survives a very long infancy. For this reason, females are considered "naturally" monogamous; they seek a committed relationship with one male to help them protect the dependent offspring.

From these assumed differences in reproductive "strategies," evolutionary psychologists claim, we can see the origins of men's and women's different psychological dispositions: Men are more aggressive, want more casual sex, and avoid commitment; females are nurturing, passive, and desire commitment (Symons, 1985).

At their most distressing extreme, some evolutionary psychologists go so far as to claim that rape is "a natural, biological phenomenon that is a product of human evolutionary heritage" (Thornhill and Palmer, 2000). To reproduce, males must have access to females. But what of the male who is unlucky or unsuccessful? In rape, the authors argue, the male circumvents females' choice and thereby increases reproductive success. Rape, they argue, is the evolutionary strategy for males who otherwise could not get a date.

To sociologists—well, to any rational creature—these evolutionary arguments are unpersuasive. They work backward, by observing some difference in sexual behavior among contemporary people and then reasoning back to its supposed evolutionary origin. Their data are selective and ignore other "natural" behaviors like altruism and cooperation. They provide more of a "just so" story, like the tongue-in-cheek ones Rudyard Kipling wrote about how elephants got their trunks or tigers their stripes.

One could take the same evidence, in fact, and construct an equally plausible evolutionary explanation for exactly the opposite results. In fact, that's exactly what primatologist Sarah Blaffer Hrdy did. (See the Sociology and Our World box on page 284).

Brain and Hormone Research

There are also some differences between male and female brains, and surely the **sex hormones,** such as **testosterone**, result in very different gendered behaviors for women and men. Or do they?

Actually, scientists disagree about what those differences mean. Once it was thought that because males' brains were bigger than females', males were smarter. But it turned out that brain size was simply a reflection of body size and did not matter. However, recent studies of the brain do suggest some differences in which side of the brain dominates and the level of connection or separation between the two halves of the brain.

Sociology and our World

Monogamous Masculinity, Promiscuous Femininity

Evolutionary psychologists argue that the size and number of reproductive cells lead inevitably to different levels of parental "investment" in children. (Males produce millions of tiny sperm; females produce only a few dozen comparatively huge eggs.) Sarah Blaffer Hrdy (1981) adds a few more biological facts to the mix. Unlike other mammals, she notes, human females conceal estrus; that is, they are potentially sexually receptive throughout their entire menstrual cycle, unlike other female mammals that go "into heat" when ovulating and who are otherwise utterly uninterested in sex. What is the evolutionary reason for this? Hrdy asks. (*Hint*: The female knows that the baby is hers, but the male can never be exactly sure.)

Could it be, she asks, that females might want to mate with as many males as possible, to ensure that all of them will provide food and protection to the helpless and dependent infant, thereby increasing its chances of survival? (Remember that infant mortality in those preindustrial cultures of origin was extraordinarily high.) Could it be that females have a natural propensity toward promiscuity to ensure the offspring's survival and that males have a natural propensity toward monogamy, lest they run themselves ragged to provide food and protection to a baby who may—or may not—be theirs? Wouldn't it be more likely for males to devise a system that ensured women's faithfulness—monogamy—and institutionalize it in marriage, and then develop a cultural plan that would keep women in the home (because they might be ovulating and thus get pregnant)? And because it often takes a couple more than one "try" to get pregnant, wouldn't regular couplings with one partner be a more successful strategy for a male than a one-night stand?

Of course, no one would suggest that this interpretation is any more "true" than the evolutionary psychologists'. But what Hrdy revealed is that one can use the same—or even better—biological evidence and construct the exact opposite "just so" story. If that's possible, it means that we should be *extremely* cautious in accepting evolutionary arguments.

The right hemisphere is associated with visual and spatial ability; the left hemisphere controls language and reading. Males are thought to be more right brained, females more left brained; and the separation between the two sides is more pronounced in males than in females. Researchers at Indiana University's medical school measured brain activity of women and men while they listened to a subject read a John Grisham novel (see Holtz, 2000). The men showed much more activity on the left side of their brains; the women showed activity on both sides. But what this means is far from clear. One could say that such brain structure means that men are better able to compartmentalize, or it could mean that women use the entire brain.

Brain research has proved inconclusive. Neuropsychologist Doreen Kimura (cited in Rivers, 2002) writes, "in the larger comparative context, the similarities between human males and females far outweigh the differences."

Perhaps the sex hormones that trigger sex development provide the causes of sex differences. Sex differentiation, the process by which males and females diverge biologically, is most pronounced at two points:

1. During fetal development, when the **primary sex characteristics** (those characteristics that are anatomically present at birth, like the sex organs themselves) develop in the embryo.

2. At puberty, when the bodies of boys and girls are transformed by a flood of sex hormones that trigger the development of **secondary sex characteristics** (breast development in girls, the lowering of boys' voices, boys' development of facial hair, and the like).

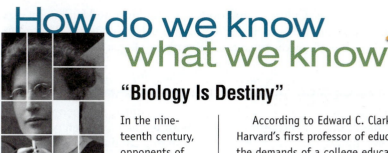

"Biology Is Destiny"

In the nineteenth century, opponents of women's equality used biological arguments to prevent women from going to work and to college, from voting, or even from serving on juries. Women were said to be too weak, irrational, or emotional, or too fragile and delicate.

Some tried to use statistical data to prove that women were not biologically capable of a college education.

According to Edward C. Clarke, Harvard's first professor of education, the demands of a college education would be too taxing for women, and if women went to college their brains would grow bigger and heavier, but their wombs would shrink.

His evidence? It turned out that college-educated women had fewer children than noncollege-educated women. And 42 percent of women admitted to mental hospitals were college educated, compared with only 16 percent of men. (Remember that in the Middle Ages, the cause of insanity for women was believed to be a detached uterus that then floated through the body poisoning it; the word *hysteria* means "wandering womb"; thus, "hysterectomies.") Could it be that college education was actually driving women crazy—and causing them to stop having babies?

As we've seen earlier, in Chapter 4, one can draw no causal inferences from even such a strange correlation. Today, we would be more likely to attribute the decrease in family size to women's expanding opportunities, not to their shrinking wombs.

The hormones responsible for these dramatic changes—testosterone and estrogen—have been held responsible as well for differences between men and women.

Much hormone research concerns the effect of testosterone on behavior, since males have much higher levels than females, and its effects seem far more noticeable. Everyone "knows," for example, that testosterone "causes" aggression. Increases in testosterone levels do cause increases in aggression. But it is also true that aggressive behavior leads to an increase in production of testosterone. So biology causes behavior, and behavior (which may be culturally induced) causes biological changes. For example, one study matched two males in athletic contests. The one whose testosterone level was higher usually won. But then they put two males with equal testosterone levels in the competition: The winner's testosterone level went up, and the loser's went down. Testosterone levels are thus responsive to changes in our social circumstances as well, so it is difficult to say that biology caused those changes (see Kemper, 1990; Sapolsky, 1997).

Biology is not necessarily destiny. Biology gives us the raw material from which we develop our identities. That raw material is shaped, molded, and given meaning within the culture in which we find ourselves. As in the example of testosterone studies, it makes far more sense to understand the *interaction* of biology and culture—to explore *both* nature *and* nurture—than to pretend that something as complicated as personal identity and social arrangements between women and men can be reduced to either nature *or* nurture.

[handwritten margin note: ex: competition between two guys winner = ↑ testosterone]

[handwritten margin note: with two guys with same level... winner = increased loser = decreased]

Exploring Cross-Cultural Variations of Sex and Gender

One way in which social scientists have demonstrated that gender behavior cannot all be biologically determined is to observe the remarkable differences in women and men among different cultures. Cultural definitions of masculinity and femininity vary significantly; thus, sex differences are "not something deeply biological." This quote is from Margaret Mead, perhaps the most famous anthropologist to study these cultural differences.

In her landmark book *Sex and Temperament in Three Primitive Societies* (1935), Mead described three South Seas cultures that had remarkably different ideas about what it meant to be a man or a woman. In two cultures, women and men were seen as very similar. Among the Arapesh, for example, both women and men were kind, gentle, and emotionally warm. Fathers and mothers shared child rearing, and everyone seemed "trustful" and felt "cherished." Among the Mundugamor, by contrast, both women and men were equally "violent, competitive, aggressively sexual, jealous." Women showed little "maternal instinct," and they tried to avoid having babies and then breast-feeding them.

The Tchambuli, on the other hand, were more like people in the United States, in that they believed that women and men were very different. One sex was more "charming, coquettish and graceful" and spent their days gossiping and shopping; they wore their hair long and loved dressing up with feathers and shell necklaces. They were the men. The women were dominant, energetic economic providers. They wore their hair short, wore no adornments, and were efficient and business-like. They ran economic and political life.

So, which one was "biological"? Well, if you were to have asked them, they would all say that their way was the "natural" one. All cultures, Mead argued, develop cultural explanations that claim that their way is the natural way to do things. But all arrangements are equally culturally based.

The Value of Cross-Cultural Research

Cross-cultural research explores both universality of gender difference and gender inequality and also the remarkable variety in our cultural prescriptions of masculinity and femininity and the proper relations between them. It shows that the question is not biology or culture—nature or nurture—but both. Our biological sex is one factor, the raw material of gender identity. But it is shaped, molded, and given meaning only within a culture. How much inequality does a culture have? How different do they think men and women are? Is there any room for change? If gender identity and inequality can vary so much, it can also be changed.

Contemporary anthropologists still observe two cultural universals, a gendered division of labor and gender inequality. Why does every known society organize itself so that men are assigned to do some tasks and not others, while women are assigned to do some tasks and not others? And why would they then rank the tasks that men do as more valuable and distribute resources and rewards disproportionately to men?

Sociologists used to believe that a gendered division of labor was *functional*—that as societies became more complex, dividing work from family life made more sense, and because females had and nursed the babies, they should remain at home and do all the house-based tasks while the males went off to hunt or fish.

It turned out that prehistoric societies were far more cooperative than we earlier thought. Archeologists suggest that whole villages—men, women, and older children—would all participate in hunting (see Zihlman, 1989). And everyone would tend

Cultural variations in gender differences and inequalities imply that our differences stem not only from biology, but also from cultural forces that shape our identities. In some societies, males take on roles and identities that are often traditionally associated with females, and vice versa. Male beauty contest among the Wodaabe in Niger. ▼

the hearths, prepare meals, and raise children. And even if it could be shown that such a division of labor was once an efficient way to organize social life, the entry of women into every area of public life has certainly made it an anachronism.

Why is every contemporary society also a male-dominated society? Later in this chapter, we will describe the dynamics of gender inequality in the world today and also examine some of the efforts to reduce or eliminate that inequality. Cross-cultural researchers offer several theories to explain the universality of gender inequality.

In the mid-nineteenth century, German philosopher Frederich Engels, the collaborator of Karl Marx, observed that the three foundations of modern society—private property, the modern nation state, and the nuclear family—all seem to have emerged at the same time. He claimed that private property both caused male domination and helped shape all modern political institutions.

Originally, Engels wrote, all families were large communal arrangements, with group marriages and gender equality. But the idea of private property brought with it several problems. How do you know what property is yours? How do you make sure your children can inherit it? How do you ensure an orderly transfer of property if you want to sell it or give it away?

The solution to these questions was the modern *nuclear family,* with a father at the head, establishing which children were his, and modern law that guaranteed the orderly transfer of property. These laws required enforcement, which led to the formation of nation states and police. In this way, the creation of private property brought with it the modern family and the modern state.

Some contemporary anthropologists have studied why gender inequality seems so universal. Karen Sacks (1974), for example, examined what happens when a market economy is introduced in a traditional culture. She found that the more people get involved in producing for a market, instead of for themselves, the more gender unequal the culture became. One reason is that women enter the market economy at the bottom of the wage scale, whereas before, their income was defined by their husband's income. Another reason has to do with male resistance to women's entry into the wage economy, resulting in a backlash of more strident enforcement of traditional gender roles (Kimmel, 2003).

Marvin Harris (1977) argued that warfare and the preparations for war are the main causes of male domination because warfare demands that there be a core group of highly valued fathers and sons to carry out its military tasks. Males come to control the society and develop patriarchal religion—monotheism—to justify their domination.

What determines women's status?

- *Size and strength*. The more a society needs and values physical strength and highly developed motor skills, the greater the level of gender inequality (see Kimmel, 2003). Larger family size also leads to a perception of greater gender difference. This is because if the family is small, as in a nuclear family, males and females will cross over and perform each other's tasks because there is no one else to do them (Bacon, Barry, and Child, 1957).

- *Women's economic activity*. Women's economic autonomy is perhaps the chief predictor of gender equality (Sanday, 1981). The more property a woman controls—especially after she gets married—the higher her status.

- *Child care*. When the females are entirely responsible for child care, their status tends to be lower. Sociologist Scott Coltrane (1996) found that the closer the relationship between father and son, the higher the status of women is likely to be because men's participation in domestic life indicates that the sexes are seen as more similar.

▲ The berdache is a great example of how cultures blur gender roles—in some cultures a person of one sex will adopt the social role of the opposite sex. Most berdaches are males who take on the female gender identity.

ex:
Navaho
have 3 genders
— the 3rd being
the nadle for
those who
have an
ambiguous sex at
birth (can act
male or
female)

Blurring the Boundaries of Gender

Another major contribution of cross-cultural research has been to challenge the simple dichotomy of two biological sexes (male and female) and two gender identities (masculinity and femininity). In fact, anthropologists suggest that there may be far more genders out there than we know. Some societies recognize more than two genders—sometimes three or four. The Navaho appear to have three genders—one for masculine men, one for feminine women, and one called the *nadle* for those whose sex is ambiguous at birth. One can be born or choose to be a nadle; they perform tasks for both women and men and dress appropriately, depending on the tasks they are performing. And they can marry either men or women.

Numerous cultures have a clearly defined gender role for the *berdache*. A berdache is a member of one biological sex who takes the social role of the other sex, usually a biological male who dresses and acts as a woman. In most cases, they are not treated as freaks or deviants but are revered as special and enjoy high social and economic status; many even become shamans or religious figures (Williams, 1986). There are fewer female berdaches, although one Native American culture permits parents to decide that, if they feel they have produced too many daughters, they may therefore raise one as a son.

In Albania, centuries of clan-based honor killings and blood feuds have left a significant shortage of men in rural areas. Thus, in some families in which there are no sons, a daughter is allowed to become a "sworn virgin." She renounces all sexual relations and socially "becomes" a man. She inherits the family property and dresses like a man, and in the evenings she hangs out in the cafes drinking with the men (Young, 2000).

Rituals of Gender—And What They Tell Us

Many cultures develop elaborate rituals to demarcate men from women. Take circumcision, for example. The surgical removal of the boys' foreskin has long been practiced by Jews and Muslims and became the standard medical practice in the United States during the twentieth century. In fact, circumcision is the single most common surgical procedure in the United States today, although the United States is the only country in which it is performed routinely and for secular or hygienic reasons. Female circumcision, or cliterodectomy, is the surgical removal of the clitoris. It is quite different from male circumcision, which may only slightly affect sexual functioning and has no effect on reproduction. Female circumcision is designed to completely eliminate the possibility of women's sexual pleasure, while most often leaving intact their reproductive ability. The World Health Organization estimates that between 100 and 140 million girls and women have undergone some form of circumcision (World Health Organization, 2001).

In some cases, the function of gender rituals is to blur the boundaries between women and men. Take the rather curious ritual called *couvade*, which means "covering." Couvade is a ritual that men practice when their wives are pregnant. They observe the same food rituals as their wives and even seclude themselves during the delivery (hence the term). Some men even claim to experience the pain of childbirth and get painful cramps. Couvades have been noted in peoples as diverse as North and South American Indians, Africans, Indians, the Basques of Spain and of France, the Chinese, and in Papua New Guinea, and they are still seen and studied around the world today (Khanodbee, Sukratanachaiyakul, and Gay, 1993; Klein, 1991; Masoni et al., 1994).

Why would cultures develop such elaborate—and, in some cases, cruel and painful—rituals? Anthropologists point to one commonality among all the cultures that perform them: They are all very highly male dominated. In fact, the more gender unequal the culture, the more likely it is that there are such elaborate rituals.

How do these rituals express gender inequality? In the case of male circumcision, it cements the bonds between father and son and ensures that the son has undergone a marking that will grant him the privileges of being a male in that culture. Female circumcision is obvious; women's sexual agency and ability to experience pleasure is destroyed so that women will be more compliant and reliably under the control of men.

And couvade? Anthropologists believe that through couvades men claim paternity in cultures that do not have strict legal marriage ceremonies and in which sexual fidelity may be less than predictable. Thus, they assert their rights to the baby (Paige and Paige, 1981).

Becoming Gendered: Learning Gender Identity

How do we become gendered? How do little biological males and females grow up to be adult men and women? In a sense, our entire society is organized to make sure that happens, that males and females become gendered men and women. From large-scale institutions like family, religion, and schools, to everyday interactions like the kinds of toys we play with and the television programs we watch—we are constantly inundated with messages about appropriate gender behavior.

In a critique of biological research on gender differences, Harvard biologist Ruth Hubbard writes:

> If a society puts half its children into short skirts and warns them not to move in ways that reveal their panties, while putting the other half into jeans and overalls and encouraging them to climb trees, play ball, and participate in other vigorous outdoor games; if later, during adolescence, the children who have been wearing trousers are urged to "eat like growing boys" while the children in skirts are warned to watch their weight and not get fat; if the half in jeans runs around in sneakers and boots, while the half in skirts totters about on spike heels, then these two groups will be biologically as well as socially different. (1990, p. 69)

And what if the half in jeans and sneakers, eating heartily, were female, she seems to want us to ask, and the ones in frilly dresses and high heels and on constant diets were males? Would there be complete gender chaos, or would we simply come to believe that boys and girls were naturally like that?

"Sex brought us together, but gender drove us apart."

Gender Socialization

Gender socialization is the process by which males and females are taught the appropriate behaviors, attitudes, and traits for their biological sex. Gender socialization begins at birth and continues throughout our lives. Before you know anything else about a baby, you know its sex. "It's a boy!" or "It's a girl!" is the way we announce the newborn's arrival. Even at the moment of birth, researchers have found, boys and girls are treated differently: A girl is held closer, spoken to in a softer voice about how pretty she is; a boy is held at arm's length, and people speak louder about how strong he looks.

From infancy onward, people interact with children based at least as much on cultural expectations about gender as on the child itself. In one experiment, adults were told that the baby was either a boy or girl, and the adults consistently gave gender-stereotyped toys to the child—dolls and hammers—regardless of the child's reaction to them. However, the babies were assigned at random, and the boys were often dressed in pink and the girls in blue. In another experiment, adults were shown a videotape of a 9-month-old infant's reaction to a jack-in-the-box, a doll, a teddy bear, and a buzzer. Half the adults were told it was a boy; half were told it was a girl. When asked about the child's emotional responses, the adults interpreted the exact same reaction as fear if they thought the baby was a girl and anger if they thought it was a boy (Condry and Condry, 1976).

All through childhood boys and girls are dressed differently, taught to play with different toys, and read different books; and they even watch different cartoon shows on TV. As children, girls are rewarded more for physical attractiveness, boys for physical activity. Although boys and girls play together as toddlers, they are increasingly separated during childhood and develop separate play cultures.

Sociology and our World

The M–F Test

In 1936, social psychologist Lewis Terman, the creator of the IQ test, turned his attention to gender. Terman sensed that parents were anxious about their children, and, with his student, Catherine Cox Miles, Terman tried to identify all the various traits, attitudes, behaviors, and preferences that could codify masculinity and femininity. Gender identity became the successful adoption of this bundle of traits and attitudes in their famous study, *Sex and Personality* (1936).

They believed that masculinity and femininity were end points on a continuum and that all children could be placed along that continuum, from M to F. The "job" of families, schools, and other agents of socialization was to make sure that boys ended up on the M side and girls ended up on the F side. The M–F test was perhaps the single most widely used means to determine successful acquisition of gender identity and was still being used up until the 1960s.

After you took the test, the researchers could place you on the continuum from M to F. At parent–teacher conferences, parents could be counseled on how to help their "feminine" son or "masculine" daughter move back to the gender-appropriate side. Terman and Miles were especially concerned that boys who scored high on the F side would turn out to be homosexual: "If they showed undue feminine tendencies special care should be exercised to give them opportunity to develop masculine characteristics" (Terman and Miles, 1936).

This often means that boys play on one side of the playground and girls play on the other. In a study of children's play, sociologist Barrie Thorne (1993) found that girls who attempt to cross over to the boys' side are labeled "tomboys," and they may have a much easier time being accepted by the boys than a boy who crosses over to the girls' side. He is likely to be labeled a "sissy" and will be shunned by both boys and girls.

In this way, boys and girls not only learn gender difference, but they learn gender inequality: The consequences are different if girls move "up" in the hierarchy or if boys try to move "down." This is the double message of gender socialization: You learn difference and inequality at the same time. "If I were a girl," one third grader said, "everybody would be better than me, because boys are better than girls."

Even today, we think of gender identity in terms of marked differences between men and women. Sandra Lipsitz Bem (1993) defined **gender polarization** to describe that male–female distinction as the organizing principle of social life, touching virtually every other aspect of human experience. As Table 9.1 shows, popular ideas of gender identity suggest a pattern of opposites (Bem, 1993).

After all the differential socialization boys and girls receive, what, then, are the real psychological differences between women and men? When social psychologists Eleanor Maccoby and Carol Jacklin (1987) surveyed more than 1,600 empirical

TABLE 9.1

Sex-Stereotyped Traits	
MASCULINE TRAITS	FEMININE TRAITS
Dominant	Submissive
Independent	Dependent
Rational	Emotional
Assertive	Receptive
Strong	Weak
Analytical	Intuitive
Active	Passive
Competitive	Cooperative
Brave	Timid
Sexually aggressive	Sex object

Source: From "Sex-Stereotyped Traits" by Sandra Bem from *Gender, Sex, and Sexuality: Contemporary Perspectives* by Gerda Siann.

How do we know what we know?

The Gender of Violence

The only trait for which there is significant gender difference is violence—from early childhood to old age, in virtually every culture at all times. Here is how the National Academy of Sciences put it: "The most consistent pattern with respect to gender is the extent to which male criminal participation in serious crimes at any age greatly exceeds that of females, regardless of the source of data, crime type, level of involvement, or measure of participation." Men, the authors conclude, are "always and everywhere" the more violent sex (Gottfredson and Hirschi, 1990).

While this may tempt some to return to biological explanations, biology begs as many questions as it answers. Male violence is not uniform: Males can be quite obedient and quiet, in the presence of their bosses or their teachers, even when they are angry or unhappy. Male violence seems to be activated toward some people and not others. Why would that be true if we were biologically driven to be violent?

Let's look at it another way. Let's ask about the variations in levels of violence. Surely, some cultures, such as Switzerland or Norway, are less violent than others—why would that be so, if all males are "hardwired" to be violent?

Cross-cultural research on societies with little violence finds that those cultures have a very different definition of manhood than cultures with lots of violence. In societies in which men are required to display a stoic, brave front, levels of violence tend to be high; where males are permitted to acknowledge being afraid, levels of violence tend to be lower. For example, anthropologist Joanna Overing compared the warrior tribe, the Shavante, who define masculinity as extremely aggressive and hierarchical, with their neighbors, the Piaroas, who define both masculinity and femininity as the ability to cooperate with others in daily life. The Shavante have high levels of violence and greater gender inequality than the Piaroas. The higher women's status, the lower the amount of violence (in Howell and Willis, 1983).

studies, they found "a surprising degree of similarity" between the sexes and in how they are raised, especially in the first few years of life. They found only four areas with significant and consistent gender differences:

1. Girls have somewhat higher verbal ability.

2. Boys have somewhat better visual and spatial ability.

3. Boys do somewhat better on mathematical tests.

4. Boys were significantly more aggressive than girls.

A recent review of all available research on gender differences found little or no difference on virtually every single characteristic or behavior (Hyde, 2005).

The Social Construction of Gender

Sociologists speak of gender as socially constructed. The **social construction of gender** means that we construct our gender identities all through our lives, using the cultural materials we find around us. Our gender identities are both voluntary—we choose to become who we are—and coerced—we are pressured, forced, and often physically threatened to conform to certain rules. We don't make up the rules we have to play by, but we do bend them and shape them to make them feel like they're ours.

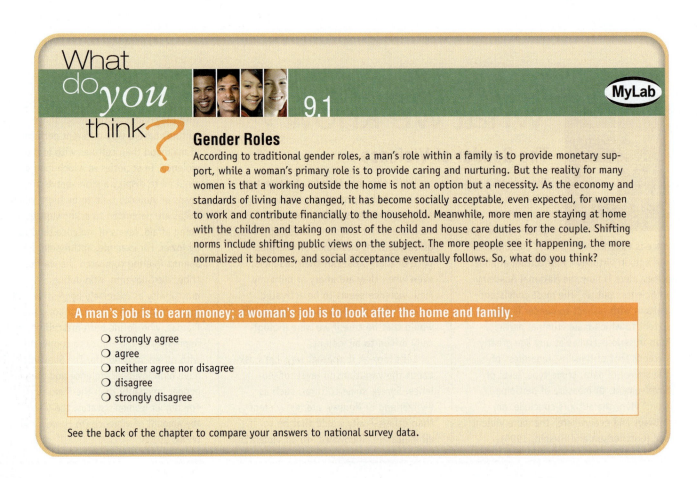

What do *you* think?

9.1

MyLab

Gender Roles

According to traditional gender roles, a man's role within a family is to provide monetary support, while a woman's primary role is to provide caring and nurturing. But the reality for many women is that a working outside the home is not an option but a necessity. As the economy and standards of living have changed, it has become socially acceptable, even expected, for women to work and contribute financially to the household. Meanwhile, more men are staying at home with the children and taking on most of the child and house care duties for the couple. Shifting norms include shifting public views on the subject. The more people see it happening, the more normalized it becomes, and social acceptance eventually follows. So, what do you think?

A man's job is to earn money; a woman's job is to look after the home and family.

○ strongly agree
○ agree
○ neither agree nor disagree
○ disagree
○ strongly disagree

See the back of the chapter to compare your answers to national survey data.

Socialization is pervasive and consistent. Sociologists believe that its very thoroughness is important to examine. If the traits and behaviors we observe among women and men were so "natural" and biologically based, why would we need such constant supervision to make sure we do them right? And why would we punish those who don't do them right so harshly?

Consider our lives to be a dramatic play, says the sociologist Erving Goffman (1974). We need props and lots of rehearsing to get it right, and then we try it out on the public stage and the audience lets us know if we are doing it well—or not. Think of how many times you've rehearsed a line, using different inflections or emphases, before you actually said it. In large part, then, gender identity is a performance. We use our bodies, language, and actions all to communicate to others that we are acting our part effectively.

Psychologists use the term **gender roles** to define the bundle of traits, attitudes, and behaviors that is associated with biological males and females. Roles are blueprints that prescribe what you should do, think, want, and look like, so that you can successfully become a man or a woman.

Many psychologists and sociologists criticized the gender role (or sex role) model. Social psychologist Joseph Pleck (1981) argued that the male sex role was so internally contradictory—one must be both emotionally inexpressive and aggressive and also passionate, for example—that it could only lead to confusion and stress for men who tried to live up to it.

Sociologists have suggested that the gender role model ignores several important dimensions of gender identity and gender inequality. For one thing, it seems to assume that the two gender roles are independent and equal: "his" and "hers." But sociologists point out that masculinity and femininity are not independent; we know what it means to be a man or a woman by reference to the other. Nor are they equal: Masculinity—and especially the traits associated with it—is more highly valued than femininity (Stacey and Thorne, 1985).

Nor does the term *role* adequately capture gender in its complexity. It makes as much sense to speak of "sex roles" as it does to speak of "race roles" or "class roles"—which is to say, not very much sense at all.

Gendered Institutions. Sociologists see another dimension to gender: an institutional level. Gender is not a "possession," something that you "get" through socialization and "have" for the rest of your life. It is a dynamic in all of our interactions. And it's part of the institutions we inhabit and the organizations we create. The positions we occupy—such as, for example, soldier or nurse—demand that we act in a certain way, and these ways of acting are also gendered. Soldiers are supposed to be stoic and aggressive, no matter whether that soldier is male or female; nurses are supposed to act caring and nurturing, regardless of whether that nurse is male or female. (As a result, male nurses and female soldiers have to constantly prove that they are masculine or feminine, respectively [see Williams, 1992].)

Observing how institutional arrangements are gendered often helps explain whether more men or women occupy those positions. In 2005, Lawrence Summers, then president of Harvard University, caused a big stir by suggesting that the reason that there were so few women at the top ranks of science and engineering professorships might be due to biology (Summers, 2005).

But consider the question sociologically. Most professors—no matter what their field, even sociology!—complete their formal professional training by their mid-to-late 20s, after which they typically become assistant professors. The next 7 years, until they earn tenure, is often the most intense work time of their lives, when they have to devote 12 to 16 hours a day to work. By the time they "arrive," they are often in their mid-30s, and only then do they finally have time for a social life, to get married and have children.

Obviously, this arrangement works better for men, who may have wives who do the housework and child care, than it does for women, who might want to spend time developing a romantic relationship and having and raising children. It is therefore not surprising that there are more male than female full professors. Nor is it surprising that so many of those women who pursue their careers do not have children. The surprise is often that *any* mothers can balance both family and career as well as they do.

Gender is a foundation of our identity, and it is also woven into the fabric of social structures. It is one of the ways in which social activities are organized. Like race, age, class, and sexuality, both aspects of gender—individual and institutional—are bases of gender inequality.

Gender Inequality on a Global and Local Scale

Discrimination against women is a global problem. Just about every country in the world treats its women less well than it treats its men (Kimmel, Lang, and Grieg 2000).

FIGURE 9.1 The State of Women

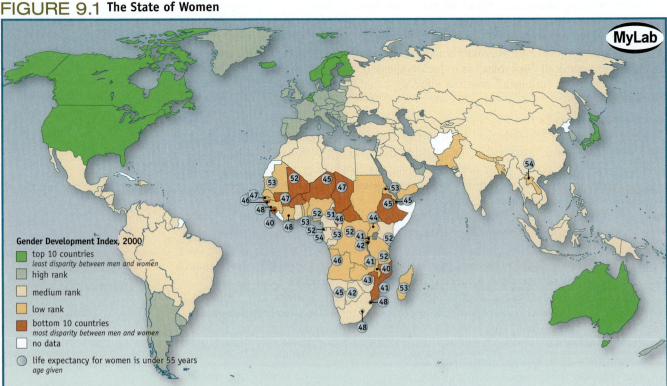

Source: From *The Penguin Atlas of Women in the World* by Joni Seager, copyright © 1997, 2003 by Joni Seager, text. Copyright © 1997, 2003 by Myriad Editions Ltd., maps & graphics. Used by permission of Penguin, a division of Penguin Group (USA) Inc.

In developing countries, problems appear more fundamental and pervasive. Significant gender gaps are found in everything from literacy to education to employment to income to health in the developing world, and these gaps are larger in nonindustrialized countries. Women are disproportionately represented among the world's poor. They are often denied access to critical resources, such as credit, land, and inheritance. Their labor is far less rewarded. Their health care and nutritional needs are underserved. They have far less access to education (Figure 9.1) and support services. Their participation in decision making at home and in the community can be minimal but is routinely lower than men's (Figure 9.2; United Nations, 2000) (UNDP, 2006). As a result, gender inequality can be said to hurt women somewhat more in poorer nations than it does in wealthier ones.

However, this is not to say that gender discrimination in industrial countries is an insignificant problem. When the World Economic Forum measured the global gender gap in 2005, publishing an international ranking of countries based on measures like women's economic opportunity and participation, political empowerment, educational attainment, and health and well-being, many wealthy countries ranked quite poorly in overall scores (Figure 9.3). Of 58 countries studied, Japan ranked 38, Switzerland 34, Italy 45. The United States ranked only 17, behind Sweden (1), Norway (2), Denmark (4), Canada (7), the United Kingdom (8), Australia (10), France (13), the Netherlands (14), and others (Figure 9.4; World Economic Forum, 2005). Within that, the United States ranked 46 on economic opportunity for women and 42 on women's health and well-being.

FIGURE 9.2 Women in Government

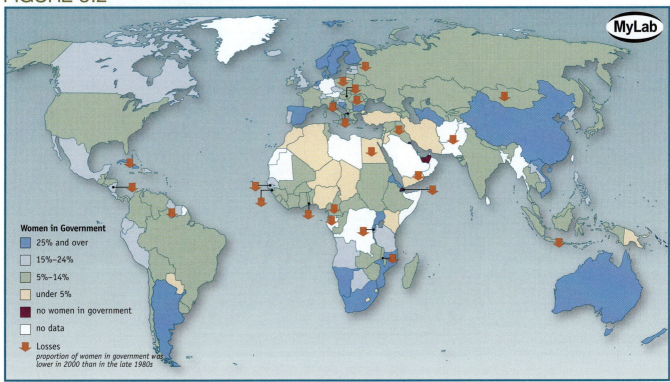

Source: From *The Penguin Atlas of Women in the World* by Joni Seager, copyright © 1997, 2003 by Joni Seager, text. Copyright © 1997, 2003 by Myriad Editions Ltd., maps & graphics. Used by permission of Penguin, a division of Penguin Group (USA) Inc.

FIGURE 9.3 **Women's Empowerment: Measuring the Global Gender Gap**

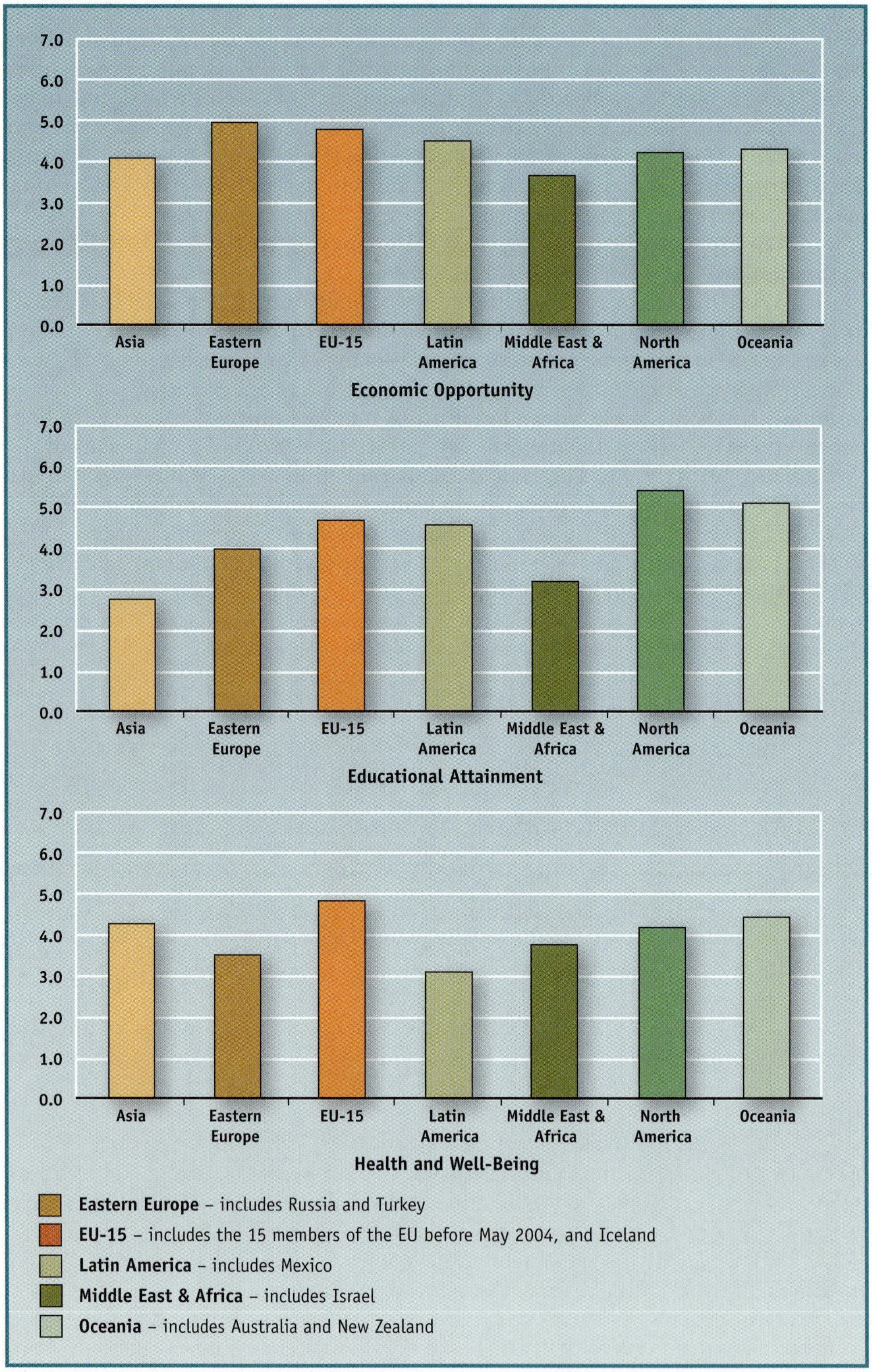

7.0
6.0
5.0
4.0
3.0
2.0
1.0
0.0
Asia
Eastern Europe
EU-15
Latin America
Middle East & Africa
North America
Oceania
Economic Opportunity
Educational Attainment
Health and Well-Being
Eastern Europe – includes Russia and Turkey
EU-15 – includes the 15 members of the EU before May 2004, and Iceland
Latin America – includes Mexico
Middle East & Africa – includes Israel
Oceania – includes Australia and New Zealand

Source: Augusto Lopez-Claros and Saadia Zahidi, "Women's Empowerment: Measuring the Global Gap." Geneva: World Economic Forum, 2005, available at: www.weforum.org.

Even U.S. women who are well off by world standards are badly harmed by discrimination based on sex—and so are their families. The U.S. **gender wage gap**—the gap between the median wages for women and for men—costs American families $200 billion every year (Murphy and Graff, 2005; Hartmann, Allen, and Owens, 1999). If working women earned the same as men for the same jobs, U.S. poverty rates would be cut in half. Nearly two-thirds of all hungry adults in America are women; globally, seven out of 10 of the world's hungry are women and girls (UN World Food Program, 2004). More women around the world are working than ever before, but women face a higher unemployment rate than men, receive lower wages, and number 60 percent of the world's 550 million working poor—those who do not earn enough to lift themselves and their families above the poverty line of $1 a day (International Labor Organization, 2004). Taken together, trends like these have come to be known as the **feminization of poverty**—a worldwide phenomenon that also afflicts U.S. women.

In the United States, women of color are even more burdened by gender inequality because gender inequality is usually compounded by racial inequality. In all the indicators above, the racial gap is wide. Like White women, women of color also perform what sociologists call the "second shift," the housework and child care that need to be done after the regular work shift is over. But minority women also tend to hold the lowest-paying, least-rewarding jobs, often without health care benefits or sick days (Sklar et al., 2001). Recent immigrants may face an additional layer, as cultural expectations derived of paternalistic cultures further compound the burdens of gender-based poverty and racism (UNDP, 2006).

Moreover, the global economy means the economic condition of both women and men in the United States is linked to that of people in other parts of the world. Driven by U.S.–based multinational corporations, all workers have become part of an international division of labor. (See Chapter 13) Corporations scanning the globe for the least expensive labor available frequently discover the cheapest workers are women or children. As a result, the global division of labor is taking on a gender dimension. Women workers, usually from the poorest countries in the world, provide lowest-wage labor to manufacture products sold in wealthier industrial countries (UNDP, 2006; Oxfam International, 2004).

Globalization has also changed the dynamics of global gender inequality. Just as globalization tends to unite us in increasingly tight networks through the Internet and global cultural production, it also separates us. Globalization has dramatically affected geographic mobility as both women and men from poor countries must migrate to find work in more advanced and industrial countries. This global geographic mobility is extremely sex segregated: Men and women move separately. Men often live in migrant labor camps, or dozens pile into small flats, each saving to send money back home and eventually bring the family to live with them in the new country. Women, too, may live in all-female rooms while they clean houses or work in factories to make enough to send back home (Hondagneau-Sotelo, 2001).

Some women and girls are kidnapped or otherwise lured into a new expanding global sex trade, in which brothels are stocked with terrified young girls who

FIGURE 9.4 Gender Equality

Overall rank, out of 58

	Rank
Sweden	1
Norway	2
Iceland	3
Denmark	4
Canada	7
Britain	8
Germany	9
Australia	10
France	13
Netherlands	14
United States	17
Spain	27
Austria	28
Russia	31
China	33
Switzerland	34
Argentina	35
South Africa	36
Japan	38
Italy	45
Indonesia	46
Brazil	51
Mexico	52
India	53
South Korea	54
Egypt	58

7 = complete equality of the sexes, 2004

Source: From "Sexual Equality," *The Economist,* May 28, 2005. © The Economic Newspaper Limited, London. Reprinted with permission.

borrowed from the traffickers enough money to pay their transportation, believing they were going to work in factories. They are forced into prostitution to repay these debts, and their families are often threatened should they try to escape (Human Rights Watch, 2000; International Labor Organization, 2001). Global sex trafficking and global sex "tourism" are among the ugliest elements of globalization, and ones that the advanced nations are increasingly policing.

Although gender inequality is a worldwide phenomenon, its expressions can and do vary from country to country and from region to region within countries. In some countries, like Saudi Arabia, women may not own or drive cars, but in other Muslim countries, like Pakistan and the Philippines, women have been heads of state.

▲ **This billboard in Nigeria indicates a growing awareness of the problems and issues surrounding the growing and profitable global sex trade.**

Gender Inequality in the United States

In the United States, gender inequality can be seen in every arena of social life—from the workplace to school to families, to even the most intimate and personal aspects of our lives, like to those whom we choose to love.

Did *you* know?

In the nineteenth century, the assistants in companies who wrote letters, kept appointment calendars, and otherwise organized office life were called "clerks." This was a highly skilled position and was reserved only for men. In the twentieth century, they're called secretaries, the positions are filled almost entirely by women, and they're paid less.

In the 1940s, by contrast, women were hired as keypunch operators, the forerunner to computer programmers, because it seemed to resemble clerical work. In fact, however, it "demanded complex skills in abstract logic, mathematics, electrical circuitry and machinery," which the women did routinely. Once programming was declared to be "intellectually demanding," it became attractive to men, who entered the field and drove wages up and women out. Today it is a largely male-dominated field (Donato, 1990).

The Gendered World of Work

The work we do is "gendered." We have definite ideas of what sorts of occupations are appropriate for women and which are appropriate for men. These ideas have persisted despite the fact that the workforce has changed dramatically in the past century. The percentage of women working has risen from around 20 percent in 1900 to more than 60 percent today. And this percentage holds for women who have children—even if they have children under 6 years old. It's also true for all races, and for every single occupation, from low-paid clerical and sales jobs to all the major professions. Today, women represent a majority of clerical and support workers and also a majority of students in medical school and law school (American Bar Association, 2006; American Medical Association, 2006; U.S. Equal Opportunity Commission, 2005).

Yet traditional ideologies persist about women and work. Women who are successful are often thought to be "less than" real women, while men who are successful are seen as "real men." Such ideology translates into practices: Women are paid less, promoted less, excluded from some positions, and assigned to specific jobs deemed more appropriate for them.

Gender discrimination in the workplace was once far more direct and obvious: Women were simply prohibited from entering certain fields. Until the late 1960s, classified advertising was divided into "Employment—Male" and "Employment—Female." Women were discouraged from "taking slots away from men" if they applied for jobs, or they might be asked in a job interview whether they planned to marry and have children (because that would mean they would leave the job). Can you imagine a male applicant being asked questions like that? In the summer of 1968, the EEOC ruled 3–2 that it violated the Civil Rights Act for employers to separate male and female "help wanted" ads in newspapers, except where sex was a bona fide occupational qualification.

A recent case became famous by exploring the other side of the coin. In 1995, the Hooters restaurant chain was sued by several men who argued that its hiring policy violated equal employment laws. Hooters countered that the chain doesn't really sell food; it sells "female sex appeal" (Baden, 1996). Eventually, the case settled out of court, with Hooters paying $3.75 million to the men and their attorneys and adding a few men as bartenders—but not as waiters (Jones, 1997).

Sex Segregation in the Workplace. The chief way that gender inequality is sustained in the workforce is through sex segregation. Sex segregation "refers to women's and men's concentration in different occupations, industries, jobs, and levels in workplace hierarchies" (Reskin, 1996, p. 94). Because different occupations are seen as more "appropriate" for one gender or the other, then the fact that one job is paid more than another is seen as resulting from the job, not the gender that does it.

How many of you have worked as a babysitter when you were a teenager? If your experience is like that of my students, most of the women have, many of the men have not. And the women were paid between $5.00 and $10.00 an hour, about $20 to $50 a day. Now, how many of you have also shoveled snow or mowed lawns? Most of the men have done this, but few of the women have. Snow shovelers and lawn mowers are paid somewhere around $25 a house and make up to $100 to $150 a day. Why?

Many of you are saying that shoveling snow and mowing lawns is "harder." And by that you mean requiring more physical exertion. But in our society, we usually pay those who use their brawn far *lower* wages than we pay those who use their brains— think of the difference between an accountant and a professional lawn mower. And besides, the skills needed for babysitting—social, mental, nurturing, caring, and feeding—are generally considered much more valuable than the ability to lift and move piles of snow. And most people would agree that the consequences of bad babysitting are potentially far worse than those of bad lawn mowing! When grown ups do these tasks—as lawn mower and baby nurse—their wages are roughly equivalent. What determines the difference is simple: Girls babysit, and boys mow lawns. That is how sex segregation hides the fact that gender discrimination is occurring.

Sex segregation is so pervasive that economists speak about a "dual labor market" based on gender. Men and women rarely compete against each other for the same job at the same rank in the same organization. Rather, women compete with other

TABLE 9.2

The Most Male- and Female-Dominated Occupations.	
MALE-DOMINATED OCCUPATIONS	**PERCENTAGE OF WOMEN EMPLOYED**
Construction managers	6.4%
Engineering managers	5.9%
Firefighters	5.1%
Installation, maintenance, and repair	4.5%
Machinists	4.4%
FEMALE-DOMINATED OCCUPATIONS	
Dental hygienists	98.8%
Preschool and kindergarten teachers	98.1%
Child care workers	94.5%
Occupational therapists	92.7%
Registered nurses	92.2%
Payroll clerks, bookkeepers, accounting clerks	91.8%*
Maids and housekeepers	90.0%

* Average of three categories within 0.3% of each other.
Source: Bureau of Labor Statistics, Annual Averages, 2004

Professions like teaching are often marked by a level of gender imbalance—female teachers outnumber male teachers. Sex segregation is pervasive and sustains inequality; it's no coincidence that teachers earn relatively low salaries. ▼

women, and men compete with other men, for jobs that are already coded as appropriate for one and not the other (Table 9.2). And while we might think that different sexes are "naturally" predisposed toward certain jobs and not others, that is not the same everywhere. While most dentists in the United States are male, in Europe dentists are mostly female. In New York City, only 25 women are firefighters, out of a force of 11,500, while in Minneapolis, 23 percent of firefighters are women, as is the fire chief. The issue is less about the intrinsic properties of the position that determine its wages and prestige and more about which sex performs it. So widespread is this thinking that in occupations from journalism, to medicine, to teaching, to law, to pharmacy, sociologists have noted a phenomenon dubbed **feminization of the professions,** in which salaries drop as female participation increases (Menkel-Meadow, 1987; Wylie, 2000).

The Wage Gap. No matter where you look, women earn less than men. In 2005, the median annual income for men working full time was $41,386; for women it was $31,858, or 77 percent of men's income (DeNavas-Walt, et al., 2006). On average, a woman brings home about $184 less per week than a man. Women of color fare considerably worse (Figure 9.5).

Ironically, the gap is magnified at the management level. For every dollar earned by a White male manager, a White female manager earns just 59 cents; a Black woman manager gets only 57 cents, and a Latina manager an even smaller 48 cents (Becker, 2002). And women of all racial and ethnic backgrounds pay an enormous

FIGURE 9.5 The Wage Gap by Gender and Race

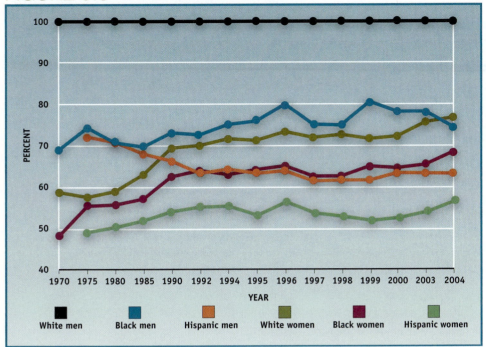

Note: Median annual earnings of Black men and women, Hispanic men and women, and White women as a percentage of White men's median annual earnings

Source: U.S. Current Population Survey and the National Committee on Pay Equity.

price for taking any time out of the full-time workforce (Crittenden, 2001; Rose and Hartmann, 2004).

The wage gap has been remarkably consistent. In biblical times, female workers were valued at 30 pieces of silver, male workers at 50—a 40 percent difference (Rhode, 1997). In the United States, since the Civil War women's wages have ranged between 50 percent and 66 percent of men's. In the late nineteenth century, one woman thought of a novel way to cope with this inequality:

> I was almost at the end of my rope. I had no money and a woman's wages were not enough to keep me alive. I looked around and saw men getting more money and more work, and more money for the same kind of work. I decided to become a man. It was simple. I just put on men's clothing and applied for a man's job. I got good money for those times, and I stuck to it. (cited in Mathaei, 1982, p. 192)

In recent years, the wage gap has been closing, but women's wages still average about 70 percent of men's. It turns out that this is not because women's wages have been rising so much, but rather because men's wages have been falling, and falling faster than women's (Bernhardt, Morris, and Handcock, 1995). In 2003–2004, real wages for full-time male workers fell just over 2 percent, versus a 1 percent decline for women (U.S. Census Bureau, 2005).

Glass Ceilings and the Glass Escalator. Gender inequality also extends to promotions. Women often hit a "glass ceiling," a barrier beyond which they cannot go, despite the fact that they can see others above them. The glass ceiling refers to "those artificial barriers . . . that prevent qualified individuals from advancing

Did *you* know?

Every year in early April, the president of the United States declares "National Pay Inequity Awareness Day." Why in early April? Because the average woman in a full-time job would need to work for a full year and then more than three additional months all the way until April of the next year to catch up to what a man earned the year before.

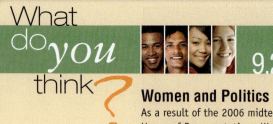
Women and Politics

As a result of the 2006 midterm elections, the United States has its first female speaker of the House of Representatives. We also have a female secretary of state, but as of this writing, we have never had a female president. While women are gaining more seats in politics here in the United States, the gender distribution is still very unequal, with local and state governments tending to have more female representatives than the national government. Still, attitudes toward women in politics vary and change over time. So, what do you think?

1. Most men are better suited emotionally for politics than are most women.
   ○ Agree
   ○ Disagree

2. If your party nominated a woman for president, would you vote for her if she was qualified for the job?
   ○ Yes
   ○ No
   ○ Wouldn't vote

See the back of the chapter to compare your answers to national survey data.

---

upward within their organization into management level positions" (Martin, 1991, p. 1). For example, women hold less than 14 percent of all corporate board seats. The 30 highest-paid women in corporate America earn only 7.7 percent of what the 30 highest-paid men do (Anderson, et al., 2006).

One reason the glass ceiling persists is because of the stereotypes about ambitious women. In a famous Supreme Court case (*Price Waterhouse v. Hopkins*, 1989), a woman was not promoted to partner of a prestigious accounting firm, even though she had outperformed all the male candidates who were promoted. Her supervisors said she wasn't ladylike enough and advised her "to walk more femininely, talk more femininely, dress more femininely, wear makeup, have her hair styled and wear jewelry." The Court ordered that she be compensated and made partner.

The "glass ceiling" is different for men when they enter traditionally female-dominated occupations. As we note in the chapter on the economy and work, sociologist Christine Williams found that male librarians, nursery school teachers, and nurses do not hit a glass ceiling but rather ride a "glass escalator" to the top—in part as a way to preserve masculinity. Male nurses and librarians are promoted to administrative positions much more rapidly than their female colleagues (Williams, 1992, 1995).

Sexual Harassment at Work. Sexual harassment is also a form of gender discrimination in the workplace. **Sexual harassment** creates an unequal work environment by singling out women for different treatment. There are two types of sexual harassment. The first type is called quid pro quo harassment, and it occurs when a supervisor uses his (or her) position to try to elicit sexual activity from a subordinate by threatening to fire, or promising to promote, or even just repeatedly pressuring a subordinate for a date or for sex. The second type is called hostile environment, and it occurs when a person feels threatened or unsafe because of the constant teasing or threatening by other workers. This type of harassment is far more common but more difficult to prove. It seems to happen most often when male workers resent the "invasion" of women into a formerly all-male work environment.

Although most cases of sexual harassment happen between male supervisors and female employees, courts also recognize that women can harass men. The key is that someone uses his or her superior occupational rank to coerce someone else. In 1999, the Supreme Court also recognized that men can sexually harass another man, even if all the men are heterosexual.

Currently, in the United States, the Equal Employment Opportunity Commission receives about 5,000 sexual harassment claims a year.

Balancing Work and Family. Women also face discrimination if they try to balance work and family life. If employees who get pregnant, bear children, and take care of them are less likely to get promoted, then women who want to balance work and family will face painful choices. And men may experience such discrimination, too. Men who say they want a better balance between work and family, or want to take parental leave, are often scoffed at by their colleagues and supervisors as not sufficiently committed to their careers; they may be put on an informal "daddy track" and passed over for promotion or high-profile accounts (Kimmel, 1993).

Though nearly all of us, women and men, work for a living outside the home, women also do the great majority of work *inside* the home. Sociologist Arlie Hochschild (1989) calls this the **second shift**—the housework and child care that also need to be done after a regular working shift is over. Housework and child care are largely women's responsibilities. Seeing housework and child care as "women's work" illustrates gender inequality, the "gender politics of housework"; women do not have a biological predisposition to do laundry or wash dishes.

Men's share of housework increased somewhat during the twentieth century, largely in response to the increasing numbers of women working outside the home. In the 1920s, 10 percent of working-class women said their husbands spent "no time" doing housework; by the late 1990s, only 2 percent said so (Pleck, 1997). But an international study of men's share of housework found that U.S. men spend no more time on housework today than they did in 1985 and do only 4 more hours of housework per week than they did in 1965 (Institute for Social Research, 2002). Today, U.S. women spend 60 percent more time on chores than men do—an average of 27 hours a week. International comparisons of seven countries—the United States, Sweden, Russia, Japan, Hungary, Finland, Canada—revealed that Swedish men do the most housework (24 hours per week) while Japanese men clock the least time (4 hours weekly). Swedish women spend 33 hours a week on housework, and Japanese women spend 29 hours. However, men and women in every nation surveyed reported that routine housework was the least enjoyable use of their time (Institute for Social Research, 2002).

The impact of gender inequality in the family on women's equality in the workplace is significant. If women are responsible for housework and child care, they are pulled away from their workplace commitments, have less networking time, and may be perceived as having less ability to relocate, all important factors in career advancement (Allen et al., 2002). They may also be less rested and more stressed, which can also affect their ability to get raises and promotions (Blair-Loy, 2003; Hochschild, 1989).

Gender Inequality in School

"Math class is hard." Those were the very first words uttered by Barbie when Mattel introduced the talking Barbie in 1992. Her hundreds of millions of owners were learning all about gender—and gender inequality.

From the earliest ages, our educations teach us far more than the ABCs. We learn all about what it means to be a man or a woman. This is what sociologists refer to as the *hidden curriculum*—all the "other" lessons we're learning in school. In nursery schools and kindergarten classes, we often find the heavy blocks, trucks, and airplanes in one corner and the miniature tea sets in another. Subjects are often as gender coded as the outfits toddlers wear. From elementary school through higher education, male students receive more active instruction than do females (Sadker and Sadker, 1994). Teachers call on boys more often, spend more time with them, and encourage them more. Many teachers expect girls to hate science and math and love reading, and they expect boys to feel exactly the opposite. This led researchers to describe a "chilly classroom climate" for girls.

In response, some pundits have asked, "What about the boys?" This question suggests that all the initiatives developed to help girls in science and math, in sports, and in acceptable classroom behavior actually hurt boys. It's not girls but the ideology of masculinity that often prevents boys from succeeding in school. Educational reforms are hardly a winner-takes-all game: What's good for girls is usually good for boys, too.

Close observation by ethnographers in classrooms can reveal the ways in which boys and girls approach their educations differently. Listen to how one Australian boy described his feelings about English and math class:

> I find English hard. It's because there are no set rules for reading texts . . . English isn't like math where you have rules on how to do things and where there are right and wrong answers. In English you have to write down how to feel and that's what I don't like.

A girl in the same class felt completely different about it:

> I feel motivated to study English because . . . you have freedom in English—unlike subjects such as math or science—and your view isn't necessarily wrong. There is no definite right or wrong answer and you have freedom to say what you feel is right without being rejected as a wrong answer. (Martino, 1997)

Education is often hailed as the major way to get ahead in our lives. Gender inequality in education makes that promise more difficult for everyone to achieve.

Gender equality in education is often uncomfortable. One teacher decided to treat boys and girls exactly equally; and, to make sure she called on boys and girls equally, she always referred to the class roster, on which she marked who had spoken. "After two days the boys blew up," she told a journalist. "They started complaining and saying that I was calling on the girls more than them." Eventually, they got used to it. "Equality was hard to get used to," the teacher concluded, and the boys "perceived it as a big loss" (Orenstein, 1994, p. 27).

They were uncomfortable, but they got used to it. Today, state and local governments work to eliminate gender inequality in schools because discrimination, stereotypes, and harassment hurt both girls *and* boys. Gender inequality in education actually ends up producing the differences we think are so natural.

Gender Inequality in Everyday Life

Gender difference and gender inequality also have a profound impact on our everyday lives, in our relationships, friendships, marriages, and family life. During the eighteenth or nineteenth century, only men were thought capable of the emotional depths and constancy that true intimacy demanded. These days, though, intimate life is seen largely as the province of women. Women are seen as the relationship experts, capable of the emotional expression and vulnerability that today define intimacy.

How did this change? Sociologists believe that the answer has far less to do with men being from Mars and women from Venus and far more to do with our history. The Industrial Revolution drove a wedge between home and work, emotional life and rational life. For the first time, most men had to leave their homes for work that was competitive and challenging; success in that dog-eat-dog world required that they turn off their emotions and become competitors. Women's sphere remained the emotional refuge of home and hearth. Men learned to separate love and work, while women's work *was* love. Women are "expected, allowed and required to reveal certain emotions, and men are expected or required to deny or suppress them" (Tavris, 1999, fn 43).

As a result, women have come to be seen as the experts on love and friendship. (Men became the experts on sex, which we discuss in Chapter 10.) Sociological research on friendship finds that women talk more with their friends, share their feelings more, and actually have more friends. Seventy-five percent of women could identify a best friend; only 33 percent of men could do so (Rubin, 1986). Men tend not to sustain friendships over time but rather pick up new ones in new situations. As sociologists and psychologists understand intimacy to be based on verbal and nonverbal sharing of feelings, mutual disclosure, vulnerability, and dependency, then men's friendships are "emotionally impoverished."

Yet other elements of masculinity—such as reliability and consistency, practical advice, and physical activity—also provide a solid foundation for friendship. Few sociologists would suggest that women have a monopoly on those qualities that make good friends.

As with friendship, women are seen as the love experts, so much so that sociologist Francesca Cancian speaks of "the feminization of love" (1987). That is because our society so positively values talking and expressing our feelings, but we also downplay "practical help, shared physical activities, spending time together, and sex," which men are more comfortable with. Of course, close loving relationships require a good deal of both emotional sharing and practical activity. The separation of spheres leaves both women and men unfulfilled. "Who is more loving," Cancian asks rhetorically, "a couple who confide most of their experiences to each other but rarely cooperate or give each other practical help, or a couple who help each other through many crises and cooperate in running a household but rarely discuss their personal experiences?"

Friendship and love are fragile because they are not secured by any social institutions; in other words, there are no formal rules for friendship or love, just an emotional bond. Marriage, by contrast, is a formal contract, a set of mutual and equal obligations.

Marriage is a deeply gendered institution. Consider how we think of it. A woman devises some clever scheme to "trap" a man into marriage. When she succeeds, her friends throw her a shower to celebrate her triumph. The groom's friends throw a raucous party, often with strippers or prostitutes, to mark his "last night of freedom."

According to this model, marriage is something she wants and he resists—as long as he can. She wins, he loses. Yet the sociological research suggests something quite different. In the 1970s, sociologist Jessie Bernard (1972) identified two types of marriage—"his" and "hers." And, she argued, "his is better than hers." Marriage benefits men more than it does women. Married men are happier and healthier than either single men or married women. They live longer, earn more money, and have more sex than single men; they have lower levels of stress and initiate divorce less often than married women (Gove, 1972; Gove, Hughes, and Style, 1983). They also remarry more readily and easily.

Why would this traditional definition of marriage benefit men more than women? Because it is based not only on gender differences between women and men but also on gender inequality. In the gender division of labor, she works at home,

How Do You Know You Are Loved?

Sociologist Cathy Greenblat asked this question of women and men who were about to get married. She also asked them how they knew that they loved the person they were going to marry. Before marriage, the answers were different but perfectly symmetrical. The men "knew" that they loved their fiancées because they were willing to do extraordinary things to demonstrate their love—spend their last dollar on flowers, drive all night in a blinding snowstorm because she was upset. Women "knew" their fiancés would do remarkable things to prove their love. They knew they loved their future husbands because they wanted to "take care" of them, to nurture and support them, because they felt tender and loving toward them. Happily for the men, that's exactly how they felt loved by their fiancées—they felt taken care of, nurtured, and supported.

So far, so good. Greenblat then interviewed 25 couples who had been married for at least 10 years. She asked them if they still loved their spouses and if they believed their spouses still loved them. What she found surprised her.

The women said they were sure they still loved their husbands, but they weren't sure, any longer, if their husbands loved them. The men said they knew their wives loved them, but many were no longer sure they still loved their wives. Still parallel but strikingly unequal. What had happened?

Greenblat reasoned that the answer had less to do with different genders and more to do with the organization of domestic life. Being married, living in the same house with someone, day after day, gives women ample opportunity to express love as caring and nurturing. But it's pretty difficult to express love if your definition of it is going far out of your way to do something heroic and extraordinary. Domestic life is more routine than that.

It's not that husbands are from Mars and wives are from Venus. It's that modern household arrangements sustain her ways of loving and his ways of being loved. What gets lost is his way of loving—and her way of feeling loved (Greenblat, 1998).

and he doesn't; outside the home, he works, and so does she (although perhaps not for as many hours). And she provides all the emotional, social, and sexual services he needs to be happy and healthy. "Marriage is pretty good for the goose much of the time," writes a science reporter surveying the field, "but golden for the gander practically all of the time" (Angier, 1999).

Of course marriage is also good for women. Married people live longer and healthier lives, have more and better sex, save more money, and are less depressed than unmarried people (Centers for Disease Control, 2006). But as long as there is gender inequality in our marriages, it's a better deal for men.

The Politics of Gender

Because sociologists study the links between identity and inequality—whether based on race, class, sexuality, age, or gender—sociologists also study the various movements that have been organized to challenge that inequality and enhance the possibilities of those identities. Gender politics includes those who are uncomfortable with the limitations placed on them by gender roles as well as more concerted social movements that would redress more structural and institutional forms of inequality.

Opposition to Gender Roles

Many men and women have found the traditional roles that were prescribed for them to be too confining, preventing them from achieving the sorts of lives they wanted.

Both women and men have bumped up against restrictive stereotypes or arbitrary rules that excluded them. Historically, women's efforts to enter the labor force, seek an education, vote, serve on a jury, or join a union served as the foundation for contemporary women's efforts to reduce discrimination, end sexual harassment or domestic violence, or enable them to balance work and family life. Women soon understood that they could not do these things alone, and their opposition to gender roles became political: They opposed gender inequality.

Many men, however, continue to find traditional definitions of masculinity restrictive. Beginning in the 1970s, they sought "liberation" from parts of that role—as "success object" or "emotionless rock." Today, some men seek a deeper and richer emotional and spiritual version of masculinity. For example, the evangelical Christian group Promise Keepers embraces a traditional nineteenth-century vision of masculinity as responsible father and provider—as long as their wives also return to a traditional nineteenth-century definition of femininity, staying home and taking care of the children. The "mythopoetic" men's movement uses myths and poetry (hence the name) to enable men to achieve a deeper and emotionally richer inner life.

On the other hand, many "men's rights" groups blame women for their plight. The women's movement has been so successful, they argue, that today men are the victims of reverse discrimination, of out-of-control political correctness (see Baber, 1992; Farrell, 1993). Despite all available empirical research indicating that men, especially middle-class White men (who are the men who join these groups), have lost little of their privileged position, their anger and distress do suggest that the gender arrangements we inherited from earlier generations enable neither women nor men to live the full and productive lives they say they want.

The Women's Movement(s)

Change, however, requires political movements, not only individual choices. The modern women's movement was born to remove obstacles to women's full participation in modern life. In the nineteenth century, the "first wave" of the women's movement was concerned with women's *entry* into the public sphere. Campaigns to allow women to vote, to go to college, to serve on juries, to go to law school or medical school, or to join a profession or a union all had largely succeeded by the middle of the twentieth century. The motto of the National Woman Suffrage Association was, "Women, their rights and nothing less! Men, their rights and nothing more!"

In the 1960s and 1970s, a "second wave" of the women's movement appeared, determined to continue the struggle to eliminate obstacles to women's advancement but also equally determined to investigate the ways that gender inequality is also part of personal life, which includes their relationships with men. Second-wave feminists also focused on men's violence against women, rape, the denigration of women in the media, and women's sexuality and lesbian rights, as well as wage disparities and the glass ceiling. Their motto was, "The personal is political."

Today, a "third wave" of the women's movement has emerged among younger women. While third-wave feminists share the outrage at institutional discrimination and interpersonal violence, they also have a more playful relationship with mass media and consumerism. While they support the rights of lesbians, many third wavers are also energetically heterosexual and insist on the ability to be friends and lovers with men. They are also decidedly more multicultural and seek to explore and challenge the "intersections" of gender inequality with other forms of inequality, such as class, race, ethnicity, and sexuality. They are equally concerned with racial inequalities or sexual inequalities and see the ways in which these other differences construct our experiences of gender. Third-wave feminists also feel more empowered than their

Third-wave feminists are diverse in terms of age, race, and even gender. Just look at the turnout at the World March of Women in 2000. ▶

foremothers; they often feel there is no need for feminism because they can now do anything they want. Their motto could be, "Girls rule!"

There are also men who are opposed to gender inequality. These "profeminist" men believe not only that gender equality is a good thing for women but that it would also transform masculinity in ways that would be positive for men, enabling them to be more involved fathers, better friends, more emotionally responsive partners and husbands.

Feminism

The political position of many young women today, however, is "I'm not a feminist, but. . . ." Most young women subscribe to virtually all the tenets of feminism—equal pay for equal work, right to control their bodies and sexuality—but they believe that they are already equal to men and therefore don't need a political movement to liberate them.

But what is feminism as a way of thinking and seeing the world? Feminism rests on two principles—one empirical observation and one moral stand. The empirical observation is that women and men are not equal; that is, that gender inequality still defines our society. The moral stand is that this inequality is wrong and should change. That's really all it takes. A feminist once said that "Feminism is the radical idea that women are people" (Kramarae and Treichler, 1997). Or, as Rebecca West famously remarked, "I myself have never been able to find out precisely what feminism is: I only know that people call me a feminist whenever I express sentiments that differentiate me from a doormat." One can, of course, be a feminist and like men, want to look attractive, and shave one's underarms and wear mascara. Or not. Feminism is about women's choices and the ability to choose to do what they want to do with no greater obstacles than the limits of their abilities.

There are several major strands of feminism. Each emphasizes a different aspect of gender inequality and prescribes a different political formula for equality.

Liberal Feminism. **Liberal feminism** follows classical liberal political theory and focuses on the individual woman's rights and opportunities (Kraditor, 1981). Liberal feminists want to remove structural obstacles (institutional forms of discrimination in the public arena) that stand in the way of individual women's entry and mobility in their occupation or profession or the political arena. Liberal feminists have been at the forefront of campaigns for equal wages and comparable worth, as well as reproductive choice. The Equal Rights Amendment, which nearly passed as a constitutional amendment in the 1970s, is an example of a liberal feminist political agenda. The amendment states simply that: "Equality of rights under the law shall not be denied or abridged by the United States or by any State on account of sex."

Liberal feminists have identified and sought to remove many of the remaining legal, economic, and political barriers to women's equal opportunity. Critics, however, claim that the focus on removing barriers to individual rights ignores the root causes of gender inequality, that liberal feminists tend to be largely White and middle class, and that their focus on career mobility reflects their class and race background (Dworkin, 1985, 2002; hooks, 1981, 1989).

Radical Feminism. **Radical feminism** states that women are not just discriminated against economically and politically; they are also oppressed and subordinated by men directly, personally, and most often through sexual relations (Brownmiller, 1976; Dworkin, 1985). Radical feminists often believe that patriarchy is the original form of domination and that all other forms of inequality derive from it. To radical feminists, it is through sex that men appropriate women's bodies. And they are really angry about it.

Radical feminists have been active in campaigns to end prostitution, pornography, rape, and violence against women. Many radical feminists argue that it is through "trafficking" in women's bodies—selling their bodies as prostitutes or making images of that trafficking in pornography—that gender inequality is reproduced (MacKinnon, 1988). Pornography provides a rare window into the male psyche: This is how men see women, they argue. "Pornography is the theory, rape is the practice," is a slogan coined by radical feminist writer Robin Morgan, who argues that women possess an essential, intuitive bonding that could confront male power and transform gender relations. All women are sisters, Morgan says, and "sisterhood is powerful" (1976).

Radical feminists have been successful in bringing issues of domestic violence and rape to international attention. They have created a growing worldwide concern for a new and revived sex slave marketplace, in which young, mostly Third World, women are often drugged and kidnapped and sold into sexual slavery throughout the world.

However, radical feminism relies too much on unconvincing blanket statements about all men and all women, without taking into account differences among men and among women. Thus, it's often "essentialist," claiming that the single dividing line in society is between men and women. That is, of all feminists, it may be radical feminists who believe that men are from Mars and women from Venus. Their claims about universal sisterhood have not been convincing to Black feminists who feel that when radical feminists say "women," they really mean "White women" (see hooks, 1981).

Multicultural Feminism. Does liberal feminism or radical feminism apply equally to all women? Do Black women or Latino women or older women or rural women have the same set of issues and problems as middle-class suburban White women?

These divisions among women are often dismissed by liberal feminists who want women to be seen as individuals, and by radical feminists who believe that all women face the same oppression *as women*.

Multicultural feminism argues that the experience as people of color cannot be extracted from the experience as women and treated separately. "Where does the 'Black' start and the 'woman' end?" said one of my students. Multicultural feminists emphasize the historical context of racial and class-based inequalities. For example, sociologist Patricia Hill Collins (1998) shows how the treatment of slaves in the antebellum South (before the Civil War) was also part of a differential treatment of African women and African men. Slavery was not only racial inequality; it was also gender inequality, woven into it and inextricable from it.

bell hooks (1989) argues that the focus on the family, the workplace, or sexuality as the sites of gender inequality does not track perfectly for Black women. For Black women, the family and sexuality may have been sources of power and pride, not oppression, and the workplace may not be an arena of expressing your highest aspirations.

The impact of multicultural feminism has been enormous. Today, most sociologists are following the lead of third-wave feminists and exploring the "intersections" of gender, race, class, age, ethnic, and sexual dimensions of inequality. Each of these forms of inequality shapes and modifies the others.

Recently, I was having a conversation with a Black lesbian. She told me that when she is with other African American women, she always feels like an outsider because she is lesbian. But when she is among other lesbians, she always feels like an outsider because she is Black. "How can I shed one part of my identity in order to claim the other part?" she asked.

Gender Inequality in the 21st Century

There is little doubt that around the world gender inequality is gradually being reduced. The International Conference on Women sponsored by the United Nations in 1985 proclaimed a universal declaration of women's rights as human rights, including the right to reproductive control and a strong condemnation of female genital mutilation.

Living in times of great historical transformation, we often forget just how recent are the changes we today take for granted. There are still women who remember when women could not vote, drive a car, serve on a jury, become doctors or lawyers, serve in the military, become firefighters or police officers, join a union, or go to certain colleges. All these changes happened in the twentieth century. They have come a long way, baby.

At the same time, today, there is significant backlash against gender equality (see Faludi, 1991). Some people believe that women's rights are simply morally wrong, that gender equality violates some theological or eternal truth, or that it would violate our biological natures. Many men have resorted to theological or biological arguments to try and force women to return to their traditional positions of housewives and mothers (Dobson, 1988, 2004).

The struggle for gender equality has a long history, filled with stunning successes and anguishing setbacks. But for women (and their male allies) who believe in gender equality, there is no going back.

1. *What is the difference between sex and gender?* Sex is the biological characterization of individuals as male or female. It is based on such things as chromosomes, hormones, and physical characteristics. Gender is the social construction of what it means to be male or female. Gender differences are not universal, and gender categories and meanings vary by culture, over time, within a society, and as individuals age. Gender identity is one's own understanding of one's self as male or female and is derived in a large part from socialization. Gender inequality is almost universal, with men having power over women in most societies.

2. *How are biological differences related to gender and gender inequality?* Biological differences between men and women have been used throughout history to justify inequality. There are three biological arguments used to explain gender differences and justify the resulting inequality. Evolutionary imperative theory holds that differences between the sexes are based on reproductive strategies. According to this theory, the main goal of organisms is to reproduce. Male and female differences have evolved over time to meet these reproductive needs. Theories about brain structure and chemistry hold that men and women use different sides of their brain more dominantly, which leads to different abilities, talents, and desires. This is used to justify inequality in the home and the workplace. Theories of hormonal differences look at how primary sex characteristics are developed in the fetal environment and how secondary sex characteristics develop during puberty. The sociological view is that biology does not equal destiny and that sex does not have to determine gender roles; gender is a result of biology and culture.

3. *How does gender vary across cultures?* According to Margaret Mead's research, each group or culture thinks its way of distinguishing and defining gender is the right way and the natural way. Mead says all cultures develop cultural explanations for gender differences and cultural standards for gender norms. Cross-cultural research looks at the universality and variety of gender among cultures. There is a universal division of labor by gender, which some consider functional and others consider a source of conflict derived from male domination. There is also universal gender inequality. Women's status in a society is determined by the value the society places on

physical strength and family size, by women's economic autonomy, and by the allocation of responsibility for child care. Some societies have a third or even more gender categories, such as the berdache, and cultural rituals distinguishing men from women.

4. *How do we learn to be male or female?* Popular ideology suggests that male and female are opposites. Males and females receive different socialization based on their sex category, which in turn affects growth and development. Gendered socialization refers to how we are taught to be male or female. This continues from birth to death, and individuals act on cultural expectations for gender. Gender polarization refers to society's organization by gender, which touches every other aspect of life. Gender is constructed within the context of a group and is ongoing and changing over time. A gender role is the attitudes, behaviors, and traits associated with being male or female.

5. *How does gender inequality manifest globally?* Gender inequality manifests in different forms in different cultures. Discrimination against women occurs everywhere but is more stark in developing countries. But even women in wealthy countries experience inequality. Women comprise two-thirds of hungry adults and 60 percent of the working poor worldwide. Women of color experience increased gender inequality as it is compounded by the intersection with race. Geographic mobility occurs when people from poor countries have to migrate to richer countries to find work, but men and women tend to migrate and live separately. The global sex trade is a form of gender oppression in which girls and women are lured or kidnapped into slavery to serve men from wealthier countries.

6. *What does gender inequality look like in the United States?* Sixty percent of American women work outside the home. More women than men are receiving college educations, yet traditional ideas still persist, and ideology translates into practice. Workplaces tend to be sex segregated, which in turn leads to inequality, as sex segregation hides gender discrimination. The wage gap is pervasive and consistent but seems to be closing since men's wages have been falling. The glass ceiling and glass escalator phenomena aid or deter individuals in their climb up the work hierarchy. Women are more likely to experience sexual harassment at work, which takes the

form of quid pro quo or hostile environment. Women are also more responsible for balancing the load of work and family than are men. Gender inequality also exists in school and is embedded in the hidden curriculum.

7. *What is the politics of gender?* Gender politics includes opposition to gender roles as too oppressive, restrictive, and arbitrary. Women's opposition to restrictions became political as they banded together to fight gender inequality. Men often also find their own gender roles restrictive, and some believe the fight for women's rights has led to reverse discrimination. The U.S. women's movement began in the nineteenth century with the first-wave feminists, who fought for entry into the public sphere, including the right to vote and attend college.

The second wave of feminism occurred in the 1960s and 70s, when women were fighting obstacles to advancement and were focusing on gender inequality in their own relationships. The third wave of feminism is occurring today among the younger women who interact with and through mass media and consumerism. They tend to focus on multiculturalism and believe that the second wave of feminism is dead. Many young women do not identify as feminists but believe in the principles of feminism. They feel equal to men. Liberal feminism focuses on individual work to remove obstacles to women's freedom. Radical feminists believe inequality stems from patriarchy, and multicultural feminists believe that all women's experiences are not the same and are affected by intersections of race, class, sexuality, and so on.

Key Terms

Evolutionary imperative (p. 283)
Feminism (p. 308)
Feminization of poverty (p. 297)
Feminization of the professions (p. 300)
Gender (p. 280)
Gender identity (p. 281)
Gender inequality (p. 282)
Gender polarization (p. 291)

Gender roles (p. 293)
Gender socialization (p. 290)
Gender wage gap (p. 297)
Intersections or intersectionality (p. 282)
Liberal feminism (p. 309)
Multicultural feminism (p. 310)
Patriarchy (p. 282)
Primary sex characteristics (p. 284)

Radical feminism (p. 309)
Secondary sex characteristics (p. 284)
Sex (p. 280)
Sex hormones (p. 283)
Sexual harassment (p. 302)
Social construction of gender (p. 292)

What does *America* think?

9.1 Gender Roles

This is actual survey data from the General Social Survey, 2004.

A man's job is to earn money; a woman's job is to look after the home and family. In 2004, about 22 percent of respondents either agreed or strongly agreed with this statement. About 65 percent disagreed, including 35 percent who strongly disagreed. Men were more likely than women to agree with the statement.

CRITICAL THINKING | DISCUSSION QUESTIONS

1. How do you think these responses would be different if the survey were taken in the 1950s? How have historical events and social movements contributed to the greater acceptance of women working outside the home and men working in the home?

2. What do you think explains the gender differences in survey results? How might a conflict theorist explain the differences?

9.2 Women and Politics

This is actual survey data from the General Social Survey, 2004.

1. **Most men are better suited emotionally for politics than are most women.** In 1972, slightly more than half of respondents said they disagreed with this statement. There was virtually no gender difference in responses. In 2004, more than three-quarters of respondents disagreed, with females being slightly more likely to disagree than were males.

2. **If your party nominated a woman for president, would you vote for her if she was qualified for the job?** This question asks about potential voting behavior, and the responses are very different from those above. In 1974, 80 percent of all respondents said they would vote for a qualified female presidential candidate. In 1998, the latest date for which statistics are available, that number had risen to above 90 percent. In both years, there was very little gender difference.

CRITICAL THINKING | DISCUSSION QUESTIONS

1. How would you explain the responses above? Why do you think the researchers asked about emotional suitability for politics? Do you think if gender was not a factor in the question that emotions would have been considered?

2. Why do you think there was virtually no gender difference in responses? Were you expecting that finding? Why or why not?

3. More respondents said they would vote for a female president than said that women were as emotionally suited as men for politics. What do you think explains that difference?

▶ Go to this website to look further at the data. You can run your own statistics and crosstabs here: **http://sda.berkeley.edu/cgi-bin/hsda?harcsda+gss04**

REFERENCES: Davis, James A., Tom W. Smith, and Peter V. Marsden. General Social Surveys 1972–2004: [Cumulative file] [Computer file]. 2nd ICPSR version. Chicago, IL: National Opinion Research Center [producer], 2005; Storrs, CT: Roper Center for Public Opinion Research, University of Connecticut; Ann Arbor, MI: Inter-University Consortium for Political and Social Research; Berkeley, CA: Computer-Assisted Survey Methods Program, University of California [distributors], 2005.

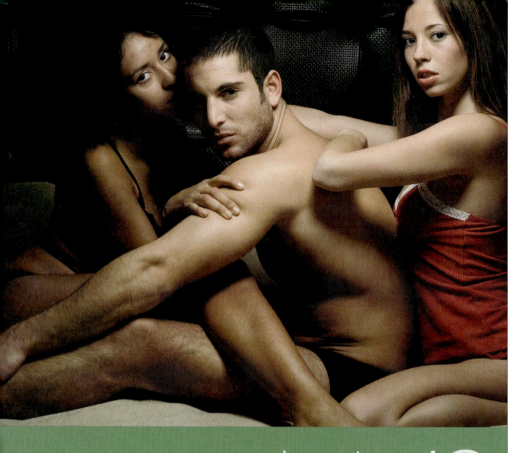

chapter 10

OF ALL OUR EXPERIENCES, sex may be the most private. One common synonym is "intimacy," which gives you a pretty good idea of how private we think it is. We rarely discuss our sexual experiences honestly with family and friends. We consider our drives and desires to be irrational, out-of-control impulses, anarchic and unruly. Many of our desires we consider too shameful to even utter.

And yet sex is everywhere we look. We are constantly bombarded with sexual images. Advertisers work from the motto "sex sells." References to sex and the sexual body are sprinkled liberally through our daily conversations. Sex is online, in books and magazines, on TV, and in movies and music.

We think of our sexual identity as fixed and permanent, something we *are*, not something we become. It's a biological drive; something in our bodies just takes over, and we can barely control it.

And yet we worry about gay or lesbian teachers luring unsuspecting heterosexual children toward a "homosexual lifestyle." We offer

Sexuality

therapies of various kinds to help gays and lesbians "convert" to heterosexuality.

Sex is as private and individual, and sex is everywhere we look. Sexuality is fixed at birth, and we can change our sexual orientation by learning a new one. Well, which is it?

To the sociologist, sex is both. It's private and public. Sex is a central part of our identity and it evolves and changes over the course of our lives. What we desire, what we do, and what we think about what we do are all social. What we learn is sexy other cultures might find disgusting—and we

Sex is a central part of our identity and it evolves and changes over the course of our lives. . . . It turns out that there are few things *more* social than sex.

might find what they do a turnoff as well. We learn sex in our culture—how to do it, why, with whom, and in what ways. It turns out that there are few things in our lives that are *more* social than sex.

Studying Sexuality: Bodies, Behaviors, and Identities

As you will recall from the gender chapter, scientists draw a distinction between **sex**, referring to one's physiology (typically, but not always, male or female), and *gender*, which refers to the social and cultural meanings associated with being male, female, or something else. Sex is biological, standard across the human species, but gender is a social construction that differs from culture to culture and across time.

When discussing sexuality, we usually try distinguishing desire (physical attraction), behavior (sex), and identity (sexuality). When we discuss "sex" in the context of sexuality, we are not referring to one's biological sex but rather sexual behavior, or "sexual conduct"—the things people do from which they derive sexual meanings. Think of sex as whatever people do to experience sexual pleasure.

The term **sexuality** also refers to the identities we construct that are often based on our sexual conduct. Our identities may derive from the biological sex of the person whom we desire or with whom we have sex; that is, we may consider ourselves heterosexual, gay, bisexual. Or our identities may derive from some particular practice such as group sex or sex only with members of a different race. Sexual identity often intersects with other sources of identity—race, class, ethnicity, age, gender—and these together may form a coherent unit, or they may collide and different parts may become salient at different times.

Because sexual desire, sexual behavior, and sexual identity are so social, they are subject to values about their "correctness" and norms governing their enactment and even their expression. Some behaviors and identities are pronounced proper and others immoral or unnatural. There is therefore significant inequality based on sexual identity and sexual behavior; in many cultures, having the "wrong" desires, doing the "wrong" things, or "being" the wrong sexuality can threaten where you live and work and even threaten your life.

Sexual behavior is, in this sense, no different from all the other behaviors in our lives. We learn it from the people and institutions and ideas around us, and assemble it into a coherent narrative that comes to be our sexuality. Sexual conduct is learned in the same ways and through the same processes as every other facet of our identity; "it is acquired and assembled in human interaction, judged and performed in specific cultural and historical worlds," writes sociologist John Gagnon (1977, p. 2).

Every culture develops a **sexual script**, a set of ideas and practices that answer the basic questions about sex: With whom do we have sex? What do we do? How often? Why? These scripts form the basic social blueprint for our sexual behaviors and identities (Gagnon and Simon, 1967). Over the course of our childhood and adolescence, even through adulthood, our understanding of our culture's sexual scripts begins to cohere into a preference. This is your **sexual socialization**.

There are four ways in which sexuality can be seen as socially constructed:

1. Sexuality varies enormously from one culture to the next. Anthropologists have catalogued a wide variety of sexual attitudes and behaviors around the world.

2. Sexuality varies within any one culture over time. Historians have pointed out the ways in which Victorian

We experience socialization around sexuality as we do any other set of behaviors and identities. And socialization by our peers teaches us what sorts of behaviors are approved—and which are not. ▼

sexual morality developed in the nineteenth century and the ways it has been challenged and eroding in the twentieth and twenty-first centuries. What was considered erotic in colonial America might feel very different today.

3. Sexuality varies among different groups in society. Race, ethnicity, age, and religion—as well as gender—all construct our sexualities. Sexual behaviors and attitudes vary by race or by whether you come from a big city or a small town.

4. Sexual behavior changes over the course of your life. What you might find erotic as a teenager may not be a preview of your eventual sexual tendencies; sexual tastes develop, mature, and change over time.

Sociologists chart these four types of variations as they study the different elements of sex—our behaviors and our identities—and the patterns of inequality that are established through them.

Desires and Behaviors

At first glance, desire, or finding someone attractive, seems to be purely instinctive: When you see an attractive person, you experience an immediate "gut reaction" of interest, without even thinking about it, even if you have no intention of doing anything about it. Some people think attraction is a purely olfactory affair: We sense another's pheromones, which trigger a chemical reaction that we experience as attraction.

But if desire were instinctive, the standards of physical attractiveness would be the same across human cultures, and with a few exceptions (big eyes, a symmetrical face), they are not. They change dramatically from culture to culture. Among the Ainu of northern Japan, women used to tattoo their chins blue to make them more attractive, and Native American men used to pull their "ugly" facial hair out by the roots.

Even within the same culture, the standards of physical attractiveness can change within just a few years. In the Renaissance, blackened teeth were considered the height of attractiveness. Fifty years ago, people thought that muscular men were ugly and ridiculous; it was the slim, sophisticated man who set hearts fluttering. Today, any man who wants to be considered attractive had better join a gym. Women who can't fit into a size 4 dress might consider themselves unattractive today; 50 years ago, chubby was considered sexy.

In many cases, desire is a function of social class. Fifty years ago, fat meant that you were wealthy enough to afford expensive steaks and chops, while muscle meant that you were a lower-class laborer. Today, fat means that you are poor and live on fast food, and muscle means that you can afford a gym. What about the blackened teeth? Bad teeth meant that you could afford sugar, which was then an extremely expensive luxury item. If you couldn't afford sexy cavities, you might just blacken your teeth artificially.

Social institutions such as education and the mass media present images of "attractive" middle-class or wealthy people and ridicule or minimize "ugly" working-class or poor people, creating models of desire that we almost always adhere to. Of course, there are exceptions, but they are often labeled deviant.

Sexual behavior, or any behavior that brings sexual pleasure or release (typically, but not always, involving sex organs), also seems, at first glance, to be limited by physiology: After all,

Everyone knows "sex sells"— and it is used to sell everything. Sex has never been as private as we imagine it was, but it is more public now than ever. ▼

there are only a finite number of things you and a partner can do with your sex organs. But again, behavior differs widely from culture to culture. Some practices, like oral–genital and genital–genital contact, occur everywhere, but others are extremely rare.

Even within the same society, different groups have vastly different incidences of specific sexual activities. In the United States, S&M, or sadomasochism (deriving sexual pleasure from inflicting or receiving pain), is much more popular among White and Asian Americans than among African Americans.

Like sexual desire, sexual behavior is monitored and policed by social institutions, which are constantly giving us explicit messages about what is desirable and what is bad, wrong, and "deviant." If you dislike someone or something, you are likely to use an all-purpose insult accusing him, her, or it of engaging in a certain "deviant" sexual behavior, and the hand gesture that you might use while driving to indicate your displeasure at a bad driver was originally an invitation to engage in another sort of "deviant" sexual behavior. Autoeroticism (sex without a partner) is so taboo that most people believe it to be extremely rare, even though it is actually very common (90 percent of men and 40 percent of adult women admit to doing it [Laumann and Michaels, 2000]). In 2005, a 17-year-old male honor student in Georgia was sentenced to ten years in prison for having consensual oral sex with a 15-year-old, even though a significant majority of males his age and 54 percent of females her age have also engaged in the same practice. (Centers for Disease Control, 2005; Curtis and Gilreath, 2007). Figure 10.1 illustrates some attitudes toward various sexual activities.

In the contemporary United States, genital–genital contact is often presented as the most natural, normal, and fulfilling sexual behavior; other behaviors are often considered "not really sex" at all. When former President Bill Clinton claimed that he "did not have sexual relations" with Monica Lewinsky, he wasn't lying, exactly: he just wasn't classifying what they did as "sexual relations"—nor would most Americans (Sanders and Reinisch, 1999). Definitions vary considerably and are based on a number of sociological factors. Forty-two percent of women consider it unfaithful if a partner looks at a sexually explicit website, while only one-quarter of men do (ABC News, 2004).

Sexual behavior refers not only to what you do sexually, but with whom you do it, how, how often, when, where, and so on. Sexual customs display a dizzying array that, taken together, imply that sexual behavior is anything but organized around reproduction alone. Where, when, how, and with whom we have sex varies enormously within cultures as well as from one culture to another.

For example, Ernestine Friedel, an anthropologist, observed dramatic differences in sexual customs between two neighboring tribes in New Guinea (1975). One, a highland tribe, believes that heterosexual intercourse makes men weaker and that women threaten men with their powerful sexuality. Many men who would otherwise be interested in women prefer to remain celibate rather than risk the contact. As a result, population remains relatively low, which this culture needs because they have no new land or resources to bring under cultivation.

Not far away, however, is a very different culture. Here, people enjoy sex and sex play.

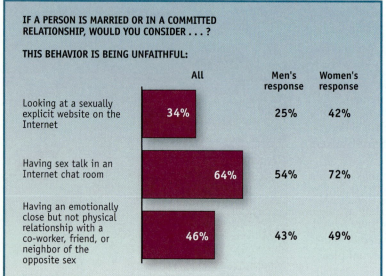

FIGURE 10.1 **Attitudes about Extramarital Sexual Activity**

IF A PERSON IS MARRIED OR IN A COMMITTED RELATIONSHIP, WOULD YOU CONSIDER . . . ?

THIS BEHAVIOR IS BEING UNFAITHFUL:

	All	Men's response	Women's response
Looking at a sexually explicit website on the Internet	34%	25%	42%
Having sex talk in an Internet chat room	64%	54%	72%
Having an emotionally close but not physical relationship with a co-worker, friend, or neighbor of the opposite sex	46%	43%	49%

Source: General Social Survey, 2004.

Men who have sex with women worry about whether their partners are sexually satisfied, and they get along relatively well. They have higher birth rates, which is manageable because they live in a relatively abundant and uncultivated region, where they can use all the hands they can get to farm their fields and defend themselves.

American sexual behavior looks something like this: Take the typical American couple, Mr. and Mrs. Statistical Average. They're White, middle-aged, heterosexual, and married. They have sex once or twice a week, at night, in their bedroom, alone, with the lights off, in the "missionary position"—the woman on her back, facing the man who lies on top of her. The encounter—from the "do you want to?" to kissing, foreplay, and intercourse (always in that order) and finally to "Goodnight, sweetheart"—lasts about 15 minutes.

Now consider other cultures: Some cultures never have sex outside. Others believe that having sex indoors would contaminate the food supply because they live in one large room. Some cultures have sex two or three times a night, others perhaps once a month—or less. Some cultures practice almost no foreplay at all but go directly to intercourse; others prescribe several hours of touching and caressing, in which intercourse is a necessary but sad end to the proceedings.

While for us, kissing is a virtually universal initiation of sexual contact—"first base," as it is often known—other cultures find it disgusting because of the possibility of exchanging saliva. "Putting your lips together?" say the Siriono of the Brazilian Amazon. "But that's where you put food!"

Among heterosexuals in our culture, men are supposed to be the sexual initiators, and women are supposed to be sexually resistant. We've all heard stories about men giving women aphrodisiacs to make them more sexually uninhibited. How different are the Trobriand Islanders, where women are seen as sexually insatiable and take the initiative in heterosexual relations. Or a culture in Brazil where the women commit adultery, not men, but they justify it by saying that it was "only sex." The men in that culture secretly give the women anaphrodisiacs to reduce their sexual ardor. These are but a few examples. When questioned about them, people in these cultures give the same answers we would. "It's normal," they'll say. And they've developed the same kind of self-justifying arguments that we have. Sexual norms can take many forms, but none is more "natural" than any other.

Sexual behavior can occur between people of the same gender or different genders, alone or in groups. It can be motivated by love or lust, money or reproduction, anger, passion, stress, or boredom. For example, some cultures forbid same-sex behavior and endorse only sexual activity between men and women. Some cultures develop elaborate rituals to credit the behaviors the culture endorses and to discredit those of which it disapproves.

Same-sex activity is treated differently from culture to culture (Figure 10.2). In 1948, anthropologist Clyde Kluckohn surveyed North American Indian tribes and found same-sex behavior accepted in 120 of them and forbidden in 54 (this is not to say that it did not occur; it was simply considered bad or wrong). In the West, same-sex marriage has become legal only recently, but some traditional cultures (Lango in East Africa, Koniag in Alaska, and Tanala in Madagascar) have permitted it for thousands of years.

In a number of cultures, relations between two men or two women are privileged as better, higher, and more spiritual—or at least different—than relations between a man

Did you know?

Despite a 2003 Supreme Court decision declaring them unconstitutional, sodomy laws are still on the books in 13 states and the U.S. military. Some laws specify behaviors, but usually they just outlaw "the crime against nature" and assume that you'll figure out that it means any behavior that cannot result in a pregnancy. Three states still forbid the "crime against nature" only for same-sex partners, but the others forbid it for anyone, including heterosexuals (even married heterosexuals). Jail terms range from 60 days (Florida) to 10 years (Oklahoma, gay people only). But the harshest sentence in America is in Idaho: The crime against nature can get you life in prison (American Civil Liberties Union, 2007). Globally, sodomy is only illegal in most of Africa and parts of the Middle East and Asia Pacific; it is punishable by death in Nigeria, Sudan, Pakistan, and Afghanistan, as well as the United Arab Emirates, Yemen, Iran, and Saudi Arabia (International Lesbian and Gay Association, 2006). Because the military is unaffected by the Supreme Court decision, sodomy remains illegal for all U.S. military service members.

and a woman. In ancient Greece, bonds of affection between soldiers were praised, and older men commonly sought out mentoring and sexual relationships with young men. In medieval Persia, poets who wanted to describe God's love for humanity used the metaphor of the male lover and his male beloved. In these cultures, men were still expected to marry women and have children, and most did. The boundaries for acceptable sexual conduct did not end at their marriage and family relations.

Perhaps the most interesting example of institutionalized same-sex behavior occurs among the Sambia of New Guinea, where all older men of the community are required to spend several years in ongoing sexual relationships with young men who are just reaching puberty. According to tribal myth, same-sex behavior is a physiological necessity—without it, the boy will not mature into adulthood. And, as tribal elders point out, it works—every boy engaging in same-sex behavior becomes a man. The male elders expressed shock and surprise when anthropologist Gilbert Herdt asked them if they were homosexual. Not at all, they said. The boys need to become men so they can marry and have children (Herdt, 1983).

Sexual Identities

Norms about sexual behavior govern not only our sexual conduct but also how we develop a sexual identity. Our sexual identities cohere around a preference—for a type of person or a specific behavior. These preferences are more flexible than we typically think. We may feel that our preferences are fixed, inflexible, and polar opposites. But in reality, each of us finds ourselves on a continuum of preferences and behaviors.

Take, for example, sadomasochism or S/M. While this preference for specific behaviors is often understood as "deviant" sexual behavior, most Americans have experienced erotic stimulation of some kind from either inflicting or receiving pain (biting, scratching, slapping). Some percentage will find that they like that experience so much that they want to do it again, and a smaller percentage will actually incorporate it into

FIGURE 10.2A Male Homosexuality

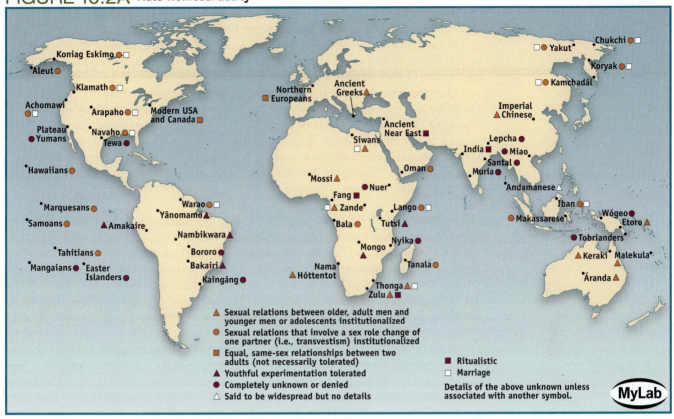

Legend:

- ▲ Sexual relations between older, adult men and younger men or adolescents institutionalized
- ● Sexual relations that involve a sex role change of one partner (i.e., transvestism) institutionalized
- ■ Equal, same-sex relationships between two adults (not necessarily tolerated)
- ▲ Youthful experimentation tolerated
- ● Completely unknown or denied
- △ Said to be widespread but no details

- ■ Ritualistic
- □ Marriage

Details of the above unknown unless associated with another symbol.

FIGURE 10.2B Female Homosexuality

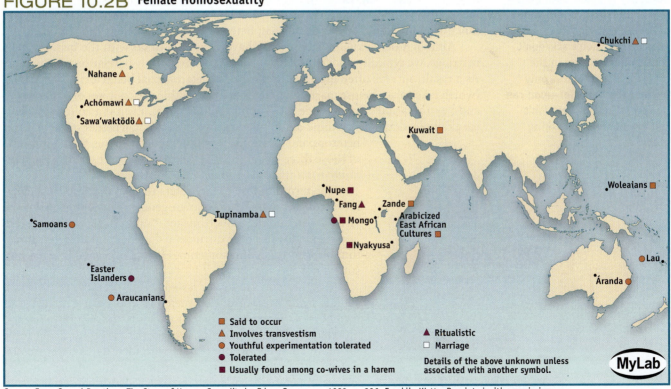

Legend:

- ■ Said to occur
- ▲ Involves transvestism
- ● Youthful experimentation tolerated
- ● Tolerated
- ■ Usually found among co-wives in a harem

- ▲ Ritualistic
- □ Marriage

Details of the above unknown unless associated with another symbol.

Source: From *Sexual Practices: The Story of Human Sexuality* by Edgar Gregersen, 1983, p. 296. Franklin Watts. Reprinted with permission.

their sexual script, as a preference. An even smaller percentage will find that they *really* like it, enough to make it a requirement of sexual conduct, and a tiny fraction will find that they can be aroused only through this behavior.

In that way, sexual behavior is rarely an either/or proposition—either you like it or you don't. Most people experience it a little bit, but they don't make it the defining feature of their sexual identity.

One doesn't experience sexual identity as something you fashion deliberately from the cultural norms of your society. In fact, your sexuality is more likely to feel more "natural" than any other facet of your identity—perhaps even deeper than your sense of masculinity or femininity. Sexual identity refers specifically to a coherent organization of sexual desires and behaviors. (Sociologists rarely use the term sexual "preference" because that term denotes too much individual choice and not enough "natural" predisposition.)

Heterosexuality and Homosexuality. Typically, we understand **sexual identity** (or, sometimes, orientation) to refer to an identity that is organized by the gender of the person (or persons) to whom we are sexually attracted. If you are attracted to members of the opposite sex, you are presumed to be heterosexual; if you are attracted to members of your own sex, you are presumed to be gay or lesbian. If you are attracted to both, you are bisexual. For all these orientations, the organizing principle is how your gender contrasts with or complements the gender of your potential partners.

Worldwide, the most common sexual identity is **heterosexuality,** sexual behavior between people of different genders. *Hetero* comes from the Greek word meaning "different." (Typically this means men and women, but in cultures with three or more genders, it could also mean that sex between a man or woman and someone of that third gender.) In most cultures, heterosexuality is considered "normal," which means that it is seen as occurring naturally. In most cultures, heterosexuality is also "normative," meaning that those who do not conform to it are often seen as deviant and subject to sanction. Although it is seen as normal, heterosexuality is learned within culture.

Although our sexual behavior may have very little to do with the institution of marriage, we typically understand heterosexual behavior only in relation to marriage. As a result, surveys often list only three types of heterosexual behavior: "premarital" (which takes place before marriage); "marital" (sex within the confines of a marriage); and "extramarital" (sex outside the confines of marriage). Even if a college student, for example, doesn't even think about marriage when deciding whether or not to have heterosexual relations, it will be understood as fitting into one of those three categories. (To be more accurate, we use the term *nonmarital* instead of *premarital* elsewhere in this book.)

The term **homosexuality** refers to sexual desires or behaviors with members of one's own gender. This comes from the Greek word *homo*, which means "same." As we have seen, homosexuality has been documented in most cultures, but sometimes it is praised, and sometimes it is condemned or even presumed not to exist.

Whether you are gay or lesbian, heterosexual, or bisexual, sounds straightforward: Gay men and lesbians are attracted to members of the same sex, heterosexuals to the opposite sex, and bisexuals to both. But again, sexual orientation turns out to be far more complex. Many people who identify as heterosexual engage in same-sex practices, and many who identify as gay engage in heterosexual practices. Their identity is derived from the people and institutions around them and assembled into a

Sexuality is about both behaviors and identities, but they are often difficult to separate. The current "don't ask/don't tell" policy on gays in the military discriminates only against the behavior—you can be gay as long as you don't tell anyone or do anything about it. ▼

Sociology and our World

"Gay" or "Homosexual"— What's in a Name?

Many people use the term *homosexual* to refer to gay people. But gay people do not. Of 5,000 gay organizations, clubs, and other venues in the United States, not one has the word *homosexual* in the title. In a poll conducted by the gay magazine *The Advocate* in 1999, readers were asked, "What should we call ourselves?" Fewer than 3 percent of the respondents said "homosexual." What's wrong with *homosexual*?

In the 1950s and 1960s, *homosexual* was a medical term, used to describe a type of mental illness. Then came the counterculture revolution of the late 1960s, and with it the Gay Liberation Front, a group that did not agree with such diagnoses. They were perfectly normal, they believed; the problem was an oppressive society. They rejected the term *homosexual* as an emblem of their oppression and called themselves "gay" instead—just as, at the same time, African Americans rejected the term *Negro* and insisted on *Black*. Ever since, if you think of your sexual orientation as normal and natural, you call yourself gay. If you think of your sexual orientation as sick and evil, you are likely to call yourself a homosexual.

coherent narrative and experiences that don't fit are left out: The lesbian who has sex with men may explain it as "trying to fit in" rather than evidence she is "really" bisexual, and the heterosexual man who enjoys same-sex activity may explain it as "fooling around," irrelevant to his heterosexual identity.

Oddly, most cultures around the world have gotten along fine without any sexual identities at all. There were desires and behaviors, but the very idea that one's desire or behavior was part of the foundation of one's identity dates to the middle of the nineteenth century, when the terms *heterosexual* and *homosexual* were first used as nouns (describing identity) rather than as adjectives (describing behaviors).

That distinction between behaviors and identities is crucial in some cultural prohibitions. In some cases, it is the identity that is the problem, not the behaviors: You can do pretty much what you want; just don't make it the basis of your identity. In other cases it is the behaviors that are troubling, not the identity. The Roman Catholic Church's official position on homosexuality—love the sinner, hate the sin—is an example of the latter.

Can sexual orientation change? Though some gay men and lesbians have sought various treatments to help them "convert" to heterosexuality, such techniques almost always fail (see Duberman, 1991). One can surely stop the behaviors, but the orientation most often remains intact. Recent religious "conversion therapies" replace psychiatric models with theological ones but produce similar results (Wolkomir, 2005).

Bisexuality. We're so used to the gay-straight dichotomy that we often believe that you have to be one or the other: Gay/straight sounds as natural and normal as young/old, rich/poor, Black/White. But what about **bisexuality**—a sexual identity organized around attraction to both women and men?

First, bisexuality in not indiscriminate, even though a bisexual magazine is entitled *Everything That Moves*. The old joke that you double your chances of a date on Saturday night is wrong. You're attracted to men in some circumstances, and women in others. You fall in love with men, but feel a sexual attraction only to women, or vice versa. Or you've had sex only with women, but you wouldn't say no if Brad Pitt called. The variety of experiences differs considerably.

Second, few understand you. Tell a date that you are bisexual, and you will get weird looks, a lecherous request to "watch" sometime, or outright rejection.

Sociology and our World

The Invention of Heterosexuality

Why do we have sexual orientations at all? In *The Invention of Heterosexuality* (1987), Jonathan Katz discusses the era before 1880, when people were not assumed to be heterosexual, gay, lesbian, or bisexual. You got married to have children, whether or not you were attracted to your spouse or even in the opposite sex at all, and usually your parents made the choice for you. Same-sex behavior was considered a sin, like adultery or masturbation—and, like those, were the sort of thing that anyone might be tempted to do.

By about 1920, people were assumed to be heterosexual, or not. Most people were attracted to the opposite sex, and they would never engage in same-sex behavior—by definition they could not be tempted. What changed in just 40 years?

Katz argues that the increasing division of labor, the move to cities, widespread immigration, and the rise of the educated middle class changed the way we got married. No longer did parents choose their children's spouses—you entered a marriage "marketplace" and made your own decision. But medical science believed that intercourse was damaging to your health, and children were an economic burden on city dwellers: So why get married at all?

The answer was: You got married because you were physically attracted to your spouse, and to the opposite sex in general, and to *only* the opposite sex. You had a "heterosexual" identity, as opposed to the small number of "homosexuals" who were attracted *only* to the same sex. A heterosexual–homosexual dichotomy developed, and it is still at work today, in statements like: "You can't be gay! You're married!"

Your straight friends believe that you are really straight, but "confused" or "experimenting" or going through a phase, like the acronym LUGs (Lesbian Until Graduation). Your gay friends believe that you're really gay but too frightened to admit it. You may be welcome at the campus gay organization—after all, it's really called the *LGBT,* for lesbian, gay, bisexual, and transgendered—but you find yourself categorized as gay or lesbian. The classes in LGBT studies on campus are mostly about gay and lesbian people.

Third, in spite of the jokes and the invisibility, you may also have a great deal of pride. Bisexuals often argue that they are more spiritual, or more psychologically developed, than gay or straight people, because they look at a person's character and personality rather than at trivial details like gender. They may be exaggerating a bit: Most bisexuals are just as attracted to certain physical types, and not as attracted to others, as gay and straight people. They just include some men and women in the category of "people to whom I'm attracted."

Identifying as a bisexual requires a coming-out process, a realization that both your same-sex and opposite-sex relations "count." Few organizations exist specifically for bisexuals, and scholars have not paid them much attention. Within the last decade, however, things have been changing. Courses about bisexuality have been taught on several college campuses. There have been anthologies, scholarly studies, and conferences. But bisexuals still have a long way to go before the average person stops assuming automatically that a new acquaintance must be gay or straight (Burleson, 2005; Fox, 2004; Rust 1995, 1999; Storr, 1999; Tucker, 1995; Weinberg, Williams and Pryor, 1994).

Identities as Behaviors. There are other sexual identities based more on sexual behaviors than the gender of your partner. For example, some people may experience erotic attraction to specific body parts (partialism) or to objects that represent sexual behaviors (fetishism). Or they may become sexually aroused by the presence of real or imagined violence and power dynamics (sadomasochism) or find that they can be aroused only when having sex in public (exhibitionism) or when they observe others having sex (voyeurism). While many of these behaviors are present in routine sexual experiences—the fear of getting caught, wearing sexy clothing, biting and pinching—only a small percentage of the population makes them the only activities in their sexual repertoire.

In recent years, the scandal of pedophilia has rocked the Catholic Church, as thousands of people have revealed their priests sexually abused them as children, and the Church officials knew about it and did nothing. Some people in this culture mistakenly believe that pedophiles are gay because so many of the children abused by the priests were boys. However, **pedophilia** is actually the erotic attraction to children, who may be of either or both genders. Most of the pedophile priests were not "gay"—that is, they were not interested at all in sexual activity with other adult men.

We know little about pedophiles because they are subject to such severe social disapproval that social scientists are reluctant to research them, and there are very few pedophile organizations. Most pedophiles are male, and most are interested only in girls, though some are interested in boys, and some are interested in both. Contrary to common misconceptions, they do not usually grab children from the streets. They establish friendships with the children that become sexual only gradually, over time. And they are not usually murderers. They believe that they are in a romantic relationship and would not mistreat the children in any way—except for the sex.

Pedophiles themselves claim pedophilia is an orientation, as innate and essential to their identity as being gay, lesbian, heterosexual, or bisexual, and therefore they are an oppressed minority group. But even if pedophilia is a sexual orientation, does that mean that pedophiles should be accepted as a minority group? In our culture, we assume that one precondition for engaging in sexual activity is consent, so any sexual orientation that requires a nonconsenting partner is unacceptable. And we believe that only adults are capable of giving consent.

Asexuality. Everybody has a sexual orientation, right? Regardless of whether you are currently sexual, everybody is attracted to men, women, or both. Not necessarily. Some people state they have no sexual desire for anyone. They aren't gay/lesbian or heterosexual; they're **asexual**. About 10 percent of men aged 15 to 44 have never had sex in their lives (Centers for Disease Control, 2005).

Friends, family, and the medical establishment are quick to diagnose them as confused, conflicted, suffering from a hormone deficiency, or traumatized by child abuse. But they counter that asexuality is not a problem that needs to be cured: It is a perfectly valid sexual orientation. Asexuals have their own organizations, websites, slogans, coming-out stories, and lots of merchandise to buy (Harris, 2006).

We've seen asexuals before—in nineteenth-century Britain, for example. The great fictional detective Sherlock Holmes was a "confirmed bachelor," with no interest in getting married. And he was not alone: Victorian England was full of writers, adventurers, businessmen, and clergymen who never married (not many laborers and craftsmen; only the upper class could afford to stay unmarried). Why the overabundance of bachelors? Some may have been gay, but the majority were straight. They liked women, they just didn't want to marry or have sex with them. The reason? Perhaps they were afraid. The best medical science of the era advised that too much sex would destroy your brain, making you mentally ill; even occasional sex had a debilitating effect.

Did *you* know?

Having sex isn't a natural act. It's a social one. And there's considerable variation in what people "count" as "having sex." Is showering together sex? Deep kissing? Oral sex?

Research published in the *Journal of the American Medical Association* (JAMA) surveyed students at a large Midwestern university. While 99 percent of them agreed that heterosexual intercourse counts as sex, nearly three-fifths thought oral sex didn't count, and one in five thought anal sex didn't count (Sanders and Reinisch, 1999). A Gallup poll of Americans found similar rates. On the other hand, a 2004 survey found more than one-third believed deep kissing *does* count as sex (Rawlings et al, 2004).

Men are more likely to count deep kissing than women. In fact, definitions of sex vary by gender and other factors, like age and nationality. Men are more likely than women to count genital touching, and younger people include fewer erotic behaviors as sex than older ones do.

▲ Most scientists now agree that sexual identity is the result of the interaction of biological, cultural, and social influences. But one thing is clear: in industrialized countries, there is increased acceptance of all sexual identities. The founding charter of the European Union prohibits discrimination based on sexual identity.

At the same time, large numbers of women were choosing not to marry. Married women were not considered for most jobs, so if you wanted any kind of career, you had to stay single. Domestic partnerships between two women, often lifelong, were so common that they had their own name—Boston marriages. No doubt some of the women involved in these relationships were lesbians, but many liked men. They just didn't want to deal with the career suicide that came with marriage.

The Interplay of Biology and Society

Where does sexuality come from? We know that orientation is pretty stable by about the age of 5 (maybe earlier—we just can't interview newborns very effectively), and unchangeable—you like who you like throughout your life, regardless of how much society approves or disapproves. But were you born with a sexual orientation, or did it evolve during those five years? Because heterosexual identity has so much social prestige, there's been little research on how people "become" heterosexual. Research, instead, typically is directed to explain the experiences of the "other." But we can take the research on gay people and expand it to include other orientations.

Many scientists claim that sexual orientation is the result of biology: chromosomes, brain chemistry, differences in our pubertal hormones. Some researchers have claimed they've discovered the "gay gene" our the "gay brain," but these studies are based on small samples with very large margins for error. Cross-cultural studies seem to indicate that about 5 percent of every human male population and 3 percent of every human female population is going to have exclusive same-sex interests, regardless of how much their culture praises or condemns same-sex activity. (And same-sex behavior is extremely common in the animal kingdom, which dispels evolutionary arguments.)

Sociologists generally believe that sexual orientation is both biologically based and socially constructed. One probably has an innate, biologically based interest in a certain sex, but the way that interest is understood, the ways we learn to act on it, to feel about it, and to express it are all learned in society.

Researching Sexuality

Human beings are curious about sex, and we have been conducting "sex research" since the beginning of time. In the Middle Ages, adventurous aristocrats collected anecdotes about sexual activity for their personal gratification, and religious leaders collected them for a (presumably) more spiritual reason, using confessions about sexual activity as a window into immorality of all sorts (Foucault, 1979). By the eighteenth century, sex was seen as draining the body of its energy, and the general belief was that any sexual behavior that was not procreative (especially masturbation) should be avoided entirely.

Early Sex Research

In the late nineteenth century, sex research was gradually taken over by scientists, who sought to observe sex without moral condemnation. Four of the most famous sex researchers at the turn of the twentieth century were European.

Richard von Krafft-Ebing (1840–1902) was interested in sexual perversions; his major book *Psychopathis Sexualis* (1886, 1998) ("sexual psychopathology") was a study of sex crimes. It was Krafft-Ebing who first observed and labeled fetishes and "perversions," which he defined as any nonprocreative sexual activities or any activity in which women took an active role: Women should never experience sexual desire of any kind. He believed that all perversions and fetishes were caused by masturbation.

Havelock Ellis (1859–1939) came to very different conclusions from Krafft-Ebing. His six-volume *Studies in the Psychology of Sex* (1896–1910), the largest sex research ever undertaken, argued that masturbation was harmless, same-sex behavior was perfectly normal, and women had a strong sex drive and could actually have orgasms of their own. Unlike his contemporaries, Ellis believed that sex was normal, natural, and "good." Sexual pleasure, he wrote, is "the chief and central function of life—ever wonderful and ever lovely."

Ellis's ideas were contradicted by his contemporary, Sigmund Freud. While he also believed that sexual desire is among the great driving forces of life, Freud argued that civilization requires that we redirect our sexual energies toward productive pursuits. This process of redirection he called sublimation. Freud believed that same-sex desire was caused by a developmental abnormality, the failure of the child to fully identify with the same-sex parent (because this was much easier for girls than for boys, there were far fewer lesbians than gay men). However, he did believe that gay men and lesbians were capable of being fully functioning and happy members of society.

Magnus Hirschfeld (1868–1935) was the first systematic collector of sexual data in Germany. Hirschfeld believed that people are born bisexual—capable of experiencing sexual pleasure with both women and men. As they develop, they lose their same-sex desire and become exclusively heterosexual. On the other hand, he believed that gay men (but not lesbians) were a third sex, with masculine bodies but feminine spirits, so their interest in other men was actually a type of heterosexuality.

In 1903, Hirschfeld undertook the first sex survey in history, and he found that 2.2 percent of the German population was gay. Hirschfeld founded the Institute of Sex Research in Berlin in 1919, began a scholarly journal, and held international conferences. Both gay and Jewish, Hirschfeld was increasingly a target of Nazi persecution, and in 1933, his offices were stormed by Nazi troops and all his books and papers destroyed.

Modern Sex Research

After World War II, the center of sex research moved from Europe to the United States. At Indiana University, a zoologist named Alfred Kinsey (1884–1956) had been asked to teach a new course on sexuality and marriage. Realizing there was little reliable information, he set about gathering data on American sexual behavior.

The Kinsey Reports. A scientist, Kinsey was determined to study sexual behavior, unclouded by morality. Eventually he and his colleagues at the Institute for Sex Research collected sexual histories from 18,000 Americans. His books were for many years the definitive works on American sexual behavior (Kinsey et al., 1948, 1953).

So as not to confuse behaviors with identities or ideology, Kinsey asked what sorts of "outlets" people used to have orgasms: masturbation, oral sex, anal sex, or coitus? With male or female partners? How often? Under what circumstances?

Did *you* know?

Some of America's most prominent health reformers of the nineteenth century were preoccupied with curtailing sexual activity. They believed changes in diet could and should stop adolescent boys from masturbating, which would weaken their bodies and drain their brains. No one was more obsessed than J. H. Kellogg, who invented the corn flake to reduce sexual impulses among young American men. In his advice manual, *Plain Facts for Old and Young* (1888), he warned parents of 39 signs that young men might be masturbating. (These included acne, slouching posture, using tobacco, desire for solitude, confusion, and talking back to one's parents.) Worried parents were counseled to take some rather chilling steps to stop their children, including bandaging the genitals, covering the sex organs with small cages, tying their children's hands to the bedposts, or, more drastically, circumcising the boys "without administering an anesthetic" or, for girls, applying carbolic acid directly on the clitoris. "It is better to endure any physical discomfort than to sacrifice one's chastity," wrote one physician (Kellogg, 1888; see Kimmel, 1996, pp. 129–131).

Kinsey's results were surprising, and his books caused enormous controversy. What he exposed was a wide gulf between Americans' professed morality and their actual behaviors. Among his most shocking findings were:

1. The higher your socioeconomic class, the more sex you have. People at the time believed that the working class was more sexually active and aware ("earthy"), but Kinsey found that the middle class had sex more often and with a greater variety of techniques and "outlets."

2. The clients of prostitutes were not only college boys and soldiers on leave. Seventy percent of men had visited a prostitute, with older men far more likely to visit.

3. Women enjoy sex. The "common knowledge" of the era taught that women did not enjoy sex and engaged in it only to please their husbands. However, women were as interested in sex as men, and most had orgasms (although primarily through masturbation).

4. Extramarital affairs are not extremely rare. Twenty-six percent of married women and 50 percent of married men had had at least one extramarital partner.

But by far the most controversial finding concerned same-sex behavior. In the 1950s, it was assumed that homosexuality was a severe, and extremely rare, psychiatric disorder. Kinsey found a great deal of variation in practices, so much that he classified his respondents along a seven-point continuum, from 0 (exclusively heterosexual outlets) through 6 (exclusively same-sex outlets); his scale is illustrated in Figure 10.3.

Kinsey found that about 5 percent of the men in his sample were ranked at 6 (only same-sex experiences), 13 percent had more gay than heterosexual experiences, and 37 percent had had at least one same-sex experience to orgasm in adulthood (adolescent "experimentation" didn't count). Only 45 percent of the adult men in the sample ranked at 0 (exclusively heterosexual behavior).

Among women, less than 3 percent were ranked at 6 (only same-sex experiences), and 13 percent had had at least one same-sex experience to the point of orgasm. However, 28 percent reported same-sex outlets that did not lead to orgasm, so only 66 percent ranked at 0 (exclusively heterosexual behavior).

FIGURE 10.3 The Kinsey Scale

RATING	DESCRIPTION
0	Exclusively heterosexual
1	Predominantly heterosexual, only incidentally homosexual
2	Predominantly heterosexual, but more than incidentally homosexual
3	Equally heterosexual and homosexual
4	Predominantly homosexual, but more than incidentally heterosexual
5	Predominantly homosexual, only incidentally heterosexual
6	Exclusively homosexual
X	Asexual

The National Health and Social Life Study. In the early 1990s, a team of researchers at the National Opinion Research Center (NORC) at the University of Chicago undertook the most comprehensive study of sexual behavior in American history (Laumann et al., 1994). Their findings were as controversial as Kinsey's but in the opposite direction: Instead of huge amounts of nonprocreative sexual activity, they found much smaller amounts than Kinsey did.

Only 25 percent of men and 10 percent of women reported having had an extramarital affair—less than half of Kinsey's percentages. The percentage of people with exclusive same-sex experiences stayed the same, about 5 percent of men and less than 3 percent of women, but the percentage with both same-sex and heterosexual experiences declined dramatically. It seemed that no one but gay men and lesbians was having same-sex experiences anymore.

Why such different findings? Is it possible that after all the changes in American culture since the 1950s—the birth control pill, the sexual revolution, feminism, gay liberation, the legalization of abortion—we had actually become more sexually conservative?

Not really. Kinsey did not draw a random sample of Americans to survey, as NORC did. He drew "convenience" samples of groups he believed he could persuade to take the survey. His respondents included a large number of college students, prisoners, psychiatric patients, and even his own personal friends. It is possible that they had more variety in their sexual experiences to begin with.

The historical context of the study may also have determined the behavior. Many of the men in his sample had been in the military during World War I and World War II, when visiting a prostitute was a common form of recreation for soldiers and sailors on leave. In the 1990s, a relatively small proportion of the men were veterans of any war.

The same-sex behavior may have declined because, with the rise of gay liberation, straight men were more sensitive to being labeled gay than their 1940s counterparts, so they were less likely to engage in recreational sex with each other. In the same way, gay men were likely to "come out" at an early age and not experience so much social pressure to sleep with women. So, paradoxically, sexual orientation and behavior were more closely aligned in the 1990s than they had been in the 1940s.

Americans had been shocked by the high rates of variant sexual behaviors reported by Kinsey; in the 1990s, they were equally shocked at the relatively low rates of variant sexual behaviors found by the NORC study. Critics of both studies believed that people would not tell the whole truth: Kinsey's critics believe respondents would omit instances of unconventional sexual behavior to make their life history sound more "normal," and the NORC study's critics believe that they would invent instances of unconventional sexual behavior because they were afraid of being labeled "prudes" in an era of sexual liberation.

But the NORC researchers built in elaborate statistical checks to catch people who were untruthful, and untruthful surveys were discarded from the analysis. It appears, after all, that Americans are relatively modest and sexually conservative, having their sexual experiences with committed partners "appropriate" to their age and sexual orientation.

American Sexual Behavior and Identities

You might not personally be a fan of any specific sexual behavior, but how do you feel about people who are? Would you invite them to Thanksgiving dinner, or would you refuse to shake their hands at a party? During the last 30 years, the General Social Survey has asked a number of questions about attitudes toward various sexual behaviors, and while disapproval of interracial and same-sex relationships has declined considerably, most attitudes have remained fairly stable. For instance, today about 95 percent of respondents state that sex between teenagers is "always wrong" or "almost always wrong," a percentage that has barely budged since 1972.

But such consistency in attitudes may be deceiving. For one thing, there is often a wide gap between those moral positions we take with regard to other people's behaviors and those we take with regard to our own behaviors. Many of the respondents (all 18 or older) state that teenage sex is wrong, when they themselves engaged in it.

Homosexuality

Homosexuality has always been a contentious topic in the United States and worldwide. Homosexual marriage rights are currently being debated around the world. Several U.S. states have provisions for marriagelike civil unions between members of the same sex, and many other states have passed constitutional amendments explicitly banning gay marriage. The issue of gay marriage is informed by morality and values and by feelings about same-sex relationships and same-sex sexual behavior. Often, people have trouble seeing beyond their personal moral values to larger issues such as civil rights. So, what do you think?

Do you think homosexual sexual relations are:

○ Always wrong
○ Almost always wrong
○ Sometimes wrong
○ Not wrong at all

See the back of the chapter to compare your answers to national survey data.

Also, attitudes may describe a position without telling us much about how someone actually applies that moral position in his or her everyday life. Take, for example, attitudes about homosexuality. In the 1970s, 75 percent of Americans believed that same-sex behavior was "always wrong" or "almost always wrong." If these respondents happened to discover that a co-worker or relative was gay, they might have been horrified, cutting all contact with the person. Their negative attitude could predict negative behavior.

Today, 50 percent of Americans believe that same-sex behavior is "always wrong" or "almost always wrong," but they are likely to be polite and tolerant to gay co-workers or relatives and even make gay friends. In other words, their negative attitude does not necessarily predict negative behavior.

The Gender of Sexuality

How do Americans construct their sexual identities? The single most important organizing principle of sexuality is gender. Men and women are raised to have very different attitudes toward sexual desire, behavior, and identity. One might say that there are "his" and "her" sexuality.

For many years, it was assumed that only men experienced sexual desire at all; women were interested in romance and companionship but not sex. Women who flirted with men were not expressing sexual desire but trying to "snare" men into marrying them or buying them something. Thus, when Queen Victoria of England signed a law prohibiting same-sex activity among men, she didn't even think to expand it to female same-sex activity; why would a woman engage in sexual behavior at all unless she was trying to seduce a man? (It was Queen Victoria, after all, who is rumored to have commented that a British wife's duty to her husband is to "lie back and think of England"!)

Even in the twentieth century, many doctors assumed that women lacked sexual desire. One study of gynecology textbooks published between 1943 and 1972 found that most asserted that women did not experience orgasms. One textbook writer claimed that "sexual pleasure is entirely secondary or even absent" in women; another described women's "almost universal frigidity."

Although today many people agree that women have some degree of sexual desire, they consider it inappropriate to express openly. Men are expected to express how "horny" they are; women are not. Men who have a lot of sex are seen as "studs," and their status rises among their peers. Women who have a lot of sex are seen as "sluts," and their status falls. "Women need a reason to have sex," commented comedian Billy Crystal. "Men just need a place."

Whether gay or heterosexual, sexual behaviors, desires, and identities are organized more by the gender of the actor than by the genders of those toward whom he or she might be erotically inclined. That is to say, on all available measures, gay and straight men are far more similar to each other than either is to gay or straight women. Men are socialized to express a "masculine" sexuality, and women are socialized to express a "feminine" sexuality, regardless of their sexual orientation.

In our culture, the sexual double standard encourages men to pursue sex as an end in itself, to seek a lot of sex with many different partners, outside of romantic or emotional commitment. And women are taught to consider sex with one partner and only in the context of an emotional relationship. As a result we see the highest rates

How do we know what we know?

How Many Sex Partners Do People Have?

For decades, sex researchers have noticed a strange thing: Men and women reported different numbers of partners. A recent survey found that men reported a median number of seven sexual partners over the course of their lives, while the median number of partners for women was four. How can this be? After all, it's a mathematical impossibility for men to average almost twice the number of partners that women average.

Perhaps one reason is what we might call the "stud versus slut" effect: Men might overestimate their numbers to appear more like a stud; women might underestimate their numbers to appear less like a slut. So men might exaggerate, and women might minimize.

It might also be that men are picking partners from outside the surveyed population—for example, going to prostitutes, or having sex in other countries when they travel—in numbers far greater than women.

There's also the problem of retrospective analysis: People's memories don't tell you what actually happened but reveal more about what they believe or want to have happened—or what they believe should have happened. That is, asking people about the past tells you more, sometimes, about the present.

All of these may contribute to the disparity. But it turns out that this difference shows up only among some groups and only when they are asked some types of questions. For the 90 percent of Americans who have had 20 or fewer lifetime partners, the male–female ratio is close to 1—that is, they report the same number of partners. And if you ask men and women how many different partners they had in the past year, the ratio again is close to 1.

The entire discrepancy is a result of measurement error among the remaining 10 percent—that is, those who have had more than 20 partners over their lifetime. Four-fifths of these people tend to report their numbers in round numbers (25, 50, 100, and so on), and men tend to round up and women tend to round down. When you have had that many partners, most people just don't keep an exact tally.

It may simply be that these forces—normative expectations for studs and sluts, a "prostitute effect," or gendered memory for only those with the most partners—are in operation only for some groups and only when they are asked certain questions.

(*Source:* Morris, 1993.)

▲ In the United States, women's and men's sexualities are increasingly similar. On the popular television show, *Sex and the City* (1998–2004), all four gal pals were depicted as sexually active, and one, Samantha, at left, was as predatory as any male.

of sexual activity among gay men (masculine sexuality times two), and the lowest rates among lesbians (feminine sexuality times two). Gay men have an average of over 30 partners during their lifetime, while lesbians have fewer than three. Gay men have the lowest rates of long-term committed relationships, straight men the next, then straight women, and finally, lesbians have the highest rates. Thus, it appears that men—gay or straight—place sexuality at the center of their lives, and that women—gay or straight—are more interested in affection and caring in the context of a long-term love relationship.

In recent years, there has been increased convergence in women's and men's sexual attitudes and behaviors. Women's sexuality is becoming increasingly similar to men's; in fact we might even speak of a "masculinization" of sex. The **masculinization of sex** includes the pursuit of pleasure for its own sake, the increased attention to orgasm, increased numbers of sexual partners, the interest in sexual experimentation, and the separation of sexual behavior from love. These are partly the result of the technological transformation of sexuality (from birth control to the Internet) and partly the result of the sexual revolution's promise of greater sexual freedom with fewer emotional and physical consequences (see Rubin, 1990; Schwartz and Rutter, 1998).

Sexual behaviors have grown increasingly similar. Among teenage boys, sexual experience has remained virtually the same since the mid-1940s, with about 70 percent of all high-school-aged boys having had a sexual experience (the rates were about 50 percent for those who went to high school in the late 1920s). But the rates for high school girls have changed dramatically, up from 5 percent in the 1920s to 20 percent in the late 1940s to 55 percent in 1982 and 60 percent in 1991 to 63.3 percent in 2002. About one in five teenagers has had a sexual experience before age 15 (Figure 10.4). And the age of the first sexual experience has steadily declined for both boys and girls (Centers for Disease Control, 2005; Finer, 2007; Lewin, 2003; Rubin, 1990; Schwartz and Rutter, 1998).

Similarly, although the rates of not having sex have declined for both girls and boys, they have declined more rapidly for girls. The number of teenagers who have had more than five different sexual partners by their eighteenth birthday has increased for both sexes; the rate of increase is greater for girls as well. (Centers for Disease Control, 2005; Lewin, 2003).

Convergence on Campus: Hooking Up

One place where one can observe the political ramifications of the gender convergence in sexual behavior is on campus, where a culture of "hooking up" has virtually erased the older pattern of "rating-dating-mating" observed by sociologist Willard Waller decades ago.

Hooking up is a deliberately vague blanket term; one set of researchers defines it as "a sexual encounter which may nor may not include sexual intercourse, usually occurring on only one occasion between two people who are strangers or brief acquaintances" (Lambert, 2003, p. 129). While that seems to cover most cases, it fails to include those heterosexuals who hook up more than once or twice, or "sex buddies" (acquaintances who meet regularly for sex but rarely if ever

FIGURE 10.4 Trends in Heterosexual Experience among Teens

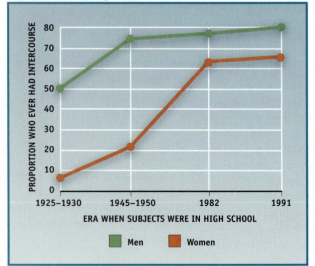

Source: "Trends in Heterosexual Experience among Teens" from The Gender of Sexuality: Sexual Possibilities by Pepper Schwartz, 1998. Used by permission of Alta Mira Press.

associate otherwise), or "friends with benefits" (friends who do not care to become romantic partners, but may include sex among the activities they enjoy together). In a sense, the patterns of heterosexual students have begun to look more like the patterns observed among their gay and lesbian peers.

On many campuses, the sexual marketplace—gay and straight—is organized around groups of same-sex friends who go out together to meet appropriate sexual partners in a casual setting like a bar or a party. Party scenes feature hooking up as the standard mode of sexual interaction. In collaborative research I have undertaken with other sociologists at Stanford, Indiana, Ithaca, and Arizona, we have found that for heterosexual students, hooking up covers a multitude of behaviors, including kissing and nongenital touching (34 percent), manual stimulation of the genitals (19 percent), oral sex (22 percent), and intercourse (23 percent). Almost all hooking up involves more alcohol than sex: Men averaged 4.7 drinks on their most recent hookup, women 2.9 drinks.

▲ On many campuses, a "hooking up" culture prevails. People hook up with others within a large social network, fueled by alcohol, for vaguely defined sexual encounters that may, or may not, lead to an actual relationship.

While "hooking up" is a mutual and consensual activity for heterosexual students, it is up to the women to negotiate whether it proceeds to a deeper level of intimacy. Women tend to be more ambivalent about the hookup culture; some report feeling sexy and desirable; others feel it's cheap and rarely leads anywhere. On many campuses, women's initiative is typically to begin a conversation called the "DTR"— "define the relationship"—or, more simply, "the talk." "Are we a couple or not?" she asks. And, as one report worries, when she asks, "he decides."

Convergence on Campus: Just Saying No

If hooking up culture is the dominant campus sexual culture, then "abstinence pledgers" may represent a counterculture. Abstinence campaigns encourage young people to take a "virginity pledge" and refrain from heterosexual intercourse until marriage (the campaigns assume that gay and lesbian students do not exist).

At first glance, such campaigns appear to be successful. One study found that the total percentage of high school students who say they've had heterosexual sex had dropped from more than 50 percent in 1991 to slightly more than 45 percent in 2001. Teen pregnancy and abortion rates have decreased somewhat, and birth rates have dropped from 6 percent to about 5 percent of all births. Proponents point to the success of abstinence-based sex education and elaborate publicity campaigns in a 10 percent drop in teen sexual activity.

Abstinence campaigns do appear to have *some* effect, but they do not offset the other messages teenagers hear. Sociologist Peter Bearman and Hannah Brickner (2001) analyzed data from over 90,000 students and found that taking a virginity pledge does lead an average heterosexual teenager to delay his or her first sexual experience—by about 18 months. And the pledges were effective only for students up to age 17. By the time they are 20 years old, over 90 percent of both boys and girls are sexually active.

The pledges were not effective at all if a significant proportion of students at the school was taking them. That is, taking the pledge seems to be a way of creating a "deviant" subculture, or a counterculture, what Bearman called an "identity

movement"—add "virgins" to the Goths, jocks, nerds, preppies, and rappers. When pledgers did have heterosexual intercourse, they were *far less likely* to use contraception.

Another survey of 527 never-married heterosexual students at a large Midwestern university found that 16 percent had taken virginity pledges but that 61 percent of them had broken their pledge before graduating from college. Pledgers were less likely to use condoms, although they were just as likely to practice oral sex as nonpledgers (Lipsitz, Bishop, and Robinson, 2003).

Because abstinence-based programs are often used instead of actual sex education, few people really know exactly what "counts" in keeping your pledge. In one recent survey of 1,100 college freshmen, 61 percent believed they were still abstinent if they had participated in mutual masturbation; 37 percent if they have had oral sex; and 24 percent if they have had anal sex. On the other hand, 24 percent believed that kissing broke their abstinence pledge (Bearman and Bruckner, 2001, Lipsitz et al., 2003).

▲ On America's college campuses, more than half of all sexual assaults take the form of "date rape," in which a woman is assaulted while on a date with a man. Getting a woman so drunk that she cannot consent—or say no—to sex is a prelude to assault, not lovemaking.

Rape and Sexual Assault

Although women's and men's sexualities are becoming more similar, there remain some important differences. One of the most important is in the area of nonconsensual sexual activity, a form of sexual assault. On many college campuses, more than half of all sexual assaults take the form of "date rape," in which a woman is assaulted while on a date with a man. Some studies have estimated the rates to be significantly higher. Some men may take advantage of a woman while she is intoxicated and unable to resist, or they may simply be unaware that she "really means it" if she says no: They have been raised on media images of women who violently resist a man's advances, only to melt into his arms at the last minute.

While women comprise the largest proportion of victims of sexual assault, male victims are not uncommon: About 23 percent of women and 4 percent of men state that they have been forced to have sex against their will. Male perpetrators are more common in assaults against women (21.6 percent were assaulted by men, and 0.3 percent by women), but in assaults against men, the gender balance is about equal (1.9 percent were assaulted by men, 1.3 percent by women).

What Else Affects Sexuality?

Gender may be the most central force shaping our sexual identity and behavior, but other identities shape them as well. For example, Blacks hold more liberal sexual values than Whites and have slightly more sex partners, but they also masturbate less frequently, have less oral sex, have less anal sex, and are slightly less likely to have same-sex contacts than Whites (Laumann et al., 2000). Hispanics are also more sexually liberal in their attitudes than Whites, and they masturbate more often than both Whites and Blacks (Laumann et al., 2000). Yet they also have less oral sex and have fewer sex partners, either same sex or opposite sex, than do Whites or Blacks (Centers for Disease Control, 2005; Laumann et al., 2000). Of all the large ethnic groups in the United States, Asian Americans are the least sexually liberal, masturbate less often, and have fewer sex partners of either same or opposite sex (Laumann and Michaels, 2000).

Age affects our sexuality, both directly and indirectly. After a certain age, younger people tend to have more sex than older ones, although there are variations by race and ethnicity (Centers for Disease Control, 2005). The aging body responds differently to sexual stimuli, and our sexual interests shift over time. And as we age we are more likely to be married or partnered—with children. And few things diminish sexual activity more than having children. Couples—gay and straight—with children report far less sexual activity than couples without children. There is less time, less freedom, and less privacy—and greater fatigue.

It turns out that politics also affects sex. The more equal women and men are, the more satisfied women and men are with their sex lives. In a recent survey of 29 countries, sociologists found that people in countries with higher levels of gender equality—Spain, Canada, Belgium, and Austria—reported being much happier with their sex lives than those in countries with lower levels of gender equality, like Japan. The reason has to do with women's pleasure: "Male-centered cultures where sexual behavior is more oriented toward procreation tend to discount the importance of sexual pleasure for women," said sociologist Ed Laumann (Laumann and Michaels, 2000).

Within each country, the greater the level of equality between women and men, the happier women and men are with their sex lives. It turns out that those married couples who report the highest rates of marital satisfaction—and the highest rates of sexual activity in the first place—are those in which men do the highest amounts of housework and child care (Laumann and Michaels, 2000).

Sexual Inequality

Our sexual identities and sexual behaviors are the bases for significant social inequality. Although heterosexuals and homosexuals both express their sexuality through gender, there are some important differences between them. Only heterosexuality is credited as a "legitimate" sexual behavior.

Sexual desire, behavior, and identity are policed by social institutions through two distinct practices. **Homophobia** is an attitude, a socially approved dislike of gay men and lesbians, the presumption that they are inferior to straight people. **Heterosexism** is the institutionally based inequality that may derive from homophobia. As a set of practices rather than an ideology, heterosexism may be more pervasive.

Gay men and lesbians encounter heterosexism constantly. Sometimes it is in specific norms and laws that reflect these institutional practices. Sometimes it is the simple assumption and gays and lesbians do not exist. In class, the professor may ask "Guys, what do you look for in a girlfriend?" as if none of the guys in the class could possibly be gay. When an attractive person of the opposite sex passes on the street, their straight friend nudges them to look, even if the friend knows that they are gay, because, at that moment, the whole world is straight. These examples of "invisibility" can have a profound psychological impact.

Gay men and lesbians are criminals in the 14 states with antisodomy laws, and they are permitted to marry in only one state, (although they may marry in Canada and in most European countries). Most religious bodies in the United States do not permit them to become members. They can be fired from most jobs and evicted from most apartments with no legal recourse. (In Europe all members of the European Union subscribe to laws that prevent any discrimination against gays and lesbians.) Every year there are thousands of hate crimes directed against them, not to mention harassment, jokes, defamation (e.g., using "gay" as an all-purpose term for anything bad), physical and sexual abuse. One recent study of homophobia estimated that

Did *you* know ?

The vocal antigay statements of some Christian denominations sometimes make us think that all organized religion is antigay, but in fact religious bodies were instrumental in the gay liberation movement of the 1970s, and today a number of Christian churches permit gay members and clergy, including the Episcopal Church, the United Church of Christ, the Disciples of Christ, the Lutheran Church (ELCA), the Presbyterian Church in America, and the American Baptists. In all, about 30 percent of Protestants in the United States belong to gay-friendly denominations.

2 million lesbian, gay, and bisexual middle and high school students have been the "frequent" targets of homophobic harassment in school, often by the teachers and staff (Bochenek and Brown, 2001).

The systematic devaluation of same-sex desire and behavior, the stigma attached to being gay, becomes a crucial element in one's identity (Plummer, 1992). Homophobia constricts gay and lesbian experience because gays are painfully aware that they are not seen as equal—only because of the gender of their partner. But we are often less aware of the power of homophobia to structure the experiences and identities of heterosexuals. Heterosexuals, especially men, spend a significant amount of time and energy making sure that no one gets the "wrong" idea about them. For men, the stakes are enormously high: Being "accused" of being gay, even for a moment, implies that they are less than fully masculine.

In an interview in 2001, Eminem was asked why his raps almost always included derogatory references to "faggots." In response, he said:

> The lowest degrading thing you can say to a man. . . is to call him a faggot and try to take away his manhood. Call him a sissy, call him a punk. "Faggot" to me doesn't necessarily mean gay people. "Faggot" to me just means taking away your manhood. (cited in Kim, 2001, p. 5)

Because they mistakenly assume that all gay men are feminine and lesbians masculine, heterosexuals also demonstrate that they are "not gay" by exaggerating gender-stereotyped behavior. In this way, homophobia reinforces the gender of sex, keeping men acting hypermasculine and women acting ultrafeminine. "Heterosexuality as currently construed and enacted (the erotic preference for the other gender) requires homophobia," write sex researchers John Gagnon and Stuart Michaels (1989).

Sexual Minority Communities

In response to sexual inequality, people with minority sexual orientations often band together, both to find suitable partners and to escape the hostility of the mainstream society. If there are enough of them and they manage to find each other, they can form

Sociology and our World

The Heterosexual Questionnaire

In the 1980s, a young writer named Michael Rochlin composed a questionnaire to illustrate the impact of homophobia on the way heterosexuals understand sexuality. Among the questions:

1. What do you think caused your heterosexuality?
2. When and how did you first decide you were a heterosexual?
3. Is it possible your heterosexuality is just a phase you may grow out of?
4. Is it possible your heterosexuality stems from a neurotic fear of others of the same sex?
5. To whom have you disclosed your heterosexual tendencies? How did they react?
6. Why do you heterosexuals feel compelled to seduce others into your lifestyle?
7. Why do you insist on flaunting your heterosexuality? Can't you just be what you are and keep it quiet?
8. A disproportionate majority of child molesters are heterosexuals. Do you consider it safe to expose your children to heterosexual teachers?
9. With all the societal support marriage receives, the divorce rate is spiraling. Why are there so few stable relationships among heterosexuals?

their own subcultures, with their own gathering places, social hierarchies, norms, values, and group cohesion (that is, a feeling that "we belong together"). Sometimes they can even work to change social disapproval. Gay men and lesbians have probably been the most successful at creating social change. Thirty years ago, the mass media commonly carried articles about crazy "homosexuals." How could anybody engage in such behavior? Today it is just as likely to carry articles about crazy homophobes. How could anyone be so prejudiced? This is a big change in a short time. What happened?

As early as the nineteenth century, there were gay neighborhoods in some large cities, such as Paris, Berlin, and New York, but most people with same-sex interests believed that they were alone (Chauncey, 1993). Medical science believed there were probably only a few thousand homosexuals, mostly in psychiatric hospitals. That changed during World War II, where gay and lesbian soldiers found each other and realized that there were many more than anyone thought (the Kinsey Report of 1948 helped also). However, they still faced oppression.

If a man sat next to you in a bar and offered to shake hands, he could be an undercover police officer, who would count the handshake as a "homosexual overture" and arrest you. An arrest for "homosexuality" could get you fired, kicked out of your apartment, sent to prison, or sent to a psychiatric hospital (where you could be subject to electroshock therapy and forced castration). In the 1950s, gay men and lesbians began forming organizations such as the Mattachine Society, One, Incorporated, and the Daughters of Bilitis, to petition for the end of police harassment.

The 1969 Stonewall riots, three days of resistance to police harassment in New York City, led to the formation of the Gay Liberation Front. More gay rights groups followed, until by 1975, there were hundreds: student groups, religious groups, political groups, social groups—groups for practically any interest you could imagine, in practically every city and town in the United States, until a whole new social movement emerged, the gay rights movement. They were not apologetic. They were loud, in-your-face, "out and proud"; staging sit-ins, marches, and media "zaps"; shouting rather than whispering, demanding rather than asking: We are not crazy! We are not criminals! We are an oppressed minority!

And they were extremely successful. During the next few years, sodomy laws were thrown out in half of the U.S. states, the American Psychiatric Association removed homosexuality from its list of disorders, a dozen Christian denominations voted to allow gay people full membership, and a new term, *homophobia,* was coined to describe antigay prejudice (Armstrong, 2005).

In 1977, the top-rated TV sitcom, *Three's Company,* was based on the premise that a straight guy, Jack Tripper (John Ritter), could pretend to be gay so a conservative landlord would let him share an apartment with two girls. (That premise would have been impossible a few years earlier.) By 2004, *Queer Eye for the Straight Guy* choreographed complete makeovers for straight men (to make them more appealing to women), courtesy of five "fabulous" gay culture experts.

Why was the gay rights movement so successful? One answer may be the connections with nongay people: It arose simultaneously with the youth counterculture of the late 1960s, when millions of college-aged people were protesting all sorts of injustices, from the Vietnam War to racial inequality. The gay rights activists were mostly college aged, members of that same counterculture. One of their early slogans was "We are your children." Political and social leaders were faced, for the first time, with gay men and lesbians who looked and acted like other young people, who could indeed be their children.

The modern gay and lesbian movement is about more than removing discrimination against homosexuals. It is also about the right to live openly as parents, workers, and neighbors. ▼

Try It   The Pink Triangle Experiment

Submitted by Jerome Rabow and Pauline Yeghnazar, *UCLA/CSUN*.

OBJECTIVE: This activity encourages the development of a greater understanding of heterosexist privilege and the role prejudice and discrimination play in our everyday lives.

STEP 1: Research

Take a moment to review some of the gay pride symbols by searching for information in your library or on the Internet. Your instructor may also share information on pride symbols and their development. Your instructor may also assign you to read an article published about the Pink Triangle Experiment (see the note at the end of the box).

STEP 2: Plan

Your instructor will either assign this as an individual project or as a partner project. You will be asked to choose one of the gay pride symbols and wear it for the day (your instructor may assign a longer time period) on your campus (most students choose to wear a pink triangle). Your instructor will either provide you with symbols to choose from or have materials on hand for you to make a symbol to wear (it should be the size of a lapel pin or only slightly larger). Should you be uncomfortable wearing a symbol, you should choose to partner with another student who plans to wear the symbol for the day. Be sure to follow the directions of your instructor.

If you choose not to wear a pin but partner with a pin wearer, you will want to plan to be with this person for at least part of the time he or she wears the symbol. As you wear the symbol on campus, keep notes on comments made to you throughout the day.

STEP 3: Write

At the end of the day (the end of the assignment), write a one-page paper on your experiences. Be sure to include answers to the following:

▶ Describe the most powerful moment or incident in your wearing of the symbol.
▶ Explain the who, what, when, and where of your experience and be sure to include comments on how you felt about wearing the symbol.
▶ What was the most difficult part of doing this assignment?
▶ For non-symbol-wearers, include a discussion of your observations and conversations with your partner and discuss your concerns about wearing the symbol.
▶ Include a conclusion where you discuss overall what you thought about this project and what it indicates about our society and culture. Do you think you would have received different reactions had you worn the symbol in your community? In your church? Where do you think you would be most welcomed? Least welcomed? Why?

STEP 4: Discuss

Be prepared to turn in your comments in class and to share your thoughts about this assignment. What do you think this has to do with prejudice and discrimination in our society?

A more detailed description of this assignment can be found in Rabow, Jerome, Jill M. Stein, and Terri D. Conley, "Teaching Social Justice and Encountering Society: The Pink Triangle Experiment," *Youth and Society, 30* (1999): 483–514.

In fact, the gay rights movement may have been too successful to remain a counterculture or a subculture; it is now part of the mainstream culture. Many strictly gay social institutions are struggling to survive. Gay bookstores are going out of business because gay-themed books are available at every bookstore. Gay political organizations are losing members, now that protection from antigay discrimination can be openly discussed at any town council meeting. A proposed gay college died on the drawing board: You can take gay studies courses just about anywhere. Why join a gay church, when gay people are welcomed in the church down the street? It is not that antigay prejudice and discrimination no longer exist but that they can now be fought more effectively within mainstream social institutions. It may be true that the more successful a social movement is, the less it is felt to be needed.

Sexuality as Politics

Sex has always been political—that is, people have always been arguing about what we *should* be able to do—and with whom, how, under what circumstances. It has often been the task of religion to regulate sexual activity, and it is increasingly the task of the state to do so. For example, laws regarding the age of consent, extramarital sex, the relationship of sex and commerce (regulating prostitution), reproductive rights, all involve the state in intimate decision making. Historically, the state sought to regulate sexual behavior to ensure clear lines of inheritance (barring children born out of wedlock from inheriting property) and to cement the connection between church and state.

Contemporary sexual politics involve political, scientific, and religious issues. Often these collide, as when scientific breakthroughs enable a wider range of sexual choices free of reproductive complications (such as the morning after pill); often they coincide, as when the state seeks to protect children from predatory pedophiles.

Although there are many issues about which sociological research adds significant clarity and perspective, we will examine only three here: sex tourism, pornography, and birth control and sex education. All have become globalized; all have been shaped by the Internet; and all reproduce inequalities based on gender, race, and ethnicity.

Sex Tourism: The Globalization of Sex

For centuries, wealthy men have sought sexual adventures with "exotic" strangers in foreign countries. During the nineteenth and early twentieth centuries, North Africa was the preferred destination for gay men in search of sex partners unrestrained by European homophobia; tourists included many famous writers and businessmen. In many major cities, prostitution catered largely to foreign men who were in town alone for business. Travel agencies always used pictures of bikini-clad women frolicking on the beach—to sell their locations to straight male customers. But in recent years, some companies are now selling sex tourism explicitly, advertising the charms of young men and women from the impoverished countries of Asia and inviting wealthy Americans and Europeans to pay them a visit.

In some respects, **sex tourism** represents the globalization of prostitution. Like other global industries, well-organized groups direct the flow of the "consumer" (wealthy men) to the "commodities" (poor men and women). Like prostitution, there is far less "choice" on the part of the locals and far more coercion than typically meets the eye. The tourists seem to be men and women who are being friendly and flirtatious, but the locals are usually victims of kidnapping and violence. According to the U.S. State Department, as many as 4 million people each year are lured by traffickers to destinations all over the world with promises of high-paying legitimate employment, only to end up as prostitutes and "rent boys."

Sex tourism uses the Internet to advertise its wares. For example, www.exotictours.com promises that on their tours, "you will be with girls who want to make you happy and will honestly consider a marriage offer." Part of a recent Chinese itinerary promised that on your first night, "girls will fight to get into the taxi with you. After picking out your night's entertainment, it's back to the hotel."

Current concern within the European community about sex trafficking, however, reveals a less erotic side of these transactions. In some Eastern European countries and new nations of the former Soviet Union, as well as Africa, young girls and boys are abducted or lured to European cities to serve as virtual sex slaves, paying off debts incurred in transporting them to their new homes. In the United States, the CIA estimates that 50,000 young women and girls are smuggled into the country every year (Jones, 2001).

Global trafficking in women and men is big business. More than $1 billion per year is spent by sex tourists worldwide. Southeast Asia is a major market, as traffickers take advantage of local economic conditions to lure girls to the city. Sometimes, they just kidnap them. ▼

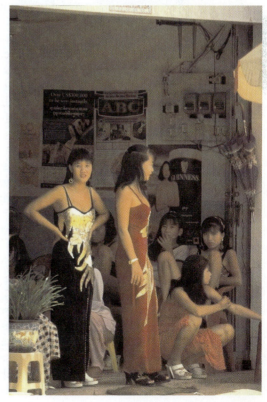

Some countries, such as Thailand, have become destinations of choice for sex tourists (mostly middle-aged men from Germany and the United States) and have well-developed sex tourism industries. This industry was begun in the 1960s, when Thailand contracted with the U.S. military to provide "rest and recreation" services for troops stationed in Vietnam (Nagel, 2003). Proprietors take advantage of high unemployment and traditional attitudes about women to ensure a steady "supply" and use the exoticism of the "Orient" and traditional stereotypes about docile and compliant Asian women to ensure a steady "demand" from their heterosexual customers.

Sex tourism thus expresses the unequal relationships between countries who "sell" sex and countries who can "buy" it, as well as the inequalities between men and women, both globally and locally. Sociologist Joane Nagel notes how the geography of sex trafficking expresses its inequality: Men, women, and children from Latin America, Asia, Eastern Europe, and Africa are moved to the United States, from Nepal to India, from Burma to Thailand, from India and Pakistan to the Middle East (Nagel, 2003). "Prostitution and related activities, which are inherently harmful and dehumanizing," according to President George W. Bush, "contribute to the phenomenon of trafficking in persons, as does sex tourism, which is an estimated $1 billion per year business worldwide" (Bush, 2003).

Pornography

Pornography refers to a visual or written depiction of sexual activity with no "redeeming social value." Of course, what counts as "redeeming social value" is in the eye of the beholder. Many of the greatest classics of world literature, such as James Joyce's *Ulysses* (1922), D. H. Lawrence's *Lady Chatterley's Lover* (1928), and Kurt Vonnegut's *Slaughterhouse Five* (1969) have been banned as pornographic. Information about birth control was banned as pornography in the 1920s; and, in 1956, the Mattachine Society was cited for pornography simply because its publication used the word *homosexual*.

The debates about pornography have traditionally pitted conservatives against liberals. Conservatives believe that any sexually explicit material is morally wrong and socially corrosive: It cannot help but lead to social decay. Liberals believe that adults should be able to make their own decisions about what they want to view and read.

In the late 1970s, this well-entrenched debate about pornography was transformed by feminist women. Women Against Pornography (WAP) claimed that heterosexual pornography was less about sex than about sexism; it was male domination turned into erotica (gay male pornography was ignored because it did not involve women). As one supporter said, heterosexual pornography "makes sexism sexy" (Stoltenberg, 1990). WAP claimed that heterosexual pornography itself was a form of censorship—it silenced women. They claimed that violence against women was caused, in part, by pornography, because when men see degrading sexual acts in pornography, it appears that women like them. In some cases, these radical feminists joined with moral conservatives in political efforts to reduce the harm caused by pornography. Other feminists disagreed. They claimed that the censorship of heterosexual pornography, whether by conservatives of feminists, would silence women's empowering efforts to express their sexuality (see Dworkin, 1981; FACT, 1985).

Social science research has attempted to assess the impact of pornography on viewers, almost always heterosexual men. Experiments have found small differences in both behavior and attitudes between men who viewed significant amounts of violent heterosexual pornography in a laboratory setting and those who did not. Men who viewed the violent heterosexual pornography held more negative views about women and were also more likely to acquit rape defendants in mock trials. However, further investigation by the researchers found that it was the violence in the videos, and not the sexually explicit scenes, that caused the change in attitudes and behaviors (Donnerstein and Linz, 1990).

In a famous study, sociologist Berl Kutchinsky observed the effects of legalizing pornography. Despite predictions that it would lead to a marked increased in sex crimes, rates of sexual assault and of child sexual abuse actually decreased in Denmark. (Kutchinsky, 1990). This decline was not caused by the availability of pornography, of course, but rather both the legalization of pornography and the reduction in sex crimes were caused by liberal social policies and the increased political participation of women. Research on the other side of the political spectrum found that municipalities that banned pornography in the 1990s did not witness an appreciable decrease in arrests for rape or child sexual assault (Kimmel and Linders, 1996).

In recent years, pornography has become a global industry, especially through the Internet. The Internet is now the single largest outlet for sexually explicit materials in the world (Fisher and Barak, 2001). An increasing number of straight women and lesbians also say they enjoy and use pornography.

Internet pornography raises new issues. On the one hand, the Internet offers new possibilities to try out new sexual identities; sometimes, individuals pretend to be something or want something just for fun. On the other hand, the Internet makes tracing the origins of the material more difficult, and, as a result, distribution of child pornography has grown enormously.

Sex Education and Birth Control

Should we educate children about sexuality? Many people believe that teaching about sex encourages young people to experiment with sex, when otherwise they would not have considered it. Others, however, believe that young people are going to experiment with sex anyway, and that adequate sex education would enable young people to make safer and more responsible sexual choices.

There is evidence supporting both positions. Students who have had sex education tend to engage in sexual activity at a slightly earlier age than those who do not. However, there is also evidence that those who have adequate sex education have lower rates of abortion, sexually transmitted infections (STIs), and pregnancy rates (Alan Guttmacher Institute, 2001; Dailard, 2001; Darroch et al, 2000; Kaiser Family Foundation, 2000; Kirby, 2001; Landry, Kaeser, and Richards, 1999).

In the past decade, a new form of sex education in the United States has been heavily promoted by the federal government. While two-thirds of all public school districts have policies to teach sex education, more than one in five of them (23 percent) require that abstinence be promoted as the sole option for unmarried people and another 34 percent teach abstinence as the preferred option. (Landry et al., 1999). In this context, birth control and condoms are mentioned only in terms of their failure rates. In 2003, the federal government devoted $117 million to abstinence education. By 2007, states such as Ohio, Montana, New Jersey, Wisconsin, Rhode Island, and Connecticut had turned down federal money, arguing that they would rather

Sex education is controversial in the United States—but not in other industrialized countries. The evidence is clear that the more young people know about sex, the lower the rates of teen pregnancies, STIs, and abortions. ▼

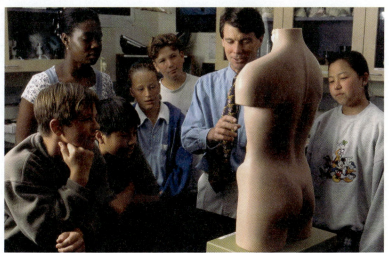

TABLE 10.1

Evangelical Christians and Sex Education Approval Percentages		
TOPIC	PERCENTAGE SAYING IT SHOULD NOT BE TAUGHT AT ALL	
	EVANGELICALS	NONEVANGELICALS
That teens can obtain birth control pills from family planning clinics and doctors without permission from a parent	42	20
Oral sex	41	20
Homosexuality and sexual orientation	37	18
Masturbation	27	13
How to put on a condom	26	9
How to use and where to get contraceptives	21	7

Don't know/refused responses are not shown.

Source: National Public Radio, Kaiser Family Foundation, and Kennedy School for Public and International Affairs, "Sex Education in America," 2004.

Family planning often empowers women to control their own lives. In the developing world, family planning and effective birth control (including condoms) is also a major strategy in reducing the spread of HIV. ▼

teach sensible sex education and reduce unwanted pregnancies and increased rates of sexually transmitted infections than teach abstinence only.

Most sociologists believe that a comprehensive sex education program should emphasize abstinence as one of a set of options available to young people and that the more information young people have, the most likely they will make the safest and most responsible choices. Parents seem to agree. Only 7 percent of Americans say that sex education should not be taught in schools (Kaiser Family Foundation, 2004). The majority of Americans, including evangelical Christians, believe that sex education and birth control should be taught (Table 10.1).

A similar debate has swirled for decades around the politics of birth control and abortion. Does the widespread availability of birth control encourage heterosexuals to have sex because the reproductive consequences can be minimized? Or does birth control simply encourage heterosexuals to have more *responsible* sex, minimizing the health risks and possibilities of unwanted pregnancy?

While moralists and political leaders take different positions, the sociological evidence is clear that information about birth control and its availability does not increase the amount of sex people have nor even the onset of sexual activity among young people. However, national as well as global studies show that the widespread availability of birth control, especially when coupled with comprehensive sex education, results in far lower rates of teen pregnancy and sexually transmitted infections (STIs) (Alan Guttmacher Institute, 2001).

Many people have religious objections to certain types of birth control because they believe that life begins at the moment an egg is fertilized, and some methods (such as the intrauterine device or IUD, and the morning after pill) prevent the implantation of the fertilized egg on the uterine wall. They also oppose abortion because abortion destroys a human embryo or fetus after implantation.

The opposition to abortion has transformed the global politics of birth control. Currently, for example, the United States refuses to fund any birth control clinic or information service anywhere in the world if the practitioners even mention abortion as a potential option for women facing unwanted pregnancies. As a result, most birth control information is now delivered through nonprofit organizations such as the Planned Parenthood Federation and often funded by private agencies, such as the Bill and Melinda Gates Foundation, The Ford Foundation, and the John D. and Catherine T. MacArthur Foundation. Despite significant political debate, there is little scientific argument that contradicts the proposition that increased availability and use of birth control in the developing countries would greatly enhance the standard of living in those societies.

The global politics of birth control has become more evident in light of the global AIDS epidemic. One of the primary methods to reduce risk of transmission of the HIV virus that causes AIDS is the condom, which has typically been marketed as a form of birth control for heterosexual men. Inadequate information about, or access to, birth control has become, in many countries, a matter of life and death.

Sexuality in the 21st Century

Sexuality is a foundation of identity, just as race or class or gender. And it is a basis for inequality—the unequal distribution of rewards and punishments, of resources and recognition. And like race, class, or gender, it is both increasingly important and decreasingly unequal. Our multicultural society makes these bases of identity ever more important in identifying who people are. But those same processes, and the political mobilization of formerly marginalized groups, lead to reforms that make different people more equal.

Attitudes may change more slowly than social movements might hope, but they change faster than the policies our countries derive to keep things the same. Gay men and lesbians still face enormous discrimination, but most industrial societies are far less homophobic than they were just a decade ago. For example, membership in the European Union requires adherence to policies that prohibit all discrimination against people based on sexual orientation.

Changing attitudes will eventually lead to changed policies. In some cases, it may simply be a function of age. While 75 percent of people over 60 oppose legalizing gay marriage, 75 percent of people under 30 support legalizing it. Movements for equality may not ever completely succeed in eradicating prejudice and discrimination, whether based on race, class, gender, or sexuality. But they can reduce homophobia and remove the legal barriers that individuals face based on their membership in marginalized groups.

 Chapter Review

1. *What is sexuality?* Sociologists distinguish among sexual desire, behavior, and identity, all of which are learned, along with cultural standards and sexual scripts. Sexuality is socially constructed; it varies between cultures, over time, by group, and over the life course. Desire is affected by cultural standards of beauty and is also a function of social class; different groups assign different meanings to beauty.

2. *What are sexual identities?* Sexual identities cohere around a preference and are affected by cultural norms and identities. Sexual identity is most strongly organized around the gender to which one is attracted. Heterosex-

uality is most common. Identity does not always align with behavior, however. In addition, sexual identity is not always as clear as heterosexual or homosexual; some individuals identify as bisexual. Sociologists believe sexual identity is both biologically based and socially constructed.

3. *How do we research sexuality?* Scientific research into sexuality began in nineteenth-century Europe. Early researchers included Krafft-Ebing, who studied sex crimes and concluded that masturbation caused perversion. Ellis countered that with his research, saying masturbation was harmless. Hirschfeld believed people were

born bisexual. In the United States, the Kinsey reports were the first large-scale investigation into sexual behavior. Kinsey found a gulf between what people professed morally and how they behaved. He also found that those from a higher socioeconomic status had more sex, 70 percent of male respondents had visited a prostitute, affairs were not uncommon, women enjoyed sex, and there were high numbers of same-sex sexual experiences. The National Health and Social Life Study in the 1990s found much lower incidences of those same behaviors.

4. *What are the characteristics of sexual behavior and identity among Americans?* Men and women are raised with different attitudes toward desire, behavior, and identity. There is a double standard with regard to men, who are socialized to see sex as an end in itself, and women, who are socialized to see sex as part of a relationship. In recent years, men's and women's sexual behaviors and attitudes have increasingly converged. On college campuses, hooking up is the new form of dating. The campus sexual marketplace is organized around same-sex groups interacting in casual settings. One important gender difference occurs in nonconsensual sex where women are more likely to be victims and men more likely to be perpetrators. Societies with higher gender equality report greater satisfaction with sex.

5. *How does inequality manifest with regard to sexuality?* Heterosexuality is considered the norm, and the most legitimate form of sexuality. Homophobia, a presumption that homosexuals are inferior, and heterosexism, or institution-based unequal practices, are both encountered frequently. Homosexuality is illegal in some states, and homosexuals can not marry in most of the United States. Gay people are discriminated against, are stigmatized, and are sometimes the victims of hate crimes. Like other minority groups, homosexuals formed a subculture, which arose with other social movements in the 1960s. Homosexuality has now become a part of mainstream culture, and those negative repercussions are declining.

6. *How does globalization reproduce sexual inequality?* Sex tourism is a global industry serving wealthy men traveling in foreign countries. This has gone on for centuries and has now become an industry. In the globalization of prostitution, sex workers are often victims of kidnapping and violence. Young people are abducted and forced into slavery. This phenomenon reinforces inequality between countries and inequality between men and women. Pornography is another globalized phenomenon whose definition is changing and subjective. Pornography, prostitution, and sex tourism have all increased with the ease of the Internet and globalization.

Key Terms

Asexual (p. 325)
Bisexuality (p. 323)
Heterosexism (p. 335)
Heterosexuality (p. 322)
Homophobia (p. 335)
Homosexuality (p. 322)

Hooking up (p. 332)
Masculinization of sex (p. 332)
Pedophilia (p. 325)
Pornography (p. 340)
Sex (p. 316)
Sex tourism (p. 339)

Sexual behavior (p. 317)
Sexual identity (p. 322)
Sexual script (p. 316)
Sexual socialization (p. 316)
Sexuality (p. 316)

What does America think?

10.1 Extramarital Sex

These are actual survey data from the General Social Survey, 2004.

How wrong do you think it is to have sex with a person other than one's spouse? In 1973, 70 percent of respondents said it was always wrong to have sex with a person other than one's spouse. In 2004, those numbers were higher, at slightly over 80 percent. In both years, and in the years in between, more women than man were likely to say it was always wrong, and more men than women to say it was never wrong.

CRITICAL THINKING | DISCUSSION QUESTIONS

1. The gender difference in responses is not large, but it is interesting. What do you think explains the gender difference?
2. Why do you think the number of respondents who said extramarital sex was always wrong has increased in the past 30 years?

10.2 Homosexuality

These are actual survey data from the General Social Survey, 2004.

Do you think homosexual sexual relations are always wrong, almost always wrong, sometimes wrong, or not wrong at all? The majority of respondents to the General Social Survey questions from 1973 to 2004 reported that they thought homosexual relations were almost always wrong. However, those numbers have declined significantly over the past 30 years, while the number of respondents who reported thinking homosexual relations were not wrong at all increased dramatically. Gender differences were almost nonexistent, but there are interesting differences when we look at the data by social class.

CRITICAL THINKING | DISCUSSION QUESTIONS

1. Social class differences in attitudes toward homosexuality are quite striking. How do you explain these differences? What part does social location and socialization into the class structure play?

▶ Go to this website to look further at the data. You can run your own statistics and crosstabs here: **http://sda.berkeley.edu/cgi-bin/hsda?harcsda+gss04**

REFERENCES: Davis, James A., Tom W. Smith, and Peter V. Marsden. General Social Surveys 1972–2004: [Cumulative file] [Computer file]. 2nd ICPSR version. Chicago, IL: National Opinion Research Center [producer], 2005; Storrs, CT: Roper Center for Public Opinion Research, University of Connecticut; Ann Arbor, MI: Inter-University Consortium for Political and Social Research; Berkeley, CA: Computer-Assisted Survey Methods Program, University of California [distributors], 2005.

chapter 11

OUR SOCIETY IS OBSESSED WITH YOUTH. Supermodels are over the hill at age 25, and actresses over 40 are rarely cast as anything but grandmothers. Television, movie, and print advertisements are aimed directly at the 18- to 35-year-old demographic and ignore the interests, tastes, and wallets of anyone older. You can buy hundreds of products designed to eliminate baldness, gray hair, wrinkles, crows' feet, paunches, all of the characteristics of age, but not a single one that promises "distinguished-looking gray hair" or "healthful wrinkles of a senior citizen." We compliment people by saying they are *young-looking*, as if it is the exact equivalent of *strong, healthy*, and *attractive*.

At the same time, our society is growing older. You can hardly pick up a newspaper or magazine without seeing a headline about the **Graying of America**. The proportion of Americans over 65 increases every year, while the proportion under 35 shrinks. Retirement is no longer a few years at the end of life: When the average person will live to see 80, some can expect to spend as much as

Age: From Young to Old

a quarter of our lives over age 65. Today, 13 percent of Americans 65 and older (4.6 million people) are still working, and there's talk of raising the official retirement age to 67 or even 70 (U.S. Census Bureau, 2004–2005).

We tend to think either that we're witnessing the "Graying of America" or the "Youth-Obsessed America." But to a sociologist, it's really both. We're graying and youth obsessed at the same time.

We tend to think either that we're witnessing the "Graying of America" or the "Youth-Obsessed America." But to a sociologist, it's really both. We're graying and youth obsessed at the same time.

Age and Identity

What does *old* mean, anyway? Sociologists believe that age is less a biological condition than a social construction. Depending on the norms of their society, a 15-year-old may play with toy soldiers or fight in real wars, a 20-year-old may receive a weekly paycheck or a weekly allowance, 40-year-olds may be changing the diapers of their children or their grandchildren, and a 60-year-old may be doddering and decrepit or in the robust prime of life. It is not the passing of years but the social environment that determines the characteristics of age.

Prior to the twentieth century, people became adults astonishingly early. Girls were allowed to marry at age 14 or even earlier, though most would not go through puberty until sometime after their eighteenth birthday. Jewish boys were considered adults at age 13. The Anabaptists of Reformation Europe disapproved of baptizing infants, as the Catholics did, so they baptized only "adults," by which they meant anyone over the age of 14.

Today, people seem to postpone adulthood until halfway through their lives. We regularly say "He's 23 years old—just a baby," and even 30-year-olds are often considered immature rather than real grownups. Middle age starts in the 50s, and old age—who knows? The boundaries are pushing upward every year.

With so much change and so much redefinition, one would expect age to diminish in importance as a social category. What does it matter if you graduate from college at age 20 or age 50? If you date someone 20 years older? If your boss at work is 20 years younger? Why should the number of years you've been alive make any difference whatever?

Yet age remains one of our major social identities; we assess ourselves and each other—positively and negatively—based on age as frequently as on class, race, ethnicity, gender, and sexuality. These judgments result in social stratification, for distributing rewards and punishments, and for allocating status and power.

To the sociologist, age is a basis for identity and a cause of inequality. As an identity, sociologists differentiate between your **chronological age**—a person's age determined by the actual date of birth—and **functional age**—a set of observable characteristics and attributes that are used to categorize people into different age cohorts. An **age cohort** is a group of people who are born within a specific time period and therefore assumed to share both chronological and functional characteristics.

Traditionally, the sociological study of aging was called **gerontology**, which is defined in the *American Heritage Dictionary* as the "scientific study of the biological, psychological, and sociological phenomena associated with old age and aging." However, sociologists now understand that such a study, while essential, tells only half the story. While age is a facet of identity at all moments through the life cycle, most of the inequality based on age occurs at the upper *and lower* ends of the life span—that is, among the young and the elderly. In high-income countries like the United States, older people often wield a great deal of political power, but they still must battle negative stereotypes and limited social services. Children, teenagers, and young adults often lack any power, prestige, and resources, but they are seen as filled with potential, and we strive to look like them. And while we tout compassion for our elders and commitment to our kids, our social and economic policies often shortchange or harm both of these vulnerable groups. Today, the study of age and aging in sociology requires that we study both identity and inequality among both the young and the old—as well as everyone in between.

The Stages of Life

All societies—whether tribal, agrarian, or industrial—have always divided the **life span** into stages, seasons, or age groups (Neugarten, 1996; Benston and Schaie, 1999). Each stage is expected to have its own **age norms**—distinctive cultural values, pursuits, and pastimes that are culturally prescribed for each age cohort. For instance, "children" in our society might be expected to share a fondness for comic books and chocolate milk that differentiates them from teenagers' penchant for pizza and music magazines or an adult's daily dose of financial news and All-Bran cereal. Life stages create predictable social groupings, allowing us to know in advance what to expect from strangers and new acquaintances and how to respond to them: We may serve chocolate milk at a party for children, for instance, but not at a party for adults, and we would think that a child who preferred CNN to the Cartoon Network (or an adult who preferred the Cartoon Network to CNN) was a little bit strange.

From ancient times through the early modern period of the seventeenth century, the rough division into childhood, adulthood, and old age was sufficient. Philosopher Thomas Hobbes (1588–1679) wrote that life was "nasty, brutish, and short." Most people died during infancy or childhood; those who survived to see puberty were thrown into adulthood instantly. The few who managed to get through the next 20 years without succumbing to disease, war, accidents, feuds, or childbirth were considered elderly. The heroine of Jane Austen's famous novel *Emma* (1815) is asked how she will occupy herself in old age if she fails to marry, and she replies that she has an active mind and will find as much to do "at forty or fifty as at one-and-twenty."

Beginning about 1800, advances in sanitation, nutrition, and medical knowledge pushed up the average life expectancy in the United States and Western Europe. (**Life expectancy** is the average number of years that people born in a certain year could expect to live.) At the same time, the Industrial Revolution required that most children would grow up to work in factories and offices rather than on farms. They had to go to school to learn to read, write, and do basic arithmetic, and many of them stayed in school well into their teens. They weren't children anymore, but they weren't adults, either.

New stages of life were coined to accommodate the changes. According to the *Oxford English Dictionary,* the term *adult* entered the English language around 1656. **Adolescence** gained its current meaning, a life stage between childhood and adulthood, in the late nineteenth century. The adjective *teen-age* appeared during the 1920s, and the noun *teenager* in 1941. The stages advanced as well: Adulthood started near the end of the teens, and elderly meant over 60, then over 65.

Today, increasing affluence, better nutrition, and more sophisticated medical expertise have increased the average life expectancy (in rich countries). Now, we often become adults at 25 or 30, and "elderly" means well over 70. With such a longer life expectancy, we need more life stages than "childhood," "adolescence," "adulthood," and "old age." We now divide adulthood and old age into new stages roughly ten years apart:

- 25–35: young adulthood
- 35–45: "young" middle age
- 45–55: middle age
- 55–65: "old" middle age

Did you know?

Perhaps the most famous riddle of all time contains a metaphor of life stages. In ancient Greece, a monster called the Sphinx accosted travelers near the city of Thebes and asked them, "What is the animal that walks on four legs in the morning, two legs at noon, and three legs in the evening?" Anyone who gave a wrong answer was devoured!

Many tried to answer—all unsuccessfully—until a stranger named Oedipus stepped forward with the solution: "Man. He crawls on his hands and knees as a child, walks on two legs as an adult, and uses a cane in old age."

▲ Many cultures celebrate rituals that mark the end of one life stage and the beginning of another. An example of such a ritual is this Quineañera (a young woman's celebration of her fifteenth birthday) in Salina, Kansas.

- 65–75: "young" old age
- 75–85: "old" old age
- 85 and over: "oldest" old age (Moody, 1998)

Of course, the boundaries of these life stages are subject to lots of variation and change.

In most societies, the transitions between life stages are occasions of great importance, marked by important milestones, ceremonies, and rituals. Many nonindustrial societies require grueling rites of passage, such as weeks in a sweat lodge or embarking on some "spirit quest" in the wilderness. Today the many transitional stages of late childhood and adolescence are marked by bar mitzvahs, religious confirmations, high school and college graduations, coming-out parties (for young women entering fashionable society at age 18), and *quinceañeras* (for 15-year-old girls in Hispanic communities).

There are also a seemingly endless number of milestones, especially for the middle class: a first part-time job, a first full-time job, getting a driver's license, being allowed to vote or to drink alcohol, owning a first car, moving into a first apartment. Middle-class adulthood has fewer milestones, and many involve watching children go through the life stages. Late adulthood and the transition to old age are marked by a flurry of retirement ceremonies and often accompanied by cross-country moves.

Childhood

When you look at paintings and sculptures from medieval Europe, you may notice a curious phenomenon: Children are portrayed as miniature adults. The artists could certainly look around and see that a 10-year-old differed from a 30-year-old in shape, proportion, and features, but they were responding to a society that did not differentiate childhood as a separate stage of life. Children worked alongside the adults, boys mostly in the fields, girls mostly at home. They were smaller, so they received easier tasks to do, but there was no conception that childhood should be free of cares or responsibilities. The "miniature adults" had little free time for play and few toys and games to play with; only a tiny percentage went to school. They were not protected from knowledge about sex and death, as modern children are. At night, around the fire, they sang the same songs and listened to the same folktales as the adults, many of them sexually suggestive and very violent. Because they were not considered innocent, when they committed crimes, they received the same penalty as adults, including the death penalty. They could even be tried for witchcraft and burned at the stake (Ariès, 1962; deMause, 1976).

While some scholars disagree, Ariès (1962) and deMause (1976) argue that the Western concept of childhood, as a distinct stage of life, didn't emerge until the Industrial Revolution of the eighteenth century. Now most children would require training outside the home before they could go to work, so schools and apprenticeships became common, and books, toys, and games designed to train children in adult social norms began to appear in large numbers. When Dante wrote *The Divine Comedy* in the thirteenth century, he assigned unbaptized babies to limbo, a place between heaven and hell, but he put older children into hell along with everyone else. By the eighteenth century, Protestant theologians were arguing that children were innocent by nature, so they could not be held accountable for their

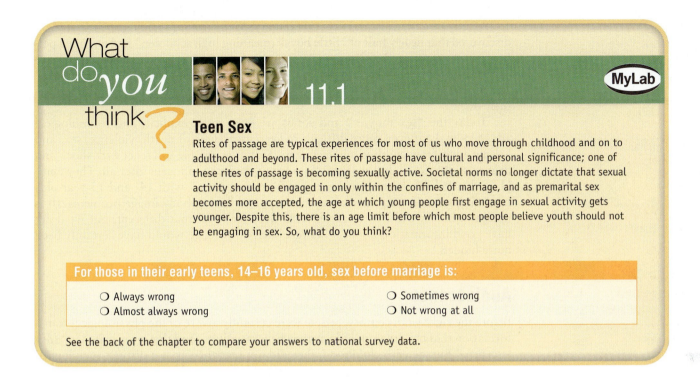

What do *you* think? 11.1

MyLab

Teen Sex

Rites of passage are typical experiences for most of us who move through childhood and on to adulthood and beyond. These rites of passage have cultural and personal significance; one of these rites of passage is becoming sexually active. Societal norms no longer dictate that sexual activity should be engaged in only within the confines of marriage, and as premarital sex becomes more accepted, the age at which young people first engage in sexual activity gets younger. Despite this, there is an age limit before which most people believe youth should not be engaging in sex. So, what do you think?

For those in their early teens, 14–16 years old, sex before marriage is:

○ Always wrong   ○ Sometimes wrong
○ Almost always wrong   ○ Not wrong at all

See the back of the chapter to compare your answers to national survey data.

sins and would invariably go to heaven. English common law agreed: Because children were innocent, they could not distinguish between right and wrong, and so they should not receive adult penalties for their crimes. By the nineteenth century, childhood was being conceptualized as a time of freedom and innocence. Child labor laws went into effect to ensure that children would not be put to work, and compulsory education, the YMCA, Boy and Girl Scouting, and high school sporting activities ensured that their lives would ideally consist of nothing but school and play.

There were gender differences in this new understanding of childhood. Boys were given time to play among themselves and receive the education and skills they needed for an adulthood in the world of factories and offices, while for many years girls stayed miniature women. They rarely went to school or played outside; they were expected to work alongside their mothers and older sisters in child care and keeping house. Even today, most boys' toys are about teamwork (balls and sports games), building or managing (construction sets, erector sets, Legos, blocks), and conquest (war toys, action figures), skills necessary for real-world businesses, while girls' toys are often about child care (dolls and stuffed animals), keeping house (kitchen sets, toy appliances), and beauty (makeup, jewelry-making, nail and hair care sets).

One of the major elements of our beliefs about childhood as a stage of life is that it is "innocent." Thus, we believe that children's actions do not carry the same consequences as those of adults (and so we often prosecute juvenile crime differently from adult crimes). We also believe that children must be shielded from information about sex and death. In the middle and upper classes, adults began to strictly censure their own behavior, as well as classroom lessons, toys, and children's media, to ensure that children would not lose their "innate" innocence. (The working classes and the poor, who lived in more crowded surroundings, were less able to control what their children saw and heard.)

Most of the concerns over childhood exposure to sex and death (or violence) began near the end of the nineteenth and beginning of the twentieth centuries. In his

1929 study of a typical American community, *Middletown*, sociologist Robert Lynd discovered that nearly half of "little boys" (meaning high schoolers) had attended petting parties (in those days "petting" meant kissing). This statistic was so contrary to his conception of childhood innocence that he blamed it on imitating "sex movies" and "sexually explicit songs," certainly nothing that the teenagers would think of on their own.

Today the "sex movies" and songs are even more explicit, and technological advances make it even more difficult to keep awareness of death, violence, sex, and kissing away from children and teenagers. However, people still react with shock and dismay to the possibility that childhood may not be so innocent after all. They complain that "children are growing up so fast these days," with 14- and 15-year-olds becoming sexually active, wearing makeup, and having body image problems. (It is unclear whether children of earlier eras were really all that different, but we don't have good information about it because such knowledge would have certainly been more hidden.)

Adolescence

Before the eighteenth century, people were certainly aware of the physiological transformation that children undergo as they become adults, and they even called it "adolescence." But, as with childhood, they did not recognize it as a distinct sociological stage. Through the eighteenth century, teenagers were also considered "miniature adults." Then they were considered "big kids," just as innocent and carefree. In fact, through the early twentieth century, they were expected to have the same pastimes and interests as younger children. But as labor became more specialized, children required more specialized training, not only in the 3 Rs (readin', writin', and 'rithmetic), but in Latin, algebra, bookkeeping, and world history: They had to go to high school. Between 1880 and 1940, the high school graduation rate increased from 2 percent to 50 percent, and the college graduation rate from under 2 percent to 9 percent. Faced with a deferment of adulthood from the early teens to the late teens or even later, adolescence became a new life stage between childhood and adulthood, with its own norms, values, pastimes, and pursuits.

Young Adulthood

Young adulthood is a transitional stage from adolescence, marking the beginning of our lives as fully functioning members of society. As with other life stages, its lower boundary has been gradually moving forward through the life span, from 18 to 25 to 30 and beyond. Many people still think of themselves (and are treated by others) as "aging adolescents" well into their thirties (see Arnett, 2004). On the TV sitcom *Seinfeld*, Jerry and George agree that it's "time to grow up" and act like young adults by getting married and having children (they already have jobs and their own apartments). They are about 40 years old.

Age 40 might be a bit out of the ordinary, but the boundary is moving forward because we're postponing most of the milestones that separate young adulthood from adolescence. Sociologists have identified five milestones that define adulthood: (1) establishing a household separate from our parents; (2) getting a full-time job so we are no longer financially dependent; (3) getting married; (4) completing our education; and (5) having children. Major structural changes in the economy, as well as media images that encourage us to stay young longer, have pushed the age at which we complete these from about 22 to close to 30 (see Arnett, 2004).

In 1950, close to half of all women in the United States were married for the first time by age 20 (and men a few years later). By 1975, the median age (when half were married) was 21, and today it's risen to about 25 (Settersten, Furstenberg, and Rumbaut, 2005).

We're starting families later, too. In 1970, the average age for women at the birth of their first child was 21.4 in the United States (men weren't asked). In 2000, it was around 25. One of the reasons for the delay is greater gender equality. Since 1970, the percentage of women graduating from college has nearly doubled, and the number in the labor force has gone up by nearly 40 percent (Arnett, 2004).

The age at first birth differs by race: 22.3 for African Americans, 25.9 for Whites, and over 30 for Asian Americans. Among Hispanic Americans, the age ranges from 22 for Puerto Rican and Mexican women to 27 for Cuban women (Centers for Disease Control, 2002). It also differs significantly by state, from 22.5 in Mississippi to 27.8 in Massachusetts. Both of these correlations probably reflect the lurking variable of socioeconomic class: Well-educated, wealthy and middle-class women are more likely to finish college or start their careers before they think about having children, while poor and working-class women are likely to start having children in their late teens or early twenties. We see the same pattern globally: In wealthy countries, women put off starting their families for several years after adolescence. The average age of a mother when she gives birth for the first time is 29 in Switzerland. But in West Africa, 55 percent of women have children in their teens (National Center for Health Statistics, 2006).

An extended period of education and training between childhood and adulthood has been required since the Industrial Revolution, but even today, for about 80 percent of the U.S. population, that training mostly ends at high school graduation, around the age of 18. So why is settling down to jobs, houses, and life partners rarely occurring at age 18 or even at age 22 for everyone anymore? The media have even invented a new term, **twixters,** for people in their twenties, years past their high school or college graduation but still culturally adolescent: living with their parents, having fun, and trying to discover "what they want to do when they grow up." (They also call it "KIPPERS," somewhat less positively: "KIPPERS" stands for "Kids in Pockets, Eroding Retirement Savings.")

Putting off all adult responsibilities may be a response to increased longevity: If I'm going to live 20 years longer than my grandparents did, then maybe I have 20 more years to "grow up." But it is also a response to the fluid nature of contemporary adulthood. Most people no longer select a career in their teens, find a job shortly after high school or college, and stick with it for the next 50 years. They change jobs every couple of years and switch careers three or four times in the course of their lives, going back to school for more training between and during each change; thus, "deciding on a career" is not a once-in-a-lifetime event restricted to adolescents but a lifelong process. What used to be strictly adolescent concerns now occupy people of every age.

Also, most people no longer go on lots of dates through high school and college, decide on "the one," and then marry and stay married for the rest of their lives. Of first marriages, 43 percent end in divorce, and 75 percent of people who divorce go on to remarry. Mate selection is not restricted to dances in the gym after high school football games but, like getting a job, is a lifelong process. The milestones that once spelled the entrance to adulthood, definitively and finally, now occur throughout life, so it is little wonder that people feel like adolescents at age 30, 40, 50, or even as old as 60. (Just watch Mick Jagger sometime.)

▲ "Twixters" or "adultoles-cents": Young people today take longer to make the transition from adolescent to adult than ever before. "Thirty is the new twenty."

Sociology and our World

Milestones of Adulthood

When students are asked to name some of the milestones between childhood and adulthood, they usually mention the ability to drive a car, vote, buy alcohol, and marry. But the legal age for these activities varies from state to state and from country to country, so you could get on an airplane as a legal "child" and get off as a legal "adult." Here are some of the more variable milestones:

- *Graduate from high school*. In Belgium, Germany, and the Netherlands, compulsory education ends at age 18. In the United States, it's 17. In most countries, it's 15 or 16. But you can leave school at age 12 in Afghanistan, Burundi, and Nicaragua, at 11 in Chad and Jamaica, at 10 in Iran, and at 9 in Angola and Myanmar (OECD, 2004).
- *Get a job*. The United States is one of 120 countries that have adopted the guidelines set by the International Labour Organization (ILO): Fifteen is the minimum age for most jobs and 18 for jobs likely to jeopardize "health, safety, or morals." But Sri Lanka and Turkey have set the minimum age for full-time work at 14, Paraguay at 13, and Peru and Zaire at 12. Many countries allow "light work" much earlier; in Thailand, at age 10 (International Labour Organization, 2006).
- *Lose your virginity*. The age of consent for sexual activity varies in the United States depending on whether you are a boy or a girl and on whether your partner is a boy or a girl. In New Hampshire, it's 16 for heterosexual and 18 for same-sex partners, regardless of their gender. In Montana, it's 14 for girls and 17 for boys in heterosexual relationships and illegal for same-sex partners at any age. Globally, the laws are even more varied. It's 14 (for everybody) in Iceland, 15 in France, and 16 in Venezuela. In Malta, it's

12 for girls and 18 for boys (gay or straight). In Burkina Faso, it's 13 for heterosexual partners and 21 for same-sex partners (male or female). (Avert, 2007; http://www.avert.org/aofconsent.htm.)

- *Get married*. In the United States, the minimum age for marrying in most states is 16 with parental consent and 18 without parental consent. It's higher in only one state, Nebraska (19). In most states, 14- or 15-year-olds can marry with the permission of a parent or guardian *and* a judge. Only five states—Mississippi, Alabama, Oregon, Rhode Island, and South Carolina—and the District of Columbia expressly forbid young teens (under 14, 15, 16, or 17, depending on gender and locale) to marry (Stritof and Stritof, 2003).
- *Drink alcohol*. The minimum age for purchasing or drinking alcoholic beverages in the United States used to vary from state to state, but now it's 21 everywhere. Most other countries set the minimum age at 16 to 18. Denmark has no minimum age for drinking, but you have to be 16 to buy alcohol in stores and 18 to buy it in pubs and restaurants. The United Kingdom allows children aged 5 and older to drink alcohol at home, but you must be 16 to order a beer at the pub. And a few countries, including China, Jamaica, and Spain, have no age restrictions at all: Drink all you want. (See Alcohol Problems and Solutions, 2007).
- *Join the army*. The minimum age for compulsory or volunteer service is 15 in Tanzania, 16 in Canada, 18 in the United States, 19 in Brazil, and 20 in Chad. In Norway, it's 18 in peacetime, 16 in wartime, 17 for male volunteers, 18 for female volunteers. In Bolivia, it's 14 for compulsory, 18 for volunteers. In Uganda "no one under the apparent age of 13 may be conscripted," but journalists have documented cases of 9- and 10-year-olds being taken from their homes and forced to bear arms (CIA, *World Factbook*, 2006).

Middle Age

Because they're starting young adulthood later, people are also starting middle age later, in their 50s instead of their 40s, but eventually they are bound to notice some physiological changes, not all of them positive: graying or balding hair, a decline in sexual potency, diminished muscularity, a drop in strength and endurance, and decreased metabolism coupled with an expanding waistline. But these changes do not begin at the same moment in everyone, and many can be forestalled by diet, exercise, and other lifestyle choices. Using sunscreen limits wrinkles; vision and hearing problems can be corrected; regular exercise can make the drop in strength and endurance so gradual as to be unnoticeable (who really cares that your speed in the mile run has decreased by 10 seconds during the last 10 years?). Many people who live relatively

How do we know what we know?

The "Midlife Crisis"

Two best-selling books of the 1970s, *Seasons of a Man's Life* (Levinson et al., 1978) and *Passages* (Sheehy, 1976) popularized the belief that middle-aged men (and to a lesser extent, women) go through a developmental "crisis" characterized by a pressure to make wholesale changes in their work, relationships, and leisure. For men, stereotypical responses to this pressure might include divorcing their wives to date younger women, pursuing lifelong ambitions, changing jobs, buying sports cars, and taking up adventurous and risky hobbies.

The idea of *midlife crisis* was embraced by a large segment of mainstream American culture. Middle-aged people found the concept intuitively compelling as a way of understanding changes in their own feelings and behaviors. Others employed it as a useful explanation of erratic behavior in their middle-adult parents or friends. Thirty years later, it remains a popular concept, the subject of pop psychology books and websites offering help for people (especially men) who struggle with the symptoms of the "crisis": depression, angst, irrational behavior, and strong urges to seek out new partners.

Despite the popular belief that male midlife crisis is universal and based on chronological age, careful research clearly demonstrates that this so-called crisis is not typical. Most men do not experience any sort of crisis in their middle-adult years. Disconfirming research became available shortly after the concept was introduced (Costa and McCrae, 1978; Valliant, 1978), and more recent research finds no empirical support for midlife crisis as a universal experience for either men or women (Wethington, 2000). Midlife does present a series of developmental challenges, and some middle-aged men do respond in ways that fit the stereotype. However, people go through challenges and crises in every life stage. The triggers are usually changes in work, health, or relationships rather than a mere accumulation of birthdays.

In the largest study to date on midlife, sociologist Elaine Wethington (2000) supported the findings of previous studies in demonstrating that midlife crisis is far from inevitable. However, she also found that more than 25 percent of those over age 35 surveyed (all residing in the United States) *believed* that they have had such a crisis. On further investigation, about half of these reports reflected only a time of stressful life events, not a sustained period of loss of balance and searching.

Belief in midlife crisis may partially hinge on what's called *confirmation bias*, whereby a single case or a few cases of the expected behavior confirm the belief, especially when the behavior is attention getting or widely reported. Less obvious disconfirming behavior is easier to ignore. In other words, if we happen to know a man who spent the year after his forty-fifth birthday getting a divorce, dating a 22-year-old, buying a sports car, and taking up skydiving, we might believe in the midlife crisis, even though we know a dozen other middle-aged men who have done none of these things.

healthy lifestyles experience decline mostly as a state of mind, an increasing awareness that they have passed the midway point of their lives.

Some of these changes are class and race related. Difficult manual labor obviously ages one more rapidly than working in an office, and painting houses will age you more quickly than painting on a canvas.

There may also be changes in workplace status and in roles as parents and partners. People may come to an understanding that their youthful dreams will never be realized: They will never be a great novelist or a rock star or drive an RV across the country. They will never hit it big. The lives they have now are, most likely, the lives they are going to have forever.

If there is a developmental task of middle age, then, it is this: acceptance. One must accept one's life as it is, and "put away childish things"—like the dreams that you will drive a Ferrari, sleep with a rock star or supermodel, be a multimillionaire, or get to say "you're fired" on national television. Many adults have a difficult time achieving that acceptance; indeed, the constant emphasis on youth and glamour makes it increasingly difficult.

In earlier generations, parents hoped that they would live long enough to see their children marry. Today they often live to see their grandchildren and great-grandchildren marry (or establish domestic partnerships). But the increase in longevity and the delay in childbearing means that many middle-aged adults find themselves in the **sandwich generation,** caring for dependent children and aging parents at the same time. For instance, say a woman has a child when she is 33 years old and her own mother is 63. She will have a toddler around the house during her mother's retirement years, and a child requiring care as her mother requires care. When her child goes off to college, she will be 51 years old, and her mother will probably still be living at 81. The sandwich generation is often stressed, worried, strapped, and squeezed. According to the General Social Survey, 70 percent felt stressed, compared to 61 percent of those without dual care responsibilities. On the other hand, 95 percent felt satisfied with their lives—about the same percentage as everyone else (General Social Survey, 2006).

Old Age

A hundred years ago, half of the population of the United States was under 23 years old, and only 4 percent was 65 or older. But the number of older Americans has increased dramatically: In 2009, they numbered 39.5 million, or more than 12.8 percent of the population (American Community Survey 2009). Between 1963 and 1976, the postwar baby boom grew into the largest generation of adolescents and young adultsthat the world had ever seen, and the echoes from that baby boom continue to resound across the United States and Europe (Figure 11.1). Jerry Gerber and his coauthors (1990) argue that in the next few decades, the dramatic growth in the proportion of people over age 65 will produce an "age-quake" with similar radical social transformations.

The projected increase of the population as a whole between 2000 and 2050 is 49 percent, but for the elderly it is 147 percent. By 2050, they will number 86.7 million, more than the entire U.S. population in 1900. They will comprise 21 percent of the population of the United States and about 20 percent of the population of the world (U.S. Census Bureau, 2000). The fastest-growing segment will be people 85 and older. There were 4.9 million in the United States in 2004, and by 2050, there will be 19 million (5 percent of the total population). (Table 11.1).

Two factors have led to the increase in the percentage of the population that is elderly and the gradual "graying of America." First, the birth rate has been declining for more than a century. In agricultural societies, children help out with jobs around the farm, so they are an economic asset. In industrialized societies, where people work as wage laborers in offices and factories, children can't help out, so they become an economic liability. (They still have to be fed and clothed, after all.) Also, the twentieth century saw more women working outside the home and therefore unable to raise a large number of children, and advances in birth control technology served to limit unexpected pregnancies. Although birthrates vary by race, ethnicity, region, and other sociological factors, overall there has been a downturn in births for all women during their peak childbearing years (Centers for Disease Control, 2003). The U.S. birthrate is at its lowest level since national data have been available and is 153rd in the world (CIA, *World Factbook*, 2006) (Table 11.2).

Second, while the birthrate has been going down, life expectancy has been going up. In the United States, it shot up over 20 years during the first half of the century, from 47.3 in 1900 to 68.2 in 1950 (Figure 11.2). During the last half of the century, it increased another 9 years or so, to 77.6 (National Center for Health Statistics, 2005). And the United States actually lags behind most of the wealthy nations, including Canada, France, Germany, New Zealand, Spain, the United Kingdom, and Japan. Andorra, a tiny country in the Pyrenees between France and Spain, currently has the highest life expectancy in the world (83.5 years) (U.S. Census Bureau, 2006).

Some of the increases were quite dramatic, depending on race and gender. Even occupation plays a role: People with high-prestige jobs live longer than those with low-prestige jobs, even after they are retired (Bassuk, Berkman, and Amick, 2002).

Advanced medical treatment also means that some of the major killers of elderly persons are decreasing. Between 2002 and 2003, the annual death rate from heart disease dropped from 240.8 to 232.1 per 100,000, and the death rate from cancer dropped from 193.5 to 189.3 per 100,000 (however, the death rate for Alzheimer disease was up 5.9 percent, hypertension 5.7 percent, and Parkinson disease 3.4 percent) (National Center for Health Statistics, 2006). Death rates for diabetes, along with the number of cases, are climbing (National Center for Education Statistics, 2006).

In poor countries, life expectancy did not rise significantly during the twentieth century. In fact, in sub-Saharan Africa, it actually decreased: In Malawi it is 37.6, in Botswana 39.3, and in Uganda 42.9 (World Health Organization, 2003). Not that people are dying of age-related illnesses like heart disease and cancer at the age of 37 or 39; malnutrition and disease, especially HIV, keep most people in these countries

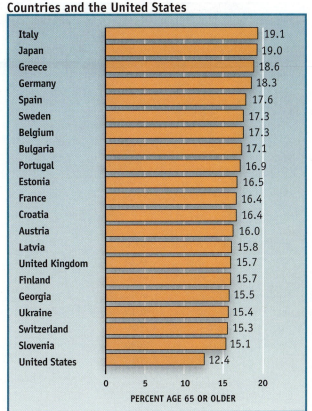

FIGURE 11.1 The World's 20 "Oldest" Countries and the United States

Country	Percent Age 65 or Older
Italy	19.1
Japan	19.0
Greece	18.6
Germany	18.3
Spain	17.6
Sweden	17.3
Belgium	17.3
Bulgaria	17.1
Portugal	16.9
Estonia	16.5
France	16.4
Croatia	16.4
Austria	16.0
Latvia	15.8
United Kingdom	15.7
Finland	15.7
Georgia	15.5
Ukraine	15.4
Switzerland	15.3
Slovenia	15.1
United States	12.4

Source: U. S. Census Bureau, International Database.

TABLE 11.1

REGION	YEAR	65 YEARS OR OLDER	80 YEARS OR OLDER
Percent of Population in Older Ages by Region, 2000, 2015, and 2030			
Asia	2000	5.9	0.9
	2015	7.8	1.4
	2030	12.0	2.3
Europe	2000	14.7	3.0
	2015	17.6	4.7
	2030	23.5	6.4
Latin America/Caribbean	2000	5.6	1.0
	2015	7.6	1.5
	2030	11.5	2.5
Middle East/North Africa	2000	4.4	0.6
	2015	5.5	0.9
	2030	8.4	1.4
North America	2000	12.4	3.3
	2015	14.7	3.9
	2030	20.0	5.4
Oceania	2000	10.1	2.3
	2015	12.4	3.1
	2030	16.3	4.4
Sub-Saharan Africa	2000	2.9	0.3
	2015	3.1	0.4
	2030	3.6	0.5

Source: U.S. Census Bureau, International Data Base.

Did you know?

According to the *Guinness Book of World Records*, the oldest verifiable person in the world was Jeanne Calment, a lifelong resident of Arles, France, who died on August 4, 1997, at the age of 122 years, 164 days. Her secret: She was "never bored." She took up fencing at age 85, rode a bicycle at age 100, and released a rap CD at 121. She finally gave up smoking at the age of 120, but not because she was worried about the long-term health consequences: She was blind and unable to see the cigarettes to light up.

from living to see middle age. Things are getting higher and lower, better and worse at the same time.

There are three life stages among the elderly. The "young old," ages 65 to 75, are likely to enjoy relative good health and financial security. They tend to live independently, often with a spouse or partner. The "old old," ages 75 to 85, suffer many more health and financial problems. They are more likely to be dependent. The "oldest old," ages 85 and higher, suffer the most health and financial problems (Belsky, 1990). However, these experiences vary enormously by class. For the lower classes, aging is often a crisis, in some cases a catastrophe. Working-class and poor people have the greatest number of health problems and the lowest rates of insurance, the least savings and retirement benefits, and the greatest financial needs.

As medical advances limit age-related health problems and more people plan on living for many years after retirement, the "old old" and even the "oldest old" may find themselves enjoying—or "enjoying"—the same quality of life as the "young old" of the earliest elderly life stages.

How long will people live in 2100 or 2500? If we calculate the data based on life expectancy between 1900 and 2000 and extrapolate it for several hundred years, we come up with a life expectancy of over 200. However, advances in medicine, sanitation, and nutrition can only go so far: Eventually the body wears out. Most scholars believe that the upper limit of life expectancy is 100, although a small percentage, blessed with the right genes, lifestyle, and luck, could live to see 120.

Aging and Dying

In 2005, a writer for *USA Today* asked people about their fears of growing old. Fifty-two percent responded "winding up in a nursing home"; 69 percent said "losing mental abilities"; 36 percent said "being alone"; 59 percent said "not being able to drive/travel"; and 49 percent said "not being able to work/volunteer." These myths about growing old have little basis in reality (Manning, 2005):

■ *Living in a nursing home.* The vast majority of elderly people maintain their own homes and apartments, and a large percentage live with relatives. Only about 5 percent live in continuous long-term care facilities (LTCFs) or nursing homes. This fear is really about losing independence, and it is true that about 20 percent of people over age 70 are unable to care for themselves without assistance (Kinsella and Phillips, 2005). However, most are nearing the end of their lives. A person who dies at the age of 80 will spend less than 3 years in a dependent state (Freedman, Martin, and Schoeni, 2002).

- *Losing mental abilities.* Alzheimers is one of several different root causes of senility, a gradual or sudden loss of cognitive function (thinking, reasoning, and memory). But less than 5 percent of the elderly develops any of the types (American Psychiatric Association, 2007). Some decline in learning and memory does occur after 70, but usually it is more of a nuisance than a tragedy, forgetting where you left your keys rather than forgetting your children's names. Even "nuisance" memory loss can be combated by continuing to learn and seek out new experiences. Seventy-three thousand elderly people are currently enrolled in college (National Center for Education Statistics, 2003). Some scholars believe that lifelong education will become as important as education for the young.

- *Being alone.* Some degree of loneliness is inevitable as long-term family and friends die or move away, but 71 percent of elderly men and 44 percent of elderly women live with a spouse or romantic partner, and a sizeable percentage live with relatives other than their spouses: 21 percent of White, 43 percent of African American, 49 percent of Hispanic, and 59 percent of Asian elderly (Wilmoth, DeJong, and Himes, 1997; Fields and Casper, 2001). Many others live with nonrelatives.

- *Having nothing to do.* This is usually a characteristic of income rather than age: It takes money to do things. The poor are likely to have nothing to do regardless of their age, but middle-class and affluent elderly tend to be more active in sports, hobbies, and religious and community groups than the middle-aged who are busy with their children and careers.

Nearly one-fourth (24 percent) of those surveyed by the *Washington Post* named "dying" as their number one fear about growing older, but only recently has death been associated with old age (Levine, 1999). From ancient societies through the European Middle Ages, poor nutrition, sanitation, and health care meant that the end of life often came in childhood, young adulthood, or middle age. The elderly (which meant anyone over 40) were not viewed as waiting for an inevitable decline and death but as very lucky to have cheated death for so long.

Today we see a similar pattern in many nonindustrial countries. The leading causes of death offer a clue. In Bangladesh, they are pneumonia, respiratory failure, accidental poisoning, and diarrhea. These diseases and accidents afflict young bodies more often than old and are fatal only when the immune system is compromised by poor nutrition and health care is inadequate.

TABLE 11.2

Selected Birthrates Worldwide

RANK	COUNTRY	BIRTHRATE (BIRTHS/1,000 POPULATION)
1	Niger	50.73
2	Mali	49.82
3	Uganda	47.35
34	Haiti	36.44
50	Iraq	31.98
93	India	22.01
103	Mexico	20.69
107	World	20.05
117	South Africa	18.20
133	Turkey	16.62
134	Brazil	16.56
153	United States	14.14
169	Australia	12.14
173	France	11.99
183	Canada	10.78
186	United Kingdom	10.71
207	Japan	9.37
222	Germany	8.25
223	Hong Kong	7.29

Source: CIA, *World Factbook*, 2006.

FIGURE 11.2 Life Expectancy at Birth, United States

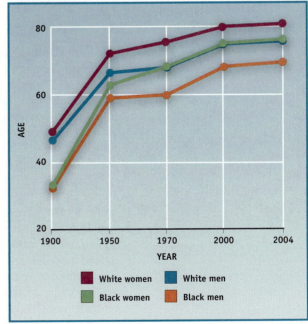

Source: Data from Centers for Disease Control and Prevention, 2006.

Sociology and our World

Why Women Live Longer Than Men

Because women live longer than men, the elderly are more likely to be female. In the United States, the ratio of men to women is about 8:10 for those 65 to 75, and by 85 it decreases to 4:10 (*The Economist,* 2005).

But why do women live longer? Physicians have speculated that women have stronger constitutions and more immunity to disease. They are less likely to fall victim to heart disease because testosterone increases the level of "bad" cholesterol (low-density lipoprotein) while estrogen increases the level of "good" cholesterol (high-density lipoprotein). British researcher David Goldspink (2005) found that men's hearts weaken much more rapidly as they age: Between the ages of 18 and 70, their hearts lose one-fourth of their power, but healthy 70-year-old women have hearts nearly as strong as 20-year-olds (but don't worry, regular cardiovascular exercise can slow or stop the decline).

Because the gap is decreasing, one cannot attribute this difference to biology. What sociological reasons might account for women living longer? Between the ages of 18 and 24, men are four to five times more likely to die than women, mostly from accidents: During this period of late adolescence and early adulthood, men often prove their masculinity through reckless and risky behavior, while women do not. At every age, men spend more time in the public sphere, where they are more likely to get into accidents, commit violent crimes, be victimized by crime, and be exposed to illnesses and hazardous material. Meanwhile, women spend more time at home. So, as gender inequality lessens and more women work outside the home, we would predict that the gap will decrease.

The problem is that the gap is decreasing everywhere, in both gender-polarized and gender-egalitarian countries: 5.80 years in Norway and 5.70 years in Sri Lanka, 7.95 years in France and 4.31 years in Mongolia. In fact, it seems to be shrinking more rapidly in gender-polarized countries: 2.51 years in Ethiopia, 1.81 years in Pakistan. And in seven countries, including Bangladesh, Malawi, Namibia, and Afghanistan, men are living longer than women.

Sociologists explain this by pointing out that rich and poor countries are diverging far more than women and men are in those countries. In poor countries, both women and men are increasingly susceptible to poor nutrition or health care, problem pregnancies, HIV, or violence and war. In wealthy countries, better health care and nutrition mean that both women and men are living longer. By 2040, European and American women will live to be about 100, and men will live to be 99 (Woods, 2005, p. 14).

In the United States, the leading causes of death are heart disease, cancer, stroke, and emphysema. These diseases are rare among the young; they come primarily in old age, as the body wears out (National Center for Health Statistics, 2006). Thus, we can conclude that death is very common among children and young adults in Bangladesh but very rare in the United States. In fact, the death rate in the United States is 1.0 or less per thousand for people under age 35 and about 2.0 per thousand for 35- to 45-year-olds. In the 45 to 55 age range, it jumps up to 4.32 per thousand, and in the 55 to 64 age range to 100.4 per thousand.

The rates and causes of death vary tremendously by age, sex, and race. Among 15- to 19-year-old men, for instance, the death rate is 0.55 per thousand for Asians and 0.89 for Whites. It nearly doubles to 1.32 per thousand for African Americans and 1.48 for Native Americans, while for women of all races, it's 0.40. We have to conclude that among teenage boys, African Americans and Native Americans tend to lead more hazardous lives than Whites or Asians, perhaps due to impoverished living conditions and the need to prove their masculinity through risky behavior. The leading cause of death is accidents for everyone except the African American men, who are more likely to die from assaults (National Center for Health Statistics, 2006).

Among 35- to 44-year-old men, the death rate is 1.6 for Asians, 2.34 for Whites, 3.75 for Native Americans, and 4.57 for African Americans. However, in this age cohort, women have a similar discrepancy: 0.67 for Asians, 1.26 for Whites, 2.24 for Native Americans, and 2.75 for African Americans. The leading cause of death is cancer for all women and Asian men, accidents for White and Native American men, and HIV for black men (National Center for Education Statistics, 2006).

Globally, leading causes of death vary from what we experience in the United States. Common diarrhea is the sixth leading cause of mortality throughout the world, killing roughly 1.8 million people each year.

Tuberculosis, largely a treatable disease in the United States, is the seventh leading cause of death around the world (World Health Organization, 2003). Living conditions, clean water, access to medicine and medical care, and other sociological factors affect these rankings.

Death is an individual event, but it is also a sociological phenomenon. Whether people die unexpectedly or not, a huge network of legal, social, economic, and religious structures come into play to establish memorials, negotiate inheritances and financial affairs, assist with the grieving process, and make sense of the death.

Psychologist Elisabeth Kübler-Ross (1969, 1981) counseled many people with incurable diseases and concluded that people faced with imminent death go through five stages. It is the job of counselors to guide them through the stages to the last stage, acceptance:

1. *Denial.* At first they cannot believe they are going to die. They think, "Obviously the doctor made a mistake." They avoid the topic and situations that remind them of it.

2. *Anger.* In this stage, they acknowledge that they will die but see their death as unjust: "I don't deserve this."

3. *Negotiation.* Next people try to bargain with God, or fate, or even with the disease itself: "Give me one more year with my family. Don't take me until after Christmas."

4. *Depression.* People become resigned to death, but they grieve because they have no power to change the fact that their life is about to end.

5. *Acceptance.* In this final stage, people come to terms with their death. They put their affairs in order. They may express regret at what they didn't do when they had the chance.

Since these stages were first proposed, though, sociologists have pointed out that this process varies among different groups, as do the meanings attached to dying (see Riley, 1983). Other cultures have a different view of death: For some it is simply the next phase of life and to be welcomed; for others, it is a "fact" and accepted more readily. Just as different groups view death differently, different cultures have developed different rituals to commemorate death.

Every culture treats death as a special event, and death and mourning are often linked to religious beliefs. There is archeological evidence that the earliest humans stained the bodies of the dead with red ochre before

Life stage rituals, including death, incorporate different cultural traditions. Here dancers perform a Dragon Dance in front of a coffin during a traditional Han funeral. ▼

Try It   Thinking Sociologically about the Lifespan

Modified from an activity submitted by Sharon Barnartt, *Gallaudet University*

OBJECTIVE: This activity will give you an opportunity to examine the life span by creating a visual graphic of the life span.

STEP 1: Plan

Think back to your grandparents' (or other people who are two generations older than you are) cohort and note the year(s) they were born. You will be choosing one of these years as a reference point for your life span graphic. You will be exploring what the various stages of the life span would have been like for one of your grandparents. Be sure to explore all stages of the life span including childhood, adolescence, young adulthood, middle age, and old age. Think about what social roles would have been expected of a person living in a particular stage at a particular time.

STEP 2: Research

Spend some time researching the various stages of the life span based on the time line you have chosen. There are

numerous sources available, but if possible consider interviewing your parents or grandparents.

STEP 3: Design

Design a life span graphic using poster board, magazine photos, clip art, and any other graphics that you think would help others understand the life span. Be creative and make sure you include a time line or graphic that illustrates the various stages.

STEP 4: Discuss

Be prepared to share your life span poster in class. As part of the discussion, examine what impact expected longevity would have had on someone during your time period and today. How has increased life expectancy changed the social expectations of "old age"? Do you think we treat the elderly better now than we did in the past? Explain.

burial, perhaps signaling some belief in an afterlife. Bodies are prepared for some type of removal from the world of the living, through either burial, cremation, or some other event. Ancient Egypt developed sophisticated mechanisms for embalming because only a fully intact body could pass over to the afterlife. Most cultures require some form of funeral and public mourning by relatives and the larger community. In some, mourners are required to be immensely sad, while in others the immediate family is supposed to celebrate the life passed with merriment and song and a big feast. Chinese funerals can be raucous, multiday affairs, with lots of ritual wailing and bands playing bad music to scare ghosts away. Often people buy paper houses, appliances, cars, and fake money to burn for the deceased to use in the afterlife. Chinese also celebrate *qing ming*, which is the day when people clean their ancestors' graves and burn fake money. Chinese are pragmatists . . . even in the afterlife!

What's important sociologically is that death is a process, not an event. Death may be the cessation of biological life, but its meaning changes dramatically from culture to culture. It is as much a cultural process as birth, maturation, and aging. Understanding how a group of people experience and explain death can provide a lens through which one can view the entire society.

Age and Inequality

Many societies place great value on the wisdom and authority that elders provide (Etzioni, 2005); *old* is a term of respect in Japanese, bestowed upon people who are not elderly at all. But in the West, and especially in the United States, *old* means feeble, fragile, worn out, and outdated. On *The Simpsons*, Grandpa Simpson is constantly the butt of jokes about his faulty memory, old-fashioned ideas, long-winded anecdotes, and inability to chew his food or control his bodily functions. The parents on *Lost* and *24* are not only intrusive, they're actually threatening; on *Lost*, Locke's father cons him into donating a kidney, steals his inheritance, and tries to kill him. Alex's father holds her hostage; her mother is insane. Ironically, Hispanic fathers (like Hurley's dad on *Lost* and Betty's father on *Ugly Betty*) fare much better; they're almost cool.

Physician Robert Butler, the first head of the National Institute on Aging, coined the term **ageism** in 1969 to refer to differential treatment based on age (usually affecting the elderly rather than the young). For instance, a housing development near his home in metro Washington, D.C., did not allow people over 65 to purchase homes. Many jobs are closed to people over 65 or even over 40 because potential employers believe that they are physically and mentally inferior to young people and therefore unable to handle the fast pace of the contemporary workplace. Some potential employers also believe that they have too few productive years to warrant investing in their training.

The declining status of the aged is not universal. For example, many cultures defer to the elderly; some even worship them. Among urban African Americans, sociologist Elijah Anderson found, being an "old head" is a venerable and venerated status, a sign that one had attained wisdom by surviving in a hostile world (Anderson, 1986).

The declining status of the elderly in the West can be traced back to the effects of the Industrial Revolution. In agrarian societies, elderly people couldn't do a lot of strenuous work, but because they had spent most of their lives working at the same tasks that the young people were currently doing, they had a great deal of knowledge about techniques and procedures to impart. They knew exactly when to plant and when to harvest, what herbs to use to improve the taste of the stew, how to cure a cough. Because social norms didn't change much from generation to generation, they had experienced precisely the same situations as the young people, and their accumulated wisdom regarding courtship or child rearing was invaluable.

Then the Industrial Revolution arrived, scientific knowledge began to advance at an astonishing speed, and social norms began to change every few years. Suddenly the knowledge that the elderly had acquired 30 years ago was obsolete, and their advice seemed painfully old fashioned.

In the factories and offices, older people did not train the younger. Children worked at jobs that their parents and grandparents knew nothing about, and the boss was a stranger rather than an older relative. The only option for older people was to apply for the same jobs as the younger people, but they were not as strong or agile, they had less education, and they wouldn't be able to offer employers 30 years of uninterrupted service. Thus, they gradually became less valuable. Just as children were weeded out of the work world through child labor and compulsory education laws, the elderly were weeded out through increased educational requirements and mandatory retirement laws.

Social institutions created a justification for this inequality by portraying the elderly as if they were children, irrational, cranky, irresponsible, lacking in common sense, and dependent, as contrasted with exuberant, energetic, progressive, intelligent young adults.

Hollywood pitched in, portraying young adults as extremely attractive and older people as unattractive, undesirable, and repugnant. An obsession with young adulthood has been relatively stable in movies, television, and print for the last century. In 1940, the top Hollywood heartthrob was probably Cary Grant, star of *My Favorite Wife* and *Philadelphia Story*, age 36. Twenty years later, it was probably Rock Hudson, star of *Magnificent Obsession* and *Pillow Talk*, age 35. In 1987, *People* magazine bestowed the honor of "sexiest man alive" on Harry Hamlin, age 36. In 2004, the honor went to Jude Law, age 32; in 2005 to Mathew McConaughey, age 36.

Age and Poverty

In 1959, 33 percent of elderly men and 38 percent of elderly women in the United States were living below the poverty level. Today, seniors as a whole are more affluent than ever before, in wealth (accumulated net worth) if not in annual income. In 2000, elderly households had a median net worth of $108,885, while households of those under 35 had a much smaller median net worth of $7,240. Of elderly people, 81 percent owned their own home in 2000, as opposed 68 percent of all householders (U.S. Census Bureau, 2001).

However, many elderly people lack the savings, investments, or pensions to be self-supporting after retirement. Most rich nations provide extensive benefits to their elderly populations, but the United States does not. Consequently, the poverty rate for senior citizens in the United States is about 10 percent—much higher than it is in other rich nations. The old are both richer and poorer than they ever have been.

In old age, inequalities based on race and gender are magnified. While they are age 18 to 64, African Americans and Hispanics are twice as likely to fall beneath the poverty threshold as their White non-Hispanic counterparts, but in the over 65 age group, they are *three* times as likely. Elderly women of all races are more likely to be poor than elderly men, and three times more likely when they reach the "oldest old" life stage of 85 and up (U.S. Census Bureau, 2001). When disenfranchised gender and racial categories are combined, the income inequality becomes more pronounced: 27.4 percent of elderly African American women and 21.7 percent of elderly Hispanic women are poor.

But these are only the percentages that fall below the official poverty threshold, $8,825 for an individual over age 65, and $11,133 for a couple (U.S. Census Bureau, 2001). A much higher proportion of elderly people are below 150 percent of the poverty threshold: nearly half of African American and Hispanic and a quarter of White individuals (Figure 11.3).

The **Social Security** program, begun in 1940, improved the financial situation of the elderly. Retired workers receive a monthly stipend based on how much they contributed to the program through their lives. Those who worked consistently throughout adulthood (for employers who participate) might receive $2,000 per month, but gaps in employment history decrease the stipend to a few hundred dollars.

Age inequalities are often compounded by inequalities of class, race, and gender. ▼

However, people who worked consistently throughout adulthood often receive pensions or other retirement provisions and so are less dependent on Social Security as their primary source of income. People who were poor during their adulthoods, unemployed, or working in low-income jobs that don't participate in the program, will receive the lowest stipends, even though they need the money the most. In old age, the rich get richer and the poor get poorer.

Another source of elderly income is the pension, a monthly stipend for those who have worked for the same employer for a specified number of years. The frequent job and career changes of contemporary workers mean that few stay in one place long enough to acquire a pension, and even when they do, the United States has one of the lowest pension benefits of all wealthy countries. Palme (1990, p. 93) calculated how well a pension replaces the worker's wage. In the United States, the minimum pension replaced only 53 percent of the worker's salary, far lower than

France (84 percent), Canada (85 percent), or Australia (100 percent) but higher than Japan (21 percent).

Today, the number of companies offering traditional pension plans and other retiree benefits, such as health care, is shrinking rapidly (Figure 11.4). Within two decades, barely one in eight retirees will be getting a guaranteed pension, and health insurance, offered by just 20 percent of companies in 2005, may disappear entirely (Gleckman and Miller, 2005).

Social Isolation

Loneliness is common among all life stages, but as people age, they are particularly vulnerable to social isolation, limited regular interaction with family, friends, and acquaintances (Goldscheider, 1990). Children may leave home and return to visit only occasionally. Retirement closes off work as a source of interaction. The elderly sometimes move to assisted living quarters, nursing homes, or retirement communities hundreds or thousands of miles from home and their long-standing social connections, and health and financial problems limit their ability to establish new ones. Family, friends, and spouses or life partners precede them in death, and negative stereotypes limit their interactions with the younger generation. Many experience social disengagement, a gradual withdrawal from feeling connected to their immediate communities or to the wider world. They may stop watching the news or reading newspapers, and they may keep up only with celebrity gossip.

Because women tend to live longer and spend more time without marital partners, they tend to feel the impact of social isolation longer than men. However, they are often more emotionally prepared for it because many did not work outside the home, or worked only part time, and therefore spent many hours alone through their lives. When the AARP conducted a poll of elderly heterosexual couples, 83 percent of the men and 67 percent of the women believed that their spouses were prepared to live alone (AARP, 2001).

Retirement

Work not only provides money and an opportunity for social interaction, it brings social prestige, personal identity, and a purpose in life. Its end, therefore, can have a devastating impact. We all have heard of people who were in good health yet died within months of their retirement. Perhaps the most poignant story is of cartoonist Charles Schulz, creator of the *Peanuts* comic strip, who died the day he drew Charlie Brown and Snoopy for the last time. (He had announced his retirement because he had cancer.)

Retirement is also a mark of social status. High-status professionals, managers, and sales workers are less likely to retire because their jobs are less physically demanding and more flexible than those of laborers, machine operators, and low-status clerical workers (Hayward and Grady, 1990).

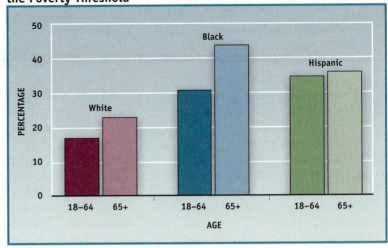

FIGURE 11.3 Individuals Living below 150 Percent of the Poverty Threshold

Source: U. S. Census Bureau, Current Population Survey, 2003.

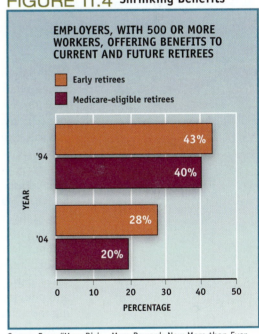

FIGURE 11.4 Shrinking Benefits

Source: From "More Risk—More Reward: Now More than Ever, Retirees are on Their Own" by Howard Gleckman and Rich Miller, *Business Week,* July 25, 2005.

However, the idea of retirement as an abrupt transition from work to leisure belongs to the past. Today it is hard to determine who is a retiree and who is not. Many elderly people continue to work, at least on a part-time basis, by necessity or to add social contacts and give their life a sense of purpose. Elder and Pavalko (1993) found that 30 percent of their sample retired abruptly, 8 percent did not retire at all, and 62 percent had other sorts of transitions: They worked part time, found new jobs, retired for a few months and then returned to work, or held "bridge jobs" between their old employment and retirement.

These trends are on track to increase. When AARP asked baby boomers how they envision their retirement, 79 percent said they plan to work in some capacity during their retirement years (AARP, 2001). A nationwide survey of all U.S. workers found that 68 percent plan to continue working in some capacity after retirement (Employee Benefits Research Institute, 2004). Many organizations have instituted phased retirement, a gradual decrease in duties and responsibilities over several years rather than a sudden "farewell" (Gardyn, 2001; Walsh, 2001). Universities have long had such a system: Emeritus faculty have no official teaching duties, but they keep their offices and can continue their research, and they may occasionally give lectures or teach seminars as long as they live.

Elder Care

Before the twentieth century, family members were expected to take care of their elderly parents, grandparents, aunts, and uncles. The few elderly people with no surviving relatives, or with relatives not interested in caring for them, might find their way into a convent or monastery, but more likely they would end their days as beggars. Today, family members still provide about 80 percent of elder care, providing services estimated at $257 billion per year (National Family Caregivers Association, 2007). However, the birthrate is decreasing, so a much larger proportion of the elderly population has no close relatives, and the increased life expectancy means an increased incidence of health problems severe enough to require professional care. So who is taking on that burden?

Many industrialized societies have institutionalized elder care through a series of nursing homes, hospitals, and other institutions. While the general quality of care is acceptable, it depends significantly on class. In many places, poorly paid staff at underfunded and overcrowded institutions leads to neglect and even elder abuse. In some cases, patients are treated as "inmates" serving a life sentence and are overmedicated and undervalued. Even the best nursing homes "deny the personhood of age" by seeing the aging process as "inevitable decline and deterioration," according to feminist writer Betty Friedan (1993, p. 516).

While these stories may provide fodder for tabloid TV and newspapers, often serving to increase the guilt of the younger generation that placed the elderly there in the first place, the elderly are just as likely to experience abuse and neglect if they stay with their families as if they are in institutions. And most Americans do care about the elderly. According to a survey from the National Alliance for Caregiving (2004), 40 percent of family caregivers worry about the well-being of the person they care for nearly every day, more often than they worry about their children, their job, retirement savings, their partner's health, the stock market, or terrorism. Yet they must constantly juggle caregiving with their work and personal commitments: 80 percent work full time in addition to their caregiving, and 40 percent are raising children under 18 (Chatzky 1999; National Alliance for Caregiving, 2004; Velkoff and Lawson, 1998).

Few have siblings to help out (31 percent believe that caregiving has increased family tension).

They are "squeezed from all sides," negotiating with doctors, outside specialists, part-time caregivers, and their own family, coordinating their own lives and everyone else's lives, feeling guilt and stress over their loved one's decline, and worrying that their loved one is receiving inadequate care. Half of the family caregivers surveyed report that their care recipient had missed meals or suffered poor nutrition, a third were involved in accidents that required emergency room care, and 22 percent were home alone when an emergency occurred. Half of the surveyed caregivers believed that their care recipient needed 10 or more hours of extra care per week.

Most caregivers also have full-time jobs, and so they must "outsource" caregiving while they work. Of those with full-time jobs, 43 percent spend more than $500 per week for that extra care, and 20 percent spend more than $1,000 per week. And since Medicare covers less than 20 percent of elder care costs, they often subsidize the additional care themselves, with enormous economic consequences: Women who assume caregiver roles are more than 2.5 times more likely to live in poverty than noncaregivers, and the proportion increases dramatically when they are non-White (Donato and Wakabayashi, 2006).

Other economic consequences are more subtle: Caregiving limits the types of outside jobs one can take and the opportunities for advancement. Thirty-seven percent of women caregivers must go from full-time to part-time work, and 35 percent give up working entirely in order to meet their caregiving responsibilities (National Alliance for Caregiving, 2004). This absence from wage work affects not only current earnings but also Social Security and pension benefits down the road.

Boomers, Busters, and Boomlets: The Generations of Youth

Many GIs returning from World War II took advantage of low-interest student loans, cheap suburban housing, and a hugely expanding economy to enter the middle class, marry, and have children—lots of children. A postwar baby boom, lasting from 1945 to about 1964, created a big bulge in the populations of Europe and North America. This created the biggest age cohort in our history—77 million in the United States. As the **baby boomers** passed through childhood, America became a nation wholeheartedly dedicated to child rearing, with new schools and libraries, a surge in children's television and other forms of mass media, and new techniques of child rearing: Dr. Spock's *Baby and Child Care*, first published in 1946, sold more than 50 million copies, putting it in almost as many homes as the Bible (CNN, 1998).

As the first wave of baby boomers, born in the late 1940s through the early 1950s, passed through their adolescence beginning around 1960, America shifted its emphasis from childhood to adolescence. There was a surge in youth-oriented magazines, movies, television programs, and songs. College attendance soared. The "now" generation, the counterculture, was wholeheartedly dedicated to social and political change, transforming norms, expectations, and ideas. It was an era of expansion—an expanding economy, expanding social rights, and expanding consciousness. The Civil Rights movement, the women's movement, and the gay/lesbian movement all started or increased their momentum while the baby boomers were college students and young adults.

The first boomers hit middle age around 1980, and America shifted its emphasis again, from adolescence to middle age. A new era of conservatism began, with concern for the "midlife crisis," and the "now generation" became the "me generation."

In the first years of the twenty-first century, this wave of baby boomers is reaching retirement age, and they promise to have an enormous impact on the Social Security system, health care, and ideas about what it means to be old. They are "staying young" (through exercise, attitude, and plastic surgery), redefining what is appropriate at different stages in the life course, and revising the expression "Act your age!" by answering "What age?" Once being over 65 was considered "over the hill," the "sunset years." But they've been transformed into "the golden years" and even the "power years" (Dychtwald, 2005).

Boomers are often portrayed as a single group with a shared history and similar demographic characteristics. They are White, well educated, liberal, affluent, innovative, and obsessed with self-discovery, stereotyped as Dustin Hoffman in *The Graduate* (1967), Peter Fonda in *Easy Rider* (1968), or Ryan O'Neal and Ali McGraw in *Love Story* (1970). But they are actually a very diverse group. About 30 percent are people of color (12 percent Black, 10 percent Hispanic, 4 percent Asian and 4 percent "other"). Twelve percent of early and 15 percent of late boomers are immigrants (including 86 percent of all foreign-born Latinos and 57 percent of foreign-born Asians in the country). The economic disparities between White and non-White boomers are as profound as in any other generation. Many members are poor or conservative. The baby boom lasted for 20 years, after all, so the earliest boomers are a full generation removed from the latest (and could even be their parents) (Hughes and O'Rand, 2004).

Generation X (Baby Busters)

The generation that followed the baby boom cohort (those born 1945 to 1954) has been called baby busters, or also **generation X** (from Douglas Coupland's 1991 book). There weren't many of them. A society can maintain a stable population with a fertility rate of 2.1; that is, 2.1 lifetime births per woman (the 0.1 because typically 5 to 10 percent of a population does not reproduce). But since 1970, the fertility rate in rich countries has been lower than 2.1, sometimes considerably lower.

In 2006, the United States was the highest of any rich country, at 2.05; the fertility rate was 1.98 in France, 1.79 in the United Kingdom, and 1.32 in Japan (Hong Kong was the lowest, at 0.98) (Population Reference Bureau, 2007). These countries are stable rather than depopulating because population is determined by many factors besides fertility, including infant mortality, longevity, and immigration.

Still, a stable population after years of enormous expansion means school closings, sharp declines in college enrollment, and a decrease in television, movies, and other mass media aimed at children or families. The 10-year-old boomers of 1963 could spend their evenings watching the kid-friendly *My Favorite Martian, Beverly Hillbillies, Ozzie and Harriet,* and *My Three Sons;* even *The Flintstones* was on prime time. In 1973, 10-year-old gen-Xers could watch the more adult-oriented *All in the Family, The Mary Tyler Moore Show, Maude, The Bob Newhart Show,* and *M*A*S*H.* Gen-X often felt like an afterthought for the "me generation."

Like the boomers, gen-Xers are often seen as a homogeneous group of White, middle-class, affluent liberals, but they are predictably as diverse as their parents: 35 percent are Black, Hispanic, or Asian. They are, however, dominated by single men: In 1972 to 1973, unmarried males outnumbered unmarried females by a ratio of 54 to 46; by 1994 to 1995, the ratio had increased to 62 unmarried males and 38 unmarried females (Paulin and Riordon, 1998).

Although they are often derided as slackers and whiners, gen-Xers really are worse off economically than their boomer parents. The average individual income dropped dramatically between the early 1970s and the 1990s, especially during the 1980s when the first gen-Xers were entering the work world. Female income dropped less sharply than the male (and actually increased a little during the 1980s), but this had more to do with a sharp drop in men's income than any rise in the women's. The income decline was compounded by race. Young African Americans lost three times more income than Whites between 1972–1973 and 1984–1985, and four times more between 1984–1985 and 1994–1995 (Paulin and Riordan, 1998).

Gen-Xers also experienced a decline in educational opportunity and attainment (Paulin and Riordan, 1998). In 1972–1973 over 50 percent of young unmarried persons were college graduates, but by 1984–1985 this had dropped to 30 percent. More X-ers were living at home after college, and more were going to college part-time, combining working and education. The costs of independence were simply out of reach of many, if not most, college-age people.

Generation Y (A Baby Boomlet)

The sheer number of baby boomers born at the end of the baby boom meant that during their young adulthood, between about 1975 and 1995, a new wave of births occurred, a 60-million-strong "echo boom" or "baby boomlet." This cohort, known as **generation Y,** is three times the size of generation X; they began to reach young adulthood in the mid-1990s. They have received a lot of media attention, and many clever journalists have conjured up a variety of names for them: "the millennial generation" (because most will come of age after 2000), "generation next," "nexters," "generation Y," "boomlets." In the United Kingdom, they are the "new mills"; in Canada, "the echoes."

A sizeable proportion of gen-Yers (35 percent) are minorities (Figure 11.5). This trend, plus high rates of immigration, will increase the proportion of minority children in America's schools, colleges, and workplaces in coming years (U.S. Census Bureau, 2000).

Generation Y is the first generation to fully experience the transformation of American households: Three in four have working mothers, and one in four lives in a single-parent household. (In 1965, according to the U.S. Census Bureau, 25 percent of mothers were working, and 8 percent of children lived in single-parent households.)

This is also the first generation to embrace the widening impact of the information revolution. Generation Y grew up with PCs at home. They can download music and play games on the Internet, and they find Web surfing perfectly ordinary. Today, 91 percent of college students, the leading edge of generation Y, own their own computers; 95 percent go online regularly; and 36 percent own mobile Web-access devices (Harris, 2004). They have instant messaging, cell phones, Blackberries, and blogs. Baby boomers grew up with three or four television stations; generation Y has hundreds.

FIGURE 11.5 Racial and Ethnic Composition of the Baby Boom and Baby Boomlet (Gen Y) Generations

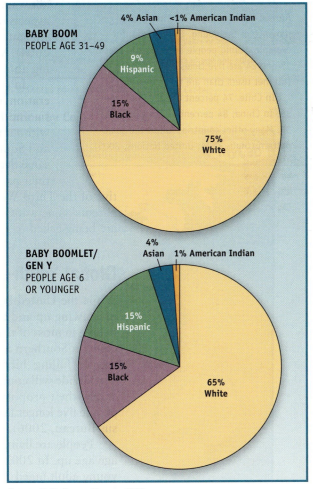

Source: U. S. Census Bureau, 2000.

nomena ove
study attitud
Have people
conservative
I could o
comparing t
various poir
instance, I t
in Pasadena
to have the
issue tested
every 10 ye
30-year-old:
olds. This m
difficulties:

▲ Although often stereotyped as lazy slackers, American teenagers are also industrious, productive, and hard-working.

▲ Globally, nearly 250 million children aged 5–17 are in the workforce, many doing adult jobs. Thirty percent of child laborers are under 10 years old. These girls are working in a carpet factory in Morocco.

jobs. Twenty-eight percent of White teenagers worked during the school year and 38 percent during the summer, a significantly larger percentage than for African Americans (13 percent and 20 percent) or Hispanic youth (15 percent and 20 percent). Boys are employed slightly more often than girls.

The average adolescent worker earned $5.57 per hour in 1998, slightly above minimum wage, for about 17 hours per week during the school year and 23 hours during the summer. Among the most common jobs for boys were stock handlers and baggers, cooks, cashiers, and farm workers; for girls the most common jobs were cashiers, sales clerks, waitresses, and child care providers. A small percentage of adolescents were self-employed, most commonly in jobs also available to younger children, such as mowing lawns (Bureau of Labor Statistics, 2000).

Globally, the statistics are much different. In 2000, 246 million children aged 5 to 17 were in the workforce, one out of every six. Thirty percent of them were under 10 years old. The largest numbers appear in Asia and the Pacific, but sub-Saharan Africa has by far the highest percentage of children under age 15 in the work force (22.0 percent), followed by Asia (15.3 percent). By comparison, Europe has only 0.3 percent of children under 15 in the labor force (International Labour Organization, 2006) (Figure 11.8). These children and adolescents are not working for spending money: They are contributing to family finances, often providing a major source of income. Their jobs differ considerably from the teen workers in the United States: 70 percent are in agriculture, 8 percent in manufacturing, 8 percent in retail trade, and only 7 percent in service industries, including domestic work and child care.

Many child laborers work long hours that prohibit them from going to school or having a leisure life; according to the International Labour Organization, over half work for 9 or more hours per day, 7 days a week, with no holidays. About 70 percent work for no pay, and the others receive a fraction of what adults would receive; one international study (International Labour Organization, 2006) found them being paid a sixth of the standard adult wage. Three-quarters (184 million) work under hazardous conditions, exposed to dangerous chemicals or using dangerous tools. They do not receive sufficient exposure to fresh air and have little freedom of movement. They may be beaten and abused. Over 20 percent suffer physical injuries; many others suffer irreparable psychological harm.

Their situations vary, and not all are unpleasant or exploitive, but for every 16-year-old studying college chemistry from behind a counter at the family shop, there are a dozen 4-year-olds tied to rug looms to keep them from running away.

The New Slavery. Global trafficking transports people far from their homes for forced, bonded, and illegitimate labor. There are about 30 million victims worldwide (nearly three times as many as were victimized by the African slave trade of 1500–1830), including over 1 million children (International Labour Organization, 2006). Most are seeking an escape from poverty; they are likely to be from disenfranchised tribal groups, castes, or minority groups. Many are refugees. They may be lured from their homes with the promise of good jobs or an education overseas, but some are sold by their parents, and some are kidnapped outright. They are crammed onto boats or trucks with insufficient food, water, and air, and transported thousands of miles from home. When their "employers" are threatened with discovery, the children are abandoned in border regions or killed (International Labour Organization, 2006).

The destination of these children differs depending on region and local culture, but it follows the general trend of globalization: Raw materials and labor flow from the less-developed countries to the more developed:

- From Latin America to North America
- From Russia and Eastern Europe to Western Europe
- From West Africa to Western Europe and the Middle East
- From Cambodia, Myanmar, and Vietnam to Thailand
- From Thailand to Australia and New Zealand
- From Nepal and Bangladesh to India
- From India to the Middle East and Western Europe

When the children finally reach their destination, the "good job" turns out to be poorly paying or unpaid domestic, factory, or farm work. They are not permitted to leave their jobs, and if they do, they have nowhere to go. They are in a strange country where they do not speak the language. Their parents are a continent away and have no resources to get them back. They cannot seek other help because they are in the country illegally, with no papers, and the authorities are usually corrupt. They are virtual slaves—if they are lucky. Trafficked children are more likely than others to fall prey to the worst forms of child labor defined by the International Labour Organization (2006).

The Worst Forms of Child Labor. Forced and bonded labor occupies 5.7 million children and adolescents. A little over 1 million have been trafficked, transported to other regions or countries, and the rest work close to home (International Labour Organization, 2006).

FIGURE 11.8 Regional Variations in Child Labor

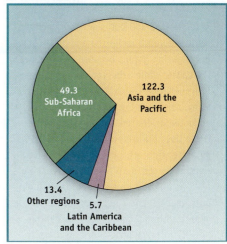

Source: © International Labour Organization 2006. Reprinted by permission.

Most jobs in forced and bonded labor are technically legal, on farms and in factories, but 1.8 million work in the global sex trade, as prostitutes or performers in pornographic videos. Most are girls, but an estimated 10 to 30 percent are boys. Procurers prefer children to adults because they are easy to control, and can be promoted to potential clients as virgins and therefore disease free (International Labour Organization, 2006).

Another 600,000 are employed in criminal activities other than the sex trade (of course, a sizeable percentage do both). Usually their jobs involve drug manufacture or distribution, but they can also engage in pickpocketing, shoplifting, car theft, and burglary. Most are boys. Procurers prefer them to adults because they can move about freely, cause less suspicion, and receive lenient punishment when they are caught (International Labour Organization, 2006).

Adolescents and children have been commandeered for armed conflicts in Africa, Asia, Latin America, and the Pacific. Some countries permit the conscription of 13- or 14-year-olds, and others simply fail to regulate its conscription process (in Bolivia, 40 percent of the armed forces are under 18 years old). Intertribal conflicts and terrorism also draw upon underaged operatives. Most are boys, but a sizeable number of girls are conscripted as well. A few become soldiers, and the others become servants or camp prostitutes (Human Rights Watch International Labour Organization, 2006).

Getting Older *and* Getting Better? Youth and Age in the 21st Century

Recently, a student came to my office wondering why she was getting a C in the class, when she had gotten straight A's before. In fact, she was getting C's in all her classes this semester, and she couldn't understand why. Had anything in her life changed this semester, I asked? Nothing except turning 21. Well, that and the fact that she was working full-time now, in addition to a full course load, partly because at age 21 she was no longer covered under her family's health plan. I suggested that she might consider cutting back on her work hours. No, she said, she needed the money. Okay, then how about cutting back on her courses? No, she said, she needs them to graduate. Well, then, I asked, can you learn to be happy with C's?

Faced with what appeared to be an impossible decision, she looked me straight in the eye and said, "It sucks to be old." (And, given the continued inequality based on age, it probably sucks to be young as well.)

The status of elders may rise as baby boomers start hitting retirement age, and because boomers grew up at the start of the information revolution, they will have the computer expertise that previous cohorts of the elderly lacked. Aging will continue to change.

But more than that, young people and old people are constantly changing the meaning of age in our society. In the future we will certainly live longer lives, and children will delay assuming full adult responsibilities for longer and longer periods— that is, we will be both old and young for a longer amount of time. It remains to be seen whether living longer will enable all of us to also live better or whether the rich will live longer and happier lives and the poor will live shorter, unhappy lives.

1. *What is "old" and "young"?* Sociologists view age as a social construction, meaning it is not the number but the social environment that determines what age means. Age of marriage and other social expectations depends on the meanings society gives to age. Children used to be viewed as adults very early; today they are postponing adulthood until much later. Age is one of society's major social identities and is a basis for inequality. Most inequality based on age affects either the very young or the very old. All societies divide members by age, and individuals are sorted into age cohorts, groups in which people experience similar life experiences and norms for behavior. With increased life expectancy and laws about child labor, age groups and definitions have changed. Transitions between age stages are often marked by rites of passage and other milestones, although the tasks and milestones of age groups are now blurred and have lost some meaning.

2. *How are ages sorted?* The Western concept of childhood developed with the Industrial Revolution and the societal changes it brought. The new social order required people to work outside the home, and schooling was required to socialize young people into the world of work. This socialization was different by gender; boys were prepared for factory work, girls for work in the home. As labor became more specialized, children needed more training and began to go to high school, creating a new life stage, adolescence. Young adulthood is a transitional stage, marked by milestones such as establishing a household, having a full-time job, getting married, completing education, and having children. Middle-aged individuals are dealing with changes in workplace and parenting status. Many middle-aged people are in the sandwich generation, caring for children and parents simultaneously. Currently, the fastest-growing segment of the U.S. population is among those in old age, a situation referred to as the "graying of America."

3. *How is age related to inequality?* While many societies revere those in old age, most Western societies do not. These attitudes can lead to ageism, or differential treatment based on age. The status of the elderly in the West is derived from social changes brought about by the Industrial Revolution. Social norms changed quickly, and the knowledge of older people became less relevant. Their decreased importance in the workplace led to differential treatment in society, which is justified by the creation of a cultural ideology portraying old people as inept children. As society changed, the place of the elderly changed. While more older Americans are wealthier than ever before, many are also living in or near poverty and lack the resources to make ends meet. As in any group, inequality is magnified when intersected with minority status.

4. *How are the generations distinguished?* The biggest age cohort in U.S. history is the baby boomers, those born roughly between 1945 and 1964. Because they are such a large group, their presence changed society in many ways. When they were children, the nation was focused on child rearing. When they were adolescents, the culture focused on that stage of life. The boomers themselves changed the landscape of society with their active participation in the Civil Rights, women's, and gay rights movements. When the boomers became middle aged, the concerns of society shifted into a new era of conservatism. Now the boomers are redefining what it means to be old. The baby boomers were followed by generation X, a smaller cohort. Because they are smaller, the culture focused less on them, and individuals in this generation experienced a decline in their standard of living. The children of the baby boomers, generation Y, followed and are a larger population. They are also the first generation to embrace new technology and new media as ways of living.

5. *How does inequality manifest among the young?* While older individuals have power as a group and own more wealth than the young, the young are relatively powerless. The poverty rate for children is higher than that for any other group. Many children have no health insurance, and when they turn 18, over half of them have no health insurance, as they are kicked off their parents' policies. Often, children have to work in order to survive. While child labor is regulated in countries such as the United States, globally one in six children works. Many are taken into global slavery and sold as sex workers or put into other criminal activities.

What does *America* think?

11.1 Teen Sex

This is actual survey data from the General Social Survey, 2004.

For those in their early teens, 14 to 16 years old, sex before marriage is: always wrong according to 70 percent of all respondents in 2004. Women were more likely than men to report thinking it was always wrong. Another 17 percent of respondents thought it was almost always wrong. Ten percent thought it was sometimes wrong, and almost 4 percent thought it was not wrong at all. Middle-class respondents seemed to be more conservative in their views on teen sex, while upper-class respondents seemed to be the most liberal.

CRITICAL THINKING | DISCUSSION QUESTIONS

1. Why do you think women are more conservative in their views toward teen sex than men?
2. How do you explain the social class differences in responses about attitudes toward teen sex?

11.2 Adult Children and Older Parents: The Sandwich Generation

This is actual survey data from the General Social Survey, 2004.

As you know, many older people share a home with their grown children. Do you think this is generally a good idea or a bad idea? According to 2004 GSS survey results, almost half of respondents thought it was a good idea, and almost half thought it was a bad idea. About one-fifth said it depends. There was very little difference among responses when separated by class or gender, but there was significant disparity when separated by race. White respondents were least likely to think it was a good idea and most likely to think it was a bad idea. About half of Black respondents thought it was a good idea. The category of "other" had the highest percentage of respondents thinking it was a good idea.

1. How would you account for the racial differences in responses? The largest numbers of individuals in the category of "other" are of Hispanic or Asian descent. Can you think of any cultural explanations for the disparity? Why do you think there was very little difference based on gender or social class?

▶ Go to this website to look further at the data. You can run your own statistics and crosstabs here: **http://sda.berkeley.edu/cgi-bin/hsda?harcsda+gss04**

REFERENCES: Davis, James A., Tom W. Smith, and Peter V. Marsden. General Social Surveys 1972–2004: [Cumulative file] [Computer file]. 2nd ICPSR version. Chicago, IL: National Opinion Research Center [producer], 2005; Storrs, CT: Roper Center for Public Opinion Research, University of Connecticut; Ann Arbor, MI: Inter-University Consortium for Political and Social Research; Berkeley, CA: Computer-Assisted Survey Methods Program, University of California [distributors], 2005.

chapter 12

ALMOST DAILY, WE HEAR some political pundit prophesy the end of the family. The crisis of the family is so severe that in 2000, the U.S. Congress passed a Family Protection Act, as if the family were an endangered species, like the spotted owl. Divorce and remarriage have never been more common. Millions of children are growing up with single parents or in blended households. Millions of young adults are putting off marriage until their 30s, or cohabiting instead of getting married, or opting to stay single. People are selecting house-hold arrangements today that would mystify our ancestors. Even the conservative U.S. Bureau of the Census has given in and added the category "cohabiting partners" to the old litany of single, married, widowed, or divorced.

On the other hand, the family has never been more popular. Suddenly, everyone seems to want one: single people, gay men and lesbians, even the elderly and widowed. Prime-time TV, which used to make fun of the nuclear family with shows like *Married . . . with Children,* is overloaded with moms, dads, and kids. And the wedding industry generates sales of about $50 billion every single year.

The Family

The family is in crisis. The family has never been more popular.

The gay marriage debate is a good example of both sides of the argument. Opponents say it would wreak "a potentially fatal blow to the traditional family," leading "inexorably to polygamy and other alternatives to one man/one woman unions" (Dobson, 2004). At the same time, gay couples across the country have been eager to pledge their love and commit-ment by getting married. And millions of supporters believe matrimony should not be limited to only some couples

Is the family in crisis—or has it never been more popular, or more supported? We believe both—in part, sociologists understand, because both are true.

but open to everyone who wants to enter into it. How much more popular can the idea of marriage get?

The great novelist Thomas Wolfe said "you can't go home again." A few years earlier, the poet Robert Frost wrote that "Home is the place where, when you have to go there, they have to take you in." We believe both statements—in part, sociologists understand, because both are true. The family has never been more popular in part *because* it is in crisis—and all the cultural media, from TV to movies to pop songs, are trying to reassert its predominance in an increasingly individualized and global world. And the family is in crisis in part *because* of those institutional forces, like the global marketplace and its ideology of individualism, which constitute the dominant ideology around the world.

One thing is certain: The family is hardly a separate realm from the rest of society. It is a political football, tossed around by both liberals and conservatives, who appeal to it abstractly and develop policies that shape and mold it concretely. It is the foundation of the economy. And it is the basic building block of society. Always has been. Probably always will be.

What is the family? Where did it come from? Is it still necessary? How do sociologists understand the forces the hold it together and the forces that pull it apart?

The Family Tree

Unlike most animals, human beings are born helpless. For the first few years of their lives, they require round-the-clock care, and for the first decade, they require nearly constant supervision, or they won't survive to adulthood. But even after they learn basic survival skills, humans are still not qualified to make their own way in the world—an adult has to provide for all of their needs for 10 or 15 years or more. You are born into a group—and your survival depends on it. This is, of course, the family.

Families as Kinship Systems

Every human society has divided the adults into cooperative groups who take charge of the care and feeding of the children. This is the origin of the **family,** defined as "the basic unit in society traditionally consisting of two parents rearing their children" but also "any of various social units differing from but regarded as equivalent to the traditional family"—such as single parents with children, spouses without children, and several generations living together. Families also refer to those related to you through blood or marriage, extended back through generations.

Families provide us with a sense of history, both as individuals and as members of a particular culture. Families themselves are part of **kinship systems,** cultural forms that locate individuals in the culture by reference to their families. Kinship systems are groupings that include all your relatives, mapped as a network from closest (mother, father, siblings) to a little more distant (cousins, aunts, uncles) to increasingly distant (your great-uncle twice removed). Your kinship system can be imagined as a "family tree." Tracing your family tree is especially popular these days because it provides a sense of history.

Family trees can be organized in several ways to ground you in that history, depending on how you trace your descent, where you live, and whom you marry. These different ways of constructing a family tree give you a different cognitive map of the world and your place in it. Your line of descent can be:

- **Matrilineal:** through your mother's side of the family
- **Patrilineal:** through your father's side of the family
- **Bilineal:** through both your parents' sides

In many cases, your surname (last name) provides a minihistory of your ancestry. In some languages, it is literally in your name, like Johnson or Stevenson in English, Jonasdottir in Icelandic, Petrov in Russian. These names suggest different ways of tracing your family tree and lineage.

▲ **Families are kinship systems that anchor our identities in shared history and culture.**

Culture and Forms of the Family

Families are not simply an expression of love between people who want to have children. They are fundamental cultural institutions that have as much to do with economics, politics, and sex as they do with raising children. As the fundamental unit of society, the social functions of the family and the regulation of sexuality have always been of interest to sociologists.

For one thing, families ensure the regular transfer of property and establish lines of succession. For another, families restrict the number of people you can have sex with. In prehistoric times, a mighty hunter might spend three weeks tracking down and killing a single mastodon. He didn't want to go through all of that time and expense to feed a child that his next-door neighbor had produced. But how could he be sure that his next-door neighbor *wasn't* the father of the children his best girlfriend had given birth to? To solve this problem, almost every society has established a type of marriage—a relationship that regulates sexual activity to ensure **legitimacy,** that is, to ensure that men know what children they have produced (women have an obvious way to know). Families then bear the economic and emotional burden of raising only the children that belong to them (Malinowski, [1927] 1974).

No society allows its members to marry or have sex with anyone they might take an interest in, but the specifics of who can marry whom vary from place to place and over time. The most common arrangement is **monogamy,** marriage between two people. Most monogamous societies allow men and women to marry each other because it takes one of each to make a baby, but same-sex monogamy is surprisingly common. Historian John Boswell found evidence of same-sex marriages existing alongside male-female marriages even in early Christian Europe (1995).

Many societies have instituted some form of **polygamy,** or marriage between three or more people, although most of those allow monogamy as well. The most common form of polygamy is **polygyny,** one man with two or more women, because a man can have children with several

Did *you* know?

The family form mentioned most often in the Bible is polygyny (multiple female partners). In fact, all of the patriarchs—Abraham, Isaac, Jacob, and Joseph—had numerous wives and concubines (sexual partners to whom they were not married to). Solomon was reputed to have had 1,000 wives, products of his many political alliances.

women at the same time. Among the Yoruba of northern Nigeria, women can have only one husband, but *they* can have as many wives as they want, so they practice a type of same-sex polygyny: One woman marries two or more women (Roscoe, 2001). **Polyandry,** one woman marrying two or more men, is rare, but it has been documented in Tibet and a few other places where men are absent for several months of the year.

Only a few societies practice **group marriage,** two or more men marrying two or more women, with children born to anyone in the union "belonging" to all of the partners equally. Group marriages appeared from time to time in the 1960s counterculture, but they rarely lasted long (Hollenbach, 2004).

Marriage does more than ensure that the proper people are responsible for the upbringing of the child; it ensures that when the child grows up, he or she will know who is off limits as a marriage partner. Almost every human society enforces **exogamy:** Marriage to (or sex with) members of your family unit is forbidden. This is the incest taboo, which Sigmund Freud argued was the one single cultural universal. (Without it, lines of succession and inheritance of property would be impossible!)

Of course, who counts as family varies from culture to culture and over time. Mom, Dad, brother, sister, son, or daughter are always off limits, except in a few cases of ritual marriage (the ancient Egyptian pharaohs married their sisters). But uncles and nieces commonly married each other through the nineteenth century, and first cousins are still allowed to marry in most countries in Europe and twenty-six of the U.S. states. In the Hebrew Bible, God struck Onan dead because he refused to have sex with his widowed sister-in-law and thereby produce an heir for his brother. But nowadays an affair with one's sister-in-law would be thought of as creepy at best. *The Brady Bunch Movie* (1995) plays with the idea that Greg and Marcia Brady are brother and sister by adoption, not by blood, so they could legally become interested in each other, date, and marry. But they won't; again, creepy.

At the other end of the spectrum, sometimes your entire clan, totem, or kinship group is often off limits. For this reason, groups of friends usually refrain from dating within the group. Until recently, Koreans were legally forbidden from marrying anyone with their same last name. Unfortunately, nearly a quarter of the population has the last name *Kim* (Yong-Shik, 2001).

The Family Unit

Family units come in an enormously varied number of types, from the father-mother-kids model that we see on evening sitcoms to longhouses where everyone in the tribe lives together in a gigantic mass. However, individual families are usually differentiated from others with a separate dwelling, their own house, apartment, cabin, or tent. Even when the entire tribe lives together in a single longhouse, each family gets its own cooking fire and personal space to differentiate it from the other families and signify that they belong together.

Chances are that you will occupy at least two different family units during your lifetime. While you are a child, you belong to a **family of origin**—the family you are born into—with your biological parents or others who are responsible for your upbringing. When you grow up, if you marry or cohabit with a romantic partner, you now also belong to a **family of procreation,** which is the family you choose to belong to in order to reproduce. Often we consider any adults you are living with as a family of procreation, even if none of them is actually doing any procreating. In modern societies, it is customary to change residences to signify that you have moved to a new family unit, but most premodern societies didn't differentiate: Either new wives moved in with their husbands' family, or new husbands moved in with their wives' family, or everyone kept right on living together (Fox, 1984; Stone, 2000).

Families usually have some rationale, real or imaginary, for being together. They, and everyone else in the community, assume that they "belong" together because of a common biological ancestry, legal marriage or adoption, some other bond of kinship, or the connection to others by blood, marriage, or adoption. Sometimes they can't prove biological ancestry, but they still insist on a common ancestor in the distant past, human, god, or animal. When all else fails, they create symbolic kinship, blood brothers, aunties, and "friends of the family."

The Development of the Family

When our son was 5 years old, we were wandering through the ethnological exhibits at the Museum of Natural History. There were lifelike dioramas of other cultures—Eskimo, Polynesian, Amazonian—and also displays that portrayed the evolution of modern society through the Neolithic, Paleolithic, and Pleistocene ages. In each case, the diorama had exactly the same form: In the front, a single male, poised as a hunter or fisherman. Behind him, by a fire toward the back of the tableau, sat a single woman, cooking or preparing food, surrounded by several small children.

It wasn't until we passed into the hall of the animals, however, that anything seemed amiss. The dioramas kept to form: A single male—lion, gorilla, whatever—standing proudly in front, a single female and offspring lounging in the back waiting for him to bring home fresh meat.

"Look, Dad," Zachary said. "They have families just like we do."

I started to simply say "uh huh," the way parents do, half listening to their children. But something made me stop short. "Uh, actually, they don't," I said. "Most of these animals actually live in larger groupings, extended families and cooperative bands. And lionesses do most of the hunting (and caring for the young) while the males lounge about lazily most of the day."

Nor was every family throughout human history a nuclear family. Indeed, the nuclear family emerged only recently, within the past few thousand years. For most of human existence, our family forms have been quite varied and significantly larger, including several generations and all the siblings all living together.

Until my son pointed it out, though, I had never noticed that these exhibits in the museum were not historically accurate reflections of human (or animal) history, but normative efforts to make the contemporary nuclear family appear to have been eternal and universal, to read it back into history and across species—in a sense, to rewrite history so that the family didn't have a history but instead to pretend it had always been the way it is.

Nothing could be further from the truth. Families have developed and changed enormously over the course of human history.

Families evolved to socialize children, transmit property, ensure legitimacy, and regulate sexuality. They also evolved as economic units. Because children went to work alongside the adults, they contributed to the economic prosperity of the family; in fact, the family became a unit of economic production. Property and other possessions were passed down from the adults of the family to the children. Occupation, religion, language, social standing, and wealth were all dependent on kinship ties.

In all agrarian societies, including Europe and America as late as the nineteenth century, the household has been the basic economic unit. Production—and consumption—occurred within the household. Everyone participated in growing and eating the crops, and the excess might be taken to market for trade.

There was no distinction between family and society: Family life *was* social life. Families performed a whole range of functions later performed by social institutions. The family was not only a site of economic production and consumption. It was:

- *A school.* Any reading and writing you learned was at your parents' knee.
- *A church.* The head of the household led the family prayers; you might see the inside of a "real" church or temple once or twice a year.
- *A hospital.* Family members knew as much as there was to know about setting broken bones and healing diseases
- *A day care center.* There were no businesses to take care of children, so someone in the family had to do it.
- *A police station.* There were no police to call when someone wronged you, so you called on your family to take care of the situation.
- *A retirement home.* If you had no family to take care of you in your old age, you would end up in debtor's prison or begging on the streets.

Obviously, all these functions cannot be met by the nuclear family model. (That model includes the biological parents and their children, although it can also include their children from other marriages.) The most common model in the premodern era was the extended family, in which two or three generations lived under the same roof or at least in the same compound. No one left the household except to marry into another family, until the group got too big for the space available and had to split up. And even then, they would build a new house nearby, until eventually everyone in the village was related to everyone else.

The Origins of the Nuclear Family

Just as families are no longer concerned exclusively with socializing children, marriage developed far more functions than simple sexual regulation, ensuring that parents and children know who each other is. Marriage could also validate a gentleman's claim to nobility and establish that a boy had become a man. It could form a social tie between two families or bring peace to warring tribes. In the Middle Ages, European monarchs often required their children to marry the child of a monarch next door, on the theory that you are unlikely to go to war with the country that your son or daughter has married into (it didn't work—by the seventeenth century, all of the European monarchs were second or third cousins, and they were always invading each other).

Marriage has also come to represent a distinctive emotional bond between two people. In fact, the idea that people should select their own marriage partner is actually a very recent phenomenon. For thousands of years, parents selected partners to fulfill their own economic and political needs or those of the broader kinship group. Arranged marriages are still the norm in a number of countries. People still fall in love—romantic love is practically universal across human societies—but not necessarily with the people they intended to marry. The tradition of courtly love, praised by the troubadours of medieval France, was expressly about adultery, falling in love with someone else's spouse (De Rougemont, 1983).

Only about 200 years ago did men and women in Western countries begin to look at marriage as an individual affair, to be decided by the people involved rather than parents, church, and state.

Romantic love is virtually universal, found in all cultures. Hindu couple in South Asia. ▼

Like the **companionate marriage,** in which individuals choose their marriage partners based on emotional ties and love, the nuclear family is a relatively recent phenomenon. It emerged in Europe and the United States in the late eighteenth century. Its emergence depended on certain factors, such as the ability of a single breadwinner to earn enough in the marketplace to support the family and sufficient hygiene and health so that most babies would survive with only one adult taking care of them.

Historians like Carl Degler (1980) trace the new nuclear family, as it emerged in the White middle class between 1776 and 1830, and Christopher Lasch (1975) suggests the theory of "progressive nucleation" to explain how it gradually superseded the extended family and became the norm. During the nineteenth century, industrialization and modernization meant that social and economic needs could no longer be met by kin. It became customary for children to move far from their parents to go to school or look for work. With no parents around, they had to be responsible for their own spouse selection, and when they married, they would have to find their own home. Eventually adult children were expected to start their own households away from their parents, even if they were staying in the same town. When they had children of their own, they were solely responsible for the child rearing; the grandparents had only small and informal roles to play.

The change was not always beneficial: In every generation, husbands and wives had to reinvent child-rearing techniques, starting over from scratch, with many possibilities for mistakes. As Margaret Mead stated (1978), "Nobody has ever before asked the nuclear family to live all by itself in a box the way we do. With no relatives, no support, we've put it in an impossible situation."

The nuclear family is also a more highly "gendered" family—roles and activities are allocated increasingly along gender lines. On the one hand, because the nuclear family was by definition much smaller than the extended family, the wife experienced greater autonomy. On the other hand, in her idealized role, she was increasingly restricted to the home, with her primary role envisioned as child care and household maintenance. She became a "housewife."

Women were seen as morally superior to men (though physically and intellectually inferior), and the homes they made as nurturing and supportive, as opposed to the "cold, cruel world" of the workplace, the home was supposed to be, as de Tocqueville put it, a "haven in a heartless world." The home was a space for feelings, the workplace a space of unemotional, sometimes brutal logic. The sentimental connotations of "home" and "mother" began during this period (cited in Janara, 2001, p. 551).

Because the home was seen as the "women's sphere," middle-class women's activities outside the home began to shrink. The husband became the "breadwinner," the only one in the family who was supposed to go to work and provide economic support for the household. (Of course, families of lesser means could not always survive on the salary of a single earner, so wives often continued to work outside the home.) But the middle-class wife, now called "the little woman," was supposedly so sweet, fragile, and innocent that only her husband was supposedly tough enough to handle the sordid world of business (Welter, 1966).

As the attention of the household, and especially the mother, became increasingly centered on children, they were seen as needing more than food, clothing, education, and maybe a spanking now and then. They were no longer seen as "little savages," barbarians who needed civilizing, or corrupt sinners who would go to Hell unless they were baptized immediately. Instead, they were "little angels," pure and innocent, born "trailing clouds of glory" as they descended from heaven (instead of trailing fire and brimstone as they ascended from that other place). Therefore they had to be kept

Did you know?

In the American colonies, single people were penalized if they remained single too long. Maryland imposed a tax on bachelors (Lauer and Lauer, 2003). Even today, federal and state income tax laws offer substantial cuts for married people, in the hopes that single people will get the message and head for the altar.

▲ The nuclear family, with its strict division of household labor, is a relatively recent historical invention—and does not apply to all cultures, even in the United States. In the Chicano family, everyone cooks, so everyone eats.

innocent of the more graphic aspects of life, like sex and death, and they needed love, nurturing, and constant care and attention. The number of children per family declined, both because they would no longer be providing economic support for the family and because each child now required a greater investment of time and emotional energy.

In modern societies, children don't often work alongside their parents, and the family has become a unit of consumption rather than production; its economic security is tied to the workplace and the national economy. Instead, the major functions of the family are to provide lifelong psychological support and emotional security. The family has been so closely associated with love and belonging that friends and even groups of co-workers express their emotional intimacy by saying they are "a family."

Family and Ethnicity

The contemporary American nuclear family—the breadwinning husband, his homemaker wife, and their 2.2 children, who live in a detached single-family house in a suburb we call Anytown, USA—developed historically. But even today, it is only one of several family forms. Families vary not only from culture to culture but also within our society—by race and ethnicity. As each racial and ethnic group has a different history, their family units developed in different ways, in response to different conditions. For example, how can we understand the modern African American family outside the deliberate policies of slavery whereby families were broken up, and husbands, wives, and children deliberately sold to different slave owners, so as to dilute the power of family as a tie of loyalty to something other than the master?

Sociologists are interested in the diversity of family forms by race and ethnicity. Some of these differences are now so well documented that to enumerate them sounds almost like a stereotype. And, to be sure, each ethnic group exhibits wide variation in their families (not all Catholic families have nine kids, but most American families with nine kids are Catholic). Sociologists are also interested in the process by which one family form became the standard against which all other family forms were measured—and found wanting. In addition, although these family adaptations are seen largely among ethnic minorities, they are also seen among the White working class, which suggests that they are less "ethnic" adaptations to a White family norm and more "class" adaptations to a middle- and upper-class family norm. As each ethnic group develops a stable middle class, their families come to resemble the companionate-marriage nuclear family of the White middle class. It may be the case not that the nuclear family is inevitable, but that it is *expensive*—and that without significant governmental support, it does not flourish.

The European American Family

This family form that became the dominant model was itself the product of a variety of social factors that are unlikely to return. Based initially on the Anglo-Irish family of the seventeenth century, the European American family has also taken on characteristics from each of the large immigrant groups, especially those that arrived in the late nineteenth century. Many of these immigrant families were Catholic and did not use birth control, so their families tended to be larger than those of the Protestant immigrants, who did practice birth control.

But the contemporary family is also the result of deliberate social policies beginning in the first decades of the twentieth century. These policies held up a specific model as normal and natural and then endeavored to fulfill that vision by prohibitions on women's entry into the workplace or pushing them out once they found their way there, ideologies of motherhood and birth control to limit family size, a "eugenics" movement that demanded that all new immigrants conform to a specific standard of marriage and family, and a new educational and child-rearing ideology that specified how parents should raise their children. American families have always been subject to deliberate policies to encourage certain types of families and discourage others, a process that continues today.

The end of World War II saw the largest infusion of government funding toward the promotion of this new nuclear family—the interstate highway system that promoted flight to the suburban tract homes, the massive spending on public schools in those suburbs, and policy initiatives coupled with ideologies that pushed women out of manufacturing work and back into the home, while their veteran husbands were reabsorbed into the labor force or went to college on the GI Bill.

The family form that finally emerged in the 1950s—idealized in classic situation comedies of the 1950s and early 1960s like *Father Knows Best* and *Leave It to Beaver* on that newly emergent and culturally unifying medium, television—was far less a naturally emergent evolutionary adaptation and far more the anomalous result of deliberate social planning.

The Native American Family

Prior to the arrival of the Europeans, most Native Americans lived in small villages where extended families dominated; you could trace a blood relationship with almost everyone you knew, and most social interaction—from food distribution to village government—depended on kinship ties and obligations. Strangers were considered enemies unless they could be somehow included in the kinship network (Wilkinson, 1999). One of the primary means of creating kinship alliances was exogamy, the requirement that people marry outside of their clan. Marriages created allies, which were useful in any disputes with other clans in the tribe.

Native American families are, themselves, quite diverse. Most marriages are monogamous, but some tribes permitted polygyny, and a few permitted men to sleep with other women when their wives were pregnant or lactating. Many tribes, such as the Zuni and Hopi in the Southwest and the Iroquois in the Northeast, were matrilineal. Hopi children were raised by their mothers and uncles (and, to an extent, their fathers). Girls continued to live with their mothers throughout their lives. When they married, they brought their husbands home with them. When boys entered puberty, they moved into the men's ceremonial house. Eventually most of them married women of other clans and moved in with their wives' family.

The father had limited authority in the family: He was considered a guest in his wife's home, and her brothers or cousins made all of the major economic and child-rearing decisions. Children went to their uncle, not their father, for approval of their life choices.

Still, children—especially boys—learned a lot from their fathers. Although uncles had the greatest authority over their life decisions, their biological fathers taught them their occupational skills, hunting, herding animals, or growing crops.

Native American family and kinship systems were developed to provide for people's fundamental needs, such as producing enough food and defending against

▲ Native Americans are often torn between the social norms of their traditional culture and those of the dominant society. This grandfather shows his grandson how to mend fishing nets.

outsiders. Although kin often shared strong emotional bonds, families did not develop primarily out of people's desire for love, intimacy, and personal fulfillment but out of the desire to survive.

Native Americans are often torn between the social norms of their traditional culture and those of the dominant society (Garrett, 1999; Yellowbird and Snipp, 1994). One-third marry outside their ethnicity, and the extended family model of the tribal society is common only on the reservations. In the cities, most Native Americans live in nuclear families (Sandefur and Sakamoto, 1988).

As with other minority groups, social problems such as poverty put significant strains on both extended and nuclear families (Harjo, 1999; Strong, 2004).

The African American Family

Before slavery was abolished, most slaves in the United States and elsewhere were prohibited from legal marriages. It was common practice to separate husbands and wives, and children and parents, on arrival and to make sure they were sold to different plantations, which, slave owners reasoned, would keep them more obedient and less likely to maintain any attachments other than to the plantation. As a result, slaves created their own permanent marital bonds, developing strong kinship ties similar to those in the extended family models of West Africa. Mutual aid and emotional support remained centered in kinship long after slavery (Strong, 2004).

Since the early 1970s, economic changes have resulted in a massive loss of blue-collar jobs (disproportionately held by minorities), and as a result the nuclear family model has become even less common. African Americans have lower marriage rates and higher divorce rates than other ethnic groups (Clarkwest, 2006) and a greater percentage of single mothers. Over half of African American families consist of only one parent, usually the mother.

The completely self-sufficient nuclear family model is difficult enough with two parents, but only one parent, trying to provide full-time emotional and financial support, is often severely overextended. As a survival mechanism, many African American communities have adopted the convention of "fictive kinship"—that is, stretching the boundaries of kinship to include nonblood relations, friends, neighbors, and co-workers, who are obligated to help out in hard times and whom one is obligated to help out in turn (Stack, 1974).

Fictive kinship can also extend to women who have children with the same man. Far from considering each other competition or "home wreckers," they often consider each other kin, with the same bonds of obligation and emotional support due to sisters or sisters-in-law. When a woman has children with several different men, each of whom has children with several different women, the bonds of fictive kinship can extend across a community.

The Asian American Family

Asian Americans trace their ancestry to many different cultural groups in more than twenty languages, so they brought many different family systems to the United States with them. The more recent the immigration, the more closely their family system reflects that of their original culture. But even third- and fourth-generation families, who are demographically almost identical to White middle-class nuclear families (same percentage of married couples, two-parent families, and male heads of household), show some differences in orientation and family style.

Suzuki (1985) studied Chinese American and Japanese American families and found that the roles and responsibilities of various family members are based on the Confucian principles that have informed Chinese society for 2,000 years. They are more collectively based than Euro-American families, emphasizing the family as a unit rather than a group of individuals. Grown-up Euro-American children may reject their parents' wishes, saying "I have to live my own life," but Chinese and Japanese American children are more concerned about not bringing shame or dishonor to the family. If Mom and Pop say that they should go to medical school, they're going to medical school, regardless of how much they might long to audition for *American Idol*.

Euro-American families tend to be democratic, with every member having a voice in such decisions as what to have for dinner or where to go on vacation. In contrast, Chinese and Japanese American families are more hierarchical. Parents and older siblings exert full authority over children and younger siblings and require respect and obedience from them. The only exceptions are made for gender—in some situations, boys may have authority over their mothers and older sisters.

The Hispanic Family

Like Asian Americans, Hispanic Americans trace their ancestry to many different cultures with different languages, religions, and different family systems: Cuban families are very different from Puerto Rican families, which are very different from Chicano families, and so on (Baca Zinn, 1995; Carrasquillo 1994). Also like Asian Americans, the more recently Hispanic Americans have arrived in the United States, the more closely their family system resembles that of their original culture.

Demographically, Hispanic families fall somewhat between Euro-American and African American families. Most are nuclear families, but they do have characteristics of extended families, with grandparents, aunts, uncles, and more distant relatives living close together, visiting each other frequently, and bearing some of the responsibilities for child rearing and emotional support.

They tend to be hierarchical by age and gender, like Asian American families, but here, too, Hispanic families exhibit significant variation. Chicano and Puerto Rican families are more egalitarian than Dominican and Cuban families; and those from South America are somewhat more likely to be middle class, smaller, and more egalitarian than those from the Caribbean.

Gender equality also increases with length of residence in the United States. The longer the family has been in the United States, the more egalitarian it will tend to be. The families of second- and third-generation immigrants tend to be more egalitarian than families of older generations (Chilman, 1999; Wilkinson, 1999). This is probably the result of social mobility rather than ethnicity—the longer the residence in the United States, the more likely is the family to belong to the middle class.

Forming Families

Sociologists study the variations in the family form and also the processes by which we form families. To most of us, it probably seems pretty straightforward: After a few years of dating, you become increasingly serious with one special someone, you fall in love, you gradually realize that this one is "it," and you decide to marry. Historically, this has been a process known as courtship, the intensification and institutionalization of an intimate relationship from meeting to mating to marrying. And it is so common, so casually assumed, we often have no idea just how unusual and recent this process is.

Courtship and Dating

In the famous musical *Fiddler on the Roof*, a drama that centers on the breakdown of a traditional Jewish family in a small Russian village in the late nineteenth century, as each of the three daughters chooses to marry an increasingly troublesome man, the girls' parents reminisce about their courtship. "The first time I met you was on our wedding day," Golde tells her husband, Tevye. That was not uncommon. So he asks if she loves him. "Do I what?!?" she answers.

Courtship was largely unknown in ancient society, despite the efforts of Hollywood movies to show true, but unrequited love, in Rome, Greece, or Egypt. Marriages were arranged, and children often were betrothed (promised, engaged) as toddlers. But even in the days when marriages were arranged by parents, children often had a voice in the selection process, and they found ways to meet and evaluate potential partners so they could make their preferences known. By the turn of the twentieth century, they were classmates at coed high schools, and they formed romantic bonds with people that their parents didn't even know.

The custom of dating, engaging in recreational activities in pairs rather than groups and with the goal of establishing or strengthening a romantic commitment, did not arise until the 1920s. Children of working-class immigrants in major American cities were trying to distance themselves from the old-fashioned supervised visits that their parents insisted on, and fortunately they enjoyed both a great deal of personal freedom and a wide range of brand-new entertainment venues (Bailey, 1989).

By the 1930s, the custom had spread to the middle class. College-aged men and women participated in a process called "rating and dating," whereby they were rated on their desirability as a date and would ask or accept dates only with people of similar ratings. Dating was based on physical attractiveness, social desirability, and other qualities—not family name and position. Most importantly, dating was supervised and scrutinized by one's peer group, not one's parents (Nock, 2003).

College and high school became the time of unparalleled freedom for American youth and were increasingly taken up by dating and courtship. Campus wits joked that girls were attending college just to get their "Mrs." degree. By the 1950s, parents were eagerly awaiting their son or daughter's first date as a sign of their entry into adulthood. There were many stages: casual dating, going steady (dating only one person), being pinned (wearing a class ring or pin as a sign of commitment), and finally becoming engaged. Boys and girls were supposed to begin dating early in high school and date many people over the period of years, perhaps going steady several times, until they found "the one" to marry. But not for too many years: "Still dating" in the late 20s was considered sad and slightly unwholesome. In the 1970s, the increased incidence of divorce sent many

On campuses, the preferred mode of social and sexual interaction is "hooking up," which usually consists of some form of sexual activity with someone you know who is connected to your social network, and is not expected to lead to a relationship. ▼

Dating in Japan

In 1955, parents arranged 63 percent of all marriages in Japan. In 1998, the percentage had dropped to 7 percent (Retherford, Ogawa, and Matsukura, 2001). Yet, relative to the United States, Japan has not developed a strong dating culture. You're not expected to bring a date to every recreational activity, and if you're not dating anyone at the moment, your friends don't feel sorry for you and try to fix you up. The expectation that dating leads to marriage is also absent. Japanese television and other mass media don't glorify marriage and ridicule or pity single people, as American television often does (Ornstein, 2001).

Outside of high school and college, there are few places where single men and women meet and interact. Forty-five percent of heterosexual women over the age of 16 say that they have no male friends at all. However, practically all of the heterosexual women with one or more male friends have engaged in premarital sex (probably with the male friends) (Retherford et al., 2001).

With no societal push to marriage and premarital sex available, it is no wonder that they don't feel pressured into getting married right away, or at all. In 2001, schoolgirls around the world were asked whether they agreed with the statement that "everyone should be married." Three-quarters of American schoolgirls agreed. But 88 percent of Japanese schoolgirls disagreed (Coontz, 2007).

---

people in their middle years into the world of dating again, until there was little stigma about dating at the age of 30, 40, or 50.

Today it seems that everyone is dating. Kindergarteners go on "play dates," married couples go on dates, and the recently widowed or divorced are encouraged to date again almost immediately. Internet dating sites are among the Web's most popular, and your potential dates are neatly categorized by age, gender, race, and sexual orientation. And yet it also seems that no one is dating. On campuses, the preferred mode of social and sexual interaction is "hooking up," which is so loose and indiscriminate that its connection to dating and mating has been lost.

Marriage

Marriage is the most common foundation for family formation in the world. The marriage of two people—a woman and a man—is universal in developed countries, although there are significant variations among different cultures.

Marriage is not identical to a nuclear family, although the two tend to go together. One can imagine, for example, marriage as a relationship between two people who are, themselves, embedded in an extended family or a communal child-rearing arrangement (such as the kibbutz). Sociologically, its universality suggests that marriage forms a stable, long-lasting, and secure foundation for the family's functions—child socialization, property transfer, legitimacy, sexual regulation—to be securely served.

Marriage is also a legal arrangement, conferring various social, economic, and political benefits on the married couple. This is because the state regards marriage—that is, stable families—as so important that it is willing to provide economic and social incentives to married couples. As a result, people who have been legally excluded from marrying—the mentally ill, gays and lesbians—have sought to obtain that right as well.

Marriage is certainly not the only living arrangement for people in society. In America between 1900 and 2000, the number of adults living alone increased by 21 percent, single parents and children by 11 percent,

Did you know?

American men are more eager to marry than American women. From 1970 to the late 1990s, men's attitudes toward marriage became more favorable, while women's became less so. By the end of the century, more men than women said that marriage was their ideal lifestyle (Coontz, 2005).

FIGURE 12.1 Households by Type, 1970–2003

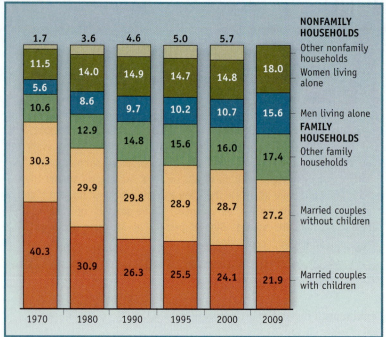

	1970	1980	1990	1995	2000	2009	
NONFAMILY HOUSEHOLDS							
Other nonfamily households	1.7	3.6	4.6	5.0	5.7		
Women living alone	11.5	14.0	14.9	14.7	14.8	18.0	
Men living alone	5.6	8.6	9.7	10.2	10.7	15.6	
FAMILY HOUSEHOLDS	10.6						
Other family households		12.9	14.8	15.6	16.0	17.4	
Married couples without children	30.3	29.9	29.8	28.9	28.7	27.2	
Married couples with children	40.3	30.9	26.3	25.5	24.1	21.9	

Source: Current Population Survey, U. S. Census Bureau, 2004.

To some, gay marriage is an indication that the family is falling apart; to others, that it has never been stronger and more desirable. A very "traditional" church wedding—in a gay and lesbian church. ▼

unmarried partners by 63 percent, and unmarried partners with their children by 89 percent. In several developing countries, marriage is also occurring later and bringing with it numerous positive social outcomes. In industrialized countries like the United States, the implications of the shift toward later marriage and less marriage are a source of extensive sociological research and social debate.

Multigenerational households (adults of more than one generation sharing domestic space) increased by 38 percent between 1990 and 2000, until today they comprise about 3 percent of all households. In about two-thirds, the grandparents are in charge of the family, sharing their home with their grown children and grandchildren (or only their grandchildren), while in about one-third, the grown children are in charge of the family, sharing their home with both their parents and their children (Figure 12.1).

Marriage varies widely by race, ethnicity, education, and income. Nearly two-thirds (63 percent) of White women over 18 who make more than $100,000 a year are married, while only 25 percent of Black women over 18 who earn less than $20,000 per year are married (Center for Changing Families, 2007).

Marriage, itself, has changed. It no longer signifies adulthood or conveys the responsibilities and commitment that it once did. In a society where pop stars marry and divorce within a day but couples who have been together for 30 years are forbidden from marrying, it is, in some people's eyes, discredited and corrupt. People are putting off marriage, cohabiting, or opting for singlehood. On the other hand, marriage has become more desirable than ever before, bringing together couples from varying backgrounds and repeat performers and inspiring many who've been excluded to fight for the right to marry. Some of these changes are temporary, like delayed marriage and, in most cases, cohabitation (which usually leads to marriage). Others, like singlehood, have become more permanent and less transitory.

Delayed Marriage. Early marriage—usually arranged by parents—is still the rule in Sub-Saharan Africa and South and Central Asia. In Southern Asia, 48 percent of young women—nearly 10 million—are married before the age of 18. In Africa, it's 42 percent; in Latin America and the Caribbean, 29 percent. More than half of all girls under 18 are married in some countries, including Afghanistan, Bangladesh, and India. In Ethiopia and some areas of West Africa, some girls are married as early as age 7 (UNFPA, 2005). However, the prevalence is decreasing significantly around the world. Since 1970, the median age of first marriage has risen substantially worldwide—for men from 25.4 years to 27.2 and for women from 21.5 to 23.2 (UNFPA, 2005).

In the United States, young people are experiencing longer periods of independent living while working or attending school before marriage. A 25-year-old American man today is far more likely to be single and childless than he would have been 50 years ago—or even 25 years ago. Among 25-year-old women, the fastest-growing demographic status is single, working, childless, head of household (Fussell and Furstenberg, 2004). The United States still has one of the industrial world's *lowest* age for first marriage (Table 12.1).

Differences among Black, White, and foreign-born populations in education and labor market opportunities have narrowed since the 1960s, creating more similarities in the lives of people of color and their White peers (Fussell and Furstenberg, 2004). However, significant educational and economic inequalities, in addition to cultural differences, mean that different groups will continue to vary in the ages of first marriage (Guzzo, 2003; Martin, 2004).

Staying Single. Not long ago, people who were "still not married" by their late 20s were considered deviant. Men were considered "big babies," who "refused to grow up" and "settle down." Women were "old maids," thought to be too unattractive or socially inept to attract a husband.

But singlehood has become commonplace, if not exactly respectable. Just over half of all Americans aged 15 (50.7 percent) and over are not married or cohabiting (U.S. Census Bureau, 2009, 1-Year Estimates). Sixty-three percent of all unmarried Americans have never been married. Although the percentage of single people is rising for all Americans, those rates vary considerably by race and ethnicity. Between 1970 and 2000, the proportion of White adults who had never married rose from 16 percent to 20 percent, 19 percent to 28 percent among Hispanics, and 21 percent to 39 percent among African Americans (U.S. Census Bureau, 2006).

In Europe, the proportion of women who have never married ranges from 7 percent in Bulgaria to 36 percent in Iceland. The proportion of men is substantially higher.

Women are more likely to be single than men. In fact, the majority of American women (51 percent) is living without a spouse (U.S. Census Bureau, 2006). Single women are better educated, are better employed, and have better mental health than single men (Fowlkes, 1994; Marks, 1996). But for both men and women, being single is an ambivalent experience. Sometimes singles are autonomous and free; sometimes they are lonely and disconnected. Often, they are both (Gordon, 1994). Singles may have financial independence, but they also have sole financial responsibility for their lives and futures. And singles are still living in a society of couples, so they are often the "third wheel" at social events. Friends and family may assume that they are unhappy and expend all of their efforts on trying to hook them up, but as they get older, it may become increasingly difficult to locate uncoupled people at all. It is no wonder that singleness comes with some adjustment problems.

Cohabiting. Cohabitation refers to unmarried people in a romantic relationship living in the same residence. A few decades ago, when nonmarital sex was illegal in most states, cohabitation was virtually impossible—landlords wouldn't rent to people unless they were related by blood or marriage. Hotel managers could lose their license if they rented rooms to unrelated people. Today, cohabitation has become commonplace, largely lacking in social disapproval (Smock, 2000). Except among the very conservative, it is no longer considered "living in sin" or even "shacking up." Almost half of people 25 to 40 years of age in the United States have

▲ While the age of marriage is increasing worldwide, child marriages are still common in many countries. This photo depicts the bride and groom at a child wedding in Rajasthan, India.

TABLE 12.1

Age at First Marriage		
	MEN	**WOMEN**
Poland	26.9	23.7
United States	27.4	25.8
France	29.7	27.7
Austria	30.5	28.1
Netherlands	31.0	29.1
Sweden	32.4	30.1
Denmark	32.8	30.3
Switzerland	35.0	31.3

Source: Trends in Europe and North America: The Statistical Yearbook of the Economic Commission for Europe 2003.

cohabited, and 60 percent of all marriages formed in the 1990s began with cohabitation (Teachman, 2003).

Globally, cohabitation is common in liberal countries—in Sweden, it is four times as prevalent as in the United States. That is largely because those countries provide universal health care and education to everyone, so you don't need to get married to be covered by your spouse's health plan or to ensure your children can go to university. However, it is rare in more conservative countries and remains illegal in some countries.

We don't know exactly how many cohabiting couples there are in the United States because the U.S. Census doesn't ask about emotional bonds or sexual activities and therefore can't distinguish between romantic partners and nonromantic roommates (Babe and Allen, 1992; U.S. Census Bureau, 2004). However, in 2003, there were 4.6 million households consisting of two adults who were not related by blood or marriage (U.S. Census Bureau, 2004). Four out of ten opposite-sex unmarried partner households included at least one minor child (U.S. Census Bureau, 2006).

Is cohabitation a stage of courtship, somewhere between dating and marriage, sort of the equivalent of "going steady" among high school students? Many scholars and cohabiters think so—in the 1980s, it was even called "trial marriage." Women cohabiters are more likely to desire marriage than men (Blumstein and Schwartz, 1983), but about 25 percent do not expect to marry the man they are currently living with. Their biggest inhibiting factor is not his willingness but his socioeconomic status: They want to marry someone with greater economic potential. Some look at it as a "trial marriage," some as an experience that might or might not lead to marriage with their current partner (like dating), and others as a stable, nonmarital alternative that they could happily pursue for the rest of their lives (Fowlkes, 1994; Seltzer, 2001).

But for some cohabiters, their living situation has nothing to do with marriage. More than one million elderly Americans cohabit—for a significant financial reason. While the government strongly encourages marriage among the young and middle-aged with tax cuts and other benefits, elderly men and women receiving Social Security cannot marry without losing a significant percentage of their combined individual incomes (Brown, Lee, and Bulanda, 2006; Chevan, 1996).

Younger people benefit financially from being married, but marriage comes with legal restrictions, such as sexual fidelity or child support, that they may not want, at least until they decide that they are "meant for each other" (Spain and Bianchi, 1996). They may also believe in postponing marriage until they have a significant amount of money in the bank, enough to buy a house or at least finance a big wedding (Seltzer, 2000).

Race and social class have an impact on who will cohabit and who will marry. Despite the popular assumption that cohabitation is a lifestyle of the rich and famous—or at least the affluent and educated—it is actually more common among working-class and poor people with less education and financial resources (Bumpass and Lu, 2000; Casper and Bianchi, 2002). One in ten adult Hispanic women currently cohabit, and 9 percent of White women, but only 6 percent of African American women (Fields and Casper, 2001; Figure 12.2).

A lot of research has been conducted on the emotional stability of cohabiting couples. Some research finds that cohabiting women are more prone to depression than married women, especially if there are children involved. Maybe they are more prone to stress because they know that their unions can dissolve more easily than marriages; if they

Almost half of people 25–40 in the United States have cohabited, and 60 percent of all marriages formed in the 1990s began with cohabitation. ▼

FIGURE 12.2 Married Couple and Unmarried Partner Households

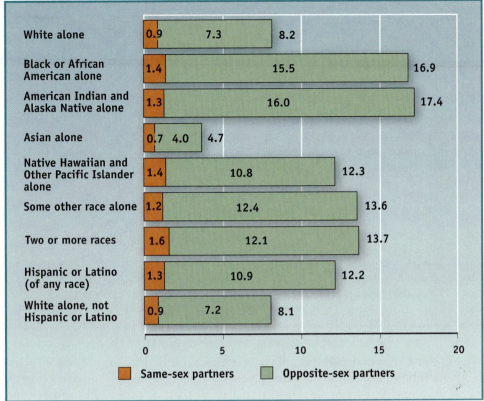

	Same-sex partners	Opposite-sex partners	Total
White alone	0.9	7.3	8.2
Black or African American alone	1.4	15.5	16.9
American Indian and Alaska Native alone	1.3	16.0	17.4
Asian alone	0.7	4.0	4.7
Native Hawaiian and Other Pacific Islander alone	1.4	10.8	12.3
Some other race alone	1.2	12.4	13.6
Two or more races	1.6	12.1	13.7
Hispanic or Latino (of any race)	1.3	10.9	12.2
White alone, not Hispanic or Latino	0.9	7.2	8.1

■ Same-sex partners   ☐ Opposite-sex partners

Source: U. S. Census Bureau, 2003.

dissolve, there will be no legal means of distributing household resources equitably, and no spousal support after the "divorce."

Explanations of Nonmarital Choices. Sociologists offer numerous explanations for the increases in delayed marriage, singlehood, and cohabitation. First, these changes are partially explained by new practices, such as courtship and dating. After all, arranged marriages usually take place when the children are younger. But courtship and dating are linked to the worldwide increase in the status of women. While it's true that arranged marriages affected both boys and girls, increased individual choice of marriage partners enables more women to seek educational and economic advancement and rests on increasing choices for women.

Second, these changes tend to be associated with higher levels of education—for both males and females. For decades, many young people, especially in industrialized countries, have been seeking and gaining more education to compete in the global marketplace. The higher the level of education, the later people get married. In China, for example, which currently accounts for more than 20 percent of young people in the developing world, schooling has increased, and adolescent labor has decreased. The average age at marriage began to rise, and the vast majority of males and females now marries after age 20 ("Age at First Marriage and Divorce," 2007).

Third, these changes are partially explained by changing sexual behaviors and attitudes, especially increased acceptance of "premarital sex." For a long time, sexual activity before marriage was referred to as "premarital" because it was assumed that the couple involved would be in a serious, committed relationship and intend to marry. However, some people engage in sexual relations during a casual dating relationship, when marriage has not yet become a topic of discussion. Some view sex as an appropriate conclusion to a first date. Still others "hook up" and don't even go as far as dating. Others never intend to marry, or they lack the right to marry, but they still have sex, sometimes in committed relationships, sometimes not. Therefore, a more precise term might be **nonmarital sex**—sex that is not related to marriage.

In wealthy countries, especially in northern Europe, nonmarital sex has become increasingly acceptable, even during the teen years. These countries provide sex education and health care services aimed at equipping young people to avoid negative consequences of sex by encouraging contraceptive use. In the United States, public attitudes toward nonmarital sex have changed significantly over the past 20 years. In a national survey in the early 1970s, 37 percent of respondents said that nonmarital sex is always wrong. By 1990 this number had fallen to 20 percent (Michael et al., 1994). However, social and political institutions have changed more slowly. As a result, rates of teen pregnancy and sexually transmitted diseases are much lower in Europe than in the United States, although their rates of sexual activity are no higher. Teen abortions are also low, even though abortion services are widely available (Guttmacher Institute, 1999).

Biracial Marriage

Through most of the history of the United States, marriage or sexual relations between men and women of different races were illegal. At a time when "race science" taught that races differed dramatically in their intelligence and morality, scholars feared that **interracial marriage, or miscegenation,** would lead to children inferior to both mother and father. The evil "half-breed" was a standard fictional type up to the twentieth century. Not until the Supreme Court's *Loving v. State of Virginia* decision of 1967 were men and women of different races permitted to marry in all U.S. states.

Social barriers still place dating, courtship, and marriage within clear racial categories. However, interracial marriage is evolving from virtually nonexistent to merely atypical. Today, 5 percent of the population of the United States claims ancestry in two or more races, and 22 percent of Americans have a relative in a mixed-race marriage (Pew Research Center, 2007). Blacks are twice as likely as Whites to have an immediate family member in an interracial marriage, while Hispanics fall in the middle of those two groups. The most common interracial couple in the United States is a White husband married to an Asian wife (14 percent of all interracial couples).

Euro-Americans are least likely to intermarry: Only 3.5 percent of White, non-Hispanic individuals are married to someone of another race. And non-Hispanic Whites, along with people over 65, are less accepting of interracial dating than are African Americans, Hispanics, and younger people of all races (Pew Research Center, 2003; Figure 12.3).

For Black–White couples, the most common pattern (73 percent) is a White woman and an African American man. Among cohabiting couples, there is even a sharper gap: Five times as many Black men live with White women as White men with Black women. Oddly, in the mass media, Black man–White women couples are almost nonexistent. Instead, we see a proliferation of White men and Black women, from Joey and Chandler dating a famous paleontologist (who happens to be a young Black woman) on *Friends* to Rose and her husband on *Lost*.

For Asian–White couples, the most common pattern (over 75 percent) is White men and Asian women. The difference is less severe in cohabitation: Twice as many White men are living with Asian women as Asian women living with White men. Asian–Black pairings are rare, but they are even more unbalanced than interracial pairings involving Whites. Black husband–Asian wife patterns outnumber Asian husband–Black wife by 6 to 1.

There is little imbalance among Hispanics. Just under 18 percent of married Hispanic women have non-Hispanic husbands, and just over 15 percent of married Hispanic men have non-Hispanic wives.

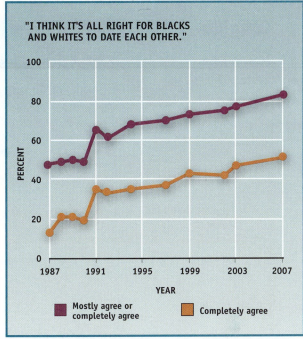

FIGURE 12.3 **Acceptance of Interracial Dating**

"I THINK IT'S ALL RIGHT FOR BLACKS AND WHITES TO DATE EACH OTHER."

Source: From "Trends in Political Values and Core Attitudes: 1987–2007: Political Landscape More Favorable to Democrats," released March 22, 2007. Reprinted by permission of Pew Research Center for the People and the Press.

Same-Sex Marriage

Same-sex couples have been cohabiting for hundreds of years, although sometimes societal pressures forced them to pretend that they were not couples at all. In the seventeenth and eighteenth centuries, for example, middle-class men often "hired" their working-class partners as valets or servants, so they could live together without question. Sometimes they pretended to be brothers or cousins. In the eighteenth and nineteenth century, it was so common for women to spend their lives together that there was a special name for their bonds, "Boston marriages."

Recent research allows us to paint a portrait of the typical lesbian or gay couple, at least the ones who are open (all following data are from Ambert, 2005; Bianchi and Casper, 2000; Black et al., 2000):

1. *They're urban.* More than half of lesbian or gay male couples live in just 20 U.S. cities, including "gay meccas" like Los Angeles, San Francisco, Washington, D.C., New York, and Atlanta.

2. *They're well educated.* They tend to have higher educational attainments than men and women in heterosexual marriages.

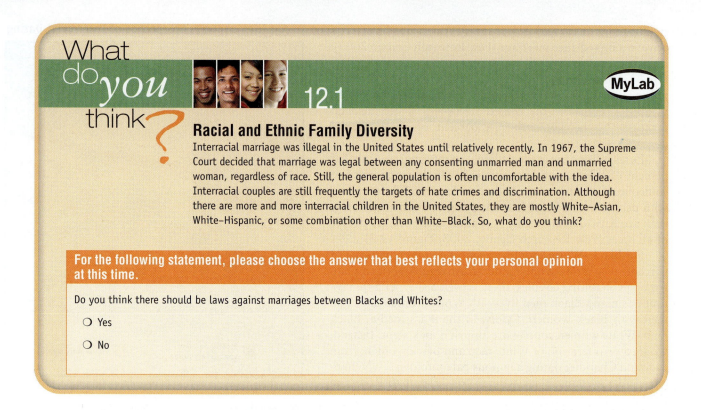

MyLab

What do *you* think ?

12.1

Racial and Ethnic Family Diversity

Interracial marriage was illegal in the United States until relatively recently. In 1967, the Supreme Court decided that marriage was legal between any consenting unmarried man and unmarried woman, regardless of race. Still, the general population is often uncomfortable with the idea. Interracial couples are still frequently the targets of hate crimes and discrimination. Although there are more and more interracial children in the United States, they are mostly White–Asian, White–Hispanic, or some combination other than White–Black. So, what do you think?

For the following statement, please choose the answer that best reflects your personal opinion at this time.

Do you think there should be laws against marriages between Blacks and Whites?

○ Yes

○ No

---

3. *They are less likely to have children.* Fifty-nine percent of married couples versus 22 percent of lesbian couples and 5 percent of gay male couples are living with children of their own. Most are the products of previous heterosexual marriages, although artificial insemination and adoption are increasingly common.

4. *They are less likely to own their own homes than married couples.*

5. *They tend to be more egalitarian.* They are more likely to share decision making and allot housework more equally than married couples and have less conflict as a result (Allen and Demo, 1995; Carrington, 2002).

Did *you* know ?

Latin Americans are more tolerant of gay and lesbian families than North Americans are. No Latin American country has explicit prohibitions against gay and lesbian adoptions such as those in many European countries and parts of the United States. Many judges in Latin America have already granted adoptions to lesbian and gay citizens. Clinics and doctors in many Latin American countries have been providing access to assisted reproduction to lesbians since the 1990s (Sarda, 2000).

And they are not permitted to marry in the United States. As of 2006, 26 states had a constitutional amendment restricting marriage to one man and one women, 19 states had a law (not affecting their constitution) restricting marriage to a man and a woman, and the United States is debating a federal constitutional amendment to ban gay marriage (HRC, 2007). Nineteen states have constitutional amendments that bar gay or lesbian couples from emergency health care, inheritance, and more than 1,000 other rights that heterosexual couples enjoy (HRC, 2007). As of mid-2007, five states provided the equivalent of state-level spousal rights to gay couples and three states plus Washington, D.C., provided some statewide spousal rights (Figure 12.4).

However, reserving marriage and domestic partnerships to men and women applies only in the United States. As of this writing, same-sex couples can marry or enter into civil partnerships with the same rights as heterosexual couples in most European countries and can enter into civil partnerships with most of the same rights as heterosexual couples in nine others, including Brazil, France, Israel, South Africa, and Switzerland.

FIGURE 12.4 State Prohibitions on Marriage for Same-Sex Couples

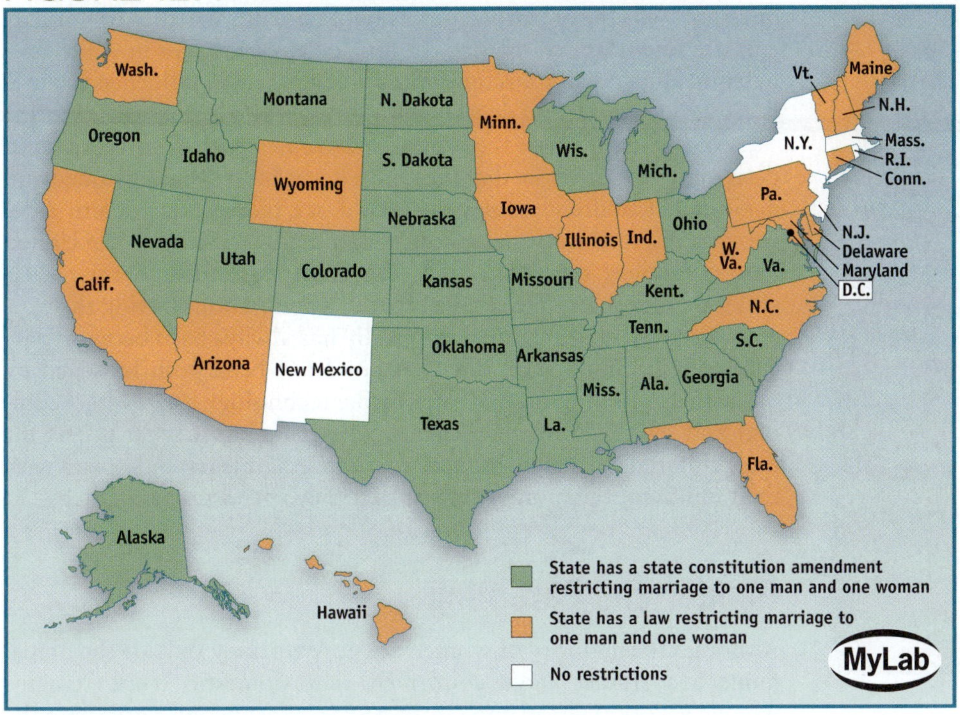

Legend:
- State has a state constitution amendment restricting marriage to one man and one woman
- State has a law restricting marriage to one man and one woman
- No restrictions

MyLab

Source: "State Prohibitions on Marriage for Same-Sex Couple" from *Human Rights Campaign,* November, 2006.
© Human Rights Campaign. Reprinted with permission.

Parenting

In the movie *The Day the Earth Stood Still* (1951), a mysterious stranger rents a room at a boardinghouse. When one of his fellow boarders finds that she has no one to look after her son for the afternoon, the stranger volunteers. Mom hesitates; she doesn't want to inconvenience him. He insists that it would be a pleasure—he loves little boys. Mom happily agrees.

Imagine a remake of that movie today. Mom would insist on fingerprints, an FBI profile, a letter from the local police chief, and a state child care license. During the past 50 years, the answer to the question, "Who should watch the children?" has become more and more narrow, from any handy teenager or adult to licensed childcare professionals to Mom and Dad, or maybe just Mom. Today, 40 percent of all children 5 and under are cared for by a relative and 11 percent by a combination of relatives and non-relatives. Almost 25 percent of all preschoolers are in organized child care facilities—13 percent at day care centers and 6 percent in preschools (*Who's Minding the Kids?*, 2005). Just as children have never been so important in our cultural values, parents have never been considered so important in the lives of their children. Many people believe that biological reproduction gives you a sudden proficiency in child care, and anyone other than the biological parent will do a shoddy job at best. More people have wanted to become parents than ever before, including some who would rarely have considered parenting just 20 or 30 years ago: teenagers, 50-year-olds, gay and lesbian couples, infertile heterosexual couples. Ironically, even though parents are thought to be so utterly decisive in the outcomes of their children's lives, we also seem to believe that it's all hereditary, and socialization plays a very minor role in how our children turn out. Of course, to a sociologist, both sides are true: Parental socialization of children

▲ More people are able to become parents today than ever before, including fifty-year-olds, gay and lesbian couples, and infertile heterosexual couples. In 2006, Lauren Cohen, 59, of New Jersey, became the oldest woman in the United States to give birth to twins.

is enormously important, and parents also overvalue their role. The questions, as you've learned in this book, are not whether or not parents are important or biology trumps socialization, but in which arenas and under what circumstances does parental influence make a decisive difference, and does it do this in all groups, around the world?

And while it's true that children have never been so valued and desired, it's equally true that they have never been so undervalued and neglected. Children around the world are facing poor health care, compromised education, and the lack of basic services. In the United States, families get virtually no financial assistance to raise their children, although they receive a lot of advice about having them.

The core relationship of the family has always been between parents and children. Yet today that bond has been both loosened by other forces pulling families apart (like technology and overscheduling) and tightened by ideas that only parents know what is best for their children. It may be the case that the less time parents spend with their children, the more we insist that they spend time together.

Gender and Parenting

Although the majority of women are now working outside the home, numerous studies have confirmed that domestic work remains women's work (Gerstel and Gross, 1995). Most people agree with the statement that housework should be shared equally between both partners, and more men in male–female households are sharing some of the housework and child care, especially when the woman's earnings are essential to family stability (Perry-Jenkins and Crouter, 1990). But still, the women in male–female households do about two-thirds of the housework (Bianchi et al., 2000). That includes child care: Mothers spend much more time than fathers interacting with their children. They do twice as much of the "custodial" care, the feeding and cleaning of the children (Bianchi, 2000; Pleck, 1997; Sayer, 2001). A survey of American secondary students revealed that 75 percent of girls but only 14 percent of boys who planned to have children thought that they would stop working for awhile, and 28 percent of girls but 73 percent of boys expected their partner to stop working or cut down on work hours (Bagamery, 2004).

Over 5 million women are stay-at-home mothers, staying out of the workforce to care for their children (under the age of 15). However, there are only about 143,000 stay-at-home fathers (U.S. Census Bureau, 2006).

On the other hand, American fathers are more active and involved parents than ever before. Today's new fathers (those between 20 and 35 years old) do far more child care than their own fathers did and are willing to decline job opportunities if they include too much travel or overtime (Pleck and Masciadrelli, 2004).

Single-Parent Families

During the first half of the twentieth century, the primary cause of single-parent families was parental death. By the end of the century, most parents were living, but living elsewhere. Currently 12.2 million people in the United States, 10 million women and 2.2 million men, are single parents, raising children while unmarried. Single-parent families have become more common in all demographic groups, but the greatest increases have been among less-educated women and among African American

How do we know what we know?

The Opt-Out Revolution

The popular view that children require round-the-clock care from Mom, not Dad or day care, has led millions of women to quit their jobs or take time off to raise their children—an "Opt-Out Revolution."

But is such a revolution really taking place? How do we know? Sociologist Kathleen Gerson and her colleagues examined the evidence that women were "opting out" of the workforce to be full-time mothers. What they found was that while it was true that between 1998 and 2002, the proportion of employed women with children under the age of one declined 4 percent from 59 percent to 55 percent, it was also true that 72 percent of mothers with children over the age of one are either working or looking for work.

One would expect that highly educated women with high-paying jobs would be the most likely to opt out, because they can afford to, but in fact they are less likely. Among mothers with children under the age of six, 75 percent of those with postgraduate degrees are working, as opposed to 65 percent of those with high school diplomas only. It turns out that one can see "opting out" only if one freezes time—at any one moment, there are, indeed, women who are leaving the labor force to raise their children. But they don't stay out; they go back to work soon after. And many would go back to work even sooner—if their husbands did a little more child care.

(*Source:* Kathleen Gerson, New York University, PR Newswire.)

---

families (Sidel, 2006). In 2002, 16 percent of White, non-Hispanic children were living in mother-only families, as were 25 percent of Hispanic children and 48 percent of Black children. Sometimes the parents are cohabiting, but most often one parent lives elsewhere and does not contribute to the day-to-day emotional and economic support of the child. Sometimes the other parent is not in the picture at all.

Most people are not single parents by choice. The pregnancy may have been an unexpected surprise that prompted the father to leave, or the relationship ended, leaving one parent with custody. Young, unprepared mothers predominate: In 2002, 89 percent of teenage mothers were unmarried but only 12 percent of mothers aged 30 to 44 (U.S. Census Bureau, 2000). And yet an increasing number of women are choosing single motherhood, either through fertility clinics and sperm banks or through adoption. In 1990 alone, 170,000 single women over 30 gave birth. White, college-educated women led this trend. The number who became mothers without marrying doubled during the 1980s; for those in professional and managerial jobs, it nearly tripled (Bock, 2000; DeParle, 1993; Hertz, 2006; Mattes, 1994).

Single mothers predominate both because it is easier for a father to become absent during the pregnancy and because mothers are typically granted custody in court cases. Although mothers predominate, the gender disparity varies from country to country. Among the countries for which data are available, Belgium has the smallest proportion of women who are the single parent ("only" 75 percent—that is, 25 percent of single parents are the fathers) with Norway, Sweden, and Finland close behind. Estonia has the largest (95 percent). Those countries in which women's status is higher would tend to have lower percentages of women who are single parents.

Grandparenting

Your kids grow up and go off to college, and your parenting is done. When they have kids of their own, you are not involved except for birthday cards and occasional visits at Thanksgiving. For good or bad, that's the nuclear family model. For good or bad, it is increasingly inaccurate. The number of grandparents raising their grandchildren has grown from 2.2 million in 1970 to nearly 4 million today.

Of this last group, grandparents raising their grandchildren alone, they tend to be African American, living in urban centers, and poor. Twenty-seven percent of children being raised by grandparents (and 63 percent being raised by grandmothers alone) are living in poverty. They tend to be working full time: 72 percent of grandfathers and 56 percent of grandmothers, as opposed to 33 percent and 24 percent, respectively, who aren't raising their grandchildren.

What happened to the parents? Often the father has abandoned the child, and the mother is incompetent, in prison, or on drugs. Courts are much more likely to grant custody of a child to a blood relative than to a legal stranger. Grandparents can even legally adopt their grandchildren, in effect becoming their parents.

Adoptive Parents

When Angelina Jolie and Madonna each adopted babies from orphanages in Africa, they were ridiculed for trying to save the world one baby at a time. These Hollywood celebrities were not an elite vanguard but latecomers to a well-worn trend in the industrial world. In the United States alone there are 1.5 million adopted children—over 2 percent of all children (Fields, 2001).

Historically, adoption was considered an option to resolve an unwanted pregnancy—that is, it was about the biological mother. For centuries, all over Europe, foundling hospitals (hospitals that received unwanted newborn babies) enabled mothers to anonymously leave babies at a back door or on the steps, and nuns would find willing families to raise the children as their own. Today, however, the interest has shifted to the adoptive families, as more and more people who want to have children use various services to adopt babies. Adoption has shifted from being about helping "a girl in trouble" to "enabling a loving family to have a child."

There are many different types of adoptions, including:

- *Foster care adoption:* adoption of children in state care for whom reunification with their birth parents is not feasible for safety or other reasons.
- *Private adoption:* adoption either through an agency or independent networks.
- *Inter-country adoption (ICA):* adoption of children from other countries by U.S. citizens. The top three countries for international adoption in 2006 were China (6,500 adoptions), Guatemala (4,135), and Russia (3,706) (U.S. Department of State, 2007).
- *Transracial adoption:* adoption of a child of a different race from the adopting parents; this involves about 10 to 15 percent of all domestic adoptions and the vast majority of ICA.

Motivations for adoption vary. The couple may be incapable of conceiving a child themselves; they may be infertile or gay. Some single women adopt, while others use assisted reproductive technologies to become pregnant. In some cases, fertile couples adopt because they choose to adopt.

Adoption seems to have largely beneficial effects for all concerned (birth parents, adoptive parents, and adoptees). However, a sizeable minority of birth parents characterize their adoption experiences as traumatic, and many birth parents and

In the United States, there are 1.5 million adopted children—over 2 percent of all children. Movie star Angelina Jolie has adopted three, including daughter, Zahara, and son, Maddox (here with Jolie's partner, Brad Pitt). ▼

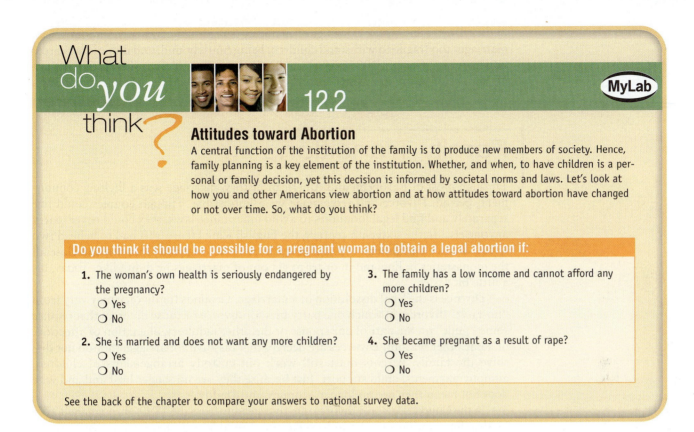

What do *you* think? 12.2 · MyLab

Attitudes toward Abortion

A central function of the institution of the family is to produce new members of society. Hence, family planning is a key element of the institution. Whether, and when, to have children is a personal or family decision, yet this decision is informed by societal norms and laws. Let's look at how you and other Americans view abortion and at how attitudes toward abortion have changed or not over time. So, what do you think?

Do you think it should be possible for a pregnant woman to obtain a legal abortion if:

1. The woman's own health is seriously endangered by the pregnancy?
   ○ Yes
   ○ No

2. She is married and does not want any more children?
   ○ Yes
   ○ No

3. The family has a low income and cannot afford any more children?
   ○ Yes
   ○ No

4. She became pregnant as a result of rape?
   ○ Yes
   ○ No

See the back of the chapter to compare your answers to national survey data.

adoptees spend significant time trying to locate each other and experience some reunions or closure in their relationships.

The number of adoptions by nonrelatives has declined sharply since 1970. The availability of birth control and legal abortion has meant that fewer women are having unwanted children, and adoption is still stigmatized in the United States; it is seen, as one sociologist put it, as "not quite as good as having your own" (Fisher, 2003).

Not Parenting

In the United States, the media are constantly telling us that children are the meaning of life. No woman can be truly happy or fulfilled unless she has given birth, and no man can be secure in his masculinity unless he is a father. When we see a childless couple, we think that something has gone wrong—obviously they are physically unable to conceive. However, childlessness is becoming increasingly common. In 1976, about 10 percent of women aged 40 to 44 (near the end of their childbearing years) had never conceived a child. By 2000, the percentage had grown to 18 percent (U.S. Census Bureau, 2007).

Education is an important predictor of childlessness: The more education a woman has, the more likely she is to bear no children. Race is also significant: Hispanic women are much less likely to expect no children than White and Black women. The longer they put off children, the more likely they are to opt out of having children altogether, perhaps because they become accustomed to a child-free lifestyle.

However, people have many reasons for remaining "child-free by choice," from concern about overpopulation to a desire to concentrate on their career to just not liking children. In one study, women said they enjoyed the freedom and spontaneity in their lives, while some others gave financial considerations, worries about stress, marriages too fragile to withstand children, being housebound, and diminished career opportunities (Gerson, 1985). Men usually cite more practical considerations, including commitment to career and concern about the financial burden (Lunneborg, 1999).

Family Transitions

Through most of European and American history, marriage was a lifelong commitment, period. Divorce and remarriage were impossible. Though couples could live separately and find legal loopholes to avoid inheritance laws, they could never marry anyone else. In the sixteenth century, the English King Henry VIII had to behead two wives, divorce two others, found a new Church (the Anglican Church), and close all the monasteries in England in order to get out of marriages he didn't like. Today, it's a little bit easier.

Divorce is the legal dissolution of a marriage. Grounds for divorce may vary from "no-fault" divorces in which one party files for divorce or those divorces that require some "fault" on the part of one spouse or the other (adultery, alienation of affection, or some other reason). Divorces are decrees that dissolve a marriage; they do not dissolve the family. Parents must still work out custody arrangements of children, alimony payments, child support. Just because they are no longer husband and wife does not mean they are no longer Mommy and Daddy.

In the United States, the divorce rate rose steadily from the 1890s through the 1970s (with a dip in the Depression and a spike after World War II). During the past 25 years, it has fallen significantly, along with marriage rates overall. The annual national divorce rate is at its lowest since 1970, while marriage is down 30 percent and the number of unmarried couples living together is up tenfold since 1960 (*Time*, 2007, p. 6).

These trends are led by the middle class. At the lower end of the scale, however, the picture is reversed, leading some sociologists to describe a "divorce divide" based on class and race (Martin, 2006). Among college-educated women who first married between 1975 and 1979, 29 percent were divorced within 10 years; for those first married between 1990 and 1994, only 16.5 percent were. Yet for high school dropouts, 38 percent of those first married between 1975 and 1979 were divorced within a decade—and 46 percent were between 1990 and 1994. For those with a high school diploma, divorce rates for those years rose from 35 to 38 percent (Martin, 2006; Figure 12.5). And the figures mask the fact that a larger percentage of poorer women avoid divorce by never marrying in the first place.

Whatever these different sociological dimensions, some commentators broadly blame divorce for nearly every social ill, from prostitution (where else are divorced men to turn?) to serial murder (evidently watching their parents break up has kids reaching for the nearest pickax). More moderate voices worry that quick-and-easy divorce undermines the institution of the family, forcing the divorced adults to start courting again when they should be engaged in child rearing and teaching children that dysfunction is the norm.

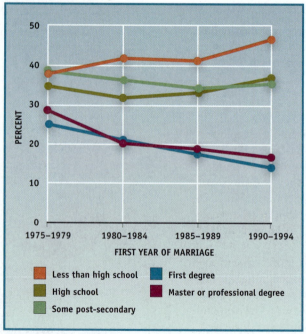

FIGURE 12.5 **More Education, Less Divorce**

Legend:
- Less than high school
- High school
- Some post-secondary
- First degree
- Master or professional degree

X-axis (FIRST YEAR OF MARRIAGE): 1975–1979, 1980–1984, 1985–1989, 1990–1994
Y-axis (PERCENT): 0 to 50

Source: Adapted from "Trends in Marital Dissolution by Women's Education in the United States" by Steven P. Martin, *Demographic Research,* December 13, 2006, Vol. 15, #20, pp. 537–560, © 2006 Steven P. Martin. Reprinted by permission.

Sociologists understand that both statements are, at least, partially true. Some people believe that the easy availability of divorce weakens our belief in the institution of marriage. On the other hand, sociologists often counter that divorce makes families stronger by allowing an escape from damaging environments and enabling both parents and children to adapt to new types of relationships.

Who usually wants the divorce? On the average, men become more content with their marriages over time, while women become less content; the wife is usually the one who wants out. A study of divorces that occurred after age 40 found that wives initiated two-thirds of them (Coontz, 2005).

The Consequences of Divorce

Married couples opt for divorce for all sorts of reasons, and the divorce itself can be easy or hard, so it is understandable that research on the impact of divorce on the husband and wife is mixed. Some studies find that people are happier after their divorce than before (Wilson and Oswald, 2005). Others find psychological scars that never heal unless the divorcees remarry (Johnson and Wu, 2002). Still others find that individual attitudes make the difference in well-being after a divorce (Amato and Sobolewski, 2001; Wood, Goesting and Avellar, 2007).

Economically, there is clearer evidence about losses and gains. In a large majority of divorces, women's standards of living decline, while men's go up. Those men who are used to being the primary breadwinner may suddenly find that they are supporting one (plus a small amount for child support) on a salary that used to support the whole family. Those women who are more accustomed to being in charge of the household, with a secondary, part-time, or even no job, may suddenly find that their income must stretch from being a helpful supplement to supplying most of the family's necessities.

It is crucial to remember that the breadwinning husband with an income-supplementing or stay-at-home wife has rarely been an option for many minority families. Black women, for example, have a longer history of workforce participation than women of other races (Page and Stevens, 2005). Divorce plays an even bigger economic role for Black households than for Whites in the United States, partly because of this difference. While family income for Whites falls about 30 percent during the first 2 years of divorce, it falls by 53 percent for Blacks (Page and Stevens, 2005). Three or more years after divorce, White households recoup about one-third of the lost income, but the income of Black families barely improves. This may have to do with the fact that when divorce occurs, the probability of Black mothers working does not change, while recently divorced White women have an 18 percent greater probability of working (Page and Stevens, 2005).

After a divorce, children are still more likely to live with the mother, while the father visits on specified days or weeks. Not only do the children have to handle this new living situation, but many will soon move to a new home, enroll in a new school, and face the stress and depression of a mother who has suddenly entered or reentered the workforce as the primary breadwinner. And that's when the divorce is amicable. At times there is open hostility between the mother and father, with each telling the children how horrible the other is or even trying to acquire full custody, with many potential negative outcomes (Coontz, 1988).

Psychologist Judith Wallerstein (2000) studied 131 children of 60 couples from affluent Marin County, California, who divorced in 1971. She followed these children through adolescence and into adulthood, when many married and became parents of their own. She found a sleeper effect: Years later, their parents' divorce is affecting the children's

Divorce is rarely a "pleasant" experience, but its impact varies significantly by race, gender, and class. Women's standard of living declines more sharply than men's (which may even rise). Poor and minority women's standards of living decline even more, and they recoup that lost income more slowly than white women do—if at all. ▼

relationships. They fear that their relationships will fail, fear betrayal, and, most significantly, fear any change at all. Divorce, she argued, was bad for children—both immediately and later in their lives. Couples, politicians argued, should, indeed, stay together, "for the sake of the children."

However, Wallerstein's findings have been quite controversial—and, in fact, her findings have been disconfirmed by most sociological studies. After all, Wallerstein studied only children who came to see her as a therapist—that is, she based her findings on those children who were already having difficulties *before their parents divorced*. And she studied children only in wealthy ultra-liberal Marin County, California—the suburban county just north of San Francisco where the Grateful Dead live. She attributed their subsequent problems in relationships to their parents' divorce, when it is just as plausible that it was the conflict between the parents that led to both the divorce *and* the children's problems. Staying together might have been the worst imaginable outcome.

Sociological research consistently finds that children are more resilient and adapt successfully to their parents' divorces. Mavis Hetherington (2002), for example, studied more than 2,500 children from 1,400 families over a period of 30 years and found that the fear of a devastating effect of divorce on children is exaggerated, with 75 to 80 percent of children coping reasonably well. Other scholars agree that, although parental divorce increases the risk of psychological distress and relationship problems in adulthood, the risks are not great (Amato, 2003; see also Ahrons, 2004).

Perhaps the outcome of divorce depends less on whether one gets a divorce and more on how civilly the parents behave toward each other and how much ongoing investment they maintain in their children's lives. That is to say, what's better for children is explained less well by whether the parents are married or divorced and better by the quality of the relationships the parents have with their children—and with each other.

Blended Families

In the first episode of the popular teen sitcom *Drake and Josh,* two high school boys with opposing personalities find that Josh's father intends to marry Drake's mother, so they will become brothers. They accept their new arrangement with no stress or conflict. Their other parents are never mentioned. Drake calls his new Dad "Dad" and defers to his authority. Josh's new Mom never lets on that she has been parenting him for only a few months. In fact, there is only one clue that they were once separate: They have decided to keep their original last names.

Sociology and our World

The Social Value of Sons?

Gordon Dahl and Enrico Moretti (2004) found families with only male children are significantly more durable than those with only female children. In Vietnam, parents of a girl are 25 percent more likely to divorce than parents of a boy. The Asian preference for male children is well known, but the trend also appears in the United States: Parents of one girl are 4.4 percent more likely to divorce than parents of one boy. Parents with three girls are nearly 9 percent more likely to divorce than parents with three boys.

Even in the matter of courtship, when men discover that the woman they are dating is pregnant, they are more likely to stay with her if she is carrying a boy. When they begin dating women who are already mothers, they are more likely to marry women with sons than women with daughters.

Evidently the preference for sons is not limited to Asia. Many American men feel that their lives are incomplete or that they are insufficiently masculine unless they have sons, so much so that their decision to marry or stay in an unhappy marriage is often based less on the wife than on the offspring.

Of course, this twenty-first-century revision of *The Brady Bunch* is a highly idealized view of blended families. When a divorced person remarries, the other parents are usually in the picture, and their partner's teenage children do not easily refer to them as "Mom" or "Dad." There are often considerable tensions about the blended partner's parenting rights and obligations. Sooner or later, a child is bound to yell, "I don't have to listen to you! You're not my real father (or mother)!"

At least half of all children will have a divorced and remarried parent before they turn 18 (Ahrons, 2004). They face different issues, depending on how old they are, the role that their biological parents have, whether it's Mom or Dad who remarries, and whether it's the custodial parent. Usually they must adjust to a new residence and a new school and share space with new siblings. In many families, finances become a divisive issue, placing significant strains on the closeness and stability of blended families (Korn, 2001; Martinez, 2005). Several studies have found that children in blended families—both stepchildren and their half-siblings who are the joint product of both parents—do worse in school than children raised in traditional two-parent families (see Ginther, 2004).

While the dynamics of blended families tend to be similar across class and race, the likelihood of blending families tends to be far more common among the middle classes, where parents have sufficient resources to support these suddenly larger families. Lower-class families may be "blended" in all but name: They may cohabit with other people's children but not formalize it by marrying.

Violence in Families

The famous French sociologist Alexis de Tocqueville spoke of the family as a "haven in a heartless world," but for some the family is a violent nightmare. In many families, the person who promised to love and honor you is the most likely to physically assault you; the one who promised to "forsake all others" is also the most likely to rape you; and the one who is supposed to protect you from harm is the one most likely to cause that harm.

Intimate Partner Violence

Intimate partner violence (IPV) represents violence, lethal or nonlethal, experienced by a spouse, ex-spouse, or cohabiting partner; boyfriend or girlfriend; or ex-boyfriend or -girlfriend. It is commonly called "domestic violence," but because some does not occur in the home, IPV is the preferred term. IPV is the single major cause of injury to women in the United States. More than 2 million women are beaten by their partners every year. Nearly one in five victims of violence treated in hospital emergency rooms was injured by a spouse, a former spouse, or a current or former boyfriend or girlfriend (Bachman and Salzman, 1994; Kellerman and Marcy 1992; Rhode, 1997; Straus and Gelles, 1990).

Globally, the problem of family violence is widespread. A study released in 2006 by the World Health Organization found that rates of IPV ranged from a low of 15 percent of women in Japan to a high of 71 percent of women in rural Ethiopia. (Rates in the European Union and United States were between 20 and 25 percent.) In 6 of the 15 sites of study, at least 50 percent of

Intimate partner violence (IPV) is the single major cause of injury to women in the United States. More than 2 million women—of all races and classes—are beaten by their partners every year. Some scars may never completely heal. ▼

FIGURE 12.6 Nonfatal Intimate Partner Victimization Rate by Gender and Race, 1993–2004

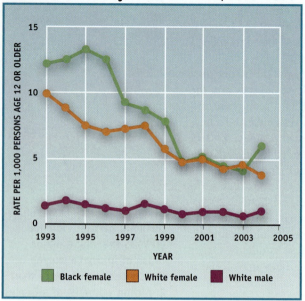

Source: U. S. Department of Justice, Bureau of Justice Statistics, 2000.

the women had been subjected to moderate or severe violence in the home at some point. Perhaps more telling, the majority of the 25,000 women interviewed in the study said that it was the first time they had ever spoken of the abuse to anyone (García-Moreno et al., 2006).

In the United States, IPV knows no class, racial, or ethnic bounds. Yet there are some differences by class, race, ethnicity, and age. For example, poor women experience significantly more violence than higher-income women, and younger women, aged 16 to 24, are far more likely to experience violence than older women. And one of the best predictors of the onset of domestic violence is unemployment.

A few studies have found rates of domestic violence to be higher in African American families than in White families (Hampton, 1987; Hampton and Gelles, 1994). Black females experienced domestic violence at a rate 35 percent higher than that of White females, and Black males experienced domestic violence at a rate about 62 percent higher than that of White males (Rennison and Welchans, 2000; Figure 12.6).

Among Latinos the evidence is contradictory: One study found significantly less violence in Latino families than in Anglo families, while another found a slightly higher rate. Rates were directly related to two factors, the strains of immigrant status and the variations in ideologies of male dominance (Klevens, 2007).

In many cases, however, these racial and ethnic differences disappear when social class is taken into account. Sociologist Noel Cazenave examined the same National Family Violence Survey and found that Blacks had *lower* rates of wife abuse than Whites in three of four income categories—the two highest and the lowest. Higher rates among Blacks were reported only by those respondents in the $6,000 to $11,999 income range (which included 40 percent of all Blacks surveyed). Income and residence (urban) were also the variables that explained virtually all the ethnic differences between Latinos and Anglos. The same racial differences in spousal murder can be explained by class: Two-thirds of all spousal murders in New York City took place in the poorest sections of the Bronx and Brooklyn (Straus and Cazenare, 1990).

Gay men and lesbians can engage in IPV as well. A recent informal survey of gay victims of violence in six major cities found that gay men and lesbians were more likely to be victims of domestic violence than of antigay hate crimes.

The single greatest difference in rates of IPV is by gender. According to the Bureau of Justice Statistics, 85 percent of all victims of domestic violence are women (see Kimmel, 2002). The gender imbalance of intimate violence is staggering. Of those victims of violence who were injured by spouses or ex-spouses, women outnumber men by about 9 to 1. Eight times as many women were injured by their boyfriends as men injured by girlfriends.

Intergenerational and Intragenerational Violence

In addition to violence between domestic partners, there is also a significant amount of intergenerational and intragenerational violence in families. Intergenerational violence refers to violence between generations, such as parents to children and children to parents. Intragenerational violence refers to violence within the same generation—that is, sibling violence.

How do we know what we know?

Gender Symmetry in IPV

Despite dramatic gender differences, there are some researchers and political pundits who claim that there is "gender symmetry" in domestic violence—that rates of domestic violence are roughly equal by gender (see, for example, Brott, 1994). One reason this symmetry is underreported is because men who are victims of domestic violence are so ashamed they are unlikely to come forward—a psychological problem that one researcher calls "the battered husband syndrome" (Steinmetz, 1978).

But a close look at the data suggests why these findings are so discordant with the official studies by the Department of Justice and the FBI. Those studies that find gender symmetry rely on the "conflict tactics scale" (CTS) developed by family violence researcher and sociologist Murray Straus and his colleagues over 30 years. The CTS asked couples if they had ever, during the course of their relationship, hit their partner. An equal number of women and men answered "yes." The number changed dramatically, though, when they were asked who initiated the violence (was it offensive, or defensive), how severe it was (did she push him before or after he'd broken her jaw?), and how often the violence occurred. When these three questions were posed, the results shifted back: The amount, frequency, severity, and consistency of violence against women are far greater than anything done by women to men.

There were several other problems with the CTS as a measure (see Kimmel, 2002). These problems included:

1. *Whom did they ask?* Studies that found comparable rates of domestic violence asked only one partner about the incident. But studies in which both partners were interviewed separately found large discrepancies between reports from women and from men.
2. *What was the time frame?* Studies that found symmetry asked about incidents that occurred in a single year, thus equating a single slap with a reign of domestic terror that may have lasted decades.
3. *Was the couple together?* Studies that found gender symmetry excluded couples that were separated or divorced, although violence against women increases dramatically after separation.
4. *What was the reason for the violence?* Studies that find symmetry do not distinguish between offensive and defensive violence, equating a vicious assault with a woman hitting her husband to get him to stop hitting the children.
5. *Was "sex" involved?* Studies that find symmetry omit marital rape and sexual aggression; because a significant amount of IPV occurs when one partner doesn't want to have sex, this would dramatically change the data.

Of course, women can be—and are—violent toward their husbands and partners. Criminologist Martin Schwartz estimates that women commit as much as 3 to 4 percent of all spousal violence. But research such as this requires that we look more deeply at the questions asked. Sometimes, the answers are contained in the questions.

Sibling violence goes beyond routine sibling rivalry. Earlier reports found that as many as 80 percent of American children had engaged in an act of physical violence toward a sibling (Straus and Gelles, 1990). In a recent sociological study, David Finkelhor and his colleagues (2006) found that 35 percent of all children had been attacked by a sibling in the previous year. Of these, more than a third were serious attacks (Figure 12.7).

The consequences of sibling violence can be severe. Children who were repeatedly attacked were twice as likely to show symptoms of trauma, anxiety, and depression, including sleeplessness, crying spells, thoughts of suicide, and fear of the dark (Butler, 2006). Finkelhor and his colleagues found that attacks did not differ by class or race, or even by gender, although boys were slightly more likely to be victims than girls. They occurred most frequently on siblings aged 6 to 12 and gradually tapered off as the child entered adolescence.

Sometime, children use violence against their parents. About 18 percent of children used violence against their parents in the past year—about half of which was considered "nontrivial," serious enough to cause pain or injury (Agnew and Huguley,

FIGURE 12.7 Leave Your Brother Alone!
Sibling Violence

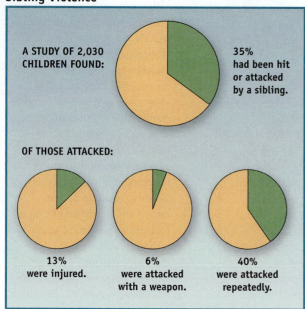

A STUDY OF 2,030 CHILDREN FOUND:

35% had been hit or attacked by a sibling.

OF THOSE ATTACKED:

13% were injured.

6% were attacked with a weapon.

40% were attacked repeatedly.

Source: From "Beyond Rivalry, a Hidden World of Sibling Violence" by Katy Butler, *The New York Times,* February 28, 2006. Reprinted with permission.

1989; Cornell and Gelles, 1982; Straus, Gelles, and Steinmetz, 1980). Rates of child-to-parent violence decrease as the child ages; it is more often younger children who hit their parents. Injuries to parents are rare, but they do happen. If the parent reacts to a child's violence with violence, the child has learned a lesson that could last a lifetime.

The rates of parental violence against children are significantly more serious. In recent years, American society has also been vitally concerned about the problem of child abuse (violence against children) and child sexual abuse (the sexual exploitation of children). The Keeping Children and Families Safe Act of 2003 defines child abuse and neglect as, at minimum: (1) Any recent act or failure to act on the part of a parent or caretaker which results in death, serious physical or emotional harm, sexual abuse or exploitation; or (2) an act or failure to act which presents an imminent risk of serious harm. This definition of child abuse and neglect refers specifically to parents and other caregivers. A "child" under this definition generally means a person who is under the age of 18 or who is not an emancipated minor.

According to the Department of Health and Human Services, rates of victimization and the number of victims have been decreasing in the first decade of the twenty-first century. An estimated 872,000 children were determined to be victims of child abuse or neglect for 2004 (the last year for which there are data). More than 60 percent of child victims were neglected by their parents or other caregivers. About 18 percent were physically abused, 10 percent were sexually abused, and 7 percent were emotionally maltreated. (A child could be a victim of more than one type of maltreatment.) The United States has rates that are significantly higher than rates in other English-speaking countries such as Australia, Canada, and Great Britain, partly, but not entirely, due to the higher rates of child poverty in the United States (poverty is a significant risk factor).

Rates of child abuse and child sexual abuse vary significantly by class but less by race or ethnicity. According to some research (Daly and Wilson, 1981), living with a stepparent significantly increases the risk of both abuse and sexual abuse. Yet other research, using the conflict tactics scale, found little difference—in generally very high rates overall. In one study, 63 percent of children who lived with both genetic parents and 47 percent of those who lived with a stepparent and 60 percent of those who lived with a foster parent were subject to violence, and about 10 percent were subjected to severe violence in all three categories (Gelles and Harrop, 1991).

Globally, the problem of child abuse and neglect is equally serious—and includes forms of abuse that are not found in the economic north. In 2006, the United Nations commissioned the first global investigation into child abuse. They found that between 80 and 98 percent of children suffer physical punishment in their homes, with a third or more experiencing severe physical punishment resulting from the use of implements.

Despite these global differences, it is equally true that Americans are far more accepting of violence against children than they may realize. Over half of all American parents (55 percent) believe that corporal punishment, including spanking, is acceptable; and one-third of parents have used corporal punishment against their adolescents (Straus, 2005). These numbers are significantly less than the 94 percent who supported the use of corporal punishment in 1968 and the two-thirds who used it with adolescents in 1975 (Straus, 2005). But it is still the case that nearly all parents—94 percent—used corporal punishment with toddlers, and they did so, on average, three times a week.

There is actually little empirical evidence that spanking serves any developmental purpose, but there is a wealth of evidence that spanking is developmentally harmful. The American Academy of Pediatrics recommends that parents avoid spanking (2007). In fact, 94 percent of all studies of the effects of corporal punishment on children showed a relationship between such forms of punishment and aggression, delinquency in childhood, crime and antisocial behavior as an adult, low levels of empathy or conscience, poor parent–child relations, and mental health problems such as depression (Gershoff, 2002).

Family violence is often difficult to remedy through policy initiatives. Globally, fewer than 10 percent of all countries even have laws against certain forms of child abuse, let alone programs to offer aid and support to victims and to prosecute perpetrators (*Rights of the Child,* 2006). In the United States, policymakers have long taken the approach that what happens "behind closed doors" is a private matter, not a social problem that can be remedied only through public policy. Rates of all forms of family violence are dramatically underreported; fear of retaliation, shame, and a general cultural acceptance of violence all greatly reduce the likelihood of reporting. And the continuum of violence, from spanking a child to murdering a spouse, is part of a culture that does not universally condemn violence but sees some instances of violence as legitimate and even appropriate and sees perpetrators as entitled to use violence.

The Family in the 21st Century: "The Same as It Ever Was"

In the first line of his novel *Anna Karenina,* the great Russian novelist Leo Tolstoy wrote, "Happy families are all alike; every unhappy family is unhappy in its own way." How unsociological! Families, happy or unhappy, are as varied as snowflakes when viewed close up and as similar around the world as all the sand in the desert.

Families are as old as the human species. We've always had them; indeed we couldn't live without them. And families have always been changing, adapting to new political, social, economic, and environmental situations. Some expectations of family may be timeless, yet families have always been different, and new relationships, arrangements, and patterns are emerging all over the world today, just as they always have been. As the musician David Byrne sang in the 1980s, the family is "the same as it ever was."

Yes, it's probably true that family is still the place where, when we go there, they have to take us in. But even if we can go home again, it's never the same.

Chapter Review

1. *How do sociologists define family?* A family is a basic unit of society. Family is also a cultural institution; the functions of the family include socializing new members and regulation of sexual activity, property ownership, and marriage. The definition of family changes over time; the nuclear family is a relatively new phenomenon. Agrarian families were extended, and the household formed the basic economic unit of society, performing all societal functions that are now handled by other institutions. The nuclear family developed in Europe and the United States in the late eighteenth century as a result of industrialization and modernization. The nuclear family model was very gendered, and the home became the women's sphere and work men's.

2. *How do families develop?* Dating emerged in the United States in the 1920s when children of immigrants shed old customs and teens had unprecedented freedom. Dating

sometimes leads to marriage, the most common family formation. Marriage in the United States varies by race; White women are more likely to marry than others. Not everyone marries; increasingly people are choosing to postpone marriage, to cohabit, or to remain single. Choices are influenced by education, changing sexual mores, and the women's movement. Attitudes toward interracial marriage are also changing, which is reflected in increased rates of such marriages. Also, same-sex couples cannot marry in most states but do form partnerships and cohabit.

3. *How important is parenting?* Parenting is becoming more desirable in the United States, and more importance is being placed on parents and parenting. At the same time, children are more undervalued and neglected than before. Parenting is gendered; although most women work outside the home, they still do most of the housework and particularly the housework having to do with caring for the children. Fathers are becoming more active parents. Also, there has been an increase in single-parent families, mostly headed by mothers. Grandparents are also raising grandchildren; this is most likely for African American grandmothers. Not everyone chooses to have children; more highly educated individuals are less likely to parent than those in other groups.

4. *What transitions do families go through?* Although marriage used to mean a lifelong commitment, today divorce is common and easy to get. The effects of divorce on children are widely debated. While parental divorce increases the risk of distress and later relationship problems, most children are found to be resilient. After a divorce, the woman's standard of living typically decreases; this is even more striking among African American women. As people remarry, blended families are becoming more common, especially among those in the middle class, although unofficial blended families are prevalent in all groups.

5. *What forms does family violence take?* Family violence takes many forms. One is intimate partner violence (IPV). IPV affects people from all groups but is more likely to occur among the poorer socioeconomic strata. Eighty-five percent of IPV victims are women. Violence also occurs between and within generations. In sibling violence, which tends to taper off after age 12, boys are more likely than girls to be victims. Children do abuse parents, but parental abuse of children is a far greater social problem. In the United States, views on corporal punishment as abuse vary, but negative attitudes toward it have strengthened over time. Globally, child abuse is prevalent and includes things such as genital mutilation and sexual slavery.

Key Terms

Bilineal descent (p. 383)
Cohabitation (p. 395)
Companionate marriage (p. 387)
Exogamy (p. 384)
Extended family (p. 386)
Family (p. 382)
Family of origin (p. 384)

Family of procreation (p. 384)
Group marriage (p. 384)
Intimate partner violence (IPV) (p. 409)
Kinship systems (p. 382)
Legitimacy (p. 383)
Matrilineal descent (p. 383)
Miscegenation (p. 398)

Monogamy (p. 383)
Multigenerational households (p. 394)
Nonmarital sex (p. 398)
Patrilineal descent (p. 383)
Polyandry (p. 384)
Polygamy (p. 383)
Polygyny (p. 383)

What does America think?

12.1 Racial and Ethnic Family Diversity

These are actual survey data from the General Social Survey.

Do you think there should be laws against marriages between Blacks and Whites? The overwhelming majority of respondents said "no" to this question in the 2002 survey. More Black (95.1 percent) than White (89.6 percent) respondents said "no." The numbers were very different when the question was asked 30 years earlier in 1972, when about 60 percent of respondents said "no." In the 1972 survey, the race categories were limited to "White" (of whom 60.7 percent said "no") and "other" (of whom 66.7 percent said "no"). Most respondents were White.

1. Why do you think almost 10 percent of the population still thinks interracial marriage should be illegal, including 9 percent of black respondents?
2. Part of doing sociology is placing things in historical context. What historical changes have taken place in the past 30 years that might explain how views toward interracial marriage have changed?

12.2 Attitudes toward Abortion

These are actual survey data from the General Social Survey, 2004.

1. **Do you think it should be possible for a pregnant woman to obtain a legal abortion if the woman's own health is seriously endangered by the pregnancy?** In 2004, 86 percent of respondents said "yes," and 14 percent said "no." These results are almost identical to 1972 responses. The percentage of respondents saying "yes" peaked in 1991 at 91.5 percent.

2. **Do you think it should be possible for a pregnant woman to obtain a legal abortion if she is married and does not want any more children?** In 2004, 41.8 percent of respondents said "yes," and 58.2 percent said "no." The percentage of people saying "yes" peaked 1994 at 48 percent, but otherwise, the data were almost identical to 1972, and attitudes have remained pretty steady since then.

3. **Do you think it should be possible for a pregnant woman to obtain a legal abortion if the family has a very low income and cannot afford any more children?** The responses from 2004 showed 41 percent of respondents saying "yes" and 59 percent saying "no." The response for those saying "yes" was rather lower than 1972 and again peaked in 1994.

4. **Do you think it should be possible for a pregnant woman to obtain a legal abortion if she became pregnant as a result of rape?** In 2004, 76.2 percent of respondents said "yes," and 23.8 percent said "no." The response for those saying "yes" was lower than it was in 1972 and peaked in 1991.

CRITICAL THINKING | DISCUSSION QUESTIONS

1. What do you think lies behind the variation of responses in approval toward abortion based on the reason for abortion? The highest approval was for the pregnant woman's health, next for rape victims, lower for married women who do not want children, and lowest for women who want to abort because they are poor. What societal values does this ranking reflect?
2. Why do you think the results break down by gender the way they do?

▶ Go to this website to look further at the data. You can run your own statistics and crosstabs here: **http://sda.berkeley.edu/cgi-bin/hsda?harcsda+gss04.**

REFERENCES: Davis, James A., Tom W. Smith, and Peter V. Marsden. General Social Surveys 1972–2004: [Cumulative file] [Computer file]. 2nd ICPSR version. Chicago, IL: National Opinion Research Center [producer], 2005; Storrs, CT: Roper Center for Public Opinion Research, University of Connecticut; Ann Arbor, MI: Inter-University Consortium for Political and Social Research; Berkeley, CA: Computer-Assisted Survey Methods Program, University of California [distributors], 2005.

chapter 13

AMERICANS SPEND AN AVERAGE OF 1,804 HOURS per year working. That's 200 hours more than in France or Sweden, over 300 more than in Germany, but 550 hours less than Korea (OECD, 2007). An American who works full-time from age 18 to age 65, with three weeks off for vacations and holidays each year, will spend about 91,000 hours doing things that are more likely to be boring, degrading, and physically exhausting than they are fun, interesting, and exciting. Why do we do it? It depends on whom you ask.

Ask a janitor or a sales clerk, and you are likely to hear: *for the money*. No one gets a free ride: food, clothing, and shelter all come with price tags. Work is, well, *work*, not play. Unless you win the lottery, you just have to find some way to get through each day. Maybe you can think about your real life, after hours, with family, friends, and leisure.

Economy and Work

Ask a photojournalist or a trial lawyer, and you are likely to hear: *for the satisfaction*. A job is a "calling," the fulfillment of talent, skill, training, and ambition, not something you *do* but something you *are*. Even when the work day is supposedly over, you are constantly getting new ideas or thinking about problems. There is no "after hours." This *is* your life.

Clearly, our motivations for working are not either/or, but both. For most of us, it's a combination of the two. The janitor and the sales clerk probably find some degree of worth, meaning, and satisfaction in their jobs in addition to paychecks, and the photojournalist and the trial lawyer would be far less likely to consider their jobs a "calling" if they weren't paid.

A job provides both identity and financial support. And the degree to which it provides each is a key to an understanding of the economy as a major institution of reproducing social inequality.

A job provides both identity and financial support. And the degree to which it provides each is a key to an understanding of the economy as a major institution of reproducing social inequality.

Theories of the Economy

We all need material resources. On the most basic level, physical survival requires the big three: food, shelter, and clothing. But an adequate quality of life requires much more, including transportation, communication, education, medical care, and entertainment. A vast array of goods and services is available to meet these needs: cars, cell phones, college classes, day care, diapers, DVD players, magazine subscriptions, microwave ovens, postage stamps, and psychiatric appointments. One person or household could never produce everything, so we must organize collectively to produce and distribute resources. The result is an economy.

An **economy** is a set of institutions and relationships that manages natural resources, manufactured goods, and professional services. These resources, goods, and services are called **capital.** The major economic theories of the world diverge on the question of whether the people serve the economy or the economy serves the people. British empiricists like John Locke (1676) and Thomas Hobbes (1658) pointed out in the seventeenth century that resources are limited, and no economy has yet been able to ensure that every member of the society has food, shelter, and clothing, let alone everything necessary for an adequate quality of life. Therefore people must compete with each other. We are motivated by rational self-interest, a desire to meet our own material needs even though we see others going without. Economies form when individuals band together to protect their common resources from outsiders or to make their competition more congenial and predictable. If asked why they work, they will answer, like the janitor and sales clerk: *for the money.*

Locke and Hobbes stressed separation, competition, and individual isolation as results of rational self-interest. But other theorists, like Adam Smith (1776), argued that social life involves much more than individuals striving for social gain: People cooperate as often as they compete. There are many good samaritans, many altruistic acts, many collective struggles over fairness and justice. If you ask them why they work, they will answer, like the photojournalist and the trial lawyer: *for the satisfaction.*

Karl Marx (1848) believed that both answers were true—and therein lay the problem. Marx believed that an economic system based on private property divided people into two unequal and competing classes: The upper class worked because they achieved satisfaction by owning all the goods and services and controlling politics and social life. The working class worked because they had to—because they were, in effect, slaves to the upper classes. Eventually, he believed, if the workers controlled and owned everything, everyone would work for the pleasure of it.

Max Weber ([1904] 2001) believed that capitalism originated in a desire for personal spiritual fulfillment and to "make the world a better place," while Émile Durkheim ([1897] 1997) argued that in modern societies, we are all interdependent: Every person must depend on hundreds or thousands of others for goods and services. Thus, economies are not an isolating, divisive force at all, but a unifying force. They foster strong social ties and create social cohesion, or *organic solidarity.*

There is some truth to all these theories. Every economic system requires some degree of competition and some degree of cooperation. An economy is essential to the common good, but it also serves to emphasize or exacerbate the gap between rich and poor, middle class and working class, having a house and having an apartment, driving a car and taking the bus. It produces both identity and inequality.

Economic Development

The first human societies, tens of thousands of years ago, were nomadic hunter-gatherer groups of 20 to 40 people. They had few rules about the production and distribution of capital. Sometimes a particularly talented or interested person might specialize in a task, like making pottery or spears, but otherwise everyone worked together to provide food, shelter, and clothing, and there were few other material resources available (nomads can't own a lot) (Panter-Brick, Layton, and Rowley-Conwy, 2001). Then came the Agricultural Revolution.

The Agricultural Economy

Around 10,000 years ago, people living along the great rivers in Mesopotamia, Egypt, and China learned how to plow the land and grow regular, predictable crops of rice, wheat, or corn. No longer nomadic, they could acquire more goods. And because agriculture is far more productive (more food produced per hour of work) than hunting and gathering, not everyone had to be involved in providing food, shelter, and clothing for the group. Farmers could use their surplus crops to pay professional potters, builders, or priests. A division of labor began.

Sometimes a village might have a surplus of pottery makers and start exchanging its pottery with a village downstream, which had a surplus of spear makers. **Markets,** regular exchanges of goods and services, began, and with them the economy became a social institution. The agricultural economy, with its characteristics of permanent settlements, job specialization, and intergroup trade, lasted for thousands of years, through the great empires of Greece, Rome, China, and Mesoamerica (Cameron and Neal, 2002; Cipolla, 1994; North and Thomas, 1976).

The Industrial Economy

Before 1765, all work was done by human or animal muscle, except for an occasional windmill or waterwheel. Then James Watt marketed the first reliable, high-functioning steam engine, and the era of the machine began. Within a century, hundreds of new machines powered by steam or electricity appeared, including lithographs, telegraphs, steam locomotives, sewing machines, slot machines, lawn mowers, and refrigerators. By 1900, there were typewriters, phonographs, electric stoves, and automobiles. The **Industrial Revolution,** or the era of the machine, transformed economics, politics, and social life, first in Europe and North America, and eventually in the rest of the world. **Industrial economies,** economies based on factory production, differed from agricultural economies in five ways (Hobsbawm, 2000; Oshima, 1986; Stearns, 2001):

1. *Power.* Machines were powerful: They could do 100 times the work of human or animal muscles. And they were production oriented. Before the Industrial Revolution, most work had been about growing or hunting food. Now natural resources were less important than the products that could be manufactured from them.

2. *Centralization.* Manufacturing required bulky, expensive machines unfeasible for home use, so most jobs moved away from family farms to centralized offices and factories. For the first time, people had leave home in the morning and *go to work,* juggling two distinct worlds.

▲ Industrialization ushered in large-scale factories, assembly-line production, and more routinized labor, and thus transformed the experience of work itself. [Assembly line at a generator factory of the Ford Motor Company].

3. *Specialization.* In the influential *Principles of Scientific Management* (1911), Frederick Taylor proposed that production would be more efficient if it were broken up into a series of single tasks, with each worker responsible for performing one task in the most efficient manner possible. Instead of a toy maker hammering, sewing, and painting every toy from start to finish, perhaps taking two entire days to complete one doll, it would be more efficient for one person do nothing but affix arms. Where 20 start-to-finish toy makers could produce 10 dolls in a day, 20 specialized toy makers could produce 600.

In 1910, Henry Ford's Model T automobiles were selling for $780 each. Automobiles have many more parts than dolls, and they must be connected with minute precision. But when Ford put Taylorism to work in his plant in Highland Park, Michigan, in 1914 with an assembly line, productivity increased tenfold, and the price dropped to $360. Without **mass production,** or *Fordism,* the goods and services of the Industrial Revolution would be out of reach for the vast majority of the population.

4. **Wage labor.** Instead of being paid for the end result of their labor, workers got a regular paycheck in exchange for performing a specific task. Usually they never saw the end result. They received the same pay, no matter how successful their product was, while the handful of people who owned the factories kept all of the profits. The owners were able to manipulate the political system for their own purposes, setting the stage for many conflicts, some deadly, as workers fought to improve their working conditions.

5. *Separation of work and home.* The family farm was both home and workplace. But the coming of the industrial factory meant that home and work were separate, with enormous consequences for both realms.

Consumption and the Modern Economy

As more efficient machines and factory assembly lines made manufacturing increasingly simply, the emphasis of industrial economies shifted from **production** (how to get more goods out there) to **consumption** (how to decide from among the goods available). Advertising became an essential part of business rather than an afterthought. Products received brand names, trademarks, slogans, and spokespeople. General stores were replaced by department stores like Harrod's in London and Wanamaker's in the United States. In 1904, Macy's, on Herald Square in New York City, was advertised as "the largest store on Earth," with nine stories, 33 elevators, four escalators, and a system of pneumatic tubes. "Window shopping," looking through shop windows for items that one would like to possess, became a common pastime (Lancaster, 1995).

In 1912, Thorstein Veblen coined the term **conspicuous consumption** to mark the shift from the Protestant ethic described by Max Weber, where prestige came from savings and thrift, to a new form of prestige based on accumulating as many possessions as possible and showing them off. Veblen argued that the real symbols of wealth were those that made it look as though you didn't have to work: Fashions like long fingernails, high heels, and tight skirts for women were a sign that they were pampered and didn't need to work; and wealthy men were shown sailing, skiing, and otherwise experiencing the leisure that only true wealth can bring.

With industrialization came the decline of agriculture as a livelihood. In 1700, before the Industrial Revolution, 60 percent of all workers in the United States were involved in agriculture, or the three F's (farming, fishing, and forestry). As late as 1900, it was 30 percent. Today, the three F's occupy less than 1 percent of the American workforce. Of course, there is little need for more workers. In 1880, a typical farmer could grow enough food to sustain five people (about the size of the typical farm family). Today's high-tech agribusiness specialists can feed about 80 people apiece.

The Postindustrial Economy

Industrial economies flourished for over two hundred years (Mathias and Pollard, 1989). Industrialized—or "developed"—nations remain the world's economic leaders. Perhaps the simplest way to determine how rich or poor a country is would be to compare the percentage of its labor force involved in agriculture to the percentage in industry. In Switzerland, it's 5 percent agriculture, 26 percent industry. In Bangladesh, it's 63 percent agriculture, 11 percent industry.

Today, jobs are shifting to the services sector, although unevenly, with developed economies seeing far greater increases in employment in services (Figure 13.1; OECD, 2007). The figure below takes the year 2000 as its base, and calculates all the shifts in the three sectors relative to their employment rate in 2000. The drop in agriculture in steep, while the rise in services is modest and industry is relatively flat. Overall, the year 2007 marked the first time the world's biggest source of employment was the service sector, rather than agriculture or industry (International Labor Organization, 2007). Some 40 percent of the world's workers are employed in the services sector, compared with 38.7 percent in agriculture and 21.3 percent in industry. Ten years ago, 43.1 percent of employees worked in agriculture, and only 35.5 percent worked in services (International Labour Organization, 2007).

FIGURE 13.1 **Change in Employment by Broad Economic Sector, 1960–2004**

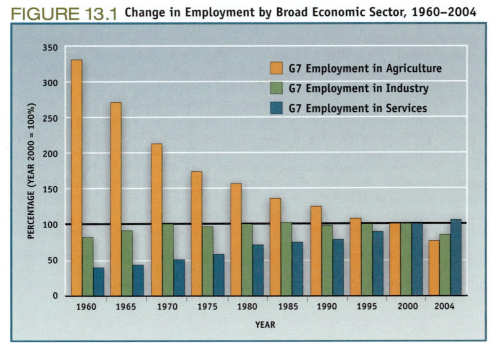

Note: G7 = The world's seven most developed countries: United States, United Kingdom, Japan, France, Germany, Italy, and Canada.
Source: "Employment by Broad Economic Sectors, ISIC Rev. 3, 1960–2004" from *OECD Labour Force Statistics Online,* Updated March 2006. Copyright © OECD, 2006. Reprinted with permission.

This trend began in the 1960s, as automated machinery substantially reduced and sometimes eliminated the need for human labor in production, resulting in **postindustrial economies.** Three social changes characterize "postindustrial" economies: knowledge work, rootlessness, and globalization (Bell, 1976; Kumar, 1995; Vallas, 1999).

Knowledge Work. Postindustrial economies shift from production of goods to production of ideas. In 1940, during the peak of the industrial economy, roughly half of all U.S. workers were working in factories. Today, with automation, outsourcing, and the decline of production, it is about 7 percent. Factories that once employed a thousand assembly-line workers may now require only a dozen or so line managers. Blue-collar jobs (production of various types) now comprise about a quarter of the American workforce, while 33 percent are white collar (management and the professions) and 43 percent are pink-collar (predominantly female) service and office/clerical jobs (Bureau of Labor Statistics, 2004). This shift has affected more than work—it has had an impact on attitudes, lifestyles, and worldviews.

Often postindustrial economies are called knowledge economies. A **knowledge economy** is less oriented around the actual production of a commodity and more concerned with the idea of the commodity, its marketing, its distribution, and its relationship to different groups of consumers. For example, a toy company may require very few people to attach doll arms on the assembly line, but it requires many people to conduct market research, direct TV commercials, design tie-in websites, negotiate with government and parental groups, and acquire global distribution rights. Postindustrial workers work not in factories, but in R&D (research and development), finance, investment, advertising, education, and training. They manipulate words and numbers rather than tools. Ideas, information, and knowledge have become the new forms of capital (Adler, 2001).

Because knowledge-based workers now design, develop, market, sell, and service, they need classes in public speaking, technical writing, global business management, and Java programming. That is, they need to go to college—at least. The proportion of American workers doing jobs that call for complex skills has grown three times as fast as employment in general, and other economies are moving in the same direction, raising global demand for educated workers (*Economist*, 2006). But the United States is losing ground compared to other countries' high school graduation rates: The high school graduation rate for U.S. 35- to 44-year-olds is fifth in the world and for 25- to 34-year-olds is tenth in the world (*U.S. News and World Report*, 2005).

What happens to people with limited education in a postindustrial economy? Fifty years ago, they would have become blue-collar workers. Assembly-line work did not require a lot of education, and it paid nearly as much as white-collar jobs. Blue-collar and white-collar workers lived in comparable houses in the same neighborhoods, sent their children to the same schools, took the same vacations. But now instead of assembly-line work, they are stuck in low-paying service jobs. They cannot afford houses in the same neighborhoods as the white-collar workers. Often, they cannot afford houses at all. The gap between "comfortable" and "barely getting by" shrank during the industrial economy, but now it is growing again (Krugman, 2002).

Rootlessness. Industrial economies moved workers from home to factories, and postindustrial economies move them out into the wide, wide world. The production of ideas does not require all of the workers to be in the same building or even on the same continent. A decade ago, they could phone in their ideas and fax their presentations; now they can transmit entire volumes by IM, e-mail, Internet, and other digital media.

"Rush-hour traffic" is quickly becoming a meaningless term because many white-collar workers don't have to be in some physical location called "work" every day

Try It Bringing Globalization Home

Modified from an activity submitted by Amy Agigian, *Suffolk University*

OBJECTIVE: Think about how your own life is embedded in the global processes of commerce, trade, production, and consumption.

STEP 1: Plan
Develop a written inventory of all the items you have on your person and list the country of origin. List only the labels you can easily read and access. Be prepared to share your list in class.

STEP 2: Develop
Your instructor may take a tally of how many items are from each country and place information in the classroom for everyone to see. After the tally is complete, take a few minutes to write your responses to the following questions:

1. Did anything surprise you about the list?
2. Why do you think so many goods are being produced outside the United States?
3. What impact does this have on you and your everyday life?
4. How does this affect people living in the countries where the goods are being produced? Do you think they are being paid a living wage? Why or why not?
5. What is globalization, and what role do you play in it?

STEP 3: Discuss
Be prepared to participate in a class discussion that further explores some of the questions asked above.

---

between 9 a.m. and 5 p.m. They are on the road constantly, en route between home, office, meetings, and the airport. Service workers *are* stuck in some physical location, but their day might begin at 11 a.m., 4 p.m., or midnight, or they could work a "split shift," with four hours in the morning and four in the evening. So the streets are always crowded.

Even time becomes meaningless to the postindustrial worker. Clients and co-workers live in every part of the globe, so there is no "quitting time": Work can happen any time of the day or night. As a result, the 200-year-old distinction between home and work, livelihood and leisure, is fading away.

Globalization. In addition to knowledge economies, postindustrial economies are often called *global economies* (Hirst, 1997). They have produced a global division of labor, interconnecting workers but also dividing them along socioeconomic lines. As we saw in Chapter 1, globalization is a process of interaction and integration among the people, companies, and governments of different nations, a process driven by international trade and investment and aided by information technology. This process has effects on the environment, on culture, on political systems, on economic development and prosperity, and on human physical well-being in societies around the world.

Globalized production refers to the fact that corporations derive raw materials from all over the world and use manufacturing and assembly plants in many different countries, using international labor forces. Global distribution insures that these products are marketed and distributed all over the world as well. The products we buy are likely made of materials from several countries, assembled in another country, packaged and distributed from yet another, with advertising campaigns and marketing schemes drawn from yet another.

During the Industrial Revolution, the raw materials may have been drawn from other countries, but the entire manufacturing and marketing processes were located in the industrial country. Now, however, the process is fragmented, and each economic function may be located in another country, or several countries. This has also led to **outsourcing,** the contracting out to another company of work that had once been done internally by your company. Initially, technology and IT were outsourced to cheaper call centers in developing nations like India and China. Then, production line jobs began to move overseas where labor was cheaper and factories could be built without bowing to environmental regulations. Now even white-collar jobs like sales and service have also been outsourced.

Although research, development, production, and distribution occur in many different countries, the "knowledge labor" tends to occur in the wealthy countries of United States, Europe, or Japan, while the unskilled and semiskilled factory work takes place in poor countries like Mexico, Sri Lanka, or Tanzania. Even on the global level, the gap between rich and poor is increasing as globalization reinforces or even increases the stark inequalities of income and wealth around the world (Figure 13.2).

By linking different national economies together and by transforming labor into a global exchange, globalization rapidly increases the integration of the economies of the world. At the same time, resistance to globalization is likely to remain national or local or regional, with either socialist ideas about the nationalization of wealth or traditional religions as the only reference points of resistance.

Globalization links owners and managers into an interlocking system of a managerial elite; often managers from Sri Lanka and Belgium will have more in common with each other (consumption patterns, tastes in art and music, and so on) than either will with the working class in his or her own country. However, while the elite at the top become more integrated and cohesive, the working classes will remain fractured and distant from each other, asserting local, regional, and cultural differences as a way to resist integration. In this way, also, the globalizing rich become richer and the globalized poor become poorer.

FIGURE 13.2 World Wealth Levels in the Year 2000

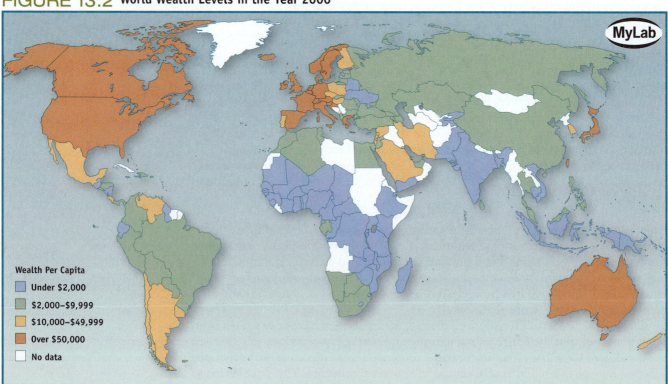

Wealth Per Capita
- Under $2,000
- $2,000–$9,999
- $10,000–$49,999
- Over $50,000
- No data

Source: From *World Distributing Household Wealth,* World Institute for Development Economic Research of United Nations University, December 2006. Reprinted with permission.

Sociology and our World

Jihad versus McWorld

Globalization is bringing the world together and pulling it apart at one in the same moment—and that may make the world unsafe for democracy. In *Jihad vs. McWorld* (1995), Benjamin Barber argues there are two possible futures arising out of globalization: "jihad," or holy wars, and "McWorld," his coinage for the complex sociopolitical outcomes of globalization.

Jihad involves a "retribalization" of many of the world's people by violence and bloodshed. These holy wars, waged in the name of numerous narrowly defined faiths, splinter societies. They pit tribe against tribe, people against people, culture against culture, and reject the idea of civic cooperation or interdependence.

The other tide is "McWorld"—the "onrush of economic and ecological forces that demand integration and uniformity and that mesmerize the world with fast music, fast computers, and fast food—with MTV, Macintosh, and McDonalds" (Barber, 1992, p. 1). McWorld forces nations into a single, homogeneous unit that is bound together by technology and global commerce.

Jihad and McWorld work with equal force but in opposite directions, according to Barber. Jihad is driven by sectarian hatreds and McWorld by all-encompassing markets; the one reinstates ethnic divisions from inside and the other neutralizes national borders from outside. But Barber argues they have one thing in common: Neither offers much hope that democracy is on the march in the world today or will have many legs to stand on in the globalized future.

Economic Systems

All societies must deal with three fundamental economic questions: (1) production, (2) distribution, and (3) consumption. An **economic system** is a mechanism that deals with the production, distribution, and consumption of goods and services in a particular society.

Capitalism

The economic system called **capitalism**—a profit-oriented economic system based on the private or corporate ownership of the means of production and distribution—arose in the Netherlands and Britain during the Protestant Reformation of the seventeenth century, when private investors began to fund the wealth-accumulating journeys of traders, explorers, and eventually colonists. Individual companies competed with each other for customers and profits with no government interference.

When the Industrial Revolution began, economists gave these practices an ideological basis. In opposition to the prevailing mercantilism, which argued that a nation's wealth was best measured by the amount of gold it could accumulate, capitalists argued that a nation's wealth should be measured by the amount of goods and services that it produced. The best way to produce a lot of goods and services was to create markets through private trade (Heilbroner, 1986). Classical capitalism has three components:

1. Private ownership of the means of production (natural resources and production machinery).

2. An open market, with no government interference. Kings and queens (and later prime ministers and presidents) should "*laissez-faire,*" or keep their hands off.

3. Profit (receiving more than the goods cost to produce) as a valuable goal of human enterprise.

In the United States, most people believe that the *political system* of democracy would be impossible without the *economic system* of capitalism. In fact, democracy and capitalism often contradict each other. Capitalism, after all, frees individuals to pursue their own private interests in the marketplace; it promotes unconstrained liberty. Democracy, on the other hand, constrains individual liberty in the name of the common good. For instance, in capitalism, it makes sense for a factory to toss its toxic waste into the nearest river: The money saved on proper waste disposal can go into the stockholders' pockets, maximizing profits. But in democracy, concern for the common good (unpolluted rivers) requires the factory to dispose of its toxic waste properly, limiting its individual liberty and reducing its profits.

As a result of the tension, capitalism in democratic countries has developed in different ways, in an attempt to balance individual liberty and the common good, or as it is sometimes framed, freedom and responsibility.

Laissez-Faire Capitalism. This is the original form of capitalism, theorized by Adam Smith, who argued that societies prosper best through individual self-interest ([1776] 1937, p. 508). Though it seems selfish on the surface, an entire nation full of people pursuing their own narrowly defined self-interests actually produces "the greatest good for the greatest number of people." Thus, in laissez-faire capitalism, property and the means of production should all be privately owned. Expansion and accumulation are expected forms of "progress." Markets should be able to compete freely to sell goods, acquire raw materials, and hire labor. No government interference is necessary: The "invisible hand" of supply and demand creates a self-regulating economy.

Laissez-faire dominated in Europe and North America through the nineteenth century, but it fell into dispute during the worldwide economic crisis and depression of the 1930s, when the "invisible hand" proved ineffective at staving off disaster. As a result, the government had to step in to stabilize the market and stimulate the economy. Today, the relationship between the government and economy is no longer a question of whether or not the government should be involved in economic life: Today the questions are how much should the government be involved? In what sectors? In what ways?

State Capitalism. State capitalism requires that the government use a heavy hand in regulating and constraining the marketplace. Companies may still be privately owned, but they must also meet government-set standards of product quality, worker compensation, and truth in advertising. In turn, the government provides some economic security to companies to avoid catastrophic losses and controls foreign imports to help local companies compete in world markets. This system is still common in the rapidly developing countries of the Pacific Rim, such as Japan, South Korea, and Singapore.

Welfare Capitalism. Most contemporary capitalist countries, including the United States, give the government even more control over private investors than state capitalism. While there is a market-based economy for most goods and services, there are also extensive social welfare programs, and the government owns some of the most essential services, such as transportation, health care, and the mass media (Barr, 2004; Esping-Anderson, 1990; Stephens and Huber, 2001). This is called welfare capitalism.

The U.S. economy incorporates elements of all three forms of capitalism. Many companies seek to operate with as little government regulation as possible, and set up corporate headquarters so they do not have to pay taxes in the United States (laissez-faire). Companies like Wal-Mart resist the unionization of their workers and undermine minimum wage regulations. Other industries, like the airlines and automobile manufacturers, agree to fare regulation or automotive emission controls in return for a more stable economic environment (state capitalism) and the promise that if they go bankrupt, as Chrysler did in 1979, the government will bail them out. And the massive public sector—federal, state, and local bureaucracies and political systems—work as a kind of welfare capitalism, attempting to ensure that everyone obtains at least a minimum standard of living (welfare capitalism).

Socialism

Although capitalism became the dominant economic system in the West by end of the eighteenth century, it was not without its detractors. Utopians argued that it would be more equitable to cooperate instead of compete, so that everyone could share the goods and services. In the nineteenth century, many socialist communes were founded in the United States, where all property was commonly owned and all decisions made as a body. However, no one tried it on a national level.

Later, Karl Marx argued that the pursuit of rational self-interest was inhumane and oppressive. The *bourgeoisie* (owners) kept most of the goods and services for themselves, while the *proletariat* (workers) had no choice but to work for them at wages barely high enough to ensure survival, with no share of the profits. Marx hypothesized that the huge economic gap between the groups would cause increasing hostility and resentment and would eventually result in violent revolution.

Marx proposed to adapt socialism to national governments by ensuring that workers rather than owners controlled the means of production and that everyone would be treated fairly. Strong government controls would be put into place to ensure equitable distribution of resource.

Socialism as an economic system is the exact opposite of laissez-faire capitalism, offering:

- *Collective ownership*. Private property is limited, especially property used to generate income. Goods and services are available equally to all, regardless of individual wealth.
- *Collective goals*. Capitalism celebrates profit as the entrepreneurial spirit, but socialism condemns profit as greed. Individuals should not attempt to make profits for themselves; they should concentrate on the common good.
- *Central planning*. Socialism operates through a "command economy." The government controls all production and distribution.

On the national level, many countries, both rich and poor, have socialist economies, but they allow for a degree of entrepreneurship, some profit, and differences in individual wealth, resulting in a democratic socialism that looks and feels much like welfare capitalism (Lichtheim, 1982; Rose and Ross, 1994). In Sweden, for instance, about 12 percent of economic production is "nationalized" (state controlled), and the rest is in private hands. High taxation, aimed especially at the

▲ The relationship between corporations and government is complex and depends on the industry. Some companies are less regulated than others. In Europe, all utilities are government controlled, but the trend in the U.S. is toward privatization. Some public utilities are either heavily regulated or the company is actually a partnership between government and private interests.

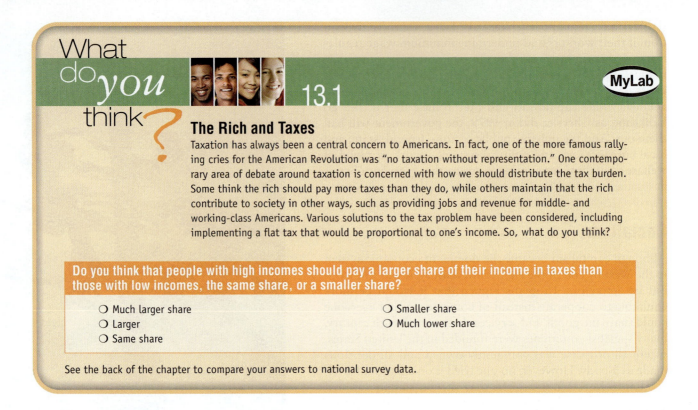

The Rich and Taxes

Taxation has always been a central concern to Americans. In fact, one of the more famous rallying cries for the American Revolution was "no taxation without representation." One contemporary area of debate around taxation is concerned with how we should distribute the tax burden. Some think the rich should pay more taxes than they do, while others maintain that the rich contribute to society in other ways, such as providing jobs and revenue for middle- and working-class Americans. Various solutions to the tax problem have been considered, including implementing a flat tax that would be proportional to one's income. So, what do you think?

Do you think that people with high incomes should pay a larger share of their income in taxes than those with low incomes, the same share, or a smaller share?

○ Much larger share
○ Larger
○ Same share

○ Smaller share
○ Much lower share

See the back of the chapter to compare your answers to national survey data.

rich, funds a wide range of social welfare programs for everyone, including universal health and child care. Scholars differ on whether this economy should be classified as socialist or capitalist.

Even in nominally capitalist countries, socialists often occupy high political positions. From 1948 to 1960, Milwaukee, Wisconsin, had a socialist mayor (Frank Ziedler), and the mayors of Paris (Bertrand Delanoë) and London (Ken Livingston) and the president of Spain (Jose Luis Rodriguez Zapatero) belong to socialist political parties.

Communism

Many people confuse the two economic systems, but communism is *not* socialism. Marx believed that socialism was a necessary transition from the oppression of capitalism to the ideal economic system of communism. **Communism** is an economic system based on collective ownership of the means of production and is administered collectively, without a political apparatus to ensure equal distribution. It's utopian, and Marx believed that communism could be achieved only after many years of socialism.

Socialism requires strong government intervention, but in a communist state, government is abolished. Socialism retains a difference between high-status and low-status work, so the janitor receives a lower salary than the physician, but in the communist paradise, the principle of distribution will become "from each according to his or her ability, to each according to his or her need." Thus, the janitor and the physician will receive the same stipend for personal expenses. Neither will lack anything, so both will be happy and content. Social inequalities will disappear, along with crime, hunger, and political strife.

Strangely, communist ideas did not take hold in industrialized, capitalist countries where the gap between owners and workers was most evident, but in agricultural countries, usually after revolutions or civil wars, such as in Russia (1917), China (1949), Vietnam (1954), Cuba (1959), and Yemen (1969). These countries usually called themselves socialist rather than communist because the government had not yet "withered away."

But as time passed, the government never withered away. Bureaucracy and regulation actually expanded, until the governments were stronger and more centralized than in capitalist countries. And social and class divisions remained strong (Muravchik, 2002; Pipes, 2001). What happened?

Sociologists explain that social stratification isn't simply a matter of economics. It involves power and status as well as wealth, so eliminating income disparities will not result in paradise. In fact, the communist governments created a new class of political elite. In the Soviet Union, about 10 percent of the population in 1984 belonged to the Communist Party. Called the *nomenklatura*, they got to shop in the best stores, send their children to the best schools, vacation at exclusive resorts, and travel abroad (Taylor, 1987; Voslensky, 1984).

The worker's paradise that Marx envisioned never happened and probably never could. After half a century of trying, most of the communist governments of the world have shifted to some form of capitalism. Today there are only five communist countries left (China, Cuba, Laos, North Korea, and Vietnam), and all except North Korea are busily decentralizing government controls and encouraging entrepreneurship (Hall, 1994; Oh and Hassig, 2000; Schopflin, 1993). Communists still hold positions of local political power in capitalist countries, but overall, on a large scale, communism does not seem to work.

The American Economy

What is the American "economic system"? While it is surely not socialist, it's also not a pure capitalist system either. How did the American economy develop?

Early American Economic Development

The United States has experienced the same movement from an agricultural to an industrial to a postindustrial economy as the rest of the world. Its economic roots lie in the seventeenth- and eighteenth-century Europeans of the Protestant Reformation, who sought to do good work, and they showed that they were good by making a profit and resisting the temptation to spend it on leisure pleasures. In England and the Netherlands, groups of stockholders formed charter companies that acquired the rights to the natural resources in the New World and sent colonists over to do the trapping, fishing, and farming. When quick profits did not materialize, the stockholders generally turned the charters over to the colonies. Soon they created an independent agricultural economy, with a few support industries like sawmills and shipyards.

The U.S. Constitution can be read as an economic charter. The entire nation is conceived as a single "common market," so there are no tariffs or taxes on interstate commerce, and there are uniform standards of currency, weights and measures, post offices and roads, patents, and copyright. The federal government can regulate international commerce, but it has little power to regulate the economic activity of individual states.

The Impact of Industrialization: Displacement and Consolidation

The new nation was formed at the start of the Industrial Revolution, as the agricultural economy was gradually superseded by the new industrial economy, and new institutions were developing to match industrial complexity (Atack, 1994). By 1860, 16 percent of the U.S. population lived in urban areas, and a third of the nation's income came from manufacturing. But most industries were located in the Northeast, while the South remained rural and agricultural, dependent on unpaid slaves rather than wage-labor employees, exporting raw materials and importing manufactured goods. The gap between North and South is reminiscent of the gap between rich, industrialized countries and poor, agricultural countries today.

The Civil War (1861–1865) was, in the economic sense, a clash between the two economic systems, and the Northern victory and the abolition of slavery sealed the industrial future of the United States. Industry surged ahead. Industrialization has also meant the gradual displacement of small shopkeepers and artisanal craft workers. Colonial America was a nation of small businessmen—whether farmers in the countryside or shopkeepers in the towns. Industrialization means consolidation, as big supersized stores undercut small shops and agribusinesses gobble up small farms.

Today, the opening of a Wal-Mart, the world's largest employer, usually means the closing of several dozen small shops nearby. Pushed down from the lower middle class into the working class, or impoverished, these small shopkeepers and farmers lose more than their stores; they lose their sense of independence and economic autonomy, which often makes them politically resentful and potentially a force for reaction.

Consolidation. This impulse towards consolidation began in earnest in the late nineteenth century, often referred to as the Gilded Age. A handful of so-called robber barons—Rockefeller, Ford, Carnegie, Vanderbilt, Gould, and Morgan—lived the opulent lives of royalty and exercised almost total control over the American economy (Chernow, 1998, 1990; Schmitz and Kirby, 1995). They managed to accumulate huge fortunes almost overnight because there were no federal regulations to limit price fixing, false advertising, underpaying and overworking employees, or establishing monopolies: At one point Rockefeller controlled 90 percent of the oil reserves in America, and Carnegie controlled 25 percent of the steel (Conte and Karr, 2001). Nor was there any shame in admitting an interest in money for its own sake: In contrast to the ideas of European intellectuals of the day, Americans embraced money making as a virtue.

During the first decades of the new century, progressive politics created many regulatory agencies, including the FDA (Food and Drug Administration), the FTC (Federal Trade Commission), and the ICC (Interstate Commerce Commission), designed to give consumers and employees an even break. But robber barons still amassed, spent, consumed, and speculated with abandon, resulting in an unstable stock market and a series of short-lived crashes and depressions. Then came the catastrophic stock market crash of 1929, which forced hundreds of banks to close, bankrupted thousands of businesses, and increased the unemployment rate to 25 percent.

It seemed obvious that the federal policy of hands-off or laissez-faire economics hadn't worked, so President Franklin Roosevelt launched the New Deal, a huge amount of government intervention into state and local economies. Many of the most important laws and institutions that we take for granted in contemporary America started with the New Deal (Gilbert and Howe, 1991; Quadagno, 1984), including:

- Minimum wage, providing a floor below which wages cannot go
- Social Security, which provides pensions to the elderly and disabled based on payments they made when part of the workforce

- Regulation of the stock market by the government (the Security and Exchange Commission, or SEC)
- Insurance of bank deposits by the government (the Federal Deposit Insurance Corporation, or FDIC)

After World War II, the economy was booming. Because the war never made it to U.S. soil (except for Pearl Harbor), factories could continue production without costly reconstruction efforts, and industries that had produced supplies for the war could change, with little effort, to companies producing consumer goods. At the same time, millions of returning GIs, furnished with low-cost GI loans, were buying cars, houses, and television sets and marrying and starting families, creating a new generation of consumers. The GDP more than tripled between 1950–1970 (U.S. Department of Commerce, 2007).

Farmers fared poorly: Small farms simply could not compete with big business. But blue-collar workers found themselves in demand, with salaries as high as what most white-collar workers earned, and labor unions were able to negotiate long-term contracts and benefits (Conte and Karr, 2001).

The Postindustrial Economy: Technology and Globalization

The returning GIs also took advantage of low-cost college loans and acquired college diplomas and technical degrees, feeding the Cold War obsession with maintaining technical superiority over the Soviet Union. The results were a technological revolution, increased automation, and a postindustrial economy. By 1956, the number of white-collar workers in the United States was greater than the number of blue-collar workers. The postindustrial economy had begun. But it was not until the 1980s, when high-tech industries made microprocessing technology cheap enough for everyday use, that the production of knowledge surpassed the production of goods (Conte and Karr, 2001).

Today, in the advanced nations, information technologies have enabled companies to race down the "information superhighway." But still, in many countries, the majority of the population does not yet have a paved road, let along a superhighway; and few on the superhighway stop to pick up hitchhikers.

Corporations

Industrial and postindustrial economies would be impossible without corporations. The **corporation** is a business that is treated legally as an individual. It can make contracts, incur debts, sue, and be sued, but its obligations and liabilities are legally distinct from those of the owners: If you sue a corporation and are awarded $1,000,000 in damages, none of the money comes from the personal bank account of the CEO. Incorporating (that is, creating a corporation) thus separates individual investors from the profits or losses of their business and gives them the freedom to take more risks than they would otherwise.

Corporations have become so common in the American workplace that when new college graduates are said to have "gone corporate," it means the same thing as "getting a job." Corporations impact the experience of employment, patterns of consumption, American and global politics, and almost every aspect of everyday life.

Corporate capitalism has developed in four stages: family, managerial, institutional corporations, and multinational (Micklethwait and Woodridge, 2003).

Family Corporations. Even in agricultural economies, farmers, merchants, and artisans usually passed their tools and workshops on to their children, and in the early days of capitalism, entrepreneurs followed their lead by sharing their investments, customers, production, and profits with relatives. By the nineteenth century, entrepreneurs were putting their relatives into most of the managerial positions in their companies. John D. Rockefeller (1839–1937) got his start in the oil business in partnership with two nonrelatives, but eventually he bought them out and handed the reigns of Standard Oil over to his son and grandsons. When they distributed stock only to family members as well, they could create huge entrepreneurial dynasties but still keep it all in the family.

Managerial Corporations. As companies grew, there were not enough qualified family members available to fill all of the necessary positions, or children and grandchildren didn't want to participate in the family business, so entrepreneurs began to hire outside managers. Eventually outsiders displaced family members in almost all managerial positions. The owners sold shares in the company's assets (stocks) to strangers who sought to share also in the company's profits, and the company became an entity separate from the family, just as work separated from home early in the Industrial Revolution.

Through most of the twentieth century, the corporate world has been the domain of a new relationship, different family and friends. Co-workers come together not because of kinship ties, nor because they like each other (they may, or they may not), but solely in the interest of personal and corporate profit. Corporations have developed their own culture, distinct from social worlds of family and friends, with their own procedures and practices, stated and unstated norms, values, goals, and vocabulary.

Managerial corporations were larger, more versatile and stronger than family run businesses, and more stable as well—as anyone who has ever tried to work with a family member can tell you. On the other hand, the larger and more impersonal forces of the corporation spelled the end of the workplace as an extension of family life.

Did *you* know?

Among the largest of the megacorporations, AOL Time Warner has 84,000 employees and received revenue of $10.5 billion in the first quarter of 2005 alone. Chances are that you conduct some business with one of its companies several times a day, including HBO, New Line Cinema, DC Comics, CNN, Castle Rock Productions, Warner Brothers Records, the WB TV station, *Sports Illustrated*, the Atlanta Braves, Cartoon Network, and *People*.

Institutional Corporations. During the last half of the twentieth century, corporations began to hold shares in *other* corporations. The same people would serve on boards of directors of several companies at once, until many corporations were interconnected through a small network of power players. Their decision-making practices changed because they were concerned not only with their own company but with all of the companies in which they had a stake. Competition changed to cooperation in the pursuit of profits. The result was a maze of major, minor, and subsidiary corporations, connected not through legal documents but through boardroom small talk, golf games, and handshakes.

The networks of corporations began acting less like businesses and more like enterprise webs—central cores that link an array of business interests and continuously contract with similar webs all over the world (Chandler and Mazlish, 2005).

Multinational Corporations

Some corporations remain centered in the United States, with overseas offices and production plants clearly dependent parts of the central operation. But most, especially the largest, operate globally; they are called transnational or **multinational corporations,** because they are no longer clearly located anywhere. Instead of a "home office," they operate through a network of offices all over the world. Even employees who are officially assigned to an office in one location may live in a dozen cities, or even a dozen countries, working together through e-mail, Web conferencing, and cell phones.

The products of multinational corporations do not really "come from" anywhere, in spite of the "Made in America" or "Made in Japan" labels. A toy may be designed by engineers living in Belgium, Switzerland, and South Africa through teleconferencing at an office in Brazil, while the parts are outsourced to a manufacturer based in Japan but with the factories located in India and Thailand; assembly occurs in a factory in Mexico, and the marketing campaigns are devised in the United States. The toy is sold in 128 countries, and the television commercials appear in 32 languages. Where is it made? Notice that my hypothetical toy is not assembled in factories in Germany, France, or Japan, and the engineers are not from Mexico or Thailand. "Outsourcing" and "offshoring" are not random: They are based on a clear economic division between First World and Third World, or between core and periphery in world-system theory. Core countries do the high-profit "tertiary economic activity," the knowledge-based design and marketing, and relegate the primary and secondary economic activity (agriculture and manufacturing) to cheap labor in peripheral countries. Every episode of *The Simpsons* is written and storyboarded in the United States, then outsourced to Korea for the tedious work of animation.

▲ Gone are the days when a group of local artisans created children's toys—or anything else. Even the simple "Made in Japan" label of the 1960s is obsolete. Today, toys designed in the United States are likely to be assembled in China from parts produced in Thailand and India.

To sociologists, like Bonacich and Appelbaum (2000), the multinational corporation illustrates how modern corporations are both national and international, global and local, at the same time. They studied the global production of clothing sold in America. They found that two-thirds of it was "outsourced," produced in peripheral countries, where factory workers could be paid a small percentage of U.S. wages (in China, workers are thrilled to get $40 per month). They note a **race to the bottom:** Manufacturers and retailers like Wal-Mart and Kmart will go wherever on earth they need to, to maximize profits by paying the lowest possible wages.

It used to be said that "what's good for General Motors is good for America." It meant that the success of companies led to prosperity for people in their home countries. But today, that old adage is ringing false. In Europe, as well as Japan, the United States, and elsewhere, people are witnessing record corporate profits while workers' wages are stagnant or even dropping. In the United States, median incomes have been flat since 2000, while corporate profits have nearly doubled (Gross, 2006). What's going on?

Globalization. It has "decoupled" the old win-win relationship between corporate and national interests. Corporate interests making profits may no longer benefit the entire society. In fact, those profits may actually hurt most people. In the past, fatter profits led companies to hire more workers and offer higher wages. This is no longer true. In today's global economy, multinational companies are not really attached to a home country any more, so they don't put their profits back into it in the form of more hiring or better benefits. Increased profits are just as likely to result in cutbacks and layoffs as they are to increase hiring. They are not "sharing the wealth," so to speak—at least not at home.

The world's 40 biggest multinationals now employ 55 percent of their workforces in foreign countries and earn 59 percent of their revenues abroad (*Economist*, 2006). In Europe, the trend is quite pronounced. Only 43 percent of all jobs at companies in France's CAC 40 (France's stock market index) are actually based in France. In Germany, just over half (53 percent) of employees of companies listed in its DAX 30 are based in Germany. But this is also happening more and more in the United States. Already, more than one-third of General Motors' employees don't work in America (*Economist*, 2006).

Because the big multinational corporations are maximizing profits abroad, they are not spending in home countries on jobs and wages. What's more, the threat of further outsourcing continues to keep wages down at home. Even in countries with very strong unions, such as France or Germany, workers have been pressed to accept pay and benefit cuts—if they want to keep jobs at all (Gross, 2006).

What are companies doing with the profit gains? Some are investing in foreign operations—because that's increasingly where their markets are and profits are coming from. For now, in the United States, a bigger slice of the increase in national income has gone to corporate profits than in any economic recovery since 1945 (*Economist*, 2006).

Work, Identity, and Inequality

Since the beginning of human society, our working lives have occupied the majority of our waking hours. From sunup to sundown, people in nonindustrial cultures have hunted and gathered, planted and sown, fished and farmed to provide for their society's members. This is still true today for most of the world's population. In contemporary industrial societies, it was only in the early twentieth century that we have cut the working day to eight hours. And political movements in Europe are suggesting cutting the work week from 40 to 35 hours, and the work day to seven or even six hours a day. In that sense, we work fewer hours today than ever before.

At the same time, we constantly hear how we are working longer and harder than ever before. Top-level managers in corporations and young lawyers in large firms often log 100-hour work weeks. Countless CEOs boast about virtually living in their offices. Americans are working harder and longer than residents of all but six other countries (Figure 13.3).

Sociologists understand that both these phenomena are true: The organization of our economies makes it possible for us to work fewer hours and also often makes it necessary for us to worker longer hours.

Sociologists bring to this conversation two important considerations: a historical perspective, comparing working life over time; and a comparative context, looking at how different societies organize working life and also how different groups within society may orient themselves to working life. For example, notice how the annual number of hours has varied over the centuries: We work about the same number of hours today that a thirteenth-century peasant worked. But in between, the number of hours rose considerably; today's rates are about half of the number in the mid-nineteenth century (Table 13.1).

And why do we do it? Sociologists also argue that we work *both* because we want to and because we have to.

FIGURE 13.3 **Average Annual Working Hours of Selected Countries**

Country	Hours
Korea	2354
Greece	2053
Czech Republic	2002
Poland	1994
Mexico	1909
New Zealand	1809
United States	1804
Italy	1801
Japan	1775
Slovak Republic	1739
Canada	1737
Australia	1730
United Kingdom	1672
Switzerland	1659
Ireland	1638
France	1546
Belgium	1534
Germany	1437
Netherlands	1367
Norway	1360

HOURS PER YEAR PER PERSON EMPLOYED

Source: From *OECD Factbook 2007: Economic, Environmental and Social Statistics*. Copyright © OECD, 2007. Reprinted with permission.

Consider these two statements, each by a famous American president:

1. "Far and away the best prize that life offers is the chance to work hard at work worth doing."

2. "It's true that hard work never killed anybody, but I figured, why take the chance?"

The first quote is by Theodore Roosevelt in his annual Labor Day speech in 1903; the second by Ronald Reagan at a speech in Washington in 1987 (both in *Columbia Dictionary of Quotations,* p. 1003).

Most of us don't necessarily believe one and not the other: We believe both are true—at different times in our lives and under different circumstances. To the sociologist, what is most interesting is the circumstances under which you live to work and the circumstances under which you simply work to live.

TABLE 13.1

Annual Hours over Eight Centuries

TIME	TYPE OF WORKER	ANNUAL HOURS
13th century	Adult male peasant, U.K.	1,620 hours
14th century	Casual laborer, U.K.	1,440 hours
Middle ages	English worker	2,309 hours
1400–1600	Farmer-miner, adult male, U.K.	1,980 hours
1840	Average worker, U.K.	3,105–3,588 hours
1850	Average worker, U.S.	3,150–3,650 hours
1987	Average worker, U.S.	1,949 hours
1988	Manufacturing workers, U.K.	1,855 hours
2000	Average worker, Germany	1,362 hours

Source: Compiled by Juliet B. Schor (1991) from various sources; Germany figure from OECD data.

How We Work

In the early days of mass production, the assembly line basically imagined workers as machines. People were simply trained to do a task with scientific precision and then asked to do it repeatedly. No one really cared whether the workers felt challenged, bored, intimidated, or humiliated. As industrialization progressed, social scientists, management scientists, and even kinesiologists began to research how we respond to the workplace, to co-workers, to bosses, and to labor itself. Happier workers, who felt less bored and more valued, it turned out, were more productive—and that spelled higher profits.

The Hawthorne Effect. The earliest experimental study of work productivity was conducted between 1927 and 1932 at the Western Electric Hawthorne factory in Chicago. Researcher Elton Mayo chose six female assembly-line workers and assigned an observer to watch them, ask for their input, and listen to their complaints. Then he made a variety of environmental changes, including breaks of various lengths, different quitting times, different quotas, a day off, and a free lunch. To his surprise, almost every change increased productivity. And when he changed things back to the default, productivity increased again (Mayo, 1933)!

Mayo concluded that the changes themselves weren't responsible for the increase in productivity. It was that the workers had some input. The workers chosen for the experiment had no boss telling them the "proper" procedure. They were allowed to work in their own way; in fact, the observer displayed a keen interest in their individual work styles. They were treated as intelligent, creative individuals rather than as mindless machines.

The "Hawthorne Effect" or the "Somebody Upstairs Cares Syndrome" soon became a standard in management textbooks: People work better and faster when they feel valued.

Theory X and Theory Y. In 1960 Douglas McGregor published *The Human Side of Enterprise,* about two theories of work. Theory X assumes that people naturally dislike work, so they will slack off unless they are coerced and threatened. On the assembly line, a line supervisor must be watching them at all times. In white-collar jobs, they must fill out time sheets, goals statements, and allocation lists. While they must have a little more freedom, supervisors should still monitor their activities closely.

Theory Y is based on the assumption that people naturally like work, so they will do it if they feel they are a valued part of a team (as in the Hawthorne Effect). The job of the supervisor is to create team spirit, solve problems, and offer advice, not monitor productivity. On the assembly line, there should be suggestion boxes and team meetings. White-collar workers might go on retreats where they fall backwards into each other's arms to learn trust.

McGregor argued that both theories are valid and can increase productivity, depending on the task and the maturity and responsibility of the workers. The biggest mistake of management is to implement Theory X all the time and never consider the possibility of Theory Y.

Manufacturing Consent. Sociologist Michael Burawoy (1980) wondered why so many people work so hard, making only their managers rich. It's not a desire for promotion because people work just as hard at dead-end jobs. It's not fear of being fired. Why don't they slack off or rebel against the oppressive system? Why do they care? To find out, he took a blue-collar job at "Allied Corporation," and carefully observed both management and workers. He found that management engaged in three strategies designed to **manufacture consent,** by which workers came to embrace a system that also exploited them. Manufacturing consent is the production of values and emotions (in addition to the actual things they produce) that bind workers to their company:

- *Piece-rate pay system.* The workers competed with each other to produce the highest quotas. Though the "prizes" were only minor pay raises, workers devoted a lot of time to "making out," strategizing new ways to increase their production. Even Burawoy found himself working harder.
- *Internal labor market.* Increasing job mobility within the company gave the workers the illusion that their dead-end jobs had potential.
- *Collective bargaining.* Unions gave workers the illusion that they, as individual workers, held power.

The ideas in *Manufacturing Consent* have been applied to many jobs, white collar as well as blue collar. For instance, in academia, promotion and tenure are based to a great extent on publications, but often tenure committees look only at the number of publications, not the quality. So professors find their own way of "making out." They publish a lot of short articles that do not involve extensive research rather than working on a big, meaningful project.

Types of Jobs

There are several different types of jobs, often categorized by the color of the collar you are thought to wear. Of course, these color codings are not always followed, but the job categories remain relatively stable.

White-Collar Jobs. White-collar work is knowledge-based work, with the day spent manipulating symbols: talking, speaking, reading, writing, and calculating, but not lifting boxes, assembling products, or welding parts together. Most white-collar jobs require considerable education, usually a bachelor's degree and often today a master's degree. In 1900, only about 16 percent of American workers had white-collar jobs, but today the figure is nearing half (Bureau of Labor Statistics, 2003).

Because white-collar jobs offer the highest salaries and the most opportunity for advancement, many sociologists, including C. Wright Mills (1951) have argued that white-collar workers are more in agreement with capitalism than blue- or pink-collar workers. However, contemporary scholars note that, in the postindustrial economy, most white-collar jobs are becoming more regimented and bureaucratic, and white-collar workers are experiencing a decay in autonomy, creativity, and advancement potential similar to that of the blue-collar workers as they shift downward to service (Fraser, 2001).

Perhaps the first type of white-collar job you think of is a "professional." The term initially, before the Industrial Revolution, referred to the clergy—universities like Harvard, Yale, and Princeton were founded to train future ministers. Law and medicine were considered skilled trades, like carpentry, entered through an apprenticeship rather than a college degree, and the only requirement for becoming a teacher was knowing how to read. (In the Middle Ages, the barber was often the village doctor.)

In the twentieth century, doctors, lawyers, and teachers became professionals, followed later by scientists, engineers, librarians, architects, artists, journalists, and entertainers. Professions can generally be distinguished from other jobs by four characteristics:

1. *Theoretical knowledge.* You must have not only technical training in a skill, but a theoretical understanding of a field. Architecture became a profession only when it became less about constructing buildings and more about understanding the dynamics of inhabited space.

2. *Self-regulating practices.* Other jobs have procedures, but professions observe a code of ethics.

3. *Authority over clients.* Based on their extensive training, professionals are qualified to advise their clients and expect them to obey directions. You expect that your doctor knows more than you do about your rash.

4. *Community orientation.* Rather than merely seeking personal income, the professional has a duty to the community.

Alongside the professionals are the white-collar workers in business. Perhaps, as President Calvin Coolidge said, "the business of America is business." Business administration remains the most popular college major, comprising nearly a quarter of all bachelor's degrees awarded in 2005 (Digest of Educational Statistics, 2006). Yet less than 14 percent of American workers are actually employed in management, business, and financial occupations. Of these, 57 percent are men and 43 percent women; 87 percent are White, 7 percent Black, 6 percent Hispanic, and 4 percent Asian (the percentage adds up to more than 100 percent because Hispanic persons can be of any race) (U.S. Census Bureau, 2004).

Sales is usually considered white collar because it is knowledge work, persuading people to buy things, but sometimes it is categorized with service jobs because of its low salary and low prestige. Seventeen percent of American workers are in sales, about equally divided between men and women. Most are White, with 10 percent Hispanic, 9 percent Black, and 4 percent Asian (Bureau of Labor Statistics, 2003).

Blue-Collar Jobs. The term *blue collar* was first coined in 1951 for jobs involved with production rather than knowledge, because factory workers traditionally wore

Did *you* know ?

Real white collars were invented by a woman named Hannah Montague in 1827. They were detachable, so they could be washed separately from the shirts to save laundry time. By the end of the century, 25 million white collars were being manufactured in the United States every year. Too expensive for manual laborers, they became a status symbol for the new middle class.

blue jumpsuits. In 1900, 60 percent of American workers were blue collar. Today it is less than a quarter (Bureau of Labor Statistics, 2003). There are several types of blue-collar jobs—like natural resource and construction, factory work, and skilled crafts work.

Natural resource and construction work includes farming, fishing, and forestry, plus the construction trades (electricians, bricklayers, plumbers), and also auto and airplane repair, heating, air conditioning, and refrigeration. About 10 percent of American workers are involved. Of there, 95 percent are men, and only 5 percent are women. Eighty-eight percent are White, 21 percent Hispanic, 7 percent Black, and 2 percent Asian (Bureau of Labor Statistics, 2006).

About 13 percent of American workers have jobs in production, which includes not only traditional factory jobs but driving buses, trucks, taxis, and cars and piloting trains and airplanes. Like natural resources and construction, these jobs are heavily male oriented (76 percent men, 24 percent women). Of production workers, 88 percent are White, 19 percent Hispanic, 14 percent Black, and 2 percent Asian (Bureau of Labor Statistics, 2006).

Pink-Collar Jobs. The term *pink collar* was coined by Louise Kay Howe in 1977, in her book *Pink Collar Workers: Inside the World of Woman's Work*. Howe found that jobs in offices, restaurants, and stores—such as secretary, waitstaff, or sales clerk— were often held by women. Today they are still stigmatized as "women's work," and therefore most are low paying and low prestige. Some highly experienced and lucky

Sociology and our World

Labor Unions

A hallmark of blue-collar employment has been the labor union. In the early days of industrialized economies, owners spent as little as they could on workers. The work day lasted 12 hours or more, often under horrible conditions, with no days off, no benefits, and poverty-level wages. Workers had no rights and no political influence, so if they were injured on the job or if they complained, they were fired.

Soon workers discovered that if they banded together in **labor unions** modeled on the medieval guilds, they could redress the balance of power through collective bargaining, appealing to owners as a group. Only a few labor unions appeared during the eighteenth and nineteenth centuries, and because they were local or limited to a single occupation, they were not successful at creating large-scale change. Then the American Federation of Labor (AFL) was founded to coordinate the activities of many different occupational unions, so that, for instance, steelworkers could assist railroad conductors. Later the AFL merged with the Committee for Industrial Organization and became the extremely influential AFL-CIO.

During the first decades of the twentieth century, organized labor used work slowdowns, work stoppages, and strikes to fight for many of the benefits that we take for granted today: the 40-hour work week, overtime pay, a minimum wage, unemployment insurance, worker's compensation for on-the-job injuries, child labor laws, and worker safety and health codes. All of these were opposed by the companies and granted only grudgingly after the government intervened (Fernie and Metcalf, 2005; Hannan and Freeman, 1987; Lichtenstein, 2002).

Union membership increased rapidly during the 1930s and 1940s, until by 1950, more than a third of all nonfarm workers in the United States belonged to unions. Membership declined after 1970, sometimes sharply, both because blue-collar employment was declining and because federal regulations to protect workers made a great deal of union negotiation obsolete. In 2004, only 12.5 percent of American nonfarm workers belonged to unions. The largest unionized segment of the population is government employees (36 percent). For nongovernment, private-sector employees, the percentage is 8 percent, the lowest in a century (Hirsch and Macpherson, 1997).

Globally, unionization varies tremendously, from 2 percent (Gabon) to 70 percent (Iceland). Overall, rich countries tend to be more heavily unionized, at 30 percent or more. But union membership is in decline almost everywhere (International Labor Organization, 2007).

pink-collar workers can work their way up to the salary of a white-collar job, but most barely make a living wage, like the factory workers of the nineteenth century.

Many of the most dominant pink-collar jobs are in clerical and sales work. These are jobs in office production: typists, file clerks, data entry clerks, receptionists, secretaries, administrative assistants, and office managers, plus cashiers, insurance agents, and real estate agents. In 1900, clerical and office work occupied only 7.5 percent of the U.S. working population. Today it is 26 percent, though the percentage is declining as more and more white-collar workers are asked to do their own administrative tasks. These jobs are heavily female oriented (75 percent women, 25 percent men). Eighty-one percent of workers are White, 13 percent Black, 11 percent Hispanic, and 3 percent Asian (Bureau of Labor Statistics, 2006).

Service Work. Service work wears both pink and blue collars. This category includes food preparation and service, personal services (hair stylists, launderers, child care workers), and maintenance workers (janitors, garbage collectors), plus police officers and firefighters. Of American workers, 17 percent have service jobs; of there, 57 percent are women, and 43 percent men, 77 percent are White, 18 percent Hispanic, 16 percent Black, and 4 percent Asian (Bureau of Labor Statistics, 2006). Service work is also age oriented: It includes the oldest and the youngest workers, like the retirees who greet you at Wal-Mart and the local teenagers who are flipping your burgers at a fast food restaurant.

Service jobs are the lowest paid, the least prestigious, and the ones with fewest—if any—health and retirement benefits. Many service jobs sit at the minimum wage.

As of July 2007, the minimum wage in the United States is $5.85 per hour. (That's the federal mandate; some states may have higher rates.) That's about $40 a day. Maybe that could barely sustain a teenager living at home, with only entertainment expenses to worry about, but a person living alone, without parental support, could never acquire adequate food, clothing, and shelter for $5.85 per hour (and don't even think about children!). Yet today nearly two million adults (aged 16 and over) earn minimum wage or less (Bureau of Labor Statistics, 2005), including 9 percent of service workers and 8 percent of office workers. Nearly 40 percent of minimum wage workers are working full-time.

Nearly one in seven workers (especially Black and women workers) spend at least half of the their work lives stuck at or near minimum wage (Carrington and Fallick, 2001.) These workers, plus the 25 million more who earn a dollar or two an hour above the minimum wage (Sklar, Mykyta, and Wefald, 2001), are called the working poor.

The real value of the minimum wage (that is, its equivalent in the contemporary workplace) rose through the 1960s to a high of $7.18 (in 1968). It fell steadily during the Reagan and Bush presidencies, to a low point of $4.80 (in 1989). Under President Clinton it rose again to $5.89. But under George W. Bush it fell to a low of $5.85 (*State of Working America*, 2004–2005).

All the while, worker productivity, corporate profits, and CEO pay have all surged. If the minimum wage had kept pace with productivity increases, it would now be $13.80 per hour. If it had kept pace with the domestic profits of corporations, it would be $13.02 per hour. If it had kept pace with the profits of the retail industry (which employs over half of minimum wage workers), it would be $20.46 per hour (Sklar, Mykyta, and Wefald, 2001).

An obvious solution would be to raise the minimum wage—to at least $8.00 per hour, the minimum necessary for a single full-time worker to acquire adequate food, clothing, shelter, and transportation (but not health insurance, which most low-income jobs don't offer anyway). Opponents argue that raising the minimum wage will hurt

How do we know what we know?

The Poor Work Harder than the Rich

One of the most enduring myths in Western culture is the myth that people are poor because they don't work hard enough. Consistently, sociologists have debunked this myth by surveys of hours worked, comparisons that show the minimum wage doesn't even come close to helping people live above the poverty line, and other methods. Recently, though, sociologists and journalists have gone deeper into the working lives of working people and found something somewhat startling: Poor people work much harder than rich people.

Sociologist Katherine Newman (1999) sent teams of her graduate students into minimum-wage jobs, like flipping burgers in a fast food restaurant she called "Burger Barn." The researchers were surprised to see just how honest and hard-working the workers were, but what's more, they noted how workers had to scramble frantically to try and put a few dollars aside for the future because they had neither health benefits nor retirement plans. The workers were proud to work, in fact, preferring to make it on their own than rely on public assistance.

And journalist Barbara Ehrenreich (2001) went even further: She took six months and worked in a variety of entry-level jobs that define low-wage service work in the global economy. She worked as a cleaning woman in Maine, as a waitress in Key West, and as an "associate" in a Wal-Mart in Minneapolis. At Wal-Mart, she had to stay late (and off the books) to clean up and arrive early (off the books) to set up. Working two jobs, she could not afford rent on an apartment and ended up, as did the other women she worked with, living out of a car or in a run-down weekly rate motel, eating soup out of cans she cooked on a hot plate and wearing an adult diaper because she was not permitted to take bathroom breaks during her shift. She often relied on the kindness of strangers, as her co-workers were always offering to share what little they had. Only the working poor, she sadly concluded, actually believe in the Protestant work ethic—that if you work hard enough, you can make it in America. The middle class has long since abandoned such illusions.

"Most civilized nations," Ehrenreich concludes, "compensate for the inadequacy of wages by providing relatively generous public services such as health insurance, free or subsidized child care, subsidized housing and effective public transportation." What, she wonders at the end of the book, does that say about us?

---

businesses, thereby fueling inflation, increasing unemployment, and ultimately harming low-skill workers. But several studies reveal that the costs to businesses, even small businesses, would be minimal. Retail businesses with fewer than 20 employees would stand to lose 1.0 percent of their current net receipts. Large social service agencies (with 500 or more employees) would lose the most, 10.1 percent of net receipts. But they would save on recruitment, training, and retention costs; reduce turnover and absenteeism; and improve quality of work, all positively affecting profits (Sklar et al., 2001).

About 70 towns and universities around the country have recently legislated "living wage" ordinances, and they are in the works in another 80. The highest of the minimum "living wages" is $11.00 per hour with health insurance (Santa Cruz, CA) and $12.25 per hour without health insurance (Santa Monica, CA) (Sklar et al., 2001, pp. 70–72). But a number of states, including Arizona, Colorado, Louisiana, Missouri, Oregon, and Utah have banned local living wage ordinances (Murray, 2001).

Alternatives to Wage Labor

Working for wages is not the only way that people work. In fact, much of our labor is not for wages at all. Economists have identified several "alternatives" to the wage-labor system.

Working off the Books. Many people depend on informal, under-the-table, off-the-books work for a substantial part of their income. The informal economy—also called the "underground economy" and the "gray market"—includes several types of activities. Although some people are uncomfortable thinking of crimes as drug dealing, prostitution, shoplifting, gambling, car theft, and burglary as part of the underground economy rather than individual aberrations, studies of arrests have found that most perpetrators think of themselves as "taking care of business." They "go to work" as deliberately as someone with an office job. They follow rules, procedures, protocols, and a code of ethics; they take occupational risks (such as being injured or going to prison).

"Informal" does not mean "unorganized." Nationally and globally, billions of dollars of goods, services, and money changes hands through complex networks of crime families, gangs, corrupt officials, smugglers, and money-laundering specialists (Portes, Castells, and Benton, 1989).

Another type of underground economy comes into play when the workers are foreign nationals with no work visas, so they cannot work legally in their host country. They therefore arrive at an off-the-books arrangement with their employers. Illegal immigrants, who are not permitted to be in the United States at all, are particularly vulnerable to unscrupulous entrepreneurs who offer sweatshop working conditions at well below minimum wage. Although some manage to find white-collar jobs or are self-employed, the majority of illegal immigrants take service jobs, including house cleaning, gardening, and food preparation. The average household income of illegal immigrant families is less than $24,000 per year, considerably less than the $46,000 of legal residents (Wasow, 2006).

Most often, however, neither the work nor the worker is illegal; the underground economy comes into play only because the money is undeclared and therefore untaxed. A waiter receives an average of $30 in tips every night, but at income tax time, he reports only his official salary, not the extra $7,500. A collector buys a vase at a garage sale for $5 and sells it on eBay for $100, pocketing the money but forgetting about it at tax time. People fix cars, do laundry, mow lawns, babysit informally for friends and neighbors, adding perhaps $60 to their pocketbooks this week and $80 next week, resulting in an extra $4,000 at the end of the year that the IRS doesn't know about.

The size of the informal economy varies among countries and regions (Figure 13.4). In sub-Saharan Africa, the informal economy accounts for more than 40 percent of the region's gross domestic product; in the high-income countries of the OECD, it is about 18 percent. Pennar and Farrel (1993) estimated that undocumented income alone (excluding crime and the work of illegal aliens) constitutes 10 to 15 percent of the regular economy. That's more than $1 trillion per year, and $100 billion in lost taxes. (*Economist*, 2006).

All socioeconomic classes participate in the informal economy, but the $95 profit that the collector made on the eBay vase is a negligible contribution to a middle-class income (and the IRS is unlikely to be terribly concerned about it). But money earned off the books and under the table may easily double a $5.15 per hour minimum wage income. The working poor are likely to depend on the informal economy for their everyday survival (Newman, 1999).

Unpaid Work. For most of human history, all work was unpaid. People provided their own food, clothing, housing, and entertainment. For jobs that were too big for one person or household, favors could be

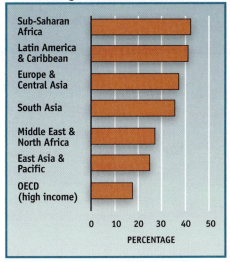

FIGURE 13.4 Informal Economy as Percentage of GDP, 1999–2000

Source: IFC, 2005; From "The Flicker of a Brighter Future" by Luanda and Lusaka. © *The Economist* Newspaper Limited, London, September 7, 2006. Reprinted with permission.

The informal economy includes work most often paid in cash or services with no benefits, and often includes workers in restaurants and bars, housecleaners, and child care workers. ▼

called in from friends and family. Sometimes people bartered something they had for something they needed. With the advent of capitalism, most of the goods and services that families or groups used to provide for themselves, from clothing to entertainment to police protection, increasingly became someone's job and required pay.

But we still do a tremendous amount of unpaid work. The line between labor and leisure blurs around the edges: Somebody, somewhere is getting paid to do most of the activities that we do for free. Yet economics ignores this unpaid work.

The best example is taking care of our own household, doing the dusting, vacuuming, dishwashing, food preparation, and so on. It is denigrated as "women's work," assumed to be the domain of full-time "housewives," even though husbands, unmarried partners, relatives, and friends all sometimes stay home to take care of the household, while someone else "goes to work" to provide the financial support. Before capitalism, there was no division between work and home: Everything took place at or near home. Men and women had different tasks to perform in most cultures, but nobody theorized that one group was doing the "real" work, while the other enjoyed a life of sleeping-in and watching soap operas. But as the division between home and work grew, and men began to work in the public arena for wages, they began to perceive themselves as "breadwinners," solely responsible for the economic vitality of the household, for "putting food on the table."

The idea that unpaid household labor had nothing to do with "real" economy was set in stone as early as the 1920s, when official decisions were handed down that only transactions in which money changes hands should be included in measures of U.S. productivity. When the first estimates of gross domestic product were developed in 1930s, calculations were limited to the total monetary value of goods and services that were sold (Crittendon, 2001).

Domestic labor lost the status of "work" and became a part of the heterosexual marital bond. Presumably women found household maintenance similar to wrapping a present—a joyful "labor of love," technically work, but worth it to please their husbands. The image still persists today, but it is counterbalanced by another image: the housewife as Stepford Wife, brainwashed by a patriarchal system that considers her worthless, sad, lonely, unfulfilled, tragically "wasting her life" (Friedan, 1963).

Near the end of the twentieth century, some economists began to realize that household labor, or **human capital,** does make a significant impact on the economy. In 1995, the World Bank found that 59 percent of the wealth in developed countries consists of human capital, 25 percent of natural resources (land, minerals, and water), and 16 percent of manufactured goods.

In the wealthiest countries, human capital accounts for 75 percent of the producible forms of wealth (World Bank, 1995). The value of unpaid work (not only household labor, but home repair, auto repair, and other informal work) was estimated to be the equivalent of 35 percent of the monetary GDP in Germany, 40 percent in Canada, 46 percent in Finland, and 48 to 64 percent in Australia (Ironmonger, 1996).

Self-Employment. Entrepreneurship has always been the hallmark of the American dream. In some socioeconomic classes, parents send their children off to sell seeds or magazine subscriptions to their neighbors nearly as soon as they can walk, to put them on the road to self-made fame and fortune. Even today, in the age of corporate dominance, 7.5 percent of the working American population listed self-employment as their primary source of income (Bureau of Labor Statistics, 2004). Their jobs range from blue-collar carpet and floor installing to white-collar management analysis and professional photography. Men are more likely to be self-employed than women (8.8 percent versus 6.0 percent) and Whites (8.8 percent) more likely than African Americans (4.1 percent) or Hispanics (5.5 percent) (Bureau of Labor Statistics, 2004). Differences in education, access to credit and capital, and intergenerational links, such as family wealth and history of entrepreneurship, largely account for the lower rates of self-employment among Blacks and Hispanics as compared with Whites (Dunn and Holtz-Eakin, 2000; Fairlie and Woodruff, 2005; Lofstrom, 2002).

Often self-employed people start small businesses and become employers of their own: More than 19 million Americans work for companies employing fewer than 20 employees, and another 18.4 work for companies with more than 20 but fewer than 100 employees. These small businesses are a continued source of energy for the American economy. They produced 75 percent of the new jobs that appeared between 1990 and 1995 (Bureau of Labor Statistics, 2004). They tend to hire more older workers and part-timers, so they tend to be points of entry into the economy for new groups.

During the past decade or so, women have been leading the way in small businesses (perhaps due to their frustration with corporate culture). Between 1997 and 2006, the estimated growth rate in the number of women-owned firms was nearly twice the growth rate of male-owned firms, and their employment and revenues grew faster than male-owned firms. Today nearly half of all privately held businesses in the United States, 10.4 million, are women owned. They employ over 12.8 million people and generate $1.9 trillion in annual sales (Center for Women's Business Research, 2007).

The trend is even more pronounced for women of color (Figure 13.5). Between 1997 and 2006, the number of firms they owned grew by nearly 120 percent, while employment grew by nearly 62 percent, and sales by nearly 74 percent. In 2006, they owned 1.4 million U.S. firms—over 20 percent of all women-owned firms. They employed nearly 1.1 million people and generated nearly $161 billion in sales (Center for Women's Business Research, 2007).

Part-Time Work. In 2005, about 25 percent of the American workforce was employed part-time (fewer than 35 hours per week) (Bureau of Labor Statistics, 2006). The percentage has remained fairly stable for the last 40 years, ranging between 14 percent (in 1968) and 19 percent (in 1994). Women are more than twice as likely as men to work part-time (OECD, 2006; State of Working America, 2005–2006). Globally, part-time workers are becoming increasingly common, ranging from 6 percent of the workforce in Greece to 36 percent in the Netherlands. However, women remain the primary part-time workers: They account for 73 percent of part-time employment in wealthy nations (OECD, 2007).

Many people work part-time by choice, because they want to attend to other commitments (part-time jobs have been traditional for high school and college students for years). However, over a quarter want full-time work, but are prevented by the lack of suitable jobs or transportation or child care problems, or by employers who keep them just below the 35-hour-per-week limit to avoid paying full-time salaries and benefits. Two-thirds of people working at or below minimum wage are part-time (Tilly, 1996). Often, to make ends meet, they must take a part-time job in addition to a full-time job, or two or three part-time jobs.

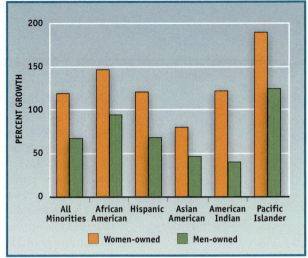

FIGURE 13.5 Women-of-Color Entrepreneurs

Source: From *Center for Women's Business Research,* 2007. Reprinted with permission.

Contingent and "On Call Work." Many employers have discovered the economic benefit of replacing permanent employees with employees hired to do a specific project or for a specific time period, or to be "on call," working only when their services are needed. According to the Department of Labor (2001), about 4 percent of the American workforce are contingent, nearly 2 percent work "on call," and 1.5 percent are contract workers or "temps" (Bureau of Labor Statistics, 2005).

Because there is no presumption of permanent employment, employers need not offer retirement pensions, cost-of-living raises, or paid holidays, vacations, sick leave, or health insurance (55 percent of traditional employees receive health insurance from their employees, but only 30 percent of on-call workers, 20 percent of contingency workers, and 10 percent of temporary workers do). They need not find more work for employees who have finished their duties early or pay overtime if their duties take longer than expected. They can lay off employees at any time without investing in expensive severance packages.

The characteristics of these workers vary widely. Independent contractors tend to be middle aged, White, and male, while temporary workers tend to be young, ethnic minority, and female. Of independent contractors, 83 percent state that they prefer their arrangements, while 44 percent of temporary workers would prefer permanent jobs (Bureau of Labor Statistics, 2005).

A large percentage of independent contractors, on-call workers, and contingency workers have white-collar jobs in management, the professions, or sales, but temporary workers are over represented in low-skill, low-paying jobs (37 percent are in offices or service jobs). Their average weekly full-time pay was $414, but most do not work full time (Bureau of Labor Statistics, 2005).

Unemployment

Even when the economy is functioning as smoothly as possible, there are always some people out of work, looking for work, or unable to work. Some people work only during some times of the year and not others; others are in between jobs, looking for some new position; others cannot find work in their field or are somehow disqualified from some jobs.

Social scientists typically distinguish among three different types of unemployment; the first two tend to be more temporary than the last:

1. *Seasonal unemployment* refers to the changes in demand for workers based on climate or seasonal criteria. For example, demand for agricultural labor drops dramatically after the harvest, and demand for workers in the tourist industry peaks only during "high season" for tourists.

2. *Cyclical unemployment* is a response to normal business cycles of expansion and contraction. During periods of economic expansion, demand for labor increases, and the unemployment rate goes down. But during recessions and economic downturns, demand for labor goes down and people are laid off or downsized, and unemployment rates increase.

3. *Structural unemployment* refers to more permanent conditions of the economy. In some cases, it may be caused by a mismatch—say, between the skills needed by employers and the skills possessed by workers or between the geographic locations of employment and the location of potential workers. Structural unemployment can benefit corporations, who can hold labor costs down in a "buyer's market." In the 1980s and 1990s, more than 10 million American workers lost their jobs due to structural shifts in the economy, including the transformation

of the auto and steel industries, the rise of high-technology jobs, and the offshore movement of many jobs.

Countries measure unemployment by counting people who are actively looking for jobs. The unemployment rate takes that number as a percentage of all employable workers. In 2007, the unemployment rate in the United States was 4.4 percent. (Some cyclical and seasonal variations mean that manufacturing jobs are declining while some retail jobs are increasing) ("Employment Situation Summary," July 2007.)

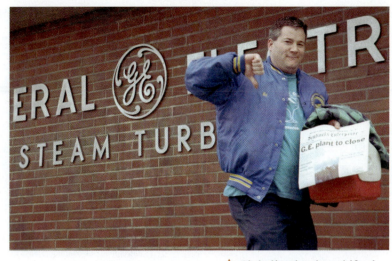

▲ Globalization has shifted much industrial production to the developing world, and many manufacturing plants in the United States and Europe have closed.

Globally, while more people are working than ever before, so, too, are more people unemployed than ever before. The International Labour Organization (ILO) estimates that 6.3 percent of the workforce is unemployed, or more than 195 million people at the end of 2006, an all-time high (International Labour Organization, 2007). The Middle East and North Africa have the highest unemployment rate in the world (12.2 percent), while the unemployment rate decreased slightly in Latin America and the Caribbean, to 8 percent in 2006. The developed economies and the EU saw rates decline, from 7.1 percent in 2004 to 6.2 percent in 2006 (International Labour Organization, 2006). Almost half of the unemployed are the world's young people aged 15 to 24, who are more than three times as likely as adults to be out of work (International Labour Organization, 2007).

What can society do to help the unemployed? What *should* it do? Most industrial countries recognize that very few people want to be unemployed, and most actively seek work, and so they offer some financial support to enable the unemployed to find work. This short-term income is *unemployment compensation*. Unemployment compensation is organized on a state-by-state basis, and each state has its own regulations. In most cases, an applicant for unemployment compensation must have already been working for at least 20 weeks and be actively seeking work.

Unemployment compensation is different from "welfare," which is direct payments from the government to people in need. In the past decade, American welfare policy has been increasingly tied to employment, so that one might be ineligible for welfare if one is not actively looking for work.

Diversity in the Workplace

Domestic comedy movies from the 1950s often begin at a suburban train station, where a crowd of White middle-class men, all dressed in identical gray suits, prepare for their work day in the big city. And, in fact, the middle-class work world in 1950 was nearly that homogeneous. In 1950, White men occupied over 90 percent of white-collar jobs in the United States. Today they occupy 50 percent of managerial, 42 percent of sales, and 41 percent of professional jobs (Bureau of Labor Statistics, 2006). Women and ethnic minorities are catching up (Figure 13.6).

During the next 50 years, the number of Hispanics and Asian Americans in the United States will triple, while the White non-Hispanic population will increase a mere 7 percent. The United States will be a "majority minority" country, with more than half

FIGURE 13.6 Labor Force Participation Rates by Sex and Region, 1996 and 2006

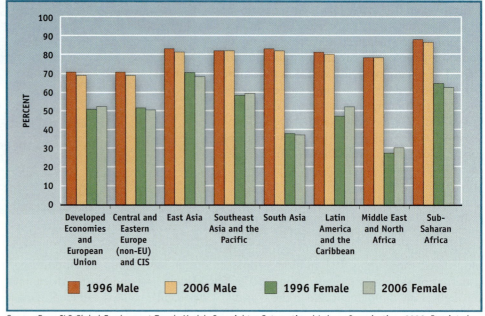

Source: From ILO Global Employment Trends Model. Copyright © International Labour Organization, 2006. Reprinted with permission.

TABLE 13.2

Increasing Racial Diversity in the U.S. Labor Force

	1995	2005	2020
White, non-Hispanic	76%	73%	68%
Hispanic	9%	11%	14%
African American	11%	11%	11%
Asian-American	4%	5%	6%

Source: Workforce 2020: Work and Workers in the 21st Century by Richard Judy and Carol D'Amico, 1997. Reprinted with permission of the Hudson Institute.

the population belonging to ethnic minority groups (Friedman, 2006; U.S. Census Bureau, 2004). The upward trends in minority population, predict a corresponding increase in racial diversity in the workforce (Table 13.2). Coupled with increases in women's workforce participation, this means that White men may soon become a minority in the workplace.

Racial Diversity

Higher representation does not mean equality in the workplace. The salaries of people of color consistently lag behind those of White men. For every dollar that White men earn, Black and Hispanic men earn 65 cents, Black women 58 cents, and Hispanic women 48 cents. In 2004, 34.9 percent of all of the discrimination cases filed with the U.S. Equal Employment Opportunity Commission were about race—the proportion has barely budged over the past decade. Two problems are becoming increasingly common in the racially diverse workforce—tokenism and the glass ceiling.

When only a few members of a minority group occupy a job, they often believe (and are treated as if) they were hired as **tokens,** as representatives of their group rather than individuals. They are hypervisible: Everything they say or do is taken as what group members *always* say or do. If they get angry, for instance, their co-workers will conclude that everyone in the group gets angry easily. Their failures will be taken as evidence that the group as a whole is incompetent. Under constant pressure to reflect well upon their group, tokens must be on guard at all times. They must consistently outperform their co-workers just to be perceived as equal (Catalyst, 1999; Moss-Kanter, 1977; Yoder, 1991).

Think about a time when you were the only member of some group in a larger group. You could have been the only woman or man, White person or person of color, straight or gay or bisexual, old or young, Christian, Muslim, or Jew—whatever set you apart. Let's say you were the only Latino. At some point, someone turns to you, innocently enough, and asks, "Well, how do Latinos feel about this?" At that moment, you become invisible as an individual, but you are hypervisible only as a member of the group. Of course, the only sensible answer is, "How should I know? I'm just an individual. I can only answer for myself. But I bet there are sociologists who have surveyed Latinos, and we can find out what most of them think about the question."

Gender Diversity

In 1900, less than 20 percent of American women (aged 15 and over) worked outside the home. Today over half do, and the percentage is increasing worldwide.

Surprisingly, women's employment is highest in poor countries, where everyone who can work does: 82.8 percent of women in Mozambique, 80.4 percent in Cambodia, and 74.7 percent in Kenya work outside the home. In wealthy OECD countries, where women in male–female households have the option of staying home, workforce participation of women (aged 20 to 64) ranges from 76 percent (Denmark) to 71 percent (United States) to 60 percent (Japan). However, for college-educated women, the percentages are much higher: 89 percent in Denmark, 82 percent in the United States, and 63 percent in Japan.

The increase in the number of women in the workforce during the last 50 years has been called the "quiet revolution," because its consequences have been gradual, but wide-sweeping—a transformation of consumer patterns, workplace policies,

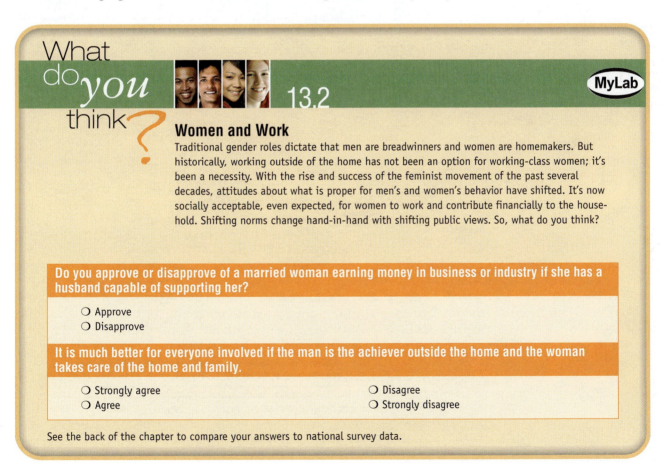

What do you think? 13.2

MyLab

Women and Work

Traditional gender roles dictate that men are breadwinners and women are homemakers. But historically, working outside of the home has not been an option for working-class women; it's been a necessity. With the rise and success of the feminist movement of the past several decades, attitudes about what is proper for men's and women's behavior have shifted. It's now socially acceptable, even expected, for women to work and contribute financially to the household. Shifting norms change hand-in-hand with shifting public views. So, what do you think?

Do you approve or disapprove of a married woman earning money in business or industry if she has a husband capable of supporting her?

○ Approve
○ Disapprove

It is much better for everyone involved if the man is the achiever outside the home and the woman takes care of the home and family.

○ Strongly agree   ○ Disagree
○ Agree   ○ Strongly disagree

See the back of the chapter to compare your answers to national survey data.

dating and relationships, parenting, household maintenance, and self-concepts for both men and women. But that transformation is incomplete. Men and women are still not equal, either in the workplace or at home.

As we saw in Chapter 9, inequality in the workplace has several distinctive characteristics, whether by gender or any other factor. Sex segregation concentrates women and men in different jobs and then explains those differences in terms of individual preferences (women and men simply want different jobs) rather than in terms of structural opportunities and barriers. About half the world's workers are in sex-segregated occupations. In the United States, men comprise 98 percent of construction workers and 97 percent of airline pilots, for instance, while women comprise 76 percent of cashiers and 75 percent of clerical workers. While the overall sex segregation declined significantly in the 1970s, there is evidence of a recent slowdown and resegregation of jobs within broad occupations (Charles and Grusky, 2004; Padavic and Reskin, 2002), including banking and financial services (Skuratowicz and Hunter, 2004).

Another effect of inequality is the **pay gap** between men and women. Typically, we think of the pay gap in terms of the percentage of men's wages that women earn—that is, we read about women earning 81 cents for every man's dollar (Figure 13.7). Yet we could also turn that around and discuss the extra money men get—just for being men. We could also say that men earn $1.23 for every woman's dollar—that is, men get a bonus, a "masculinity dividend" just for being men (Connell, 1995).

FIGURE 13.7 For Women, Equal Pay? No Way

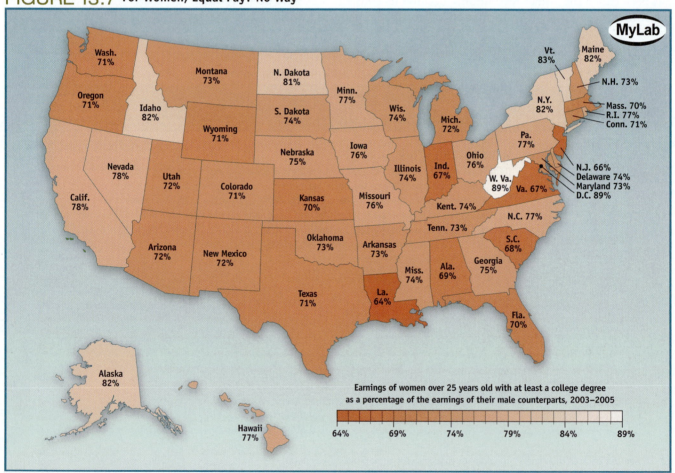

Earnings of women over 25 years old with at least a college degree as a percentage of the earnings of their male counterparts, 2003–2005

Source: From "For Women, Equal Pay? No Way," *Time,* April 27, 2007.

In 2005, the median weekly earnings for full-time workers was $722 for men and $585 for women. The gap is noticeable across all racial divisions (Table 13.3). The gap varies considerably by geographic location and by age—it is much smaller among young workers (25–34) than middle-aged and older ones (Bureau of Labor Statistics, 2006).

The gender wage gap is a global phenomenon. In most economies around the world, women still earn 90 percent or less of what their male co-workers earn (International Labour Organization, 2007). Even in typically "female professions" worldwide—jobs such as teaching and nursing—wage inequality persists for women (ILO, 2007).

A third dynamic of gender inequality is the "glass ceiling." While women have been making small gains consistently for half a century, White men still control nearly all of the top jobs in corporate America. Women comprise more than half of all managers and professionals, but less than 15 percent of the Fortune 500 corporate officers, only 5.2 percent of the top earners, and only 1.2 percent of the CEOs (Catalyst, 2003). Women of color fare worse: They comprise only one corporate officer of every 100 (Catalyst, 2003). The Glass Ceiling Commission observes: "The world at the top of the corporate hierarchy does not yet look anything like America." (Compare this to the "glass escalator" effect that men in gender-nontraditional positions experience [see Williams, 1995].)

Work–Family Dynamics. Our family lives also reinforce workplace gender inequality. In 2002, for the first time, the majority (51 percent) of married male–female couples in America were dual income (perhaps not surprisingly because the middle-class lifestyle that used to be feasible on one income now takes two). As women break into the ranks of the top earners, salary differences sometimes upset the traditional designation of the male partner as the "breadwinner": more than 25% of all women in dual-wage households earn more than their husbands (Bureau of Labor Statistics, 2005). Women make up 39 percent of America's top wealth holders (Konig, 2005).

However, household maintenance is still widely assumed to be a woman's job. A Western woman spends an average of 10 hours per week on household maintenance and a man about five hours. Sociologists have found that living arrangements don't change the average much: Two women living together will still spend about the same amount of time, as will two men. When men and women marry, the woman will perform 50 percent more housework than the man, even if they are both working full-time outside the home (Couprie, 2007). Once children arrive, the gap actually grows. American mothers do three times as much housework as men, spending 17 hours a week on average, while fathers spend just six (Seward, Yeatts, Amin, and Dewitt, 2006).

TABLE 13.3

The "Masculinity Dividend": Median Weekly Pay Gap between Men and Women, 2005

	MEN	WOMEN
White	$743	$596
Black	$599	$499
Hispanic	$489	$429

Source: Bureau of Labor Statistics, 2006.

Sexual Diversity

The workplace originated in a heterosexual division of labor: the male husband/father/breadwinner and the female wife/mother/domestic worker. Early decisions about wages and benefits assumed a single breadwinner for the entire family—and assumed that he was not only male but heterosexual. Many companies continue to assume that all of their employees, stockholders, and customers are heterosexual. There are no federal regulations barring discrimination on the basis of sexual orientation, so employers can refuse to hire gay men and lesbians or fire them at any time. As a result, most gay or lesbian employees must pretend that they are heterosexual, but even those who are out tend to bump up against what they call a "lavender ceiling."

As recently as the 1970s, help wanted ads in newspapers were coded for "Male" and "Female." Interviewers would routinely ask women about their marital status and family lives—whether they had children or were planning to have them any time soon. Today, those questions are out of bounds. And yet working mothers still experience more workplace prejudice than working fathers. In one study, 196 undergraduates were asked to judge a fictitious resumé for an entry-level job as an immigration lawyer. Different groups got resumés from male and female applicants, some with children, some without. The respondents were just as likely to recommend hiring men with and without children, but they were more likely to recommend childless women than women with children. They were also less likely to consider women with children to be good candidates for promotion (Biernat and Fuegen, 2001).

Corporate culture is built around the assumption of heterosexuality, with conversations and jokes from the boardroom down to the loading dock focused on husbands and wives, boyfriends and girlfriends, and the attractiveness of various movie stars. Employees who refuse to participate are perceived as cool, distant, and snobbish, not "team players." Employees who mention same-sex partners, interests, and experiences are perceived as "problems." As a result, they are passed over at promotion time. In spite of the stereotype that all gay men are sophisticated interior designers living in Manhattan high-rise apartments, for example, gay and lesbian salaries lag far behind those of heterosexual workers (Raeburn, 2004).

Some changes have occurred recently, mostly through the efforts of gay and lesbian workplace activists. Of the Fortune 500 companies, 253 now offer benefits for same-sex partners, and 410 (86 percent) include sexual orientation in their nondiscrimination policies. However, nondiscrimination policies have been mandated for women and ethnic minorities for decades, and glass ceilings are still intact. Not one of the Fortune 500 CEOs is openly gay or lesbian (Human Rights Campaign, 2006).

Working Parents

The United States ranks number eight among wealthy nations in the percentage of mothers in the labor force, with 60 percent of all mothers and 53.3 percent of mothers with children under 1 year old are in the workforce, (Cohary and Sok, 2007). In other nations, the percentage ranges from 76 percent (Sweden) to 32 percent (Czech Republic). Sixty-four percent of American working mothers are White and 36 percent are women of color (OECD, 2006; U.S. Census Bureau, 2000).

For many years, working mothers have been struggling to make corporate culture see children not as "problems" or distractions, but as part of "business as usual." As parents, they want more flexibility in their hours and in their career paths, more options, updated criteria for success.

Recently some men have joined them, reframing the issue from "women's right to work" to "parenting and the workplace." A 1998 study by the AFL-CIO found that balancing work and family commitments was the top concern for both sexes, nearly 50 percent of women and 45 percent of men. A study of generation Xers by the Radcliffe Institute (2001) found that more men than women would trade some of the prestige and salary of a potential job for more free time to spend with their families.

On the other hand, employers could probably benefit significantly from accommodating working parents of either sex. The skills one learns from parenting, including communication, emotional availability, multitasking, efficient organization, and patience, are valuable in the twenty-first century workplace (Crittenden, 2005). Levine (1997) found that "working fathers," or fathers heavily invested in their children's daily lives, perform better and are more comfortable in a diverse workplace than the traditional "breadwinners."

Work and Economy in the 21st Century

The workplace as we know it today was created by the needs of an industrial economy. But now we are moving into a postindustrial, knowledge-based economy. The stereotypic office workplace, 9 to 5 workday, and single-field career are all becoming obsolete. What sorts of new arrangements will arise to take their place?

In the future, only a small percentage of workers will do a single job throughout their lives, changing only to move up to positions of greater authority (such as teachers becoming principals). Instead, they will develop a portfolio of skills and credentials that they will use to move horizontally, between jobs in many different career fields. Sometimes they will even occupy different jobs simultaneously.

The increased flexibility means that workers will have more control over their work and more creativity. However, they will have no job security because employers will be able to hire and fire them at will. And productivity will suffer because training and recruitment will be never ending: Workers will devote more time and energy to learning new skills and finding work than actually *doing* work.

In the future, we'll be more mobile. At present, such mobility is an option only for white-collar workers; the blue and pink collars are left behind. Also, it is unclear what benefits the white-collar employees will receive as mobility becomes more common. Greater flexibility, perhaps? More creativity? Greater autonomy? They are working and playing at playing at the same moment, answering personal and professional e-mails, watching movies while checking figures, surfing the Web while videoconferencing. Does this blurred boundary between work and leisure increase the quality of either? Or does it eat into private lives, cause higher stress, and create an army of slaves to e-mail?

In the future, will we be working more and enjoying it less, or working less and enjoying it more? To the sociologist, the answer is both. It depends on whom you talk to, where they live, and what they do for a living.

Chapter Review

1. *What is the economy?* The economy is a set of institutions and relationships that manages natural resources, manufactured goods, and professional services.

2. *How do economies develop?* Before the Agricultural Revolution, societies had few rules, and everyone worked together. Later, people grew predictable crops with permanent settlements and surplus that led to a division of labor and the development of markets. The invention of the steam engine ushered in the industrial economy, centralizing jobs, specializing workers, and moving to a model of paid labor. This in turn leads to increased production which brings increased consumption. Postindustrial economies are characterized by knowledge work, rootlessness, and globalization and occur when jobs shift from production to service orientation.

3. *What economic systems are there?* Economic systems deal with production, distribution, and consumption. Capitalism is based on profit, competition, and ownership of private property. Socialism is characterized by

collective ownership, collective goals, and central planning. Communism is collective ownership with little government intervention. There are very few real communist economies.

4. *How did the U. S. economy develop?* The American economy moved from agricultural to industrial to postindustrial. After the Industrial Revolution, shopkeepers and artisans were displaced as mass production provided cheaper goods. After the stock market crash of 1929, government intervened in local economies, which led to minimum wage laws, Social Security, and regulation of the stock market. A technological revolution began after World War II, which led to a postindustrial economy where the production of knowledge surpassed the production of goods.

5. *What are corporations?* Corporations are businesses that are legally treated as individuals. Thus, individual investors and managers are separated from the profit or loss of the business. Corporate capitalism developed in four stages. Initially, investments, customers, and profits were shared with relatives in family corporations. When the family was unable to meet the needs of the company, entrepreneurs began to hire outside managers in managerial corporations that were larger and more stable. Companies began to hold shares in other companies, and institutional corporations developed that were interconnected through a small network of powerful individuals. Now, the most common type of corporation is multinational.

6. *How are work, identity, and inequality interrelated?* Work is a central activity of human life, and sociologists argue whether we work because we have to or because we want to. The Hawthorne effect studies state that when workers feel more control over their work, they are more satisfied with their jobs. This is similar to theory Y, which is based on the assumption that people naturally like work and will do it if they feel they are valued. Theory X is the opposite; it assumes that people naturally dislike work and will work well only if they are coerced. Buroway's theory of manufacturing consent holds that management engages in strategies to make workers embrace the system that exploits them.

7. *How does diversity manifest in the workplace?* White-collar work used to be dominated by White men, but this is no longer the case, as women and ethnic minorities are gaining. As the ethnic composition of the United States changes, so will the workplace composition. However, higher representation does not mean equality. Pay for women and minorities still lags. More American women work outside the home than ever before, and globally, women's employment is highest in the poor countries where work is not a choice. Women's increased participation in the workplace has led to the "quiet revolution," which is changing consumer, home, and work patterns.

Key Terms

Capital (p. 418)
Capitalism (p. 425)
Communism (p. 428)
Conspicuous consumption (p. 420)
Consumption (p. 420)
Corporation (p. 431)
Economic system (p. 425)
Economy (p. 418)
Human capital (p. 442)

Industrial economies (p. 419)
Industrial Revolution (p. 419)
Knowledge economy (p. 422)
Labor unions (p. 438)
Manufacture consent (p. 436)
Markets (p. 419)
Mass production (p. 420)
Multinational corporations (p. 432)
Outsourcing (p. 423)

Pay gap (p. 448)
Postindustrial economies (p. 422)
Production (p. 420)
Race to the bottom (p. 433)
Socialism (p. 427)
Tokens (p. 446)
Wage labor (p. 420)

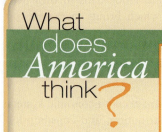

What does *America* think?

13.1   The Rich and Taxes

This is actual survey data from the General Social Survey, 2002.

Do you think that people with high incomes should pay a larger share of their income in taxes than those with low incomes, the same share, or a smaller share? In the 2002 General Social Survey, 23 percent of respondents said the rich should pay a much larger share of their income in taxes. Almost 44 percent said the rich should pay a larger share. Thirty-one percent thought the current share paid was adequate. When broken down by race, there was a significant difference between Black and White respondents, with Black respondents being much more likely (32 percent) to think that the rich should pay a much larger share of their income in taxes.

CRITICAL THINKING | DISCUSSION QUESTIONS

1. Why do you think the survey responses broke down by race the way they did?
2. How do you think responses might differ if they were broken down by social class?
   Go to the website and check for yourself. How did your prediction compare to the data?

13.2 Women and Work

This is actual survey data from the General Social Survey.

1. **Do you approve or disapprove of a married woman earning money in business or industry if she has a husband capable of supporting her?** In 1972, 65 percent of respondents approved of a married woman earning money. More women than men approved. In 1998, the numbers were a bit higher, with almost 77 percent of respondents approving and the gender difference in response disappearing.
2. **It is much better for everyone involved if the man is the achiever outside the home and the woman takes care of the home and family.** In 1977, 18 percent of respondents strongly agreed, with slightly more men than women agreeing. Only 34 percent of respondents disagreed or strongly disagreed. In 2004 the numbers shifted. Only 9 percent of respondents strongly agreed, with no gender difference, and 58 percent disagreed or strongly disagreed.

CRITICAL THINKING | DISCUSSION QUESTION

1. Why do you think a significant number of people still think a woman's place is in her home?
2. What do you make of the lack of variance in the answers by gender?

▶ Go to this website to look further at the data. You can run your own statistics and crosstabs here: **http://sda.berkeley.edu/cgi-bin/hsda?harcsda+gss04**

REFERENCES: Davis, James A., Tom W. Smith, and Peter V. Marsden. General Social Surveys 1972–2004: [Cumulative file] [Computer file]. 2nd ICPSR version. Chicago, IL: National Opinion Research Center [producer], 2005; Storrs, CT: Roper Center for Public Opinion Research, University of Connecticut; Ann Arbor, MI: Inter-University Consortium for Political and Social Research; Berkeley, CA: Computer-Assisted Survey Methods Program, University of California [distributors], 2005.

chapter 14

THERE ARE TWO OLD SAYINGS about politics:

"Everybody wants to change the world."
"You can't fight city hall."

Which is true? In some ways, we have more political power than ever before. The Internet gives us constant access to political discussion and protest. Local groups constantly organize to change things. Yet we also have less power than ever. Every week, it seems, a new scandal reveals how the big money behind big corporations seem to dictate public policy. Labor strikes no longer work. Worldwide protests against wars and invasions have little impact on policymakers.

Politics and Government

We're more politically aware than ever. Round-the-clock news stations broadcast every detail of major and minor political disputes. C-Span lets us glimpse every moment of every session of Congress. Telephone and

Internet polls chart changes in public opinion minute by minute. Yet we're also less politically engaged than ever. Party membership is down. Voting is down—even in elections full of hot-button issues.

We're more politically polarized than ever before. The divisions between Democrat and Republican have never been greater. No journalist half a century ago would have thought to divide the country into red and blue states. Yet we're also less politically coherent than ever before. Legislation that passes one year is rescinded the next. Few voters pull the lever for a straight party line any longer. Liberals vote for conservative candidates, conservatives vote for liberal candidates, and

We are both more politically aware and more apathetic, more empowered and more disenfranchised, and the world is both more and less democratic than ever. Understanding this dynamic is sociology's unique contribution to the study of politics.

many people just give up on labels and vote for a mixed bag of Republicans, Democrats, independents, and Greens.

Finally, in some ways, the world is more democratic than ever before. People everywhere celebrate democracy as an ideal, and virtually every nation claims, in its constitution or in its official name, to be a democracy—including the People's Republic of China, the Islamic Republic of Iran, the Democratic People's Republic of Korea. Yet many of these countries are authoritarian regimes, ruled by political or theocratic elites rather than the "consent of the governed." And many democracies are also corrupt or run like individual fiefdoms, so the world sometimes seems less democratic than ever before.

Which is it? More or less power? More or less aware? More or less politically aligned? More or less democratic?

To the sociologist, the answer to these questions isn't one or the other. It's both. The processes and dynamics of how we can be both more *and* less aware, powerful, or democratic is sociology's unique contribution to the study of politics.

Politics: Power and Authority

Politics is the art and science of government. Politics is about about power, the ability to make people do what you want them to do—whether they want to do it or not. And it is about **government**—the organization and administration of the actions of the inhabitants of communities, societies, and states. And politics is about authority—**power** that is perceived as legitimate by both power holders and those who are subjected to it. If politics is working well, it is through government that power is transformed into authority.

If you have a lot of power, you can coerce (force) others, through violence, monetary means (like fines for speeders on the highway), or loss of liberty (detention for students who talk in class). If you have very little power, you must beg, plead, or wheedle (the way children get permission to stay up past their bedtime). If you have no power at all, you might need to resort to trickery, the way sit-com heroes like Bart Simpson do.

Sociologists have always wondered about power: how we get it, how we use it, why some of us have so much of it and some of us have so little (Faulks, 2000; Lukes, 1986; Orum, 2000). Back in the nineteenth century, Marx saw power as purely a characteristic of social class. The owners of the means of production had a tremendous amount of power. They had complete control over the workers' tasks, schedules, and salaries; they could pay their workers enough to live comfortably, or just enough to keep them alive, or even less and let them starve to death. Meanwhile the workers had no power at all. They had no control over their wages or working conditions and could vote only for candidates who were handpicked by the factory owners. Their only means of getting more were trickery and theft.

Class, Status, and Power

No society has ever been built around pure coercion. A few have come close—the slave society of the antebellum South, for example, or Romania under Nicolai Ceausescu—but they are always vastly inefficient because they must expend almost all of their resources on keeping people in line and punishing dissidents. And even there, the leaders must supplement coercion with other techniques, like persuasion and indoctrination.

That's why Max Weber (1978 ed.) argued that power is not a simple matter of absolutes: Few of us have total power over others, so force won't work. And few of us have no power at all, so we rarely have to resort to trickery. Most often, people do what we want them to do willingly, not because they are being coerced or tricked. Drivers who obey the speed limits are probably not worried about being fined—after all, hundreds of cars are zooming past them at 90 mph without punishment. Instead, they have decided that they want to obey the speed limit, because they're good citizens and that's what good citizens do.

In most societies, cultures, subcultures, families, and other groups, coercion remains a last resort, while by far the most common means of exercising power is authority. **Authority** is power that is perceived as legitimate, by both the holder of power and those subject to it. People must believe that the leader is entitled to make commands and that they should obey.

Consider it this way: Although this book is admittedly fascinating, I'm sure that you would rather be doing something else instead of reading it at this moment. So why are you here? Are you being coerced? Surely, your professor is not sitting in the chair next to you, poised to mark an F on your report card the moment your attention lags. You're reading because the professor told you to and because you believe that professors are entitled to tell students to read things. Chances are that if you have been putting it off for awhile, you felt a sense of relief when you finally began to read. You believed that you were doing the right thing.

Note that the professor's authority is not transferable to situations in which you are *not* a student. If your professor accosts you on the street and says, "Go pick up my dry cleaning!" it is unlikely that you will obey. In fact, you might register a complaint with the dean. Nor is it transferable to others in your network. If you introduce your professor to your parents, and he or she then expects them to take notes as he or she pontificates about current events, you'll probably just laugh.

Weber argued that leaders exercise three types of authority: traditional authority, charismatic authority, and legal-rational authority.

Traditional Authority

Traditional authority is a type of power that draws its legitimacy from tradition. We do things this way because we have always done them this way. In many premodern societies, people obeyed social norms for hundreds, sometimes thousands, of years. Their leaders spoke with the voice of ancient traditions, issuing commands that had been issued a thousand times before. They derived their authority from who they were: the descendants of kings and queens, or perhaps the descendants of the gods, not from their educational background, work experience, or personality traits.

Traditional authority is very stable, and people can expect to obey the same commands that their ancestors did. Its remnants still exist today in many social institutions, including religion, government, and the family, where we obey some rules because we have always done so. Children obey parents; parishioners obey the clergy because they have always done so—and always will. In some cultures, the expectation of blind obedience by wives to their husbands' authority is similar. But even in ancient times, large-scale political, economic, and social changes sometimes occurred, such as invasion, war, or natural disaster, and new generations faced situations and challenges unknown to their ancestors, thus putting a great strain on traditional authority. That's when a second form, charismatic authority, would emerge.

Charismatic Authority

Charismatic authority is a type of power in which people obey because of the personal characteristics of the leader. Charismatic leaders are so personally compelling that people follow them even when they have no traditional claims to authority. Indeed, they often ask their followers to break with tradition. We read in the New Testament that Jesus frequently said "it is written, but I say unto you . . . ," contrasting traditional authority (Jewish law) with charismatic authority (his teachings).

Charismatic leaders are often religious prophets, but even when they are not, their followers can be as passionate and devout as religious believers. Some presidents, like Franklin D. Roosevelt and John F. Kennedy, developed a popularity that cannot be explained by their performance in office alone. Many other political leaders of the past and present depend, to some degree, on charisma in addition to other types of authority.

Charisma is morally neutral—as a personal quality, it can be found at all points in an ethical spectrum: Hitler, Gandhi, Osama bin Laden, and Nelson Mandela all possessed personal qualities that elicited obedience from their followers. Charismatic leaders can change societies, leading people away from the traditional rules and toward a more personal experience of authority.

But pure charisma is also unstable because it is located in the personality of an individual, not a set of traditions or laws. And because they defy other forms of authority, charismatic leaders rarely live long—they are exiled (like the Dalai Lama in 1959), assassinated (Gandhi, Kennedy), or imprisoned (Mandela). When they are gone, their followers are faced with a crisis. How do you maintain the emotional high that you felt when the leader was with you?

Weber argued that after the leader's departure, a small group of disciples will create a set of rules and regulations by which one can continue being a follower, and a set of rituals that will remind the followers of the presence of the departed leader. Thus, charismatic authority is replaced by the rules, regulations, and rituals of legal-rational authority.

Legal-Rational Authority

In the third form of authority, **legal-rational authority,** leaders are to be obeyed, not primarily as representatives of tradition or because of their personal qualities, but because they are voicing a set of rationally derived laws. They must act impartially, even sacrificing their own opinions and attitudes in obedience to the laws of the land.

Legal-rational authority begins with the rationalization of authority after the departure of the charismatic leader and has become the most common form of authority in contemporary societies. In fact, many argue that modern government would be impossible without it. Governments operate under a set of regulations flexible enough to withstand changing social situations, and traditional authority is unable to handle much change without breaking down. And no leader, however charismatic, would today be able to sway tens of millions of people of diverse socioeconomic classes, races, religions, and life situations, on the basis of their personality alone.

Power/Knowledge

Weber argued that we obey authority because we perceive it to be legitimate. But how do we get the idea that it is a good thing to obey a leader, instead of rebelling or striking out on our own? The late twentieth-century French philosopher Michel Foucault had a different idea: We obey because we cannot conceive of anything else. Power is always explicitly connected with knowledge. In fact, he wrote, they should be the same word: *power/knowledge* (Foucault, 1980).

Power/knowledge does not force us to do things, but it shapes and limits our thoughts and desires until they correspond to the dominant ideologies of our society. If you cannot think of doing something, then it is pretty hard to entertain actually doing it. For example, if you have no idea that there are forms of contraception, it would be difficult to imagine "planning" your family. If the rules of a game are firmly established, it's hard to imagine that they might be otherwise.

Authorities use three strategies to limit our own power/knowledge and thereby maintain control:

1. *Hierarchical observation.* They watch and observe what you do, sort of the way that supervisors constantly check up on salespeople in retail stores or "Big Brother" may be observing what Internet sites you are visiting when you are supposed to be working on office spreadsheets.

2. *Normalizing judgment.* "Experts" use their knowledge to determine if what we do or want to do is "normal," like the ways that employers use personality tests to decide whether or not to hire you.

3. *Examination.* Regular assessments determine if we have acquired the proper thoughts and desires—probably something like the test you'll take about this book at the end of this semester.

But Foucault did not see power/knowledge as purely repressive and prohibitive; it is also a creative force. The very actions taken by the powerful create new opportunities for resistance to it. So, for example, Foucault argues that the sexual repression of the Victorian age also created, for the first time, distinct sexual identities called "homosexuals" and "heterosexuals." (There were behaviors before, of course, but never the idea that such behaviors formed an identity. In other words, prior to that era, "homosexual" and "heterosexual" were adjectives, describing behaviors, not nouns, describing people.)

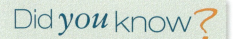

Did you know?

Today the term *politically correct* is used mostly by political conservatives to condemn what they perceive as liberal hypocrisy. Originally the term was positive, referring to honest attempts to avoid offending different groups. The efforts to change the word "mankind" to "humankind" or to eliminate the use of "Miss" or "Mrs." for women (which referred to them only in their relationship to men) were some examples.

Actually, the term is much older. It first appeared in 1793 in a Supreme Court decision (*Chisholm v. Georgia*) to distinguish between "the United States" and "the people of the United States" (the latter was politically correct).

Political Systems

Political systems determine how group leaders exercise their authority. Virtually all political systems fall into one of two categories, authoritarian or democratic.

Authoritarian Systems

In an **authoritarian political system,** power is vested in a single person or small group. Sometimes that person holds power through heredity, sometimes through force or terror.

Monarchy. One of the first political systems was the rule by a single individual, or **monarchy** (*mono* means "one," and *archy* means "rule"). In many early societies, the best hunter or the best warrior would seize control and rule until a better hunter or warrior arrived on the scene. Then leaders began to rule throughout their lives, and on their deathbed they would name one of their children as the new leader. Thus individuals from a single family began to rule from generation to generation. Denmark has had 52 kings and queens, in a family lineage extending from Margrethe II (1940–) all the way back to Gorm the Old (840–936). Japan has had 125 emperors, from Akihito (1933–) extending back to the legendary Jimmu (711–585 BCE).

The rule of a family was legitimized by traditional authority. The rulers of ancient Egypt, China, Japan, and Peru all claimed that their families descended from the gods. Medieval monarchs derived their power from divine right: They were not literally descended from God, but their power was based on God's will. By the time of the Renaissance, most of the kings and queens of Europe were "absolute monarchs": their word was law, even when their word contradicted the law of the land. It might be illegal for the average person to commit murder, but the king or queen could call for the execution of anyone, for any reason or for no reason (so it made sense to stay on their good side).

Gradually a more egalitarian climate began to prevail. We can find traces of "rule of the people" as early as the English Magna Carta (1215), which established government as a relationship between monarchy and the people. But it wasn't until the seventeenth and eighteenth centuries that Enlightenment philosophers like John Locke began to suggest that kings and queens, however noble, may be as human as everybody else (Marshall, 1994). If they were evil or incompetent, they should be removed from office. During a relatively short period, the English Civil War and revolutions in France, America, and Haiti either deposed hereditary rulers or made them answerable to parliaments of elected officials (Birn, 1992; Wedgewood, 1990; Winks and Kaiser, 2003). Other kingdoms became "constitutional monarchies" peacefully, adopting constitutions and electing parliaments with the full support of the kings or queens. A constitutional monarchy may still have a hereditary ruler, but he or she functions as a symbol of the country and a goodwill ambassador, while elected officials make the everyday political decisions based on the principles embedded in a constitution.

Today only a few absolute monarchies remain, such as Kuwait, Saudi Arabia, and Swaziland, but even they often legislate a system of checks to keep the rulers from overstating their power. In Saudi Arabia, for instance, King Abdullah bin Abdulaziz al-Saud receives no direct input from the Saudi people—there are no political parties or elections—and he cannot be deposed. But he is answerable to the ulema, the body of Muslim clerics who help him interpret Islamic law, and if he committed a severe offense, he could be asked to abdicate in favor of another member of the Saudi royal family.

Oligarchy. **Oligarchy** is the rule of a small group of people, an elite social class or often a single family. For instance, in Renaissance Italy, the city-state of Venice had a population of about 200,000. It was originally a republic, ruled by an elected official, the Doge. But gradually the Maggior Consiglio, the equivalent of the parliament, took more and more power. Members of the Maggior Consiglio were required by law to belong to one of a few aristocratic families (Norwich, 1989). As a simple guide, if monarchy is like the rule of the father in a household, oligarchy is more like the rule of the father and all his brothers. (Oligarchies tend to be patriarchal, and thus the use of the male family members.)

Dictatorship. A **dictatorship** is rule by one person who has no hereditary claim to rule. Dictators may acquire power through a military takeover, or they may be elected or appointed. Many people are surprised to find out that three of the most ruthless dictators of the twentieth century acquired their power legitimately. King Victor Emmanuel of Italy appointed Mussolini prime minister in 1922. That same year, in the Soviet Union, Joseph Stalin was elected president of the Communist Party. German president Paul von Hindenburg appointed Adolph Hitler as chancellor in 1933. Afterwards, however, they took over the press, dismantled parliament, outlawed political opposition, exiled or executed their enemies, and generally ignored the democratic ideals that gave them their power in the first place (Kilpatrick, 1983).

▲ Although dictators rule by violence, they often have significant popular support. Adolf Hitler arriving at a rally in Nuremberg in 1936.

Totalitarianism. **Totalitarianism** is when political authority is extended over all other aspects of social life—including culture, the arts, and social relations. Any political system may become totalitarian when no organized opposition is permitted and political information is censored. Secret police and paid informers closely monitor the people to ensure that they remain loyal to a rigidly defined ideology. Propaganda, misinformation, and terror are used to ensure obedience (Arendt, 1958).

In North Korea, for instance, pictures of "Dear Leader" Kim Jong-il are everywhere, and political messages are broadcast over loudspeakers, constantly reminding citizens that they owe allegiance to the state. Government-controlled schools and mass media present only official versions of events, and very little knowledge of the outside world is permitted. No labor unions or other political groups are permitted, and even social groups are closely monitored. Friends and family members are encouraged to spy on each other, reporting momentary lapses into disloyalty. Some 200,000 people are held in concentration camps as "political dissidents" (Martin, 2004).

No doubt many absolute monarchs would have preferred totalitarian regimes, but they lacked the cameras, radios, telephones, and other equipment necessary to closely monitor their citizens and to quickly locate and punish dissidents. Only in the twentieth century did the technology become available.

Other than the brutal attempts to control the thoughts and behaviors of their citizens, modern totalitarian governments have little in common. They can start out as democracies (Nazi Germany), constitutional monarchies (Italy under Mussolini), or socialist states (the Soviet Union under Stalin). They span economic systems, although free-enterprise capitalism is uncommon because it is difficult to control. They tend to be more common in rich nations than in poor nations because they are expensive to maintain (North Korea expends 25 percent of its resources on the military).

Democracy

The great British statesman Winston Churchill once commented that democracy is the worst form of government—except for all the others. Democracy is messy and noisy, and order is difficult because in its basic idea, democracy gives a political voice to everyone.

Democracy (from *demos*, or people) puts legislative decision making into the hands of the people rather than a single individual or a noble class (Dahl, 1989; Finley, 1973). The concept originated in ancient Greek city-states like Athens and Sparta, in which all questions were put to a vote in an assembly, and every adult male citizen had voting rights. City officials were selected by lottery (Hansen, 1999).

Pure democracy, or **participatory democracy,** with every person getting one vote and the majority ruling, can work only in very small, homogeneous units, like classrooms, families, communes, clubs, churches, and small towns. If many people participate, it becomes impossible to gather them all together for decision making. If the population becomes heterogeneous, simple majority rule obliterates the needs of minorities. In ancient Greece, women, children, foreigners, and slaves were excluded from citizenship, so almost all of the voters at assemblies shared a socioeconomic status, language, belief system, and political agenda. If 10 percent of the citizens had been Persian rather Greek, their opinions would have vanished at every majority vote (Schumpeter, 1942).

The idea of democracy vanished when ancient Greece became part of the Roman Empire (510–23 BCE). It reappeared during the Enlightenment (1650–1800), when philosophers began to argue that all human beings have natural rights, including the right to select their own political leaders. Because nation-states were too big for participatory democracy, they developed the theory of **representative democracy,** in which citizens elect representatives to make the decisions for them. Representative democracy requires an educated citizenry and a free press. High-speed communication and transportation are also helpful; during the nineteenth century, it took weeks to calculate the popular votes in presidential elections and months before everyone in the country was informed of the results. However, there are often several steps between the people and the decisions, such as an electoral college, to minimize chaos while things get counted.

In 1900, there were only a few democracies in the world, and none with **universal suffrage** (voting for all adults, both men and women). Today 70 percent of the world's nations are democracies, more than twice the percentage just 20 years ago, and another 14 percent are constitutional monarchies, all with universal suffrage. The remaining 16 percent of the world's nations are a mixture of colonies, territories, absolute monarchies, communist states, Islamic republics or other forms of theocracy (rule by a religious group), military juntas, and dictatorships, plus one ecclesiastical state (Vatican City) and two states with no central government (Somalia, which is in chaos after 20 years of civil war; and Iraq, which is under American occupation as of this writing).

The appeal of democracy as a political ideal has become nearly universal. The first national election in Iraq in 2005. ▼

How do we know what we know?

Measuring Democracy

We generally agree that democracy is a "good thing" and that the more democratic a society is, the better life is. But we don't really agree about how to measure democracy. After all, a society in which the majority rules could be one with no tolerance for anyone not in the majority or one with lots of tolerance. Social scientists have developed three different methods to measure democracy:

1. Survey-based data identify public perceptions of democracy. These surveys ask questions related to democracy, human rights, and responsive government. Two surveys that use these surveys are the Global Barometer Surveys and World Values Surveys, which now contain data on 43 countries (see Inglehart, 1997).

2. Standards-based data use specific political ideals as their basis and measure the extent to which those ideals have been realized. These ideals might include the constraints on executive behavior, the extent of "polyarchy" or rule by many different people, competitiveness of the nomination process, or the extent of violations of individual rights (torture, terror, political imprisonment, disappearances). Freedom House offers a seven-point scale of political and social liberties that have measured different countries since 1972.

Another standards-based measure was offered by Finnish researcher Tatu Vanhanen, who measures contestation and participation. Contestation is measured by the smallest political parties' share of the vote, and participation is measured by voter turnout. These are multiplied together and divided by 100 to yield an "index of democratization" for 187 countries (Vanhanen, 2000).

3. Events-based data count specific events that promote or impede democracy. These might include both negative acts of discrimination, such as corruption and violations of human rights, and positive events, like voter turnout and free and fair elections. Events can be tallied from newspapers or magazines or from NGO networks and human rights testimonies.

(*Source:* Landman, 2003)

But even these countries are experiencing strong pressure toward democratization from both home and abroad. Globalized mass media constantly put rich people on display as examples of "ordinary" citizens of the United States, Japan, or Western Europe, thereby associating democracy with wealth, privilege, and power. International humanitarian agencies often associate democracy with freedom and condemn autocracies as necessarily oppressive. The only way to resist the pressure is to strictly censor outside media, thereby transforming the state into a totalitarian regime.

Because every state, even the most authoritarian, claims to be democratic, it may be useful to look not at official government structures but at how the government actually works. Even when the democratic institutions are functioning properly, the egalitarian ideals of democracy often fall short. In **illiberal democracies** such as Singapore, officials are elected by the people, but they pay so little attention to the constitution and other laws and to the opinions of their constituents that the country might as well be an oligarchy (Zakaria, 2004). But even the most scrupulously observed democratic ideals can sometimes fall prey to corruption, bureaucracy, marginalization of minority groups, and exclusion of the poor.

Problems of Political Systems

Democracies are messier than authoritarian systems; populations in open societies are more difficult to control. But both authoritarian and democratic systems are prone to the same types of problems.

Corruption. An international agency called Transparency International (www.transparency.org/) ranks nations on a scale of 0 (not corrupt) to 10 (highly corrupt) on the basis of three variables:

1. Outside interests donate large sums of money to elected officials.

2. New members of parliament or Congress obey special interest groups rather than the views of the people they are supposed to represent.

3. Officials misuse government funds or the power of their office for personal gain.

Corruption seems to have little to do with whether the country is democratic or authoritarian. For instance, Papua New Guinea, which rated a 10 on democratic institutions, ranked a 7.9 in corruption, and Kuwait, which rated a –7 on democratic institutions, ranked 4.7 in corruption. Instead, corruption seems to be characteristic of poor nations, where there are few economic opportunities, so people use their political influence to make money or exercise illicit power.

Sometimes it is hard to blame these public officials because the systems they work in are also corrupt. Or "corrupting"—for example, when they are paid little or nothing, so they must make do with outside income and bribes. In many countries, a bribe is approximately the equivalent of a tip, an unofficial fee to ensure that your visa application is processed sometime this year.

In recent years, showcase trials of political lobbyists like Jack Abramoff have revealed the extent of "legitimate corruption" in the United States, where massive expenditures by lobbyists for various industries supply expensive travel junkets and other expensive "gifts" to lawmakers on committees that affect those industries.

Bureaucracy. As nations become larger and more complex, more and more levels between the people and the decision making are formed, creating **bureaucracy.** In the United States, most people who operate the government are never elected by anyone and not directly accountable to the people, and there are many possibilities of mismanagement, inefficiency, and conflict of interest (Etzioni-Halevy, 1983). The administrative staffs of organizations often wield enormous influence over policies, as do lobbyists and other interested groups.

Bureaucracies, Weber argued, were inherently antagonistic to democracy. In a democracy, after all, one is elected to a fixed term (and with contemporary "term limits," these are increasingly short terms). This means that elected officials do not become "entrenched" but are constantly subordinate to the will of the people. By contrast, bureaucracies are staffed by people who are appointed, often for a "life tenure," which means that they are accountable to no one but the bureaucracy itself. Bureaucracies therefore almost always suffer from "bureaucratic entrenchment" (1978).

Sociologist Robert Michels argued that all institutions are subject to what he called the "iron law of oligarchy." An oligarchy is the rule by a specialized elite, who come to power because of their technical expertise, and they tend to remain in power because they are seen as indispensable. They consolidate their power, and the public becomes marginalized because they cannot muster the technical expertise to replace the elite. No matter how democratic or authoritarian they may have been in the beginning, they all tend toward oligarchy (Michels, 1966).

Class, Race, Gender, and Power. The rich have far more political clout than the poor. Every U.S. president elected in the past 100 years has been wealthy when elected, and most were born into wealth. Today millions of dollars are necessary to successfully finance the campaigns of presidents, governors, senators, and even local

Exploring Women and Politics in the United States and the World

Developed by Katherine R. Rowell, *Sinclair Community College* (based on suggestions in the chapter).

OBJECTIVE: Examine the issue of women and politics in the United States and the world.

STEP 1: Plan
You will need access to the Internet or library resources to complete this activity. You will also want to use a search engine like Google to find the information required for this activity.

STEP 2: Research
1. Using various sources, find out what countries do not allow women to vote (include only those countries that allow men to vote). Make a list of these countries and note your sources and date of the information. Did anything surprise you, or did you note any type of pattern?
2. Using various resources, identify how many countries have had a woman as the head of state in the past

10 years. List the country, the name of the leader, and the dates for which she held office (include those in leadership currently). Also, make a list of how many U.S. senators, congressional representatives, and governors are women. Again, provide a citation for your sources.

STEP 3: Review and Reflect
After reviewing the information you gathered in steps 2 and 3, take a moment to write a brief reflection (paragraph) on what impact that gender stratification and socialization has on the role women play in government in the United States and in the world. Do you think the role women play in government is changing? Why or why not?

STEP 4: Discuss
Be prepared to share the information from previous steps in class.

▲ Political campaigns have become so costly that often only the wealthiest can mount one. Billionaire Michael Bloomberg spent tens of millions of his own money to run for mayor of New York City in 2002.

officials like mayors: Grassroots door knocking and envelope stuffing can never compete with high-tech prime-time TV commercials and glossy full-page magazine ads. Members of the middle class rarely rise higher than the local school board or local civil service, and the working class are virtually excluded from elected office altogether.

In recent years, several enormously wealthy men have spent hundreds of millions of their own dollars to run for public office—and win. Billionaire Michael Bloomberg, the current mayor of New York City, and Jon Corzine, a U.S. senator who became governor of New Jersey, had no political experience before running for elected office but used their business acumen as an asset, promising to run the government like a successful business. (This idea of applying a business model to government is always attractive because government bureaucracies tend to make people feel the government is entrenched and unresponsive, and hence, undemocratic.) Billionaire real estate developer and TV celebrity Donald Trump could easily win elective office—although it would probably decrease his political power to do so because he would not be able to easily say "you're fired" to anyone with whom he disagreed.

Corporations and special interest groups spend millions, sometimes billions, of dollars on lobbying and political action committees (PACs), often leaving the average citizen's concerns far behind. As a result, the average citizen often feels that neither party is doing what is needed, that no one is listening to "people like me." Minorities feel particularly slighted by their parties and by the party system (Kittilson and Tate, 2004).

The representation of minorities in elected offices is tiny. There has never been a U.S. president who was female, an ethnic or racial minority, or openly gay. Of 535 seats in Congress, 15 percent are occupied by women, 8 percent by African Americans, 5 percent by Hispanics, and less than 1 percent each by Asians and gay people. Most minorities occupy seats in the lower House of Representatives, not the Senate; in fact, African American men are overrepresented in the House (Kittilson and Tate, 2004). On the state and local level, the situation is similarly unequal. For instance, men outnumber women in local legislatures by a margin of about 4.8 to 1 (Rule and Hill, 1996).

Similar processes occur in democracies around the world. Although the representation of women in national legislatures has been increasing steadily during the past 50 years, it approaches equality in only a few wealthy European countries (43 percent in Sweden, 37 percent in Finland, 31 percent in Germany). The world average is 14 percent. Several nations (Britain, India, Israel, Pakistan) have had female presidents or prime ministers—twice in India. Non-Whites (Black, Indian, Pakistani, and others) comprise 8 percent of the population of Britain but only 2 percent of the members of Parliament and only about 1 percent of MPs are gay or lesbian (Kittilson and Tate, 2004).

The commonsense explanation for the underrepresentation of minorities in high government positions is simple: discrimination. Either minorities lack the financial resources to successfully run for office or else voter prejudice keeps them from being elected. Prejudices about the "qualifications" of various minorities to adequately represent the majority often induce people to vote for "majority" candidates.

This, though, begs another question: If the minorities cannot adequately represent the majority, how can the majority claim to adequately represent the minorities? If democracy is defined as the rule of the majority, what happens to those who are not in the majority? Will there be, as some sociologists predicted, a "tyranny of the majority," in which power becomes a zero-sum game and the winners get it and the losers don't, or will there be protections of the minorities to ensure they are not trampled politically? (Of course, middle-aged wealthy White men, who dominate all elective office, are the statistical *minority* of all voters. By a landslide.)

Perhaps the most eloquent document in world history to address this problem is the Bill of Rights—the first set of amendments to the U.S. Constitution. The founders worried about the tyranny of the majority and, through our Constitution, put into place a wide variety of protections for individual rights. Thus, even if you disagree with the majority, you have certain basic rights (free speech, ability to practice your religion, to dissent, and the like) that no majority can take away.

Discrimination does not, however, explain what happens in countries with multiple electoral systems, combining "winner take all" (the U.S. practice) with proportional representation (or PR). In a **proportional representation** system each party would receive a proportion of the legislative seats and thus would be more likely to govern "from the center" and build coalitions. This would tend to increase minority representation because coalitions of minority groups can form a majority. Countries that use proportional representation elect many times more women to their legislatures than winner-take-all systems (Rule and Hill, 1996). Proportional representation also drives the need for a coalition government. To muster the required votes, the party with the most seats must align itself with one or more of the smaller parties. There are always efforts to make democracies more democratic. They are always being reformed and always in need of reform.

Citizenship

One question that characterizes all systems is: Who gets to participate? Who decides? To participate in the political process, you must be a citizen. Throughout most of human history, people were born into a tribe or cultural group, and they belonged to it forever, no matter where they happened to live. In ancient Rome, only people of Roman ancestry could become citizens. It didn't matter that your ancestors had lived in Rome for five generations, or that your first language was Latin; citizenship, and with it the opportunity for political participation, was forever beyond your grasp. Well into the twentieth century, Jews were excluded from citizenship in most European countries, even if their ancestors had lived there for 500 years.

The idea of universal citizenship didn't take hold until the nineteenth century (Holston, 1999; Jacobsohn, 1996; Steenbergen, 1994). When the United States was founded, a Black person counted as three-fifths of a White person for statistical purposes, but Black men were denied **suffrage** (the right to voting and representation) until 1865. Women (Black and White) didn't acquire suffrage until 1920 (Figure 14.1).

By the twentieth century, most nations recognized two rights to citizenship: the right of blood, whereby you become a citizen automatically if your father or mother is a citizen, regardless of where they happen to be living; and the right of territory, whereby you become a citizen automatically if you are born in a country, regardless of where your parents live. For instance, if you are born in Helsinki to American parents, you could embrace either Finnish or American citizenship, or both, becoming a dual citizen. Most countries allow foreigners with no right of blood or right of the territory to become naturalized citizens, but there are restrictions: Usually you must speak the language and have a job or vital skills that will make you attractive to employers. Sometimes you must meet nationality and racial quotas (the United

Citizenship is the foundation of political participation. In the United States, the number of naturalized citizens has been steadily climbing, to 702,589 in 2006. A naturalization ceremony in Miami, 2007. ▼

FIGURE 14.1 The Year in Which Women Achieved the Right to Vote on an Equal Basis with Men

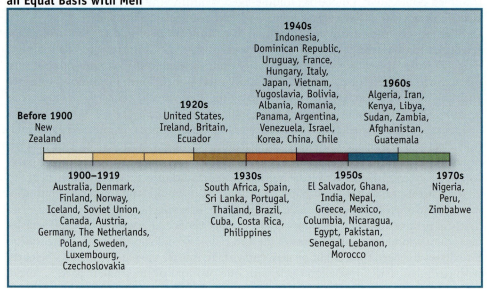

1940s
Indonesia, Dominican Republic, Uruguay, France, Hungary, Italy, Japan, Vietnam, Yugoslavia, Bolivia, Albania, Romania, Panama, Argentina, Venezuela, Israel, Korea, China, Chile

1960s
Algeria, Iran, Kenya, Libya, Sudan, Zambia, Afghanistan, Guatemala

Before 1900
New Zealand

1920s
United States, Ireland, Britain, Ecuador

1900–1919
Australia, Denmark, Finland, Norway, Iceland, Soviet Union, Canada, Austria, Germany, The Netherlands, Poland, Sweden, Luxembourg, Czechoslovakia

1930s
South Africa, Spain, Sri Lanka, Portugal, Thailand, Brazil, Cuba, Costa Rica, Philippines

1950s
El Salvador, Ghana, India, Nepal, Greece, Mexico, Columbia, Nicaragua, Egypt, Pakistan, Senegal, Lebanon, Morocco

1970s
Nigeria, Peru, Zimbabwe

Source: Adapted from Lisa Tuttle, *Encyclopedia of Feminism,* 1986.

States barred non-Whites from becoming citizens well into the 1930s), educational restrictions (a high school diploma or the equivalent), and age limits (no one over 40) (Aileinikoff and Klusmeyer, 2001; Castles and Davidson, 2000). A number of countries do not permit naturalization (though you can become a permanent resident), and a few "holdout" countries like Japan do not even recognize the right of citizenship by virtue of being born there. Citizens must be of Japanese ancestry (Tarumoto, 2003).

The Political System of the United States

In the American political system, citizens are protected as individuals from the exercise of arbitrary control by the government, but individual citizens have little impact on changing the system. Individuals must band together at every level—local, state, and national—to hope to sway policies. And even then, it is only through one's elected representatives that change can be accomplished. The system is so large and complex that organized bureaucratic political parties dominate the political landscape.

Political parties are groups that band together to petition for political changes and to support candidates to elected office. Most of the world's democracies have many parties: Germany has 6, Japan 7, France 19, Italy 30, and Argentina 49. Usually, however, only two or at most three dominate in parliament or congress. British elected officials traditionally belong to either the Labour Party or the Conservative Party; there are many other parties, but the most successful, the Liberal Democrats, occupy only 9.6 percent of the seats in Parliament.

American Political Parties

The United States was founded on a **two-party system:** The Federalists, led by Alexander Hamilton, distrusted the newly enfranchised populace and argued for a strong, centralized government; the Republicans, led by Thomas Jefferson and James Madison, held a more agrarian small-town ideal and argued for a decentralized government with limited power. These morphed in the first decades of the nineteenth century based on their positions on central government, immigration, and slavery. In the years after the Civil War, the modern two-party system of Democrat and Republican was consolidated. By the 1880s, Republicans and Democrats received 100 percent of electoral votes and very nearly 100 percent of popular votes.

With only two major political parties, the United States is something of an anomaly among democratic nations. Sociologists generally attribute the fact that most other countries have many more political parties to America's winner-take-all electoral system. With legislative representation based on proportional voting, as in Europe, for example, smaller parties can gain seats, have influence, and even be included in coalition governments. In the United States, it doesn't make sense to spend money and launch major campaigns if you are a third (or fourth, and so on) party because if you don't win, you get nothing, no matter how many votes you received. However, that fact hasn't stopped some Americans from starting smaller political parties.

Republicans and Democrats tend to have different platforms (opinions about social and economic concerns) and different ideas about the role of government in the first place. According to conventional thinking, the Republicans run "against" government, claiming that government's job should be to get out of the way of individuals and off the back of the average taxpayer. Democrats, by contrast, believe that only with active government intervention can social problems like poverty or discrimination be solved. It is the proper role of government to provide roads, bridges, and other infrastructure, as well as services such as welfare, health insurance, and minimum wages to those who cannot fend for themselves.

Both sides point to the other side's failures as evidence that their strategy is better. Republicans argue that overspending on welfare has made poor people lazy and dependent, unable and unwilling to help themselves, victims, as President Bush said, of the "tyranny of low expectations." Democrats point to the devastating human toll of Hurricane Katrina, for example, which was made infinitely worse because of Republican policies of cutting funding to reinforce the levees surrounding New Orleans, while they offered massive tax cuts to the wealthy.

To a sociologist, however, this question—whether the government should intervene in personal life or not—is a good example of how framing the issue as "either/or" misses the most important issues. It's always both—and both parties believe that the government should both intervene in private life and stay out of it. It is rather *where* they want to stay out of your life and *where* they want to intervene that is the question.

The Republicans want to stay out of your personal life when you are at work. They want to lower taxes, enable you to keep more of what you earn. When you come home, though, they very much want to intervene: They want to tell you what gender you may love and marry and what gender is off limits; they want to control your decisions about pregnancy and birth control; and they want to control what you can even *know* about sex. They're likely to favor of censorship and strict controls on the Internet.

The Democrats see it exactly the other way around. They want to leave you alone when you are in the privacy of your own home, believing that you should be able to make decisions about when, how, and with whom you make love. They trust that you can make good decisions about what books you read, but that you must pay for these freedoms and your privacy by ensuring that others have access to the same freedoms that you have. The Republicans want to stay out of your wallet, but get into your bed; the Democrats are picking your pocket, but leave you alone at night.

Sociology and our World

Third Parties

Since the 1920s, third parties in the United States have sometimes run successful campaigns on the local level, but American politics on the national level have been dominated by the Democrats and the Republicans.

Although no third party candidate has won a presidential election since 1860, some have received a surprising amount of popular support: Progressive Robert M. LaFollette won 17 percent of the popular votes in 1924, American Independent George Wallace 13 percent—and 46 electoral votes—in 1968, and Independent (with no party affiliation) Ross Perot 19 percent in 1992. In 1948, the first election after World War II and the death of Franklin Roosevelt, two candidates ran on smaller party slates: South Carolina senator and ardent segregationist Strom Thurmond ran as a "Dixiecrat" for the State's Rights Party and Henry Wallace ran on the Progressive Party ticket. Thurmond received 2.41 percent of the vote and Wallace 2.37 percent—not much of a difference. But Thurmond actually carried four states (Louisiana, Alabama, Mississippi, and South Carolina) and received 39 electoral votes.

Many voters are hesitant about voting for a third party candidate, believing that not only are they "throwing their votes away," but they are also "election spoilers," compromising the chances of an otherwise worthy candidate. In 2000, for instance, liberal Republican candidate George W. Bush won the critical state of Florida by less than 600 votes, and Democrats blamed Green Party candidate Ralph Nader for taking away liberals who would otherwise have voted for Al Gore (Sifry, 2003).

During the 2004 presidential elections, three other parties received ballot access; that is, they met the regulations for putting their candidates on the ballot in enough states to have a chance at winning. The Constitution Party's Michael Peroutka won 144,000 popular votes; the Green Party's David Cobb 120,000; and the Libertarians' Michael Badnarik 397,000. But the most votes a third party candidate has received in recent presidential elections is 2.8 million, going to Green candidate Ralph Nader in 2000.

Party Affiliation: The Politics of Race, Class, and Gender

What makes people affiliate with—that is, join, support, or vote for—Republicans, Democrats, or a third party? Surprisingly, it's not often the issues, and rarely the "great divide" of government intervention versus hands off. The answer is that people are socialized into party affiliation. They vote to express their group identity. If you were to tell me your educational background, class, race, and gender, I would probably be able to predict who you are going to vote for with an amazing amount of accuracy (Burdick and Broadbeck, 1977; Popkin, 1994). Party affiliation tends to follow from:

1. *Class.* Poor, working-class, lower-middle-class, and blue-collar trade unionists tend to be Democrats, while wealthy, upper-middle-class, white-collar individuals tend to be Republicans. In 2004, the Republican Bush beat the Democrat Kerry among households earning over $50,000 per year, but Kerry beat Bush among low-income and blue-collar households. (See Figure 14.2 for all data cited here.)

2. *Education.* Generally, the higher educational levels go Democratic, and the lower Republican. However, in 2004, Kerry beat Bush among *both* the least-educated and the most-educated voters.

3. *Race.* Since the 1930s, most racial and ethnic minorities have been Democratic. However, the percentages are declining as more minorities become wealthy, upper middle class, and white collar. In 2000, 90 percent of Blacks and 67 percent of Latinos voted Democratic. In 2004, it was 88 percent of Blacks and 67 percent of Latinos.

4. *Gender.* Women are more likely than men to vote Democratic, but again the percentages are declining (54 percent in 2000, 51 percent in 2004). The decrease

occurs primarily among White women: 44 percent voted for Kerry in 2004 as compared to 75 percent of women of color.

Early sociologists predicted that a two-party system would lead to a concentration on the middle ground, where most voters are found, excluding more radical views. And because everyone is in the middle, there's no need to participate, leading to voter apathy. The opposite has happened. We are more polarized than ever before. At election time, the other party's candidates are characterized not merely as less competent but also as villains intent on destroying America.

Voters are increasingly dissatisfied with both parties. Many voters, especially younger ones, identify as independents. Twenty-six percent of American voters, including nearly 47 percent of voters under 30 years old, identify as independents (Greenberg, 2003). They tend to vote about the same as the rest of the population (in 2004, 48 percent voted for Bush, 49 percent for Kerry), but third-party voting is increasing. In 1998, Jesse Ventura (an independent running for governor of Minnesota), got 46 percent of the under-30 and only 29 percent of the over-30 voters.

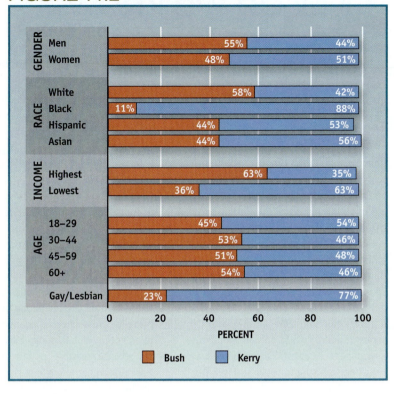

FIGURE 14.2 Who Voted How in 2004?

However, there is also evidence for increasing voter apathy. Only about 34 percent of eligible Americans are registered to vote (U.S. Census Bureau, 2006). Registration rates of voting-age citizens dropped significantly between 1996 and 2000 in almost every group. Of registered voters, only 58.3 percent voted in the 2000 presidential election, one of the most controversial and hotly contested in history. And this turnout was the highest since 1990. The United States has one of the lowest percentages of voter turnout of all democracies. In many of the others, average turnout is 80 to 90 percent of eligible voters. For example, in Iceland 87 percent of eligible voters actually vote; in Israel it's 84 percent, and in Russia its 69 percent.

Several theories have been proposed about the low voter turnout. Conservatives argue that people are satisfied with the status quo and see no need for change. Liberals counter that people feel alienated from politics due to influence peddling by special interest groups and large corporations. The answer is that both are true. Some people refrain from voting because they are pretty happy; others don't vote because they are so disaffected they don't see how it would change anything. But both agree that people who feel they have less at stake in the election—that is, less to lose or less to gain—are less likely to vote, and thus the higher your socioeconomic status, the more likely you are to go to the polls.

Interest Groups

Parties are not the only organized groups that influence political decisions. Individuals, organizations, and industries often form **interest groups** (also known as *special interest groups, pressure groups,* and *lobbies*) to promote

Did *you* know ?

Twenty-seven of the world's democracies make voting compulsory. Usually nonvoters face no penalty, or they can get off with just an explanation and a fine (the equivalent of $2.50 in Switzerland, $25 to $250 in Austria, $400 in Cyprus). In some countries, they face a fine plus "disenfranchisement": loss of voting privileges in Belgium and Singapore, loss of some government services in Peru. In Chile, Egypt, and Fiji, they can go to prison (International Institute for Democracy and Electoral Assistance).

How do we know what we know?

The Case of Polling

"Dewey Defeats Truman" was the headline of the *Chicago Daily Tribune* on the day after the 1948 presidential election. Preelection polls had predicted that Dewey would win by a 5 to 15 percent margin. In fact, Truman defeated Dewey by 4.4 percent of the vote. In the 2000 election, preelection polls showed Al Gore beating George W. Bush in Florida. Exit polls in 2004 found John Kerry beating Bush in Ohio. How did the media get it so wrong?

Every election is preceded by a series of polls. Private polling agencies, newspapers, TV networks, and individual candidates all sponsor polls to track the way that the election is shaping up.

Polling is nearly as old as the United States. In the 1820s, newspapers began to do straw polls to test the mood of the electorate. (The term comes from an old trick used by farmers, who would throw a few sticks of straw into the air to see which way the wind was blowing. The "straw poll" was designed to tell which way the political wind was blowing.)

Polls are surveys of likely voters, culled from county or state lists of registered voters. Pollsters like Gallup, Harris, Roper, and Zogby rely on preelection polls to discern the general sentiments of the electorate, and predict its outcome. These are watched daily, even hourly, to show trends among likely voters. They also use exit polls in which voters are asked for whom they voted as they leave the polling place. Again, exit polls are carefully stratified to ensure that age, race, class, gender, and other factors are accurately represented. And, of course, the elections themselves are polls in which people indicate a preference for a candidate. But this time, the answers actually count! Why are polls sometimes wrong?

Typically polls are conducted by sampling from the telephone book, and these are cross-checked against registered voters. But this may bias the sample because wealthier people often have several telephone numbers (increasing the likelihood they will be called) but the extremely wealthy have unlisted phone numbers (so they will never be called). This is called sampling error, in which a random sample is actually not random.

In election polls, pollsters use stratified sampling to construct a sample of likely eligible voters who well represent the different factions and groups that make up the electorate. A stratified sample divides the electorate up into discrete groups by age, gender, race, class, education, and a host of other factors.

But young people are more likely to have only cell phones, which are often not listed in the phone book. And some people have answering machines while others don't. This may result in a response rate error.

Finally, most polls have a margin of error of about 3 to 4 percent—which, in the case of tight elections, is enough to be terribly misleading.

In the case of the 1948 presidential election, several things may have caused the polls' error. The preelection polls were so overwhelming predicting that Dewey would win that one pollster, Elmo Roper, announced he wouldn't even do any more polls. This may have left Republicans feeling overly confident, so they were less aggressive in the final weeks, while Truman's supporters marshaled every possible vote they could. In the six weeks before the election, Truman traveled 32,000 miles and gave 355 speeches. Experts still weren't convinced. In October, 1948, *Newsweek* asked 50 key political journalists who they believed would win. All 50 predicted Dewey would win.

Political skill, Winston Churchill once said, "is the ability to foretell what is going to happen tomorrow, and to have the ability afterwards to explain why it didn't happen."

Key polling organizations include:

Pew Research Center for the People and the Press (http://people-press.org)

The Gallup Organization (http://www.gallup.com)

---

their interests among state and national legislators and often to influence public opinion. *Protective groups* represent only one trade, industry, minority, or subculture: Labor unions are represented by the AFL-CIO, African Americans by the NAACP, women by NOW, and conservative Christians by Focus on the Family. *Promotional groups*, however, claim to represent the interests of the entire society: Greenpeace tries to preserve the planet's ecology, and Common Cause promotes accountability in elected officials (Grossman and Helpman, 2001; Miller, 1983).

Increasingly, interest groups do not try to represent an entire political agenda. Instead, they fight for or against a single issue, like gun control. As the number of "hot-button" issues has become more visible in the media, the number of interest groups has increased, especially now that the Internet provides an easy, risk-free place for mobilization: Potential members need only push a button indicating that they support the cause and key in their credit card number to make a donation.

Interest groups are very visible in Washington. They often have a staff of full-time professional lobbyists who influence politicians for a living. In fact, many people believe that interest groups have too much power and can buy votes in any election by pumping money into their campaign—or the campaigns of their opponents. For example, the medical risks of smoking were known to physicians for more than 20 years before Congress mandated that warning labels should appear on cigarette boxes. Why? It's likely that it was because lobbyists for the tobacco industry were effective in preventing it, by promising big campaign contributions to those legislators who went along with them. As a result of widespread public suspicion, interest groups are also subject to severe restriction. They must be registered, and they must submit detailed reports of their activities.

But how much power do interest groups really have? University of Washington sociologist Jon Agnone (2007) studied the number of proenvironmental bills passed by Congress each year between 1960 and 1994 and found no correlation with the intensity of proenvironmental lobbying. Talking to politicians made no difference in the way they voted. However, each major environmental protest increased proenvironmental legislation by 2.2 percent. Evidently big, showy gestures get more results than conversations.

One of the more controversial contemporary versions of an interest group is the **political action committee** (PAC). These are lobbying groups that work to elect or defeat candidates based on their stance on specific issues. Most PACs represent interests of large corporations—business and industry; there are no poor people's PACs. However, you can find many smaller special-interest PACs on the Internet.

PACs work by soliciting contributions, which they then contribute to the campaigns of their chosen candidates. Prior to the 2004 presidential election, for instance, PACs raised $376 million (an increase of 19 percent over 2001) and contributed $106 million of it to federal candidates. Because the total campaign contributions received by George Bush and John Kerry combined amounted to $665 million, this was a sizeable sum. And it was all "soft money," outside the limits imposed by federal election law (Federal Election Commission, 2006). By June 2006, disbursements to federal candidates had increased by 27 percent over 2004 (Federal Election Commission, 2006). Even in nonelection years, PAC contributions to candidates has been growing steadily, with sharper increases over the past decade (Federal Election Commission, 2006; Figure 14.3). In 2006, the top three PACs—the National Association of Realtors, National Beer Wholesalers Association,

▲ Interest groups organize to lobby around specific issues. These Greenpeace polar bears are protesting against global warming.

FIGURE 14.3 PAC Contributions to Candidates in Nonelection Years

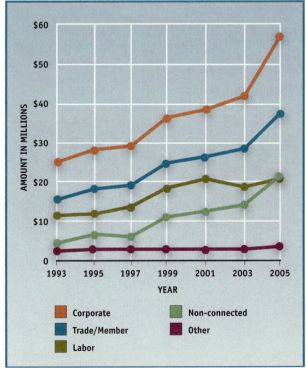

Source: Federal Election Commission.

and Trial Lawyers of America—each contributed more than $2 million to selected candidates and committees (Federal Election Commission, 2006).

Political Change

Political life is not merely a matter of orthodox social institutions: political parties, voting, and elections. History shows us that some groups find their objectives or ideals cannot be achieved with this framework—or are actively blocked by it. They need to develop "unorthodox" political action. Some types of efforts for political change, social movements and revolutions, are internal; others, like war and terrorism, are attempted from outside the society.

Social Movements

When people seek to effect change, they may engage in political revolutions, but more commonly they start **social movements**—collective attempts to further a common interest or secure a common goal through action outside the sphere of established institutions. They may try to influence public opinion with advertising campaigns or by convincing a celebrity to act as their spokesperson. They may try to get legislators' attention through marches, sit-ins, media "zaps" (invasions of televised media events), Internet protests, boycotts, or work stoppages. Or they may try more colorful (and illegal) methods of getting their points across, like animal-rights activists who splash blood on actors wearing fur coats (McAdam, 1996; Meyer, Whittier, and Robnett, 2002; Morris and Mueller, 1992; Tarrow, 1998).

Like representative democracy, social movements require an educated populace and adequate communication and transportation technology to get the word out, so they did not appear in any great numbers until the nineteenth century. But today there are thousands of social movements, dedicated to supporting every imaginable political agenda. Many social movements are international and rely heavily on use of information technology to link local campaigners to global issues. They are as evident a feature of the contemporary world as the formal, bureaucratic political system they often oppose.

Social movements often innovate new tactics to get attention for their positions. Members of People for the Ethical Treatment of Animals protest against killing animals to make fur coats. ▼

Social movements vary by the types of issues around which they mobilize, their level of organization, and their persistence over time. They can be arrayed on a variety of continua: For example, they range from the most militant and doctrinaire, which demand strict adherence to a fully developed party line, to those that are more expansive and inclusive, absorbing people from a wide variety of backgrounds and with different political positions. Or movements may range from broadly messianic movements involving total social transformation to locally based and extremely locally focused movements.

Some social movements change over the course of their lives. Some become more limited in focus, others more expansive. Some morph into political parties to sustain themselves over time. Movements such as the labor movement or the Civil Rights movement began as more limited in focus, trying to better working conditions, raise the minimum wage, or ensure the right to vote, but both became broad-based movements that have been sustained over time by large organizations and a wide variety

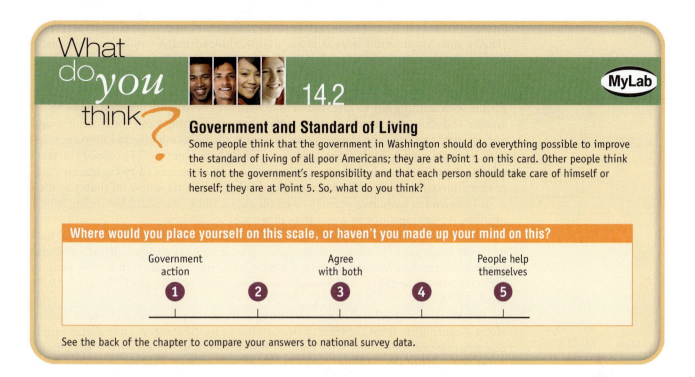

What do you think? 14.2

Government and Standard of Living

Some people think that the government in Washington should do everything possible to improve the standard of living of all poor Americans; they are at Point 1 on this card. Other people think it is not the government's responsibility and that each person should take care of himself or herself; they are at Point 5. So, what do you think?

Where would you place yourself on this scale, or haven't you made up your mind on this?

Government action		Agree with both		People help themselves
1	**2**	**3**	**4**	**5**

See the back of the chapter to compare your answers to national survey data.

of issues. As they were successful, they expanded their scope and their horizons and began to press for more sweeping changes.

Today, some organized social movements like the labor movement are in decline. Others, though, like the Civil Rights, women's, and environmental movements have continued to press for reforms in a wide variety of arenas.

Revolutions

Revolution, the attempt to overthrow the existing political order and replace it with a completely new one, is the most dramatic and unorthodox form of political change. Many social movements have a revolutionary agenda, hoping or planning for the end of the current political regime. Some condone violence as a revolutionary tactic; many terrorists are hoping to start a revolution. Successful revolutions lead to the creation of new political systems (in France, Russia, Cuba, and China), or brand new countries (Haiti, Mexico, and the United States). Unsuccessful revolutions often go down in the history books as terrorist attacks (Defronzo, 1996; Foran, 1997).

Earlier sociologists believed that revolutions had either economic or psychological causes. Marx believed that revolutions were the inevitable outcome of the clash between two social classes. As capitalism proceeded, the rich would get richer and the poor would get poorer, and eventually the poor would become so poor that they had nothing else to lose, and they would revolt. This is called the **immiseration thesis**— you get more and more miserable until you lash out.

Talcott Parsons (1956) and other functionalists maintained that revolutions were not political at all and had little to do with economic deprivation. They were irrational responses by large numbers of people who were not sufficiently connected to social life to see the benefits of existing conditions and thus could be worked into a frenzy by outside agitators.

This theory is clearly wrong. Revolutions are almost never caused by mass delirium but by people who want a change in leadership. A number of sociologists after

Parsons, especially Charles Tilly (1978, 2006), William Gamson (1975), Jeffrey Paige (1975), and Mayer Zald (David et al., 2005), showed that revolutions were just a type of social movement, rationally planned, with mobilization strategies, grievances, and specific goals in mind.

But Marx was also wrong—especially about which groups will revolt. It is not people with nothing left to lose, but people who are thoroughly invested in the social system and have something at stake. Don't expect a revolt from the homeless and unemployed but from the lower middle classes in the cities and the middle-rung peasants in the countryside. Political scientist Ted Robert Gurr (1971) coined the term **relative deprivation** to describe how misery is socially experienced by constantly comparing yourself to others. You are not down and out: You are worse off than you used to be (downward mobility), or not as well off as you think you should be (rising expectations), or, perhaps, not as well off as those you see around you.

Revolutions do not take place in advanced societies where capitalism has had time to create huge gaps between rich and poor. The major revolutions of the twentieth century occurred in Mexico, Russia, China, Cuba, and Vietnam—that is, in peasant societies where capitalism was vestigial or nonexistent (Paige, 1981; Skocpol, 1979; Wolf, 1979).

Sociologists typically distinguish among different types of revolutionary events, along a continuum from the least dramatic change to the most. A **coup d'état** simply replaces one political leader with another but often doesn't bring with it any change in the daily life of the citizens. (Some coups do bring about change, especially when the new leader is especially charismatic, as in Argentina under Perón.)

A **political revolution** changes the political groups that run the society, but they still draw their strength from the same social groups that supported the old regime. For example, the English Revolution between 1640 and 1688 reversed the relationship between the king and aristocracy on the one hand, and the elected Parliament on the other, but it didn't change the fact that only property owners were allowed to vote.

Finally, a **social revolution** changes, as Barrington Moore (1966) put it, the "social basis of political power"—that is, it changes the social groups or classes that political power rests on. Thus, for example, the French Revolution of 1789 and the Chinese Revolution of 1949 swept away the entire social foundations of the old regime—hereditary nobility, kings and emperors, and a clergy that supported them—and replaced them with a completely new group, the middle and working classes in the French case, and the peasantry in the Chinese case.

War and the Military

In Hebrew and Arabic, the standard word for *hello* and *goodbye* is *shalom* or *salaam*, meaning "peace." War was so common in the ancient world that the wish for peace became a clichéd phrase, like the English *goodbye* (an abbreviated version of the more formal "God be with you"). By some estimates, there were nearly 200 wars in the twentieth century, but they are increasingly hard to pin down. The old image of war, in which two relatively evenly matched groups of soldiers from opposing states try to capture each other's territory, has become increasingly meaningless in the days of long-range missiles, smart bombs, and ecoterrorism. However, war still occurs as a standard, perhaps inevitable characteristic of political life: In his classic *On War* (1832), Carl von Clausewitz wrote, "War is not an independent phenomenon, but the continuation of politics by different means."

Worldwide, there are 19,670,000 soldiers. Every country has an army, navy, or air force, with the exception of some small islands, Panama, and Costa Rica. The percentage of military personnel is often very high, often as much as 1 percent of the total population. In the United States it's 4.6 per 1,000 people, but in Russia it's 10.6, in Greece 15.0, and in Israel 27.4. Military service excludes children, most middle-aged and elderly people, and many other categories, so this is a substantial percentage of the eligible young adult population.

The United States spends more money on its military than any country in the world; in 2004, it spent $370 billion. China spent "only" $67 billion, France $45 billion, Saudi Arabia $18 billion. If we look at expenditures per capita, we find that Israel leads with $1,451 per person, but the United States is number two at $1,253.

The frequency of war suggests that it is an inevitable problem of human societies, but extensive research has found no natural cause and no circumstances under which human beings will inevitably wage war. In fact, governments worldwide expend considerable time and energy to mobilize their people for warfare (Brown, 1998; Stoessinger, 2004). They offer special privileges to those who enlist in military service, glorify warfare as "freedom fighting," schedule parades and exhibitions of military power, and portray enemies or potential enemies as monsters out to destroy us.

Sociologist Quincy Wright (1967) identified five factors that serve as root causes of most wars:

1. *Perceived threats*. Societies mobilize in response to threats to their people, territory, or culture. If the threats are not real, they can always be manufactured. The possibility that Saddam Hussein possessed weapons of mass destruction, aimed at the United States, was the justification for the U.S. invasion of Iraq in 2002.

2. *Political objectives*. War is often a political strategy. Societies go to war to end foreign domination, enhance their political stature in the global arena, and increase their wealth and power. For example, the United States entered the Spanish American War in 1898 to ensure American influence and dominance in Latin America.

3. *"Wag the dog" rationale*. When internal problems create widespread unrest at home, a government may wage war to divert public attention and unify the country behind a common, external enemy. During World War I, many countries entered because they were on the brink of collapse and revolution.

4. *Moral objectives*. Leaders often infuse military campaigns with moral urgency, rallying people around visions of, say, "freedom" rather than admitting they fight to increase their wealth or power. They claim that wars are not acts of invasion but heroic efforts to "protect our way of life." The enemy—whether Germany in World War I (the "Hun") or Iraq in the early twenty-first century—is declared "immoral," and morality and religion are mobilized for the cause.

5. *Absence of alternatives*. Sometimes, indeed, there is no choice. When your country is invaded by another, it is hard to see how to avoid war. The United States adopted a strictly isolationist policy during World War II, until Pearl Harbor.

Terrorism

Terrorism means using acts of violence and destruction against military or civilian targets (or threatening to use them) as a political strategy. For instance, an individual or group interested in acquiring independence

A perceived threat is often a justification for war—whether it turns out to be true or not. In February 2003, at the United Nations, the U.S. government presented its case for the invasion of Iraq by showing maps of chemical and biological weapons storehouses. After the invasion, no such weapons were ever found. ▼

for the Basque people of northern Spain might engage in terrorism in the hope that the Spanish government will acquiesce to their demands for autonomy. Frequently, however, terrorism has no specific political goal. Instead, it is used to publicize the terrorist's political agenda or simply to cause as much damage to the enemy as possible. Interviews with terrorists who bomb abortion clinics reveal that they do not believe that their actions will cause the Supreme Court to reverse the *Roe v. Wade* decision; they simply want to kill abortion doctors. Similarly, when al-Qaeda orchestrated the 9/11 attacks, they did not expect Americans to embrace their extremist form of Islam en masse; they simply wanted to hurt Americans (Hoffman, 1998; Juergensmeyer, 2003).

Terrorism can be used *by* the regime in power to ensure continued obedience and to blot out all dissent. For example, Stalin in the Soviet Union, Pol Pot in Cambodia, Saddam Hussein in Iraq, and the apartheid regimes in South Africa all used terrorist violence to maintain control. Because totalitarian states can only survive through fear and intimidation, many make terrorism lawful, a legitimate tool of government.

But usually we think of terrorism as the actions *against* the existing regime. Usually terrorists have little or no political authority, so they use terror to promote or publicize their viewpoints, just as nonviolent groups might use marches and protests. Terrorists often believe that their cause is just, but they lack the legitimate means (movements, parties) to effect the sorts of changes they want. Most terrorists are recruited and mobilized in the same way as members of social movements. They simply see violence as a legitimate political tactic.

While terrorism is not new, recent technological advances have made weapons easier to acquire or produce and communication among terrorist groups easier, so that terrorism is increasingly common. According to the U.S. National Counterterrorism Center, in 2006 there were 14,000 terrorist attacks worldwide, resulting in 20,000 deaths (Figure 14.4). Those figures represent a 25 percent increase in attacks and a 40 percent increase in deaths over 2005. Of the 14,000 global total, 45 percent—6,600 attacks, with 20,000 deaths—occurred in Iraq. Afghanistan saw a 50 percent increase in terrorist attacks from 2005. But 2006 saw more than 700 killed by terrorists in Sudan, 520 in Thailand, 115 in Russia, and 97 in Nigeria (National Counterterrorism Center, 2007).

FIGURE 14.4 Terrorist Attacks and Deaths by Region

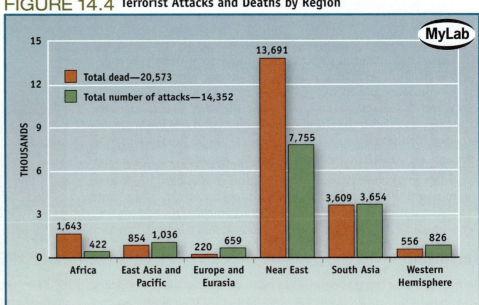

Source: National Counterterrorism Center: Report of Terrorists Incidents, April 30, 2007.

Sociology and our World

A Tale of Two Terrorists

In 1992, an American GI returning from the Gulf War wrote a letter to the editor of a small, upstate New York newspaper complaining that the legacy of the American middle class had been stolen by an indifferent government. Instead of the American dream, he wrote, most people are struggling just to buy next week's groceries. That letter writer was Timothy McVeigh from Lockport, New York. Three years later, he blew up the Murrah Federal Building in Oklahoma City in what is now the second-worst act of terrorism ever committed on American soil.

McVeigh's background and list of complaints were echoed, ironically, by Mohammed Atta, the mastermind of the September 11 attack and the pilot of the first plane to hit the World Trade Center. Looking at these two men through a sociological lens sheds light on both the method and the madness of the tragedies they wrought.

McVeigh emerged from a small legion of White supremacists, mostly younger, lower-middle-class men, educated through high school. They are the sons of skilled industrial workers, of shopkeepers and farmers. But global economic shifts have left them little of their fathers' legacies. They face a spiral of downward mobility and economic uncertainty. They complain they are squeezed between the omnivorous jaws of global capitalism and a federal bureaucracy that is, at best, indifferent to their plight.

Most of the terrorists of September 11 came from the same class and recited the same complaints. Virtually all were under 25, educated, lower middle class, and downwardly mobile. Many were engineering students for whom job opportunities had dwindled dramatically. And central to their political ideology was the recovery of manhood from the emasculating politics of globalization.

Both Atta and McVeigh failed at their chosen professions. McVeigh, a business college dropout, found his calling in the military during the Gulf War, where his exemplary service earned him commendations; but he washed out of Green Beret training—his dream job. Atta studied engineering to please his authoritarian father, but his degree meant nothing in a country where thousands of college graduates were unemployed. After he failed to find a job in Egypt, he moved to Hamburg, Germany, where he found work as a draftsman—humiliating for someone with engineering and architectural credentials—at a German firm involved with eliminating low-income Cairo neighborhoods to provide more scenic vistas for luxury tourist hotels. Defeated, humiliated, emasculated, a disappointment to his family, Atta retreated into increasingly militant Islamic theology.

The terrors of emasculation experienced by lower-middle-class men all over the world will no doubt continue, as they struggle to make a place for themselves in shrinking economies and inevitably shifting cultures. Globalization feels to them like a game of musical chairs, in which, when the music stops, all the seats are handed to others by nursemaid governments. Someone has to take the blame, to be held responsible for their failures. As terrorists they didn't just get mad. They got even.

Democratic societies reject terrorism in principle, but they are especially vulnerable to terrorists because they afford extensive civil liberties to their people and have less extensive police networks (as compared with totalitarian regimes). This allows far more freedom of expression, freedom of movement, and freedom to purchase terrorist weaponry. The London subway attacks of July 2005 and airport attacks in Glasgow, Scotland, of 2007 were possible only because people are free to move about the city at will; in a totalitarian state they would be subject to frequent searches and identification checks, and they would not be allowed in many areas unless they could prove that they had legitimate business. And the absence of checking and monitoring duty means that democratic countries have smaller police forces to respond to emergencies.

Terrorism is always a matter of definition. It depends on who is doing the defining: One person's terrorist might be another's "freedom fighter." Had the colonies lost the Revolutionary War, the patriots would have gone down in history books as a group of terrorists. The same group can be labeled terrorist or not, depending on who their foes are: In the 1980s, when they were resisting the Soviet Union, the Taliban groups in

Did *you* know?

Two former terrorists have won the Nobel Peace Prize. In 1946, Menachim Begin participated in the bombing of the British government offices at the King David Hotel in Jerusalem. Ninety-one people were killed. Later he became prime minister of Israel, and in 1978 he won the Nobel Peace Prize for his efforts to stabilize relations with Egypt. Yasser Arafat, president of the PLO (Palestinian Liberation Organization), publicly disavowed responsibility for any of the group's attacks on Israeli civilians. In 1994, he shared the Nobel Peace Prize with Israeli Prime Minister Yitzhak Rabin and foreign minister Shimon Peres for their "efforts to create peace in the Middle East."

Afghanistan were portrayed in the media as "freedom fighters," but in 2001, when they were resisting the United States, they were portrayed as terrorists.

Everyday Politics

Most political activity does not occur in political caucuses and voting booths, through large-scale social movements, or even through the violence of war, terrorism, and revolution. Politics happens in everyday situations that have nothing to do with candidates.

Being Political: Social Change

In 1969, Carol Hanish wrote an article for the book *Feminist Revolution* (1969/1979) titled "The Personal Is Political," arguing that even the most intimate, personal actions make a political statement: "Personal problems are political problems," she concluded. Or, to put it another way, every problem is a political problem. For example, in the area of social inequality, you are making a political statement when:

- Someone makes a racist, sexist, or homophobic comment, and you agree, disagree, or stay silent.
- You make a friend who belongs to a different race, gender, or sexual orientation, or who doesn't.
- Your new doctor belongs to a different race, gender, or sexual orientation, and it bothers you, or it doesn't bother you, or you don't notice.
- You worry about whether to use the term *Black* or *African American, Hispanic* or *Latino, gay* or *homosexual,* and when you don't worry about it.
- A company exploits the workers in its foreign factories, but you buy its products anyway, or refuse to buy its products, or don't know about it.

In short, you are "being political" all the time.

Everyday politics is not a replacement for organized political groups. In fact, the two complement each other. Small, seemingly inconsequential everyday acts have a cumulative impact, creating grassroots support for the legislative changes for which political groups lobby. These acts also express political identity, enhance solidarity, and promote social change (Scott, 1987).

Frequently, groups with little formal power still attempt to resist what they perceive as illegitimate or dictatorial authority. How can they demonstrate their resistance when they have so little power and could risk so much by doing so? Everyday resistance can be found in symbolic and cultural expressions: what language you speak, what music you listen to, how you raise your children, or what holidays you celebrate. For example, when Estonia was under Soviet occupation in the 1980s, citizens would pretend they spoke only Estonian or put signs on hotels in Russian that said "No Vacancy" (Suny, 1985). In France and Spain, schools in Brittany, Catalonia, or the Basque country schools often teach subjects in the local language rather than French or Spanish, to preserve local traditions.

Civil Society: Declining, Increasing, or Dynamic?

In the best-selling book, *Bowling Alone* (2000) political scientist Robert Putnam looked at **civil society**—that is, the clubs, churches, fraternal organizations, civic organizations, and other groups that once formed a third "zone" between home and work.

In 1950, most middle-class men belonged to the Elks, Masons, Odd Fellows, Kiwanis, Toastmasters, or Chambers of Commerce, while middle-class women belonged to garden clubs, literary clubs, civic improvement societies, and the PTA. These groups provided places for friendships to be forged, opinions expressed, and political changes pursued. They were the primary schools of democracy—but no longer.

In the mid-1970s, two-thirds of the adult American population regularly attended club meetings. In the mid-1990s, it was one-third. The number who had attended a public meeting on local or school affairs fell by a third.

The raw numbers of civic groups has actually increased, from around 8,000 in 1950 to just over 20,000 in 2000. But the new groups are not grassroots "third places," but advocacy groups involving far fewer people and little real contact. Skocpol (1979) estimates that in 1955, 5 percent of the adult American population was doing work for one or more of the largest voluntary associations. Today professionals do all of the work, and the "members" mail in checks. There are no local offices. Group members rarely if ever meet each other in person. The national leaders spend all of their time lobbying and fund-raising in Washington, not in communities with like-minded people.

What are the causes of the decline in civil society?

1. *Increased mobility.* Civil society meant joining local, home-town groups with people you had known all of your life. Today fewer of us have home towns anymore. We grow up moving as our parents' jobs change, and we spend our adult years moving from town to town with our own job changes. Why bother to push for political change in this town, when we will be living somewhere else in two or three years?

2. *Mass communication.* TV and computers connect us on a national and global level but tend to eliminate the local. One newscast looks pretty much like all the others, and the 5 o'clock news is followed by prime-time programming that is identical everywhere in the United States and available around the world. Location is even less relevant to the Internet. The result is that we feel less connected to political issues; we wonder why we should bother to push for political change in one location, when our interests, concerns, and activities take place on a global stage.

3. *Commuting.* With Americans working longer and driving longer distances to and from work (with traffic jams that seem to occur at every hour of the day or night), there are fewer hours left at the end of the day to devote to club meetings.

4. *Two-income families.* In earlier generations, most middle-class women did not work outside the home, so they had enough free time to take leadership roles in community and civic volunteerism. Today most middle-class women have full-time jobs (and that extra-long commute home), so they have little time to spare for volunteering.

Despite those factors that reduce civic engagement, we still need friends, community, and a sense of the civic. Civility may change because of long commutes and two-career families, but it hasn't been eliminated. Mobility means that we are unlikely to forge significant social contacts with relatives (too far away), co-workers (they live on

In earlier generations, most middle-class women did not work outside the home, so they had enough free time to take leadership roles in community and civic volunteerism. Today many more middle-class women have full-time jobs, so they have less time to volunteer. ▼

the other side of town), or neighbors (rather, the strangers who live next door). We are likely to seek out friends in clubs and organizations, just as our parents and grandparents did 50 years ago. Only now we go about it differently (Norris, 2002).

In the twenty-first century, civic engagement by young adults (15- to 25-year-olds) increased. They are less likely to participate in traditional avenues of political engagement: 85 percent have never participated in a protest march or demonstration, 82 percent have never written a letter to a newspaper or magazine, and 81 percent have never contacted a public official. However, over half have helped raise money for a charitable cause, and 41 percent have walked or bicycled for a charitable cause. They are making their political viewpoints known through grassroots, day-to-day involvement rather than through attempting to influence political leaders. Political activism is taking on some new forms—stretching the concept of civic engagement (Rimmerman, 2001):

1. *Shift to the marketplace.* Young people use their power as consumers. Over half have refused to buy something because of "the conditions under which it was made" or made the decision to buy something because they liked the values of the company that made it (Grimm, 2003; Neuborne, 1999).

2. *Preference for hands-on activity.* Young people prefer helping to raise money for a cause—especially through mass activities like "AIDS Walk" or "Race for the Cure." These events allow them to participate in a group, and they can actually "see" themselves making a difference (Grimm, 2003; "Inside the Mind," 2001).

3. *Preference for supportive activity.* They don't protest against something; they prefer to rally for something. Instead of protesting the deficiency in funds for AIDS research, they march to raise money for AIDS research (Grimm, 2003).

If we divide young people up by generation, we see some significant patterns emerging. Generation X, the oldest of the young, is alienated, cynical, self-centered, the "slackers," and least likely to participate in civil society. Generation Y, the children of the baby boomers, is much more socially aware and committed. And a large percentage of generation Y is still under 18 and therefore excluded from most studies of political engagement. Does this mean participation will increase and expand into still new venues as gen-Y become young adults? What do you think?

Political Life in the 21st Century

The great Greek philosopher Aristotle once wrote that "man is by nature a political animal." We are also political animals "by nurture"—because social life requires it. Politics remains a contentious arena, in which people organize together, formally and informally, to fight for their positions and influence the policies that, in turn, influence their lives. It is an arena in which the divisions among people—by class, race, gender, and age—are most evident, and the arena in which the power of some groups over other groups is declared to be legitimate because "the governed" consented to it.

And politics also remains an arena in which we habitually congratulate ourselves for the development and maintenance of a democracy, in which we all feel somewhat connected to each other because we all are able to participate in the political process. It is rarely a question of whether politics unites us or divides us—indeed, politics *both* unites and divides. The questions remain, as always—united toward what goals, inspired by what vision, and divided by what factors?

1. *How do power and authority manifest in politics?* Politics is about power. Usually power is exercised through authority; authority is situation specific. Weber delineated three types of authority. Traditional authority is stable through time, and people obey because they always have. When traditional authority is challenged, charismatic authority often emerges, when people obey due to the personal characteristics of the leader. When a group begins to create rules, legal-rational authority ensues. This is kind of authority is viewed as impartial, with rationally derived rules that people obey because the authority is thought to be legitimate. Foucault argued that power is always connected to knowledge and that it is both repressive and creative at once.

2. *What are the different political systems?* Political systems are either authoritarian or democratic. In authoritarian systems, power is vested on one person or a small group of people. A dictatorship is a totalitarian political authority that extends to all of social life. In contrast, in a democracy, power is vested in the people. Democracy can be participatory (which works in smaller groups) or representative, which requires educated citizens and a free press. Seventy percent of the world governments are democracies. Some nations call themselves a democracy but are actually full of corruption or ruled by bureaucracies. Weber said bureaucracies are antagonistic to democracy and lead to leadership by an unelected elite. Additionally, inequality manifests in politics in many ways. The rich have more power than the poor, corporations have more power than individuals, and minorities are underrepresented among elected government officials.

3. *Describe the U.S. political system.* The U.S. political system is large, complex, and dominated by powerful, organized, bureaucratic political parties. The modern U.S. political system, which emerged after the Civil War, is a two-party system. Democrats and Republicans have different platforms. For example, Republicans favor small government, while Democrats favor a more active government. Americans are socialized into a particular political party affiliation, and it becomes a marker of group identity. Party affiliation is correlated strongly with class, education, and gender. Americans are polarized by party and, at the same time, exhibit extensive voter apathy. Voters are also swayed by interest groups, which have great influence on legislators and on the public and often focus on a single issue.

4. *How does political change happen?* Social movements are collective attempts to secure a common goal. They may be global and tend to rely heavily on information technology. Social movements vary by type of issue, by level of organization, and by their persistence over time. Political change also occurs through revolution, where a political system is overthrown and replaced. When successful, a revolution leads to a new political system. When they are unsuccessful, revolutionaries are called terrorists. Marx believed revolution stemmed from class conflict. The functionalists believed it was irrational. Other sociologists see it as just another type of social movement. War develops from perceived threats, political objectives, to divert attention, to achieve moral objectives, or because there is no other choice.

5. *How does politics manifest in everyday life?* Politics plays out in our everyday personal lives; we make political statements with our personal actions. Everyday politics has a cumulative impact; it is an expression of identity; it enhances solidarity and helps promote social change. Civil society is the zone between home and work. It's declining due to several factors, including increased personal mobility that leads to weaker ties, mass communication that promotes global issues but ignores or eliminates local issues, and increasingly busy personal lives. Political activism is evolving into new forms. Younger people are using the marketplace to wield their power as consumers, and civic groups tend to be more hands-on and more in support of an issue rather than against it.

Key Terms

Authoritarian political system (p. 460)	Civil society (p. 480)	Government (p. 456)
Authority (p. 457)	Coup d'état (p. 476)	Immiseration thesis (p. 475)
Bureaucracy (p. 465)	Democracy (p. 462)	Interest groups (p. 471)
Charismatic authority (p. 458)	Dictatorship (p. 461)	Illiberal democracies (p. 463)

What does America think?

14.1 International Organizations and American Governmental Power

These are actual survey data from the General Social Survey, 2004.

International organizations are taking away too much power from the American government. Only 9 percent of respondents in the 2004 General Social Survey strongly agreed with this statement. Another 26 percent agreed. Those from the lower class were most likely to agree (39.1 percent). Thirty percent of respondents disagreed, and only 3 percent strongly disagreed. Those in the upper class were most likely to disagree (53 percent).

CRITICAL THINKING | DISCUSSION QUESTIONS

1. What role, if any, do you think international organizations should play in decisions made by the U.S. government? How would you explain a social class difference in response to this question?

2. Why do you think political party affiliation often correlates with social class? What party-associated values or beliefs might contribute to one's view on the power of international organizations?

14.2 Government and Standard of Living

These are actual survey data from the General Social Survey, 2004.

Some people think that the government in Washington should do everything possible to improve the standard of living of all poor Americans; they are at Point 1 on this card. Other people think it is not the government's responsibility and that each person should take care of him- or herself; they are at Point 5. Where would you place yourself on this scale, or haven't you made up your mind on this? Only 17 percent of respondents picked the first choice, government action. There was a huge disparity between those in the lower and upper classes, though. Most respondents agreed that both the government and the individual were responsible for improving the standard of living.

CRITICAL THINKING | DISCUSSION QUESTIONS

1. The disparity between lower- and upper-class respondents with regard to opinions on this question is very large. What do you think explains this disparity?
2. Where do you place yourself on the social class ladder? How does your position inform your own opinion on improving standard of living?

▶ Go to this website to look further at the data. You can run your own statistics and crosstabs here: **http://sda.berkeley.edu/cgi-bin/hsda?harcsda+gss04**

REFERENCES: Davis, James A., Tom W. Smith, and Peter V. Marsden. General Social Surveys 1972–2004: [Cumulative file] [Computer file]. 2nd ICPSR version. Chicago, IL: National Opinion Research Center [producer], 2005; Storrs, CT: Roper Center for Public Opinion Research, University of Connecticut; Ann Arbor, MI: Inter-University Consortium for Political and Social Research; Berkeley, CA: Computer-Assisted Survey Methods Program, University of California [distributors], 2005.

chapter 15

IS THERE A GENE that makes us religious? Is a belief in God encoded in our DNA? Or is it the other way around: Does faith in science undermine our religious beliefs?

These questions are part of global debate about religion and science. Many people think of religion and science as competitors, even as enemies. After all, both seek answers to life's big questions, but they use very different methods and come up with different answers.

There weren't always two major sources of knowledge available in the world. Every society has religion, but only a few societies have science. Science is far more recent. When medieval religious authorities wrote that tree frogs would die if exposed to rain, they weren't reporting on the results of a scientific experiment. In fact, they didn't ever go out and look at any frogs in the rain. They relied on anecdotes, classical authors, or logical deduction. Frogs are associated with the earth; water is the opposite of earth; so obviously water kills frogs.

Around 1400, philosophers started to use what would be called the "scientific method," systematic,

Religion and Science

experimental studies that uncover the facts of the natural world. Unfortunately, the facts they uncovered often disagreed with religious doctrine. The sun doesn't revolve around Earth. The equatorial regions are not too hot to support life. Earth is much more than 6,000 years old. The Church conceded some points, but not others, and the competition between religion and science began.

Even though science and religion seek to do so many of the same things and often come to different conclusions, they are not necessarily rivals in society. Strong religious belief and deep scientific knowledge can coexist. In fact, the United States is simultaneously one of the most scientifically advanced and one of the most deeply religious countries in the world.

Strong religious belief and strong scientific knowledge can coexist. In fact, the United States is simultaneously one of the most scientifically advanced and one of the most deeply religious countries in the world.

The same individual is often involved in both religion and science. Most religious professionals have to keep up with advances in medicine, psychology, and sociology to minister to their congregations effectively, and many, if not most, scientists attend religious services regularly.

Comparing Religion and Science

Sociologists view science and religion as similar institutions. Both are *organized and coherent systems of thought that are organized into social institutions*. Both make claims to "truth." Both make claims to govern our conduct: Science governs our conduct toward the natural world, regulating how we are able to understand it, and religion orients people toward social interaction in this world as an expression of its beliefs in the next world. Both have professionals who devote many years to study and training to acquire the credentials necessary to speak as experts. This special access to the truth is established and reinforced by the universities and seminaries that they must attend and the separate subcultures they inhabit, churches on the one hand and labs on the other.

However, there are also many differences between the two institutions. **Religion** is a set of beliefs about the origins and meaning of life, usually based on the existence a supernatural power. It is primarily concerned with the big questions of existence, such as: What is the meaning of life? Where did I come from? Where am I going?

In a sense, the emphasis of science is more methodological. **Science** is the accumulated systematic knowledge of the physical or material world, which is obtained through experimentation and observation. Religion deals with big questions of existence; science deals with smaller questions of classification or processes. Scientific journals are full of articles about the cell walls of mollusks and the effect of a certain quantity of electricity on a strontium compound. Only a few branches of science consider ultimate questions of existence, and even then they don't focus on the individual. They ask, "Where did the universe come from?"

Religion acquires its ideas through **revelation**: God, spirits, prophets, or sacred books give us the answers to the questions of existence. On the other hand, science acquires its knowledge through **empirical verification**: Information is developed, demonstrated, and double-checked using an experimental method. Science bases its claims on what has been shown this way, rather than asking you to believe something on faith. Occasionally, religion may seek to offer proof of the truth of its claims—through miracles, for example—but even these may be a matter of faith. Scientific types believe it when they see it; religious types are more likely to see it when they believe it.

Religion distinguishes between the physical world (chaotic, uncertain, full of suffering), and a spiritual world (orderly, permanent, and full of joy). Although the two worlds are nearly opposite, few religions teach that there is no bridge between them: Gods and spirits pass between them, and often mortals visit the other world through visions, dreams, and spirit journeys. When we die, we can go there permanently, if we behave according to the rules of the religion. Meanwhile, we can experience the **sacred,** that which is holy or divine, and we can see the spiritual in the midst of our **profane,** or secular, everyday lives.

Science is interested in only the physical world. It concedes that a spiritual world may exist, but it is undetectable to scientific research. No systematic experiments have demonstrated its existence, or the existence of spiritual beings like ghosts, or spiritual powers like ESP. The parapsychologists who study such matters have had mixed, unreliable results.

Religion changes over time. There are new interpretations of the revealed message, new emphases, or even new revelations: For over 100 years, Black men were forbidden from entering the priesthood in the LDS (Church of Jesus Christ of Latter-Day Saints)—a strident restriction, because every adult male in the church is a priest—but in 1978, a divine message indicated that they could. During the Civil War, the Southern Baptists split from the American Baptists over the issue of slavery: They believed that it was God's will for Africans to be slaves. But you won't find many Southern Baptists supporting slavery today.

Science also changes over time. Scientific discoveries that are accepted as empirically demonstrated one day may be replaced by new discoveries, also empirically verified. For many years, the best scientific studies found that Mars had a relatively mild climate, water, and oxygen—everything necessary for intelligent life to evolve. Then better scientific studies revealed that Mars is much too cold and dry to support life.

However, neither religion nor science changes overnight. Neither has a smooth, uncontroversial change from one set of beliefs to another. Instead, they advance by dramatic breaks with accepted wisdom. In religion, these breaks generally come when a new prophet or **charismatic leader** draws people away from established institutions, as Martin Luther led people away from the Roman Catholic Church to become Protestants, and John Wesley from the Anglican Church to become Methodists. In science, these breaks come from scientists who challenge accepted assumptions and begin to draw followers into newer empirical areas of scientific exploration.

Classical Theories of Religion

Religion is a **cultural universal**—that is, it exists in every single culture. No human society has yet been discovered that lacks an organized, coherent system of beliefs about a spiritual world. However, religions vary tremendously. Some have no gods, some have many, and some have only one. Some believe in a heaven or a hell, some in reincarnation, some in both, and some do not believe in an afterlife at all. Sociologists are less interested in debating the truth of religious doctrine than in the function of religion. Why do all societies have one? What does it do for the society?

Durkheim and Social Cohesion

For Emile Durkheim, religion served to *integrate* society, to create a sense of unity out of the enormously diverse collection of individuals. Religion provides a sort of social glue that holds society together, binding us into a common destiny and common values.

But how? Durkheim went back to the origins of society. He surmised that primitive cultures were so overcome by the mystery and power of nature—lightning striking a tree, for instance—that they would come together as a group. These events were seen as sacred—holy moments that evoked that sense of unity. Cultures then try to recreate these moments in **rituals**—solemn reenactments of the sacred events. Rituals would remind individuals that they are part of a whole that is greater than its parts.

Durkheim's emphasis on what holds a society together is important to sociologists who study modern societies, where the greater complexity and diversity poses many challenges to social unity. Sociologist Robert Bellah (1967) suggested that modern, secular societies develop a **civil religion** in which secular rituals—such as reciting the Pledge of Allegiance, the singing of the national anthem at professional sports events, lighting fireworks on the Fourth of July—create the intense emotional bonds among people that used to be accomplished by religion.

Marx and Social Control

Whereas Durkheim saw the positive aspects of religion as social glue, other classical sociologists have explored its use as a form of control. As we've seen, religion attempts to answer basic questions of human existence, which are profound and terrifying, but also provides a way to organize one's life in preparation for the next world. Yet a successful transition to the next life requires obeying specific cultural norms: Do not eat pork (if you're Jewish or Muslim), do not drink alcohol (if you're Muslim or Pentecostal). In Mark Twain's *Adventures of Huckleberry Finn* (1885), Huck is racked with guilt over the "sin" of helping a runaway slave. Because he is from the pre–Civil War South, he has been taught that slavery is God's will, that slaves are the property of their masters, and that helping a runaway will send him to hell. Religion offers a spiritual justification for why you should obey the rules and not try to make any changes.

Karl Marx believed that religion kept social change from happening by preventing people from revolting against the miserable conditions of their lives. In feudal society, Marx argued, religion served as a sort of ideological "blinder" to the reality of exploitation. Because the lords of the manor owned everything, including the rights to the labor of the serfs, anyone could tell that there was brutal inequality. So how could the lords stay in power? How come the serfs didn't revolt?

Marx believed that religion provided a justification for inequality. For example, the belief in the "Great Chain of Being," in which all creatures, from insects to kings, were arranged on a single hierarchical arrangement ordained by God, obviously justified the dominion of those at the top over those at the bottom. Marx called religion "the opiate of the masses," a drug that made people numb to the painful reality of inequality. Religion is what keeps change from occurring.

Weber and Social Change

Max Weber, in contrast, argued that religion could be a catalyst to change. Weber's earliest work wondered why capitalism developed in Western Europe in the way that it did. After all, he noted, capitalist economic activity (profit-maximizing buying and selling) had certainly existed as the dominant economic form of life in other times and places—notably in ancient China, ancient India, and among the ancient Jews. But none of these societies sustained capitalist activity. Only Western Europe in the fifteenth and sixteenth centuries broke out of feudalism, its established social order, developing instead a type of capitalism that was self-sustaining. Why?

Weber reasoned that it might have had something to do with the impact of religious ideas on economic activity. In the other three cases, religious ideas interfered with economic life, restrained trade, and made it more difficult for capitalism to become a self-sustaining system. He noticed that Protestant countries (Britain,

Holland, Germany, the United States) had advanced earlier and further than Catholic countries such as Italy, Portugal, Spain, and France.

Perhaps the Protestant Reformation had freed individuals from constraints and enabled each individual to develop his or her relationship to God directly, without priests or churches as intermediaries. The Protestant Church was simply the gathering together of equal individuals, each man being "his own church." In its most extreme forms, such as Puritanism or Quakerism, there were no priests at all but simply the gathering of congregants.

The Protestant image of God was also more abstract and distant, less personal and intimately involved in the day-to-day life of believers. But while Catholicism offered certainty—believers were certain they were going to heaven if they fulfilled the sacraments—Protestantism offered only insecurity; one could never know God's plan. This insecurity led Protestants, especially Calvinists, to begin to work exceptionally hard in this life to reduce the insecurity about where they might be going when they die (because that could not be known). Thus, Weber argued, individuals began to work harder and longer, to approach economic life rationally, through careful calculation of costs and benefits, and to resist the temptation to enjoy the fruits of their labor—which led to rapid and dramatic accumulation of capital for investment. And this accumulation eventually enabled capitalism in the West to become self-sustaining.

Weber was pessimistic about the future of this economic activity. Without the original ethical and religious foundation, Weber predicted, we would become trapped in an "iron cage" of routine, senseless economic acquisition. The very activities that we believed would give meaning to our lives would turn out to eventually leave us empty.

All three of these classical theorists shared several sociological insights. First, although we may experience our religious beliefs as individuals, religion is a profoundly social phenomenon. And they all believed that **religiosity,** the extent of one's religious belief, typically measured by attendance at religious observances or maintaining religious practices, would decline in modern societies. None would have predicted that religion would be as important to Americans as it is today.

Religious Groups

Because religion is so profoundly social, there are many forms of religious organizations. Some are small scale, with immediate and very personal contact; others are larger institutions with administrative bureaucracies that rival those of complex countries. These differ not only in size and scale but also in their relationship to other social institutions, the level of training for specific roles within the religion, and the levels of administration (Table 15.1).

Cults

The simplest form of religious organization, a **cult,** forms around a specific person or idea drawn from an established religion. It is often formed by splitting off from the main branch of the religion. Cults are distinguished by the measure of loyalty they extract from members. Typically small, they are also composed of deeply fervent believers. Some cults prophesize the end of the world and are called "doomsday cults."

Did *you* know?

Most religions are pretty serious business. When you're discussing the big questions, there's not much room for jokes. But one religion, the Church of the Reformed Druid, got its start as a joke. Back in 1963, at Carleton College in Northfield, Minnesota, all students were required to attend Lutheran religious services—unless they belonged to another church. Isaac Bonewitz and his friends didn't belong to any church, so they invented one, the Church of the Reformed Druid, with the most bizarre beliefs and rituals that they could think of, and held regular, crazy meetings. It worked—the requirement to attend religious services was repealed.

Then something remarkable happened. Members didn't want to disband. They had found spiritual meaning in the invented beliefs and practices. The church still exists today (Adler, 1997).

TABLE 15.1

Types of Religious Organizations				
	CULT	**SECT**	**DENOMINATION**	**ECCLESIA**
Size	Small	Small	Large	Universal
Wealth	Poor	Poor	Wealthy	Extensive
Beliefs	Strict	Strict	Diversity tolerated	Diversity tolerated
Practices	Variable	Informal	Formal	Formal
Clergy	Untrained	Some training	Extensive training	Extensive training
Membership	Emotional commitment	Accepting doctrine	Birth/decision to join	By belonging to a society

Members of cults leave behind their membership in older religious institutions and often live on the margins of society. Thus they typically run afoul of local and national governments. And that may mean violent repression. During the 1980s, the Branch Davidians, led by David Koresh, broke off from the Seventh Day Adventist Church. They moved to a compound outside Waco, Texas; amassed a small arsenal of weapons; and began teaching that the end of the world was approaching. In 1993, their compound was stormed by federal agents from the Bureau of Alcohol, Tobacco, and Firearms. The government claimed that the cult had broken numerous laws, that Koresh was keeping people hostage and sexually abusing his followers. To the cult's supporters, the government was interfering in religious freedom. After a week-long standoff, a gun battle, and a fire, all 82 Branch Davidians and several federal agents were killed (see Report to the Deputy Attorney General on the Events at Waco, Texas, 1993).

Cults can develop murderous messianic tendencies as well. In 1995, a cult called Aum Shinrikyo (Supreme Truth) released sarin gas on the Tokyo subway during the morning rush hour, killing 12 people and injuring thousands of others. The cult's leader had stockpiled enough poison gas to kill millions before the attack; he was captured in 2004.

Does globalization increase or decrease the number of cults? Both. Globalization and technological advances such as the Internet have had contradictory effects. On the one hand, the Internet facilitates recruitment and enables cult members to remain connected despite large distances. On the other hand, cults often require intense interpersonal interaction. Cults often use very modern techniques to express their antimodernist views, using the information superhighway to "restore" the traditional world that has been displaced.

Cults are often held together by a charismatic personality, no matter how bizarre their ideas. Marshall Applewhite, at left, was the leader of the Heaven's Gate cult. He convinced 38 followers to commit suicide so that their souls could take a ride on a spaceship that they believed was hiding behind the comet carrying Jesus. ▼

Sects

A **sect** is a small subculture within an established religious institution. Like cults, they break from traditional practices, but unlike cults they remain within the larger institution. For example, the Jehovah's Witnesses are usually classified as a Christian sect. Sects typically arise when some members of an established religious institution believe that the institution is drifting from its true mission, becoming sidetracked by extraneous, more "worldly" pursuits. Thus the sect seeks to remain true to the initial mission by demanding more of its members than does the established institution. Sects control membership criteria and set their own behavioral standards for members. Sect members often think of themselves as the only true believers and regard the mainstream membership as apostate (falling away from the faith).

Many sects are short lived. This is generally the case either because the initial *charismatic leader*—a person whose extraordinary personal qualities touch people deeply enough to motivate them to break with tradition—leaves the group or because they encourage reforms within the established religious institution. For instance, "traditionalist" sects in the Roman Catholic Church reject attempts at modernization like services in English. On the other side of the political spectrum, a sect called the People of the Church believes that women should be allowed to enter the priesthood and that celibacy should be optional.

Some sects become "established sects" and develop their own formal institutional arrangements within a larger institutional framework (see Yinger, 1970). In Christianity, the Latter-Day Saints or the Amish are established sects. In Judaism, we can look at the Hasidic Jews, and in Islam, the Druze of Lebanon.

Denominations

A **denomination** is a large-scale, extremely organized religious body. It has an established hierarchy, methods for credentialing administrators, and much more social respect than either a cult or a sect. Members of cults and sects are often subject to prejudice and discrimination in the mainstream society, but members of denominations are usually considered "normal." The various Pentecostal churches were considered cults or sects as long as their members were mostly poor, urban, and African American; but once they began to gain White middle-class converts, they quickly became denominations.

In the United States, the overwhelming majority of the population belongs to one of the denominations of Christianity. The largest is the Roman Catholic Church (23 percent). Nearly 70 percent of all Americans claim membership in a Protestant denomination (chiefly Methodist, Baptist, Presbyterian, or Lutheran). There are 5.9 million Jews in the United States, 3 million Muslims, 2 million Buddhists, and 1 million Hindus.

With some 2,000 cults, sects, and denominations in the United States, how do you decide which one to join? Most people adopt the religion of their parents and stay with it throughout their lives, with little conscious choice. Many denominations accept new members at birth or offer membership at such a young age that one could scarcely be said to carefully weigh alternatives. A third of the U.S. population has changed denominations, but they usually do not walk into a strange church or temple and say "I want to join you." They adopt the religion of a friend or romantic partner.

Ecclesiae

There is one more formal religious organization, the **ecclesiae,** or religion so pervasive that the boundary between state and church is nonexistent. In such societies, the clerical elite often serve as political leaders or at least formal advisors to political leaders. Everyone in the society

The International Society of Krishna Consciousness (or Hare Krishnas) is considered a cult in the United States. In India, however, it is an established Hindu sect. ▼

OBJECTIVE: Explore the four types of religious organizations.

STEP 1: Research

Using various Internet resources and library resources, find two examples (not mentioned in your textbook) of each of the four religious organizations noted in your book, including cult, sect, denomination, and ecclesia. In your examples, include an explanation for why your example is a particular type of organization. Include a discussion of the size, wealth, beliefs, practices, training of clergy, and type of membership. Note the sources for each of your examples and write up your responses in an easy-to-read format (your instructor may ask that you develop a chart).

STEP 2: Discuss

Bring your responses to class and be prepared to share your examples. Did anything surprise you about the class discussion? Were there examples similar to yours? Did anyone have your example in a different category?

STEP 3: Review

Your instructor will conclude this activity by discussing how religious organizations change over time. You will be challenged to think of examples of religious organizations that have changed over time.

belongs to that faith by birth, not individual decision, and those who do not belong to the faith cannot become citizens. Until the French Revolution, the clergy in France was one of the two pillars on which the monarchy rested (the other was the nobility). Today, the Muslim clerics in Saudi Arabia, the Shi'ite mullahs in Iran, and the Buddhist priests in Thailand are nearly identical with political leadership.

Such merging of politics and religion is not inevitable. Some societies with established state churches remain remarkably free of clerical influence in political matters. In Sweden, for instance, the Lutheran Church has official status, but it exerts virtually no influence on political decision making.

Religions of the World

Sociologists are not only fascinated by religion as a cultural universal; they are also interested in the remarkable diversity of religious belief and practice. In most places, local, traditional religions have given way to **world religions,** religions with a long history, well-established traditions, and the flexibility to adapt to many different cultures.

Western Religions

Three of the world's major religions, Judaism, Christianity, and Islam (plus a few smaller ones) are called Western religions because they originated in the Middle East. They all trace their spiritual ancestry to the same event: About 2000 BCE, a nomadic tribe living in ancient Mesopotamia recognized that their god, Yahweh, was not specific to their tribe, but was the god of all the world. They eventually founded Judaism (after Judea, where they settled), and they tried to follow God's law as revealed in the Torah, his sacred book. Christianity arose 2,000 years later out of a protest against the "corruption" of Judaism, and Islam 600 years after that as a protest to the "corruption" of both, so all three religions share many beliefs and practices.

Sociology and our World

The "Church" of Scientology

What is Scientology? Is it a cult? A religion? A hoax?

Scientology was founded in 1952 as a self-help system by a science fiction writer, L. Ron Hubbard. Hubbard believed that he had found both the vision of a pure and whole life, as well as the method of achieving it. He gradually came to believe that he had founded a new religion and declared Scientology a church.

Some critics, however, argue that Scientology is nothing more than a cult of personality surrounding Hubbard and his followers and that they seek recognition as a religion only because they seek to avoid paying taxes. A May 1980 *Reader's Digest* article quotes Hubbard as saying, "If a man really wants to make a million dollars, the best way would be to start his own religion." Because church members are paid for each recruit they bring into the organization, and each branch pays fees to the international center, most countries in Europe classify scientology as a for-profit business, although Germany considers it a dangerous cult. In the late 1990s, Great Britain denied it classification as a tax-exempt religion, and the United States granted that status.

Scientology claims more than 10 million followers, though less-partisan observers estimate the numbers to be somewhere between 100,000 and 500,000 worldwide. In the United States, there are about 55,000 practitioners.

They are exclusive: They have the one true faith; all others are invalid. They are evangelistic: They want you to choose their faith. There is only one god (although sometimes there are intermediaries, like saints and angels). There is usually a heaven and a hell, where we will experience eternal joy or torment. There is a sacred book, usually revealed by God, which followers are expected to read and obey. Believers are expected to attend regular worship services, held on the holiest day of the week (Friday for Muslims, Saturday for Jews, Sunday for Christians). And finally, a messiah is coming to save us. (For Christians, he has already come, but he's coming back, and the Shi'ite is the only Muslim denomination that believes this.)

Judaism and Christianity spread west, through Europe, while Islam spread east and south, throughout the Arabian Peninsula and into India and Central Asia. Today, of course, all three religions have adherents worldwide.

Judaism believes that the covenant between God and Abraham around 2000 BCE became the foundation of Jewish law, as recorded in the Pentateuch (first five books of the Bible). Judaism flourished in the ancient world; it is estimated that 10 percent of the population of the Roman Empire was Jewish. Today there are about 15 million Jews in the world (0.2 percent of the world's population), divided into three branches: Orthodox, who follow traditional Jewish law very strictly; Reformed, who attempt to modernize dress, dietary laws, and worship practices (for instance, synagogue services are conducted in the usual language of the country, not in Hebrew); and Conservative, who rebelled against the overmodernization of the Reformed branch.

Christianity was founded 2,000 years ago by the disciples of Jesus, who declared him to be the son of God. Christians revere the Jewish Bible (which they call the Old Testament), as well as the New Testament, a collection of writings recounting the life of Jesus and the history of early Christianity. Today, Christianity is the world's largest single religion, with 2.1 billion adherents (about one-third of all the world's people), although it is divided into so many different denominations with widely varying beliefs and practices that it is often treated as a group of religions. There are three main branches, Roman Catholicism, Eastern Orthodoxy, and Protestantism, as well as many sects.

Islam was founded about 1,400 years ago when God grew displeased with the corruption of the teachings of his earlier prophets and gave his last prophet,

FIGURE 15.1 **World Religions, 2005**

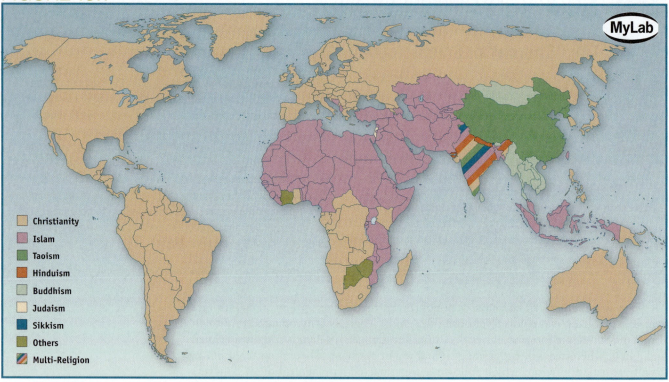

MyLab

Christianity
Islam
Taoism
Hinduism
Buddhism
Judaism
Sikkism
Others
Multi-Religion

Source: "World Religions" from Maps of the World website, www.mapsoftheworld.com. Reprinted with permission.

Mohammed, a new sacred text, the Koran. Islam means "Submission to God," and Muslim, "one who has submitted to God." Islam is far more communal than Christianity, especially its Protestant variety, and requires the fusion of religion and government. Only a Muslim government is seen as legitimate. There are two main branches, Shi'ite and Sunni, which differ in a number of beliefs and practices; for instance, Shi'ite Muslims revere holy men, or imams. In Iraq under Saddam Hussein, the Shi'ite majority was severely persecuted. Today about 20 percent of the world's population is Muslim. Like Christianity, the numbers have increased dramatically, from 529 million to 1.3 billion (Figure 15.1).

All three of these religions are divided into various denominations and sects, based on interpretations of their religious texts. Some interpret these texts liberally and thus enable religious belief to casually coexist with modern life. Others are more demanding. At the extreme ends of all these religions are fundamentalist groups, which claim to be the purest and truest followers of their religion. **Fundamentalism** tries to return to the basic precepts, the "true word of God," and live exactly according to His precepts.

However, even within a fundamentalist group, there is much debate about what precisely God expects of his followers, and there is little agreement between fundamentalist groups. For example, al-Qaeda's interpretation of **jihad,** or holy war, to mean acts of terrorism against non-Muslims, is viewed with horror by most fundamentalist Muslims. Some fundamentalist Christians believe that going to the movies is immoral, while others play movies during "fellowship hour." Some Orthodox Jews will not push the buttons on an elevator on the Sabbath because they believe that the restriction against working on the Sabbath extends to elevator buttons.

All fundamentalist groups are selective in the application of their chosen texts. Even if you believe that the Bible is literally true, you must decide which parts are applicable to today's world and which are not. To the sociologist, references to scripture are important because they suggest a search for a coherent and consistent way to live ethically in a world of ambivalence and contradiction. To be selective in our use of these religious texts is human; to understand that search is sociological.

Eastern Religions

Three other major religions of the world, Hinduism, Buddhism, and Confucianism (plus some minor ones), are called "Eastern" because they arose in Asia, although, like the Western religions, they have adherents around the world. They have many beliefs and practices in common, some of which might baffle people raised in a Western religion. They are **syncretic religions:** It is perfectly acceptable to practice Buddhism, Hinduism, Confucianism, Taoism, and any other religion you want, all at the same time. There are many gods (although often religious scholars interpret them as emanations of a single god). There is no heaven or hell, just an endless series of reincarnations until you achieve enlightenment (except in Confucianism). There is no specific sacred book, although sometimes there are vast libraries of sacred texts to be revered. And there are no regular worship services. Temples are used for special rituals.

Hinduism developed from many indigenous religions in India around 1500 BCE. Unlike the Western religions, which rely on sacred texts (and therefore presume that believers can read), Hinduism is based largely on oral tradition, passed on from one generation to the next by storytellers. However, there are also many sacred texts, notably the Vedas and the Upanishads. There are many gods, but most people, most of the time, revere one of the main three, Brahman (who creates life), Vishnu (who preserves or maintains life), and Shiva (who destroys or renews life). Some of the avatars or incarnations of Vishnu are also popular, especially Krishna (portrayed as a blue-skinned youth) and Ganesha (portrayed as an elephant-headed man). Enlightenment is available only after countless incarnations, so most Hindus do not hope for it to happen in this lifetime; instead, they try to behave in a moral fashion to ensure a favorable reincarnation. Today there are nearly one billion Hindus (14 percent of all religious adherents) mostly in South Asia and in Indian communities around the world.

Just as Protestantism developed as a reaction to the "corruption" of Catholicism, **Buddhism** developed as a reaction to the "corruption" of Hinduism. It was founded by Siddhartha Gautama (560–580 BCE), later called the Buddha, or "The Enlightened One." While Hinduism taught that enlightenment could come only after countless lifetimes of reincarnation, the Buddha taught that enlightenment was possible in this lifetime, through the "Tenfold Path" of physical and spiritual discipline. Today there are two main branches of Buddhism. Hinayana ("The Small Cart"), which still follows strict discipline, is common primarily in Southeast Asia and Tibet. The need for discipline led Hinayana Buddhists to found the first monasteries, and in some countries, monks comprise up to a third of the population. Mahayana ("The Large Cart") does not emphasize strict discipline and thus has fewer monks. There are 376 million

Buddhist priests practice meditation and a strict physical and spiritual discipline to reach enlightenment. These Thai priests pray before their tea ceremony. ▼

FIGURE 15.2 **World Religions by Percent of Adherents, 2005**

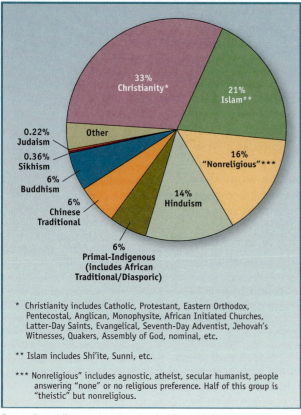

* Christianity includes Catholic, Protestant, Eastern Orthodox, Pentecostal, Anglican, Monophysite, African Initiated Churches, Latter-Day Saints, Evangelical, Seventh-Day Adventist, Jehovah's Witnesses, Quakers, Assembly of God, nominal, etc.

** Islam includes Shi'ite, Sunni, etc.

*** Nonreligious" includes agnostic, atheist, secular humanist, people answering "none" or no religious preference. Half of this group is "theistic" but nonreligious.

Source: From Adherents.com. Reprinted with permission.

Buddhists (6 percent of all adherents), mostly in East Asia, although many Westerners have become interested in Buddhist teachings.

The philosopher K'ung Fu Tzu or Confucius (551–479 BCE) lived in China about the same time as the Buddha in India. The faith he founded, **Confucianism,** remained the official religion of China until the People's Republic officially became atheist in 1949 and also had a strong impact on other Asian countries, especially Japan and Korea (Figure 15.2).

Confucianism does not have much to say about gods or the afterlife. Instead, it establishes a strict social hierarchy. Confucius put forth Five Constant Relationships: ruler–subject; husband–wife; father–son; elder brother–younger brother; elder friend–junior friend. In each, one person is subordinate to the other, but the deference due the superior person cannot be taken for granted. Rather, it must be earned. Confucianism sees Heaven and Earth as linked realms that are constantly in touch with each other. People in Heaven are the ancestors of those on Earth. It is hard to determine the number of adherents because officially no religions are practiced in mainland China, but it is safe to say that every aspect of Chinese culture owes a debt to Confucianism.

Eastern religions tend to be somewhat more tolerant of other religions than Western religions. Without the privileged access to revealed truth—by which conversion of nonbelievers is a mission of love—there is not as much need for coerced conversion, or the bloody religious wars that have appeared for millennia in the West. It is the certainty of religious doctrine that might contribute, sociologically speaking, to the higher levels of religious persecution and discrimination in the West.

Contemporary Religion: Secularization or Resurgence?

Early sociologists believed that as societies became more modern, religion would decline. Individuals, and society as a whole, would no longer need it, and so society would become increasingly secular. **Secularization**—the process of moving away from religious spirituality and toward the worldly—was assumed to be the future of religion around the world.

Marx believed that as capitalism developed, we would all become rational individuals, interested only in self-interest and the bottom line. Capitalism, he wrote, would "drown the heavenly ecstasies of religious fervor" in the "icy water of egotistical calculation" (Marx [1848] in Kimmel, 2006). Weber believed that religious ideas had a way of becoming applied in the everyday world and that this process made religious ideas less mysterious and special, which in turn, led to their becoming less meaningful to us. And Durkheim thought religion would decline because society itself would perform the functions of religion—ensuring group cohesion and providing meaning and social control.

The secularization thesis was so well accepted that it became a sort of truism; no one contradicted it because it seemed so "right." Over the years, sociologists have amassed a large amount of empirical data to support the theory of secularization.

However, it turns out that secularization has not occurred—at least not as sociologists had originally predicted it. For one thing, religion has not declined worldwide, despite the dramatic modernization of societies and the technological breakthroughs of the past century. Religious adherence is prospering in a wide variety of different societies.

In fact, the majority of countries in the world, the majority of the global population, is experiencing a religious resurgence (Berger, 1999; Moghadam, 2003). Religiosity is generally increasing in the former Communist countries of Eastern Europe, Central Asia, and the Caucasus, as well as Latin American, Africa, China, Southeast Asia, and the Middle East (Moghadam, 2003; Riesebrodt, 2000).

In Eastern Europe, the number of atheists and nonreligious people has been declining steadily since 1990 (Moghadam, 2003). In Russia, belief in God has risen sharply, to roughly 60 percent of the population today (Moghadam, 2003). In Central Asia and across the Caucasus, there has been a steady decline in the nonreligious and atheist population. China is seeing a steady rise in Buddhism, the country's largest faith, but also in traditional folk religions (Gargan, 2002) and in Christianity, particularly Protestantism. Some 10 million people belong to the state-sanctioned Catholic Church and 15 million to the official Protestant church, and an estimated 2 million Chinese a year are being baptized as Protestants (Lakshmanan, 2002). While data are scarce for Africa, Islam is an increasingly strong force in several countries, and Christianity is on the rise. The number of Catholics alone in Africa has increased from an estimated 16 million in 1955 to 120 million in 2000 (Jenkins, 2003). In fact, Christianity is not only the world's largest religion today, but, in some regions, particularly in the developing world, it is the fastest-growing religion as well. Increasingly, trends such as this rapid growth of Christianity in the global South and increased Muslim immigration to Western nations are shaping both public attitudes and government policies around the world (Table 15.2).

In the developing world, religion continues to hold enormous sway over the society. For many years, sociologists believed that a society's adherence to religious beliefs was one of the major cultural barriers to modernity. But religion offers an alternative to modern society, which people may regard as corrupt—and corrupting. For example, Buddhism or Confucianism proposes radical disengagement with the material world (transcendence), and others offer a parallel spiritual world that enables you to live in the world but not succumb to it (like, for example, orthodox Judaism). Other religions, such as some groups of fundamentalist Muslims or Christians, demand fervent engagement with the world as a way to redirect society away from such corruption.

From a European perspective, the secularization thesis is more valid than it is in the United States; religious affiliation, belief in God, and church attendance in Europe are but a fraction of what they were a century ago. Religious participation has declined steadily since the 1960s (Banchoff, 2007). Were it not for one very big exception, one might say that the more industrially and technologically developed a society is, the lower its rates of religious beliefs. In those industrial countries where the government provides the most extensive social safety net (health care, retirement benefits), rates of church attendance have decreased most dramatically. Even in Italy, the seat of the Roman Catholic Church, religious participation has declined in the past 30 years, although less sharply and consistently than elsewhere in Europe (Banchoff, 2007).

The big exception to this rule is the United States. While scientific and economic progress has continued virtually unabated, so has religious affiliation. The United States has five times fewer nonbelievers than even the state of Israel, let alone European

TABLE 15.2

Global Trends in Religious Resurgence

Religiosity is declining in most OECD countries, except the United States. It is resurgent in the Middle East and Southeast Asia, Eastern Europe except Poland, and in the developing world except India.

DECLINING (SELECTED COUNTRIES)	RESURGENT (SELECTED COUNTRIES)
Australia	Russia
Britain	China
Canada	Brazil
France	Nigeria
Germany	South Africa
Netherlands	Bosnia
Norway	Yugoslavia
Poland	Kazakhstan
India	United States

Source: Assaf Maghadam, "A Global Resurgence of Religion?" Weatherhead Center for International Affairs, Harvard University, August 2003.

countries (Zuckerman, 2005). The United States always has been a strongly religious country—and we continue to be. The United States stands alone among wealthy, industrialized countries in its embrace of religion. Nearly six in ten Americans say religion plays a *very* important role in their lives (Pew Global Attitudes Project, 2002).

Religion in the United States

Around the time America was founded, Thomas Jefferson confidently predicted that people would eventually think of the Bible as a book of myths, like Greek mythology. Yet faith in the literal truth of the Bible remains strong, and the United States remains one of the world's most churchgoing societies. Why have rates of religious belief and participation declined in every other industrialized country but the United States?

One factor might be that the United States has been, since its inception, more than simply a nation of immigrants, but actually a nation of *religious* immigrants. Since the Pilgrims were kicked out of England, the United States has always been a haven for those who were constrained from practicing their religion elsewhere—European Jews, Chinese Christians, Russian Orthodox believers, and so on. As some nations become increasingly secular, those who are religious may seek a haven in the United States. As a result, increased religiosity and increased secularism coexist.

Another factor is that the United States has been swept by several waves of increased religious passion. There were two Great Awakenings, one in the 1720s and one in the 1820s, which witnessed a democratization of religion, as itinerant preachers spread the news that God was less impressed with fancy churches and ornaments than by sincere beliefs of individuals. In the early twentieth century, the Pentecostal Revival, another significant spiritual "awakening," invited poor, non-white, and otherwise disenfranchised people to leave traditional Methodist and Presbyterian churches to hold meetings in storefronts and private houses. Just as the Industrial Revolution freed individuals' enterprise, these revivals of religious experience had the effect of freeing individuals from the hold of organized churches and making religion feel "American" (Table 15.3).

Still a third factor has been the way that American religious institutions have grown as providers of social support and cultural interaction. In Europe, churches are often tourist attractions, but locals rarely set foot inside. During my first trip to London, I thought it might be a good idea to attend a service in Westminster Abbey. But services are held in the Abbey only on Sundays; every other day they're held in a tiny basement chapel—with about 30 people in attendance. Even the great cathedrals of Europe, like Notre Dame in Paris, or St. Peter's in Rome, or the Cathedral of Seville, have sparse attendance at mass—and then the congregation is composed largely of tourists.

American churches, by contrast, are almost always full. Churches are often the social and cultural center of the town. Every night there are groups that meet there, from Alcoholics Anonymous to Bible study to social gatherings for divorced parents. Religious institutions not only run parochial schools, but many organize preschool and day care facilities (these are provided by the government in European countries). Churches sponsor soccer leagues and wilderness retreats,

Church attendance in all industrialized countries except the United States is at or near all-time lows. Even in Italy, home of the Pope, Church attendance is significantly less than it has been in several centuries. At this evening mass in St. Peter's Basilica in Rome, many of the people are actually tourists. ▼

picnics and bingo nights. They have become the social—as well as the spiritual—hub of American communities, especially important as other civic supports, from Kiwanis and bowling leagues to public services, have declined (Table 15.4).

Perhaps one of the other reasons religion is so strong is, ironically, *because* of its separation from political life. The separation of church and state, the prohibitions on school prayer, and the general global trend toward secularization make religiosity something of a rebellion against the dominant culture. Portraying oneself as a minority, whose status is as a victim of state persecution, is almost always a good way to recruit new members.

Finally, it may be that the assumptions that one had to choose between a religious and a secular life were invalid. Americans hold religious beliefs in ways that can fit readily into an otherwise secular life. For Americans, it is not a question of religion *versus* business, but religion *and*. American religious beliefs are modified so that we can be both sacred and secular. Christian bookstores are open on Sundays; children come to church dressed in their soccer uniforms (Gibbs, 2004).

Many observers consider this the **Third Great Awakening** in American history, a religious revival that further democratizes spirituality, making a relationship with the sacred attainable to even greater numbers of Americans, with even less effort or religious discipline. For example, while more Americans are deeply religious, they commit to religious organizations only as long as they like them; one in three Americans has switched denomination, according to a Gallup Poll (Wolfe, 2003).

Even though many of us claim to be highly religious, our knowledge of the dominant U.S. religions is rather limited. Over half of Americans (58 percent) cannot name even five of the Ten Commandments, and just under half know that Genesis is the first book of the Bible. Even fewer can explain the meaning of the Holy Trinity (a theological concept taught by almost all Christian denominations). And 12 percent of Americans believe that Joan of Arc was Noah's wife (she was really an early-fifteenth-century war heroine and political martyr) (McKibben, 2005).

It may be that the dramatic rise of evangelical Christianity in the United States—nearly 40 percent of Americans identify themselves as "born-again" Christian or evangelical—has less to do with its doctrinal rigidity and more to do with how well it sits with other "American" values. Evangelical Christianity uses market-savvy approaches

TABLE 15.3

Top Ten Religions in the United States

1. Christianity
2. Nonreligious/secular
3. Judaism
4. Islam
5. Buddhism
6. Agnostic
7. Atheist
8. Hinduism
9. Unitarian Universalist
10. Wiccan/Pagan/Druid

Source: American Religious Identity Survey, Kosmin and Mayor, 2001.

TABLE 15.4

What Do U.S. Churches Do? Social Services among Hispanics

DOES YOUR CHURCH OR HOUSE OF WORSHIP HELP MEMBERS IN NEED WITH . . .	ALL HISPANICS	CATHOLIC	EVANGELICAL	OTHER PROTESTANT
Food or clothing	84%	83%	90%	89%
Finding a job	56	52	74	65
Financial problems	63	58	82	73
Finding housing	50	45	67	61
Taking care of children	57	52	75	72
Language or literacy training	57	57	56	53

Note: Based on Hispanics who attend religious services.
Source: Pew Forum on Religion and Public Life, 2007.

▲ Evangelical megachurches have "supersized" religion in the United States. At Willow Creek Community Church, in South Barrington, IL (outside Chicago), about 17,000 attend weekly services.

to expanding its congregations; employs high-level technologies in megachurches; and, most importantly, is strongly personal and therapeutic. In America, God is intimately involved in the minutest details of your everyday life. (Forget that old idea of a distant, abstract, and judgmental God; in the American version, God is close enough to be your best friend.) "While more Americans than ever consider themselves born again, the lord to whom they turn rarely gets angry and frequently strengthens self-esteem" according to sociologist Alan Wolfe (2003, p. 3).

One indication of this intimacy comes from a 2004 survey in which Americans were asked to whom they might want to place a 15-minute telephone call. George W. Bush received 11 percent, Abraham Lincoln and Albert Einstein got 5 percent, and many others, like Bill Gates, Marilyn Monroe, Elvis Presley, and Martha Stewart received a few. But 60 percent of respondents wanted to call God. Three of five respondents believed God was sort of a human being and amenable to a phone chat.

When some religious figures have declared the Harry Potter series or even Halloween to be sacrilegious because they involve magic and witchcraft, writers soon turn out a Christian alternative like "Shadowmancer" who solves problems by prayer (see Smith, 2004). Rather than fight against media's "corrupting" influence, religious themes have been incorporated into media, like TV shows. Religious organizations develop and market their own products, from best-selling novels, like Tim LaHaye and Jerry B. Jenkins's *Left Behind* series, and Christian rock CDs by groups like Audio Adrenaline.

Like our consumer economy, some evangelical religious organizations have "supersized," so that today, many Americans worship in megachurches such as Chicago's Willow Creek Community Church (17,000 weekly attendance) or Bellevue Baptist Church outside Memphis (10,000 attendees and another 8,000 in Bible study groups each week). If these mainstream pop-culture renditions of Protestantism seem either too remote or too commercial, other smaller churches offer a relaxed experience in "house churches" where ministers are likely to wear blue jeans and speak to congregants informally (see Leland, 2004). All are relatively "seeker friendly," offering spiritual redemption and psychological therapy in the same package. With congregations numbering in the tens of thousands on any given Sunday, American megachurches are less somber religious affairs and more like a mixture of arena rock concerts and old-time tent preaching.

However, it is important to remember that Christians—even American born-again Christians—do not all agree on major issues. In a recent survey, sociologists Andrew Greeley and Michael Hout found that conservative Christians are not all likely to vote Republican (class matters here, and poorer Protestants are less likely to vote Republican than wealthier ones); do not universally oppose abortion (only 14 percent oppose it in all circumstances and 22 percent are prochoice); and a large majority support sex education in school (Greeley and Hout, 2006).

Did *you* know?

The world's first Islamic superheroes battle evil in the comic book, *The 99*. Named for the 99 attributes Muslims believe are embodied in God, the comics aim to reach the growing Muslim markets in many countries worldwide. Its creator says existing superheroes are either Judeo-Christian archetypes—individuals with great power who are disguised (Batman, Superman, Spiderman), or Eastern archetypes of small characters who depend on one another to become powerful (like Yu-Gi-Oh or Pokemon). *The 99* offers an Islamic model: By combining the virtues that each superhero will represent, the team builds collective power that expresses the divine.

Religious Experience and Religious Identity

Religions don't vary only by denomination; we vary in our level of religious affiliation and in the intensity of our beliefs. Rates vary from country to country; and, within the United States, different groups express different levels of religiosity. For example, age matters: The older are more religious than the young. And where you live matters: The rural are more religious than the suburban, and the suburban are more religious than the urban (the major exception to this is urban Blacks, who have high rates of religiosity, as we will discuss below). And sex matters: Although they have long been excluded from leadership positions in several major religions, women remain more religious than men. Women attend religious services more frequently and report higher levels of religiosity (intense religious feelings) than do men. But why would women be more likely to adhere to a spiritual discipline that portrays them as second-class citizens?

Many researchers point to more psychological explanations: Women are socialized to be kinder and gentler, qualities often associated with religion; or the fact that women are primarily involved in childrearing, which also extracts those values from women. But sociological research suggests that women's structural location, specifically their absence from the labor force, better explains higher levels of religiosity. Men who are not in the labor force exhibit equally high levels of religiosity, and women's levels decline significantly when they enter the paid labor force (deVaus and McAllister, 1987).

Most Western religions not only prohibit women from leadership but also condemn homosexuality as contrary to divine law. Though actual references to homosexuality in the Bible are few, those who condemn homosexuality point to a passage in Leviticus (18:22) that reads, "And with a man you shall not lie with as a man lies with a woman; it is an abomination." Despite this, several religious denominations have begun to include gay men and lesbians, including some Protestant denominations, conservative and reform Judaism, and most non-Western religions. The consecration of an openly gay priest as an Episcopal bishop in 2005 has split the American Episcopal Church from other national synods and threatens to tear the church in two.

Both denominational affiliation and rates of religiosity also vary by race and ethnicity as well (Figure 15.3). In the United States, more than 92 percent of Blacks and Hispanics practice some religious denomination, while only about 88 percent of Whites do. Of those, more than 67 percent of Hispanics are Catholic, while only 22.4 percent of Whites and a mere 4.25 percent of Blacks are. Almost 83 percent of Blacks are Protestant, as compared with 57 percent of Whites and 19.6 percent of Hispanics (Pew Forum on Religion and Public Life, 2007).

"I don't belong to an organized religion. My religious beliefs are way too disorganized."

Did you know?

The historical association of religiosity and femininity has troubled theologians at various times as they sought ways to bring men back into religious institutions. At the turn of the twentieth century, an entire evangelical movement, called Muscular Christianity, proclaimed Jesus as a he-man, a sort of religious Rambo, not the kind, sweet, angelic image of many mainstream churches. Jesus was no "dough-faced lick-spittle proposition," quipped Billy Sunday, a professional baseball player turned evangelist preacher and leader of the Muscular Christians, "but the greatest scrapper that ever lived" (cited in Kimmel, 1996, p. 171). Today, PromiseKeepers use similar images of Jesus as a real man in their efforts to bring men back into the fold.

FIGURE 15.3 **Denominational Distribution by**
Race/Ethnicity, 2007

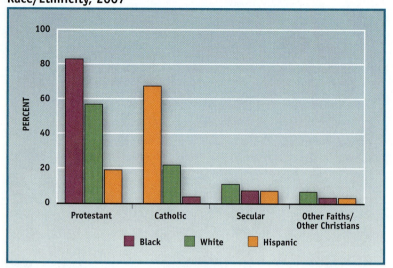

Source: "Changing Faiths: Latinos and the Transformation of American Religion," Pew Forum on Religion & Public Life and Pew Hispanic Center, 2007. Reprinted by permission.

When it comes to religious observance, 84 percent of U.S. Blacks say religion is very important in everyday life, while only 68 percent of Hispanics and 39 percent of Whites feel the same way. Sixty-two percent of Blacks and 50 percent of Hispanics believe the Bible is the literal word of God, while only 31 percent of Whites do. Eighty percent of Whites believe that miracles still occur today as they did in ancient times; fewer Hispanics (75 percent) hold the same belief. Religiosity also varies by other sociological factors, including education and income; across all racial and ethnic groups, greater education and higher household incomes both correlate with more secular beliefs (Pew Forum on Religion and Public Life, 2007) (Table 15.5).

Most churches in the United States are populated by Whites *or* Blacks; rarely do they worship together. As Dr. Martin Luther King Jr. once put it, "The most segregated hour of Christian America is 11 o'clock on Sunday morning." Just as the White church has been, for centuries, an important social institution, so too has the Black church evolved as one of the central institutions of the African American community.

Actually, to speak of a singular "Black church" in America is a bit misleading; the "Black church" is really the vast array of Black churches, usually Protestant, that have developed over the course of U.S. history. The massive importation of African slaves in the seventeenth and eighteenth centuries was coupled with efforts to crush their traditional African-based religions (which were seen as a threat to their enslaved status) and to convert them to Christianity. Often slaves were required to attend church with their White masters but relegated to the balconies of the church.

Gradually, however, slaves began to appropriate parts of the service, especially identifying with the Biblical stories of the Jews, who were slaves in Egypt, and their eventual liberation in the book of Exodus. After the Civil War, they established their

TABLE 15.5

Religious Tradition among Hispanics by Education and Household Income[†]						
		AMONG HISPANICS . . .				
	ALL HISPANICS	CATHOLIC	EVANGELICAL	MAINLINE PROTESTANT	OTHER CHRISTIAN	SECULAR
Education						
Less than high school degree	39%	42%	34%	30%	37%	33%
High school degree	47	44	54	56	52	49
Four-year college degree	10	9	10	12	9	17
Household Income						
Less than $30,000	43	46	39	29	45	41
$30,000–$49,999	19	18	24	21	26	21
$50,000 or more	17	14	21	24	11	25

[†]21% of respondents did not provide information on their household income.
Source: Pew Forum on Religion and Public Life, 2007.

own churches, which quickly became the cultural and social centers of the newly arrived free Blacks to the northern cities and in the small southern towns where the descendents of former slaves settled.

Sociologist E. Franklin Frazier (1974) studied the Black church in America and especially noted how it answered secular as well as sacred needs for its community. The Black church was far more expressive than the more staid White churches and often integrated elements of traditional and long-suppressed African religion into its services, including singing, dancing, and especially call-and-response styles of preaching and praying. But he was especially impressed with the way that these churches became a training ground for activist ministers who began the Civil Rights movement—Jesse Jackson, Al Sharpton, Martin Luther King Jr. himself—and were consistently inspired by Biblical stories of nonviolent resistance.

Today the Black church remains influential, both as a source of religious inspiration and for political mobilization (Battle, 2006; Billingsley, 1999) Ministers like Jesse Jackson mounted serious campaigns for the presidency; ministers are often powerful orators who inspire and mobilize. The Black church's contribution to American society has been enormous, including being the origins of soul and gospel music (Sam Cooke and Aretha Franklin got their start in gospel groups).

▲ The Black church often integrated elements of traditional and long-suppressed African religion into its services, including singing and dancing, and especially call-and-response-styles of preaching and praying. These women are members of the Temple of Deliverance Church of God and Christ in Memphis.

Religion on Campus

It is on college campuses that science and religion most often clashed. Many of the nation's first colleges and universities, such as Harvard and Yale, were originally designed for the training of ministers, but they soon expanded into other fields, and even at church-related colleges today, only a small percentage of students major in religion. Public universities are often so careful to maintain the separation of church and state that they usually have no departments of religious studies and often no courses devoted to any religion.

The higher your level of educational attainment, the less devout you will be in practicing your religion. That means that the professors, who usually have PhDs, tend to number among the nation's unfaithful. But their students are often quite religious. They may come from strict religious backgrounds; most likely they never hear of conflicting scientific data like evolution and the age of Earth until they enroll in Biology 101, and they certainly have never been asked to read and discuss the works of atheists like Karl Marx. Yet religious belief and practice have never been stronger on college campuses. After a decline during the 1980s, religion has been regaining ground. More students are enrolling in religion courses and majoring in religion; more are living in dormitories or houses where spirituality and faith are parts of daily life; and groups are springing up where students can discuss religious ideas as a means of understanding the world in addition to (or instead of) science (Finder, 2007).

While church attendance among college students is lower than that of the nation as a whole (in part because services are held on Sunday morning, not an attractive time slot after a Saturday night of partying), the first national survey on the spiritual lives of college students (2004) found that more than two-thirds of college freshman pray, and almost 80 percent believe in God. Nearly 50 percent of freshman say they are seeking opportunities to grow spiritually (Higher Education Research Institute, 2004). Perhaps that's why the popularity of nondenominational Christian organizations has surged on campus in recent years. Membership in the long-established Campus

New Age beliefs have certainly benefited from increased globalization because followers can now travel the world in search of meaningful rituals. Indeed, travel companies have developed that cater especially to the spiritual nomads, who travel the world seeking meaning (Gooch, 2002). The rapid development and number of these groups also suggests that we are, in essence, a spiritual nation—with a spirituality that covers vast areas of our mental landscape and welcomes multiple beliefs but does not go very deep. The trend in industrialized countries is that the decline in "traditional" religion is accompanied by a rise in New Age spirituality (Moghadam, 2003). The United States is seeing a rise in both.

Religion as Politics

Religion has always been "political"—indeed, manifesting the vision of one's religious beliefs in the political arena is often an essential part of the religion. The great religious leaders, like Moses, Jesus, and Muhammad, found out firsthand that existing authorities find new religious beliefs threatening to their political control.

In the twentieth century, religion has been embroiled in political debates on all sides of the political spectrum. In the former Soviet Union or in China today, just *professing* religion could be threatening to social control by the Communist party, providing an alternative authority structure. In twentieth-century Latin America, **liberation theology** within the Catholic Church was a source of popular mobilization against ruthless political dictators. Liberation theology focuses on Jesus not only as savior but specifically as the savior of the poor and oppressed and emphasizes the Christian mission of bringing justice to the poor.

Most commonly, religious mobilization has aimed to move society to the political right, to restore a conservative agenda of a "Christian America" or an "Islamic Republic." In contemporary America, the mobilization of the Christian right has had an enormous effect on everyday life, from the sorts of books one can read in

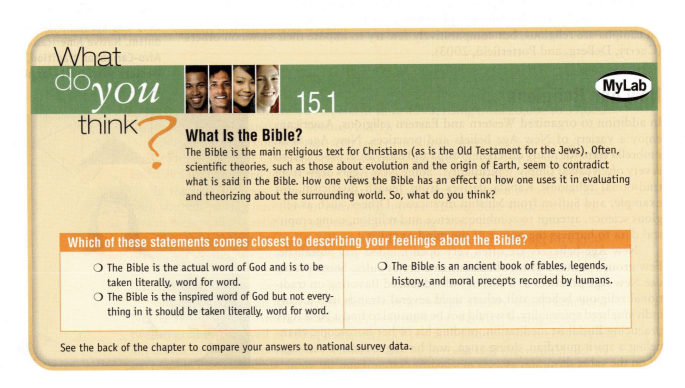

What do *you* think? 15.1 — MyLab

What Is the Bible?

The Bible is the main religious text for Christians (as is the Old Testament for the Jews). Often, scientific theories, such as those about evolution and the origin of Earth, seem to contradict what is said in the Bible. How one views the Bible has an effect on how one uses it in evaluating and theorizing about the surrounding world. So, what do you think?

Which of these statements comes closest to describing your feelings about the Bible?

○ The Bible is the actual word of God and is to be taken literally, word for word.

○ The Bible is the inspired word of God but not everything in it should be taken literally, word for word.

○ The Bible is an ancient book of fables, legends, history, and moral precepts recorded by humans.

See the back of the chapter to compare your answers to national survey data.

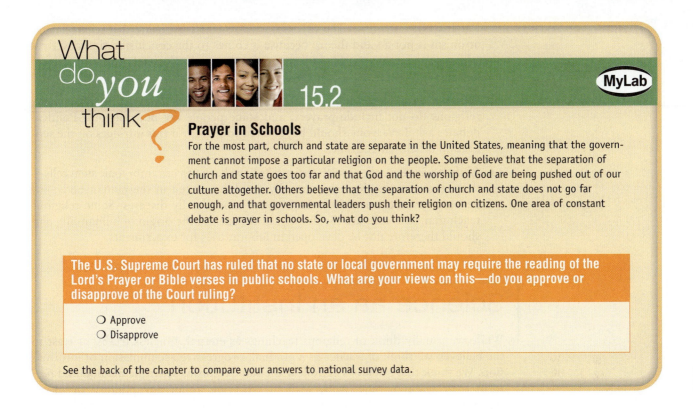

MyLab

Prayer in Schools

For the most part, church and state are separate in the United States, meaning that the government cannot impose a particular religion on the people. Some believe that the separation of church and state goes too far and that God and the worship of God are being pushed out of our culture altogether. Others believe that the separation of church and state does not go far enough, and that governmental leaders push their religion on citizens. One area of constant debate is prayer in schools. So, what do you think?

The U.S. Supreme Court has ruled that no state or local government may require the reading of the Lord's Prayer or Bible verses in public schools. What are your views on this—do you approve or disapprove of the Court ruling?

○ Approve
○ Disapprove

See the back of the chapter to compare your answers to national survey data.

classrooms and libraries, to whom one can fall in love with. A few Muslim countries have instituted shari'a, or the Islamic law outlined in the Koran, which, when strictly interpreted, includes such penalties as cutting off the hand for robbery and death by stoning for adultery. Yet there is evidence that in industrial societies higher rates of religiosity also correlate with higher rates of homicide, juvenile mortality, infections with sexually transmitted diseases, teen pregnancies, and abortion. While religion is surely not the cause of these social problems, perhaps people in the United States feel the protection of the sacred realm more acutely than those in more secular Britain, and so they are more likely to take risks. Or, perhaps, high levels of religiosity lead to social policies that constrain people from more secular protections (Paul, 2005).

The secular side also exerts an influence. While we often hear about religious institutions being intolerant of political diversity, it is also common for secular politics to be intolerant of religious diversity. In the United States, Jehovah's Witnesses have been fined or jailed for refusing to salute the flag. In 2003, French President Jacques Chirac proposed banning the wearing of any religious symbols in French public schools—including Catholic crucifixes, Jewish yarmulkes, Muslim chadors, and Sikh turbans (Sciolino, 2004).

Although the constitutional principle of the separation of church and state was meant to protect liberty and ensure democracy in the United States, it also enabled religion and science to develop and expand separately. In recent years, however, the boundaries between the two have become increasingly blurry, and several political debates currently strain their happy coexistence:

1. *Evolution and creationism.* The majority of U.S. students, and their parents, do not accept the theory of evolution. They propose scientific creationism as an alternative theory that suggests that all current animal and plant species appeared on

Earth at the same time. The vast majority of scientists believe that scientific creationism is not a valid theory because it comes to the conclusion first and then tries to find data that fit. Should creationism be taught alongside evolution in public schools?

2. *School prayer.* Many public schools begin the day with a prayer. However, some religions do not include prayers, and some people are not religious. Political debates ask if everyone should be required to pray or if this infringes on the separation of church and state.

3. *Embryonic stem cell research.* Scientists have begun to use embryonic stem cells—those that can develop into virtually any kind of cell in the human body—to develop new treatments for some of our most deadly diseases. Some religions teach that stem cells are the domain of the sacred, the origin of human life, and should therefore not be developed in laboratories for experiments.

Science as an Institution

While we usually think of religious teachings as eternal, timeless truths, at least to the believer, we think of science as a gradual, progressive accumulation of information. We think that scientists all follow the same rigorous scientific method and perform their research objectively, without worrying about any political or moral implications. We think that scientific breakthroughs are the result of individual genius, a greater-than-the-rest scientist who applies existing research and generates a revolutionary application or theoretical revelation.

Sociologists, however, see science quite differently. Sociologists see communities of scientists working within a particular field, accumulating tidbits of knowledge within a specific theoretical framework, and often censuring those who discover different results. Scientists create rules that govern who gets to do research and who does not. Scientific breakthroughs are the result of the collapse of the old framework under the accumulated weight of new evidence, and the old guard releases its control over the field.

Sociologists observe the interactions among scientists, ranging from the way they interact within a scientific laboratory to the ways they form and sustain scientific communities, groups of scientists working on similar or related problems in a number of different settings. Other sociologists take a more institutional approach, focusing on the role of the scientist and scientific institutions within a society.

Types of Science

Just as there are many different religions, there are many different types of science in the world. Scientists usually practice only one and know little about the others:

1. Biological sciences study living organisms, including microorganisms (microbiology), animals (zoology), plants (botany), physiology, and biochemistry. Medicine and agriculture are applied branches of biological science.

2. The physical sciences study nonliving processes, including the basic physical laws of existence (physics), organic and inorganic matter (chemistry), Earth sciences (geology, meteorology, and oceanography), and the stars and planets (astronomy). The various types of engineering are applied branches of physical science.

3. Mathematics provides the quantitative foundation of all other sciences. Most research is purely theoretical, but there is an applied branch, computer science.

4. Social sciences concern human beings, their mental processes (psychology), culture (anthropology), social structures (sociology), history, economics, and political science. There are several applied branches, including social work and criminal justice.

The Norms of Science

Like all social institutions, science has norms that govern interactions among scientists and relationships between scientists and the rest of society and between scientific institutions and other social institutions. These norms are understood to govern these relationships and set the standards for scientific research. However, as with many other institutional norms, they are honored and ignored in about equal measure.

Objectivity.   The most important norm of science is **objectivity,** in which judgments are based on empirical verification, not on personal feelings or opinions. Scientific knowledge must be based on objective criteria, not on political or personal preferences. Scientists must check their personal lives at the laboratory door, and differences in class, race, and nationality should make no difference in procedure or results. Anyone using the scientific method should be able to arrive at the same conclusions—regardless of his or her personal characteristics.

But how often have you heard the results of research dismissed because of exactly those characteristics? Can we trust social scientific research done by people who do not have the experience they are studying? Would a White person simply be too biased to arrive at any reliable conclusions about Black people? Or would a Black or White person be too biased to reliably research his or her own group?

While a scientific universalism provides one pole, the social response to "advocacy research" provides the other. **Advocacy research** is undertaken to provide the research necessary to support or promote a particular position. One "knows" what one wants to find before undertaking the research, and one intends to use findings to further a cause or group. At the turn of the last century, for example, a research field called phrenology examined the size and shape of people's heads and purported to find factual evidence that women and non-White racial groups were intellectually inferior to White men; therefore, they concluded, gender and racial inequality were "natural." (See Chapter 8.) In the twentieth century, the field of eugenics sought to scientifically breed out "inferior" qualities of Jews and other immigrant groups to create a more "pure" breeding stock of Americans. While for empirically based objective science, seeing is believing, for advocacy research, it's exactly the opposite: Believing is seeing.

Common Ownership. A second norm of science is that scientific knowledge should be open to everyone. Research results should be public knowledge; data should always be shared with colleagues. Technological advances in applied science can be patented, but the pure research, the science behind the technology, is available to all. Einstein never tried to patent his theory of relativity, nor could he have.

The most common method of providing this access is through publication in scholarly journals. Although there is no

Private corporations inject enormous amounts of money into research for new drugs, but they are guided by the marketplace—not human needs or the interests of the scientific community—and seek to control access to their discoveries in order to increase profits. ▼

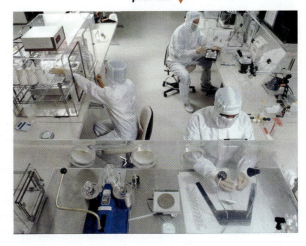

How do we know
what we know?

The Gay Brain

Advocacy research and the questions it raises have become well refined. Take the case of Simon LeVay, a neuroscientist and brain researcher. In the early 1990s, LeVay performed some experiments to determine if sexual orientation had a biological basis (LeVay, 1991, 1994). He examined the brain tissues of 19 gay and bisexual men (all had died of AIDS), and 16 men and 6 women whom he presumed were heterosexual (six of the men and one of the women had died of AIDS). There were no significant differences except in the anterior hypothalamus, a part of the brain about the size of a grain of sand that regulates body temperature, growth, and metabolism.

LeVay found that the anterior hypothalamus of the presumably heterosexual men was approximately twice the size of that of the women and presumably gay men. Was this evidence that, at least in men, sexual orientation was a matter of brain chemistry?

But several questions about the methodology were raised. It turned out that the differences were not uniform, and the sources of his data varied. All the gay men in his sample died of AIDS, a disease known to affect the brain. And all the brains of gay men were preserved in a formaldehyde solution that was of a different strength than the solution in which the brains of heterosexual men were preserved, because of the fears of HIV transmission. Formaldehyde has a definite impact on tissue structure.

Maybe what LeVay was measuring was the combined effect of HIV infection and formaldehyde density, not gay and straight brains. An effort to replicate LeVay's findings failed (Yahr, 1993).

Perhaps the most important question for us, however, is: Does it matter what Simon LeVay's sexual orientation is? Does it change your view of the research to know that LeVay is gay? If so, does it change your view of the research to know that virtually all the prior research undertaken to demonstrate that difference was done by heterosexual researchers? Who is more biased?

Scientists work hard to ensure that their biases are kept in check and that the individual characteristics of the scientist do not "interfere" with their research. But sociologists also understand that the questions one decides are worth asking, and the conclusions one finds (or at least hopes to find) are conditioned by the social lives that scientists—like all the rest of us—actually live.

Did you know?

Nearly 20 percent of all human genes in the human genome are protected by patents, which effectively grant ownership rights for a period of time. Although U.S. and European laws prohibit anyone from patenting a gene as it exists in the human body, institutions have claimed that their unique way of isolating a gene or of developing a specific therapeutic use for it entitles them to patent protection. Of the more than 4,300 genes covered by patents, 63 percent are owned by corporations. (The rest belong to universities.) Most of the patented genes are associated with cancer (Jensen and Murray, 2005; Westphal, 2005).

law that requires publication, scientists feel obliged by the norm of common ownership to publish their studies and to make their data available to anyone who wishes to replicate their studies. For example, the data sets of the General Social Survey are available at cost from NORC (the National Opinion Research Center), so that all social scientists can benefit from their use.

However, this norm of common ownership is constantly being threatened or undermined. As public money for basic research has shrunk in recent years, two "interested" parties have filled the funding gap: the military and private industry. Much scientific research about nuclear fission or on chemical or biological weapons is not published in scholarly journals at all, to avoid giving terrorists and other enemies access to it.

Technological innovations are always privately owned, but it is becoming increasingly difficult to distinguish between pure science and technology. Private corporations, like the pharmaceutical industry, have begun to spend increasing amounts of money on research and development (R&D) of new products. The need is great, and the potential for extraordinary profits is enormous. But the interests of the private company and the scientific community often conflict: The company wants to keep the results of its research private, lest competitors gain access to the information, and scientists want to disseminate those findings widely because of their potential benefit to the public and to future scientific research.

These two interests came to a boil in 2001, as two teams raced to complete the mapping of the human genome. One team was funded by a private company, and the other was part of a government laboratory. Many believed that if the private company "won" the race, they would "own" the map of the human genome and could establish patents on human genetic sequences. (Eventually the two groups compromised and shared the publication of the map of the human genome.)

As scientific projects become increasingly complex, government, universities, and private companies will increasingly share the funding costs and the results. The norm of common ownership will be increasingly difficult to follow.

Disinterestedness. Another important norm of science is **disinterestedness.** Scientific research should not be conducted for personal goals, such as fame or glory, and certainly not for money, but for the pursuit of scientific truth.

Unfortunately, this norm is constantly undermined. As we have seen, the new partnerships between universities and private corporations push scientists away from performing basic research and more toward applied research. Second, the enormous amount of money that is possible if one has a financial interest in discoveries that can be big business—drugs, energy, weapons, for example—also lures science away from the disinterested pursuit of truth.

▲ Social dynamics, such as the power of scientific networks, different access to prestigious journals, collegial connections, and in-group recommendations for large research grants—and not overt prejudice—are more likely to explain the relative absence of women and some minorities (like African Americans) in science.

Scientific Networks

Popular images of scientific work often depict the mad scientist, his hair wild and unkempt, his eyes glazed over in demented genius, working all day and all night alone in his laboratory. All of a sudden, he has his revelation, his "Eureka!" moment, and he makes a new discovery. Such a view is unrealistic. Science is work, and like most forms of work, it is a collaborative effort, requiring the interaction of many different people with different roles, tasks, and social locations.

Sociologists around the world are interested in "the network of communication and social relationships between scientists working in given fields or in all fields" (Ben-David, 1984, p. 3). These scientists develop rules of conduct, and those who do not accept these rules are excluded from scientific networks. Established scientists control research by acting as gatekeepers: They edit and review articles for scientific journals and decide who receives research grants. If you don't do science by their rules, you don't get to do science.

In that sense, science is no different from any other workplace. Those at the top of the scientific hierarchy are the gatekeepers, making sure that scientific research conforms to what *they* think is worthy. In other words, scientific communities are like religious elites: They decide what the doctrine says, how you are to think about it, and what you can and cannot know.

These sociological dynamics better explain the continued lack of women, for example, at the highest reaches of science and engineering professorships, as well as the abundance of Asian men, but not Latino or African American men, in those positions. And those groups are consistently paid less than White males. In one study, even after accounting for seniority, experience, and age, female scientists earned 23 percent less than their male counterparts ("Mind the Gap," 2006). This is not the result of individual malevolence; indeed, many university departments claim to be eager to hire women and minorities. But the work they believe qualifies as breakthrough science and the unexamined prejudices they may harbor often conspire to form

TABLE 15.6

	FEMALE (%)	MALE (%)	WHITE (%)	ASIAN (%)	BLACK (%)	HISPANIC (%)
Working Scientists: Employment in Science and Engineering by Gender and Race						
All science and engineering	27	73	75	14	4.3	4.3
Biological/life scientist	43.3	56.5	76	14	3.7	4.2
Computer and information scientist	27.6	72.4	71	18.2	5	3.9
Mathematical scientist	60	40	76.5	11.6	7.4	3
Physical sciences	28.5	71.5	79	12.2	2.7	4
Engineers	11	89	77	12.5	3.3	5

Source: Adapted from National Science Foundation, 2006.

barriers that are difficult to overcome. Changing the gender and racial composition of the scientific community will take more than simply adding a few women or minorities; it will require changing the structure of the enterprise itself.

Scientific Breakthroughs

Scientific breakthroughs happen much the same ways that religions change. In religion, everyone is taught to believe the same thing and interpret the sacred teachings the same way, but occasionally someone comes along who begins to interpret them a little differently and manages to convince others through sheer strength of character (what Weber called "charisma"). "You have heard . . . ," said Jesus, "but I say unto you . . . ," and his followers took his word over other teachings.

Often the charismatic leaders who seek to change religious teachings are branded as heretics and condemned by religious authorities. Sometimes they are exiled or even executed.

In a pathbreaking study of the history of science, Thomas Kuhn (1962), a theoretical physicist, proposed that science changes in a similar way. Instead of scientific progress being gradual and linear, it is erratic and often unpredictable. Long periods of dull routine science are punctuated by dramatic breakthroughs, just as long periods of religious stability are broken by revivals, reformations, and Great Awakenings.

Kuhn observed that, most of the time, scientists accept prevailing theories as true and organize their experiments *within* the existing framework. At any one time, there is a prevailing paradigm, or model, and scientists work within the paradigm. This is what Kuhn calls "normal" science. Normal science follows social customs: Older, more established scientists train younger ones to work within the existing fields of knowledge. These younger scientists extend the reach of the paradigm, but they seldom dare to challenge the paradigm itself. If they do, they often find they don't get published, receive research grants, or get tenure.

Yet sometimes, scientists doing normal science find results they cannot explain by existing theories. Initially, the scientific establishment discredits these "anomalies" (findings that differ from the norm) and gives the cold shoulder to the scientists. But eventually, these anomalies are too numerous and too significant to ignore. And then, the old paradigm is replaced by a new one, one that can explain the older research

Sociology and our World

Is Pluto a Planet?

In August 2006, astronomers "demoted" Pluto from its status as the ninth planet to a new status as "dwarf planet." It is too small (one-fifth the size of Earth's moon), and its orbit is influenced by Neptune's. While some may mourn Pluto being kicked out of the solar system, the decision also reveals how science works. Scientists are constantly testing their theories against empirical findings, refining and even rejecting theories as the evidence no longer supports earlier reasoning. In science, if new information does not support prevailing theory, the theory is revisited—and revised or refined. Religious knowledge, by contrast, must always refer to the received wisdom of a canonical text like the Bible and therefore is more likely to interpret the evidence to fit the theory.

and the new findings as well. In this way, long periods of normal science are punctuated by these scientific breakthroughs.

The Role of the Scientist and Society

Until the sixteenth century, individual members of the Church or nobility financed scientific research. This form of private support for science (as well as the arts) is called patronage, and it enabled many influential scientists to conduct their research in the absence of government or university jobs. Gradually, in the seventeenth and eighteenth century, European scientists were increasingly supported by the government, through subsidies and grants. Groups of scientists joined together into colleges and universities, under government sponsorship, to pursue their increasingly complex and expensive research. By the twentieth century, most scientific breakthroughs were made by professors, working in state-funded laboratories on university campuses.

Take, for example, the history of the Nobel Prize. During the nineteenth century, European scientists were heavily supported by the government. But two world wars, with a depression between, all but eliminated the money for government support in Europe. At the same time, the development of graduate training in the sciences and the space race with the Soviet Union after World War II propelled the United States into scientific leadership in the world. As a result, the number of European scientists who have won a Nobel Prize in the sciences has fallen, while the number of Americans has grown dramatically (www.Nobelprize.org). (We should point out, however, that many of the American Nobel laureates have been immigrants, who received their training in Europe and came to the United States to escape Nazi or Communist regimes.)

Today, scientific research around the world is supported both by governments, through grants for research, and by private companies, which employ scientists to develop new products—everything from new types of paint to robots that can land on the moon, from flavoring for soda to genetically modified crops that grow faster, stronger, or more plentifully even in adverse climates.

Typically, private enterprise and government fund different aspects of research. The government funds basic science—that is, scientific research that has no immediate application other than the furtherance of knowledge. Private companies are interested in developing new products, and they fund research that has possibilities for commercial application. In addition, large-scale scientific research requires so much money in start-up costs that global scientific cooperation has become the norm, as different groups, operating in different countries, often specialize in some smaller piece of the larger puzzle.

Of course these government and private foundations often overlap. For example, the search for a cure for HIV or cancer will both be a breakthrough of basic research and also will have immediate application in the treatment of illness.

Recently, however, foundations, states, and university consortiums have stepped in to many high-profile areas where neither government nor private companies have been willing to go. For example, in 2005, the Bill and Melinda Gates Foundation gave $750 million toward basic vaccine science and development, pursuing the prevention and treatment for diseases afflicting poor countries of low priority to for-profit drug companies. Within the United States, the state of California has floated a $3 billion bond issue to fund stem cell research in the wake of the Bush administration's cutoff in 2001 of federal funding for such cutting-edge research on religious grounds. The state of New Jersey has already begun to allocate millions to stem cell research. Several universities have set up privately funded stem cell research programs, including University of California, San Francisco (which raised $11 million), Stanford ($12 million), and Harvard (which hopes to raise $100 million).

Science and Religion in the 21st Century

As a society, we are becoming increasingly scientific. Human beings are curious about the world and always want to understand it better; science gives them that opportunity. On an almost daily basis, scientists change how we understand the world—from the furthest reaches of the universe to the tiniest subatomic particles.

We are also becoming increasingly religious. Human beings are also spiritual beings, and religion helps us navigate our way through the spiritual world. Some religious institutions may decline in membership, but others are growing dramatically, and new ones are constantly arising.

And then there is the "science of religion" and the "religion of science." Some scientists are attempting to explain religion scientifically, proposing that there is a "God gene," or that human beings, unlike other species, are either biologically programmed or evolutionarily adapted to believe in the supernatural (see, for example, Dennett, 2006; Harris, 2004). Evolutionary biologist Richard Dawkins (2007) argues that morality results largely from genetic instincts evolved because humans benefit from cooperation and that religion itself is a by-product of mental abilities evolved for other reasons. Children, he argues, are "wired" to believe what their parents tell them because so much of what parents impart is useful or essential information. But this programming is vulnerable to error, becoming an avenue for useless information that gets passed along for no other reason than tradition.

At the same time, some evangelical ministers use scientific skepticism (one can never be absolutely certain that scientific discoveries are the truth) to question biological facts like evolution or geological facts like the age of Earth. A 2006 *Time* magazine poll found that nearly two-thirds (64 percent) of Americans say they would continue to believe what their religion teaches—even if scientists proved it to be wrong (Masci, 2007).

Some scholars predict a long period of tension between religion and science, followed by the triumph of one over the other. However, it seems just as likely that religion and science will coexist, as the growth of both religious ideas and scientific progress in the United States seems to suggest. Politically, there is always a danger that either religious fanatics or antireligious totalitarians will seize control of a country, as in Iran or Afghanistan as well as the former Soviet Union and China. But even there, it seems impossible to eradicate religion or science. In Iran today, science is undergoing a dramatic increase, just as under Soviet rule, many continued to practice their religions. Science and religion may even "need" each other: As Albert Einstein once commented, "Science without religion is lame, and religion without science is blind" (cited in Lazare, 2007, p. 26). It seems that the human quest to know and understand one's world, and one's place in it, is as basic and unquenchable as human life itself.

Chapter Review

1. *How do religion and science compare?* Religion and science have been in an ongoing global debate about life's big questions and the different methods of discovering answers. Historically, religion has provided the dominant view; the dominance of science is relatively new. Scientific findings and facts are often not in sync with religious facts, yet science and religion continue to coexist. Science and religion have similarities; they are both organized and coherent systems of thought leading to truth. Religion focuses on larger questions, while science focuses on the smaller ones. Both change over time.

2. *What does religion do?* While religion is a cultural universal, it varies between cultures. Durkheim focused on how religion serves as social cohesion by integrating individuals into society and holding society together. Rituals help remind people they are part of something bigger. Conflict theorists such as Marx saw religion as a tool of social control. It gave people a reason to adhere to norms and prevented revolt. Weber studied the relationship between the Protestant ethic and capitalism and the impact of religious ideas on economic activity; he said religion was a catalyst for social change.

3. *What forms do religious groups take?* The simplest form of religious organization is a cult. Cults usually form around a specific charismatic leader, engender significant loyalty, are small, and often live on the margins of society. A sect also breaks from established religious institutions but is a subculture, not a counterculture. Denominations are large-scale, extremely organized structures with an established hierarchy that garner social respect. The United States is overwhelmingly of the Christian denomination. Ecclesiae are state religions, where the boundary between the state and the church is nonexistent.

4. *What are the religions of the world, and how does religion manifest in modern society?* Judaism, Christianity, and Islam originated in the Middle East and are referred to as Western religions. The three share many beliefs and practices; they are exclusive, evangelistic, and monotheistic. All three are divided into denominations and sects, and all have extreme groups and members who are fundamentalists. Hinduism, Confucianism, and Buddhism arose in Asia. They also have much in common, such as having more than one god and believing in reincarnation. Early sociologists thought religion would be replaced by secularization, but that has not occurred. Religious expression varies dramatically between societies. It has a stronger hold in developing countries. Europe is more secularized, and the United States is more religious.

5. *What does religion look like in the United States?* The United States is one of the world's most church-going societies. As a nation of religious immigrants, the United States has gone through waves of increased religious passion. Americans have democratized religion, and religious institutions provide social support and cultural interaction. American beliefs are modified to be sacred and secular at the same time. The United States is going through another religious revival with the evangelical movement, which fits American values. Americans claim high religiosity but have low knowledge levels of religion. There are differences in religiosity; women are more religious than men, and rural dwellers are more religious than urban. Religion also varies by race; Hispanics are overwhelmingly Catholic, and Blacks are overwhelmingly Protestant. Blacks and Whites maintain separate churches; Black churches have historically also been used for political mobilization.

6. *How does science function as an institution?* There are many types of science, but all are governed by scientific norms such as objectivity, common ownership, and a lack of personal interest in the outcome of research. Sociologists look at scientists the way they look at any workplace. There are gatekeepers, which results in gender and racial inequality within the disciplines. Sociologists also look at the role of scientists in society, including their sources of financial support from private foundations or government.

KeyTerms

Advocacy research (p. 511)
BCE and CE (p. 494)
Buddhism (p. 497)
Charismatic leader (p. 489)
Christianity (p. 495)
Civil religion (p. 490)
Confucianism (p. 498)
Cult (p. 491)
Cultural universal (p. 489)
Denomination (p. 493)
Disinterestedness (p. 513)

Ecclesiae (p. 493)
Empirical verification (p. 488)
Fundamentalsim (p. 496)
Hinduism (p. 497)
Islam (p. 495)
Jihad (p. 496)
Judaism (p. 495)
Liberation theology (p. 508)
New Age (p. 507)
Objectivity (p. 511)
Profane (p. 489)

Religion (p. 488)
Religiosity (p. 491)
Revelation (p. 488)
Rituals (p. 490)
Sacred (p. 489)
Science (p. 488)
Sect (p. 492)
Secularization (p. 498)
Syncretic religions (p. 497)
Third Great Awakening (p. 501)
World religions (p. 494)

What does *America* think?

15.1   What Is the Bible?

These are actual survey data from the General Social Survey, 1998.

Which of these statements comes closest to describing your feelings about the Bible? Thirty percent of respondents felt that the Bible was the literal word of God. Almost half believed it was God inspired, and 17 percent thought it was a book of fables. Social class differences were significant; the higher one's social status the less likely one was to believe the Bible was the word of God.

CRITICAL THINKING | DISCUSSION QUESTION

1. Why do you think social class differences were so striking? What might lead someone from the lower class, for example, to have stronger views on the Bible being literal than someone from the upper class?

15.2 Prayer in Schools

These are actual survey data from the General Social Survey, 2004.

The U.S. Supreme Court has ruled that no state or local government may require the reading of the Lord's Prayer or Bible verses in public schools. What are your views on this—do you approve or disapprove of the Court ruling? Overall, almost 37 percent of respondents approved of the ruling, while 63 percent disapproved of the ruling. Men were more likely than women to approve of the ruling.

CRITICAL THINKING | DISCUSSION QUESTION

1. Why do you think men were more likely than women to approve of the ruling?

▶ Go to this website to look further at the data. You can run your own statistics and crosstabs here: **http://sda.berkeley.edu/cgi-bin/hsda?harcsda+gss04**

REFERENCES: Davis, James A., Tom W. Smith, and Peter V. Marsden. General Social Surveys 1972–2004: [Cumulative file] [Computer file]. 2nd ICPSR version. Chicago, IL: National Opinion Research Center [producer], 2005; Storrs, CT: Roper Center for Public Opinion Research, University of Connecticut; Ann Arbor, MI: Inter-University Consortium for Political and Social Research; Berkeley, CA: Computer-Assisted Survey Methods Program, University of California [distributors], 2005.

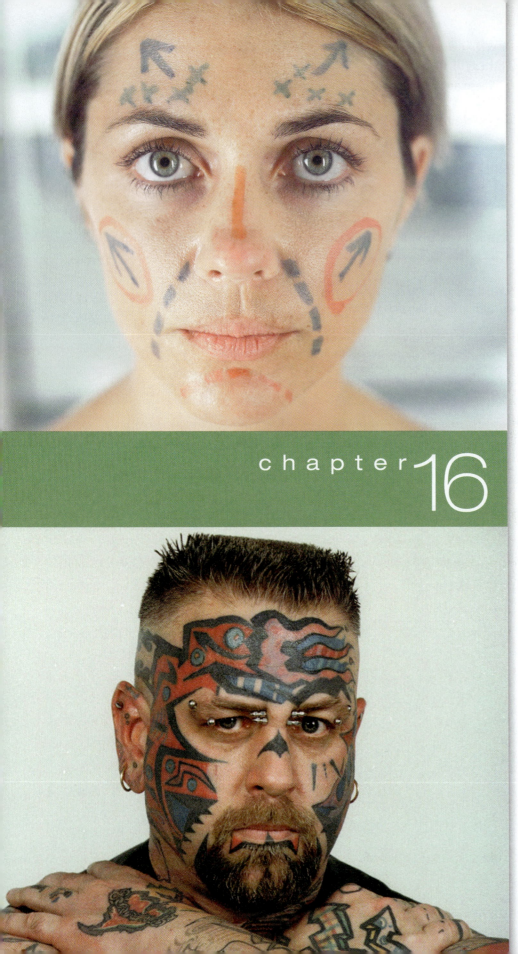

chapter 16

ON A WARM SUMMER NIGHT, August 7, 2007, Barry Bonds hit the 756th home run of his career, passing Hank Aaron as the all-time Major League Baseball home run leader (Saduharo Oh of the Yomiuri Giants in Japan remains the world record holder with 822 in his career). Hitting a 90-plus-mile-an-hour fastball 400 feet in the air takes a significant amount of power—but also eye–hand coordination, catlike reflexes, and remarkable agility.

Perhaps it also takes drugs. For the last few years of his career, Bonds has been plagued by accusations that he took anabolic steroids to increase his size, bulk, and power. Some have suggested that his record have a permanent asterisk affixed to note that it was not accomplished naturally. Photographs of his early years compared with his later career show a body that has changed as much as Michael Jackson's face over the same amount of time.

The public debate about Bonds's

The Body and Society: Health and Illness

achievement almost inevitably turns on either/or questions: Did he take steroids or not? Did he "really" break the record or not? But to the sociologist, the lines are never as clear. After all, virtually every athlete uses some form of chemical elixir—from Gatorade to surgery—to enhance performance. And steroids may increase size and power, but they do nothing about speed or eye–hand coordination.

There are few things more personal and private than our bodies, and few things that are more shaped by social processes. Our bodies are ourselves, as the women's health handbook told us, but they are also profoundly social.

More than that, these debates indicate something deeply social about our bodies. On the one hand, we may experience them as private possessions, over which we exercise complete control. From childhood, we're taught that no one can touch our bodies without permission and that respecting others means respecting the sanctity of their bodies. That our body is our own property is the foundation principle of many laws, including all crimes against a person, child abuse, rape laws, and women's reproductive rights.

But on the other hand, our bodies are subject to enormous social control—what we can and cannot do to them, with them, and for them. How we present our bodies; the risks we are permitted to pose to them; the responsibility we bear for injury, disability, or disease—all are subject to social scrutiny and control.

Is the body an individual possession or a social space? To the sociologist, it's both. There are few things more personal and private than our bodies and few things that are more shaped by social processes. Our bodies are ourselves, as the women's health handbook told us, but they are also profoundly social.

The Social Construction of the Body

"I used to hate my body. Now, instead, I hate the forces that conspire to make me hate my body."

© The New Yorker Collection 2000 William Haefeli from cartoonbank.com. All Rights Reserved. Reprinted by permission.

When sociologists talk about the body, we do so in three distinct ways. First we discuss the ways in which we construct our identity through our bodies: what we think is beautiful, for example, or the ways we adorn and transform them to fit with cultural norms. Second, we discuss the ways in which our interactions are *embodied*—that is, the ways in which we use our bodies in interacting with others. And, third, we discuss the ways that social institutions use those bodies—in work or family life, for example, disciplining and training bodies to participate in social life (Lorber and Moore, 2007; Weitz, 2002).

The Sociology of Beauty

What we think of as beautiful is less a matter of individual perception and more about ever-shifting cultural standards. Standards of beauty vary enormously from culture to culture, and, within the United States, among different racial and ethnic groups, ages, and even classes. In general, standards of women's beauty vary depending on economic trends and the status of women: When the economy goes up, women's standards become increasingly "feminine," exaggerating biological differences to suggest that male breadwinners can afford to have their wives stay at home. When women's status rises, men tend to become more interested in their own upper-body muscles, and beards and mustaches increase. In some Islamic cultures, women are believed to be so sexually alluring (and men so unable to control themselves when confronted with temptation) that they wear burkhas, which keep their entire bodies covered.

In the United States, women's beauty is placed at such a high premium and the standards of beauty are so narrow that many women feel trapped by what feminist writer Naomi Wolf (1991) called the "beauty myth"— a nearly unreachable cultural ideal of feminine beauty that "uses images of female beauty as a political weapon against women's advancement." By this standard, women are trapped in an endless cycle of cosmetics, beauty aids, diets, and exercise fanaticism (Wolf, 1991, pp. 10, 184; see also Rodin, Silberstein, and Streigel-Moore, 1985; Streigel-Moore, Silberstein, and Rodin, 1986).

Weight and Height. The body shape and weight that is considered ideal also varies enormously. And it appears that standards are becoming harder and harder to achieve. For example, in 1954, Miss America was 5' 8" and weighed 132 pounds. Today, the average Miss America contestant still stands 5' 8", but now she weighs just 117 pounds. In 1975, the average female fashion model weighed about 8 percent less than the average American woman; by 1990 that disparity had grown to 23 percent. And though the average American woman today is 5' 4" tall and weighs 140 pounds, the average model is 5' 11" and weighs 117 pounds. Forty-two percent of girls in first through third grades say they want to be thinner, and 81 percent of 10-year-olds are afraid of being fat. Almost half of 9- to 11-year-olds are on diets; by college the percentage has nearly doubled (Gimlin, 2002).

Just as the gap between rich and poor has been growing, so too has the bifurcation between the embodied haves and have-nots. For example, Europeans are getting taller—but Americans are not. Dutch men now average over six feet tall; women average about 5' 8". (American men average 5' 10" and women 5' 4"). Researchers believe

Sociology and our World

White or Wrong?

Over the past decade, a whiter skin industry has been flourishing across Asia. Women believe that the whiter your skin, the more beautiful you are. In the Philippines, Malaysia, Hong Kong, Taiwan, and South Korea, 4 in every 10 women use a whitening cream daily. One cream is called "White Perfect." An ad for another asks, "White or Wrong?"

And the whitening does not stop at the face. Also crowding the shelves of pharmacies and supermarkets are creams that whiten darker patches of skin in the armpits and "pink nipple" lotions that bleach away brown pigment. Some of the most effective bleaching agents may be risky to one's health.

Small groups of women in Asia are bucking the trend. In Japan, for example, some young women have been regulars at tanning salons for a decade.

Why would Asians, who are divided by language, ethnicity, and religion, share a cultural preference for ever-whiter skin? Social class may play a role. Lighter complexion may be associated with wealth and higher education levels because those from lower classes—laborers, farmers—are tanned from exposure to the sun. Another hypothesis is that waves of lighter-skinned conquerors and colonizers reset the standard for beauty. More recently, films and advertising have clearly played a role (Fuller, 2006).

FIGURE 16.1 The Battle of the Bulge

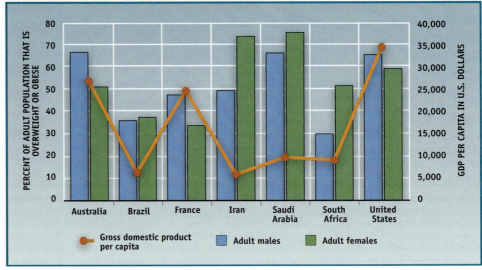

Source: "Overweight and Obese Adults" from "The Battle of the Bulge" by Kelly D. Brownell and Derek Yach, *Foreign Policy,* December 2005. Reprinted by permission.

that this has to do with nutrition and general health of the population. (Researchers are careful to screen so that only native-born citizens who speak English at home are included, thus preventing bias from immigrant groups that are somewhat shorter than average, like Chinese or Mexicans.) In addition, the Dutch have the best pre- and post-natal health care in the world—and it's free for all citizens.

These differences are more important than predicting basketball games. Tall people have significant advantages: They get married sooner, get promoted more quickly, and receive higher wages. Taller boys are the first ones to get dates. One recent study found that a 6' worker earns $166,000 more over a 30 year period than a 5' 5" co-worker—that's $800 per inch per year (Bilger, 2004). The tall get richer, and the rich get taller.

About weight, too, there is a significant irony. Wealthy countries worry about obesity; poor countries worry about malnutrition and starvation. Developing countries, particularly those that are realizing economic gains due to globalization, are in between, seeing waistlines expand with economic development that includes urbanization, less exercise, and high-fat foods that are cheap and readily available (Figure 16.1).

But within the developed countries, the rich are significantly thinner than the poor. The wealthier you are, the more likely you are to eat well and exercise regularly; poorer people eat more convenience foods with high fats and suffer more weight-related illnesses, like diabetes.

In the United States, we're both fatter and thinner. In 1990, 11.3 percent of Americans were obese; by 2000 it was nearly 20 percent; in 2006, it was 32 percent. (Obesity is measured as having a body mass index [BMI] of over 30; [Centers for Disease Control, 2007]). About one out of three Americans under age 19, and about two-thirds of all adults, qualify as overweight or obese (Hellmich, 2006). And about 5 percent of Americans are "morbidly obese," which is so obese that they qualify for radical surgery (Crister, 2003).

Within the Americas, the United States is by far the fattest country (International Obesity Task Force, 2007), but that weight gain was unevenly distributed throughout our society. The average American is a

Did *you* know ?

Body mass index, or BMI, is a new term to most people. However, it is the measurement of choice for many physicians and researchers studying obesity. BMI uses a mathematical formula that takes into account both a person's height and weight. BMI equals a person's weight in kilograms divided by height in meters squared (BMI = kg/m²).

bit chubbier, but overweight Americans are *much* heavier now than ever. According to the National Health and Nutrition Examination survey, America's BMI has moved towards the extremes; that is, the thin are getting thinner, and the fat are getting fatter. We're either exercising obsessively or sedentary couch potatoes, eating tofu and organic raw vegetables or Big Macs and supersized fried foods.

The five states with the highest levels of obesity are Mississippi, where nearly 30 percent of the population is obese, followed by Alabama, West Virginia, Tennessee, and Louisiana. The five states with the lowest levels are Colorado, at 16.7 percent, Massachusetts, Vermont, Rhode Island, and Connecticut (Centers for Disease Control, 2007).

Inequalities of class, race, and gender fuel these trends. Among Mexican American women, for example, those below the poverty line have a 13 percent higher obesity rate than those above it. About 16 to 26 percent of Hispanic and Black Americans have diabetes, one of the possible medical consequences of obesity, compared with 12 percent of Whites (Crister, 2003, pp. 4–5) (Table 16.1).

Once a modest girth was a sign of prosperity; today it is the poor who are more likely to be heavy. Diets of cheap fast food coupled with significantly less exercise lead to unhealthier lives. Many poor people don't know that exercise is good for their health. In 2000, 37 percent of people whose income was less than $25,000 agreed with the statement "There are so many conflicting reports, I don't know if exercise is good or bad for me," compared with 14 percent of those making between $50,000 and $75,000 and 12 percent of those making more than $75,000. Two-thirds of those making more than $50,000 said they "would definitely exercise more if I had the time," while less than half (46 percent) of those under $25,000 said they would (cited in Crister, 2003, p. 71). Among young people, the best predictors of being overweight are how much exercise one gets and what types of food one eats (Crister, 2003).

Globally, obesity is a growing health problem, the mirror image of hunger and starvation. The World Health Organization claims that there are now as many overnourished people as undernourished around the world; they call obesity "the dominant unmet global health issue" (Crister, 2003, p. 1; see also Newman, 2004). The World Health Organization gathered information about obesity from 36 different countries between 2000 and 2004 and found that 29 of them—including New Zealand, Mexico, Finland, Israel, Canada, Australia, Ireland, Peru, Sweden, Belgium, and Brazil—have fewer obesity-related public health problems than does the United States (World Health Organization, 2007).

Obesity is coupled with starvation and malnourishment in many developing societies as well. Recent surveys in India find consistently high levels of malnourishment among children and dramatically increasing obesity, despite record levels of economic development. Over half of all Indian children between 10 and 16 years old are either obese or malnourished (Sengupta, 2006).

Despite their connection, we think of starvation and obesity very differently. We have pity for the hungry and donate significantly to charities that minister to hunger. We have contempt for the obese and believe it is their fault that they are fat. Both hunger and obesity are

TABLE 16.1

U.S. Obesity: Percent by Race and Class			
	ANNUAL INCOME		
	$10,000 OR LESS	20–25,000	50,000 OR MORE
White	19	20	16
Black	33	27	23
Hispanic	26	18	22

Source: Adapted from Crister, 2003.

Obesity has become a global problem, not restricted to industrialized consumer societies. And imported images of the beautiful body, as in the poster looking over this Chinese teenager's shoulder, also become the standard against which everyone is measured. ▼

▲ Most girls are preoccupied with body image and their weight—at least most middle-class White girls are (body image varies by class and race). At one end of the continuum are fad diets and efforts to stay fit and in shape. At the other end lie dangerous, and potentially lethal, eating disorders, such as anorexia.

physical responses to a changed environment. The hungry can no longer consume their own food because of the transformation of subsistence agriculture and overfarming of arid land; the obese are also responding to a new dietary environment of supersized fast foods, the use of cheaper saturated fats in fast foods, and the partnering of fast food companies with school lunch programs.

Feeding and Starving the Female Body. Current standards of beauty for women combine two images—dramatically thin and also muscular and buxom—that are virtually impossible to accomplish. Research on adolescents suggests that a large majority consciously trade off health concerns in their efforts to lose weight. As a result, increasing numbers of young women are diagnosed with either anorexia nervosa or bulimia every year. **Anorexia nervosa** involves chronic and dangerous starvation dieting and obsessive exercise; **bulimia** typically involves "binging and purging" (eating large quantities and then either vomiting or taking enemas to excrete them). These are serious problems, often requiring hospitalization, which can, if untreated, threaten a girl's life. To a sociologist they represent only the farthest reaches of a continuum of preoccupation with the body that begins with such "normal" behaviors as compulsive exercise or dieting.

It is important to remember that rates of anorexia and bulimia are higher in the United States than in any other country—by far. Estimates in the United States calculate that 3.7 percent of American women suffer from anorexia at some point in their lifetime; up to 4.2 percent struggle with bulimia at some point in life (U.S. Department of Health and Human Services, 2006). In Europe, about 0.3 percent of women suffer from anorexia and around 1 percent from bulimia—more than ten times less than the United States (Hoek and van Hoeken, 2003). By contrast, many non-Western societies value plumpness, and throughout Europe and the United States, non-White girls are far less likely to exhibit eating disorders than are White and middle-class girls. Recent increases have been observed among young middle- and upper-class Japanese women (Efron, 2005).

While some stereotypic understandings would have it that such a dramatic emphasis on thinness afflicts only middle- and upper-class White girls and women, the evidence suggests that these standards also define working-class and Black ideals of the feminine body. Largeness "was one accepted—even revered—among Black folks," lamented an article in *Essence* magazine in 1994, but it "now carries the same unmistakable stigma as it does among Whites" (Gregory, 1994). And a study the following year found that Black adolescent girls demonstrated significantly higher drive for thinness than did White adolescent girls. The media coverage of Oprah's dramatic weight loss and the depiction of ultra-thin African American models and actresses may have increased Black women's anxieties about their weight; indeed, it may be a perverse signal of assimilation and acceptance by the dominant culture that "their" ideal body type is now embraced by the formerly marginalized (Fitzgibbon and Stolley, 2000; Schreiber et al., 1995).

Pumping up the Male Body. Men have become increasingly concerned with their bodies, especially fitness and weight. While men have long been concerned about appearing strong, the emphasis on big muscles seems to increase as an obsession during periods when men are least likely to actually have to use their muscles in their

Try It Body Image and Eating Disorders

Developed by Katherine R. Rowell, *Sinclair Community College.*

OBJECTIVE: Examine the research on body image and eating disorders.

STEP 1: Research

Take some time to read some of the reviews of body image research available on the Internet. Websites like the Social Issues Research Centre and the Media Awareness Network are good places to start.

STEP 2: Develop

Participate in an online body image survey by going to the Monash University website and searching for "open learning psyII." Click on the top result. (Please note that some instructors may also ask you to look at the collated data for this project and answer some questions about the data; directions for this option will be given in class.)

Answer the following questions on a separate sheet of paper:

1. What does body image research suggest about gender and body image?
2. What did you think about this survey? How accurate do you think it might be? What are some of the potential problems with an online survey?
3. What differences would you expect to find between men and women on this survey? Explain.
4. How might you study the topic of body image?
5. What if anything does this have to do with eating disorders? Cite some sources for this question.
6. How does all of this relate to sociology?

STEP 3: Discuss

Bring your responses to class and be prepared to share and discuss your thoughts on this assignment.

---

work (Gagnon, 1971; Glassner, 1988). Today, successful new men's magazines like *Men's Health* encourage men to see their bodies as women have been taught to see theirs—as ongoing works-in-progress. In part, this coincides with general concerns about health and fitness, and in part it is about looking young in a society that does not value aging. But more than that, it also seems to be about gender.

Men's bodily anxieties mirror those of women (see Bordo, 2000). While women are concerned with breast size and weight, men are concerned with muscularity—that is, both are preoccupied with those aspects of the male and female body that suggest and exaggerate innate biological differences between the sexes. It would appear that the more equal women and men become in the public sphere, the more standards of beauty would emphasize those aspects that are biologically different.

Many men experience what some researchers have labeled **muscle dysmorphia**, a belief that one is too small, insufficiently muscular. Harvard psychiatrist Harrison Pope and his colleagues call it the **Adonis complex**—the belief that men must look like Greek gods, with perfect chins, thick hair, rippling muscles, and washboard abdominals (Pope, Phillips, and Olivardia, 2000).

Take, for example, those two icons of ideal femininity and masculinity, GI Joe and Barbie. Their proportions are so unrealistic that if they existed in real life, they couldn't function. But they've also changed over time. Barbie's measurements have changed dramatically, in part because of pressure by feminists. In the 1990s, she went from measuring 38-18-34, to the "Happy to Be Me" Barbie in 1998 who measured 36-27-38. In 2003, Mattel launched the "It's a New Barbie World" for a younger "tween" audience; she measured 30-19-32—somewhat more supermodelish, but also less curvy. "Barbie may only be a doll," wrote one irate mom to the company, " but when some little girl's best friend and role model is a doll, we have to consider what will become of young girls when they grow up" (Hand, 2003).

The standards for men are increasingly impossible. In 1974, GI Joe was 5' 10" tall and had a 31-inch waist, a 44-inch chest, and 12-inch biceps. Strong and muscular, but

performed worldwide in 2004, second only to the Americas. Asians, South Americans, and Arabs are also undergoing cosmetic procedures in increasing numbers. As in the United States, these procedures are becoming increasingly affordable to the middle class and are being sought by men as well as women. The popularity of different procedures, however, does vary by country.

- In Japan, South Korea, Singapore, Colombia, Russia, and Romania, eyelid surgery is the top operation.
- In Brazil, Argentina and Germany, liposuction is the most popular.
- In Spain, Italy, Great Britain, Sweden, Norway, and Slovenia, breast augmentation is the procedure performed most frequently.
- In Jordon, Lebanon, Cyprus, Turkey, Taiwan, and France, nose reshaping tops the list.

Why eyelid surgery across Asia? Why nose work in the Middle East? Perhaps we are seeing an emerging global standard of beauty due to globalization. Not only are people living and working in more multinational settings, but also Western images long exported worldwide by magazines, movies, and television have been accelerated in recent years by the addition of satellite TV and the Internet. Like globalization in other arenas, some influence goes both ways, but the dominant tendency is for beauty standards to trend from West to East (Guteri and Hastings, 2003; Lewis, 2005).

Changing Identity by Changing the Gendered Body: Transgenderism. Transgenderism is an umbrella term that describes a variety of people, behaviors, and groups whose identities depart from normative gender ideals of masculinity or femininity. Transgendered individuals develop a gender identity that is different from the biological sex of their birth; they array themselves along a continuum from those who act in public as members of the sex other than the sex they were born, to those who chemically (through hormone therapy) or surgically transform their bodies into the body of the other gender. Transgenderism implies no sexual orientation—transgendered individuals identify as heterosexual, homosexual, bisexual, or asexual.

Think of gender identity and behavior along a continuum from "our culture's definition of masculine" to "our culture's definition of feminine." Some people feel constrained by gender role expectations and seek to expand these by changing their behavior. Though there are significant penalties for boys who are effeminate ("sissies") and some, but fewer, penalties for girls who are "tomboys," many adult men and women continue to bend, if not break, gender norms in their bodily presentation. Some may go as far as to use the props of the opposite sex to challenge gender stereotypes; some people find erotic enjoyment in this, while others do it to "pass" into a forbidden world. Again, this runs along a continuum: At one end are women who wear man-tailored clothing and power suits to work; at the other end are those men and women who wear full cross-gender regalia as a means of mockery and the pleasure of transgression. Transvestites regularly dress in the clothing of the opposite sex, for play or in everyday life.

Some people, though, feel that their biological sex doesn't match their internal sense of gender identity. Transgendered people may feel a "persistent discomfort and sense of inappropriateness about one's assigned sex (feeling trapped in the wrong body)" as the diagnosis for transsexualism in the American Psychiatric Association's *Diagnostic and Statistical Manual*

Transgendered individuals may have one biological sex and present as the other gender, or they may seek to surgically make their biological sex and socially presented gender the same. Either way, they make clear that gender is an embodied performance. Here, Italian actor and transgender political candidate Wladimiro Guadagno poses on a movie set. ▼

(DSM III-R) puts it. And rather than change their gender, they want to change their biological sex to match their felt gender identity. After two years of therapy and radical hormone therapies to mute or reverse secondary sex characteristics (like body hair, voice, breasts), some of these people undergo sex reassignment surgery (SRS), by which the original genitalia are surgically removed and new realistic medical constructions of vaginas and penises are created. What more evidence of "social construction of gender" could one ask for?

Historically, transgenderism was quite rare; in 1980, only about 4,000 people in the world had undergone these surgical interventions, almost all of them males seeking to become females. New medical and surgical procedures facilitated both male-to-female and female-to-male transsexual operations, and the inclusion of sex-change operations as procedures to be covered by Medicare (1978) and the listing of transsexualism in the DSM-III in 1980 allowed for insurance coverage for SRS. The increased visibility of transgendered people within the gay and lesbian movement has also increased the viability of SRS as an option.

Typically, transgenderism is experienced as a general discomfort that becomes increasingly intense during puberty; that is, with the emergence of secondary sex characteristics. As one female-to-male transgendered person told an interviewer:

> I hated the changes in my body . . . I couldn't stand it . . . It affected my identity. I became very upset and depressed. As a matter of fact, by this time in my life, I spent most of my time in my room . . . I thought about suicide . . . . (Devor, 1997)

While transgenderism remains relatively uncommon, the implications of such procedures are enormous. Once, a discrepancy between one's biological sex and what one experienced internally as one's gender would privilege the body, as if it contained some essential truth about the person. If such conflicts were to be resolved by therapeutic interventions, they would "help" transsexuals accept their body's "truth" and try and adjust their feelings about their gender. Transgenderism enables us to dissolve what is experienced as an arbitrary privileging of the body-at-birth and give more weight to who we feel we are, bringing us close to a world in which we can choose our gender because we can change our sex.

The "Disabled" Body

According to the Americans with Disabilities Act of 1990 (ADA), a **disability** is "a physical or mental impairment that substantially limits one or more major life activities." A person is considered to have a disability if he or she:

> has difficulty performing certain functions (seeing, hearing, talking, walking, climbing stairs and lifting and carrying), or has difficulty performing activities of daily living, or has difficulty with certain social roles (doing school work for children, working at a job and around the house for adults). A person who is unable to perform one or more activities, or who uses an assistive device to get around, or who needs assistance from another person to perform basic activities is considered to have a severe disability.

Disabilities are not always visible, nor are they necessarily "disabilities," in that many disabled people could live full and "normal" lives if only the larger society would cooperate. Disabilities do not reside solely in the bodies of the person but rather emerge through a relationship with the society. For example, the standard design of streets and sidewalks makes it extremely difficult for people in wheelchairs or walkers to use the same sidewalks as other people. The standard design of buses means that people in wheelchairs cannot use them. Is that their fault? Disabilities are the result of an interaction between the person and the society.

▲ People with disabilities are today living full and productive lives—and even incorporating their disabilities into their self-presentation. Comedian Josh Blue, who was born with cerebral palsy, won the reality TV competition on *Last Comic Standing* in 2006.

Nearly 20 percent of all Americans have one or more disabilities. Seven percent of boys and 4 percent of girls between the ages of 5 and 15 have disabilities; 43 percent of women and 40 percent of men age 65 and older have disabilities. There are 2.7 million people in wheelchairs in America, and 9.1 million who use a cane, crutches, or a walker. There are 1.8 million who are unable to see and 1 million who are unable to hear; another 7.8 million have difficulty hearing a normal conversation.

One of our family members is a good example. Diagnosed with rheumatoid arthritis at age 2, she came perilously close to death several times in early childhood. As a result of the medication she has taken for 25 years, several other systems failed, and she is now blind as well. She has had spinal fusion surgery twice to compensate for deteriorating discs and complete knee replacements in both knees. She also graduated near the top of her class in high school and majored in psychology at Princeton, where her books were read to her on tape or offered in Braille.

The number of Americans with a physical or mental disability has increased in recent years. This is due to several factors. First, advances in medical technologies mean that many people who might not have survived with their disabilities are now living longer lives. In addition, those medical breakthroughs are enabling the survival of people born with disabilities that would earlier have been fatal. Third, life expectancy continues to rise for everyone, and some disabilities, such as arthritis, are age related.

Most disabilities are not present at birth: They are the result of accidents, disease, and war. About 2.5 million veterans receive compensation for service-related disabilities. Some disabilities are the result of industry and pollution. The highest rates of disability by county in the United States are in coal mining regions; the highest rates in cities are in those cities near oil refineries. Globally, poorer countries have higher rates of disability, caused by malnutrition as well as accidents and disease. In Brazil, 14.5 percent of the population is disabled; in Ecuador, about 12 percent; in Panama, more than 11 percent (Inter-American Development Bank, 2007). Across the developing world, 10 percent of the population is disabled, according to the World Health Organization.

Disabilities are unevenly distributed by race and class within the United States as well. (Figure 16.2) African Americans have significantly higher levels of disability than Whites, but Asians and Latinos have lower rates than Whites. The poor have more disabilities than the rich. Disabilities not only reflect existing social inequalities by race and class, but disabilities are, themselves, the basis for further discrimination. People with disabilities are employed at about half the rate as people without disabilities—about 37.5 percent of the disabled compared with 74.4 percent without, and they earn about $3,000 less per year (*DiversityInc*, 2006). The Americans with Disabilities Act made it illegal to discriminate against people with disabilities in public accommodations. As a result, buses were adapted to accommodate people in wheelchairs, ramps replaced high curbs at streetcorners, and landlords built ramps to accommodate disabled tenants. "Black people fought for the right to ride in the front of the bus," said one disability activist. "We're fighting for the right to get on the bus" (cited in Shapiro, 1993, p. 128.)

Many people find themselves feeling uncomfortable and even angry around people with disabilities, as if somehow the disability is contagious.

FIGURE 16.2 People with Disabilities by Race and Ethnicity

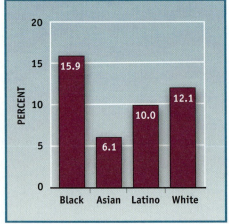

Black: 15.9
Asian: 6.1
Latino: 10.0
White: 12.1

(PERCENT)

Source: U.S. Census Bureau.

When the actor Christopher Reeve fell off his horse and was paralyzed from the neck down, he became a vocal campaigner for the disabled; the actor who played Superman showed superhuman courage as he became one of the most visible campaigners for the rights of the disabled.

People with disabilities are increasingly integrated into society. In addition to their efforts to overcome discrimination, they actively participate in sports like wheelchair basketball tournaments, marathon races, and the paralympics. In 2006, Josh Blue, who has cerebral palsy, won the television competition *Last Comic Standing*. Our family member mentioned above has sailed in regattas for the blind and won races in New Zealand and Newport, Rhode Island.

Healthy Bodies, Sick Bodies

A major concern of sociologists has been to understand health and illness, from the personal experience of being sick to the institutional arrangements that societies develop to care for the sick, and the political issues that surround health care, such as health insurance and prescription drug coverage.

The World Health Organization (WHO) defines **health** as a state of complete mental, physical, and social well-being, not simply the absence of disease. But when social scientists measure health, they typically do so using a "negative health standard"; that is, we are healthy when we are not sick. Statistically, the presence of a fever, pain, or illness that interferes with our daily lives means we are not healthy. Anyone who has ever been sick can tell you that it transforms your daily life.

Health and Inequality

Health and illness are among the most profoundly social experiences we have. For one thing, not everyone gets sick with the same illnesses in the same ways. Health and illness vary enormously by nationality, race, gender, and age.

The study of the causes and distribution of disease and disability is called **epidemiology**. This includes all the biomedical elements of disease and also social and behavioral factors that influence the spread of disease. The focus on these social and behavioral factors is called **social epidemiology**.

All health researchers begin with baseline indicators, such as the **mortality rate**, which is the death rate as a percentage of the population, and the **morbidity rate**, which indicates the rates of new infections from disease. Epidemiologists then attempt to understand the *incidence* of a disease—that is, how many new cases of a disease are reported in a given place during a specified time frame—and the *prevalence* of a disease, which usually refers to the distribution of the disease over different groups of the same population. For example, when a new disease like SARS is discovered or a new epidemic of the flu breaks out, epidemiologists tracking the spread of the disease will try to observe its effect on different groups (race, age, region) to assess the risks of different groups and even suggest policies that may inform the sorts of precautions people might take.

Measures of health care include:

- *Life expectancy:* an estimate of the average life span of people born in a specific year.

> ## Did *you* know?
>
> Around the world, scientists are marrying technology with biology to develop "bioartificial" organs that may transform millions of lives. In the United States, an artificial lung is in preclinical testing, an artificial pancreas and kidney have been tested in rats, and an artificial kidney is in early human trials. In Germany, a bioartificial liver is in early human trials. A computerized eye for the blind is in human testing in Belgium. Several universities around the world are testing artificial ears for the deaf (Arnst, 2003).

- *Infant mortality rate:* the number of deaths of infants under 1 year of age per 1,000 live births in a given year.
- *Maternal mortality rate:* the number of deaths of pregnant or new mothers either before, during, or immediate following childbirth, per 1,000 births in a given year.
- *Chronic diseases:* long-term or life long diseases that develop gradually or are present at birth (rates are calculated in proportion to the population—number per 1,000, 100,000, or 1 million).
- *Acute diseases:* diseases that strike suddenly and may cause severe illness, incapacitation, or even death.
- *Infectious diseases:* diseases that are caused by infectious agents such as viruses or bacteria.

Age and Health. Our health changes as we age. Not only does our general health decline, but our susceptibility to various illnesses shifts. For example, men aged 25 to 44 are twice as likely to die of HIV or unintentional injuries than they are to die of heart disease or cancer. By age 45 to 64, though, these two leading causes of death for young men barely scratch the surface, and heart disease and cancer are about 20 times more likely to be the cause of death.

Breakthroughs in medical technologies and treatments, as well as increased attention paid to health, mean that life expectancy will continue to increase at roughly the same rate as today. As our population gradually ages, the divisions between the "young old" and the "old old" will sharpen, and people will come to expect to live into their 80s and 90s as a matter of course. The burden of health care will fall disproportionately on the younger members of society.

Race, Class, and Health. In the United States and throughout the world, the wealthier you are, the healthier you are. People in more developed countries live longer and healthier lives, and in every country, the wealthy live longer and healthier lives. Of course, wealthy people are not immune to illness simply because they are wealthy. But they have better nutrition, better access to better-quality health care, and better standards of living—and these all lead to healthier lives.

Just as being wealthy is a good predictor of being healthy, so too is being poor a good predictor of being ill. Lower-class people work in more dangerous and hazardous jobs, with fewer health insurance benefits, and often live in neighborhoods or in housing that endangers health (peeling lead-based paint, exposed and leaky pipes that attract disease-bearing rodents or insects, unsanitary water and food supplies, for example). Stated most simply, inequality kills.

In the United States, men with fewer than 12 years of education (a broad measure of class position) are more than twice as likely to die of chronic ailments such as heart disease and almost twice as likely to die of communicable diseases than those with 13 or more years of education. Women with family income under $10,000 per year are three times more likely to die of heart disease and nearly three times as likely to die of diabetes than those with incomes above $25,000. White men earning less than $10,000 a year are 1.5 times more likely to die prematurely as those earning $34,000 of more (Isaacs, 2004).

Poor urban Blacks have the worst health of any ethnic group in the United States, with the possible exception of Native Americans. One-third of all poor Black 16-year-old girls in urban areas will not reach their sixty-fifth birthdays. High rates of heart disease, cancer, and cirrhosis of the liver make African American men in Harlem less likely to reach age 65 than men in Bangladesh (Epstein, 2003). Latinos die of several leading causes of death at far higher rates than do Whites, including liver disease, diabetes, and HIV. Racism itself is harmful to health: The stress

Sociology and our World

Race and Illness: The Tuskegee Experiment

Few scientific "experiments" reveal the racial aspects of health care better than the infamous Tuskegee experiments. Begun in 1932, 399 poor African American men who had been diagnosed with late-stage syphilis by the U.S. Public Heath Service were told that they had "bad blood" and could obtain free medical care, transportation to and from the Tuskegee Institute medical center for treatment, and even hot meals on days of their examination—all for simply joining a social club called "Miss Rivers' Lodge."

In fact, they were not treated at all but were deliberately left untreated so that the doctors could observe the ravages of the disease when left unchecked. "As I see it," one of the doctors explained, "we have no further interest in these patients until they die." The nature of the experiment was concealed from the men, because health officials feared they would refuse to participate if they knew. They were required to have painful spinal taps and were denied penicillin after it had become the best treatment option. After 25 years, all the patients who were still alive received a letter from the United States Surgeon General thanking them for their continued participation.

The Tuskegee Experiment lasted for 40 years. By its end, 28 of the men had died directly from the disease, 100 were dead of related complications, 40 of their wives had been infected, and 19 of their children had been born with congenital syphilis. The shocking indifference to human life, the callous contempt for these African American men's health and well-being, exposed a level of racism in America's public health system that was reminiscent of the experiments carried out on concentration camp inmates by the Nazi doctors. To this day, many Black Americans do not trust the health care system. In 1997, President Bill Clinton apologized to the eight surviving members of the study by saying, "The United States government did something that was wrong—deeply, profoundly, morally wrong. It was an outrage to our commitment to integrity and equality for all our citizens . . . clearly racist" (Jones, 1993).

---

brought about by discrimination and inequality may contribute to the higher rates of stress-related diseases, hypertension, and mental illness (Brown, 2003; Jackson and Stewart, 2003).

While new scientific research suggests some medicines may be more or less effective depending on the patient's race, poverty explains far greater health disparities. As health care costs and the number of Americans living in poverty or in the ranks of the working poor all increase, health and health care disparity depends on inability to pay—for screening and preventive care, treatment and follow-up, as well as safe and healthy living conditions. Thus, those who need health care the most actually have the least access and the poorest care. In addition, those at the bottom end of the socio-economic ladder are also less likely to have health insurance, and, if they do, their insurance is more likely to place strict constraints on spending. Most have no insurance at all. America is paying a huge price in terms of health inequalities for its growing class inequalities. (See Asch, et al., 2006; Kawschi, et al., 2005).

Gender and Health. Not only do class, race, and age affect health and illness, but so, too, does gender. Before the twentieth century, women's life expectancy was slightly lower than men's, largely due to higher mortality rates during pregnancy and childbirth. Through the twentieth century, though, women have been increasingly outliving men, so that today American women's life expectancy is 80 years and men's is 78 years. In the highly developed countries, women outlive men by about five to eight years, but they outlive men by less than three years in the developing world. (Japanese women have a life expectancy of over 85 years, the highest in the world.) In general life expectancy for both women and men has been increasing at a rate of 2.5 years per decade—with no end in sight.

TABLE 16.2

Ratio of Male to Female Death Rates for the 15 Leading Causes of Death in the United States

ALL RACES, MALES	PERCENT*
1. Heart disease	27.2
2. Cancer	24.3
3. Unintentional injuries	6.1
4. Stroke	5.0
5. Chronic lower respiratory diseases	5.0
6. Diabetes	3.0
7. Influenza and pneumonia	2.3
8. Suicide	2.2
9. Kidney disease	1.7
10. Alzheimer's disease	1.6

Source: Centers for Disease Control, 2005. (www.cdc.gov/men/lcod.htm)

ALL RACES, FEMALES	PERCENT*
1. Heart disease	27.2
2. Cancer	22.0
3. Stroke	7.5
4. Chronic lower respiratory diseases	5.2
5. Alzheimer's disease	3.9
6. Unintentional injuries	3.3
7. Diabetes	3.1
8. Influenza and pneumonia	2.7
9. Kidney disease	1.8
10. Septicemia	1.5

Source: Centers for Disease Control, 2005. (www.cdc.gov/women/lcod.htm)

But why do women in the advanced countries outlive men now? For one thing, improvements in prenatal and maternal health care during pregnancy and childbirth save many lives. But another reason may be the gender of health. Norms of masculinity often encourage men to take more health risks and then discourage them from seeking health care services until after an illness has progressed. As health researcher Will Courtenay put it:

> A man who does gender correctly would be relatively unconcerned about his health and well-being in general. He would see himself as stronger, both physically and emotionally than most women. He would think of himself as independent, not needing to be nurtured by others. He would be unlikely to ask others for help. . . . He would face danger fearlessly, take risks frequently, and have little concern for his own safety. (Courtenay, 1998, p. 21)

Or, as one Zimbabwean man put it, "real men don't get sick" (cited in Courtenay, 1998, p. 21).

In Table 16.2, you can see the ratio of male to female age-adjusted death rates for the 15 leading causes of death for the total population in the United States in the year 2000. Note that the two causes of death that have the highest male-to-female ratio, the highest differential by sex, are those most closely associated with gendered behavior, not biological sex: unintentional injuries and suicide.

Another reason for the disparities between women's and men's health has been the success of the women's health movement. Beginning in the 1970s with a critique of a male-dominated health care industry that seemed relatively uninterested in women's health issues, the women's health movement has brought increasing awareness to certain illnesses such as breast cancer that overwhelmingly affect women (a tiny number of men get breast cancer per year). In addition, the movement has also spurred new interest in women wresting control over pregnancy, labor, and childbirth from the medical establishment, sparking increased interest in natural childbirth, a wider variety of reproductive and neonatal health care options, and the breast-feeding of newborn babies.

The Global Distribution of Health and Illness

Globally, the problem of health and inequality is enormous. The wealthier the country, the healthier its population. In the poorest countries, high rates of poverty also mean there are high rates of infectious diseases, malnutrition, and starvation. In Haiti, for example, a newborn baby has only a 50–50 change of surviving to age 5.

The cause of death for most people in the developed world is chronic diseases, such as heart attacks, cancers, and others; over one-half of all deaths in the developing world are the result of infectious diseases or complications during pregnancy and childbirth to either the mother or the baby (Figure 16.3).

But even some wealthy countries do not manage to safeguard health for their citizens or take care of the ill or fragile in their populations. Despite the fact that the U.S. health care system is among the world's most advanced, the United States does not rank particularly high on many of the most basic health indicators. We rank seventeenth in life expectancy, and twenty-first in infant mortality (United Nations, 2005).

In fact, when comparing wealthy countries, there is considerable variation in the levels of health achieved. To look at the amount of money spent on health care, one would think the United States is the healthiest country in the industrialized world. Today, U.S. health expenditures equal $6,102 per person per year, while Japan spends just $2,249 (in U.S. dollars). Australia spends $3,120. Yet life expectancy in Japan is the highest in the ten most industrialized countries of the world, and life expectancy in the United States is lowest of all these countries. Australia, eighth in spending, enjoys the third highest life expectancy of the top ten countries. Canada spends $3,165 per capita, yet the average Canadian's life expectancy is also more than two years longer than the average American's. Moreover, on many measures of health care quality, the United States ranks at the bottom when compared with other developed countries, including Canada, Britain, and Australia (Table 16.3).

Sickness and Stigma

Our experience of illness may be individual, but the way we understand our illness and the way we act are deeply socially patterned. In a still relevant formulation, sociologist Talcott Parsons (1951) described what he called the **sick role** to describe not how we "get" sick, but how we learn to "be" sick.

The Sick Role. According to Parsons, the individual is not responsible for being sick. Getting sick is not a moral failure; the origins of illness are seen as coming from outside the individual's control. As a result, the sick individual is entitled to certain privileges, including a withdrawal from normal responsibilities, and to expect others to exhibit compassion and sympathy, often in the form of caretaking behaviors. However, such rights and privileges of the ill are not indefinite; they are temporary. The sick person must actively make an effort to get better, by seeing a doctor, taking medication, and doing whatever therapies a medical expert prescribes (Parsons, 1951).

Other sociologists refined the idea of the sick role. Elliot Freidson specified three different types of sick roles (Freidson, 1970):

- The most typical is the *conditional* sick role. This concerns individuals who are suffering from an illness from which they will recover. As long as the sick person plays his or her part (tries to get better), then other aspects of the role (relief from work or family obligations, expectation of compassion) will be forthcoming.
- The *unconditionally legitimate* sick role concerns those people who have either long-term or incurable illnesses, such as certain forms of cancer, and who are unable to get better by their own behavior. They are therefore entitled to occupy the sick role for as long as they are ill with no moral disapproval.
- Finally, there is the *illegitimate* sick role. This may concern those people who do nothing to improve their situation or people who are believed to be ill because of something they themselves did. Those who suffer from sexually transmitted diseases (STDs) may be seen by some as bringing the disease on themselves and therefore are not entitled to play the sick role. Initially, those suffering from

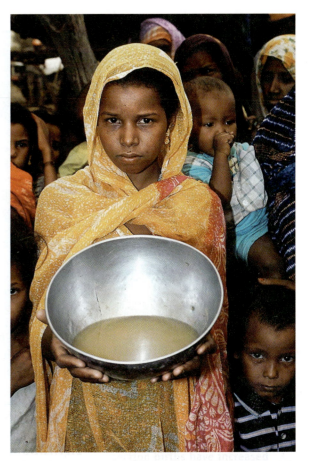

▲ Globally, health varies with wealth: the poorer the country, the poorer its citizens' health. This girl in Mauritania holds a bowl of water from the village well, its only source of drinking water. In the developing world, the major cause of death is infectious disease, many of which are transmitted by unclean water.

chapter 17

EDUCATION, AS WE OFTEN HEAR, IS "THE GREAT EQUALIZER." By studying hard, staying in school, and applying yourself, you can gain the knowledge and skills you need to get ahead. Education can enable a poor person to get out of poverty, can catapult you into ranks of the wealthy and powerful. It's the purest form of meritocracy; the smartest cream always rises to the surface. Sometimes, when you hear parents or teachers talk admiringly about education, it sounds as though getting a college degree is like winning the lottery.

Talk to others, and it sounds as if you're in prison. Education is the best predictor of your eventual position in the socioeconomic hierarchy—but the best predictor of your education turns out not to be your motivation or intelligence but your parents' level of education. Education keeps you where you are, keeps the structures of inequality (based on class, race, or gender) in place. In fact, education is what makes that inequality feel like a meritocracy, so you have no one to blame.

So why do it? It depends on whom you ask. Teachers often subscribe to the meritocracy idea and contend that education builds critical

Education

reasoning skills and the ability to grapple with issues, weigh evidence, and make informed decisions in a changing society. It is valuable in itself. Students are often more cynical and more interested in learning the skills they will need to get or keep a job.

Does education level the playing field and facilitate mobility, or does it freeze things where they are and maintain the status quo? Should education teach you how to think, or how to make a living? Is it the road to the good life, or does it turn us into overintellectualized snobs, corrupting goodness and simple virtues?

Education is both one of the best ways to enhance your upward mobility and career opportunities and one of the legitimizing institutions that maintain social inequality.

How do sociologists understand education? It's both. Education is intrinsically interesting, and you can gain useful skills to build your job credentials. It is a path of mobility and one of the central institutions involved in the reproduction of structured social inequality.

The Sociology of Education

Every day in the United States 72.7 million people gather in auditoriums, classrooms, and laboratories, in the open air and in online chat rooms, to learn things from 4.5 million teachers, teaching assistants, lab assistants, instructors, and professors (*Digest of Educational Statistics*, 2006). They can learn an endless variety of subjects: Babylonian cuneiform and nuclear physics, short-story writing and motorcycle repair, conversational Portuguese and managerial accounting, symphony conducting and cartoon animation, existential philosophy and the gender politics of modern Japan.

Most people spend a quarter of their lives (or even more) becoming *educated*. If you live to be 70, you will devote 19 percent of your life to preschool, elementary school, and high school, and another 6 percent to college (assuming you graduate in four years). A PhD might easily take another eight years. You would then finish your education at age 30, with 43 percent of your life over.

Education doesn't end at high school, college, or graduate school. Many people return to school after they received their degree, for additional degrees, courses, and certificates. Some want to learn a new skill or develop a new interest. And many others depend on education for their livelihood: They become teachers, administrators, and service personnel; they write and publish textbooks; they build residence halls and manufacture three-ring binders; they open restaurants and clothing shops in college towns to draw student business. In the United States, we spend $550 billion a year on elementary and secondary schools and another $200 billion on colleges and universities (Department of Education, 2006).

Why do we do it? How does it work? How does it both enable and restrict our own mobility?

Education as a Social Institution

Sociologists define **education** as a social institution through which society provides its members with important knowledge—basic facts, job skills, and cultural norms and values. It provides socialization, cultural innovation, and social integration. It is accomplished largely through schooling, formal instruction under the direction of a specially trained teacher (Ballantine, 2001).

Like most social institutions, education has both manifest (clearly apparent) and latent (potential or hidden) functions. The manifest function is the subject matter: reading and writing in grade school, sociology and managerial accounting in college. Latent functions are by-products of the educational process, the norms, values, and goals that accrue because we are immersed in a specific social milieu: Students taking ancient Greek probably differ from those taking managerial accounting in their conceptions of what's important in life, how people should behave. Education teaches both a subject and a **hidden curriculum:** individualism and competition, conformity to mainstream norms, obedience to authority, passive consumption of ideas, and acceptance of social inequality (Gilborn, 1992).

In addition to teaching a subject matter and various sorts of hidden norms and values, education establishes relationships and social networks, locating people within social classes. Randall Collins (1979) notes that the United States is a **credential society:** You need diplomas, degrees, and certificates to qualify for jobs; you can only open a medical practice if you have a M.D. degree, regardless of how smart you are; and you have to pass the state bar exam to practice law, regardless of how much law you know. Diplomas, degrees, certificates, examination scores, college majors, and the college you graduate from say "who you are" as much as family background. They tell employers what manners, attitudes, and even skin colors the applicants are likely to have. They provide gatekeeping functions that restrict important and lucrative jobs to a small segment of the population.

The History of Education

For most of human history, there were no schools. Your parents taught necessary skills, or they hired you a tutor (the philosopher Aristotle tutored the young Alexander the Great). Sometimes people with special skills opened academies, where you could pay tuition to study philosophy, music, or art. But there was no formal, structured system of education.

In many cultures, schools developed out of a need to train religious leaders. In ancient Babylonia, priests-in-training went to school so they could learn to read sacred texts and write the necessary rituals. In India, *gurukuls,* connected to temples and monasteries, offered instruction in Hindu scriptures, theology, astrology, and other religious topics. They were tuition free, but still it was primarily wealthy children who could be excused from working alongside their parents long enough to profit from them (Ghosh, 2001). In China, education was propelled by tradition rather than religion. For 2,000 years, beginning with the Han dynasty (206 BCE to 200 CE), Chinese citizens who wanted to become civil servants on any level had to pass a series of "imperial examinations." Examinations were theoretically open to anyone, but only the wealthy could afford to spend the years of preparation necessary for even the lowest exam (Chaffee, 1985; Gernet, 1982).

European schools also developed in connection with monasteries or cathedrals to teach priests and other religious workers necessary subjects, like Latin, theology, and philosophy. We still call the highest academic degree a PhD, or doctor of philosophy. When the Protestant Reformation began to teach that all believers, not just priests, should be able to read and interpret the Bible, many churches began to offer all children instruction in reading and writing. By the sixteenth century, formal schooling for children was available in many European countries, though only the wealthy had enough money and free time to participate (Bowen, 1976; Boyd, 1978).

The United States was among the first countries in the world to set a goal of education for all of its citizens, under the theory that an educated citizenry was necessary for a democratic society to function. A free public education movement began in 1848, and soon there were free, tax-funded elementary schools in every state, with about half of young people (ages 5 to 19) attending (Urban and Wagoner, 2003). They often attended for only a few years or for only a few months of the year, squeezed in between their duties at home, and instruction was very basic—"reading, writing, and arithmetic." By 1918, every state had passed a mandatory education law, requiring that children attend school until they reached the age of 16 or completed the eighth grade, and a variety of new subjects were available, including higher levels of mathematics, science, social studies, foreign languages, art and music, and "practical subjects" like bookkeeping and typing. By the mid-1960s, a majority of American adults were high school graduates. Today about seven out of ten have high school diplomas.

Why did the educational curriculum expand so much, from basic subjects to everything under the sun? As industry expanded in the mid-nineteenth century, occupations became more differentiated, and work skills could no longer be passed down from parents to children. There was a great need for specialized education in the skills necessary for the modern workforce, especially English composition, mathematics, and the sciences. Abstract learning in subjects such as history and Latin did not provide immediate work skills, but they did signify that the student had the cultural background necessary to move into the middle class (Willis et al., 1994). They were not only the key to advancement; they were the key to impressing people.

What do *you* think? 17.1

MyLab

Complete Formal Schooling

Americans in general place a high value on education. One's life chances are directly related to one's education, as are one's income, social group, and even one's potential marriage partner pool. In the United States, children are required by law to go to school until they are 16 years of age, and according to the U.S. Department of Education, 85 percent of 25- to 29-year-olds in 2005 had completed high school. So, what do you think?

How important is it that young people should complete formal schooling?

○ Extremely important
○ Quite important
○ Somewhat important
○ Not too important
○ Not at all important

See the back of the chapter to compare your answers to national survey data.

John Dewey (1859–1952) was a proponent of "progressive education"—constantly updating what the schools teach to make learning relevant to people's lives. During the first half of the twentieth century, policy makers and employers sought to ensure that education coincided with the country's economic profile and employment demands.

As education became universal, more and more scholars began experimenting with how people learn. Was rote memorization effective? Problem solving? Practical experience? Pragmatism taught the value of practical experience—actually using a foreign language for everyday conversations, for instance, instead of translating passages from great works of literature. During the 1960s, affect, or feelings, became nearly as significant in educational theory as cognition, or intellect. Students learned self-esteem, how to recognize and handle emotions, how to manage conflict, often to the detriment of more practical skills. A backlash in the 1980s and 1990s moved the curriculum "back to basics," and rote memorization returned as an appropriate way to learn.

Before the Civil War, abolitionist Frederick Douglass (c1818–1895) stated that learning to read and write would be the "road to liberation" for oppressed minorities. Educational theorist Horace Mann (1796–1859) believed that education could be "the great equalizer" eliminating class and other social inequalities as everyone gained access to information and debate (Cremin, 1957). For this goal to be met, however, all citizens in the country must be educated. On the college level, the United States is indeed the best-educated country in the world, with the highest graduation rate (one in four adults now has a bachelor's degree) and boasts the majority of the world's best universities (*Economist*, 2005). Yet on the high school level, we have more dropouts and underpreparedness than any other industrialized country. We are falling behind in math, science, and problem-solving skills.

Some groups have consistently enjoyed more educational success than others. Women received less elementary and secondary education than men through the nineteenth century and were all but excluded from higher education until the early twentieth century. The vast majority of high school dropouts come from low-income families, and the vast majority of college students come from high-income families.

Research confirms the funneling effect of the educational system. The high school graduation rate is significantly lower among minorities: 78 percent of Whites, 56 percent of African Americans, and 52 percent of Hispanic Americans graduate from high school (Greene and Winters, 2005). The states with the highest graduation rates are often the states with the highest White populations: 85 percent in Iowa, North Dakota, and Wisconsin, but only 56 percent in Georgia and 53% in South Carolina (Figure 17.1).

The Hispanic dropout rate is particularly troubling. For third-generation Hispanics, it was 15.9 percent in 2001, almost double the rate of White non-Hispanics (8.2 percent) and even of new Hispanic immigrants (8.6 percent) (Greene and Winters, 2005). There are many causes for this disparity: low incomes, a language barrier, and low-quality schooling that discourages participation.

▲ Educational opportunity and retention are organized by class and race. Lower income and minority students are far more likely to drop out than middle class and white students. The highest dropout rate is among lower income Hispanic girls.

Education and Globalization

Around the world, education is closely tied to economic success. In low- and middle-income nations like India, Uganda, and Malawi, boys and girls may spend several years in school, but their learning is limited to the practical knowledge they need to farm or perform other traditional tasks. They don't have time for much else.

FIGURE 17.1 High School Dropouts, Age 25 and over, 2004

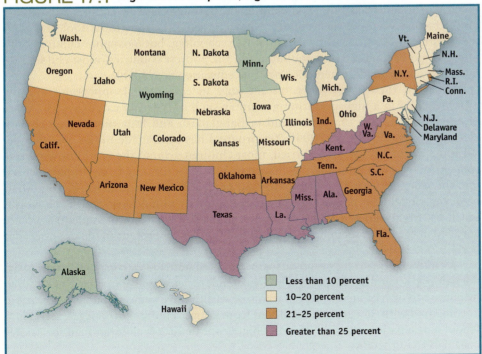

Less than 10 percent
10–20 percent
21–25 percent
Greater than 25 percent

Source: Frey, William H., Amy Beth Anspach & John Paul Dewitt, *The Allyn & Bacon Social Atlas of the United States.* Published by Allyn & Bacon, Boston, MA. Copyright © 2008 by Pearson Education. Reprinted by permission of the publisher.

Try It Developing an Educational Profile

Developed by Katherine R. Rowell, *Sinclair Community College.*

OBJECTIVE: Develop an educational profile for one of the 50 states using Kids Count data from the Annie E. Casey Foundation.

STEP1: Plan

Imagine the following scenario: You have just been asked to serve as an educational consultant to the new governor of your state. As part of your first duty, you have been asked to brief the governor on the state of education for children through high school (another person is working on the college report). The governor needs brief detailed information to make some decisions about funding and policy.

Your instructor may assign each student in your class a state to explore for this activity; others may identify teams of students to work on one state. Your assignment is to create a detailed educational profile for your state. In other words, in as much detail as possible develop a visual and statistical educational profile of your assigned state and be prepared to share your information with your classmates. (There are numerous methods of presenting this information, and your instructor may require a brief report or a PowerPoint presentation.)

STEP 2: Research

Most if not all the information that you may need for this profile can be found on the Annie E. Casey Foundation website. Explore this website to develop your educational profile to be submitted to the governor. Please note that while this website has a lot of educational data, you may also want to check the Internet for additional government-specific resources from your specific assigned state.

STEP 3: Discuss

Present your profile in class. As noted in Step 2, there may be various methods of presenting this profile. Some instructors may ask you to submit a written report, others may expect a brief presentation, and some may ask you to submit a PowerPoint presentation that can be posted for students in your class to read at a later time.

After completing the educational profile, take a moment to answer the following question and submit with your final report: What policy changes would you recommend to the governor? Be sure to explain your thoughts.

For instance, India has outlawed child labor, but many Indian families still depend on the factory wages of their children, leaving them little time for school. In Egypt, the constitution guarantees five years of free schooling, but most poor children can't afford to go beyond the bare minimum. In the poorest countries, most children do not go to school at all, whether or not free education is available.

Globally, there is considerable inequity in educational opportunity (Table 17.1). A child in a high-performing country such as Norway can expect 17 years of education, double that of a child in Bangladesh and four times as much as a child in Niger (UNESCO, 2004). Yet progress has been made in the past decade. With the major exception of Africa, most children around the world now receive some primary education, and the chance of a child continuing from primary school into the secondary grades is more than 80 percent in most countries. Beyond that, however, enrollment percentages drop dramatically in most regions of the world. In China, Malaysia, and Mexico, for example, the 90 percent of students who are enrolled at the lower secondary level drops to under 50 percent in the upper grades (UNESCO, 2004).

A child's family background or socioeconomic status is a strong predictor of participation in secondary education. In Swaziland, for example, 78 percent of children from the top fifth of households in terms of wealth have some secondary education, as compared with 38 percent of children from poorer families. In Senegal, secondary school participation rates are 25 times higher for better off children than for poorer ones (UNESCO, 2004).

Gender also determines educational opportunity. One in three children worldwide lives in a country that does not ensure equal access to education for boys and

TABLE 17.1

Percentage Currently Attending School, by Region

| | WEIGHTED[a] AVERAGES | | | | | |
| | AGES 10–14 | | AGES 15–19 | | AGES 20–24 | |
REGION	BOYS	GIRLS	BOYS	GIRLS	BOYS	GIRLS
Africa						
Eastern/Southern Africa	74.1	70.6	52.2	39.4	16.4	9.1
Western/Middle Africa	66.1	57.6	48.1	34.3	24.2	12.2
Asia[b]						
South-central/South-eastern Asia[c]	81.0	76.0	47.1	37.3	16.9	9.8
Former Soviet Asia[d]	98.4	98.9	56.1	54.4	13.2	11.7
Latin America and Caribbean						
Caribbean/Central America	80.0	77.8	50.9	44.2	21.3	16.5
South America	92.9	93.1	60.5	61.7	22.0	23.8
Middle East						
Western Asia/Northern Africa	81.0	67.6	47.7	37.4	17.5	10.3
TOTAL—All regions	79.8	74.6	50.4	41.2	18.7	12.2

[a] Weighting is based on United Nations population estimates for year 2000 (World Population Prospects: The 2000 Revision).
[b] Eastern Asia not included; no DHS available.
[c] India's DHS does not include current enrollment data for 18–24-year-olds and has been removed from this table.
[d] Former Soviet Asia includes former Soviet Republics in South-central and Western Asia.
Source: From *Growing Up Global: The Changing Transitions to Adulthood in Developing Countries* by Cynthia B. Lloyd. Reprinted with permission from the National Academies Press. Copyright © 2005, National Academy of Sciences.

girls. And in all countries without gender parity, it is girls who are disadvantaged (UNESCO, 2004). Gender disparity is even more widespread at the secondary level; in fact, the magnitude of inequity increases by educational level. Ironically, while disadvantages for girls in secondary education are common in low-income countries, girls tend to outnumber boys in high-income countries, including the United States (UNESCO, 2004).

As a result, the literacy rate is extremely low in poor countries. Among the Arab states, 19.8 percent of men and 41.1 percent of women were not literate as of 2006. Globally, 60 percent of Africans, 70 percent of Asians, and 85 percent of Latin Americans are literate (UNESCO, 2006). When most citizens cannot read and write at ordinary levels, they cannot compete in the global marketplace, and their nations remain impoverished (Figure 17.2).

A number of developing nations have begun intensive efforts to improve education, from grade school through university and professional schools. India has the world's youngest population, with 500 million people aged 18 and younger. If they could be educated, they would prove a formidable economic force. Government spending on education has grown rapidly. As a result, almost 90 percent of all Indian children are enrolled in school. The literacy rate is up to 63 percent—from 53 percent in 1995. The number of Indians attending colleges and universities almost doubled in

Some developing countries have made enormous strides in education. China now boasts very high enrollments in primary grades and almost 96 percent literacy. And yet enrollment drops considerably after ninth grade, especially in poorer regions, and there are large gender gaps. ▼

FIGURE 17.2 Projected Illiteracy Rates, 2015

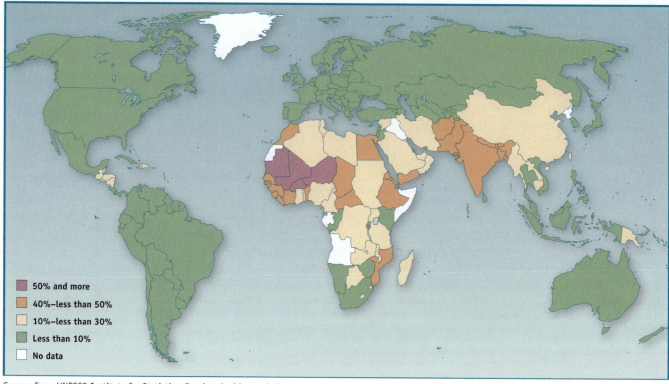

50% and more

40%–less than 50%

10%–less than 30%

Less than 10%

No data

Source: From UNESCO Institute for Statistics. Reprinted with permission.

the 1990s. However, there is still a high dropout rate—75 percent of Indian students drop out after eighth grade, and 78 percent of girls and 48 percent of boys fail to graduate from high school (*Economist*, 2005).

In the 1980s, China also planned for universal education for grades 1 through 9 by 2000. As a result, there was an immense expansion of the educational system. Enrollment is high—at least through grade nine—and the literacy rate among young adults (age 12 to 40) is now 96 percent. There has also been a massive university expansion, especially at the doctoral level: Between 1999 and 2003, nearly 12 times as many doctorates were awarded as in 1982 through 1989 (*Economist*, 2005).

However, enrollment in China is still low, and there is still a large gender gap: Many more boys than girls are being educated. The curriculum depends to a large extent on rote learning and memorization rather than reasoning and problem solving. And authoritarian political control inhibits new scientific research if the government doesn't like it.

Intelligence(s) and Literacy

One of the primary goals of education is to "make people smarter," or at least to develop their innate intelligence. But is there a single human capacity called intelligence? If so, can it really be modified by education and training, or is it a permanent, unchangeable part of the human brain or spirit?

Though these questions remain unanswered, the tests we have devised to measure the intelligence quotient (IQ) are highly correlated with success in school. Of course, they were *designed* to predict success in school. Some scholars contend that they are measuring the social, economic, and ethnic differences that correlate with success rather than intelligence itself. In other words, they do not prove that some people are smarter, or even that smarter people are more likely to succeed in school. They prove that our school system is biased.

A few scholars do believe that different levels of success in school among different ethnic groups is not due to bias or inequality after all. They are due to differences in intelligence, which IQ tests measure just fine. Remember the controversy that *The Bell Curve* caused (see Chapter 8)? Richard Herrnstein and Charles Murray (1994) argued that differences in IQ between Blacks and Whites in the United States had a biological basis. However, a team of Berkeley sociologists completely disproved this claim, showing that the differences on IQ tests result from social and cultural differences (Fischer et al., 1996).

Maybe it's time to look at intelligence in another way. In *Frames of Mind: The Theory of Multiple Intelligences* (1983), psychologist Howard Gardner argues that intelligence is not a single characteristic. You may get A's in science class and struggle to keep a C in English. You may be a whiz at remembering people's names and faces but unable to drive five blocks without getting lost. Gardner defines intelligence as a set of skills that make it possible for a person to solve problems in life; the potential for finding or creating solutions for problems, which involves gathering new knowledge; and the ability to create an effective product or offer a service that is valued in a culture.

In all, Gardner tabulates seven different kinds of intelligence (he added an eighth in 1997). Everyone has different levels in different combinations—a sort of intelligence "profile" (Table 17.2).

Critics argue that this theory of intelligence is vague and undefined. Aren't dancing and musical ability talents rather than types of intelligence? Is the ability to understand other people's emotions intelligence, or sensitivity? Intelligence should be revealed when people must confront an unfamiliar task in an unfamiliar environment, not be strengthened or weakened by culture, as multiple intelligence theory argues.

How would one go about using multiple intelligence theory in the classroom? Doesn't it undercut the value of "core knowledge"—a common collection of "essential facts that every American needs to know"? Certainly, it makes national standards difficult to measure, as well as classifying students' skills and abilities across subjects. And it is impractical—overcrowded classrooms with few resources can barely handle the basic mathematical and verbal aptitudes, let alone bodily-kinesthetic, interpersonal, intrapersonal, and naturalistic. Nevertheless, multiple intelligence theory has become the basis of curricula in thousands of schools across the country.

TABLE 17.2

Gardner's Eight Types of Intelligence

- **Linguistic**—sensitivity to meaning and order of words
- **Logical-mathematical**—the ability in mathematics and other complex logical systems
- **Spatial**—the ability to "think in pictures," to perceive the visual world accurately, and recreate (or alter) it in the mind or on paper
- **Musical**—the ability to understand and create music
- **Bodily-kinesthetic**—the ability to use one's body in a skilled way, for self-expression or toward a goal
- **Interpersonal**—the ability to perceive and understand other individuals' moods, desires, motivations
- **Intrapersonal**—the understanding of one's own emotions
- **Naturalist**—the ability to recognize and classify plants, minerals, animals

Source: Gardner, 1997.

Did you know?

"Everybody knows Albert Einstein flunked math." This was offered and repeated constantly when I was a child, to reassure underachievers that our time would someday come. A Google search found more than 500,000 references to it, and it even made it into "Ripley's Believe it or Not!" newspaper column.

Except it isn't true. When showed the column in 1935, he laughed. "I never failed in mathematics," he replied, correctly. "Before I was 15 I had mastered differential and integral calculus." Einstein's mathematical genius was one of his many intelligences—and was pronounced at an early age (Isaacson, 2007).

Cultural Literacy

Is there a set of information that everyone should know, or is it all a matter of personal preference? Is the person who can discuss Shakespeare's *The Tempest* but has never seen an episode of *Star Trek* really better educated than the person who can argue the merits of Kirk versus Picard but looks for the remote when Shakespeare's play is performed on PBS? More qualified for a white-collar job? Better able to select a candidate on Election Day?

E. D. Hirsch Jr. thinks so. A University of Virginia professor of humanities, Hirsch caused some controversy with his *Cultural Literacy: What Every American Needs to Know* (1988). He argued that the modern school curriculum, with its emphasis on diversity, is depriving children of the background that they need to be effective American citizens. They learn trivia, rather than a sound core curriculum.

So what do Americans need to know? Hirsch obliged with his over 600-page *Dictionary of Cultural Literacy* (2003). He doesn't reveal much about his criteria for inclusion: He selected items that are not too broad or too narrow, that appear frequently in national periodicals, and that have found "a place in our collective memory." It sounds like an outline of the "hidden curriculum," a reproduction of elite knowledge, and indeed there is little about minorities, very little about non-Western cultures. *Star Trek* is mentioned, as well as Batman, and the *Peanuts* comic strip. However, most of the entries have to do with "high culture," elite knowledge. For example, here are some things that every educated person should know:

- "The Ballad of Reading Gaol," a poem by Oscar Wilde.
- Absurdist playwright Samuel Beckett.
- Francois Rabelais, who wrote the sixteenth-century masterpiece *Gargantua and Pantagruel*.
- Thomas Aquinas, whose *Summa Theologica* is a classic of medieval theology.
- Novelist Sir Walter Scott.
- William Gladstone, prime minister of England during the Victorian era.

OK, tell the truth: How many did you know? How many did your *instructor* know? Why are these more important to know than, let's say, the lyrics to a Bob Dylan song or who Lord Voldemort is?

And what about **scientific literacy,** which is, according to the National Academy of Sciences, the "knowledge and understanding of the scientific concepts and processes required for personal decision making, participation in civic and cultural affairs, and economic productivity." Scientific literacy has doubled over past two decades, but still, only 20 to 25 percent of Americans are scientifically savvy and alert, according to Jon D. Miller, director of the Center for Biomedial Communications at Northwestern University Medical School (Dean, 2005). Miller's research finds that:

- Most American adults do not understand what molecules are.
- Fewer than a third can identify DNA as the key to heredity.
- Only about 10 percent know what radiation is.
- One in five believes the sun revolves around Earth.

He attributes this ignorance to poor education. Many high schools require only a year of two of "general science" that does not provide adequate instruction in everyday scientific concepts. Colleges are little better, often requiring only two or three "general interest courses" to fill their science requirements.

Low scientific literacy undermines our ability to take part in the democratic process today. One can't be an effective citizen without it, given that we are facing such issues as:

- Stem cell research
- Infectious diseases
- Nuclear power
- Global warming
- Evolution

Did *you* know?

Most colleges and universities require "general education" courses in the broad areas of natural sciences, physical sciences, social sciences, and humanities. But many general education courses are not broad surveys at all but specialized seminars in a tiny, sometimes arcane, subfield of knowledge. Here are a few general education courses that should have no trouble attracting students:

- Physics for Poets (D'Youville College)
- Philosophy and *Star Trek* (Georgetown University)
- Surfing and Culture (Plattsburgh State University)
- Foods of the World (Rochester Institute of Technology)
- Campus Culture and Drinking (Duke University)
- The American Vacation (University of Iowa)
- Ghost Hunting 101 (Lane Community College)

Sources: http://encarta.msn.com/college_article_OddCourses/Top_10_Odd_College_Courses.html; http://www.degreetutor.com/library/choosing-degree/weird-classes; http://media.www.fsunews.com/media/storage/paper920/news/2006/05/15/Lifestyles/Seven.Unusual.College.Courses-2353619.shtml

Education and Inequality

If education doesn't make you smarter, at least it makes you richer. The higher your level of education, the higher your income will likely be. Look, for example, at Table 17.3.

The same holds true in other countries as well. While men at all levels of education earn more than equally educated women, and Whites earn more than racial and ethnic minorities, the relative earnings of all people of greater education are higher than those with lesser educational attainment (OECD, 2006).

But is this because educated people get paid more or because people who are already in the upper classes have enough resources to make sure their children go further in their educations, and because upper-class people value education more and therefore push their children?

Education and Mobility

Most of us believe that education is a ticket to social mobility. Over the course of American history, different groups of immigrants—for example, Jews, Koreans, and Cubans—have successfully used educational advancement as a vehicle for social mobility for the entire ethnic group. But education is also one of the primary vehicles by which society reinforces social inequalities based on race, ethnicity, class, and gender. As long as we believe that education is a strict meritocracy—the best get ahead—we believe that different educational outcomes (some groups do better than others) are based on characteristics of those individuals or those groups: They try harder and do more homework, or their culture rewards educational achievement more than other groups.

While this is partly true, sociologists also study a different dynamic, a hidden curriculum, through which education not only creates social inequalities but makes them seem natural, normal, and inevitable (Bowles, 1976; Lynch, 1989; Margolis, 2001). Of course, some teachers and administrators are racist, sexist, heterosexist, or classist and deliberately introduce stereotypes, marginalization, and exclusion into their lesson plans. But the problem goes much deeper than that. Educators need not *try* to reproduce social inequalities. They are reproduced in textbooks, in test questions, and in classroom discussions.

However, the most important lessons of the hidden curriculum take place outside the classroom, on the playground, in the cafeteria, in the many informal interactions that take place during every school day, from kindergarten through college. There students learn which of their peers are "supposed" to dominate and which are "supposed" to be bullied, beaten, laughed at, or ignored. They learn about gender hierarchies (call a boy a "girl" to humiliate him, or "gay" to humiliate him even more). They learn about racial hierarchies (there are far more bad words for every ethnic minority group than for White people). They learn about social status (the most popular group usually has the richest parents). The lessons they learn will influence their future decisions, whether they are in the boardroom or the courtroom, whether they are

TABLE 17.3

Mean Income by Years of Education, 2004		
	MEN	WOMEN
Less than ninth grade	$21,659	$17,023
Some high school	$26,277	$19,162
High school graduation	$35,725	$26,029
Some college	$41,895	$30,816
Associate's degree	$44,404	$33,481
Bachelor's degree	$57,220	$41,681
Master's degree	$70,530	$51,316
Professional degree	$100,000	$75,036
Doctorate	$82,401	$68,875

Source: Digest of Education Statistics, 2005.

▲ In addition to the formal curriculum in class, students also participate in a "hidden curriculum" in which they learn social lessons about hierarchy, peer pressure, and how to act around the opposite sex.

applying for a job or doing the hiring, regardless of how often the formal curriculum includes units on diversity.

Inequality and the Structure of Education

The types of schools and the uneven distribution of resources for schools result in often dramatic differences in student achievement.

Private versus Public Schools. Today one in nine American children (about 6 million) attend private schools (U.S. Department of Education, 2003). White students are twice as likely to attend private schools as Black students, and their numbers are increasing: Only 60 percent of White students were enrolled in public school in 2001–2002, 7 percentage points less than a decade before (Figure 17.3).

Nearly three-fourths of the 27,000 private schools in the United States are run by religious bodies. The Roman Catholic Church runs the most (8,000), and interdenominational fundamentalist Protestants come in a close second, but there are also schools affiliated with Presbyterians, Mormons, Lutherans, Orthodox Jews, and many others. There are usually no restrictions about the religious background of the students, but religious instruction is required, along with chapel and other religious services.

Most of the 6,000 secular private schools are prestigious (expensive), modeled after British boarding schools, with many advantages in educational quality and school-based social networks. They draw an elite group of students, and their graduates go on to equally prestigious and expensive private universities.

Many people believe that a private school provides better education and send their children if they can afford it. Forty-seven percent of U.S. members of Congress and 51 percent of U.S. senators with school-age children sent them to private schools. In Florida, nearly 40 percent of lawmakers, nearly four times the state average, send their school-aged children to private schools—and when the lawmakers are on education committees, the percentage rises to 60 percent (*St. Petersburg Times*, 2005). Even public school teachers believe that private schools are superior—nationwide, more than one in five public school teachers choose private schools for their own children, almost twice the national average (Council for American Private Education, 2005).

Other than the prestige, what is the attraction of private education? Advocates argue that smaller class sizes and lower student–teacher ratios facilitate learning. Discipline is better, and thus there is a more focused and orderly environment for learning. And private schools are safer (Chubb and Moe, 1990; Coleman, Hoffer, and Kilgore, 1982; West, 2001).

FIGURE 17.3 Race/Ethnicity of Students by Type of Schooling

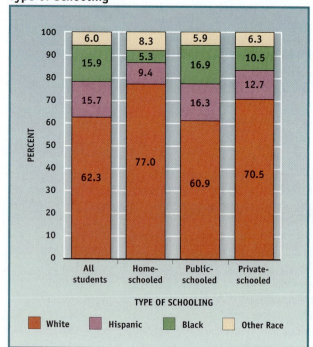

Source: Frey, William H., Amy Beth Anspach & John Paul Dewitt, *The Allyn & Bacon Social Atlas of the United States.* Published by Allyn & Bacon, Boston, MA. Copyright © 2008 by Pearson Education. Reprinted by permission of the publisher.

Wealthy versus Poor School Districts. Parents say they switch to private schools—or want to—because of the

How do we know what we know?

Does Private School Make a Difference?

Studies of students attending public and private schools do find some greater performance. But was it because of the type of school they attended? Christopher and Sarah Lubienski (2006) analyzed data from 2003 National Assessment of Educational Progress, which looked at achievement rates for 166,736 fourth grade students at 6,664 schools and 131,497 eighth grade students attending 5,377 schools. This included students at both public and private schools and included secular private schools and Christian schools.

They found that the rather modest differences in achievement between students in public and private schools were actually explained by demographic variables, such as parents' education, income, and other factors. When they controlled for these factors, the differences between public and private schools disappeared, meaning that there were no appreciable differences as a result of the type of school you went to. In fact, the relationship reversed when comparing public and Christian schools: When demographic variables were controlled, students at public schools had significantly higher achievement than students at Christian schools.

Similar results have been found in other countries. In a 2002 study of public and private schools in ten countries in Latin America (Somers, McEwan, and Willins, 2004), raw test scores favored private schools. But when socioeconomic status was taken into account, the advantage shrank (just as the Lubienskis found). When the "peer effect"—the influence of other students and school environment—was factored in, the overall difference was zero: Public and private school children performed equally well.

---

crumbling buildings, overcrowded classrooms, bare-bones curriculum, and poor instruction in many public schools today. Unfortunately, those parents most able to afford private schools probably live in districts where the public schools are actually pretty good. Because education is funded largely by local property taxes, wealthier neighborhoods and communities have more money to spend on schools than poorer ones. Public schools in wealthy neighborhoods can afford state-of-the-art labs and libraries, small classes, and highly paid teachers. It is the poor neighborhoods that have the crumbling buildings, overcrowded classrooms, and overworked, underpaid teachers. The pattern holds up in every city and every state, reproducing the same class privileges that we find in the public/private school divide (Oakes, 1990).

Racial Segregation. The Supreme Court's *Brown* v. *Board of Education* decision (1954) outlawed the practice of **segregation**—requiring White and non-White students living in the same district to attend separate schools. In 1954, nearly 100 percent of Black students were attending intensely segregated (predominantly minority) schools. Busing programs began to decrease segregation in favor of **integration,** in which the school's ethnic distribution is more balanced.

Integration in U.S. classrooms peaked in 1988, then began to reverse when the 1991 Supreme Court ruling allowed the return of neighborhood schools. In spite of the increased diversity of the nation as a whole, school districts began to resegregate. In 1998, more than 70 percent of Black students attended intensely segregated schools. The most dramatic (and largely ignored) trend affects Hispanic Americans. In 1968, a little more than 20 percent of Hispanic students were enrolled in intensely segregated schools. In 1998, more than a third were, an increase of 13.5 percentage points. Hispanics face serious levels of segregation by race and also poverty, with particularly large increases in segregation in the West, the nation's first predominantly minority area in terms of public school enrollment (Orfield, 2004).

Segregation is strongly associated with poverty for all groups: Nearly 90 percent of intensely segregated Black and Latino schools have student bodies with concentrated poverty (Orfield, 2004). Concentrated poverty means students with worse health care, lower nutrition, less-educated parents, more frequent moves, weaker preschool skills, and often limited English skills. They have two strikes against them in their quest for educational excellence already, and then they must contend with outdated textbooks, inadequate facilities, overcrowded classrooms, and, often, inexperienced, uncredentialed teachers.

Bilingual Education

Up to the 1960s, public education in the United States was always conducted in English (except for classes designed to teach foreign languages). Children were not allowed to use another language in the classroom, and often they were punished for speaking another language in the hallways or in the schoolyard. Immigrants, Native Americans, and others who came to school with poor or no English were lost.

In 1968, Congress passed the Bilingual Education Act, asserting that these children were being denied equal access to education and that school districts should "take affirmative steps to rectify the language deficiency." These steps included courses in ESL (English as a second language) and often classroom instruction in the student's native language on the primary level.

In recent years, critics of bilingual education have argued that the programs are costly and inefficient; that there simply aren't enough qualified teachers fluent in Navajo, Somali, and Thai to go around; and that students tend to do poorly in tests of both English and their native language. But often the question boils down to melting pot versus multiculturalism. Should everyone be learning English as quickly as possible, or is there room for Navajo, Somali, and Thai in our schools and in our society?

Many researchers have concluded that bilingual education helps students to learn English. A long-awaited, federally commissioned report was supposed to summarize existing data to determine whether bilingual education helps students who speak other languages to read English, but its release has been cancelled by the government. It is known that the researchers involved conclude that it helps (*New York Times*, 2005).

While they don't offer instruction *in* other languages, other countries around the world do teach languages other than the native tongue beginning early. Denmark has compulsory second language learning at age 11. In Sweden, it begins in the lower grades. France is initiating second language training for children under 5. But in the United States, despite increasing domestic diversity, globalism, and children's early language-acquisition abilities, language education remains weak.

Maybe it is a matter of globalization. No longer is German the language of science or French the language of the arts. No longer is Russian the other "big" language, the way it was during the Cold War era. Now English is the universal second language. Whether you live in Beijing or New Delhi, Caracas or Rome, chances are you either speak English or are scrambling to learn. Thus, Americans wonder, why learn their language, when they are learning ours?

Tracking

Tracking, or grouping students according to their ability, is common in American schools. Some schools do not have formal tracking, but virtually all have mechanisms for sorting students into groups that seem to be alike in ability and achievement (Oakes, 1985).

Whether the tracking is formal or informal, strong labeling develops. Individuals in the low-achievement, non–college-preparatory, or manual track come to be labeled "dummies" or "greasers" by both teachers and other students and even among themselves. They are not only labeled, they are treated as if they are stupid or incompetent, thus affecting their self-image and ultimately affecting their achievement in a self-fulfilling prophecy. The negative impact of tracking mostly affects minority students (Oakes, 1990).

The term self-fulfilling prophecy was coined by Merton (1949) for a curious phenomenon: When you expect something to happen, it usually does. We've seen this before with racial stereotypes (Chapter 8). Rosenthal and Jacobson (1968) found it among San Francisco schoolchildren. Farkas and colleagues found that girls and Asian Americans got better grades than boys, Blacks, and Latinos, even when they all had the same test scores (Farkas, 1996; Farkas et al., 1990a; Farkas, Sheehan, and Grobe, 1990b). They concluded that girls and Asian Americans signaled that they were "good" students—they were eager to cooperate, quickly agreed with what the teacher said, and demonstrated they were trying hard. These characteristics, coveted by teachers, were rewarded with better grades.

In addition, because the funds go mostly toward the educational needs of the high-track students, the low-track students receive poorer classes, textbooks, supplies, and teachers. Gamoran and colleagues (1995) confirmed Oakes's finding that tracking reinforces previously existing inequalities for average or poor students but found it has positive benefits for "advanced" students.

The correlation between high educational achievement and race is not lost on the students. In a speech before the Democratic National Convention in 2004, Barack Obama denounced, "the slander that a Black child with a book is 'acting White.'" He was paraphrasing research by Berkeley anthropologist John Ogbu, which demonstrates that even people who suffer from stereotyped images often believe them. Minority children, especially boys, believe that good school performance is a challenge to their ethnic identity or a betrayal. They *are supposed to* perform poorly. (Ogbu and Fordham, 1986; Fordham, 1991; Ferguson, 2002).

Pedro Noguera (2004) found a positive correlation between self-esteem and school achievement: Students who feel good about themselves perform better. Only one group showed no correlation: African American boys. They are so disconnected from school that raising their self-esteem has no effect on how well they do.

▲ Grades reflect both students' achievement and teachers' expectations. In one study, girls and Asian Americans received better grades than other students—even when their test scores were the same. The researchers concluded that this was because they conformed to teachers' perceptions of how good students behave.

Gender Inequality in School

Among the first words ever spoken by the first talking Barbie were "Math class is tough!" Education not only reproduces racial inequality, it reproduces gender stereotypes. In the hidden curriculum, teachers, administrators, and peers require us to conform to narrow definitions of what it means to be a "boy" or a "girl," and they punish deviance, subtly or not. However, education also allows us to move

How do we know what we know?

The Racial Achievement Gap

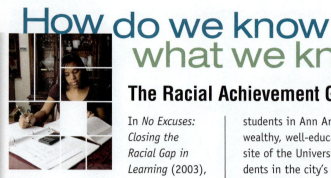

In *No Excuses: Closing the Racial Gap in Learning* (2003), Abigail and Stephan Ternstrom argue that African American educational under-achievement stems from a variety of factors:

- Low birth weight, which can impair intellectual development.
- High number of single-parent families led by young mothers unprepared to give children good educational guidance.
- Inadequate funding.
- Difficulty recruiting good teachers to work in schools attended primarily by Blacks.

By contrast, Ronald Ferguson (2001) studied middle- and upper-middle-class students in Ann Arbor, Michigan, a wealthy, well-educated community, the site of the University of Michigan. Students in the city's three high schools had an average SAT score in 2004 of 1165, over 100 points higher than the national average. In 2003, they had 44 National Merit finalists. Eighty-five percent of high school seniors go on to four-year colleges and universities. Quite an elite bunch!

Even in middle-class college-bound high schools, African American students typically had a C average, White students a B. African Americans typically scored 100 points below White students on the SAT. Why?

Some of the reasons Ferguson found were environmental: Even in the same community and the same schools, the African American students were less affluent: 21 percent were upper middle class or upper class, compared to 73 percent of the White students. But there was more. The parents of African American students lacked access to the networks White parents had to trade information about the best teachers, classes, and strategies for success. They felt less entitled, less able to be demanding and advocate for their children.

Teachers often misread signals from the Black students. In high-stress, high-achievement schools, students who are trying hard and not doing well perceive themselves as failures. It's better to act as though you are simply uninterested in doing well than to acknowledge that you are struggling. Teachers see laziness and indifference, lower their expectations, and give students less support—which Ferguson found matters a great deal to minority students. They then try harder to pretend that they are uninterested, resulting in a self-fulfilling prophecy.

---

beyond stereotyping: The classroom is perhaps the only place where a boy can be praised for being quiet and studious and a girl can be praised for knowing the answer.

In their book, *Failing at Fairness* (1994), David and Myra Sadker documented some of the subtle ways teachers reinforce both gender difference and gender inequality. They named it the "chilly classroom climate" for girls.

One fifth grade classroom Sadker and Sadker studied was having a particularly noisy and active discussion about who was the best president in American history. So the teacher warned students to raise their hands; otherwise, she would call on someone else. Then one boy enthusiastically called out:

Stephen:	I think Lincoln was the best president. He held the country together during the war.
Teacher:	A lot of historians would agree with you.
Mike:	[Seeing that nothing happened to Stephen, calls out.] I don't. Lincoln was okay, but my Dad liked Reagan. He always said Reagan was a great president.
David:	[Calls out.] Reagan? Are you kidding?
Teacher:	Who do you think our best president was, Dave?
David:	FDR. He saved us from the Depression.
Max:	[Calls out.] I don't think it's right to pick one best president. There were a lot of good ones.
Teacher:	That's interesting.
Kimberly:	[Calls out.] I don't think that presidents today are as good as the ones we used to have.
Teacher:	Okay, Kimberly. But you forgot the rule. You're supposed to raise your hand. (Sadker and Sadker, 1994, p. 42–43)

Before seeing a videotape of this class, the teacher insisted that she treated boys and girls exactly the same.

The class materials used often reflect stereotyped differences between women and men, boys and girls. In 1975 the Department of Health, Education, and Welfare surveyed 134 textbooks and found that "boy-centered" stories outnumbered "girl-centered" stories by a five to two ratio. Adult male characters outnumbered females by three to one (by four to one in fairy tales). Male subjects of biographies outnumbered female subjects by six to one.

Because of these disparities, there has been an effort to increase the number of active girls in schoolbooks and also in children's media. No longer does Batman only have Robin as his assistant; now Dora the Explorer vies with the Powerpuff Girls, and all superhero shows have at least one female hero.

There have also been dramatic changes outside the classroom. Title IX legislation forbids discrimination against girls and women in all aspects of school life. As a result, many elementary and secondary schools have increased funding for girls' sports, allowing more girls the opportunity to participate. And, contrary to some expectations, girls have shown they love sports.

The visible and successful campaign for gender equality in school has produced a backlash. "What about the boys?" some complain (Hoff-Sommers, 2000). These critics argue that it is boys, today, who are the victims of reverse discrimination and that all the initiatives developed to help girls in science and math, in sports, and in classroom decorum actually hurt boys.

And there is some evidence that from elementary schools to college, boys perform worse than girls. From the earliest ages, girls are now more connected to school; they get higher grades and more class honors and are less likely to repeat a grade or get suspended. Boys are nine times more likely to be diagnosed with attention deficit and hyperactivity disorder (ADHD) and somewhat more likely to be diagnosed as retarded, learning disabled, and emotionally disturbed (see, for example, Pollack, 1998).

But is this because the boys are the victims of reverse discrimination? After all, the reforms instituted to enable girls to do better—more attention to different learning styles, new teacher training, different classroom techniques—all benefit boys too. In reality, it's not girls, but ideas of masculinity that too often prevent boys from succeeding in school. Masculinity is often associated with indifference to and contempt for school, especially reading and languages. In many studies, boys consistently label English and foreign languages as "feminine" subjects (Mac and Ghaill, 1994; Martino, 1994, 1997). As Catherine Stimpson, Dean of the Graduate School at New York University, put it "Real men don't speak French," (quoted in Lewin, 1998). It turns out that certain norms of masculinity make it difficult for both boys and girls to succeed.

Schooling for Gender Identity

One of the chief lessons taught in school is what it means to be a man or a woman. Gender conformity—adhering to normative expectations about masculinity or femininity—is carefully scrutinized. We get messages everywhere we look—in the content of the texts we read, the rules we are all supposed to follow, and the behaviors of teachers and administrators as role models. But it is most significantly taught by peers, who act as a sort of "gender police," enforcing the rules. Often we learn it by a sort of negative reinforcement: Step out of line, even the tiniest bit, and your friends and other students will let you know, clearly and unequivocally, that you have transgressed. Do it again, and they may begin to doubt you as a potential friend. Do it consistently, and you will be marginalized as a weirdo, a deviant, or, most importantly, as gay.

▲ Bullying has become an increasingly important problem in schools. More than 1 million school children a year are bullied. More than just a problem of individual bullies and victims, sociologists point to bullying as a social experience that can compromise educational goals. Challenging bullying must involve changing school culture.

Every American teenager knows that the most constant put-down in our high schools and middle schools these days is "that's so gay." Ordinarily this gay-baiting—calling people or something they do "gay" as a way of ridiculing them or putting them down—has little to do with sexual orientation: Calling someone's shirt or hairstyle or musical preference "gay" doesn't typically mean that you suspect he or she might actually be homosexual. It means that you don't think the person is acting sufficiently masculine. "Dude, you're a fag," is the way one kid put it (Pascoe, 2005).

The constant teasing and bullying that occur in middle schools and high schools have become national problems (Juvonen, 2005; Olweus, 1993). Bullying is not one single thing but a continuum stretching from hurtful language through shoving and hitting to criminal assault and school shootings. Harmful teasing and bullying happen to more than 1 million school children a year. The evidence of bullying's ubiquity alone is quite convincing. In one study of middle and high schools students in midwestern towns, 88 percent reported having observed bullying, and 77 percent reported being a victim of bullying at some point during their school years. In another, 70 percent had been sexually harassed by their peers; 40 percent had experienced physical dating violence, 66 percent had been victimized by emotional abuse in a dating relationship, and 54 percent had been bullied.

Another national survey of 15,686 students in grades 6 through 10 published in the *Journal of the American Medical Association* (JAMA) found that 29.9 percent reported frequent involvement with bullying—13 percent as bully, 10.9 percent as victim, and 6 percent as both (Nansel et al., 2001). One-quarter of kids in primary school, grades 4 through 6, admitted to bullying another student with some regularity in the three months before the survey (Limber et al., 1997). And yet another found that during one two-week period at two Los Angeles middle schools, nearly half the 192 kids interviewed reported being bullied at least once. More than that said they had seen others targeted (Juvonen et al., 2003).

Many middle and high school students are afraid to go to school; they fear locker rooms, hallways, bathrooms, lunchrooms, and playgrounds, and some even fear their classrooms. They fear being targeted or bullied in hostile high school hallways. Among young people 12 through 24, three in ten report that violence has increased in their schools in the past year, and nearly two-fifths have worried that a classmate was potentially violent ("Fear of Classmates," 1999). More than half of all teens know somebody who has brought a weapon to school. And nearly two-thirds (63 percent) of parents believe a school shooting is somewhat or very likely to occur in their communities ("Half of Teens," 2001).

Did *you* know?

Bringing a weapon to school varies only a little bit by race: 15.2 percent of African Americans report bringing a weapon to school, 16.5 percent of Hispanics report bringing a weapon, and 17.9 percent of White students report bringing a weapon (*Contexts*, 2005, p. 37).

School Reform

Schools are one of the major ways in which people hope to move up in the social hierarchy, obtaining knowledge and skills to better their class position. And, at the same time, schools are one of the major ways that social inequalities are reproduced, in which class, or race, or gender inequality is legitimated. How can schools be more responsive to the people they are intended to serve?

Sociology and our World

Random School Shootings

Bullying and homophobic harassment were two of several precipitating factors in the tragic cases of random school shootings that have taken place in American schools. Since 1992, there have been 29 cases of such shootings in which a boy (or boys) opens fire on his classmates. In my research project on these shootings, I've discovered several startling facts. First, all 29 shootings were committed by boys. All but one took place in a rural or suburban school—not an inner-city school. All but one of the shooters were White.

And they all had a similar story of being bullied and harassed every day, until school became a kind of torture. Why? It was *not* because they were gay, but because they were *different* from the other boys—shy, bookish, honor students, artistic, musical, theatrical, nonathletic, "geekish," or weird. It was because they were not athletic, overweight or underweight, or because they wore glasses.

Faced with such incessant torment, some boys withdraw, some self-medicate, some attempt suicide. Many try valiantly, and often vainly, to fit in, to conform to these impossible standards that others set for them. And a few explode. Like Luke Woodham, a bookish, overweight 16-year-old in Pearl, Mississippi. An honor student, he was teased constantly for being overweight and a nerd. On October 1, 1997, Woodham opened fire in the school's common area, killing two students and wounding seven others. In a psychiatric interview, he said, "I am not insane. I am angry. I killed because people like me are mistreated every day. I am malicious because I am miserable."

Fourteen-year-old Michael Carneal was a shy freshman at Heath High School in Paducah, Kentucky, barely 5 feet tall, weighing 110 pounds. He wore thick glasses and played in the high school band. He felt alienated, pushed around, picked on. Over Thanksgiving, 1997, he stole two shotguns, two semiautomatic rifles, a pistol, and 700 rounds of ammunition and brought them to school hoping that they would bring him instant recognition. "I just wanted the guys to think I was cool," he said. When the cool guys ignored him, he opened fire on a morning prayer circle, killing three classmates and wounding five others. Now serving a life sentence in prison, Carneal told psychiatrists weighing his sanity that "people respect me now" (Blank, 1998).

And then there was Columbine High School in Littleton, Colorado. The very word *Columbine* has become a symbol; kids today often talk about someone "pulling a Columbine." The connection between being socially marginalized, picked on, and bullied every day propelled Eric Harris and Dylan Klebold deeper into their video-game-inspired fantasies of a vengeful bloodbath. On April 20, 1999, Harris and Klebold brought a variety of weapons to their high school and proceeded to walk through the school, shooting whomever they could find. Twenty-three students and faculty were injured and 15 died, including one teacher and the perpetrators.

On April 16, 2007, Seung Hui Cho, a 23-year-old student at Virginia Tech, murdered two students in a dorm, waited about an hour, and then calmly walked to an academic building, chained the entrance, and started shooting methodically. In the end, he killed 30 students and faculty before shooting himself—the deadliest shooting by an individual in our nation's history. While obviously mentally ill, he had managed never to be ill "enough" to attract serious attention. In the time between the shootings, he recorded a video in which he fumed about all the taunting, teasing, and being ignored he had endured and how this final conflagration would even the score.

In a national survey of teenagers' attitudes, nearly nine of ten teenagers (86 percent) said that they believed that the school shootings were motivated by a desire "to get back at those who have hurt them" and that "other kids picking on them, making fun of them, or bullying them" were the immediate causes. Other potential causes such as violence on television, movies, computer games or videos, mental problems, and access to guns were significantly lower on the adolescents' ratings (Gaughan, Cerio, and Myers, 2001).

Privatization

One of the most popular types of school reform during the last few decades has been privatization, allowing some degree of private control over public education. There are two types of privatization, vouchers and charter schools.

The **voucher system** uses taxpayer funds to pay for students' tuition at private schools. The idea has been floating around for decades. It was first proposed by economist Milton Friedman in 1955, based on the idea of the free market: If there is

TABLE 17.4

Charter School Scores: Percent of Fourth Graders at or above Basic Level

	MATH		READING	
	CHARTER SCHOOLS	OTHER PUBLIC	CHARTER SCHOOLS	OTHER PUBLIC
RACE				
White	84	**87**	71	**74**
Black	50	**54**	37	**40**
Hispanic	58	**62**	**45**	43
INCOME				
Eligible for public lunch	53	**62**	38	**45**
Not eligible	80	**88**	70	**76**
LOCATION				
Central city	58	**68**	50	**52**
Urban fringe/large town	78	**80**	64	**66**
Rural/small town	**84**	80	64	**67**

Source: From "Charter Schools Trail in Results, U.S. Data Reveals" by Diana Jean Schemo, *The New York Times,* August 17, 2004. Reprinted by permission.

competition for a product or service, quality will increase. However, it is controversial: A school district in Wisconsin instituted the first voucher program in 1990, and 15 years later only two more states (Ohio and Florida) and the District of Columbia have followed suit, with a total of only about 36,000 students. Voters have defeated proposed voucher programs in many states, including California, Michigan, Texas, South Carolina, and Indiana.

Charter schools are publicly funded elementary or secondary schools that set forth in their founding document (charter) goals they intend to meet in terms of student achievement. In return, these schools are privately administered and exempt from certain laws regarding education. They encompass a wide range of curricula and style, from no-nonsense, "back-to-basics" reading, writing, and mathematics to technology-rich science and math schools to intimate academies modeled on the more elite private schools. The first charter school was authorized in Minnesota in 1991, and they have been proliferating ever since. Now there are 3,400 charter schools in 40 states, with about 1 million students (Center for Education Reform, 2007).

But do charter schools work? In the first national study, fourth graders attending charter schools performed worse than their peers in traditional public schools in almost every racial, economic, and geographic group (Table 17.4). Charter schools are also more segregated than public schools, especially for African American students (Orfield, 2004). Obviously this may not be due to the intent or desires of academic leaders, but to flaws in state policies, enforcement, and the method of approving schools for charters.

Homeschooling

About 1.1 million students ages 5 through 17 were homeschooled in the United States in spring 2003, an increase of almost a quarter million since 1999 (National Center for Education Statistics, 2004). They are homeschooled in all grades, from kindergarten through twelfth grade.

Why do parents homeschool their children? The most important reason cited was concern about the environment of traditional schools (31 percent). Almost as many said that they wanted to provide the religious or moral instruction missing in traditional schools (30 percent). Only 16 percent said that they were dissatisfied with the academic instruction at the other schools (Figure 17.4).

Thus, homeschooling is a phenomenon largely of the political far left and the far right. Liberals might complain about classroom conduct, watered-down academics, and the lack of attention to individual learning styles; conservatives and religious homeschoolers complain about having a required multicultural curriculum, with no school prayer, and teaching evolution.

No Child Left Behind

In January 2002, President George W. Bush signed Public Law 107-110, the Elementary and Secondary School Act, better known as "No Child Left Behind" (NCLB). The 670-page law outlines a top-down approach to school performance, with a number of sweeping, even revolutionary, provisions:

- Students in elementary school (grades 3 through 8) must take annual tests to ensure that they have met minimal standards of competency in reading and math.
- Students in schools that are falling behind can transfer to better schools on the government's tab.
- Every child should learn to read and write English by the end of the third grade.

The cost of enforcing this law is immense: The Department of Education budget increased from $14 billion to $22.4 billion to handle it. And the goals, though broadly defined, become difficult to enforce. Teachers complain that they must spend an excessive amount of class time preparing students for the reading and math tests, while ignoring other essential subjects like history and science. They complain that the program doesn't target the students who need the most help and even forces them to dumb down accountability measures that were already in place.

School districts complain that the law tends to reproduce the same inequalities that it is intended to combat. It treats every school district alike, ignoring special challenges faced by districts with many impoverished or non-English-speaking students or students with learning disabilities.

The administration says that the programs are successful, pointing to a (small) rise in math and reading test scores. But 40 states have requested exemptions from part of the NCLB, and 20 states are debating whether to drop out and forego the federal funding. Others are setting absurdly low standards to make targets easy to meet or are passing laws giving priority to their existing school accountability programs. In 2005, Connecticut Attorney General Richard Blumental (backed by a Republican governor) sued the federal government for not allocating enough money to finance the law (an "unfunded mandate"). New Jersey and Maine are expected to follow. The National Education Association (NEA), the nation's largest teachers' union, has also joined several school districts in challenging inadequate funding in court (Dobbs, 2005).

FIGURE 17.4 Parental Reasons for Having Children Homeschooled, 2003

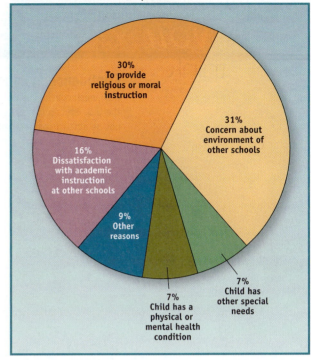

30%
To provide religious or moral instruction

31% Concern about environment of other schools

16% Dissatisfaction with academic instruction at other schools

9% Other reasons

7% Child has a physical or mental health condition

7% Child has other special needs

Source: Frey, William H., Amy Beth Anspach & John Paul Dewitt, *The Allyn & Bacon Social Atlas of the United States.* Published by Allyn & Bacon, Boston, MA. Copyright © 2008 by Pearson Education. Reprinted by permission of the publisher.

MyLab

What do you think? 17.2

Confidence in Education

How much confidence do you have in our educational system? There are those who think that the U.S. educational system is in a state of crisis. These individuals worry that our students will not be able to compete with those of other countries in the global economy. Other individuals and agencies are more optimistic, and are working hard to develop strategies to improve the system. So, what do you think?

As far as the people running the education system are concerned, would you say you have a great deal of confidence, only some confidence, or hardly any confidence at all in them?

○ A great deal
○ Only some
○ Hardly any

The Sociology of Higher Education

In 1949, there were 2,400,000 college students in the United States. Fifty years later, there were 16,000,000. The population of the country had doubled during that period, but the proportion of the population going to college increased by 800 percent. About one in four Americans now has a college degree. And it is not merely a matter of intellectual interest: Today people need bachelor's degrees, and sometimes master's degrees, to get jobs that would have required a high school diploma or less 50 years ago. What happened?

In 1949, college degrees were simply unnecessary. A high school diploma qualified you for almost every job, and if you needed additional training, you could apply directly to a law or medical school. The wealthy went to college to "become educated," learn the social skills, and build the social networks necessary for an upper-class life (Altbach, 1998; Lucas, 1996; Rudolph, 1990).

After World War II, GI loans brought many of the returning soldiers to college for the first time. Most were the first in their families to attend college, and they weren't quite sure what to expect. Some studied "liberal arts" such as English, history, and philosophy, but most wanted courses directly related to the jobs they would get afterward. Colleges filled the need with job-oriented majors and courses. Employers, faced with a glut of applicants more qualified than usual, began to require more advanced degrees for entry-level jobs: Why hire someone with just a high school diploma for the typist job, when there were a dozen applicants with college degrees? Majors and career paths became more specialized: Why hire someone with an English degree for the advertising job, when there were a dozen applicants who majored in advertising? Today most students still major in one of the liberal arts, but job-oriented majors are very popular.

Preparing for College

Although college is rapidly becoming a necessity for middle-class and even working-class lives, the quality of American higher education is in question. Student readiness and achievement are both low.

Among industrialized countries, American 15-year-olds rank 24 out of 29 in math literacy and problem-solving ability (Program for International Student Assessment, 2003). They fall behind all Scandinavian countries, Korea, Japan, Canada, Australia, New Zealand, Slovakia, the Czech Republic, in fact all of Western Europe except Portugal and Italy. Just over one-third of American high school graduates have college-ready skills. More than half (53 percent) of all college students are required to take remedial English or math (American Diploma Project, 2004).

Because they are unprepared for college, it is understandable that they are not prepared to graduate within the traditional four years. Smaller college endowments (which mean less scholarship money) and a widening gap between federal grant stipends and tuition costs mean that most students must work, part-time or full-time, and classes and studying compete with their work schedules. Only a little over 50 percent of all college freshmen actually receive a bachelor's degree within six years of enrolling (Greene and Winters, 2005). The six-year rate varies from a high of 66 percent in Massachusetts and 64 percent in Maryland to a low of 39 percent in New Mexico, 37 percent in Louisiana, and 20 percent in Alaska. At historically Black colleges, the six-year graduation rate is 42 percent (*Journal of Blacks in Higher Education*, 2007).

On the other hand, there is also evidence that we are no less prepared than we used to be. For example, the average Scholastic Aptitude Test (SAT) scores are about the same today as they were in 1976. As you can see in Table 17.5, contrary to popular opinion, scores on the SAT test, taken by most high school students who intend to go to college, have not been in a downward spiral. During the last 30 years, the mean score on the verbal section has stayed about the same, and the mean score on the math section has actually increased.

Could it be that American students are doing about the same as they have been for decades—but that the rest of the world is catching up?

Higher Education and Inequality

High school graduation is only the rim of the funnel of educational privilege. Of those minorities and lower- and working-class persons who graduate from high school, few go on to college. Of those who do attend college, few graduate from college. And so on. By the time they turn 26, 59 percent of people from affluent families but just 7 percent of people from low-income households have a bachelor's degree (Education Trust, 2006). The system itself transforms social privilege into personal merit, justifying and perpetuating the inequality it is supposed to combat and correct.

The class barrier to higher education is actually increasing. The proportion of students from upper-income families attending the most elite colleges declined dramatically after World War II, but it is growing again. Only 3 percent come from the bottom quartile of the income, and only 10 percent come from the bottom half.

TABLE 17.5

Average SAT Scores of High School Seniors in the United States, 1976–2004		
	VERBAL	**MATH**
1976	511	520
1980	506	515
1984	511	518
1988	512	521
1992	504	521
1996	507	527
2000	507	533
2004	512	537

Source: College Entrance Examination Board, 2005.

Did you know?

When you receive a four-year college degree, you typically become a Bachelor of Arts or Bachelor of Science. But bachelor is also a term for an adult, unmarried man. What's the connection? In the Middle Ages, were unmarried men all supposed to have advanced degrees?

Actually, there is no connection. In the original Vulgar Latin (Latin spoken by the common people), *baccalaris* meant a poor unmarried "farmhand" and *baccalaureus* meant "advanced student" (from *bacca laureus*, the laurel branch used to honor degree holders). Both words entered the English language in the late fourteenth century, but because they sounded almost the same, they both became *bachelor*.

Sociology and our World

The Chosen

Sociologist Jerome Karabel graduated from Harvard University and now teaches at the University of California at Berkeley (and served on the admissions committee), so he may be the ideal person to write *The Chosen: The Hidden History of Admission and Exclusion at Harvard, Yale, and Princeton* (2005). He examined a century of admissions decisions at these three Ivy League schools to determine who gets in—and how.

Prior to the 1920s, all applicants who met high academic standards were accepted. The administration of these schools became concerned about the increasing numbers of well-qualified Jewish applicants (20 percent of the Harvard freshman class of 1918): How could they maintain a Protestant majority if they admitted everyone with a rash of A's? Instead, they established admissions committees and limited the "super bright" to about 10 percent of available spots. For the rest, grades were less important than "character": manliness, congeniality, leadership potential, and other qualities that they believed lacking in Jewish men.

Other universities followed the example of the Big Three, and for the rest of the century, admissions committees from the top to the bottom tier of universities regularly rejected applicants whom they believed belonged to an "undesirable" race, ethnic background, religion, or socioeconomic status. "Character" was further delineated by looking at applicants' extracurricular activities and soliciting letters of recommendation. That system is still in place today. Virtually every student reading this book is part of a system that was designed initially to keep some people out. Though no admissions committee would dare ask about an applicant's race or religion today, they still weed out applicants with the wrong "character," and that rarely means the children of wealthy alumni.

But it is not just elite colleges. Across the spectrum, colleges are drawing more members from upper-income households and fewer from average or below-average income households. Because the income gap between the college educated and the noncollege educated was 66 percent in 1997 (up from 31 percent in 1979) (Lexington, 2005), it seems that the universities are reproducing social advantage instead of serving as an engine of mobility.

The poorer students are priced out of the market for higher education by soaring tuition increases (which means that financial aid is extending farther up the income ladder than it used to). We might think, "Oh, there are always scholarships for the smart ones," but being smart is not a replacement for having money. Seventy-eight percent of the top achievers from low-income families go to college. But 77 percent of the *bottom* achievers from high-income families also manage to get in (*Business Week*, 2003).

Student Life

Sociologists do not simply look at educational institutions and the ways in which they reinforce existing relationships based on class, race, ethnicity, or gender. Schools also offer several different cultures, all competing and colliding with each other. For example, there is the culture of professionalism among teachers and professors, by which the standards for academic success at the nation's elite universities have been raised consistently. Professors at major universities are rarely rewarded for excellence in teaching but more often for publication in specialized scholarly journals that only other specialists can read and understand.

Students also develop a subculture that their professors (and their parents!) often find foreign and even a bit disconcerting. According to this stereotype, student life revolves around drinking, partying, playing video games and online poker, watching pornography on the Internet, sports, and sleeping. At many colleges, it appears that academic life—studying, homework, reading in the library, doing research—is almost an incidental afterthought, the least important part of a student's day. And occasionally, a professor goes "underground" and lives in a dorm or fraternity or sorority house for a semester and writes an exposé of campus life, designed to shock adults into paying attention to student culture (see Moffatt, 1989; Nathan, 2005).

Occasionally, anthropologist's get the idea to study the "foreign" culture that is living right under their noses. In the late 1980s, anthropologist Michael Moffatt moved into the dorms at Rutgers and wrote a scathing expose of campus life (Moffatt, 1989)—a world of indiscriminate drunken sex, copious drinking, no studying but lots of sleeping, and a lack of serious intellectual engagement. College, he wrote, is really about the pursuit of "fun."

▲ On many college campuses, classroom education takes a backseat to social life. Studying, going to the library for research, and even attending classes are often lower priorities than achieving social (and athletic) goals.

Actually, college students have been accused of being lazy, drunken sex fiends since, well, since there have been college students. In the late eighteenth century, Princeton students were disciplined after assaulting and beating up professors whose lectures they didn't like (Horowitz, 1987). In the late nineteenth century, the famous American essayist Henry Adams remembered mostly the "fantastic" amount of drinking during his Harvard days (he graduated in 1858). And essayist Edmund Wilson remembered his Princeton days before World War I as a time "of prevalent drunkenness, cheating in examinations, intellectual cowardice and repression, indiscriminate mockery, general ignorance, and the branding as a 'sad bird' anyone who tried to rise above it" (in Dabney, 2005).

Moffatt's description seemed a bit over the top to Northern Arizona University anthropologist Cathy Small. She wanted to understand why students didn't come to her office hours, didn't seem to do the readings for her classes, and fell asleep and ate during class time. In the fall of 2002, she enrolled in her own university, and spent a year in the dorms as an incoming first-year student. She told virtually no one that she was a professor. And she published the results under a pseudonym to try to conceal her identity, but journalists figured it out within a week of the book's publication (Nathan, 2005).

Small found students to be amazingly busy: Most work at part-time jobs for at least 15 hours a week, juggle five courses, and try to join campus activities to pad their college resumés to gain a competitive advantage in the job market. Sure, they drink and sleep, hook up and party down. And they expect their colleges to both "educate and entertain" them.

Small found that the biggest differences between campus life today and when she was a student in the 1970s were the virtual lack of any free time in the lives of her students, the absence of a sense of campus "community," and the absence of any impact by faculty on the lives of students. Students today are so overscheduled that they cut corners—as she did when confronted with massive work demands. She interprets plagiarism and cheating to be simple time-saving maneuvers by students with impossible demands. Students also never discussed intellectual, political, or philosophical issues outside of class, and rarely, if ever, discussed anything that happened in class with their friends.

As a result of her ethnographic fieldwork, Small has reduced the amount of homework she assigns and spends more time discussing issues that students find relevant. She says today she has far more empathy for their efforts to juggle so many different demands. "A lot of the assumptions that professors and administrators make about student life," she says, "are just wrong" (in Farrell and Hoover, 2005, p. 36).

TABLE 17.6

Student Life by the Numbers

In 2005, the National Survey of Student Engagement, administered by the Center for Postsecondary Education and Indiana University, surveyed more than 48,000 college seniors. Here's how they spend their time (the numbers indicate percentages of students)

ACTIVITY	0 HOURS/WEEK	1–5	6–10	11 OR MORE
Studying and preparing for class	0	20	25	55
Working for pay	56	6	9	29
Activities outside of class (organizations, publications, student government, sports)	43	30	12	15
Relaxing and socializing	2	33	29	35

Source: National Survey of Student Engagement, 2006.

Recent surveys support Small's observations, consistently finding that students are working harder and longer today than they ever did (Table 17.6). Students study harder, and nearly half have paid jobs outside of school. Students also have far less sex and drink far less than observers—and students themselves—imagine (Perkins, 2002). As with most sociology, it isn't the case that students are complete party-going alcohol-sodden, sex-addicted sports fans or serious academic nerds who live to study. They're both—although preferably not at the same time.

Education, Inc.

One of the dominant recent educational trends, in primary and secondary education as well as in higher education, has been the spread of the marketplace. For centuries, colleges and universities were a sort of refuge from the market, a place where the pursuit of dollars didn't interfere with the pursuit of knowledge. Not anymore.

For-Profit Universities

Traditional universities are not-for-profit organizations. However, an increasing number of proprietary or **for-profit universities** have arisen in recent years. They have some advantages over traditional universities: The cost is comparatively low, the university rather than the professors owns the curriculum, and students can graduate relatively quickly. They omit or severely curtail the traditional social activities of a college; their facilities are usually very limited; and their degrees lack the prestige of a degree from a traditional university. However, most students today are far more interested in developing practical, job-related skills than in a "total college experience," and they have found proprietary schools a viable alternative. Each school has developed its own practical market niche:

- Strayer concentrates on telecommunications and business administration.
- Cardean University offers online business education, including MBAs.
- Concord Law School, owned by Kaplan (in turn owned by the *Washington Post*) has one of largest law school enrollments in the United States.

The University of Phoenix, the largest for-profit university in the United States, is also the largest university in the United States, period. It has 280,000 students on 239 campuses and various satellite campuses around the world, including some in China and India, and enrollment is growing at 25 percent per year.

It is the brainchild of John Sperling, a Cambridge University–educated economist turned entrepreneur. While teaching at a state university, he noticed that the curriculum was designed for "traditional" 18- to 22-year-old students and ignored adult learners. But in the new economy, people 10 or 20 years past high school often decide that they need college, and those with degrees often return to update their skills or retool their resumés. He decided to found a new university catering to working adults, with convenient class schedules, many centers in conveniently located areas instead of one giant central campus (beginning in the 1990s, entire degrees could be taken online), and an emphasis on practical subjects that will help them build careers.

▲ College is no longer the sole domain of traditional-age students. Adult learners over 23 years old now make up about 10 percent of all college students—and more than 90 percent at some for-profit schools.

Nontraditional students now account for 95 percent of the Phoenix student body. They are over 25 years old, hoping to enhance their job possibilities rather than broaden their intellectual interests, and not particularly interested in immersing themselves in the traditional college environment. In some ways, the University of Phoenix has proved more successful than traditional colleges in meeting the needs of nontraditional students.

However, as institutions for higher learning, for-profits strip the university of its other functions. There are no science labs and no faculty members do research, nor are professors protected by tenure or any forms of academic freedom. Faculty members are paid only to teach, and they are paid hourly wages that don't approach the salaries of professors at most colleges and universities. In a sense, these private universities separate the different dimensions of higher education and concentrate on some while ignoring others.

The Marketization of Higher Education

The marketing success of for-profit universities has led to a trend to "marketization" in traditional universities. Public universities have shifted from state institutions to state-supported institutions to state-assisted institutions. For example, at the University of Virginia, the state's share of the operating budget decreased from 28 percent in 1985 to 8 percent in 2004. Higher education becomes a business, "the education industry," with the same goals statements and five-year plans of any other business. Students become "clients," and their grades "product."

As universities transform themselves into competitive commercial operations, they increasingly must ask the "clients" to pay "fees," particularly when they are out-of-state and foreign students. In the United States, international students contribute some $13 billion a year to the education industry (*Economist*, 2005). In this respect, the United States has been the market leader for the past 50 years. However, the Institute for International Education reports that the foreign student population declined in 2003–2004 for the first time in 30 years. Applications from foreign students to American grad schools fell by 28 percent in 2004, and actual enrollment dropped 6 percent (*Economist*, 2005).

The biggest reason for the decline in lucrative student enrollment is foreign competition. The number of foreign students is up by 21 percent in Britain, 23 percent in

FIGURE 17.5 Distribution of Foreign Students by Host Country/Territory, 2002–2003

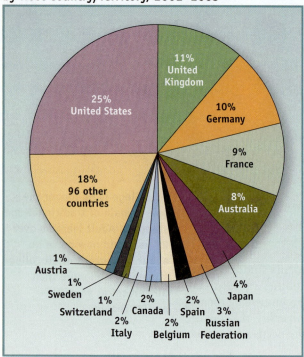

25% United States

11% United Kingdom

10% Germany

9% France

8% Australia

18% 96 other countries

1% Austria

1% Sweden

1% Switzerland

2% Italy

2% Canada

2% Belgium

2% Spain

3% Russian Federation

4% Japan

Source: From UNESCO Institute for Statistics. Reprinted with permission.

Germany, and 28 percent in France (Figure 17.5). Both Australia and New Zealand are actively trying to turn their educational systems into an export industry (*Economist,* 2005).

McSchool

Marketization is spreading to elementary and secondary schools as well. There has been significant publicity concerning the food industry's takeover of school lunch programs—selling high-fat, low-nutrition fast foods—and the dominance of sodas, snacks, and candy in school vending machines across the country. Some, including the U.S. Surgeon General, have linked this marketing strategy to an obesity epidemic among American kids.

But that's just one aspect of larger incursion of the profit motive into public education. To keep strapped school districts functioning amid increasing enrollments and widening budget deficits, to pay for unfunded government mandates, to subsidize sports and other enrichment programs that might otherwise have to shrink or be cancelled, elementary and high schools are opening their doors to hundreds of thousands of dollars in corporate money annually.

In 2004, a New Jersey elementary school became the first school in the country to sell naming rights to a corporate sponsor, when it allowed a $100,000 illuminated corporate advertisement to be affixed to its gym. Three high schools in Texas have sold the naming rights to their football stadiums for more than a million dollars (the sponsors are a bank, a communications company, and a health care provider). In Massachusetts, lawmakers recently authorized the placement of ads on school buses to the tune of $600,000 a year (*Economist,* 2005).

Across the United States, corporate sponsors' logos appear on sports fields, gyms, libraries, playgrounds, and classrooms. School events are paid for by corporations and carry their names. Corporations advertise on book covers, in hallways, on school websites, and on teaching materials. There are brand-name menus in school cafeterias. Coupons for brand-name sodas, chips, burgers, and pizza are given as rewards for reading. Some school districts have even hired full-time marketing directors whose job it is to raise money for the schools by selling ads.

Education in the 21st Century

Americans have always had the optimistic faith that education leads to a secure future, to happiness, to success. Chances are that you have this faith. That's why you are here, enrolled in a college class, reading this book.

But the first country in the world to institute mass education for all of its citizens may be the first to sell it out: literally, to corporate interests, but also to those millions who found that education did not lead to a secure future after all, were denied education, or found that it did not lead to a secure future at all.

Like every social institution, education is always going to be both a tool of liberation and a tool of oppression. Some members of underprivileged groups will acquire the skills necessary to move up in the social hierarchy of our society. Most will not. Some members of majority groups will acquire the skills necessary to combat injustice. Most will not. Inequality will certainly be criticized in uncounted thousands of lesson plans and essay-exam questions. But it will also be made to appear natural and inevitable.

Chapter Review

1. *How does sociology view education?* Sociologists view education as both a path to mobility and a central institution with regard to reproducing social structure. The manifest function of education is to teach the subject matter, and the latent functions of education are to teach norms and values and to establish relationships and social networks.

2. *How does globalization affect education?* Education is related to economic success. Inequality in educational opportunities mirrors inequality between countries. One's family background is the best predictor of educational attainment, but other factors play a role. For example, worldwide, girls are more poorly educated and more likely to be illiterate than boys. This is compounded in poor countries which have low literacy rates.

3. *How does education reproduce inequality?* Higher levels of education are correlated with higher income. Most people believe that education leads to mobility, but sociologists see education as being a primary vehicle for reproducing race, ethnic, class, and gender inequalities despite a widespread belief in meritocracy. Sociologists are also interested in the hidden curriculum, which creates inequality and makes it seem natural. Inequality is reproduced in books, tests, class, and discussions; and much of it takes place outside the classroom with peers. Types of schools and district resources equal dramatic differences in achievement. Whites are more likely than Blacks to attend private schools, which provide prestige, are safer, and focus on an environment of learning. Wealthier public school districts reproduce class privilege through better schools.

4. *How does inequality manifest in education?* Segregation is illegal but still widespread and is associated with poverty. Although research shows that bilingual education helps students learn English, it is not widespread or widely supported. Tracking also leads to inequality and is common. Tracking leads to labeling, unequal treatment, and self-fulfilling prophecies. Education also reproduces gender stereotypes through treatment, expectations, and class materials.

5. *How do sociologists view higher education?* One in four Americans has a college degree. However, preparation for college is inadequate in many ways. Most students also have to work at least part-time, which affects educational achievement and graduation rates. In addition, fewer minority and poor individuals go to college. Family income is the best predictor of college enrollment and success. Schools offer a variety of cultural experiences. For example, the culture of the professors and administration focuses on education, and the culture of student life focuses on social activities.

6. *How is education affected by the market?* Traditional universities are nonprofit, but an increasing number of for-profit institutions are developing. For-profit universities have advantages; the cost is low, the university owns the curriculum, and students can graduate quickly. On the downside, professors are paid less and have less security and prestige, social lives of students suffer, and the degree holds less prestige. For-profit colleges have spurred marketing of traditional universities, which also spills over into elementary and secondary schools that have corporate sponsors.

chapter 18

ON APRIL 20, 1999, two seniors at Columbine High School in Littleton, Colorado, Eric Harris and Dylan Klebold, walked through their school corridors, guns blazing, murdering their classmates. When their rampage was over, 12 students and one teacher lay dead, many others had been wounded, and the shooters had taken their own lives.

This horrific mass murder was only one of nearly 30 such "rampage" school shootings in our nation's schools since the early 1990s. While virtually all other crimes of violence have decreased in the United States since 1990, these alone have increased. Why?

While some have blamed permissive parents, permissive gun laws, and psychological problems, nearly everyone agreed that the media had something to do with it. Then-President Clinton suggested that it was the Internet because Klebold and Harris had visited many violent racist websites. Others suggested it was violent video games or violent TV shows and movies.

The debate about Columbine repeats the debate our society has had for decades: Do the media *cause* violence, or do the media reflect the

Mass Media

violence that already exists in our society?

Think of how many times we have heard variations of this debate: Does gangsta rap, or violent video games, or violent movies, or violent heavy metal music lead to increased violence? Does violent pornography lead men to commit rape? Or do these media merely remind us of how violent our society already is?

The sociologist approaches this debate differently. To the sociologist, one does not choose between these two positions. It's both: The media both reflect the society in which they were created and also affect our behaviors and

The media both reflect the society in which they were created, and also affect our behaviors and attitudes. If they didn't reflect our society, then they wouldn't make any sense. And if they didn't have some effect on our attitudes or behavior, then they wouldn't "work."

attitudes. If they didn't reflect our society, then they wouldn't make any sense. And if they didn't have some effect on our attitudes or behavior, then they wouldn't "work"—which means that the entire advertising industry would be out of business.

Sociologists understand that the media had an effect on Dylan Klebold and Eric Harris's rampage at Columbine, but we also understand that the media no more caused it than watching *Law and Order* repeats increases the conviction rate. Sociologists are rarely interested in "whether or not," but rather "how" and "in what ways."

What Are the Mass Media?

Media (the plural of *medium*) are the ways that we communicate with each other. If I am talking, I am using the medium of speech. I could also sing, gesture, and make smoke signals. In the Canary Islands, people used to communicate through the medium of whistling. Right now I am writing, or more precisely typing, using alphabetic symbols instead of sounds.

Technological innovations like the printing press, the radio, the television, and the personal computer have created **mass media**, ways to communicate with vast numbers of people at the same time, usually over a great distance. Mass media have developed in countless directions: There are books, newspapers, magazines, motion pictures, records and tapes, CDs and DVDs, radio and television programs, comic strips and comic books, and a whole range of new digital media. New forms of mass media are constantly being developed, and old forms are constantly falling into disuse.

Sometimes the new forms of mass media can revive or regenerate the old. Teenagers used to keep their diaries hidden in their rooms, with little locks to deter nosy siblings. Today they are likely to publish them on the Internet as blogs.

Sociologists are interested in the access to media by different groups with different resources and also in the effects of media—how they affect our behaviors and attitudes, how they bring us together or drive us apart, how they shape the very rhythm of our days.

For example, do your parents ever tell you that video games, MP3s, iPods, and the Internet rot your brain and make you passive and stupid? I'd bet that your grandparents said the same thing to your parents about television. They even called it the "boob tube" or "the idiot box." And *their* parents said the same thing about comic books and the radio. And *their* parents said the same thing about nickelodeons (machines that display moving pictures when you turn a crank) and "penny dreadfuls" (cheap, garishly printed books about crime and murder).

Mass media have allegedly been rotting brains for well over a hundred years. Every generation worries that its children are becoming mass media zombies with no initiative or imagination. Yet every generation is smarter, more literate, and better informed than the one before.

Who decides what gets put on television anyway? Or in movies, video games, or comic books? Are they tapping into the tastes and interests of the audience, or do they actually create new tastes and new interests?

Both. The media tap into our culture just as the media help to create it. The media provide a common language, a common set of reference points from which we draw in our daily conversations. At the same time, the media "segment" us into definable groups, based on class or age or race or gender.

Some media events unite us: When Hurricane Katrina struck in the summer of 2005, or the World Cup soccer tournament was played in the summer of 2006, the whole world was watching. Yet at the same time, the media world is divided into hundreds, maybe thousands, of separate audiences, markets, and special interest groups with little or nothing in common. For example, in my classes, I might refer to a song by Bruce Springsteen, which students under 30 and students of color find quaint, anachronistic, or just plain "White"; when I refer to Nelly or Shakira, students over 30 and some White students get a blank look. In a class in which students are varied by age or race, we struggle for a common language of media references.

This market segmentation occurs at the global level as well. Around the world, the staggering inequality between countries, and also within many countries, is reflected in media access and use. The vast majority of the world's people cannot afford media, so media production and consumption are strongly oriented toward the wealthier members of the world's population.

▲ Through media segmentation, some groups are connected to global cultural trends while others remain wedded to more local forms. These Argentine fans greeting Ricky Martin in 2006 may have more in common with American fans than they do with the rural poor in Argentina.

Types of Mass Media

There are many types of mass media. All have experienced enormous growth since the nineteenth century, and today media animate—and some would say dominate—our everyday lives.

Print Media. People have been keeping written records for 5,000 years, on clay tablets, papyrus scrolls, the wooden tablets of Easter Island, and eventually books. But everything had to be copied by hand, so anything written was extremely rare and expensive. In *The Canterbury Tales* (1386), the Clerk is so obsessed with books that he owns 20 of them!

The printing press, which appeared in China in the eighth century and Europe in the fifteenth, changed the way we record and transmit information (Eisenstein, 1993). The new technology allowed media to be produced more quickly, more cheaply, and in larger numbers. Reading shifted from a privilege of upper-class males to a much wider population, and the literacy rate in Europe jumped from less than 1 percent to between 10 and 15 percent.

But even during the 1800s, most people owned only two or three books—the family Bible, an almanac, and maybe a book of poetry. In the first decades of the twentieth century, reading became a mass middle-class activity (Radway, 1999). People read cheap paperbacks, newspapers, and magazines.

The newspaper and the magazine were originally vehicles for general interest readers (the word *magazine* originally meant a storehouse where you would keep your excess flour or corn). In the nineteenth century, both flourished. Newspapers became a staple of middle-class life in the developed world (in the United States, over 11,000

Tap into your creativity and master 19 new projects

BEAD &BUTTON

Your complete beading resource

Apr 2007 • Issue 76

ALL PROJECTS FULLY TESTED

5 bracelets for spring
Dress up a chevron chain with flowers p. 96

Seed bead netting accents a peyote cuff p. 72

Daisy chain necklace p. 108

Bead **fringe** spills from a pendant's center p. 116

Floral **peyote** bracelet p. 104

Stitch a pearl necklace this weekend p. 84

Use your favorite colors to customize a bracelet pattern

PLUS:
Chain mail bracelet p. 68
St. Petersburg chain lariat p. 75
Basic techniques p. 124

$5.95 • $7.50 Canada

▲ **While mass general-interest magazines have declined, there are thousands of special-interest magazines—for every imaginable hobby. These magazines unite small communities, but "buttonhole" them into separate and definable niches.**

were being published in 1880), and mass-market magazines similarly reached an increasing range of readers, bringing novels, political and cultural information, artwork, and soon photography, plus tips, advice, and contemporary musings to millions of literate people in various countries of the world.

Today, the 13,000 magazines published in the United States are largely specialized publications, of interest to only a selected audience (Tebbel and Zuckerman, 2005). The number of daily newspapers in the United States has shrunk over the past century, to about 2,030 in 1935, 1,780 in 1955, and 1,457 in 2002, due in part to the consolidation of media empires like Rupert Murdoch's and the Hearst Corporation and in part to competition from radio, television, and the Internet (journalism.org). Newspapers seem to have been hit harder by the development of new media than books or magazines; however, most newspapers are now available online (worldwide, more than 5,000), and 45 percent of U.S. adults who went online indicated that they had visited a newspaper site during the last week (*Harris Poll*, 2004).

New technologies and new literate audiences have actually spurred sales of magazines and books. Today, despite widespread worries that the Internet has made the book obsolete, book publishing is a $23 billion a year industry in the United States alone, with sales increasing every year ("Bound for Success," 2006). And magazine publishing is a $35 billion business, with hundreds of new titles launched every year. In the first four months of 2006 alone, 101 new magazines were launched.

Sociology and our World

Do Women's Magazines Oppress Women or Liberate Them?

In 1963, Betty Friedan published *The Feminine Mystique*, a blockbuster bestseller that many say launched the modern women's movement. Friedan argued that women's magazines are the main way that culture brainwashes women into believing that their highest value is in fulfilling their femininity, that true happiness can only come from catching a man, marrying him, and becoming a homemaker and mother.

Some 40 years later, the discussion continues, but now some best-selling authors are blaming women's magazines for leading women astray—in the opposite direction. These critics now say women's magazines brainwash women into wanting careers and independence, leading them away from the homes and families that represent their true pursuit of happiness (Crittenden, 1999; Shalit, 1999).

Which is it? Are women's magazines instruments of women's oppression by keeping women in the home—or by forcing them to seek fulfillment outside of the home? Are they guidebooks to fulfillment by encouraging women to marry and be mothers—or to build careers, businesses, and individual success in the world?

To the sociologist, the answer is not one or the other—it's both. From the very beginning, American women's magazines have presented readers with competing messages and have asked them to select which ideas to accept and which to resist and to resolve conflicting messages in their own ways (Aronson, 2002i).

That diversity of perspectives remains true today. Women's magazines remain highly profitable and popular; four women's titles—*Good Housekeeping, Family Circle, Women's Day*, and *Ladies' Home Journal*—rank among the top ten best-selling magazines in the nation. The major magazines also have international editions published in dozens of countries around the world. And modern versions still carry at least some of the competing messages that readers have long expected and enjoyed. See for yourself: Look at any popular women's magazine—*Glamour, O, Jane, Latina, Marie Claire, Cosmopolitan*—or check out even the great-grandmothers like *Good Housekeeping* or *Ladies' Home Journal*. See if you notice competing perspectives among the articles, the ads, and the editorials.

Globally, one can discern the difference between rich and poor nations by their newspaper circulation. Norwegians are the most avid newspaper readers in the world, with 554 issues sold per 1,000 people, more than one per household. It's 257 in Australia, 218 in the United States, and 122 in Russia. But look at the poor countries: 24 subscriptions per 1,000 people in Algeria, 6 in Bangladesh, 4 in Benin. Ethiopia is the lowest, at 0.3 (UNESCO, 2000). Obviously the newspapers in these countries are not suffering greatly from Internet competition: Most people are too poor to afford newspapers and unable to read them anyway (Ethiopia has a 36 percent literacy rate).

Blogs: Online Print Journalism. A **blog**, short for "Weblog," is essentially an online personal journal or diary where an author can air his or her opinions directly to audiences. Some call it "personal journalism." Others call it "citizen journalism." Some say it doesn't qualify as journalism at all. Blogs, you might say, put the "me" back in "media."

Blogs have become amazingly popular: There are about 12 million of them (Lee, 2006; Nussbaum, 2004; Rich, 2006), with a new blog getting started every 5.8 seconds (Belo, 2004, Pew Study of Internet and American Life, 2004;). About 57 million Americans—39 percent of all U.S. Internet users—read blogs (Lee, 2006). A majority of bloggers are young people under 29 (Nussbaum, 2004), but many are also written by professors, journalists, scientists, and other adults of various professions. The "blogosphere" is a continually globalizing space; bloggers speak an array of languages (but English and Japanese are dominant; Figure 18.1). Some blogs resemble the editorial page of a newspaper, and others offer gossip, photography, or video content.

There is controversy about both the definition and the growing power of blogs. Are blogs the first form of journalism to truly harness the democratic potential of the World Wide Web? Are they the way ordinary citizens can speak up, voicing their views without having to get past media company gatekeepers, editors, or advertisers? Blogs became so influential in both fund raising and opinion making in the hotly contested 2004 U.S. presidential campaign that today it is considered a strategic essential for political candidates to have a "blogmeister" on staff. The most-linked-to American blogs are connected to many more sites than are the newspapers usatoday.com and latimes.com, the wire service reuters.com, or National Public Radio's website, npr.org (Technorati, 2006). In 2006, Farsi, the language of Iran, also widely spoken in Afghanistan, moved into the top ten languages of the blogosphere, suggesting the potential importance of blogs and bloggers in world affairs (Technorati, 2006).

On the other hand, traditional news journalism, whether print, broadcast, or online, must meet established standards of fairness and accuracy. Bloggers are under no obligation to be scrupulous and diligent in their research, news gathering, and reporting. They never need admit when their reports are fraudulent, unfair, or wrong. In fact, quite the contrary—and to some that's the whole point. The writer Andrew Sullivan, a former national magazine editor turned popular blogger, told the *Washington Post* that he sees his blog as "a way you can throw ideas around without having to fully back them up, just to see what response you get" (Rich, 2006). Given their growing influence, blogs are of significant interest to sociologists—and not just to those who write them.

FIGURE 18.1 **Blog Globalization: Blog Posts by Language**

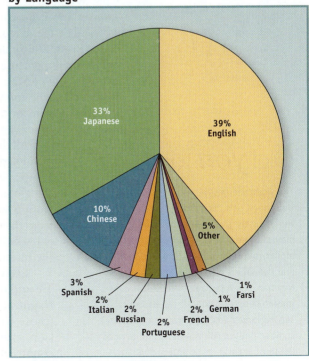

33% Japanese
39% English
10% Chinese
5% Other
3% Spanish
2% Italian
2% Russian
2% Portuguese
2% French
2% German
1% Farsi
1%

Source: Technorati, 2007. Reprinted by permission of Technorati, Inc., www.technorati.com

Radio, Movies, and Television. Before 1880, if you wanted music, you had to make it yourself or hire someone. Individuals who could play the piano or the violin were a big hit at parties because without them there would be dead silence. That all changed when Thomas Edison recorded his voice. Within a few decades, the gramophone (a machine that enabled you to listen to recorded music) was a staple of American life. And, at the same time, entrepreneurs sought to harness the power of transmitting sound via invisible "radio waves" and make them profitable. And movies were born with a 12-minute clip of *The Great Train Robbery* in 1903—and the media world changed forever.

The problem was, after the initial purchase, listening to the radio would be free; how could producers make any money? Eventually someone came up with the idea of sponsors: A company would pay for the production in exchange for regular advertising "plugs." The first commercial radio station, KDKA, opened in Pittsburgh in 1920. By 1923, 7 percent of American households had radio receivers; by 1935, 65 percent.

Movies offered no such commercial resistance. By the mid-1930s, over half of the U.S. population went to the movies—every week. And this would include, typically, two full-length features, newsreels, serial dramas, cartoons shorts—and commercials. And television, introduced in the late 1940s, was geared to commercial sponsorship of shows. With variety shows and commercial spots every few minutes, the connection between selling products and consuming media was indelibly tightened. (European television and radio are state sponsored and, until the 1980s, had no commercials at all.)

The irony of American television is that between 1955 and 1985, television was arguably the most popular form of mass media in the United States. Virtually everyone was watching—and everyone was watching the same channels. There were only three national networks, NBC, ABC, and CBS. Whole generations were defined by their preferred television programs: *I Love Lucy* in 1955, *Bonanza* in 1965, *All in the Family* in 1975.

Today, the average American home has more television sets than people (Associated Press, 2006). But television is so fragmented that even the top-rated shows draw only a small percentage of viewers. Only 15 percent of all households with TVs tune in to *CSI:Crime Scene Investigation*, the top-rated show, compared to 74 percent who watched *I Love Lucy*, the top-rated show in the 1950s (Hof, 2006). Today viewers can choose from among hundreds of channels, and the traditional networks lose numbers every year in favor of specialized niche channels.

All these media have experienced increased audience and amazing new technologies. Movies are seen not only in theaters but on DVDs, televisions, computer downloads, and even on cell phones. Nearly half (46 percent) of the global movie market comes from DVD sales and rentals, 28 percent from television (network, cable, and pay-per-view), and only 26 percent from the box office (*ABN Amro*, 2000). Digital and satellite radio stations carry hundreds of digital channels, many of which are also streamed over the Internet, and boast deeper playlists than traditional radio.

Each new form of media brings the world closer together—satellite TV and radio broadcast shows around the world. And yet media also can fragment us into niches and exacerbate the gap between rich and poor (those who have media access and those who do not). Globally, television is similar to the newspaper, saturating rich countries, rare in poor countries. In the United States, there are 740 television sets per 1,000 people, less than half that in South Korea, but that's more than enough to immerse the population in the latest game shows and reality series. Among poorer countries though—with 58 TVs per 1,000 people in India and 3.5 in Mozambique, for example—there is no unifying national television culture (CIA World Factbook, 2005).

Games, Gambling, and Porn: Guy Media. Worldwide, more than 300 million people play video games. The global video game market totaled more than $40 billion in 2006, outselling box office receipts for movies, books, CDs, and DVDs by a landslide. (Movies, in second place, made $14 billion globally.) Over 225 million computer games—nearly two games *per household*—are sold every year. Three-fifths of Americans age 6 and older play video games regularly—and three-fifths of those players are men. Some games, like Halo, GTA, and Madden sports games, are played almost exclusively by males; others, like Sims, are far more gender equal (Roberts et al., 1999; Trend, 2007).

Young males are also the primary players of online poker. Daily on college campuses, hundreds of thousands of young men are playing for millions of dollars. According to PokerPulse.com, which tracks online poker games, some 88,000 players were betting almost $16 million in online poker every day when the first World

▲ Many new media forms are marketed to, and enjoyed by, different groups. There are "his" and "her" video and computer games, but, as a genre, it's mostly "his."

How do we know what we know?

Does Watching Pornography Cause Rape?

What effect does viewing pornography have on men's attitudes and behaviors? Does watching porn cause rape? Social scientists (both social psychologists and sociologists) have tried to address this question from several different perspectives.

Early researchers showed men some porn clips and then asked them to either serve as jurors in a mock rape trial or to take a survey measuring rape myths (cultural beliefs about rape such as "women say no when they mean yes" and "women like it when you force them to have sex"). This research found that watching pornography increased the likelihood that male jurors would acquit a defendant in a rape trial and that they would support rape myths. But these effects were not very long lasting and vanished within a day or two.

Research by psychologist Dolf Zillman (1993) tried to measure if watching pornography actually increased men's aggression toward women. But his methodology reflected flawed assumptions. He measured aggression by how sexually aroused the men were—they wore a rubber band fitted with electrodes around the penis that measured arousal. Yet surely sexual arousal is not the same thing as sexual aggression.

Ed Donnerstein and his colleagues (1985) showed college age men three sets of images: (1) violence alone (no sex), like slasher movies; (2) sex alone (no violence, soft-core porn); (3) sexually violent material from hard-core porn. Men who watched the second set of images, sex alone, showed no changes in attitudes or behaviors. But the images of both violence and sexual violence together changed both attitudes and behaviors—and in virtually identical ways. Donnerstein concluded that it was the violence in the pornography, not the sex, that caused the changes.

Finally sociologists Murray Straus and Larry Baron (1993) noticed a correlation between rape and pornography consumption. In the 1980s, they found that the states that had the highest subscription rates per capita of *Playboy, Penthouse,* and *Hustler* magazines also had the highest per capita rape rates.

But, Straus and Baron cautioned, correlation does not mean causation. Subscribing to a magazine may not cause rape. In fact, they found, those states (Wyoming, Montana, Alaska) also had the highest ratio of single men to single women—that is, the largest number of unattached males. And they also had the highest per capita subscription rates to *Field and Stream*—and no one was suggesting that reading *Field and Stream* might contribute to rape.

Poker Tournament was held in 1997. Today, those figures have increased by a factor of ten—1.8 million players bet $300 million online every single day. The single largest group of online poker players is young men, 14 to 22 years old, according to the National Annenberg Risk Survey (NARSY) in 2003 and 2004. One in eight college guys is betting on poker games online at least once a week (see Conley, 2005).

Pornography is a massive media category worldwide. In the United States, gross sales of all pornographic media range between $10 and $14 billion a year for the whole industry—more than the NFL, the NBA, and Major League Baseball combined, or, in media terms, with revenues greater than ABC, NBC, and CBS combined. Sales and rentals of videos and DVDs alone gross about $4 billion a year. More than 200 new pornographic videos are produced every week. Adult bookstores outnumber McDonald's restaurants in the United States—by a margin of at least three to one. On the Internet, pornography has increased 1,800 percent, from 14 million web pages in 1998 to 260 million in 2003 (Williams, 2004). One study found that the adult entertainment is the number one thing people do online, outpacing even e-mail and search engine use (Grover, 2006).

What often concerns parents is the time boys spend using these media. They claim that these media have replaced social interaction with these solitary activities. What is of interest to sociologists, though, is that the use of these new media is so heavily gendered, and that young males seem to use them not in place of social interaction but as a form of interaction itself. Young males play video games together, play poker online together, and even watch pornography together. How does this new medium of interaction change the patterns of friendships and interaction?

The Internet. There was a home computer on the market as far back as 1975: the Altair 8800, which came unassembled, with a price of $5,000 (in today's dollars, that would be $18,000). Personal computers were a business tool, not a mass medium. But with the development of the World Wide Web in the 1980s, the computer had transformed the world yet again. Later called the Internet, online usage grew 300,000 percent per year: There were 10,000 network hosts in 1987, and 1,000,000 in 1992. By 2007, every country in the world, with a very few exceptions (Monserrat, the Isle of Man, Palau), was online (Abbate, 2000; Campbell-Kelly, 2004; *World Internet Statistics*).

As of 2007, the Internet was accessed by 76 percent of the population of Sweden, 70 percent of the United States, 67 percent of Japan. Beyond the core countries, penetration is considerably smaller: 16 percent in Colombia, 13 percent in Venezuela, 11 percent in Saudi Arabia, 10 percent in South Africa, 7 percent in Pakistan. In poor countries, Internet access remains an overwhelmingly elite activity, available to well under 1 percent of the population. But even there, change is coming. In 2000, Somalia had 200 users; today it has 90,000, an increase of 44,900 percent (*World Internet Statistics*).

The Internet became so integral to middle-class lives, both at home and at work, that it is hard to believe that it is only 20 years old, and most people in the world grew up without

Personal computers, now nearly universal in the industrialized world, are the centerpiece of our interface with media—they store information, give access to the Web, store music, video, movies, TV, and old love letters. The first general-purpose computer, called the Electronic Numerical Integrator and Computer (ENIAC), was built by the U.S. Army in the 1940s. It weighed 30 tons, was eight feet high, three feet deep, and 100 feet long, and contained over 18,000 vacuum tubes that were cooled by 80 air blowers. And it mainly stored information. ▼

it. Today if you have the money and the technical inclination, you can gain access to the Internet not only through home computers, but through laptops, BlackBerries, cell phones, and iPods (Figure 18.2). Libraries no longer catalog their books on little white cards; if you ask for a "card catalog" by mistake, younger librarians will not know what you are talking about, and older ones will direct you to a computer catalog. This book has been written primarily through online newspaper articles, journal articles, databases, and websites. We've set foot inside a library only to pick up books from interlibrary loan—and we ordered them online.

I often collaborate with other sociologists all over the world. Not that long ago, I'd write my section of our research paper, send it by "snail mail" and wait two months for a reply. Then I'd work on it again and send it off again. A paper would take us a year to write. At the end of the project, we'd often schedule a telephone call, but I was often so busy watching the second hand tick away on the clock, measuring how much the call was costing, that I could barely focus on the conversation. Today, I send a draft as an e-mail attachment in the evening. By the next morning, my European collaborators have replied. If we work well, what used to take us a year now takes less than a week. And we conclude our collaboration with a phone call on Skype, the Internet-based telephone service.

The Internet has not only transformed mass media but is a new form of mass media in its own right. A website is its own medium, like nothing that has ever come before, with text, graphics, and sounds combined in a way that no previous medium could do. Information is scattered across hundreds of sites in dozens of countries; and because there is little or no regulation of its content, it often becomes difficult to distinguish fact from opinion and opinion from diatribe.

The Internet has been accused of facilitating increased isolation—all those millions of teenagers who spend the time they should be doing their homework in chat rooms, playing online poker, or blowing up the galaxy on online games, downloading songs and pornography. But at the same time, it's also a new form of community, a virtual town square, where you offer intimate details about yourself and your romantic (and sexual) desires, meet your friends on Friendster or Facebook, and interact with like-minded members of your virtual network. As President George W. Bush noted, "With the Internet, you can communicate instantly with someone halfway across the world and isolate yourself from your family and neighbors." It's not either/or—it's both (Bumiller, 2006).

Saturation and Convergence: The Sociology of Media

We live in an age saturated by the media. The average American home today has 3 television sets, 1.8 VCRs, 3.1 radios, 2.6 tape players, 2.1 CD players, 1.4 video game players, and at least one computer. American kids between 8 and 18 spend seven hours a day interacting with some form of electronic media—which may explain why

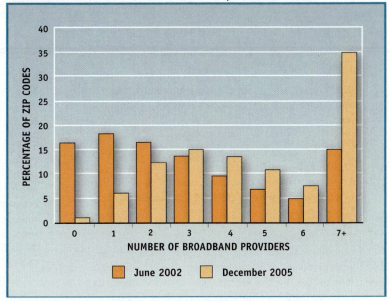

FIGURE 18.2 Percentage of Zip Codes by Number of Broadband Internet Providers Available, 2002 and 2005

Source: Frey, William H., Amy Beth Anspach and John Paul Dewitt, *The Allyn & Bacon Social Atlas of the United States.* Published by Allyn & Bacon, Boston, MA. Copyright © 2008 by Pearson Education. Reprinted by permission of the publisher.

Try It Media Literacy and Sociology

Developed by Katherine R. Rowell, *Sinclair Community College*
(based on suggestions in the chapter).

OBJECTIVE: Learn about the issue of media literacy and apply some basic principles while using a sociological lens.

Directions:

STEP 1: Review
Spend some time reviewing what is meant by media literacy by exploring the website created by the Center for Media Literacy.

STEP 2: Research
Choose one type of media (books, newspapers, movies, advertisements, music, websites, and the like) to explore further using the five key questions of media literacy as noted by the Center for Media literacy. Then find three examples of this media type to analyze (for example, if you choose to explore websites, you will need to analyze three different sites; or, if you choose movies, you will need to analyze three different movies). Then answer the following questions (developed by the Center for Media Literacy, 2005) for each one:

1. Who created this message? (For example, who created this movie, book, or the like?)
2. What creative techniques are used to attract my attention?
3. How might other people understand this message differently than I do?

4. What values, lifestyles, and points of view are represented in, or omitted from, this message?
5. Why is this message being sent?

STEP 3: Analyze
Compare and contrast the following information to your textbook (be sure to look over the conclusion to the chapter again): How do the five core concepts of media literacy compare to the sociological perspective of media? How are they similar? How are they different? Why are both perspectives important in understanding the media? Do you think media literacy is important? Why or why not? You will need to write your responses to this step in a one-page paper.

The Center for Media Literacy argues that there are also five core concepts of media literacy.

1. All media messages are constructed.
2. Media messages are constructed using a creative language with its own rules.
3. Different people experience the same media message differently.
4. Media have embedded values and points of view.
5. Most media messages are organized to gain profit and/or power.

STEP 4: Discuss
Be prepared to share the information from steps 2 through 4 in class. Your instructor will inform you of any other expectations.

---

40 percent of 8- to 13-year-olds said they did not read any part of a book on the previous day, a figure that shoots up to 70 percent of kids 14 to 18.

TV is omnipresent: 58 percent of families with children have the TV on during dinner, and 42 percent are "constant television households"—that is, they have a TV on virtually all day, whether or not anyone is actually watching it. And while once restaurants and bars were a way to escape the isolation of being in front of the boob tube, now those restaurants and bars are as likely to have TVs mounted on the walls so you don't miss a second.

Not long ago, the various types of mass media used to be vastly different, using distinct forms of technology. Now they are all digital. Even if a real book appears at the end of the production process, it is still written, edited, and produced in the form of word processing documents, spreadsheets, jpgs, mpgs, and wav files, and stored as computer files. The gap between forms of mass media is shrinking constantly. We can already access the Internet from our television sets, watch TV on our computers, and play video games on either. The difference is just a matter of social context: We tend to watch TV in a group, and the computer is a solitary device.

Someday soon, analysts believe, one machine will serve as a reception point for almost every mass medium (Consoli, 2005).

Convergence is not only happening in technology: The media objects themselves are converging. An increasing number of media objects have appeared simultaneously as movies and comic books, or as comic books and video games, and especially as both television series and Internet sites. *Lost,* the drama about airplane crash survivors in the South Pacific, is not only a television series; additional material, including interviews and new clips, appears as a podcast (a webfeed), accessible on the Internet, iPods, cell phones, and other devices (it can even be accessed on television, if you have Web TV!) (Davis, 2005).

Scholars have only just begun to speculate on the sociological implications of media convergence, but one effect is certain. Older people have always complained that the preferred mass media of their youth were far superior to the mass media today. Reading books was far superior to listening to the radio: You were active, engaged, and you had to use your imagination. Then: Listening to the radio was far superior to watching television, for the same reasons: active, engaged, used imagination. Then: Watching television was far superior to playing video games: active, engaged, used imagination. When every mass medium appears on flickering computer screens, there will be no nostalgic "active, engaged, imaginative" medium to look back on.

Both the cognitive demands that new media require from their viewers, and their effects, seem actually to be *more* engaging than those of previous generations. Surely, computer games require more manual dexterity and eye–hand coordination, as well as the ability to hold several different plotlines in your head simultaneously, while a TV show or radio show—not to mention sitting quietly and reading a book—required less physical connection. Radio and TV stories are far more complex than 20 years ago. The "good old days" of media may not have demanded any more from the consumer and certainly did not leave you as dizzy from so many choices.

Media Production and Consumption

How do the media produce what they produce? For whom? What is the relationship between the producers and their audiences? How are audiences created and maintained? These are questions that animate the sociological investigations into both the production and the consumption of media.

For years, there seemed to be a strict division between production and consumption. A group of writers, editors, directors, actors, artists, and supporting personnel, all working for corporate executives in high-rise offices, produces and distributes the books, magazines, and television programs. The books, magazines, and television programs appear in their respective mass media, and we consume them. We have little input; a million irate letters failed to save *Star Trek* from cancellation in 1967.

This boundary is being increasingly blurred. (Think of the long history of TV shows about TV or radio shows—from *Mary Tyler Moore* to *Frasier* to *Martin* to *30 Rock* to *Studio 60 on the Sunset Strip*—in which the plot centers around the corporate "suits" arguing against the irresponsible creative types.) Audiences increasingly run the show. Viewers of *American Idol,* for example, determine through their voting how the show turns out.

These days, media producers are all consumers themselves. The people who write, act in, and direct television programs go home every night and watch television

In today's interactive media environment, the line between consumer and producer is becoming blurred—at least for those consumers with access to the technology. Network television stations add additional content as well as provide opportunities for interactions among fans of their most popular TV shows.

Source: Screen capture "Heroes" from the NBC website, www.nbc.com/Heroes, accessed October 24, 2007. Reprinted by permission.

themselves. The writers of *Lost,* for example, scour Internet chatrooms and message boards to determine the popularity of plot twists and even to get new ideas. Consumers are not just sitting idly by, consuming media as if they were popcorn; they create their own fan fiction, blogs, chatrooms, message boards. Consumers are also producers, using the same technologies to write books and magazines and produce movies.

However, the distinction between mass media production and consumption is still useful, particularly as we try to figure out exactly what happens as a message goes from my brain into words, sounds, and pictures (is encoded), is transmitted over a long distance through a mass medium, and then gets into your brain (is decoded). It's not at all like talking to you or showing you pictures face-to-face. To paraphrase Marshall McLuhan, the medium changes the message. Actually, the medium changes everything.

Culture Industries

Like any other industry, mass media are characterized by industrial patterns such as hierarchy and bureaucracy. But the goal of most industries is to provide a product that you

Sociology and our World

Minorities in Media

Television helps sell products to everyone, majority and minority alike, so we would expect television executives to make a concerted attempt not to offend minorities by including them in the sitcoms, cop shows, and commercials. However, while most ensemble shows are far more diverse than they might have been in the past, they are still disproportionately White and middle class. A report from *Children Now* (2005) found that 73 percent of prime time characters in the 2003–2004 season were White, 16 percent African American, 6.5 percent Hispanic, 3 percent Asian, and 1.5 percent other. Only African Americans were close to representing their real numbers. Sixty-five percent of prime-time characters were male and only 35 percent female, obviously disproportionately high for the men. Children, teenagers, and young adults were highly overrepresented: Only 16 percent of male and 6 percent of female characters were over 50 years old. Those youth, the most racially diverse population in America, are represented as even more predominantly White than other age groups—77 percent of prime-time characters

under 18 are Caucasian. The report doesn't mention GLBT people at all, but in 2006–07, the Gay and Lesbian Alliance Against Defamation counted 9 gay men and lesbians out of a total of 679 prime-time lead or supporting characters, or 1.3 percent, again an under representation (GLAAD, 2006).

Even when members of the minority group appear in a media text, the way they are presented sometimes reinforces negative ideologies. They may display negative stereotypes. On television, Latinos have begun to appear more frequently in prime time, but they tend to be cast disproportionately in low-status occupations and are four times more likely than other groups to portray domestic workers (*Children Now,* 2005). In popular video games, seven out of ten Asian characters are fighters; eight out of ten Black characters are sports competitors. Nearly nine out of ten Black women were victims of violence. Nearly 80 percent of Black men are shown as physically and verbally abusive (*Children Now,* 2001). Even those women and minority characters who are shown in authoritative positions, like district attorneys or police chiefs, are mostly seen but not heard, having few lines and/or little influence in the flow of the plot.

can use. The goal of the media is either to convince you that you need someone else's product or to entertain you sufficiently that you will be positively motivated to purchase someone else's product.

Much of the arts—classical music, visual arts, dance—remain shrouded in an aesthetic sensibility that makes it difficult to see their more sociological elements. Many of us subscribe to a notion of "art for art's sake"—the work of art is produced by an individual artist as an expression of his or her unique vision.

Sociologists often challenge such romantic views, generally by focusing on the more mundane elements of artistic production. In *Art Worlds,* for example, Howard Becker (1984) showed that much of the life of a painter or a musician is bureaucratic and routine; he or she goes to work, practices routine material, deals with money and sales receipts, talks on the phone, in a way that is quite similar to that of an office worker. In *Making News* (1978) Gaye Tuchman found that what gets seen, heard, and read as "the news" has less to do with human judgments about newsworthiness, importance, or social value than with the organizational structures within which reporters and editors do their jobs (see also Becker et al., 2000; Berkowitz, 1990; Gans, 1979; Tuchman, 1978).

In addition, sociologists examine the **culture industries**—the mass production of cultural products that are offered for consumption. Instead of crafting an individual work of creative genius, movie studios and radio stations are like assembly lines, producing cultural products as if they were loaves of bread. They may recycle the same tired images and themes over and over again because they are cheap and have been successful in the past. If you've seen one cowboy movie (or one episode of *CSI: Miami*), you've seen them all. Every sitcom covers the same territory, with the same jokes. As a result of taking in such material over time, some sociologists have argued, consumers become passive and uncritical. They absorb the simplistic, repetitive images with no questions asked, never having their preconceptions, stereotypes, and ideologies challenged (Horkheimer and Adorno, 1944; Steinert, 2003).

The concept of culture industries is helpful in explaining why so many mass media promote old-fashioned, even oppressive, ideologies. For instance, in a free-market economy, the producers must make the product appealing to as many potential consumers as possible. Therefore they select the themes and situations that are familiar to people, never challenging a preconception, a stereotype, or an ideology. Sociologist Todd Gitlin coined the phrase "the logic of safety" to describe the continuing tendency of media producers to repackage time-tested themes and formulas to capture established media audiences and markets, thus minimizing programming risks and maximizing profits (Gitlin, 2000). In so doing, the mass media also reinforce and may actually promote acceptance of inequalities.

But media production and media consumption are more complex than the kind of "hypodermic needle" idea that Horkheimer and Adorno's original "culture industries" idea proposed. Producers cannot churn out exactly the same old images audiences have seen before; some originality, some tweak, some spin is needed to attract an audience. Some mass media producers do have artistic visions in their own right, and sometimes they do challenge preconceptions, stereotypes, and ideologies.

What's more, media consumers are not the passive zombies Horkheimer and Adorno feared. Rather, audiences are active; we participate in the process of making meaning out of media. We actively interpret the words, images, and/or sounds that are referred to as the **media text**. Stuart Hall (1980) coined the term **encoding/decoding** to capture this dynamic relationship between how media texts construct messages for us and how, at the same time, people actively and creatively make sense of what they see, hear, and read. Encoding and decoding are connected because they are processes that focus on the same media text, but a particular decoding does not necessarily follow from a specific encoded message. As audiences, we tend to take what we want from the media text and ignore everything else. We "misread" it. We create meanings that producers might never have intended. For example, soap operas and romance novels are formulas often said to reproduce gender stereotypes that are oppressive to women. Yet scholars such as Radway (1984) and Ang and Hermes (1991) have found that women audiences read and use these media in a variety of independent and self-affirming ways. The writer of the classic television comedy *M*A*S*H*, Larry Gelbart, left his own hit show after only a few seasons because the message he thought he had encoded was not what audiences decoded when they watched. A chronicle of the daily life of a surgical unit during the Korean War, Gelbart wanted the show's message to be that war was futile. But fans kept writing to say the show made war look like fun and that they couldn't wait to sign up for the army. Gelbart's content intentions were defeated by his active viewing audiences.

Multicultural and global viewers of mainstream media can be particularly active audiences. Katz and Liebes (1990) studied international audiences for the hit American prime-time drama *Dallas* and discovered that groups from different cultural backgrounds produced a variety of different ways of relating to the series and retelling stories from it. They may find their own ways into media texts that would seem to marginalize them. Gillespie (1995) found young Punjabis living in London who watched Australian soap operas; they identified with personal and familial struggles and used them to explore and resolve related tensions in their own lives and communities. Shively (1992) found that Native American viewers of classic John Wayne westerns identified not with the "Red Indian" characters, but with Wayne, because it was he who represented preservation of autonomy. Gay men and lesbians tend to be particularly skilled at taking and making their own messages from mainstream media, probably as a result of the pervasiveness of heterosexual norms in media messages (see Eldridge, Kitzinger, and Williams, 1997).

Multicultural Voices

The Mohawk, one of the "Five Civilized Tribes," once occupied a huge area of Quebec, Ontario, and New York. Today there are only about 3,000 speakers of Mohawk left, mostly older people. Children are rapidly losing sight of their ethnic identity because Native Americans are invisible in the mass media of the United States and Canada. So what did the tribal elders do? They started a website where you can learn some common Mohawk words and phrases, listen to traditional songs, learn about tribal traditions, and order many different CDs not available on amazon.com: *Music from Turtle Island, Yazzie Girl.*

Gay adolescents used to be stuck in limbo. They rarely knew any other gay people, teenagers or adults. Their teachers and parents assumed that everyone in the world was straight. No organizations existed in their small towns, or they were afraid to contact them. So while their friends were happily planning dates and proms, they were doomed to years of loneliness and silence. Not anymore. An Internet search for "LGBT youth" yields hundreds of websites: Gay Youth UK, OutProud, the Gay Youth Corner, Toronto Coalition for LGBT Youth. Then there is *XY,* a glossy magazine with articles on sports, fashion, music, and celebrities.

Thus, mass media can be more democratic, spreading ownership and consumption of media to more and more

Mass media can allow access to more and more people and enable previously voiceless minorities access to connection and visibility. Univision, the leading Spanish-language media conglomerate in the United States, creates its audience as it caters to it. ▼

people and enabling previously voiceless minorities access to connection and visibility. For another example, Black Entertainment Television (BET) and Black-owned record companies, digital media companies, and magazines have identified and sustained a new media market and also, in the process, helped to create that market. Ethnic media markets have grown robustly in the United States in the twenty-first century. About 51 million Americans, 24 percent of the adult population, are either primary or secondary consumers of ethnic media today (Project for Excellence in Journalism, 2006).

Media Consolidation

But media can also, simultaneously, be less democratic, as those at the top can concentrate increasing amounts of media power. **Media consolidation** refers to the increased control of an increasing variety of media by a smaller and smaller number of companies. A small number of companies control virtually all the media in the United States today, and huge conglomerates own or hold large stakes in a variety of media. This consolidation raises fears about what gets produced and also about the quality and reliability of media products, particularly news.

During the past two decades, media ownership has rapidly become concentrated in fewer and fewer hands. Time and Warner Brothers merged into the world's biggest media company in 1989. Ten years later, Viacom and CBS set a new record for the largest corporate merger ever. Then the AOL–Time Warner merger in 2000 was several times bigger than that. Today's media consolidation raises fears about the access to the diverse sources of news and opinions that citizens in a democracy need to make informed decisions about how to vote and how to live. When a small group of people controls how information circulates, the spectrum of available ideas, opinions, and images seems likely to narrow. Moreover, big media companies will prefer programming and voices that conform to their own financial interests, and they are in a position to block most smaller, independent companies from rising to offer alternatives.

Any major music store in America is filled with thousands of selections from dozens of different labels in dozens of different musical categories: country, rap, house, bluegrass, Latin, rock, reggae, folk, R&B, and on and on and on. But do you think the producers of the $37 billion worldwide music business are as various as their products appear? The truth is just five gigantic corporate conglomerates own all the different record labels, and so they distribute 95 percent of all music carried in record stores in the United States. They are called "the big five," and only one of them is a U.S. company. Warner is an American firm, but the others are Bertelsmann (Germany), EMI (U.K.), Universal Music Group (Canada), and Sony (Japan). They show us that the distribution of media products may have spread around the globe, but ownership has become more centralized with media globalization.

But as this example may suggest, the links between consolidation and diverse content are far from clear. Gamson and Latteir (2004) found that sometimes media giants homogenize content, and sometimes they don't. Sometimes these corporations stifle dissent, and sometimes they open up extra space for new people to be visible and vocal. It depends on numerous factors, not the least of which are the financial rewards owners can reap for doing one or the other at particular times in particular markets.

Journalistic integrity is yet another concern stemming from corporate media conglomeration. Now that a few gigantic corporations own most media producers in the United States, news is no longer produced by companies engaged primarily in journalism. When Time Inc. merged with Warner Communications and then AOL, the percent of its revenues from journalism dropped from 100 percent to 5 percent—even though the company still controlled 35 percent of all magazines in the United States (Hargreaves, 2005).

The Importance of Advertising

Advertising is a form of mass media and also a kind of media text (Figure 18.3). Advertising can appear as phrases, pictures, songs, cartoons, or short films ("commercials"), but its purpose is always the same: to convincing prospective consumers that they want or need a product—soap, soda, sportscars—but also services (like monster.com for job seekers) and other media ("Must See TV"). Occasionally advertisements merely discuss the qualities of the product. But usually ads try to associate the product with a desirable quality or activity (Fox, 1997; Marchand, 1986; Samuel, 2002). The flavor of a soda is not nearly as important as the surge in popularity you experience with just one sip. Who cares about the nutritional content or taste of the cereal purveyed by the wizened old general store proprietor?

Advertising is an engine of media production; most media depend on advertising to survive and profit. Since most of these mass media forms themselves are free (like TV) or cheap (like newspapers or magazines), ads pay for most of the cost of production as well as the profits. As a rule, the more the medium depends on advertising for its revenue, the more it will shy away from challenging preconceptions and stereotypes (Pipher, 2000; Williamson, 1994). I have never seen an interracial couple on any television commercial, though they are increasingly common in real life (see Chapter 12, Family). Rarely, if ever, would you see a lesbian couple in an ad for some household product. This is probably because advertisers fear that someone, somewhere, might get offended and refuse to buy the product.

FIGURE 18.3 **Advertising Expenditures Worldwide**

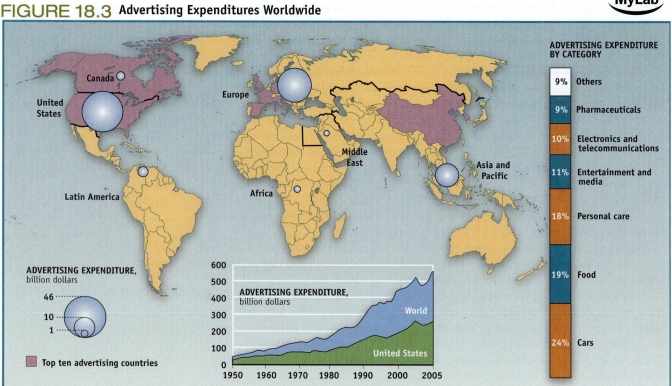

Source: "Consumption Appeal" by Emmanuelle Bournay from *Vital Waste Graphics* 2, 2006, which appears on the UNEP/GRID-Arenda, http://maps.grida.no/go/graphic/consumption_appeal. Reprinted by permission.

Sociologists bring the same sorts of questions to advertising that they bring to other forms of mass media: What is the relationship between producers and consumers? Why do so many media texts promote stereotypes and oppressive ideologies? If consumers aren't passive zombies, under what conditions do media messages influence our attitudes, ideas, even behavior? The questions become more important for two reasons. First, we consume many more ads than anything else, dozens every day, hundreds every week. They are everywhere. And second, ads present by far the most pervasive stereotypes of any form of mass media: Almost every commercial shows affluent nuclear families in huge suburban houses, with Dad reading the newspaper and Mom in the kitchen. Dad does not mop the floor, and whenever he cooks dinner, he botches the job and takes the kids out to a fast-food restaurant.

How does a steady diet of such images affect our ideas about how life works or how it should work? Do most consumers really desire such a life, or are the commercials imputing desire where none existed before? Do mass media reflect or create desire?

Celebrities

Every year, Gallup surveys Americans about the living man and woman that they admire most. In 2005, the top ten men included George W. Bush, Bill Clinton, Jimmy Carter—and Bono, the singer from the rock group U2 who has been working tirelessly to end poverty in Africa. The top ten women included Hillary Clinton, Laura Bush, Margaret Thatcher—and actress Angelina Jolie, an Oscar-winning actress and partner of Hollywood heartthrob Brad Pitt, who also does a lot of humanitarian work.

The surprising part is that more performers did not make the top ten. Actors and singers are among the most common mass media products. Many Americans cannot name their own senators and representatives, but nearly all of them know who Tom Cruise is and even about how in 2005 he jumped on the couch and howled on *The Oprah Winfrey Show*. Celebrity news often makes the front page of newspapers in the United States and Europe, particularly in Britain. Why? Celebrity stories sell papers—and magazines, and products.

Mass media created celebrity. There were professional performers before, of course. But even the most diligent theatergoer might see the same actor only twice in a given year. With the advent of radio, listeners could hear their favorite comedians or singers every week. With movies, you could *see* your favorite performers almost as often. Celebrity magazines grew up around the American film industry, developing the thirst for details on the smallest doings of stars.

Television, however, is even more intimate than movies: You can see your favorite performers every week, in your own living room. These people are not simply performers; they are *celebrities,* famous not necessarily because of their talent or accomplishments but because they appear so often in mass media texts that audiences feel that they know them personally (Dyer, 1987; Gamson, 1994). And, in some ways, you do: In talk shows, magazine interviews, and fan articles, you learned every detail of their everyday lives, sometimes more intimately than your real friends. Of course, celebrities are not your friends; the intimacy is one-sided. You think you know everything about them, but they know nothing about you. Thus, the relationship between celebrity and audience is paradoxical. They are neither friends nor strangers; Richard Schickel (1985) calls them "intimate strangers."

The mass media crave celebrities—they sell papers and magazines, we watch them on TV. The media also create a cult of celebrity, drawing us to certain people sometimes for no other reason than the fact that they are featured and photographed. Paris Hilton, like Zsa Zsa Gabor, is "famous for being famous." ▼

A Hungarian-born socialite named Zsa Zsa Gabor (1917–) was probably the first celebrity created purely by media exposure. She was technically an actress, with a string of bad movies to her credit. But she didn't become one of the most recognizable people in the world because of her movies. She appeared on talk shows to talk about her marriages, her diamonds, her appearances at posh functions, her jet-set lifestyle. She became "famous for being famous."

Today, that's increasingly common. Celebrity itself has become the product—rather than a device for marketing films or music. Now there are "faux celebrities" everywhere—from the winners (and runners-up) of reality shows like *Survivor, The Bachelor, Joe Millionaire,* and others, to Anna Nicole Smith, to Jack and Kelly Osbourne, to Paris Hilton. Celebrities and their agents have now begun to collaborate with photographers and publications, staging shots that then appear to be intrusions in their private lives in exchange for more control over their image and a share of the profits.

Consuming Media, Creating Identity

Whatever the producers may intend, consumers use media texts for their own ends. Through our consumption of media, we actively create our identities. In fact, it is largely *through* our media consumption that we know who we are and where we fit in society. Consumers have five broad goals in consumption:

1. *Surveillance, to find out what the world is like.* This is the main reason that we consume news and information programs, nonfiction books, magazines, and newspapers. However, we also acquire information from fiction. The best-selling novel

The Da Vinci Code is both a mystery and a guided tour of modern Paris and the art of its famous museum, the Louvre.

2. *Decision making, to acquire enough information on a subject to make a decision.* I may research housing markets online before deciding to move, or read Roger Ebert's movie review in the *Chicago Sun-Times* to decide what movie to see. The success of most advertising depends on my getting information at the right moment: That Pizza Hut commercial may be all the information I need to decide what to have for dinner tonight.

3. *Aesthetics.* Media objects are works of art because they create a particular vision of reality. I can appreciate the theme, style, and technique of *SpongeBob SquarePants* as easily as (maybe even more easily than) *Macbeth*.

4. *Diversion.* If we're being entertained, the reasoning goes, we are not engaged in big, important, useful work. What are we being diverted from? From improving ourselves, thinking about our problems, saving the world. We are wasting our time. However, diversion performs an important function. It's like a short vacation. By stepping outside of everyday reality for a moment, we are refreshed and better prepared to think about that big, important, useful work.

5. *Identity.* Consuming mass media texts allows us to create and maintain a group identity. If you belong to the upper class, chances are you will not listen to country-western music (or will keep the CDs hidden when company comes around), because your class identity requires that you like classical music instead. Men are "supposed" to like movies with lots of car chases, and women are "supposed" to like movies with lots of crying and hugging, so they will attend these sorts of movies to signify their gender identity.

There is no single, definitive meaning in media texts. Media texts may emphasize or "prefer" certain, hegemonic meanings over others, but, ultimately, meaning is in the mind of the beholder. Readers and viewers interpret what they see in different ways; they notice, follow, value, and understand things in different ways and so "create" the meaning of a media text for themselves. No single meaning is "correct": There are always multiple possibilities. John Fiske (1989) suggests three possible types of readings:

1. *Dominant/hegemonic.* The reader or viewer is fully complicit with the "preferred reading" (Hall, 1980). He or she completely agrees. In fact, the viewer may not even notice that it's there. All people are White, middle-class, and affluent, as they seemed in the cereal commercial. Every Mr. does have a Mrs. There may be a few exceptions, but it goes without saying that a man in a business suit in a suburban kitchen would fit this description.

2. *Ironic.* The reader or viewer notices the ideology put forward in the preferred reading, but distances him- or herself from it. Isn't this commercial ridiculous? Fortunately, he or she has moved beyond such limited ideas. The producers of the commercial may be idiots, but he or she realizes that not all yuppies in business suits are White and suburban and male, and not every Mr. has a Mrs., so there is no reason to portray them using this absurd, oppressive stereotype.

3. *Oppositional/resistant.* The reader or viewer believes that the text itself undermines the hegemonic ideology. Effectively, it disputes its own apparent claims. Sure, the announcer says the every Mr. has a Mrs., but he's the one so concerned about the taste and quality of the cereal. Who says the past was better than the present? The old geezer doesn't look as snappy as the yuppie and doesn't have the choices the yuppie has about what he wants and why.

We never consume media texts in a vacuum: We discuss them with family, friends, and co-workers. We join clubs and chat rooms. We take classes and get degrees. We understand media content within social groups, with whom we share certain strategies for interpreting and using media content. We consume the media text within an **interpretive community** (Fish, 1980; Lewis, 1992).

Interpretive communities are groups that guide interpretation and convey the preferred meanings of mass media texts. In subtle ways, they offer rewards for "correct" meanings and punishments for "incorrect" meanings. Sometimes the rewards and punishments are formal, like a grade in school. Usually, however, they are informal, approval or ridicule—just try to defend a "chick flick" if you are a guy, enjoy folk music if you are Black, or say the typical summer blockbuster is a mess of mindless explosions among teen or twenty-something friends!

▲ Media also create interpretive communities, groups that cohere around similar media tastes and create a subculture. At Comic-Con International in 2005, a group of Bat-people pose as some Ghostbusters look on.

Your friends represent an interpretive community; so does your school, your region, your age group, and your country. Back in the 1960s, Van Williams starred in a superhero adventure series, *The Green Hornet*. Martial arts expert Bruce Lee played his chauffeur and valet, certainly a subsidiary role—except in Hong Kong, where it ran as *The Bruce Lee Show*. The interpretive community of Hong Kong preferred a resistant reading that made Bruce Lee the star.

Interpretive communities also produce fans. A **fan** is someone who finds significant personal meaning through allegiance to a larger social group: a sports team, for example. In the media, fandom refers to a heightened awareness of and allegiance toward a specific text—a story, a series, a performer—so that the fan gains satisfaction by belonging to an interpretive community. There are varying levels of fandom, a continuum of fans from those who just enjoy a media text; to those who spend money on books, DVDs, clothing, fan clubs, and conventions; to those who devote a good deal of their lives to the text; to, finally, those whose lives center around it and seem to be unable to live without it.

Fandom is a public affiliation, not just a private love. It is a public proclamation of identity, a choice that your allegiance to some media product reveals a core element of yourself. It was important for fans of Harry Potter to buy the latest installment in the series the second it went on sale—in part to display publicly to other fans (or themselves) the strength of their allegiance. Rap and hip-hop fans may express their affiliation through clothing, jewelry, verbal affections, social interactions. "Deadheads" will bedeck themselves in tie-dyed shirts (preferably with skulls on them) and, if they are male, wear their hair long. The hard core *Star Trek* fan might write fan fiction (sometimes complete novels), start websites, organize conventions, use the hand gesture and expression "live long, and prosper," even walk around with Mr. Spock's pointed ears.

The word *fan* comes from *fanatic*, and in the popular imagination, fans are crazy and escape into a world of fantasy. Actually, most fans are in touch with reality. They have understandable sociological reasons for their fandom: An interpretive community of fellow fans allows them to hold responsible positions, acquire prestige, and obtain social capital that they could not obtain in mainstream culture (Harris, 1998; Hills, 2002; Lewis, 1992).

Fandom is a good example of the ways the media both create and reflect audience desires. Movie studios, television producers, and record producers offer websites and merchandise schemes to entice and sustain existing fans. These and other devices reflect the fandom of those who already like a particular star or show. But they also set the standard for "true" fandom: Suddenly you can't be a "real" fan unless you subscribe to these magazines, wear these clothes, and purchase these products. The media both meet "demand" (offering services) and create the very demand they then service.

Regulating Media

The fact that media can be both more and less democratic at the same time—creating access and concentrating power—means that eventually media will encounter government regulation. Currently there are laws that attempt to prevent the concentration of media in one company's hands, but they generally mean that one company can't own *all* the newspapers or *all* the radio stations in any metropolitan area. But they can, legally, own the biggest newspaper in *every* metropolitan area, and the largest-circulation magazine and the most popular radio station. Laws designed to prevent too much concentration in media ownership have been relaxing steadily since the 1990s (Croteau and Hoynes, 2003).

The other way in which the media is regulated has to do with the effects of media consumption on consumers. One side of the argument goes like this: If you watch a violent act in a mass media text, you will be more likely to commit a violent act yourself. It may validate your preexisting propensity to violence through group socialization, just as you are more likely to litter if you see someone else littering, or else it may create a propensity to violence where none existed before. (The same argument is used for sex: Watching a sexually explicit act will either incite your pre-existing desire or create a new desire.)

We've heard the argument before. Psychological experiments have demonstrated that people who view aggressive behavior of any sort, either on film or in real life, are slightly more likely to become aggressive themselves—for a few minutes. But then the effect fades away. Despite what many pundits and public figures suggest, most studies have failed to find a causal link between violent media and long-term violent behavior or violent crime (Comstock and Scharrer, 1999; Huesmann and Eron, 2006).

There was no indication that watching a violent movie, or a hundred violent movies, would make people more violent (Felson, 1996). For one thing, as with any media content, people's varying identities, and their social and cultural contexts, shape the meanings they see in media and how they respond to them. In 1997, the largest ever study of media content conducted by several major universities—the National Television Violence Study—concluded that exposure to violence in the media was unlikely to cause violent behavior in most cases, but it may lead many people to think that violence is more pervasive than it is in society and cause them to be afraid (National Television Violence Study, 1997).

Yet we hear the argument every time a new form of mass media arrives. And every time there is a new tragedy, we hear it again (Trend, 2007). When Eric Harris and Dylan Klebold opened fire on their classmates at Columbine High School, everyone wondered: Why did they do it? Many commentators put the blame on the violent video game *Doom*, which was reputed to contain a layout of a high school, and on the movie *The Basketball Diaries*, in which Leonardo DiCaprio fantasizes about wearing a black trench-coat and shooting his classmates. However, an estimated 10 million people have played *Doom*, and about one million saw *The Basketball Diaries*, without shooting anyone.

On a societal level, it sometimes looks as if violent media actually decrease violence. Between 1978 and 1988, hundreds of movies appeared involving psycho-slashers who killed groups of teenagers in creatively gruesome ways: the *Friday the 13th, Nightmare on Elm Street, Halloween,* and *Sleepaway Camp* series, plus *Prom Night, Graduation Day, Funhouse,* and nearly 200 others. They appealed mostly to teenagers.

By 1998, those teenagers were grown up. And according to the FBI, the number of serial killers in the United States remained relatively stable—there were 30 to 40. The violent crime rate had actually decreased from 44.1 to 36.0 per 1,000 people, the lowest rate ever. Between 1994 and 2005, violent crime rates have steadily declined, reaching the lowest level ever recorded in 2005 (U.S. Department of Justice). Did watching Freddie, Michael, and Jason decrease violent tendencies, or is there no valid social scientific connection whatever?

And what are we to do about it? In the days before mass media, adults and children were exposed to everything—good, bad, and in between. The first fairy tales told in front of the fireplace were for everyone (and they had a lot more sex and violence than today's sanitized versions). Adults and children alike listened to folk songs with bawdy lyrics. But people weren't alarmed about these messages until they couldn't control the quantity or supervise the transmission of them. The mass media are seen as different; they are produced by strangers, probably transmitting insidious messages into children's heads when their parents aren't paying attention.

Worries about the media consumption by children has come in two forms. One argument is that media incite or create violence (and sexual behavior) because children are presumed to be highly impressionable. If they see a cartoon mouse hit a cartoon cat with a frying pan, the next thing you know, they'll be trying it out on baby brother. The other worry is that children are not constitutionally able to handle "mature" themes: They will be confused, distressed, upset, and perhaps psychologically scarred for the rest of their lives (Dorr, 1986; Trend, 2007).

All media are censored—the question is not whether or not there is censorship but rather what should be censored and why. Books have frequently been banned. James Joyce's *Ulysses,* now considered one of the greatest works in Western literature, was banned in the United States for years because it presumably contained explicit sexual situations (there really aren't any). References to drugs and gay men got Allen Ginsberg's "Howl" banned in 1956, but now it appears in anthologies assigned to freshman English classes. Few books are banned outright anymore, but when it's a matter of consumption by children, books are quickly and easily removed from school libraries.

In the 1930s, movies were censored for such things as premarital sex, homosexuality, graphic violence, criminals who get away with it, bad words, and disrespect toward the U.S. government and organized religion. In the late 1960s, a new rating system was introduced: G (for all audiences), PG (parental guidance suggested), R (no one under 17 without a parent or guardian present), and X (no one under 17, period).

Even television cartoons have been carefully watched and controlled. In the 1970s, child advocates noticed that the old Bugs Bunny and Daffy Duck cartoons being shown on Saturday mornings featured a lot of anvils dropped on people's heads and bombs exploding in people's faces. In real life, they would be killed by such encounters. Even without the violence, cartoon characters were often irreverent and disrespectful to authority figures. By the 1980s, censorship resulted in new shows

While almost everyone agrees that some images are harmful to children, not everyone agrees what those images are. Some have criticized the Public Broadcasting System for "promoting homosexuality" (the friendship between Bert and Ernie on *Sesame Street,* Tinky Winky, the purple Tellytubby, and Buster's unproblematic visit to a lesbian couple in Vermont on a spinoff from *Arthur).* ▼

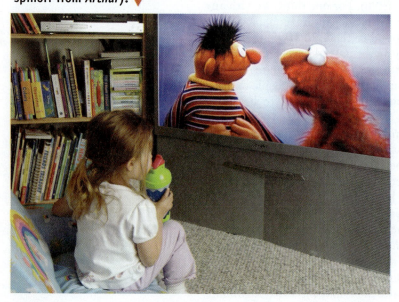

like *Smurfs* and *Care Bears,* with characters hugging, learning, and finding nonviolent solutions to their problems. Whatever the potential social value of such messages, children of the 1980s recall them as excruciatingly dull (Hendershot, 1999).

With each new medium, there is renewed concern about controlling the harmful effects of its content, especially when it comes to children. Since the 1990s, there has been considerable concern about sexuality and, particularly, violence in video games. Critics of video game content argue that levels of violence and cruelty are at least as bad as on TV shows and that these images are even more threatening because video games allow users to act out the violence personally.

These debates have resulted in different controls in different countries. In the United States, Canada, and the United Kingdom, for example, video game companies have agreed to a basic, voluntary rating system. Some other countries have taken stronger actions. In China, new laws seek to restrict play of any video game to only three hours. After that, game programming will make in-game characters lose their abilities. (After a five-hour break, full powers will be automatically restored.)

For sociologists, censorship raises questions about context more so than content. What is considered "too violent," under what conditions, and who decides? History has shown that censorship laws reflect the interests of whoever is in power to declare them. In Stalinist Russia, material with Christian themes was banned; in southern New Mexico in 2001, Harry Potter books were burned by a Christian group for purveying anti-Christian messages (BBC, 2001). In 2004, Harry Potter topped the list of the most frequently banned books, seeing 26 challenges to remove it from bookshelves in 16 states (American Library Association). Nobody wants a society with no limits at all on what is permissible to communicate to children—or to the rest of us. Nor do many of us want a world in which someone else is always making decisions about what is permissible for us to consume. The issue for sociologists is not whether or not there is censorship—there is, and always has been, and always will be. To the sociologist, the question is more about where we draw the line as a society about who can see and say what, what the criteria are for judgment, and who gets to make those decisions. That is: Censorship, like virtually every other social process, is about power, inequality, and choice.

Globalization of the Media

A few years ago, I was visiting Morocco, and I stayed in a fourteenth century Moorish castle converted into a hotel. My room was furnished with ornate tile work, panels inlaid with lapis lazuli, fringed pillows. It was like moving into another world. I opened an ornately appointed armoire, and found that it hid a large television set— evidently they didn't want modern conveniences to interfere with the lush fantasy of the room. I turned on the TV. What were they watching in this ancient, mysterious country? *Beavis and Butthead.*

American movies were being shown around the world as early as the 1920s, but the immersion has increased dramatically during the last 20 years. *The Simpsons* is broadcast in Central and South America, Europe, South Africa, Israel, Turkey, Japan, South Asia, and Australia. On any given night, *The Bold and the Beautiful* is playing in Romania, *CSI* in Germany, *Sex and the City* in Spain, *Fairly Oddparents* in the Philippines. In China, the most popular programs are *Friends* and *Seinfeld.*

The mass media have become truly global in nature. CNN broadcasts via 23 satellites to more than 212 countries and territories in all corners of the globe. Major sporting events are seen by hundreds of millions of people worldwide. The 2006 World Cup, for example, was watched by a cumulative television audience of more than 26 billion viewers across the globe (FIFA, 2007). The Internet is growing more global every day, allowing millions of users from all over the world to come online to seek and share information, post opinions and creative work, and shop for items previously available only to those who physically traveled to other countries.

In the 1960s, the path-breaking media scholar Marshall McLuhan predicted that the rise of global electronic media would bring the world closer together. He coined the term **global village** to describe an environment in which people everywhere could make their voices heard to one another, thus compelling "commitment and participation" and making human beings "irrevocably involved with, and responsible for, each other" (McLuhan and Fiore, 1967, p. 24). Four decades later, is that what globalization means?

What Is Media Globalization?

Media globalization has two main concerns. First, there is the technological innovation that allows us to communicate instantaneously over vast distances. In many countries today, there is no need to be physically close by to work together; images, sounds, the thoughts of almost anyone, from anywhere, can potentially be available to billions of people. Technology is giving increasing numbers of people the power to produce culture. And technology is making it as easy to communicate with someone on another continent as it is with someone down the hall.

But media globalization also concerns the cultural products that are available around the world. In that area, sociologists are finding that McLuhan's vision of a global village is far from today's reality. Commercial interests, rather than humanitarian ideals of education, understanding, or equality, are driving media globalization. Large media conglomerates from a few wealthy industrialized nations are dominating global markets. In fact, both media production and consumption are strongly oriented toward the wealthier members of the world's population. As a result, the global media often function to highlight and help reproduce global inequality (Croteau and Hoynes, 2003).

Cultural Imperialism

The media products of the West, especially of the United States, are so dominant in global markets that some sociologists call it **cultural imperialism**. Imperialism is economic control of one country by another. Cultural imperialism, then, is cultural control of one country by another. One culture's art, music, television, and film are defined and controlled by another. And from Latin America to Asia to the Middle East, the West, but particularly the United States, is decried for its pervasive cultural dominance around the world.

Cultural imperialism is not simply the cultural domination of poor countries by rich ones, however. Western and American media products certainly do have a very strong presence in poorer nations, but Europeans and Canadians complain of American media dominance too—and quite loudly. In Europe, for example, American movies make up anywhere from 54 to 92 percent of movies shown in theaters, while European films make up only 3 percent (Croteau and Hoynes, 2003). Of all movies shown on European television, over 50 percent are made in America (De Bens, Kelly, and Bakke, 1992). In Canada, 95 percent of films in theaters are American movies. U.S. firms control music distribution. Eighty percent of magazines sold are from the United States, as are two-thirds of all books. (Croteau and Hoynes, 2003; Escobar and Swardson, 1995)

The overwhelming majority of music in the global marketplace is sung in English—usually by Americans. In Japan, songs sung in English make up 50 percent of radio playlists. In Germany, it's 80 percent. In Brazil, where the people speak Portuguese, nearly three-quarters of songs on the radio are sung in the English language (Barnet and Cavanaugh, 1994; Croteau and Hoynes, 2003).

Of the top-grossing films of all time at the international box office, all of the top ten were American films (Figure 18.4).

The issue is not jealousy of American lifestyles or dislike of global media products like MTV, Hollywood films, English-language pop music, and American soap operas. The cultural imperialism thesis holds that this kind of Western media dominance, driven by the relentless desire for profits, will shape all the cultures of the world and ensure their Westernization. Playing everywhere and blocking out opportunities for local productions, this media dominance will substitute American values like individualism and consumerism for the local values of countries where media products are sold. Eventually, cultural distinctiveness will be eroded, threatening national and cultural identity. Other nations will be so thoroughly indoctrinated with U.S. cultural, political, and economic images and ideals that they will forget who they are.

U.S. cultural products are having an immense impact around the world, but sociologists are finding that for a number of reasons the cultural imperialism thesis offers

▲ **Media globalization means both the technological innovations that allow us to communicate instantly over vast distances and the stock of media images that circulate around the world. Both could connect us to one another—or reinforce existing inequalities. Even in Oaxaca, Mexico, E.T. phones home.**

Did *you* know?

The Middle Eastern Broadcasting Company in Dubai currently broadcasts a dubbed version of *The Simpsons* called *Al Shamsoon* to most of the countries in the Persian Gulf. In the Arabic version, Homer becomes Omar, and Bart is Badr. Some scenes have to be cut to avoid offending conservative Muslim censors: no girls in bikinis, no bacon for breakfast, and no alcohol. Homer cannot be shown drinking or talking about beer, and his after-work hangout, Moe's Tavern, no longer exists.

FIGURE 18.4 Top Ten Grossing Films of All Time at the International (non–U.S.) Box Office

RANK	U.S. FILMS	YEAR	TOTAL GROSS REVENUE (MILLIONS OF U.S. DOLLARS)
1	Titanic	1997	1,235
2	Lord of the Rings: The Return of the King	2003	696
3	Harry Potter and the Sorcerer's Stone	2001	651
4	Harry Potter and the Chamber of Secrets	2002	604
5	Lord of the Rings: The Two Towers	2002	581
6	Jurassic Park	1993	563
7	Lord of the Rings: The Fellowship of the Ring	2001	547
8	Finding Nemo	2003	513
9	Independence Day	1996	505
10	Star Wars: Episode I: The Phantom Menace	1999	491

Source: From *The Human Development Report*, 2004.

only a partial picture. For now anyway, U.S. products are dominating some media and markets, while other media continue to be locally produced. Plus, different audiences still interpret foreign fare differently, and there are apparent limits to the appeal of Western—particularly U.S.—culture in other countries. Finally, different countries have created local variations of American or Western programs, giving imported formats a local resonance. Media globalization has induced successful "fusions" in film, television, and, perhaps especially, music, which circulate and sell well in originating countries and beyond. Many locally produced fusions have been so popular that they have allowed local producers to successfully compete with much larger media conglomerates.

Overall, then, it's not a question of domination or resistance, global or local, but both. Ironically, the relentless drive for corporate profits—the very basis for fears of cultural imperialism in the first place—is so far forcing media companies to adapt their products to speak to local customs and audiences.

How do we know what we know?

Interfering Variables

Most countries import a substantial number of their movies from abroad, usually Hollywood. Look at the percentage of films imported from abroad between 1990 and 1995, according to the *UNESCO World Culture Report*. If we take level of globalization as the dependent variable, could we hypothesize that imported films are the independent variable—that is, that greater the number of imported films, the higher the level of globalization?

Ethiopia	99%	Russia	72%
Australia	93%	France	63%
Norway	92%	Bangladesh	43%
Sweden	86%	Iran	47%
Mexico	83%	Japan	36%
Cuba	79%	United States	22%
Turkey	77%	India	14%

Actually, no. Is Cuba really more globalized than France, or Ethiopia more than Australia? Sometimes variables that we hadn't counted on will *interfere* with the data, eliminating the effect of the independent (globalization) on the dependent (imported movies). Religion, for example: Conservative Muslim countries may disapprove of the excessive sexual content of Hollywood movies and not import many. Or poverty: Some countries may be too poor to produce many films at home.

Media in the 21st Century: New Media, New Voices

Developments such as satellite TV and the Internet have allowed local groups to develop a voice that they never had before, no matter how strictly local governments may control media access. For instance, before around 1990, the West heard a single, monolithic Arab "opinion" on everything from Israel to Islam, even though there were 18 predominantly Arab countries stretching from Morocco to Iraq, with people from all ethnic groups, social classes, religions, and political persuasions. Minority opinions were censored. Now they are talking, and through approved channels. And their voices are fragmented. For instance, among Morocco's 15 online newspapers and news websites are the progressive feminist *Femmes du Maroc* (published in French) and the socialist *Libération*. Saudi Arabia forbids its citizens from publishing or accessing any information that disagrees with official policy, but there are hundreds of clandestine groups, including over 500 on Yahoo.com.

Al Jazeera, an independent television network based in Qatar (on the Persian Gulf), is one of the most popular media sites in the world, with several specialized channels devoted to sports, music, and children's programs and over 50 million regular viewers (it is available in the United States via satellite). Its main claim to infamy is its dedication to presenting alternatives to official policies of the Arab world. Several Arab countries have claimed that the network is too pro-Israel or pro-U.S. On the other hand, after the 9/11 attacks, when Al Jazeera broadcast statements from Osama bin Laden, many Westerners claimed that it was merely a front for terrorists. Journalists have had their credentials revoked in both Arab and Western countries, and when an English-language version of its website premiered in 2003, hackers immediately rerouted visitors to a picture of an American flag (Lynch, 2005; Rugh, 2004)

New media today are helping other cultures to preserve and help "alternative" voices to be heard. In the United Kingdom, for example, Sianel Pedwar Cymru, the Welsh fourth channel, is helping to support Welsh language and culture. In Mexico, the Zapatistas movement was able to bypass established media to communicate with the world via the Internet. Broadcasting among the Bedouin tribes of the Sahara has helped revive a sense of collective identity (Abu-Lughod, 1989; Williams, 2001).

In 2005, two new television networks were launched, each with a different approach to the same goal: bringing alternative voices to the public. One is Independent World Television (IWT), the brainchild of Canadian documentary filmmaker Paul Jay. IWT seeks to be an independent voice, free of corporate control over editorial content. The network is to be financed by Jay and other contributors and will allow no corporate ownership, underwriting, or advertising.

Telesur ("Telesouth") is a homegrown Latin American television network that seeks to challenge Western media dominance and present a Latin American perspective to Latin American viewers. The new network is being financed mainly by Venezuela, which is footing 51 percent of the bill. But Telesur is also being supported by the governments of Uruguay (10 percent), Cuba (19 percent), and Argentina (20 percent).

Some are calling Telesur "the Latin American Al Jazeera." Others say it will be little more than a mouthpiece for the governments that are paying its bills (Adams, 2005). A sociological perspective would suggest that both are true. Sociologists might be concerned about government control but fascinated by the idea of people speaking for themselves.

I sometimes show excerpts of old TV programs or films in my classes. They're short, they require little background information, and they illustrate whatever sociological issue we are covering in the lecture. But there are always two or three students who rebel against the idea of "wasting" valuable class time on something as inconsequential as a mass media text. "What difference does it make? It's just a TV show," they say.

Sociologists don't see it that way. Media both unite and fragment us. They both marginalize and free us. They both reproduce patterns of inequality and challenge them. But a TV show is never just a TV show.

Chapter Review

1. *What are the mass media?* Mass media are ways we communicate with large numbers of people; they are spurred by technological innovation and both reflect and create culture. Sociologists are interested in access to and the effects of media. Mass media include print media, radio, TV, and movies, as well as the Internet.

2. *How are media production and consumption related?* The production and consumption of media used to be divided but are now more interactive as producers consume and consumers produce. The media is considered a culture industry—a hierarchical and bureaucratic industry. This explains why so many mass media promote old or oppressive ideologies. Sociologists call this the "logic of safety," or using time-tested formulas. But consumers are involved in both interpreting and creating meaning. Multicultural and global viewers are especially active and interpret through their particular lens.

3. *How are advertising and celebrity related to the media?* The purpose of advertising is to convince consumers they want or need a product or service by associating the product with a desirable quality or activity. Sociologists are interested in advertising because we consume more ads than anything else, and ads are full of stereotypes and lead to questions about consumer desire. Mass media created celebrity; now celebrity itself is a product that we consume.

4. *What role does the consumption of media play in creating identity?* We often figure out who we are and where we fit into society through our consumption of media. Consumers are doing five things: surveillance to find out what the world is like, decision making through information gathering, appreciating aesthetics, being diverted for fun, and creating and maintaining a group identity. You can interpret media in different ways. In the dominant/hegemonic reading, the reader agrees with the preferred reading. In the ironic reading, the reader sees the ideology but distances him- or herself. In the oppositional or resistant reading, the reader sees the text as disputing its own ideology.

5. *How are the media regulated?* There are some laws regarding monopolies, particularly with newspapers, but these laws are relaxing. Another way of regulating media is through examining the effects of consumption on viewers. There are claims that all new media lead to violence or the destruction of society, but these claims tend not to be backed up empirically. Worry about the effects on people, especially children, leads to attempts at censorship. Censorship varies over time and by culture and place and is usually propelled by concerns over sex and violence. Sociologists are interested in how censorship is determined by power, inequality, and choice.

6. *What is the interrelation of globalization and the media?* The mass media are truly global. Media globalization involves technological innovations that allow production and consumption and develop media as a global product. Global media work to perpetuate the dominance of the powerful and both highlight and increase global inequality. Some call the dominance of Western media cultural imperialism or cultural control. But there is resistance to the possible homogenization of cultures, and the media are reflecting that by adapting to local audiences. The media today help spread culture, help preserve local culture, and let alternative voices be heard.

Key Terms

Blog (p. 591)
Cultural imperialism (p. 611)
Culture industries (p. 599)
Encoding/decoding (p. 599)

Fan (p. 606)
Global village (p. 610)
Interpretive community (p. 606)
Mass media (p. 588)

Media (p. 588)
Media text (p. 599)
Media consolidation (p. 601)

What does America think?

18.1 Confidence in Press

These are actual survey data from the General Social Survey, 2004.

As far as the people running the press are concerned, would you say you have a great deal of confidence, only some confidence, or hardly any confidence at all in them? The GSS survey results for 2004 indicate that almost 44 percent of the population has hardly any confidence in the press. Almost half of respondents had only some confidence in the press. Those in the upper class were most likely to reporting having a great deal of confidence in the press and at the same time were also the group most likely to report having very little confidence in the press. The percentage of respondents reporting confidence in the press has steadily declined since 1972 for all social class categories.

CRITICAL THINKING | **DISCUSSION QUESTION**

1. Take a good look at the social class differences in responses. They are complex. How do you explain them?

18.2 Free Press

These are actual survey data from the General Social Survey, 2002.

Which of these three statements comes closest to your feelings about balancing freedom of the press and the right to privacy? In the 2000 General Social Survey, just over 20 percent of respondents felt there should complete freedom of the press, even if the press sometimes invades the privacy of public figures. Sixty-four percent of the respondents felt the press should develop a code of ethics to keep it from invading the privacy of public figures. Almost 15 percent of respondents thought the government should keep the press from printing stories that invade the privacy of public figures. Respondents who identified as lower class were least likely to support complete freedom of the press.

CRITICAL THINKING | **DISCUSSION QUESTION**

1. Respondents in the middle class were least likely to favor government censoring of the press, while those in the lower class were most likely to favor it. How do you explain these social class differences?

▶ Go to this website to look further at the data. You can run your own statistics and crosstabs here: **http://sda.berkeley.edu/cgi-bin/hsda?harcsda+gss04**

REFERENCES: Davis, James A., Tom W. Smith, and Peter V. Marsden. General Social Surveys 1972–2004: [Cumulative file] [Computer file]. 2nd ICPSR version. Chicago, IL: National Opinion Research Center [producer], 2005; Storrs, CT: Roper Center for Public Opinion Research, University of Connecticut; Ann Arbor, MI: Inter-University Consortium for Political and Social Research; Berkeley, CA: Computer-Assisted Survey Methods Program, University of California [distributors], 2005.

chapter 19

Sociology of Environments: The Natural, Physical, and Human Worlds

ON AUGUST 23, 2005, the summer's twelfth tropical depression formed over the Bahamas. Soon it was upgraded to a Category 1 hurricane named Katrina. In a busy hurricane season, most of the world didn't pay much attention as it made landfall in Florida, caused little damage, weakened into a tropical storm, and blew off into the Gulf of Mexico. But then the warm water strengthened it into a Category 5, with winds of 175 miles per hour, the most intense hurricane to ever hit the gulf. On August 28, New Orleans Mayor Ray Nagle ordered a mandatory evacuation of the entire city. By the morning of August 29, only 20 percent of the 1.3 million residents remained, mostly those too poor or sick to move. Shortly after landfall, a storm surge breached the levees in several places. Four-fifths of the entire city was under water.

So far this doesn't sound very much like the introduction to a chapter in a sociology textbook. Read on.

We think of people and the natural and built environments in which they live as separate, even conflicted, realms. Sociologists are interested in the dynamic relationships among the human, the physical, and the urban environments.

During the subsequent days and weeks, news reports described a city in chaos, with snipers, rapes and murders, people dying of hunger and exposure, bodies lying unattended in the streets. (Later it turned out that many of the reports were exaggerated or even made up.) National Guard and federal troops were mobilized, but were they in New Orleans to distribute food and water or to keep looters away from the pricey boutiques on Canal Street? Why did they take so long to arrive? Most of the survivors were poor and African American. And the spin of the news reports—African Americans "looting" but White people "searching for food"— suggested that the disaster was bringing long-hidden prejudices to light.

We think of human beings, the cities they live in, and the physical world of tropical depressions as separate realms, sometimes even conflicted ones. As the events leading up to and following Hurricane Katrina demonstrate, they are related, even interdependent. The hurricane, the flooding of New Orleans, and the aftermath are parts of the same story. Cities "create" the countryside. "Natural disasters" have human causes as well as human consequences. All three environments—the human, the urban, and the natural—constrain and construct human action, help create and sometimes help destroy each other. Sociologists are vitally interested in the dynamic relationships among the human, the physical, and the urban environments.

The Human Environment

Humans are a social species. We want—and need—to be around other people most of the time. People who go off by themselves on purpose are often considered strange, socially inept, or even psychologically disturbed. Every time a serial killer or mass murderer is apprehended, newshounds rush to broadcast a neighbor saying, "He was a loner, kept to himself most of the time," as if somehow being alone explains murderous thoughts.

A major part of our environment is the mass of other people around us, simply doing what people do: being born and growing up, moving into town and leaving town, getting sick and getting well, living and dying. **Demography** is the scientific study of human populations and one of the oldest and most popular branches of sociology. Demography is used to calculate health, longevity, and even political representation, as the census is the basis for allocation of congressional seats. Demographers are primarily concerned with the statistics of birth, death, and migration (Yaukey and Anderton, 2001).

Being Born

Demographers use two birth measurements: **fertility** (the number of children that a woman has) and **fecundity** (the maximum number of children that she could possibly have). Women are physically capable of having a child every nine months, so in the years between menarche (the onset of menstruation) and menopause (the end of menstruation) they could give birth over 20 times (their fecundity). However, in the United States, women have an average of 2.08 children each (their fertility) (Hamilton, et al, 2006; U.S. Census Bureau). (Figure 19.1) (Men are not counted because they could produce thousands of children if they found enough partners. King Sobhuza II of Swaziland [1899–1982] fathered 210 children with his 70 wives.)

Demographers measure fertility with the number of live births in the country per year. They measure fecundity with the **fertility rate,** the number of children that would be born to each woman if she lived through her childbearing years with the average fertility of her age group. Poor countries often have a fertility rate of four or more (it's 6.84 in Somalia), while in rich countries, the fertility rate often drops to less than two (1.61 in Canada) (CIA World Factbook). Very high fertility rates spell trouble: Children do not contribute to the economy until they are older, but they must be fed, clothed, educated, and given health care, thus putting a severe strain on already impoverished families. Women with so many children cannot participate in the labor force, putting even more strain on the family economy. As the children grow into adulthood, there will not be enough jobs to accommodate them, resulting in widespread unemployment. On the other hand, more children means more potential support for aging and infirm parents.

However, very low fertility rates are also a problem, suggesting that the population is aging faster than it can be replenished with new births. Fewer people participate in the workforce as they grow old or retire, but at the same time they continue to require housing, food, transportation, and health care, again putting a strain on the economy. The low number of births means that in about 20 years there will not be enough adult workers to fill critical jobs in business and technology, putting the country at an economic disadvantage. On the other hand, lower birth rates mean that adults have far more geographic and occupational mobility.

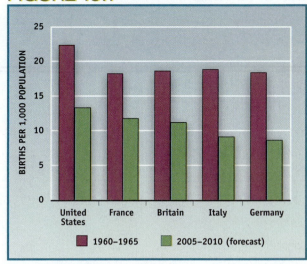

FIGURE 19.1 The Birth Dearth

Source: "The Birth Dearth" from "German Demography: Cradle Snatching," *The Economist,* March 18, 2006, p. 55.

Dying

Of course, everyone dies sooner or later, but the **mortality rate,** or the number of deaths per year for every thousand people, can tell demographers a great deal about the relative health of the country. In the United States, the mortality rate is 8.25; every year, a little over eight people in every thousand die. Most wealthy nations range between 8 and 12.

Strangely, poor nations can have either higher or lower mortality rates. A low mortality rate, as in Guatemala (6.81) or Tonga (5.35), does not necessarily mean that the people there enjoy a high **life expectancy** (the average number of years a person can expect to live). In fact, in Guatemala, it's rather low, 64.31 for men and 66.21 for women. It usually means that the fertility rate is so high that the proportion of older people in the population goes down. In the United States, about 12 percent of the population is 65 or older. It's 3.3 percent in Guatemala and 4.2 percent in Tonga (CIA World Factbook).

A higher mortality rate, as in Afghanistan (20.99) or Zambia (20.23), usually signifies that, due to famine, war, or disease, many people do not live to see old age. AIDS is causing a significant decline in population growth in many low-income countries. In some sub-Saharan African countries, 10 percent or more of the adult population is infected with HIV—37 percent in Botswana, which also has the highest mortality rate

FIGURE 19.2 Infant Mortality Rate in the World

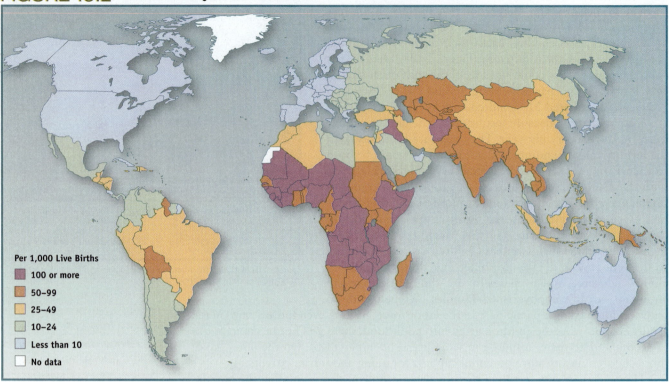

Per 1,000 Live Births
- 100 or more
- 50–99
- 25–49
- 10–24
- Less than 10
- No data

Source: From Maps of the World website, www.mapsoftheworld.com. Reprinted with permission.

in the world (29.36). Most people cannot afford the expensive medications necessary to keep HIV from developing into AIDS, so their life expectancy is low (CIA World Factbook). The majority are in their prime childbearing years, which also contributes to the population decline. They are also in their prime economic years, so these countries are experiencing reversals in economic and social development.

Demographers are especially interested in the **infant mortality rate,** the number of deaths per year in each thousand infants up to one year old (Figure 19.2). As you might expect, the infant mortality rate is extremely low in wealthy countries (4.31 in France), and extremely high in poor countries, especially in sub-Saharan Africa: It's 70.49 in Nigeria and 192.5 in Angola (that is, one out of five babies born die during their first year of life). Because infants are more vulnerable to disease and malnutrition than adults or older children, the infant mortality rate correlates with the effectiveness of the country's health care, the level of nutrition, and innumerable other quality of life factors. In Angola, for instance, fewer than half of all children have been immunized for measles, only 30 percent have access to adequate sanitation, and only 10 percent sleep under mosquito netting (to guard against malaria) (UNICEF, 2003). The infant mortality rate serves as a proxy for the overall health of the country and can guide policy makers in their allocation of funds for hospitals, medical care, and pregnancy counseling.

Moving In, Moving Out

In addition to people being born and dying, demographers are interested in their physical movements, as they leave one territory (*emigrating*) and take up permanent residence in another (*immigrating*). People emigrate and immigrate either voluntarily or involuntarily. Most wealthy countries have sizeable populations of voluntary immigrants. In 2000, the United States granted citizenship to 898,000 foreign nationals.

Canada was second (214,600 new citizenships), followed by several European countries and Australia (OECD 2004).

Over 46 million people living today emigrated from their home territory involuntarily. Thirty million were lured or abducted into forced labor or the global sex trade, and 16 million are refugees, victims of political strife, war, or natural disasters. Iran hosts the most refugees (nearly two million), followed by Germany, Bosnia, Pakistan, and Rwanda (UNESCO 2002).

Voluntary migrants usually have two sets of motives for their move, called *push factors* (reasons they want to leave their home territory in the first place) and *pull factors* (reasons they want to settle in this particular territory). The most common push factors are a sluggish economy, political and cultural oppression, and civil unrest—not enough to force them to leave, but enough to make their lives at home miserable. A slight downturn in one country's economic fortunes often leads to a rise in immigration in others. The most common pull factors are the opposite: a good economy, political and cultural tolerance, and civil stability. Because rich countries offer superior jobs and education and a great degree of political and cultural tolerance, they tend to receive the most voluntary migrants. Most Scandinavian countries offer citizenship, health benefits, and educational access the second you land on their shores, so they have become magnets for enterprising migrants from Turkey and Pakistan.

Another extremely important pull factor is having someone you know in the territory you intend to immigrate to. People don't like to start out afresh in areas where they know no one and where possibly no one speaks their language or understands their culture, so when they have a choice, they often move to where family and friends are already located. Many relocate to follow a romantic partner.

On arrival, new immigrants tend to cluster in the same neighborhoods, both because racism and discrimination prevent the easy mobility they had imagined and because they come with few financial resources, and old friends and relatives offer free places to stay and possibly even jobs. The nineteenth- and early twentieth-century immigrants to New York didn't live scattered all over the city but in carefully defined neighborhoods—Greek, Hungarian, Irish, Polish, and so on. Sometimes entire villages relocate to the same neighborhood in the new country.

Many refugees cannot afford to leave their home countries, or else authoritarian governments forbid them to leave. It takes the concerted efforts of humanitarian agencies to get them out. When China took control of Tibet in 1959, thousands of Tibetans moved into exile in neighboring India. Many others have followed since. Church and secular agencies around the world created programs to relocate them, until today the 140,000 Tibetan refugees are living in host countries around the world. There are 5,000 in about 30 cities in the United States and Canada.

There have been four major flows of immigration in modern history (Pagden, 2001):

1. Between 1500 and 1800, as Europe began to establish colonial empires around the world, millions of English, French, Spanish, and Portuguese citizens emigrated to the sparsely settled regions of North and South America, South Africa, and Oceania. Some were forced to leave as punishment for a crime, but most chose to leave voluntarily, drawn by the promise of wealth or political freedom in the colonies.

▲ Many refugees cluster in places where their ethnic group has gained a foothold. There are 18,000 Hmong, political refugees from Laos, in the United States, almost all in a few cities in Minnesota, Wisconsin, and California. Here, Hmong third graders join a class in St. Paul, Minnesota.

2. At about the same time, Europeans transported over 11,000,000 East and West Africans to their New World colonies in North and South America and the Caribbean to work as slaves. Eventually they came to form a substantial part of the population of the United States, the Caribbean, and many regions of South America, especially Brazil. Because they maintained so much cultural continuity with their African homeland, they are now sometimes called "The African Diaspora," and the two regions (Africa and the New World) are studied together in Africana Studies departments of universities (Gomez, 2004; Thornton, 1998).

3. Beginning in about 1800, East Asians began to emigrate from China and to a lesser extent other countries, with motives similar to those of the Europeans who settled the New World (Takaki, 1998). They immigrated to major cities in the United States, Latin America, Africa, and the Middle East. Today Brazil has the largest population of Japanese ancestry (1.5 million) outside of Japan, and 50 percent of the population of the United Arab Emirates consists of South Asian nationals (CIA World Factbook). In fact, because there are even more South Asian migrants—25,000,000—than African forced migrants, culture scholars have begun to refer to an "Indian Diaspora" on the model of the African Diaspora (Bates, 2001).

4. Between about 1880 and 1920, millions of Southern and Eastern Europeans emigrated as they faced increasing political and economic strife as their countries modernized. These included the political traumas of unification in Italy, pogroms and forced conscription in Russia, and economic depression across Europe. High school textbooks in the United States tend to portray only immigrants arriving at Ellis Island, but they also settled in Canada, South Africa, Australia, New Zealand, and Latin America. By 1914, 30 percent of the population of Argentina was foreign born, speaking Italian, Russian, Polish, Czech, English, Yiddish, and German. In some districts, the percentage was as high as 50 percent (Shumway, 1993).

Did *you* know?

Most people know that Australia was originally a penal colony to thin out the population of Britain's overflowing jails, but did you know that the province of Georgia was founded in 1732 as a penal colony for British criminals (mostly debtors)? Later, criminals were transported to other cities in the South, where plantation owners could bid on them along with the African slaves. It is estimated that a quarter of all British colonists during the eighteenth century, some 50,000 people, arrived that way (Coleman, 1991).

Studying Immigration

The **immigration rate** is the number of people entering a territory each year for every thousand of the population. The **emigration rate** is the opposite, the number of people leaving per thousand. However, few territories are so terrible that they cannot attract at least a few immigrants, or so wonderful that no one ever decides to emigrate (although some authoritarian states forbid their citizens from emigrating). Therefore demographers study the changing population by examining the **net migration rate,** the difference between the immigration and emigration rates in a given year.

Because rich countries offer the greatest educational and job opportunities and the most freedom from oppression, more people want to move to them than to leave, so they tend to have positive net migration rates (5.9 in Canada, 3.31 in the United States, 2.18 in Germany). A negative net migration rate means that more people are emigrating than immigrating, suggesting that the country is too poor to offer many jobs or else is undergoing a political crisis (Iran, –2.64; Mexico, –4.57). The lowest net migration rate in the world is in Micronesia, where 21 more people per thousand leave than arrive every year. With one-fifth of the population unemployed, palm trees and ocean breezes haven't been sufficient incentive to stick around (CIA World Factbook 2006).

Internal migration means moving from one region to another within a territory. The average American moves 11 times during his or her life—more for young, middle-class professionals. Most of these migrations occur within the same city or to adjacent cities, as people seek bigger and better residences while staying "close to home." A surprising percentage occur across county lines, however. In the United States, demographers classify as "significant" only those moves out of the county. This is not always an accurate measure. For instance, if you move from Upland, California, to Needles, on the Arizona border, the 219 miles will not be considered "significant" because you're still in San Bernardino County. But if you move a mile down the road to Claremont, you've changed to Los Angeles County, and demographers will take notice.

Young college-educated people are more likely to move out of the county—75 percent of the single ones and 72 percent of the married ones moved between 1995 and 2000. Married or single, they have fewer long-term responsibilities to tie them to a place, no kids to take out of school or houses to put up on the market. Also, people looking for jobs that require a college degree often conduct a national job search instead of a local search; over 20 percent of people who moved significant distances in 1999–2000 said they moved because of a "new job" or "job transfer," by far the most popular reason (Schachter, 2001).

Internal and international migration are regulated by similar push and pull factors: People want jobs and freedom. Two million African Americans moved from the rural South to the urban North between 1900 and 1940, to escape stagnating rural economies and oppressive Jim Crow laws. Another five million moved north between 1940 and 1970 (Lemann, 1992). Since World War II, there has been an ongoing migration of young gay men and lesbians from small towns to big cities, to escape from the homophobia and heterosexism back home (Weston, 1995). This simultaneous push (discrimination) and pull (attraction of a community) created and sustain the now well-established gay ghettos in San Francisco, New York, Miami, Atlanta, and other major cities (see Levine, 1979).

Today most internal migration flows from the cities of the Northeast and the Midwest, where economies are stagnating—the so-called Rust Belt, from the reliance on heavy industry and especially the homes of the steel and auto industries—toward places with high economic prospects, the Sun Belt of the New South—Texas, Tennessee, Georgia, Florida—and the Southwest, especially Arizona, California, and Nevada (Table 19.1). Between 1990 and 1997, 4 percent of the population of Pittsburgh moved away, while Atlanta added 22 percent. The trend continued in 2000 through 2004, with huge gains for Sun Belt cities like Phoenix, Las Vegas, Dallas, and Atlanta, and big losses for Boston, Detroit, and Chicago (U.S. Census Bureau).

▲ Internal migration has shifted a significant proportion of the population from the industrial Northeast and Midwest (the "Rust Belt") to the South and Southwest (the "Sun Belt"). Some cities have declined, while others, like Raleigh, North Carolina, have boomed.

TABLE 19.1

Biggest Population Gains and Losses, 2000–2004			
GAINS		**LOSSES**	
Riverside–San Bernardino, CA	325,842	New York, NY	−844,058
Phoenix, AZ	194,392	Los Angeles, CA	−471,118
Las Vegas, NV	168,463	Chicago, IL	−252,997
Tampa, FL	145,580	San Francisco, CA	−243,934
Atlanta, GA	124,106	San Jose, CA	−174,295

Note: Los Angeles is second in losses, but adjacent counties are first in gains—these changes may simply be a matter of people moving to the suburbs and just outside city limits
Source: Frey, 2005.

▲ Migration takes place because people may be pushed out of their communities by discrimination or pulled to a welcoming community elsewhere. In the 1970s, "gay ghettoes" emerged in most major American cities, notably San Francisco (shown, the Castro district) and New York.

An influx of new immigrants, either internal or international, can provide new talent for the community, but it also puts a strain on the local infrastructure, as utility companies, school districts, real estate, and retailers try to deal with the influx. Meanwhile, the territories losing population experience a loss of talent, failed businesses, deserted downtowns, and a "sinking ship" feeling.

Population Composition

Comparing births and deaths, emigration and immigration, can give demographers only a partial understanding about what's going on in a country or region. They also want to know the **population composition**—that is, the comparative numbers of men and women and various age groups. The male:female ratio is never 50:50. Due to physiological differences in X and Y chromosomes, 106 boys tend to be born for every 100 girls. A significantly lower birth ratio suggests that environmental pollution is having an impact on the human body at the chromosomal level (Davis, Gottlieb, and Stampninsky, 1998). A significantly higher ratio, especially in countries where boys are strongly preferred over girls—for instance, China (109), South Korea (110), and Guam (114)—suggests to demographers that women are more likely to choose abortions if they find that they are carrying girls. Some may even engage in the once common but now outlawed practice of infanticide (killing the newborn).

After birth, the ratio of men to women decreases in every age group because men are more likely to die in accidents, warfare, and of certain diseases. If the ratio is too high or not high enough, demographers conclude that the country is especially unpleasant or unattractive for men or women. During the middle years of life (ages 15 to 64), the highest disproportion of men to women occurs in countries that draw a substantial number of male foreign workers (there are 2.28 men for every woman in Qatar). On the other side of the coin, countries that lose many men to foreign employment tend to have a disproportionate number of women (there are 0.92 men for every woman in Puerto Rico). The greater the disproportion, the more likely that men and women interested in heterosexual unions will not be able to find appropriate partners.

The distribution of people of different age groups can best be represented by a graph called a **population pyramid,** which shows five- or ten-year age groups as different-sized bars, or "blocks" (Figure 19.3). Many poor countries, like Mexico, have "expansive pyramids" that look like real pyramids. They have a broad base to signify a high fertility rate, and every "block" gets smaller as the age group shrinks due to accident, disease, or other mortality factors, until the highest block (the elderly) is very small. Rich countries often have "constrictive pyramids." The base is not very broad because the fertility rate is not very high, but there's a big block of middle-aged and older people. Some countries, like Italy, even look somewhat top heavy because the middle and apex of the pyramid is bigger than the base; there are many more people over 30 than children. A few countries have "stationary pyramids," which look like pillars. Because few people in each age group die of accident or disease, every block is about the same size, beginning to shrink only a little beginning with the 60-year-olds. Demographers predict that while the United States is slightly constrictive now, it will be more stationary by 2030 (Young, 1998). In the United States, the higher fertility rates of

Did *you* know?

The situation of women (both a "surplus" of women and severe gender discrimination) in many countries in Asia and the former Soviet Union has created a cottage industry of "mail-order wives." American men are invited on websites to select foreign brides who are "unspoiled by feminism." In 2001, the U.S. government issued over 17,000 "fiancée" visas, most for women who had never met their future husbands in person. About half of the brides were from Asia and half from Eastern Europe and the former Soviet Union.

immigrants help account for a less-constrictive pyramid than in some other wealthy countries ("As They Don't Like It," 2005).

Population pyramids can also be divided by gender, with men on one side and women on the other. If one of the blocks is larger on one end than the other, it means that men or women far outnumber the other sex in that age group. In the United States, women begin outnumbering men around the age of 70, but in India, they begin outnumbering men around the age of 40.

Demographers use population blocks to determine current and future social service needs of the society. In the United States, the baby boomer block has been a bulge in the pyramid, working its way upward since the 1950s, allowing demographers to predict a need for more child-oriented facilities, then more colleges and universities, and now more facilities for elderly people.

Population Growth

Cities and countries grow or shrink for a variety of reasons: **natural population increase** (the number of births every year subtracted by the number of deaths), immigration and emigration, and changing boundary lines when territories are annexed or lost. But the world as a whole grows for only one reason, natural increase, and it is growing fast, at a rate of 1.3 percent per year. As of this writing, there are 6.5 billion people living on Earth, but by the time this book is published, it will probably be 6.75 billion. If you are 20 years old today, you can expect to see the world's population reach 8 billion before your fortieth birthday, and 9 billion long before you retire (Cohen, 1995).

How did we get so many people? And what are we going to do with them?

For thousands of years, children meant prosperity. They started working alongside their parents as soon as they could walk, thus adding to the family's economic productivity. In the absence of Social Security and retirement communities, they meant the difference between being taken care of in old age and being thrown out onto the street. Women were pregnant as often as they could be. With a high infant mortality rate and virtually no effective medical care, only about half of the babies born survived to age 14 (Kriedte, 1983), so it was prudent to have as many children as possible to ensure that one or two would survive to maturity.

FIGURE 19.3 U.S. Population Pyramid Summary 2000, 2025, 2030

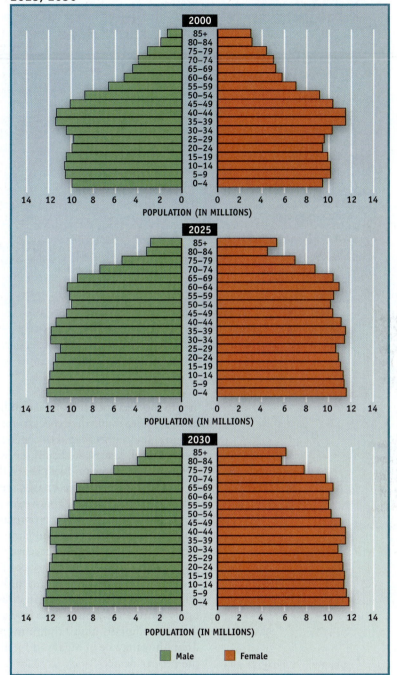

Source: U.S. Census Bureau, International Data Base, 2007.

Try It  Understanding Population Pyramids

Developed by Katherine R. Rowell, *Sinclair Community College.*

OBJECTIVE: Understand population data and apply them to potential policy issues.

STEP 1: Plan

Understanding the distribution of population within a country by age and sex is important in understanding future issues that may develop. This activity requires you to examine the population pyramids of three developed (mostly wealthy) countries and compare them to three developing (mostly poor) countries. To compare and contrast, choose the year 2000 for information on the population of the countries you choose.

STEP 2: Research

Go to the International Database of the U.S. Census Bureau (www.census.gov/ipc/www/idb) and choose your six countries (keep in mind three are to be developed, and three should be developing, based on year 2000).

For each country, either print out the pyramid or save the diagram in a document file.

STEP 3: Compare

Write a one-page paper comparing and contrasting the pyramids. Did you notice any patterns? What seem to be the main population issues facing the developed countries? What seem to be the main issues facing the developing countries? What do you think the future holds?

Take a look at the information provided by the Population Reference Bureau website (www.prb.org) and search for the World Population Clock, 2006.

How does this information compare to your overall thoughts? Based on world population data, what population issues do you see in the world? Explain in a short paragraph.

STEP 4: Discuss

Be prepared to turn in your work for this activity in class and to discuss and share your results.

In modern societies, most children survive to adulthood, so it is imprudent to give birth to more than you expect to raise. And, far from meaning endless prosperity, they are an economic burden. For the first 20 years or so of their lives, parents provide their room, board, braces, medicine, school supplies, books, toys, and probably an allowance, while at least in the middle classes the children contribute little or nothing to the family budget (they may have a part-time job, but it's usually for their own spending money). When they grow up, they move away and contribute no money to their household of origin; in fact, many modern parents resist the idea of their children's giving them anything at all. However, a significant minority of young middle-class adults—even after they go to college—continue to live at home, relying on financial support (familial cleaning, catering, and laundry services) and other forms of life support.

Fewer children, therefore, make more economic sense than lots of children. But tell that to men and women in cultures where a household with ten children is infinitely more prestigious than a household with just one—or, heaven forbid, none. Even if they grudgingly admit that it might be a good idea to limit the number of their children, they may be unaware of birth control techniques, or they are unable to acquire the proper devices.

Even where urban populations find children an economic liability, in the absence of social safety nets like Social Security and elderly care facilities, people may want large families to ensure care in their old age. High fertility may be encouraged for religious or political reasons. Also, if women's opportunities are limited, childbearing, especially at an early age, is one of the few roles open to them.

Low infant mortality plus the prestige of large families meant that beginning about 1750, the world's population started to inch upward (Table 19.2). Then the inch became a foot. Not only the population itself, but the rate of increase started to climb. It was this climb that sparked the growth of demography as a field of sociological study.

In 1900, the world's population was about 1.7 billion. During the twentieth century, it quadrupled to over 6 billion, due to plummeting infant and maternal mortality rates (the result of improved health care for both pregnant women and their infants and of better neonatal nutrition) and dramatically increased longevity. Although the peak slowed a bit after 1970, due to a declining fertility rate in rich countries and the world pandemic of HIV/AIDS, we are still gaining 77 million people each year, or the equivalent of the entire population of the United States every four years.

Ninety-six percent of the population growth is taking place in poor countries. Somalia, one of the poorest countries in the world, adds 3.38 percent to its population every year. This means that the people having the most children are precisely the ones least economically capable of providing for them. Many rich countries, on the other hand, have a stable population, and some are in decline. Demographers consider a population growth rate of 0.4 percent or so stable, but in 40 of the 42 countries in Europe, the growth rate is lower than that, and in some it is actually shrinking. The birth rate and immigration rate are too low to replace those who die and emigrate.

How High Can It Go?

Thomas Robert Malthus (1766–1834), an English economist and clergyman, was one of the first to suggest that population growth might spin out of control and lead to disaster (1798). Though the population of England was only about 6 million at the time, **Malthusian theory** held it would increase by geometric progression, doubling in each generation—a man and a woman would have four children, and those four would have eight, and those eight sixteen, and so on. However, because farm land has a limited fertility, even with new technology, food production can only increase by arithmetic progression—20 tons becomes 40, then 60, then 80, and so on. Eventually—and quite rapidly—there would be more people than food, leading to starvation on a global level.

While in principle his theory made sense, Malthus failed to foresee several cultural trends. First, the birth rate in England began to drop around 1850 as children were increasingly seen as an economic liability and people began to use birth control. Also, Malthus underestimated human ingenuity—irrigation, fertilizers, pesticides, and selective breeding have greatly increased farm productivity. So the population did not increase quite as fast as he thought, and there has been no global starvation. Yet. In rich countries, the problem is often quite the opposite—we consume far more than we need to survive.

Karl Marx was highly critical of Malthus's basic assumption that population growth would be a source of hardship for the masses. He argued that unequal distribution of resources was a far more significant factor. To Marx, the problem was that the rich get richer and the poor get babies. The political question was not how to reduce the number of babies but how to get the poor some of those riches.

But Marx has been criticized for failing to take uneven population growth into account as a contributing factor in global inequality. For example, India is the second most populous country in the world, with a little over a billion people in 2005. Its population increases by 18 million per year, with an expected 50 percent increase by 2050. It currently faces a severe water shortage. This is not a resource that can be redistributed. As its population increases, its quality of life will get lower, resulting in a widened inequality gap in high-income countries.

TABLE 19.2

World Population Milestones
■ 1 billion in 1804
■ 2 billion in 1927 (123 years later)
■ 3 billion in 1960 (33 years later)
■ 4 billion in 1974 (14 years later)
■ 5 billion in 1987 (13 years later)
■ 6 billion in 1999 (12 years later)

Source: United Nations Population Division. Fact Monster/Information Please® Database, © 2005 Pearson Education, Inc. All rights reserved.

Migration and fertility rates also affect the age demographics of a society. Russia loses 0.37 percent of its population every year, becoming older and grayer. ▼

In 1968, Paul Ehrlich published *The Population Bomb,* which put a modern take on Malthus. He argued that even a moderate 1.3 percent population increase would soon spin out of control. Before the year 3000, he predicted, Earth's population would grow to 60 million billion, or 100 people for each square yard of the world, including the oceans and mountaintops. Of course, we would run out of food and usable water long before that. Ehrlich predicted that the first mass starvations would begin in the 1990s. He turned out to be slightly off as well. Millions of people are malnourished across the world, but not nearly as many as he predicted. Erlich later argued that an increased population combined with an alarming depletion of natural resources can only lead to chaos. His solution was a global effort to achieve **zero population growth**—where the number of births does not exceed the number of deaths. This would involve not only global stability in population but a decrease in poor countries and a redistribution of resources to those countries.

Demographic Transition

Frank Notestein (1945) argued that population growth is tied to technological development. **Demographic transition theory** holds that the population and technology spur each other's development. This transition has three stages:

1. *Initial stage.* The society has both a high birth rate and a high death rate, so the population size remains stable or else grows very slowly. Preindustrial societies were all at this stage.

2. *Transitional growth stage.* Industrialization leads to a better food supply, better medical care, and better sanitation, all resulting in a decrease in mortality at all age levels. However, the sociological prestige of large families has not decreased, so the birth rate remains high, and the population explodes. This is what Malthus observed, and it precipitated his theory of exponential growth.

3. *Incipient decline stage.* Social forces and cultural beliefs catch up with technology. Both the birth and death rates are low, so population growth returns to minimal levels. Zero population growth is rare, but many industrialized countries like Germany are coming close.

This theory has been criticized for two reasons. First, it always works in the same direction, from high fertility/high mortality to high fertility/low mortality as technology increases, and then to low fertility/low mortality as social norms catch up. However, there have been many instances in history where the mortality rate moved from low to high, such as the periods immediately after the fall of the Roman Empire and the Mayan Empire. In contemporary sub-Saharan Africa, the high rate of HIV infection is offsetting the birth rate and causing countries to move backward, from stage two to stage one (high fertility/high mortality).

Second, it is not technology that causes a decrease in the mortality rate—but rather the sociology, the changes in personal and public health practices. Several major medical discoveries in eighteenth and nineteenth centuries led to little change in the mortality rate. But when the public accepted the germ theory of disease, and therefore they began to sterilize implements, pasteurize their milk, immunize their children, wash their hands, and bathe regularly—then the mortality rate declined.

Decreasing the Rate of Flow

A number of organizations and nations have come together to try to decrease the population explosion. In the United States, Population Connection promotes the

Life Expectancy

You can go online or to an encyclopedia and find the life expectancy for men and women and different ethnic and occupational groups in every country in the world. But how do we know that a baby born today is likely to live to be 61, or 66, or 78, or 100? It's not easy.

First we have to find the crude death rate, the percentage of people of each age who were alive last year but are dead this year. For instance, if last year's records indicated that there were 1,000,000 people of age 30, and this year there are 900,000 people of age 31, then 30-year-olds have a 90 percent chance of seeing their thirty-first birthday, and their crude death rate is 10 percent. From this we can construct a life table, a list of the probabilities that persons of age X will live to see age $X+1$, $X+2$, and so on. To find the life expectancy of the population, we take the mean of all the probabilities for a person of age 0 (a newborn baby).

Notice that the measure of life expectancy cannot predict the future. If the life expectancy in the country is 75, that doesn't mean that newborn babies will live for 75 more years, or that people who are 30 now have 45 years left to live. It is really a measure of how long people are living at this moment in time.

replacement level of only two children per family. The organization's website contains updates and policy briefs about different pressing environmental issues and has branches on many college campuses.

Several countries have started protocols intended to decrease overpopulation. In China, a family planning law was mandated in 1980. Although known worldwide as a "one child per couple" law, it is actually calculated by neighborhoods rather than couples: Each neighborhood has a maximum number of births it can have per year. If a couple wants to have a child, they must apply for a "pregnancy permit." They may be permitted to have more than one, if the neighborhood has not met its quota, and if there are extenuating circumstances (such as if they work on a farm, if their first child was a girl, if their first child is disabled, and so on), or they may not be permitted to have a child at all. Illegal pregnancy means losing privileges, paying fines, and even losing their jobs. Globally, some commentators worried about compromising personal freedom, and others worried about women accidentally getting pregnant and then being forced to have an abortion. However, the measures have been successful. China has reduced its growth rate to 1.1 percent per year, half that of other poor nations.

The Urban Environment

In the U.S. farming town of Dekalb, Illinois, only 65 miles from downtown Chicago, live people who have never ventured to the city. Not to go to a Cubs game or the Art Institute, not to shop at Macy's. When questioned, they seem surprised—who in their right mind would want to go into Chicago? It's crowded, dirty, ugly, expensive, and dangerous. Meanwhile, in the high-rise condos of Chicago's Gold Coast live people who have never ventured more than five miles west of the Loop. When they are questioned, they also seem surprised—where else is there to go? They're surrounded by nonstop excitement, cultural diversity, artistic innovation, and economic promise. Beyond Chicago there is nothing but small towns stuck in the 1930s, populated by narrow-minded bigots.

We think of cities as the capitals of civilization—culturally alive, commercially dynamic, exciting. We also think of cities as the centers and incubators of many of

Sociology and our World

Bare Branches

What happens when men are told constantly that they are worthless, a disgrace to their ancestors, and a failure to their country, unless they produce sons? And then modern medical techniques allow them to determine the sex of their children early in the pregnancy, early enough for an abortion? And strict birth control policies allow only one child per couple, unless it's not a son—then they can keep trying?

A lot of sons get born, and not very many daughters.

And, 20 years later, there's a new generation of young men who have been told constantly that they are worthless unless *they* produce sons. Except now there are fewer women around for them to produce the sons with.

In China they are called "bare branches," these men who do not produce sons, mostly not due to physiological malfunction or lack of heterosexual interest, but due to the lack of female partners. (The phrase refers to the bare branch on the family tree.) And their numbers are increasing. Nationwide, 2,000,000 more boys than girls are being born every year. By 2020, that will mean 40 million more young adult men than women (Lim, 2004), a population the size of Spain. The Chinese government fears widespread rape, prostitution, and other sex crimes, but unless it can change 2,500 years of Confucian teachings and give these men a purpose in life besides having sons, the psychological consequences may outweigh the sociological.

---

our most central social problems—crime, poverty, racial and ethnic antagonism, more crime. But it's not one or the other—it's both. The two sets of social issues are linked and interacting. To a great extent, one cannot exist without the other.

The City: Ancient to Modern

When people depend on farming for sustenance and don't have cars, they must live within walking distance of their farmland. Throughout most of human history, and in many undeveloped countries today, they have lived in villages scattered across the farmlands, with a population of only a few hundred, so small that everyone knows everyone else and is probably related through blood and marriage. Between 8,000 and 5,000 BCE, technological innovations in agriculture began to produce food surpluses, so some people could take on nonfarming jobs, mostly as priests and artisans. They could live in larger settlements—but not too much larger because 99 percent of the population had to be within walking distance of the fields or cattle. Many archaeologists name Çatalhöyük, in modern-day Turkey, as the first city. In 7000 BCE, it was home to 10,000 people—a tiny village today, but then by far the most populous settlement in the world (Mumford, 1968; Yoffee, 2005).

Most ancient cities grew up along major rivers, where enough food could be produced to feed a large nonfarming population. It still took up to 75 farmers to feed one nonfarmer, so these cities had to be small by modern standards. Most had no more than 10,000 residents. At the end of the first century BCE, a few cities in China and India reached a population of 300,000, and Rome was probably unique throughout the ancient world for its population of nearly one million.

The number of "large" cities stayed about the same throughout the Middle Ages and the Renaissance. For all of their fame as centers of Western civilization, European cities were surprisingly small. Of the ten most populous cities in the world in 1500, four were in China, three in the Middle East, and two in India. Only one was in Europe: Paris, reaching number eight with a population of 185,000 (about the size of Dayton, Ohio, today). Beijing, China, number one, had a population of 672,000 (about the size of Memphis, Tennessee, today) (Chandler, 1987).

When the Industrial Revolution began around 1750, agricultural productivity increased exponentially, farming jobs began to diminish (a trend that continues today), and manufacturing took precedence. Factories needed hundreds of workers all in the same place, so thousands of people left the farms to move to the city (another trend that continues today). England and Western Europe became urbanized first, and then the United States.

The Founders conceived of the United States as a nation of "gentlemen farmers," living on rural estates with their families and servants, with only a few towns scattered about. In 1790, only 5.1 percent of the population was urban. New York, the biggest city, had a population of 33,000. Philadelphia had 28,500 people, and Boston 18,000 (U.S. Census Bureau, 1998). These were small towns even by eighteenth-century standards; compare them to Paris, which had a population of 525,000 in 1790.

The former colonial empires in Africa, Asia, and Latin America urbanized more slowly. By 1900, nine of the ten most populous cities in the world were located in Europe or the United States; the most populous, London, had a population of 6,400,000, ten times the population of Beijing in 1500. Today we can tell rich from poor countries by the percentage of the population that lives in urban areas rather than rural areas: 97 percent in Belgium, 90 percent in the United Kingdom, 79 percent in Japan, as opposed to 31 percent in Mali, 25 percent in Vietnam, and 16 percent in Ethiopia (United Nations, 2006).

Ironically, where urbanization is high, people moving from rural areas have their choice of many cities, but where urbanization is low, there are fewer choices. Thus, poor countries with a high rural population are more likely to have megacities (cities with populations of 5,000,000 or more). Only six of the world's 40 megacities are in the United States or Western Europe, but over half are in poor countries (Table 19.3).

Estimates of the population of the city itself are often misleading because suburbs and adjacent cities can double or triple the urbanized population, and in some regions the cities have blurred together into gigantic megacities. For instance, Chicago has an "official" population of about 2.9 million, but the PMSA (Primary Metropolitan Statistical Area), including all of the outlying suburbs and cities, brings it up to 8.6 million. Thus sociologists more often use "urban agglomerations"—a central city and neighboring communities linked to it, for example, by continuous built-up areas or commuters.

The number of people in a city is not always a good measure of what it feels like to live there. Does it feel crowded? Are the houses crammed together, or are there wide spaces between them? Is every inch of land built up, or are there open areas, such as parks, lawns, and public squares? Are the streets narrow and clogged with cars? A better measure of how crowded a city feels is **population density**, the number of people per square mile or kilometer. Generally, older cities will have a larger population density, because they were constructed before the automobile allowed cities to spread out. Older neighborhoods will be more dense than newer neighborhoods.

▲ Cities, both ancient and modern, are often situated near major waterways—for trade, hygiene, and agriculture. This 1853 painting depicts the 9th century Assyrian palaces of Ashurnasirpal II.

TABLE 19.3

World's Largest Cities (Urban Agglomerations), 2007

Tokyo	Japan	33,400,000
Seoul	South Korea	23,200,000
Mexico City	Mexico	22,100,000
New York	USA	21,800,000
Mumbai	India	21,300,000

Source: www.citypopulation.de/World.html

▲ Urban demographers measure population density, which considers both the number of people and the area of the city itself. Some new expanding cities, like Mumbai, India, are extremely crowded, as people stream to the city from the countryside.

The most densely populated cities in the world are constricted; that is, there is no place for them to expand outward. Malé, capital of the Maldive Islands, is the most densely populated city on Earth, with 48,007 people per square kilometer (the total population of 81,000 is crammed onto a small atoll in the Indian Ocean). By contrast, New York has a population density of 10,292 (except on the island of Manhattan, which goes up to 25,849).

The more recently the city was founded, the lower the population density: Oklahoma City, founded in 1889, has a population density of 836 per square kilometer. Though cities with low population densities don't seem crowded, they have a downside. Everything is scattered, so it takes time and gas to get anywhere. If you live on one side of Oklahoma City and work on another, you can drive up to 90 miles.

Fortunately, most people don't. The average commute in Oklahoma City is 18.6 minutes, well below the national average of 25 minutes, and far lower than the 38.6 minutes in New York City or 30.3 minutes in Philadelphia (U.S. Census Bureau, 2002).

The Countryside

The U.S. Census Bureau used to define *urban* as living in an incorporated area with a population of 2,500 or more. However, so many people live in unincorporated areas adjacent to big cities or small towns that have been engulfed by big cities, that many demographers suggest a change from a simple dichotomy of city and countryside to a rural–urban continuum, nine levels from #1 (county in a metropolitan area with 1,000,000 people or more) to #9 (counties not adjacent to a major metropolitan area and with no city over 2,500). By that figure, 93.9 percent of the U.S. population was rural in 1800, 60.4 in 1900, and only 19 percent in 2000 (Northeast-Midwest Institute, 2002).

The decline of rural populations can be attributed to the decline of farm jobs, a move into the cities, and an expansion of the cities, so the farmland of 100 years ago—or even 30 years ago—is today's gated condominium community. Sociologists noticing the decline of rural areas theorized that the "survivors" in the countryside would lose their civic spirit and small-town values. Public perception of rural areas became increasingly negative. Coupled with the ideas of strong communities and kinships are also assumptions about closed-minded, backward "hicks" who are afraid of modern life and antipathetic to progress and science, as in televisions shows from *The Beverly Hillbillies* to *My Name Is Earl*.

However, in another trend, many small towns and rural areas have bounced back. Many city dwellers have found rural areas a pleasant alternative to the crowds, crime, and the feeling of isolation of the big city. Satellite TV and the Internet make the countryside as wired as the big city, and interstate highways mean that those who live there can still enjoy the big city's cultural attractions easily (only a few places in the United States are more than two hour's drive from a sushi bar) (Doyle, 2004).

Globalization increasingly impoverishes the countryside, both by concentrating agricultural enterprises into larger and larger agribusinesses and by locating engines of industrial development in or near urban areas. Poverty and hunger are the ironic consequences of farm foreclosures and economic concentration in urban areas. Rural areas have higher rates of poverty than do urban areas, and rural Americans are more likely than city dwellers to use food stamps—despite the relative proximity to farms (National Rural Health Association, 2006). Rural areas in the United States also have increasingly higher suicide rates than cities—with all their urban alienation (National Association for Rural Mental Health, 2007).

Yet the scale and speed of migration from the countryside to cities has slowed in rich countries like the United States and in the European Union compared with poor and developing ones, especially in Asia and Africa. The United Nations reports that today's global urban population of 3.2 billion will rise to nearly 5 billion by 2030, when three out of five people worldwide will live in cities. (U.N. World Urbanization Prospects, 2005). This surge of migrants will generally come into urban environments whose minimal infrastructure, squalid slums, and air and water pollution already make them fundamentally difficult and dangerous places to live and work. Already over 90 percent of the urban population of Ethiopia and Uganda, two of the world's most rural countries, live in slums, as do nearly 60 percent of city dwellers in South Asia and 30 percent in Latin America. The city of Delhi draws 75 percent of its drinking water from the Yamuna River, into which untreated city sewage is dumped, right along with farm and industrial waste (*Economist*, 2007).

Suburbs

Before the twentieth century, members of the upper classes always had at least two houses, one in the city and the other in the country, for weekend and summer visits (one of the most popular magazines for the upper class is entitled *Town and Country*). Everyone else had to live a mile or two at most from where they worked (don't believe the stories your grandparents tell about walking 20 miles to work and back, in three feet of snow, uphill in both directions). Once Henry Ford's mass production made automobiles affordable, people could live much farther from work, as much as five or ten miles, and, once limited-access highways grew up, 20 or more miles. What's more, the rapid migration of large numbers of Blacks from the rural South to northern cities in the decades after the Civil War, especially to cities that were home to expanding industries like automobiles and steel, led to racial fears of crime and violence. The White middle classes began moving out of the cities altogether, into outlying areas called **suburbs,** where their houses were separate from the others, with front and back yards, just like upper-class estates, instead of the cramped apartments and townhouses of the cities. The expression "a man's home is his castle" arose during this period (Jackson, 1987). And the natural boundaries (rivers and the like) were the moats that were to protect these miniestates from the now-dangerous cities.

The first mass-produced suburb, Levittown, opened in an unincorporated area on Long Island in 1951. By the time it was finished in1958, there were 17,311 houses, plus shopping areas, churches, and recreation centers.

Suburbia has also received its share of detractors. Folksinger Malvina Reynolds complained that the suburbs were made of "Little Boxes," that were "all made out of ticky-tacky, and they all look just the same," not only the houses but the people: identical families, White, middle-class, heterosexual, husband, wife, 2.5 kids. Many comedies of the 1950s begin with long lines of cars driven by identically dressed wives, who drop identically dressed husbands off at the train station for their identical commutes into the city. Suburbs were criticized as deadening, soul destroying, isolated. They stifled creativity. They created a generation of robots—of "men in gray

Did *you* know?

The world's first suburb was probably Brooklyn, New York, founded as a village in 1834 just across the river from Manhattan, an easy commute by ferry, yet set in a rustic, rural environment. By 1860, this suburb had been incorporated into a city, and in 1898, Brooklyn voted to become a borough of New York. Today Brooklyn is the fourth most populous "city" in the United States, with 2.5 million residents (Jackson, 1987; Snyder-Grenier, 2004).

▲ We often think that the great suburban boom in the 1950s was spurred by the do-it-yourself nuclear family, but it actually was supported by the single largest infusion of federal funds toward that end: the GI Bill (which promised interest-free loans and educational subsidies for returning veterans), the interstate highway system, massive roads, and school construction.

flannel suits" and "Stepford wives." But people still moved there in huge numbers.

Why? Safety, or assumed safety—because cities were increasingly seen as crime infested, poor, and populated by more "dangerous" minorities. Comfort—one could have a larger home, with all the new technological amenities, like televisions and barbecue pits. Ease of life—including the ability to have a car. Suburbs promised "the good life," and Americans followed the call.

During the 1960s, suburbs grew four times faster than cities due to the "White flight" of White, middle-class residents. (The history of the American suburb is intimately connected to the history of Black migration to large Northern cities.) Jobs and amenities went with them. Downtown stores closed one by one as gigantic suburban shopping malls opened. Downtown movie palaces (with one movie playing) closed as gigantic multiplexes opened next to the shopping malls (12 or more movies playing on peanut-sized screens). Downtown businesses relocated to "business parks" in the suburbs. Because the middle classes and the poor rarely saw each other anymore, they often had enormous misconceptions about each other.

Once suburban areas had their own jobs and amenities, they were no longer simply "bedroom communities," empty during the day as the workers trekked into the city for their jobs, but cities in their own right, called "edge cities," with their own economic focus (often high tech). Sometimes they are called "beltway cities," because they are clustered around the interstate highways that loop around major cities. You might live in the edge city of Grand Prairie, Texas, and work in Fort Worth, 22 miles away, though you are actually in a suburb of Dallas, 13 miles away. But it hardly matters because you depend on the nearby edge cities of Irving and Arlington to shop. Downtown is just for jury duty.

The Sociology of Commuting: Separate and Unequal

In 1900, rich and poor walked to work; in cities, they took streetcars and trolleys. Then the automobile arrived and quickly engulfed every other mode of transportation. If you were middle class or working class, you drove your own car; if you were poor, you took the bus. Only very large, very congested cities still had streetcars or trolleys (the last of Los Angeles's famous Red Cars stopped running in 1961), along with light-rails to transport commuters to and from the suburbs, like the Long Island Railroad in New York or the BART (Bay Area Rapid Transit) in San Francisco.

As more and more jobs moved out of the cities into the suburbs, middle-class suburbanites found their commute easier. But poorer people who lived in the suburbs without cars had a problem. The suburbs had new, sleek buses running direct routes many times a day. City buses were all old and decrepit, and their routes were "local" (with many stops), with infrequent, inconvenient hours (often they stopped running at 6:00 p.m.). Even more annoying, the suburban and city routes didn't intersect well. They were set up as distinct systems, and the ones in the suburbs received the greater amounts of money (Bullard and Johnson, 1997).

A colleague recently told me of this experiment. He asked the Chicago Metro Transit to plan a trip from a fictitious "job" at the Oak Mill Mall in the near-north Chicago suburb of Niles to a fictitious "home" at 3501 S. Lowe Avenue (actually an

Commuting to work exaggerates class, race, and gender inequalities. The average driving commute in California is 26 minutes per day—it nearly doubles to 47 minutes if you take public transportation. ▼

Sociology and our World

Celebration, Florida

Celebration, Florida, is a "created suburb," laid out by the Disney Corporation in a rural area a short commute from Orlando and opened in 1996. Disney "imagineered" a small town right out of its own nostalgia movies. According to its website, Celebration is a " place where memories of a lifetime are made, it's more than a home; it's a community rich with old-fashioned appeal and an eye on the future" and "people are connecting in ways that build vibrant, caring, and enduring traditions."

Such vibrant, caring, and enduring traditions come with a hefty price tag (bungalows start at $443,000 and cottages at $524,000), and there are more regulations than in a convent or military barracks. Every new resident must abide by a "Declaration of Covenants" that dictates everything from how long cars may be parked on the street to the number of occupants per bedroom (two). Residents are seen as "representatives" of the Disney vision of America, performers just as much as the costumed Mickeys and Goofys who roam Disney World.

Much of Celebration seems geared more toward tourists than to its residents. The Market Street shopping area contains six upscale restaurants and 14 shops selling jewelry, dolls, and gifts—but there is no grocery store, drugstore, or gas station. The list of activities and civic organizations includes a nondenominational community church, a Rotary Club, Little League, the D.A.R. (Daughters of the American Revolution), and a chapter of the Republican Party (but not the Democratic Party).

Some 8,000 people believe that it is worth being on constant display to live in a clean, well-maintained, safe community. And they are not alone. Disney may be the most famous example, but some 40,000,000 Americans are now living in privately owned communities that regulate how long you can park in the street and with whom you can share your bedroom (Ross, 2001).

---

inner-city police station). The distance was 19 miles, about the average suburban commute. Even with heavy traffic, driving such a distance takes about 40 minutes. But using public transportation proved quite a challenge. Assuming that he got off work at 9:00 p.m., when the malls close, he would need to take three buses and a metro rail, with four chances of missed connections. If everything worked like clockwork, he could reach his bus stop by 11:00 p.m., and walk the remaining two blocks, making it home by 11:10, more than three times longer than it takes a commuter in a car. If he was unlucky and missed a connection, he would be stranded, because he was catching the last bus of the day.

Revitalizing Downtown

During the 1980s and 1990s, many cities fought back, trying to revitalize their downtowns with hip shops, restaurants, and entertainment venues that would attract suburbanites looking for an evening of fun. Some especially hip young professionals even moved back in search of diversity and excitement, buying cheap houses and renovating them. Sometimes they take over whole downtown neighborhoods, raising the property values so much that poor and even middle-class people can no longer afford to live there (a process called **gentrification**). More commonly, cities annexed the suburbs, and any outlying areas that might become suburbs, so they could charge property tax. For example, one day in 1970, Indianapolis annexed all of Marion County, city, suburb, and farmland, in a plan with a name right out of *Matrix*: "Unigov."

Suburbs and edge cities are increasingly difficult to distinguish from inner cities. They have their own problems with traffic, crime, congestion, and pollution. Edge cities often have greater ethnic diversity than inner cities, in spite of "White flight" (Palen, 1995). For instance, the edge city of Hawthorne, California, between Los Angeles and Long Beach, is 44 percent Hispanic and 33 percent Black. The problems of poverty, unemployment, high rents, and inadequate housing are no longer confined to the inner city. In Hawthorne, 20 percent of the residents are below poverty level, and 74 percent rent rather than own their homes.

As suburbs expanded outward, it was inevitable that they would meet the suburbs of adjacent cities, until they all combined into one gigantic city, a **megalopolis.** Megalopolises span hundreds of miles. You can drive from Nashua, New Hampshire (north of Boston), to Fairfax, Virginia (south of Washington, DC), through ten states and a bewildering number of city and county jurisdictions, without ever hitting unincorporated territory.

Megalopolises face enormous structural problems. Their sheer size compounds the problems of air and water pollution, traffic congestion, crime, and joblessness. Civic improvement projects are often stalled by red tape, as different jurisdictions argue over whose responsibility it is. The sociologists and social commentators who worried about the loss of social identity as people moved from villages to cities are even more worried about loss of social identity in a megalopolis. What happens to civic pride? Do residents have any sense of place at all, or is every place identical to them? Do they have any sense of guardianship—who peers through windows to make sure there are no vagrants outside or keeps tabs on the neighbors and alerts the police to suspicious activity? Is the megalopolis just another word for urban anomie (Gottmann and Harper, 1990)?

Sociology and the City

Many early sociologists were fascinated and appalled by life in cities. Ferdinand Töennies (1855–1936) theorized that families, villages, and perhaps neighborhoods in cities formed through *gemeinschaft,* or "commonality" (1957). They shared common norms, values, and beliefs. They had an instinctive trust; they worked together because they cared for each other. Instead, cities and states formed through *gesellschaft,* or "business company." They had differing, sometimes contradictory, norms, values, and beliefs. They had an instinctive mistrust. They worked together toward a definite, deliberate goal, not because they cared for each other but because everyone was acting to his or her own self-advantage. Siblings operate through gemeinschaft—they care for each other no matter what. But business partners operate through gesellschaft—they might not like each other or the product that they're selling. In a memorable scene from the musical *Chicago* (2002), Velma Kelly and Roxy Hart acknowledge that they hate each other, but they decide to form a musical act together anyway; personal feelings are irrelevant if there's money to be made.

Most sociologists today translate gemeinschaft and gesellschaft as "community" and "society," as two underlying motives for cementing bonds between people. Moving to the city undermines kinship and neighborhood, the traditional sources of social control and social solidarity. As a society industrializes and becomes more urban, gemeinschaft is ripped apart, and what emerges is a new society based on gesellschaft, where instinctive community is unknown or a sentimental dream out of Hallmark cards and *The Cosby Show.* In short, the personal freedom that the city provides comes at the cost of alienation.

The concepts of gemeinschaft and gesellschaft have been used most frequently to compare small towns and villages, where presumably everyone is one big happy family, with big cities, where presumably interpersonal connections are based on manipulation and fear. However, they can also be used to compare the "big happy family" of inner cities with the "isolation" of the suburbs.

Shortly after Töennies, Emile Durkheim took his own look at villages and cities and theorized that village life was so much nicer because there was little division of labor. Almost everyone did the same work; they shared norms and values. Durkheim called this **mechanical solidarity,** a connection based on similarity. In the cities, by contrast, everyone was different: They worked at different jobs, they had different norms and values, they disagreed on what was right and wrong. What held them together was what he called **organic solidarity**—connections based on interdependence. Organic solidarity was more stable (if not as "nice") than mechanical solidarity because this interdependence meant that each individual was necessary to the functioning of the whole.

After working with the villagers of the Yucatan, anthropologist Robert Redfield (1941) decided that the division was not a matter of settlement size or division of labor, but between rural (or "folk") and urban social networks. Folk societies are certainly characterized by homogeneity and a low division of labor, but more importantly, the social networks are based on family. Family is everything. There are no friends or acquaintances. People who are not related to you by blood or marriage are by default enemies, unless you create sorts of fictional kinship ties in clans (presumed descent from a common ancestor) or in the common tradition of "blood brothers."

In urban societies, family is less important. Geographic mobility is greater, as is the emphasis on "chosen" communities—workplaces, neighborhoods—over kinship. You might call your mother on her birthday and see the entire family over the Christmas holidays. "Secondary relationships"—friendships, work relationships—are more significant. In villages, kinship ties ensured that the person walking toward you would not rob or murder you. In cities, there was no such guarantee. There had to be rules of courtesy, and there had to be laws. The origins of the rituals such as shaking hands (to show you had no weapons) begin in these new environments of strangers. Urban societies are more diverse, heterogeneous, and in constant flux.

In "The Metropolis and Mental Life" (1902), the great German sociologist Georg Simmel worried about the overstimulation of the city environment. You are surrounded by so many sights and sounds, so many other humans, that you can't pay attention to everything. So, you pay attention to nothing. You develop a "blasé attitude." It is not that you are cold and unfeeling; it's that you have only enough brain cells to concentrate on your immediate concerns. If someone falls to the sidewalk in front of you, you might pass him or her by, assuming that someone in authority will provide the necessary assistance; anyway, it's none of your business.

On the other hand, in *The Death and Life of Great American Cities* (1961), urban analyst Jane Jacobs found that busy streets were not a source of overstimulation at all. Life happened on the street: Children played there; neighbors sat on stoops to gossip with each other; there was a sense of solidarity and belonging. In contrast, in the suburbs no one knew anyone else, and the streets were deserted except for people hurrying from their cars into their houses. Even deviance is under control in the city. Although many strangers are coming and going all the time, they are under constant scrutiny by people in the houses, who are making sure that nothing bad happens. The more gazing through windows, the less deviant activity occurs. But in the suburbs, no one is peering through windows, and deviance can go undetected.

Cities presented problems that villages never faced, in building and street construction, transportation, distribution of food and other goods, social stratification, and deviance and social control—not to mention sanitation. However, they provided the leisure for creative thought, at least in the upper classes. If it weren't for cities, there would be no literature, art, or science. Some people find alienation in the city, a sense that no one knows you or cares what happens to you, but others find community, a belonging that they could never find in the villages (Abrahamson and Carter, 1996). (This is reminiscent of the good news and bad news about college choice. The good news in a small college is that everyone knows you. The bad news is that . . . everyone knows you.)

Sociologists from Durkheim to Simmel to contemporary planner Jane Jacobs argued that, although frequently criticized as alienating and impersonal, urban neighborhoods are teeming with life and foster the development of cohesive communities. ▼

Human Ecology

Looking at the spatial patterns of the city, sociologists noted that they share many characteristics in common with biological ecosystems. Both are based on the cooperative efforts of many specialized groups to distribute resources, eliminate waste, and maintain life. Even groups that seem scary and destructive serve a function: Predators are necessary to eat the herbivores and keep their population down, or else there would be so many of them that they would destroy the entire forest. In the same way, criminal activity demonstrates to the law-abiding population the limits on their behavior and creates a sense of "normalcy." Both human and biological systems are also extremely interdependent. A tiny problem with the smallest element can have catastrophic consequences for the whole. Just as the extinction of a "minor" species can destroy an entire ecosystem, the destruction of the roads leading into a city can lead to starvation and chaos in just a few days.

Human ecology arose as a discipline of the social sciences that looks at the interrelations of human beings within a shared social environment—the physical size and shape of the city, its social and economic dynamics, and its relationship to other cities and the natural world.

Urbanization. One of the most influential early studies of human ecology was Louis Wirth's "Urbanism as a Way of Life" (1938), drawing Durkheim and Töennies together to suggest that the move from villages to cities is not merely a change of residence but a change in the way people think and feel. He argued that people lose their kinship ties when they move from villages to cities; and, in the city, the size of the population, density, and social diversity make new social ties impossible to find. Therefore, they do not interact with people on more than a superficial level, resulting in loneliness and a feeling of rootlessness. Being around so many people leads to sensory overload, but now it makes city dwellers feel stressed and bad-tempered—this is why when you walk down the street in a village, passersby will say "hello" to you, but in a city they pretend that you don't even exist.

Wirth also explained the rise of crime in the cities. With no kinship ties, there is no consensus about what norms should be followed, and even when an act occurs that most people agree is deviant, they cannot rely on informal networks to maintain social control. They must call social service agencies or the police. (Such ideas echo those of Sutherland and Coleman, cited in Chapter 6, Deviance and Crime.) However, these agencies are not as effective as informal ties, because formal mechanisms rely only on punishment and sanctions for those who get caught; so crime and other forms of deviance soar. Again, human ecology can explain both why cities are terrible places compared to villages and why suburbs are terrible places compared to cities.

The Urban Village. Herbert Gans (1962, 1968) disagreed with these human ecologists. He found that social networks are around the same size in both the city and the small town. You do not try to make friends with the 5,000,000 people around you. You find community in a series of smaller worlds, people who share your tastes, interests, and socioeconomic background, just as you would in a village. Even slums, which to outsiders seem so threatening and merciless, can provide a strong sense of belonging to people.

Gans (1968) found five types of people in the city:

- Cosmopolites—artists and intellectuals.
- Young, single professionals—people who would later be called Yuppies (young urban professionals, a term coined in the 1980s).
- Ethnic villagers—immigrants.

- The deprived—poor, often ethnic minorities.
- The trapped—poor elderly people.

Concentric Zones. Sociologists Robert Park and Ernest Burgess (1925) studied how human ecology affected the use of urban space in the city. Inequalities of race and class (later sociologists added gender and sexual orientation) affected the distribution of resources. They believed that cities develop according to "concentric zones" of activity. These look much like the different zones in an archery target. Zone 1, the center of the city, is the political and cultural heart of the city, site of the most important businesses and government facilities and retail trade.

Zone 2 is an area of manufacturing and wholesale trade, providing the goods to sell in zone 1. It is also a zone of "social disorganization." Park and Burgess noted a large immigrant population (during this period immigrants were presumed sources of social disorganization). There are many transients and "hobos." Because no one has a sense of responsibility for the community, deviant activities such as crime, prostitution, and drunkenness, which would be swiftly dealt with in other zones, are allowed to flourish.

As people become upwardly mobile, they move away from the city core into zone 3 (working-class residential) and then into zone 4 (middle-class and upper-class residential). Or, if they are downwardly mobile, they move into a zone closer to the city core. Zone 5 is a commuter zone.

The concentric zone theory may have characterized Chicago, at least for a period before middle-class flight to the suburbs.

▲ The television series *Friends* exemplified the idea of the urban village. The six main characters live in New York, but they inhabit a small neighborhood on the Upper West Side. They run into each other and patronize the same coffee shop (Central Perk) day in and day out. They virtually ignore anyone outside of their circle of friends.

Global Urbanization

For many years, urbanization was considered a sign of development, a sure sign that the nation was becoming richer and more prosperous. Recent trends suggest a more complicated picture (Figure 19.4). In 2000, 75 percent of the population of Latin America lived in urban areas, about the same as in the industrialized United States. Nearly half lived in cities with over one million inhabitants, and there were seven cities with more than 5 million: Mexico City, São Paulo, Buenos Aires, Rio de Janeiro, Bogotá, Lima, and Santiago. But the vast numbers of individuals moving to the city did not find sudden wealth.

Nearly half of the population of Latin America (43.4 percent) lives in poverty, many in urban areas. More than one-third of urban dwellers live in slums. These vast neighborhoods in these cities lack adequate sanitation, housing, utilities, and police protection.

The gap between rich and poor is more noticeable in these urban centers than anywhere else in the world. In Rio de Janeiro, neighborhoods catering to tourists have a homicide rate of about 4 per 100,000. But in the favelas, slums only a few blocks away, the homicide rate can be as high as 150 per 100,000, among the highest in the world (Vander Schuerer, 1996).

Many cities around the world have global rather than local ties (Chase-Dunn, 1985). They are command centers not only of their own countries but also of the global economy. They are intimately involved in innovation and creation, producing not manufactured goods but information. They are more interdependent on each other than on the countries where they happen to be located. And they share a common culture of consumption. In New York, London, Tokyo, and, to a lesser

FIGURE 19.4 Urban Population of the World

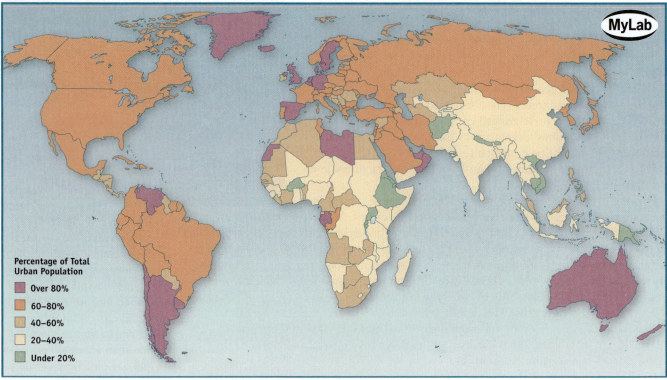

Percentage of Total Urban Population

- ■ Over 80%
- ■ 60–80%
- ■ 40–60%
- ■ 20–40%
- ■ Under 20%

Source: From Maps of the World website, www.mapsoftheworld.com. Reprinted with permission.

extent, the second tier of global cities—Jakarta, Milan, Singapore, Rio de Janeiro—businessmen and women armed with high-tech communication devices hold meetings in board rooms, read the *Financial Times* in English, and relax with American mass culture.

In 1991, Saskia Sassen introduced the term "global city." She noted that New York, London, and Tokyo are actually located in three different countries on three different continents, with two languages in common use, so one might expect significant cultural differences. However, they have so many multinational ties that their exact location is meaningless. There are 2,500 foreign banks and financial companies in New York, employing one-quarter of all of the city's financial employees. National boundaries make little sense when the horizon of expectation for a city resident is the entire world.

The Natural Environment

Sociologists understand that the natural environment—the physical world, or more precisely, animals, plants, and the material substances that make up the physical world—is also organized into **ecosystems,** which are interdependent systems of organisms and their environment. Even if you have lived in Los Angeles your whole life and have never seen an open space other than a vacant lot, you are still participating in biological and geological ecosystems. You still breathe the air of the natural world. You drink its water, eat its food, and depend on its natural resources as raw materials for your manufactured products. Local natural disasters like fires and floods can disrupt your life as quickly as human warfare, and there are global environmental changes, slow-moving disasters, that threaten to disrupt all human life on the planet.

Early sociologists often theorized that the social world was a subcategory of the natural world. Herbert Spencer (1820–1903) argued that biological, social, psychological, and moral systems are all interrelated (2002). Others tried to analyze the impact of social life on the natural world. Ellsworth Huntington argued that Northern Europeans were so "advanced" because they lived in a tough climate, with harsh winters and the need to grow crops (1915/2001). Because they had to struggle to survive, they became industrious and hardworking. Meanwhile, people in tropical climates never had to worry about winter, and they could pick fruit right off the trees, so they became fat and lazy. He was wrong; sustenance in the tropics is no easier than in the north. There were "primitive" hunter-gatherers in the cold climates and advanced technological civilizations in the tropics.

After the first few decades of sociological thought, however, social sciences tended to ignore the environment, leaving it to the biologists, the geologists, and maybe the geographers. Sociology was about people, they figured, so why bother to worry about air and water pollution? Supplies were limitless, and even if they weren't limitless on Earth, we would soon be moving into space to mine the asteroid belt.

Then, during the 1970s, people began to envision Earth not as an infinite space, but as a small, fragile community, "Spaceship Earth" (Schnaiberg, 1980). If we weren't going to be going to other planets, we had to make do with Earth, and it wouldn't last forever. Keep digging up iron and pumping out oil, and eventually there won't be any left. And, if we weren't going to be moving out to other planets, we had to make sure Earth stayed amenable for human life. The two most public environmental concerns

How do we know
what we know?

Indexes

Which city has the highest level of air pollution? It's difficult to tell because there are so many types of pollutants: suspended particles, sulfur dioxide, nitrogen dioxide, carbon monoxide, and so on, with many different concentrations. Sulfur dioxide becomes hazardous for sensitive groups at a concentration as low as 0.145 ppm (parts per million), but carbon monoxide has to reach a concentration of 9.5 ppm before it has a negative effect on health. Particulate matter (solids suspended in gas, as in smoke) is not even measured in ppm, but in micrograms per

cubic meter, and the hazardous proportion varies depending on the size of the particle.

When the different parts of a phenomenon are measured in different ways, sociologists and other scientists often construct an index to look at them all together. First, they must *standardize* the parts. Instead of looking at parts per million or micrograms per cubic meter, for instance, they classify each concentration as low, medium, and high. Then they must *weigh* the parts. If some of the pollutants represent a greater hazard than others, then they should be worth more, perhaps getting a doubled score. The Environmental Protection Agency has

created an air quality index based on the concentrations of seven pollutants: nitrogen dioxide, sulfur dioxide, carbon monoxide, two sizes of particulate matter, and ozone (calculated two ways):

0–50	Good
51–100	Moderate
101–150	Unhealthy for sensitive groups
151–200	Unhealthy
201–300	Very unhealthy
301–500	Hazardous

So, according to these indices, what U.S. city has the worst air pollution problem? Bakersfield, California, with 142 days over 100 in 2003. Riverside, California, comes in second with 141. Los Angeles had 112. But cities elsewhere were considerably lower: New York City 14, Philadelphia 22, Memphis 13. (see www.airnow.gov)

of the 1970s were conservation, avoiding the depletion of natural resources, and pollution, avoiding "fouling our nest" (Schnaiberg, 1980).

At the same time, some sociologists began to criticize the discipline for being too "anthropocentric," or focused on human beings (Catton and Dunlap, 1978). They began to look at the social production of conservation and pollution, how issues were framed as problems, how public perceptions and public policy could change, and the success or failure of environmental movements (Buttel, 1987). They looked into the role of technology in causing and potentially solving environmental problems (Bell, 2004; Hannigan, 1995; King, 2005). Finally, they looked at the problems themselves, what impact they were having on social relations, and how they might change social life in the future.

Energy

In 1900, even if your house was wired for electricity, you couldn't do much with it besides turn on electric lights. In 1930, you might have an electric telephone and radio; in 1960, an electric refrigerator, oven, and television set. In 2005, you would have a microwave oven, two or three television sets, a stereo system, several cell phones, a DVD-VCR combo, a personal computer or two, and, in the garage, at least two cars. Our energy needs have skyrocketed. Sociologists want to know: What are the social implications of dependence on oil and the search for sustainable energy sources, like solar and hydroelectric? What sorts of political arrangements and business environments promote reliance of which types of energy (Rosa, Machlis, and Keating, 1988; Smil, 2005)?

The United States is by far the world's largest energy consumer, but not when consumption is calculated on a per capita basis (total amount of energy consumed divided by the population). In 2003, the United States consumed 339 million BTU (British thermal units) of energy per capita; those countries with higher per capita rates tended to be either very cold (Norway), oil-producing nations (Kuwait, Norway, Qatar, United Arab Emirates), or small, underpopulated remote countries with very small and very wealthy populations where any essential service requires lots of energy to transport and provide (Netherlands Antilles, U.S. Virgin islands, Gibraltar).

Only about 15 percent of energy consumed in the United States in 2005 came from renewable sources like nuclear, hydroelectric, geothermal, solar, or wind generators. The other 85 percent of our energy came from nonrenewable resources, especially oil and natural gas, by-products of millions of years of fossilization that stayed in the ground, undisturbed, until very recently. This is similar to global rates of consumption; worldwide, only 13.1 percent of the energy supply is from renewable sources like tide, solar, wind, and geothermal (*Economist,* 2007).

Americans are 5 percent of the world's people, yet the United States consumes at least 25 percent of every type of energy. Americans use about 20 million barrels of oil per day, far more than any other country in the world. Most wealthy countries use less than 2 million. At current levels of consumption, presuming no dependence on foreign oil, we have enough for 20 years (Roberts, 2005). And Americans use 64.4 billion cf (cubic feet) of natural gas per day, again far more than any other country in the world, twice as much as number two (Russia, with 38.8 billion cf). At current levels of consumption, we have enough for 34 years.

In addition, the United States produces 2.638 tetrawatt-hours of nuclear energy per million population per year, about the same as Bulgaria produces with six nuclear reactors. Sweden has 11 nuclear reactors and produces 7.288 tetrawatt-hours of nuclear energy per million population per year. Because we have invested so little in nuclear power in the past decades, our plants are old and inefficient, and there has been little effort to remain competitive.

Vanishing Resources

Globally, forests are being depleted at the rate of one acre per second, depriving the world of a gigantic natural storage capacity for harmful carbon dioxide. Forests are unique in their capability to convert CO_2 during photosynthesis into carbon compounds that are then stored in wood, vegetation, and soil humus, a process called "carbon sequestration." Through this natural process, the world's forests store about one trillion tons of carbon—about one-and-a-half times the total amount found in the atmosphere. Deforestation, the clearing of these forests for crops and development, accounts for about 25 percent of all human-made emissions of carbon dioxide in the atmosphere—roughly the same amount as is produced by the United States, the world's largest polluter. Deforestation is often accomplished by burning, contributing to as much as 10 percent of the greenhouse effect (Bonnicksen, 2000). And, of course, the products that the forests might provide are also gone forever. The depletion of tropical rain forests is particularly disturbing because they cover only 7 percent of Earth's surface but account for up to 80 percent of the world's plant species, most of which have not been tested for medicinal effect.

Deforestation also results in the loss of topsoil because the cleared land is quick to erode. Covering huge stretches of land with concrete buildings and roads also increases erosion because there is nowhere for rainwater to go but onto undeveloped land. (Concrete also absorbs heat, as you will know if you have ever tried to walk barefoot over concrete in the summertime, thus leading to an increase in global warming.) An estimated 26 billion tons of topsoil is being lost per year, transforming arable land into desert. The process of desertification can be seen in many parts of the world, especially sub-Saharan Africa.

Desertification, combined with the increased water use necessary for an increased population, means that the world is quickly losing groundwater—water tables are falling in large swaths of many countries around the world, including the Great Plains and Southwest of the United States, most states in India, the entire northern half of China, and throughout the north of Mexico (Brown, 2005).

A final natural resource that we are quickly depleting is animal and plant species. We don't know exactly how many species there are—new ones are being discovered every day. But we do know that species are becoming extinct at a rate 1,000 times greater than before technological civilization, at a rate of 100 per day, usually as their natural environment is destroyed and they cannot adapt to their new surroundings. The U.S. Fish and Wildlife Service lists 1,120 endangered animals, including such "common" animals as the brown bear, the fox, the otter, the prairie dog, and the red squirrel, as well as 748 endangered plants. Only a few hundred species have a specific economic or aesthetic value to humans, but we won't know which ones do and which do not if they disappear before we can test them. More important, however, is the contribution every species, even the most seemingly insignificant, makes to the delicate interbalance of an ecosystem. When an insect species goes instinct, the plant that it pollinated will die out soon, and then all of the animals that subsisted on that plant.

Environmental Threats

The natural environment is not only natural—it is "social" in that there is a constant interaction between the natural and the built environments, between people and the places where they live (and don't live), between nature and culture. The environment is today threatened by several human-created problems.

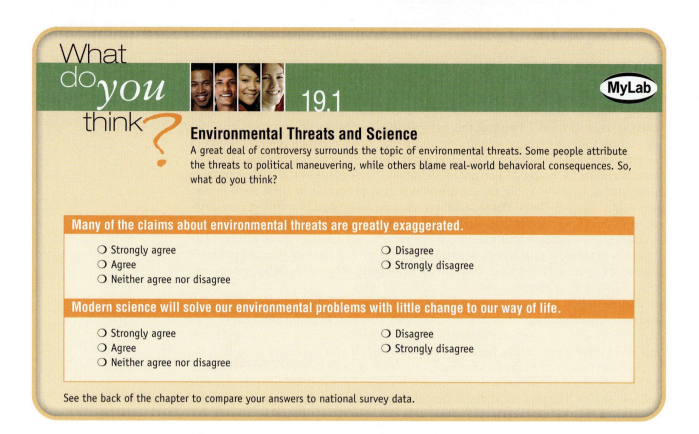

What do *you* think?

19.1

Environmental Threats and Science

A great deal of controversy surrounds the topic of environmental threats. Some people attribute the threats to political maneuvering, while others blame real-world behavioral consequences. So, what do you think?

Many of the claims about environmental threats are greatly exaggerated.

○ Strongly agree
○ Agree
○ Neither agree nor disagree

○ Disagree
○ Strongly disagree

Modern science will solve our environmental problems with little change to our way of life.

○ Strongly agree
○ Agree
○ Neither agree nor disagree

○ Disagree
○ Strongly disagree

See the back of the chapter to compare your answers to national survey data.

Pollution. There are three major sources of water pollution: domestic waste, industrial waste, and agricultural runoff. Indoor plumbing in urban areas means a huge amount of human waste, which is usually treated with toxic chemicals and then dumped into the nearest river. Many industrial processes require huge amounts of water, which is then dumped, along with more toxic chemicals. The petroleum industry is particularly problematic; every year billions of gallons of oil are routinely deposited into the ocean during tank cleaning and other operations. Agricultural runoff includes not only topsoil but toxic pesticides and fertilizers. When it all ends up in the water supply, it can cause a huge number of unspecified health problems in humans. Even tiny changes in freshwater or saltwater habitats can kill microorganisms, undersea plants, and fish, as well as every animal that feeds on them.

Air pollution is concentrated in urban areas, the result of carbon monoxide, sulfur dioxide, and nitrogen oxide from cars, heaters, and industrial processes. These gases have a profound impact on the lungs and circulatory system; breathing the air in downtown Tokyo is the equivalent of smoking a pack of cigarettes every day. The gases have similar negative effects on every animal trying to breathe the same air, and when toxic gases combine with water molecules in the air, they can return to Earth as acid rain; enter lakes, rivers, and oceans through groundwater runoff; and destroy the ecosystems. Or they can rise up to the ozone layer, a band of oxygen isotopes 10 to 30 miles from Earth's surface, and bond with them, thus eliminating their effectiveness in shielding Earth from ultraviolet radiation. These invisible rays cause skin cancer, cataracts, and damage to the immune system and contribute to an increased production of carbon dioxide, which contributes to global warming.

Garbage. In 2003, the United States produced 236,000,000 metric tons of municipal solid waste, or MSW (household waste and waste from civic maintenance, like mowing

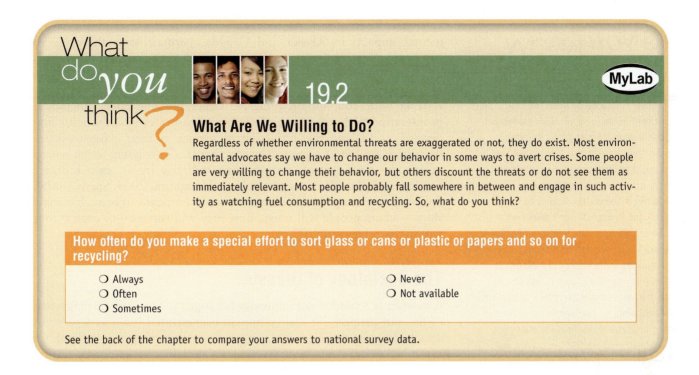

What Are We Willing to Do?

Regardless of whether environmental threats are exaggerated or not, they do exist. Most environmental advocates say we have to change our behavior in some ways to avert crises. Some people are very willing to change their behavior, but others discount the threats or do not see them as immediately relevant. Most people probably fall somewhere in between and engage in such activity as watching fuel consumption and recycling. So, what do you think?

How often do you make a special effort to sort glass or cans or plastic or papers and so on for recycling?

○ Always
○ Often
○ Sometimes

○ Never
○ Not available

See the back of the chapter to compare your answers to national survey data.

parks and sweeping streets). Fourteen percent was incinerated, and 30.6 percent recycled or composted, but 54.5 percent went into garbage dumps. (BBC, 2005)

Many other countries are not as good at recycling. In poor countries, it typically doesn't happen at all: 100 percent of waste goes into landfills. But even rich countries have a spotty record: 42 percent of municipal waste is recycled in Germany, but only 12 percent in the United Kingdom, 11 percent in Iceland, and 7 percent in Australia (BBC, 2005).

Landfills pose two major problems. First, most of the garbage isn't biodegradable. Petroleum-based products, plastics, and styrofoam stay there forever, which means that the landfills fill up. A third of American landfills are already full, and by 2020, four-fifths of them will be full. There will be no place to put the garbage anymore.

When the garbage is biodegradable, it degrades into toxic chemicals, which seep into the groundwater and increase water pollution or into the air to increase air pollution. Degrading waste also increases the world's heat level, contributing to global warming.

A particularly problematic kind of waste comes as a by-product of nuclear energy. Nuclear reactors produce waste that will be radioactive for thousands of years.

Global Warming. Since the nineteenth century, the global temperature has increased by about 0.6 degrees Celsius (1.08 degrees Fahrenheit), primarily because carbon dioxide, aerosols, and other gases released by human technology are prohibiting heat from escaping, resulting

Garbage is among the most immediate environmental concerns, especially in countries with high levels of consumption. The United States dumps more than half of its garbage in landfills, but by 2020, 80 percent of those landfills will be "land-full." ▼

in a greenhouse effect. Many regions are already seeing an environmental impact: in Alaska and Canada, permafrost is thawing; 90 percent of the world's glaciers are in retreat. Because most of the world's major cities are on or near the ocean, a rise in the sea level due to melting glaciers and ice sheets could be catastrophic, like Hurricane Katrina with 200 million refugees. Other possible effects include a proliferation of hurricanes and extreme weather events, droughts and desertification, and the extinction of species as their ecosystems are destroyed. And most scientists believe that it is only going to get worse: during the next century, temperatures will rise by at least 1 degree Celsius, and possibly 5 degrees Celsius (Houghton, 2004; Speth, 2005). Sociologists attempt to calculate the social ramifications of such climate shifts—where people will move, how they will survive—or even *if* they will survive (Figure 19.5).

The Sociology of Disaster

A disaster is a sudden environmental change that results in a major loss of life and property. It can be human orchestrated, such as a terrorist attack, or it can originate in nature, such as an earthquake or flood. Or it can be both. Bioterrorism would involve unleashing a deadly disease like anthrax and causing a "natural" epidemic. The only operative term is "sudden," so that it comes upon people with little or no warning (Figure 19.6).

For many years, sociologists were not much interested in disasters. They were interested in the social upheaval of wars and migration more than in fires and floods. The Johnstown Flood of 1889 received little note.

FIGURE 19.5 World Temperature Increases, 2001–2005

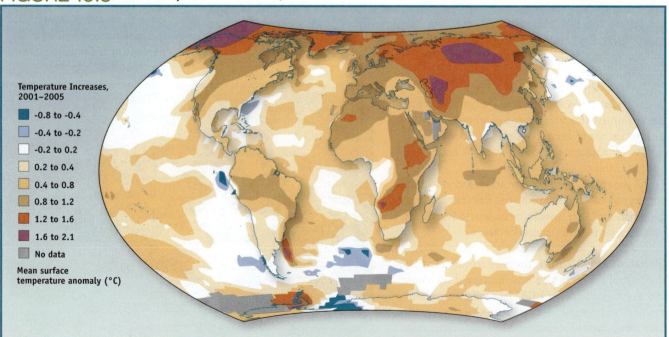

Temperature Increases, 2001–2005

- -0.8 to -0.4
- -0.4 to -0.2
- -0.2 to 0.2
- 0.2 to 0.4
- 0.4 to 0.8
- 0.8 to 1.2
- 1.2 to 1.6
- 1.6 to 2.1
- No data

Mean surface temperature anomaly (°C)

Source: Hugo Ahlenius, United Nations Environmental Programme/GRID-Arendal, 2006. www.grida.no. Used by permission.

But with so many things that could go wrong and are going wrong, sociologists are taking note (Erikson, 1995; Wisner, 2003).

One of the earliest sociological studies of a disaster was Kai T. Erikson's *Everything in Its Path* (1978), about the human response to a dam that burst and flooded Buffalo Creek in Logan County, West Virginia. One might expect survivors to experience long-term psychological trauma after losing many of their loved ones and everything they owned, but Erikson probed more deeply to investigate how they lost their individual and communal identity: The "furniture of self" had vanished.

In 1995, a week-long heat wave in Chicago was responsible for over 700 deaths. This was not a sudden catastrophe, so why were so many people unprepared? Eric Klineberg (2003) investigated the social conditions that led to and compounded the disaster. He found the obvious, that many poor and elderly people—and most of them Black women—had no air conditioning. Some were not aware of the neighborhood "cooling systems" or were afraid to go to them. Others did not realize that they were in danger; the news media downplayed the disaster, treating it as little more than a human-interest story.

The Asian tsunami of December 2004 that killed over 200,000 people may be too recent for a significant number of sociological studies, but they are certainly forthcoming, as is the study of the aftermaths of Hurricane Katrina and Rita, as well as theorizing about the meaning of disaster in a sociology that has been too frequently concerned with societies as orderly and cohesive.

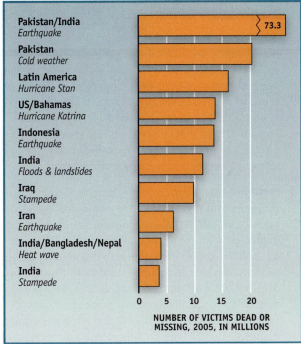

FIGURE 19.6 Catastrophes: Biggest Insurance Losses and Worst Human Costs

NUMBER OF VICTIMS DEAD OR MISSING, 2005, IN MILLIONS

Source: From "Catastrophes: Biggest Insurance Losses and Worst Human Costs," *The Economist*, March 4, 2006. Copyright © 2006 by the Economist Newspaper Group. Reproduced with permission of Economist Newspaper Group in the format Textbook via Copyright Clearance Center.

Environments in the 21st Century

What do we do now? Do we sit alone in our room, waiting for the next hurricane, earthquake, tornado, nuclear accident, or biological pandemic, or a more gradual catastrophe caused by global warming, air pollution, desertification, or overpopulation? Do we play video games, eat nachos, and await the Apocalypse?

If Katrina and its aftermath have taught us anything, it is that we should be prepared. With foresight and planning, we can avoid some catastrophes altogether and lessen the impact of others. And one of the most important tools we have is a recognition of how the physical, urban, and human worlds interconnect. The connections between the natural world, social life, and the ways that technology shapes and transforms both arenas is the heart of sociological investigation. Nature is nurture— that is, the natural world does not exist except in relationship to the social and built worlds. City and countryside create each other; people are part of the ecosystem and also its greatest threat. Ignoring the interconnection nearly always leads to disaster. Recognizing and working with it may lead to a future.

Did *you* know?

With the exception of 9/11 terrorist attacks, the top ten most costly catastrophes in U.S. history have all been natural disasters—five of them hurricanes—and *all* of them have occurred since 1988 (Steinberg, 2000). According to environmental historian Ted Steinberg, this has far more to do with the political capacity of cities and states to prepare for and respond to natural disasters than some mysterious increase in the severity of the events. They may be disasters, but politics makes them calamities.

1. *What is the human environment?* Humans are social; other people are part of our environment. Sociologists called demographers study the social environment by examining birth, death, and infant mortality rates as indicators of the overall health of a population. They also look at immigration and emigration of a territory and the push and pull factors that compel people to move. Immigration has both positive and negative consequences, such as the spread of culture and the strain on resources.

2. *How does a population grow?* Cities and countries grow through natural growth (births minus deaths), changing boundaries, and population movement. The highest population growth is in the poorer countries. Malthusian theory holds that population growth is geometric and leads to inequality. Marx disagreed and said it is the unequal distribution of resources among the increased population that leads to inequality. Zero population growth was Erlich's solution and entails a global effort to curtail population growth. Many organizations and nations are trying to stem population growth, which demographic transition theory shows is tied to technology.

3. *How do urban, rural, and suburban areas compare?* Cities develop along with emigration resulting from technological and agricultural advances. Richer countries have a higher concentration of people in cities; poorer countries have fewer cities, but they tend to be megacities. Rural areas often have more poverty, exacerbated by globalization, which results in jobs moving to cities. The invention of the automobile led to the development of suburbs because people could drive to work and escape the negative aspects of urban living. Also, as minorities move into cities, wealthier White residents often move outward.

4. *What do sociologists know about cities?* Sociologists study both the pros and cons of cities by examining what holds people together, including the common bonds of community and the interdependence inherent within. Durkheim distinguished between mechanical solidarity, based on connection, and organic solidarity, based on interdependence. Sociologists also look at the difference between urban and rural areas in terms of social networks. In urban groups, family networks often hold less importance while secondary relationships like work and friends become more important. In addition, Georg Simmel found that cities were so overstimulating that people tend to ignore other people and events, which can lead to alienation and its associated problems.

5. *What are the effects of urbanization?* Wirth found that migrating from rural to urban areas changes the way people think and feel and leads to rootlessness and crime. Gans disagreed; he found urban dwellers have social networks, or urban villages, comparable to rural ones. Burgess studied the effect of human ecology on the use of space and found that race and class affected the distribution of resources. He developed a concentric zone model of cities. While urbanization leads to positive developments in richer countries, it often leads to poverty and crime in poorer ones. Globalization causes cities in developed countries to be very similar with regard to culture.

6. *How are the natural and social worlds connected?* In the 1970s people began to focus on conservation and pollution, and sociologists began to pay attention to the interrelationship of society and nature. With technological developments, energy needs increase. The United States, at 5 percent of the world's population, consumes 25 percent of its energy resources. Worldwide, natural resources are vanishing as forests are being depleted for crops and development, and loss of topsoil is leading to desertification. Sociologists also focus on how the natural environment is affected by the social world through things such as pollution, garbage, and global warming and the ways in which people combat these problems with technology.

Key Terms

Demographic transition theory (p. 628)
Demography (p. 618)
Ecosystems (p. 640)
Emigration rate (p. 622)
Fecundity (p. 618)
Fertility (p. 618)
Fertility rate (p. 619)
Gentrification (p. 635)
Human ecology (p. 638)

Immigration rate (p. 622)
Infant mortality rate (p. 620)
Internal migration (p. 622)
Life expectancy (p. 619)
Malthusian theory (p. 627)
Mechanical solidarity (p. 636)
Megalopolis (p. 636)
Mortality rate (p. 619)
Natural population increase (p. 625)

Net migration rate (p. 622)
Organic solidarity (p. 637)
Population composition (p. 624)
Population density (p. 631)
Population pyramid (p. 624)
Suburbs (p. 633)
Zero population growth (p. 628)

19.1 Environmental Threats and Science

These are actual survey data from the General Social Survey, 2000.

Many of the claims about environmental threats are greatly exaggerated. Less than 30 percent of respondents agreed or strongly agreed with this statement, and almost 43 percent disagreed or strongly disagreed. Those in the middle and upper classes were most likely to disagree, while those in the lower class were most likely to agree. Age and race differences were not significant.

Modern science will solve our environmental problems with little change to our way of life. Almost 50 percent of respondents disagreed or strongly disagreed with this statement, while only 22 percent agreed or strongly agreed. Those in the upper class were most likely to disagree.

CRITICAL THINKING | DISCUSSION QUESTION

1. Why do you think there are social class differences in the survey responses?

19.2 What Are We Willing to Do?

These are actual survey data from the General Social Survey, 2000.

How often do you make a special effort to sort glass or cans or plastic or papers and so on for recycling? Almost 33 percent of respondents said they always recycle, while 24 percent said they often recycle. Those in the upper class were much more likely to say they always recycle (50 percent), and those in the lower class were more likely to say they never recycle (16.2 percent), although that percentage was still relatively low.

CRITICAL THINKING | DISCUSSION QUESTION

1. What do you think explains the social class differences in responses?

▶ Go to this website to look further at the data. You can run your own statistics and crosstabs here: **http://sda.berkeley.edu/cgi-bin/hsda?harcsda+gss04**

REFERENCES: Davis, James A., Tom W. Smith, and Peter V. Marsden. General Social Surveys 1972–2004: [Cumulative file] [Computer file]. 2nd ICPSR version. Chicago, IL: National Opinion Research Center [producer], 2005; Storrs, CT: Roper Center for Public Opinion Research, University of Connecticut; Ann Arbor, MI: Inter-University Consortium for Political and Social Research; Berkeley, CA: Computer-Assisted Survey Methods Program, University of California [distributors], 2005.

Glossary

AARP   New name for the American Association of Retired Persons, the largest and most influential lobbying group for older people in America.

achieved status   Status or social position based on one's accomplishments or activities.

adolescence   Term coined by psychologist G. Stanley Hall (1904) to name the years coinciding with puberty as a distinct—and perilous—life stage.

Adonis complex   Term coined by psychiatrist Harrison Pope and his colleagues for the belief that men must look like Greek gods, with perfect chins, thick hair, rippling muscles, and washboard abdominals.

advocacy research   Scientific research pursued to support or promote a particular position.

affirmative action   Programs and policies developed to ensure that qualified minority group members are not discriminated against in the workplace, school admission, and the like. Affirmative action policies generally apply to race, ethnicity, and gender, among other categories.

age cohort   A group of people who are born within a specific time period and therefore assumed to share both chronological and functional characteristics, as well as life experiences.

age norms   Distinctive cultural values, pursuits, and pastimes that are culturally prescribed for each age cohort.

ageism   Term coined by a physician to refer to differential treatment based on age—usually the elderly rather than the young.

agents of socialization   The people, groups, or institutions that teach people how to be functioning members of their society.

alternative medicine   Any of a variety of systems of healing or treating disease, including chiropractic, herbal treatments, homeopathy, meditation, and yoga, that are not included in the Western medicine curricula and may not have been scientifically tested for safety or effectiveness.

anorexia nervosa   A potentially fatal syndrome characterized by chronic and dangerous starvation dieting and obsessive exercise.

anticipatory socialization   The process of learning and adopting the beliefs, values, and behaviors of groups that one anticipates joining in the future.

apartheid   A race-based caste system that mandated segregation of different racial groups. In South Africa it was a political system institutionalized by the White minority in 1948 and remained in effect until 1990.

ascribed status   Status that is assigned to a person and over which he or she has no control.

asexual   Having no sexual desire for anyone.

assimilation   Occurs when a two groups come into contact and the minority group abandons their traditional culture to embrace the dominant culture.

authoritarian political system   When power is vested in a single person or small group. Sometimes that person holds power through heredity, sometimes through force or terror.

authority   Power that is perceived as legitimate, by both the holder of power and those subject to it. For a leader to exercise power, the people must believe he or she is entitled to make commands and that they should obey; indeed, that they want to obey.

baby boom   Population bulge that occurred in Europe and North America following World War II, creating the biggest cohort in U.S. history.

BCE and CE   Secular abbreviations for contemporary calendars. CE refers to the "common era" and BCE to "before the common era" instead of referring to the birth of Jesus as the marker.

bilineal descent   Tracing one's ancestry through both parents, rather than only the mother (see *Matrilineal*) or only the father (see *Patrilineal*).

bisexual   Feeling attracted to and preferring sexual partners of both sex.

blogs   Short for "weblogs"; online opinion sites.

bourgeoisie   Popularized by Karl Marx, term for the upper-class capitalists who owned the means of production. In Marx's time, they owned factories instead of farms. Today the term is also used to refer to upper-class managers who wield a lot of power.

broken windows theory   Philip Zimbardo's proposition that minor acts of deviance can spiral into severe crime and social decay. Atmosphere and context are keys to whether deviance occurs or spirals.

Buddhism   Founded by Siddhartha Gantana, later called the Buddha, it teaches that enlightenment is possible in this lifetime, through the Tenfold Path. There are two main branches—Hinayana and Mahayana. Today there are 376 million Buddhists, mostly in East Asia.

bulimia   A potentially fatal syndrome characterized by food "binging and purging" (eating large quantities and then either vomiting or taking enemas to excrete it).

bureaucracy   Originally derived from the French word *bureau*, or office, a formal organization characterized by a division of labor, a hierarchy of authority, formal rules governing behavior, a logic of rationality, and an impersonality of criteria.

bureaucratic personality   Robert Merton's term to describe those people who become more committed to following the correct procedures than they are to getting the job done

canon   The officially recognized set of foundational sociologists.

capital   Natural resources, manufactured goods, and professional services.

capitalism   An economic system in which free individuals pursue their own private interests in the marketplace. In laissez-faire capitalism, markets freely compete without government intervention. State capitalism requires that the government use a heavy hand in regulating and constraining the marketplace; and welfare capitalism creates a market-based economy for most goods and services, yet also has social welfare programs and government ownership of essential services.

caste system   A fixed and permanent, stratification system to which you are assigned to at birth.

causality   The term used when one variable causes another to change.

charismatic authority   Authority derived from the personal appeal of a specific leader.

charismatic leader   A person whose extraordinary personal qualities touch people enough to break with tradition and follow him or her.

charter schools   Privatization-oriented school reform initiative in which schools are financed through taxpayer funds but administered privately.

Christianity   The world's largest religion today, it was founded 2,000 years ago by disciples of Jesus, who declared him to be the son of God.

chronological age   A person's age determined by the actual date of his or her birth.

civil religion   Robert Bellah's term for secular rituals that, much like religious practices, create intense emotional bonds among people.

civil society   The clubs, churches, fraternal organizations, civic organizations, and other groups that once formed a third "zone" between home and work.

class   A group of people sharing the same social position in society. Class is based on income, power, and prestige.

class system   System of stratification in which people are ranked according to their economic position.

cluster sample   A sampling technique used when "natural" groupings are evident in the population. The total population is divided into these groups (or clusters), then a sample of the groups is selected. Then the required information is collected from the elements within each selected group.

coercive organization   One in which membership is not voluntary, with elaborate formal rules and sanctions and correspondingly elaborate informal cultures.

cohabitation   Once called "shacking up" or "living in sin," now more often called just "living together," the sociological term for people who are in a romantic relationship but not married living in the same residence.

colonialism   A political-economic system under which powerful countries establish, for their own profit, rule over weaker peoples or countries and exploit them for natural resources and cheap labor.

communism   Envisioned as the ideal economic system by Karl Marx, communism would produce and distribute resources "from each according to his or her ability, to each according to his or her need," erasing social inequalities along with crime, hunger, and political strife.

companionate marriage   The (comparatively recent) idea that people should select their own marriage partner based on compatibility and mutual attraction.

confirmation bias   Occurs when a single case or a few cases of an expected behavior confirms a belief while less-obvious disconfirming behavior is ignored.

conflict theory   Sociological paradigm that views society as organized by conflict rather than consensus and sees that norms and values are not equally distributed or accepted among members of a society. This theory tends to focus on inequality.

confounding variables   The things that might get in the way of an accurate measurement of the impact of one variable on another.

Confucianism   Ethical and philosophical system developed from the teachings of the Chinese sage Confucius that focuses primarily on secular ethics and the cultivation of the civilized individual to create a civilized and peaceful society.

conspicuous consumption   Thorstein Veblen's term to describe a new form of prestige based on accumulating and displaying possessions.

consumer crime   Crime in which the perpetrator uses a fake or stolen credit card to buy things for him- or herself or for resale. Such purchases cost both retailers and, increasingly, "e-tailers" over $1 billion per year, or nearly 5 cents for every dollar spent online.

consumption   The purchase and use of goods and services.

content analysis   Research method in which one analyzes artifacts (books, movies, TV programs, magazine articles, and so on) instead of people.

control group   In an experiment, the comparison group that will not experience the manipulation of independent variable (the experimental group). Having a control group enables sociologists to compare the outcomes of the experiment to determine if the changes in the independent variable had any effects on the dependent variable.

control theory   Travis Hirschi's theory that people perform a cost-benefit analysis about becoming deviant, determining how much punishment is worth the degree of satisfaction or prestige the deviance will confer.

corporation   A business that is treated legally as an individual. It can make contracts, incur debts, sue, and be sued, but its obligations and liabilities are legally distinct from those of its owners.

correlation The term for the fact of some relationship between two phenomena.

countercultures Subcultures that identify themselves through their difference and opposition to the dominant culture.

coup d'état The violent replacing of one political leader with another, it often doesn't bring with it any change in the daily life of the citizens.

credential society A society based more on the credentialing aspects of education than any substantive knowledge.

crime A deviant act that lawmakers consider bad enough to warrant formal laws and sanctions.

cross-sectional study A study that compares different age groups at one moment in time.

crowd An aggregate of individuals who happen to be together but experience themselves as essentially independent.

cult The simplest form of religious organization, characterized typically by fervent believers and a single idea or leader.

cultural capital French sociologist Pierre Bourdieu's term for the cultural articles—an idea, an artistic expression, a form of music or literature—that function as resources that people in the dominant class can use to justify their dominance.

cultural diffusion The spreading of new ideas through a society, independent of population movement.

cultural diversity Describes both the vast differences between the cultures of the world as well as the differences in belief and behavior that exist within cultures.

cultural imperialism The deliberate imposition of one' country's culture on another country.

cultural relativism A position that all cultures are equally valid in the experience of their own members.

cultural universals Rituals, customs, and symbols that are evident in all societies.

culture Both the material basis for social life and the sets of values and ideals that we understand to define morality, good and evil, appropriate and inappropriate.

culture industries The idea that American media productions are industrial products like any other product, a mode of production that empties them of original or complex content and soon renders their audiences passive and uncritical.

culture lag The relatively gradual process by which nonmaterial elements of culture catch up with changes in material culture and technology.

culture of poverty Oscar Lewis's theory that poverty is not a result of individual inadequacies but larger social and cultural factors. Poor children are socialized into believing that they have nothing to strive for, that there is no point in working to improve their conditions. As adults, they are resigned to a life of poverty, and they socialize their children the same way. Therefore poverty is transmitted from one generation to another.

culture shock A feeling of disorientation when the cultural markers that we rely on to help us know where we are and how to act have suddenly changed.

cybercrime The growing array of crimes committed via Internet and the World Wide Web, such as Internet fraud and identity theft.

data The plural of '*datum*', data are systematically collected and systematically bits of organized information.

deductive reasoning Reasoning that logically proceeds from one demonstrable fact to the next. It often moves from the general to the more specific.

deinstitutionalization The mental health movement of the 1970s that relocated mental health patients into halfway houses and community-based organizations in an effort to help them reintegrate into society.

democracy Derived from the Greek word *demos* (people); puts legislative decision making into the hands of the people rather than a single individual or a noble class.

demographic transition theory Frank Notestein's (1945) theory that the population and technology spur each other's development.

demography The scientific study of human populations, it's one of the oldest and most popular branches of sociology. Demographers are primarily concerned with the statistics of birth, death, and migration.

denomination A large-scale, extremely organized religious body with established hierarchy and methods for credentialing administrators.

dependent variable The variable whose change depends on the introduction of the independent variable.

detached observation A perspective that constrains the researcher from becoming in any way involved in the event he or she is observing. This reduces the amount that the researchers' observations will change the dynamic that they are watching.

deviance Breaking or refusing to follow a social rule. The rule can be societywide or specific to a particular group or situation.

dictatorship Rule by one person who has no hereditary claim to rule. Dictators may acquire power through a military takeover, or they may be elected or appointed.

differential association Edwin H. Sutherland's theory suggesting that deviance occurs when an individual receives more prestige and less punishment by violating norms than by following them.

differential power Phrase defining significant differences in access to economic, social, and political resources; is one of the four characteristics that a group must have to be considered a minority group.

disability According to the Americans with Disabilities Act, "a physical or mental impairment that substantially limits one or more major life activities."

discrimination A set of actions based on prejudice and stereotypes.

disinterestedness The scientific norm that stipulates scientific research should not be pursued for personal goals but in pursuit of scientific truth.

dramaturgy   Erving Goffman's conception of social life as like a stage play wherein we all work hard to convincingly play ourselves as "characters," such as grandchild, buddy, student, employee, or other roles.

drug   Any substance that, when ingested into the body, changes the body's functioning in some way.

dyad   A group of two people, the smallest configuration defined by sociologists as a group.

ecclesiae   Religious institutions so pervasive that the boundary between state and church is nonexistent and in which the clerical elite also serves as the political elite.

economic system   A mechanism that deals with the production, distribution, and consumption of goods and services in a particular society.

economy   A set of institutions and relationships that manages capital.

ecosystem   An interdependent system in which the animals, plants, and the material substances that make up the physical world live.

education   A social institution through which society provides its members with important knowledge—basic facts, job skills, and cultural norms and values. It provides socialization, cultural innovation, and social integration. It is accomplished largely through schooling, formal instruction under the direction of a specially trained teacher.

ego   Freud's term for the balancing force between the id and the superego; it channels impulses into socially acceptable forms.

emigration rate   Outflow of people from one society to another.

empirical verification   The scientific way of learning answers to questions, in which knowledge is developed, demonstrated, and double-checked through experiments.

encoding/decoding   Model for media interpretation that focuses on the relationship between how media construct meaning and how people make sense of what they see, hear, and read.

epidemiology   The study of the causes and distribution of disease and disability.

ethnic groups   A group that is set apart from other groups by language and cultural traditions. Ethnic groups share a common ancestry, history, or culture.

ethnicity   Social category that depends on an assumption of inherent cultural differences to rate and organize social groups.

ethnocentrism   The use of one's own culture as the reference point by which to evaluate other cultures; it often depends on or leads to the belief that one's own cultures is superior to others.

ethnography   A type of field method in which the researcher inserts him or herself into the daily world of the people he or she is trying to study, to understand the events from the point of view of the actors themselves.

ethnomethodology   The study of the social knowledge, codes, and conventions that underlie everyday interactions and allow people use to make sense of what others say and do.

evolutionary imperative   The term used to imply that the chief goal of all living creatures is to reproduce themselves.

exogamy   The insistence that marriage to (or sex with) members of your family unit is forbidden. This is the incest taboo, which Sigmund Frued argued was the one single cultural universal.

experimental group   In an experiment, the group that will have the change introduced to see what happens. *See* Control Group.

extended family   The most common model in the premodern era, the family model in which two or three generations lived under the same roof, or at least in the same compound: grandparents, parents, unmarried uncles and aunts, married uncles and aunts, sisters, brothers, cousins, and all of their children.

extraneous variables   Variables that influence the outcome of an experiment but are not the variables that are actually of interest.

face work   In dramaturgical theory, the possible performance of ourselves, because when we make a mistake or do something wrong, we feel embarrassed, or "lose face."

fads   Short-lived, highly popular, and widespread behaviors, styles, or modes of thought.

family   The basic unit in society, it traditionally consists of two parents rearing their children, but may also be any of various social units differing from but regarded as equivalent to the traditional family, such as single parents with children, spouses without children, and several generations living together.

family of origin   A child's biological parents or others who are responsible for his or her upbringing.

family of procreation   The family one creates through marriage or cohabitation with a romantic partner. Today, we consider any adults you are living with as a family of procreation, even if none of them is actually doing any procreating.

fan   Someone who finds significant personal meaning through a heightened awareness of and allegiance toward a specific media text—a story, a series, a performer. Fandom is a public affiliation, a public proclamation that your allegiance to some media product reveals a core element of your identity.

fashion   A behavior, style, or idea that is more permanent and often begins as a fad.

fecundity   The maximum number of children a woman could have during her childbearing years.

femininities   Term that recognizes the multiple meanings that female gender might contain. Making the term plural indicates how different groups of women might have different identities and enables us to see how conflicts between different groups—say, for example, Whites and Blacks or rich and poor—may also be expressed in gender terms.

feminism   A system of beliefs and actions that rests on two principles: gender inequality defines our society; and inequality is wrong and must change.

feminization of poverty   A worldwide phenomenon that also afflicts U.S. women, this term describes that women's overrepresentation among the world's poor and tendency to be in the worse economic straits than men in any given nation or population.

feminization of the professions The phenomenon in which salaries drop as female participation increases, revealing that it is less the intrinsic properties of the position that determine its wages and prestige and more which sex does it.

fertility The number of children that a woman bears.

fertility rate The number of children that would be born to each woman if she lived through her childbearing years with the average fertility of her age group.

folkways Relatively weak and informal norms that are the result of patterns of action. Many of the behaviors we call "manners" are folkways.

for-profit universities These institutions of higher learning are proprietary and are characterized by lower tuition costs and a faster path to degrees for students. Facilities are usually limited, and faculty is not tenured.

functional age A set of observable characteristics and attributes that are used to categorize people into different age cohorts.

fundamentalism The extreme end of many religions, fundamentalism tries to return to the basic precepts, the "true word of God," and live exactly according to his precepts.

gender A socially constructed definition based on sex category, based on the meanings that societies attach to the fact of sex differences.

gender identity Our understanding of ourselves as male or female and what it means to be male or female, perhaps the most fundamental way in which we develop an identity.

gender inequality Gender inequality has two dimensions: the domination of men over women, and the domination of some men over other men and some women over other women.

gender polarization Term coined by sociologist Sandra Bem to describe that male–female distinction, understood in a pattern of opposites, is the organizing principle of social life.

gender roles Psychology-based term to define the bundle of traits, attitudes, and behaviors that are associated with biological males and females. Roles are blueprints that prescribe what you should do, think, want, and look like, so that you can successfully become a man or a woman.

gender socialization Process by which males and females are taught the appropriate behaviors, attitudes, and traits for their biological sex. It begins at birth and continues throughout their lives.

gender wage gap The significant and remarkably consistent gap between earnings of men and women. The gap between White men and women of color is larger than between White men and White women.

generalizability Also called external validity or applicability, the extent to which the results of a study can be generalized to other circumstances.

generalized other The organized rules, judgments, and attitudes of an entire group. If you try to imagine what is expected of you, you are taking on the perspective of the generalized other.

generation X Also called "baby bust," the generation that followed the baby boom, which was much smaller in number and experienced lesser educational and professional opportunity and income than boomers.

generation Y Also called the "Echo Boom" or "Baby Boomlet," the children of the baby boomers who make up nearly as large a cohort as did their parents and are characterized by being technology, brand, and market savvy.

genocide The planned, systematic destruction of a racial, political, or ethnic group.

gentrification The process by which poorer urban neighborhoods are "upgraded" through renovation and development, often pushing out long-time residents of lesser means who can no longer afford to live there.

gerontology Scientific study of the biological, psychological, and sociological phenomena associated with old age and aging.

global commodity chains Worldwide networks of labor and production processes, consisting of all pivotal production activities that form a tightly interlocked "chain" from raw materials to finished product to retail outlet to consumer. The most profitable activities in the commodity chain (engineering, design, advertising) are likely to be done in core countries, while the least profitable activities (mining or growing the raw materials, factory production) are likely to be done in peripheral countries.

global inequality Systematic differences in wealth and power among countries, often involving exploitation of the less powerful by the more powerful countries.

global village Marshall McLuhan's term for his vision of the way global electronic media would unite the world through mutual interaction and involvement.

globalization A set of processes leading to the development of patterns of economic, cultural, and social relationships that transcend geographical boundaries; a widening, deepening, and speeding up of worldwide interconnectedness in all aspects of contemporary life.

government The organization and administration of the actions of the inhabitants of communities, societies, and states.

graying of america Term for the current sociological trend in which birthrates have been going down while life expectancy has been going up, resulting in an increasing proportion of elderly people.

group Collection of individuals who are aware that they share something in common and who interact with one another on the basis of their interrelated roles and statuses.

group cohesion The degree to which individual members of a group identify with each other and with the group as a whole.

group marriage Rare marriage arrangement in which two or more men marry two or more women, with children born to anyone in the union "belonging" to all of the partners equally.

groupthink   Irving Janis' term for social process in which members of a group attempt to conform their opinions to what they believe to be the consensus of the group, even if, as individuals, they may consider that opinion wrong or unwise.

hardcore members   The small number of group members, the "inner circle," who wield a great deal of power to make policy decisions.

hate crime   A criminal act committed by an offender motivated by bias against race, ethnicity, religion, sexual orientation, or disability status.

health   A state of complete mental, physical, and social well-being, not simply the absence of disease, according to the World Health Organization.

heterosexism   Institutionally based inequalities that may derive from homophobia.

heterosexuality   The most common sexual orientation worldwide, it is sexual attraction between people of different genders.

hidden curriculum   Means of socialization through which education not only creates social inequalities, but makes them seem natural, normal, and inevitable.

Hindusim   Developed in India around 1500 BCE, it believes in many gods, but most of the time people revere one of the main three: Brahman (creator of life); Vishnu (preserver of life); Shiva (destroyer or renewer of life). Today there are 900 million Hindus, mostly in South Asia and in Indian communities worldwide.

homophobia   A socially approved dislike of gay men and lesbians.

homosexuality   Sexual desire toward members of one's own gender.

hooking up   A sexual encounter that may nor may not include sexual intercourse, usually occurring on only one occasion between two people who are strangers or brief acquaintances.

human capital   Unpaid household labor.

human ecology   A social science discipline that looks at the relations among people in their shared environments.

hypothesis   A testable explanation for an event or phenomenon, that assumes a relationship between two or more variables.

id   Sigmund Freud's label for that part of the human personality that is pure impulse, without worrying about social rules, consequences, morality, or other people's reactions.

identifiability   Term used to describe that minority group members share (or are assumed to share) physical or cultural traits that distinguish them from the dominant group.

illiberal democracies   Societies that select leaders through free elections but in which officials pay so little attention to the constitution and other laws and to the opinions of their constituents that the country might as well be an oligarchy.

immigration rate   The number of people entering a territory each year for every thousand of the population.

immiseration thesis   Marx's theory that, as capitalism proceeded, the rich would get richer and the poor would get poorer, and eventually the poor would become *so* poor that they had nothing else to lose and would revolt.

impression management   Erving Goffman's term for our attempts to control how others perceive us, by changing our behavior to correspond to an ideal of what they will find most appealing.

independent variable   In an experimental study, the agent of change, the ingredient that is added to set things in motion.

inductive reasoning   Research in which one reasons to a conclusion about all or many members of a class based on examination of only a few members of that class. Loosely, it is reasoning from the specific to the general.

industrial economies   Economies based on factory production and technologies.

industrial revolution   Transformation of the economy due to a large-scale shift from home-based craft work by individuals to machine-based mass production in factories.

infant mortality rate   The number of deaths per year in each thousand infants (up to one year old).

in-group   A group with which you identify and that you feel positively toward, producing a "we" feeling.

in-group heterogeneity   The social tendency to be keenly aware of the subtle differences among the individual members of your group (while believing that all members of out-groups are exactly the same).

institution   An organization or association created and sustained by patterned social relationships established for the promotion of some object, especially one of public or general utility.

institutional discrimination   The most subtle and pervasive type of discrimination, it is deeply embedded in such institutions as the educational system, the business world, health care, criminal justice, and the mass media. These social institutions promote discriminatory practices and traditions that have such a long history they just "seem to make sense," and minority groups become the victims of systematic oppression, even when only a few people, or none at all, are deliberately trying to discriminate.

integration   The physical intermingling of the races organized as a concerted legal and social effort to bring equal access and racial equality through racial mixing in institutions and communities.

interest groups   Also called special interest groups, pressure groups, and lobbies, these groups promote their interests among state and national legislators and often influence public opinion. There are two kinds: Protective groups represent only one trade, industry, minority, or subculture; promotional groups seek to represent the interests of the entire society.

internal migration   Moving from one region to another within a territory.

interpretive communities   Groups that guide interpretation and convey preferred readings of media texts.

intersections or intersectionality   Denotes the study of the "intersections" of gender, race, class, age, ethnic, and sexual

dimensions of inequality. Each of these forms of inequality shapes and modifies the others.

interviews   Research method in which a researcher asks a small group of people open-ended questions.

intimate partner violence (IPV)   Violence, lethal or nonlethal, experienced by a spouse, ex-spouse, or cohabiting partner; boyfriend or girlfriend; or ex-boyfriend or girlfriend. It is commonly called "domestic violence," but because some does not occur in the home, IPV is the preferred term.

Islam   Founded about 1400 years ago when God was displeased by the corruptions of earlier prophets and gave his last prophet, Mohamed, a new sacred text, the Koran. It requires the fusion of religion and government and has two main branches—Shi'ite and Sunni.

jihad   A holy war

Judaism   The first monotheistic religion; believes the covenant between God and Abraham took place around 2000 BCE and became the foundation of Jewish law. Today there are about 15 million Jews worldwide.

kinship systems   Social systems that locate individuals by reference to their families, that is by common biological ancestry, legal marriage, or adoption.

knowledge economy   One defining element of the postindustrial economy in which ideas, information, and knowledge have become new forms of capital.

labeling theory   Howard Becker's term stresses the relativity of deviance, naming the mechanism by which the same act is considered deviant in some groups but not in others. Labels are used to categorize and contain people.

labor unions   A group of workers who act collectively address common issues and interests.

language   An organized set of symbols by which we are able to think and communicate with others, and the chief vehicle by which human beings create a sense of self.

latent functions   The unintended consequences of an action or event.

laws   Norms that have been organized and written down. Breaking these norms involves the disapproval not only of immediate community members, but also of the agents of the state, who are charged with punishing such norm-breaking behavior.

leader   All groups have leaders, people in charge, whether they were elected, appointed, or just informally took control.

legal-rational authority   Form of authority where leaders are to be obeyed not primarily as representatives of tradition or because of their personal qualities but because they are voicing a set of rationally derived laws. They must act impartially, even sacrificing their own opinions and attitudes in obedience to the laws of the land.

legitimacy   Social arrangements that ensure men know what children they have produced (women usually know). Families then bear the economic and emotional burden of raising only the children that belong to them.

liberal feminism   One of the three main branches of feminism today; focuses on the individual woman's rights and opportunities.

liberation theology   A movement within the Catholic Church in Latin America that was a source of popular mobilization for social change. Liberation theology stressed the nobility of the poor and promoted a religious response to hunger, disease, and poverty.

life expectancy   The average number of years a person can expect to live; varies greatly by country and region.

life span   The average or the maximum amount of time an organism or object can be expected to live or last.

Likert scale   The most common form of survey coding; arranges possible responses from lowest to highest.

literature review   Reading and summary of other research on or closely related to the topic of a study.

longitudinal study   A study that compares the same group (cohort) at various points in time as they age.

looking-glass self   Cooley's term for the process of how identity is formed through social interaction. We imagine how we appear to others and thus develop our sense of self based on the others' reactions, imagined or otherwise.

macrolevel analysis   Analysis of the large scale patterns or social structures of society, such as economies or political systems.

majority group   A group whose members experience privilege and access to power because of their group membership. With regard to race, lighter-colored skin usually means membership in the majority group.

Malthusian theory   Developed by the English economist and clergyman Thomas Robert Malthus (1766–1834), the theory held that population would increase by geometric progression, doubling in each generation—a man and a woman would have four children, and those four would have eight, and those eight sixteen, and so on, leading to mass starvation, environmental disaster, and eventual human extinction.

manifest functions   The intended consequences of an action or event.

manufacture consent   Michael Burawoy's term for the strategies by which companies get workers to embrace a system that also exploits them.

markets   Regular exchanges of goods and services within an economy.

masculinities   Term that recognizes the multiple meanings that male gender might contain. Making the term plural indicates how different groups of men might have different identities and enables us to see how conflicts between different groups—say, for example, Whites and Blacks or rich and poor—may also be expressed in gender terms.

masculinization of sex   The pursuit of sexual pleasure for its own sake, increased attention to orgasm, increased numbers of sexual partners, interest in sexual experimentation, and separation of sexual behavior from love. That is partly the result of the technological transformation of sexuality (from birth control to the Internet) and partly the result of the sexual revolution's promise of greater sexual freedom with fewer emotional and physical consequences

mass media   Ways to communicate with vast numbers of people at the same time, usually over a great distance. Mass media have developed in countless directions: books, newspapers, magazines, motion pictures, records and tapes, CDs and DVDs, radio and television programs, comic strips and comic books, and a whole range of new digital media.

mass production   The manufacture of goods in large quantities, generally using standardized designs and assembly-line techniques.

master status   An ascribed or achieved status presumed so important that it overshadows all of the others, dominating our lives and controlling our position in society.

material culture   The things people make, and the things they use to make them—the tools they use, the physical environment they inhabit (forests, beaches, mountains, fertile farmlands, or harsh desert).

matrilineal descent   Tracing one's ancestry through the mother, her mother, and so on.

matrix of domination   An interlocking system of control in which each type of inequality reinforces the others, so that the impact of one cannot be fully understood without also considering the others.

McDonaldization   The homogenizing spread of consumerism around the globe.

mechanical solidarity   Durkheim's term for a traditional society where life is uniform and people are similar. They share a common culture and sense of morality that bonds them.

media   The plural of *medium*, they are the ways that we communicate with each other.

media consolidation   The ongoing trends in media ownership in which only a handful of very large companies own and control the vast majority of media around the world.

media text   The words, pictures, and/or sounds that convey ideas in any mass medium.

medicalization   The current social tendency to assign virtually all aspects of health and illness an exclusively medical meaning.

megalopolis   A term coined by Jean Gottmann in 1961 to describe the integration of large cities and sprawling suburbs into a single organic urbanized unit, such as "Bo Wash" the Boston to Washington DC corridor that includes New York and Philadelphia, as well as the suburbs.

mental illness   "Any of various psychiatric disorders or diseases, usually characterized by impairment of thought, mood, or behavior," according to the *American Heritage Science Dictionary* (2002).

meritocracy   Social system in which the greater the functional importance of the job, the more rewards it brings, in salary, perks, power, and prestige.

microlevel analysis   Analysis of small-scale social patterns, such as individual interactions or small group dynamics.

midlife crisis   Popular belief that middle-aged men (and to a lesser extent, women) go through a developmental crisis at midlife characterized by wholesale changes in their work, relationships, and leisure activities.

minority group   A group one is born into, which has a distinguishable identity and whose members have less power and access to resources than other groups in society because of that group membership.

miscegenation   Early term for interracial marriage, it carries a pejorative inflection.

modernism   In sociology, it challenged tradition, religion, and aristocracies as remnants of the past and saw industry, democracy, and science as the wave of the future.

modernization theory   W. W. Rostrow's theory focusing on the conditions necessary for a low-income country to develop economically. Arguing that a nation's poverty is largely due to the cultural failings of its people, Rostrow believed poor countries could develop economically only if they give up their "backward" way of life and adopt modern Western economic institutions, technologies, and cultural values that emphasize savings and productive investment.

monarchy   One of the first political systems; rule by a single individual (*mono* means "one," and *archy* means "rule").

monogamy   The most common arrangement, it means marriage between two people. Most monogamous societies allow men and women to marry each other because it takes one of each to make a baby, but same-sex monogamy is surprisingly common.

morbidity rate   The rates of new infections from disease.

mores   The plural of *mos*, these are informally enforced norms based on strong moral values, which are viewed as essential to the proper functioning of a group.

mortality rate   The number of deaths per year for every thousand people.

multicultural feminism   One of the three main branches of feminism today; argues that the experience of being a woman of color cannot be extracted from the experience of being a woman. Multicultural feminists emphasize the historical context of racial and class-based inequalities.

multiculturalism   The doctrine that several different cultures (rather than one national culture) can coexist peacefully and equitably in a single country.

multigenerational households   Adults of more than one generation sharing a domestic space.

multinational corporations   Also called "transnational corporations," giant companies that are not clearly located in any one country but operate through a network of offices all over the world.

muscle dysmorphia   A belief that one is insufficiently muscular.

natural population increase   Simple calculation of the number of deaths every year subtracted from the number of births.

net migration rate   The difference between immigration and emigration rates in a given year.

network Often conceived as a web of social relationships, a type of group that is both looser and denser than a formal group but connects people to each other, and, through those connections, with other people.

New Age An umbrella term for many groups that practice and develop a distinct spirituality. New Age groups draw on organized religions and even traditions like astrology and a belief in life in outer space.

nonmarital sex Sexual relations outside marriage.

nonmaterial culture Often just called "culture," the ideas and beliefs that people develop about their lives and their world.

normative organization Voluntary organization wherein members serve because they believe in the goals of the organization.

norms The rules a culture develops that define how people should act and the consequences of failure to act in the specified ways.

objectivity The scientific norm that stipulates scientific knowledge must be based on objective criteria, not political agendas or personal preferences.

occupational crime The use of one's professional position to illegally secure something of value for oneself or for the corporation.

oligarchy Rule of a small group of people, an elite social class, or often a single family.

organic solidarity Emile Durkheim's term for a modern society where people are interdependent because of the division of labor; they disagreed on what was right and wrong but shared solidarity because the division of labor made them dependent on each other.

organization A formal group of people with one or more shared goals.

organizational crime Illegal actions committed in accordance with the operative goals of an organization, such as antitrust violations, false advertising, or price fixing.

out-group One to which you do not belong and toward which you feel either neutral or hostile; the "they" who are perceived as different from and of lower stature than ourselves.

out-group homogeneity The social tendency to be believe that all members of an out-group are exactly the same (while being keenly aware of the subtle differences among the individual members of one's own group).

outsourcing Also called "offshoring," the term refers to the practice of hiring out any phase(s) of product development to lower-wage countries.

overt racism Systematic prejudice applied to members of a group in clear, manifest ways, such as speech, discrimination, or a refusal to associate with members of that group.

paradigm An example, pattern, or model, especially an outstandingly clear or typical example or archetype.

participant observation Sociological research method in which one observes people in their natural habitat.

participatory democracy Also called "pure democracy," a political system in which every person gets one vote and the majority rules.

patriarchy Literally, "the rule of the fathers"; a name given to the social order in which men hold power over women.

patrilineal descent Tracing one's ancestry through the father, and his father, an so on.

pay gap The consistent, worldwide difference between what men are paid and what women are paid for their labor.

pedophilia Erotic attraction to children of either or both genders.

peer groups Our groups of friends and wider groups of acquaintances who have an enormous socializing influence, especially during middle and late childhood.

pluralism Maintains that different groups in a stable society can treat each other with mutual respect and that minority cultures can maintain their own distinctiveness and still participate in the greater society without discrimination.

Political Action Committee (PAC) Lobbying groups who work to elect or defeat political candidates based on their (the candidates) stances on particular issues.

political revolution Changes the political groups that run the society, but they still draw their strength from the same social groups that supported the old regime.

politics The art and science of government.

polyandry Rare form of polygamy in which one woman marries two or more men.

polygamy Marriage between three or more people. (See *Polyandry* and *Polygyny*.)

polygyny The most common form of polygamy, a marriage between one man and two or more women.

popular culture The culture of the masses, the middle and working class, that includes a wide variety of popular music, nonhighbrow forms of literature, any forms of spectator sports, and other popular forms of entertainment, like television, movies, and video games.

population composition The comparative numbers of men and women and various age groups in an area, region, or country.

population density The number of people per square mile or kilometer.

population pyramid Type of graph that shows five- or ten-year age groups as different-sized bars, or "blocks."

pornography A visual or written depiction of sexual activity with no "redeeming social value." Of course, what counts as "redeeming social value" is in the eye of the beholder.

postindustrial economies Economies that shift from the production of goods to the production of ideas.

postmodernism A late-twentieth-century worldview that emphasizes the existence of different worldviews and concepts of reality, rather than one "correct" or "true" one. Postmodernism emphasizes that a particular reality is a social construction by a particular group, community, or class.

poverty line Estimated minimum income required to pay for food, shelter, and clothing. Anyone falling below this income is categorized as poor.

power The ability to extract compliance despite resistance or the ability to get others to do what you want them to do, regardless of their own desires.

predictability The degree to which a correct prediction of a research outcome can be made.

prejudice A set of beliefs and attitudes that cause us to negatively prejudge people based on their social location.

primary deviance Any minor, usually unnoticed, act of deviance committed irregularly that does not have an impact on one's self-identity or on how one is labeled by others.

primary group One such as friends and family, which comes together for expressive reasons, providing emotional support, love, companionship, and security.

primary sex characteristics Those anatomical sex characteristics that are present at birth, like the sex organs themselves, which develop in the embryo.

primary socialization A culture's most basic values, which are passed on to children beginning in earliest infancy.

production The creation of value or wealth by producing goods and servies.

profane Anything in our everyday lives that is non-religious in subject matter, form or use, or is marked by contempt or irreverence for what is sacred.

proletariat Popularized by Karl Marx, the term for the lower classes who were forced to become wage laborers or go hungry. Today, the term is often used to refer to the working class.

property crime A crime committed on property, such as burglary, car theft, or arson, where there is no force or threat of force against a person.

proportional representation In contrast to the winner-take-all system used in the United States, proportional representation gives each party a proportion of the legislative seats based on the number of votes its candidates garner.

purposive sample Sample in which respondents are not selected randomly and are not representative of the larger population but are selected precisely because they possess certain characteristics that are of interest to the researcher.

qualitative methods Inductive and inferential means to drawing sociological understanding, usually about less tangible aspects of social life, such as the actual felt experience of social interaction.

quantitative methods Numerical means to drawing sociological conclusions using powerful statistical tools to help understand patterns in which the behaviors, attitudes, or traits under study can be translated into numerical values.

race Social category, still poorly defined, that depends on an assumption of biological distinction to rate and organize social groups.

race to the bottom Bonacich and Appelbaum's term for outsourcing jobs to wherever manufacturers and retailers can pay the lowest possible wages so as to maximize profits.

racism A particularly powerful form of prejudice that includes not only a belief in general stereotypes but also a belief that one race (usually White) is inherently superior to the others. Racism is a prejudice that is systematically applied to members of a group.

radical feminism One of the three main branches of feminism today; moves beyond discrimination economically and politically to argue that women are oppressed and subordinated by men directly, personally, and most often through sexual relations.

random sample A sample chosen by an abstract and arbitrary method, like tossing a piece of paper with each person's name on it into a hat, or selecting every tenth name in a telephone book or every thousandth name on the voter registration list. In this way, each person has an equal chance of being selected.

reference group A group toward which one is so strongly committed, or one that commands so much prestige, that we orient our actions around what we perceive that group's perceptions would be.

relative deprivation Describes how misery is socially experienced by constantly comparing yourself to others. You are not down and out: You are worse off than you used to be (downward mobility), or not as well off as you think you should be, (rising expectations) or, perhaps, not as well off as those you see around you.

religion A set of beliefs about the origins and meaning of life, usually based on the existence a supernatural power.

religiosity The extent of one's religious belief, typically measured by attendance at religious observances or maintaining religious practices.

representative democracy System in which citizens elect representatives to make the decisions for them; requires an educated citizenry and a free press.

resocialization Learning a new set of beliefs, behaviors, and values that depart from those held in the past.

retirement In the developed world, the time when people cease employment and become eligible to collect benefits accrued and/or designated for old age. Formal retirement ages vary from country to country.

revelation A religious way of learning answers to fundamental questions of existence; God, spirits, prophets, or sacred books reveal what we need to know.

revolution The attempt to overthrow the existing political and social order of a society and replace it with a new one.

rites of passage Culturally specific rituals that mark the transitions between life stages.

rituals Enactments by which members of a culture engage in a routine behavior to express their sense of belonging to the culture.

role Behavior expected of people who have a particular status.

role conflict What happens when we try to play different roles with extremely different or contradictory rules at the same time.

role exit The process we go through to adjust when leaving a role that is central to our identity.

role performance The particular emphasis or interpretation each of us gives a social role.

role strain The experience of difficulty in performing a role.

sacred A place, time, object, or person in which the worlds of the spiritual and the worldly come together.

sample A limited group of research subjects whose responses are then statistically developed into a general theme or trend that can be applied to the larger whole.

sandwich generation Popular term for middle-aged adults who are caring for both their young children and their aging parents.

Sapir-Whorf hypothesis A theory that language shapes our reality because it gives us a way to talk about the categories of life that we experience.

scapegoat A convenient, weak and socially approved target for economic or social loss or insecurity.

science The accumulated systematic knowledge of the physical or material world, obtained through experimentation and observation.

scientific literacy According to the National Academy of Sciences, it is the "knowledge and understanding of the scientific concepts and processes required for personal decision making, participation in civic and cultural affairs, and economic productivity."

second shift The term coined by sociologist Arlie Hochschild to describe how working women typically must work both outside the home for wages and inside the home doing domestic management and childcare.

secondary analysis Analysis conducted on data previously collected from others for other reasons.

secondary deviance The moment when someone acquires a deviant identity, occuring when he or she repeatedly breaks a norm, and people start making a big deal of it, so the rule breaking can no longer be attributed to a momentary lapse in judgment or justifiable under the circumstances but is an indication of a permanent personality trait.

secondary group Co-workers, club members, or another group that comes together for instrumental reasons, such as wanting to work together to meet common goals. Secondary groups make less of an emotional claim on one's identity than do primary groups.

secondary sex characteristics Those sex characteristics, such as breast development in girls and the lowering of voices and development of facial hair in boys, that occur at puberty.

secondary socialization Occurring throughout the life span, it is the adjustments we make to adapt to new situations.

secondhand smoke The tobacco smoke that is inhaled by nonsmokers as a result of other people smoking; led to public health campaigns to ban smoking in movie theaters, airplanes, restaurants, bars, and all public offices and buildings.

sect A small subculture within an established religious institution.

secularization The process of moving away from religion and toward the worldly.

segregation The practice of physically separating Whites from other races by law and custom in institutions and communities.

self-fulfilling prophecy Term coined by Robert K. Merton in 1949 to name the phenomenon that when you expect something to happen, it usually does.

sex A biological distinction; the chromosomal, chemical, and anatomical organization of males and females.

sex hormones Testosterone and estrogen, the hormones that trigger development of secondary sex characteristics, such as breast development in girls and the development of facial hair in boys.

sex tourism Effectively the globalization of prostitution, a well-organized business whereby the flow of "consumers" (wealthy men) is directed to the "commodities" (poor men and women). Like prostitution, there is far less "choice" on the part of the locals and far more coercion than typically meets the eye. The tourists seem to be men and women who are being friendly and flirtatious, but the locals are usually victims of kidnapping and violence.

sexual behavior Any behavior that brings sexual pleasure or release (typically, but not always, involving sex organs).

sexual harassment A form of gender discrimination in the workplace that singles out women for differential treatment. There are two types: "quid pro quo," which occurs when a supervisor uses his (or her) position to elicit sexual activity from a subordinate; and the more common "hostile environment," which occurs when a person feels threatened or unsafe because of constant teasing or threatening by other workers.

sexual identity Refers to an identity that is organized by the gender of the person (or persons) to whom you are sexually attracted. Also called *sexual orientation*.

sexual script Set of ideas and practices that answer basic questions about sexual identity and practices: With whom do we have sex? What do we do? How often? Why?

sexual socialization The process by which your sexual scripts begin to cohere into a preference and sexual identity.

sexuality Identities we construct that are often based on our sexual conduct and often intersect with other sources of identity, such as race, class, ethnicity, age, or gender.

social construction of gender We construct our gender identities all through our lives, using the cultural materials we find around us. Our gender identities are both voluntary—we choose to become who we are—and coerced—we are pressured, forced, and often physically threatened to conform to certain rules.

social controls   As Walter Reckless theorized, people don't commit crimes even if they could probably get away with them due to social controls. There are *outer controls*, family, friends, teachers, social institutions, and authority figures (like the police) who influence (cajole, threaten, browbeat) us into obeying social rules; and *inner controls*, internalized socialization, conscious, religious principles, ideas of right and wrong, and my self-conception as a "good person."

social Darwinism   A model of social change that saw each succeeding society as improving on the one before it.

social epidemiology   The focus on these social and behavioral factors that influence the causes and distribution of disease and disability.

social interaction   The foundation for societal groups and relationships and the process of how people behave and interact with each other.

social mobility   The movement from one class to another, it can occur in two forms: *intergenerational* – that is, your parents are working class, but you became lower, or your parents are middle class, but you became upperclass; and *intragenerational* – that is, you move from working to lower, or from middle to upper, all within your lifetime.

social movements   Collective attempts to further a common interest or secure a common goal through action outside the sphere of established institutions.

social revolution   Revolution that changes the social groups or classes that political power rests on.

Social Security   The U.S. government program wherein citizens contribute a small portion of their earnings while working, then collect a cash supplement after retirement. The program has been credited with preventing tens of millions of elderly from living in poverty and hunger.

social stratification   Taken from the geological term for layers of rock or "strata," the ranking of people into defined layers. Social stratification exists in all societies and is based on things like wealth, race, and gender.

social structure   A complex framework composed of both patterned social interactions and institutions that together both organize social life and provide the context for individual action.

socialism   Economic system in which people are mean to cooperate rather than compete, share goods and services, own property collectively, and make decisions as a collective body.

socialization   The process by which we become aware of ourselves as part of a group, learn to communicate with others, and learn how to behave as expected.

society   An organized collection of individuals and institutions, bounded by space in a coherent territory, subject to the same political authority, and organized through a shared set of cultural expectations and values.

socioeconomic status (SES)   Your social connections, your taste in art, your ascribed and attained statuses, and more.

Because there are so many components, sociologists today tend to prefer the concept of *socioeconomic status* to that of social class, to emphasize that people are ranked through the intermingling of many factors, economic, social, political, cultural, and community.

sociological imagination   The ability to see the connection between our individual identities and the social contexts (family, friends, and institutions) in we which we find ourselves.

sociology   The study of human behavior in society.

solidarity   Term for one's awareness of membership in a definable category of people, so that there is a clearly defined "us" and "them."

status   One's socially defined position in a group; it is often characterized by certain expectations and rights.

stereotypes   Generalizations about a group that are oversimplified and exaggerated and that fail to acknowledge individual differences in the group.

stigma   An attribute that changes you "from a whole and usual person to a tainted and discounted one," as sociologist Erving Goffman (1963) defined it. A stigma discredits a person's claim to be normal.

stigmatized identity   An identity where the individual loses his or her claim to be normal. This leads to a perception that a person or group is somehow responsible for their illness and that it is their fault.

strain theory   Robert K. Merton's concept that excessive deviance is a by-product of inequality within societies that promote certain norms and versions of social reality yet provide unequal means of meeting or attaining them. Individuals respond to this strain either by conforming or by changing the goals or means of obtaining goals accepted by society.

stratified sample   Sample in which research subjects are divided into proportions equal to the proportions found in the population at large.

structural functionalism   A sociological paradigm that contends that all social life consists of several distinct, integrated levels that enable the world—and individuals who are within in—to find stability, order, and meaning.

subculture   Group within a society that creates its own norms and values distinct from the mainstream and usually its own separate social institutions as well.

subjectivity   The complex of individual perceptions, motivations, ideas, and emotions that give each of us a point of view.

subordinate   Individual or group that possesses little or comparatively less social power.

subtle racism   Systematic prejudice applied to members of a group in quiet or even unconscious ways; a simple a set of mental categories that one may possess about a group based on stereotypes.

suburb   A residential community outside of a city but always existing in relationship to the city.

suffrage   The right to vote.

superego Freud's term for the internalized norms, values, and "rules" of our social group that are learned from family, friends, and social institutions.

superordinate Individual or group that possesses social power.

surveys Research method in which one asks a sample of people closed-ended questions and tabulates the results.

symbol Anything—an idea, a marking, a thing—that carries additional meanings beyond itself to other who share in the culture. Symbols come to mean what they do only in a culture; they would have no meaning to someone outside.

symbolic interactionism Sociological perspective that examines how individuals and groups interact, focusing on the creation of personal identity through interaction with others. Of particular interest is the relationship between individual action and group pressures.

syncretic religions Religions that do not forbid one's practicing other religions at the same time, such as Buddhism, Hinduism, Confucianism, Taoism, and others.

taboos The strongest form of norms, these are prohibitions viewed as essential to the well-being of humanity

terrorism Using acts of violence and destruction (or threatening to use them) as a political strategy.

tertiary deviance Occurs when members of a group formerly labeled deviant attempt to redefine their acts, attributes, or identities as normal—even virtuous.

the sick role Talcott Parsons described the social expectations for both the sick individual and those with whom the individual interacts. The sick role is a social contract where the sick person has to try to get better in order to receive the social benefits of being sick.

third great awakening What some term a current religious revival in the United States that further democratizes spirituality, making a relationship with the sacred attainable to even greater numbers of Americans, with even less effort or religious discipline.

time-series study A study that involves tracking a variable over time.

token Representative of a traditionally disenfranchised group whose hypervisibility results in constant pressure to reflect well on his or her group and to outperform co-workers just to be perceived as equal.

tokenism When a single member of a minority group is present in an office, workplace, or classroom and is seen as a representative of that minority group rather than as an individual.

total institution An institution that completely circumscribes your everyday life, cutting you off from life before you entered and seeking to regulate every part of your behavior.

totalitarianism A political system in which no organized opposition is permitted and political information is censored.

tracking Common in American schools, this system groups students according to their scholastic ability. Tracking can be formal or informal, but virtually all schools have mechanisms for sorting students into groups that seem to be alike in ability and achievement. Labeling is often a by-product of tracking.

traditional authority Dominant in premodern societies, including ancient Egypt, China, and Mesoamerica, the form of authority that people obey because, they believed, their society had always done things that way; derives from who the leaders are: the descendants of kings and queens, or perhaps the descendants of the gods, not from their educational background, work experience, or personality traits.

transgenderism Transgendered people have felt a "persistent discomfort and sense of inappropriateness about their assigned sex (feeling trapped in the wrong body)" as the diagnosis in the American Psychiatric Association's *Diagnostic and Statistical Manual* (DSM III) puts it, and rather than change their gender, they change their biological sex to match their felt gender identity.

twixters Popular term coined to name people in their twenties who still live culturally as job-free, home-free, spouse-free, responsibility-free adolescents.

two-party system State in which two political parties dominate. Other parties may exist, but they are largely inconsequential.

underclass About 4 percent of the U.S. population, this group has no income, no connection to the job market, little education, inadequate nutrition, and substandard housing or none at all. They have no possibility of social mobility and little chance of achieving the quality of life that most people would consider minimally acceptable.

universal suffrage Granting of the vote to any and all citizens who meet specified, universal criteria, such as legal citizenship and a minimum age.

utilitarian organization Organization like the college we attend or the company we work for, whose members belong for a specific, instrumental purpose or tangible material reward.

values If norms tell us *how* to behave, values tell us *why*. Values constitute what a society thinks about itself and so are among the most basic lessons that a culture can transmit to its young.

verstehen Max Weber's term for "intersubjective understanding," or the ability to understand social behavior from the point of view of those the sociologist is observing.

violent crime A crime of violence or one in which violence is a defining feature. According to the FBI, violent crime consists of four offenses: murder and nonnegligent manslaughter, forcible rape, robbery, and aggravated assault.

voucher system First proposed in 1955, a free-market approach to school reform in which taxpayer funds are used to pay for students' tuition at private school, ostensibly upping competition and increasing quality in public schools.

wage labor The arrangement by which workers get a regular paycheck in exchange for performing a specific task, rather than being paid for the end product of their labor.

white-collar crime Edward Sutherland's term for the illegal actions of a corporation or people acting on its behalf, by using the authority of their position to commit crime.

world religions Those religions with long histories, well-established traditions, and the flexibility to adapt to many different cultures.

world system theory Immanuel Wallerstein's theory that the interconnectedness of the world system began in the 1500s, when Europeans began their economic and political domination of the rest of the world. Because capitalism depends on generating the maximum profits for the minimum of expenditures, the world system continues to benefit rich countries (which acquire the profits) and harm the rest of the world (by minimizing local expenditures and therefore perpetuating poverty).

zero population growth Paul Erlich's (1968) modern solution to the Malthus's concerns, it entails a global effort to ensure that the number of births does not exceed the number of deaths, providing global population stability, a decrease in poor countries, and a redistribution of resources to those countries.

References

"A World of Opportunity" in *The Economist,* September 8, 2005.

AARP. "Baby Boomers Envision Their Retirement," 2001. Washington, D.C.: AARP.

Abbate, Janet. *Inventing the Internet.* Boston: MIT Press, 2000.

Abbott, Andrew, "Status and Status Strain in the Professions," *American Journal of Sociology,* 86, pp. 819–835.

Abbott, Andrew. *The System of Professions: An Essay on the Division of Expert Labor.* Chicago: University of Chicago Press, 1988.

ABC News, "Poll: American Sex Survey." October 21, 2004; Available at: http://abcnews.go.com/print?id=156921

Abrahamson, Mark, and Valerie Carter. *Urban Enclaves: Identity and Place in America.* New York: St. Martins Press, 1996.

Abu-Lughod, L. "Bedouins, Cassettes, and Technologies of Public Culture." *Middle East Report,* 159 (1989): 7–11.

Adams, David. "Latin America's Balanced/Biased Voice." *St. Petersburg Times,* August 8, 2005.

Adger, Neil Saleemul Huq, Katrina Brown, Declan Conway and Mike Hulme, 2002. "Adaptation to Climate Change: Setting the Agenda for Development Policy and Research." Norwich, UK: University of East Anglia, Tyndell Centre for Climate Change Research, working paper, 16, April.

Adler, Jerry. "The New Naysayers." *Newsweek,* September 11, 2006.

Adler, Margot. *Drawing Down the Moon: Witches, Druids, Goddess-Worshippers, and Other Pagans in America Today.* New York: Penguin, 1997.

Adler, Paul S. "Market, Hierarchy, and Trust: The Knowledge Economy and the Future of Capitalism." *Organization Science* March–April, 2001: 214–234.

"Age at First Marriage and Divorce" available at http://www.wvdhhr.org/MCFH/adohealthprofile/nationalstatedata/Age_at_First_Marriage_and_Divorcelist.asp

Agnew, Robert, and Sandra Hughley. "Adolescent Violence Towards Parents." *Journal of Marriage and the Family,* 5(1), 1989, 699–711.

Agnone, Jon. "Amplifying Public Opinion: The Policy Impact of the U.S. Environmental Movement," *Social Forces,* 85: 1593–1620.

Ahrons, Constance. *We're Still Family: What Grown Children Have to Say about Their Parents' Divorce.* New York: HarperCollins, 2004.

Aileinikoff, Thomas Alexander, and Klusmeyer, Douglas B. *Citizenship Today: Global Perspectives and Practices.* New York: Carnegie Endowment for International Peace, 2001.

Alan Guttmacher Institute. *Teenage Sexual and Reproductive Behavior in Developed Countries: Can More Progress Be Made?* New York: Alan Guttmacher Institute. 2001.

Alan Guttmacher Institute. "Abortion Common among All Women, Even Those Thought to Oppose Abortion." 1996; accessed at www.agi-usa.org/pubs/archives/prabort2.html

Alcohol Problems and Solutions, 2007. "Legal Drinking Ages Around the World." Available at: http://www2.potsdam.edu/hansondj/LegalDrinkingAge.html

Alan Guttmacher Institute. "Abortion in Context: United States and Worldwide." Available at: http://www.guttmacher.org/pubs/ib_0599.html

Allan, Emilie Andersen and Darrell J. Steffensmeier, "Youth Underemployment and Property Crime: Differential Effects of Job Availability and Job Quality on Juvenile and Young Adult Arrest Rates." *American Sociological Review,* 54 (1989): 107–23.

Allegretto, Sylvia. "U.S. Government Does Relatively Little to Lessen Child Poverty Rates." Washington, D.C.: Economic Policy Institute, 2006.

Allen, K. R., and Demo, D. H. "The Families of Lesbians and Gay Men: A New Frontier in Family Research." *Journal of Marriage and the Family,* 57 (1995): 111–127.

Allen, Tammy D., Lillian T. Eby, Shane S. Douthitt, and Carrie L. Noble. "Applicant Gender and Family Structure: Effects of Perceived Relocation Commitment and Spouse Resistance." *Sex Roles,* December, 2002.

Allport, Gordon. *The Nature of Prejudice.* New York: Anchor, 1954.

Altbach, Philip. *American Higher Education in the Twentieth Century: Social, Political, and Economic Challenges.* Baltimore, MD: Johns Hopkins University Press, 1998.

Amato, Paul R. "Reconciling Divergent Perspectives: Judith Wallerstein, Quantitative Family Research, and Children of Divorce." *Family Relations,* 52, 4 (2003): 332–339.

Amato, Paul R. "The Consequences of Divorce for Adults and Children." *Journal of Marriage and Family,* 62(4), 2000 pp. 1269–1287.

Amato, Paul R., and Juliana M. Sobolewski. "The Effects of Divorce and Marital Discord on Adult Children's Psychological Well-Being." *American Sociological Review,* vol. 66, 2001, pp. 900–921.

Ambert, Anne-Marie. "Same-Sex Couples and Same-Sex-Parent Families: Relationships, Parenting and Issues of Marriage." Ottawa, Canada: The Vanier Institute of the Family, 2005.

American Academy of Pediatrics. "Discipline." Available at: http://www.aap.org/publiced/BR_Discipline.htm

American Civil Liberties Union. Lesbian, Gay, Bisexual, Transgender Project, 2007. www.aclu.org/lgbt/index.html

American Diploma Project, *Ready or Not: Creating a High School Diploma That Counts* 2004. Available at: http://www.achieve.org/node/552.

American Library Association, "Most Frequently Challenged Books of 2004." www.ala.org/bbooks/challeng.html.

American Medical Association. *Physician Characteristics and Distribution in the U.S., 2000.* Washington, D.C.: American Medical Association, 2000.

American Psychiatric Association, 2007. "Mental health of the Elderly." Available at: http://healthyminds.org/mentalhealthofelderly.cfm

American Society of Plastic Surgeons, "Cosmetic Surgery Procedures." Available at: www.plasticsurgery.org

Americans with Disabilities Act of 1990, available at: http://www.ada.gov/pubs/ada.htm

Amnesty International, "Facts and Figures" online www.therepert.amnesty.org/eng.

Anderson, C. A., Benjamin, A. J., Jr., and Bartholow, B.D., "Does the Gun Pull the Trigger? Automatic Priming Effects of Weapon Pictures and Weapon Names." *Psychological Science* 9 (1998): 308–314.

Anderson, Christy, and David M. Burns. "Patterns of Adolescent Smoking Initiation Rates by Ethnicity and Sex." *Tobacco Control*, 2000, 9 (Suppl II).

Anderson, E. "The Code of the Streets." *Atlantic Monthly*, 273, May 1994, pp. 81–94.

Anderson, Elijah. *Code of the Street: Decency, Violence, and the Moral Life of the Inner City*. New York: W. W. Norton, 2000.

Anderson, Elijah. *Streetwise: Race, Class and Change in an Urban Community*. Chicago: University of Chicago Press, 1992.

Anderson, Elijah. "Of Old Heads and Young Boys: Notes on the Black Experience." A paper commissioned by the National Research Committee on the Status of Black Americans, 1986.

Anderson, Sarah, John Cavanaugh, Chuck Collins, and Eric Benjamin. *Executive Excess, 2006*. Washington, D.C.: Institute for Policy Studies, 2006.

Andrew, John W. *Lyndon Johnson and the Great Society*. New York: Ivan R. Dee, 1999.

Andrews, Kenneth T. *Freedom Is a Constant Struggle: The Mississippi Civil Rights Movement and Its Legacy*. Chicago: University of Chicago Press, 2004.

Ang, Ien, and Joke Hermes. "Gender and/in Media Consumption." In *Mass Media and Society*, James Curren and Michael Gurevitch, eds. London: Arnold Press, 1991.

Angier, Natalie. *Woman: An Intimate Geography*. Boston: Houghton-Mifflin, 1999.

Appelbaum Richard P., and Jeffrey Henderson. *States and Development in the Asian Pacific Rim*. Newbury Park, CA: Sage, 1992.

Archer, J., "Violence between Men," in J. Archer, Ed., *Male Violence*. pp. 121–140. London: Routledge, 1994.

Arendt, Hannah. *The Origins of Totalitarianism*. New York: Harcourt, 1973. (Originally published in 1958.)

Ariès, Phillippe. *Centuries of Childhood: A Social History of Family Life*. New York: Knopf, 1962.

Armstrong, Elizabeth. *Forging Gay Identities*. Chicago: University of Chicago Press, 2005.

Arnett, Jeffrey Jensen. *Emerging Adulthood: The Winding Road from the Late Teens through the Twenties*. New York: Oxford University Press, 2004.

Arnst, Catherine. "Off-the-Shelf Body Parts." *BusinessWeek*, August 25, 2003: 106–107.

Aronson, Amy. *Taking Liberties: Early American Women's Magazines and Their Readers*. Westport, CT: Praeger Press, 2002.

"As They Don't Like It: Europe's Demographic Disaster Is Self-Inflicted but Not Terminal." *The Economist*, October 20, 2005.

Asch, Solomon. "Opinions and Social Pressure." *Scientific American*, vol. 193, no. 5 (1955): 31–35.

Asch, Steven, Ever Kerr, Joan Keesey, John Adams, Claude Setodji, Shaistas Malik, and Elizabeth McGlynn. "Who Is at Greatest Risk for Receiving Poor Quality Health Care?" *New England Journal of Medicine*, 354(11), March 16, 2006, 1147–1156.

Asian American Cultural Center, University of Illinois at Urbana-Champaign. Vol. 3, No. 11, October 31, 2005. Available at www.odos. uiuc. edu/aacc/news/archives/2005/aacc_2005_10_31.html

Astin, Alexander, Helen Astin, and Jenifer Lindholm. *The Spiritual Life of College Students* (Los Angeles: Higher Education Research Institute, UCLA, 2005). Available at: www.spirituality.ucla.edu.

Atack, Jeremy. "Tenants and Yeomen in the Nineteenth Century." In Morton Rothstein and Daniel Field, eds., *Quantitative Studies in Agrarian History*, pp. 3–29. Ames: Iowa State University Press, 1994.

Atkinson, Michael. *Tattooed: The Sociogenesis of a Body Art*. Toronto, Ont.: University of Toronto Press, 2003.

Auyero, Javier. *Poor People's Politics: Peronist Survival Networks and the Legacy of Evita*. Durham, NC: Duke University Press, 2000.

Avert, 2007. "Worldwide Ages of Consent" available at http://www.avert.org/aofconsent.htm

Ayres, Irving, and Peter Siegelman. "Race and Gender Discrimination in Bargaining for a New Car." *American Economic Review*, 85(3), 1995, 304–321.

Baber, Asa. 1992. *Naked at Gender Gap*. New York: Birch Lane.

Baca Zinn, Maxine. "Social Science Theorizing for Latino Families in the Age of Diversity," In: R.E. Zambrano (ed.), *Understanding Latino Families: Scholarship, Policy, and Practice*. Thousand Oaks, CA: Sage Publications, 2005 pp. 177–189.

Bachman, R., and L. E. Saltzman. "Violence against Women: A National Crime Victimization Survey Report" (NCJ No. 154348). Washington, DC: U.S. Department of Justice, 1994.

Backman, Clifford R. *The Worlds of Medieval Europe*. Oxford, U.K.: Oxford University Press, 2002.

Bacon, Margart, Herbert Barry, and Iruin Child, "A Cross-Cultural Survey of Some Sex Differences in Socialization." *Journal of Abnormal Social Psychology*, 53, 1957.

Baden, John. 1996. "Perverse Consequences (P.C.) of the Nanny State" in *Seattle Times*, January 17, p. 1.

Bagamery, Anne. "Hearing Tomorrow's Workers." *International Herald Tribune*, April 14, 2004.

Bailey, Beth L. *From Front Porch to Back Seat: Courtship in Twentieth Century America*. Baltimore, MD: Johns Hopkins University Press, 1989.

Baldus D.C. et al., "Race Discrimination and the Death Penalty in the Post Furman Era: An Empirical and Legal Overview, with Preliminary Findings from Philadelphia." *Cornell Law Review*, (1998): 1638.

Ballantine, Jeanne H. *The Sociology of Education: A Systematic Analysis*. Upper Saddle River, NJ: Prentice-Hall, 2001.

Balz, Dan, and Richard Morin "Nation Is Divided on Drawdown of Troops" in *The Washington Post*; June 27, 2006: p. A.1.

Banchoff, Thomas, ed. *Democracy and the New Religious Pluralism*. New York: Oxford University Press, 2007.

Barber, Benjamin. *Jihad vs. McWorld: How Globalization and Tribalism Are Reshaping the World*. New York: Crown, 1995.

Barnes, P. M., E. Powell-Griner, K. McFann, and R. L. Nahin. "Complementary and Alternative Medicine Use among Adults." National Center for Health Statistics, 2004.

Barnet, Richard J., and John Cavanagh. *Global Dreams: Imperial Corporations and the New World Order*. New York: Simon & Schuster, 1994.

Baron Larry, and Murray Straus. *Four Theories of Rape*. New Haven, CT: Yale University Press, 1993.

Barr, Nicolas. *The Economics of the Welfare State*. New York: Oxford University Press, 2004.

Bartholow, B. D., Anderson, C. A., Carnagey, N. L., and Benjamin, A. J., Jr., "Interactive Effects of Life Experience and Situational Cues on Aggression: The Weapons Priming Effect in Hunters and Non-Hunters." *Journal of Experimental Social Psychology*, 41 (2005): 48–60.

Bassuk, Shari S., Lisa F. Berkman, and Benjamin C. Amick II. "Socioeconomic Status and Mortality among the Elderly: Findings from Four U.S. Communities." *American Journal of Epidemiology*, 155, 6 (2002): 520–533.

Bates, Crispin, ed. *Community, Empire, and Migration: South Asians in Diaspora*. New York: Palgrave Macmillan, 2001.

Battle, Michael. *The Black Church in America: African American Christian Spirituality*. London: Blackwell, 2006.

Bauder, David. "More TVs Than People in Average Home." *Associated Press*, September 1, 2006. http://www.ap.org/

BBC News, "'Satanic' Harry Potter Books Burnt." BBC News, December 31, 2001. Available at http://news.bbc.co.uk/1/hi/entertainment/arts/1735623.stm

Bearman, Peter S., and Hannah Bruckner. "Promising the Future: Virginity Pledges and First Intercourse." *American Journal of Sociology*, 106(4), 2001: 859–912.

Becker, Elizabeth. 2002. "Study Finds a Growing Gap between Managerial Salaries for Men and Women" in *The New York Times*, January 24, p. 18.

Becker, Howard. *Art Worlds*. Berkeley, CA: University of California Press, 1984.

Becker, Howard S. *Outside: Studies in the Sociology of Deviance*. New York: The Free Press, 1966.

Becker, Lee, Wilson Lowrey, Dane Claussen, and William Anderson. "Why Does the Beat Go On?" *Newspaper Research Journal*, Fall 2000: 1–11.

Bell, Daniel. *The Coming of Post-Industrial Society: A Venture in Social Forecasting*. New York: Basic Books, 1976.

Bell, Michael Mayerfield. *An Invitation to Environmental Sociology*. Thousand Oaks, CA: Pine Forge Press, 2004.

Bellah, Robert N. "Civil Religion in America." *Journal of the American Academy of Arts and Sciences*, 96(1) (Winter, 1967): 1–21.

Bellah, Robert N., et al. *Habits of the Heart*. New York: Harper, 1985.

Belo, Roberto "Blogs Take on the Mainstream." BBC.co.uk website, December 31, 2004, available at: http://news.bbc.co.uk/1/hi/technology/4086337.stm

Belsky, J. K. *The Psychology of Aging: Theory, Research and Intervention*. Pacific Grove, CA: Brooks/Cole, 1990.

Bem, Sandra Lipsitz. *Lenses of Gender: Transforming the Debate on Gender Inequality*. New Haven, CT: Yale University Press, 1993.

Ben-David Joseph. *The Scientist's Role in Society: A Comparative Study*. Chicago, IL: University of Chicago Press, 1984.

Benjamin, C. I. Ravid. "From Geographical Realia to Historiographical Symbol: The Odyssey of the Word 'Ghetto'" in *Essential Papers on Jewish Culture in Renaissance and Baroque Italy*. New York: Schocken, 1992.

Berger, Johannes. "The Capitalist Road to Communism: Groundwork and Practicability." *Theory and Society*, 15.5(1986): 689–694.

Berger, Peter L., and Thomas Luckmann. *The Social Construction of Reality: A Treatise in the Sociology of Knowledge*. New York: Anchor Books, 1966.

Berger, Peter. "The Desecularization of the World: An Overview." In *The Desecularization of the World*, Peter L. Berger, ed., Washington, DC: Ethics and Public Policy Center, 1999.

Berkowitz, Dan. "Refining the Gatekeeper Metaphor for Local Television News." *Journal of Broadcasting & Electronic Media*, Winter 1990, 55–68.

Bernard, Jessie. *The Future of Marriage*. New York: World, 1972.

Berner, Robert, and Adrienne Carter, "Swiping Back at Credit-Card Fraud" in *Business Week*, July 11, 2005, p. 72.

Bernhardt, Annette, Martina Morris, and Mark S. Handcock. "Women's Gains or Men's Losses? A Closer Look at the Shrinking Gender Gap in Earnings." *American Journal of Sociology*, 101 (1995): 302–328.

Bettencourt, B. A., and Kernaham, C., "A Meta-Analysis of Agression in the Presence of Violent Cues: Effect of Gender Differences and Aversive Provocation." *Aggressive Behavior* 23 (1997): 447–456.

Bianchi, S. M. "Maternal Employment and Time with Children: Dramatic Change or Surprising Continuity?" *Demography*, 37 (2000): 401–414.

Bianchi, S. M., and Casper, L. M., "American Families." *Population Bulletin*, 55, 4 (2000): 1–43.

Bianchi, S. M., Milkie, M. A., Sayer, L. C., and Robinson, J. P. "Is Anyone Doing the Housework? Trends in the Gender Division of Household Labor." *Social Forces*, 79 (2000): 191–228.

Bieber, Irving, et al. *Homosexuality: A Psychoanalytic Perspective*. New York: Basic Books, 1962.

Biernat, Monica, and Kathleen Fuegen. "Shifting Standards and the Evaluation of Competence: Complexity in Gender-Based Judgment and Decision Making." *Journal of Social Issues*, 57(4), 2001, 707–724.

Bilger, Burkhard. "The Height Gap." *The New Yorker*. April 5, 2004, 38–45.

Billingsley, Andrew. *Mighty Like a River: The Black Church and Social Reform*. New York: Oxford, 1999.

Birdsong, David, Ed. *Second Language Acquisition and the Critical Period Hypothesis*. Mahwah, NJ: Lawrence Erlbaum, 1999.

Birn, Raymond. *Crisis, Absolutism, Revolution: Europe, 1648–1789*. New York: Harcourt, 1992.

Black, D., et al., "Demographics of the Gay and Lesbian Population in the United States: Evidence from Available Systematic Data Sources." *Demography*, 37 (2000): 139–154.

Blackwell, J. E. "Persistence and Change in Inter-Group Relations: The Crisis upon U." *Social Problems*, 29 (1982): 325–346.

Blair-Loy, Mary. 2003. *Competing Devotions: Career and Family among Women Executives*. Cambridge, MA: Harvard University Press.

Blank, J. "The Kid No One Noticed." *U.S. News and World Report*, December, 1998, 27.

Blau, Judith R., and Peter M. Blau, "The Cost of Inequality: Metropolitan Structure and Violent Crime." *American Sociological Review*, Vol. 47, no. 1 (February, 1982): 114–29.

Blau, Peter. *Exchange and Power in Social Life*. New York: Wiley, 1964.

Blau, Peter M., and Otis Duncan. *American Occupational Structure*. New York: John Wiley & Sons, 1967.

Blumstein, Philip and Pepper Schwartz. *American Couples*. New York: William Morrow, 1983.

Bochenek, M., and A. W. Brown. *Hatred in the Hallways: Violence and Discrimination against Lesbian, Gay, Bisexual, and Transgender Students in U.S. Schools*. New York: Human

Rights Watch, 2001. Available online at: www.hrw.org/reports/2001/uslgbt/toc.htm

Bock, Jane, "Doing the Right Thing? Single Mothers by Choice and the Struggle for Legitimacy." *Gender & Society*, 14, 1 (2000): 62–86.

Bogardus, Emery S. 1925 "Social Distance and its Origins." *Sociology and Social Research*, 9, 216–225.

Bogardus, Emery S. 1933. "A Social Distance Scale." *Sociology and Social Research*, 22, 265–271.

Bonacich, Edna, and Richard P. Appelbaum. *Behind the Label: Inequality in the Los Angeles Garment Industry*. Berkeley: University of California Press, 2000.

Bonnickesen, Thomas. "Forests Can Give Us Breathing Room on Kyoto Rules," *Houston Chronicle*, November 15, 2000.

Booth, Alan, and Paul R. Amato. 2001. "Parental Predivorce Relations and Offspring Postdivorce Well-being." *Journal of Marriage and the Family* 63:197–212.

Bordo, Susan. *The Male Body*. New York: Farrar Straus, and Giroux, 2000.

Boswell, John. *Same-Sex Unions in Premodern Europe*. New York: Vintage, 1995.

Bouffard, J. A. "The Influence of Sexual Arousal on Rational Decision Making in Sexual Aggression." *Journal of Criminal Justice* 30(2) 2002: 121–134.

"Bound for Success" *Foreign Policy*, May–June, 2006, pp. 26–7.

Bourdieu, Pierre. *Distinction: A Social Critique of the Judgment of Taste*. Cambridge, MA: Harvard University Press, 1984.

Bourgois, Phillipe, *In Search of Respect: Selling Crack in El Barrio*. New York: Cambridge University Press, 1995.

Bowen, James. *A History of Western Education: Civilization of Europe, Sixth to Sixteenth Century*. New York: Palgrave Macmillan, 1976.

Bowles, Samuel. *Schooling in Capitalist America: Educational Reform and the Contradictions of Economic Life*. New York: Basic Books, 1976.

Boyd, Elizabeth A., Richard A. Berk, and Karl A. Hamner. "Motivated by Hatred or Prejudice: Categorization of Hate-Motivated Crimes in Two Police Divisions." *Law and Society Review* 30, 4(1996): 819–850.

Boyd, W., and E. King. *History of Western Education*. Lanham, MD: Littlefield Adams, 1978.

Boykoff, Maxwell T., and Jules M. Boykoff. "Balance as Bias: Global Warming and the U.S. Prestige Press." *Global Environmental Change* 14 (2004): 125–136.

Brewer, Marilyn, and Miller, N. 1984. "Beyond the Contact Hypothesis: Theoretical Perspectives on Desegregation." In N. Miller & M. Brewer (Eds.), *Groups in Contact: The Psychology of Desegregation*. New York: Academic Press.

British Broadcasting Company, "Recycling Around the World," June 25, 2005, available at: http://news.bbc.co.uk/2/hi/europe/4620041.stm

Broder, John, and Carl Hulse, "Republicans Denounce Ex-Lawmaker." *New York Times*, November 30, 2005, A-29.

Brodkin, Karen. *How Jews Became White Folks and What That Says about Race in America*. New Brunswick, NJ: Rutgers University Press, 1998.

Brohman, John. "Postwar Development in the Asian NICs: Does the Neoliberal Model Fit Reality?" *Economic Geography* 72.2(1996): 107–130.

Brooks, David. "Nonconformity Is Skin Deep." *The New York Times*, August 27, 2006.

Brott, Armin. "The Battered Statistic Syndrome." *Washington Post*, July, 31, 1994.

Brown, Lester R. *Outgrowing the Earth: The Food Security Challenge in an Age of Falling Water Tables and Rising Temperatures*. New York: Norton, 2005.

Brown, Michael E., ed., *Theories of War and Peace*. Cambridge, MA: MIT Press, 1998.

Brown, Susan L., Gary R. Lee, and Jennifer Roebuck Bulanda. "Cohabitation among Older Adults: A National Portrait." *The Journals of Gerontology Series B: Psychological Sciences and Social Sciences*, 61 (2006): S71–S79.

Brown, Tony N., "Critical Race Theory Speaks to the Sociology of Mental Health: Mental Health Problems Produced by Racial Stratification." *Journal of Health and Social Behavior*, 44 (September 2003): 292–301.

Brownmiller, Susan. *Against Our Will*. New York: Simon and Schuster, 1976.

Buchanan, Pat. *The Death of the West: How Dying Populations and Immigrant Invasions Imperil Our Country and Civilization*. New York: Thomas Dunne Books, 2002.

Bullard, Robert, and Glenn Johnson, eds. *Just Transportation: Dismantling Race and Class Barriers to Mobility*. Gabriola Island, British Columbia: New Society Publishers, 1997.

Bumiller, Elisabeth. "Bush Urges Graduates to Use Science to Protect Human Dignity." *New York Times*, May 7, 2006, 34.

Bumpass, Larry, and H. Lu.. "Trends in cohabitation and implications for children's family contexts in the United States." *Population Studies*, 54, 2000, pp. 29–41.

Burawoy, Michael. *Manufacturing Consent*. Chicago: University of Chicago Press, 1980.

Burdick, Eugene, and Arthur J. Brodbeck. *American Voting Behavior*. Westport, CT: Geenwood Press, 1977.

Bureau of Labor Statistics, "Highlights of Women's Earnings in 2005," Report 995. Washington, D.C.: U.S. Department of Labor, 2006.

Bureau of Labor Statistics, "Employed persons by Industry, Sex, Race, and Occupation," Washington, D.C.: 2006. U.S. Department of Labor. Available at: http://www.bls.gov/cps/cpsaat17.pdf

Bureau of Labor Statistics, "Wives Who Earn More than Their Husbands, 1987–2003," Table 25, *Annual Economic Supplement*. Washington, D.C.: U.S. Department of Labor, 2005. Available at http://www.bls.gov/cps/wlf-table25-2005.pdf

Bureau of Labor Statistics, "Contingent and Alternative Employment Arrangements, February 2005." Washington, D.C.: U.S. Department of Labor, 2005.

Bureau of Labor Statistics, "Characteristics of Minimum Wage Workers: 2005." Washington, D.C.: U.S. Department of Labor, 2006. Available at www.bls.gov/cpsminwage2005tbls.htm.

Bureau of Labor Statistics, "Small Business Research Summary." Washington, D.C.: U.S. Department of Labor, 2004.

Bureau of Labor Statistics, 2004. "Annual Averages of Occupations." Washington, D.C.: Department of Labor.

Bureau of Labor Statistics, 2000. "Report on the Youth Labor Force, 2000." Washington, D.C.: Department of Labor.

Burleson, William E. *Bi America: Myths, Truths and Struggles of an Invisible Community*. London: Harrington Park Press, 2005.

Bush, George W. "The Trafficking in Persons." National Security Presidential Directive issued on February 25, 2003. Cited at: http://feminist. com/violence/spot/tourism.html

Butler, Katy. "Beyond Rivalry: A Hidden World of Sibling Violence." *New York Times*, February 28, 2006.

Butler, Robert. "Age-ism: Another Form of Bigotry." *The Gerontologist*, 9 (1969): 243–246.

Buttel, Frederick H. "New Directions in Environmental Sociology." *Annual Review of Sociology*, 13 (1987): 465–488.

Califano, J. A. "A Punishment-Only Prison Policy." *America* (February, 1998): 3–4.

Cameron, Rondo, and Larry Neal. *A Concise Economic History of the World*. New York: Oxford University Press, 2002.

Campbell, A., Muncer, S., and Odber, J., "Aggression and Testosterone: Testing a Bio-Social Model." *Aggressive Behavior* 23 (1997): 229–238.

Campbell-Kelly, Martin. *From Airline Reservations to Sonic the Hedgehog: A History of the Software Industry*. Cambridge, MA: MIT Press, 2004.

Cancian, Francesca. *The Feminization of Love*. New York: Cambridge University Press, 1987.

Candland, D. K. *Feral Children and Clever Animals: Reflections on Human Nature*. New York: Oxford University Press, 1993.

Cannon, Angie. "DWB: Driving While Black." *U.S. News and World Report*, March 15, 1999, p. 72.

Capron, Christiane, and Michel Duyme. "Assessment of Effects of Socioeconomic Status on IQ in a Full Cross-Fostering Study." *Nature*, August 17, 1989, 552–553.

Cardoso, Fernando, and Ernesto Faletto. *Dependency and Development in Latin America*. Berkeley: University of California Press, 1978.

Carrasquillo, Hector. "The Puerto Rican Family." In *Minority Families in the United States: A Multicultural Perspective*, Ronald L. Taylor, ed., pp. 82–94. Englewood Cliffs, NJ: Prentice Hall, 1994.

Carrington, Christopher. *No Place Like Home : Relationships and Family Life among Lesbians and Gay Men*. Chicago: University of Chicago Press, 2002.

Carrington, William J., and Bruce C. Fallick. "Do Some Workers Have Minimum Wage Careers?" *Monthly Labor Review*, May 2001:18, 25.

Carter, Susan B. ed., *Historical Statistics of the University States*. New York: Cambridge University Press 2006.

Casper, Lynne M., and Suzanne M. Bianchi. *Continuity and Change in the American Family*. Thousand Oaks, CA: Sage Publications, 2002.

Castles, Stephen, and Alistair Davidson. *Citizenship and Migration: Globalization and the Politics of Migration*. New York: Routledge, 2000.

Catalyst. *Women of Color in Corporate Management: Three Years Later*. New York: Catalyst, Inc., 2003. Accessed at www.catalystwomen.org

Catton, William, Jr., and Riley E. Dunlap. "Environmental Sociology: A New Paradigm." *The American Sociologist*, 13 (1978):41–49.

Center for Changing Families, online briefing, July 2, 2007.

Center for Communication and Social Policy, University of California, Santa Barbara. *The National Television Violence Study*. Thousand Oaks, CA: Sage, 1997.

Centers for Disease Control, 2006. "Deaths, percent of total deaths, and death rates for the 15 leading causes of death in 10-year age groups, by race and sex: United States, 2003." National Center for Health Statistics, available at: http://www.cdc.gov/nchs/data/dvs/lcwk2_2003.pdf

Centers for Disease Control, Advance Data No. 362, September 15, 2005.

Centers for Disease Control "First Birth Rates by Age of Mother, According to Race and Hispanic Origin." Available at: http://www.cdc.gov/nchs/data/statab/t991x02.pdf

Centers for Disease Control. *Healthy People, 2010*. Atlanta: Center for Disease Control, 2006.

Centers for Disease Control. "Overweight" 2007. Available at: http://www.cdc.gov/nchs/fastats/overwt.htm

Centers for Disease Control and Prevention, "Leading Causes of Death in Females, United States, 2004." Washington, D.C.: CDC, 2005.

Centers for Disease Control and Prevention, "Leading Causes of Death in Males, United States, 2004." Washington, D.C.: CDC, 2005.

Center for Educational Reform. "Charter Schools by State." 2007. available at: http://www.edreform.com/upload/ncsw-numbers.pdf

Center for Women's Business Research, "Women-Owned Businesses in the United States, 2006: A Fact Sheet." Washington, D.C.: Center for Women's Business Research, 2007.

Central Intelligence Agency, *The World Factbook, 2006*. Washington, DC: Central Intelligence Agency, 2007. Available at https://www.cia.gov/library/publications/the-world-factbook

Central Intelligence Agency, *The World Factbook, 2007*. Washington, DC: Central Intelligence Agency, 2007. Available at https://www.cia.gov/library/publications/the-world-factbook

Chaffee, John. *The Thorny Gates of Learning in Sung China: A Social History of Examinations*. New York: Cambridge University Press, 1985.

Chambliss, William J. *Power, Politics and Crime*. Boulder, CO: Westview Press, 2000.

Chandler, Alfred Jr., and Bruce Mazlish. *Multinational Corporations and the New Global History*. Cambridge, U.K.: Cambridge University Press, 2005.

Chandler, Tertius. *Four Thousand Years of Urban Growth: An Historical Census*. Lewiston, NY: Edwin Mellen Press, 1987.

Charles, Maria, and David B. Grusky. *Occupational Ghettos: The Worldwide Segregation of Women and Men*. Stanford, CA: Stanford University Press, 2004.

Chase-Dunn, Christopher. "The System of World Cities." In *Urbanization in the World Economy*, M. Timberlake, ed., pp. 269–292. Beverly Hills, CA: Sage, 1985.

Chasin, B. H. *Inequality and Violence in the United States: Casualties of Capitalism*. New York: Humanities Press, 1997.

Chatzky, Jean Sherman. "The Big Squeeze." *Money*, October 1, 1999.

Chauncey, George. *Gay New York*. New York: Basic Books, 1993.

Chen, Shaohua, and Martin Ravalon. "How Have the World's Poorest Fared Since the Early 1980s?" Paper prepared for The World Bank, 2006.

Chernow, Ron. *The House of Morgan: An American Banking Dynasty and the Rise of Modern Finance*. New York: Atlantic Monthly Press, 1990.

Chernow, Ron. *Titan: The Life of John D. Rockefeller Sr*. New York: Random House, 1998.

Cherry, Conrad, Betty A. DeBerg, and Amanda Porterfield. *Religion on Campus*. Chapel Hill: University of North Carolina Press, 2003.

Chesney-Lind Daly, Meda. "Women and Crime: The Female Offender." *Signs* 12: 78–96.

Chevan, A. "As Cheaply as One: Cohabitation in the Older Population." *Journal of Marriage and the Family*, 58 (1996): 656–667.

Children Now. *Fall Colors: Prime-Time Diversity Report 2003–2004*. Oakland, CA: Children Now, 2005.

Children Now. *Fair Play: Violence, Gender and Race in Video Games*. Oakland, CA: Children Now, 2001.

Chilman, Catherine Street. "Hispanic Families in the United States: Research Perspectives." In *Family Ethnicity: Strengths in Diversity*, Harriet Pipes McAdoo, ed. Newbury Park, CA: Sage, 1999.

Christakis, Dimitri A. "Early Television Exposure and Subsequent Attention Problems in Children." *Pediatrics*, April, 2004.

Chubb, John, and Terry Moe. *Politics, Markets, and America's Schools*. Washington, DC: The Brookings Institution, 1990.

Cipolla, Carlo M. *Before the Industrial Revolution*. New York: Norton, 1994.

Clark, David D., "Analysis of Return Rates of the Inmate College Program Participants." State of New York Department of Correctional Services, 1991.

Clark, Nancy, and William H. Worger. *South Africa: The Rise and Fall of Apartheid*. Nashville, TN: Longmans, 2004.

Clarkwest, Andrew. "African American Marital Disruption in the 20th Century: What Changed? What Did Not?" Ann Arbor: Institute for Social Research, University of Michigan, 2006. Working paper.

Clausewitz, Claus von. *On War*. Michael Howard and Peter Paret, trans. Princeton, NJ: Princeton University Press, 1984. (Originally published in 1832.)

"Cleaning Up," a special report in *The Economist*, June 2, 2007, pp. 3–6.

Cleveland, Alice Ann, Jean Craven, and Maryanne Danfelser. *Universals of Culture*. Intercom, 1992–1993.

Cloward, Richard A., and Lloyd E. Ohlin. *Delinquency and Opportunity: A Theory of Delinquent Gangs*. New York: The Free Press, 1960.

CNN, "Benjamin Spock, 1903–1988." Obituary, broadcast, March 15 1988.

Cohany, Sharon R., and Emy Sock, "Trends in Labor Force Participation of Married Mothers of Infants." *Monthly Labor Review Online*, Vol. 130, no. 2 (February, 2007). Available at: http://www.bls.gov/opub/mlr/2007/02/art2exc.htm.

Cohen, Albert R. *Delinquent Boys: The Culture of the Gang*. New York: The Free Press, 1955.

Cohen, Joel E. *How Many People Can the Earth Support?* New York: Norton, 1995.

Cohen, Patricia. "As Ethics Panels Expand Grip, No Research Field Is Off Limits." *New York Times*, February 28, 2007, 1, 15.

Cole, David. "When Race Is the Reason," *The Nation*, March 15, 1999, pp. 22–24.

Cole, T. B. "Rape at U.S. Colleges Often Fueled by Alcohol." *Journal of the American Medical Association* 296 (August 2, 2006): 504–5.

Coleman, James, Thomas Hoffer, and Sally Kilgore. *High School Achievement: Public, Catholic, and Private Schools Compared*. New York: Basic Books, 1982.

Coleman, Kenneth, ed. *A History of Georgia*. Athens: University of Georgia Press, 1991.

Collins, Patricia Hill. *Fighting Words: Black Women and the Search for Justice*. Minneapolis: University of Minnesota Press, 1998.

Collins, Patricia Hill. 1990. *Black Feminist Thought: Knowledge, Consciousness, and the Politics of Empowerment* New York: Routledge.

Collins, Randall. *The Credential Society: A Historical Sociology of Education and Stratification*. New York: Academic Press, 1979.

Coltrane, Scott. *Family Man: Fatherhood, Housework, and Gender Equity*. New York: Oxford University Press, 1996.

Columbia Dictionary of Quotations, Robert Andrews, ed. New York: Columbia University Press, 1993.

Commission on Women in the Profession, American Bar Association 2006. *Charting Our Progress: The Status of Women in the Profession Today*. Chicago: American Bar Association.

Computer Security Institute and Federal Bureau of Investigation. *Computer Crime and Security Survey*. 2005. Available at: http:// www.cpppe.umd.edu/Bookstore/Documents/2005CSISurvey .pdf

Comstock, George, and Erica Scharrer. *Television*. San Diego, CA: Academic Press, 1999.

Condry, J., and S. Condry. "Sex Differences: A Study in the Eye of the Beholder." *Child Development*, 47, 1976.

Conley, Kevin. "The Players." *The New Yorker*, July 11, 2005.

Connell, R. W. *Masculinities*. Berkeley: University of California Press, 1995.

Conrad, Peter, and Joseph W. Schneider. *Deviance and Medicalization: From Badness to Sickness*. Philadelphia: Temple University Press, 1992.

Consoli, John, "Nielsen: TV Viewing Grows." *Mediaweek*, September 21, 2006. Available at: http://www.mediaweek.com/ mw/news/recent_display.jsp?vnu_content_id=1003154980

Consoli, John. "Media Convergence Catching Hold." *Media Week*, March 5, 2005.

Conte, Christopher, and Albert R. Karr. "An Outline of the U.S. Economy," chapter 3. International Information Programs, U.S. Government. Available at http://usinfo.state.gov/products/ pubs/oecon/

Cookson, Peter W. Jr., and Caroline Hodges Percell. *Preparing for Power: America's Elite Boarding Schools*. New York: Basic Books, 1985.

Cooley, Charles Horton. *Human Nature and the Social Order*, (1902). New York: Transaction, 1983.

Cooley, Charles Horton. *Social Organization: A Study of the Larger Mind* (1902). New York: Transaction, 1983.

Coontz, Stephanie. *Social Origins of Private Life: A History of American Families, 1600–1900*. New York: Verso, 1988.

Coontz, Stephanie. *Marriage: A History*. New York: Viking, 2005.

Cooper, Frederick. *Colonialism in Question: Theory, Knowledge, History*. Berkeley: University of California Press, 2005.

Corbin, Juliet, and Anselm L. Strauss. "Managing Chronic Illness at Home: Three Lines of Work." *Qualitative Sociology*, 8 (3) (1985): 224–227.

Cornell, Claire, and Richard Gelles. "Adolescent to Parent Violence." *Urban and Social Change Review*, 15 (1982): 8–14.

Coser, Lewis A. *The Functions of Social Conflict*. Glencoe, IL: The Free Press, 1956.

Costa, P. T., and McCrae, R. R. "Age Difference in Personality Structure: A Cluster Analytic Approach." *Journal of Gerontology*, 31 (1978): 564–570.

Costello, B. J., and P. R. Vowell, "Testing Control Theory and Differential Association: A Reanalysis of the Richmond Youth Project Data." *Criminology* 37(4) (1999): 815–842.

Coult, Allan. *Cross-Tabulations of Murdock's World Ethnographic Sample*. Columbia: University of Missouri Press, 1965.

Council for American Private Education, "Benefits of Private Education" 2005, available at: http://www.capenet.org/bene-fits4.html#fn11

Coupland, Douglas, *Generation X: Tales for an Accelerated Culture*. New York: St. Martin's Press. 1991.

Couprie, Helene, "Time Allocation within the Family: Welfare Implications of Life in a Couple." *Economic Journal*, January, 2007: 1–12.

Courtenay, William.H. "College Men's Health: An Overview and a Call to Action" in *Journal of American College Health* 46(6), 1998.

Covington, Dennis. *Salvation on Sand Mountain*. New York: Penguin, 1996.

Craig, Kellina M., and Craig R. Waldo. "So, What's a Hate Crime Anyway? Young Adults' Perceptions of Hate Crimes, Victims and Perpetrators." *Law and Human Behavior*, 20, 2(April 1996): 113–129.

Crary, David. "Bible Belt Leads U.S. in Divorces." Associated Press, November 12, 1999; accessed at www.ncpa.org/pd/social/pd111999g.html

Cremin, Lawrence A. *The Republic and the School: Horace Mann on the Education of Free Men*. New York: Teachers College, 1957.

Crittenden, Danielle. *What Our Mothers Didn't Tell Us: Why Happiness Eludes the Modern Woman*. New York: Simon & Schuster, 1999.

Crittenden, Ann. *If You've Raised Kids, You Can Manage Anything*, New York: Gotham, 2005.

Crittenden, Ann. *The Price of Motherhood*. New York: Owl Books, 2002.

Crompton, Rosemary. *Class and Stratification: An Introduction to Current Debates*. Cambridge, U.K.: Polity, 1993.

Cross, Harry, Genevieve Kenney, Jane Mell, and Wendy Zimmerman. *Employer Hiring Practices: Differential Treatment of Hispanic and Anglo Job Seekers*. Washington, DC: The Urban Institute Press, 1990.

Croteau, David, and William Hoynes. *Media/Society: Industries, Images, and Audiences*. Thousand Oaks, CA: Pine Forge Press, 2003.

Cumings, Bruce. *Korea's Place in the Sun*. New York: W. W. Norton, 1998.

Cummings, H. J. "Permanent Temps." *Chicago Tribune*, June 8, 2004: 12.

Currie, Elliot. *Confronting Crime: An American Challenge*. New York: Pantheon, 1985.

Curtis, Michael Kent, and Shannon Gilreath. "Transforming Teenagers into Oral Sex Felons: The Persistence of Crime against Nature after *Lawrence v. Texas*." Unpublished law review paper, Wake Forest School of Law, 2007.

Dabney, Lewis. *Edmund Wilson: A Life*. New York: Farrar, Straus & Giroux, 2005.

Dahl, Gordon, and Enrico Moretti. "The Demand for Sons: Evidence from Divorce, Fertility, and Shotgun Marriage." Washington, D.C.: National Bureau of Economic Research, Paper # 10281, Feb. 2004.

Dahl, Robert A. *Democracy and Its Critics*. New Haven and London: Yale University Press, 1989.

Dailard, C. "Sex Education: Politicians, Parents, Teachers and Teens." *The Guttmacher Report on Public Policy*, 4 (1) (2001): 9–12.

Dalakar, Joseph. 2001. "Poverty in the United States: 2000." *Current Population Reports Ser*. P60, No. 214. Washington, DC: U.S. Government Printing Office.

Daly, Kathleen, "Neither Conflict Nor Labeling Nor Paternalism Will Suffice: Intersections of Race, Ethnicity, Gender, and Family in Criminal Court Decisions." *Crime and Delinquency* 35 (1989): 136–168.

Daly, Kathleen, and Chesney-Lind, M., "Feminism and Criminology." *Justice Quarterly* 5 (1988): 497–538.

Daly, Martin, and Margaret Wilson. "Child Maltreatment from a Sociobiological Perspective." *New Directions for Child Development*, 11 (1981), 93–112.

Daly, Martin, and Margo Wilson. *The Truth about Cinderella: A Darwinian View of Parental Love*. New Haven, CT: Yale University Press, 1999.

Darroch, J. E., et al., "Changing Emphases in Sexuality Education in U.S. Public Secondary Schools, 1988–1999." *Family Planning Perspectives* 32 (5) (2000): 204–211, 265.

Davidson, Lance C. *Ludicrous Laws and Mindless Misdemeanors*. New York: Wiley, 1998.

Davis, Devra Lee, Michelle B. Gottlieb, and Julie R. Stampnitzky. "Reduced Ratio of Male to Female Births in Several Industrial Countries: A Sentinel Health Indicator?" *Journal of the American Medical Association*, 279, 13 (April 1998).

Davis, Gerald, Doug McAdam, W. Richard Scott, and Mayer Zald, *Social Movements and Organization Theory*. New York: Cambridge University Press, 2005.

Davis, James A., Tom W. Smith, and Peter V. Marsden. *General Social Surveys 1972–2004*: [Cumulative file] [Computer file]. 2nd ICPSR version. Chicago, IL: National Opinion Research Center [producer], 2005. Storrs, CT: Roper Center for Public Opinion Research, University of Connecticut/Ann Arbor, MI: Inter-university Consortium for Political and Social Research/Berkeley, CA: Computer-assisted Survey Methods Program, University of California [distributors], 2005.

Davis, Karen. "Aiming High: Targets for the U.S. Health System" annual president's report, *The Commonwealth Fund*, April 2006; available at: http://www.commonwealthfund.org/about-us/aboutus_show.htm?doc_id=334742

Davis, Kingsley, and Wilbert E. Moore. 1945. "Some Principles of Stratification." *ASR* 10(2, 1945):242–49.

Davis, Wendy. "Yahoo! Creates Original Reality Show for the Web." *Online Media Daily*, December 14, 2005.

Dawkins, Richard. *The God Delusion*. Boston, MA: Houghton-Mifflin, 2007.

Dawkins, Richard. *The Selfish Gene*. New York: Oxford University Press, 1990.

De Bens, Els, Mary Kelly, and Marit Bakke. "Television Content: Dallasification of Culture?" In *Dynamics of Media Politics: Broadcast and Electronic Media in Western Europe*, Kareen Siune and Wolfgang Treutzschler, eds., pp. 75–100. London: Sage Press, 1992.

De Rougemont, Denis. *Love in the Western World*. Princeton, NJ: Princeton University Press, 1983.

Dean, Cornelia, "Scientific Savvy? In U.S., Not Much," *New York Times*, August 30, 2005.

Defronzo, James. *Revolutions and Revolutionary Movements*. Boulder, Co: Westview Press, 1996.

Degler, Carl N. *At Odds: Women and the Family in America from the Revolution to the Present*. New York: Oxford University Press, 1980.

DeGolia, Rachel. "Moving beyond Political Deadlock: Health Reform Initiatives in the States." Universal Healthcare Action Network, 2007. Available at www.uhcan.org

Deloitte. 2004 Global Security Survey. 2004 http://www.deloitte.com/dtt/cda/doc/content/dtt_financialservices_2005GlobalSecuritySurvey_2004-07-21.pdf

Deloitte. 2005 Global Security Survey. 2005 http://www.deloitte.com/dtt/cda/doc/content/dtt_financialservices_2005GlobalSecuritySurvey_2005-07-21.pdf

deMause, Lloyd. *The History of Childhood*. London: Souvenir Press, 1976.

DeNavas-Walt, Carmen, Bernadette D. Proctor, and Cheryl Hill Lee, 2006. *Income, Poverty, and Health Insurance Coverage in the United States: 2005*. Washington, D.C.: U.S. Bureau of the Census.

Dennett, Daniel C. *Breaking the Spell: Religion as a Natural Phenomenon*. New York: Viking, 2006.

DeParle, Jason. "Census Reports a Sharp Increase in Never-Married Mothers; Puncturing Stereotypes of Out-of-Wedlock Births." *New York Times*, July 14, 1993.

Deux, Kay, and Lawrence S. Wrightsman. *Social Psychology*, 5th edition. New York: Thomson/Brooks Cole, 1988.

deVaus, David, and Ian McAllister. "Gender Differences in Religion: A Test of the Structural Location Theory." *American Sociological Review,* 52 (1987): 472–481.

Devor, Holly. *FTM: Female-to-Male Transsexuals in Society.* Bloomington, IL: Indiana University Press, 1997.

Digest of Educational Statistics, Table 254, "Bachelor's Degrees Conferred by Degree-Granting Institutes, by Discipline and Division, Selected Years, 1970–71 through 2004–05." Washington, D.C.: National Center for Education Statistics, 2006.

"Diversity and Communication Values in Families," *Journal of Family Communication,* 3, 2003.

Diversity Inc. "Second Generation Latinos." September, 2005.

Dixon, John. *Searching for Aboriginal Languages: Memoirs of a Field Worker.* Chicago: University of Queensland Press, 1983.

Dobbs, Lou, "The Generation Gap." *U.S. News & World Report,* May 23, 2005: 58.

Dobbs, Lou, "The Imbalance of Trade." *U.S. News & World Report,* March 30, 2004: 44.

Dobbs, Michael. "NEA, States Challenge 'No Child' Program." *The Washington Post,* April 21, 2005, A21.

Dobson, James. *Marriage under Fire: Why We Must Win This Battle.* Colorado Springs, CO: Multnomah Publishers, 2004.

Domhoff, G. William. *Who Rules America? Power and Politics*, 4th edition. Boston: McGraw-Hill, 2002.

Domhoff, G. William. *Who Still Rules America.* Englewood Cliffs, NJ: Prentice Hall, 1986.

Donato, Katherine, "Programming for Change? The Growing Demand among Computer Specialists." *Job Queues, Gender Queues,* B. Reskin and P. Roos, eds. Philadelphia: Temple University Press, 1990.

Donato, Katherine, and Chizuko Wakabayashi. "The Consequences of Caregiving: Effects on Women's Employment and Earnings." *Population Research and Policy Review,* 24(4), 2005: 467–488.

Donnerstein, Edward, and Daniel Linz, "Mass Media, Sexual Violence and Male Viewers" in *Men Confront Pornography,* Michael Kimmel, ed. New York: Crown, 1990, pp. 219–232.

Donnerstein, Edward., *The Question of Pornography.* New York: Free Press, 1985.

Donohue, John, and Steven Levitt, "The Impact of Legalised Abortion on Crime." *Quarterly Review of Economics,* May, 2001.

Dorr, Aimee. *Television and Children.* Beverly Hills, CA: Sage, 1986.

"Dossier: Red-State Values." *American Prospect,* January 4, 2006.

Douglass, Frederick. *Narrative of the Life of Frederick Douglass, American Slave* (1845). John W. Blessingame, Fohn Ro McKivigan, Peter P. Hinks, eds. New Haven, CT: Yale University Press, 2001.

Doweiko, Harold. *Concepts of Chemical Dependency,* 3rd ed. Pacific Grove, CA: Brooks-Cole, 1996.

Doyle, Rodger. "Middle of the Country: As Farming Declines, Rural America Adapts to Survive." *Scientific American* (August 2004): 27.

Doyle, Roger. "Ethnic Groups in the World." *Scientific American,* September 1998, p. 30.

"Dreams Only Money Can Buy" in *Business Week,* April 14, 2003, p. 66.

Dreier, Peter, John Mollenkopf, and Todd Swanstrom, 2005. *Place Matters: Metropolitics for the Twenty-First Century.* Lawrence, KS: University Press of Kansas.

"Drug War Facts." Common Sense for Drug Policy (CSDP), 2006. www.csdp.org

Du Bois, W. E. B. *The Philadelphia Negro* (1899). Elijah Anderson, Islabel Eaton, eds. Philadelphia: University of Pennsylvania Press, 1998.

Duberman, Martin. *Cures.* New York: Dutton, 1991.

Dudenhefer, Paul. "Poverty in the Rural United States." *Focus* 15.1(1993): 37–46.

Dunn, T., and D. Holtz-Eakin. "Financial Capital, Human Capital and the Transition to Self-Employment: Evidence from Intergenerational Links." *Journal of Labor Economics,* 18 (2000): 282–305.

Durkheim, Emile [1899]. *The Division of Labor in Society.* New York: The Free Press, 1997.

Durkheim, Emile. *Division of Labor in Society.* New York: The Free Press, 1964a. Orig. 1893.

Durkheim, Emile. *The Rules of Sociological Method.* New York: The Free Press, 1964b. Orig. 1895.

Dworkin, Andrea. *Heartbreak: The Political Memoir of a Feminist Militant.* New York: Basic Books, 2002.

Dworkin, Andrea. *Intercourse.* New York: Free Press, 1985.

Dworkin, Andrea. *Pornography: Men Possessing Women.* New York: Dutton, 1981.

Dychtwald, Ken. *The Power Years.* New York: Wiley, 2006.

Dyer, Richard. *Heavenly Bodies: Film Stars and Society.* New York: St. Martins, 1987.

Ebaugh, Helen Rose Fuchs. *Becoming an Ex: The Process of Role Exit.* Chicago, IL: University of Chicago Press, 1988.

Eberstadt, Nicholas, "Why Poverty Doesn't Rate." *The Washington Post,* September 3, 2006: B01.

Economic Mobility Project, *Economic Mobility: Is the American Dream Alive and Well?* The Pew Charitable Trusts, 2006.

Economic Policy Institute. *The State of Working America.* Washington, D.C. 2007.

Economic Policy Institute. *The State of Working America 2004–05.* Ithaca, NY: Cornell University Press, 2005.

Economist, "The Flicker of a Brighter Future." September 7, 2006: 51.

Economist, "The World Is Our Oyster." October 5, 2006: 35–37.

Economist, 2005, "Why Women Live Longer Than Men." January 13, npl.

Economist, "Nollywood Dreams." July 27, 2006: 48.

Economist, "Going Global: Why Street Things Are Getting Nastier." February 26, 2005, p. 29.

Education Trust. "Funding Gaps, 2006." Available at: http:// www2 .edtrust.org/EdTrust/Press+Room/Funding+Gap+2006.htm

Edwards, S. S. M., "Neither Bad Nor Mad: The Female Violent Offender Reassessed." *Women's Studies International Forum* 9 (1986): 79–87.

Efron, Sonni. "Eating Disorders on the Increase in Asia," 2005. Available at www.dimensionsmagazine.com/news/asia/html

Ehrenreich, Barbara. *Nickel and Dimed: On (Not) Getting by in America.* New York: Owl Books, 2001.

Eisenstein, Elizabeth. *The Printing Revolution in Early Modern Europe.* New York: Cambridge University Press, 1993.

Ekman, P., and Wallace V. Friesen, "A New Pan Cultural Facial Expression of Emotion." *Motivation and Emotion,* 10(2), 1986: 886–891.

Ekman, Paul, and Wallace V. Friesen. *Facial Action Coding System: A Technique for the Measurement of Facial Movement.* Palo Alto, CA: Consulting Psychologists Press, 1978.

Elder, Glenn, and Pavalko, Elizabeth. "Work Careers in Men's Later Years: Transitions, Trajectories and Historical Change." *Journal of Gerontology,* 48(4), 1993: S180–S191.

Eldridge, J., J. Kitzinger, and K. Williams. *The Mass Media and Power in Modern Britain*. Oxford, U.K.: Oxford University Press, 1997.

Ellin, Abby. "God on Campus." *Link, The College Magazine,* November 1997.

Elliot, Jane. *The Eye of the Storm*, DVD, 1970.

Ellis, Havelock. *Studies in the Psychology of Sex* (1910). Charleston, SC: BiblioBazaar, 2007.

Employee Benefits Research Institute, 2000. "2000 Retirement Confidence Survey," Washington, D.C.

Ericson, Richard V., and Keven D. Haggerty. *Policing the Risk Society*. Oxford, UK: Clarendon Press, 1997.

Erikson, Erik. *Identity and the Life Cycle: Selected Papers*. Chicago: University of Chicago Press, 1959.

Erikson, Kai T. *A New Species of Trouble: The Human Experience of Modern Disasters*. New York: Norton, 1995.

Erikson, Kai T. *Everything in Its Path: Destruction of Community in the Buffalo Creek Flood*. New York: Simon & Schuster, 1978.

Erlich, Paul. *The Population Bomb*. New York: Ballantine, 1968.

Esbensen, F. A., and Winfree, L. T., Jr. "Race and Gender Differences between Gang and Non-Gang Youth: Results From a Multi-Site Survey." *Justice Quarterly*, 15, (1998): 505–525.

Escobar, Gabriel, and Anne Swardson. "From Language to Literature, a New Guiding Lite." *Washington Post*, September 5, 1995, 1, A 18.

Esping-Anderson, G. *The Three Worlds of Welfare Capitalism*. Princeton, NJ: Princeton University Press, 1990.

Etzioni, Amitai. "What Society Owes Older Generations." *The American Scholar*, Spring, 2005, pp. 32–40.

Etzioni, Amitai, "Going Soft on Corporate Crime." *Washington Post*, April 1, 1990: C3

Etzioni, Amitai. *A Comparative Analysis of Complex Organization: On Power, Involvement, and Their Correlates*. Rev. and enlarged ed. New York: Free Press, 1975.

Etzioni-Halevy, Eva. *Bureaucracy and Democracy: A Political Dilemma*. London: Routledge and Kegan Paul, 1983.

Evans, Peter B., and James E. Rauch, "Bureaucratic and Growth: A Cross-National Analysis of the Effects of 'Weberian' State Structures on Economic Growth." *American Sociological Review*, 64(5) (1999): 748–765.

"Facts on Disabilities" in *DiversityInc*, October, 2006, p. 28.

Fairlie, Robert W., and Christopher Woodruff, "Mexican-American Entrepreneurship." Paper presented at the Tenth Annual Meeting of the Society of Labor Economists, San Francisco, June, 2005.

Faludi, Susan. *Backlash: The Undeclared War against American Women*. New York: Crown, 1991.

Farber, Susan L. "Identical Twins Reared Apart." *Sciences*, 215, 4535 (February, 1982): 959–960.

Farkas, G. *Human Capital or Cultural Capital? Ethnicity and Poverty Groups in an Urban School District*. New York: Aldine, 1996.

Farkas, G., D. Sheehan, and R. P. Grobe. "Coursework Mastery and School Success: Gender, Ethnicity, and Poverty Groups within an Urban School District." *American Educational Research Journal*, 27(4) (1990b): 807–827.

Farkas, G., R. P. Grobe, D. Sheehan, and Y. Shuan., "Cultural Resources and School Success: Gender, Ethnicity, and Poverty Groups within an Urban School District." *American Sociological Review*, 55 (1990a): 127–142.

Farrell, Elizabeth, and Eric Hoover. "Getting Schooled in Student Life." *Chronicle of Higher Education*, July 29, 2005, 36.

Farrell, Warren. 1993. *The Myth of Male Power*. New York: Simon and Schuster.

Fass, Sarah, and Nancy K. Cauthen, "Who Are America's Poor? The Official Story." National Center for Children in Poverty, 2006. Available at www.nccp.org/publications/pub_684.html

Faulks, Keith. *Political Sociology: A Critical Introduction*. New York: New York University Press, 2000.

"Fear of Classmates." *USA Today*, April 22, 1999, p. A1.

Featherman, D., and R. Hauser. *Opportunity and Change*. New York: Academic Press, 1978.

Federal Election Commission, "PAC Activity Increases." Washington, DC: August 30, 2006.

Federal Trade Commission, *Consumer Fraud and Identity Theft Complaint Data*, January–December 2006.

Felson, Richard. "Mass Media Effects on Violent Behavior." In *Annual Review of Sociology*, vol. 22, John Hagen and Karen S. Cook, eds., pp. 103–128. Palo Alto, CA: Annual Reviews, Inc.

Feminist Anti-Censorship Taskforce. *Caught Looking*. New York: FACT Collective, 1985.

Ferguson, Ann Arnett. *Bad Boys: Public Schools in the Making of Black Masculinity*. Ann Arbor: University of Michigan Press, 2001.

Ferguson, Ronald. "Cultivating New Routines that Foster High Achievement for All Students: How Researchers and Practitioners Can Collaborate to Reduce the Minority Achievement Gap." *ERS Spectrum*, 19.4, Fall 2001.

Fernie, Sue, and David Metcalf. *Trade Unions: Resurgence or Decline?* New York: Routledge, 2005.

Ferrell, Jeff, and Eugene Stewart-Huidobro. *Crimes of Style: Urban Graffiti and the Politics of Criminality*. Boston: Northeastern University Press, 1996

Festinger, Leon. *When Prophesy Fails*. New York: Harper and Row, 1957.

Fields, Jason, and Lynne M. Casper. "America's Families and Living Arrangements: March 2000." *Current Population Reports*, 2001: P20–537.

Fields, Jason. "Living Arrangements of Children." *Current Population Reports*, U.S. Census Bureau, April, 2001, p. 9.

FIFA.com, "2006 World Cup Broadcast Wider, Longer and Farther than Ever Before." February 6, 2007. Available at: http://www.fifa.com/aboutfifa/marketingtv/news/newsid=111247.html

"Filmspace: Behind the Scenes," ABN AMRO, Sept. 12, 2000.

Filoux, J. C. "Inequalities and Social Stratification in Durkheim's Sociology." In *Emile Durkheim: Sociologist and Moralist. S. P. Turner, ed.* London: Routledge, 1993.

Finder, Alan. "Matters of Faith Find a New Prominence on Campus." *New York Times*, May 2, 2007: A16.

Finer, Laurence B. "Trends in Premarital Sex in the United States, 1954–2003." *Public Health Reports*, 122 (Jan–Feb., 2007): 73–122.

Finkelhor, David, Heather Turner, and Richard Ormrod. "Kid Stuff: The Nature and Impact of Peer and Sibling Violence on Younger and Older Children." *Child Abuse and Neglect*, 20 (2006), 1401–1421.

Finley, M. I. *Democracy Ancient and Modern*. New Brunswick, NJ: Rutgers University Press, 1985.

Firebaugh, Glen. "Empirics of World Income Inequality." *American Journal of Sociology*, 104.6(1999): 1597–1630.

Firebaugh, Glen. "Does Foreign Capital Harm Poor Nations? New Estimates Based on Dixon and Boswell's Measures of Capital Penetration." *American Journal of Sociology*, 102.2(1996): 563–575.

Firebaugh, Glen, and Dumitru Sandu. "Who Supports Marketization and Democratization in Post-Communist Romania?" *Sociological Forum*, 13.3(1998): 521–541.

Firebaugh, Glen, and Frank D. Beck. "Does Economic Growth Benefit the Masses? Growth, Dependence, and Welfare in the Third World." *American Sociological Review*, 59.5(1994): 631–653.

Fischer, Claude, Michael Hout, Martin Sanchez Jankowski, Samuel R. Lucas, Ann Swidler, and Kim Voss. *Inequality by Design*. Princeton: Princeton University Press, 1996.

Fish, Stanley. *Is There a Text in This Class? The Authority of Interpretive Communities*. Cambridge, MA: Harvard University Press, 1980.

Fisher, Allen. "Still 'Not Quite as Good as Having Your Own'? Toward a Sociology of Adoption." *Annual Review of Sociology*, 2003, 335–361.

Fisher, William A., and Azy Barak. "Internet Pornography: A Social Psychological Perspective on Internet Sexuality." *Journal of Sex Research*, 38(4) (November, 2001): 312–324.

Fiske, John. *Reading the Popular*. New York: Routledge, 1989.

Fitzgibbon, Marian, and Melinda Stolley. "Dying to Be Thin—Minority Women: The Untold Story." *Nova*, 2000. Available at www.pbs.org/wgbh/nova/thin/minorities.html

Foner, Eric. "Hiring Quotas for White Males Only." *The Nation*, 924, June 26, 1995.

Foote, Christopher, and Christopher Goetz, "Testing Economic Hypotheses with State-Level Data: A Comment on Donohue and Levitt (2001)." Federal Reserve Bank of Boston working paper, November, 2005.

Foran, John. *Theorizing Revolutions*. New York: Routledge, 1997.

Fordham, Signithia. *Blacked Out: Dilemmas of Race, Identity, and Success at Capital High*. Chicago: University of Chicago Press, 1996.

Foucault, Michael. *The History of Sexuality*, volume 1. New York: Pantheon, 1979.

Foucault, Michel. *Power/Knowledge: Selected Interviews & Other Writings 1972–1977*. Colin Gordon, ed. New York: Pantheon Books, 1980.

Fowlkes, M. R. "Single Worlds and Homosexual Lifestyles: Patterns of Sexuality and Intimacy." In *Sexuality across the Life Course*, A. S. Rossi, ed., pp. 151–184. Chicago: University of Chicago Press, 1994.

Fox, James Alan, "Demographics and U.S. Homicide." In *The Crime Drop in America*. Blumstein and Wallman, eds. New York: Cambridge University Press, 2000, pp. 288–318.

Fox, Robin Lane. *Pagans and Christians*. New York: Knopf, 1987.

Fox, Robin. *Kinship and Marriage: An Anthropological Perspective*. New York: Cambridge University Press, 1984.

Fox, Ronald C., ed. *Current Research in Bisexuality*. London: Harrington Park Press, 2004.

Fox, Stephen R. *The Mirror Makers: A History of American Advertising and Its Creators*. Urbana: University of Illinois Press, 1997.

Frazer E. Franklin. *The Negro Church in America*. New York: Schocken Books, 1974.

Fraser, Jill Andresky. *White Collar Sweatshop: The Deterioration of Work and Its Reward in Corporate America*. New York: W. W. Norton, 2001.

Freedman, Vicki A., Linda G. Martin, and Robert F. Schoeni. "Recent Trends in Disability and Functioning among Older Adults in the United States." *Journal of the American Medical Association*, 288, 24 (2002): 3137–3146.

Freedom House. "Freedom in the World, 2007," available at: http://www.freedomhouse.org/template.cfm?page=351&ana_page=333&year=2007

Freeman, Richard B., "Does the Booming Economy Help Explain the Drop in Crime?" Perspectives on Crime and Justice: 1999–2000 Lecture Series. Washington, D.C.: U.S. Department of Justice, 2000.

Freidson, Elliot. *Profession of Medicine*. New York: Dodd, Mead, 1970.

Freud, Sigmund. *Letters of Sigmund Freud, 1873–1939* (Ernst Freud, ed.). London: Hogarth Press, 1961.

Frey, William H. *Metro America in the New Century: Metropolitan and Central City Demographic Shifts Since 2000*. Washington, DC: Brookings Institute, 2005.

Friedan, Betty. *The Fountain of Age*. New York: Simon and Schuster., 1993.

Friedan, Betty. *The Feminine Mystique*. New York: Dell, 1963.

Friedel, Ernestine. *Women and Men: An Anthropologist's View*. New York: Holt, Rinehart, 1975.

Friedman, Michael J., "Minority Groups Now One-Third of U.S. Population." USInfo.state.gov, July 14, 2006.

Friedman, Thomas. *The Lexus and the Olive Tree: Understanding Globalization*. New York: Farrar Straus and Giroux, 2000.

Frogner, B. K., and G. F. Anderson. *Multinational Comparisons of Health Systems Data, 2005*. New York: The Commonwealth Fund, 2006.

Fuller, Margaret. *Woman in the Nineteenth Century* (1845). Donna Dickenson, ed. New York: Oxford University Press, 1994.

Fuller, Thomas. "Glamour at a Price in Asia: Use of Skin Whiteners Raises Safety Concerns," *International Herald Tribune*, May 31, 2006.

Fussell, Elizabeth, and Frank Furstenberg. "The Transition to Adulthood during the 20th Century: Race, Nativity and Gender." In *On the Frontier of Adulthood: Theory, Research and Public Policy*, Richard R. Settersten Jr., Frank F. Furstenberg, and Ruben G. Rumbaut, eds. Chicago: University of Chicago Press, 2006.

G. B. Schreiber, K. M. Pike, D. E. Wilfley, and J. Rodin. "Drive for Thinness in Black and White Preadolescent Girls." *International Journal of Eating Disorders*, 18(1) (1995).

Gagnon, John. "Physical Strength, Once of Significance." *Impact of Science on Society*, 21 (1), 1971: 31–42.

Gagnon, John, and Stuart Michaels. "Answer No Questions: The Theory and Practice of Resistance to Deviant Categorization." Unpublished manuscript, 1989.

Gagnon, John, and William Simon. *Sexual Conduct*. Chicago: Aldine, 1967.

Gamoran M. Nystrand, M. Berends, and L. LePore. "An Organizational Analysis of the Effects of Ability Grouping." *American Educational Research Journal*, 32 (4) Winter 1995: 687–715.

Gamson, Joshua. *Claims to Fame: Celebrity in Contemporary America*. Berkeley: University of California Press, 1994.

Gamson, Joshua, and Pearl Latteir. "Do Media Monsters Devour Diversity?" *Contexts*, 3, 3 (2004): 26–32.

Gamson, William. *The Strategy of Social Protest*. New York: Dorsey Press, 1975.

Gans, Herbert J. *Deciding What's News: A Study of CBS Evening News, NBC Nightly News, Newsweek, and Time*. New York: Random House, 1979.

Gans, Herbert. *People and Places*. New York: The Free Press, 1968.

Gans, Herbert. *The Urban Villagers*. New York: The Free Press, 1962.

Garbarino, James. *Lost Boys: Why Our Sons Turn Violent and How We Can Save Them*. New York: Anchor Books, 2000.

García-Moreno, Claudia, Henrica A. F. M. Jansen, Mary Ellsberg, Lori Heise, and Charlotte Watts. *WHO Multi-Country Study on Women's Health and Domestic Violence against Women*. Geneva: World Health Organization, 2006.

Gardner, Howard. *Frames of Mind: The Theory of Multiple Intelligences*. New York: Basic Books, 1983.

Gardyn, R. (2000) Retirement Redefined. *American Demographics*, 22 (11), 16–18.

Gargan, Edward. "The Temples of Bloom; Chinese Revive Folk Tradition." *Newsday*, August 19, 2002: A8.

Garner, David. "The 1997 Body Image Survey Results" in *Psychology Today*, January 1997, 30(1): 30–47.

Garrett, M. T. "Understanding the 'Medicine' of Native American Traditional Values: An Integrative Review." *Counseling & Values* 43(2), 1999: 84–99.

Gates, Jeff. "Statistics on Policy and Inequality." Global Policy Forum, www.globalpolicy.org/socecon/inequal/gates99.htm (1999).

Gaughan, E., J. Cerio, and R. Myers. *Lethal Violence in Schools: A National Survey Final Report*. Alfred, NY: Alfred University, 2001.

Gay and Lesbian Alliance Against Defamation, "Where We Are on TV: GLAAD's Eleventh Annual Study Examines Diversity of the 2006–2007 Prime-Time Television Season." GLAAD, August 24, 2006. Available at http://www.glaad.org/eye/ontv/06-07/overview.php.

Gelles, Richard, and John Harrop, "The Rise of Abusive Violence among Children with Nongenetic Caretakers." *Family Relations*, 40(1), January 1991, 78–83.

General Accounting Office, "Death Penalty Sentencing: Research Indicates Pattern of Racial Disparities," Washington, D.C., 1990.

General Social Survey, 2006. Chicago: National Opinion Research Center, University of Chicago.

Gerber, Jerry, Janet Wolff, Walter Klores, and Gene Brown. *Lifetrends: The Future of Baby Boomers and Other Aging Americans*. New York: Macmillan, 1990.

Gereffi, Gary, and Miguel Korzeniewicz, eds. *Commodity Chains and Global Capitalism*. Westport, CT: Praeger, 1993.

Gernet, Jacques. *History of Chinese Civilization*. J. R. Foster, trans. Cambridge, U.K.: Cambridge University Press, 1982.

Gershoff, T. E. "Corporal Punishment by Parents and Associated Child Behaviors and Experiences: A Meta-Analytic and Theoretical Review." *Psychological Bulletin*, 128(4), 2002: 539–579.

Gerson, Kathleen. *Hard Choices: How Women Decide about Work, Career and Motherhood*. Berkeley: University of California Press, 1985.

Gerstel, Naomi, and Harriet Engel Gross, "Gender and Families in the United States: The Reality of Economic Dependence." In *Women: A Feminist Perspective*, Jo Freedman, ed., pp. 92–127. Mountain View, CA: Mayfield, 1995.

Ghosh, Suresh. *The History of Education in Ancient India*. New Delhi: Munshiram Manoharlal Publishers Ltd, 2001.

Gibbs, Nancy. "And on the Seventh Day We Rested?" *Time*, August 2, 2004: 90.

Gigli, Susan. 2004. "Children, Youth and Media around the World: An Overview of Trends & Issues," paper presented at the 4th World Summit on Media for Children and Adolescents, Rio de Janeiro, Brazil, April 2004, available at: http://www.comminit.com/trends/ctrends2004/trends-24.html

Gilbert, Jess, and Caroline Howe. "Beyond State vs. Society; Theories of the State and New Deal Agricultural Policies." *American Sociological Review*, 56 (1991): 204–220.

Gilborn, D. "Citizenship, 'Race', and the Hidden Curriculum." *International Studies in the Sociology of Education*, 2 (1992): 57–73.

Gillespie, Mary. *Television, Ethnicity and Cultural Change*. London & New York: Routledge, 1995.

Gilligan, Carol. *In a Different Voice: Psychological Theory and Women's Development*. Cambridge, MA: Harvard University Press, 1982.

Gilman, Charlotte Perkins. *Herland* (1915). Denise D. Knight, ed. New York: Penguin, 1999.

Gilman, Charlotte Perkins. *The Yellow Wallpaper* (1899). Robert Shulman, ed. New York: Oxford University Press, 1899.

Gilman, Charlotte Perkins. *Women & Economics* (1898). Michael Kimmel, Amy Aronson, eds. Berkeley, CA: University of California Press, 1998.

Gimlin, Debra. *Body Work: Beauty and Self-Image in American Culture*. Berkeley: University of California Press, 2002.

Ginther, Donna K. "Family Structure and Children's Educational Outcomes: Blended Families, Stylized Facts, and Descriptive Regressions." *Demography*, 41, 4 (November 2004): 671–696.

Gitlin, Todd. *Inside Prime Time*. Berkeley: University of California Press, 2000.

Gladwell, Malcolm, "The Cool Hunt." *The New Yorker*, March 17, 1997.

Glassner, Barry. *Bodies*. New York: Putnam, 1988.

Glassner, Barry. *The Culture of Fear*. New York: Basic Books, 1999.

Gleckman, Howard, and Rich Miller, "More Risk—More Reward." *Business Week*, July 25, 2005, p. 37.

Glueck, Sheldon, and Eleanor Glueck. *Unraveling Juvenile Delinquency*. New York: The Commonwealth Fund, 1950.

Goffman, Erving. *The Presentation of Self in Everyday Life*. New York: Overlook, 1974.

Goffman, Erving. *Stigma: Notes on the Management of a Spoiled Identity*. Englewood Cliffs, NJ: Prentice-Hall, 1963.

Goffman, Erving. *The Presentation of Self in Everyday Life*. New York: Anchor Books, 1959.

Goldscheider, Frances. "The Aging of the Gender Revolution: What Do We Know and What Do We Need to Know?" *Research on Aging*, 12 (1990): 531–545.

Goldschneider, Francis K., and Linda J. Waite, "New Families, No Families? The Transformation of the American Home." A RAND Study. Berkeley: University of California Press, 1991.

Gomez, Michael A. *Reversing Sail: A History of the African Diaspora*. New York: Cambridge University Press, 2004.

Gooch, Brad, "Spiritual Retreats: Om-ward Bound." *Travel & Leisure*, October 5, 2002.

Goode, Erich. "The Ethics of Deception in Social Research: A Case Study." *Qualitative Sociology*, 19 (1996a): 11–33.

Goode, Erich. *Deviant Behavior* (7th Edition). Englewood Cliffs, NJ: Prentice-Hall, 2004.

Goode, Erich. "Sexual Involvement and Social Research in a Fat Civil Rights Organization." *Qualitative Sociology* 25, Winter, 2002, pp. 501–534.

Goode, Erich. "Gender and Courtship Entitlement: Responses to Personal Ads." *Sex Roles*, 34(3–4), 1996b, 141–169.

Goode, William J., "A Theory of Role Strain." *American Sociological Review*, 25 (1960): 483–496.

Gordon, Michael. *The American Family in Socio-Historical Perspective*. New York: St. Martin's, 1994.

Gottfredson, G. D., and Gottfredson D. C. *Gang Problems and Gang Programs in a National Sample of Schools*. Ellicott City, MD: Gottfredson Associates, Inc., 2001.

Gottfredson, Marvin, and Travis Hirschi. *A General Theory of Crime*. Stanford, CA: Stanford University Press, 1990.

Gottfredson, Michael R., and Travis Hirschi, "National Crime Control Policies." *Society*, Vol. 32, no. 2 (January–February, 1995): 30–36.

Gottman, Jean, and Robert Harper, eds. *Since Megalopolis*. Baltimore: The Johns Hopkins University Press, 1990.

Gottman, John, and Levinson, Daniel. "What Predicts Change in Marital Interaction over Time? A Study of Alternate Models." *Family Process*, 38 (2) (1999): 143–158.

Gould, S. J. "Ghosts of Bell Curves Past." *Natural History* (February 1995): 12–19.

Gove, Walter R., Hughes, M., and Style, C. B. 1983. "Does Marriage Have Positive Effects on the Individual?" *Journal of Health and Social Behavior*, 24, pp. 122–131.

Gove, Walter R. "The Relationship between Sex Roles, Marital Status and Mental Illness." *Social Forces*, 51, 1972.

Granovetter, Mark. *Getting a Job: A Study of Contacts and Careers*, 2nd edition. Chicago, IL: University of Chicago Press, 1995.

Granovetter, Mark. "The Strength of Weak Ties." *American Journal of Sociology*, 78, 6 (May 1973): 1360–1380.

Gray, John. *Men Are from Mars, Women Are from Venus*. New York: HarperCollins, 1992.

Greeley, Andrew, and Michael Hout. *The Truth About Conservative Christians*. Chicago: University of Chicago Press, 2006.

Greenberg, Anna, "New Generation, New Politics: As Generation Y Steps into the Polling Booths, How Will Political Life Change?" *The American Prospect*, October, 2003, 3–4.

Greenblat, Cathy. "How Do You Know You're in Love?" Unpublished manuscript, Rutgers University, 1998.

Greene, Jay P., and Marcus Winters. *Public High School Graduation and College-Readiness Rates: 1991–2002*. New York: Manhattan Institute, 2005.

Greene, Judith, and Kevin Pranis, *Gang Wars* Washington, D.C.: Justice Policy Institute, 2007.

Greene, Judith A., "Zero Tolerance: A Case Study of Police Policies and Practices in New York City." *Crime and Delinquency*, 45 (2) (April 1999): 171–187.

Greenwald, A. G., and S. D. Farnham. "Using Implicit Association Test to Measure Self-Esteem and Self Concept." *Journal of Personality and Social Psychology*, 79 (2000): 1022–1038.

Greenwald, A. G., D. E. McGhee, and J. K. L. Schwartz. "Measuring Individual Differences in Implicit Cognition: The Implicit Association Test." *Journal of Personality and Social Psychology*, 74 (1998): 1464–1480.

Gregory, Deborah. "Heavy Judgment." *Essence*, August 14, 1994.

Griffin, Gary A., and Harry F. Harlow, "Effects of Three Months of Total Social Deprivation on Social Adjustment and Learning in the Rhesus Monkey." *Child Development*, Vol. 37, no. 3 (Sept., 1966): 533–547.

Grimm, Matthew. "Bout Your G-G-Generation—Generation Y." *American Demographics*, September, 2003, pp. 38–41.

Gross, Daniel, "Invest Globally, Stagnate Locally." *The New York Times*, April 2, 2006: 2.

Grossman, Gene M., and Elhanan Helpman. *Special Interest Politics*. Cambridge, MA: MIT Press, 2001.

Grover, Ronald. "The Pornographers vs. the Pirates." *Business Week*, June 19, 2006: 68–69.

Grusky, David B., ed. *Social Stratification: Class, Race, and Gender in Sociological Perspective*. Boulder, CO: Westview Press, 2000.

Gupta, Dipankar. *Interrogating Caste: Understanding Hierarchy and Difference in Indian Society*. New York: Penguin Books, 2000.

Gurr, Ted Robert. *Peoples Versus States: Minorities at Risk in the New Century*. Washington, DC: U.S. Institute of Peace, 2000.

Gurr. Ted Robert. *Why Men Rebel*. Princeton, NJ: Princeton University Press, 1971.

Guteri, Fred, and Michael Hastings. "The Global Makeover." *Newsweek*, International Edition, November 1, 2003.

Guzzo, Karen Benjamin. "How Do Marriage Market Conditions Affect Entrance into Cohabitation vs. Marriage?" Unpublished paper, Dept. of Sociology, University of Pennsylvania, September, 2003.

Hagan, John, and Patricia Parker, "White Collar Crime and Punishment: The Class Structure and Legal Sanctioning of Securities Violations." *American Sociological Review*, Vol. 50, no. 3 (June, 1985): 302–16.

Hagan, John, and Ruth D. Peterson. *Crime and Inequality*. Palo Alto, CA: Stanford University Press, 1995.

Hagist, Christian, and Laurence Kotlikoff. "Who's Going Broke? Comparing Growth in Healthcare Costs in Ten OECD Countries." NBER Working Paper No. 11833, December, 2005.

"Half of Teens Have Heard of a Gun Threat at School." *USA Today*, November 27, 2001, 6D.

Hall, G. Stanley. *Adolescence: Its Psychology and Its Relations to Physiology, Anthropology, Sociology, Sex, Crime, Religion, and Education*. New York: D. Appleton and Company, 1904.

Hall, J. A. "After the Fall: An Analysis of Post-Communism." *British Journal of Sociology*, 45(4) (1994): 14–23.

Hall, Stuart. "Encoding/Decoding" In *Culture, Media, Language: Working Papers in Cultural Studies, 1972–1979*. pp. 3–36. London: Hutchinson, in association with the center for Contemporary Cultural Studies, University of Birmingham, 1980.

Hamamoto, Darrell Y. *Monitored Peril: Asian Americans and the Politics of TV Representation*. Minneapolis: University of Minnesota Press, 1994.

Hamilton, Brady E., Joyce A. Martin, and Stephanie J. Ventura, "Births: Preliminary Data for 2005" Atlanta: Centers for Disease Control, 2006.

Hamilton, James. *All the News That's Fit to Sell: How the Market Transforms Information into News*. Princeton, NJ: Princeton University Press, 2003.

Hampton, R. L., "Family Violence and Homicides in the Black Community: Are They Linked?" In *Violence in the Black Family: Correlates and Consequences*. Lexington, MA: Lexington Books, 1987.

Hampton, R. L., and Richard Gelles. "Violence towards Black Women in a Nationally Representative Sample of Black Families." *Journal of Comparative Family Studies*, 25(1), 1994, pp. 105–119.

Hand, Jennifer. "Barbie's New Scene Looks Like an Eating Disorder." *UCLA Daily Bruin*, November 5, 2003.

Hannan, Michael T., and John Freeman. "The Ecology of Organizational Founding: American Labor Unions, 1836–1985." *American Journal of Sociology*, 92 (1987): 910–943.

Hannigan, John. *Environmental Sociology: A Social Constructionist Perspective*. New York: Routledge, 1995.

Hansen, M. H. *The Athenian Democracy in the Age of Demosthenes*. Norman, OK: University of Oklahoma Press, 1999.

Hargreaves, Ian. *Journalism: A Very Short Introduction*. London and New York: Oxford University Press, 2005.

Harjo, Suzan Shown. "The American Indian Experience." In *Family Ethnicity: Strength in Diversity*, Harriette Pipes McAdoo, ed. Newbury Park, CA: Sage, 1999.

Harlow, Harry F., and Stephen J. Suomi, "Social Recovery by Isolation-Reared Monkeys." *Proceedings of the National Academy of Sciences of the United States of America*, Vol. 68, no. 7 (July, 1971): 1534–1538.

Harlow, Harry F., Margaret K. Harlow, Robert O. Dodsworth, and G. L. Arling, "Maternal Behavior of Rhesus Monkeys Deprived of Mothering and Peer Associations in Infancy." *Proceedings of the American Philosophical Society*, Vol. 110, no. 1 (February, 1966): 58–66.

Harlow, Harry R., Robert O. Dodsworth, and Margarget K. Harlow, "Total Social Isolation in Monkeys." *Proceedings of the National Academy of Sciences of the United States of America*, Vol. 54, no. 1 (July, 1965): 90–97.

Harris Interactive, 2004. "360 Youth College Explorer Study." Rochester, NY: March.

Harris Interactive, "A Third of Americans with Tattoos Say They Make Them Feel More Sexy," September, 2003, available at: http://www.harrisinteractive.com/news/allnewsbydate.asp?NewsID=691

Harris,Cheryl, ed. *Theorizing Fandom: Fans, Subculture, and Identity*. London: Hampton Press, 1998.

Harris, Lynn. "Asexual and Proud!" Salon.com, May 26, 2006. Accessed at www.Salon.com.

Harris, Marvin. *Cannibals and Kings*. New York: Random House, 1977.

Harris, Sam. *The End of Faith: Religion, Terror and the Future of Reason*. New York: W. W. Norton, 2004.

Hartmann, Heidi, Katherine Allen, and Christine Owens, "Equal Pay for Working Families." Institute for Women's Policy Research, Publication #C344, June, 1999.

Hartney, Christopher. "U.S. Rate of Incarceration: A Global Perspective" National Council on Crime and Delinquency, 2006.

Hayward, M. D., and W. R. Grady, "Work and Retirement among a Cohort of Older Men in the United States, 1963–1983." *Demography*, 27(3) (1990): 337–356.

Healy, J. *Endangered Minds: Why Children Don't Think and What We Can Do about It*. New York: Simon & Schuster, 1990.

Heilbroner, Robert L. *The Nature and Logic of Capitalism*. New York: W. W. Norton, 1986.

Hellmich, Nanci. "33% of Kids Tip Scales Wrong Way." *USA Today*, April 5, 2006, A-1.

Hemenway, David, Harvard School of Public Health. Quoted in Wirzbicki, Alan, "Gun Control Efforts Weaken in the South." *The Boston Globe*, September 4, 2005. Online at www.boston.com/news/nation/article/2005/09/07/gun.control/

Hendershot, Heather. *Saturday Morning Censors: Television Regulation Before the V-Chip*. Durham, NC: Duke University Press, 1999.

Henshaw, S. K., and K. Kost, "Abortion Patients in 1994–1995: Characteristics and Contraceptive Use." *Family Planning Perspectives* 28:4, July/August, 1996; accessed at www.agi-usa.org/pubs/journals/2814096.html

Henshaw, S. K., and G. Martire. "Abortion and the Public Opinion Polls: 1. Morality and Legality." *Family Planning Perspectives*, 14:2, March/April, 1982: 53–60.

Herdt, Gilbert. *Guardians of the Flute*. Chicago: University of Chicago Press, 1983.

Hernnstein, Richard, and Charles Murray. *The Bell Curve: Intelligence and Class Structure in American Life*. New York: The Free Press, 1996.

Herskovits, Melville. *The Anthropology of the American Negro*. New York: Columbia University Press, 1930.

Hertz, Rosanna. *Single by Chance, Mothers by Choice*. New York: Oxford University Press, 2006.

Hertz, Tom. "Trends in the Intergenerational Elasticity of Family Income in the United States." *Industrial Relations*, 46(1) (January 2007), pp. 22–50.

Hetherington, Mavis. *For Better or for Worse: Divorce Reconsidered*. New York: W. W. Norton, 2002.

Higher Education Research Institute, "The Spiritual Life of College Students." Los Angeles: UCLA Higher Education Research Institute, 2005.

Higher Education Research Institute, "The Changing American College Student." Los Angeles: UCLA Higher Education Research Institute, 2004.

Hill, G., and S. Hill. *Black on Television*. Lanham, MD: Scarecrow Press, 1985.

Hills, Matt. *Fan Cultures*. New York: Routledge, 2002.

Hirsch, Barry T., and David A. Macpherson. *Union Membership and Earnings Data Book: Compilations of the Current Population Survey*. Washington, DC: Bureau of National Affairs, 1997.

Hirsch, E. D. *Cultural Literacy: What Every American Needs to Know*. New York: Vintage, 1988.

Hirsch, E. D., Joseph F. Kett, and James Trefil. *Dictionary of Cultural Literacy*. Boston: Houghton Mifflin, 2003.

Hirschi, Travis. *Causes of Delinquency*. Berkeley: University of California Press, 1969.

Hirst, Paul. "The Global Economy—Myth and Realities." *International Affairs*, 73 (1997): 409–425.

Hobsbawm, E. J. *The Age of Revolution, 1776–1848*. New York: Anchor, 1962.

Hobsbawm, Eric J. *The Age of Capital*. London: Widenfeld and Nicholson, 2000.

Hochschild, Arlie. *The Second Shift*. New York: Viking Press, 1989.

Hoek, H., and D. van Hoeken, "Review of the Prevalence and Incidence of Eating Disorders." *International Journal of Eating Disorders*, 34 (2003): 383–396.

Hof, Robert D. "Who Needs Blockbusters?" *BusinessWeek*, July 17, 2006, 88.

Hoffman, Bruce. *Inside Terrorism*. New York: Columbia University Press, 1998.

Hoff-Sommers, Christina. *The War against Boys*. New York: Simon & Schuster, 2000.

Hofmann, Wilhelm, Bertram Gawronski, Tobias Gschwendner, Huy Le, and Manfred Schmitt. "A Meta-Analysis of the Correlation between the Implicit Association Test and Explicit Self-Report Measures." *Personality and Social Psychology Bulletin*, 31, 10 (October, 2005): 1369–1385.

Holahahn, John, Allison Cook, and Lisa Dubay, 2007. "Characteristics of the Uninsured: Who Is Eligible for Public Coverage and Who Needs Help Affording Coverage?" Prepared for the Kaiser Family Foundation. Available at: http://www.kff.org/uninsured/upload/7613.pdf

Hollenbach, Margaret. *Lost and Found: My Life in a Group Marriage Commune*. Albuquerque: University of New Mexico Press, 2004.

Holston, J. A. *Cities and Citizenship*. Chicago: University of Chicago Press, 1999.

Holtz, Robert Lee, "Women Use More of Brain When Listening, Study Says." *Los Angeles Times*, November 29, 2000.

Home Office (Great Britain). Statistics on Race and the Criminal Justice System. London: The Home Office, 2005 http://www.homeoffice.gov.uk/rds/pdfs05/s95race04.pdf.

Hondagneu-Sotelo, Pierrette. *Domestica: Immigrant Workers Cleaning and Caring in the Shadows of Affluence*. Berkeley: University of California Press, 2001.

hooks, bell. *Talking Back: Thinking Feminist, Thinking Black*. Boston: South End Press, 1989.

hooks, bell. *Ain't I a Woman? Black Women and Feminism*. Boston: South End Press, 1981.

Hoover, Stewart, Lynn Schofield Clark, and Lee Rainie, 2004. "Faith Online." Report of the Pew Center on the Internet and American Life.

Hopkins, Terence, and Immanuel Wallerstein. *The Age of Transition: Trajectory of the World System, 1945–2025*. London: Zed Books, 1996.

Horkheimer, Max, and Theodor W. Adorno. "The Culture Industry: Enlightenment as Mass Deception." *Dialectic of Enlightenment*. John Cumming, trans. New York: Herder and Herder, 1972. (Originally published in 1944.)

Horowitz, Helen Lefkowitz. *Campus Life: Undergraduate Cultures from the End of the Eighteenth Century to the Present*. Chicago: University of Chicago Press, 1987.

Houghton, John. *Global Warming: The Complete Briefing*. New York: Cambridge University Press, 2004.

Hout, Michael. "Status, Autonomy and Training in Occupational Mobility." *American Journal of Sociology*, 89(1984): 1379–1409.

Howe, Louise Kay. *Pink Collar Workers: Inside the World of Woman's Work*. New York: Putnam, 1977.

Howell, J. C., Egley, A., Jr., and Gleason, D. K. 2002. *Modern Day Youth Gangs*. Bulletin. Youth Gang Series. Washington, DC: U.S. Department of Justice, Office of Juvenile Justice and Delinquency Prevention.

Howell, James C. "The Impact of Gangs on Communities." *National Youth Gang Center Bulletin*, August 2006. Available at: http://www.iir.com/nygc/publications/NYGCbulletin_0806.pdf

Howell, Signe, and Roy Willis, eds. *Societies at Peace*. New York: Routledge, 1983.

Hrdy, Sarah Blaffer. *Mother Nature: A History of Mothers, Infants, and Natural Selection*. New York: Pantheon, 1999.

Hrdy, Sarah Blaffer. *The Woman That Never Evolved*. Cambridge, MA: Harvard University Press, 1981.

Hsiang-Shul, Chen. *Chinatown No More: Taiwan Immigrants in Contemporary New York*. Ithaca, NY: Cornell University Press, 1992.

Hubbard, Ruth. "The Political Nature of Human Nature." In *Theoretical Perspectives on Sexual Difference*, Deborah Rhode, ed. New Haven, CT: Yale University Press, 1990.

Huesmann, L. Rowell, and Leonard Eron. "Rhodes Is Careening Down the Wrong Road," American Booksellers Foundation for Free Expression, www.abffe.com/mythresponse.htm

Hughes, Mary Elizabeth, and Angela M. O'Rand. *The Lives and Times of the Baby Boomers*. New York: Russell Sage Foundation, 2004.

Human Rights Campaign. "State Prohibitions on Marriage for Same-Sex Couples," 2007.

Human Rights Campaign. *Domestic Partner Benefits Employer Trends and Benefits Equivalency for the GLBT Family*, 2006.

Human Rights Watch, 2007. "Facts about Child Soldiers," available at: http://hrw.org/campaigns/crp/fact_sheet.html

Humphreys, Jeffrey. 2006. "The Multicultural Economy 2006," *Georgia Business and Economic Conditions*, 66(3), University of Georgia.

Humphreys, Laud. *Tearoom Trade: Impersonal Sex in Public Places*. New York: Transaction, 1970.

Huntington, Ellsworth. *Civilization and Climate*. Honolulu: University Press of the Pacific, 2001. (Originally published in 1915.)

Hyde, Janet. "The Gender Similarities Hypothesis." *The American Psychologist*, 60(6), 2005, 581–592.

Ignatiev, Noel. *How the Irish Became White*. New York: Routledge, 1996.

Inglehart, R. *Modernization and Postmodernization: Cultural, Political, and Economic Change in 43 Societies*, Princeton, NJ: Princeton University Press, 1997.

"Inside the Mind of Gen Y." *American Demographics*, September, 2001.

Institute for Social Research, 2002. "Husbands Are Doing More Housework while Wives Are Doing Less." Available at: http://www.umich.edu/news/index.html?Releases/2002/Mar02/chr031202a

Inter-American Development Bank. "Latest Disability Prevalence Rates in LAC," 2007. Available at: www.iabd.org/sds/soc/site_6215_e.htm.

International Helsinki Federation for Human Rights. *Report: Human Rights in the OSCE Region*, 2006.

International Institute for Democracy and Electoral Assistance. "Compulsory Voting." Available at: http://www.idea.int/vt/compulsory_voting.cfm

International Labour Organisation, *Global Employment Trends for Women 2004*. Geneva, Switzerland: International Labor Organization, March, 2004.

International Labour Organisation. *Annual Report 2005–06*. Geneva, Switzerland: ILO, 2007.

International Labour Organisation. *Global Employment Trends Brief, January 2007*. Geneva, Switzerland: ILO, 2007.

International Labour Organisation, 2006. "Facts on Child Labor." Available at: http://www.ilo.org/wcmsp5/groups/public/—-dgreports/—dcomm/documents/publication/wcms_067558.pdf

International Labour Organisation. "Every Child Counts: New Global Estimates on Child Labour." April 2002.

International Labour Organisation. *Global Estimates on Child Labour, 2000–2004*. Geneva: International Labour Office. Available at: http://www.ilo.org/dyn/declaris/DECLARATIONWEB.DOWNLOAD_BLOB?Var_DocumentID=6233

International Lesbian and Gay Association World Legal Survey 2006. Available at: www.ilga.info/Information/Legal_survey/ilga_world_legal_survey%20introduction.htm

International Obesity Task Force. *Global Obesity Map*. London: IOTF, 2007.

"Internet Use Statistics," September 2007. Available at: http://www.internetworldstats.com/stats.htm

Ironmonger, Duncan. "Counting Outputs, Capital Inputs and Caring Labor: Estimating Gross Household Product." *Feminist Economics* 2 (3), 1996: 37–64.

Irwin, Katherine. "Legitimating the First Tattoo: Moral Passage through Informal Interaction." *Symbolic Interaction*, 24, 2001, pp. 49–73.

Isaacs, Stephen L., "Class—The Ignored Determinant of the Nation's Health." *New England Journal of Medicine*, 351, 11 (September 9, 2004): 1137–1142.

Isaacson, Walter. *Einstein: His Life and Universe*. New York: Simon and Schuster, 2007.

Jackall, Robert. *Wild Cowboys: Urban Marauders and the Forces of Order*. Cambridge, MA: Harvard University Press, 1997.

Jackson, Kenneth. *Crabgrass Frontier: The Suburbanization of America*. New York: Oxford University Press, 1987.

Jackson, Pamela Braboy, and Quincy Thomas Stewart. "A Research Agenda for the Black Middle Class: Work Stress, Survival Strategies, and Mental Health." *Journal of Health and Social Behavior*, 44 (September, 2003): 442–455.

Jacobs, Jane. *The Death and Life of Great American Cities*. New York: Vintage, 1961.

Jacobsohn, J., S. Dunn, and Williams College. *Diversity and Citizenship: Rediscovering American Nationhood*. Lanham, MD: Rowman & Littlefield, 1996.

Janara, Laura. "Democracy's Family Values: Alexis de Tocqueville on Anxiety, Fear and Desire." *Canadian Journal of Political Science*, 2001, 34: 551–578.

Jang, S. J., "Race, Ethnicity and Deviance: A Study of Asian and Non-Asian Adolescents in America." *Sociological Forum*, 17(4) 2002: 647–680.

Jankowski, Martin Sanchez. *Islands in the Street: Gangs and American Urban Society*. Berkeley: University of California Press, 1991.

Jenkins, Philip. *The Next Christendom: The Coming of Global Christianity*. New York: Oxford University Press, 2003.

Jensen, Kyle, and Fiona Murray. "The Landscape of Patents and Patent Applications Over the Human Genome." *Science*, 310 2005: 239–240.

Johnson, David R., and Jian Wu. "An Empirical Test of Crisis, Social Selection, and Role Explanations of the Relationship Between Marital Disruption and Psychological Distress: A Pooled Time-Series Analysis of Four-Wave Panel Data." *Journal of Marriage and Family*, vol. 64, 2002, pp. 211–224.

Johnson, Steven. *Everything Bad Is Good for You*. New York: Riverhead Books, 2005.

Jones, Arthur. "Global Sex Trade Prospers." *National Catholic Reporter*, May 25, 2001.

Jones, Del. 1997. "Hooters to Pay $3.75 Million in Sex Suit." *USA Today*, October 1, p. 1A.

Jones, Edward E., Amerigo Farina, Albert H. Hastorf, Hazel Markus, Dale T. Miller, and Robert A. Scott. *Social Stigma: The Psychology of Marked Relationships*. New York: W. H. Freeman, 1986.

Journal of Blacks in Higher Education, "Black Student College Graduation Rates Inch Higher but a Large Racial Gap Persists," 2007. Accessible at www.jbhe.com/preview/winter07preview.html.

Journal of Blacks in Higher Education, "Black Student College Graduation Rates Remain Low, But Modest Progress Begins to Show," news item, 2007, available at: http://www.jbhe.com/features/50_blackstudent_gradrates.html

Journalism.org. "The State of the News Media, 2004," available at: http://www.stateofthenewsmedia.org/narrative_newspapers_audience.asp

Juergensmeyer, Mark. *Terror in the Mind of God: The Global Rise of Religious Violence*. Berkeley: University of California Press, 2003.

Juvonen, Jaana, Sandra Graham, and Mark Schuster, "Bullying among Young Adolescents: The Strong, the Weak and the Troubled." *Pediatrics*, 112(6), December 2003, 1231–1237.

Kaiser Family Foundation, "Sex Education in America: General Public/Parents Survey" January, 2004. Available at: http://www.kff.org/newsmedia/upload/Sex-Education-in-America-General-Public-Parents-Survey-Toplines.pdf

Kaiser Family Foundation, *Generation M: Media in the Lives of 8- to-18-Year Olds*. Menlo Park, CA: Henry J. Kaiser Family Foundation, 2004.

Kaiser Family Foundation. *Sex Education in America: A View from Inside the Nation's Classrooms*. Menlo Park, CA: Henry J. Kaiser Family Foundation, 2000.

Kanter, Rosebeth M. *Men and Women of the Corporation*. New York: Basic Books, 1977.

Karabel, Jerome. *The Chosen: The Hidden History of Admission and Exclusion at Harvard, Yale, and Princeton*. Boston: Houghton Mifflin, 2005.

Karsten, Marge *Management, Gender, and Race in the 21st Century*. Lanham, MD: University Press of America, 2006.

Katz, E., and T. Liebes. *The Export of Meaning*. New York: Oxford University Press, 1990.

Katz, Jack. *The Seductions of Crime*. New York: Basic Books, 1988.

Katz, Jonathan. *The Invention of Heterosexuality*. New York: Dutton, 1987.

Katz, Lawrence, Steven Levitt, and Ellen Shustorovich, "Prison Conditions, Capital Punishment, and Deterrence." *American Law and Economics Review*, Vol. 2, No. 2 (2003): 318–343.

Katz, Michael. *The Underserving Poor*. New York: Pantheon, 1990.

Kawachi, Ichior, Normal Daniels, and Dean E. Robinson, "Health Disparities by Race and Class: Why Both Matter." *Health Affairs* 24, No. 2 (2005): 343–352.

Keach, Karoline. *In the Shadow of the Dreamchild*. London: Peter Owens, 1999.

Keay, Douglas, "AIDS, Education, and the Year 2000: An Interview with Margaret Thatcher." *Woman's Own*, September 23, 1987: 14.

Kellerman, A. L., and J. A. Marcy. "Men, Women and Murder: Gender Specific Differences in Rates of Fatal Violence and Victimization." *Journal of Trauma*, 33, (1) 1992.

Kelling, George L., and William H. Souza. *Do the Police Matter? An Analysis of the Impact of NYC's Police Reforms*. New York: Manhattan Institute, Civic Report no. 22, December, 2001.

Kellogg, J. H. *Plain Facts for Old and Young*. Burlington, IA: I. F. Segner, 1888.

Kempadoo, Kamala, Jyoti Saghera, and Bandana Pattanaik, eds. *Trafficking and Prostitution Reconsidered: New Perspectives on Migration, Sex Work, and Human Rights*. Boulder, CO: Paradigm Publishers, 2005.

Kemper, Theodore. *Testosterone and Social Structure*. New Brunswick, NJ: Rutgers University Press, 1990.

Kennedy, Randall. *Nigger: The Strange Career of a Troublesome Word*. New York: Pantheon, 2002.

Kerbo, Harold R. *Social Stratification and Inequality: Class Conflict in Historical and Comparative Perspective*. New York: McGraw-Hill, 1996.

Khanobdee, C., V. Sukratanachaiyakul, and J. T. Gay. "Couvade Syndrome in Expectant Thai Fathers." *International Journal of Nursing Studies*, 30:2 (April, 1993).

Killias, M., and Haas, H., "The Role of Weapons in Violent Acts: Some Results of a Swiss National Cohort Study." *Journal of Interpersonal Violence* 17 (2002): 14–32.

Kim, Richard. "Eminem—Bad Rap?" *The Nation*, March 13, 2001, p. 4.

Kim, Won. "Asian Americans Are at the Head of the Class." *DiversityInc*, July/August, 2006, p. 40.

Kimmel, Michael. "What Do Men Want?" *Harvard Business Review*, April, 1993.

Kimmel, Michael. *Manhood in America: A Cultural History*. New York: The Free Press, 1996.

Kimmel, Michael. "'Gender Symmetry' in Domestic Violence: A Substantive and Methodological Research Review." *Violence Against Women*, 8(11), 2002: 1332–1363.

Kimmel, Michael. *The Gendered Society*. New York: Oxford University Press, 2003.

Kimmel, Michael. *Guyland: The Inner Lives of Young Men, 18–26*. New York: HarperCollins, 2008, forthcoming.

Kimmel, Michael, James Lang, and Alan Grieg. 2000. "Men, Masculinities and Development" New York: United Nations Development Program (UNDP).

Kimmel, Michael, and Annulla Linders. "Does Censorship Make a Difference?: An Aggregate Empirical Analysis of Pornography and Rape." *Journal of Psychology and Human Sexuality,* 8(3), 1996.

Kimura, Doreen. *Sex and Cognition*. Cambridge, MA: MIT Press, 1999.

King, Leslie. *Environmental Sociology: From Analysis to Action*. Lanham, MD: Rowan & Littlefield, 2005.

Kinloch, Graham C. *The Comparative Understanding of Intergroup Relations: A Worldwide Analysis*. Boulder, CO: Westview Press, 1999.

Kinsella, Kevin and David R. Phillips. *Global Aging: The Challenge of Success*. Washington, DC: Population Reference Bureau, 2005.

Kinsey, Alfred. *Sexual Behavior in the Human Male*. Philadelphia: Saunders, 1948.

Kinsey, Alfred. *Sexual Behavior in the Human Female*. Philadelphia: Saunders, 1953.

Kirby, D. *Emerging Answers: Research Findings on Programs to Reduce Teen Pregnancy*. Washington, DC: Campaign to Prevent Teen Pregnancy, 2001.

Kirp, David. "After the Bell Curve." *The New York Times Magazine*, July 23, 2006: 15–16.

Kitsuse, John. "The New Conception of Deviance and Its Critics" in *The Labelling of Deviance: Evaluating a Perspective,* edited by Walter A. Gove. Thousand Oaks, CA: sage Publications, 1980. pp. 381–392.

Kittilson, Miki C, and Katherine Tate (2004). "Political Parties, Minorities and Elected Office: Comparing Opportunities for Inclusion in the U.S. and Britain." University of California, Irvine: Center for the Study of Democracy. Paper 04–06 (http://repositories.cdlib.org/csd/04–06).

Klein, H. "Couvade Syndrome: Male Counterpart to Pregnancy." *International Journal of Psychiatry Medicine*, 21:1 (1991).

Klevens, Joanne. "Overview of Intimate Partner Violence among Latinos" *Violence Against Women*, 13(2), 2007, 111–122.

Klineberg, Eric. *Heat Wave: A Social Autopsy of Disaster in Chicago*. Chicago: University of Chicago Press, 2003.

Kohlberg, Lawrence. *Stages of Moral Development as a Basis for Moral Education*. Center for Moral Education, Harvard University, 1971.

Kohlberg, Lawrence, and Carol Gilligan. 1971. "The Adolescent as Philosopher." *Daedalus*, 100, 1051–1086.

Kohn, Melvin, "Social Stratification, Parents' Values, and Children's Values" (with Carrie Schoenbach), pp. 118–151 in Dagmara Krebs and Peter Schmidt (Eds.), *New Directions in Attitude Measurement*. Berlin and New York: Walter de Gruyter, 1993.

Kohn, Melvin, "Social Structure and Personality: A Quintessentially Sociological Approach to Social Psychology." *Social Forces* 68 (September, 1989.): 26–33.

Kohn, Melvin, "Social Stratification and the Transmission of Values in the Family: A Cross-National Assessment" (with Kazimierz Slomczynski and Carrie Schoenbach). *Sociological Forum* 1 (Winter, 1986): 73–102.

Kohn, Melvin, "On the Transmission of Values in the Family: A Preliminary Formulation," pp. 3–12 in Alan C.Kerckhoff (Ed.), *Research in Sociology of Education and Socialization: A Research Annual*, Vol. 4. Greenwich, CT: JAI Press, 1983.

Kohn, Melvin. *Class and Conformity*. Chicago, IL: University of Chicago Press, 1977.

Kohn, Melvin, "Social Class, Occupation, and Parental Values: A Cross-National Study" (with Leonard I. Pearlin). *American Sociological Review* 31 (August, 1966): 466–479.

Kohn, Melvin, "Social Class and Parent-Child Relationships: An Interpretation." *American Journal of Sociology* 68 (January, 1963): 471–480.

Kohn, Melvin, "Social Class and the Allocation of Parental Responsibilities" (with Eleanor E. Carroll). *Sociometry* 23 (December, 1960): 372–392.

Kohn, Melvin, "Social Class and the Exercise of Parental Authority." *American Sociological Review* 24 (June, 1959): 352–366.

Kohn, Melvin, "Social Class and Parental Values." *American Journal of Sociology* 64 (January, 1959): 337–351.

Kolata, Gina. "With No Answers on Risks, Steroid Users Still Say 'Yes.' " *The New York Times*, December 2, 2002.

Konig, Susan, "Courting High Net Worth Women." *On Wall Street*, February 2005.

Korn, Donald Jay. "Yours, Mine, OURS." *Black Enterprise*, October 2001.

Kosmin, Barry A., and Egon Mayer, principal investigators, *American Religious Identification Survey*. New York: CUNY Graduate Center, 2001.

Kozol, Jonathan. *Death at an Early Age: The Destruction of Hearts and Minds of Negro Children in the Boston Public Schools*. Boston: Houghton-Mifflin, 1967.

Kraditor, Aileen. *The Ideas of the Woman Suffrage Movement, 1890–1920*. New York: Norton, 1981.

Krafft-Ebing, Richard von, *Psychopathia Sexualis* (1886). New York: Arcade Publishing, 1998.

Kramarae, Cheris, and Paula A. Treichler. *A Feminist Dictionary*. Urbana: University of Illinois Press, 1997.

Kraybill, D. B. *The Fiddle of Amish Culture* (rev. ed.). Baltimore, MD: The Johns Hopkins University Press, 2001.

Kriedte, Peter. *Peasants, Landlords, and Merchant Capitalists*. New York: Cambridge University Press, 1983.

Kristof, Nicholas. "Marriage: Mix and Match." *The New York Times*, March 3, 2004, A23.

Krugman, Paul, "Graduates versus Oligarchs." *The New York Times*, February 22, 2006, A-31.

Krugman, Paul. "The End of Middle-Class America." *The New York Times Magazine*, October 20, 2002: 62–67, 76–78, 141.

Kubler-Ross, Elisabeth. *On Death and Dying*. New York: Touchstone, 1969.

Kubler-Ross, Elisabeth. *Living with Death and Dying*. New York: Touchstone, 1981.

Kuhn, Thomas. *The Structure of Scientific Revolutions*. Chicago: University of Chicago Press, 1962.

Kumar, K. *From Post-Industrial to Post-Modern Society: New Theories of the Contemporary World*. Oxford, U.K.: Blackwell, 1995.

Kupers, Terry. *Prison Madness.* New York: Wiley, 2003.

Kurdek, L. A. "The Allocation of Household Labor in Gay, Lesbian, and Heterosexual Married Couples." *Journal of Social Issues,* 49(3) (1993): 127–140.

Kurki, Leena, "International Crime Survey: American Rates About Average." *Overcrowded Times,* 8 (5) (1997): 4–7.

Kutchinsky, Berl. "Legalized Pornography in Denmark," in *Men Confront Pornography,* edited by Michael Kimmel. New York: Crown, 1990, pp. 233–246.

La Veist, Thomas, and Amani Nuru-Jeter. "Is Doctor-Patient Race Concordance Associated with Greater Satisfaction with Care?" *Journal of Health & Social Behavior,* 43, 3 (September, 2002): 296–306.

Lakshmanan, Indira A. R. "China Cracks Down on Growing Faiths." *Boston Globe,* March, 2, 2002: A8.

Lambert, Tracy. "Pluralistic Ignorance and Hooking Up." *Journal of Sex Research,* 40(2), May, 2003: 129.

Lancaster, B. *The Department Store: A Social History.* London: Leicester University Press, 1995.

Landman, Todd. *Map-Making and Analysis of the Main International Initiatives on Developing Indicators on Democracy and Good Governance.* Essex, U.K.: Human Rights Centre, University of Essex Final Report, 2003.

Landry, D. J., L. Kaeser, and C. L. Richards, "Abstinence Promotion and the Provision of Information about Contraception in Public School District Sexuality Education Policies." *Family Planning Perspectives,* 31(6) (1999): 280–286.

Lane, Harlan. *The Wild Boy of Aveyron.* Cambridge, MA: Harvard University Press, 1979.

Lasch, Christopher. "The Family and History." *New York Review of Books,* 8, November 13, 1975: 33–38.

Lauer, Robert H., and Jeanette C. Lauer. *Marriage and Family: The Quest for Intimacy,* 5th ed. New York: McGraw-Hill, 2003.

Laumann, Edward, John Gagnon, Robert Michael, and Stuart Michaels. *The Social Organization of Sexuality: Sexual Practices in the United States,* 2nd ed. Chicago: University of Chicago Press, 1994.

Laumann, Edward, and Robert Michael eds. *Sex, Love, and Health in America: Private Choices and Public Policies.* Chicago: University of Chicago Press, 2000.

Lazare, Daniel. "Among the Disbelievers." *The Nation,* May 28, 2007, 27–28.

Leach, Karoline, *In the Shadow of the Dreamchild: A New Understanding of Lewis Carroll.* New York: Peter Owen, 1999.

Lee, Felicia. "Survey of the Blogosphere Finds 12 Million Voices." *The New York Times,* July 20, 2006.

Leland, John. "Hip New Churches Sway to a Different Drummer." *The New York Times,* February 18, 2004, A-1, 17.

Lemann, Nicholas. *The Promised Land: The Great Black Migration and How It Changed America.* New York: Vintage, 1992.

Lemert, Edwin. *Human Deviance, Social Problems and Social Control.* Englewood Cliffs, NJ: Prentice-Hall, 1972.

Lenski, Gerhard. *Power and Privilege: A Theory of Social Stratification.* Chapel Hill: University of North Carolina Press, 1984.

LeVay, Simon. *The Sexual Brain.* Cambridge, MA: M.I.T. Press, 1994.

LeVay, Simon. "A Difference in Hyopthalamic Structure between Homosexual and Heterosexual Men." *Science,* 253, August 30, 1991.

Levine, James A. *Working Fathers.* New York: Perseus Books, 1997.

Levine, L. W. *Highbrow/Lowbrow: The Emergence of Cultural Hierarchy in America.* Cambridge, MA: Harvard University Press, 1988.

Levine, Martin. "Gay Ghetto." *Journal of Homosexuality,* 4(4), Summer 1979.

Levine, Susan. "Laughing through Their Years." *The Washington Post,* May 29, 1999, C-1.

Levinson, Daniel. *The Seasons of a Man's Life.* New York: Alfred Knopf, 1978.

Levitt, Steven, and Stephen Dubner. *Freakonomics.* New York: William Morrow, 2005

Lewin, Tamar. "Boys Are No Match for Girls in Completing High School." *The New York Times,* April 19, 2006: A12.

Lewin, Tamar. "One in Five Teenagers Has Sex before 15, Study Finds." *The New York Times,* May 20, 2003.

Lewin, Tamar. "American Colleges Begin to Ask, Where Have All the Men Gone?" *The New York Times,* December 6, 1998, A-1.

Lewis, Lisa A. *The Adoring Audience; Fan Culture and Popular Media.* New York: Routledge, 1992.

Lewis, Oscar. *Five Families: Mexican Case Studies in the Culture of Poverty.* San Francisco: HarperCollins, 1965.

Lewis, Wendy. "Global Trends Emerging in Aesthetic Medicine." *Cosmetic Surgery Times,* November–December, 2005.

Lexington. "Minding About the Gap," *The Economist,* June 11, 2005, p. 32.

Liazos, Alexander, "Nuts, Sluts, and Perverts: The Poverty of the Sociology of Deviance." *Social Problems,* Vol. 20, no. 1 (Summer, 1972): 103–20.

Lichtenstein, Nelson. *State of the Union: A Century of American Labor.* Princeton, NJ: Princeton University Press, 2002.

Lichtheim, George. *Marxism.* New York: Columbia University Press, 1982.

Liebman, J. S., J. Fagan, and V. West. "A Broken System: Error Rates in Capital Cases, 1973–1995." http://papers.ssrn.com/papers.taf?abstract_id=232712 (June 12, 2000).

Liebow, Elliot. *Tally's Corner.* Boston: Little, Brown, 1968.

Lifton, Robert Jay. *The Nazi Doctors: Medical Killing and the Psychology of Genocide.* New York: Basic Books, 1986.

Likert, Rensis. 1932. "A Technique for the Measurement of Attitudes," *Archives of Psychology* 140: pp. 1–55.

Lim, Louisa. "China Fears Bachelor Future." BBC News International Edition. April 4, 2004.

Limber, S. P., P. Cunningham, V. Florx, J. Ivey, M. Nation, S. Chai, and G. Melton. "Bullying among School Children: Preliminary Findings from a School-Based Intervention Program." Paper presented at the Fifth International Family Violence Research Conference, Durham, NH, June, 1997.

Lind, Michael. "Are We Still a Middle-Class Nation?" *Atlantic Monthly,* 293.1(2004): 120–129.

Lipsitz, Angela, Paul D. Bishop and Christine Robinson, "Virginity Pledges: Who Takes Them and How Well Do They Work?" Presentation at the Annual Convention of the American Psychological Association, August 2003.

Livingston, J. *Crime and Criminology.* Englewood Cliffs, NJ: Prentice-Hall, 1992.

Loehlin, John C., and Robert C. Nichols. *Heredity, Environment, and Personality.* Austin: University of Texas Press, 1976.

Lofland, John. "Collective Behavior: The Elementary Forms." In *Collective Behavior and Social Movements,* Russell Curtis Jr. and Benigno Aguirre, eds. Boston: Allyn and Bacon, 1993.

Lofstrom, Magnus. "Labor Market Assimilation and the Self-Employment Decision of Immigrant Entrepreneurs." *Journal of Population Economics,* 15(1) (2002): 83–114.

Lombroso, Ceasare. *Crime and Its Remedies* (1911). New York: Gryphon, 2000.

Lorber, Judith, and Lisa Jean Moore. *Gendered Bodies: Feminist Perspectives*. New York: Oxford University Press, 2007.

Loving v. Commonwealth of Virginia 388 U.S. 1, 87 S.Ct. 1817 (June 12, 1967).

Lubienski, Sarah T. and Christopher Lubienski. "School Sector and Academic Achievement: A Multi-Level Analysis of NAEP Mathematics Data." *American Educational Research Journal*, 43 (4), 651–698.

Lucas, Christopher J. *American Higher Education: A History*. New York: Palgrave Macmillan, 1996.

Luchau, Peter. "By Faith Alone? Church Attendance and Christian Faith in European Countries." *Journal of Contemporary Religion*, 22, 1 (January, 2007): 35–48.

Lukes, Steven. *Power*. New York: New York University Press, 1986.

Lunneborg, Patricia. *The Chosen Lives of Child-Free Men*. Westport, CT: Bergin & Garvey, 1999.

Luxembourg Income Study. "Relative Poverty Rates for the Total Population, Children and the Elderly." Luxembourg: 2007 Available at: http://www.lisproject.org/keyfigures/poverty-table.htm

Lynch, Kathleen. *The Hidden Curriculum: Reproduction in Education, a Reappraisal*. London: Falmer Press, 1989.

Lynch, Marc. *Voices of the New Arab Public: Iraq, Al-Jazeera, and Middle East Politics Today*. New York: Columbia University Press, 2005.

Lynd, Robert S., and Helen Merrill Lynd [1929] *Middletown: A Study in Modern American Culture*. New York: Harvest Books, 1959.

Mac an Ghaill, Mairtin. *The Making of Men: Masculinities, Sexualities and Schooling*. Buckingham, U.K.: Open University Press, 1994.

Maccoby, Eleanor and Carol Jacklin. *The Psychology of Sex Differences*. Stanford, CA: Stanford University Press, 1987.

MacKinnon, Catharine. *Feminism Unmodified: Discourses on Life and Law*. Cambridge: Harvard University Press, 1987.

Mahoney, Kathleen A., John Schmalzbauer, and James Youniss, "Religion a Comeback on Campus." *Liberal Education* (Fall, 2001).

Males, Mike. *The Scapegoat Generation: America's War on Adolescents*. San Francisco, CA: Common Courage Press, 1996.

Maler, Mike. *Ten Myths about the Next Generation*. San Francisco, CA: Common Courage Press, 1998.

Malinowski, Bronislaw. [1927] *Sex and Repression in Savage Society*. New York, Plume, 1974.

Malthus, Thomas Robert. *An Essay on the Principle of Population* (1798). New York: Oxford University Press, 1999.

Manning, Anita. "Aging Gracefully Is the Biggest Concern." *USA Today*, October 23, 2005, A-7.

Manza, Jeff. "Democratic Reversal? The Political Consequences of Felon Disenfranchisement." *American Sociological Review*, 67, 2002, pp. 777–803.

Manza, Jeff, and Chrisopher Uggen. *Locked Out: Felon Disenfranchisement and American Democracy*. New York: Oxford University Press, 2006.

Marchand, Roland. *Advertising the American Dream: Making Way for Modernity*. Berkeley: University of California Press, 1986.

Marchioso, Kathleen. "From Sambo to Brute: The Social Construction of African-American Masculinity." *The Edwardsville Journal of Sociology*, 1 (2001). Available at: www.sieu.edu/sociology

Margolis, Eric, ed. *The Hidden Curriculum in Higher Education*. New York: Falmer Press, 2001.

Marks, N. "Flying Solo at Midlife: Gender, Marital Status and Psychological Wellbeing." *Journal of Marriage and the Family*, 58 (1996): 917–932.

Marshall, John. *John Locke: Resistance, Religion and Responsibility*. Cambridge, U.K.: Cambridge University Press, 1994.

Martens, Jens, "A Compendium of Inequality: The Human Development Report 2005." Global Policy Forum, 2005.

Martin, Bradley. *Under the Loving Care of the Fatherly Leader: North Korea and the Kim Dynasty*. New York: St. Martins, 2004.

Martin, Jack K., Bernice A. Pescosolido, and Steven A. Tuch. 2000. "Of Fear and Loathing: The Role of 'Disturbing Behavior'" Labels, and Causal Attributions in Shaping Public Attitudes Toward People with Mental Illness." *Journal of Health and Social Behavior* 41: 208–223.

Martin, Joyce A., Brady E. Hamilton, Paul D. Sutton, Stephanie J. Ventura, Fay Menacker, and Sharon Kirmeyer "Births: Final Data for 2004." Atlanta: National Center for Health Statistics, Centers for Disease Control, 2006.

Martin, Lynn. *A Report on the Glass Ceiling Initiative*. Washington, DC: U.S. Department of Labor, 1991.

Martin, Steven. "Growing Evidence for a 'Divorce Divide'? Education, Race and Marital Dissolution Rates in the U.S. Since the 1970s." Russell Sage Foundation, 2006.

Martin, Steven. "Reassessing Delayed and Forgone Marriage in the United States." Working paper, Maryland Population Research Center, June 2004.

Martinez, Michael. "Blended Families Face Difficult Financial Decisions." AP Business Wire, June 17, 2005.

Martino, Wayne. "Gendered Learning Experiences: Exploring the Costs of Hegemonic Masculinity for Girls and Boys in Schools." *Gender Equity: A Framework for Australian Schools*. Canberra: Publications and Communications, Department of Urban Services, ACT Government, 1997.

Martino, Wayne. "Masculinity and Learning: Exploring Boys' Underachievement and Underrepresentation in Subject English." *Interpretation*, 27(2), 1994.

Marx, Karl. *Capital* (1867). David McLellan, ed. New York: Oxford University Press, 1998.

Marx, Karl. *The Eighteenth Brumaire of Louis Napoleon*. New York: Monthly Review Press, 1965.

Masci, David. "How the Public Resolves Conflicts between Faith and Science." Pew Forum on Religion and Public Life, Aug. 27, 2007. Available at: http://pewforum.org/docs/?DocID=243

Masoni, S., A. Maio, G. Trimarchi, C. dePunzio, and P. Fioretti. "The Couvade Syndrome." *Journal of Psychosomatic Obstetric Gynecology*, 15:3 (September, 1994).

Massey, Douglas S., and Nancy A. Denton. *American Apartheid*. Cambridge, MA: Harvard University Press, 1993.

Mathaei, Julie. *An Economic History of Women in America*. New York: Schocken, 1982.

Mathias, Peter, and Sidney Pollard. *The Cambridge Economic History of Europe, Vol. 8: The Industrial Economies: The Development of Economic and Social Policies*. Cambridge, U.K.: Cambridge University Press, 1989.

Mattes, Jane. *Single Mothers by Choice: A Guidebook for Single Women Who Are Considering or Have Chosen Motherhood*. New York: New York Times Books, 1994.

Mayo, Elton. *The Human Problems of an Industrial Civilization*. New York: MacMillan, 1933.

McAdam, Doug, ed. *Comparative Perspectives on Social Movements: Political Opportunities, Mobilizing Structures, and Cultural Framings*. Cambridge, U.K.: Cambridge University Press, 1996.

McAdam, Doug. *Freedom Summer*. New York: Oxford University Press, 1990.

McAll, Christopher. *Class, Ethnicity, and Social Inequality*. Montreal: McGill-Queen's University Press, 1990.

McGregor, Douglas. *The Human Side of Enterprise* (1960). New York: McGraw-Hill, 2005.

McKibben, Bill. "The Christian Paradox." *Harper's Magazine*, August, 2005.

McLanahan, S., and E. Kelly, "The Feminization of Poverty: Past and Future." MacArthur Foundation Working Paper series. Available at http://www.onlin.wustl.edu/macarthur/working%20papers/wp-mclanahan3.htm

McLaughlin, Margaret L., Kerry K. Osborne, and Christine B. Smith, "Standards of Conduct on Usenet." In Steven G. Jones, ed., *Cybersociety*, pp. 90–111. Thousand Oaks, CA: Sage, 1995.

McLuhan, Marshall and Quentin Fiore. *The Medium Is the Message*. New York: Bantam, 1967.

Mead, Herbert. *Mind, Self, and Society*. Chicago: University of Chicago Press, 1934.

Mead, Margaret. "Interview" in *New Realities*, June, 1978.

Mead, Margaret. *Sex and Termperament in Three Primitive Societies*. New York: William Morrow, 1935.

Mechanic, David and David A. Rochefort, "Deinstitutionalization: An Appraisal of Reform." *Annual Review of Sociology*, 16 (1990): 301–327.

Medical World News. "Abortion Clinic's Toughest Cases." March, 9, 1987: 55–61.

Meissner, Christian A., John C. Brigham, and David A. Butz, "Memory for Own- and Other-Race Faces." *Applied Cognitive Psychology* 19 (Jan., 2005): 545–567.

Menkel-Meadow, Carrie, "The Comparative Sociology of Women Lawyers: The 'Feminization' of the Legal Profession." Menlo Park, CA: Institute for Social Research, 1987.

Merton, Robert K. "Discrimination and the American Creed." In *Sociological Ambivalence and Other Essays*, pp. 189–216. New York: The Free Press, 1976. (Originally published in 1949.)

Merton, Robert K. *Social Theory and Social Structure*. New York: The Free Press, 1957.

Merton, Robert K. *Theoretical Sociology*. New York: The Free Press, 1967.

Merton, Thomas King. *Social Theory and Social Structure*. New York: Free Press, 1968.

Meyer, David S., Nancy Whittier, and Belinda Robnett, eds., *Social Movements: Identity, Culture, and the State*. Oxford, U.K.: Oxford University Press, 2002.

Meyer, J. W., and Brian Rowan. "Institutional Organizations: Formal Structure as Myth and Ceremony." *American Journal of Sociology*, 83 (1977): 340–363.

Michael, R. T., Gagnon, J. H., Laumann, E. O., and Kolata, G. *Sex in America: A Definitive Study*. Boston: Little, Brown, 1994.

Michels, Robert. *Political Parties*. New York: The Free Press, 1966.

Micklethwait, John, and Adrian Woodridge. *The Company: A Short History of a Revolutionary Idea*. New York: The Modern Library, 2003.

Milgram, Stanley. 1963. "Behavioral Study of Obedience." *Journal of Abnormal and Social Psychology* 67: 371–378.

Milgram, Stanley *Obedience to Authority; An Experimental View*. New York: Harper and Row, 1974.

Miller, Matthew, and Tatiana Serafin, editors, "The 400 Richest Americans" in *Forbes*, September 21, 2006.

Miller, Stephen. *Special Interest Groups in American Politics*. Piscataway, NJ: Transaction Publishers, 1983.

Miller, Walter B., "Lower Class Culture as a Generating Milieu of Gang Delinquency." In Marvin E. Wolfgang, Leonard Savitz, and Norma Johnston, eds., *The Sociology of Crime and Delinquency*. New York: Wiley, 1970. Originally published in *Journal of Social Issues*, 14: 5–19, 1958.

Mills, C. Wright. *White Collar: The American Middle Classes*. New York: Oxford University Press, 1951.

Milner, Jr., Murray. *Freaks, Geeks, and Cool Kids: American Teenagers, Schools and the Culture of Consumption*. New York: Routledge, 2006.

"Mind the Gap." *The Economist*, September 9, 2006, 76.

Mishel, Lawrence, and Roy Joydeep. *Rethinking High School Graduation Rates and Trends*. Washington, D.C.: Economic Policy Institute, 2006.

Moffatt, Michael. *Coming of Age in New Jersey*. New Brunswick, NJ: Rutgers University Press, 1989.

Moghadam, Assaf. "A Global Resurgence in Religion?" Paper No. 03–03, Weatherhead Center for International Affairs, Harvard University, 2003.

Montagu, Ashley. [1942] *Man's Most Dangerous Myth: The Fallacy of Race*. Lanham, MD: Altamira Press, 2000.

Moore, Barrington. *Social Origins of Dictatorship and Democracy: Lord and Peasant in the Making of the Modern World*. Boston: Beacon Press, 1966.

Moore, J. W., and Hagedorn, J. M. *Female Gangs: A Focus on Research*. Bulletin. Youth Gang Series. Washington, DC: U.S. Department of Justice, Office of Juvenile Justice and Delinquency Prevention, 2001.

Moore, Molly. "Micro-Credit Pioneer Wins Peace Prize," *Washington Post*, October 14, 2006: A1.

Morgan, Richard. "The Men in the Mirror." *Chronicle of Higher Education*, September 27, 2002, p. A 53.

Morgan, Robin. *Sisterhood Is Powerful*. New York: Random House, 1976.

Morris, Aldon D., and Carol McClurg Mueller, eds. *Frontiers in Social Movement Theory*. New Haven, CT: Yale University Press, 1992.

Morris, Martina. "Telling Tails Explain the Discrepancy in Sexual Partner Reports." *Nature* 365(6445) (1993): 437–440.

Morsch, James. "The Problem of Motive in Hate Crimes: The Argument against Prescriptions of Racial Motivation." *Journal of Criminal Law and Criminology*, 82, 3 (Autumn, 1991): 659–689.

Moss-Kanter, Rosabeth. *Men and Women of the Corporation*. New York: Basic Books, 1977.

Mowry, George. *The Era of Theodore Roosevelt and the Birth of Modern America*. New York: Harper, 1958.

Mullen, B., and Hu, L., "Perceptions of In-Group and Out-Group Variability: A Meta-Analytic Integration." *Basic and Applied Psychology* 10 (1989): 291–301.

Mumford, Lewis. *The City in History: Its Origins, Its Transformations, and Its Prospects*. New York: Harvest Books, 1968.

Muravchik, Joshua, "Marxism." *Foreign Policy* 133 (Nov–Dec, 2002): 36–38.

Murdock, George P. In *The Science of Man in the World Crisis* Linton, ed. 1945.

Murphy, Evelyn and E.J. Graff. *Getting Even: Why Women Don't Get Paid Like Men and What To Do About It*. New York: Simon and Schuster, 2005.

Murray, Bobbi. "Living Wage Comes of Age." *The Nation*, July 23/30, 2001.

Mustard, David B. "Racial, Ethnic, and Gender Disparities in Sentencing: Evidence from the U.S. Federal Courts." *Journal of Law and Economics*, 44 (2001): 285–314.

Nagel, Joane. *Race, Ethnicity and Sexuality: Intimate Intersections, Forbidden Frontiers*. New York: Oxford University Press, 2003.

Nagourney, Eric. "Surgery Remains 'Macho' Field, Survey Finds." *The New York Times*, April 18, 2006.

Nansel, T. R., M. Overpeck, R. S. Pilla, W. J. Ruan, B. Simons Morton, and P. Scheidt. "Bullying Behaviors among U.S. Youth: Prevalence and Association with Psychosocial Adjustment." *Journal of the American Medical Association*, 285(16), 2001, 2094–2100.

Nathan, Rebekah. *My Freshman Year*. Ithaca, NY: Cornell University Press, 2005.

National Alliance for Caregiving, 2004. "National Caregiving Report." Washington, D.C. Available at: http://www.caregiving.org/data/04finalreport.pdf

National Association for Rural Mental Health, "Suicide Rates in Rural Areas," available at: http://www.highplainsmentalhealth.com/news.asp?ID=73

National Center for Education Statistics 2004. "1.1 Million Homeschooled Students in the United States in 2003." Available at: http://nces.ed.gov/nhes/homeschool/

National Center for Education Statistics. "Program for International Student Assessment (PISA)," 2003. Available at: http://nces.ed.gov/surveys/pisa/

National Center for Women and Policing, *Equality Denied: The Status of Women in Policing, 2001*. Washington, DC: National Center for Women and Policing, April, 2002.

National Counterterrorism Center. *Report on Terrorist Incidents 2006*. Washington, DC: April 30, 2007.

National Family Caregivers Association, 2007. "National Caregiving Statistics." Available at: http://www.nfcacares.org/who_are_family_caregivers/care_giving_statstics.cfm#1

National Highway Traffic Safety Administration, "Motor Vehicle Traffic Crash Fatality Counts and Estimates of People Injured for 2006." DOT HS 810 837, September, 2007, available at: http://www.nhtsa.dot.gov/

National Public Radio, Kaiser Family Foundation and Kennedy School of Government. *Sex Education in America*. January, 2004.

National Retail Federation, *National Retail Security Survey*, 2007.

National Rural Health Association, "Farm Bill Reauthorization: Implications for the Health of Rural Communities." Issue paper, November, 2006.

National Science Foundation. Table H-19: "Employed Scientists and Engineers, by Sector of Employment, Broad Occupation, Sex, Race/Ethnicity, and Disability Status: 2003." Washington, D.C.: National Science Foundation, 2006.

National Urban League. *The State of Black America*. Washington, D.C.: 2006.

National Youth Gang Center, *National Youth Gang Survey Analysis*, 2007.

Neilsen, Francois, and Arthur S. Adelson. "The Kuznets Curve and the Great U-Turn: Income Inequality in U.S. Counties, 1970 to 1990." *American Journal of Sociology*, 62.1(1997): 12–26.

Neugarten, Bernice. *The Meanings of Age*. Chicago: University of Chicago Press, 1996.

"New Thinking about an Old Problem," *The Economist*, September 17, 2005: 36.

Newman, Cathy. "Why Are We So Fat?" *National Geographic*, August, 2004.

Newman, Katherine. *No Shame in My Game: The Working Poor in the Inner City*. New York: Alfred A. Knopf, 1999.

Newton, Michael. *Savage Girls and Wild Boys: A History of Feral Children*. New York: Thomas Dunne Books, 2003.

Nisbet, Robert A. *The Social Bond: An Introduction to the Study of Sociology*. New York: Alfred A. Knopf, 1970.

Nock, Steven. "The New Chronology of Union Formation: Strategies for Measuring Changing Pathways." Paper prepared for Office of the Assistant Secretary for Planning and Evaluation, HHS, November 2003.

Noguera, Pedro. "The Trouble with Black Boys." Paper presented at Harvard University Graduate School of Education, May, 2004.

"Nollywood Dreams." *The Economist*, July 29, 2006.

Norris, Pippa. *Democratic Phoenix : Reinventing Political Activism*. Cambridge, U.K.: Cambridge University Press, 2002.

North, Douglas and Robert Paul Thomas. *The Rise of the Western World: A New Economic History*. Cambridge, U.K.: Cambridge University Press, 1976.

Northeast-Midwest Institute, Rural Population as a Percent of State Total by State, 2001. Available at: http://www.nemw.org/poprural.htm

Norwich, John Julius. *A History of Venice*. New York: Vintage, 1989.

Notestein, Frank. "Population—The Long View," in P. W. Schultz, ed., *Food for the World*. Chicago: University of Chicago Press, 1945.

Nussbaum, Emily. "My So-Called Blog." *New York Times Magazine*, January 11, 2004, 32.

O'Hare, William P. and Sarah Savage. "Child Poverty in Rural America." National Center for Children in Poverty, Columbia University, Summer, 2006.

Oakes, Jeannie. *Keeping Track: How Schools Structure Inequality*. New Haven, CT: Yale University Press, 1985.

Oakes, Jeannie. "Multiplying Inequalities: The Effects of Race, Social Class, and Tracking on Opportunities to Learn Mathematics and Science." Santa Monica, CA: Rand Corp., 1990.

Oates, Stephen B. *Abraham Lincoln: The Man Behind the Myths*. New York: Perennial, 1994.

OECD Observer. "Day Care for Mothers," March, 2006.

OECD, *OECD Factbook 2007: Economic, Environmental, and Social Statistics*. Paris: OECD, 2007.

OECD. *Women and Men in OECD Countries*. Paris: OECD, 2007.

OECD. *OECD Education at a Glance: OECD Indicators 2006*. Paris: OECD, 2006.

Offer, Daniel, Marjorie Kaiz Offer, and Eric Ostrov. *Regular Guys*. New York: Plenum, 2004.

Ogbu, John. *Black American Students in an Affluent Suburb: A Study of Academic Disengagement*. New York: Lawrence Erlbaum Associates, 2003.

Ogbu, John and Signithia Fordham, "Black Students' School Success: Coping with the Burden of 'Acting White,'" *The Urban Review*, 18:3 (1986), 176–206.

Ogburn, William F. *Social Change with Respect to Culture and Original Nature*. New York: Dell, 1966. (Originally published 1922.)

Oh, Kongdan, and Ralph C. Hassig. *North Korea: Through the Looking Glass*. Washington, DC: The Brookings Institution Press, 2000.

Olweus, Dan. *Bullying at School: What We Know and What We Can Do*. New York: Blackwell, 1993.

"Online Pokerpulse Estimates," available at: http://www.pokerpulse.com/currentCL.php

Orenstein, Peggy. *Schoolgirls*. New York: Doubleday, 1994.

Orenstein, Peggy, "Parasites in Pret-a-Porter." *The New York Times Magazine*, July 1, 2001: 31–35.

Orfield, Gary. "Brown at 50: King's Dream or the Plessy Nightmare." Harvard Civil Rights Project, Harvard Graduate School of Education, 2004.

Organization for Economic Cooperation and Development, 2004. "Education at a Glance, 2004." Available at: http://www.oecd.org/document/11/0,3343,en_2649_201185_33712011_1_1_1_1,00.html

Organization for Economic Cooperation and Development, 2004. "OECD Economic Survey of the Czech Republic." Available at: https://www.oecd.org/dataoecd/43/61/33963950.pdf

Orum, Anthony M. *An Introduction to Political Sociology*, 4th ed. Englewood Cliffs, NJ: Prentice-Hall, 2000.

Oshima, Harry T., "The Transition from an Agricultural to an Industrial Economy in East Asia." *Economic Development and Cultural Change*, 34, 4 (July 1986): 783–809.

Oxfam International. *Trading Away Our Rights: Women Working in Global Supply Chains*. London: Oxfam, 2004.

Padavic, Irene, and Barbara F. Reskin. *Women and Men at Work*. Thousand Oaks, CA: Pine Forge Press, 1994/2002.

Pagden, Anthony. *Peoples and Empires: A Short History of European Migration, Exploration, and Conquest, from Greece to the Present*. New York: Modern Library, 2001.

Page, Marianne, and Ann Huff Stevens, "The Economic Consequences of Absent Parents." *Journal of Human Resources*, 39, 1 (Winter, 2004), pp. 80–107.

Page, Susan. "Most in Poll Want Plan for Pullout from Iraq," *USA Today*, June 27, 2006, p. A8.

Paige, Jeffrey. *Agrarian Revolutions*. New York: The Free Press, 1975.

Paige, Karen, and Jeffrey Paige. *The Politics of Reproductive Ritual*. Berkeley: University of California Press, 1981.

Palen, J. John. *The Suburbs*. New York: McGraw-Hill, 1995.

Palme, Joakim. *Pension Rights in Welfare Capitalism*. Stockholm: Swedish Institute for Social Research, 1990.

Panter-Brick, Catherine, Robert H. Layton, and Peter Rowley-Conway. *Hunter-Gatherers: An Interdisciplinary Perspective*. Cambridge, U.K.: Cambridge University Press, 2001.

Paoletti, J. O. "The Children's Department." *Men and Women: Dressing the Part*. Washington, DC: The Smithsonian Institution Press, 1989.

Paoletti, J. O. "'Pink or Blue? What Color for Your Baby?' The Gendering of Infants' and Toddlers' Clothing in America." *The Material Culture of Gender/The Gender of Material Culture*. Winterthur, DE: The Henry Francis du Pont Winterthur Museum, 1997.

Paoletti, J. O. "Clothing and Gender in American Children's Fashions, 1890–1920. *Signs*, 13 (Autumn 1987): 136–143.

Parillo, Vincent. "Diversity in America: Past, Present, and Future." Paper presented to the Eastern Sociological Society, 24 February, 2006.

Parillo, Vincent, and Christopher Donoghue. "Updating the Bogardus Social Distance Studies: A New National Study." *The Social Science Journal*, 422, (2005), pp. 257–271.

Park, Robert E., Ernest Burgess, and Robert McKenzie. [1925]. *The City: Suggestions for Investigation of Human Behavior in the Urban Environment*. Chicago: University of Chicago Press, 1967.

Parsons, Talcott. *The Social System*. New York: The Free Press, 1951.

Pascoe, P. J. " 'Dude, You're a Fag.'" *Sexualities*, 8(3) 2005, pp. 329–346.

Passel, Jeffrey S., and Roberto Suro, "Rise, Peak, and Decline: Trends in U.S. Immigration 1992–2004." Pew Hispanic Center Reports on Immigration, September 2005.

Paul, Gregory. "Cross-National Correlations of Quantifiable Societal Health with Popular Religiosity and Secularism in the Prosperous Democracies," *Journal of Religion and Society* 7, November, 2005. Available at: http://moses.creighton.edu/JRS/2005/2005-11.html

Paulin, Geoffrey, and Brian Riordan. "Making It on Their Own: The Baby Boom Meets Generation X." *Monthly Labor Review*, February, 1998. pp. 10–21.

PBS/Frontline: *Merchants of Cool*. Airdate February 27, 2001.

Pennar, K., and C. Farrel, "Notes from the Underground Economy." *Business Week*, February 15, 1993: 98–101.

Perkins, H. Wesley, ed. *The Social Norms Approach to Preventing School and College Age Substance Abuse: A Handbook for Educators, Counselors, and Clinicians*. San Francisco: Jossey-Bass, 2003.

Perry-Jenkins, M., and Crouter, A. C. "Implications of Men's Provider Role Attitudes for Household Work and Marital Satisfaction." *Journal of Family Issues*, 11(2) (1990): 136–156.

Pescosolido, Bernice A., Jack K. Martin, Bruce G. Link, Saeko Kikuzawa, Giovanni Burgos, Ralph Swindle, and Jo Phelan. *Americans' Views of Mental Health and Illness at Century's End: Continuity and Change*. Bloomington, IN: Indiana Consortium for Mental Health Services Research, 2000.

Peter, Laurence J., and Raymond Hull. *The Peter Principle: Why Things Always Go Wrong*. New York: William Morrow, 1969.

Peterson, D., Miller, J., and Esbensen, F. "The Impact of Sex Composition on Gangs and Gang Delinquency," *Criminology*, 39(2) (2001): 411–439.

Pettigrew, Thomas F. "Intergroup Contact Theory." *Annual Review of Psychology*, Vol. 49 (1998): 65–85.

Pettit, Becky, and Bruce Western, "Mass Imprisonment and the Life Course: Race and Class Inequality in U.S. Incarceration." *American Sociological Review*, Vol. 69 (April 2004): 151–169.

Pew Forum on Religion and Public Life. *Changing Faiths: Latinos and the Transformation of American Religion*. Philadelphia, PA: The Pew Charitable Trusts, 2007.

Pew Forum on Religion and Public Life, 2007. "Hispanics Transforming Nation." Available at: http://pewforum.org/news/display.php?NewsID=13310

Pew Forum on Religion and Public Life, 2003. *Religion and Politics: Contention and Consensus*. Available at: http://pewforum.org/publications/surveys/religion-politics.pdf

Pew Global Attitudes Project, "Among Wealthy Nations . . . U.S. Stands Alone in its Embrace of Religion." Pew Research Center, 2002. Available at: http://pewglobal.org/reports/display.php?ReportID=167

Pew Research Center on the People and the Press. "Acceptance of Interracial Dating." Available at: http://people-press.org/reports/pdf/312.pdf

Philipp, Steven F. "Race and Gender Differences in Adolescent Peer Group Approval of Leisure Activities." *Journal of Leisure Research*, 30(2), 1998, 214–232.

Phinney, Jean S., Debora L. Gerguson, and Jerry D. Tate. "Intergroup Attitudes among Ethnic Minority Adolescents: A Causal Model." *Child Development*, Vol. 68, no. 5 (October, 1997): 955–969.

Piaget, J. *The Child's Construction of Reality*. London: Routledge and Kegan Paul, 1955.

Piaget, J. *The Origins of Intelligence in Children*. London: Routledge and Kegan Paul, 1953.

Piaget, J. *The Moral Judgment of the Child*. London: Kegan Paul, Trench, Trubner and Co., 1932.

Piaget, J. *The Child's Conception of the World*. London: Routledge and Kegan Paul, 1928.

Pipes, Richard. *Communism*. London, UK: Weidenfeld and Nicolson, 2001.

Pipher, Mary. *Can't Buy My Love: How Advertising Changes the Way We Think and Feel*. New York: Free Press, 2000.

Pizzo, Stephen, and Paul Muolo. *Profiting from the Bank and Savings and Loan Crisis*. New York: HarperCollins, 1994.

Pleck, Elizabeth, Joseph Pleck, M. Grossman, and Pauline Bart, "The Battered Data Syndrome: A Comment on Steinmetz's Article." *Victimology*, 2, 1978.

Pleck, Joseph H. "Paternal involvement: Levels, sources, and consequences." In M. E. Lamb (Ed.), *The Role of the Father in Child Development* (3rd ed., pp. 66–103). New York: John Wiley, 1997.

Pleck, Joseph. *The Myth of Masculinity*. Cambridge, MA: M.I.T. Press, 1981.

Pleck, Joseph H., and Masciadrelli, Brian. "Paternal Involvement in U.S. Residential Fathers: Levels, Sources, and Consequences." In *The Role of the Father in Child Development*, 4th ed., M. E. Lamb, ed., pp. 222–271. New York: Wiley, 2004.

Plummer, Ken. "Speaking Its Name: Inventing a Lesbian and Gay Studies." In Ken Plummer, ed., *Modern Homosexualities*, London: Routledge. pp. 3–25, 1992.

Pollak, Otto. *The Criminality of Women* [1950]. Westport, CT: Greenwood, 1978.

Pollack, William. *Real Boys: Rescuing Our Sons from the Myths of Boyhood*. New York: Owl Books, 1999.

Pomer, Marshall. "Intergenerational Occupational Mobility in the United States: A Segmentation Perspective." *Work and Occupations*, 10(1983): 497–501.

Pope, Harrison, Katharine Phillips, and Roberto Olivardia. *The Adonis Complex: The Secret Crisis of Male Body Obsession*. New York: The Free Press, 2000.

Popenoe, David. *Disturbing the Nest: Family Change and Decline in Modern Societies*. New York: Aldine Press, 1988.

Popenoe, David. *Life Without Father*. New York: The Free Press, 1996.

Popenoe, David. *Promises to Keep*. New York: Roman & Littlefield, 1996.

Popenoe, David and Barbara Dafoe Whitehead, *Should We Live Together? What Young Adults Need to Know about Cohabitation Before Marriage*. New Brunswick, NJ: The National Marriage Project, 1999.

Popkin, Samuel L. *The Reasoning Voter: Communication and Persuasion in Presidential Campaigns*. Chicago: University of Chicago Press, 1994.

Population Reference Bureau, 2007. "Fertility Rates for Low Birth-Rate Countries, 1995 to Most Recent Year." Available at: http://www.prb.org/pdf07/TFRTable.pdf

Population Reference Bureau, "Female-Headed Households With Children, by Race/Ethnicity, 1970–2002," Washington, D.C., 2003. Available at: http://www.prb.org/pdf/DiversityPoverty CharacterizeFemaleHeadedHouseholds.pdf

Portes, A., M. Castells, and L. A. Benton. *The Informal Economy: Studies in Advanced and Less Developed Countries*. Baltimore, MD: Johns Hopkins University Press, 1989.

Potok, Mark 2006. *The Year in Hate. 2005*. Montgomery, AL: Southern Poverty Law Center. Available at: http://www.splcenter.org/intel/intelreport/article.isp?aid=627

Project for Excellence in Journalism. *The State of the News Media 2006*. Washington, D.C.: Project for Excellence in Journalism, 2006.

Publishing Statistics from Para Publishing, available at:http://para-publishing.com/sites/para/resources/statistics.cfm

Pullum, Geoff. *The Great Eskimo Vocabulary Hoax and Other Irreverent Essays*. Chicago: University of Chicago Press, 1991.

Quadagno, Jill. "Welfare Capitalism and the Social Security Act of 1935." *American Sociological Review*, 49, 1984: 632–647.

Quinney, Richard. *Class, State, and Crime: On the Theory and Practice of Criminal Justice*. New York: David McKay, 1977.

Radcliffe Public Policy Center, *Life's Work: Generational Attitudes toward Work and Life Integration*. Cambridge, MA: Radcliffe Institute of Advanced Study and Harris Interactive Inc., 2001.

Radcliffe-Brown, A. R. *Structure and Function in Primitive Society*. London: Cohen and West, 1952.

Radelet, M. L., and H. A. Bedau. *In Spite of Innocence: Erroneous Convictions in Capital Cases*. Boston: Northeastern University Press, 1992.

Radway, Janice. *A Feeling for Books: The Book-of-the-Month Club, Literary Taste, and Middle-Class Desire*. Chapel Hill: University of North Carolina Press, 1999.

Radway, Janice. *Reading the Romance: Women, Patriarchy, and Popular Literature*. Chapel Hill: University of North Carolina Press, 1984.

Raeburn, Nicole C. *Changing Corporate America from the Inside Out: Lesbian and Gay Workplace Rights*. Minneapolis: University of Minnesota Press, 2004.

Ranis, Gustav, and Syed Akhtar Mahmood. *The Political Economy of Development Policy Change*. Oxford, U.K.: Blackwell, 1991.

Rawlings, M. Keith, R. J. Graff, R. Calderon, S. Casey-Bailey, and M. Pasley, "Patient and Provider Differences in what they perceive as having 'had sex': Implications for HIV/AIDS prevention" Poster 889, 42nd Annual Meeting of the Infectious Diseases of America, Boston, MA: September, 2004.

Redfield, Robert. *Folk Cultures of the Yucatan*. Chicago, IL: University of Chicago Press, 1941.

Redstockings. *Feminist Revolution* (1969). Second edition. New York: Random House, 1979.

Reisberg, Leo. "Enrollments Surge at Christian Colleges." *Chronicle of Higher Education*, March 5, 1999: A42.

Rennison, M., and W. Welchans. *Intimate Partner Violence*. U.S. Department of Justice, Office of Justice Programs, Bureau of Justice Statistics. May 2000, NCJ 178247, Revised 7/14/00.

Reskin, Barbara. "Sex Segregation in the Workplace." In *Women and Work: A Handbook*, P. Dubeck and K Borman, eds. New York: Garland, 1996.

Resnick, Stephan A., and Richard D. Wolff. *Knowledge and Class: A Marxian Critique of Political Economy*. Chicago: University of Chicago Press, 1987.

Retherford, Robert D., Noah-iro Ogawa, and Rikiya Matsukura, "Late Marriage and Less Marriage." *Population and Development Review*, 27 (1) (2001): 65–78.

Rhode, Deborah. *Speaking of Sex: The Denial of Gender Equality*. Cambridge, MA: Harvard University Press, 1997.

Rich, Carole. *Writing and Reporting News*. Belmont, CA: Thomson Publishing, 2006.

Riesebrodt, Martin. "Secularization and the Global Resurgence of Religion." Paper presented at the Comparative Social Analysis Workshop, University of California, Los Angeles, March 9, 2000.

Rights of the Child, Notes by the Secretary General of the United Nations. New York, 29 August 2006.

Riley, John W. Jr. "Dying and the Meanings of Death: Sociological Inquiries." *American Review of Sociology*, 9 (1983): 191–216.

Rimmerman, Craig. *The New Citizenship: Unconventional Politics, Activism, and Service.* Boulder, CO: Westview Press, 2001.

Ritzer, George. *The McDonaldization of America.* Thousand Oaks, CA: Pine Forge Press, 1996.

Rivers, Caryl. "Pop Science Book Claims Girls Hardwired for Love." *Women's E-News*, June 29, 2002.

Roberts, D. F. "The Dynamics of Racial Intermixture in the America Negro—Some Anthropological Considerations." *American Journal of Human Genetics*, 7 (December, 1975): 361–367.

Roberts, Donald, Ulla Foehr, Victoria Rideout, and Mollyann Brodie. *Kids and Media @ the New Millennium: A Comprehensive Analysis of Children's Media Use.* Menlo Park, CA: The Henry J. Kaiser Foundation, 1999.

Roberts, Paul. *The End of Oil: On the Edge of a Perilous New World.* New York: Mariner Books, 2005.

Roberts, Sam. "51% of Women Are Now Living Without Spouse." *The New York Times*, January 16, 2007, p. A-1.

Rodin, Judith, Lisa Silberstein, and Ruth Streigel-Moore. "Women and Weight: A Normative Discontent." *Psychology and Gender*, T. B. Sonderegger, ed. The Nebraska Symposium on Motivation. Lincoln: University of Nebraska Press, 1984.

Roediger, David. *The Wages of Whiteness: Race and the Making of the American Working Class.* New York: Verso, 1991.

Roethlisberger, Fritz J., and William J. Dickson. *Management and the Worker.* Cambridge, MA: Harvard University Press, 1939.

Rogers, J. W., and M. D. Buffalo, "Fighting Back: Nine Modes of Adaptation to a Deviant Label." *Social Problems* 22 (1974): 101–118.

Rosa, Eugene, A., Gary E. Machlis, and Kenneth M. Keating. "Energy and Society." *Annual Review of Sociology*, 14 (1988): 149–172.

Roscoe, Will, ed. *Boy-Wives and Female Husbands: Studies of African Homosexualities.* London: Palgrave Macmillan, 2001.

Rose, Brad, and George Ross, 1994. "Socialism's Past, New Social Democracy, and Socialism's Futures." *Social Science History*, Vol. 18, no. 3 (Autumn, 1994): 439–469.

Rose, Stephen J., and Heidi I. Hartmann. "Still A Man's Labor Market: The Long-Term Earnings Gap." Washington, D.C.: Institute for Women's Policy Research, 2004.

Rosenhan, David. "On Being Sane in Insane Places." *Science, 179,* 1973, pp. 250–258.

Rosenthal, Robert, and Lenore Jacobson. *Pygmalion in the Classroom.* New York: Holt, Rinehart and Winston, 1968.

Ross, Andrew. *The Celebration Chronicles: Life, Liberty, and the Pursuit of Property Value in Disney's New Town.* New York: Ballantine Books, 2000.

Rossi, Alice. *Gender and the Life Course.* Chicago: Aldine, 1985.

Rostow, W. W. *Process of Economic Growth.* New York: W. W. Norton, 1962.

Rubin, Lillian. *Erotic Wars: What Happened to the Sexual Revolution?* New York: Farrar, Straus & Giroux, 1990.

Rubin, Lillian. *Just Friends.* New York: Harper and Row, 1986.

Rudolph, Frederick. *The American College and University: A History.* Athens, GA: University of Georgia Press, 1990.

Rugh, William A. *Arab Mass Media: Newspapers, Radio, and Television in Arab Politics.* Westport, CT: Praeger, 2004.

Rule, Wilma, and Steven Hill. "Ain't I a Voter?: Voting Rights for Women." *Ms.*, September–October 1996.

Rust, Paula Rodriguez. *Bisexuality and the Challenge to Lesbian Politics.* New York: New York University Press, 1995.

Rust, Paula Rodriguez. *Bisexuality in the United States: A Social Science Reader.* New York: Columbia University Press, 1999.

Sacks, Karen. "Engels Revisited: Women, Organization of Production, and Private Property." *Women, Culture, and Society.* Stanford, CA: Stanford University Press, 1974.

Sadker, Myra, and David Sadker. *Failing at Fairness: How Schools Shortchange Girls.* New York: McGraw Hill, 1995.

Sampson, Robert J. "Open Doors Don't Invite Criminals." *The New York Times*, March 11, 2006, A15.

Samuel, Lawrence R. *Brought to You by Postwar Television Advertising and the American Dream.* Austin, TX: University of Texas Press, 2002.

Sanday, Peggy Reeves. *Female Power and Male Dominance: On the Origins of Sexual Inequality.* New York: Cambridge University Press, 1981.

Sandefur, Gary D., and Arthur Sakamoto. "American Indian Household Structure and Income." *Demography, 25(1) (1988): 71–80.*

Sanders, Stephanie, and June Machover Reinisch. "Would You Say You 'Had Sex' If . . ." *JAMA*, 281, January 20, 1999, pp. 275–277.

Sapolsky, Robert. *The Trouble with Testosterone.* New York: Simon and Schuster, 1997.

Saporito, Bill. "Are Your Secrets Safe?" *U.S. News & World Report*, February 10, 2005.

Sarda, Alejandra. "My God How We Loved Each Other: Love Relations among Argentine Women in the 50s and 60s," paper presented at the "Future of the Queer Past" conference, Chicago, IL, 2000.

Sasseen, Jane. 2006. "White-Collar Crime: Who Does Time?" *Business Week*, February 6, p. 60.

Sassen, Saskia. *The Global City: New York, London, Tokyo.* Princeton, NJ: Princeton University Press, 1991.

Saunders, Peter. *Social Class and Stratification.* London: Routledge, 1990.

Saxton, Alexander. *The Indispensable Enemy: Labor and the Anti-Chinese Movement in California.* Berkeley: University of California Press, 1971.

Saxton, Alexander. *The Rise and Fall of the White Republic: Class Politics and Mass Culture in Nineteenth-Century America.* New York: Verso, 1990.

Sayer, L. S. *Time Use, Gender, and Inequality: Differences in Men's and Women's Market, Nonmarket, and Leisure Time.* Ph.D. Dissertation, University of Maryland, 2001.

Scalia, Antonin. Dissent in *J.E.B. v Alabama*, 114 S Ct. 1436 (1994).

Schachter, Jason, "Why People Move: Exploring the March 2000 Current Population Survey." Washington, D.C.: U.S. Bureau of the Census, 2001. Available at: http://www.census.gov/prod/2001pubs/p23-204.pdf

Schaffner, Laurie. *Girls in Trouble with the Law.* New Brunswick, NJ: Rutgers University Press, 2006.

Scheff, Thomas. *Being Mentally Ill: A Sociological Theory*, 2nd ed. New York: Aldine, 1984.

Scheper-Hughes, Nancy. *Death Without Weeping: The Violence of Everyday Life in Brazil.* Berkeley: University of California Press, 1992.

Schickel, Richard. *Intimate Strangers: The Culture of Celebrity.* Garden City, NY: Doubleday, 1985.

Schlesinger, Arthur. "Biography of a Nation of Joiners." *American Historical Review*, 50(1), (October 1944), pp. 1–25.

Schmitz, Christopher, and Maurice Kirby. *The Growth of Big Business in the United States and Western Europe 1850–1939.* Cambridge, U.K.: Cambridge University Press, 1995.

Schnaiberg, Allan. *The Environment: From Surplus to Scarcity.* New York: Oxford University Press, 1980.

Schodolski, Vincent J., "Inconceivable." *San Diego Tribune,* January 7, 2006.

Schopflin, George. *Politics in Eastern Europe.* New York: Blackwell, 1993.

Schor, Julie. *The Overworked American: The Unexpected Decline of Leisure.* New York: Basic Books, 1991.

Schumpeter, Joseph. *Capitalism, Socialism, and Democracy* (1942). New York: Harper and Row, 1962.

Schwartz, Pepper, and Virginia Rutter. *The Gender of Sexuality.* Thousand Oaks, CA: Pine Forge Press, 1998.

Schwendinger, Herman, and Julia R. Schwendinger. *Sociologists of the Chair: A Radical Analysis of the Formative Years of North American Sociology (1883–1922).* New York: Basic Books, 1974.

Sciolino, Elaine. "French Sikhs Defend Their Turbans and Find Their Voice." *The New York Times,* January 12, 2004: A4.

Scott, James. *Weapons of the Weak: Everyday Forms of Peasant Resistance.* New Haven, CT: Yale University Press, 1987.

Scott, Janny, and David Leonhardt. "Does Class Still Matter?" *New York Times Upfront,* 138.6 (2005): 10–16.

Scott, Robert. *The Making of Blind Men.* New York: Russell Sage Foundation, 1969.

"Secrets of Success." *The Economist,* September 8, 2005.

Selden, Steven. *Inheriting Shame: The Story of Eugenics and Racism in America.* New York: Teachers College Press, 1999.

Seltzer, J. A. "Families Formed Outside of Marriage." In *Understanding Families in the New Millennium: A Decade in Review.* Lawrence, KS: NCRF and Alliance Communication Group, 2001.

Sengupta, Somini. "India Prosperity Creates Paradox; Many Children Are Fat, Even More Are Famished." *The New York Times,* December 31, 2006, 8.

Sennett, Richard, and Jonathan Cobb. *The Hidden Injuries of Class.* New York: Norton, 1993.

Settersten, Richard A., Frank F. Furstenberg, and Ruben Rumbaut. *On the Frontier of Adulthood: Theory, Research, and Public Policy.* Chicago: University of Chicago Press, 2005.

Seward, Rudy Ray, Dale E. Yeatts, Iftekhar Amin, and Amy Dewitt, "Employment Leave and Fathers' Involvement with Children: According to Mothers and Fathers." *Men and Masculinities,* 8 (2006): 405–427.

Shah, Anup. "Poverty Facts and Stats" at Global Issues Website, 2007; available at http://www.globalissues.org/TradeRelated/Facts.asp

Shalit, Wendy. *A Return to Modesty: Discovering the Lost Virtue.* New York: The Free Press, 1999.

Shapiro, Joseph. *No Pity: People with Disabilities Forging a New Civil Rights Movement.* New York: Random House, 1993.

Shattuck, R. *The Forbidden Experiment: The Story of the Wild Boy of Aveyron.* New York: Kodansha International, 1980.

Sheehy, Gail. *Passages.* New York: Bantam, 1976.

Sheldon, William H., Emil M. Hartl, and Eugene McDermott. *Varieties of Delinquent Youth.* New York: Harper, 1949.

Shilling, Chris. "Culture, the Sick Role and the Consumption of Health." *British Journal of Sociology,* 53 (4)(2002): 621–638.

Shively, JoEllen, "Perceptions of Western Films among American Indians and Anglos," *American Sociological Review* 57 (1992): 725–734.

Shumway, Nicholas. *The Invention of Argentina.* Berkeley: University of California Press, 1993.

Sidel, Ruth. *Unsung Heroes: Single Mothers and the American Dream.* Berkeley, CA: University of California Press, 2006.

Siegel, Larry J. *Criminology: Theories, Patterns, and Typologies.* Belmont, CA: Wadsworth, 2000.

Sifry, Micah L. *Spoiling for a Fight: Third Party Politics in America.* New York: Routledge, 2003.

Sikes, Gina. *8 Ball Chicks.* New York: Anchor, 1998.

Simmel, Georg. [1902] "The Metropolis and Mental Life." In *Georg Simmel on Individuality and Social Forms,* edited by Donald Levine. Chicago: University of Chicago Press, 1971.

Simmel, Georg. *Conflict and the Web of Group Affiliations* (1908). New York: Free Press, 1956.

Singer, Natasia. "Who Is the Real Face of Cosmetic Surgery?" *The New York Times,* August 16, 2007, G1, 3.

Sklar, Holly, Laryssa Mykyta, and Susan Wefald. *Raise the Floor.* New York: Ms. Foundation for Women, 2001.

Skocpol, Theda. *States and Social Revolutions: A Comparative Analysis of France, Russia, and China.* Cambridge, U.K.: Cambridge University Press, 1979.

Skuratowicz, Eva, and Larry W. Hunter "Where Do Women's Jobs Come from? Job Resegregation in an American Bank." *Work and Occupations* 31 (1) (2004): 73–110.

Smelser, Neil., ed. *Karl Marx on Society and Social Change.* Chicago: University of Chicago Press, 1975.

Smil, Vaclav. *Energy at the Crossroads: Global Perspectives and Uncertainties.* Cambridge, MA MIT Press, 2005.

Smith, Adam. *The Wealth of Nations* (1776). Robert B. Reich, ed. New York: Modern Library, 2000.

Smith, Christian. *Mapping American Adolescent Subjective Religiosity and Attitudes of Alienation toward Religion: A Research Report.* Galva, IL: Association for the Sociology of Religion, 2003.

Smith, Dinitia. " 'Harry Potter' Inspires a Christian Alternative." *The New York Times,* July 24, 2004: B-7.

Smock, Pamela J. "Cohabitation in the United States: An Appraisal of Research Themes, Findings, and Implications." *Annual Review of Sociology,* 26 (2000): 1–20.

Smolak, L., and R. Striegel-Moore. "The Implications of Developmental Research for Eating Disorders." In *The Developmental Psychopathology of Eating Disorders: Implications for Research, Prevention, and Treatment,* M. Smolak, P. Levine, and R. Striegel-Moore, eds., Mahwah, NJ: Lawrence Erlbaum, 1996.

Snyder, Howard N., and Metissa Sickmund, "Juvenile Offenders and Victims," National Center for Juvenile Justice, U.S. Department of Justice, March, 2006.

Snyder, Laura. "Four Surprising Ways to Make Love Last." Accessed at http://webcenters.netscape.compuserve.com/love/content.jsp?file=love/fun/makelovelast

Snyder, Mark. *Public Appearances, Private Realities: The Psychology of Self-Monitoring.* New York: W. H. Freeman, 1987.

Snyder-Grenier, Ellen M. *Brooklyn: An Illustrated History.* Philadelphia: Temple University Press, 2004.

Sollors, Werner, ed. *Interracialism: Black–White Intermarriage in American History, Literature, and Law.* New York: Oxford University Press, 2000.

Solon, Gary. "Intergenerational Income Mobility in the United States." *American Economic Review,* 82.3 (1992): 393–408.

Somers, M.-A., P. J. McEwan, and J. D. Willins. "How Effective Are Private Schools in Latin America?" *Comparative Education Review,* 48(1) (2004): 48–69.

Spain, Daphne, and Suzanne M. Bianchi. *Balancing Act: Motherhood, Marriage, and Employment among American Women.* New York: Russell Sage, 1996.

Spencer, Herbert. *Principles of Biology.* Honolulu, HI: University Press of the Pacific, 2002.

Speth, James Gustave. *Red Sky at Morning: America and the Crisis of the Global Environment.* New Haven, CT: Yale University Press, 2005.

Spitzer, Steven, "Toward a Marxian Theory of Deviance." *Social Problems, 22* (1975): 638–657.

Spock, Benjamin. [1946] *Baby and Child Care.* New York: Pocket Books, 2004.

Stacey, Judith, and Barrie Thorne. "The Missing Feminist Revolution in Sociology." *Social Problems,* 21 (1985): 301–316.

Stack, Carol. *All Our Kin.* New York: Harper and Row, 1974.

Stamm, K., F. Clark, and P. R. Eblacas, "Mass Communication and Public Understanding of Environmental Problems: The Case of Global Warming." *Public Understanding of Science, 9* (2000): 219–237.

Stearns, Peter. *Consumerism in World History.* New York: Routledge, 2001.

Steenbergen, B. V. *The Condition of Citizenship.* Thousand Oaks, CA: Sage, 1994.

Steinberg, Ted. *Acts of God: The Unnatural History of Natural Disaster in America.* New York: Oxford University Press, 2000.

Steinert, Heinz. *Culture Industry.* Cambridge, U.K.: Polity Press, 2003.

Steinmetz, Susan. "The Battered Husband Syndrome." *Victimology,* 2, 1977–1978, pp. 499–509.

Stephens, John D., and Evelyne Huber. *Development and Crisis in the Welfare State: Parties and Policies in Global Markets.* Chicago, IL: University of Chicago Press, 2001.

Stewart, Janet Kidd. "Generation Broke." *Chicago Tribune,* November 28, 2004. p. 5.

Stiggelbout, Anne M., and Gwendoline M. Kiebert. "A Role for the Sick Role." *Canadian Medical Association Journal,* 157(4) (1997): 383–389.

Stoessinger, John G. *Why Nations Go to War.* New York: Wadsworth, 2004.

Stoltenberg, John. "Pornography and Freedom." In *Men Confront Pornography,* edited by Michael Kimmel. New York: Crown, 1990, pp. 60–71.

Stone, Linda. *Kinship and Gender: An Introduction.* Boulder, CO: Westview Press, 2000.

Storch, G. "Claim of 12 Million Battered Husbands Takes a Beating." *Miami Herald,* 7 August 1978.

Storr, Mel. *Bisexuality: A Critical Reader.* New York: Routledge, 1999.

Straus, Murray, and Richard Gelles, eds. *Physical Violence in American Families.* New Brunswick, NJ: Transaction Publishers, 1990.

Straus, Murray, Richard Gelles, and Susan Steinmetz. *Behind Closed Doors: Violence in America's Families.* New York: Anchor, 1980.

Straus, Murray. "Children Should Never, Ever, Be Spanked No Matter What the Circumstances." In *Current Controversies about Family Violence,* 2nd ed., D. R. Loseke, R. J. Gelles, and M. M. Cavanaugh, eds. Thousand Oaks, CA: Sage Publications, 2005.

Straus, Murray. *Beating the Devil Out of Them: Corporal Punishment in American Families and its Effects on Children* (2nd ed.). New Brunswick, NJ: Transaction, 2001.

Streigel-Moore, Ruth, Lisa Silberstein, and Judith Rodin. "Toward an Understanding of Risk Factors for Bulimia." *American Psychologist,* 41, 1986, 246–263.

Stritof, Sheri, and Bob Stritof. *Your Guide to Marriage.* New York: Adams Media, 2003.

Strong, Bryan. *The Marriage and Family Experience,* 9th ed. Belmont, CA: Wadsworth, 2004.

Summers, Lawrence. "Remarks at NBER Conference on Diversifying the Science and Engineering Workforce." January 14, 2005. Available at http://www.president.harvard.edu/speeches/2005/nber.html.

Sumner, William Graham. *Folkways: A Study of the Sociological Importance of Usages, Manners, Customs, Mores, and Morals* (1906). Mineola, NY: Dover Publications, 2002.

Suny, Ronald. "Some Notes on National Character, Religions and Way of Life of the Armenians." Paper presented at the Lelio Basso Foundation, Venice, Italy, 1985.

Sutherland, Edwin H., "White Collar Criminality." *American Sociological Review,* Vol. 5, no. (February, 1940): 1–12.

Suzuki, Bob. "Asian-American Families." In *Marriage and Family in a Changing Society,* James Henslin, ed., pp. 104–119. New York: Free Press, 1985.

Swidler, Ann. "Culture in Action: Symbols and Strategies." *American Sociological Review,* 51(2), April 1986, 273–286.

Symons, Donald. "Darwinism and Contemporary Marriage." *Contemporary Marriage: Comparative Perspectives on a Changing Institution.* Kingsley Davis, ed., New York: The Russell Sage Foundation, 1985.

Szasz, Thomas S. *The Myth of Mental Illness.* New York: Harper & Row, 1974.

Töennies, Ferdinand. *Community and Society: Gemeinschaft und Gesellschaft.* Tr. Charles P. Loomis. New York: Harper and Row, 1957.

Takaki, Ronald. *Strangers from a Different Shore.* Boston: Little, Brown, 1989.

Tarrow, Sidney. *Power in Movement: Social Movements and Contentious Politics.* Cambridge, U.K.: Cambridge University Press, 1998.

Tarrow Sidney. *Contentious Politics.* Boulder, CO: Paradigm Publishers, 2006.

Tarumoto, Hideki. "Multiculturalism in Japan: Citizenship Policy for Immigrants." *International Journal on Multicultural Societies,* 5.1 (2003): 88–103.

Tatum, Beverly Daniel. *Why Are All the Black Kids Sitting Together in the Cafeteria? A Psychologist Explains the Development of Racial Identity.* New York: HarperCollins, 1997.

Tavris, Carol. *The Mismeasure of Women.* New York: Peter Smith, 1999.

Taylor, Frederic Winslow. *Principles of Scientific Management.* New York: Harper & Brothers, 1911.

Taylor, Michael. *The Possibility of Cooperation.* New York: Cambridge University Press, 1987.

Teachman, J. "Premarital Sex, Premarital Cohabitation, and the Risk of Subsequent Marital Dissolution among Women." *Journal of Marriage and Family,* 65 (2003): 444–455.

Tebbel, John, and Mary Ellen Zuckerman. *The Magazine in America, 1741–1990.* Oxford, U.K.: Oxford University Press, 2005.

Technorati, "Blog Posts by Language—Q4, 2006," available at: http://korlieng.exteen.com/20070513/technorati-chart

Terman, Lewis, and Catherine Cox Miles. *Sex and Personality.* New York: McGraw-Hill, 1936.

"The World Goes to Town." Special section of *The Economist* on Global Urbanization, May 5, 2007, pp. 3–11.

The American Heritage Science Dictionary. Boston: Houghton Mifflin, 2002.

The Gallup Poll Monthly, Number 396, September 1998, Survey GP9809035, September 21, 1998, Q. 15, p. 47.

The Harris Poll, May 8, 2004. Available at: http://www.harrisinteractive.com/harris_poll/index.asp?PID=464

The National Health Care for the Homeless Council, "America's Dirty Little Health Care Secret: For Millions, That's the

Way It Is." *Health Care for the Homeless Mobilizer*, May 24, 2007. Available at: http://www.nhchc.org/2007mobilizerpdf/Mobilizer 052407SinglePayer.pdf

The New York Times. "Immigration Flows and Homicide Trends." March 11, 2006.

"The State of Divorce: You May Be Surprised," *Time*, May 28, 2007.

Thernstrom, Abigail, and Stephan Thernstrom. *No Excuses: Closing the Racial Gap in Learning*. New York: Simon and Schuster, 2003.

Thomas, W. I., and D. S. Thomas. *The Child in America*. New York: Alfred A. Knopf, 1928.

Thompson, Michael, and Dan Kindlon. *Raising Cain: Protecting the Emotional Life of Boys*. New York: Ballantine Books, 2000.

Thornberry, T. P., Krohn, M. D., Lizotte, A. J., Smith, C. A., and Tobin, K. *Gangs and Delinquency in Developmental Perspective*. New York: Cambridge University Press, 2003.

Thorne, Barrie. *Gender Play: Boys and Girls in School*. New Brunswick, NJ: Rutgers University Press, 1993.

Thornhill, Randy, and Craig T. Palmer. *A Natural History of Rape: Biological Bases of Sexual Coercion*. Cambridge, MA: MIT Press, 2000.

Thornton, John. *Africa and Africans in the Making of the Atlantic World, 1400–1800*. New York: Cambridge University Press, 1998.

Tierney, John. "What's So Funny? Well, Maybe Nothing." *The New York Times*, March 13, 2007: F1, F6.

Tilly, Charles. *From Mobilization to Revolution*. Reading, MA: Addison-Wesley, 1978.

Tilly, Chris. *Half a Job: Bad and Good Part-Time Jobs in a Changing Labor Market*. Philadelphia, PA: Temple University Press, 1996.

Tocqueville, Alexis de. *Democracy in America* (1835). New York: Library of America, 2004.

"Tongue-Tied on Bilingual Education." Editorial in *The New York Times*, September 2, 2005.

Traver, Amy. "Becoming a 'Chinese-American' Parent: Parents' Cultural Decision-Making and Inter-Country Adoption from China." 76th Annual Meeting of the Eastern Sociological Society, Boston, MA, February 26, 2006.

Trend, David. *The Myth of Media Violence: A Critical Introduction*. London: Blackwell, 2007.

Tsukashima, Ronald Tadao, "Chronological, Cognitive, and Political Effects in the Study of Interminority Group Prejudice." *Phylon*, 44, 3 (1983): 217–231.

Tuchman, Gaye. *Making News: A Study in the Construction of Reality*. New York: Macmillan Publishing Company, 1978.

Tucker, Naomi. *Bisexual Politics: Theories, Queeries, and Visions*. Binghamton, NY: Haworth Press, 1995.

Turkheimer, Eric, Brian D'Onofrio, Hermine Maes, and Lindon Eaves, 2005. "Analysis and Interpretation of Twin Studies Including Measures of the Shared Environment." *Child Development*, 76(6), November/December 2005, 1217–1233.

Turkheimer, Eric, Andreana Haley, Mary Waldron, Brian D'Onofrio, and Irving Gottesman. "Socioeconomic Status Modified Heritability of IQ in Young Children." *Psychological Science*, 14(6) (November 2003): 623–628.

U.S. Census Bureau. "Percentage of Childless Women 40 to 44 Years Old Increases Since 1976, Census Bureau Reports." Available at: http://www.census.gov/Press-Release/www/releases/archives/fertility/001491.html

U. S. Census Bureau. "Population of the 24 Urban Places: 1790" June, 1998. Available at: http://www.census.gov/population/documentation/twps0027/tab02.txt

U.S. Census Bureau, "Median Household Income." April, 2001.

U.S. Census Bureau, "The 65 Years and Over Population: 2000." Washington, DC: U.S. Bureau of the Census, October 2001,

available at: http://www.census.gov/prod/2001pubs/c2kbr01-10.pdf

U.S. Census Bureau, Census 2000 Brief. *The Two or More Races Population, 2000*. November, 2001. Available at http://www.census.gov/prod/2001pubs/c2kbr01-6.pdf

U.S. Census Bureau. "Average Travel Time to Work of Workers 16 Years and Over Who Did Not Work at Home," 2002. Available at: http://www.census.gov/acs/www/Products/Ranking/2002/R04T160.htm

U.S. Census Bureau. "Marital Status of Women at First Birth by Age: 2002."

U.S. Census Bureau. *2004 American Community Survey*. Washington, D.C.: U.S. Census Bureau, 2004.

U.S. Census Bureau, "More Diversity, Slower Growth: Census Bureau Projects Tripling of Hispanic and Asian Populations in 50 Years; Non-Hispanic Whites May Drop to Half of Total Population." Washington, D.C.: U.S. Department of Commerce, March 18, 2004.

U.S. Census Bureau. "American Community Survey (2005 supplement to the 2000 Census)." Washington, D.C.: United States Census Bureau, 2006.

U.S. Census Bureau. "Father's Day, 2006." Available at: http://www.census.gov/PressRelease/www/releases/archives/facts_for_features_special_editions/006794.html

U.S. Census Bureau. "Voting and Registration in the Election of 2004." Population report P20-556, Washington, D.C.: Bureau of the Census, 2006.

U.S. Census Bureau, 2006. "Life Expectancy at Birth by Region, Country, and Sex: 2002, 2025, and 2050." Available at: http://www.census.gov/ftp/pub/ipc/www/idbsum.html

U.S. Census Bureau, "Poverty: 2005 Highlights." *Current Population Survey Annual Social and Economic Supplement*, 2006.

U.S. Census Bureau, "Income Poverty and Health Insurance Coverage in the U.S.: 2005." *Current Population Reports, August* 2006.

U.S. Census Bureau, 2006. "Population Estimates by Sex and Age, July." Available at:. http://www.census.gov/popest/national/asrh/NC-EST2006/NC-EST2006-02.xls

U.S. Department of Commerce, Bureau of Economic Analysis. "Current Dollar and 'Real' Gross Domestic Product." Posted 7/27/07.

U.S. Department of Education, National Center for Education Statistics, Projections of Education Statistics to 2013 (NCES 2004–013) (Washington, D.C., 2003).

U.S. Department of Education. *Digest of Educational Statistics 2006*. Washington, D.C.: Institute for Education Sciences, 2006. Available at: http://nces.ed.gov/programs/digest/d06/

U.S. Department of Education. "Fiscal Year Budget, 2007" archived at: http://www.ed.gov/about/overview/budget/budget07/summary/edlite-appendix3.html

U.S. Department of Health and Human Services. "Eating Disorders: A Midlife Crisis for Some Women." *Health Reports*, 2006. Available at www.healthfinder.gov.

U.S. Department of Justice, "Crime in the United States," 2005. Available at www.fbi.gov/ucr/ojcius

U.S. Department of Justice, Bureau of Justice Statistics, Federal Bureau of Investigation, 2005. *Hate Crime Statistics, 2005*. Available at: http://www.fbi. gov/ucr/hc2005/index.html

U.S. Department of Justice, Bureau of Justice Statistics. "Crime and Victims Statistics." 2005. Available at: http://www.ojp.usdoj.gov/bjs/cvict.htm

U.S. Department of Justice, Bureau of Justice Statistics. "Violent Victimization of College Students, 1995–2002." 2005. Available at: www.ojp.usdoj.gor/bjs/pub/pdf/vvcs02.pdf

U.S. Department of Justice, "Report to the Deputy Attorney General on the Events at Waco, Texas, February 28 to April 19, 1993," October 8, 1993. Available at: http://www.usdoj.gov/05publications/waco/wacotocpg.htm

U.S. Department of Justice, Bureau of Justice Statistics. *Trends in Criminal Victimization 1973–2005*. Available at http://www.ojp.usdoj.gov/bjs/cvict.htm

U.S. Department of Labor, Bureau of Labor Statistics. *A Profile of the Working Poor, 2003*. Report 983, March, 2005.

U.S. Department of State. "Immigrant Visas Issued to Orphans Coming to the U.S." Available at: http://travel.state.gov/family/adoption/stats/stats_451.html

U.S. Equal Opportunity Commission, 2005. "Occupational Employment in Private Industry by Race/Ethnic Group/Sex and by Industry, United States, 2005." Available at: http://www.eeoc.gov/stats/jobpat/2005/national.html

U.S. Supreme Court. *Price Waterhouse v. Hopkins*. 87 S Ct. 1167 (1989).

Uchitelle, Louis. *The Disposable American: Layoffs and Their Consequences*. New York: Alfred Knopf, 2006.

Uggen, Christopher. "Ex-Offenders and the Conformist Alternatives: A Job-Quality Model of Work and Crime. *Social Problems*, 46(1), February, 1999: 127–151.

UNAIDS, "HIV Data" 2006. Available at: http://www.unaids.org/en/HIV_data/default.asp

UNESCO, "Human Rights of Migrants," Paris: UNESCO, NGLS Roundup 89, March 2002.

UNESCO, "World Culture Report," 2000.

UNESCO Global Education Digest 2004: Comparing Education Statistics across the Globe. Montreal: UNESCO, 2004.

UNESCO Institute for Statistics. *Literacy Rates, Youth (15–24) and Adult (15+), by Region and Gender*. September 2006 Assessment.

UNICEF. "Immunizing Angola's Children against Measles." July, 2003; available at: http://www.unicef.org/immunization/angola_13042.html

United National Development Program. *Taking Gender Equality Seriously*. New York: UNDP, 2006.

United Nations. *2006 Report on the Global AIDS Epidemic*. New York: United Nations, 2006.

United Nations. *World Youth Report*. New York: Author, 2005.

United Nations. World Urbanization Prospects Report, 2005. Available at: http://www.economist.com/images/20070505/ CSU158.gif

United Nations. Department of Economic and Social Affairs. "World Urbanization Prospects, 2005." New York: United Nations, 2006. Available at: http://esa.un.org/unup/index. asp?panel=1

United Nations. Population Fund (UNFPA). "Child Marriage Fact Sheet." Available at: http://www.unfpa.org/swp/2005/presskit/factsheets/facts_child_marriage.htm

Urban, Wayne J., and Jennings L. Wagoner. *American Education: A History*. New York: McGraw-Hill, 2003.

Vallas, Steven P., "Rethinking Post-Fordism: The Meaning of Workplace Flexibility." *Sociological Theory*, 17 (1999): 68–101.

Valliant, G. E. *Adaptations to Life*. Boston: Little, Brown, 1978.

Van Amersfoort, Hans. 1982. *Immigration and the Formation of Minority Groups: The Dutch Experience, 1945–1975*. New York: Cambridge University Press.

Van Kesteren, J.N., P. Mayhew and P. Nieuwbeerta. "Criminal Victimization in Seventeen Industrialized Countries: Key Findings from the 2000 International Crime Victims Survey." The Hague, Ministry of Justice, WODC. 2000.

Van Vugt, William E. *Britain to America: Mid Nineteeenth-Century Immigration to the U.S.* Urbana: University of Illinois Press, 1999.

Vanahen, Tatu. "A New Dataset for Measuring Democracy, 1810–1998." *Journal of Peace Research*, 37(2) (2000): 251–265.

Vanderschueren, Franz. "From Violence to Justice and Security in Cities." New York: UN-Habitat, 1996. Available at: http://www.unhabitat.org/downloads/docs/1899_49562_franz_paper.pdf

Veblen, Thorstein. *The Theory of the Leisure Class* (1899). New York: Prometheus, 1998.

Velkoff, V., and V. Lawson, "International Brief: Gender and Aging Caregiving." Washington, DC: U.S. Department of Commerce, iB/98-3, December 1998.

Verhaag, Bertram. *Blue Eyed*, [videorecording/DVD]. Denkmal Filmproductions; a Claus Stigal & Bertram Verhaag production; written and directed by Bertram Verhaag. 1996.

Villarroel, Maria, Charles Turner, Elizabeth Eggleston, Alia Al-Tayyib, Susan Rogers, Anthony Roman, Philip Cooley, and Harper Gordek, "Same Gender Sex in the United States: Impact of T-ACASI on Prevalence Estimates," *Public Opinion Quarterly*, 70(2), Summer 2006, 166–196.

Voci, A., "Perceived Group Variability and the Salience of Personal and Social Identity," in W. Stroebe and M. Hewstone, eds., *European Review of Social Psychology*, vol. 11 (2000): 177–221.

Von Ornsteiner, J. Buzz. "Pitfalls of the 'Sick Role.'" *Body Positive*, November, 2000. Available at www.thebody.com/content/art_30636.html.

Voslensky, Michael. *The Soviet Ruling Class*. New York: Doubleday, 1984.

Wacquant, Loic. "The 'Scholarly Myths' of the New Law and Order Doxa." *The Socialist Register*, 2006: 93–115.

Wacquant, Loic. *Body and Soul: Notebooks of an Apprentice Boxer*. New York: Oxford University Press, 2003.

Walch, Timothy. *Immigrant America: European Ethnicity in the U.S.* New York: Garland, 1994.

Walker, J. J. Senger, F. Villaruel, and A. Arboleda. *Lost Opportunities: The Reality of Latinos in the U.S. Criminal Justice System*. National Council of La Raza. 2004. Available at: http://www.nclr.org/content/publication/detail/27567/

Waller, Willard. "The Rating and Dating Complex," *The American Sociological Review*, 2 (October, 1937): 727–734.

Wallerstein, Immanuel. "The Development of the Concept of Development." *Sociological Theory*, 2 (1984): 102–116.

Wallerstein, Immanuel. *World-Systems Analysis: An Introduction*. Durham, NC: Duke University Press, 2004.

Wallerstein, Immanuel. *The Capitalist World-Economy*. Cambridge U.K.: Cambridge University Press, 1979.

Wallerstein, Immanuel. "The Rise and Future Demise of the World Capitalist System: Concepts for Comparative Analysis." *Comparative Studies in Society and History*, 16.4 (1974): 387–415.

Wallerstein, Judith. *The Unexpected Legacy of Divorce: A 25 Year Landmark Study*. New York: Hyperion, 2000.

Walsh, Mary Williams. "No Time to Put Your Feet Up as Retirement Comes in Stages." *The New York Times*, April 15, 2001.

Walton, John, and Charles Ragin. "Global and National Sources of Political Protest: Third World Responses to the Debt Crisis." *American Sociological Review*, 55.6 (1990): 876–890.

Warrick, J. "The Warming Planet; What Science Knows." *The Washington Post*, November 11, 1997: A1.

Wasow, Bernard. 2006. "Illegal Immigrants, Our Low-Income Taxpayers" in *Mother Jones*, May 26.

Waters, Mary. *Ethnic Options: Choosing Ethnic Identities in America*. Berkeley: University of California Press, 1990.

Weber, Max. *Economy and Society* (2 volumes). Berkeley: University of California Press, 1978.

Weber, Max. (1958). *From Max Weber*. Translated and edited by H. H. Gerth and C. Wright Mills. New York: Oxford University Press.

Weber, Max. *The Protestant Ethic and the Spirit of Capitalism* (1904, 1905). New York: Routledge, 2004.

Wechsler, Henry, and Bernice Wuethrich. *Dying to Drink: Confronting Binge Drinking on College Campuses*. Emmaus, PA: Rodale Press, 2002.

Wedgwood, C. V. *The Thirty Years' War*. New York: Routledge, 1990.

Weich, Ronald, and Carlos Angulo, "Justice on Trial: Racial Disparities in the American Criminal Justice System." Washington, D.C.: Leadership Conference on Civil Rights, 2000.

Weinberg, Martin S., Colin J. Williams, and Douglas W. Pryor. *Dual Attraction: Understanding Bisexuality*. New York: Oxford University Press, 1994.

Weiss, Gregory L., and Lynn E. Lonnquist. *The Sociology of Health, Healing, and Illness*. Upper Saddle River, NJ: Prentice-Hall, 2000.

Weiss, Karen. *(Re)Defining Sexual Victimization: An Analysis of Victims' Excuses and Justifications*. Ph.D. dissertation, SUNY Stony Brook, 2006.

Weitz, Rose. *The Politics of Women's Bodies: Sexuality, Appearance, and Behavior*. New York: Oxford University Press, 2002.

Weitzman, Lenore J. "The Economic Consequences of Divorce Are Still Unequal: Comment on Peterson." *American Sociological Review*, 61.3 (1996): 537–539.

Welter, Barbara. "The Cult of True Womanhood." *American Quarterly* (Summer 1966): 151–174.

West, Carrell M. *Why Providence Parents Send Their Children to Private Schools, and What Would Bring Them Back*. Providence, RI: Taubman Center for Public Policy, Brown University, September 2001.

Weston, Kath. "Get Thee to a Big City: Sexual Imaginary and the Great Gay Migration." *GLQ* 2.3 (1995): 253–277.

Westphal, Sylvia Pagan. "Human Gene Patents Surprisingly High, a New Study Shows." *The Wall Street Journal*, October 14, 2005.

Wethington, Elaine. "Multiple Roles, Social Integration, and Health." In K. Pillemer, P. Moen, E. Wethington, and N. Glasgow, eds. *Social Integration in the Second Half of Life*. Baltimore, MD: The Johns Hopkins University Press, 2000.

Who's Minding the Kids? Childcare Arrangements Winter 2002. U.S. Census Bureau. Current Population Reports, 2005.

Whyte, William Foote [1943] *Street Corner Society: The Social Structure of an Italian Slum* 4th ed. Chicago: University of Chicago Press, 1993.

Wilkinson, Doris. "Family Ethnicity in America." In Harriette Pipes McAdoo, ed., *Family Ethnicity: Strength in Diversity*. Newbury Park, CA: Sage, 1999.

Williams, Christine. *Still a Man's World: Men Who Do "Women's Work."* Berkeley, CA: University of California Press, 1995.

Williams, Christine. "The Glass Escalator: Hidden Advantages for Men in the 'Female Professions.' " *Social Problems*, 39(3), 1992.

Williams, Jessica. "Facts That Should Change the World: America Spends $10billion Each Year on Porn." *New Statesman*, June 7, 2004.

Williams, Kevin. *Understanding Media Theory*. New York: Oxford University Press, 2003.

Williams, Robin Jr. *American Society: A Sociological Interpretation*, 3rd ed. New York: Alfred Knopf, 1970.

Williams, Walter. *The Spirit and the Flesh*. Boston: Beacon, 1986.

Williamson, Judith. *Decoding Advertisements*. London: Marion Boyars Publishers, 1994.

Willis, George, William H. Schubert, Robert V. Bullough, Craig Kridel, and John T. Holton, eds. *The American Curriculum: A Documentary History*. Westport, CT: Praeger, 1994.

Willis, P., *Learning to Labor*. New York: Columbia University Press, 1977.

Wilmoth, Janet M., Gordon F. DeJong, and Christine C. Himes, "Immigrant and Non-Immigrant Living Arrangements in Later Life." *International Journal of Sociology and Social Policy*, 17 (1997): 57–82.

Wilson, Chris M., and Oswald, Andrew J. "How Does Marriage Affect Physical and Psychological Health? A Survey of the Longitudinal Evidence," *The Warwick Economics Research Paper Series (TWERPS) 728*, University of Warwick, Department of Economics, 2005.

Wilson, James Q. *Thinking about Crime*. New York: Alfred Knopf, 1985.

Winks, Robin W., and Thomas E. Kaiser. *Europe, 1648–1815: From the Old Regime to the Age of Revolution*. Oxford, U.K.: Oxford University Press, 2003.

Wirth, Louis. "Urbanism as a Way of Life: The City and Contemporary Civilization." *American Journal of Sociology* 44, 1938, pp. 1–24.

Wirzbicki, Alan, "Gun Control Efforts Weaken in the South." *The Boston Globe*, September 4, 2005.

Wisner, Ben. *At Risk; Natural Hazards, People's Vulnerability, and Disasters*. New York: Routledge, 2003.

Wolf, Eric. *Peasant Wars of the Twentieth Century*. New York: Harper and Row, 1978.

Wolf, Naomi. *The Beauty Myth*. New York: William Morrow, 1991.

Wolfe, Alan. *The Transformation of American Religion: How We Actually Live Our Faith*. New York: Free Press, 2003.

Wolkomir, Michelle. *The Sacred and Sexual Struggles of Gay and Ex-Gay Christian Men*. New Brunswick, NJ: Rutgers University Press, 2005.

Wollstonecraft, Mary. *Vindication of the Rights of Women* (1792). New York: W. W. Norton, 1988.

Wong, Morrison G., "Post-1965 Asian Immigrants: Where Do They Come From, Where Are They Now, and Where Are They Going?" *Annals of the American Academy of Political and Social Science*, 487 (September, 1986): 150–168.

Wood, Robert G., Brian Goesling, and Sarah Avellar. "The Effects of Marriage on Health: A Synthesis of Recent Research Evidence." Washington, D.C.: Department of Health and Human Services, 2007. Available at: http://aspe.hhs.gov/hsp/07/marriageonhealth/

Woods, Richard. "Women Take Lead as Lifespan Heads for the Happy 100s." *The Sunday Times* (London), October 30, 2005, p. 14.

World Bank. *World Development Indicators 2006*. Available at www.devdata.worldbank.org

World Bank, *Monitoring Environmental Progress*. Washington, DC: Author, 1995.

World Economic Forum. *Women's Empowerment: Measuring the Gender Gap*. Geneva: World Economic Forum, 2005.

World Health Organization, "Obesity" 2007, available at: http://www.who.int/topics/obesity/en/

World Health Organization. "The World Health Report, 2003." Geneva: World Health Organization.

World Health Organization. *Female Genital Mutilation: A Student's Manual*. Geneva: World Health Organization, 2001; available at http://www.who.int/reproductive-health/publications/rhr_01_17_fgm_student_guide/fgm_student_manual.pdf

"World's Largest Cities." Available at http://www.citypopulation.de/World.html

Wright, Lawrence. *Twins and What They Tell Us about Who We Are*. New York: John Wiley, 1999.

Wright, Quincy. *A Study of War*. 2nd ed. Chicago: University of Chicago Press, 1967.

Wright, Richard. *Black Boy*. New York: Harper Brothers, 1945.

Wylie, Cathy. "Trends in the Feminization of the Teaching Profession in OECD Countries 1980–1995." International Labor Office, 2000.

Yahr, P. "Sexually Dimorphic Hypothalamic Cell Groups and a Related Pathway That Are Essential for Masculine Copulatory Behavior." In *The Development of Sex Differences and Similarities in Behavior*, M. Haug, R. Whalen, C. Aron, and K. Olsen, eds. Dordrecht, The Netherlands: Kluwer Academic Publishers, 1993.

Yaukey, David, and Douglas L. Anderton. *Demography: The Study of Human Population*. Long Grove, IL: Waveland Press, 2001.

Yellowbird, Michael, and C. Matthew Snipp. "American Indian Families." In *Minority Families in the United States: A Multicultural Perspective*, Ronald Taylor, ed Englewood Cliffs, NJ: Prentice-Hall, 1994, pp. 179–201.

Yinger, J. Milton. *The Scientific Study of Religion*. London: Macmillan, 1970.

Yinger, John. *Closed Doors, Opportunities Lost*. New York: Russell Sage Foundation, 1995.

Yoder, J., "Rethinking Tokenism: Looking beyond Numbers." *Gender and Society*, 5 (1991): 178–192.

Yoffee, Norman. *Myths of the Archaic State: Evolution of the Earliest Cities, States, and Civilizations*. Cambridge, U.K.: Cambridge University Press, 2005.

Yong-Shik, Choe. "Surnames: Microcosmic Icon of Korea's Confucian Order." *Korea Now*, April 7, 2001.

Young, Antonia. *Women Who Become Men: Albanian Sworn Virgins*. New York: Berg, 2000.

Young, T. Kue. *Population Health: Concept and Methods*. New York: Oxford University Press, 1998.

Zakaria, Fareed. *The Future of Freedom: Illiberal Democracy at Home and Abroad*. New York: W. W. Norton, 2004.

Zehr, S. C. "Public Representations of Scientific Uncertainty about Global Climate Change." *Public Understanding of Science*, 9 (2000): 85–103.

Zeune, Gary D. "Are You Teaching Your Employees to Steal?" *Business Credit*, April, 2001.

Zihlman, Adrienne. "Woman the Gatherer: The Role of Women in Early Hominid Evolution." In *Gender and Anthropology*, Sandra Morgen, ed. Washington, DC: American Anthropological Association, 1989.

Zimbardo, Philip G. "The Human Choice: Individuation, Reason, and Order versus Deindividuation, Impulse, and Chaos." *Nebraska Symposium on Motivation*, 17, 237–307, 1969.

Zimring, Franklin E., and Gordon Hawkins. *Crime Is Not the Problem: Lethal Violence in America*. New York: Oxford University Press, 1997.

Zuckerman, Phil. "Atheism: Contemporary Rates and Patterns." In *The Cambridge Companion to Atheism*, Michael Martin, ed. Cambridge, U.K.: Cambridge University Press, 2005.

Name Index

Holtz-Eakin, D., 443
Homer, 58
Hondagneau-Sotelo, Pierrette, 297
hooks, bell, 309, 310
Hoover, Eric, 579
Hoover, Stewart, 152
Hopkins, Terence, 236
Horkheimer, Max, 599
Horowitz, Helen Lefkowitz, 579
Houghton, John, 646
Hout, Michael, 226, 261, 502
Howe, Caroline, 430
Howe, Louise Kay, 438
Howell, J. C., 173
Howell, James C., 174
Howell, Signe, 291
Hoynes, William, 88, 607, 611
Hrdy, Sarah, 143, 283, 284
Hsiang-Shul, Chen, 117
Hu, L., 84
Hubbard, L. Ron, 495
Hubbard, Ruth, 289
Huber, Evelyne, 426
Hudson, Rock, 363
Huesmann, L. Rowell, 607
Hughes, 78
Hughes, M., 305
Hughes, Mary Elizabeth, 368
Huguley, Sandra, 411
Hull, Raymond, 97
Humphreys, Jeffrey, 266
Humphreys, Laud, 115
Hunter, Larry W., 448
Huntington, Ellsworth, 641
Hussein, Saddam, 477, 478, 496
Hyde, Janet, 292

Ignatiev, Noel, 250
Imus, Don, 251
Inglehart, R., 463, 506
Ironmonger, Duncan, 442
Irwin, Katherine, 529
Isaacs, Stephen L., 534
Isaacson, Walter, 563

Jackall, Robert, 188
Jacklin, Carol, 291
Jackson, Andrew, 263
Jackson, Jesse, 505
Jackson, Kenneth, 633
Jackson, Michael, 39, 521
Jackson, Pamela Braboy, 535
Jacobs, Jane, 637
Jacobsohn, J., 467
Jacobson, L., 260, 569
Jacobson, Lenore, 113–114
Jagger, Mick, 353
James, Jesse, 172
James, Lebron, 60
Janara, Laura, 387
Janis, 87
Jankowski, Martin Sanchez, 116, 173
Jay, Paul, 613

Jefferson, Thomas, 13, 140, 469, 500
Jenkins, Jerry B., 502
Jenkins, Philip, 499
Jensen, Kyle, 512
Jimmu, 460
Johansson, Scarlett, 41
Johnson, David R., 407
Johnson, Glenn, 634
Johnson, Lyndon, 219, 256
Johnson, Steven, 155
Jolie, Angelina, 404, 603
Jones, 84, 535
Jones, Arthur, 339
Jones, Del, 299
Jones, Edward E., 540
Jones, Nora, 60
Jones, Quincy, 39
Joplin, Janis, 529
Joyce, James, 340, 608
Joydeep, Roy, 267
Juergensmeyer, Mark, 478
Juvonen, Jaana, 572

Kaeser, L., 341
Kaiser, Thomas E., 460
Kanter, Rosebeth M., 94
Karabel, Jerome, 578
Karatz, Bruce, 219
Karr, Albert R., 430, 431
Katz, E., 600
Katz, Jonathan, 324
Katz, Lawrence, 195
Katz, Michael, 223
Kawachi, Ichior, 535
Keating, Kenneth M., 642
Keay, Douglas, 70
Keiter, William, 87
Kellerman, A. L., 409
Kelling, George L., 188
Kellogg, J. H., 327
Kelly, E., 222
Kelly, Mary, 611
Kempadoo, Kamala, 237
Kemper, Theodore, 285
Kennedy, John F., 263, 265, 458
Kennedy, Randall, 274
Kerbo, Harold R., 206
Kerry, John, 55, 470, 471, 472, 473
Khanobdee, C., 288
Kiebert, Gwendoline M., 538
Kilgore, Sally, 566
Kilpatrick, 461
Kim, Richard, 336
Kim, Won, 268
Kim Jong-il, 461
Kimmel, Michael, 249, 280, 281, 287, 294,
    303, 327, 341, 410, 411, 498, 503, 544
Kimura, Doreen, 284
Kindlon, Dan, 162
King, 49
King, E., 557
King, Leslie, 642
King, Martin Luther, Jr., 504, 505

Kinloch, Graham C., 259
Kinsella, Kevin, 358
Kinsey, Alfred, 327–329
Kipling, Rudyard, 283
Kirby, D., 341
Kirby, Maurice, 430
Kirp, David, 105, 106
Kitsuse, John, 177
Kittilson, Miki C., 466
Kitzinger, J., 600
Klebold, Dylan, 573, 587, 588, 607
Klein, H., 288
Klevens, Joanne, 410
Klineberg, Eric, 647
Kluckohn, Clyde, 319
Klusmeyer, Douglas B., 468
Kohlberg, Lawrence, 146–147, 149
Kohn, Melvin, 151–152
Kolata, Gina, 528
Konig, Susan, 449
Koresh, David, 492
Korn, Donald Jay, 409
Korzeniewicz, Miguel, 236
Kosmin, Barry A., 501
Kost, K., 130
Kotlikoff, Laurence, 550
Kozol, Jonathan, 152
Kraditor, Aileen, 309
Krafft-Ebing, Richard von, 327
Kramarae, Cheris, 308
Kraybill, D. B., 2005
Kriedte, Peter, 625
Kristof, 53
Kristof, Nicholas, 247
Krohn, M. D., 173
Krugman, Paul, 218, 422
Kübler-Ross, Elisabeth, 361
Kuhn, Thomas, 514
Kumar, K., 422
Kupers, Terry, 540
Kutchinsky, Berl, 341

LaFollette, Robert M., 470
LaHaye, Tim, 502
Lakshmanan, Indira A. R., 499
Lambert, Tracy, 332
Lancaster, B., 420
Landman, Todd, 463
Landry, D. J., 341
Lane, Harlan, 142
Lang, 178
Lang, James, 294
Lasch, Christopher, 387
Latteir, Pearl, 601
Lauer, Jeanette C., 387
Lauer, Robert H., 387
Laumann, Edward, 318, 328, 334, 335
La Veist, Thomas, 547
Law, Jude, 364
Lawrence, D. H., 340
Lawson, V., 366
Lay, Kenneth, 185
Layton, Robert H., 419

Subject Index

Domestic labor, 442
Doubt, role exit and, 80
Dramaturgical model, 24
Dramaturgy, 73–74
Drugs
    definition of, 542
    recreational, 541–542
    therapeutic, 542
Durkheim's views, 16–18
    on religion, 489–490
Dyads, 81
Dying, 360–362
    stages of, 361

Eating disorders, 526, 527, 528
Ecclesiae, 493–494
Economic development, 419–425
Economic systems, 425–429
    capitalism, 425–427
    communism, 428–429
    socialism, 427–428
Economies, 418–434
    agricultural, 419
    American, 429–434
    corporations and, 431–434
    definition of, 418
    global, classification of, 230–232
    industrial, 419–420
    industrialization and, 430–431
    modern, 420–421
    postindustrial, 421–425, 431
    theories of, 418
    in 21st century, 451
    world, 235
Ecosystems, 640
"Edge cities," 634
Education, 554–584. See also School(s)
    as agent of socialization, 152
    bilingual, 568
    completing formal schooling and, 558, 584
    confidence in, 576, 584–585
    cultural literacy and, 563–564
    gender identity and, 571–572
    gender inequality in school and, 569–571
    globalization and, 559–564
    higher. See College campuses; Higher education
    history of, 557–559
    home schooling and, 574–575
    intelligence and literacy and, 562–563
    "marketization" of, 581–582
    mobility and, 565–566
    No Child Left Behind Act and, 575
    political party affiliation and, 470
    privatization and, 573–574
    racial achievement gap and, 570
    school reform and, 572
    as social institution, 556–557
    structure of, inequality and, 566–568
    tracking and, 568–569
    in 21st century, 582–583
Educational profile, 560

Efficiency in bureaucracies, 95
Ego, 147–148
Elder care, 366–367
Elderly people, poverty among, 222
"Elderly" status, 77
Elected office. See Political office
Electronic Numerical Integrator and Computer (ENIAC), 594
Elementary and Secondary School Act of 2002, 575
Embryonic stem cell research, political debate over, 510
EMI, 601
Emigration, 620–622
Emigration rate, 622
Emma (Austen), 349
Emotional problems, 541, 552–553
Empirical verification, 488
Employment, 434–445. See also Workplace entries
    balancing work and family and, 303
    blue-collar, 437–438
    of children, 231, 349, 373–376
    contingent and "on call" work and, 444
    forced and bonded labor, 375–376
    gender inequality in, 298–304
    gender wage gap and, 297, 300–301
    glass ceiling and glass escalator and, 301–302
    global economies and, 230–231
    Hawthorne Effect and, 435
    industrial economies and, 420
    knowledge work and, 422
    labor unions and, 438
    manufacturing consent and, 436
    part-time, 443
    pink-collar, 438–439
    poverty and, 221
    self-employment and, 442–443
    service work and, 439–440
    sex segregation in, 299–300
    sexual harassment and, 302–303
    social mobility and, 227–228
    Theory X and Theory Y and, 435–436
    in 21st century, 451
    unpaid work and, 441–442
    white-collar, 436–437
    working off the books and, 440–441
    working poor and, 440
Encoding/decoding, 598–599
Energy, 642
English
    as official language, 48, 66
    as a second language, 568
Enron, 183, 185
Environments. See also Cities; Human environment; Natural environment
    in 21st century, 647
Epidemiology, 533
Equal Rights Amendment, 309
ESL (English as a second language), 568
Ethics in research, 132–133
Ethnic cleansing, 30

Ethnic groups, 262–275. See also specific groups
Ethnic identity, sexuality and, 334–335
Ethnicity, 262. See also Minority groups; Race; Race and ethnicity; specific groups
    "choosing," 271
    conflict based on, 271–272
    families and, 388–391
    race versus, 244–245
    social mobility and, 228–229
Ethnic Options (Waters), 271
Ethnocentrism, 42
Ethnography, 115–117
Ethnomethodology, 75
Eugenics, 250
European Americans, 263
    families of, 388–389
Everyday work, 539
Everything in Its Path (Erikson), 647
Evolution, political debate over, 509–510
Evolutionary imperative, 283
Exchange as pattern of social interaction, 75
Exogamy, 384
Experiment(s), 111, 112–114, 126
    field, 134
Experimental group, 112
Extended family, 386
Extramarital sex, 320, 344–345
Extraneous variables, 112

Facebook, 91
Face work, 74
Fads, 59–60
Failing at Fairness (Sadker), 570
Fair Housing Act of 1968, 254
Fairness of others, perceptions of, 33, 36–37
Family(ies), 380–414
    as agent of socialization, 151–152
    balancing work with, 303
    blended, 408–409
    culture and forms of, 383–384
    development of, 385–386
    divorce and, 406–409
    ethnicity and, 388–391
    extended, 386
    family unit and, 384–385
    forming, 391–401
    intergenerational and intragenerational violence in, 410–413
    interracial, 400, 414–415
    intimate partner violence in, 409–410
    as kinship systems, 382–383
    marriage and. See Marriage
    nuclear, 287, 386–388
    of origin, 384
    parenting and. See Parenting
    of procreation, 384–385
    single-parent, 402–403
    in 21st century, 413
Family corporations, 431–432
Fans, 606–607
Fashions, 60

Traditional authority, 457–458
Transgenderism, 530–531
Transracial adoption, 404
Tuskegee experiments, 535
Twixters, 353
Two-party system, 468–469

Ulysses (Joyce), 340
Underclass, 214–215
Underemployment, 227
"Underground economy," 441
Unemployment, 444–445
Unemployment compensation, 445
Unions, 438, 472
U.S. Constitution, 429
Universal Music Group, 601
Universal suffrage, 462
Universities. *See* College campuses; Higher
    education
University of Phoenix, 581
Unpaid work, 441–442
Upper middle class, 213–214
Upper upper class, 212–213
Urbanization, 638
    global, 639–640
"Urbanization as a Way of Life" (Wirth), 638
Urban village, 638–639
Utilitarian organizations, 92–93

Validity, 110
Values, 51–55
    American, 52–54
    changing and contradictory, 54–55
    of criminal subcultures, 180–181
    emerging, 54
    inconsistent, 51
Variables, 111–112
    confounding, 112
    dependent, 110
    extraneous, 112
    independent, 110
Veblen's views, 20
Verbal communication, 75. *See also*
    Language
Verstehen, 107
Viacom, 601
Video games, 593
Violence
    in adolescence, 159

bullying and, 572
    in families, 409–413
    gender and, 291
    intimate partner, 409–410
    school, 572, 573
    sibling, 410
Violent crime, 183
Virginia Tech, 573
Voting. *See also* Suffrage
    compulsory, 471
Voucher system, 573–574

Wage gap, gender, 297, 300–301, 448–449
Wage labor, 420. *See also* Employment;
    Workplace *entries*
Wal-Mart, 427, 430, 433, 440
War, 477
Ward's views, 20
Warner Brothers, 601–602
Water pollution, 644
Wealth, distribution of, global economies
    and, 232
Weber's views, 18–19
    on religion, 490–491
    on social class, 210–212
Weight, 523–526
Welfare capitalism, 426
Western Electric study, 96
White Americans, 248–251. *See also*
    Ethnicity; Race; Race and ethnicity
    history of, 249–251
    terminology for, 274
White-collar crime, 183
White-collar jobs, 436–437
*Why Are All the Black Kids Sitting Together
    in the Cafeteria?* (Tatum), 245
"Wild Boy of Aveyron," 142
Willow Creek Community Church (Chicago,
    Illinois), 502
Woman in the Nineteenth Century (Fuller), 21
Women. *See also* Gender *entries;* Sex *entries;*
    Sexual *entries*
    determinants of status of, 287
    early focus on, 21–23
    employment of, 438
    feminism and, 308–310
    lesbian. *See* Homosexuality; Sexual orien-
        tation
    life span of, 360

"mail-order wives" and, 624
    maternal "instinct" and, 143
    maternal mortality rate and, 534
    matrilineal descent and, 383
    microcredit and, 226
    in political office, 302, 313
    poverty among, 222
    sexual harassment of, 302–303
    in sociology, 34
    women's movements and, 307–308
Women and Economics (Gilman), 22
Women's magazines, 590
Women's movements, 307–308
Work. *See* Employment; Workplace *entries*
Work-family dynamics, gender and, 449
Working class, 214
Working parents, 450–451
Workplace as agent of socialization,
    156–157
Workplace crime, 183–185
Workplace discrimination, 450
Workplace diversity, 445–451
    gender, 447–449, 453
    racial, 446–447
    sexual, 449–450
    working parents and, 450–451
WorldCom, 183
World economy, 235
World March of Women 2000, 308
World Poker Tournament, 593–594
World religions, 494–500
    contemporary, 498–500
    Eastern, 497–498
    Western, 494–497
World system theory of global inequality,
    235–237

"The Yellow Wallpaper" (Gilman), 22
Young adulthood, 352–353
Youth
    global, 370–371
    inequality and, 371–376
    poverty and, 372–373
    in 21st century, 376
Youth gangs, 173–174

Zero population growth, 628

Credits

Value/SuperStock; **p. 286** © Carol Beckwith & Angela Fisher/HAGA/The Image Works; **p. 288** © National Anthropological Archives, Smithsonian; **p. 291** © Charles & Josette Lenars/CORBIS; **p. 298** © AP Images/Sunday Alamba; **p. 299** © Ellen B. Senisi; **p. 308** © Cleve Bryant/PhotoEdit.

Chapter 10: p. 314 (top) © Welsh/zefa/CORBIS; **p. 314 (bottom)** © Jacques M. Chenet/CORBIS; **p. 316** © Randy Faris/CORBIS; **p. 317** © Rommel Pecson/The Image Works; **p. 322** © AP Images/Susan Walsh; **p. 326** © vario images GmbH & Co.KG/Alamy; **p. 331** John Davis © Dorling Kindersley; **p. 332** © HBO/Courtesy Everett Collection; **p. 333** © Everynight Images/Alamy; **p. 334** © AP Images/Victor R. Caivano; **p. 337** © Rachel Epstein/The Image Works; **p. 339** © WAY GARY/CORBIS SYGMA; **p. 341** © Jonathan Nourok/PhotoEdit; **p. 342** © Kapoor Baldev/Sygma/CORBIS.

Chapter 11: p. 346 (top) © Evan Agostini/Getty Images; **p. 346 (bottom)** © George Shelley/CORBIS; **p. 350** © AP Images/Ryan Soderlin/Salina Journal; **p. 353** © C. J. Burton/Time & Life Pictures/Getty Images; **p. 355** © Michelle Pedone/Photonica/Getty Images; **p. 361** © Christophe Boisvieux/CORBIS; **p. 364** © Robin Nelson/PhotoEdit; **p. 370** © Charles Gullung/zefa/CORBIS; **p. 372** © Motofish Images/CORBIS; **p. 374 (left)** © David Young-Wolff/PhotoEdit; **p. 374 (right)** © JP Laffont/Sygma/CORBIS.

Chapter 12: p. 380 (top) © Banana Stock/SuperStock; **p. 380 (bottom)** © Jamie Chomas/Nonstock/Jupiterimages; **p. 383** © Karan Kapoor/Getty Images; **p. 386** © Dinodia/The Image Works; **p. 388** © Jose Carillo/PhotoEdit; **p. 390** © Lawrence Migdale/Photo Researchers, Inc.; **p. 392** © T. Kruesselmann/zefa/CORBIS; **p. 394** © Rick Friedman/CORBIS; **p. 395** © Robert Fried Photography; **p. 396** © Jim Bastardo/Getty Images; **p. 402** © Erik Freeland/CORBIS; **p. 403** © Jim Pickerell/The Stock Connection; **p. 404** © AP Images; **p. 407** © David Young-Wolff/PhotoEdit; **p. 409** © Robin Nelson/PhotoEdit; **p. 411** © Carlos Serrao/Getty Images.

Chapter 13: p. 416 (top) © Jon Feingersh/Masterfile; **p. 416 (bottom)** © Gideon Mendel/CORBIS; **p. 420** © Bettmann/CORBIS; **p. 427** © Mason Morfit/Taxi/Getty Images; **p. 433** © AP Images/David Zalubowski; **p. 440** © Peter Hvizdak/The Image Works; **p. 441** © Bill Aron/PhotoEdit; **p. 445** © AP Images/Gail Oskin; **p. 450** © Ariel Skelley/CORBIS.

Chapter 14: p. 454 (top) © Ali Jarekji/Reuters; **p. 454 (bottom)** © Mark Richards/PhotoEdit; **p. 461** © Heinrich Hoffmann/Timepix/Time & Life Pictures/Getty Images; **p. 462** © AP Images/Odd Anderson; **p. 463** © Stella/Getty Images; **p. 466** © EZIO PETERSEN/UPI/Landov; **p. 467** © AP Images/Lynne Sladky; **p. 472** © W. Eugene Smith/Time & Life Pictures/Getty Images; **p. 473** © DARREN WHITESIDE/Reuters/Landov; **p. 474** © AP Images/Ed Andrieski; **p. 477** © AP Images/Elise Amendola; **p. 481** © Ernst Grasser/Getty Images.

Chapter 15: p. 486 (top) © Bob Sacha/CORBIS; **p. 486 (bottom)** © David Joel/Getty Images; **p. 492** © AP Images/San Francisco Examiner and Houston Post; **p. 493** © AP

Images/Elise Amendois; **p. 497** © Dinodia/The Image Works; **p. 500** © Marion Kaplan/Alamy; **p. 502** © JOHN GRESS/Reuters/CORBIS; **p. 505** © Arlene Gottfried/The Image Works; **p. 506** © Andersen Ross/Brand X/CORBIS; **p. 507** © Claudia Kunin/CORBIS; **p. 511** Copyright © Bartee Photography, Inc./Phototake – All rights reserved.; **p. 512** © Scott Camazine & Sue Trainor/Photo Researchers, Inc.; **p. 513** © Stephen Derr/Getty Images.

Chapter 16: p. 520 (top) © ER Productions/CORBIS; **p. 520 (bottom)** © AP Images/John Miller; **p. 525** © REUTERS/Guang Niu/File/Landov; **p. 526** © Richard T. Nowitz/CORBIS; **p. 528** © AP Images/Frank Hormann; **p. 530** © TIZIANA FABI/AFP/Getty Images; **p. 532** © Chris Gordon/Getty Images for The South Beach Comedy Festival; **p. 537** © Lauren Goodsmith/The Image Works; **p. 539** © Image Source Limited/Phototake Royalty Free; **p. 543** © Spencer Grant/PhotoEdit; **p. 544** © ACE STOCK LIMITED/Alamy; **p. 547** © Journal-Courier/Steve Warmowski/The Image Works; **p. 549** © Steven Rubin/The Image Works; **p. 551** COURTESY: MARY BOONE GALLERY, NEW YORK.

Chapter 17: p. 554 (top) © Kevin Moloney for The New York Times; **p. 554 (bottom)** © Najlah Feanny/CORBIS; **p. 559** © Ellen B. Senisi/The Image Works; **p. 561** © Rhoda Sidney/The Image Works; **p. 566** © Sean Justice/Getty Images; **p. 567** © Adrian Sherratt/Alamy; **p. 569** © Blend Images/Alamy; **p. 570** © Michael Newman/PhotoEdit; **p. 572** © ACE STOCK LIMITED/Alamy; **p. 579** © Heide Benser/CORBIS; **p. 581** © Stock4B/Getty Images.

Chapter 18: p. 586 (top) © Darrin Klimek/Digital Vision/Getty Images Royalty Free; **p. 586 (bottom)** © David Paul Morris/Getty Images; **p. 589** © AP Images/Natacha Pisarenko; **p. 590** Courtesy of Kalmbach Publishing Co. and Bead & Button magazine, BeadAndButton.com; **p. 593 (top)** © Stockbyte/Getty Images; **p. 593 (bottom)** © AP Images/Michael Schmelling; **p. 594** © Jerry Cooke/Bettmann/CORBIS; **p. 598** © NBCU Photo Bank; **p. 600** © Ann Johansson/CORBIS; **p. 603** © Jean Baptiste Lacroix/Getty Images; **p. 606** © AP Images/Denis Poroy; **p. 608** © Jonathan Nourok/PhotoEdit; **p. 611** © David H. Wells/CORBIS; **p. 612** © Frank Leather/Eye Ubiquitous/CORBIS.

Chapter 19: p. 616 (top) © Jenny Hager/The Image Works; **p. 616 (bottom)** © Jose Fuste Raga/CORBIS; **p. 621** © Melanie Stetson Freeman/The Christian Science Monitor via Getty Images; **p. 623** © Jeffrey Greenberg/PhotoEdit; **p. 624** © AP Images/Marcio Jose Sanchez; **p. 627** © Françoise De Mulder/Roger Viollet/The Image Works; **p. 629** © Tom Merton/Digital Vision/Getty Images Royalty Free; **p. 631** © Stapleton Collection/CORBIS; **p. 632** © Dinodia/The Image Works; **p. 634 (top)** © Oregon State Archives; **p. 634 (bottom)** © Spencer Ainsley/The Image Works; **p. 637** © Robert Brenner/PhotoEdit; **p. 639** © Warner Bros/Courtesy Everett Collection; **p. 641** © REUTERS/Ivan Alvarado/Landov; **p. 645** © Louie Psihoyos/CORBIS.